PENG

A NEW HANDE~~BOOK OF~~

John Hinnells was born in Derby, England. He married Marianne
in 1965 and they had two sons, Mark Julian and Duncan Keith
William. Tragically Marianne died of cancer in 1996. After
studying, practising and teaching art, he began his theological
studies in 1961 at King's College, London, following this with
postgraduate studies at King's and the School of Oriental and
African Studies, London University. In 1967 he was appointed
Lecturer in Religious Studies at the University of Newcastle upon
Tyne, and then in 1970 he moved to Manchester, where he was
made Professor of Comparative Religion in 1984. He was
seconded to the Open University as Visiting Senior Lecturer in
the History of Religions from 1975 to 1977. He was Dean of the
Faculty of Theology at Manchester from 1987 to 1988. In 1993
he was appointed Professor of Comparative Religion in London
University and the founding head of the Department for the
Study of Religion at the School of Oriental and African Studies.
Although he has edited a number of books on the history
of religions generally and has initiated four important series
of books, his own research and writings are in the field of
Zoroastrianism, particularly Mithraism and the Parsis. In
addition to convening the first, the second and the fourth
International Congresses of Mithraic Studies (Manchester, 1971;
Tehran, 1975; Rome, 1990), he has undertaken research of
Mithraic sites in most European countries and made a number of
visits to the Indian subcontinent for his publications on the Parsis
in British India. He has also lectured in Hong Kong, Australia,
Sweden, America, Canada, Iran and Pakistan. In 1975 he
delivered the Government Research Fellowship Lectures in
Bombay and in 1985 the Ratanbai Katrak Lectures in the
University of Oxford. He is a Fellow of the Society of Antiquaries
and of the Royal Asiatic Society, and a member of several learned
societies. In 1997 he was appointed Visiting Professor in

Religious Studies at the University of Derby. He has been elected to the Council of the Society for South Asian Studies, and Chairman of the Association of University Departments of Theology and Religious Studies.

John Hinnells has edited *Who's Who of Religions* (1996), *The Penguin Dictionary of Religions* (second edition, 1997) and *A New Handbook of Living Religions* (1997), all for Penguin. His books on Zoroastrianism include *Persian Mythology* (Newnes, 1983) and *Zoroastrians in Britain* (Oxford, 1996), and he is the author of some fifty research articles. He also acts as an advisor for Penguin's publishing in religion and non-western classics.

A NEW HANDBOOK
OF LIVING RELIGIONS

EDITED BY JOHN R. HINNELLS

PENGUIN BOOKS

This book is dedicated to
my late wife
Marianne Grace Hinnells 1943–1996
as a token of deep and abiding love

PENGUIN BOOKS

Published by the Penguin Group
Penguin Books Ltd, 27 Wrights Lane, London W8 5TZ, England
Penguin Putnam Inc., 375 Hudson Street, New York, New York 10014, USA
Penguin Books Australia Ltd, Ringwood, Victoria, Australia
Penguin Books Canada Ltd, 10 Alcorn Avenue, Toronto, Ontario, Canada M4V 3B2
Penguin Books (NZ) Ltd, 182–190 Wairau Road, Auckland 10, New Zealand

Penguin Books Ltd, Registered Offices: Harmondsworth, Middlesex, England

First published by Blackwell Publishers by arrangement with Penguin Books 1997
Published in Penguin Books 1998
1 3 5 7 9 10 8 6 4 2

Printed in England by Clays Ltd, St Ives plc

Contents

The Contributors

Dr Purushottama Bilimoria, School of Social Inquiry, Deakin University, Australia

Professor Mary Boyce, Professor Emerita of Iranian Studies, University of London

Dr W. Owen Cole, Religious Studies Department, Chichester Institute of Higher Education

Professor Brian E. Colless, Religious Studies Department, Massey University, New Zealand

Professor John E. Cort, Department of Religion, Denison University, Ohio

L. S. Cousins, formerly Department of Comparative Religion, University of Manchester

Professor Harold Coward, Centre for Studies in Religion and Society, University of Victoria, British Columbia

Professor Peter Donovan, Religious Studies Department, Massey University, New Zealand

The late **Professor Kendall W. Folkert**, Department of Religion, Central Michigan University

Professor Armin W. Geertz, Department of the Study of Religions, University of Aarhus, Denmark

Professor John R. Hinnells, Department for the Study of Religions, School of Oriental and African Studies, University of London

Professor Ursula King, Department of Theology and Religious Studies, University of Bristol

Dr Kim Knott, Department of Theology and Religious Studies, University of Leeds

Dr Denis MacEoin, formerly of the University of Newcastle upon Tyne

Professor J. Gordon Melton, Institute for the Study of American Religion, Santa Barbara, California

Professor David Reid, Seigakuin University, Japan

Professor Michael Saso, Institute of Asian Studies, Beijing

Dr Aylward Shorter, Tangaza College, The Catholic University of Eastern Africa, Nairobi, Kenya

Dr Ossie Stuart, freelance writer and researcher on ethnicity, race and identity

Professor Harold W. Turner, formerly of Selly Oak Colleges, Birmingham

Dr Alan Unterman, Department of Religions and Theology, University of Manchester

Professor Andrew Walls, Centre for the Study of Christianity in the Non-Western World, University of Edinburgh

Simon Weightman, Department for the Study of Religions, School of Oriental and African Studies, University of London

Professor Alford T. Welch, Department of Religious Studies, Michigan State University

Professor Raymond Brady Williams, Department of Religious Studies, Wabash College, Indiana

Acknowledgements

The Editor gratefully acknowledges permission to reproduce copyright material in this book.

Figure 2.1: from the late J. M. Hornus, by permission. Figure 2.4: from a drawing by June Reed, for *The Work of William Perkins* (ed. I. Breward), Sutton Courtenay Press, 1969. Figures 2.7, 2.8 and 2.9: based on D. B. Barratt, *World Christian Encyclopedia*, Oxford University Press, 1982. Figures 3.2 and 3.5: after Kenneth Cragg, *Islam and the Muslim* (figs 5 and 10), Milton Keynes, The Open University Press, 1978 (Man's Religious Quest, Units 20–21). Figure 3.3(a): from A. Kuran, *The Mosque in Early Ottoman Architecture*, University of Chicago Press, 1968. Figure 4.4: from an architect's plan kindly provided by Faribourz Nariman. Figures 5.10 and 5.11 are based, by permission, on S. M. Bhardwaj, *Hindu Places of Pilgrimage in India*, University of California Press, 1973, pp. 81 and 89. Figures 13.4 and 13.5: drawings by Ben Rwegoshora. Figures 15.1 and 15.2: drawn from J. Gordon Melton, *A Directory of Religious Bodies in the United States*, New York, Garland, 1977.

Every effort has been made to trace the copyright holders but if any have been inadvertently overlooked the publishers will be pleased to make the necessary arrangement at the first opportunity.

Introduction to the *New Handbook*

JOHN R. HINNELLS

This *New Handbook*, which grew out of the Penguin *Handbook of Living Religions*, first published in 1984, is new in two ways. First, the various chapters have been updated in the light both of modern scholarship and of developments since the production of the first edition. Some of the chapters have been substantially revised; others have had new sections added; in the case of China the chapter has doubled in size. The chapter on North American Indians has been totally rewritten.

Secondly, nine completely new chapters have been added on cross-cultural issues. It is no longer acceptable for general introductions to religions to neglect the issue of gender and that subject is now covered in chapter 17. Contrary to the expectations of the 1970s and 1980s, and despite the evident materialism in much of the world, there is at the dawn of the third millennium a growing interest in spirituality and it was thought important that this dimension of living religion should also receive specific treatment. Chapter 18 is dedicated to it.

There is also a group of seven new chapters on the subject of religion in migration, or diaspora religion. These cover black African religion in America and Britain, and include also four comparative chapters on religions from South Asia (Buddhism, Hinduism, Indian Christianity, Islam, Jainism, Parsis, Sikhism) and their settlement in Australia, Britain, Canada and the United States. The reasons for this selection are set out in chapter 19, but may be stated briefly here. Teachers of religion have often emphasized that the subject has immediate relevance in the West because of the local presence of Asian religions. Although there have been many books on Asian migration to the West, few have studied the religions of these communities, which have been neglected as though religion were something left behind in the old country. When religion has been mentioned, it has typically been viewed as marginal to the main history of that tradition, as though 'real' Islam were something found in the Middle East, or 'real' Hinduism, Zoroastrianism, Jainism, Sikhism, etc. were to be found only in Asia. Yet there are almost as many Muslims in the West as in Saudi Arabia; there are indications that America could become a fertile centre for future theological developments in several religions; and many western-based Sikhs, Hindus and other faith members return with honour to the old country on visits and affect the communities there. In short, the diaspora communities can no longer be seen as peripheral to the story of their religions. Further, their presence in the West has affected the West. There have been converts to Islam, inter-faith dialogue has affected Christianity, branches of Christianity have been inspired to discover some of their contemplative, healing or charismatic traditions from African and Asian groups. Western society has to face the challenges posed by multi-religious societies – to its legal and medical professions, for example. A book on living religions, indeed the study of religion generally, should now include the fact of the global dispersion of religions previously more geographically restricted. This is the first book to attempt an international comparison of how seven major religions have migrated to four different countries. Future editions of the *Handbook* may extend this comparison, though doubtless the story and method of study will be different then. It is hoped that this volume will inspire others to carry the subject further. (Readers seeking specific information about the various diaspora sects and groups mentioned in these chapters are referred to *A New Dictionary of Religions*, published by Blackwell and Penguin in 1995.)

Thanks are due to many people. Gillian Bromley has worked with characteristic care and efficiency on the copy-editing and it has been a pleasure to work with her. I am very grateful to Professor John Cort for agreeing to update the chapter on Jains, following Professor Folkert's death in India. Indeed, I am grateful to all the authors, each of whom has been cooperative and understanding of what has sometimes been editorial strictness regarding length, coverage, deadlines, etc. Above all I am grateful to my late wife, Marianne Grace Hinnells, who died in the last stages of the editing of this work. Indeed, much of the conclusion was word-processed at her bedside. The support and strength which she gave throughout our life together was present to the end. My work in this book is dedicated to her.

Introduction to the First Edition

JOHN R. HINNELLS

This *Handbook* is the product of scholarly collaboration on an international scale. It presents the conclusions of some of the latest academic research in a readable manner for the general public as well as for the student of religions. The book has a clear focus, namely living religions in the twentieth century. It also has a carefully thought-out structure, so that the reader is entitled to an account of the presuppositions which lie behind it.

The most fundamental of these is the importance of religion in history. Whatever any individual's personal religious beliefs may be, or even if there is some antagonism towards religion, it is difficult for anyone to deny that religions have had considerable impact on societies in all continents. Religions have often been deeply involved in political matters, in cultural developments; they have been used to legitimate, suppress or inspire regimes, philosophies and artistic movements. Religious institutions have, for good or ill, dominated or undermined secular establishments of many kinds. Individuals have been inspired by religion to live up to the highest possible personal standards, or provoked to display the basest instincts. It is not possible to understand the history of most, if not all, countries without knowledge of the religions which have flourished there and influenced, moulded or corrupted both leaders and masses.

It is often said that this is a secular age; that religion is declining. A basic conviction behind this book is that such assertions are at most half-truths, if not wholly wrong. Perhaps formal membership of some established religious institutions is declining, but this represents only one part of the religious spectrum. In other parts religion can evidently be seen to flourish in the twentieth century: in new religious movements in primal societies in Africa or in the cities of Japan; on US university campuses in the 1960s; in the powerful spirit of Islamic revivalism in the 1970s; and in the growth of 'alternative' religions or charismatic movements in various continents in the 1970s and 1980s. Religion is only seen to be declining if it is viewed from a limited and 'traditionalist' perspective. This *Handbook* is concerned with both established religions and the new movements.

With modern communications, religious institutions and people are in greater contact than ever before. Such contact produces an enormous impetus for change. This is true not only of international religions (for example Buddhism), as they have moved across political boundaries and been challenged by radical political change, but also of the traditions of 'small-scale' or primal societies, whether in Africa or the Pacific, as they have been confronted by the entry of such missionary religions as Islam and Christianity. The twentieth century can be characterized as a particularly dynamic period in the history of religions. Religious people of most generations in diverse cultures have considered 'the youth of today' as less religious than themselves. The truth is sometimes that the young are not so much less religious as religious in a different way. Living means changing; this *Handbook* is concerned with living religions as they have experienced change in the twentieth century.

However great, and valid, people's interest in modern movements may be, it would be rash, even wrong, to look at recent apart from earlier history. This is not only because religions, like people, are in some measure the products of their own history, but also because living religions commonly assert their identity with the past. Few movements, however new, stress their difference from their origins. Revival or reform movements often emphasize that they are returning to the purity of their tradition's original form. It is, therefore, necessary to understand both the history and the perceived history of the religions.

This *Handbook* is concerned with *living* religions in another sense also: how does each religion function as a vital force in the daily life of its adherents? Many books focus heavily on doctrines, making religion primarily a belief system or a cerebral activity. Right belief is an important factor in some traditions, but not in others. For a great many people in various countries religion is something which is part of the fabric of society and life. It is something 'done' and lived rather than something reasoned: however the scholars may theorize, whatever may be the 'official' teaching of a given 'establishment', the religion of the majority is often expressed mainly through custom and practice. So, whereas some books assume a 'pure' form of the 'original' religion which has been 'adulterated' by the 'superstitions' of the common people, writers in this *Handbook* give serious attention to both beliefs and practices, to the rites and customs as well as to the teachings of the religions. In recent years some scholars have used the distinction between the 'great' and the 'little' traditions to distinguish between the (inter)national or 'mainstream' formal expression of a religion and its local (e.g. village) expressions. Such a division may be inappropriate for some religions because it implies too great a gap between classical teachings and popular practices, or because there may be more than one 'great' tradition (as for example with the Eastern Orthodox, Catholic and Protestant traditions of Christianity). Nevertheless, this distinction has served a useful function in that it has drawn to people's attention the variety of expressions of religion which conventional 'theological' approaches have neglected.

A real danger for a book on religions is that it can too easily assume, wrongly, that there are always definable, separate phenomena corresponding to the labels popularly used, such as Christianity or Hinduism. In practice the divisions between religions are sometimes artificial. It is not always the case that to believe one religion is 'right' necessarily involves believing that another is 'wrong'. Dual or multiple affiliation to religious organizations does occur, for example in contemporary Japan. The impact of missionary religions on primal societies has often produced new movements which do not naturally belong under any of the conventional labels. Religion must sometimes, therefore, be studied as a regional phenomenon rather than under the conventional headings of '-isms'.

Assumptions abound in the study of religion; they are at their most dangerous when they are unrecognized. This book seeks to challenge many commonly held assumptions: that India is changeless; that Christianity is a single, easily recognized phenomenon; that religions are monolithic wholes; that Jainism and Zoroastrianism are dead religions; that Islam is a 'Near Eastern' religion; or that Buddhism is an abstract philosophy. But it is not only popular assumptions which need to be questioned or clarified; it is just as important to spell out scholarly assumptions. There are few cold facts in the study of religions: all explanation involves interpretation. Rarely do general books on religions set out what scholarly methods and assumptions lie behind their accounts. Perhaps it is assumed that the general reader does not need such information. One conviction behind this book is that it is precisely the general reader, or the non-specialist, who *does* need such an account because she or he is the most vulnerable to an unbalanced or biased account. Authors in this *Handbook* have, therefore, given a brief account of the different scholarly methods and assumptions which have influenced the study of their subject. It is equally necessary for the reader to have some idea of the nature of the sources on which such studies have been based, because the questions which can be asked, if not always answered, vary according to the type of sources available. Contributors have added a brief survey of the range of materials available in order to aid a proper understanding of the tradition.

Because the various religions differ so much from one another it is not possible to devise a single appropriate structure for all the entries. A literary straitjacket is neither desirable nor possible. But in order to give some unity and coherence to this multi-author work, authors were asked to lay out their material under the following headings, in so far as they are appropriate:

1 *Introduction*, covering: (a) a brief survey of the main primary sources; (b) an introduction to the history of the religion; (c) a survey of the main phases and assumptions of scholarly study of the religion.
2 A succinct account of the main *teachings* of the religion.
3 An outline of the main *practices* of the religion, including formal worship and 'rites of passage' (i.e. rituals thought to convey the individual from one stage of life to another, as at birth, initiation to maturity, marriage and death).
4 *Popular*, 'little' or 'local' traditions.
5 *Modern* or twentieth-century developments, not only in beliefs and practices but also with reference to major political and social changes.

In addition authors were asked to collect, where possible, appropriate data (e.g. statistics) which would make this a useful *Handbook* for the scholar as well as the layperson. Obviously this general structure and range of material had to be adapted to the nature of the respective traditions.

In addition to the study of modern developments in each of the religions or regions covered, it seemed important to include material which set these developments in a wider perspective. Thus chapters have been included on new religious movements and on the 'alternative' religions in the West. The latter subject is one which few general books cover, yet it is one which is particularly important given the vitality of such groups and the ignorance with which they are so often reported. 'Alternative' religions have proliferated to such an extent that there is a real problem in providing full coverage in any one book. The solution adopted here is to give one general chapter on the main 'families' of such religions and a substantial entry on one case, namely Baha'ism, which may be considered something of a paradigm for possible future developments. Baha'ism can be seen in origin as an Islamic reform movement, but it has grown into an autonomous, self-aware religion with missions in many countries, for example the United States, as well as in the Third World.

The sequence of chapters in a general book of this kind sometimes reflects a fundamental assumption regarding the priority of religions or a conviction relating to their supposed type. There is no such significance in the order of chapters in this *Handbook*. It is intended to be a book to be enjoyed, but in practice it is unlikely that it will be read from one cover straight through to the other. Which tradition is at the front and which at the back is, therefore, not a significant issue. The important point is rather the groupings of traditions. Because of their historical interconnectedness it was thought helpful to group together the semitic traditions of Judaism, Christianity and Islam. Similarly, Hinduism, Sikhism and Jainism needed to be together. Zoroastrianism was placed between these two groups because it is a religion which has historically and geographically stood between them. The chapter on Buddhism is placed between those on India and those on China and Japan because it spans these various Asian cultures. The traditions of Native North Americans, the Pacific and Africa (so commonly neglected in books on living religions) are grouped together, as are the chapters on different aspects of the nature and development of new or 'alternative' religious movements.

Every reader will doubtless have his or her own ideas on what should go into a book and in what proportions. Obviously there are omissions. What single book could encompass a field that is so diverse, so changing and so complex? One topic which the editor regretfully omitted was a general discussion of methods, assumptions and definitions. But, given that such methodological issues are considered in relation to the individual topics, it was decided that a general chapter on such themes would have swung the overall balance of the book too far towards the theoretical. For the interested reader a list of challenging books on this topic is included in the general bibliography (see p. 849).

As authors have taken as a priority the readability of their text and a broad view of the history and phenomena of their respective subjects, they have had to omit details which readers may find important and interesting. This is especially the case with regard to intercontinental movements such as Buddhism, Christianity and new religious movements. In such instances the reader is referred to *A New Dictionary of Religions* (Blackwell/Penguin, 1995). The two books can be used, for both pleasure and profit, independently. But they do complement each other. In various ways they are designed alike, not least in the presentation of bibliographical material. Each entry has a numbered bibliography. In the body of the text square brackets are used exclusively and consistently for bibliographical references. An Arabic numeral before the colon refers to the number of a book in the bibliography. A roman numeral after the colon refers to a chapter in that book, whereas an arabic numeral after the colon refers to pages in that book. Thus [4: v] refers to chapter 5 of item 4, whereas [4: 5] refers to page 5 of the same book. In this way references can be given to further reading on specific as well as general points without interrupting the flow of the text. The guiding

principle in the arrangement of the bibliographies is to provide the
non-specialist reader with the information necessary to find the
books in a library. Alternative editions (mainly, but not only,
American and British) have also been noted. In addition to the bibliographies, some chapters carry a few end-notes, referred to by
superior figures in the body of the chapter, or appendices of a specialist nature.

In contrast to the *Dictionary* it was decided, reluctantly, to omit
the subjects of Marxism and Humanism. The *Dictionary* is intended
to be more comprehensive than the *Handbook*. For the latter it was
thought important to allow space for more extended consideration
of the religions covered. The physical constraints of the size of the
book made it necessary to concentrate on what are generally considered the major religious traditions, from which category Marxists
and Humanists typically wish to distance themselves.

It should be noted that maps in the *Handbook* are intended to
locate important places mentioned in the text. They do not distinguish chronological periods, so that ancient and modern sites
appear on the same map.

A Note on Terminology

Two common designations have been avoided in this book. The first
is AD (= *anno Domini*, 'the year of Our Lord'), because this is taken
by many to represent a Christian orientation. Instead, the more
widely accepted CE (Christian Era) and BCE (Before [the] Christian
Era) are used throughout. The second term which has been avoided
is 'Old Testament', because this implies belief in a 'New Testament',
reflecting a Christian assessment of texts which is offensive to Jews.
Instead, the term 'Hebrew Bible' has been used, which by referring
to the language of the texts is intended to be religiously neutral. In a
book written for, and by, people of different religious positions, or of
none at all, a neutral stance is considered essential.

Western publishing conventions generally treat Judeo-Christian
scriptures differently from those of other religions. Thus books from
the Christian Bible, e.g. the Gospel according to Matthew, abbreviated to Matthew, are not printed in italics, whereas those of other
religions are. In a technical, unbiased book such practice is questionable. In this *New Handbook* the following practice has been
adopted: the name of the main scriptural work (Avesta, Bible,
Qur'an) appears in roman, because of the frequency with which
such titles appear. Sections or books within that scriptural collection
and all other texts are italicized.

Part 1

The Religions

1

Judaism

ALAN UNTERMAN

Introduction

Sources of Judaism

The primary source of Jewish religion is the Hebrew Bible, consisting of twenty-four books divided up into three sections: *Torah* (the
Pentateuch), *Neviim* (the Prophets) and *Ketuvim* (the Writings or
Hagiographa). Next in importance to the Bible is the *Babylonian
Talmud*, a collection of rabbinical traditions edited in the fifth/sixth
centuries CE, containing the main teachings of the oral Torah. Other
early rabbinical writings, such as the *Palestinian Talmud* (fourth/fifth
centuries) and midrashic commentaries on the Bible, are less
authoritative than the *Babylonian Talmud*, which itself is an
extended commentary to the *Mishnah* (a work redacted at the end
of the second century). The most influential medieval works are the
commentary of Rashi (1040–1105) on both the Bible and the
Babylonian Talmud; the great law code, known as *Mishneh Torah*, of
Maimonides (1135–1204), and the same author's philosophical
magnum opus, *The Guide for the Perplexed*, which reinterprets Jewish
theology in Aristotelian terms; and the collection of mystical traditions, known as the *Zohar*, which was written or edited by Moses de
Leon (1240–1305). (See figure 1.1.)

In the late middle ages the standard code of Jewish law and ritual
(*halakhah*), the *Shulchan Arukh* or 'Prepared Table', was written by
Rabbi Joseph Caro (1488–1575), who included the customs of
Spanish and oriental Jewry, and was added to by Rabbi Moses
Isserles (1525–72), who incorporated the customs of central and
east European Jewry. This work has shaped the practice of Jewish
communities throughout the world.

In the modern period rabbinical writings have mainly taken the
form of commentaries on pre-modern texts, and Responsa.

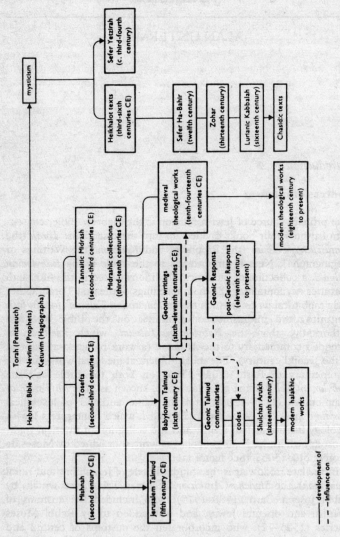

Figure 1.1 The religious literature of Judaism

Responsa literature dates back to the early post-Talmudic period, and consists of published answers to questions about matters of law or ritual. In the changing environment of modernity many new situations have arisen calling for a reinterpretation of Jewish law and its application to differing circumstances. Rabbis have dealt with such issues in Responsa, which if their author is an acknowledged halakhic expert may be collected together and published. Since the mid-nineteenth century a renewed interest in Jewish theology has been stimulated by the contact of Jewish thinkers with modern European thought. The various sub-movements within Judaism – Modern Orthodox, Conservative, Reform, Liberal, Reconstructionist and Zionist – have all produced works reflecting their own ideological understanding of Jewish existence and Jewish identity.

World Jewry

The modern religious Jew, whether affiliated to an Orthodox, Conservative, Reconstructionist, Reform or Liberal synagogue, sees him- or herself as a member of a faith community which goes back some 4,000 years to its origins in the Patriarchal period of Abraham, Isaac and Jacob. For religious Jews the past is not merely of antiquarian interest; it lives on in the rituals out of which their religious life is structured, in their beliefs, and it is constitutive of their very identity as Jews. Since the eighteenth century, when Jews began to move *en masse* out of the medieval European ghetto (segregated area) into modern society, Jews have had to grapple with the challenges to tradition presented by the norms and beliefs of a scientific understanding of man and the world (see figure 1.2). Over the last half-century they have had to readjust their outlook in the face of the Nazi-inspired Holocaust, in which about 6 million Jews were brutally killed merely because they were Jews (see figure 1.3), and in the light of the rebirth of a Jewish national home in the land of Israel after 2,000 years of exile.

Today there are nearly 14.5 million Jews in the world. The biggest demographic concentration is in the US, with just under 6 million Jews, followed by the State of Israel (over 3.5 million), and then by the countries of the Soviet Union (just under 2.2 million). The rest of the Jewish population is scattered throughout the world, with sizeable communities in France, Britain, Canada, South America and South Africa, and with much smaller concentrations in a host of other countries (see figure 1.4). Because of the political situation in the former Soviet Union, Jews there made little contribution to the cultural, intellectual and religious life of world Jewry. The two main centres of Jewish life are therefore in the North

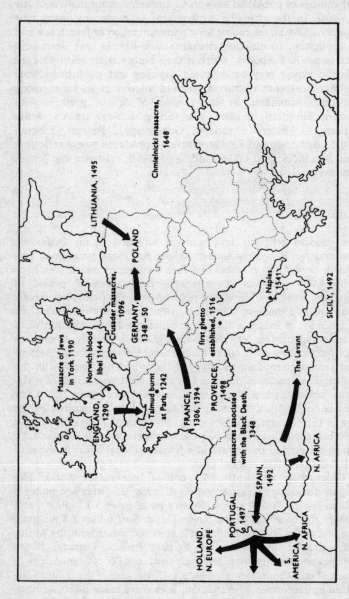

Figure 1.2 Dates of expulsions of Jews from Christian Europe and main sites of anti-Jewish persecution

LITHUANIA, 1495

POLAND

Chmielnicki massacres, 1648

Crusader massacres, 1096

GERMANY, 1348–50

Massacre of Jews in York 1190

Norwich blood libel 1144

ENGLAND, 1290

Talmud burnt at Paris, 1242

FRANCE, 1306, 1394

first ghetto

PROVENCE, 1498

established, 1516

Naples, 1541

massacres associated with the Black Death, 1348

The Levant

SICILY, 1492

N. AFRICA

SPAIN, 1492

PORTUGAL, 1497

HOLLAND, N. EUROPE

S. AMERICA

N. AFRICA

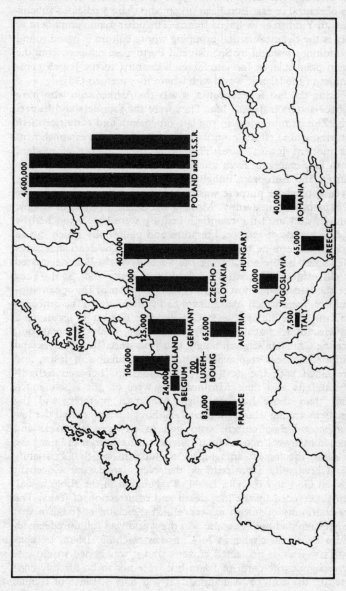

Figure 1.3 The destruction of European Jewry during the Nazi Holocaust (figures represent the minimum estimated casualties)

POLAND and U.S.S.R.
4,600,000

402,000
277,000
125,000 HUNGARY
CZECHO-SLOVAKIA
106,000 GERMANY 65,000
24,000 HOLLAND
700 BELGIUM
LUXEM-BOURG
AUSTRIA
83,000 FRANCE
760 NORWAY

40,000 ROMANIA
65,000 GREECE
60,000 YUGOSLAVIA
7,500 ITALY

American continent and in Israel. The majority of Jews in the former, and approximately half the Jews in the latter, are Ashkenazi Jews of central or east European origin who share a religious subculture with Yiddish as its lingua franca. The other main component of Jewry is the Sefardi-oriental grouping whose culture is based round the traditions brought by Spanish and Portuguese refugees from the Iberian peninsula, in the late fifteenth century, to the Jewish communities of the Islamic world with whom they merged [35].

During the last few centuries it was the Ashkenazim who were the pace-setters in Jewish life. They were the founders and leaders of the Zionist movement in the late nineteenth and early twentieth centuries, whose efforts eventually brought about the establishment of a modern Jewish state. They were the initiators of modern Jewish life, emerging from ghetto life in Germany and France to confront the European Enlightenment, and to set up reforming movements whose purpose was to adjust the religion of the Jew to the demands of modernity. Most of the Sefardim lived in Islamic countries and until the twentieth century were barely touched by the new worlds of science, literature and philosophy which did so much to undermine traditional religious life. The Nazi massacres of Jews just before and during the Second World War decimated the old established centres of Ashkenazi Jewry [20: 533]. They were the latest, and most horrific, manifestation of European anti-Semitism, from which Ashkenazim had suffered down the centuries [21: xviii]. The life of Jews in Christendom was rarely secure, and pogroms (attacks against Jews) were always likely to break out, since the Christian Church taught that Jews were Christ-killers who continued to bear responsibility for the crucifixion of Jesus, and were allied with the devil [31]. Relationships between Sefardi-oriental Jews and their Muslim hosts were on the whole much better than those between their Ashkenazi brethren and the Christians among whom they lived. Although Islam treated the Jew as a second-class citizen, who had to pay special taxes, and imposed many restrictions on his life and behaviour, it did not have the same theological antagonism to Judaism which Christianity had. Christianity saw itself as the New Israel, the Covenant between God and the Old Israel as recounted in the Bible having been superseded by the life, death and resurrection of Jesus. The very continuity of Jewish existence and the claim of Judaism that the Messiah had not yet come and the world was still unredeemed, were a continual challenge to Christian teaching. Islam, by contrast, saw Jews as protected citizens who it was hoped would one day recognize the truth of Islam but were not to be forcibly converted to the faith of Muhammad. It was only at times of Islamic fanaticism that such forced conversions of Jews were attempted. Christianity was more aggressive in its policy of converting Jews,

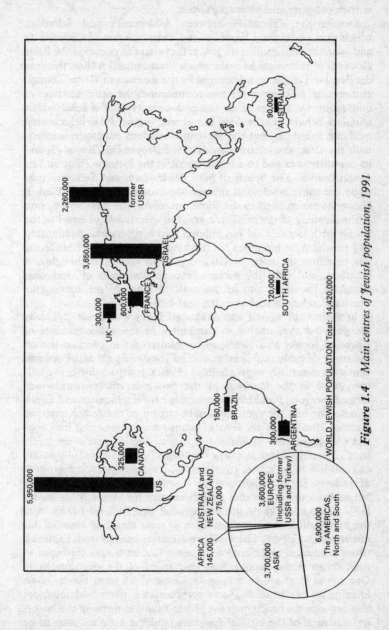

Figure 1.4 Main centres of Jewish population, 1991

90,000 AUSTRALIA

2,260,000 former USSR

3,650,000 ISRAEL

120,000 SOUTH AFRICA

300,000 UK

600,000 FRANCE

5,950,000 US

325,000 CANADA

150,000 BRAZIL

300,000 ARGENTINA

WORLD JEWISH POPULATION Total: 14,420,000

AFRICA 145,000

AUSTRALIA and NEW ZEALAND 75,000

3,700,000 ASIA

3,600,000 EUROPE (including former USSR and Turkey)

6,900,000 The AMERICAS, North and South

threatening those who resisted baptism with expulsion, confiscation of their property and ultimately death.

Despite the differences between Ashkenazim and Sefardim, which may be ascribed largely to the wider cultures of Christianity and Islam and their effect on Jewry, they share in common the basic elements of rabbinical Judaism which characterized it from the time the Second Temple was destroyed by the Romans in 70 CE. Though customs are different in the two communities the ritual practices of both follow the rulings of the sixteenth-century code of *halakhah*, or religious behaviour, the *Shulchan Arukh* (figure 1.1). Educational methods also differ, but the content of religious education is essentially the same: the intensive study of the *Babylonian Talmud* [3] and its commentaries and to a lesser extent of the Hebrew Bible and its commentaries. The beliefs of both Ashkenazim and Sefardim turn upon the same typological images: the redemptive acts of God in history as exemplified in the Bible, promising the final redemption at the dawning of the messianic age; the special role of Israel as the people with whom God has entered into a covenantal relationship and to whom he has given his teaching or Torah; the need for the Jew to affirm the unity of God, negate all idolatrous thoughts or practices, and obey the *mitzvot* or commandments of God contained in the Bible and in the oral teachings of the rabbis (the 'teachers', religious leaders in the post-biblical period).

In the middle ages it was Ashkenazi Jewry which was culturally the poor relative, unable to participate in the wider interests of Christian society and having to concentrate its intellectual life on the study of rabbinical literature. The Jews of Spain and Portugal, who were eventually to give Sefardi-oriental Jewry its distinctive culture, were at the forefront of the two great movements which formed medieval Judaism: the synthesis between Judaism and Greek philosophy; and the most important stream of the Jewish mystical tradition, the Kabbalah. Jews in Islamic lands first came into contact with philosophy in Arabic translation, and because of the tolerance of various Muslim rulers were able to participate fully in the cultural life of their host countries. The most outstanding product of medieval Jewish philosophy was *The Guide for the Perplexed*, written towards the end of the twelfth century by Moses Maimonides [17]. Maimonides grew up in Spain but fled with his family from the persecution of a fanatical Islamic sect, spending most of his mature life in Egypt. The *Guide* reinterprets biblical and Talmudic (from rabbinical traditions of the early Christian era) teachings in Aristotelian terms, emphasizing that many of the descriptions of God found there are anthropomorphisms which must not be taken literally, for any belief in God's corporeality is heresy. Maimonides also explains the function of the Jewish rituals in terms of the historical situation of the biblical Israelites, and the need for man to be refined in his moral outlook and his beliefs to perfect himself in the service of God. In another of his works Maimonides, for the first time in the history of Jewish doctrine, lays down thirteen fundamentals of Jewish belief the negation of which would lead the Jew into heresy [13]. Apart from the *Guide*, Maimonides' other major contribution to Judaism was his all-embracing halakhic (or legal) code, the *Mishneh Torah* or *Yad Ha-Chazakah*. This included theological material based on Maimonides' philosophical understanding of Judaism, and had considerable influence in raising the intellectual horizons even of those Jews who restricted their education to the *Talmud* and codes. All of the major contributions to medieval Jewish philosophy came from Spain or from areas dominated by Islam such as north Africa and the Orient. Though some Ashkenazi scholars subsequently read the philosophical works of their co-religionists, Ashkenazi culture as a whole did not absorb the ethos of free inquiry or the consequent broad-based perspective on Judaism which was current in parts of the Islamic world. The Ashkenazim in northern France and Germany, and later on in Poland, Lithuania, Hungary and Russia, developed a very intricate system of study of Talmudic literature, and turned in on themselves away from interests which were more theological and general in nature. Ashkenazi religiosity was inclined to pietism, to an awareness of humanity's finiteness and sinfulness, and to a form of mysticism in which the adept underwent a severe regimen of spiritual training leading to a vision of the divine Glory seated on the heavenly throne [27: III]. Many elements of folk religion, with strong magical overtones, were absorbed by Ashkenazim and indeed came to be accepted as normative customs on a par with the *halakhah* itself.

The great flowering of medieval mysticism, however, took place precisely in those areas which had experienced the most intense development of philosophical religion, namely in Spain and Provence. In part the Kabbalah spread as a reaction to the changes that philosophically minded intellectuals had made in the traditional Jewish outlook. They had allegorized away much of the substance of Jewish theology, and reinterpreted the halakhic rituals as spiritual ideas. The great monument of kabbalistic religion was the *Zohar* [37], written in Spain but claimed by Moses de Leon, its promulgator, to be the teachings of the second-century sage R. Simeon bar Yochai [27: v, vi]. In this work we find a reversion to the modes of Talmudic Judaism, the rituals being interpreted as the mystical contact points between humanity and the divine. The *Zohar*, however, goes beyond the strengthening of halakhic norms by interpreting them as the primary means whereby the divine substratum underlying the world is kept in harmonious relationship with it. It also advocates a whole series of new rituals of its own, emphasizes the demonic forces at work in the creation, teaches that the difference between Jew and

Gentile is a question not merely of degree but of kind, the Jew possessing a quality of soul absent from the non-Jew, and generally reinforces the sense of the magical which theologians influenced by Greek philosophy had argued was inimical to monotheistic belief.

Sefardi culture was deeply influenced by the Kabbalah of the *Zohar*, which began to circulate at the end of the thirteenth century, and by the kabbalistic teachings of Isaac Luria among a community of Spanish exiles in Safed, northern Palestine, in the late sixteenth century. While the philosophical religion of the middle ages left great works of literature to future generations, it was essentially an elitist perspective on Judaism. Kabbalah continued as a living movement within Judaism, eventually shaping exoteric religion through its special rituals and ideological assumptions about the emanations with which God created the world, the nature of the soul, the task of humanity in the world, and the means by which the messianic redemption could be brought about. At both its scholarly and its popular level, Sefardi Jewry was transformed into an amalgam of rabbinical and kabbalistic Judaism, with its central images drawn from both the Bible and *Talmud*, and the *Zohar* and Lurianic corpus.

Although kabbalistic ideas spread among the Ashkenazim they never gained the almost complete dominance that they had among the Sefardim. Ashkenazi culture had never risen to the rarefied, and somewhat dangerous, heights of this synthesis with philosophy. It had its own traditions of pietism and mysticism, and its profound system of intellectual analysis of Talmudic and halakhic texts meant that it set as much store by scholastic knowledge as by religious or mystical intuition. The only major movement among the Ashkenazim almost entirely inspired by the Kabbalah was the Chasidic movement, which began in eastern Europe in the eighteenth century. This was originally a populist revolt against the scholarly elitism of the rabbinical leadership in Ukraine and southern Poland, emphasizing the worth of the ordinary, unlettered Jew who could not engage in the very demanding life of Talmudic studies. Chasidism adapted kabbalistic teachings about the divine emanations within all creation, and singled out the inner state of the worshipper, rather than his understanding of the tradition, as the primary value in the service of God. Since the humble and simple Jew could attain to a state of *devekut*, or inner cleaving to God, he could play a central role in the spiritual scheme of things despite his ignorance [19: III; 33: 107]. In the course of time even the Chasidic movement gave way to the predominant Ashkenazi tradition of the meticulous following of halakhic norms and the study of the *Torah* as the main ideal of the religious life. Although it maintained its separate identity, and formed self-contained communities around the Chasidic rabbi or *tzaddik*, Chasidism ceased to be guided by the kabbalistic impetus and became part of Ashkenazi orthodoxy.

Attitudes to Jewish Mysticism and Judaism

In the nineteenth century modernizing Jews associated with the early stages of Reform Judaism found the elements of kabbalistic Judaism among Ashkenazi culture to be the most recalcitrant to change, and to encapsulate the ethos of what they regarded as medieval superstition and magic. They had no sympathy for its symbolism and no understanding of its contribution to Jewish spirituality. To them it represented the worst form of the narrow-minded and obscurantist ghetto religion. It was only in the twentieth century that Jewish academic scholars shook off these prejudices and began to investigate the profound religious ideas which lay behind the magical and folkloristic elements of Kabbalah. The twentieth century has also seen a reassessment of Judaism by Christian scholars, whose picture had been clouded by the negative attitude of the New Testament to the Pharisees, the spiritual ancestors of rabbinical Judaism. It was customary for Christians to think of ancient Judaism as the religion of the Bible and of modern Judaism as the religion of the Jewish people in the times of Jesus. Behind all this was the view that Judaism had somehow ceased all development and growth during the first century CE, and that at that period Pharisaic religion was as hidebound and hypocritical as the Gospel authors depict it. Although one still comes across this view in Christian writings about Judaism, it has become less common as a result of the scholarly work of both Jewish and Christian academics [18]. The nature of rabbinical Judaism in the first few centuries CE has been extensively explored, and developments during the middle ages and up to modern times have been fully charted [4]. The great complexity of Judaism, made up as it is of a variety of different strands, makes over-facile comparisons between Christianity ('the religion of love, of compassion') and Judaism ('the religion of law, of divine judgement'), which were so common in a previous age, seem singularly unfounded. Within Judaism there are elements of both faith and works, both divine love and judgement, which have come to be recognized as constituting the very fabric of the religion.

The Basic Teachings of Judaism

At the centre of Jewish belief lies the faith in one God, who has made the heaven and the earth and all that they contain (*Genesis* 1: 2), and who took the Israelites out of their bondage in Egypt, revealed his divine teaching or Torah to them, and brought them into the Holy Land. This idea of God's redemptive acts in history has coloured the Jews' view of their situation since the biblical period, and proffers the hope that one day the Messiah, or anointed one of God, will come to usher in a messianic age when the Jews will be gathered once again to the Land of Israel. The idea that Israel is a people chosen by God is associated in Jewish consciousness with the revelation of the Pentateuchal teachings to Moses and the Israelites as they wandered in the wilderness after the Exodus from Egypt (c. fourteenth century BCE; the archetype for later Judaism of God's liberation of the Jews from bondage and suffering). An oft-repeated benediction of the liturgy runs: '. . . who has chosen us from all the nations and given us His Torah [i.e. teaching]. Blessed are you, O Lord, who gives the Torah' [2: 5, 71]. The Torah of God is not merely identical with the text of the *Pentateuch*, or even with the whole Hebrew Bible, which is also considered to be divinely inspired, but includes the oral teachings of Judaism, which are thought in essence to go back to the revelation to Moses. The fact that the religion has developed since the biblical period is not unrecognized, but the traditional Jewish view is that the developments all follow the principles of interpretation laid down in that period or are consequences of rabbinical enactments whose purpose was to make fences around biblical religion in order to strengthen it as circumstances changed.

Maimonides' analysis of the thirteen fundamentals of Jewish belief, although much criticized by subsequent scholars, has come to be accepted as something like the official creed of Judaism [13; 26: 3]. It has the following structure. The first five fundamental beliefs concern God: God is the creator of all that is; God is one; God is incorporeal; God is eternal; and God alone is to be worshipped. In the middle ages both popular piety and certain elements of the mystical tradition were less than happy about the belief in the corporeality of God being regarded as heretical. The popular imagination had always tended to take the biblical and rabbinical descriptions of God more or less literally, while the mystics developed a series of meditations on the gigantic dimensions of the 'body' of God, known as *Shiur Komah* [27: 63], which were not in line with Maimonides' more philosophical approach to the subject. Since then, however, the incorporeality of God has come to be accepted by all sections of Jewry as representing authentic Jewish doctrine, and the belief that God has physical dimensions or form as heretical [13: IV].

The next four fundamental beliefs concern revelation. They are: that God communicates to humanity through the medium of prophecy; that Moses was the greatest of the prophets to whom God communicated in the most direct manner; that the whole of the Torah (i.e. the *Pentateuch*) was revealed to Moses by God; and that the Torah will not be changed or supplanted by another revelation from God. The idea of prophetic revelation was seen as a basic element of Judaism in the past, and has continued to play a central role among both Orthodox and modernizing trends in contemporary Jewry, with the exception of the Reconstructionist movement (see p. 41). The other three doctrines have led to great controversy in the modern era, with Reform Judaism emphasizing the message of the purely prophetic books of the Bible more than the *Pentateuch* with its rituals; accepting the finding of biblical criticism that the Bible in general, and the *Pentateuch* in particular, are composite texts redacted over a long period of time by different editors; and firmly espousing the view that the biblical traditions have become outdated and must give way to modern religious sensitivities. All this is considered heretical by Orthodox thinkers and is regarded as undermining the very basis of Jewish religion as a response to the revelation of God. Against this, both Reform and Conservative Jews have argued that there is room for the idea of divine inspiration within the Jewish tradition, but that this inspiration is something less than the older idea of revelation by direct communication with the prophets. What is to be identified as divinely inspired and what as purely human within the Bible and Jewish tradition is very difficult to decide, and there has been no general agreement among the different modernizing movements within Judaism [13: x, xi; 30: 223; 22: 290].

The tenth and eleventh fundamental beliefs are in God's knowledge of the deeds of humankind and his concern about them; and that he rewards and punishes people for their good or evil ways. This is meant to negate the ideas that God has withdrawn from involvement in the day-to-day running of the world, and that there is no ultimate justice. The notion of a God who is interested in the doings of both nations and individuals, and who metes out the deserts of the righteous and the wicked, characterizes the salvation-history of the Bible and is the assumption behind the commandments and laws which presuppose that Jews are free to choose how they behave and are consequently responsible for their choices. Although some radical theologians have questioned these basic assumptions about God, particularly in the light of the killing of millions of Jews by the Nazis, which seems to make a mockery of the idea of a just world and a caring God, they have remained part and parcel of mainstream Jewish thought in the modern world.

The last two of Maimonides' fundamental beliefs concern the coming of the Messiah ('anointed one'), a descendant of the line of David, the famed ancient king of Israel, who will usher in the messianic age, and the resurrection of the dead. Both of these doctrines have been considered questionable by sections of Jewry since the beginning of Jewish emancipation in the late eighteenth century.

The idea of a personal Messiah of the Davidic line was considered too particularistic and the Reform movement has preferred to talk instead about a universalistic messianic age which will dawn for all humankind [13: 384; 22: 178]. The resurrection was likewise considered a doctrine out of tune with modern ideas about the body and soul, and has been generally replaced among non-Orthodox Jews with a doctrine of the continuing existence of the soul after death. Such a doctrine is also part of traditional Judaism, where it coexists with the belief in the resurrection, and even Maimonides himself in his works devotes far more space to it than to the more formal doctrine of the resurrection. Nevertheless, in an essay about the resurrection, which Maimonides wrote to answer critics who accused him of neglecting this doctrine in favour of that of the immortality of the soul, he makes it clear that Judaism believes in the resurrection even if little can be said in philosophical support of it. The reason why he discusses the soul's immortality at greater length in his works is that more can be said about it in rational terms. It does seem clear, however, that Maimonides holds the disembodied bliss of the soul to be the ultimate state to which the righteous will attain and the resurrection to be merely a stage, albeit a doctrinally supported stage, prior to this spiritual bliss. The daily prayers offered by Jews contain references both to the Messiah and to the resurrection, and the Reform prayer-book has changed these texts in line with its own interpretation of the doctrines.

Jewish Ritual

The Hebrew language is a very concrete mode of expression, preferring to use stories or images rather than more abstract concepts to express an idea. In a parallel way Judaism expresses its beliefs and attitudes more through its ritual nexus than through abstract doctrine. The earliest work of rabbinical Judaism, the *Mishnah* (end of second century CE), is concerned with agricultural laws, benedictions, festivals, the relationship between men and women, issues of civil and criminal law and damages, ritual purity, and the temple ritual and its sacrifices. In the discussion and formulation of such issues the rabbinical sages gave expression to the ethos of Judaism. The ordinary Jew today may know little about the sophisticated analysis of Jewish theology and doctrine which went on among philosophers in the middle ages, or about the speculations of the Kabbalists. In so far as he is a traditional Jew, however, his life will be structured around the halakhic rituals which shape his approach to God, to his fellows and to the world about him. For him they are the prime repository of his faith. This is why there is such a large gap between the traditionalist and the modernist. It is not the differences in doctrine alone which divide them, but, more important, the differences in lifestyle, liturgy, festival rituals, dietary laws, marriage and divorce procedures, etc. While variations in practice between one Jewish community and another do not substantially affect the overall religious orientation, the complete modernization of the *halakhah* by Reform Judaism and some sections of the Conservative movement present a ritual structure which on occasion is almost unrecognizable to the traditionalist, and seems to express a different set of beliefs and values. In what follows we shall describe some of the more important traditional rituals, it being understood that the extent of their observance varies from very strict to very light depending on the degree of modernization of the Jews practising them.

The Jewish Year

The Jewish ritual year is a lunar year of twelve months, approximately eleven days shorter than the solar year. Leap months are intercalated at regular intervals to prevent the lunar and solar years from diverging too far, since the festivals are tied to the agricultural seasons (see figure 1.5). The year begins in late September/early October with the New Year festival (Rosh Ha-Shanah), which for Jews is a period of divine judgement in which the fate of the world in the coming year ahead is determined. Jews repent of their sins, the ram's horn (*shofar*) is blown in the synagogue (see p. 31) summoning man to an awareness of his shortcomings, and the idea of God as the divine king is emphasized in the liturgy. For the two days of this festival Jews eat sweet foods as a symbol of the good year to come, and celebrate to show that they are confident of God's mercy [33: 173; 25: 145, 156]. The day after Rosh Ha-Shanah is a fast day (Tzom Gedaliah), lasting from dawn till nightfall, commemorating a tragic event in Israel's past.

Ten days after the New Year is the Day of Atonement (Yom Kippur), a twenty-five-hour fast day beginning at dusk and lasting till nightfall on the following day. All food and drink are forbidden; no leather shoes (a sign of comfort) may be worn; nor may sexual relations take place between husband and wife. Most of the time is spent in the synagogue, seeking atonement from God for past sins, reciting the account of the entrance of the High Priest into the Holy of Holies, the most sacred area of the ancient Temple, which took place on this day, and reading from the *Pentateuch* and the *Book of Jonah*. The day is the most solemn occasion of the Jewish year, and synagogues are usually crowded with worshippers, many of whom

The Jewish calendar

Month (secular equivalent)	Days and observances
TISHRI (Sept.–Oct.)	1 New Year; 2 New Year; 3 Fast of Gedaliah; 10 Day of Atonement; 15 Tabernacles; 16* Tabernacles; 17 Intermediate festival days; 21; 22 Shemini Atzeret; 23* Simchat Torah; 29; 30 New Moon
CHESHVAN (Oct.–Nov.)	1 New Moon; 29
KISLEV (Nov.–Dec.)	1 New Moon; 25 Chanukah; 26 Chanukah; 27 Chanukah; 28 Chanukah; 29 Chanukah; 30 Chanukah, New Moon
TEVET (Dec.–Jan.)	1 New Moon, Chanukah; 2 Chanukah; 10 Fast; 29
SHEVAT (Jan.–Feb.)	1 New Moon; 30 New Moon
ADAR (Feb.–Mar.)	1 New Moon; 13 Fast; 14 Purim; 15 Shushan Purim; 29
NISAN (Mar.–Apr.)	1 New Moon; 15 Passover; 16* Passover; 17 Intermediate festival days; 20; 21 Passover; 22* Passover; 30 New Moon
IYYAR (Apr.–May)	1 New Moon; 5 Israel Independence Day; 18 Lag-Ba Omer; 28 Jerusalem Day
SIVAN (May–June)	1 New Moon; 6 Pentecost; 7* Pentecost; 30 New Moon
TAMMUZ (June–July)	1 New Moon; 17 Fast; 29
AV (July–Aug.)	1 New Moon; 9 Fast; 30 New Moon
ELUL (Aug.–Sept.)	1 New Moon; 29

Legend:
☐ festival or feast
☐ *festival day in Diaspora

Figure 1.5 The Jewish calendar

would not attend at other times. The message of Yom Kippur is that God forgives the truly penitent sinner, but for sins committed against one's fellow man one must first try to win his forgiveness before turning to God in prayer [33: 178; 25: 151, 161].

Five days later comes the festival of Tabernacles (Sukkot), an eight-day festival in Israel and a nine-day one elsewhere because of uncertainty about when the lunar month began when this was fixed by the sighting of the new moon in the Land of Israel. The Jew lives for the duration of the festival in a little shack or booth (*sukkah*) covered with branches, remembering the time that his Israelite ancestors wandered through the wilderness after the Exodus from Egypt, protected only by the mercy of God. One of the most important rituals of Tabernacles is the taking of the four species, a palm branch, willows, myrtles and a special citrus fruit, the *etrog*, which are held together and shaken during the prayers. The first day (outside Israel the first two days) of the festival and the last day (or last two days) are festive days proper and no profane work may be done. During the intermediate days work is restricted but allowed. The last day (or last two days) are celebrated as the time of the Rejoicing of the Torah (Simchat Torah) when the Pentateuchal cycle of yearly readings is completed and begun again from the beginning of *Genesis*. This ceremony is accompanied by great rejoicing in the synagogue, with singing, dancing and alcohol [33: 180; 27: xix, xx].

Some two months later Chanukah, an eight-day feast of lights commemorating the victory of the Hasmonean priests over the non-Jewish Seleucid rulers of Palestine in the second century BCE, is celebrated. On each night an extra candle is lit in the eight-branched candelabrum or *menorah*, until on the last night all eight candles are burning. The lighting is accompanied by benedictions and the singing of a hymn, 'Maoz Tzur', recounting God's saving acts during the course of Jewish history. Chanukah is not a true festival, and normal work is allowed [33: 184; 25: xxiii, xxiv]. A week after the end of Chanukah there is another daytime fast remembering a tragic event which took place in the biblical period. This is known as Asarah Be-Tevet (the tenth of the month Tevet). The month of Tevet is followed by the month of Shevat.

The next month of the Jewish year, Adar, is the most joyous month, on the fourteenth of which the carnival-like festival of Purim falls. This commemorates the events recounted in the biblical book of *Esther* – how the Jews of the Persian empire were saved from the designs of the villainous Haman. The scroll of *Esther* is read publicly in the synagogue, once in the evening and once during the day (Jewish festivals always begin in the evening before the nominated day, at sunset). Whenever Haman's name is mentioned the congregation boo and stamp their feet. Jews often dress up in fancy dress on Purim; they send gifts of food to each other and give charity to

the poor. The Purim feast is usually held in the afternoon, and Jews
are encouraged to drink alcohol to the point when they cannot distinguish between 'blessed be Mordecai' (one of the heroes of the
story) and 'cursed be Haman', signifying that divine help transcends
the normal distinctions of human understanding [33: 186; 25: XXVII,
XXVIII].

A month after Purim is the seven-day (eight outside Israel) festival of Passover (Pesach). This festival must always fall in the spring,
and commemorates the time of the Exodus of the Israelites from
Egypt. No leavened bread may be eaten during the festival and the
Jewish house is given a thorough spring-clean to remove all traces of
leaven. The staple food eaten during Passover is flat wafers of
unleavened bread (*matzah*). On the first night (outside Israel, on the
first two nights) a ritual family meal, known as the Seder, is held.
During the meal the story of the Exodus is read from a special
Haggadah text, four cups of wine are drunk, and bitter herbs symbolizing the suffering of the Israelite slaves in Egypt are eaten, as are
other ritual foods including unleavened bread. The Seder is maintained even among Jews who do not keep up other Jewish traditions,
for apart from its purely religious significance as a celebration of
God's redemption it is intimately associated with family ties, which
are extremely important for Jews [27: VII, IX].

Seven weeks after the second day of Passover the one-day (or
two-day) festival of Pentecost (Shavuot) falls. The period between
Passover and Pentecost is one of semi-mourning, and no weddings
take place. Shavuot is celebrated as the time when the Ten
Commandments were given to Moses on Mount Sinai, and the
story of the theophany on Sinai is read in the synagogue. Jews customarily stay up all night on the first night of Pentecost studying the
Torah, as if to show that they are ready to receive the word of God
once more [33: 193; 25: X]. In the modern period a number of new
festivals have been introduced in the period between Passover and
Pentecost, associated with the modern state of Israel (Israel
Independence Day and Jerusalem Day) and with the Nazi
Holocaust (Holocaust Remembrance Day). As yet these have
gained only partial acceptance as part of the Jewish ritual year.

Just over five weeks after Pentecost there is a three-week period of
intense mourning remembering the events surrounding the destruction of the First and Second Jerusalem Temples in the sixth century
BCE and the first century CE respectively. This period begins with a
daytime fast (Shivah Asar Be-Tammuz) and ends with a twenty-
five-hour fast (Tisha Be-Av), during which no leather shoes may be
worn and Jews do not sit on normal chairs but on the ground or on
low stools. Weddings are not allowed for these three weeks, and
haircuts, the eating of meat and the drinking of wine are restricted –
customs about these matters varying between different communities

[33: 194; 25: x]. The mourning, though focused upon the destruction of the Second Temple, also symbolizes the sufferings experienced in the exile during the centuries that followed. The memory of what happened thousands of years ago is, therefore, at the same time a living memory of what has been happening since. The Jewish ritual year ends with the lunar month of Elul, falling around September, which is a period of preparation and repentance leading up to the New Year festival.

Aside from the yearly cycle there is a minor festival falling at the beginning of each month (Rosh Chodesh) and, more important, there is the weekly Sabbath (Shabbat), which begins each Friday evening at sunset and lasts till nightfall on Saturday. The Sabbath is a day of complete rest, and even those types of work which are allowed on festivals (associated with cooking) are forbidden. As with other festivals, there is a special liturgy for the Sabbath, and the day is sanctified over a cup of wine (*kiddush*). Apart from attendance at the synagogue for prayers and the weekly reading from the *Pentateuch*, much of the day is spent in the family circle. On Friday night the mother lights candles before the Sabbath begins, and on his return from synagogue the father blesses his children before reciting *kiddush* and making the blessing over two loaves of the special bread (*challah*). During the three Sabbath meals hymns are sung at the table, and the best food is served. At the conclusion of the Sabbath a prayer (*havdalah*) is recited over a cup of wine, incense, and a candle flame [33: 169; 25: IV].

Rites of Passage

A child is considered a Jew if it is born of a Jewish mother; whether or not the father is Jewish is of no consequence for the religious status of the child, according to tradition. A male child is circumcised on the eighth day after its birth, if it is healthy, and is then given a Hebrew name. Circumcision, representing the entrance of the child into the covenant which God made with Abraham and his descendants, is accompanied by a celebratory meal. Up to the age of twelve for a girl, and thirteen for a boy, a child is regarded as a minor. He or she will be gradually instructed in the keeping of Jewish rituals, will be taught Hebrew and will learn to translate passages from the Bible and the prayer-book. At the age of twelve or thirteen the child is regarded as an adult who must keep the halakhic rules in their entirety. Its passage to maturity is marked by a Bar Mitzvah ceremony for a boy, and a Bat Mitzvah ceremony for a girl. The Bar Mitzvah consists of being called up in synagogue to read from the *Torah* scroll or the weekly portion from the *Prophets*. This is followed by an often elaborate party to which relatives and friends are invited. The Bat Mitzvah is a relative newcomer to the Jewish scene, having been introduced in modern times to give the girl more of a role in Jewish public life. It usually consists of a ceremony in which several girls participate together, and is more common in Reform communities than in Orthodox ones [33: VIII].

Marriage is a high point in the life of a Jew, for it signifies the setting up of a new family – the family being the basic unit of Jewish ritual. Judaism does not allow marriage with a non-Jewish spouse, and intermarriage between a Jew and a Gentile cannot be performed in a synagogue. Intermarriage is generally regarded as a tragedy for the parents and family of the Jewish partner, although it is an increasingly frequent occurrence in the modern Western world. The desire of a non-Jewish partner to be accepted by the family and community of the Jewish partner is one of the main reasons for the conversion of Gentiles to Judaism today, even though it is not considered to be a particularly good reason for conversion by the religious authorities.

Marriage usually takes place under a decorated canopy in the synagogue, with a minority of Ashkenazi Jews preferring the more traditional setting of marriage under a canopy in the open air. It is not necessary for a rabbi to perform the ceremony; any layman can do so in the presence of at least two witnesses. It has become customary for the rabbi, who is not a priest but an expert on *halakhah*, to officiate together with the synagogue cantor and to preach a short sermon containing words of encouragement to the couple. The ceremony itself consists of various benedictions over glasses of wine, the giving of a ring by the groom to the bride, the reading of the wedding document, and the breaking of a glass indicating, at the time of greatest joy, a sense of sadness at the destruction of Jerusalem [33: 150]. Marriage is considered a desirable condition for every Jew, since there is a biblical commandment, or *mitzvah*, to have children. Jews are generally discouraged from remaining single by choice, and religious literature from the biblical story of the first human couple, Adam and Eve, onwards depicts the unmarried individual as an incomplete person. If there is a breakdown of the marriage relationship a religious divorce procedure is necessary before either party is allowed to remarry, civil divorce not being recognized as a means of dissolving the marital state.

Great store is set in Judaism by respect for the aged. Children have a duty to look after their parents; indeed, the honouring of parents is one of the Ten Commandments. In established Jewish communities today old-age homes are often large and well endowed, providing a Jewish atmosphere in which people may spend the twilight of their lives. After death, which is defined in Judaism by the cessation of respiration, burial must take place immediately out of respect for the departed. Orthodox Jews do not practise cremation, and burial has to take place in consecrated ground, which means that Jews have their own cemeteries. It is customary to throw a small amount of earth from the Land of Israel on to the coffin, and some Jews who die in the diaspora (i.e. in the lands of the Jewish dispersion) are even taken to be buried in the Holy Land, particularly in Jerusalem. All this is an affirmation of the belief in the resurrection, which it is thought will take place essentially in the Land of Israel. According to a popular Jewish belief, those who die outside of Israel will have to roll over in subterranean caverns till they reach the Holy Land to be resurrected there. Next of kin have to undergo an intense period of official mourning for the first week after burial. They sit at home on low stools, with their garments rent, and do not wear leather shoes. People come to conduct prayer services in the mourners' house and to comfort them. The mourning then gradually decreases in intensity, depending on the closeness to the dead relative, allowing the mourner eventually to resume his or her normal place in the community. The ritualized mourning procedure is intended to permit the mourner to express grief, but at the same time to discourage him or her from taking the sense of loss to extremes [33: 163].

The Synagogue

The proto-synagogue began in the sixth century BCE, after the First Temple was destroyed, when many Jews were deported in captivity to Babylonia. Its role then was as a house of assembly. It developed markedly after the destruction of the Second Temple in 70 CE, eventually becoming the centre for community prayers, for the reading of a section from the *Pentateuch* on Mondays, Thursdays, Saturdays and on festivals, and for instruction in Jewish teachings. Both the Christian church and the Islamic mosque were modelled after the synagogue prototype. Until the modern period the synagogue was overshadowed by the Jewish home, which was the primary locus of ritual. In the last two centuries, however, with the growing secularization of the home, the synagogue has become more important as the place where Jewish life finds its full expression [33: 197].

The influence of the non-Jewish environment is apparent in the architecture of the synagogue building, and even in some cases in the internal layout. After Jews emerged from the medieval ghetto they looked upon the European church as a model for synagogue reform. The traditional platform at the centre of the synagogue, from which the *Torah* scroll was read, was moved up to the front, so that the congregation became more of an audience witnessing the religious activities of the rabbi and cantor. The older style of synagogue, still found in many Orthodox communities, was built on the assumption of the equal participation of all worshippers. In the newer-style synagogues the religious functionaries have adopted more of a priestly role.

When praying, Jews face towards Jerusalem, and the ark of the synagogue (a type of cupboard often set behind a curtain) in which the *Torah* scrolls are kept is set in the Jerusalem-facing wall, making it the focus of prayer. The liturgy consists of three basic prayers, to be said in the morning, the afternoon and the evening. On Sabbaths and festivals there are variations in the liturgy reflecting the special character of the day, and the services are generally much longer than on weekdays [12: VII, x]. A typical Saturday morning service including a sermon would last between two and a half and three hours, while even the longest weekday morning service takes less than an hour. Each service is built round an *amidah* (literally 'standing') prayer which consists of blessings, requests and thanksgivings. On Sabbaths and festivals the requests are replaced by special prayers for the occasion, and an additional *amidah* is also recited, modelled on the additional sacrifices brought in Temple times. The other main component of the morning and evening services is the Shema (*Deuteronomy* 6: 4–9; 11: 13–21; *Numbers* 15: 37–41), which opens with the affirmation of faith: 'Hear O Israel, the Lord is our God, the Lord is One.' The rest of the liturgy consists of benedictions, psalms, hymns and selections from the Bible. Prayers are led by the cantor or any competent layman, whose purpose is to keep the pace of prayer at a regular tempo and to recite those portions of the liturgy said when there is a quorum (*minyan*) of ten adult males [33: 209].

The traditional synagogue is run entirely by men; the women do not play a public role, lead the prayers, read from the *Torah* scroll, preach or indeed sit with the men in the main body of the building (see figure 1.6). They will usually occupy a ladies' gallery, or sit downstairs behind a partition. Reform and Conservative synagogues (known as temples in the United States) have mixed seating and involve the female worshippers to a far greater extent than Orthodox ones. Women have even been ordained as rabbis in a number of Reform communities. Another difference between traditional and Reform synagogues relates to the covering of the head during prayer. In all Orthodox and Conservative synagogues the male congregants will wear either a hat or a skull-cap during the service, and many Orthodox Jews keep their heads covered even at home or at work as a sign of respect for God in whose presence man always is. Orthodox married women will also cover their hair in synagogue with a wig, hat or scarf, some even maintaining the covering at other times as well. In many Reform congregations, particularly in the United States, the covering of the head in synagogue is not mandatory.

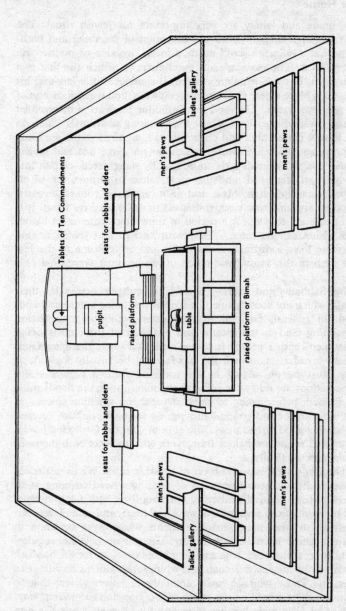

Figure 1.6 Plan of a typical synagogue

ladies' gallery

men's pews

Tablets of Ten Commandments

seats for rabbis and elders

pulpit

raised platform

table

raised platform or Bimah

seats for rabbis and elders

men's pews

ladies' gallery

men's pews

The Home

The home and family are very important for Jewish ritual. The doorpost of each door, with the exception of the toilet and bathroom, has a *mezuzah* scroll inside a metal, wooden or plastic case affixed to it. The *mezuzah* is a parchment on which the first two paragraphs of the Shema are written. It signifies to the Jew that his home is a place where God's presence dwells, and it reminds him of his religious duties. The food the Orthodox Jew eats is determined by the Jewish dietary laws. These forbid eating all animals which do not have a cloven hoof and chew the cud, all birds which are birds of prey, and all sea creatures which do not have fins and scales. *Kosher* (i.e. fit) animals have to be ritually slaughtered, certain forbidden parts removed, and the meat salted to remove the blood before it can be eaten. Meat and milk cannot be cooked or eaten together, and different kitchen utensils must be used for them. It is also necessary to wait for a period of time after eating meat before milk dishes can be eaten. The Jewish kitchen and Jewish cuisine therefore have a distinctive character, and bring home to the Jew that even in this most basic mode of life he must serve God [33: XII].

On Sabbaths and festivals the family gather together for their meals, which are accompanied by hymns and grace before and after food. In general, no food may be eaten without a benediction acclaiming God as the creator and producer of the objects being consumed, and a prayer is to be said afterwards thanking God. Before bread is consumed the hands must be ritually washed, as they must be on arising in the morning from a night's sleep. Benedictions are said after going to the toilet, when the hands must be washed, before going to sleep at night, on smelling spices, on hearing thunder and seeing lightning, on seeing a rainbow, or even on hearing good or bad news. Life at home, for the Orthodox Jew, is structured round a religious framework which affects both the individual and the family.

The Jew's dress is also subject to halakhic rules. We have already mentioned the custom for males of wearing a head covering at all times and for married women of covering their hair. Clothes must not be woven from a mixture of wool and linen, and some Jews even continue to wear the style of garments which were common in Europe before Jewish emancipation. There is no halakhic requirement to wear the black hats and long black coats, or for the Sabbath the fur-rimmed caps, silk coats and white socks which Chasidic Jews dress in. Those who do insist upon them, however, feel that to abandon them would be too much of a concession to modern ways [19: XXIV]. The male Jew has to wear a four-cornered vest-like garment with strings attached to each corner. This is a miniature version of the fringed shawl (*tallit*) worn during morning prayers, which on weekday mornings accompanies the arm and head phylacteries (*tefillin*). Phylacteries consist of leather boxes, painted black, held in place by black leather straps. In the boxes are scrolls of parchment with various passages from the *Pentateuch* inscribed on them. These specifically ritual items of apparel are based on biblical commandments, but their effect on the Jew is to remind him that his life and activities must be oriented to God and to the fulfilment of the *mitzvot*.

Popular or Folk Religion

Most of our knowledge about Judaism in the past comes from religious literature which reflects the beliefs and attitudes of its authors, an intellectual elite. There is considerable evidence, however, concerning the beliefs and outlook of the ordinary, unlettered Jew in the pre-modern period. Some of this is contained in rabbinical literature itself, having been taken over and developed from oral motifs as a means of exemplifying religious truths and values. Many of the collections of *midrashim*, or homiletic commentaries on the Bible, edited during the first millennium of the Christian era, are replete with folkloristic themes [10]. To later readers the midrashic tales, originally meant to clothe an abstract idea or ethical principle, represented the literal truth about historical events. Angels, demons, magical powers, ascents to heaven, wise animals and birds, and all the other features of folklore were thus sanctioned as part of the Jewish tradition, and were used for oral transmission and embellishment. Jewish mystical texts also reflect this pattern. They use images from popular religion to symbolize mystical doctrine, and because of the awe in which kabbalistic teachings were held by ordinary Jews many of these images were accepted literally in popular belief [27: vi]. This is exemplified by the kabbalistic practice of making a *golem* or artificial man. For the mystics this was essentially a spiritual exercise, being a certain stage in the kabbalist's inner development [28: v]. For the wider Jewish populace the making of a *golem* was a real act of magic power, and many legends circulated about wonder-working mystics and the doings of the *golems* they had created [32: 84]. The philosopher-theologians of the middle ages fought against the excesses of the popular imagination, their belief in semi-mythological beings, their literal approach both to the Bible and to rabbinical literature. They saw Jewish monotheism being qualified by the belief in angels and demons, by an interest in magic rather than in prayer and the service of God.

Over the centuries the attempts of the medieval philosophers bore fruit, and limited the extent to which folk religion developed. However, even the impact of the European Enlightenment, which has deeply affected Jews since the early nineteenth century, did not quite eradicate the belief in and practice of magic and superstition. These continued to exist side by side with the official religion in which the worship of the one, true God was taught. From early rabbinical literature onwards we find a divergence in attitude towards the *mitzvot*, some rabbis seeing the commandments as having only one purpose, i.e. enabling man to refine himself in the service of God, while other rabbis understood them as means for affecting the spiritual/physical condition of man, the environment, and even the state of higher levels of reality. The way halakhic rules were finalized often reflected the first interpretation of the *mitzvot*, and this is also the view of them that appears in medieval philosophical literature. Under kabbalistic influence the second interpretation gradually dominated the halakhic outlook, and acted as a conserving force, since any changes in ritual had to contend with the belief that the ritual was the means of maintaining harmony in the universe and therefore was sacrosanct [28: IV]. The popular approach to the *mitzvot* also invariably preferred the view of ritual in which it is operative as a quasi-magical force, and in folk religion halakhically prescribed ritual and purely magical practices coexist and are interwoven. Some newly introduced rituals were severely attacked by scholars, who believed them to be magical practices infiltrating the halakhic nexus. A case in point is the custom of slaughtering a chicken just before the Day of Atonement. The thirteenth-century Spanish talmudist, Rabbi Solomon ibn Adret, fought to eradicate this custom in his city on the grounds that it was a forbidden magical practice. A later scholar, the sixteenth-century author of the main halakhic code, the *Shulchan Arukh*, also sought to discourage this custom. Nevertheless it won widespread popular approval and the support of other rabbis, and eventually was taken up by standard works on Jewish ritual.

Magical practices were widely used by unlettered Jews for a variety of purposes. Many magical prescriptions, known as *segullot*, circulated to deal with ill health, barrenness, lack of love between a man and a woman, the evil eye, burglary, a bad memory, the need to discover whether a missing relative was still alive, witches' spells against people, children who cry continually, astrological forces, protection against bullets, difficult childbirth, unsuccessful business dealings, fire, storms at sea, imprisonment, drunkenness, etc. [10: IX, X]. Some of these belong to the sphere of folk medicine, while others involve purely magical remedies [36: VIII]. The purveyors of this magic, known as *baalei shem* (singular *baal shem*), were itinerant wonder-workers catering for a clientele of mostly poor, semi-literate

Jews. The founder of the Chasidic movement, R. Israel ben Eliezer (1700–60), began his career as a wonder-working faith-healer, hence his title Israel Baal Shem Tov [19: III]. Another semi-magical practice, found among both Ashkenazi Jews in eastern Europe and Sefardi-oriental Jews in Islamic lands, involved visiting the graves of dead holy men. A request might be written on a piece of paper and deposited inside the tomb on the site of the burial, or candles burnt. Sometimes the tomb was measured out in coloured string or candle wick. The idea behind these and similar practices was that the spirit of the deceased should intercede on behalf of the visitor, or that being in the mere presence of the mortal remains of such a saintly and powerful person would be of benefit. Criticism was directed against such practices by the rabbinical leadership, but ultimately they were unable to prevent Jews seeking out the help of the dead, even if there were ample warnings against such behaviour in early Jewish literature.

In the modern period people's exposure to scientific assumptions about the world and to secular education has meant that many of the magical procedures of the past are no longer practised. Ashkenazi Jews who still preserve the culture of the pre-modern ghetto, and who consciously reject some of the advances in the human outlook on the world, are likely to continue folk religion. This is even more true of the older generation of Sefardi-oriental Jews in Israel who have not received a modern education. For such Jews the evil eye, the machinations of demons, and the need for protective amulets against miscarriage and misfortune are part of the very reality of the world they inhabit. Magic fills the gap between their belief in God who has created heaven and earth and demands of the Jew that he fulfil the Commandments, and their immediate experience of life. There is no essential conflict between their monotheistic theology and their belief that the space between man and God is populated by a host of lesser powers at work.

Modern Movements

The nineteenth and twentieth centuries have seen some of the greatest changes in Judaism since it underwent its dramatic transformation after the destruction of the Second Temple in 70 CE. In the latter part of the eighteenth century Jews in Germany and in France began to move outside the confines of their cultural ghetto and to participate in the intellectual life of Europe. Their emancipation and acceptance as citizens, rather than as aliens, was still to come, but some managed to surmount the obstacles in the path of the Jew and attained a measure of equality with their Christian fellow country-men. One of these was Moses Mendelssohn (1729–86), who as a young boy moved on his own to Berlin, taught himself Latin, European languages and other secular subjects, and attained con-siderable renown as a German writer and philosopher. Though he encountered anti-Semitism among some of his Christian contacts, and suspicion among his less modernizing co-religionists, he believed that a new age was dawning for the Jews. He encouraged them to learn German and cease using their Yiddish dialect. He urged them to study secular subjects, acquire a trade, and prepare themselves to become part of the wider community. At the same time, however, he wanted them to preserve their Jewish traditions and himself remained an Orthodox Jew. In succeeding generations many of those who followed Mendelssohn's lead went beyond their mentor's intentions. They found that the easiest method of accep-tance into Christian society was to undergo baptism and shed their Jewish identity. The gap between Mendelssohn's view of Judaism and the somewhat liberal Christianity of their contemporaries did not seem large enough to warrant maintaining separate Jewish exis-tence with all its inherent problems [33: 71; 22: III; 23: 46; 14: 255].

Some Jews in the post-Mendelssohn era did not wish to lose their identity as Jews, but could not identify with the ghetto-type Judaism of the majority of their co-religionists. They could not believe in all of the teachings of traditional Judaism, nor did they feel comfortable with aspects of synagogue ritual. They began, in their different ways, to introduce changes which were the forerunners of those associated with the later movement known as Reform Judaism. The areas of concern were the continued use of Hebrew rather than German in services; the references in the liturgy to the return of the Jews to the Holy Land in the messianic age, which implied that Jews could not be regarded as loyal citizens of their country of residence; their preference for the use of an organ and choir in synagogue, which was not common practice in traditional communities; and the need for a regular sermon in the vernacular [22: 156].

During the first few decades of the nineteenth century new-style synagogues, known as temples, spread both in Germany and in other European countries. Their practices were opposed by the Orthodox rabbis, and both sides appealed for support to the govern-ment authorities. Gradually the reforming movement was taken over by intellectuals who began to formulate its ideological plat-form. The main assumption of this ideology was that Judaism was a historical religion developing through time, and that it had to change in line with the new conditions it was facing. A number of conferences of reforming rabbis were called in the 1840s at which there was some disagreement between those who favoured radical change, since Judaism was essentially a religion of ethical monotheism to which ritual was extraneous, and those who wished to preserve elements of the tradition. The conferences tried to dissociate themselves from those reforming movements which sought to abolish all ritual expression, but nevertheless took up a radical stance on some issues which alienated the moderates. In general the history of Reform Judaism in Germany was one of modified traditionalism, with only a small number of communities adopting a radical approach to the *mitzvot*. The same was true of Reform Judaism in Britain, which began in the 1840s. It was only with the beginning of Liberal Judaism in Britain, in the early twentieth century, that the more extreme reforming position was institutionalized [29: 161]. In the US, by contrast, the radical tendency predominated in Reform Judaism from the 1880s.

Underlying Reform Judaism was the belief that a new age of tolerance was dawning for mankind, and that Jews would be accepted by the Christian world as equals. This optimism has gradually diminished, particularly in the light of Nazi atrocities and the support they had from European anti-Semitic movements. Today Reform Judaism is strongly Zionist in orientation, whereas it was once very hostile to nationalistic elements in Judaism. There is also a much more positive approach to Jewish ritual and to more traditional themes of Jewish theology among Reform Jews in the Western world. The antagonism between Orthodoxy and Reform, which characterized the early history of the latter movement, is still very much a feature of their relationship today.

An offshoot of the more traditionalist branch of movements for reform in Judaism was the Conservative movement in the US. This was begun in the mid-nineteenth century by European Jews who wanted to modify old-style Orthodoxy in the face of the realities of American life. They did not approve of Reform Judaism, and took as their model the attitudes of the European Historical school which affirmed the validity of the Jewish past as well as the need for Jews to modernize [22: VIII, XIII]. After a slow start Conservativism began to expand at the end of the nineteenth century when the radicalness of the Reform platform made any attempt at compromise with official American Reform impossible. Conservative Judaism set up its own training college for rabbis, its own synagogue and rabbinical organizations. Today it is the biggest organized stream within North American Jewry, with branches throughout the US and Canada [30: 254]. It claims to be the authentic continuation of the rabbinical Judaism of the pre-modern period, but the many changes it has introduced into Jewish ritual and the doctrinal position of some of its proponents have led Orthodox rabbis to outright condemnation of its institutions. During the 1920s Mordecai Kaplan, a member of staff of the Conservative rabbinical seminary, developed a new, more naturalistic theology of Judaism which eventually led to the

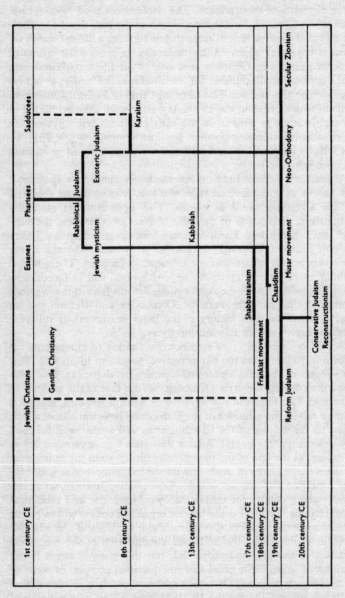

Figure 1.7 Jewish sects and movements

founding of the Reconstructionist movement as a breakaway from Conservative Judaism. Reconstructionism has adopted a more radical stance towards changes in ritual and doctrine, but its appeal has mostly been to intellectuals and it has not won a large following [33: 219; 30: 241; 23: 535]. Conservativism has found its main support among traditionally minded reformers or modernist traditionalists. Its success in North America is due, in part, to the rejection of traditional mores by Reform Judaism there. In Britain, by contrast, it has had very limited success owing both to the greater moderation of British Reform and to the nature of Orthodoxy organized into the United Synagogue in London. Many of the United Synagogue communities are very modernist in outlook, and in an American context would be considered Conservative. In Britain, however, they affiliate to an Orthodox organization.

The general response of Orthodoxy to reforms was to affirm the divine basis of Judaism and to deny that man could simply change God's teaching at his convenience. In practice, however, two different approaches were taken. Many of the leading rabbis in eastern Europe closed ranks against any changes in Jewish life, even of a minor nature, since they suspected change to be a hallmark of Reform. Hungarian Orthodoxy took a lead in this position, but it was equally strong among Chasidic groups who forbade their members to study secular subjects or even to change their style of dress. The other response was to accept modernity and the culture of European Enlightenment, but to maintain the rituals and doctrines of traditional Judaism. The most important genre of this type of synthesis was the movement of German Neo-Orthodoxy founded in Frankfurt by S. R. Hirsch. In opposition to those who saw Judaism as a historically evolving religion, Hirsch argued that it was a system of symbols, encapsulated in ritual, and that these symbols were equally valid in each age [33: 221; 22: ix].

The varied religious responses to Jewish emancipation were not felt to be satisfactory by many of the more assimilated Jews in the late nineteenth century. The problem as they saw it was that anti-Semitism was endemic in the Christian culture of Europe, and that Jews would not be accepted as equals however much they shed their Jewish identity. Under the influence of nationalist movements in central Europe Jewish thinkers started to advocate Jewish national revival, seeing the Jews not as a religious entity but as an ethnic group whose members shared historical memory and a common culture. This contrasted markedly with the Reform view that Jews were Germans, French or Britons of the Mosaic faith. Most of the nationalists, later known as Zionists, were completely secular in their outlook. They wished to see Jews established in their own homeland where they would at least be free from anti-Semitic prejudice. Jews would then be able to develop like any other nation [22:

305; 23: XIII]. The most important Zionist leader was Theodor Herzl (1860–1904), who is known as the founder of Zionism as a political movement. Herzl came to believe in Jewish nationalism after his experiences of French anti-Semitism during the notorious Dreyfus Affair in Paris in the 1890s, when a Jewish captain in the French army was falsely accused of spying. If France, the most highly cultured European country, could be the seat of such virulent anti-Jewish feeling then the idea that one day Jews would be accepted as equal members of Christian society was merely a pipe-dream. Herzl called together the various Zionist groups to attend the first Zionist congress in 1897, and spent the rest of his short life in seeking the backing of a major power for his goal of a Jewish homeland [11: III]. During the early twentieth century the Zionist movement grew, and groups of Jews went to resettle Palestine, the ancient homeland of the Jewish people, which was part of the Turkish empire and subsequently controlled by Britain under a mandate from the League of Nations. The Nazi-inspired massacres of 6 million Jewish civilians during the Second World War convinced many of the remaining Jews that a Jewish state was an absolute necessity. It also stimulated the United Nations to recognize the State of Israel, which was set up on 14 May 1948. The Arab countries of the Middle East were strongly opposed both to the existence of a non-Arab state in the centre of what they saw as essentially Arab territory, and to the mass immigration of Jews from all over the world to Israel [23: 559]. They fought a number of wars, including those of 1967 and 1973, with the aim of eliminating Israel and driving out the Jewish population. Although they had little purely military success the wars, and the political pressure backed up by the power of Arab oil, have meant that Israel has found itself constantly threatened since its inception. There has been considerable pressure on Israel to agree to the setting up of a Palestinian state in areas occupied by the Israelis since the Six-Day War (1967), but the Israeli government has not as yet agreed to such a solution to the problems of the area, despite the current peace process.

The effect of all this on world Jewry has been profound. The shock of the Nazi Holocaust has made Jews much more aware of their insecurity and the depths of prejudice against them. Support for Zionism is strong, and for many Jews in the West Zionism has filled the gap in their sense of Jewish identity left by the diminishing of purely religious belief and rituals. Israel's isolation and the Arab-inspired resolution of the United Nations equating Zionism with racism have convinced many Jews that anti-Semitic prejudice did not end with the fall of the Hitler regime. It seems to be a permanent feature of the Gentile world's relationship to the Jew, with the State of Israel the only place where Jews can live without fear that

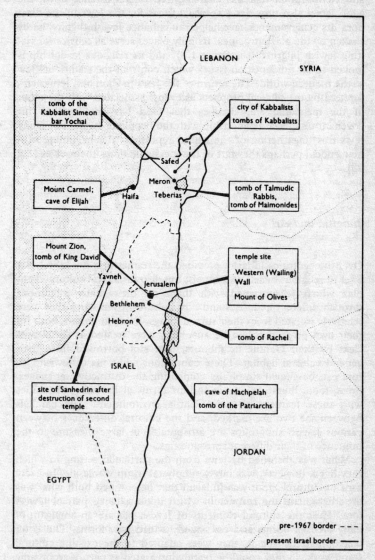

Figure 1.8 *Jewish holy sites in Eretz Israel ('the land of Israel')*

their Jewishness may one day lead to a resurgence of the alienation
and victimization that has characterized their existence down the
ages. Israel also provides a spiritual focus for the Jews in the diaspora. Its achievements have helped to enhance Jewish dignity, badly
shaken by the Nazi atrocities. Its holy places serve as centres for visiting Jewish pilgrims (see figure 1.8), and its religious leadership is
looked to for guidance on issues which confront the traditional Jew
in the modern world. The return of the Jews to Zion and Jerusalem,
foretold by the biblical prophets as events associated with the onset
of the messianic era, signifies that God has not forsaken his
covenant or special relationship with the people of Israel. For many
Jews this 'ingathering of the exiles' represents the beginning of a
new epoch, perhaps the start of the messianic times themselves [33:
90].

Judaism and Art

Over the centuries Judaism provided the framework, not merely for
a set of religious beliefs and rituals, but also for a total cultural complex which Jews carried with them on their many migrations
through different countries and host cultures. Even when they were
relatively isolated from their surroundings, living in ghettos both for
their own protection and because they were treated as social out-
casts by their Gentile neighbours, they still borrowed from their
general cultural habitat. These continuous additions to Jewish culture can be shown simply by comparing the distinctive languages,
dress, food, literature, music and art forms of Jewish communities
with these features in their Gentile environment. The parallels
between the two are marked, and the cultural differences between
various Jewish subgroups are attributable in large measure to the
influence of their different surroundings.

What was absorbed by Jews from the particular setting in which
they lived, however, was rarely simply taken up wholesale. In every
area of cultural life it was Judaism that determined both what was
absorbable and the manner in which it came to be part of Jewish
lore. Thus the cultural elements of Jewish life are an amalgam of
early Hebraic forms and continually added new forms. The latter
were Judaized, that is, they were adapted to the existing cultural
framework, so they could be readily integrated as part of an organic
whole [34: 16, 18].

Basic to the expression of Jewish artistic creativity, in its most
general sense, is the limited place of the visual in Judaism. The biblical and post-biblical antagonism to representative art, particularly

three-dimensional forms, emerges from the need to avoid idolatry, i.e. the association of any objects or representations with God himself [13: IV]. Although in the synagogue art of the early Christian period biblical scenes feature on wall paintings and on mosaics, with a large representational element of human and animal motifs, the opposition to such art was widespread both prior to and during this period. Josephus, the first-century CE Jewish historian, reports popular unrest at Roman attempts to set up figures or military insignia in Jerusalem. Early rabbinical works contain views prohibiting art even if used for purely decorative purposes, since this is an extension of the biblical injunction, contained in the Decalogue (*Exodus* 20: 4–5), not to make a graven image. In the middle ages these iconoclastic tendencies characterize much of rabbinical thought, and the revulsion at representational art was strengthened by the influence of Islamic views on the subject. Jews also clearly felt the need to distance themselves from the icons, statues and paintings of the Christian churches, which were felt to be idolatrous. This is not to say that visual art had no form of expression among Jews of the premodern period, but rather that it was severely limited. An important outlet for visual art was in the shaping of artefacts for ritual purposes, often in precious or semi-precious metals (candelabra, spice boxes, marriage rings, as well as synagogue furnishings and tapestries, scribal arts, the illumination of manuscripts, etc.). The many rituals of Judaism in the home and the synagogue, the festivals of the Jewish year, and the central place played by religious texts of all types allowed Jewish craftsmen, and Jewish patrons employing non-Jewish craftsmen, to develop distinctive art forms.

The main cultural expression of Jewish creativity was, however, not in visual art but through musical, oral and literary forms. There was less danger of idolatry in the literary and story-telling imagination, and though the religious authorities were wary of heretical ideas finding their way into untrammelled flights of fancy, they had much less control over the dissemination of this cultural form than over visual art. The poetry, hymns and aggadic (legendary) stories, and the great flowering of mystical speculation as well as the many fables of Jewish folklore, are all expressions of this emphasis on non-visual creativity [32: II]. Were the images of the Kabbalah, with its interpretation of the ten aspects of the Godhead as mother and father, son and daughter, lover and beloved, and its understanding of all reality, both human and divine, as made up out of male and female elements, to have found iconographic expression they would have posed a major problem for Jewish monotheism. As it was they remained in oral forms and, after overcoming some opposition to their wider dissemination, also in literary forms. Jewish music has characteristically been expressed in liturgical form, both in the synagogue and in the home. Hymn singing, the chanting of prayers and the reading of Hebrew scripture to a fixed musical notation have long been a basic part of Jewish life. On more joyous occasions, such as family celebrations or festivals, dancing and instrumental music (e.g. for weddings) are quite common, although the different Jewish communities were influenced by the non-Jewish musical forms of their host cultures.

The cultural preference in Judaism for the primacy of the word (whether sung, spoken or written) over the visual object has had a more general effect on Jews, in both the pre-modern and modern periods. Jewish communities have frequently been uprooted from their areas of settlement and been forced to move across provincial or national boundaries to re-establish themselves once more in a new environment. Such moves were often accompanied by anti-Jewish turmoil, in which the refugees managed to salvage little of the material possessions which they owned in their old locale. Migrations and expulsions would normally completely disrupt the cultural life of the community because of the loss of the synagogues and of the works of art. The fact that Jews had mainly a musical, oral and literary culture enabled them to survive and to carry the main forms of their culture from place to place. In the modern world the cultural bias of Judaism, favouring verbal expression, has influenced Jews even far removed from their religious roots to find creative outlets in theatre, novels, films, poetry, singing and in music rather than in sculpture and the visual arts.

Recent Developments in Jewish Life and Religion

Introduction

In the last few decades dramatic changes have taken place in Jewish life, both in the State of Israel and among diaspora Jewry. Some of these changes are reflections of the age, such as the response to a new awareness on the part of Jewish women influenced by feminism, or the efforts of Jewish law to deal with the massive development of biotechnology and new medical techniques. Others are the consequences of shifts on the world political scene, such as the break-up of the old Soviet Union and the massive migration of ex-Soviet Jews to Israel, or the new order in the Middle East brought about by the Iraqi invasion of Kuwait. The Gulf War which followed the latter led to a shake-up of old alliances in the Arab world, and subsequently to peace negotiations between Israel, the Palestine Liberation Organization (PLO) and certain Arab states.

Overshadowing many of the innovations among world Jewry one can detect the dark cloud of the Holocaust, whose power seems to increase in Jewish consciousness, paradoxically, as the number of surviving victims gradually diminishes. Interestingly, there is a marked preference among Jewish writers for the use of the Hebrew term *shoah*, 'destruction', rather than the more commonly used term 'Holocaust'. The latter refers to those sacrifices that were completely burnt after being offered up in the Temple ritual in ancient times. Using such a term to refer to the genocide of the Nazis and their allies is deemed inappropriate, for it seems to depict the Nazis as priestly figures offering up the Jews as sacrificial victims. Shoah, by its very name, simply indicates the negativity and desolation which the period of Nazi rules conjures up in Jewish consciousness.

The Shadow of the Holocaust

There are two basic explanations for the increasing role of the Shoah in Jewish life. The first is that as the remaining survivors age they remember the events of their early life better than they remember more recent events. So their memories are gradually suffused by pain. A number of prominent survivors have indeed committed suicide precisely at the point at which they seemed to have transcended their past and attained a life of peace and security. The best-known case of survivor suicide is that of the Italian Jewish writer Primo Levi [1: 454] whose death in 1987 left many people puzzled. They could not understand why a man who had successfully navigated the post-Holocaust world for forty-two years should eventually succumb to the black cloud of despair still hovering over him at the age of sixty-eight. If, however, the past becomes more real as the early memories begin to dominate, then Primo Levi's predicament is comprehensible.

The second explanation is that both survivors and non-survivors seem to be suffering from delayed Holocaust shock. This is a process whereby those affected by trauma, even indirectly, at first try to put it out of their minds in order to go on living with a semblance of normality. Eventually, however, it makes its way to the forefront of consciousness and affects all aspects of life. Thus Jewish consciousness is now having to face up to the Shoah and to its bitter lessons for the future.

Initially post-Holocaust poetry, literature, art and theology needed to affirm humanity in the face of a humanly created hell. Now it is attempting to wrestle with the trauma that hell has caused in the Jewish psyche. The response to the Shoah has moved from history and documentation on to the level of mythopoeic imagination affecting both the remaining survivors and also the next generation. Today books about the Shoah are one of the biggest growth areas within Jewish literature and within academic studies of Jewish life and history. Indeed, whole new types of Holocaust literature are being produced [8].

The fact that there has been a resurgence of anti-Semitism in Europe, and in parts of the former Soviet Union, keeps the Holocaust at the centre of Jewish concern. Although the numbers of people involved in vicious anti-Jewish incidents are small, the memory of how Fascism and National Socialism grew from insignificant beginnings is part of the stock-in-trade of post-Holocaust Jewry. One of the most disturbing features of this period is people's ignorance of what actually happened to Jews, Gypsies, homosexuals, and Slavs under Nazism. The fact that a small minority of writers and thinkers on the extreme right deny that anything like a Holocaust took place is grave cause for concern [16].

Lubavitch Messianism

The rise of contemporary messianic movements can be directly related to the Shoah and the shadow it casts over Jewish history. The Lubavitch Chasidic Movement promulgated a missionary messianism in which their leader, the Lubavitcher Rebbe M. M. Schneerson, was seen as the prime candidate for the role of messianic redeemer. Schneerson had argued that a belief in divine justice entailed the view that the post-Shoah period would herald the dawning of the messianic age. Otherwise it would seem bizarre to affirm heavenly justice. He encouraged his followers to raise the level of Jewish practice and commitment among secularized Jews. They did this by accosting them in public places and persuading them to carry out some ritual act or other, such as putting on phylacteries (*tefillin*) or shaking the palm branch on the festival of Sukkot. These missionary acts helped to initiate a return to Jewish tradition on the part of deracine Jews, who as penitents are known as *baalei teshuvah* (singular *baal teshuvah*). This return to religion was seen by Lubavitch as an important step in bringing about the advent of the Messiah.

As the Lubavitcher Rebbe grew older, however, his followers' messianism grew more urgent [15: x, xi]. Posters appeared all over Israel and in Jewish areas of the diaspora saying 'Prepare for the Coming of the Messiah' below pictures of Rabbi Schneerson. When he was ill in hospital, after suffering a series of strokes, messianism among his followers reached a fever pitch, with some Lubavitchers even wearing pagers so they could be notified as soon as their rabbi declared himself the Messiah and summoned Jews back to the Holy Land. Since his death at the age of ninety-two in New York on 12 June 1994, Lubavitch messianism has been curtailed and the movement has been left in some disarray. As with other messianic movements, however, the death of the would-be Messiah has meant that beliefs are being reinterpreted. As yet a section of his followers still expect him to return miraculously from the grave, despite the questionable Jewish nature of this belief.

Zionist Messianism

In Israel there are a number of religious/nationalist groups which can be described as essentially messianic. The largest and best-known is the Gush Emunim Movement ('Block of the Faithful') founded in 1974 [9; 15: XIX]. While not promoting any given individual as a messianic figure, Gush Emunim has seen the conquest of the whole historical Holy Land by the Israeli army in 1967 as a major step in redemption. The atrocities of the Shoah are seen as the pre-messianic catastrophes predicted by the Prophets. The setting up of the State of Israel as an independent Jewish state in 1948 is seen as the 'footprints of the Messiah', while the miraculous Six-Day War in 1967 is a sign of the immediately pre-messianic redemptive hand of the Lord.

The peace moves between the Labour government of Israel and the PLO, initiated in Oslo in the wake of the Gulf War with Iraq, are viewed with suspicion and loathing by Gush Emunim sympathizers, Lubavitchers, other nationalist messianists and right-wing secularists. The late Israeli Prime Minister, Yitzhak Rabin, who shook hands with the PLO Chairman, Yassir Arafat, outside the White House in Washington on 13 September 1993, and then signed an agreement in Cairo on 4 May 1994 for limited Israeli withdrawal from areas of the West Bank, was viewed not only as a traitor to Israel but as an infidel undermining the messianic hope. These peace moves have been bitterly opposed because the compromises and concessions of the peace agreement clearly negate the messianic promise that the Jews will return to the whole of their historic homeland in Palestine. The assassination of Rabin in 1995 by Yigal Amir, a religious student with Gush Emunim sympathies, is to be understood against this background.

A substantial minority of religious nationalists, and some secular ones, believe that any attempt to hand control of the areas of the West Bank known to Jews as Judea and Samaria over to the Palestinian Arabs must be opposed by all means available. Thus a former Chief Rabbi of Israel, Shelomoh Goren, has called upon religious soldiers in the Israeli army to disobey orders if they are asked to dismantle any Jewish settlement in the ancient areas of the Jewish Holy Land which will be returned to the Palestinians.

Traditional and Progressive Judaisms

The shadow of the Holocaust also hangs over the relations between traditional Judaism (Ultra Orthodox and Modern Orthodox), Conservative Judaism and Progressive Judaism (Reform and Liberal). The experience of common persecution has led many Modern Orthodox thinkers to see Progressive Jews, for all their 'heresies' and neglect of certain aspects of the *halakhah*, as fellow Jews with whom there is a covenant of fate and shared history even if there is not exactly a community of faith and ritual [24]. Modern Orthodox rabbis and leaders have worked together with their Progressive co-religionists on shared platforms supporting Israel and commemorating the Shoah.

The British Chief Rabbi, Jonathan Sacks, has argued for an inclusivist attitude on the part of Orthodoxy which should be willing to accept non-Orthodox Jews as mistaken co-religionists, as 'children who have grown up among Gentiles' and therefore know no better. Regarding them as not totally responsible for their religious attitudes and their rejection of the traditional teachings enables their Orthodox co-religionists still to consider them as part of the same communion and not as rebels and heretics [24: VI].

The destruction of one-third of world Jewry by the Nazi extermination programme has made Jews feel even weaker and numerically smaller than they are. It has drawn Jews together despite the religious gulf between them, although some Ultra Orthodox rabbis still maintain that 'Reform Jews who imitate the Gentiles are to be feared more than the Gentiles themselves'. It has also exacerbated the process of assimilation and intermarriage in which whole families and indeed whole communities in isolated areas disappear as they merge into the dominant, mostly Christian, culture. This rush to assimilation has been described as 'giving posthumous victories to Hitler'.

Reform in North America has responded to this high rate of intermarriage by advocating the patrilineal principle in which the children of Jewish fathers and Gentile mothers would be recognized as Jews if they were brought up as Jews, not needing conversion to the faith. This flies in the face of tradition, where Jewish identity comes from the mother rather than the father. There has, naturally, been virulent opposition to patrilineality from the Orthodox and Conservatives, and even from Reform groups outside the US.

Reform and Conservative conversions have continued to cause problems because they are not recognized by Orthodoxy, and all attempts to unite on matters of conversion with a law court (*bet din*) made up of Orthodox, Conservative and Reform members have not succeeded. Conversion is quicker, easier and more common in Reform Judaism than in other Jewish groups. This means that as non-Orthodox converts, mostly women and their children, come to represent a sizeable proportion of Reform communities, whole communities will cease to be recognized as Jewish in anything but name by Orthodox and even by Conservative Judaism. Marriage between members of such communities and members of non-Reform communities will thus become extremely problematic.

Aside from conversion, a more intractable marriage impediment exists for those who are born to a previously married mother who has not received a religious divorce (*get*) from her first husband. Since Reform rabbis will remarry someone on the strength of a civil divorce, which Orthodoxy does not recognize as having any religious significance, a growing number of Reform members are the children of such second marriages. They are regarded as *mamzerim* (illegitimate children born from an adulterous or incestuous relationship) and though their Jewishness is not in doubt they are severely restricted in whom they can marry. One American Orthodox rabbi has predicted a catastrophic situation emerging in the US, if current trends continue, where Jewry will be split into two basic Jewish groups, one of which (the Orthodox and the Conservatives) will not marry with the other (the Reform) [7].

Gender Issues

It was recognized from the middle ages that movements in the Gentile world had an effect on the religion and behaviour of Jews. Thus one medieval pietist work says: 'The behaviour of Jews in most places is just like the behaviour of the Gentiles. Thus if the Gentiles practise sexual morality so will the Jews who are born in that town' (*Sefer Hasidim*, Margoliot edn, section 1101). This has certainly been true of the feminist movement in the contemporary world. The general movement for liberation and greater equality on the part of women has made its mark on all Jews who are in direct cultural contact with the modern world, be they Orthodox, Conservative, Reform, Liberal or Reconstructionist. Modern Orthodox thinkers have begun to re-examine halakhic texts to find ways in which the situation of women can be improved within the framework of Jewish law [5]. Even Ultra Orthodox groups have opened the doors of Jewish education to women and young girls in ways that would not have been possible in the pre-modern period.

Liberal, Reform and Conservative Judaisms have not only abolished separate seating in the synagogue for men and women, they have also allowed women to study for the rabbinate and take up rabbinical positions in communities. This change of role has been condemned by Orthodox rabbis of all persuasions. Even Modern Orthodoxy itself is divided on the advisability of allowing women to organize their own separate prayer services. Some Orthodox women have felt that they are marginalized in synagogue services where they sit behind a partition and where the prayers are led by men. These women have wanted a greater involvement in prayer, and as they cannot act as cantors or prayer leaders they wish, on occasion, to have women-only services. Against this it has been objected that such innovations undermine tradition, and that women would not be able to participate in those special prayers that can only be said with a quorum (*minyan*) of males. Those Orthodox rabbis, particularly in the US, who permit women's services place restrictions on the form they may take. The British Chief Rabbi has allowed women in the communities under his aegis to meet for prayers in private homes but not in the synagogue itself, and he has not permitted them to use a *Torah* scroll for Bible readings.

Medical Ethics

Almost every modern scientific advance raises issues for Jewish law, because the *halakhah* is a system which covers all areas of life. Indeed, there has even been some contemporary discussion among Orthodox rabbis as to whether one needs to keep the divine commandments on the moon. New methods of contraception have been widely discussed in halakhic literature, as have artificial insemination, host mothers, trans-sexual surgery, organ transplants, and the use of animals, severed organs and embryos for experimentation [6]. The transplanting of organs in particular has raised the question of how to determine the moment of death. Traditionally, death has been identified as the cessation of breathing, but when bodies are kept alive on a ventilator, after brain death, the question of when an operation to remove an organ can take place becomes crucial. Moves have been set afoot among one influential group of Modern Orthodox rabbis in the US to change the classical Jewish view of death. After some discussion and argument they have agreed to accept that brain death should constitute a sufficient criterion of death for the purposes of *halakhah*. They would thus allow certain organ transplants to take place which might otherwise be prohibited if the brain-dead donor were considered to be still alive.

Bibliography

1 ABRAMSON, G. (ed.), *The Blackwell Companion to Jewish Culture: From the Eighteenth Century to the Present*, Oxford, Blackwell, 1989

2 *The Authorized Daily Prayer Book* (with tr. by S. Singer), new edn, London, Eyre & Spottiswoode, 1962; repr. 1968

3 *The Babylonian Talmud* (tr. under the editorship of I. Epstein), 18 vols, London, Soncino, 1961; in 35 vols, 1935–52

4 BARON, S. W., *A Social and Religious History of the Jews*, 2nd edn, 17 vols and index to vols 1–8, Philadelphia, Jewish Publication Society of America; New York/London, Columbia Press, 1952–76

5 BIALE, R., *Women and Jewish Law: An Exploration of Women's Issues in Halakhic Sources*, New York, Schocken, 1984

6 BLEICH, J. D., *Judaism and Healing: Halakhic Perspectives*, New York, Ktav, 1981

7 BULKA, R. P., *The Coming Cataclysm: The Orthodox–Reform Rift and the Future of the Jewish People*, Oakville, Ontario, Mosaic Press, 1984

8 ELIACH, Y., *Hasidic Tales of the Holocaust*, New York, Oxford University Press, 1982

9 FRIEDMAN, R. I., *Zealots for Zion: Inside Israel's West Bank Settler Movement*, New York, Random House, 1992

10 GINZBURG, L., *The Legends of the Jews*, 7 vols, Philadelphia, Jewish Publication Society of America, 1968; prev. publ. 1909–38

11 HERTZBERG, A. (ed.), *The Zionist Idea: A Historical Analysis and Reader*, New York, Atheneum, repr. 1971; prev. publ. New York, Doubleday, 1959

12 IDELSON, A. Z., *Jewish Liturgy and its Development*, New York, Schocken, 1967; prev. publ. New York, Holt, 1932

13 JACOBS, L., *Principles of the Jewish Faith: An Analytic Study*, London, Vallentine, Mitchell/New York, Basic Books, 1964

14 KATZ, J., *Tradition and Crisis: Jewish Society at the End of the Middle Ages*, New York, Schocken, 1971

15 LANDAU, D., *Piety and Power: The World of Jewish Fundamentalism*, London, Secker & Warburg, 1993

16 LIPSTADT, D., *Denying the Holocaust: The Growing Assault on Truth and Memory*, New York, Free Press, 1993

17 MAIMONIDES (MOSES BEN MAIMON), *The Guide of the Perplexed* (tr. S. Pines), 2 vols, Chicago, University of Chicago Press, 1974; prev. publ. 1963

18 MOORE, G. F., *Judaism in the First Centuries of the Christian Era*, 3 vols, Cambridge, MA, Harvard University Press, 1966 (repr.); first publ. 1927–30

19 RABINOWICZ, H. M., *The World of Hasidism*, London, Vallentine, Mitchell/Hartford, CT, Hartmore, 1970

20 REITLINGER, G., *The Final Solution: The Attempt to Exterminate the Jews of Europe, 1939–1945*, 2nd edn, New York, Yoseloff, 1961, repr. 1968; London, Vallentine, Mitchell, 1968

21 ROTH, C., *A Short History of the Jewish People*, rev. edn, London, East and West Library, 1969; Hartford, CT, Hartmore, 1970; New York, Hebrew Publications, 1978

22 RUDAVSKY, D., *Modern Jewish Religious Movements: A History of Emancipation and Adjustment*, New York, Behrman, 1967; 3rd edn. 1979. First publ. as *Emancipation and Adjustment: Contemporary Jewish Religious Movements*, New York, Diplomatic Press/London, Living Books, 1967

23 SACHAR, H. M., *The Course of Modern Jewish History*, New York, Dell, 1958; rev. edn 1977; prev. publ. Cleveland, World/London, Weidenfeld, 1958

24 SACKS, J., *One People? Tradition, Modernity and Jewish Unity*, London, Littman Library of Jewish Civilization, 1993

25 SCHAUSS, H., *Guide to Jewish Holy Days*, New York, Schocken, repr. 1970

26 SCHECHTER, S., *Studies in Judaism*, New York, Meridian, 1962; prev. publ. 1958

27 SCHOLEM, G. G., *Major Trends in Jewish Mysticism*, 3rd edn repr. New York, Schocken, 1954; London, Thames & Hudson, 1955

28 SCHOLEM, G. G., *On the Kabbalah and its Symbolism* (tr. Ralph Manheim), New York, Schocken, 1965

29 SHAROT, S., *Judaism: A Sociology*, Newton Abbot, David & Charles/New York, Holmes & Meier, 1976

30 SKLARE, M., *Conservative Judaism: An American Religious Movement*, new edn, New York, Schocken, 1972

31 TRACHTENBERG, J. *The Devil and the Jews: The Medieval Conception of the Jew and its Relation to Modern Antisemitism*, New York, Harper, 1966

32 TRACHTENBERG, J., *Jewish Magic and Superstition: A Study in Folk Religion*, New York, Atheneum, 1970; prev. publ. New York, Behrman, 1939

33 UNTERMAN, A., *Jews: Their Religious Beliefs and Practices*, London/Boston, Routledge, 1981

34 UNTERMAN, A., *Judaism*, London, Ward Lock Educational, 1981 (The Arts and Practices of Living Religions)

35 ZIMMELS, H. J., *Ashkenazim and Sephardim*, London, Oxford University Press, 1958

36 ZIMMELS, H. J., *Magicians, Theologians and Doctors: Studies in Folk-Medicine and Folk-Lore as Reflected in the Rabbinicial Responsa, 12th–19th Centuries*, New York, Feldheim/London, Goldston, 1952

37 *The Zohar* (tr. H. Sperling and M. Simon), 5 vols, London, Soncino, 1931–4

2

Christianity

ANDREW WALLS

Introduction

Name

The term 'Christian' was first used in Antioch in Syria *c.* 35–40 CE to designate a new religious community there which included both Jewish and non-Jewish adherents and was marked out by its attachment to 'Christos' (*Acts* 2: 26), a Greek translation of the Hebrew title 'Messiah', used by Jews to designate their expected national saviour. In this case it was applied to the prophet–teacher Jesus of Nazareth, executed in Judea, where the movement had originated, a few years earlier.

The sobriquet stuck as the movement developed and spread. It is entirely appropriate: Christianity has appeared in a profusion of different forms and expressions, but allegiance to 'Christ' is crucial to all. It is also appropriate that the word used to identify Christians is a *Jewish* technical term, since the roots of the movement lie deep in the life and writings of ancient Israel, and significant that it is a Jewish term translated into Greek. The multitudinous forms in which Christianity appears are conditioned by cultural and linguistic factors, so that translatability and transmission across cultural frontiers are leading characteristics of Christianity as a faith.

Sources

The Jewish scriptures The earliest Christians were Jews, well read in the scriptures of Israel which traditionally subsisted in three categories: the Law, the Prophets and the Writings. Although Christianity soon developed as an overwhelmingly Gentile movement, the Christian communities continued to read the Jewish scriptures, to relate these scriptures to Christ, and to use them as an authoritative source for teaching and debate. By this means the Jewish scriptures came to be designated by Christians as the 'Old Testament' (or 'Old Covenant'), representing a stage of the divine dealings with humanity prior to the coming of Christ.

The New Testament writings For the life and work of Jesus the Christ the collection of early Christian writings known as 'the New Testament' is the crucial early source. This consists of four accounts of the ministry and teaching of Jesus (called 'Gospels'); a supplement to the third of the Gospels describing the early preaching of Jesus in Jerusalem and the wider Mediterranean world (the 'Acts of the Apostles'); a collection of letters ('the Epistles'), most to congregations, a few to individuals, many of which bear the name of the early missionary Paul; and a work which combines several more letters with prophecy and interpretation of history (the 'Apocalypse' or 'Revelation' of John). These writings reflect the ideas and images of Jesus held in the early Christian communities, and indeed, brought these communities into being, as well as giving accounts of his teaching. The special status of the New Testament writings originally derived from their association in one way or another with the group of followers of Jesus known as the apostles. The members of this group were chosen by Jesus himself, and while still living they were recognized as the founders and regulators of the Christian community, in the sense that their interpretation of his person and teaching was regarded as authoritative. When the living apostles passed from the scene, their surviving writings, or those of their close associates, took on a special significance as preserving the authentic interpretation of Jesus by his chosen companions.

Taken together, the Old and the New Testaments came to be seen as representing 'the prophets and the apostles' who are viewed in early Christian literature as forming the foundation of the church, the early Christian community (*Ephesians* 2: 20). They also represented a record of a continuous series of revelations of God and of the divine purpose for humanity, of which Christ, as interpreted by those whom he appointed for the purpose, was the culmination. They thus formed a 'canon', or measuring rod, for the life and teaching of the Christian community. Broadly speaking, the principle of the canon of Scripture, and, for practical purposes, the same list of books, has united Christians ever since. In the early centuries there were for a time variations in the lists used by the churches because a few writings were recognized in some regions as having apostolic associations but were unknown elsewhere. It is also clear that some early Christian communities kept writings (sometimes claiming an esoteric apostolic origin for them) that never gained acceptance outside their local area.

Of the books in the canon which was eventually accepted there were regional doubts especially about the *Epistle to the Hebrews*, the *Revelation of John* and some of the very small letters; and some argued for the authority of one or two other books such as the apocalyptic Shepherd of Hermas. Less contentious, because their origins and purpose were generally blatantly obvious, were works meant to advance tendentious teaching by ascribing it to apostolic sources, and popular, often sensational, novellas about the Lord and his apostles. There was a vast quantity of such 'apocryphal' literature, and a good deal survives. That some of it long influenced Christian popular imagination is clear from its traces both in the medieval West and in Islamic derivatives from Christian sources in the East; but there is no evidence that any of it was ever widely taken seriously as a source of apostolic teaching.

The development of a universally recognized canon may, in fact, have been accelerated by the need to counter the influence of Marcion of Pontus, who in the middle of the second century produced a Greek version of Christianity so thoroughly indigenized that it rejected altogether the God and the scriptures of Israel. Marcion listed a canon of one gospel and ten letters of Paul. Before Marcion's time, references by Christian writers indicate their knowledge and use of most of the works that form the New Testament now used everywhere; from Marcion's time onwards we begin to find lists of the works recognized as authoritative. The process was consensual, and by the fourth century was complete. At that period both Eastern and Western sources provide lists of recognized works which agree with each other and have been in universal use since.

The application within Western Christianity over the last two centuries of Enlightenment principles of literary and historical criticism has had remarkably little effect as regards the principle or contents of the canon. It is not possible here to give an account of the literary discussions concerning the books which comprise either 'Testament', nor is it necessary for our purpose. Of the New Testament writings, all (or virtually all) come from the first century, some from within the first half of that century; all were, or were early believed to be, associated with people or communities within the apostolic circle, and were therefore seen as containing normative teaching. The principal variation among Christians concerning the canon has in fact arisen from the adoption in some Christian communities of the Alexandrine or Greek canon for the Old Testament. This includes several books in Greek – *Tobit*, *Judith*, 1 and 2 *Maccabees*, the *Wisdom of Solomon*, *Ecclesiasticus* and *Baruch*, along with some additions to other books – which were not among the sacred books read in Hebrew synagogues and which come from a later period than most of those which were so read. While some Christian communities – notably the entire Roman Catholic tradition – have accepted these additional books as Scripture, others have given them secondary status as 'apocrypha', and yet others have rejected or ignored them. The variation, however, has probably had little effect on Christian teaching and practice.

The Christian community From its earliest period, Christianity has been marked by the consciousness of shared life in a community of which Christ is the head. Almost universal in Christian thought is the conviction that God is active in the Church or Christian community. So widespread, indeed, is this conviction that it seems proper to regard the Church, the Christian community, as one of the sources of Christianity, though Christians differ widely among themselves as to the instruments by which that guidance is given and as to the relationship of these instruments to the institutional structures of the Church. While some Christians believe the Church to be entrusted by God with a tradition to transmit and develop through its accredited representatives and teachers, others deny the existence of any source of revelation independent of the scriptures, and relate the principle of active divine guidance in the Church closely to these scriptures.

These differences relate especially to the role of the apostles. In a good deal of Christian thought, the office of the apostles, those chosen companions of Jesus who transmitted to the earliest Christian community the record of his life, teaching and significance, has been perpetuated in the Church over the centuries. This perpetuation is represented in the succession of bishops, whose unanimity guarantees 'catholic', i.e. universal, truth. Other Christians hold that the office of apostle was a once-for-all institution directed to the establishment of the Church; the scriptures are now the sole reliable guide to 'apostolic' teaching, to which the institutional church should conform. A third pattern has appeared from time to time in Christian history and in recent times has gathered new strength in Pentecostal, charismatic and some forms of African Christianity. In this pattern, God continues to speak directly through prophets and inspired people, to give guidance in specific human situations.

Christian history has seen many disputes over the relative importance of Scripture, Church and direct revelation as sources of authority. In practice, all recognize the special place of the scriptures; even the minority who stress the continuance of direct revelation usually insist that such activity in no way supersedes or contradicts the scriptures, and frequently that it merely applies them in a contemporary setting. Similarly, though Christians differ in their identification of the Church, virtually all groups recognize some form of consensus as a test of authenticity, and virtually all accept that God in some way directs the life and deliberations of the Christian community.

History

Christianity has existed for two millennia. During that time, its geographical and cultural centre of gravity has shifted several times. It has adapted itself to diverse societies and both shaped and been shaped by them. In some ways it has been the most syncretistic of the great faiths, while never losing the marks of its Jewish origins. It has produced no single distinctive civilization, but has brought its sources to bear on the existing structures and traditions of a series of societies, adopting the categories of thought of those societies and addressing their concerns. The result has been successive translations in terms of different languages and cultures, and often of the subcultures within them. This in turn has involved a repeated process of cross-cultural transmission followed by cultural interpretation.

This process has also on occasion been marked by periods when the activity of translation has stagnated, bringing an end to interpretation within a particular culture. As a result, although Christianity is now spread across all six continents, its expansion does not represent a steady line of progress (as might be argued for Islam) but a pattern of advance and recession. It has a history of erosion in the successive areas of its greatest strength, areas where its cultural impact has been most profound; it has also shown the capacity to take root in areas where it has had no significant previous presence. The processes of recession in the heartlands and expansion into new areas and cultures have often been simultaneous; and on several occasions the very continuance of Christianity as a major force in the world has resulted from its moving across a cultural frontier. Christian expansion has been not progressive, but serial.

The periodization of Christian history offered below arises from this feature of serial expansion. It reflects the successive Christian encounters with successive dominant cultures. In each case the encounter described produced a deep Christian imprint upon the culture; produced a translation of the Christian tradition in terms of the forms, concerns and priorities of that tradition; and left permanent effects, which affected the later transmission of Christianity. Nevertheless it is necessary to remember that at no point (except perhaps in the very earliest period) was Christianity geographically confined to the area of any one of the dominant cultures included in this survey. Some parts of the world have Christian histories entirely unaffected by events and processes which have been formative for other Christian communities.

The Judaic phase (c.30–c.70 CE) For a short but vital period Christianity was entirely Jewish in composition and mode of life. To a contemporary observer, the early Christian community described in the opening chapters of the *Acts of the Apostles* would have appeared to be simply one more of the seemingly infinite variations of Judaism. All its members were Jewish by birth or inheritance. Their regular meeting-place was the Temple in Jerusalem, symbolic centre of the nation's worship, a building, indeed, which only Jesus could penetrate. They were zealous in attendance at 'the prayers', i.e. the Temple liturgy, and maintained all the outward marks of observant Jews: animal sacrifices, circumcision of male children, certain ceremonial food avoidances, keeping the seventh day free from work. The chief figure in the community of the followers of Jesus in Jerusalem, James, who was the brother of Jesus himself, was a well-known figure in the Temple and was nicknamed 'the Just' – i.e. righteous in the sense of careful, heartfelt fulfilment of the Law.

There were, however, important distinctive features to the community which set them apart from other observant Jews. In terms of lifestyle, the most notable were their voluntary commitment to communal ownership of property (with special provision for vulnerable groups such as widows) and frequent communal meals in one another's houses. In terms of belief, the distinctive heart of their teaching concerned Jesus of Nazareth, a prophet–teacher known by all to have been recently crucified, and declared by the group to have been raised from the dead. The group identified Jesus with scriptural figures of the Messiah, the Son of Man and the Suffering Servant.

It will be noted that these distinctive features of the early Christian community's life and belief were expressed in terms of the scriptures of Israel and Jewish experience and aspirations. The apostles, the chosen companions of Jesus, who were the recognized leaders of the movement, were the principal witnesses of the resurrection of Jesus. That resurrection was the crowning proof that he was the divinely appointed Messiah, the promised saviour of the nation. The prophetic writings indicated that 'the Age to Come' would dawn with the Messiah's coming; that era had therefore now begun, and with it the way to the moral renewal of the nation as people of God was opened. Through Jesus the Messiah, God's people might now be forgiven their past sins and shortcomings and receive an overflow of the divine presence and energy – the 'Holy Spirit' – all as the scriptures indicated. All this was entirely intelligible, however controversial, within the framework of Jewish history, Jewish experience and Jewish institutions. For many years, indeed, the apostles seem to have confined their preaching – as Jesus himself had done – to the Jewish, and indeed the Palestinian Jewish, community, expounding the Jewish scriptures and explaining their fulfilment in Jesus. On this interpretation Jesus was the linchpin of the history of the nation of Israel.

One of the signs of the Age to Come, according to several

prophecies, was that non-Jews would seek and find the salvation which God had given to Israel. So when some pagan Greeks in the Syrian metropolis of Antioch were attracted to Jesus through the talk of believers who had been expelled from Jerusalem (*Acts* 11: 19–20), their joining the community raised no difficulty in principle. Such events fulfilled Scripture by revealing that Gentiles would want to enter Israel and serve Israel's God. Jews had always welcomed proselytes, and had an established method for their reception and incorporation. This included the requirement to observe the Torah, or Jewish Law, and (for males) the rite of circumcision. It was at this point that the believers in Jesus introduced a critical innovation. After careful consideration at a meeting in Jerusalem (described in *Acts* 15), and not without some degree of controversy that did not immediately die down, it was agreed to accept Gentiles on the ground of faith in Jesus the Messiah, without circumcision and without any requirement to fulfil the ritual Law. This effectively bypassed the whole institution of the reception of Jewish proselytes. On this interpretation proselyte status was unnecessary; it was possible for Gentiles to enter Israel, the people of God, without becoming Jews or taking on even the most widely recognized marks of Jewish religious culture. The decision ensured the future ethnic and cultural diversity of Christianity; it also produced an immediate crisis of social relations. As we have seen, one of the early marks of the lifestyle of the followers of Jesus was the frequency of their shared meals. The events in Antioch, and the decision made at the assembly in Jerusalem, meant that observant ethnic Jews who were believers in Jesus could be expected to share tables with followers of Jesus who were uncircumcised Gentiles, in flagrant breach of tradition and custom, and to the scandal of other observant Jews. The bond with Jesus now took precedence over the bond of national unity and ethnic identity. It is no accident that the name 'Christians' was first bestowed in Antioch; it was there that the need of a title for a religious community that was both Jewish and Gentile first became apparent.

When the decision was taken to admit Gentiles solely on the ground of their adhesion to Jesus Messiah, without their becoming proselytes, Jerusalem was still the centre of Christianity, and the majority of Christians were still ethnic Jews. Within a very short time thereafter, the ethnic and cultural balance of the faith was overturned. In the hellenistic world beyond Antioch, Gentile Christians began to abound, and the decision of the Jerusalem assembly ensured that they did not assimilate to the original Judaic model, but developed along independent lines. Still more crucially, the Jewish state, within which that Judaic model had emerged as a potent force, ceased to exist. Even before that time the position of the Christian movement in Jerusalem had become highly insecure.

In 62 CE, James the Just was murdered; when the Jewish revolt against the Romans began a few years later, the Christians withdrew from Jerusalem. Though the evidence is fragmentary and may be read in different ways, it is possible that they found a home among other Jewish separatist religious communities in rural areas. At any rate, various writers between the second and fifth centuries bear witness to the existence in Palestine of groups of Torah-keeping Jews who acknowledged Jesus as Messiah but were outside the Christian mainstream. As regards the Christian future in the world, the fall of Jerusalem, and the destruction of the Temple and the Jewish state which ensued, brought about the end of the original, Judaic model of Christianity.

The fall of Jerusalem in 70 CE was a defining moment for the Christian movement, breaking the link between the developing Gentile forms of Christianity and the first normative model of Christianity, its first geographical and cultural centre. The movement parted from its Jewish matrix. By this time many, perhaps most, of the apostles had passed from the scene, and ethnic Jews ceased to be so important in the movement's leadership. In a short time they were no longer important even in its composition. Those mixed congregations of Jews and Gentiles, with their impressive table-sharing (celebrated, for instance, in the New Testament *Epistle to the Ephesians*; see e.g. *Ephesians* 2: 11–18), became less and less significant. Christianity became as overwhelmingly Gentile as it had once been overwhelmingly Jewish; and the Jerusalem assembly's abandonment of the proselyte mode for Gentile converts meant that the new Christian communities would reflect the dominant culture of the hellenistic–Roman world.

The transition was not without pain. Tensions mounted between Jewish and Christian communities as both groups redefined themselves in the new situation. The Judaic model of Christianity which defined allegiance to Jesus Messiah in essentially Jewish terms faded away. Over many centuries, such Jews as took on the Christian faith generally assimilated to Gentile models of Christianity; indeed, in the long period of Christian ascendancy in Europe there was seldom any other option. The recent appearance of a 'Messianic' Judaic form of Christianity, notably in North America, though significant, is exceptional in Christian history.

Nevertheless, Christianity has never lost the marks of its Jewish matrix. Its roots in the history of Israel (which Christians continue to take on as an adoptive history), its use of the scriptures of Israel, its allegiance to a Christ who belonged to the land of Palestine, have been enduring. From time to time movements inspired by a desire to affirm indigenous culture more strongly, or by anti-Semitism, or by some other cause, have sought to detach Christians from the scriptures they see as their 'Old Testament', or to erase the other marks of Jewish origin. They have never succeeded; an opposite and stronger reaction has always swept them away.

The hellenistic–Roman phase (c.70–c.500) We have already noted a new direction in Christian history arising from the action of some unnamed Jewish Christians in Antioch who began to talk about Jesus to 'Greeks', i.e., pagans of hellenistic outlook. Antioch became the centre of the first organized attempt to spread faith in Jesus through the hellenistic world. The outstanding figure in this movement was a diaspora-born rabbi called Saul. He had not been a companion of Jesus, and had at first actively opposed the Jesus movement, but he was convinced that he had seen and heard the risen Jesus and was widely recognized as an apostle. Paul contended vigorously for accepting Gentile converts on the ground of faith in Jesus without obligation to follow the Jewish Law. He urged that such converts had clearly received the divine life of the Holy Spirit, a fact which showed that God had already accepted them. He took a Gentile name, Paul (by which he is generally known), lived equally readily within Jewish and Greek culture, and, while himself remaining thoroughly hebraic in thought and instinct, encouraged Greek Christians to assert their freedom from the Jewish cultural tradition. He gloried in the organic union represented in the Christian Church between ethnic and religious communities which had previously been thought divided for ever. He travelled across Asia Minor and eastern Europe, and eventually to Rome itself, introducing Jesus to the synagogues of overseas Jewish communities like the one into which he was born. These often had a fringe of sympathetic Gentiles influenced by Judaism, who proved particularly open to Paul's message. In addition to these 'God-fearers', many pagans without a significant background in Judaism were affected through Paul and his colleagues; Paul, indeed, proved to be the 'apostle to the Gentiles'.

Jewish believers called Jesus by the pregnant title 'Messiah'; but that term meant little to anyone not raised in Israel. For the new Christians, Jesus was 'Lord', a title which was regularly applied to the cult divinities worshipped in the east Mediterranean lands to which they belonged. They were necessarily influenced by the various currents at work in those lands: strands of Greek philosophy, Roman law, mystery cults, oriental magic and astral science. All this mental furniture had to stand in the same room with the essentially hebraic faith in Jesus Messiah that the apostles had preached. And, as we have seen, it was a remarkably short time before the typical Christian leader was no longer a son of Israel nurtured in centuries of the Israelite inheritance but, by birth or ancestry, a Greek-speaking convert from paganism. This shift transformed the lifestyle of Christians and the expression of their beliefs. Observance of the

Law, animal sacrifice, circumcision, Sabbath observance, all questions of importance to ethnic Jews, disappeared. On the other hand, Christianity entered the intellectual discourse of the hellenistic world, and was necessarily applied to the intellectual, social and religious concerns of that world. Entrance into this discourse raised new questions for Christian thinking that had not confronted it in a purely Jewish milieu; for instance, what the statements about the ultimate significance of Jesus as Lord meant when translated into the Greek categories of being and substance. Similarly, new questions arose about social relations, and about the position of Christians within the body politic. Jews within the Roman empire had certain acknowledged exemptions; these could not be extended to members of this new community who worshipped the God of the Jews and preserved so many Jewish attitudes, but were not ethnic Jews.

As Christian thinking now entered a different social universe, it developed new styles, methods and techniques. The Greek translation of the Old Testament, the Septuagint, was the only alternative body of literature available in the hellenistic world which could claim a comparable antiquity with the great works of Greece. Christians, who saw in the prophets of Israel predictions of Christ, could therefore confidently affirm a special status for the translated scriptures of Israel; and this passed also to the gospels and epistles, despite their comparatively recent origin. In hellenistic Christian hands the translated scriptures became a handbook whereby a total Christian world-view could be constructed, using the categories and methods of Greek thought and debate. They also became a source book in Greek which could be used to apply a critique to the Greek heritage. By such means hellenistic Christians were able to appropriate and modify the framework of Greek culture, and make their understanding of God and Christ intelligible within it, as their Jerusalem predecessors had done within the framework of Jewish understanding.

Some of the ineradicably Jewish features of the new faith were hard to assimilate into hellenistic thought. Many Greek-speaking people took it as axiomatic that the seat of evil, whether in the world at large or in the human personality, lay in matter. They therefore desired liberation from the body as the condition of the bliss of the soul. The conviction that Christ had risen from the dead was too central to Christian teaching to be easily abandoned, but hellenistic Christians often spoke more generally of the resurrection of the body (a well-established Judaic doctrine) as though it expressed the immortality of the soul, a conception readily found in Greek thought. (Much Western Christian thought has continued to confuse the two ideas.) On this and some other questions, 'indigenizing' movements in Christian thought, which sought to make

Christianity at home in the hellenistic world, played down or rejected the most obviously Jewish features of the Christian inheritance. Such movements, however, were regularly countered by others which found ways of upholding, adapting or reinterpreting such features, taking them into new realms of discourse in the Greek world.

For this purpose the thought forms of hellenistic culture were pressed into service. It was natural to use the language and concepts of the hellenistic religious environment. Contemporary mystery religions gave currency to the idea of immortality flowing from initation into secret knowledge. Christians boldly appropriated the idea, regularly describing baptism (which followed a course of doctrinal and moral instruction, a profession of faith in Christ and testimony from others of a life consistent with it) as initiation. The concept of 'orthodoxy' – developed statements of correct belief – came to be of immense importance; and it was established by rational use of the categories and methods of Greek philosophical debate. The development and enforcement of orthodoxy was furthered by a developing pattern of Christian organization, another example of accommodation to the ways in which hellenistic society worked. The earliest Christian congregations naturally followed the pattern of the synagogue, with its corporate leadership; in the hellenistic world Christians were influenced by Greek civic organization, and the synagogue model gave place to a system of linked local hierarchies, each under a bishop. Consultation among the hierarchies of particular areas and regions helped to maintain 'orthodox' or 'apostolic' tradition. The test of Christian authenticity thus became 'catholicity', universal recognition among the Christian communities. Individuals or communities who insisted on teachings which were not approved by the hierarchies of a locality found themselves excluded.

This type of organization – strong, consultative, not over-centralized – helped Christianity to cope with another peril. Official persecution of Christians was at first spasmodic and local, but by the middle of the third century the increase in their numbers attracted direct intervention by the Roman state, and by the early years of the fourth this had reached a level of intense ferocity. Under these pressures the organizational structures seem to have held up remarkably well. In general the Roman empire was not interested in the details of religious activities, of which its territories offered an immense variety. What attracted suspicion or hostility to the Christians was their insistence that their allegiance to Christ precluded their participation in the civil religion of the state cult, which involved veneration of the emperor's 'genius' or spirit. Their frequent refusal to undertake military service was a further aggravation, a sign of a pernicious, disloyal and potentially dangerous grouping outside the usual sources of social control. All this changed with Constantine's accession to imperial power in 313 CE. He first tolerated, then favoured the Christian Church. Privilege replaced disability until under his successors Christianity by degrees effectively became the state religion of the Roman empire. Up to the early fourth century, a variety of attractions brought people into the Christian community from the declining popular religions, from philosophical rationalism and from the Eastern cults. Demonstrable moral change was a powerful attraction; so were the majesty and solemnity of Christian worship, the close, caring relationships created within the Church, and, in some circles certainly, the presentation of Christianity as a coherent philosophy, offering what Plato declared as the true aim of philosophy, the vision of God. From the fourth century onwards, however, Christian profession became the rule rather than the exception, and a period dawned in which Christianity and affairs of state were constantly intertwined.

These processes naturally had their effect on the organization and conduct of Church affairs. We have already noted the importance of the principle of 'catholicity' or universality, a natural product of the assumption that the apostles all taught the same thing everywhere, and the early practice of local and regional consultation between the linked hierarchies. Under the Christian Roman empire, both principle and practice were extended, to achieve consensus on major matters of theology or practice which might otherwise be divisive. Bishops, who represented the teaching and ruling functions of the Church, met in council, implicitly agreeing to be bound by the council's decisions. Constantine himself, concerned for imperial unity, accelerated the process, and his successors continued this policy, so that councils on occasion were held on an 'ecumenical' (i.e. world-wide) basis. All this lent colour to the idea of the Church as a corporate entity with quasi-juridical powers.

Constantine himself convened the first and most famous of the councils, held at Nicea in 325 to settle a question that was causing deep rifts: how to express the relationship of Christ to God in terms that made sense in Greek categories of thought about being and time and yet faithfully represented inherited Christian tradition. In Greek thought, a phrase such as 'Son of God' could have a wide range of meanings; what was the precise relationship of Son to Father in terms of *ousia*, 'substance'? It was impossible to answer this question using the words of Scripture alone. The formula embodied in the creed adopted at Nicea stated that the Son was of the same *ousia*, or substance, as the Father. This has been accepted as the orthodox expression of faith ever since, in Eastern and Western Christianity alike. The fourth of these 'ecumenical', or world, councils, held at Chalcedon in 451, sought to find language within contemporary Greek discourse to express the relationship of the divine and human natures in Christ. Everyone in the Christian world affirmed that Christ was both fully divine and fully human; the difficulty was to find a formula which expressed this and still made sense in Greek categories of thought. Scandal and division arose whenever the formula used by one group was adjudged by another group to imply something less than full divinity, or full humanity, or an imperfect union between them.

After Chalcedon, the Western Church, now using Latin as its medium, did not actively participate in the councils which continued to be convened in the Greek-speaking Eastern Roman empire (though councils – Western in composition – were to develop as a feature of later Latin Christianity). The Eastern (Orthodox) churches today speak of seven ecumenical councils; the Roman Catholic Church of only four in the early centuries.

Councils were an instrument to obtain consensus in contentious situations; they were also theatres of interaction between the Christian faith and the Greco-Roman intellectual tradition. Inevitably they also had a political dimension. Imperial power, losing stability, harassed by theological controversy and nervous of dissent, had an interest in securing and enforcing agreed solutions. At Nicea, the first council, bishops were present from Armenia and other places beyond the imperial boundaries. Later councils were without such extra-imperial representatives (who in any case were always vastly outnumbered by those from within the empire). Insensibly, 'ecumenical', which ought to mean 'world-wide', came in practice to mean 'empire-wide'. The Armenian church never accepted the definition of Chalcedon: it was not part of the process which produced it. A high proportion of the Christians of Egypt and Syria, provinces of the empire which believed themselves exploited and neglected by the imperial centre, and had vigorous vernacular cultures of their own, rejected Chalcedon. After the earliest 'ecumenical' councils, those parts of the Christian world for which the hellenistic Roman intellectual tradition was not determinative followed their own paths.

Outside the Church's organization, however, a cauldron of religious activity continued to boil in the hellenistic world. Church writers, both before and after the age of the councils, denominated all this activity 'the heresies', but the term covered a wide range of reference. Some of the movements, while borrowing Christian institutions or vocabulary, bore little relationship to the Christian faith. Others were radical indigenization movements which strove to bridge the gap between hellenistic culture on the one hand and the Christian faith with its Jewish scriptures on the other. Some arose from disputes on policy or practice. Yet others represented the Christian penetration of subcultures and minority cultures within the hellenistic world. Some movements which the Church at large declared heretical may simply have been local forms of Christianity.

The Roman empire was not, however, the first Christian state: the Kingdom of Armenia anticipated it by several years, and some small Mesopotamian states became Christian earlier still. Before 500, in fact, there were large numbers of Christians in areas which were quite independent of the Roman empire. There were sizeable Christian communities, for instance, in south India and south Arabia, in the Nile valley and the Sudan, in the Horn of Africa and the Caucasus. There were substantial Christian minorities in the Persian empire, with their own scholars, saints and martyrs; in this context the association of Christianity with the old enemy, Rome, worked against it. The size and significance of early Christianity outside the Roman empire is often under-estimated, and it was perhaps under-estimated within the Christian Roman empire itself. 'Ecumenical' councils in principle represented the inhabited world; the dynamics of their processes often ensured that their immediate relevance was to the Roman imperial world.

The barbarian phase (c.500–c.1100) By 500, the geographical and cultural base of Christianity lay in one of the three great world empires of the day. It had clothed itself in the intellectual garments of a sophisticated literary civilization, and taken up the tools of a high technology. From here it spread eastwards along the trade routes, southwards into parts of eastern Africa and, most significantly for the future, among the tribal peoples north of the long imperial frontiers. The expansion was made possible both by dedicated agents set apart to preach the faith and by ordinary people propagating it in the ordinary course of their work, trade and family life.

Roman attitudes to the peoples beyond the frontiers, the 'barbarians' outside the pale of Roman civilization, traditionally comprehended both fear and contempt. Christian Romans were no different in this respect; the fear that empire, and with it Christian civilization, would one day be swept away in a barbarian flood haunted many Christian thinkers. The flood eventually came, and the western half of the Roman empire collapsed under a barrage of fierce and ugly little wars. But the effect on the Christian Church was not at all what earlier writers had expected. Many of the barbarians were already Christians, if not always of a Roman kind. The archaic 'Arian' type of Christianity, long banned in the empire, was common; gradually, however, it gave place to the more developed Roman confessions. Indeed, in spite of long years of destruction and unsettlement, the peoples of northern and western Europe proved surprisingly open to both the religion and the culture of the people whose empire they had destroyed.

As the empire broke down, Christianity spread among the states which arose from its ruins; and as, in different parts of the West, various new peoples achieved dominance, Christianity spread among them also (see [5] for the example of England). There was no single means of propagation. Certainly, strong rulers sometimes built Christianity into their own expansion; Charlemagne, king of the Franks 768–814, and chief architect of the Holy Roman Empire, imposed the faith on the conquered Saxons, and Olav Trygvason (d.1000), the centralizing king of Norway, extended the number of Christians and his own power simultaneously. But conversion by coercion was far from universal. As a rule, expansion of Christianity meant that groups of people, linked by kinship, obligation or military obedience, adopted Christianity as, or at least into, their code of customary law. In these circumstances, even strong rulers had to proceed by consensus and with the support of their military elites when they listened to the preachers of Christianity. The Franks assumed the faith of the romanized Celts of Gaul whom they conquered. There were 'official' Church missions, such as that sent by Pope Gregory the Great to southern England in 597; and there were innumerable missions by small groups of monks and ascetics, driven by the desire for holiness and obedience, which were no part of any official Church strategy.

There were not many martyrs among the northern peoples. The progress of religious change was often rapid, whole communities moving behind their leaders to adopt a new code of custom. There were periods of return to the old gods, and places which long resisted the new ways: much of Sweden was unpenetrated before the eleventh century, most of Finland later still. Nevertheless, the old gods died. Many people were clearly weary and disillusioned with them. Christianity sometimes also helped the transition from an obsolete raiding lifestyle to settled farming. Inevitably, however, attitudes belonging to the old religion passed into the new. The driving motives of the old religion had been power and protection against enemies, whether natural or spiritual, in a harsh, uncertain and dangerous world. Power and protection were still needed; Christianity offered a clearer map of the spiritual universe, clarified the concept of moral offence, and in doing so extended the need for protection into the eternal world. The symbols of religion changed, the directions and motives of religious practice remained. Power and protection were still sought, but their source was now the one God, with the Church the trustee of power and its saints and ceremonies the channels. Saints and martyrs quietly replaced the local spirits.

This process coincided with an enlargement of world-view. Migration, war and resettlement had already eroded traditional kinship-based identities and many local identities: a universal ('Catholic') Christian Church offered a wider kinship. The same

Church acted as the courier for transmitting substantial elements of Roman culture and learning, now put to Christian uses. In particular, the use of Latin throughout the West for scriptures, liturgy and learning forged a powerful bond. Rome may have lost its old political significance, but its association with Peter, the chief of the apostles, gave it a special spiritual significance; and something of the old sense of identity associated with the Roman empire was preserved in the idea of an empire of Christ, in which all Christian princes and peoples owed allegiance to Christ who spoke through his apostolic representative on earth. The concept of the Christian Roman empire, revived and continued, appears in the empire of Charlemagne, whose power base lay in what is now France and Germany and whose capital was in Aachen. It is significant that he was crowned as emperor by the Pope.

The adoption of Christianity as the basis of custom, the new sense of wide kinship, the single language for learning (of which the Church was the effective agent) and worship, the multi-layered sense of affinity with Rome, all reinforced the idea of Christianity as territorial. Nonconformity to established custom was unthinkable for the peoples of the north and west; and Christianity – expressed in a single 'universal' Church which used a single language – was now the basis of custom. The territory occupied by the peoples living under Christian custom was itself Christian; it was the duty of its rulers to keep it so. The whole area from Ireland to the Carpathians formed a sweep of Christian territory, united in liturgical language and in recognition of Rome as source of heritage and of spiritual authority.

We have spoken so far of the Latin Christianity which arose in western and central Europe following the collapse of the western Roman empire. The shape it took was greatly influenced by the fact that the West had only one functioning church clearly historically associated with the apostles. It was easy, therefore, for Western Christians to see Rome as the crown of the entire system through which the power of God flowed for the salvation of humanity. Numerous factors, historical and cultural, political and theological, gave Rome a special place in the minds of Western Christians, and enforced the view of its bishop as successor of Peter and earthly representative of Christ. Eastern Christians saw the matter differently. In the eastern Mediterranean, the Roman empire still existed, the successors of Constantine still reigned in the New Rome, Constantinople, and its language was not Latin but Greek; and it could claim a number of ancient churches associated with the apostles. However, the position of Christianity in the East became transformed under the impact of the arrival of the Arabs, united and inspired by their new-found faith of Islam. By 642 Muslim Arabs had overrun Egypt and Syria. Over generations to come, much of the population of these provinces, once the very heartlands of Christianity, embraced the faith of their new rulers. In the Middle East as a whole, Christianity became and has remained the hereditary faith of a minority community. In North Africa, overset by both barbarian and Arab invasions, it died out altogether. In Constantinople, Greek-speaking Roman emperors, ruling over south-eastern Europe and Asia Minor, prolonged the hellenistic–Roman phase of Christianity for several centuries more.

Meanwhile, just as in the West, Greek Christianity spread across cultural boundaries to the 'barbarians' beyond the imperial frontiers. A significant difference from the Western process was a much greater openness to the use of vernacular languages in worship. In 988, Christianity was proclaimed the official religion in Kiev; and though it took several centuries to penetrate the countryside, the basis of Russian Christianity was laid. The balance of Eastern Christianity changed: new Slavonic churches appeared to the north, while the outlying provinces in the Mediterranean area were gradually eroded as Muslim occupation moved forward, and their Christian populations gradually followed the same path as those of Egypt and Syria. The political and cultural divide sharpened between East and West, and was reinforced by language. Eastern and Western Christians increasingly belonged to different worlds.

The local forms of Christianity associated with Egypt, Syria and the Euphrates valley, now separated from both Eastern and Western Christianity into Monophysite and Nestorian families, continued to spread beyond the old bounds of the empire. In the Persian empire, hostile pressure on Christians was sometimes intense, and the Christian communities in India seem to have been augmented by refugees from persecution in Persia. We hear of 'Persian' churches in the sixth century as far off as Sri Lanka; and Christian merchants and missionaries from the Persian lands travelled the silk route. By 550 CE there was a church among the Huns of Bactria, and in 635 a Nestorian bishop was at work in the capital of T'ang China.

The Christian heartland, however, was now in the area inhabited by those whom Greeks and Romans had called barbarians.

Another shift was taking place in the centre of gravity of Christianity, almost as remarkable in its effects as the transition from Jewish to Greek Christianity. No longer was the typical Christian city-dwelling, literate, Greek-speaking, or 'civilized' at all; typical Christians were now northern peasant cultivators. The Muslims inherited much of the legacy of Greco-Roman civilization. None the less, Christianity, more than any other factor, connected the 'barbarian' peoples north of the old frontiers to the inheritance of Greece and Rome. The Church was the principal factor in establishing literature, learning and literary habits among peoples who were essentially pre-literate. The Church maintained the creeds of the councils, and asserted orthodoxy as it knew it; and its learning and theology were inevitably shaped by the hellenistic–Roman phase of Christianity.

One factor in the expansion of Western, Eastern and Oriental Christianity alike was an institution which the different branches of Christianity adapted in different ways. Monasticism – close-knit communities of men or women, celibate, dedicated to religion, living together under rule – had originated in the hellenistic–Roman phase of Christianity. Its pioneer was a fourth-century Egyptian Copt called Antony, who began a desert community which sought to emulate the commitment to discipleship called for by Jesus in the gospels. Benedict of Nursia (480–546?) developed a style of community life more suited to the climate and conditions of western Europe. Monasticism took various forms and served various purposes. For centuries it produced the task forces of dedicated, disciplined people needed for the proclamation of the faith in new areas, and formed centres of religion, education, scholarship and philanthropy across the whole region. Some notable women achieved prominence and influence through leadership in the institution or by the way in which they exemplified its ideals. The motives which filled the monasteries were not always of the highest, but over centuries they provided a focus for those who sought to be radically Christian, to imitate the lifestyle of Christ and the apostles. In this sense monasticism was a protest movement, a protest against a society which was Christian in principle and name but not in practice. In post-Roman Western society, dominated by military elites and often violent, the monasteries provided an alternative community where a consistent Christian life might be actualized, for those who could otherwise see no such possibility. The developments of a later period were to make the Western form of the institution still more flexible, by cutting the dedicated community free of the monastery. The strikingly different figures of Francis of Assisi (1181–1226) in Italy and Dominic (1170–1221) in Spain produced 'mendicant' orders of friars whose lifestyle, though ascetic, kept them in constant interaction with wider society. Francis, who had been a wealthy man, stressed Christian service to the poorest, laid down a rule for his followers which required utter simplicity of life, delighted in the natural world as God's handiwork and took his preaching mission even to the Muslim world in Egypt. Dominic stressed purity of doctrine and confutation of error, and his 'Order of Preachers' had a substantial impact in centres of education and learning. Both figures stimulated a great expansion of public preaching. It is not surprising that in later times the orders they founded became important in the establishment of the missionary movement.

The Western phase (c.1100–c.1600) The adoption of Christianity by the barbarian peoples of the north and west, and the tortuous process of assimilation which followed, gave cohesion to a substantial area of Europe where Latin was used as the language of worship and learning and the bishop of Rome recognized as spiritual arbiter. This could be conceived as Christian territory, 'Christendom'. Since Christianity was the basis of law and custom there, all members of the community must be Christians; the responsibilities of a Christian ruler included ensuring the repudiation of idolatry, heresy and schism. Events elsewhere reinforced the European sense of Christian identity. The Western Christian pattern of development differed so much from that of the Greek-speaking Christians of the eastern Mediterranean that relationships were never easy, and often hostile. A formal breach in 1054 was followed by a thaw when it appeared that Western Christians might aid their Eastern co-religionists against the Muslims. The idea of Christianity as territorial gave substance to the idea of crusade: war conducted with a view to regaining 'rightfully' Christian territory, including the lands where Christ and his apostles had walked. But in 1204 Crusaders from the West looted Constantinople and desecrated its churches, an event which drove a wedge between West and East which lasted for centuries. It also opened the way for the final collapse of the old Christian empire of the East. After centuries of erosion, Constantinople itself fell to the Turks in 1453, and the last remaining areas of the original hellenistic Christian heartland were eclipsed. Meanwhile the Nestorian adventure in China had faded, and by the thirteenth century a Mongol dynasty was ruling in Beijing. For a short time the possibility flickered of a Western Christian mission to the Mongols, but Western Christianity was not yet able to sustain such horizons. Gradually much of the Christian presence among the tribes of Central Asia faded. Despite the persistence of Christian communities in Ethiopia and India, Christianity was becoming increasingly European in its constitution. And Europe was becoming increasingly Christian. The fifteenth century saw the last pagan strongholds in the north brought into Latin Christendom. Still more strikingly, it saw southern Spain restored to Christian rule in the most successful of all the Crusades.

The sense of Western political responsibility for Christianity was matched and enhanced by intellectual, literary and artistic developments. The initial nexus between Christianity and Western societies had been in the sphere of law and custom, and a prolonged period of interaction ensued between the Christian tradition and the principles of law, an interaction assisted by the Roman inheritance of legal codification. This took Christian theology in new directions, for instance, in exploring the idea of atonement; the early classic text by Anselm (1033–1109), *Cur Deus Homo?*, applies current assumptions about legal responsibility and compensation for offences to the significance of Christ's death.

The intellectual and artistic developments of the period, the foundations of scientific practice and the related technological advance all owe something to the discovery by Latin-speaking Westerners of the legacy of Greece. This development owed something to sporadically renewed contact with the East, but more to the knowledge of Greek texts derived from Muslim sources, notably in Spain, reflecting Greek philosophy and literature. The Greek intellectual tradition, as well as Roman legal thinking, underlies the widely different expositions of Christian belief represented in the *Summa Theologica* of Thomas Aquinas (1225–74) and the *Institutes of the Christian Religion* by John Calvin (1509–64), the most considerable encyclopedic thinkers produced by Western Christianity. A return to Greek language studies opened up access to the Christian scriptures in a new way; Desiderius Erasmus (*c.*1466–1536) produced an edition of the Greek New Testament in 1516. The most important technological development of the period, printing, played a critical part in the religious conflicts of the time, and may have done much to determine their outcome. A European artistic and literary tradition emerged over this period, its conventions and its register of symbols essentially formed by Christian influences. Rediscovery of the Greek legacy was ambivalent in its effects, for one of them was to awaken interest in pre-Christian themes from the classical period. In the political sphere, the period saw the first signs of the development of nation-states, as the consciousness of common nationality gradually became more important than allegiance to a particular ruler. As nation-states developed, each with its own distinctive features but each professing to be a Christian community, the possibility increased of Christianity taking distinctively local and national expressions within the Western framework.

Christianity had developed in Europe against a background of centuries of primal religion. European peasants retained their lively sense of spiritual forces, benevolent and malevolent, always being at hand, ready to break into daily life. Originally these forces brought bane or blessing in this life; specifically Christian teaching introduced a new dimension, the inevitability of another life, for which earthly life was a preparation. To the perils of this life was added the need of shelter from the terrors of divine judgement in the next. For both it was natural to turn to the Church, which had replaced the spirit shrines as the reservoir of spiritual power, and to its priesthood as the specialists in spiritual power. Inevitably this laid popular religion open to manipulation and commercial exploitation.

The sixteenth century brought the end of the worst abuses in most of Europe; it also brought the beginning of the end of the conditions which produced them. But the accompanying social, intellectual and religious ferment proved too much for the unitary structure of Latin Christendom.

The nature and meaning of salvation came under particularly intense discussion. In debate fuelled by the abuses to be seen in popular religion, three affirmations about salvation became the watchwords of a significant movement in the Church. First, salvation is 'by grace only' – that is, it is a matter of divine initiative, not subject to the mechanical and quantitative methods of achieving it which dominated so much of popular religion. Second, it is received 'by faith only' – that is, it is not earned by human merit. In the third place, the source of knowledge about it is to be located 'in Scripture only' – there are no hidden or privileged sources of salvation to be dispensed by experts or specialists. The conservatives of Christendom had no wish to deny the importance of grace, faith or Scripture; but they were frightened by the 'onlys', and insisted on the need to couple other factors in salvation to those of grace, faith and Scripture. These included the merits of the saints, and especially of the Virgin Mary, as a contributory means; the necessity of good deeds as a condition; and the continuing tradition of the Church as a source of authority, and the use of that tradition for the interpretation of Scripture.

From the sixteenth century onwards, Western Christianity appears in three distinguishable streams or branches. The period in which the streams become clearly distinguishable is usually called the Reformation era. In fact, there were several reformations, each with roots deep in the past, each reflecting a widespread drive against corruption and abuse, an intensification of spiritual endeavour, a revival of biblical studies and a clearer, more coherent formulation of Christian convictions.

The most conservative reformulation could claim institutional continuity with the older Christianity, by asserting not only the concept of a single, 'Catholic', that is, universal and supranational Church, but the primacy and authority in that Church of the bishop of Rome, the successor of Peter, chief of the apostles. This conservative renewal is often called the Counter-Reformation, but as a movement of reform it was not simply a response to Protestantism, and some of its greatest successes – for instance in Spain – were achieved before the Protestant movement had proceeded far. Its doctrinal expression is found in the Council of Trent (in session between 1545 and 1563) which codified Catholic doctrine with special reference to the other reformations of the sixteenth century. The outcome of the conservative or Catholic Reformation is reflected in the Roman Catholic Church.

Another formulation, usually called Protestant, had as its watchwords the three 'onlys' referred to above: salvation is by grace only, received through faith only, and the guide to it is Scripture only. By these criteria, many so-called 'Catholic' features could be identified as relative innovations, products of recent centuries, and certainly no part of the teaching of the apostles. The best way of achieving continuity with the apostles was therefore to pay attention to the apostolic scriptures. Since the Church as a whole manifestly refused to submit to the type of reformation indicated in the scriptures, it was for the Christian rulers of each nation to reform the Church within their own boundaries. As a result a series of national 'Reformed' churches appeared, similar to one another in their main teachings, but reflecting local conditions especially in their forms of church government. The increasing availability of the scriptures in various European vernaculars heightened this tendency to national expressions of Christianity.

National, regional and local movements of this type appeared in many parts of Latin Christendom. In southern Europe they made little headway. Elsewhere, the best-known representative figures are Huldrych Zwingli (1484–1531), Martin Luther (1483–1546) and John Calvin (1509–64). All were originally leaders of local reform movements, though all, and especially the latter two, came to have much wider influence. Zwingli, a Zurich priest, was the first to see the church and society of his area reformed on 'Protestant' lines. Awakened by the new movement of biblical and humanistic studies, disgusted by the supersititions of popular religion at a local shrine and distressed at the demands made on his canton for mercenaries in papal armies, he effected his reformation by a process of persuasion of the Zurich Council, while also being identified as a popular patriotic figure. Luther was a typical product of German peasant religion, and a monk who in quest of salvation had thrown himself into the penitential discipline of the contemporary Church. As a professor of biblical studies he produced ringing enunciations of the three onlys, and later a German translation of the Bible of abiding influence. Protected by the elector of Saxony, he was the great symbolic figure of the movement in Germany, and often of Protestantism as a whole. Calvin, a generation younger, was a French humanist scholar. Moving to Geneva, he found a twofold source of influence. As a pastor, he helped to make the city-state a working model of a reformed religious and civil community which many admired and sought to emulate; as a writer, he applied the humanist intellectual tradition to the exposition of the Bible and, in his *Institutes of the Christian Religion*, to the reasoned and comprehensive statement of theology in the new categories, using – a revolution in itself, this – the French language for the purpose.

Both the Catholic and Protestant reformulations retained the territorial conception of Christendom which had shaped Western Christianity since the conversion of the northern barbarians. But a third formulation arose which broke with the underlying assumption, common to both the old and the new 'Catholic' model and the 'Reformed' national churches, that membership of the Church was coterminous with membership of the civil community. This radical branch of the Reformation movement, often called 'Anabaptist', took many and various forms, but its general effect was to break the link between church and state, and to recreate the vision of the persecuted Church of early Christianity. The radicals took the Protestant affirmation of salvation to its logical conclusion, and identified the Church with the company of true believers, those who had personal faith. In the process they enabled the concept of freedom of conscience to arise, and heralded the adaptation of Christianity to the developing ideas of the modern world.

The period of reformulation was followed by a century of struggle, conflict and uncertainty. In the end, southern and central Europe opted for the conservative, 'Catholic' formulation and the maintenance of the supranational institutional church (and with it, the supranational language of worship, Latin), while northern Europe generally adopted the 'Protestant' formulation, with national churches reflecting national characteristics and governed on a national or regional basis, with worship and scriptures in the vernacular. Many areas saw deep division and there were people, like Erasmus himself, who would gladly have avoided the necessity to choose between the two strands. It has been observed that the eventual division of Europe into an area where the concept of a universal Church took precedence and one in which local, vernacular expressions of Christianity predominated follows (very roughly, and with important exceptions such as Ireland and Poland) the boundary of the old, settled provinces of the Roman empire. The radical Anabaptists, who threatened basic European assumptions about society as well as about doctrine and church government, met fierce opposition from governments everywhere, but survived in protected pockets. Their day of significance for Christian history was still to come, notably in their impact on North America.

The institutions of Western Christianity were affected in different ways by these events. As we have seen, Latin retained its place in Catholic Europe while the Protestant countries increasingly used their vernaculars for the scriptures and worship. In Catholic Europe the monastic and other orders were left in very much their traditional form; in the coming age of expanding Christendom they were to provide an essential source of missionary personnel. The Protestant reformers abandoned monasticism as open to abuse and as obscuring the sanctity of family life; they insisted that family life in society could be just as holy, just as dedicated to God, just as beneficial in its effects. The radical reformers went further. For them the Church was the holy community of dedicated people, actualized in each congregation of true believers. The Anabaptist congregation is the fully Protestant version of the monastery, with husbands, wives and children all incorporated into a community wholly committed to a Christian way of life.

In different ways each of the three manifestations in which Western Christianity was from this time forward embodied represented a radicalization of Christianity, a rejection of compromise with some of the pre-Christian concepts which had underpinned Western Christian practice for centuries. Each provided a path of adjustment to the modern world, to more complex forms of society and a wider universe of ideas (see figure 2.1).

The years that saw Western Europe become the Christian heartland also saw the balance of Eastern Christianity transformed. Bulgaria, Serbia and Russia in succession became seats of major

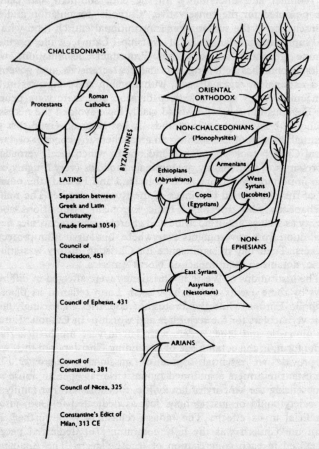

CHALCEDONIANS

Protestants

Roman Catholics

BYZANTINES

ORIENTAL ORTHODOX

NON-CHALCEDONIANS (Monophysites)

LATINS

Separation between Greek and Latin Christianity (made formal 1054)

Council of Chalcedon, 451

Ethiopians (Abyssinians)

Armenians

West Syrians (Jacobites)

Copts (Egyptians)

NON-EPHESIANS

East Syrians

Assyrians (Nestorians)

Council of Ephesus, 431

ARIANS

Council of Constantine, 381

Council of Nicea, 325

Constantine's Edict of Milan, 313 CE

Figure 2.1 *The relationships between Eastern, Oriental and Western Christianity*
Source: *from the late J. M. Hornus, by permission.*

new Christian populations. Their churches were organized on the model of that of the Roman empire of Constantinople, but they were quite prepared on occasion to withstand that empire's authority. The Greek Christianity centred in Constantinople had a late flowering in the last period of the Eastern Roman empire. Its monasteries produced spiritual and mystical writers with the power of Gregory Palamas (d.1359); its laity, theologians as profound as Nicholas Cabasilas (d.1380). (Until recently, the lay theologian was usually more characteristic of Eastern than of Western Christianity).

When, with the fall of Constantinople to the Turks, the old empire passed under Muslim rule, Russia had already known two centuries of Mongol domination. The Christian eclipse in the south, however, was not paralleled in Russia; under the Mongols the Russian Church was protected and quietly throve. The centre of gravity of Eastern Christianity moved northwards as that of Western Christianity had already done. The fall of the Second Rome in Constantinople was to be the prelude to the rise of the Third Rome in Moscow.

The maritime phase (c.1500–c.1920) From about 1500, Europe, which had so signally become the Christian continent, nurturing Christianity in a degree of geographical isolation, came into ever-increasing contact with the world beyond. Its new seaborne capacity brought it into relation with continents of whose very existence it had been ignorant. Russia, its eastern bastion, in inevitable competition with the Muslim powers to the south, extended its interests and activity across the great Asian land mass to the east, and thus into encounter with the established powers of South and East Asia. The two processes of expansion, by sea and by land, which extended over several centuries, transformed the balance between Europe and the rest of the world. Europeans assumed charge of vast areas as settlers or rulers, claiming possession of many territories and controlling the economies of still more, until, at the outbreak of the First World War in 1914, people of European origin dominated the globe. The position of Christianity was likewise transformed; after having been for so long essentially European, it became diffused across the world. It was not immediately clear that this would involve substantial modifications of the European model of Christianity, for Christian diffusion was accompanied by diffusion of the cultural norms of Europe. Nor was it always noticed that a decline had now begun of Christian allegiance in Europe itself, just as it had begun to expand elsewhere. Taken together, these developments indicated a new phase of Christian history, a further change in centre of gravity, and one which would cut many of the ties to the territorial model of Christendom so characteristic of the long association of Christianity and Europe. This phase overlaps with the last, since parts of Europe were in significant contact with the non-Western world while others were still engaged in the reformulations of Christianity described in the last section.

With the whole of the eastern Mediterranean under Turkish rule by 1500, the ancient centres of Christianity became concerned mainly with survival. Russia, however, became a centre of Christian thought and spirituality, developing an ascetic and mystical style of its own. Throne and Church were closely linked, as they had been in Constantinople; and the Tsar (or 'Caesar') was, like the Christian Roman emperors, the defender of the Church and of its orthodoxy. As Russian economic and political interests moved east, so did Russian Christianity, producing new Christian populations among some of the peoples of Siberia, outlasting the Russian presence in Alaska, and establishing a small presence beyond the limits of Russian power, for instance in Japan. In Europe itself, Russia assumed the role of protector of the Eastern Christians. Christian identity had much to do with the emergence of independent Balkan states as the Turkish empire decayed, a movement pioneered by Greece in the early decades of the nineteenth century.

Western expansion was even more dramatic, and the expansion of Western Christianity even more significant. The Iberian powers were first in the field; by 1500 Spain had set up a vast new empire, which had changed the balance of its economy, in Central and South America. By 1650 Portugal was established not only in Brazil but along the coastlines of western, central and south-eastern Africa, in parts of India, and in South-East Asia, with footholds in China and Japan. France and the northern powers, England and the Netherlands, followed, settling large tracts of North America, exploiting the commercial advantages of the Caribbean islands, and competing for the great prizes in India and beyond.

There had been little previous contact between Western Christianity and non-Christian peoples (other than the Jewish minorities); and relations with Islamic peoples were soured by centuries of warfare, crusade and folk memory. Further, the territorial model of Christendom in which all those born into the community were part of the Church, and in which Christian rulers were responsible for maintaining Christian regimes, encouraged the idea that to explore or control new territories involved setting up Christ's kingdom there. The earliest colonial expansion was thus conceived in a spirit of crusading zeal. In Spanish America the indigenous cults were forbidden and whole populations incorporated into the enlarged Christendom. The exercise, however, proved far more complex than at first envisaged. Contact with the indigenous concepts of the Americas, which was forced upon serious Christians once the indigenous languages were used for Christian purposes, exposed gaps in the theological structures formed from centuries of

European experience. The brutality and rapacity of the conquerors meanwhile called the moral status of the conquest into question; so that Christian faith, originally urged as a motive for conquest, became, with figures like Bartolomé de Las Casas (1474–1566), the principal factor mitigating its effects. Recognition of the capacity of the conquered peoples for conversion implied recognition of their full common humanity and potentially of their equal status as Christians; and acceptance, however nominally, of Christian ethical norms provided the conquerors with almost their only available source of self-criticism. Over the coming centuries conversion in Central and South America (by inducement, force and conviction), together with settlement from southern Europe and intermarriage, laid the foundations of a new Christian continent. Its moral ambiguities, however, were to return later to haunt it, and in time it appeared that there were important differences between this new Christendom and the old.

For the future of Christianity, however, it was less important that the Spanish seemed for a time to expand Christendom than that the Portuguese found the process almost impossible. Portugal's immense overseas commitments left the resources of a small country severely stretched. Portugal was not always able to overthrow the power of resistant Islam or Hinduism even in the territories that it controlled, still less in the vast hinterlands on which the Portuguese enclaves depended. The outcome was a new development, which had been foreshadowed occasionally in the Christian West by Francis of Assisi and others, but had little place in the territorial model of Christianity that Europe exemplified. This was the rise of the missionary movement: the emergence of a body of people with the task of promoting, commending and illustrating Christian teaching, but with no power of coercion. Missionaries went not only to the territories under Portuguese control, but beyond them, to the heart of the Mughal empire (where Akbar the Great invited them to his court), to China (where by sheer persistence they found for themselves a niche in the imperial court) and to Japan (where for a while they had a remarkable impact). All these missions, though their bases lay in the Portuguese enclaves, depended for their existence on the sovereign power of the host nations. Their remit could, as happened bloodily in Japan, be suddenly withdrawn. Without, probably, any such original intention, the missionary movement pointed in a different direction from that indicated by the Spanish conquests. It recognized that the extension of Christian territory was not an immediate prospect. A much longer interactive process was initiated of involvement in the life, thought and languages of the peoples of the non-Western world.

The early missions came from Catholic Europe, and depended for their maintenance on the orders, especially the mendicant orders. New orders and societies, such as the Society of Jesus (the 'Jesuits'), came into being. The missionaries came from many countries besides Portugal and Spain and their priorities and concerns were not always those of the monarchs of those countries, to whose care Rome originally committed the Church in the new territories. In fact, the overseas expansion of Europe began a process of separation between the economic and political interests of the various European nations and the religious interests of the Christian faith, which around 1500 had seemed to be identical. The gap widened as the northern, Protestant powers began their overseas expansion. This expansion was explicitly economic or strategic in motive. Propagation of the Christian faith was rarely a part of active public policy; and the largest of such enterprises, the British East India Company, explicitly avowed its religious neutrality and sought to avoid public alignment with Christianity. The church settlements so painfully worked out in the sixteenth century in the various countries of Europe could rarely be maintained in their colonies abroad. The European territorial model of Christianity proved hard to transplant outside Europe. Though the high period of the European empires in the later nineteenth century provided a degree of security for missionaries by comparison with earlier periods, the official policy of the colonial powers had other goals, which often involved the conciliation or furtherance of Islam.

The missionary movement in Protestant countries took firm shape only in the eighteenth century, at a point when the first cycle of Catholic missions had lost impetus. Protestantism had no orders, but contemporary conditions permitted the development of voluntary societies. Such associations, set up for the purpose of achieving specified religious or charitable objectives, became widely influential in western Europe during the late eighteenth century, developing greatly in the nineteenth. Societies to promote overseas missions were prime examples. Voluntary societies had no basis in the way churches had developed in Christendom: they were not subject to civil or ecclesiastical control, were able to bypass official church leadership, and depended on the vision and energy of participating activists. They could employ the skills and knowledge of laypeople, who were often prominent in directing them, and could be flexible enough to transcend the boundaries of churches. Some – and missionary societies took the lead in this respect – developed local membership networks and effective propaganda and information services which could maintain interest and participation. It was through such societies, nourished by the new streams of piety and enthusiasm, that the Protestant missionary forces were recruited, maintained and organized. As a result, the missionary movement developed not only independently of governments but to a large extent independently of official church structures. The nineteenth century saw a new cycle of Catholic missionary activity, with a new batch of orders and societies to maintain it.

Despite all this effort, in most parts of the non-Western world the statistical growth of Christianity did not appear significant, even as late as 1900. The exception was in the Americas. As well as the Spanish enterprise in the centre and south, European peoples from a variety of Christian backgrounds and traditions settled in their thousands in North America. Some of the early settlements in what became the United States were formed by people influenced by the radical wing of the Reformation who dissented from the religious settlement in their homelands, which gave their settlements a distinctive character. But in the nineteenth century, as the immigrant populations moved steadily westwards and their descendants multiplied, Christian enthusiasm expanded with them. By every token, Christian profession and activity in the United States steadily increased in the nineteenth century; even the burgeoning new cities, which in Europe were leading a recession from Christianity, experienced a marked Christian impact. Other areas of European immigration, such as Australia and New Zealand, produced nothing of this character. By 1900 the United States was replacing Europe as the principal centre of Christian activity, influencing European Christianity by means of its energy, organization and innovative methods, and supplying much of the missionary force for the rest of the world.

North American Christianity never became an extension of European Christendom. The thought of the new country as essentially Christian territory carried over from Europe, and was sometimes extremely powerful; not until the twentieth century was it seriously challenged. Unlike Europe, however, the United States had no state church: pluralism, if originally a Christian pluralism, was consciously built into its development. While different immigrant groups brought their different church structures from Europe, others arose on American soil, innovative and adaptive and, above all, mobile. The absence of the pressures of tradition, the infinite possibilities of innovation, led to many attempts to recreate a lost 'primitive' Christianity in the new setting, often restoring some lost emphasis (holiness, the return of Christ, the power of the Holy Spirit), or some neglected feature of church life or organization. Some forms of American Christianity also developed the use of the Bible as a quarry of facts which could be fitted together to form a complete theology and world-view.

The other remarkable religious development arose from the creation of Afro-America. This originated from the steady importation, over several centuries, of Africans to work as slaves in the plantations of northern, southern and Caribbean America alike. By a variety of processes, most of these adopted Christianity, Catholic in

South and Protestant in North America, and the interaction with African tradition, and the special experience of African-American people, imparted some distinctive features to their faith. The consciousness of the African connection remained, and African-American Christianity has sometimes had a significant impact on Christianity in Africa itself. In a separate development, the encounter of African religion and Catholic Christianity in South America and the Caribbean produced new religions, such as Candomblé, Umbanda, Santeria and Voodoo.

Meanwhile, European Christianity entered a slow recession over the maritime period. Its progress was steady; revival movements in both Catholic and Protestant countries regained some lost ground in the eighteenth and nineteenth centuries. Western Christianity, which had inherited from the pre-Christian past the idea of religion as transmitted custom binding the whole community, had to accommodate to the developing culture of the modern West. One of the most crucial features was the heightened sense of the importance of the individual and individual worth. Movements like Pietism (originating in seventeenth-century Germany) and the Evangelical revival (which affected Protestants on both sides of the Atlantic for much of the eighteenth and nineteenth centuries) adapted Western Christianity to the new climate by stressing the necessity of individual conversion and decision, while not breaching the principle of public recognition of Christianity by the community. Such movements introduced a distinction between the 'nominal' or 'formal' Christianity acknowledged in society and the 'real' Christianity of inward experience of renewal and active faith. The same principle of individual action could, of course, also issue in a decision to alter or reject the Christian system altogether. Thus, while Western Christianity as a whole managed to accommodate happily enough to the main features of the European Enlightenment, an alternative, rationalistic, non-Christian and often non-religious Western tradition emerged alongside it. Currents of thought, of which Marxism was the most coherent and powerful, drew from the Christian moral vision while rejecting the framework of Christian belief. Western Christianity in this period is thus marked by two features which appear opposite in tendency. On the one hand, Christianity was marked by a new activism. The theatre of Christian faith was the whole world of human activity, not the heavenly training ground of the monastery or the alternative community of the elect. On the other hand, religion increasingly moved into the sphere of private choice and private judgement.

The southern phase (from c.1920) A new phase of Christianity has developed in the twentieth century. It has seen another remarkable shift in Christianity's demographic and cultural centre of gravity. At

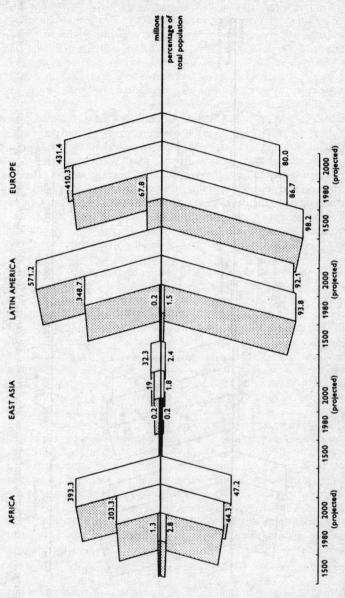

Figure 2.2 Geography and statistics of Christian profession, 1500–2000: Africa, East Asia, Latin America and Europe

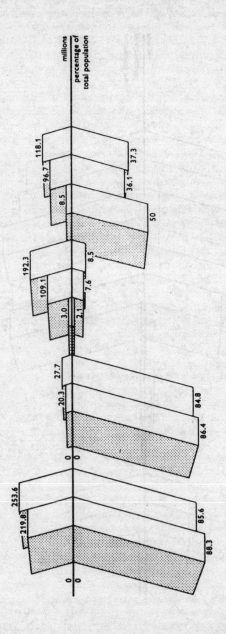

Figure 2.3 Geography and statistics of Christian profession, 1500–2000: North America, Oceania, South Asia and (former) Soviet Union

the beginning of the previous phase Christianity was the religion of nearly all the peoples of Europe and of their New World descendants, and of few others. Today it is distributed throughout the world, is characteristic of peoples of the southern continents and, generally speaking, is receding only among people of European origin. (See figures 2.2. and 2.3.)

The recession from Christianity observable in Europe in the previous phase has accelerated. In the beginning of the present phase Russia, the centre of Eastern Christianity, officially adopted an atheistic ideology, and following the Second World War other east European countries did the same. This never produced the abolition of Christianity; only in Albania, a largely Muslim country, did open religious activity actually cease under Communist rule, and Poland under Communism was the most strikingly Catholic country in Europe. But in Russia and some other countries where the Church was long subject to political supervision, generations grew up without direct influence from the Church which had once permeated society and shaped national identity. The eclipse of Communist governments has introduced religious liberty without restoring the Church to its pre-revolutionary power. It has also introduced a new pluralism, with a variety of religious influences, Eastern and Western, Christian and post-Christian, seeking to establish themselves in a situation which offers little predictability.

In the open, liberal regimes of western Europe the recession from Christianity has been more marked, especially in the second half of the century. The public and civic recognition of Christianity, often expressed in a state church, which was inherited from the earlier Christendom, has generally remained in place. Even in those countries of northern Europe where a tax is levied to support the state church and its activities, religious and philanthropic, only a small minority exercise their right to opt out. Nevertheless, the principal churches have seen a steady diminution of membership and influence and church attendance has declined sharply over the period. Meanwhile immigration from Asia has established Hindu, Muslim and Sikh communities as a highly visible feature of the European religious scene.

Christian adhesion in North America was increasing during the period when recession was beginning; any recession in the present phase of Christianity thus starts from a significantly higher Christian base. Some sections of society in Canada and the United States now show marked signs of the recession; others are vigorously resisting it, reflecting cultural divisions in the society itself. A conservative expression of Christianity is widely identified with traditional American cultural values. Decline has been most pronounced in the older churches closest to European patterns. Islam has also exercised a powerful new influence among the once overwhelmingly Christian African-American community.

For the Native American peoples, attitudes to Christianity were inevitably linked to relations with the white population, and the extent to which accommodation with them and to their lifestyle was acceptable or possible. By the twentieth century, with Native Americans displaced from their lands or confined to pockets, and the traditional ways of life for most of them impossible, Christianity was widely, though never universally, accepted. The appropriation, however, was often passive and seldom vigorous, with relatively few movements to establish distinctively Native American forms of Christianity. Even where traditional practice was maintained or revived, it usually existed in parallel with Christian profession rather than in interaction with it. Recent years have seen more signs of theological activity related to Native American culture, often in association with the question of land rights. Still more striking has been the revival of Native American religion, with elements from different local traditions fused in a pan-Indian post-Christian religion into which ecological and 'New Age' concerns are woven. The Inuit of Arctic America have, generally speaking, moved quietly into the Christian faith.

Latin America is one of the largest Christian culture areas. It was formed out of the coexistence and (in varying degrees) the coalescence of two elements: the indigenous peoples with their primal religions and the Iberian incomers, bearing a culture shaped by the conservative but reformed Catholicism of the sixteenth century. An African infusion (very considerable in Brazil and Cuba) in many parts, and later immigration from western and southern Europe and elsewhere, have increased the range of cultural and religious influences. In its origins, Latin America reflected the attempt to establish Christendom on the European model, with the state, the Catholic Church and the social hierarchies in effective alliance. Under the independent republics which succeeded the Iberian monarchies, the model was often modified, either on account of political tensions or to encourage immigration from Europe. Meanwhile, despite early Spanish attempts to eradicate the old religions, popular religion often maintained a symbiosis of indigenous and Catholic ritual and belief.

The twentieth century has seen both social upheaval (including an unprecedented degree of urbanization) and religious ferment which bears comparison with the sixteenth-century Reformation period in Europe. As in Europe at that era, a ferment of ideas and movements has produced a variety of responses. A movement within the Catholic Church reformulated both theology and church organization by giving primacy in theology to praxis or action. The Christian Gospel is primarily good news for the poor; the test of theology and church organization is how far it actualizes and demonstrates this. At one time such ideas – often called 'liberation theology' – appeared to have strong support even in the leadership of the Catholic Church, but in recent years official church statements have been careful to avoid markedly innovative theology or provocative social action. A second feature of the century has been an exponential growth of Protestantism; in some Latin American countries Protestants now form a high proportion of those Christians whose religious profession is active. The most noticable strand of Protestant Christianity is charismatic or Pentecostal Christianity, which has also proved compatible with conceptions belonging to popular Latin American world-views and with sustainable economic development. Charismatic activity was at one time prominent in the Catholic Church also, but is less noticeable in the current more conservative climate. A contemporary feature is a new stress on the indigenous cultures of Latin America and their long-suppressed religious traditions. There are some signs, as in North America, of the organized revival of these traditions in a modernized form; but there are also conscious attempts to express the Christian life and teaching in ways which take the indigenous cultures seriously. The increasing availability of the scriptures in Andean languages may take some branches of Latin American theology in new directions. Latin America has in the present century already shown the capacity to revise and reshape the inherited forms of Christianity.

The Caribbean area stands culturally between Latin America and Afro-America, and its Christianity bears the religious influences of both.

In the nineteenth century some Western observers expected the religions of Asia eventually to collapse under the impact of modernization. This has not happened: the old religions have reformulated and adjusted, and Christianity remains in most Asian countries the faith of a small minority. Taken as a whole, however, it is a statistically significant minority, and in a few countries substantial. The Philippines (which actually has a Christian majority) bears many of the features of Latin America. Korea has seen remarkably rapid Christian growth for a century. Many of the world's largest congregations are in South Korea, which also has a highly developed missionary consciousness with a remarkable number of Christian missionaries working in every part of the world. The Christian community of India, though small as a proportion of that country's total population, is remarkable both for its antiquity and continuous history and for its capacity for fresh and constructive Christian thought. India provides perhaps the most testing environment of all for Christianity, for here it risks either being an essentially foreign implant or being absorbed into Hinduism. For a long period, from Ram Mohun Roy to Gandhi, the influence of the figure and teaching of Christ was evident outside Christianity in much Hindu thought; it is now much less clear. The Christian presence is strongest in the south, where the majority of adherents come from the lower end of the caste system or fall outside it altogether, and in the upper north-east, where some of the tribal groups are over-whelmingly Christian. A great deal of current Christian activity is related to the fact that so many Christians belong in the socially dis-advantaged Dalit category. Thus, while some Indian Christian thinking is expressed in relation to the dominant forms of Hindu tradition, much is seeking an expression of Christianity in con-sciously Dalit terms. The recent development of religious liberty in Nepal has been accompanied by the emergence of a distinctively Nepali church.

China saw a movement towards Christianity early in the century, associated with the brief 'modernizing' period. This appeared to fade with the period of war and revolution that followed and the establish-ment of the new post-revolutionary China. It has recently become clear that the half-century following the success of the revolution saw substantial Christian growth. In 1950 the Christian population was estimated as well under a million; estimates of the present figure vary between 8 million and 13 million. Both Catholics and Protestants are divided into bodies with official government recognition and oth-ers without it. All have demonstrated the capacity that their situation has demanded to maintain themselves without overseas support and with minimal overseas contact.

The years following the establishment of the new China also saw many overseas Chinese becoming Christians, especially in Indonesia, Malaysia and Singapore. In Japan, however, the Christian community has remained small, despite its long history in the country, the early independence of its churches from Western control, and the distinction of some of its leaders.

The strongest impact of Christianity in Asia has been upon the tribal cultures with primal religions, often within countries where the central state authority has a Buddhist or even a Muslim ethos. There are important Christian populations in Myanmar (Burma), Thailand, south-west China, Sumatra and other parts of Indonesia, and among the Vietnamese montagnards and the forest peoples of Malaysia. The importance in Indian Christianity of the tribal groups (especially, but not only, in the upper north-east) has already been noted.

In the Middle East the period since 1920 has been marked by the collapse of the Turkish empire, the decline and withdrawal of the Western empires, the creation of the state of Israel, the emergence of Middle Eastern oil as a factor in world politics, endemic war in several countries and, frequently, an embattled Islamic conscious-ness. These factors have weighed heavily on the Christian minorities (mostly Arab) of the area, some of whom have come under severe pressure.

Speaking generally, despite the small numbers of Asian Christians relative to the total population of Asia, the period has seen Asia become a more significant factor within Christianity than at any other time since its early centuries. It is also noteworthy that much of the growth has taken place with minimal Western Christian intervention. In China and Myanmar (Burma) there has been no Western missionary presence for decades, and in some other countries it has been restricted.

Statistically, the most remarkable growth of Christian profession in this period has been in sub-Saharan Africa. On one estimate this profession has been moving in geometrical progression since the mid-nineteenth century, with the numbers of Christians doubling about every twelve years. The process has gone on over the pre-colonial, colonial and post-colonial periods, so that Africa has now one of the largest concentrations of Christians of any of the continents. There are also signs that the Christian faith is over the generations interacting with African systems of beliefs and social organization, a process likely to prove as complex in its results as the similar process in the hellenistic world many centuries earlier. For many African peoples this has already produced a major reordering of the traditional maps of the universe. Four components were characteristic of the traditional maps (though not all African peoples had all four): God, other divinities, ancestors, and power objectified in persons or artefacts. The Christian impact has greatly increased the significance of the God component (which in traditional Africa was often marginal to actual religious practice). The effect has been to marginalize the component represented by territorial or other divinities. In the general religious consciousness God has come nearer, while the old divinities – conceptually – have moved to the edges of the religious map, or become absorbed as the subordinates of God or demonized as his enemies. A great variety of thought and practice is evident on the relation of the ancestors, so substantial a part of African family life, to Christian thought and practice, and this question seems likely to provide an area of future development, and perhaps controversy.

African Christianity is not proving to be a replica of the Western model. It has to deal with realities of life which have been no part, or at least no recent part, of Western experience: ancestors, witchcraft, sorcery, healing without access to advanced medical resources. Already Africa has produced models of the Church quite different from those typical of Western Christianity. New movements abound, some following patterns recognizable in earlier Christian history, some apparently unique to Africa, but all evidence of specifically African appropriations of Christianity.

The Pacific is the other sphere of notable Christian impact, though here the movement to Christianity was already evident during the nineteenth century, when island states in Polynesia like

Tonga, Samoa and Fiji converted en masse with their rulers. Indeed, it appeared that here a new Christendom might be set up, with some states adopting Christian constitutions. A variety of causes impeded this, some of them the product of colonial conditions, such as the British importation of Indian workers to the sugar plantations of Fiji. The Christian impact on Melanesia was later, slower and more complex, with new religions often arising to combine traditional and Christian elements. In the small island of Tanna in Vanuatu, one such new religion has replaced Christianity. But in general Christianity has progressed steadily in Melanesia over the period, and is apparently doing so in the largest land mass, the island of New Guinea, which comprises Papua New Guinea and the Indonesian-governed Irian Jaya.

Australia and New Zealand, in so far as their populations reflect a European origin, have taken part in the general decline of Western Christianity. The Aboriginal population of Australia, which never assimilated to a Western model of Christianity with any enthusiasm, is, in the current revival of interest in Aboriginal culture, exploring new forms of Christian expression. The early Maori Christian story, like that of other Polynesian peoples, included a widespread movement into the Christian faith, and signs of its vigorous appropriation. The situation became complicated, and then soured, by the scale of European settlement and the effective relegation of Maori Christianity to an appendage of white churches, a process which is now being reversed.

Christianity is now much more diverse in its forms and manifestations, its geographical spread and its cultural variety, than at any previous time in its history. The only safe prediction appears to be that its southern population, in Africa, Latin America, Asia and the Pacific, areas which at present provide its centres of special significance, also holds the key to its future.

The Study of Christianity

One way of categorizing different forms of the study of Christianity would be to distinguish between 'emic' studies, in which the materials of the Christian tradition are framed within the Christian community, and 'etic' studies, conducted outside the community on some principle external to the tradition. In many periods and places, however, this merely distinguishes between apologetics designed for a specific audience and hostile polemic. Thus in the early Christian centuries, Christian writers appealed to educated hellenistic–Roman audiences by expounding Christian convictions and affirmations about God, Christ, the future life, the Christian community, and Christian practices and lifestyle in terms of contemporary metaphysics, morality and law. The process of explanation in such terms was in fact a powerful stimulus to the creation of a body of Christian theology, an intellectual construct produced by the application of rational thought to the normative sources. On the other hand, there were also descriptions of Christianity from anti-Christian sources such as that by the second-century Platonist Celsus, known to us from a reply by the Christian philosopher Origen (?185–254). Celsus sought to demonstrate the incompatibility of Christianity with the accepted axioms of contemporary thought, its disreputable oriental origins, and the social and intellectual inferiority of its membership. The Neo-Platonic attack on Christianity was continued by the third-century philosopher Porphyry, whose *Against the Christians* (in fifteen books) survives only in fragments.

The triumph of Christianity within the Greco-Roman world by the fourth century altered the parameters of study. No longer was it necessary to produce reasoned presentations of the faith to attract the attention of outsiders. (This form revived when the Christian position was no longer secure; John of Damascus, *c.*673–749, a pillar of Greek Christianity living in a multi-religious but Muslim-dominated society, expounded a system of knowledge in which Christian theology was fused with science and medicine.) Nor, under the Christian empire, are comprehensive, encyclopedic statements for the faithful common. (Origen, who lived before the Christian triumph, was unusual in compiling a work of theological exploration – *On First Principles*, he called it – for its own sake, with no obvious apologetic purpose.) Theology was active under the Christian empire, but its main concerns were to find valid ways of describing in contemporary terms the implications of traditional understandings and statements about the relationship of Christ to God, and of the human and divine aspects of Christ's being; or, with Augustine of Hippo (354–430), the greatest Western Christian thinker of the early centuries, the nature of humanity in the light of contemporary thought, anguished personal experience and the Christian affirmations about salvation. This serves to illustrate an important and recurrent aspect of Christian theology. New developments in theology rarely arise as a result of abstract intellectual activity conducted for its own sake. It is the pressure of particular situations which forces the reflective process and dictates its priorities, sometimes forcing new questions which demand answers on to the theological agenda. This introduces a local and occasional element into theology. Issues which caused convulsion in one age and place may be taken for granted or pass unnoticed in another. For the same reason, there is no finished corpus of Christian theology (even though particular groups of Christians have from time to time assumed their own to have that status). New segments of social reality pose new problems; the encounter with new or changing systems of thought requires exposition in new terms.

The most comprehensive form of the study of Christianity to emerge in the wake of the post-Constantinian triumph of Christianity in the Roman world was historical; the development of a specifically Christian philosophy of history. Eusebius of Caesarea (c.265–339) is with justification called 'the father of church history'; in fact his achievement goes some way beyond that. His *Ecclesiastical History* relates the history and chronology of the world as he knew it to the biblical history from Adam to Christ, and the trials and triumphs of the Christian Church from apostolic times to his own, that is, the days of Constantine. He thus develops a view of Christianity as the key to human history, and presents that history in terms of God's redemption of the world through Christ. It was an influential model. Augustine, who saw the beginnings of the collapse of the Western empire, turns in his greatest work, *The City of God*, to enunciate a Christian philosophy of history, the providence of God actively at work in human affairs for the salvation of the race. Writers at work in the barbarian period of Christian history, such as Gregory of Tours (538–94) and Bede (673–735), demonstrate how the redemptive activity has reached their own northern lands. In their histories the events of comparatively recent times in Gaul or England are seen as part of a chain in which the stories of early humanity, Israel, the apostles and the early Church and the Roman empire are all providentially linked with them.

Another medium of Christian study which developed at an early period, and has proved particularly durable, is the biblical commentary. The practice of sustained study of particular books of the Bible seems to have begun as early as the second century. By the third it became, with Origen and others, a major literary form in East and West alike, often as the basis of systematic preaching. It has continued to modern times, changing in method with changes in approach to textual interpretation.

We have already seen the underlying influence of Roman law in the intellectual development of Western Christianity, producing over centuries a tendency to systematize and synthesize theological thinking into comprehensive schemes. The tendency was well developed long before the diversification of Western Christianity into Catholic and Protestant streams, and continued unabated in both after that division. The chart in figure 2.4 was first drawn in 1590 to illustrate a work called *A Golden Chaine, or The Description of Theology*. It will be noted that such a description of theology can be represented as a chart, map or diagram, such are its logical interconnections, its chain-like coherence. The work illustrated is not one of intellectual speculation – it is intended for a practical purpose, as a pastoral guide for anxious people seeking salvation; but the practical religious theme can be articulated within a total world-view, an encyclopedic system. The *Golden Chaine* is from the Reformed tradition, but Roman Catholic theology has been equally hospitable to systematization. The *Summa Theologica* of the Dominican Thomas Aquinas, and the *Institutes of the Christian Religion* by the French reformer John Calvin, have already been mentioned as encyclopedic works that have stimulated Western Christian thought over centuries. Later theologians went further, extending theology (the title 'queen of the sciences' goes back a long way) to a complete system covering art and culture, politics and economics; an index, in fact, of a Christian civilization. The monumental *Church Dogmatics* of Karl Barth (1886–1968), written against the threat to a Christian understanding of the world posed by Nazi dominance in Germany, continued the tradition to the middle of the twentieth century.

The tendency to schematize should not be exaggerated; there has always been a current in the West that resisted it. Its representatives tend to work with a number of key theological concepts, or to use recurrent biblical themes as guiding principles. Eastern Christianity has always been much less prone to systematization, its theology much less compatible with maps and diagrams. The importance of tradition as a guide, and the ultimate goal of deification as the ideal of religious life, give a different tone to its scholarship.

The later study of Christianity in the West has been shaped by three streams of influence in particular: Renaissance humanism from the sixteenth century, the European Enlightenment from the later seventeenth, and evolutionary thought since the nineteenth. The later streams have not replaced the earlier; the earlier have gone on flowing, and the waters have intermingled. The three streams have influenced both emic and etic views of Christianity, and have had a deep effect both on how Western Christians have thought about and expressed their faith and on the emergence of alternatives to Christianity reflecting the conditions and priorities of the West.

The Renaissance brought a quickening of European intellectual life, a new consciousness of the resources available in Greek, and new recourse to the original languages of the Bible. The invention of printing opened new possibilities for the comparison of texts; for the first time one could ensure that all copies of a given exemplar were identical. By this time the Greek church, in which the language of the New Testament was still living speech, was in eclipse, and in no position to take advantage of these opportunities. It was therefore Western scholars, enthusiastic for the new learning, and stimulated by the recent recovery of the lost Greco-Roman past, who led the way. There was a special impetus for those who wished the church to proceed 'by Scripture only'. Reformers like Zwingli and Calvin began their careers as humanist scholars of the ancient

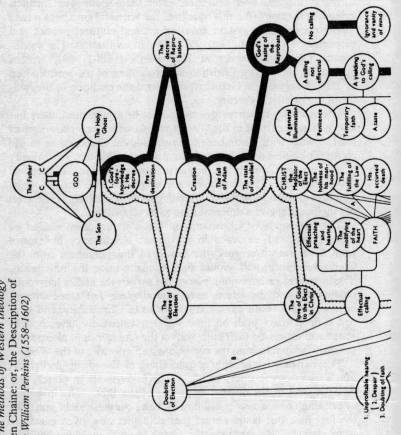

Figure 2.4 *The methods of Western theology*
Source: A Golden Chaine: or, the Description of
Theology, by William Perkins (1558–1602)

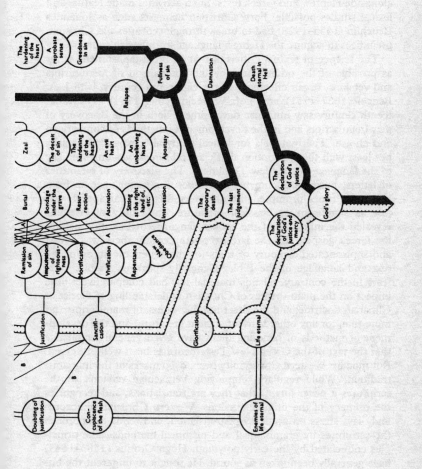

classics; and Luther was a professor of biblical studies. But reformers were not alone in the new scholarship; Erasmus, who stood
clearly neither with the old party nor the new, produced the first
printed Greek New Testament, and the conservative Spanish
Cardinal Ximenes de Cisneros (1436–1517) oversaw production of
a massive work which set the official Latin version of Scripture
alongside Hebrew and Greek texts. Such activities made textual and
lexical studies possible. Early Christian hebraists such as Johannes
Reuchlin (1455–1528) had to break through centuries-old Christian
prejudices to acquire the Hebrew language from Jewish sources.

The science of textual criticism, that is, the establishment as far
as possible of the original text by the comparison of manuscripts
and versions, began effectively in the eighteenth century, with J. A.
Bengel (1687–1751) and J. J. Wetstein (1693–1754). The nineteenth century saw immense development both in the discovery of
new manuscripts and in the development of methods of comparison
and choice. The materials for lexical study also expanded greatly,
not least with the recognition that classical Greek was only one key
to the language of the New Testament. The discovery of quantities
of letters, business documents and other non-literary papers from
hellenistic times prompted the discovery that popular speech was
just as significant as classical literature; and study of Aramaic
revealed the influence of the spoken language of Palestine behind
the Greek gospels. By the late twentieth century there was a vast
and sophisticated armoury of tools for the systematic study of the
text and language of the Bible. Generally speaking, despite early
fears to the contrary, all this material has had comparatively little
impact on the main themes of Christian understanding of Christ or
Christian doctrine; and the sheer number of extant manuscripts (far
more than for any other work of ancient literature) and the development of methods of handling them have given general confidence
that the text of the Greek New Testament has been well preserved.
But modern Western Christianity bears deep marks of the humanist
tradition. While regularly employing vernacular versions of the
scriptures it never forgets that they are translations, and recognizes
the primacy of the original versions. Western Christianity accordingly lays stress on accuracy of translation, and tends to approach
the scriptures by grammatical and historical methods. The principles enunciated by the early polymath Hugo Grotius (1583–1645)
have generally been taken as sound. He sought to undercut the bitter theological controversy of his times by seeking to establish grammatical and literary rules which would be above party strife, rather
than making theological coherence itself the aim. Nor has the
humanist tradition necessarily been a mark of scholasticism
detached from active religion; movements for deeper devotion and
spiritual renewal, such as the Pietist movement in Germany around

Philip Spener (1635–1705) and A. H. Francke (1663–1727), demanded scholarly precision about the biblical text as part of the serious business of applying the scriptures to daily life.

The Enlightenment stream of influence, however, marked Western Christianity in a still more visible way. This intellectual movement of the later seventeenth and eighteenth centuries is often taken as introducing the modern era. Among its aspects are the establishment of reason as an autonomous basis of judgement, and a developed sense of individual consciousness, of the autonomous self. Such principles implicitly challenged the 'Christendom' mode under which Western Christianity had developed; and with some Enlightenment thinkers the threat to Christianity as a whole was made explicit. For one thing, systems appeared which were meant as alternatives to the Christian interpretation of reality, claiming rationality as their hallmark; these alternatives to Christianity had generally no place for the active acknowledgement of the transcendent. For another, the Enlightenment interest in establishing universal moral principles underlying human society meant that Christianity could be viewed principally as a body of moral principles binding a society; those aspects concerned with relationship with God, the transcendent world, with salvation, in fact, became secondary. And for a third, the concern with universal principles meant that Christianity could be treated as one component within a system of knowledge, rather than being the organizing principle of that system, or even the system itself. Religion moves firmly into the sphere of the private and personal, leaving public discourse essentially secular.

All these developments had immense implications for the wider study of religion which lie outside our present purpose. Suffice it to say here that etic study of Christianity, views from the outside, developed in ways not conceivable in the old Christendom. In course of time – though it took the developments of the nineteenth century, and the influence of evolutionary thought, to effect this process fully – new divisions of the study of religion emerged. In areas such as the sociology of religion, the psychology of religion, the history of religions, Christianity became only one element among others. Such studies, moreover, did not presuppose intentional engagement in the processes of salvation, which had been the motor of earlier studies and brought passion to them.

If the Enlightenment shaped modern Europe, it reshaped Western Christianity. The new currents of thought presented a threat to the way Christianity had been conceived in European history; accordingly, Western Christianity was reconceived in line with Enlightenment concerns. The process took place most noticeably in Protestant Europe; Catholic thought, especially in southern Europe, moved less willingly and more cautiously. Nevertheless, within a remarkably short period the process of cultural translation that has marked Christian history was once more well advanced.

Christianity accommodated itself to the new stress on individual consciousness comparatively easily; indeed, some of the new movements within it, notably Evangelicalism, postively hastened this process. Where this occurred, the inherited framework of Christendom was renewed, but its nature changed; the primacy of private decision in matters of religion, with pluralism its inevitable result, was recognized. In the study and intellectual presentation of religion, stress was laid on rationality and order, and on the excellence, comprehensiveness and social efficacy of Christian morality – themes compatible with Enlightenment concerns. It was reasonable to expect that a universe created by an all-wise God would operate according to discoverable laws. Theology was thus compatible with, indeed was cognate with, scientific investigation. Christians could not accept, with the more radical Enlightenment thinkers, a closed frontier between the phenomenal and transcendent worlds, but the regular crossing-places where special divine intervention took place in the world could be identified. The miraculous was not abandoned, but the place and purpose of miracles were more defined and circumscribed. That God governed the universe according to 'laws of nature' was taken for granted; there was even a 'natural theology' to be discerned in these laws, a theology consistent with the revelation in Scripture, preliminary knowledge of the God in whom Christians sought salvation. Consistent with God's character, laws of nature had a moral dimension, with implications for the conduct of social affairs. Philosophy, science, morality and theology belonged to a single discourse after all.

Thus Western Christianity made peace with Enlightenment rationality. It was even possible to reconstruct a total view of knowledge – not quite like the old schemes where theology provided the framework, but none the less coherent expositions in which philosophy, science, literature, astronomy, political economy – those disciplines which provided the 'arts of civilization' – formed a prelude to theology. In turn, theology demonstrated the ultimate source of the body of knowledge and activity which produced civilization. Such was the teaching presented to India, with some degree of success, by the nineteenth-century missionary Alexander Duff. It was equally a model of Christianity and a model of modern knowledge, and was accepted as a sound basis for education. It was also a total alternative to traditional Indian systems of knowledge, which manifestly did not accord with scientific order; its adoption would not only establish a Christian presence in India, but bring India fully into the world of modern knowledge and in touch with resources which could enrich the country's social and economic life by undermining those stultifying influences in Indian society which arose from lack of a valid comprehensive frame of knowledge. Scottish missionaries were perhaps more imbued with Enlightenment thinking than most, but in general the Christianity brought by the missionary movement to the very different cultures of Africa and Asia was deeply influenced by the Enlightenment. Education was a regular product and accompaniment of Christian presence.

Enlightenment Christianity was based on the assumption that science and revelation were compatible. Nineteenth-century studies produced challenges to that assumption. Some of these arose from new developments, but one of the more complex had its roots in earlier Enlightenment attitudes. If history and literature were in some sense sciences, might not the methods of historical and literary criticism be applied to the Bible as they were to other ancient literature? But to do this might be to indicate inconsistencies, inaccuracies or other deficiences; if so, was this compatible with the special status which the scriptures possessed as revelation? Such difficulties had been identified before, but invariably from sources hostile to Christianity. To take them up within the Christian frame of reference was to introduce new ideas about the nature of revelation.

In the end it proved hard to agree on what was properly 'scientific' in the sphere of literary and historical criticism. The earliest battlegrounds were in the Old Testament: first, indications of multiple authorship in the Pentateuch, and then, much more seriously, a total reconstruction of Old Testament history, of which the articulation by Julius Wellhausen (1844–1918) was the most erudite and influential. It was not all trauma; one product of the study, with its stress on historical context, was a new appreciation of the prophetic literature. When the prophets were seen in their contemporary settings, their calls for justice, humanity and social righteousness were heard as hardly ever before.

Similar study applied to the New Testament at first seemed less threatening. There was clearly a literary problem in the close relations of the first three gospels (called 'synoptic' since they posited the same general view of the life of Christ). The synoptic gospels, too, clearly differed from the fourth gospel in both form and approach. The 'synoptic problem' proved intractable, but in itself did not call in question the portrait of Jesus in the gospels; while the power of the fourth gospel over Christian devotion and imagination proved unbreakable. The twentieth century, however, brought the 'quest for the historical Jesus' – a series of attempts to get behind the synoptic gospels to a supposed historical kernel within them, and uncover the figure of the 'real' Jesus, stripped of garments assumed to be laid on him by the early Church. There proved, however, to be no unanimity as to the nature of the 'historical' Jesus. Some, such as Albert Schweitzer (1875–1965), found an apocalyptic stormtrooper proclaiming the imminent end of history; others, in contrast, found a pacific exponent of a simple gospel of love. It is hard to escape the conclusion that many participants in that particular quest found only what they were in any case looking for.

In some degree the whole application of literary and historical criticism to the scriptures has suffered from similar difficulties. The use of such methods, with the stress on historical context as the key to interpretation, has become a characteristic of mainstream Western Christianity. Germany set the pace, the rest of the Protestant world following with more caution and moderation. The Roman Catholic world long held aloof, but then entered cautiously and conservatively. Over the past generation and more, Catholics have fully shared the methods and results of other Western scholars. Conservative Protestants long resisted the trend but have now developed their own tradition of historical and literary approach.

It is impossible here to follow the rapidly changing scene, with its study of historical and literary forms, of oral tradition, editorial process and community use, not to mention the still problematic application of computer technology to style. What is remarkable is the range of attitudes to be found, especially in New Testament studies. There is little ground now for extreme scepticism about the text, or even about the dating of the documents: it is clear that the New Testament is a compilation from very early Christianity, most of it from well within the first century. But as to its nature as historical record, every possible position can be adduced in the contemporary literature, from strong affirmation to extreme scepticism. In applying the results of this research, many Christian scholars remain very close to the traditional interpretations of the person of Christ, while others completely reinterpret them. The almost universal adoption of the methods of historical and literary criticism has not produced the unanimity expected by its pioneers. Eastern Christianity, meanwhile, has taken little notice of the whole enterprise.

The third stream of influence on the Western study of Christianity came with nineteenth-century evolutionary thought. The announcement of scientific evidence for biological evolution posed a potential threat not only to the biblical account of creation, but to the Christian understanding of humanity as 'made in the image of God'. Before long the biological doctrine had been widely adopted in Western intellectual circles as a general theory of social explanation. It was at first an important element in the new social sciences of anthropology and sociology, as they emerged late in the nineteenth century. From there it passed to another new discipline, that of comparative religion.

After the first shock, the proposition of biological evolution seems to have had less impact on European theology than might have been expected. The total systems of knowledge forwarded by early

Enlightenment Christianity had now been superseded. They were hardly compatible with the methods of biblical criticism already in use, and it was now hard to keep up with, and thus incorporate, the explosion of new scientific and experimental knowledge. Science and theology were now taken as autonomous explanatory systems working on different levels. It was thus not the province of theology to identify the scientific means used by God in creation. Some, however, boldly appropriated evolution for the Christian framework of explanation, seeing it as God's providentially chosen means to lead humanity nearer himself. This explanation fitted with the reconstructed history of Israel by now widely accepted; it was also an element in the approach of many early twentieth-century interpreters of comparative religion. Such fashions faded with the recognition that the principle of evolution could have only limited explanatory value outside the biological sphere. In American Christianity, however, the controversy over biological evolution has been long and fierce, with a debate between 'creationism' and 'evolution' engaging the energies of both a considerable conservative Christian constituency and anti-religious forces.

The study of Christianity as discussed so far has been largely directed by Western currents of thought and Western concerns and priorities. Accordingly, the story is very much one which belongs to Western Christianity. The trends mentioned above seem not to have greatly influenced Eastern Christianity, even in Europe. The Western concern with questions of text and authorship has not been matched in the East, where the purpose of patristic study is the acquisition of the temper of mind of the fathers, not the establishment of the correct text. The Western emphasis on historical context as the key to interpretation has little appeal where the contemporary significance of Scripture derives from its antiquity and apostolic origin.

It is clear that quite new developments in the study of Christianity can now be expected. In the post-modern West, the long hold of Enlightenment values is less assured than formerly. Current debates about the autonomous nature of texts apart from their contexts, or about the validity of ranges of meanings for different readers, break with the old axioms about historical context and interpretation by grammatical rules.

Still more important is the growing non-Western dominance within Christianity itself. The majority of Christians now belong to the southern continents, where the effects of the Enlightenment are certainly present, but amid many factors of another kind. Some Latin American thinkers have undermined the literary–historical tradition of biblical interpretation by insisting on the primacy of the context in which Scripture is *read*. Many Asian Christians belong to cultures which have their own, quite different, traditions for the

reading of classical or sacred texts, and bring these to the reading of
the Bible. There was a Western Christian debate in the 1950s and
1960s about 'demythologizing' the Christian Gospel on the ground
that the New Testament reflected a universe of spiritual powers
quite alien to modern minds. In fact, that world-view is close to the
actual experience of large numbers of Christians in the southern
continents. To them, 'demythologizing' it would be extremely puz-
zling.

Southern Christianity has long been influenced by the West.
Now, Western Christianity is receiving influences from Southern
Christianity. The best-known example is probably that of liberation
theology, which arose in Latin America, with the Peruvian Gustavo
Gutierrez as its most prominent spokesman. This movement not
only recognized the appalling poverty, injustice and exploitation of
the masses of the population in Latin America, and the Church's
part in perpetuating them, but also made the test of Christian
authenticity participation in 'praxis' (i.e. action) to produce justice.
Liberation theology often used the language of Marxist economic
analysis, but was intended as a means of Christian proclamation
and fellowship. It was to be actualized in groups of people who
shared its affirmations and worked together to achieve them (the so-
called 'base ecclesial communities'). Translations of Gutierrez' book
A Theology of Liberation (1971) into English and other languages,
followed by other similar works, brought these themes to the West
and beyond. In Latin America, liberation theology has taken various
forms; but the thought of the Christian message as essentially libera-
tive, and the impact of that liberation on political and economic
structures and interests, has been potent in many other parts of the
world.

Similarly, the enunciation by the African-American theologian
J. H. Cone of a 'black theology', reflecting the conditions under
which the majority of African Americans lived in the United States,
found echoes in South Africa. Here a whole school of black theologians framed theologies specifically directed against the ideology of
apartheid and its declared association with Christianity. These aimed
to present Christ in a way that took account of the sufferings of the
townships and the daily affronts to black dignity, and channelled the
commitment to seek justice. Since the passing of apartheid as an ideology, South African theologians have been grappling with questions
which have long occupied their colleagues in the rest of the continent, namely the relation of Christ to the African past and the issues
arising from Christianity in African culture.

Recent Western theology has been alerted to the issue of the
faiths of Asia by the size and significance of their communities in
the West now. One of the major contemporary questions becomes
the development of a theology of religions that takes account both

of these faiths and their traditions, and of the Christian affirmation of salvation through Christ. In this activity the pioneering work of the Roman Catholic theologians Karl Rahner and Hans Küng has been particularly fertile; but much of the ground-clearing was achieved by Christian theologians in India in actual dialogue with believers of other faiths.

Perhaps the most far-reaching changes in the study of Christianity may yet come from the feminist movement and the issues of gender, femaleness and the place of women (probably an actual majority of Christians). The original impetus in this direction came from Western women theologians, who brought a lively critique of the traditional conceptional vocabulary of theology; but the issues are being taken up with other emphases in different parts of the world. It is too early yet to predict the outcome.

All these considerations show that the Christian world is increasingly interactive, with influences from different continents making an impact or finding echoes in others. This process will undoubtedly have an effect on the future development of the study of Christianity, and the development of Christian thought. Meanwhile the immediate study of Christianity is still inhibited by the assumption that it is essentially a Western phenomenon. The American K. S. Latourette (1884–1968) pioneered the global writing of Christianity; the challenge he posed has yet to be fully taken up.

Teachings

The process by which Christianity interacts with culture means that Christians of a certain time and place sometimes stress things which would seem irrelevant or even repellent to Christians of another. If a Martian observer were to visit, say, a meeting in the Jerusalem Temple in about 37 CE, a session of one of the early councils, for example that of Nicea in 325 CE, a convention of Irish monks in about 600 CE, a London meeting to promote civilization and missions in Africa in 1840 and a white-robed congregation singing through Lagos streets on its way to a healing service in Nigeria in the 1990s, he would in each case be meeting representative Christians from the heartlands of their respective times. He would also be meeting Christian groups which are historically interconnected: the Greek Christianity of Nicea arose from the activity of Jerusalem believers, the old Celtic Church was ultimately of Greek origin, its missions laid the Christian foundations on which nineteenth-century British Christianity was eventually built and British missions shaped the communities in which the indigenous Nigerian forms of Christianity appeared. But he might have difficulty at first establishing what they had in common; and each of the five groups would severely disapprove of some of the others' priorities and practices. If this is the case where there is a clear historical connection, it will be no less so where the historical process had been different. The Martian, for instance, might equally well visit fifth-century Arab holy men on their pillars in the Syrian desert, and the pilgrims who visited them for prayer and counsel; an Ethiopian monastery of the tenth century; a congregation in the tsardom of Moscow emerging from the sixteenth century, with parish church as academy, concert hall, art gallery and, above all, holy place; an Orthodox Inuit community in Alaska in the nineteenth century with a Christian shaman; and a twentieth-century seminar on questions of Christianity, technology and development associated with an ancient church of India claiming foundation in apostolic times. What follows does not seek to supply a systematic account of Christian teaching. Instead, it asks what the various communities which profess Christianity have in common. What links observant messianic Jews in the Jerusalem Temple, Greek intellectuals at Nicea, ascetic monks on Iona, earnest early Victorian Protestants in Exeter Hall and the Eternal Sacred Order of the Cherubim and Seraphim in Nigeria? And what links all of these to the Arab, Ethiopian, Russian, Alaskan and Indian groups, equally representative Christians of their own time and place? This means omitting from consideration of Christian teaching matters which any one of the Martian's chosen groups, and any large group of Christians today, might consider vitally important.

Christians Worship the God of Israel

Christian worship of the God of Israel indicates the historical particularity of the Christian faith. In every phase of Christian history it has been taken for granted that the revelation of God took place by a particular process, involving a particular people, the Jews. In each phase, too, Christians have seen themselves as in some way continuous with Israel, and the biblical history of Israel as part of their own, even in the periods of Christian hostility towards the Jewish community or amid harsh theological judgements on Jewish destiny. This 'scandal of particularity', the coupling of the divine purpose for the whole world to certain events, places and people, runs right through Christianity.

It is thus Israel's God who discloses himself, the God spoken of in the Israelite scriptures: beneficent and all-powerful, universal and alone, creator and guide of his people, the One Who Does Right. Before the God of Israel, humanity falls down, with hidden face. *I am* is one translation of the name of Yahweh the God of Israel, but this does not indicate static existence; he is the God Who Acts. The earliest Christians, being Jewish, knew this deity from the history of their nation and their scriptures. The divinities of popular religion, which formed the background of hellenistic–Roman Christians, were of a different order. Jews had always abused these as no-gods, anti-God. Christians took the same attitudes, and rejected the gods of popular religion.

However, an important stream of Greek thought had also rejected, or at least reinterpreted, these beings. The God of philosophical tradition was the highest Good: without a name, often spoken of in abstract terms or described in negatives. It was natural for early Greek Christians to fuse the God of the Bible with this concept of a somewhat distant, impersonal being. When Christianity spread to the barbarian peoples, they, too, were not encouraged to identify the God of their salvation with any of the traditional deities of their fathers. So the single impersonalized word 'God' replaced all the pantheons of Greece and Rome, and of the Celtic and Germanic and many other peoples. The living God of the Hebrews thus came to be interpreted in terms derived from the Greek philosophical tradition. The mind of all European forms of Christianity has been deeply affected by this. It may be that Southern Christianity, with different influences at work within it, will express itself in quite different ways. Some of them may be closer to the dynamic hebraic vision of the God Who Acts.

The history of Southern Christianity has differed from that of the Northern at a vital point. In terms of concept and language, Northern peoples abandoned their old pantheons in their entirety, substituting for them belief in an entirely new deity with the neutral name 'God' (actual practice was less clear-cut, and the old divinities, the Celtic goddesses in particular, often lived on in disguised form in the Christian world). In Africa, the Americas and much of the Pacific, however, the bearers of Christian faith repeatedly found that the people already believed in a great God, the creator and moral governor of the universe. As a result, in most Southern Christian communities the God of Israel and of Christians has a vernacular name from a pre-Christian past. This gives a starting-point for a theology quite different from that of the earlier phases of Christian history, by recognizing the presence of the God of Israel and the Bible in the past of each people.

Jesus Christ of Nazareth has Ultimate Significance

The inescapable connection of Christianity with history ties it to a place, a time and a person. In Christian movements, Jesus Christ is not considered simply to be a particular representative of a universal: he *is* the universal. Historically, Christian groups accord him ultimate significance, and for them life involves a commitment to following him.

There is an enormous range of interpretations of that significance, depending on what constitutes the ultimate for people of the particular time and place concerned. There is an equally wide range of understandings of the implications of following Christ, affected by the priorities of the situation in which the followers find themselves. Let us take, purely as examples, the Martian's five groups. The Jerusalem Christians saw ultimate significance in the messiahship of Jesus. For them he was the long-expected saviour of Israel. He would rule it rightly, end its sufferings and make it in actuality what it already was in principle: the people of the holy and right-doing God. ('You shall call his name Jesus, for he shall save *his people* from their sins,' the angel says to the devout family to which Jesus is born: *Matthew* 1: 21 [39].) This Messiah figure was fused with two other figures from the Jewish scriptures: the Son of Man, the divine agent who would bring the whole historical process to a climax, vindicate right and show the defeat of evil; and the Suffering Servant, who voluntarily underwent a sacrificial death on behalf of his people.

The Martian's second group, the fourth-century theologians assembled at Nicea, would have fully accepted all these statements, but for them the statements about Messiah, Son of Man and Suffering Servant did not signify the ultimate. The Greek intellectual habit forced them to make distinctions. If Jesus was the divine Son (and language like this was plain enough in the scriptures), it was necessary to define the implications. For God must by definition be unchangeable, beyond pain, beyond pressures from his own creation, and Jesus was a human, historical figure who suffered and died. After agonizing debate – by no means ended at this assembly – the Nicenes decided on a formula, conditioned by the Greek intellectual vocabulary, with which to express their conviction about the ultimate significance of Jesus. He is 'of the same substance with the Father'; and they expressly renounced language which might suggest he was some sort of demigod or mixed being, higher than man but lower than God.

The Martian's remaining groups of Christians would all have been prepared to accept the Nicene conclusion. But in some cases they would do so rather formally, mainly as a decision of the Church, a chapter in a book now concluded. The Irish monks, though supporting it strenuously, were perhaps more immediately concerned with Christ as the conqueror of evil, a 'strong name' with which they confronted the evil powers abroad in the universe, and the curses, incantations and sorceries of pagan opponents. The crucified and glorified Son of God also gave inspiration and hope of victory in the relentless austerity of their own lives; the creeds which expressed these truths were formulas of power. For the early Victorian group in London, all these ideas – the exact definition of the person of Christ, the inspiration of his sufferings, the invocatory power of his name – were questions either taken for granted or rarely thought of. The principal affirmation they made about Christ concerned his completed work of atonement for human sin, appropriated by each true believer personally in faith. Otherworldly asceticism had passed away; they were seeking to bring their affirmations about Christ to bear upon a busy, complex life, church and state, home and overseas. Most of these questions are very secondary for the Nigerian charismatic group in the 1990s. For them Christ is power, ultimate power available now, triumphing over disease and all the multitudinous frustrations and privations of urban life in modern Africa. He is also exclusive power, not to be shared, as half-Christians try to share him, with the old powers of traditional Africa.

There are certain features common to the various Christian perceptions of the significance of Jesus:

1 The 'ultimate' has to be interpreted in the light of the earlier statement that Christians worship the God of Israel. If God is one and Jesus ultimate, then language used of one will penetrate that used of the other. Jewish Christians like Paul used the language of divine sonship about Jesus without apparently feeling that they were compromising the centuries of fierce monotheism in their blood. There is no hint in the transition from Jewish to Greek Christianity of any crisis over the status of Jesus or the proper titles to describe him.

2 Jesus provides the moral yardstick for the believer. It is clear that ethical instruction had a substantial place in the early Christian communities. Some of this was in a form already well known to Jewish converts: avoid theft, lies, idolatry and sexual misbehaviour. Some dealt with family and social relationships. Some expounded the fundamental of Christian ethics, the principle of love. Jesus summed up the whole of the humanity-orientated side of the voluminous Jewish law as 'You must love your fellow human as yourself'; while Paul described love as 'patient and kind; not jealous or conceited or proud; not ill-mannered, or selfish or irritable. Love doesn't keep a record of wrongs; love is not happy with evil, but is happy with the truth. Love never gives up' (1 *Corinthians* 13: 4–7) [39].

But this ethical instruction is not free-standing; it is tied to the person of Jesus. Jesus himself associated his moral teaching with the idea of the Kingdom of God, the divine rule established on earth, inaugurated or brought near by his own coming. Paul and other early Christian writers linked the ethical dynamic of love to the figure of Jesus, who abrogated his privileges as divine son and voluntarily accepted unjust suffering on behalf of others (e.g. *Philippians* 2: 2–11; 1 *Peter* 2: 18–25). Jesus is the moral absolute for all forms of Christianity.

3 The ultimate significance of Jesus attaches especially to his death and its outcome. In each of the gospels, the four accounts of the life of Christ presented in the New Testament, an amount of space which would be disproportionate in any normal biography is devoted to the last week of Jesus's life. The interpretations, doctrines and theories developed by Christians to explain the significance of the events of that week are beyond number. Their very multitude indicates how fundamental these events are in all Christian perceptions. Not for nothing has the cross become the most widespread of all symbols of Christian faith.

Three ideas occur time and again in all the doctrines and theories about the death of Christ. The first is that Jesus's death was on behalf of others. The second is its association with forgiveness, and especially with God's forgiveness of humanity. In describing this, it has been common to use the language of atoning sacrifice; but even those Christians who have depicted Jesus principally as the perfect teacher, and his death as the supreme example of self-sacrifice or patient submission and non-retaliation, link these ideas with the forgiveness of past human wrongs and the possibility of a new start. The third idea is that of resurrection. This characteristically Irano-Jewish belief, resisted even by some in Judaism, was a feature of Christianity from the start. The earliest preaching insisted that Jesus was actually alive after being actually dead. No feature of the Christian message caused more intellectual problems, or more rejection in the Greek world, and some recent trends in Western thought have found it equally hard to accommodate. But in the Christian movement as a whole, belief in the resurrection of Christ has obstinately remained a fixed point. It is fundamental to the conviction of the triumph of God and of good in the face of the crucifixion of Jesus. From it has followed the conviction of the eventual resurrection of the rest of the human race.

While the Christian belief in the resurrection of Jesus has usually stressed its historical nature, it has never been viewed solely as a past event. Most expressions of Christianity depend on the conviction that Christ is not only alive, but accessible, and this is as true of much popular Christianity as it is of Christian saints and mystics. While some stress the presence of the Lord when the Christian company gathers for worship, others concentrate on a continuing relationship in daily life. Many of the simplest, and some of the sublimest, expressions of Christian experience display the conviction of a relationship that can only be expressed in personal terms.

4 The ultimacy of Jesus is associated with the end of history and the summing-up of the universe. Sometimes this has been expressed in the idea of a judgement of the righteous and the wicked: sometimes in the reversal of the fortunes of the proud oppressor and the wretched oppressed; sometimes in the renewal of the earth and the establishment there of a righteous order directed by Christ; sometimes in an amalgam of all these things. Whatever the form, the underlying conviction is that Jesus – as Judge, Saviour, Ruler, Renewer – will bring world history to its climax, triumph over its evils and inaugurate a new age. Christian beliefs about Jesus show the inescapable commitment of Christian faith to history. Nevertheless, the significance of Jesus for Christianity is not only of past history, but of the present and future as well.

God is Active Where Believers Are

Some faiths which share with Christianity the idea of a supreme God envisage this being as distanced from the world, approached by the believer, if at all, only in emergency. By contrast, it has been a common thread of Christian belief that God is both active in the world and accessible within it. In some expressions of Christianity that accessibility is commonly mediated through the saints, but there is never doubt as to its true source.

In the traditional theology of all the main confessions, this divine activity and the accessibility of the divine presence to the believer is associated with a doctrine of the Holy Spirit. The Jerusalem Christians spoke of 'Holy Spirit' in relation to the remarkable and spectacular capacity for ecstatic utterance which marked out their community. The fact that Gentile converts received the same capacity was one of the decisive factors in persuading Jerusalem believers to recognize their authenticity. By Nicene times these phenomena had disappeared; whenever anything similar emerged, it usually met with disfavour. Christians of the fourth century, however, spoke of the Holy Spirit as the special presence of God in the Church, leading it to right corporate decisions. The Irish monks thought of the power which gave a holy person boldness to speak the word of God even before mighty chiefs or rulers. The Victorians stressed the refining influence working in the individual Christian's character and personality, overcoming his or her natural self-centredness. The Lagos believers, perhaps rather vague about distinctions between the living divine Son and the divine Spirit (and indeed, the two are closely connected in much early Christian language), stress the manifest power of healing revealed in the community and its charismatic leader.

These examples – and others could be given – show that the precise formulation of the doctrine of the Holy Spirit is affected by the world-view of each particular Christian group. Those groups whose world-view is orientated towards personal effort and piety will stress a different type of divine activity from those who emphasize corporate life. Similarly, those who think of the Church primarily in universal terms will have different priorities from those who think primarily in local terms. None the less, in some form or other, most groups of Christian believers, even the least sophisticated, will insist that the divine activity is present and continuing in the world; they will identify that activity with the Holy Spirit, even if they use language in which the Spirit alternates with Christ; and, almost certainly, that activity of the Spirit will be held to operate especially in the sphere of the Church (however that body may be conceived by that particular group) and among believers.

In traditional Christian theology the combination of the three constantly recurring factors we have mentioned, that is, the worship of the God of Israel, the ultimate significance of Jesus and the immediacy of the divine presence to believers, has given rise to the doctrine of the Trinity. Statements of this doctrine developed in the first four centuries and (usually represented in English as 'one God in three persons') have been commonly adopted by most Christian groups. Eastern and Western Christians have differed on the precise formula indicating the relationship of the Holy Spirit to the other 'persons', but this difference has not involved any question of the unity of God or the status of the three 'persons'. The formulations (which have indeed been explicitly rejected by a small minority of Christian groups) owe much to the traditions and terminology of Greek philosophy and Roman law, but the idea which underlies them does not derive from these sources. The doctrine has been a way of stating three basic convictions which go back to the earliest period of the Christian tradition and reappear throughout its history: of the One God of Israel; of the Ultimate Christ; and of the divine activity where believers are.

Christians Use the Same Sacred Writings

Christians with no ethnic relationship to Judaism adopted the Jewish scriptures as their own. The resistance to this and other

Jewish features during the hellenistic phase of Christianity has been followed by other controversies about the 'Old Testament', notably among Western Christians of the last two centuries. Some of these were disturbed over conflicts with scientific or historical studies, or embarrassed at the possible moral implications of some 'Old Testament' passages. In one form or another, however, most Christian communities have been able to accommodate their changing views and emphases to the age-old Christian appropriation of the Jewish scriptures, and with them the conviction that they relate to Christ, and reflect a process of divine revelation of which he was the climax. This way of reading the scriptures is reflected in the earliest Christian writings, and derives ultimately from Jesus himself.

The double corpus of sacred writings formed by the 'Old' and 'New' Testaments (see pp. 55–8 above) has always been regarded as regulating Church life, and as the ultimate source of Christian doctrine. It has also been the regular court of appeal for prophets and reformers. Though Church authorities have sometimes restricted or discouraged lay access to the scriptures, public reading has always been a feature of Christian worship. Private reading has also been deeply influential, especially in Western Protestantism, in recent Western Catholicism and in the churches of Africa and Latin America. In some largely oral cultures today, public Scripture reading is again becoming important, as it was before the invention of printing.

Not until the sixteenth century did the West follow the precedent of earlier Christianity, and the example of Eastern churches, in presenting the Bible in the languages commonly spoken. Since then no feature of Christian expansion has been more noticeable than the translation of the Bible. By 1995 the whole Bible was available in at least 341 languages, and parts in more than 1,700. Many of the newer churches and movements in Africa and the Pacific have remodelled the Christian inheritance they originally received through Western missionaries on the basis of their reading of the Bible. This accessibility to translation has much to do with the immense cultural adaptations which have been such a feature of Christian history. Christians frequently draw the analogy between Scripture, a divine message in human speech, and Christ, the divine in human form. Both are called 'The Word of God'.

Christians Belong to a People of God

In view of the relationship already noted, it is not surprising that Christians feel a degree of continuity with Israel, and carry over Israel's sense of being a people of God. This idea of a people of God commonly transcends time, space and race, and comprehends all believers in Christ. If we look again at the Martian's five groups of Christians, we see that each recognizes a continuity with old Israel to which only the first belongs by birth. Each also recognizes that it is part of a Christian body which stretches back in time. The later groups, although apparently so different in their preoccupations from the earlier groups, still see those earlier groups as part of their own history.

This sense of a people of God in and beyond history, analogous to and continuous with Israel, results in a doctrine of the Church. The consciousness of a universal, time-transcending, corporate body to which Christians belong is common to virtually all Christian communities. How that body is identified and expressed in time and locality, however, is another matter. Some Christians have sought to identify the universal body with a particular Christian community, with a single focus of authority and an identifiable membership. Such an 'exclusive' type of doctrine of the Church has been a feature of both very large and very small Christian communities. Others have linked the concept of the universal Church with that of various autonomous 'churches', distinguished from each other by nationality, differences on secondary matters of doctrine, or even matters of convenience. Others stress the idea of a spiritual fellowship of Christians, drawing its reality from the experience of relationship with Christ, in which external and organizational matters are comparatively unimportant. Others again combine several of these ideas. (One common combination distinguishes between a visible organization of professing Christians and an invisible fellowship of authentic Christians.) Such different understandings inevitably issue·in diverse forms of organization and often reflect influence from the cultural setting and the nature of local society.

Practices

The range of Christian practice is even more immense than the range of doctrine and equally impossible to summarize. The syncretistic nature of historical Christianity means that Christian elements appear in many different aspects of social life. Almost any of the practices found in other religions of the world may be found in Christianity – but only in certain forms of Christianity. Pilgrimage or possession, meditation or monasticism are prominent and valued features in some types of Christian tradition, but regarded as alien to the essence of the faith in others. A mere catalogue of affirmations and denials would be tedious and unhelpful. A selection of Christian practices follows, some all but universal, some used by many, but not all, Christians, some used only by small minorities. The selected practices have in common only that they are explicitly referred to in the scriptures which are accepted as foundational by all Christians.

Prayer

Prayer is generally held to be both an obligation upon Christians and a privilege arising from the accessibility of the transcendent world. The elements of public and private prayer do not greatly differ, save for what the solemnity of liturgical language may bring to the former, and the spontaneity which personal situations may impart to the latter. Both have been moulded by three influences in particular:

1 *The Jewish inheritance of Christianity.* In prayer, Israel's high transcendent God is addressed by dependent, contingent and sinful humanity. Adoration, thanksgiving and confession are thus among the elements of prayer. The biblical *Book of Psalms*, originally designed for worship in the Jewish Temple and often used in Christian churches, has deeply affected the language of adoration. Its highly personal exaltations and laments, its fierce aspirations and desperate cries for help, have also provided a fountain of expression and example for Christian private prayer.

2 *The short prayer taught by Jesus to his disciples, commonly known as the Lord's Prayer.* Occurring in the New Testament in two slightly differing forms, this has from early centuries been regularly used in public worship, even by communities which use no other fixed form of words for prayer. It is also often taught to children and to new Christians. Its few clauses form an index of basic teaching on Christian life and practice: a daring address to God as Father; an acknowledgement of God's kingly rule and of desire for conformity to his will on earth; a quiet request for the immediate necessities of life; and a plea for forgiveness coupled with readiness to forgive.

3 *Other words of Jesus, backed by their exemplification in letters of Paul, which relate to the element of asking.* This element, whether on the petitioner's own behalf or on behalf of others, is thoroughly characteristic of Christian prayer. Indeed intercession, the act of representing the needs of others to God, is encouraged by the sense of community which underlies the various forms of the doctrine of the Church.

The meditative, contemplative tradition of personal prayer is also found, but not in all forms of Christianity. Christian mysticism has left a long record of spiritual experience and a rich deposit of literature. It is most prominent in the Orthodox churches of Eastern Christianity, where deification is the recognized goal of the Christian life. Eastern spiritual writers speak constantly of a vision of boundless divine Light by which, in the words of the seventh-century Maximums Confessor, 'the mind is ravished, and loses all sensation of itself or of any other creature, and is aware of Him alone, who through love has produced this illumination'. A Syrian writer of unknown name and date, usually called Pseudo-Dionysius, was deeply influential. God, he says, is beyond affirmation, being or knowing; the divine is dark through very excess of light. It is therefore by *unknowing* that the divine is approached: inner stillness, requiring unceasing and absolute renunciation, bringing to bear the deeper powers of the soul. Pseudo-Dionysius was read in the West through a ninth-century Latin translation by the Irish monk John Scotus Erigena, and in certain Western circles was influential over centuries. Sixteenth-century Spain produced notable mystics, including Teresa of Avila (1515–82) and her disciple John of the Cross (1542–91), who combined the interior quest (involving what John called the dark night of the soul and the ascent of Mount Carmel, and Teresa the interior castle) with practical activity such as the foundation and reform of monasteries and convents. In northern (Protestant) Europe, the Quaker tradition, which affirmed God to be the inner light indwelling each person, has perhaps provided the most fertile soil for mysticism, and for early Quakers such as George Fox (1624–91) experiences of union with the divine were a matter of frequent testimony. Some strands in the Anglican, Pietist Lutheran and Methodist traditions have also fostered the mystical quest – the hymns of Charles Wesley, for instance, are full of longing for the vision of God – and the great mystical writers have been read still more widely as a stimulus to prayer and devotion. But the official attitude of the Western churches, while favourable to meditation and contemplation informed by the teaching of Church or Scripture, has been cautious about mystical experience. Some mystics – including Teresa of Avila and John of the Cross – are among those recognized by the Latin church as its saints, people of pre-eminent holiness; but others who used Dionysius' 'way of unknowing' remained suspect. Even John of the Cross lived in intermittent tension with his ecclesiastical superiors; other mystical writers such as the German Dominican Meister Eckhart (b. 1260) were denounced as dangerous; Fox was accused of blasphemy; and Western manuals of theology often refer to the mystical quest with reticence and with reference to its pitfalls. Western spirituality, unlike Eastern, has been shy about using the language of the deification of humanity; communion, rather than union, with God has been presented as the way of devotion. Western Christianity has always feared any blurring of the distinction between transcendent God and contingent humanity; it has also been reluctant to admit what cannot be tested by Scripture or Church.

The question is moving into a new phase in Asia, where some Christians are exploring the goals and modes of their own mystical and contemplative traditions in the light of those of other faiths. A succession of Christian contemplatives in India, of whom the best-known are Abhishiktananda (Henri Le Saux) and Bede Griffiths have expressed the quest for union with Christ in terms of the Hindu quest for union with the divine. (A younger contemporary, Raimundo Pannikar, in a more philosophical and scholastic approach, argued that Christ was to be found within Hindu spirituality.) Elsewhere Christians have shared the disciplines of Buddhist devotional life.

A good deal of Western and African Christianity is essentially activistic in orientation. Because of this, the great intercessor is as likely as the great contemplative to be seen as a hero of spirituality.

Christian prayer is typically addressed to the Father in the name of Christ, and its motivation and effect are associated with the divine action of the Spirit. The use or absence of fixed forms or specific postures are secondary questions, and the variety of answers to them is beyond our scope here.

Days of Observance

In the overwhelming majority of Christian communities, Sunday, the first day of the week, is accepted as a time when the community meets for worship. The custom is of great antiquity and owes something to the Jewish Sabbath. The Ten Commandments (frequently accepted by Christians as representing the permanent, as distinct from the provisional, aspect of the Jewish Law) require the seventh day to be kept holy, that is, separate. Early Christian practice was to use the first day of the week, the day associated with the resurrection of Jesus, as the special day of worship. As Christianity came to dominate society, Sunday was recognized as a 'holy-day', permitting or requiring worship, and remitting some of the duties attached to other days of the week. In subsequent Christian history, the association with the Jewish Sabbath sometimes brought an emphasis on prohibition of unnecessary activity. By reaction, others stressed the recreational opportunities of Sunday.

In nineteenth- and twentieth-century Africa, the granting of a special status to Sunday (e.g. by prohibition of public markets) has often been a milestone in the acceptance of Christianity by a particular community. A minority of Christian groups, including the Seventh-day Adventists and some other bodies of American origin, the Church of Ethiopia and many African churches, insist on a literal observance of the Ten Commandments and the special status of the Saturday Sabbath.

About other 'holy-days' there has been less unanimity. In the hellenistic phase of Christianity, Easter, which commemorates the resurrection of Jesus and occurs near the Jewish Passover festival, was a landmark in the year. It was the pre-eminent time for baptism and reception of new converts. As Christianity spread among the primal peoples of Europe, indigenous festivals were often replaced by or altered into Church festivals. In particular, the great midwinter ceremony was linked with a commemoration of the birth of Christ, to make it the festival of Christmas.

The sixteenth-century Reformation challenged the structure of festivals, and especially the saint cult with which it was associated. In some Protestant countries, such as Scotland, seasonal festivals were abolished altogether. For practical purposes today the more conservative traditions, Orthodox, Roman Catholic and Anglican, adhere to a structured Church year with numerous festivals commemorating events associated with the life of Christ and the work of salvation, some other biblical themes and events, or particular saints. Other Western-originated Christian traditions take particular note of only a few major festivals, usually Christmas, Easter and perhaps Pentecost, the festival of the Holy Spirit. The official tradition of most Western churches exalts Easter, as in early Christian times, as the main Christian festival. In popular esteem, however, this place is usually held by Christmas, which in the post-Christian West continues to bear special significance as a season of 'peace and goodwill'.

Some newer forms of Southern Christianity appear to be developing a new pattern of festivals, strongly influenced by ancient Jewish models. Many African Independent churches, for instance, have great open-air assemblies which draw inspiration from Jewish feasts like Passover or Tabernacles, but give them Christian significance, rooting them in the history and experience of the local community or of the particular church.

Giving

In all Christian communities liberality is considered to be an obligation. Three particular areas of obligation can be identified. The first is support for the Church itself: the upkeep of places of worship, provision for their services, and usually the maintenance of men (and sometimes women) with special duties of ministry. The second (not invariable, but still very common) is the extension of the work of the Church. This reflects the consciousness of a wider kinship beyond the local worshipping community which is a recurrent feature of Christianity and places an obligation to maintain the wider work of the Church beyond the immediate locality. The third is an obligation to give to 'the poor'. Paul devotes a surprising amount of attention to famine relief (*Romans* 15: 25–8; 1 *Corinthians* 16: 1–4). In modern societies this is expressed in a range of charitable objects and organizations for the relief of suffering. Most Christian bodies with anything more than a local organization sponsor or share in some such activity. Concern for 'the poor' is by no means unique to Christianity, but it has been especially characteristic of Christianity to *organize* the consequent liberality. Institutions for education, nursing or healing, for relief of famine or for assisting those on the margins of society have been prominent in one form or another in every phase of Christian history.

Some Christian bodies, both in the West and in the southern continents, practise tithing of income, based on the Jewish model described in the Hebrew scriptures, as a minimum standard of giving. Quite small Christian communities can by this means produce a remarkably high level of activity.

Bread and Wine

It is recorded that immediately before the crucifixion Jesus arranged a last meal with his disciples at which (as the host or president would do at any Jewish meal) he took bread and wine and gave thanks to God. He then spoke words linking the bread and the wine with his approaching death, and urged his disciples to repeat this meal in memory of him. In every phase of Christian history, Christians have solemnly taken bread and wine, read or recited the words of Jesus at the Last Supper, offered prayer, and eaten and drunk. There are a few Christian communities which do not follow this custom. The best known is the Society of Friends (Quakers), who in stressing the internal action of the Spirit of God have abandoned many external and traditional forms of worship and the rites thought of as sacraments (i.e. channels of divine action) by most other Christians. A number of Christian communities have substituted articles of local fare for the bread or the wine (which were, of course, the local fare of first-century Palestine); for instance, the Kimbanguist Church in Zaire uses sweet potatoes and honey.

There are immense differences in the external action of the various Christian communities in respect of the bread and wine. Some have sumptuous language, dress and music meant to indicate the very presence of the King of Heaven, and ritual to mark the high drama of his appearance among humans. Others recall the domestic simplicity of the original meal which the rite repeats, and the humble human circumstances in which the historical Jesus displayed God. There are communities, notably in the Eastern churches, where the people stand throughout as though in the heavenly courts with the risen Jesus among them. There are some Western traditions, notably the Roman and Anglican, wherein the people receive the consecrated bread and wine kneeling, as in solemn adoration of the Lord present at the feast; and other Western Protestant traditions where they sit, as though his guests, as the disciples did at the first supper and as all his people will at the ultimate heavenly feast. There have been chapters in the life of the Latin Church when only priests took the bread and wine, while the people watched; and in the Greek, when only priests have taken them regularly, the people infrequently. In each case the practice arose from a view of the significance of the bread and wine as the body and blood of Christ, and of priests as representatives of the whole Christian community. The frequency of the rite also varies; weekly or even daily in some Christian circles, annually in others.

In their different ways, all these things underline the importance which this practice has for Christians. But the significance attributed to the practice is as varied as its forms. Some interpretations use the language and ideas of expiatory sacrifice, i.e. of taking away sin, while insisting that the sacrifice represented is the death of Christ. Some associate it with a special and particular presence of Christ. Others stress the nature of the broken bread and poured-out wine as 'visible words', a representation of the work of Christ in material form. Others eschew any language which might suggest that the rite has effect in and of itself, or requires the presence of a consecrated priest, or that the self-offering of Christ needs to be repeated in some way. These insist that the practice is essentially a solemn commemoration of Christ's original self-offering. For some, the associations of the bread and wine are less of present realization than of future hope. Taking up a theme in the record of Jesus' own words at the Last Supper, they see the action as pointing to his final return in triumph. Taking the bread and wine is an indicative event for a transitional time, a reminder of the eventual reunion of the Lord with his followers (an event described in the gospels in terms of a banquet). African Christianity may be introducing yet other ideas into the action of sharing bread and wine; some African Independent churches, for instance, incorporate acts of solidarity with the ancestors, the departed members of the family.

The names given to the practice reflect these differing ideas: mass, eucharist, Lord's Supper, communion. The idea of communion, in fact, underlies them all. All, probably, think of the act as affording opportunity for heightened sharing in the accessibility of Christ to his people. And its original significance as a *shared* meal, taken together by the friends of Jesus, has never quite been lost. Centuries of separation were broken down when Jewish Christians first sat at the table with Gentile believers. From earliest times the ultimate form of discipline for Christians has always been excommunication – exclusion from the table set for the Christian family. Conversely, a welcome to the same table is the ultimate sign of acceptance. Though some forms of observing it emphasize individual reception, and thus the communion between the worshipper and the Lord, the activity also represents communion, sharing, between and among the worshippers who represent the Lord's people. Occasionally, the two strands are in tension.

The Special Use of Water

Prophecy was revived in Israel in the first century CE in the person of John the Baptist (literally, 'the Dipper'), whose appearance and impact reminded people of a prophecy that the first great prophet, Elijah, would reappear one day to herald the Messiah. John's preaching had an ethical urgency, demanding a change of heart and style of life. Those who responded were symbolically immersed in water. It seems that this rite had previously been used to symbolize the cleansing of Gentile converts to Judaism. John insisted that true-born Israelites needed the same transformation, and the same cleansing, as any pagan outsider.

Jesus continued John's movement and his followers continued to administer baptism. With them, however, baptism symbolized not only a change of heart but the coming of the Holy Spirit which was to mark the messianic age. The early Christian writings sometimes speak of 'repentance and baptism' and sometimes of 'repentance and faith', as though these were interchangeable. Baptism was an act of open identification with, i.e. faith in, Jesus. Paul saw an added symbolism: passing down into, then up out of the water recalled the death, burial and resurrection of Jesus. The believer identified with him, died to the old life, rose to a new life 'in the Spirit'. Baptism was a great symbolic entrance to the Christian community.

We cannot tell when the question of baptizing children first arose, but the practice of baptizing whole families is very understandable. As Christianity became a mass religion virtually all children in 'Christian' countries were baptized, and in time few people other than children. The original link between baptism and active faith was lost, and immersion was largely abandoned. The sixteenth-century radical reformers in the West sought to restore it by abandoning infant baptism, restoring immersion and requiring profession of faith from those of responsible age. Their successors in this 'Baptist' approach today represent a substantial minority of Western Christians, particularly strong in the United States, and with fair numbers in Russia as well as other parts of Europe. Some sections of African Christianity have also restricted baptism to actively participating adults, often administering it in a river or the sea, understanding it as marking both entrance to the Church and acknowledgement of divine power there.

The association of baptism with entrance to the Christian community makes it a 'rite of passage'. In 'Baptist' communities, the commencement of active profession of faith tends to be most frequent at adolescence. Churches which practise infant baptism have often developed other rites of confirmation or of admission to church membership to mark the passage to full responsibilities within the Christian community. Two complexes of ideas have been associated with Christian baptism from earliest times: that of repentance–faith–commitment (inherited from John), and that of bestowal of the Holy Spirit. Sometimes one and sometimes the other is most in the mind of Christians. Where the first is uppermost, baptism is the sign of the committed Christian who has taken up his or her place in the community over against 'the world', i.e. society organized in opposition to God. Where the latter prevails, baptism is principally a sign of divine activity, of God's initiative for human salvation.

The stress in northern Christianity on faith commitment as the means by which salvation is received, and the stress in Latin Christianity on the divine activity at work in the Church's recognized ordinances, has led to disputes over whether baptism *in itself* is necessary to salvation. However, virtually all Christian traditions (Quakerism, where stress on the inner light precludes all external forms and signs, is a rare exception) regard baptism as the entrance to the Church and the Christian life; and all insist that faith is an essential aspect of what happens in baptism. The question has thus been less important in practice. Early Christian understanding (endorsed in later Roman Catholic theology) accepted that formal lack of baptism was not a barrier to salvation for those who desired it but died before attaining it. The question occurred in a new form in India, where some have affirmed their faith in and devotion to Christ as Lord without accepting the baptism which would break the link with their Hindu community. It has taken on an important new dimension, still under exploration in recent decades, especially in Roman Catholic theology, with the recognition since the Second Vatican Council of God's saving activity outside the Church, and specifically within other religions.

Some African groups see a further significance in water, consecrated by prayer, as a means or sign of healing.

The Special Use of Oil

Earliest Christianity inherited the Jewish traditional practice of anointing with oil to mark the divine appointment of prophets, priest and kings. The very word 'Christ', the anointed one, reflected this idea. The former use led to the anointing of newly baptized Christians, as a sign of their entrance to a community prophetic, priestly and royal in character. This rite of 'chrismation', using consecrated ointment, remains important among Eastern Orthodox Christians, who link it with the gift of the Holy Spirit.

In Latin Christianity the prayerful use of oil for healing gradually gave place to anointing as a solemn preparation for death. The use of oil for healing has periodically been revived in various traditions, not least those which seek a literal replication of actions found in Scripture.

Cultural changes have diminished the special use of oil; for many Christian communities the symbolism of anointing has become too remote to be meaningful. Westerners have linked the sign of the endowment of the Holy Spirit rather with the laying on of hands (see below), and Africans have often seen water, rather than oil, as the appropriate vehicle or accompaniment of divine healing. Eastern Christianity, however, consistently uses oil both as marking the presence of the Holy Spirit within and for healing. The references in the Bible to anointing, with similar associations, have led to the periodical recurrence of its use, in diverse forms, throughout Christian history elsewhere.

Laying On of Hands

The laying on of hands is now no longer universal among Christians, and where it occurs it has a range of significance. The origins lie in Jewish practice, where the range was equally wide. The commonest examples in modern Christianity are as follows.

For appointment to office According to the earliest Christian writings, the apostles set aside leaders for the Church after prayer and laying on of hands, and most branches of Christianity employ this practice at the ordination or appointment of ministers and sometimes of other leaders. It signals both historical continuity and corporate solidarity.

For some major branches of Christianity it means much more, in that it is held that the authentic Church is continued through a visible line of succession of bishops reaching back to the apostles and continuing their office. This belief is strenuously resisted by many other Christians, who maintain that it undermines the fundamental principle of faith in Christ as the entrance to the Church. This difference has probably been in recent years the greatest single stumbling-block to the union of different branches of Christianity.

The question of the succession of ordaining bishops is often linked with another question, the nature of the ministry to which ordination refers. Most of the older and larger Christian traditions – Orthodox, Roman Catholic, Anglican, Lutheran – call their ordained ministers 'priests', though the word is used with interpretations varying both between and within the traditions. Many other Christian traditions, especially those of northern origin, reject the word altogether, since it might suggest that the minister in some ways offers sacrifices (raising controverted interpretations of the nature of the eucharist or Lord's Supper; see above), or mediates between God and the people. Undoubtedly both these ideas have from time to time been attached to Christian priesthood, but at others those employing the word 'priest' have stressed the distinction between the Christian ministry and the sacrificing priesthood of the Jewish Temple, not to mention other religions of sacrifice. Much recent Roman Catholic theology, for instance, stresses the priesthood of the Risen Christ in offering the effective sacrifice for sin and mediating for his people; affirms the New Testament use of the language of priesthood to apply to the totality of Christian people; and, while insisting on the necessity of a priesthood within the Church, asserts the 'prophetic' functions of preaching the Word of God and leadership as equally necessary to priesthood as the liturgical functions in worship.

For confirmation We have already seen that the development of infant baptism as the norm led to a need for another ceremony to mark the transition to full participation in the Christian community. Such rites of 'confirmation' in many communities include the laying on of hands. Since most Christians think of the Church as in a special way the sphere of the Holy Spirit, it is natural that the practice should be associated, at least symbolically, with the gift of the same Holy Spirit.

For healing Jesus commonly laid his hands on the sufferer when healing, and the early accounts of healings in his name by his followers indicate that they also did so, at least on occasion. The practice is still widespread in African Christianity, where Christian healing is a common feature, and among Pentecostals generally, and in some other American Christian traditions which similarly emphasize healing.

The Use of Tongues

The early Christian communities knew a heightened consciousness which they attributed to the gift of the Holy Spirit. One aspect of it was the capacity to utter fluently a range of sounds outside normal speech. Paul, though he possessed this capacity, seems to have thought it often overvalued, and insisted that it should be controlled and the utterances interpreted for the benefit of those without it [1 *Corinthians*: 12–14]. The phenomenon (known as 'glossolalia') seems to have soon died out. It was thus frequently thought of as special to the apostolic age and its occasional appearance thereafter was ascribed to hysterical or even diabolical sources. Since the nineteenth century, however, it has reappeared on an increasing scale. The London congregation of Edward Irving (1792–1834) experienced it, and its presence in revival movements in America and Europe early in this century led to the separate growth of Pentecostal churches, for whom the experience in normative. The name 'Pentecostal' derives from the account in the *Acts of the Apostles* of the coming of the Holy Spirit, with the gift of exalted speech, to the disciples of Jesus during the feast of Pentecost. The roots of the modern movement lie in African-American Christianity in the United States, but it has become a world-wide phenomenon. Originally principally affecting Western Protestants, it has in recent decades become part of the regular experience of a significant number of Western Christians, both Protestant and Roman Catholic (frequently called 'charismatics'), who have remained within their churches. These regard the use of tongues as an enhancement and enrichment of devotion rather than as a necessary mark of the Church. More significantly, however, 'Pentecostal' Christianity has become a feature of substantial sections of Southern Christianity, where it is the dominant strand in an expanding Latin American Protestantism, and in Africa, where in different forms it is characteristic of many African Independent (or 'spiritual') churches and of the radical Evangelical movements which are prominent in a great deal of urban religious life.

Among some churches and groups which practise it, it is regarded as a *sine qua non* of authentic spirituality, the real evidence of the presence of the Holy Spirit. To others it is a valuable, intense and liberating, but not essential, experience of divine love. In circles where it is not practised it is often regarded with reserve or dislike, as a source of disorder or division.

Christian Art and Architecture

The needs of Christian worship have obviously brought about special forms of architecture. In any society where Christians have been secure enough to build, they have usually produced distinctive buildings, instantly recognizable as churches. At the same time there is no single, universal 'shape' for a church (see figure 2.5). Some of the reasons for this are simply cultural, but different strains within Christianity have affected the nature and the scale of Christian architecture. The great cathedrals rising massively above the cold and wretched hovels of medieval European towns expressed grandeur and permanence amid hard struggle and brief, uncertain life. In modern times, the south Indian Anglican bishop, V. S. Azariah, was one of several contemporaries to plan imposing church structures in poor and famine-ridden areas. The churches were to be the shared possession of the Christian community, something in which people who held virtually no personal property could take pride of ownership. A different strand of Christianity rejects the symbols of grandeur and permanence. It sees the people of Christ (himself often homeless) as pilgrims seeking a better land. Their true symbol is the traveller's tent. The church they need is a modest – but still distinctive – building which reflects this transitional life.

Throughout Christian history attitudes to art have reflected two strains of Christianity. Neither can be identified simply with any one Christian tradition, or any particular Christian community. One strain insists that God has a right to the best, the highest and the costliest offerings of human riches, skill and labour. This instinct has been fruitful in grand conceptions, superb achievements and, it must be added, rank bad taste. With it has often gone another conviction: that the world belongs to God, that Christ redeemed the whole of human life and every human activity. One fruit of this may be the artist's belief in freedom to follow art to God's glory. Another may be the legislator's belief that there is a certain pattern of law and learning, art and music, appropriate to a Christian society.

A different strain emphasizes the poverty of even the most magnificent human offering to God, and the central Christian belief that God himself came to earth in the humble circumstances of a Palestinian peasant family. Rich adornment and complex art may also discourage the poor, while the wealthy bask in the false security of their outlay which provided it. The finest human creations all too readily call attention not to God, but to themselves, and thus lead not to adoration, but to idolatry. With this strain there also often goes a sharp mental division between this present world, the world of nature, perverted in all its courses, but transitional and temporary, and the next world, the world of spirit, God-ordered and permanent. The effect of this division is sometimes that certain activities – in this case, art – are associated with the world of nature, the 'secular' world. There is therefore little or no place for art in worship or in the religious life; it is at best a luxury, at worst a distraction. Alternatively, the activities may be regarded as legitimate

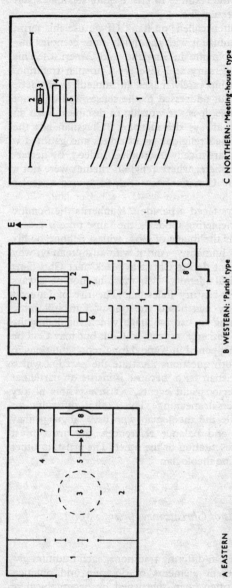

A EASTERN

1. Narthex – porch for preparation
2. Nave – no seating; congregation stands, walks
3. Dome above, painted with Christ as ruler
4. Iconostasis – screen covered with icons
5. Central door – opened during service
6. Altar
7. Chapel for preparation of bread and wine
8. Bishop's seat in semi-circular 'apse'

B WESTERN: 'Parish' type

1. Nave – seated congregation
2. Screen (in older churches) – open door
3. Choir (where service is led)
4. Sanctuary (railed)
5. Altar table
6. Pulpit (for preaching)
7. Lectern (for reading Scriptures)
8. Font (for baptism)

C NORTHERN: 'Meeting-house' type

1. Congregation seated
2. Pulpit (where service is led)
3. Bible (open for service)
4. Communion table (no rails)
5. Baptistery (covered when not in use)

Figure 2.5 Types of church building: some different uses of religious space

only in so far as they directly serve the interests of the 'sacred' world of the spirit. Either way, the result is to create quite separate styles for the religious and the secular life.

The second strain is often called 'puritan'. (If we use this term, however, we must not confuse it with the much more complex historical movement of that name in England and America.) This strain is found in every century and in every Christian tradition. Where it dominates, worship rarely makes an immediate aesthetic appeal. Such worship is not addressed to the senses and does not court easy popular response; it is the worship of disciples. Such an attitude is not, however, always destructive of Christian art; the strain has sometimes purified religious art of excess and gaudy display. Nor is it necessarily artistically uncreative. Indeed, by declaring a separate, 'secular' sphere, where religious themes were not a necessary feature, 'puritan' Christian views helped to create secular art.

Christian art has always faced a paradox. It inherits the Semitic revulsion at the idea of depicting God. At the same time it recognizes one human figure as the image of God, with a definite bodily form, identifying with all humanity. And if with all humanity, why should an African artist not depict Christ as black? Yet Christians insist on Christ's historical identity – so must he not be always depicted as a Jew of first-century Palestine? The rise of feminist expressions of Christianity has posed the question in still more acute form. It is one thing to use language which highlights the 'motherly' as well as the 'fatherly' aspects of God; but may God be depicted in art – as has happened in some daring representations in churches – as female? Both questions illustrate the paradox which runs throughout the Christian faith, because it insists on particular times and places and persons and events, yet invests this history with timeless and universal meaning. The capital difficulty for Christian art is that while the theologian who uses language may introduce qualifications and balance references, the artist must choose one mode of representation or the other. The artist, in other words, is always a front-line theologian.

The Principal Traditions of Christianity

Christianity has developed in differing traditions, each tradition giving prominence to different elements of doctrine and practice. These differences have often been sharpened by geographical or communal isolation. In the modern world at least five such 'great traditions', each associated with a particular church or group of churches, may be identified: Eastern, Oriental, Latin, Northern and African. Cultural rather than doctrinal or ecclesiastical appellations are used here, not because the questions of doctrine or practice are unimportant, but to indicate the significance of certain historical and cultural factors in producing the present shape and characteristics of the different traditions. The vast majority of Christian churches and congregations belong to one or other of these traditions; there are also several others, less notable in numbers or geographical spread, as well as, inevitably, some mixed forms. It would be misleading to describe any of the traditions as 'central' in a way which suggested that any of the others are peripheral.

The Eastern Tradition

Nomenclature Two Christian traditions share a common origin in the early Christianity of the eastern Mediterranean. Each claims to be the authentic continuation of that early Christianity, and each claims the title 'Orthodox'. 'Eastern' here identifies those Christians who think of themselves as constituting the Holy Orthodox Church, or the Orthodox Church of the East, and are called by others 'Greek Orthodox' or 'Russian Orthodox'. It is the descendant of Byzantine Christianity, itself the product of early hellenistic Christianity.

Geographical distribution Eastern Christianity has survived as the faith of a minority community in some of its old heartlands (Turkey, Syria). In other parts of these heartlands (Egypt, Lebanon) the majority of Christians today (again a minority of the total population) belong to other traditions. In Greece it has retained its ancient hold, and in all the Balkan countries except Albania, Croatia and non-Serb Bosnia it is the main religious force. But by far the largest number of Eastern Christians today are Russians. The considerable Russian diaspora has spread the faith of Holy Russia to western Europe, North America and Australia, and Greeks, Cypriots and others have increased this Eastern presence within Western societies. A spontaneous and indigenous development in East Africa has linked numbers of Kenyan and Ugandan Christians to the Eastern Church (figure 2.6).

Conditioning factors Eastern Christianity is marked by a sense of continuity, of embodying the ancient in the modern world, of being 'living antiquity'. The East had no middle ages, and the patristic period of the early Church fathers, which had ended in the West by 600 CE at the latest, lasted here until the fifteenth century. Among Greeks, for whom the very language of the faithful is the language of the apostles and their scriptures, the sense of timelessness can be overwhelming.

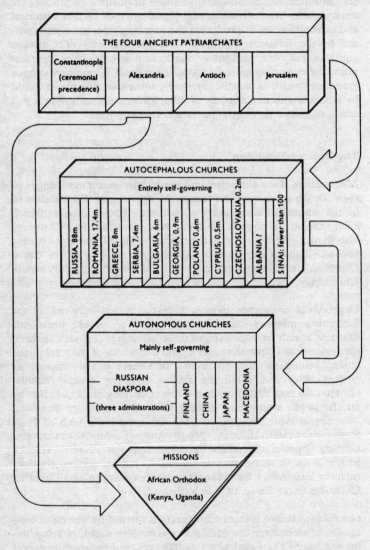

THE FOUR ANCIENT PATRIARCHATES

| Constantinople (ceremonial precedence) | Alexandria | Antioch | Jerusalem |

AUTOCEPHALOUS CHURCHES

Entirely self-governing

RUSSIA, 88m | ROMANIA, 17.4m | GREECE, 8m | SERBIA, 7.4m | BULGARIA, 6m | GEORGIA, 0.9m | POLAND, 0.6m | CYPRUS, 0.5m | CZECHOSLOVAKIA, 0.2m | ALBANIA? | SINAI: fewer than 100

AUTONOMOUS CHURCHES

Mainly self-governing

RUSSIAN DIASPORA (three administrations) | FINLAND | CHINA | JAPAN | MACEDONIA

MISSIONS

African Orthodox (Kenya, Uganda)

Figure 2.6 *Eastern Christianity today: the Orthodox Church*

Eastern Christianity has a long history of persecution and disability. In early days, Christians in the eastern Mediterranean bore the fiercest attacks of the pagan Roman state, a memory kept alive by the assiduous veneration of the martyrs. Over the long centuries of Muslim rule every inducement was given to convert from the faith, and conversion to it was well-nigh impossible. Attrition became the norm, survival the goal, fierce attachment to a glorious past the means. Russian Christians, spared Turkish over-rule, generally thought of themselves as the defenders of their persecuted brethren; but under Soviet rule they too were to know persecution, of varying degrees of ferocity. To its adherents, therefore, Eastern Christianity is, simply, Christianity; their church, not a denomination, but *the* universal and orthodox Church. It is in this light that one must view both the 1,500-year-old dispute with the Oriental churches (see below), and the gulf, enlarged by history and geography, that has until recently divided Eastern Christians from the churches of the West. From an Eastern point of view, the divisions within Western Christianity are insignificant. As the Russian thinker Alexei Khomiakov (1804–60) put it, 'the Pope was the first Protestant.'

Characteristic features Two twentieth-century developments have broken a long cultural and theological isolation. This has already had profound consequences, and may have more. One is the emigration of Eastern Christians to Western lands, where they have become a minority among Christians, a rare situation hitherto. There are particularly large communities in the United States. The other is the new readiness of Eastern Christians to engage in discussion and shared activity with other Christians, exemplified in their lively participation in the World Council of Churches.

Tradition is the guide of Eastern Christianity. The elements of the tradition, in their approximate order of importance, are: the scriptures; the ecumenical councils (the meetings of bishops in the early centuries which furnished the great creeds); the fathers of the church (the early Christian writers in Greek); the liturgy (which expresses in words and action the presence of God with his people); the canons or codified Church law; and the icons (literally 'images'), or holy pictures, which transmit sacred doctrine and history.

Eastern Christians are less given than Western Christians to the precise formulation of doctrine. Tradition is an organic fusion of all the elements mentioned, expressed in thought, word, action, line and colour. The painstaking critical studies of the fathers characteristic of Western scholarship since the Enlightenment find little favour, for what matters is not the actual words of the fathers but the cultivation of their temper of mind. The eucharist is the theatre of God's action, but the controversies over it and attempts at definition which have divided Western Christians have little place here. Icons are 'tradition' since they express, not the mind of the artist, as do other forms of painting, but the mind of the Church. The icon, a characteristic external mark of Eastern Christianity, is also a key to Eastern Christian thought. Jesus the Divine Son was himself an icon; not only the image of God, but an image of what redeemed humanity can be. The idea of redeemed humanity means that the aim of the Christian life is to be taken up into God. A saying of the fourth-century Greek father Athanasius is much quoted, that Christ 'became what we are in order that we might become what he is'. The path to deification is through the Church with its rites, especially baptism and the eucharist, with prayer and the study of Scripture, and by following the commands of Christ. In the end, humanity is not absorbed into God, but transfigured by the divine indwelling. This transfiguration of the body explains the care taken with the relics of the saints, who have known that indwelling.

Eastern Christianity has no central authority; it is a family of self-governing churches. The four ancient patriarchates (Jerusalem, Antioch, Alexandria and Constantinople) remain, though a shadow of their former selves, alongside the 'autocephalous' churches of Russia, eastern Europe and the Balkans, and 'autonomous' churches elsewhere (see figure 2.6).

The Oriental Tradition

Nomenclature 'Oriental' identifies a group of ancient churches originating within Eastern Christianity, and also describing themselves as 'Orthodox'. The Council of Chalcedon of 451 was meant to secure a consensus of teaching on the person of Christ, but its decrees were opposed by some Eastern Christians and passed unnoticed by others. This was especially the case among the non-Greek-speaking minorities of the Roman empire, and in those provinces most aggrieved at the extortion and misrule of the central imperial government. Attempts by that government to coerce submission to Chalcedon only produced greater dissidence. Political, ethnic and theological factors all therefore assisted division; the theological factors were probably matters of emphasis and approach rather than of substance.

Two main groups refused to conform to the norms of Chalcedon and central government: the Nestorian (named from a patriarch of Antioch) and the Monophysite (meaning 'one nature', a key word in this formulation of the doctrine of Christ), also called Jacobite (after a great sixth-century leader). Both were rooted in the peoples of old Christian lands, Syria and Egypt; both spread the Christian faith far outside the Roman empire. A few Oriental churches have entered into association with the Roman church while maintaining their traditional rites and liturgies. These 'Uniate' churches represent a mixed form of the Oriental and Latin traditions. (There are also eastern European Uniate churches, notably the Ukrainian Catholics.)

Geographical distribution Oriental Christianity was once a more significant part of the Christian world than it is now. The Christianity of the Persian empire was largely Nestorian, and spread across central Asia and into China; but most of it was destroyed by the Mongols in the thirteenth and fourteenth centuries. Its principal remnant, the so-called 'Church of the Assyrians', was decimated in Iraq between the First and Second World Wars. The present patriarch lives in the United States.

Monophysite Christianity has fared better. In Egypt, its first centre, most Christians today belong to the Coptic Orthodox Church, which is of this family. So is the ancient Church of Ethiopia. The still older Church of Armenia ignored Chalcedon, and belongs today, with its important offshoot in the United States, to Oriental rather than to Eastern Christianity.

The Maronite Church, the principal Christian community of Lebanon, is Uniate.

Indian Christians claim that Thomas, the apostle of Jesus, founded a church in India. It is beyond doubt that Christianity has been there from the early centuries. The oldest Christian community is rooted in a high-caste Malayalam-speaking sector of Kerala. Its history is so complex as to defy summary here. Nestorian, Jacobite and Western forces have all played a part. There are Uniate sections and one displaying Protestant influence.

Conditioning factors The Oriental churches (if we except those of India and Ethiopia) have known persecution and restriction perhaps beyond any other. Persecution has left the Nestorians only a small fragment of what they once were. The Oriental churches have not only maintained a Christian presence in a hostile environment; they have helped whole communities to survive and keep an identity. But they now represent – Ethiopia again excepted – the faith of self-conscious cultural minorities. Over the centuries, the intense conservatism which the need to maintain an identity often produces has meant that what were once vernaculars have become 'sacred' languages for church purposes. The Egyptian church uses Coptic in its services; its members speak Arabic outside. The Ethiopian church maintains the obsolete language Ge'ez (though with increasing signs of its supersession by Amharic). Even in India, liturgies are performed in Syriac. The transmission of the faith in Oriental churches has accordingly been by common worship and prayer rather than through Scripture and doctrine.

The Oriental churches, so firm in rejecting the domination of the Eastern tradition, have sometimes been a little more open to overtures from Western sources. Some of the Uniate churches, which acknowledge Rome, originated in this way, while other Oriental churches have been prepared to accept Protestant help in medical care or education, or even in the training of the ministry. But they have always been jealous of their separate identity. In Ethiopia different conditions prevailed. No persecuted minority here, the church became interlocked with the imperial state apparatus. Ethiopia's geographical isolation, the interaction of Christian with ancient African traditions, and the presence of Judaic features of rather mysterious origin have also contributed to a unique development.

Characteristic features The Oriental churches have retained their old confessions, reflecting differences from the old churches of East and West in the statement of the doctrine of the person of Christ. But their distinctive theological formulations have rarely lain at the heart of their life. Since the sixteenth century, when the maritime phase of Christian history began to bring Western Christians to the non-Western world, the Oriental churches have known the presence of Western Christians, both Catholic and Protestant, in their midst. Relations between them have often been tense, but the tensions have rarely had much to do with arguments about the formulation of the doctrine of Christ's person set out at Chalcedon. These communities have generally seen themselves as the local representatives of Christianity, rather than the guardians of some particular branch of it. Transmission of their faith has been possible only within families in communities, identified by their distinct forms of Christianity. Expansion into another culture group has long been denied them (Ethiopia being a rare exception). Their survival is itself a marvel, their conservatism an inevitable accompaniment. The idea of timeless tradition dominates them. Their claim to preserve apostolic tradition is not a formal statement, nor a theological judgement; it is a historical affirmation, soaked in the sense of direct historical connection.

The churches, however, have not all been immobile. Ethiopia and India have provided plenty of evidence of creative response to new situations. They have also kept up a notable network of communication. Until recent times the Coptic patriarch appointed the head of the Ethiopian church, and Indian churches traditionally took their bishops from Mesopotamia.

Monasticism first developed in the Egyptian desert and the Syrian hinterland, the soil on which the earliest Oriental churches developed. The monastic ideal of spiritual athleticism through ascetic discipline has remained a potent force in the Oriental churches ever since. Its object is to achieve the uninhibited worship of God in the glory of the Trinity, and thus to realize the life of heaven on earth. As in heaven, that worship is a corporate activity, and it is most likely to be attained with the fellowship of like-minded others, and in submission to freely chosen leaders. Though the monastic life involves dying to the ordinary world of humanity and its ways, it does not produce a total separation from that world; hospitality, works of charity, study and counsel are all part of the monastic regime.

The Ethiopian church has some special features, such as observance of the Sabbath, circumcision, and a vast clergy and monastic community. Emperor Haile Selassie II promoted a cautious modernization, with increasing use of the widely spoken Amharic, instead of the archaic Ge'ez, for Scripture reading, and better training of the clergy. These measures were overtaken by the revolution of 1976, which had a Marxist ethos. The end of the monarchy created a new situation for the Ethiopian church, where throne and altar had traditionally been linked. In the new, post-Marxist situation the Orthodox Church remains a significant force, though having to adjust to complex political realities and to the existence of fast-growing new churches in some of the important ethnic groups of the country, especially in the south.

The Latin Tradition

Nomenclature The Latin tradition of Christianity today is represented above all by the vast body of Christians presided over by the Pope (= *Papa*, Father) in his capacity as bishop of Rome, and known to its members as the Catholic (i.e. universal) Church, or, simply, the Church. To avoid any confusion arising from these terms it is known in many settings as the Roman Catholic Church.

The term 'Latin', however, draws attention to some of the factors which have determined the form of this tradition. It arose and was shaped by the conditions of the western Mediterranean, and its use of the language of the western Roman empire had a decisive effect. From one point of view the disruption of Western Christianity in the sixteenth century is the result of a vernacular movement, reflecting the triumph for northern Christians of the local over the universal principle in that tension between local and universal which has always marked Christianity. Accelerated change within the Catholic Church in the second half of the twentieth century has accompanied the diminished status of Latin and the rise in the importance of the vernaculars.

Geographical distribution A specifically Latin tradition, guided more by legal precedent than by speculative theology, is discernible by the fourth century. Latin Christianity developed apace thereafter, in the wake of the destruction of the western empire. The peoples of western Europe who wrought that destruction, and their successors, slowly became Christians, and were Latinized as they were Christianized. They became late Romans. They also recognized the special position of the church of Rome, the only church with which they were acquainted which could also claim to be founded by the apostles. All Europe west of a line from Scandinavia through the Carpathians to the Danube became a single Christian entity, linked by the special use of Latin and the active recognition of the bishop of Rome as the successor of Peter and representative of Christ, factors which distinguished it from the other Christian lands to the east and south. Small wonder, then, if it began to think of itself as 'Christendom'.

In the late fifteenth and sixteenth centuries 'Christendom' expanded with the beginnings of European domination in the Americas. At the same time, however, the disruption within European Christianity meant that vernacular-speaking 'Protestant' churches, still influenced by Latin models, but no longer determined by them, came to predominate throughout northern Europe. The Latin tradition was henceforth centred in the southern lands of western Europe: Portugal, Spain, France, Italy and Austria. Germany, Switzerland and the Low Countries were divided. The rise of the maritime power of Portugal and Spain, accompanied by a new zeal to spread the faith in the wake of colonization, established Latin Christianity not only in Central and South America, but on many parts of the African coastline and in parts of Asia. Missionary operations in the nineteenth and twentieth centuries spread the tradition yet more widely, and immigration from Ireland, Italy and other countries produced substantial Latin Christian enclaves in North America, Australia and other areas previously dominated by Northern or Protestant Christianity. In the same period anticlerical, secular or Marxist influences have shaken the hold of Latin Christianity on France, and on sectors of the population in other southern European countries also. Today, Latin Christian influence is virtually world-wide, and the Catholic Church has more adherents, on any method of computation, than any other single Christian body.

Conditioning factors By the use of Latin the Christianity of the western, rather than that of the Greek eastern, Roman empire was transmitted to the majority of the new Christians of the 'barbarian' phase of Christianity, and Latin rather than the European vernaculars continued to be the language of the Church. It became the language of learning also, because it was the Church which preserved learning; and it remained so long after Latin had ceased to be an ordinary spoken language. The western peoples came to a common faith and a common cultural inheritance at the same time. Over the years that faith was transmitted to peoples outside Europe – but still with that language, and within a culture necessarily shaped by it. Even vernacular translations of the scriptures were for centuries often treated with great suspicion. All this helped to create cohesiveness, the consciousness of belonging to a supranational entity. At the same time, the connection of so much that belongs to the heart of religion with a special language has often helped to concentrate power in the hands of the priesthood.

In the last few decades this central feature of Latin Christianity has changed dramatically. The liturgy is now given in the language of the worshippers and reading of the scriptures in the worshippers' language is encouraged. The eventual effect of this change on Latin Christianity is incalculable.

The Western peoples converted to Christianity en masse. Latin Christianity thus developed from an early stage as the religion of whole communities, with the Church accorded a jurisdiction over the whole of society and all its members. For a long time this was the norm; it was many centuries before it was accepted in Europe that a community might be diverse in faith. This assumption of uniformity, and the persecution of 'deviants' which it engendered, was inherited by most Protestant states after the sixteenth-century Reformation. Today there are still Catholic states in which the Church holds a position of privilege, but most Catholics now live in plural or secular societies.

The special position accorded to Rome and its bishop has enabled the development of a degree of centralization not achieved by any other religious body of remotely comparable size. It has also modified the ancient Christian custom of reaching major decisions after consideration by the bishops of different churches meeting in council. In Latin Christianity councils have not been frequent, at least in recent centuries. Since the Council of Trent, which fixed a standardized pattern of worship and doctrine after the great disruption in the Western Church in the sixteenth century, only two have met. The First Vatican Council of 1869–70 considered some of the major new movements of the nineteenth century; and the crucial Second Vatican Council, held between 1963 and 1965, brought a radical readjustment of the Church to the conditions of the modern world. This Council was called by Pope John XXIII, whose reign (1958–63) was brief and who did not live to see its work completed. It set forth a view of the Church as the whole people of God which gave new significance to laypeople; it is the Church as a people, not just its priests, who offer its worship. The central feature of the eucharist is the communion, the sharing together with the Lord, of all who participate. The function of ministers is to serve rather than to rule, and their authority is collegial, not monarchical. The Council stressed the Church's nature as a growing, developing, changing community – the 'pilgrim' Church, as it is described – rather than as a static, timeless institution. In line with this came insistence on intelligibility in liturgy and worship to enable full lay participation. This entailed not only the use of vernacular languages rather than Latin, but a new openness to variety and locality in the forms of worship. The Council urged easy access to the scriptures and commended study of the scriptures to all. It acknowledged the existence of the Church beyond the Roman communion, recognized the work of the Holy Spirit in the ecumenical movement, encouraged cooperation and conversation with other Christians and looked forward to the eventual 'reintegration' of the whole Church. It affirmed the principle of religious liberty. It indicated that the other world religions were within God's plan of salvation for humanity and that God might use them as a means of salvation. The relationship of Christians to the Jewish people (who are 'most dear to God') was defined in a positive way.

The Second Vatican Council established guidelines for Catholic thinking which emphasize respect for human freedom, for culture, for other Christian communions and for all religions. It also reflected the changing demographic balance in the Church. At this Council the influence of the indigenous bishops of Africa and Asia began to be felt; their number and weight has greatly increased since. Implicity, the Council also acknowledged the passing of the old Christendom, with much of Europe entering a post-Christian phase, Latin America in social and religious turmoil, and an important North American Catholic community which could not be regulated by old precedents. It recognized continuing change and adaptation as a necessary feature of a 'pilgrim' Church.

After the Council there were other conferences of bishops, which suggested a continuing collegial leadership in the Church. This has been less evident in the 1980s and 1990s, when signs have appeared of a returning emphasis on centralization. A recent (1994) synod of African bishops was held in Rome, rather than in Africa. Nevertheless, regional conferences of bishops in various parts of the world have been active and effective, new liturgies have developed with marked local and contemporary features, Bible reading and study in the vernacular is widely practised, and the training of priests, freed from Latin models, reflects local conditions. Dialogical relationships, both with other Christians and with those of other faiths, are well established. All in all, the Second Vatican Council ushered in more profound changes than any of its predecessors.

Latin Christianity has been deeply affected by the major disruption which it suffered in the sixteenth century, usually called the Protestant Reformation. This led to the withdrawal of many

Christians from the acknowledgement of Roman headship, and the development of another tradition of Christianity characteristic of the northern peoples. Much of the standardization of doctrine and practice which was arrived at in the wake of the disruption, notably at the Council of Trent, was expressly formulated with the positions or assertions of the Protestant leaders in mind. One result was that definitions or practices which had their origin in purely local or temporary circumstances were given permanence or significance (another feature partly modified as a result of the Second Vatican Council). The course of European history in the fifteenth and sixteenth centuries divided the West into 'Catholic' and 'Protestant' states. As these states came into conflict with one another, a religious dimension was added to patriotism, a nationalist dimension to religion. To profess the faith of one's national enemy was to render one's own loyalty to the nation suspect. Emotional reactions and deep-set repugnances that had little to do with religion became associated with the name of 'Catholic', which became a badge of national or communal identification to friend and foe alike. Some of this legacy remains today.

Characteristic features In practice Latin Christianity has been able to combine a supranational structure and a strong sense of national local identity with fair success, maintaining a firmly centralized decision-making power in major matters, but allowing scope for local particularities. The latter has enabled local cults to flourish with devotion to local saints, images or appearances; it has also enabled newly christianized societies to adapt their own institutions or reconcile old and new beliefs. In addition, the apparently rigid hierarchical structure admits of exceptions and modifications. Latin Christianity is marked by a strong emphasis on the institutional Church as the possessor, the guarantor and the interpreter of the tradition of Christ, including the scriptures. The Church is the sphere of the Spirit's activity on earth, within which the truth is taught and the divine life made actual for humanity.

No Christian tradition has sought to define doctrine, law and practice as closely as the Latin – with the exception, perhaps, of some forms of northern Christianity themselves influenced by Latin models. Hence the centuries-old insistence that the sacraments are seven in number: the rites of baptism, marriage, confirmation, eucharist, penance, anointing of the sick before death, and ordination. (Roman Catholic theology places much emphasis on sacraments as vital actions of the Church through which God works for human salvation.) Hence also the pronouncement by the First Vatican Council of the infallibility of the Pope when speaking in the name of the Church; and the succession of pronouncements over many centuries about the Virgin Mary, culminating in the declaration in 1950 of her 'assumption', i.e. that at the end of her earthly life she was taken up, body and soul, into heaven. The two latter examples indicate also the cumulative process of definition; a widely held belief often persists for centuries before it is formally defined.

The Latin tradition stresses the objective presence of the life of Christ in the Church, made available in the sacraments. The sacraments carry out what they signify; and, assuming they are carried out within the Church, they are independent of the agent who carries them out. The characteristic sign of the Church's presence, and of Christ's presence, has therefore been the celebration of the eucharist, called the mass.

The Northern Tradition

Nomenclature In the sixteenth-century disruption known as the Reformation, a section of Western Christianity abandoned Latin and the acknowledgement of Roman leadership, and produced a vernacular reformulation of Christianity. The name usually applied to it, 'Protestant', is not a particularly descriptive term, and names used by the reformers themselves, such as Evangelical or Reformed, have the disadvantage that they are now used in different senses, or to describe particular forms of Protestantism. 'Northern' is used here since, while this tradition of Christianity has spread throughout the world, it has been especially characteristic of northern Europe and its peoples, and their descendants elsewhere.

In the sixteenth century, the earliest period of its separate existence, the Northern tradition developed two forms. The first, the type for which the term Protestant is more strictly correct, sought a reformed version of that Latin church which had held the allegiance of the western European peoples since their conversion. The supremacy of the Roman see would be ended. National churches, no longer subject to pressures from outside, and using the languages of their people, would be purged of doctrines and practices out of tune with the scriptures. But these churches would still be the churches of the whole community, as the old church had been. Some reformers of this type, essentially conservative, made only the changes which seemed to them to be absolutely demanded by Scripture. Others sought to remodel the church completely in the light of the scriptures, to make it more like what they saw there of the New Testament church. Generally speaking, the Lutheran churches result from the former, and the Calvinist or Reformed from the latter process. (The English development was unique in combining rather advanced reform in doctrine with a fairly conservative form of church government. In later times Anglican doctrine has been developed in a conservative direction, to the extent that many Anglicans now prefer not to be called Protestant.) All the Protestant reformers, however, sought to reform the whole of the church within their particular state, and looked to the rulers of that state to assist in the work of reformation.

Another group sought a more radical reformation. If, as all Protestants held, faith was personal trust in Christ, then, argued these radicals, the church cannot consist of the whole population of the state, but consists only of those who have faith. So they developed 'believers' churches' – close-knit fellowships of families with personal commitment – a form of organization quite different from the Christian state with its priests or pastors instructing their parishes. The radical reformers were thus disturbing to the state as well as to the church, and Protestant reformers feared these 'Anabaptists' as much as conservative Catholics did. Baptists, Congregationalists, Mennonites and Quakers are among the modern descendants of the radical reformers.

Since the eighteenth century, the Protestant and radical streams within Northern Christianity have increasingly intermingled. One reason has been the slow erosion of the 'Christendom' idea. Intellectual developments in eighteenth-century Europe produced alternatives to Christianity, and this and other factors, by bringing religion increasingly into the sphere of private choice, secured the effective autonomy of the state from theological considerations. The new nation that became the United States specifically excluded any link between church and state; as Northern Christianity spread through the missionary movement in Africa and Asia the question hardly arose. All this cut away at the sharpest distinction between the radicals and those national churches of Europe which formed the bedrock of the Protestant Reformation: the attempt to embody a reformed church and people, united in a Christian civil society.

Another factor was the Evangelical revival of the eighteenth century, the effects of which became clearer in the nineteenth. Those influenced by it distinguished between 'nominal' Christians, taking the name because they had been born and baptized in a Christian society, and 'real' Christians, defined by personal faith commitment – a distinction similar to that made by the sixteenth-century radicals. The intensification of religious and moral life brought about by the Evangelical revival affected in differing degrees nearly all the branches of Northern Christianity then existing in Europe and North America, including the national churches of Europe. Evangelicalism penetrated them in most cases without producing secession or breaking the formal structures of these churches. (The most striking example of separation, that of English Methodism from the Church of England, took a long time to happen, and there were marks of ambiguity even when it did; and the nineteenth-century division which split the Church of Scotland in two was not solely a product of Evangelicalism, and was healed in the twentieth century.) Generally speaking, Evangelical movements claimed not to be introducing new doctrines but to be returning to the norms of New Testament Christianity and to the understanding of faith proclaimed by Luther and the other sixteenth-century reformers. The tendency of Evangelicalism was therefore to bring the Protestant and radical streams of the earlier Reformation closer together, or at least to open a channel between them.

Both the Protestant and radical streams were evident in North America from the time of the early European settlements, and the Evangelical revival affected America with particular force, its impact falling upon the white and African sectors of the population alike. By the nineteenth century the United States had produced a new stage of development for Northern Christianity. As we have seen earlier, Christianity in America (Catholic as well as Protestant, though the full significance of the former was not evident until the twentieth century) saw flourishing growth at a time when Christianity in Europe was entering recession. The frontier moved westwards in a religious as well as in a demographic and political sense.

Leading the expansion were groups rooted in the radical tradition (e.g. Baptists) or in Evangelical Protestant traditions (e.g. Methodists), but in communities shaped by American conditions and using methods and styles indigenous to America. We have seen that in Europe the voluntary society, the product of conditions which allowed free association, made possible some forms of Christian activity – notably the missionary movement – for which the churches had no infrastructure. In America, where the principle of free association was native to the political climate, the voluntary society took on a new importance. Indeed, the very distinction between church and voluntary society became blurred. Protestantism had grown out of Christendom. It had on the one hand national churches based on a reform on Protestant lines of the former 'Catholic' model of the community, and on the other 'free' or dissenting churches based on principled rejection of the claims of these national churches. In America, which had no national church, all churches could be viewed simply as free associations of members – for practical purposes voluntary societies – between which the individual or family made a personal choice.

Two other factors operated in America, and to some extent modified those described so far. One was ethnic. Groups of immigrants from particular European communities not unnaturally transplanted the models of the churches they had previously known. This meant not simply the introduction of Lutheran or Baptist or Mennonite churches, but of German or Norwegian or Finnish Lutherans, of

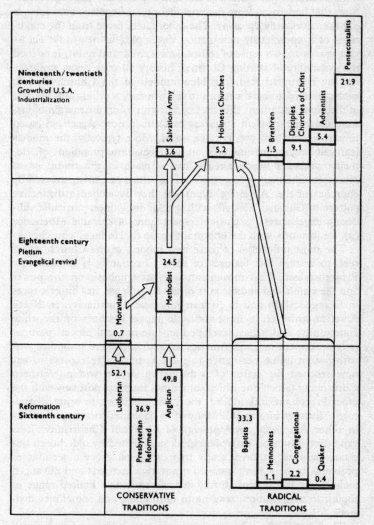

Figure 2.7 *Northern (non-Latin Western) Christianity, 1980: world figures*

Source: *after D. B. Barrett (ed.),* World Christian Encyclopedia: A Comparative Study of Churches and Religions in the Modern World, AD 1900–2000, *Nairobi, Oxford University Press, 1982.*

Swedish Baptists, of Ukrainian Mennonites. As succeeding generations assimilated to American life and the English language, structures that had arisen from national identity or linguistic convenience
did not necessarily die away. The other factor arose from the conditions of a consciously new nation developing in new ways across
vast spaces amid a sense of spiritual awakening and quest. It opened
the possibility of starting Christian history all over again, uninhibited by corrupted tradition. New models of the Church arrived,
each claiming to mark a return to the worship, teaching and lifestyle
of the New Testament churches. A few groups on the margin of historic Christianity went so far as to claim a new, American-based
revelation, but this was not the norm. More typically, the models
featured heightened emphasis on, or special interpretations of, elements of belief which already had a place in the traditions of
Northern Christianity (e.g. the coming return of Christ, stressed by
churches of the 'Adventist' type). Or they developed a distinctive
pattern of Christian lifestyle, with special disciplines, particular vali-
dating experiences, or particular paradigms of spiritual experience
(as, for instance, with the important group of 'Holiness' churches).

The most influential of these new models of the Church which
seek to restore lost features of early Christianity is undoubtedly
Pentecostalism. This movement, with its emphasis on the power
and the visible and audible gifts of the Holy Spirit, has historic roots
in Evangelicalism and in African-American Christianity. In North
America, however, its most noticable impact has been on the white
community; and it has developed an international aspect, particularly prominent in Latin America and Africa, where it meshes well
with potent influences native to these settings. Pentecostalism has
now reached the status of a distinctive stream within Northern
Christianity (albeit one which sometimes interacts postively with the
older Protestant and, indeed, the Latin traditions to bring 'charismatic' features into them). Many of its characteristics figure equally
in other American developments of Northern Christianity. It is
expansive, assertive, entrepreneurial; uninhibited by old church tradition or alien cultures; ready to treat obstacles or objections as
problems to be solved; open to innovative methods and advanced
technology; in doctrine, firmly articulated over a limited range of
topics; in organization, tending to diffuseness and sometimes division.

The especially American movement often denominated
Fundamentalist draws its membership from every branch of the
Northern tradition – old Protestant, old radical, American radical
(e.g. Adventist and Holiness groupings) and Pentecostal. It is
marked by the use of the Bible as an instrument for problem-
solving, by precisely articulated doctrinal statements, by clearly
formulated conservative social attitudes and by a stress on in-

dividual religious response. The movement is by no means mono-lithic or centralized; it is perhaps best seen as a tendency or climate rather than a discrete entity. Nor is it to be simply identified with the much wider Evangelical movement already mentioned, of which it forms a part.

Geography and distribution Southern Europe produced outstanding Protestant reformers, but they made little headway in their own lands. France hesitated over the Reformation for many years. It was northern Europe that responded. A Lutheran, conservative Reformation was adopted in many German princedoms and the Scandinavian kingdoms within the sixteenth century. More advanced forms were established in the German and Swiss city-states and in Holland and Scotland. The radicals were persecuted. Holland proved more hospitable to them than many places, and radicals entered a brief period of ascendancy in seventeenth-century England. But it was America that brought the radicals into their own. Much of the huge complex of American Protestantism is of radical origin.

Since the eighteenth century both emigration and vigorous mis-sionary activity have taken all branches of Northern, like Latin, Christianity, to all the continents.

Conditioning factors The factors which have conditioned Latin Christianity (see above) have also affected the Northern tradition.

Characteristic features Northern Christianity is essentially vernacular. The break with Latin, brought about by the desire that the faith should be widely apprehended by the people, meant the growth of local and national expressions of the faith. The diversity of Northern Christianity is a natural result. Freed from external constraint, the church government of a Tudor monarchy was unlikely to resemble that of a Swiss democracy. The waves of immigrants to America nat-urally brought their own diverse expressions of Christianity with them, and the totally new urban conditions of the nineteenth century produced new forms, attracting different social groups. The charac-teristic form of the Church in Northern Christianity is the denomi-nation. The denomination is an autonomous organization, perhaps called a church, but not in any exclusive sense. It sees itself as part of a wider Christian community, 'the Church'. It is infinitely adaptable, at the price of being infinitely diffuse.

The Northern tradition has produced a laicization within Western Christianity. The preaching of God's initiative for human salvation and of faith as the instrument by which salvation was received reduced the place of the sacramental system of the Church, to which popular religion had earlier looked for salvation. This in turn undermined the power of the priesthood, which dispenses the sacraments. The stress on Scripture as the sole norm of guidance, and the popularization of Scripture, meant that the same sources were open to laity as to ministers. Ministers openly married and had families, just like laymen. Luther insisted that a married cobbler could live as holy a life as a celibate monk; so a separate monastic class was no longer needed. Virginity, so long exalted, lost its special status of holiness.

Laicization originally meant a consecration of the 'ordinary' life of work and family. *All* Christians were called to holiness and to prepare for heaven. It has often been argued that the values this fostered favoured the accumulation and investment of capital and helped to shape the economic and industrial pattern of the West. Laicization later helped to produce secularization, when the motives for the consecration to God of ordinary life waned. In the post-Christian West, anti-religious and anti-clerical movements are strongest in the Catholic countries; the pace of secularization, and the disappearance of the overt signs of Christian attachment, have been more rapid in Protestant ones.

The African Tradition

Nomenclature At the beginning of the twentieth century there were perhaps 10 million professing Christians in Africa. In the mid-1990s one estimate puts the figure at 307 million, and it is rising steadily. Besides representatives of Oriental Christianity in Egypt and Ethiopia, some late adherents to Eastern Christianity in Kenya and Uganda, and the fruit of the missionary efforts of Latin and of Northern Christianity, the figure includes churches which cannot be called Catholic or Protestant or Orthodox. The so-called African Independent churches (sometimes called 'African instituted' or 'spiritual' churches) draw from springs deep in the heart of African culture (see chapter 13 below). They are found, to different degrees, in every part of the continent, and no one set of causes or conditions explains them. They are another example of the way the Christian faith clothes itself in different cultural garments. Many of these characteristics also appear in members of the churches which derive directly from Catholic and Protestant missions, and which comprise the majority of African Christians. In other words, a profound modification of Latin and Northern Christianity seems to be taking place in Africa, with the Independents giving some indication of the direction the modification may take.

Conditioning factors African Christianity is shaped by the fact that it arrived in conjunction with the impact of modern, Western forces upon the primal societies of Africa. The colonial period was short, the missionary period not much longer, but the effects of Western trade, technology, education and ideas, and the fundamental shift of activities and values brought about by the period of Western domination, show every sign of being permanent. Primal societies are holistic. Sacred and secular duties are not distinguished; both are submerged in all-embracing custom, sanctioned by the ancestors. The religious effect of the new developments, therefore, even the apparently 'secular' ones, has been shattering. The Christian faith has been embraced as a substitute world-view for the primal one; or, in places where transition has been less sharp, it has supplemented a partly rejected, partly retained world-view. In either case, the primal world-view, even in its broken form, poses religious questions which have no meaning in European society, and cannot be answered in terms of the Latin or Northern forms through which the Christian faith originally came to Africa.

The encounter of modern and primal societies has produced a disturbance of values and overlapping codes of practice, causing ambiguity and moral uncertainty. It has also linked people who previously had no common bond of kinship. Christianity itself has made people consciously part of a universal community. It has also frequently provided a means of knitting together the torn fabric of moral choice in African society. The extent to which churches of missionary origin have not been able to reintegrate old and new is a measure of the significance of the Independent churches.

Characteristic features The experience of African Christianity, and that of other newer Christians of the southern hemisphere, has been different from that of Europe at two vital points. In both north and south the acceptance of Christianity brought pre-literate peoples into the sphere of literary culture; but whereas for the northern peoples literary culture meant an alien language in which only religious specialists could be expected to be competent, for the southern peoples the change has favoured the growth of vernacular literature. This process has theological effects: the explanation and elucidation of the Christian faith in one's own vernacular, in dialogue with other vernacular speakers, is a wholly different matter from its recapitulation in a fixed form in an alien language, however carefully learned, by a specialist. Even more important, in the conversion of the northern countries new Christians turned from many gods to 'the One', and the Christian faith found no shadow of itself in the faiths which it displaced; but in Africa, Christian missionaries frequently found knowledge of a being, often associated with the sky, with no altars, no priests, perhaps no regular worship, but present and behind the constitution of reality. The coming of Christianity was less bringing God to the people than bringing God near. Thus, however severe the missionary judgement may have been about African society's religion and life (and it was often uncomprehendingly harsh), a traditional name for God remained as the name of the Christian God. This makes a link between old and new which leads to important questions about the relation of the old religion of Africa to the new.

In Africa salvation has a solid, material context: the power of God, Christ and the Holy Spirit is revealed in healing, in protection from evil powers, in combating frustration and fear. These themes are particularly prominent in the newer branches of African Christianity, the Independent (or 'spiritual') churches and the indigenous radical Evangelical and charismatic groups who assert Christ's saving power over against the old spiritual powers of Africa and against sin, disease and the myriad ills and frustrations of African urban life. The immediacy of salvation is a regular theme of African preaching.

African Christianity works with continuing world-views which allow for much more frequent crossing of the frontier between the transcendent and natural worlds than has been common in post-Enlightenment Western Christianity. It has to cope with the fear of witchcraft and sorcery, a desolating fact of African life. Attempts to remove this fear by means of rationalistic assurance that there is no such thing are foredoomed to failure; generalized assurances of the love and power of God are often ineffective. African Christianity (and again Independents offer an index to the views of a much wider group of African Christians) is finding ways of taking the issues of witchcraft and sorcery seriously. These ways involve visually recognizable action in the name of Christ, and make possible forgiveness and reconciliation between those separated by the objectified malice or hatred that witchcraft stands for. Similarly, with medical services in disarray in so much of Africa, the time-honoured African connection between religion and healing is taking Christian forms. African healing was always directed to the patient, not the illness, taking account of the (often suppressed) feelings of guilt likely to follow infractions of the ritual social or moral code. Many Christian healers bring a similar pastoral insight to their activity of healing through prayer. The missions from the West brought a Christianity shaped by the Enlightenment, and had some success in transplanting Enlightenment values; but the strength of Christianity in Africa may prove to be its capacity for independence of the Enlightenment.

African Christianity has to cope with this, and to argue in the light of both Scripture and experience about questions of duty to ancestors (for death does not divide the African family) and to the land. It is already showing more attention to sacred places than has been common in Northern Christianity, and in a different way from that of Latin Christianity; and an interest in uses of water as a symbol and medium of divine action beyond those seen in Christianity elsewhere.

African Christianity puts strong emphasis on the word. Christianity came with the book and the literary revolution, and in Africa is generally biblicist; but the inspired preacher, the charismatic leader who has 'utterance', is held in high honour. Among the Independents the special words of revelation received through prophecy and the use of sacred 'revealed' words are also common. By contrast, the sacraments as defined in the West are probably less significant, though shared meals have an important place in church life as in community life.

In general, African churchmen have been happy enough to retain the denominational structures inherited from the missions, and sometimes to diversify them. On the other hand, they have shown little interest in schemes of church union. The Independent churches have added thousands of new denominations, and more recently the radical Evangelicals and charismatics have added still others, as well as countless para-church movements which function almost as churches. The plethora of religious bodies does not, however, mean a harsh, exclusive sectarianism. It is associated with the tendency to produce cohesive unity where the leader is known and can be active among his people. African church order has combined complex hierarchical structures with scope for spontaneity and congregational expression.

Since the 1960s, when political systems in Africa based on the nation-state have come under strain or broken down, African churches have sometimes offered the only alternative viable forms of civil society. This has led in some cases to a mediatory role when state rule has collapsed. Direct church–state confrontations have occurred, but are usually avoided. In a few states, Christian–Muslim relations have been dominated by the issue of political power. In one respect, the experience of European and Latin American Christianity is unlikely to be repeated; almost all African states (outside the Islamic states of the north and east) are plural in religious allegiance. There are few where any one church can ever expect to be exclusive.

Other Southern Traditions

The largest single Christian culture will probably soon be the Spanish- and Portuguese-speaking mestizo complex of Latin America, and it might seem proper to devote a section to Latin American Christianity. However, most of its features either are to be found within the Latin tradition, which is the dominant strand, or (like the 'liberation theology' characteristic of many of its principal theologians) are local extensions of that tradition. Latin American Protestantism, which has seen phenomenal growth within the twentieth century, is distinguished by a marked Pentecostal strain – Evangelical, enthusiastic, stressing the immediacy of the Holy Spirit's activity – and is marked by the gift of tongues (see p. 125 above). So far, however, the Hispano-Portuguese movement in theology and life has influenced the Latin and Northern traditions of Christianity which originally produced it, rather than becoming identifiable as a separate Christian tradition.

The Pacific islands, to a greater extent even than Africa, have produced new Christian nations, where Christian profession is almost universal; but their total population is small in relation to the world population. There are movements in some respects parallel to the African Independent churches. Some of the most spectacular, however, are properly seen as movements of adjustment of traditional society to Christian and modern influences rather than as part of the Christian tradition itself. (See chapter 12 below.)

Other modern traditions might be identified but for the present small size of their Christian communities relative to the total number of Christians in the world. India and China may yet produce important versions of Christianity. The former in particular operates in a world of thought quite different from that in which Christianity has hitherto thrived, differing in all its assumptions about time, nature and the being of God. It also operates in a land with age-old traditions of renunciation, asceticism and the mystical quest, as well as one in the throes of rapid social change. An expression of Christianity which takes account of all these is likely to display striking differences from any that have gone before.

Marginal Traditions

There are movements which are only intelligible in relation to Christian faith, but which do not clearly bear the marks of historic Christianity which we have enumerated. In some cases, however, a degree of movement or fluidity is discernible, so it is best to take these movements as belonging to the margins of Christianity.

Three groups may be distinguished:

1 *Folk religions* A synthesis of Christian and pre-Christian elements is common in many rural communities. In Latin America and parts of southern Europe, for example, processions take place which are in all essentials reenactments of traditional events of pre-Christian religion associated with fertility and renewal. These include some reference to the Virgin or saints and some reinter-

pretation of old rituals. Such ceremonies very in the degree of adaptation used; some are frankly plural, while in others, notably the influential spirit movements of African origin in Brazil or the Caribbean, the Christian element is imported and relatively superficial.

2 *Hebraist movements* In many primal societies religious reformers have arisen, influenced by Christian models, who have induced in whole communities a clear break with the traditional world-view, perhaps recognizing the Christian God, but making no clear confession of the ultimate significance of Christ. The prominence in such movements of the High God (often in clear contrast to the traditional practice of local society), and the frequent identification with the God of Israel and the Scriptures, has led to the application to them of the title 'Hebraist'. There are also cases, such as the Ratana movement in New Zealand, which began as Christian movements but in which the personality of the founder has tended to replace the figure of Christ. Such movements gather round the margins of historic Christianity, and may flow backwards and forwards across these margins.

3 *Post-Christian Western denominations* Here we should perhaps distinguish between Unitarianism and a succession of nineteenth- and twentieth-century new Western movements. In Unitarianism two separate strands are noticeable: one, which is biblicist, resisting dogmatic statements which seem to go beyond biblical warrant, has modified the historic confessions about Christ, but kept contact with the main Christian tradition; the other is rationalist, endeavouring to construct a universal 'rational' religion in which the miraculous plays no part.

Some movements have produced new 'revelations' to supplement the Christian scriptures, such as *Science and Health with a Key to the Scriptures*, the textbook of Christian Science by Mary Baker Eddy (1821–1910), or *The Book of Mormon*, associated with Joseph Smith (1805–44), the founder of the Mormons (the 'Church of Jesus Christ of Latter-day Saints'); or mandatory interpretations of the scriptures, like those characteristic of the Jehovah's Witnesses since the days of their founder C. T. Russell (1852–1916). These three movements originated in American Christianity but have greatly modified the significance of Christ, compared with that characteristic of historic Christianity.

Modern Developments

If its previous history is anything to go by, Christianity is on the verge of a transformation. During the twentieth century its centre of gravity has moved from the north to the south; and its centres of present growth make it likely that this shift will continue. It is too early to predict the precise nature of the changes, but in the past such changes of centre of gravity have altered priorities, preoccupations and the way in which Christianity has been expressed. Christian thought has hitherto developed in relation to the pressing needs of particular situations. It is likely that new developments will be increasingly dictated by the situations of Africa, Latin America and Asia. A sign of this is that, since the 1960s at least, issues arising from race, poverty, institutionalized oppression and the use of the world's resources have figured on the agenda of Christian theology in a way foreshadowed, but not attained, in earlier Christianity. South Africa, where these issues long appeared in a peculiarly painful form, and which has a large Christian population, figured prominently in the debate. There is, perhaps, no country where theological activity has been more noticeable.

Such concerns arise from a widespread belief that the relief of distress – always recognized as a Christian duty – is in itself not a sufficient response to human suffering. To fulfil God's will for mankind, changes in society are necessary. The spread of this belief has made Christians more aware than before of questions posed by Marxist thought. Historically Christianity and Marxism have been hostile to each other, and the first Marxist political triumph resulted in the transformation of Holy Russia into an atheistic state. In practice, the condition of Christianity in Marxist countries has differed widely. In Cuba, where the Church was traditionally allied with the old social order, Christian adherence has halved since the revolution; in Poland it fell hardly at all. (If anything, it is the post-Communist period that has seen decline.) Marxist economic analysis for a time affected Christian theologians in Latin America. A feature of the 'theology of liberation' which developed there is the insistence that theology involves action on behalf of the poor. At one time many Latin American clergy therefore saw developing the political awareness of the poor as part of their calling.

The missionary era, which helped to transform Christianity, has practically ended. There are still thousands of Western missionaries (as well as a growing number of missionaries from Africa and Asia and especially Korea) serving 'overseas', and, while many are engaged in philanthropic work or specialized services, an increasing recognition of large numbers of 'unreached peoples' in all continents may well result in an expansion in the numbers of missionaries

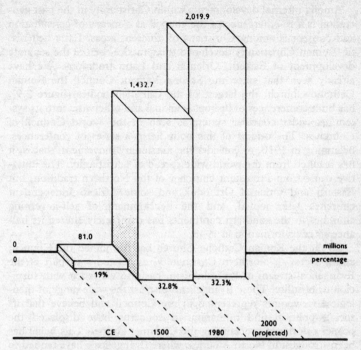

Figure 2.8 *Statistics of Christian profession as a percentage of world population*
Source: *after Barrett (ed.)*, World Christian Encyclopedia.

engaged in evangelistic enterprise. Nevertheless, if every missionary were withdrawn from Africa overnight, congregational life in the vast majority of cases would continue unaffected. Western domination of the Church is as dead as the old empires. In the 'high days' of the missionary movement, Christians looked for the collapse of all other religions. Despite the phenomenal response to Christianity since then, no one would now predict the imminent collapse of any of the major world faiths. Christians are pondering anew the significance of a plural universe of faiths, and one result has been the development at various levels of a dialogue with members of other faiths. This is an activity which demands seriousness about truth; if one begins with the assumption that all religions are the same in essence, dialogue is hardly a priority. The increased Christian awareness of issues of peace and justice has also led to a desire to discuss with representatives of other faiths the shared human responsibility for the peace and health of the world.

Among internal developments within Christianity in the past generation is a re-emergence of the council as a means of consultation and consensus among Christians of different areas. Early hellenistic–Roman Christianity developed this practice, before the separate development of Eastern, Oriental and Latin traditions. We have already seen that since the Second Vatican Council the Roman Catholic Church, the largest of the Christian bodies (figure 2.9), has built conferences of bishops, regional and otherwise, into its system. A wider conciliar system is seen in the World Council of Churches. The origins of this body lie in a series of conferences, beginning in 1910, to consider the missionary movement; that is, it has resulted from the world-wide spread of Christianity. The initiative came from Protestant churches of the Northern tradition, but Eastern and Oriental Orthodox and some African Independent churches later joined, and the development of self-governing churches in the southern continents has completely altered its balance since its formation in 1948.

So far the Roman Catholic Church has not joined the Council; and a sector of Northern Christianity, associated with part of the Evangelical stream of Protestantism, has also viewed it with suspicion or hostility. These Evangelicals distrust the wide range of theological viewpoints represented in the Council and believe that its social, political and humanitarian concerns have displaced the proper priority of proclaiming the Christian Gospel. This belief has been strongest in North America, where Evangelicals have tended to form distinct denominations, rather than (as in Europe) remaining as a wing of the older Protestant churches. Since the Lausanne Consultation on World Evangelization of 1974, however, a world conciliar movement has been developing among Evangelicals also. One fruit has been a deepening manifestation of Evangelical concern about social issues and behaviour and their relation to the Gospel.

One of the original hopes of the new conciliarism, the union of churches, arose in Northern Christianity, the most diffuse of the Christian traditions. Despite the emergence of large united churches such as the Church of South India (1947) and later the Church of North India, there has been less enthusiasm for union schemes in the southern continents. Some unions have taken place in North America, Australia and Europe; but far more significant than formal unions is the much greater degree of understanding and mutual acceptance visible between the Christian traditions than at earlier times.

The so-called 'basic Christian communities', which developed most noticeably in Latin America, are communities in which, to quote a recent joint statement, 'the poor celebrate their faith in the Liberating Christ and discover the political dimension of love'. By

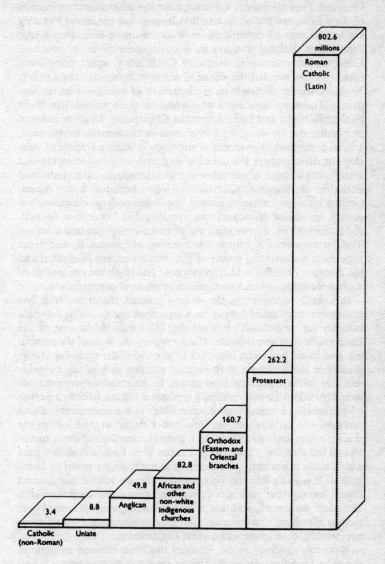

Figure 2.9 *Christianity, 1980: world figures*
Source: *after Barrett (ed.)*, World Christian Encyclopedia.

contrast, the house churches of Western Europe, in which Christians, mostly young, enjoy together the enthusiastic expression of their faith, are not often touched by political concerns; but they are an example of community in Western urban life, often a rare commodity. Related changes in worship seem to be in progress. Until recently almost all forms of Christianity, apart from some fringe groups, avoided the dance in worship, retaining it as a purely 'secular' activity or rejecting it altogether as irreligious in its tendency. There are now signs of a break in these attitudes in some parts of Western and Latin American Christianity. In areas exposed to popular culture or to the Pentecostal or charismatic movements, a strong, rhythmic movement of the body is often a feature of worship. In Africa, where the dance is so deeply entrenched in life and society, the change is still more marked. Originally, the traditional attitudes of Western Christianity were introduced to Africa. Gradually, most notably among the Independent churches but among the older churches also, dancing has become a normal, almost unnoticed, accompaniment of much congregational worship. The characteristically African combination of spontaneity and order appears in the gripping power of traditional patterns of rhythm and the dialogue of leader and respondents. The rhythmic movement of a whole congregation is a powerful expression of corporate joy.

In church organization, the older Christian traditions, with few exceptions, have relied heavily on a separated and (usually) full-time ministry (or 'priesthood'; but see p. 124) which in the case of the Latin tradition is also celibate. Ministers perform most of the preaching and in all but some branches of the Northern tradition always preside at the eucharist; they exercise pastoral care of the believers and give leadership to the local group. In their various ways the different traditions have accordingly envisaged the minister as a person of comparative learning and of some status in the community. These centuries-old expectations are now under strain: in Africa from the sheer number of Christians, which forbids hope for sufficient ministers on the traditional pattern; and in the West from economic forces which make it less easy than formerly to maintain a pattern of distribution. It is likely that the ranks of the ministry will be more varied than formerly, that such service will be increasingly combined with 'ordinary' daily work, and that ministerial duties may be spread over various members of a congregation. The developments would seem to resemble some features of earliest Christianity.

Women's entrance to the ministry has been effected in some of the older traditions. In many African churches women play a dominant part, and the Independents especially have found roles for women of notable insight or utterance. Also, attitudes to marriage and the family shaped by the conditions of Western life are being reformulated in the light of the different understanding of these institutions in Africa. Recent years have seen a new consciousness of the significance of women in Christianity. The question runs wider and deeper than that of ordination, and is voiced in different ways in many parts of the world. There are signs, especially but not only in Western Christianity, of a thorough revision of the language of worship and theology to avoid the assumption of the 'maleness' of God. It is perhaps too early to assess how radical, or how universal, these changes will be.

Attitudes within Christianity to sexuality may also be revised by the southward move. Both Eastern and Western Christianity were powerfully affected at a critical period of their growth by indigenous currents of thought which equated the material, and hence the body, with evil. Southern Christianity will doubtless be affected by the exaltation of life and the reproduction of life dear to African and Pacific societies.

Christian history has seen a constant tension between the forces which localize and indigenize it, and those which universalize it. Both forces belong to its earliest sources and message. Its present situation in the world shows both to the full. The universalizing forces are the same as ever: the worship of Israel's God, the according of ultimate significance to Christ, the sense of continuing divine activity in the Christian community, the use of the scriptures and the consciousness of a community transcending time and space. It will be surprising if the localizing forces of the southern continents do not lead it into new paths.

Bibliography

1 ABBOTT, W. M. (ed.), *The Documents of Vatican II*, New York, Association Press & Herder/London, Dublin, G. Chapman, 1966
2 ARBERRY, A. J. (ed.), *Religion in the Middle East: Three Religions in Concord and Conflict*, Cambridge, Cambridge University Press, 1969
3 ATIYA, A. S., *A History of Eastern Christianity*, London, Methuen/Notre Dame, University of Notre Dame Press, 1968
4 BARRETT, D. B. (ed.), *World Christian Encyclopaedia: A Comparative Study of Churches and Religions in the Modern World, AD 1900–2000*, Nairobi, Oxford University Press, 1982 (contains a mass of statistics, analysis and information on 223 countries, plus an atlas)
5 BEDE, *A History of the English Church and People* (tr. Leo Sherley-Price; rev. edn by R. E. Latham), Harmondsworth, Penguin, 1968
6 BEDIAKO, K. *Christianity in Africa: The Recovery of a Non-Western Religion*, Edinburgh, Edinburgh University Press, 1994
7 BOSCH, D. J., *Transforming Mission: Paradigm Shifts in the Theology of Mission*, Maryknoll, NY, Orbis, 1991

158 ANDREW WALLS

8 BROWN, P. R. L., *Augustine of Hippo: A Biography*, London, Faber/Berkeley, University of California Press, 1967
9 BRUCE, F. F., *New Testament History* (1st US edn), Garden City, NY, Doubleday, 1971 (copyr. 1969); rev. edn London, Oliphants, 1971
10 BÜHLMANN, W., *The Coming of the Third Church: An Analysis of the Present and Future of the Church* (tr. R. Woodhall), Slough, St Paul Publications, 1976
11 BUTLER, J. F., *Christianity in Asia and America after AD 1500*, Leiden, Brill, 1979 (Iconography of Religions)
12 CAMBRIDGE HISTORY OF THE BIBLE, 3 vols, Cambridge, Cambridge University Press, 1963–70:1, ACKROYD, P. R. and EVANS, C. F. (eds), *From the Beginnings to Jerome*; 2, LAMPE, G. W. H. (ed.), *The West from the Fathers to the Reformation*; 3, GREENSLADE, S. L. (ed.), *The West from the Reformation to the Present Day*
13 CHADWICK, O., *The Popes and European Revolution*, Oxford, Clarendon Press/New York, Oxford University Press, 1981
14 CHURCH HISTORY ASSOCIATION OF INDIA, *History of Christianity in India*, Bangalore, Theological Publications in India for Church History Association of India, 1982–
15 CONE, J. H., *God of the Oppressed*, New York, Seabury, 1975; London, SPCK, 1977 (an example of American 'black theology', a phenomenon also important in South Africa)
16 CRAGG, K., *The Arab Christian: A History in the Middle East*, Louisville, Westminster/John Knox Press, 1991
17 CROSS, F. L. and LIVINGSTONE, E. A. (eds), *The Oxford Dictionary of the Christian Church*, 2nd edn, London, New York, Oxford University Press, 1974 (new edn 1996)
18 CULLMANN, O., *Christ and Time: The Primitive Christian Conception of Time and History* (tr. F. V. Filson), rev. edn London, SCM, 1962; Philadelphia, Westminster, 1964
19 DAVIDSON, A. K., *Christianity in Aotearoa: A History of Church and Society in New Zealand*, Wellington, New Zealand Education for Ministry Board
20 DICKENS, A. G., *Reformation and Society in Sixteenth Century Europe*, London, Thames & Hudson/New York, Harcourt, Brace, 1966
21 DODD, C. H., *The Founder of Christianity*, London, Collins, 1971; New York, Macmillan, 1970
22 DOUGLAS, J. D. (ed.), *The New International Dictionary of the Christian Church*, Grand Rapids, Zondervan/Exeter, Paternoster, 1974
23 DOWLEY, T. (ed.), *The History of Christianity*, Tring, Lion, 1977; as *Eerdmans Handbook to the History of Christianity*, Grand Rapids, Eerdmans, 1977
24 ELLACURIA, I. and SOBRINO, J. (eds), *Mysterium Liberationis: Fundamental Concepts of Liberation Theology*, Maryknoll, Orbis, c.1993
25 FORMAN, C. H., *Island Churches of the South Pacific*, Maryknoll, Orbis, 1982
26 FREND, W. H. C., *The Early Church*, London, Hodder, 1965; Philadelphia, Lippincott, 1966
27 GARRETT, J., *To Live Among the Stars: Christian Origins in Oceania*, Geneva, World Council of Churches, 1982

28 GOPPELT, L., *Apostolic and Post Apostolic Times* (tr. R. A. Guelich), London, Black/New York, Harper & Row, 1970

29 GUTHRIE, D., *New Testament Introduction*, 3rd edn, London, Tyndale/Downers Grove, Inter-Varsity, 1970

30 HANDY, R. T., *A History of the Churches in the United States and Canada*, Oxford, Clarendon Press, 1981; prev. publ. Oxford, New York, Oxford University Press, 1976

31 HARRIS, J. *One Blood: 200 years of Aboriginal Encounter with Christianity*, Sutherland, NSW, and Claremonth, CA, Albatross Books; Oxford, Lion, 1990

32 HASTINGS, A., *African Christianity: An Essay in Interpretation*, London, G. Chapman, 1976

33 HASTINGS, A., *The Church in Africa, 1400–1950*, Oxford, Clarendon Press, 1994

34 HASTINGS, A., *A History of African Christianity, 1950–1975*, Cambridge, Cambridge University Press, 1979

35 HOLLENWEGER, W. J., *The Pentecostals: The Charismatic Movement in the Churches* (tr. R. A. Wilson), Minneapolis, Augsburg Publishing, 1972; London, SCM, 1972

36 HORNER, N. A., *A Guide to Christian Churches in the Middle East: Present-day Christianity in the Middle East and North Africa*, Elkhart, Mission Focus, 1989

37 ISHERWOOD, L., and MACEWAN, D. (eds), *Introducing Feminist Theology*, Sheffield, Sheffield Academic Press, 1993

38 ISICHEI, E., *A History of Christianity in Africa: From Antiquity to the Present*, Grand Rapids, Eerdmans, Africa Word Press, 1995

39 KELLY, J. N. D., *Early Christian Doctrines*, London, Black, 2nd edn, 1960; 5th rev. edn 1977; rev. edn New York, Harper & Row, 1978

40 KING, U. (ed.), *Feminist Theology from the Third World: A Reader*, London, SPCK/Maryknoll, Orbis, 1994

41 LANTERNARI, V., *The Religions of the Oppressed: A Study of Modern Messianic Cults* (tr. Lisa Sergio), London, MacGibbon & Kee/New York, Knopf, 1963

42 LATOURETTE, K. S., *A History of the Expansion of Christianity*, 7 vols, London, Eyre & Spottiswoode, 1938–45; New York, Harper, 1939–47; Grand Rapids, Zondervan, n.d.; London, Paternoster, 1971

43 LEHMANN, A., *Christian Art in Africa and Asia* (tr. E. Hopka, J. E. Napola and O. E. Sohn), St Louis, Concordia, 1969

44 LEWIS, C. S., *Mere Christianity*, rev. edn, London, Bles/New York, Macmillan, 1952

45 MCKENZIE, J. L., *The Roman Catholic Church*, London, Weidenfeld/New York, Holt, Rinehart, 1969

46 MCKENZIE, P. R., *The Christians: Their Beliefs and Practices*, Abingdon Press, 1988

47 MARSDEN, G. M., *Fundamentalism and American Culture: The Shaping of Twentieth Century Evangelicalism, 1870–1925*, New York, Oxford University Press, 1980 (1981)

48 MEEKS, *The First Urban Christians: The Social World of the Apostle Paul*, New Haven, Yale University Press, 1983

49 MOFFETT, S. H., *A History of Christianity in Asia*, New York, HarperCollins, 1992

50 MOORE, P., *Christianity*, London, Ward Lock Educational, 1982 (The Arts and Practices of Living Religions)

51 NEILL, S., *A History of Christianity in India*, Cambridge, Cambridge University Press, 1985

52 NEW TESTAMENT. There are many available versions in English. Good and convenient are *Today's English Version*, London, The Bible Societies, Collins, 1976 (The Good News Bible); New York, American Bible Society, 1974; and *The New Jerusalem Bible*, London, Darton, Longman & Todd, 1985

53 NIEBUHR, R., *Christ and Culture*, London, Faber, 1952; New York, Harper, 1951

54 NOLL, M. A., BEBBINGTON, D. W. and RAWLYK, G. A. (eds), *Evangelicalism: Comparative Studies of Popular Protestantism in North America, the British Isles, and Beyond, 1700–1990*, New York, Oxford University Press, 1994

55 PARKER, T. H. L., *John Calvin: A Biography*, London, Dent, 1975; Philadelphia, Westminster, 1976; Tring, Lion, 1977

56 PARRATT, J. K. (ed.), *A Reader in African Christian Theology*, London, SPCK, 1987

57 PELICAN HISTORY OF THE CHURCH (ed. W. O. Chadwick), 6 vols, Harmondsworth/Baltimore, Penguin, 1960–71; repr. London, Hodder, 1965–86: 1, CHADWICK, H., *The Early Church*; 2, SOUTHERN, R. W., *Western Society and the Church in the Middle Ages*; 3, CHADWICK, O., *The Reformation*; 4, CRAGG, G. R., *The Church and the Age of Reason, 1648–1789*; 5, VIDLER, A. R., *The Church in an Age of Revolution, 1789 to the Present Day*; 6, NEILL, S., *A History of Christian Missions*

58 SANNEH, L., *Encountering the West. Christianity and the Global Cultural Process: The African Dimension*, London, Marshall Pickering, 1993

59 SANNEH, L. *Translating the Message: The Missionary Impact on Culture*, Maryknoll, Orbis, 1990

60 SUNDKLER, B. G. M., *Zulu Zion and Some Swazi Zionists*, London/New York, Oxford University Press, 1976

61 THOMAS, M. M., *The Acknowledged Christ of the Indian Renaissance*, London, SCM, 1969; Indian edn Madras, CLS, 1970

62 TORRES, S., and EAGLESON, J. (eds), *The Challenge of Basic Christian Communities* (tr. John Drury), Maryknoll, Orbis, 1981

63 TURNER, H. W., *Religious Innovation in Africa: Collected Essays on New Religious Movements*, Boston, G. K. Hall, 1979

64 UNDERHILL, E., *Mysticism*, 6th edn, London, Methuen, 1916; many edns issued London, Methuen/New York, Dutton

65 WARE, T. (KALLISTOS), *The Orthodox Church*, Harmondsworth/Baltimore, Penguin, 1963

66 WILLIAMS, C. W. S., *The Descent of the Dove: A Short History of the Holy Spirit in the Church*, London, SCM/Longman, 1939; New York, Meridian, 1956

67 WILLIAMS, G. H., *The Radical Reformation*, Philadelphia, Westminster/London, Weidenfeld, 1962

68 WRIGHT, A. D., *The Counter-Reformation: Catholic Europe and the Non-Christian World*, London, Weidenfeld, 1982; New York, St Martin's, 1982

69 WRIGHT, N. T., *The New Testament and the People of God*, London, SPCK, 1992

70 ZERNOV, N., *Eastern Christendom: A Study of the Origin and Development of the Eastern Orthodox Church*, London, Weidenfeld/New York, Putnam, 1961

3

Islam

ALFORD T. WELCH

Introduction

For Muslims, Islam has been from the beginning much more than
what is usually meant by the Western concept 'religion'. Islam,
meaning in Arabic 'submission (to God)', is at the same time a religious tradition, a civilization and, as Muslims are fond of saying, a
'total way of life'. Islam proclaims a religious faith and sets forth
certain rituals, but it also prescribes patterns of order for society in
such matters as family life, civil and criminal law, business, eti-
quette, food, dress and even personal hygiene. Traditional Muslims
view virtually all aspects of individual and group life as being regulated or guided by Islam, which is seen as a complete, complex religious and social system in which individuals, societies and
governments should all reflect the will of God. The Western distinction between the sacred and the secular is thus foreign to traditional
Islam, although some Muslim intellectuals now call for more
attention to the sacred as a response to the world-wide spread of
secularism.

Sources

Since Islam is such a rich religious and cultural tradition that has
varied dramatically across time and place, the sources and methods
for understanding it vary equally in breadth. Until recent decades
the study and portrayal of Islam involved mainly the tasks of editing, translating and interpreting written sources. This emphasis on
the analysis of written texts meant that historical and philological
methods dominated the field of Islamic studies. During the last
quarter of the twentieth century the methods of the social sciences,

especially anthropology and sociology, have vastly enriched our understanding of Muslim societies, elevating our awareness of the importance of aspects of the Islamic tradition that previously had been largely neglected [e.g. 5; 7; 12; 19]. The history and functions of rituals in the daily lives of Muslims, the various roles of the mosque (social and political as well as religious), and the relationship of Islam to politics, national and international law, and the modern state are just a few examples. Continued sensitivity to the obvious fact that Islam is both a personal religious faith and a cumulative historical tradition (stressed for decades by Wilfred Cantwell Smith, beginning with his *Meaning and End of Religion*) has had several positive effects. One is that scholars are devoting more attention to the study of Muslim faith and piety – the essence of Islam, but in some ways the most difficult aspect of its study for outside observers. Another is that the search for knowledge of varieties of Muslim piety has increased our awareness of the importance of a number of fields that in the past had been neglected by Islamicists or treated as independent disciplines. Examples such as Islamic art and architecture [17], the many uses of Qur'an calligraphy, the rich tradition of Qur'an recitation, Islamic poetry, various ritual and literary expressions of devotion to the Prophet [42], and popular sermons – many of which are now widely available in printed and electronic forms – provide windows of insight into Muslim piety for those who know how to look and what questions to ask.

Primary written sources for the study of Islam are also vast in number and scope. In addition to writings on Islamic history, scripture, and theology, where students in religious studies would naturally seek knowledge about this tradition, an immense literature exists on a number of distinctively 'Islamic sciences', such as the study of the Sunna of the Prophet contained in hadiths (reports of his sayings and deeds); Islamic law (which governs virtually all aspects of Muslim life); the 'sciences of the Qur'an', including ways of reciting (*tajwid*); Arabic grammar (as it pertains to the sacred texts); biography (especially regarding authorities for hadiths and Islamic law); and the twin sciences of geography and astronomy (important in a practical way for determining the direction of Mecca for prayer and for the orientation of mosques). Until modern times the vast majority of major Islamic works were written in Arabic, regardless of the native tongue or ethnic background of the writer. Only a small percentage of the most important classical sources, although fortunately a growing number in recent years, have been translated into other languages. Thus, those who want to study Islam in depth must learn this so-called 'language of the angels'. Persian, Turkish and Urdu gradually became important vehicles for conveying Islamic ideas, and their significance continues to grow. In modern times, with the widespread use of printing and the vast increase in literacy throughout the world, works essential to understanding the diversity of Islam came to be written in countless languages of Asia, Africa and Europe, so that knowledge of Arabic, while still necessary, is no longer sufficient, emphasizing the need for collaborative studies among scholars with a variety of language and disciplinary specialties.

Among the many works in classical Arabic the one that all consider to be the 'first source' for Islamic belief and practice is the Muslims' scripture, the Qur'an (Arabic, al-qur'an, 'the recitation'). It is divided into 114 independent units of widely varying length called suras (from the Arabic sura, 'unit'). Each sura begins with, or is preceded by, the formula, 'In the name of God, the Merciful, the Compassionate', often followed by a longer liturgical or formulaic statement. The suras thus stand as independent units – although varying considerably in form and content – unlike the chapters of the Bible. After the first sura, al-Fatiha (the Opening), a seven-verse prayer that serves as an introduction to the Qur'an (see p. 183 below), the suras are arranged generally in order of descending length, with many exceptions and with other criteria for keeping certain groups of suras together [54: 410]. Islamic orthodoxy and modern critical scholarship agree that the contents but not the final arrangement of the Qur'an go back to Muhammad. It is also virtually certain that Muhammad began but did not complete the task of compiling a written text of the Qur'an [54: 402–4]. About twenty years after his death an official recension of the consonantal text was issued by the third caliph, 'Uthman, establishing the number, order and contents of the suras. At that time Arabic was mainly an oral language; written Arabic was largely an aid to memory, with no uniform system of vowel signs or diacritical marks (one, two or three dots written above or below consonantal forms) for distinguishing several sets of consonants that share the same form. A system of seven canonical 'readings' or vocalizations (that is, systems for adding vowels and diacritical marks) of 'Uthman's text was established in the tenth century, and gradually one of these came to be used in nearly all parts of the Islamic world. In 1923 or 1924 (1342 AH – see pp. 180, 230–2), a standard edition of the printed text, complete with signs for recitation (indicating pauses, elision, etc.), was issued in Cairo under the authority of the king of Egypt, Fu'ad I. This edition – variously designated 'the royal Egyptian edition', 'the Egyptian standard edition', etc. – has gained widespread acceptance by Muslims and Islamicists alike, although other texts and verse numbering systems are still used. No critical edition of the Qur'an exists, nor do standard translations of the Arabic text in the various 'Islamic' and European languages. Among the many English translations, those by Yusuf Ali (1934) and M. M. Pickthall (1930,

1976) are preferred by most English-speaking Muslims (neither follows the Egyptian standard verse-numbering precisely, except for the latter's 1976 Arabic–English edition). The most popular English translation by a non-Muslim is that of the Cambridge Arabist, A. J. Arberry (1955). The two-volume translation by Richard Bell (1937, 1939) is the most useful for purposes of analysis of the history of the Arabic text of the Qur'an, an issue in which very few scholars have shown any interest since the middle of the twentieth century. These latter two translations follow an inferior nineteenth-century European Arabic text and verse-numbering system; because it is so widely used, in this chapter the verse numbers according to that system are given after the Egyptian verse numbers, separated by a virgule (see [53: 410–11] on the confusing issue of Qur'an verse divisions and the various numbering systems.

Next to the Qur'an stand the multi-volume collections of accounts called hadiths (from the Arabic *hadith*, 'story, tradition') that report or allege to report sayings and deeds of the Prophet Muhammad. The hadiths provide an authoritative guide for most aspects of Muslim daily life, for which Muhammad stands as exemplar *par excellence*. Six canonical collections of hadiths were compiled in the ninth and early tenth centuries (the third century AH), and other early collections such as Ahmad b. Hanbal's *Musnad* also gained widespread respect. Among these the most highly regarded are the two called *al-Sahih*, 'the sound (hadiths)', compiled by al-Bukhari (d. 870) and Muslim (d. 875), both available in English translation [8; 37]. At least one of the other six, the *Sunan* by Abu Dawud (d. 889), as well as a later, popular compendium, the *Mishkat al-Masabih*, are also available in English [2; 43]. The traditional Muslim view is that at least the 'sound' hadiths compiled by al-Bukhari and Muslim are authentic statements going back to Muhammad's contemporaries, and that genuine Islamic life and thought must be based on the Qur'an and these hadiths. Modern scholarship is divided on the question of the extent of the authenticity of the hadiths. It is clear that many of them, including some in the collections by al-Bukhari and Muslim, grew out of legal and theological debates that occurred long after the time of Muhammad, and that others reflect later stages in the development of Islamic rituals and other practices. Regardless of the question of their authenticity as precedents for Islamic law and as historical sources for the time of Muhammad, these collections are undoubtedly extremely valuable as primary sources for classical Islam. The focus of the debate among historians concerns the extent to which these accounts represent the Islam of the third rather than the first century of the Islamic era. Some Muslim reformers have rejected the hadith reports as representing a stage in the history of Islam generations after the time of Muhammad, while others reject them simply as representing an Islam of long ago that is no longer relevant and should not be normative for Muslims today. Those who hold these modernist views are, however, a small minority of the world population of Muslims.

In addition to the Qur'an, the hadith collections, and the vast literature on both of these (commentaries, dictionaries, etc.), primary written sources for the study of Islam include historical works on the development of Islam and its spread to various parts of the world, legal and theological treatises, biographical and devotional works on Muhammad, Islamic poetry and other religious literature, and a wide variety of devotional and pilgrimage manuals, as well as mystical, philosophical and sectarian works. Fortunately, more and more of these works are being translated into English and other European languages. Examples of classical Arabic sources that are fundamental to the study of Islam and are now available in English (in addition to the Qur'an and the hadith collections mentioned above) include Ibn Ishaq's *Sirat Rasul Allah* (Life of the Messenger of God) [20]; al-Tabari's *Ta'rikh al-rusul wa-l-muluk* (History of the messengers [of God] and the rulers) [46]; Ibn Sa'd's *Kitab al-tabaqat al-kabir* (Large book of the generations) [25]; and Malik ibn Anas's *Muwatta* [32] on Islamic law. Much of al-Ghazali's magisterial *Ihya' 'ulum al-din* (Revival of the religious sciences) has been translated in individual volumes by various scholars. Several very useful anthologies of English translations of a wide variety of classical and modern Arabic source materials are also available (see [5; 41; 56]; and, for selections from Qur'an commentaries, [4; 18]).

History

Islam dates from the last ten years of the life of the Prophet Muhammad (d. 632). Born probably around 570, Muhammad was orphaned at an early age and is said to have been reared by his grandfather and then an uncle, Abu Talib. At about the age of twenty-five Muhammad gained financial security when he married Khadija, a well-to-do widow. At about the age of forty he is said to have begun seeing visions, or according to other accounts receiving revelations, which at some point he proclaimed publicly in the streets of Mecca, his native city and also the centre for commerce and religious pilgrimage for western Arabia. Fearing the economic repercussions of Muhammad's preaching against the deities worshipped by the pilgrims at Mecca's central shrine, the Ka'ba, the leading families of the city persecuted Muhammad and his followers, forcing many who did not have tribal or clan protection (usually said to have been a large majority of the Muslims at that time) to migrate to the Christian kingdom of Abyssinia, also called Ethiopia, across the Red

Sea. The Meccan plutocrats are said to have imposed a social and economic boycott against Muhammad's clan of Hashim, causing dissension within the clan. This resulted in the loss of Muhammad's clan protection when his uncle and guardian Abu Talib died in about 620 and an enemy uncle, nicknamed Abu Lahab (Father of the Blaze) and immortalized in Sura 111 where he is condemned to the hellfire, became the clan chief and then withdrew his nephew's protection. Muhammad's life was no longer safe in Mecca, so he was forced to seek refuge elsewhere. After failing to find a new home for himself and his followers in nearby al-Ta'if, he reached an agreement with representatives of Yathrib, an agricultural settlement some 445 km north of Mecca, and in 622 he and his followers made the *hijra* (migration) to this settlement, which came to be called Medina, from *madinat al-nabi*, 'the city of the Prophet'. There within the short period of ten years Muhammad, the religious leader of a small band of emigrants, rose to become the political leader of virtually all of central and western Arabia. A Muslim military defeat of a much larger force of Meccans and their confederates at a caravan watering site called Badr in 624 became a major turning-point in Muhammad's rise to power. This awe-inspiring victory over the polytheists at Badr, along with several failed attempts by the Meccans and their allies to stop Muhammad by military force, eventually followed by what turned out to be an equally impressive diplomatic feat in the signing of the Treaty of al-Hudaybiya in 628, led to the peaceful surrender of Mecca to Muhammad in 630.

After Muhammad's death in 632 the political and spiritual leadership of the Muslim community (called the *Umma* in Arabic) was assumed by a succession of caliphs or 'deputies' of the Prophet, who ruled Islam in his place in all aspects except as prophet. By the end of the reign of the second caliph, 'Umar (d. 644), the Arabs had taken control of Egypt, Palestine, Syria, Mesopotamia and the heart of ancient Iran, capturing Damascus in 635, Jerusalem in 640, what was to become Cairo in 641, Alexandria in 642 and Isfahan in 643. During the reign of the third caliph, 'Uthman (d. 656), the Arab empire expanded westwards to Tripoli, northwards to the Taurus and Caucasus mountains, and eastwards to what is now Pakistan and Afghanistan. After the death of the fourth caliph, 'Ali (d. 661), Muhammad's cousin and son-in-law, the Muslim community split, with the majority, who later came to be called Sunnis, following the Umayyad dynasty of caliphs (661–750) and then the 'Abbasid dynasty (750–1258). In 711, about a century after Muhammad began preaching in Mecca and mid-way through the Umayyad period, the Arabs entered Spain from North Africa and also crossed the Indus river into the subcontinent of India. The Arabs' furthest point of advance into western Europe is marked by their defeat at the hands of Charles Martel near Tours in 732, exactly a solar century after the Prophet's death and ten years before the birth of Charlemagne. The Arabs were forced to withdraw from France, but they and their Muslim Berber successors continued to rule in Spain for seven and a half centuries. In the east the Arab-ruled Umayyad empire spread northwards to the Aral Sea and across the Oxus river (now called the Amu-Dar'ya) to Tashkent, and eastwards to include almost the whole of what is now Pakistan and Afghanistan. During the caliphate of the 'Abbasids with their capital in Baghdad, the extent of the 'Islamic territories' in the west remained the same as under the Umayyads, while in the east Muslims gained control of northern India and the area down to the Bay of Bengal. But this vast region, from the Pyrenees to what is now Bangladesh, was soon divided into a number of independent territories, ruled for centuries by successions of Islamic dynasties, and 'Abbasid rule was eventually reduced to just part of what is now Iraq [6].

While most areas that came under Muslim control remained so, this was not the case in Europe and the subcontinent of India. In Muslim Spain the Spanish Umayyads ruled from 756 to 1031, and then several Islamic dynasties, including the Almoravids and Almohads from North Africa, ruled an ever-shrinking Muslim Spain during the period of the Christian Reconquista that culminated in the fall of Granada in 1492, when most of the remaining Muslims (and also the Jews) were forced to leave Spain. The Ottoman Turks, whose leaders, called sultans, assumed the title of caliph, crossed into eastern Europe from Anatolia in the fourteenth century and rapidly took over most of the Balkan peninsula. During the next two centuries their empire gradually encircled the Black Sea and spread north-west almost to Vienna and north-east almost to Kiev, while to the south the Ottomans gained control of Egypt, North Africa and the Fertile Crescent. During the nineteenth century the Ottomans lost most of their holdings in Europe and across northern Africa, and by the beginning of the First World War Turkey in Europe was reduced to the small area called Eastern Thrace that surrounds Istanbul. When the last Ottoman sultan, Muhammad VI, was deposed by Mustafa Kemal Atatürk, the title of caliph went briefly to a cousin and then in 1924 the caliphate was abolished altogether. The Muslim Mughals by the end of the seventeenth century controlled virtually all of the subcontinent of India, in addition to what are now Pakistan, Afghanistan, Kashmir and Bangladesh. In the eighteenth and nineteenth centuries, however, they gradually lost control of the outlying areas and eventually also of northern India. The last Mughal emperor was deposed by the British in 1858. So the Arabs and the Berbers were forced out of western Europe and the Turks out of virtually all of eastern Europe, while the Mughals lost control of India; but not before these groups had left a permanent Islamic imprint on these regions.

A distinction must be made between the rapid political and military expansion of empires ruled by Arabs and other Muslims and the spread of Islam or religious conversion, which proceeded at a much slower pace. Those areas where the rulers and the majority of the people became Muslims came to be called Dar al-Islam, the House of Islam (sometimes translated as 'the House of Peace', partly because of the root meaning of the term *islam*, which yields also the word *salam*, 'peace'). Gradually, over a period of centuries, the overwhelming majority of the people living under Muslim rule in northern Africa, the Fertile Crescent and Anatolia, who had previously espoused various forms of Christianity, converted to Islam. In contrast, all but a small percentage of the people of Iran, who had previously followed the state-sponsored Zoroastrian faith, adopted Islam, the religion of their new rulers, within just a few generations. At the opposite extreme, the Jewish people, many of whom lived under Muslim rule for many centuries, with very few exceptions remained faithful to their tradition. Since the time of the 'Abbasids, Islam has continued to spread, mostly by peaceful, missionary means, eastwards through Asia to parts of China and South-East Asia – notably Malaysia and Indonesia, where a large majority are now Muslim – and also across a wide area of Saharan Africa and sub-Saharan East and West Africa. Only on rare occasions in some parts of Africa and Asia, far fewer than in the case of Christianity, has Islam spread in accordance with the popular misconception 'by the sword', going against the clear teaching of the Qur'an that 'There shall be no compulsion in religion.'

Perhaps the most persuasive evidence of the vitality of Islam today is that it continues to be a missionary force in various parts of Asia, Africa, Europe and North America. Remarkable successes can be seen, especially in sub-Saharan West and East Africa, where Islam has the advantage of not being identified with white, European colonialists. Even more perplexing to Christians is the fact that Islam is the fastest-growing religious community in Europe and North America, with many Caucasian converts. Today, Muslims are represented in all the major races and cultures; but the vast majority live in a nearly contiguous band around the globe from the Atlantic shores of North and West Africa eastward to Indonesia in the Pacific. The largest broad ethnic community of Muslims is that of South Asia (the Indian subcontinent, where the vast majority live in Pakistan, India and Bangladesh), numbering in 1990 over 300 million or almost 30 per cent of the Muslim world population. In 1990 almost 200 million Muslims lived in South-West Asia (the Middle East, not including Egypt), 250 million in the rest of Asia (with about 175 million of these in South-East Asia and Indonesia), 145 million in northern and Saharan Africa (most of whom are native Arabic-speakers), over 100 million in the rest of Africa, and nearly 20 million in Europe (excluding Istanbul and the rest of Turkey that lies in the Balkan peninsula) and North America. The United States of America now has the largest number of Muslims of any country in the West (that is, Europe and the Western Hemisphere). Altogether the world Muslim population in 1990 was over 1 billion, with the population centre being somewhere in northern India – possibly near the famous Taj Mahal in Agra or the grand Jami' Masjid (congregational mosque) in Delhi, both built in the time of the Mughal ruler Shah Jahan (see figure 3.3 below). Shi'i Muslims (see pp. 206–7) make up about one-tenth of the world Muslim community, with their largest populations in Iran and Iraq, but with significant and long-established minorities in other countries, such as Lebanon, Kuwait and parts of India. For approximate 1990 Muslim population statistics and percentages and very general estimates for the year 2000, listed by country and arranged by geographical region, see appendix B (p. 227).

The expressions 'the Middle East', 'the Arab world' and 'the Muslim world' are often not precisely defined and, in any case, are frequently confused. The Middle East is usually taken to include the area from Egypt and Turkey to the western border of Pakistan (usually considered part of South Asia). Using this definition, about 240 million Muslims or less than 25 per cent of the world Muslim population lived in the Middle East in 1990. Of these, about 130 million lived in non-Arabic-speaking countries (Iran, Turkey and Afghanistan). The Arabic-speaking countries of South-West Asia and northern and Saharan Africa had about 190 million Muslims, or less than 20 per cent of the Muslim world population. These figures show that the popular identification of 'the Middle East' with 'the Muslim world', and of Arabs with Muslims, is far from correct. The country with the largest Muslim population is Indonesia, in East Asia. The country with the largest Arabic-speaking population is Egypt, in north-eastern Africa. (Egypt happens also to be the geographic and demographic centre of the Arab world, with about 35 per cent of all native Arabic-speakers living east of Egypt in South-West Asia, and 40 per cent living west and south of Egypt in Africa – indicating that about 65 per cent of native Arabic-speakers live on the continent of Africa.) It is also important to remember that millions of Arabs, that is, native Arabic-speakers, are Christians and some are Jews. Most of these live in the Middle East, thus disproving both of the false equations mentioned above.

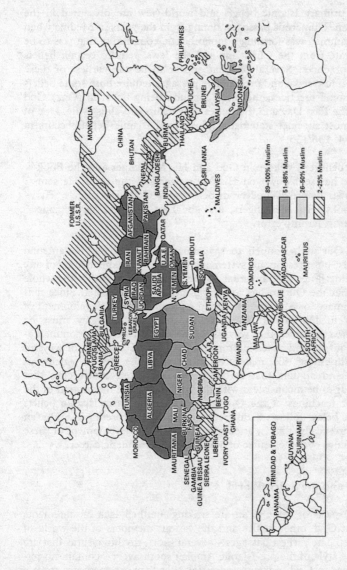

89-100% Muslim

51-88% Muslim

26-50% Muslim

2-25% Muslim

Figure 3.1 *The peoples of Islam*

Source: J. L. Esposito, Islam: The Straight Path, *New York/Oxford, Oxford University Press, 1995.*

Basic Doctrines

The primary Islamic beliefs and world-view are presented in the Qur'an. Numerous passages, dating from the years in Medina when Muhammad was forming a monotheistic community that was to be separate from the Christians and the Jews, require certain beliefs and practices. Several of what appear to be the earliest of these Qur'anic creedal and prescriptive passages require both some beliefs and some practices, the most common being belief in (One) God and the Last Day and the duties of worship and almsgiving. One of the most succinct statements of essential Islamic beliefs occurs in Sura 4. 136/135:

> O believers, believe in God and His Messenger and the Book
> He has sent down on His Messenger and the Book He sent
> down before. Whoever disbelieves in God, His angels, His
> Books, His Messengers, and the Last Day has surely gone
> astray, far into error.

The Qur'an has much to say about each of these fundamental beliefs, but presents no systematic or extended explanations of any one doctrine. Also, apparent contradictions occur within the whole of what the Qur'an has to say on any one basic belief. Since it is customary for Muslims to deny the presence of the development of ideas in the sacred text, any apparent inconsistency must be resolved in some other way. Over the centuries Qur'an commentators, jurists and other interpreters have found a variety of ways of accomplishing this, mainly by interpreting the Qur'an synchronically and arguing that certain verses abrogated earlier ones that appear to be inconsistent with the later ones. The description of the major teachings of the Qur'an and thus the basic Islamic beliefs given below follows a different approach, interpreting the Qur'an diachronically, that is, attempting to trace the development of these teachings over the course of Muhammad's prophetic career.

God and the Spirit World

Early parts of the Qur'an are striking for their lack of statements about God, other deities and the various members of the world of spirits. The earliest passages – several short, rhythmic suras that are in the style of the pre-Islamic Arabian soothsayers – contain no references to God, nor any indication that they are messages from a deity. The earliest revelations that mention Muhammad's God refer to him only as 'Lord' (*rabb*), as in the expressions 'your Lord', 'his

Lord', etc. (see the beginning of Suras 74, 87 and 96). Some time later, Muhammad's Lord began to be called 'the Merciful' (al-rahman). This name seems to have been preferred for a while (see, for instance, Suras 19 and 43, and the important statements in 13. 30/29, 25. 60/61 and 55. 1ff). At about the same time, the name 'Allah', known to the Meccan polytheists before Muhammad's time, was introduced into the revelation. The well-known verse, Sura 17. 110, which begins, 'Say: Call upon Allah or call upon the Merciful; whichever you call upon, to Him belong the most beautiful names', had the effect of replacing the dominant usage of 'the Merciful' with that of 'Allah'. Later parts of the Qur'an provide the ingredients of a rich theology in their frequent use of a wide variety of divine epithets, as for instance in the following liturgical passage at the end of Sura 59:

He is God – there is no god but He.
He is the Knower of the unseen and the visible.
He is the Merciful, the Compassionate.
He is God – there is no God but He.
He is the King, the Holy, the Peaceable, the Faithful,
    the Preserver, the Mighty, the Compeller, the Sublime.
Glory be to God, above what they associate [with Him].
He is God – the Creator, the Maker, the Shaper.
To Him belong the most beautiful names.
All that is in the heavens and the earth magnifies Him.
He is the Mighty, the Wise.

By collecting these divine epithets in the Qur'an and forming others from verbs and other terms that refer to God, later Muslims compiled slightly varying lists of the Ninety-Nine Names of God. These appear in calligraphy, sometimes on the inside covers of copies of the Qur'an, and most strikingly in devotional use, where some Muslims memorize them and recite them using strings of thirty-three or occasionally ninety-nine prayer beads.

Theologians were often concerned to express Islamic beliefs about God in more formal, even philosophical, language, and thus developed other themes, as seen in Article 2 of the document that came to be called Fiqh Akbar II:

God the exalted is one, not in the sense of number, but in the sense that He has no partner; He begetteth not and He is not begotten and there is none like unto Him. He resembles none of the created things, nor do any created things resemble Him. He has been from eternity and will be to eternity with His names and qualities, those which belong to His essence as well as those which belong to His action. Those which belong to

His essence are: life, power, knowledge, speech, hearing, sight and will. Those which belong to His action are: creating, sustaining, producing, renewing, making, and so on. [55: 188]

The doctrine that 'God is One' is so prominent in later parts of the Qur'an that it is easy to overlook the fact that earlier parts of the Islamic scripture do not explicitly reject the existence of other deities. The three goddesses whose worship flourished in and around Mecca in Muhammad's time, al-Lat, al-'Uzza and Manat, are mentioned by name in Sura 53. 19–20. In a number of passages in the Qur'an, including what appear to be a series of revisions of Sura 53, these goddesses may at first have been accepted as intercessors with God, then are designated as angels, and finally are said to be merely names invented by the Meccans' ancestors. In other Meccan parts of the Qur'an, that is, passages dating from before the Hijra in 622, deities other than Allah are demoted to the level of jinn before they are said not to exist at all (see Suras 6.100, 34. 40–2/39–41, 37. 158–66).

The existence of the jinn, those shadowy, invisible spirits of pre-Islamic Arabia that, like man, can be either good or evil, is also assumed in Meccan parts of the Qur'an, especially in the frequently occurring expression 'jinn and men', which seems to present jinn as the invisible counterpart of man. The jinn also appear in the Qur'an in mythic and legendary accounts, for instance as listeners at the gate of heaven seeking knowledge of the future (Sura 72. 8–9, one of the Qur'anic versions of an ancient Near Eastern myth explaining shooting stars), as slaves of Solomon working on the Temple (27. 39, 34. 1–14/1–13) and as the army of Iblis, the fallen angel (18. 50/48). Iblis is the Qur'anic and Islamic equivalent of the Christian archangel Lucifer, who was cast from heaven for revolting against God and became Satan, the Tempter. In some contexts, such as Sura 72, jinn become believers, while in others they are presented as evil or mischievous and are sometimes equated with 'satans', *shayatin*, the plural form of Shaytan, the Arabic equivalent of the Hebrew and English word Satan. It is significant that the jinn, demons and Iblis are not mentioned in parts of the Qur'an that date from after the establishment of distinctively Islamic beliefs and practices in Medina after the Hijra. In place of these 'lower' spirits, later parts of the Qur'an present a more exalted view of angels as invisible, abstract symbols of God's power, and a more abstract view of Satan as a symbol for evil and disbelief. This process of polarization of spiritual powers for good and evil in the world is similar to the manner in which the Qur'an treats deities other than God. The theologians in their treatises and creeds expand very little on what the Qur'an says about these spirits, but popular Islam elaborated a vast, complex spirit world that touches virtually all aspects of life in this world and in the hereafter.

The Nature and Destiny of Man

A second complex of ideas central to Islamic faith as it arose in the Qur'an and developed in later creeds and theological treatises involves the origin, nature and destiny of man. In the Qur'an the creation and judgement of man are frequently mentioned together, often with references to the resurrection. In some contexts the idea of creation is closely related to the conception and birth of each individual, as in Sura 80. 17–22/16–22:

> Woe to man! How ungrateful they are.
> From what did He create them?
> From a sperm-drop has He formed them.
> Then He makes his path easy for them.
> Then He causes them to die and buries them.
> Then, when He will, He raises them.

In other passages of the Qur'an the biblical idea of the creation of the First Man from dust or clay occurs a number of times, as in the following version of the Iblis story in 15. 28ff, which begins: 'And when your Lord said to the angels: "See, I am about to create a human being from clay, formed from moulded mud. When I have shaped him [Adam] and breathed My spirit into him, fall down all of you and bow before him."' This idea of creation occurs frequently in the context of concise statements on the human life-cycle, as in 71. 17–18/16–17: 'God caused you to grow out of the earth, then He will return you into it, and bring you forth [from it again at the Resurrection].' Then in a number of passages these two teachings regarding God's creation of man are combined into more elaborate accounts, such as in 23. 12–16:

> We created man [Adam] from an extract of clay;
> Then [later] We placed [you] as a sperm-drop into a safe receptacle;
> Then We fashioned the clot into a lump; then We fashioned the lump into bones; then We clothed the bones with flesh; then We made [you] into a new creation. So blessed be God the fairest of creators!
> After this you will surely die,
> And on the Day of Resurrection you will surely be raised up.

As for our basic nature, whether we are 'born in sin' as a result of the Original Sin of Adam and Eve (essentially a Christian belief) or are intrinsically good, the glory and crown of God's creation (a theme that occurs in the Jewish scriptures), Islam adopts what appears to be a middle view, seen in Sura 91. 7–10:

> By the soul and [Him who] formed it,
> And implanted into it its wickedness and its piety!
> Blessed is he who purifies it.
> Ruined is he who corrupts it.

Thus the potential for both good and evil is breathed into each person by God at birth. Then throughout life people are tested by their Maker, as the Qur'an says in 21. 35/36: 'And We try you with evil and good as a test; then unto Us you will be returned.' The Qur'an says that some people will choose good and will be rewarded, while others will choose evil and will be punished. Eternal reward and punishment are to be meted out by God at the Last Judgement, around which a central doctrine of the Qur'an and later Islamic theology developed. In the early stages of the development of Qur'anic creedal statements, the most frequently occurring requirement was that one 'believe in God and the Last Day'. This great eschatological event, also called the Day of Judgement, the Day of Resurrection, and sometimes simply 'the Day', is vividly described in the Qur'an, as are the pleasures of the Garden of Paradise and the torments of the hellfire, called Jahannam (cf. the Hebrew Gehenna), the Fire, etc. (22. 19–22/20–2, 56. 11–56, 69. 13–37, 76. 11–22, etc.).

The Islamic doctrine of the hereafter, with its stress on reward and punishment, seems to require the corollary belief in individual responsibility for one's faith and actions. But the ancient Arabian belief in Fate also appears in the Qur'an, along with a number of statements that clearly support the later Islamic doctrine of predestination. According to the ancient view, four things are decided for each individual before birth: the sex of the child; whether it will have a happy or miserable life; what food it will have; and its 'term of life'. This idea of a predetermined life-span occurs in the Qur'an, as in 6. 2: 'It is He who created you from clay, then determined a term, and a term is stated with Him' (cf. 3. 145/139). Man's predestination is said to involve everything in life, as in 9. 51: 'Nothing will befall us but what God has written down for us . . .' It was left for later theologians to correlate this teaching with other Qur'anic statements saying that each person is responsible for his or her own actions.

Revelation – God's Messengers and Books

The earliest parts of the Qur'an do not mention revelation or God's prophets and their scriptures. When those who later came to be called prophets are mentioned in Meccan passages they are referred to simply as 'messengers' (*rusul*; sing. *rasul*), 'ambassadors' (*mur-*

salun), etc. The context in which these messengers appear most frequently are series of so-called 'punishment-stories', where Noah, Lot and several others bring God's message to their people or tribes, are ridiculed and rejected by most of their people and then rescued by God along with their families and followers, while those who rejected them perish in a flood, fire or some other natural calamity (see Suras 7. 59ff/57ff, 11. 25ff/27ff, 26. 105–91, etc.). Details of Muhammad's experience in Mecca, such as accusations made against him by his opponents, appear frequently in stories of earlier prophets, but it is only implied that Muhammad is also such a 'messenger' and that his city, Mecca, is being threatened with the same type of terrestrial destruction. The Qur'an does not, during this period, explicitly describe Muhammad as a 'messenger of God' (*rasul Allah*) to be classed with the great messengers or prophets of the past.

It is only after the Hijra in 622 and after the Muslims' victory at the battle of Badr in 624 that the role of 'prophet' (*nabi*) became prominent in the Qur'an and Muhammad came to be included explicitly among the prophets. Prophets are said to descend from Abraham, the first monotheist and thus the first 'Muslim' (one fully surrendered to God alone), and each is said to have been given a Book or scripture (*kitab*). The Torah of Moses and the Gospel of Jesus receive special attention in the Qur'an and in later Islamic belief, but the Psalms of David and the 'scrolls of Abraham' are mentioned briefly. The teaching of the Qur'an appears to be that every prophet brought a copy of the heavenly Book, presumably in the language of his people. In Medinan parts of the Qur'an, that is, passages that date from after the Hijra in 622, Muhammad is frequently called 'the Prophet' or 'the Messenger of God', two expressions that came to be used synonymously in later revelations (see for instance their usage in Sura 33). Just what the expression 'Seal of the Prophets' (*khatam al-nabiyyin*), applied to Muhammad in 33. 40, meant to him and his followers is difficult to say. Most likely it meant that the revelations recited by Muhammad confirmed or put a seal of divine approval on certain teachings that were attributed to earlier prophets, such as Moses and Jesus, while declaring that other Jewish and Christian teachings did not come from these prophets but were invented later and surreptitiously inserted into the Torah and the Gospel. The Qur'an mentions certain later Jewish food laws and the Christian belief that Jesus is the Son of God as examples of teachings that do not derive from Moses and Jesus. Later Muslims came to interpret the expression 'Seal of the Prophets' in 33. 40 to mean that Muhammad was the 'last of the prophets', and some, against the teachings of orthodox theology, interpret it to mean 'the last and greatest of the prophets'. According to the teachings of the Qur'an and later Islamic theology, all prophets are equal. Many passages throughout the Qur'an stress Muhammad's complete humanity, his lack of supernatural knowledge or powers such as the ability to see the Unseen (al-ghayb), to foretell future events or the end of time, or to perform miracles. After his death Muhammad rapidly came to be elevated in popular belief. Many miracles are attributed to him and he is widely venerated and called upon for intercession with God. (On these later developments, see [43; 26: 309–36, 530–6].)

Basic Practices

Five fundamental rituals, called the Pillars of Islam, are regarded as essential public signs of a Muslim's submission to God (islam) and identity with the Muslim community (umma): (1) public profession of faith by recitation of the doctrinal formula called the shahada; (2) daily performance of a prayer ritual called the salat; (3) annual giving of obligatory alms called zakat; (4) fasting (sawm) during the month of Ramadan; and (5) performance of the rituals of the Great Pilgrimage, called the Hajj, in and near Mecca once in one's lifetime if health and wealth are sufficient. The last four of these are specifically prescribed in the Qur'an, but none is described there fully. The Pillars of Islam and other rituals eventually came to be regulated in detail by Islamic law (fiqh). Thus a brief introduction to fiqh is necessary for understanding the basic religious practices of Muslims.

The person most responsible for establishing the theory and structure of classical Islamic law for the majority of Muslims (the Sunnis) was Muhammad ibn-Idris al-Shafi'i (d. 819). His main contribution was in developing a system of four Sources of Islamic law (usul fiqh) that eventually came to be accepted by most Sunnis: (1) the Qur'an; (2) the Sunna (custom) of the Prophet as reported in the hadiths; (3) consensus (ijma') of the classical jurists; and (4) 'systematic original thinking' (ijtihad) of the founders of the legal schools or rites (madhahib) described briefly below. Both the third and fourth Sources must involve 'reasoning by analogy' (qiyas) based on statements in the Qur'an and the hadiths. By the time of al-Shafi'i the prominent jurists had already reached 'consensus' on many issues on which the Qur'an and the hadiths do not provide definitive answers to legal questions. Thus ijma' was well along in the process of being established as the third Source, independent of the need for emphasis on analogical reasoning (qiyas). For this reason some classical and modern writings list qiyas as the fourth Source or even equate it with ijtihad. (For an excellent summary of the early history of these technical terms see [39: 68–79].) The basic theory behind Islamic law and correct performance of the required rituals is that Muslims should first ask: What does God prescribe in the Qur'an? On practices about which the Qur'an is silent or ambiguous, they then ask: What did the Prophet Muhammad do or say? In most cases where the hadiths report conflicting views, the prominent jurists of the third century AH (ninth century CE), motivated by a strong desire for uniformity of Islamic practice, reached consensus (*ijma'*). Where they could not, mainly regarding details of law and the precise way rituals were to be performed, they agreed to disagree, thus establishing a system of multi-orthopraxis. The Pillars of Islam, for instance, must be performed precisely according to Islamic law, but Muslims have a choice as to which legal rite (*madhhab*) they follow. Once orthopraxis was established, the classical jurists declared that the 'gate of independent reasoning' (*bab al-ijtihad*), which allowed for differences among the schools and for new regulations, was closed. Thereafter, any new practice or any variation in an established one was termed an 'innovation' (*bid'a*), which came to mean heresy. (See pp. 209ff for the significance of these terms in modern debates within the Muslim community.)

Al-Shafi'i did not succeed in establishing a universal Sunni legal school or rite, partly because of the prestige of Abu Hanifa (d. 769), the champion of logical thought in Islamic law, and Malik ibn Anas (d. 795), author of the first major compendium of Islamic law, the *Muwatta*. Eventually, four Sunni legal schools or rites (*madhahib*; sing. *madhhab*) became firmly established: the Shafi'is (dominant today in lower Egypt, Syria, southern India, Indonesia and Malaysia); the Hanafis (who flourished within the Ottoman empire and are dominant today in Turkey, northern India, Pakistan, Central Asia and China; the Malikis (dominant in Saharan Africa, upper Egypt and the countries of North Africa, i.e. Morocco to Libya); and the Hanbalis, named after Ahmad ibn Hanbal (d. 855), the smallest school today (dominant mainly in Saudi Arabia). The Malikis rely more on the Sunna of the Prophet, especially 'the living tradition' in Medina at the time of the founder of this school. The Hanafis place more emphasis on creating precedents by analogy (*qiyas*), often resulting in more lenient regulations and penalties. The Hanbalis are the most strict, tending towards puritanical characteristics. The major Shi'i legal school is sometimes called Imami, sometimes Ja'fari, after the Sixth Imam, Ja'far al-Sadiq (p. 206 below). (See [39: 81–4] on the origins of the Sunni schools and p. 209 below on the influence of the Hanbalis today.)

The dates for observance of the annual practices, notably the fast during the month of Ramadan and the pilgrimage during the month of Dhu-1-Hijja, are determined by a purely lunar Islamic calendar, which was established by Muhammad during the last year of his life.

Some knowledge of the Islamic calendar is thus necessary for understanding the annual rituals in particular. A lunar year of twelve revolutions of the moon around the earth lasts about 354 days, or eleven days less than a solar year. Thus the beginning of the Islamic year, and each of the annual festivals, moves back through the solar calendar one season approximately every eight years or through the entire solar year (and the four seasons) once in about thirty-two and a half years. Probably within a decade of Muhammad's death – the decision is usually said to have been made during the caliphate of 'Umar (634–44) – the year of the Hijra, 622 (see p. 167 above), was chosen as the year 1 of the Islamic era, often designated AH from the Latin *anno Hegirae*. Contrary to popular belief, and to statements in many writings on Islam, the first day of the first month of the Islamic calendar does not correspond with the date of Muhammad's emigration from Mecca to Medina, nor with the fictional concept of a mass emigration of all the Meccan Muslims. After Muhammad's final agreement with representatives from Yathrib (later called Medina), his followers began a gradual, intermittent move from Mecca and from Abyssinia throughout the spring and summer of 622, while he is said to have remained in his native city until late summer and did not arrive in Medina until September. The Islamic calendar was set to begin on the day when Muharram (the first Islamic month) was calculated to have begun during the year of the Hijra, usually believed to coincide with 16 July 622. (On the Islamic calendar, and its relation to the Christian calendars, see appendices C and D below, pp. 229–32.)

The Shahada

The beginning and essence of being a devout Muslim is to recite with sincere 'intention' (*niyya*) the simple Islamic creed called the Shahada (confession), consisting of two statements: 'There is no god but God' and 'Muhammad is the Messenger of God'. Both occur in the Qur'an, but not together. This formula is pronounced by new converts as part of the ceremony of becoming a Muslim, and it is recited in each performance of the Salat (see below). The term in the Shahada translated above as 'God' is Allah, the Arabic proper name for God used by Christians as well as Muslims. This name probably comes from *al-ilah*, 'the god', the common Arabic noun for a deity, with the definite article. Since Christians, Jews and others agree with Muslims on the first statement of the Shahada, it is the second that distinguishes Muslims. Implying much more than casual assent that Muhammad is 'a prophet', it carries with it the conviction that Muhammad is at least the last, if not the greatest, of the prophets. His role in Islamic practice is pivotal since in theory he was the ideal Muslim and the exemplar of all proper religious life and ritual. As mentioned above (pp. 176–7), the expressions 'the Messenger of God' and 'the Prophet' occur in later parts of the Qur'an as synonymous titles for Muhammad. In later Islamic thought a distinction was made between the expressions 'messengers' (*rusul*) and 'prophets' (*nabiyyun*), which came to designate two categories of men, one being a smaller, elite group within the other. The theologians disagreed, however, as to which title designated which group.

The Salat

The earliest Islamic practice to arise was the daily prayer ritual called the Salat. Passages of the Qur'an that appear to date from before Hijra in 622 explicitly require only Muhammad to perform this ritual, and God commands him to perform it twice each day, 'in the morning and the evening', or, according to Sura 11: 114/116, 'at the two ends of the day'. This command, always addressed to Muhammad in the second person singular, is worded a variety of ways in Suras 17. 78/80, 20. 130, 40. 55/57, 50. 39/38, 52. 48–9, and in several other suras. Then in Medinan portions of the Qur'an, as rituals for the new religious community were being established, all Muslims are commanded to perform the Salat, and a third daily ritual, called simply 'the middle Salat' is mentioned in Sura 2. 238–9/239–10. Most modern historians are convinced that this third ritual was performed at midday and thus is equivalent to the present so-called noon Salat. Within a century of the Prophet's death the number of required daily Salats was increased to five. They are usually called 'morning' (*fajr*), 'noon' (*zuhr*), 'afternoon' ('*asr*), 'sunset' (*maghrib*), and 'evening' ('*isha*'), names that are somewhat misleading since they sometimes indicate the beginning of the prayer time or a specific time of the day after which the prayer ritual can be performed. That is, the morning Salat is performed from the time it is light until the sun begins to appear on the horizon; the noon Salat, from after the sun has reached its zenith until it is half-way down; the afternoon Salat, from that point until the sun starts to set; the sunset Salat, after the sun has fully set until it is dark; and the evening Salat, after it is dark. Eventually a number of hadiths arose claiming that Muhammad's followers performed the Salat five times daily during his lifetime [see 8: VIII; 37: IV], but these are contradicted by others that appear to reflect the historical development more accurately. The three daily Salats that are clearly mentioned in the Qur'an are not easily identified with the later five, partly because they did not yet have established or formal names. The expressions *salat al-fajr* and *salat al-'isha*' occur in Sura 24. 58, a fairly late Medinan verse.

The context suggests that these are the Salats 'at the two ends of the day' mentioned frequently in the Qur'an, making the latter coincide with what later came to be called the *maghrib*, the fourth rather than the fifth daily Salat. The interpretation is further complicated by hadiths that say Muhammad sometimes led the congregational evening Salat while it was still light, keeping the men in the mosque until the women had time to return to their homes before dark, but that at other times he waited until after dark 'after the women and children had gone to bed' to call the men to the mosque for this Salat. These observations on the origins of the Salat are relevant to various arguments by modern Muslims calling for reforms or a return to the way rituals were performed during Muhammad's lifetime (see pp. 209–10, 211–12 below).

To what extent the present complex ritual described below had developed during Muhammad's lifetime is difficult to determine. Some essential parts of the present Salat are mentioned in the Qur'an, for instance, the bowing (*ruku'*) in 2. 125/119, 22. 26/27, 48. 29, etc., and the prostration (*sujud*) in 2. 125/119, 4. 102/103, 25. 64/65, etc. Also, specific instructions for performing ablutions before prayer are given in 5. 6/8–9. For the first year or so after the Hijra the Muslims in Medina faced north towards Jerusalem while performing their daily prayer ritual, as was the Jewish practice. Then, at the time of the so-called 'break with the Jews' [52: 93–9], the *qibla* or 'direction worshippers face during the prayer ritual' was changed from Jerusalem to Mecca (see Sura 2. 142–50/136–45), as part of a larger process of developing Islam into an independent religious tradition, with indigenous Arabian features in some of its fundamental rituals [52: 98–9, 112–14]. The Meccan *qibla* has been an obligatory feature of the Salat ever since, whether performed in mosques, in homes or other buildings, or out in the open. This requirement in the performance of the Salat led to a unique feature of mosque architecture, a niche in the wall that indicates the direction of Mecca (see p. 187 and the mosque drawings in figure 3.3).

The beginning of the period for performing each of the five prescribed daily Salats and the time to go to the mosque on Fridays are announced by a public 'call to prayer' (*adhan*), given by the muezzin (*mu'adhdhin*). The call to prayer consists of seven short statements:

God is most great.
I testify that there is no god but God.
I testify that Muhammad is the Messenger of God.
Come to prayer.
Come to salvation.
God is most great.
There is no god but God.

The first statement is chanted four times, the last only once, and all the others twice. In the call to the morning prayer the statement 'Prayer is better than sleep' is inserted after the fifth statement, or, in one of the legal rites, at the end. The Shiʻis (see pp. 206–8) insert 'Come to the best work' after the fifth statement, and they recite the final statement twice. The worshipper must be in a state of ritual purity, accomplished by performing either the minor ablution called *wuduʼ*, for minor impurities, or the major one called *ghusl*, for major impurities. Some of the legal schools have ruled that one ablution ceremony in the morning serves for all five prayers of that day unless it has been invalidated by some impurity.

Proper observance of the Salat is a required duty of all Muslims, and its essential elements are prescribed by Islamic law and customary practice. The exact performance of the Salat varies among the various legal rites described briefly above, but a general uniformity of practice exists regarding thirteen essentials (*arkan*) – six utterances or recitations, six actions or positions, and the requirement that these twelve must proceed in the prescribed order. The description given below is based largely on the practice of the Shafiʻis, the classic definition of which is given in the *Ihyaʼ* of the great theologian al-Ghazali (see pp. 166, 205). The system used below for numbering the utterances and giving letters for the positions (see figure 3.2) makes the description of the essentials valid, however, for all the major legal rites. In addition to the thirteen essentials, there are also a large number of customary (*sunna*) elements that are recommended but not required. Considerable variation exists among the major rites on the *sunna* elements.

The Salat begins with the worshipper in (a) the 'standing position' (*qiyam*), facing the Kaʻba in Mecca. In a congregational Salat, whether performed in a mosque or elsewhere, a second call to prayer, called the *iqama*, is recited, followed by the statement, 'Worship has begun.' Then comes (1) the statement of 'intention' (*niyya*), indicating which prayer is about to be performed, followed by (2) a *takbira*, the statement, 'God is most great (*Allahu Akbar*).' Remaining standing, the worshippers then begin the first *rakʻa* or liturgical cycle with (3) recitation of *al-Fatiha* ('The Opener'), the first sura of the Qurʼan:

In the name of God, the Merciful, the Compassionate.
Praise belongs to God, the Lord of the worlds,
The Merciful, the Compassionate,
The Master of the Day of Judgement.
Thee only do we serve, and to Thee only do we pray for succour.
Guide us on the straight path,
The path of those whom Thou hast blessed, not of those
    against whom Thou art wrathful, nor of those who go astray.

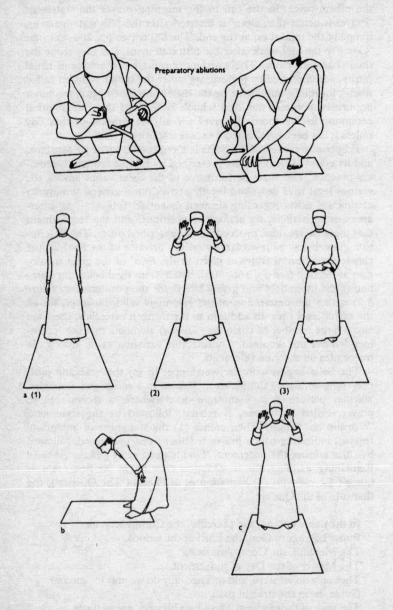

Preparatory ablutions

a (1)   (2)   (3)

b

c

Figure 3.2   *The positions of prayer*

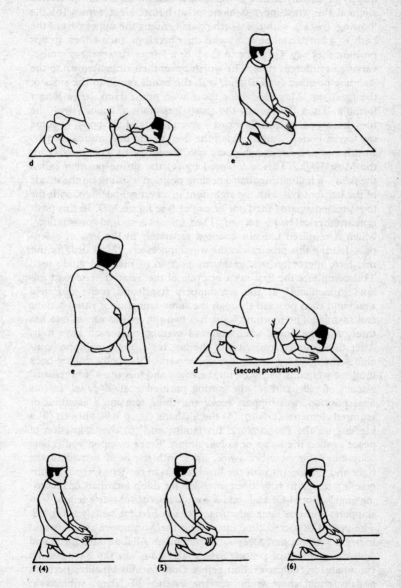

d

e

e

d (second prostration)

f (4)

(5)

(6)

This is followed by a second recitation from the Qur'an, spoken quietly or silently if in a congregation behind an *imam*, or recited aloud if the worshipper is alone or at home. Next comes (b) the 'bowing' (*ruku'*), with the worshippers bending the upper part of the body to a horizontal position with their hands on their knees. In this position they say 'Glory be to God' or a longer statement of praise, varying in different rites. The worshippers then straighten up to the standing position (*i'tidal*) and, with the hands raised to the sides of the face, say 'May God hear those who praise Him', or a longer formula. Then follows (d) the (first) 'prostration' (*sujud*), with the toes, knees, palms and forehead – seven points of the body, or some say 'seven bones' – all touching the floor or ground simultaneously. In this position the worshippers say, 'Praise be to Thee, my Lord, the Most High.' This is followed by (e) the sitting position called the *julus* – a half-sitting, half-kneeling position – sitting on the inside of the left foot but with the right foot in a vertical position, with the toes pressed against the floor or carpet (see figure 3.2). In this position another *takbira* is recited. Then follows a second 'prostration', which is required but not counted separately in the lists of essentials. During this prostration the worshippers say, 'My Lord, forgive me, have mercy on me, grant my portion to me, and guide me.' This completes the first rak'a or cycle of the Salat. The second follows immediately as the worshippers stand and recite *al-Fatiha* again and then proceed through the same sequence of ritual actions and sayings. The morning Salat has two rak'as, the sunset one has three, and the noon, afternoon and evening ones each have four. After the second prostration of the last rak'a, the worshipper concludes the Salat by raising the upper part of the body, rolling back until the weight is balanced on the knees and feet (now 'four points' instead of seven) in (f) the 'sitting position', called *qu'ud*. In this final position, worshippers recite the three remaining essential or required elements (*arkan*): (4) the Shahada (see p. 180 above); (5) a blessing on the Prophet and his family; and (6) the 'salutation of peace', called the *salam* or *taslim*, simply 'Peace be upon you (*salam 'alay-kum*)', pronounced twice, once with the head turned to the right and then again with the head turned to the left. Originally this greeting seems to have been intended for one's guardian or recording angels, but al-Ghazali said it should also be for one's fellow worshippers, and this later interpretation has become widely accepted. The period of sacred time into which the worshipper enters is said to begin with the first *takbira*, the statement 'Allahu Akbar', and end with the greeting of peace, 'Salam 'alay-kum.' In the Salat, which culminates in the prostration before God, faithful Muslims perform a daily ritual that symbolizes the essence of Islam, submission (*islam*) before God, the Almighty, and public participation in the rituals instituted by Muhammad. (See [8: VIII–XII; 37: IV] for al-

Bukhari's and Muslim's hadiths on the Salat; [9: 63–84] for al-Ghazali's description; and [25: 463–80] for the Shafi'i regulations.)

Friday Worship and the Mosque

In the early afternoon on Fridays Muslims throughout the world gather in the central or 'congregational mosque' (*masjid jami'* or *jami' masjid*, as in Delhi, India, shown in figure 3.3) in each town, or in any of several in the larger cities, for a special worship service called 'the assembly' (*al-jum'a*), which takes the place of the regular noon Salat for that day. The mosque (*masjid* in Arabic) is a unique, Islamic institution that is essentially different from the Jewish and Christian counterparts, the synagogue and the church, and most Muslims do not regard Friday as a holy day or sabbath. S. D. Goitein [20] presented compelling evidence to show that the Muslim practice of observing their weekly worship service at midday on Fridays arose not so much as an alternative to the Jewish and Christian Saturday and Sunday sabbaths as for the practical reason that Friday was the weekly market day in Medina in the time of Muhammad when people from the surrounding area came into the city and thus were available for congregational services and announcements in the mosque.

The most characteristic architectural features of the mosque are (a) one or more towers or minarets (Arabic sing., *manar*) from which the call to prayer is given five times daily, (b) a niche (*mihrab*) that indicates the direction of Mecca, towards which the worshippers face during the Friday service and for daily prayers performed in a mosque, (c) a pulpit (*minbar*), often an ornate enclosure with a staircase leading to a platform at the top, from which the Friday sermon is delivered, and (d) some type of fountain, pool or other source of water for ablutions. Some mosques, such as the elegant Eski Cami (Turkish for the Arabic, *jami'*, 'congregational', but sometimes meaning simply mosque) in Edirne, Turkey (shown in figure 3.3) and the historic, superb al-Hasan mosque–school–mausoleum complex in Cairo have (e) a raised, often ornate platform called a *dakka* or *dikka* located usually in front of the *minbar* against a wall or row of columns, but occasionally free-standing in the centre of the worship area in front of the *mihrab* (for photographs showing the relationships among the *mihrab*, the *minbar* and the *dikka* in Turkish mosques, see [21: 118, 153, 179, 186, 234, 260, and 263–5]). The primary purpose of the *dikka* is for expert, often professional, reciters (called *qurra'*) to sit on, with open copies of the Qur'an on stands in front of them, while they chant portions of the Qur'an on special occasions such as the evenings of Ramadan, the month of fasting. The *dikka* is also often used by the muezzin when

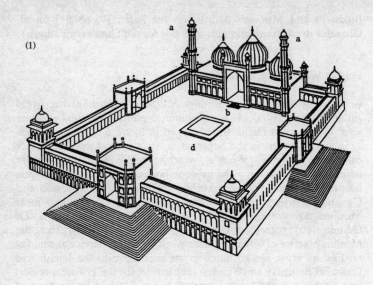

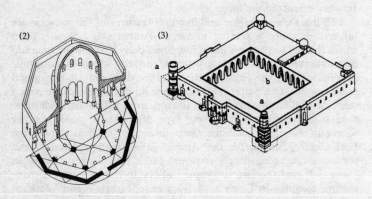

Figure 3.3 *(1) Jami' Masjid, Delhi, the largest mosque in India, built between 1644 and 1658 by the Great Mughal Shah Jahan; (2) Dome of the Rock, Jerusalem, begun 691; (3) Mosque of al-Hakim, Cairo, built 990–1013; (4) Eski Cami in Edirne, Turkey, built 1403–14*

Sources: *(1) H. Stierlin (ed.),* Islamic India, *Architecture of the World no. 8, Lausanne, Compagnie du Livre d'Art, n.d.; (2) A. Choisy,* Histoire de l'architecture *(Paris, 1899); (3) K. A. C. Creswell and J. W. Allan,* A Short Account of Early Muslim Architecture, *2nd edn, Aldershot, Scolar, 1989 (prev. publ. London, Penguin 1958); (4) A. Kuran,* The Mosque in Early Ottoman Architecture, *Chicago/London, University of Chicago Press, 1968*

(4)

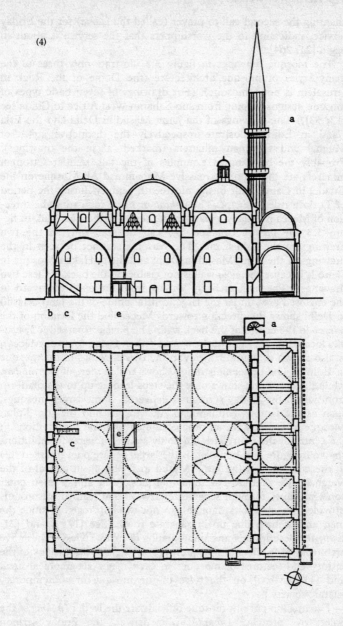

a

b c   e   d

a

b c

e

chanting the second call to prayer (called the *iqama*) for the Friday service, indicating to the worshippers that the service is about to begin [21: 264].

The mosque drawings in figure 3.3 illustrate only three of the many styles of mosque architecture (the Dome of the Rock in Jerusalem is not a mosque). (For drawings of seven basic types of mosque designs ranging from sub-Saharan West Africa to China see [17: 13].) The drawings of the Jami' Masjid in Delhi and the Eski Cami in Edirne illustrate respectively the distinctive styles of Mughal and Ottoman minarets (marked 'a' in the drawings). Probably the best-known examples of the tall, slender Ottoman minarets are those on the massive Muhammad Ali Mosque on the Citadel in Cairo, built in the nineteenth century during the period of Turkish rule of Egypt. The *mihrab* or niche indicating the direction of Mecca is usually located in the centre of the *qibla* wall. In figure 3.3 the *mihrab* (marked 'b') can be seen only in the two drawings of the Eski Cami. The reason it cannot be seen in the drawings of the Jami' Masjid in Delhi and the al-Hakim Mosque in Cairo is because the *qibla* wall is not visible (in the back of these two drawings). The high archway leading from the open courtyard to the enclosed area under the large, central dome of the Jami' Masjid in Delhi shows the direction towards Mecca and the location of the *mihrab* in the centre of the back wall. The *minbar* (marked 'c'), usually located to the right of the *mihrab* (when facing towards Mecca), is also shown in figure 3.3 only in the two drawings of the mosque in Edirne. The upper illustration shows a side view of the *minbar*, while the lower one shows only the steps leading up to the platform from which the Friday sermon is delivered. Some larger mosques, such as the famous Muhammad Ali Mosque and the Ibn Tulun Mosque in Cairo, have an ornate, domed fountain for ablutions in the centre of the courtyard. The only source of water for ablutions shown in figure 3.3, however, is the large, square pool (marked 'd') in the courtyard of the Jami' Masjid in Delhi, again typical of the Mughal style of Indo-Pakistani mosques. Men and women enter some mosques through separate doorways that lead to washrooms provided for ablutions; families do not worship together since the men and women line up in separate rows. (See [17: i] and [21: v–vii] for descriptions and photographs of many styles of these five architectural features of mosques; [17: iv–xiii] for discussions of the history and features of mosques in each major geographical area; and [17: xiv–xvi] on the roles of the mosque in contemporary Islamic society.]

The most important mosque officials are the leader (*imam*) of the Salat; the preacher (*khatib*), who delivers the Friday sermon (*khutba*); and the 'caller (to prayer)' or muezzin (*mu'adhdhin*). In smaller mosques these offices are often combined in one or two persons, while in the larger ones several imams, muezzins and some-times professional Qur'an reciters (*qurra'*) serve. The 'essentials' (*arkan*) of the Friday worship service are (1) a sermon, usually pre-sented in two parts, followed by (2) a special Salat of two rak'as called in Arabic the *salat al-jum'a*, led by the imam. It is recom-mended that a *sunna* or 'customary' Salat of two rak'as be per-formed by the worshippers individually before the service begins. Performing ablutions before the service, wearing perfume, arriving early, and reciting suras from the Qur'an and blessings on the Prophet are also considered *sunna* and meritorious. (See [8: XI, 34: VII and 25: 537–49] for canonical hadiths on the Friday worship ser-vice; [9: 144–72] for al-Ghazali's description; and [25: 480–1] for the regulations according to the Shafi'i rite.)

Alms-giving

The broad lines of the origin and early development of the Islamic institution of alms-giving during Muhammad's lifetime are fairly clear. Before the Hijra the sharing of wealth with the poor was stressed in the Qur'an as a pious act, but neither the borrowed tech-nical term *zakat* nor even the common Arabic noun *sadaqa* was used. After the Hijra, when the small Muslim community of Emigrants (*muhajirun*, those who made the Hijra from Mecca to Medina) found themselves in need of support from the new con-verts in Medina (called the Helpers), alms-giving acquired new sig-nificance as an Islamic welfare system in which those who had more income shared with those who did not have enough. But no set amount was stipulated. In response to the question posed by a group of believers, 'How much do we pay?' the Qur'an says simply (in 2. 219/217), 'The surplus! (*al-'afw*)', meaning 'whatever you do not need'. In the course of time this 'surplus' came to be interpreted differently, and a minimum assessable amount called the *nisab* was set for each type of property. The Zakat then became a tax of a cer-tain percentage of one's wealth or produce, or a specified ration of livestock. The Zakat was to be paid on food crops and fruit at the time of harvest, on livestock after a full year of grazing, and on pre-cious metals and merchandise on hand at the end of the year. The Zakat system, which varied across different geographical areas and among different legal rites, came to be carefully regulated by the Muslim religious and political leaders. With the establishment of modern secular states throughout the Islamic world, the traditional Zakat was in most cases replaced by national taxation and welfare systems. Only a few countries, such as Saudi Arabia and Libya, have maintained official Zakat systems along traditional lines. In most parts of the Islamic world today alms-giving has become a voluntary

practice carried out at the local level. Egypt and a few other countries have large national agencies that collect and distribute Zakat,
but still on a completely voluntary basis [8: xxiv; 26: 486–91; 37: v].

Fasting

During the first year after the Hijra Muhammad instituted a one-
day, twenty-four-hour fast called the *'ashura'* ('tenth'). This was
apparently the name used by the Jews of the Hijaz for the fast on the
Day of Atonement, which falls on the tenth day of Tishri. The
Qur'an does not mention the Ashura fast, but hadith accounts have
much to say about it, acknowledging that it was borrowed from the
Jews and that it was kept for a while as an Islamic fast before the
Ramadan fast was instituted. The establishment of the thirty-day
daytime-only fast of Ramadan seems to have been related to the
Muslim victory at the battle of Badr in Ramadan, 624. From the
beginning, recitation of the Qur'an had a special place in the
Ramadan activities. Later, it became customary for Muslims to
recite or read one-thirtieth of the Qur'an each night of the month.
For this reason the text has been divided into thirty equal parts,
marked with medallions in the margins of most oriental editions of
the Qur'an.

The very basic requirements of the Ramadan fast are given in the
Qur'an in a passage that appears to have been revised (that is,
Muhammad recited it differently on earlier and later occasions); or,
as the jurists say, later verses abrogated or cancelled the rulings of
earlier ones. Sura 2. 185/181, which seems to have instituted this
fast, states that it is to be kept throughout the month of Ramadan,
and that anyone who is sick or on a journey may break the fast for
those days but must make them up later. Sura 2. 187/183, which
appears to have replaced and relaxed some earlier regulations – possibly involving verses that are no longer in the Qur'an – states in
part: 'You are permitted during the night of the fast to go in to your
wives . . . and eat and drink until so much of the dawn appears that
a white thread can be distinguished from a black one [at arm's
length away]. Then keep the fast completely until night and do not
lie with them when you should remain in the mosques.' According
to later Islamic law the essentials of the fast are that it is to be kept
from just before sunrise until just after sunset during the thirty days
of Ramadan by all adult Muslims who are in the full possession of
their senses; for women, it is to be kept only on those days when
they are free from menstruation and the bleeding of childbirth. The
fast is regarded as having been broken on any day on which certain
violations occur, the exact lists of which vary among the different
legal rites. Violations are usually listed in four categories: (1) allow-

ing food, beverages, or anything else, to be swallowed intentionally (in modern times, inhaling tobacco smoke has also been prohibited); (2) intentional vomiting, even when this is done under a doctor's orders; (3) sexual intercourse; and (4) the emission of semen when caused by any type of sexual activity or thoughts. Muslims are encouraged to break their fast as soon as possible after the sun has set and to eat in the morning as late as possible before sunrise. Indecent talk, gossip, slander and anything else that would cause anger or grief to anyone should also be avoided, along with any actions that might arouse passion in oneself or someone else. Any days during Ramadan on which the fast is broken should be made up as soon as possible during the following month, Shawwal, after the completion of the 'Id al-Fitr, 'the Feast of the Breaking [of the Fast]', which usually lasts for the first three days of the month. Although carefully regulated by Islamic law and custom, fasting by its very nature becomes a voluntary act of piety on the part of the observant Muslim. (See [8: xxxi; 26: 88–123; 37: vi] for canonical hadiths on fasting; [25: 491–6] for regulations according to the Shafi'i rite.)

The Great Pilgrimage

The fifth pillar of Islam is the Great Pilgrimage or Hajj, which consists of a number of rituals performed at sacred monuments in and near Mecca. The Hajj is required of all Muslims at least once in a lifetime if they are physically able to make the trip and can afford it (see figure 3.4). From before the time of Muhammad these rituals have been divided into two groups, originally performed at different times of the year (during the great market days in the spring and in the fall), the 'umra (visitation [to Mecca]) and the hajj (pilgrimage). The 'umra rituals take place in and near the Sacred Mosque in Mecca and now can be performed at any time of the year as an independent ritual called the 'Lesser Pilgrimage' or simply the 'Umra. The hajj rituals take place outside of Mecca, beginning in the nearby town of Mina and proceeding out to 'Arafat and back. The Islamic Great Pilgrimage, also called the Hajj, combines the ancient 'umra and hajj rituals. It can be performed only on certain days of Dhu-l-Hijja, the twelfth month of the Islamic calendar (see figure 3.5). Islamic law and custom stipulate three methods of performing these two groups of ceremonies: (1) 'one by one' (ifrad), the preferred method, completing the hajj ceremonies (that is, those that occur outside of Mecca) first, and then the 'umra ones; (2) 'enjoyment' (tamattu'), performing the 'umra rituals first and then breaking the state of ritual purity or sanctification (ihram) to enjoy the pleasures of Mecca for a few days before resuming the ihram for the

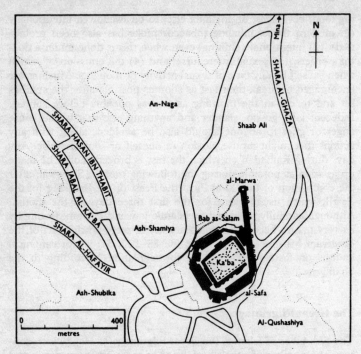

Figure 3.4   *The Sacred Mosque, Mecca*

hajj rituals; and (3) 'conjunction' (*qiran*), beginning the *'umra* rituals and then the *hajj* ones, and then completing both at the same time.

For several days and even weeks before the Hajj begins, a steady stream of pilgrims, numbering nearly 2 million in recent years, flows into Mecca. Before crossing into the *haram*, the sacred territory that surrounds Mecca, the pilgrims enter a state of ritual purity (*ihram*) by performing a major ablution (*ghusl*) and a special Salat of two *rak'as*, expressing their 'intention' (*niyya*) to perform one of the three types of pilgrimage mentioned above, and then donning a white, seamless garment, called also an *ihram*. On entering Mecca all pilgrims visit the Sacred Mosque as soon as possible and perform a sevenfold circumambulation (*tawaf*) of the Ka'ba. Then they perform a Salat of two *rak'as* and drink from the nearby sacred well called Zamzam. Those who intend to fulfil an 'Umra, either as a ceremony separate from the Hajj proper – essentially a mark of respect paid to the city, especially for those entering it for the first time – or as the *'umra* portion of a *tamattu'* performance of the Hajj, then leave the courtyard of the Sacred Mosque and climb the stairs to the hill called al-Safa, the site of an ancient sanctuary. Here

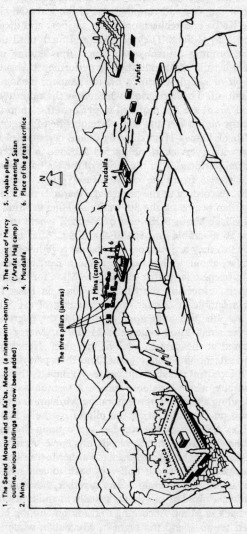

1. The Sacred Mosque and the Ka'ba, Mecca (a nineteenth-century outline, various buildings have now been added)
2. Mina
3. The Mount of Mercy ('Arafat Hajj camp)
4. Muzdalifa
5. 'Aqaba pillar, representing Satan
6. Place of the great sacrifice

N

The three pillars (jamras)

5   2 Mina (camp)
6

1 Mecca

Muzdalifa
4

'Arafat
3

Figure 3.5 *The Hajj: the route followed by the Hajji in and near Mecca (the distance from Mecca to 'Arafat is about 24 km)*

begins the second major ceremony of the 'Umra, the 'running' (*sa'y*) between al-Safa and al-Marwa, another hill about 385 metres away. First, the 'intention' to perform the 'running' ceremony is expressed and verses from the Qur'an and other pious sayings are recited. Then the pilgrims traverse 'the running course' (*al-mas'a*), walking part of the way and running part of the way. On al-Marwa they face the Ka'ba and recite more pious sayings, and then retrace their steps back to al-Safa. They go back and forth until they have traversed 'the running course' seven times, thus ending up at al-Marwa, where a ritual desacralization is performed by having their hair shaved off or simply trimmed or, for women, having a single lock of hair cut off. Those pilgrims who follow the other two methods (*ifrad* and *qiran*) are not required to perform the 'running' ceremony before the *hajj* rituals that take place outside of Mecca.

On the 7th of Dhu-1-Hijja the pilgrimage ceremonies are officially opened with a service at the Sacred Mosque in Mecca, which includes a ritual purification of the inside of the Ka'ba and a sermon or *khutba* delivered from the ornate stone pulpit (*minbar*) that stands nearby. According to the pilgrimage manuals the *hajj* portion of the rituals then begins on the 8th of Dhu-l-Hijja in Mina (a small uninhabited village about 8 km east of Mecca), where the pilgrims are supposed to assemble and spend the night. After the morning prayer on the 9th they are supposed to depart together for the great plain of 'Arafat, about 15 km further east. In fact, in recent years the crowd has been so large that many leave Mina for 'Arafat on the 8th, and others, especially the Shi'is travelling in from Iran and Iraq, simply assemble at 'Arafat on the evening of the 8th or the morning of the 9th. Just after noon on the 9th the pilgrims gather on or near the small knoll called the Mount of Mercy (*Jabal al-Rahma*), located at the eastern edge of the plain. Here they recite the noon and afternoon Salats together and then perform what has been called the central ritual of the entire pilgrimage, the 'standing' (*wuquf*) ceremony, which lasts until sunset. A sermon is delivered by one of the leading imams, commemorating Muhammad's Farewell Sermon, given on this hill during the pilgrimage he led in the last year of his life. As soon as the sun has set, cannon-fire marks the end of the *wuquf*, and the throng of pilgrims leave 'Arafat immediately and begin the 'flight' (*ifada*) back towards Mecca. They stop in the valley of Muzdalifa, about half-way back to Mina. Here they perform the sunset and evening Salats together, have a light meal and then gather a number of stones, usually in multiples of seven, for use later back in Mina. According to tradition and the Hajj manuals, the men are to spend the night in Muzdalifa, while it is customary for the women, children and elderly men to proceed on to Mina for the night.

Before dawn on the 10th the pilgrims who remained in Muzdalifa are awakened for a meal and the morning Salat. Then they depart on another 'flight' back to Mina. They proceed directly to the western end of the main street of Mina and throw seven pebbles at a stone pillar called Jamrat al-'Aqaba that represents Satan. This ancient ritual curse is intended to drive away temptation, believed in this case to commemorate Abraham's victory in overcoming the temptation of Satan. Then follows a vast ritual slaughtering of sheep, goats and camels, and the meal called the Feast of the Sacrifice (*'id al-adha*), celebrated at Mina and simultaneously by Muslims throughout the world. This meal commemorates Abraham's sacrifice of a ram after demonstrating his faith by his willingness to sacrifice his son to God. After this meal, the pilgrims have their heads shaved, or, in the case of women, have a lock of hair cut off. They are then free to bathe and put on clean, often new, clothes. But they must still perform another circumambulation of the Ka'ba back in Mecca before they are completely free of the *ihram* restrictions. Pilgrims who did not perform the 'running' (*sa'y*) ceremony between al-Safa and al-Marwa earlier must fulfil this pilgrimage obligation on the night of the 10th. These rituals back in Mecca complete the requirements (*arkan*) of the Hajj, but it is 'customary' (*sunna*) for the pilgrims to return to Mina for three days of celebration on the 11th–13th of Dhu-l-Hijja. On each of these days it is customary for pilgrims to throw seven stones at each of three pillars representing Satan. Before leaving the area of Mecca the pilgrims are encouraged to perform a final circumambulation of the Ka'ba, called 'the farewell *tawaf*'. A large number of Sunni Muslims visit Islam's second holy city, Medina, after completing the Hajj rituals in and near Mecca, while it is customary for many Shi'is, the majority of whom live in Iraq and Iran, east of the holy cities, to visit Medina first before proceeding to the plain of 'Arafat to join the Sunni Muslims at the Mount of Mercy on the 9th of Dhu-l-Hijja. (See [8: XXVI and 37: VII] for hadiths on the Hajj; [26: 496–509] for specific Shafi'i regulations.)

Other Practices and Customs

In addition to the major rituals, the last four of the so-called Five Pillars of Islam, other practices are regarded as obligatory and are regulated by Islamic law – sometimes as a group or community obligation rather than one for each individual, such as the presence of a sufficient number of mourners at funerals – while many other customs are commonly observed throughout the Islamic world as *sunna*: recommended and meritorious, but not obligatory. Eventually, religious or ethical acts came to be divided into five categories, those that are: (1) obligatory; (2) recommended and customary, but not obligatory; (3) neutral, neither good nor bad, Islamic or non-Islamic; (4) disapproved and discouraged, but not prohibited; and (5) prohibited. The legal rites and theological schools vary in their opinions on how certain practices should be classified. For instance, a more lenient legal rite such as the Hanafis places in the second and fourth categories some practices that a stricter rite such as the Hanbalis regards as belonging to the first and fifth. Complicating the matter further is the fact the Qur'an mentions many practices and customs which were debated by the later jurists and theologians, partly because statements in the Qur'an are sometimes ambiguous or are not sufficiently explicit for the purposes of later Islamic law. The Qur'an is very specific on some regulations, for instance dealing with marriage, divorce, inheritance and food laws (2: 228–32, 4. 3, 11–14/12–18, 22/26, 5. 1, 96/97, etc.). It also makes clear that certain practices, such as usury, eating pork, drinking wine and gambling are bad (2. 173/168, 3. 130/125, 5. 3, 90/92, etc.). But the Qur'an discourages or prohibits these practices in language that allows for differences in later interpretation. For instance, the strongest statement the Qur'an makes about wine and gambling (*khamr* and *maysir*: actually only one type of each that was popular in Arabia in Muhammad's time) is that they are 'the works of Satan' (5. 90/92). Distinctively Islamic regulations and customs involving marriage, divorce, circumcision, funerals and special prayers also vary in different Islamic cultures and countries. Finally, it should be mentioned that Muslims worldwide celebrate two major annual festivals, the 'Id al-Fitr (the feast of the breaking of the fast) on the first three days of the month of Shawwal, which follows Ramadan, and the 'Id al-Adha (the Feast of the Sacrifice) on the 10th of Dhu-l-Hijja, which commemorates Abraham's faith by his willingness to sacrifice his son, seen by some as the high point of the annual Great Pilgrimage to Mecca and its environs (see [8: xv] for al-Bukhari's hadiths on these two 'Ids).

Women in Traditional Islamic Practice

In addition to the numerous references to women in the preceding sections regarding special circumstances in their performance of the major Islamic rituals, some general comments are needed to help clarify one of the most misunderstood aspects of Islam. The Qur'an in many places prescribes equality between men and women in terms of the basic religious duties and rituals. For instance, Sura 33. 35 states: 'Surrendering men and surrendering women, believing men and believing women, obedient men and obedient women . . . who give alms (*zakat*) and who fast (during Ramadan) . . . will receive a mighty wage (in the afterlife).' The three pairs of Arabic terms at the beginning of this fairly late Medinan verse, when seen in light of their usage within the entire Qur'an, offer considerable insight into the growing importance of the role of women in the Muslim community during Muhammad's lifetime. In earlier passages and in most contexts throughout the Qur'an, Muhammad's followers are called 'believers' (*mu'minun*), and only the masculine plural form occurs (which in Arabic usage can include women along with men, but not women only). In some Medinan contexts, when the people are called on to 'surrender to God and His Messenger (Muhammad)', the Qur'an refers to his followers as 'those who surrender' (*muslimun*), the term that eventually came to designate those who accepted this call. The verse quoted above is one of several in later parts of the Qur'an that include also the feminine plurals, *muslimuna*, *mu'minuna*, etc., making it explicit that women as well as men are expected to perform the basic rituals.

That women worshipped in the mosque during Muhammad's lifetime and went about in public unveiled seems indisputable, as evidence from the Qur'an and the hadith collections makes clear. One fairly late passage in the Qur'an does instruct Muhammad's wives (who it says 'are not like other women') to remain in their apartments (33. 32–3), but this is a general statement on their privacy that need not be interpreted as prohibiting their participation in public worship. The Qur'an enjoins modesty in dress and behaviour for both women and men (e.g. 24. 30–1), but it does not require either to wear veils. Sura 24. 31 does instruct believing women to 'reveal of their beauty only what (normally) shows and draw their veils (*khumur*) over their bosoms', but the concern here is with modest dress and specifically with covering the chest. The reference to the *khimar* or head covering – commonly worn in Arabia by both men and women in the time of Muhammad because of the hot climate – may be incidental. The preceding verse tells men to 'lower their gaze' or look down when encountering women in public, which would hardly be necessary if women were fully veiled. Another verse, Sura 33. 59, instructs believing women 'to draw their cloaks (*jalabib*; sing. *jilbab*) around them' when they are out in public, and 33. 53 says that whenever Muslim men speak to Muhammad's wives (presumably when in his residential quarters) they should do so from 'behind a curtain (*hijab*)' – a practice that was later adopted by some of the caliphs. Nowhere in the Qur'an is veiling or the seclusion (*purdah*) of women clearly prescribed, although a number of verses such as these lend themselves to such interpretations for those who seek Qur'anic sanction for these practices. Most historians believe that it was not until after Muhammad's death and the conquest of the Fertile Crescent that the Muslim community gradually adopted these and other cultural practices of the ancient civilizations of the conquered peoples, restricting urban middle- and upper-class women to the home at most times and requiring that they be veiled in public. These practices were well established in ancient Mesopotamia and Persia, and also in some pre-Christian societies of the eastern Mediterranean area, as well as within some Byzantine and Syriac Christian communities long before the time of Muhammad. When they were adopted by Muslims, this led to changes in Islamic practice, later enforced in some instances by Islamic law, for instance encouraging women to perform the Salat in their homes, while proclaiming that prayers in the mosque were more efficacious for men [49: 4–6, 47–54].

In some aspects of Muslim family life the Qur'an and later Islamic law assign men certain responsibilities and allow them certain privileges that give the appearance of placing women in an inferior position. One example of a legal responsibility of Muslim men that seems paternalistic to many people today is that they are required to provide living expenses (*nafaqat*) for their wives, unmarried grown daughters and, in some cases, other female relatives. Al-Bukhari devotes a separate section of his *Sahih* to this male responsibility [8: LXIV; see also 15: 26–8]. Probably the most striking example of a Muslim male privilege is polygyny, allowing a man to have up to four wives (Sura 4.3), whereas polyandry, a woman's right to have more than one husband at the same time – which seems to have existed in Arabia before Islamic law was established – is strictly prohibited by Islamic law. Other examples of Muslim male privileges involve divorce: a man can divorce a wife much more easily than a woman can divorce a husband, and a man may remarry immediately after divorce, whereas a divorced Muslim woman must wait three or four months before remarrying, because of the importance of knowing the paternity of a child. (See [8: LXII; 36: VIII] for al-Bukhari's and Muslim's hadiths on marriage; [8: LXIII; 37: IX] on divorce; and [44: VI, XVI] for a modern defence of traditional practices.)

These and other issues related to Muslim family life are, however, complex and need to be understood in historical perspective. For instance, the statement in Sura 4. 11/12 saying sons are to inherit an amount twice that of daughters seems to be blatantly discriminatory. It takes on a different significance, however, when seen in light of Muhammad's historical situation, when daughters had previously inherited nothing and men were not legally responsible for the living expenses of their wives, unmarried daughters and other relatives [44: x]. The dowry (*mahr*) previously went to the bride's guardian (usually her father or a brother) rather as a purchase price, but in Islam goes to the bride and becomes her permanent property, which she can keep or spend as she likes, while, as mentioned above, her husband is completely responsible for her living expenses [44: VII].

Most historians agree that in general the Qur'an improved the rights and living conditions of Muslim women over those of the women of pre-Islamic Arabia and other geographical areas. Some of the gains were later codified into Islamic law, but this did not guarantee their implementation for all women. For instance, although it has been customary through the centuries for urban Muslim women to inherit, those living in rural and nomadic settings often have not had this right, since it would have resulted in the break-up of family agricultural lands and herds. (See pp. 220–2 on some current customs and trends regarding Muslim women.)

Unity and Diversity

Since the time of Muhammad the Muslim community has tended to split up into various groups. Often political and cultural factors were as significant as theological and philosophical ones in this process. The formative period in the development of Islamic thought, culminating in the work of al-Ash'ari (d. 935), was an exciting battleground of ideas that in retrospect can be seen as a complex dialectical process that culminated in what became Sunni orthodoxy, the established doctrines of the vast majority of Muslims. The main issues involved faith and works, predestination and free will, revelation and reason, the implications of the unity of God, the eternity of the Qur'an, and whether or not the Qur'an must be taken literally.

This dialectical process can be seen as beginning with the group that came to be called the Kharijis, the 'seceders', since they withdrew from the 'party of 'Ali' (see p. 206 below) and later from the Umayyads, claiming that the Muslim leaders at that time did not follow the Qur'an strictly and leave major decisions to God. The Kharijis, who have continued as a small sect in North Africa, also conclude that Islam should be a community of saints and that those who commit grave sins forfeit their identity as Muslims. Those who differed on this point, emphasizing the importance of proper faith over works and arguing that the decision on grave sinners should be deferred to God at the Judgement Day, came to be called Murji'is, 'postponers' or 'those who hope' [50: v]. Those who emphasized human responsibility over predestination or predeterminism came to be called Qadaris, 'determiners', meaning in their case that people determine their own fate [50: IV].

The Traditionists, that is, those who based their faith and practice strictly on the 'traditions' (*ahadith*, singular *hadith*) of the Prophet and were suspicious of the use of reason in ascertaining religious truth, rallied round Ahmad b. Hanbal (d. 855), who defended the concept of the eternity of the Qur'an as the Speech of God (*kalam Allah*), and argued for a literal interpretation of the Qur'an, including its vivid descriptions of creation and the afterlife and its anthropomorphic statements about God. This latter point involved the doctrine of God's attributes, that is, the belief that God literally sees, hears, speaks, etc., because these human attributes are ascribed to him in the Qur'an. His followers, the Hanbalis, came to reject the use of critical reason in determining doctrinal issues. Their opponents, known as Mu'tazilis, 'separatists', attempted to give equal weight to revelation and reason as sources of religious knowledge and truth, but their methods and conclusions tended to come down on the side of reason. The system of the Mu'tazilis was built around the twin emphases, 'the unity and justice of God'. The first point led them to deny the doctrines of the attributes of God, the eternity of the Qur'an and literal interpretation of the Qur'an; the second led to a denial of the doctrine of predestination. The views of the Mu'tazilis were adopted as official doctrine by the caliph al-Ma'mun (d. 833) and were imposed on the leading judges and religious teachers through an Inquisition (*mihna*) that lasted from 833 to about 849. Most of those questioned yielded to the pressure of the government and publicly affirmed the doctrine of the createdness of the Qur'an. Among the few who firmly refused was Ahmad b. Hanbal, who was imprisoned for two years for his insistence on the doctrine of the uncreatedness, and hence eternity, of the Qur'an [50: VIII; and on the Inquisition, ibid: 178–9].

A synthesis between the Traditionist–literalist position of the Hanbali theologians and the rationalist approach of the Mu'tazilis was achieved by al-Ash'ari (d. 935), who studied under the leading Mu'tazilis of his day and accepted their methods and their conclusions until he was about forty. He then 'converted' to Hanbali views and spent the remainder of his career defending them, but using the rational methods of the Mu'tazilis. Al-Ash'ari's thought can be summarized in four main points: (1) The Qur'an is uncreated and is the very speech of God, and, like his other attributes, it is eternal and is in some sense distinct from his essence. (2) The anthropomorphic statements about God in the Qur'an must be accepted, but 'without asking how', that is, without asking how God sees, hears, speaks, etc. (3) Eschatological descriptions in the Qur'an must also be accepted as they stand, but 'without asking how'. One of the key issues here involved the Qur'anic phrase 'looking to their Lord' and whether in the afterlife people will be able to 'see' God in the normal sense. (4) The Qur'anic teaching on predestination must be accepted on the basis of the formula, 'God creates the acts of a person, and the person acquires the acts,' that is, the omnipotence of

God is to be taken seriously, while people 'acquire' responsibility for their deeds by willing at the moment of acting to do them [51: ix]. The Hanbali theologians continued to distrust the Ash'aris' use of reason, but the latter group's system of theology came to be accepted by the vast majority as Sunni orthodoxy.

The extreme representatives of the Greek, rationalist outlook were the group that came to be called the 'philosophers' (falasifa). They differed from the 'theologians' (mutakallimun) not only in their view that observation and reason are the primary sources of knowledge and truth, but also in their preference for discussing traditional philosophical questions rather than theological ones. Al-Kindi (d. c.870) is usually regarded as the first major philosopher to write in Arabic, and the only great one of Arab lineage. His main accomplishment was that he adapted Greek thought and science to fit the Arab and Islamic world. His theological views were close to those of the Mu'tazilis, and, in contrast to later Islamic philosophers, he accepted the doctrine of creatio ex nihilo. The Turkish-born al-Farabi (d. 950) is regarded as the founder of Arabic Neo-Platonism. Especially favoured by the Shi'is (see below) because of his political philosophy, which is consistent with their religious beliefs, al-Farabi has received much attention and acclaim in recent times in the West, where he is sometimes hailed as the most original thinker among the Islamic philosophers. The Andalusian philosopher–physician–scientist, Ibn-Rushd (d. 1198), better known in the West as Averroës, seems to have had the greatest impact on European thought, especially among the Scholastics, such as Thomas Aquinas (d. 1274) and Albertus Magnus (d. 1280). Ibn-Rushd's main contribution lay in his meticulous commentaries on the writings of Aristotle and his conscientious grappling with the perennial question of the relation of revelation to reason [16: 66–94, 107–28, 270–92]. But the person most often deemed the greatest philosopher to write in Arabic is the Persian-born Ibn-Sina (d. 1037), known in the West by his Latin name, Avicenna. His major philosophical work, the Kitab al-Shifa' (Book of Healing), is an encyclopaedia of eleventh-century Greek and Islamic learning, ranging from logic and metaphysics to mathematics and science. The philosophical parts he later abridged into a more popular work, the Kitab al-Najat (Book of Salvation). Ibn-Sina, also a Neo-Platonist, made a major contribution to Oriental and Western philosophy, not so much for his original ideas as for his synthesis and systematic elaboration of the ideas of his predecessors, including especially al-Farabi [16: 128–62].

Mystical ideas began to flow into the stream of Islamic thought as early as the first century AH, when an ascetic pietism arose in the Muslim community. The growing emphasis on the need for obedience to divine law within official Islam was another factor leading

Muslim mystics and ascetics, who came to be called Sufis, to turn inward. Calling for a life of love and pure devotion to God, the Sufis developed a spiritual path to God, consisting of a series of 'stages' of piety (*maqamat*) and gnostic–psychological 'states' (*awal*), through which each Sufi was to pass. The 'stages' are similar to the *scala perfectionis* of the medieval Christian monks, while the 'states' resemble Hindu and Buddhist concepts, as may be partly seen in the simplified version shown in table 3.1. The Sufi emphasis on this twofold spiritual path led to a doctrine of 'annihilation' (*fana'*) of the individual in God, exemplified in the famous statement by al-Hallaj (d. 922), 'I am the Truth', Truth being one of the names or attributes of God and a cognate of the term translated in table 3.1 as 'the Reality'. The idea that there are various levels of Islamic piety, and that only a few of the elite can reach the highest goal, led to a concept of sainthood in Islam, along with the related belief that saints could perform miracles.

Table 3.1 The Sufi mystical path and the Christian *scala perfectionis*

The Sufi mystical path according to al-Sarraj's *Book of the Radiances of Sufism*	The *scala perfectionis* according to the fourteenth-century *Theologia Germanica*
I *The Law*	I *Purification*
1 Repentance	1 Remorse for sin
2 Abstinence	2 Confession of sin
II *The Way*	3 Reconciliation of life
3 Renunciation	II *Enlightenment*
4 Poverty	4 Avoidance of sin
III *The Gnosis*	5 Living life of virute and good works
5 Patience	6 Bearing trial and temptation
6 Trust in God	III *Union*
IV *The Reality*	7 Pureness and integrity of heart
7 Satisfaction	8 Love
	9 Meditation on God

The Sufi tradition within Islam also stands out for its distinctive practices. While traditional Sunni and Shi'i Muslims frown upon any use of music in religious rituals, Sufi orders throughout the Islamic world, particularly in Turkey, Iran and the Indo-Pakistani region, have developed a wide variety of ritual observances involving singing, drums and other musical instruments, and dance. Music is used in ritual processions, often commemorating the birthday (*mawlid*) of the founder of the order. Each order also developed its own distinctive ritual observance called a *dhikr*, a Qur'anic term meaning 'remembrance (of God)'. These rituals often include some form of dance, the best known in the West being that of the Turkish Mevlevi order, often called the Whirling Dervishes, whose cosmic dance around their master (*shaykh*) simulates the rotation of the planets around the sun. Sufi belief and practice sometimes degenerated into saint cults and superstition that were clearly outside the realm of traditional Islam. During the two centuries from the time of the famous al-Junayd of Baghdad (d. 910), said to be the greatest Sunni exponent of the 'sober' type of Sufism, to the even more celebrated al-Ghazali (d. 1111), said to be the most original thinker Islam produced, the Sufi movement proliferated into diverse schools, from moderate to radical in relation to Islamic orthodoxy and orthopraxis. Al-Ghazali, influenced by the moderate Sufi thought and practices of renowned masters such as al-Junayd and the Sunni, Shafi'i school of Islamic law, achieved significant reforms and made major contributions in the development of both the Sufi and the Sunni traditions. Al-Ghazali rejected any literal interpretation of the Sufi concept of 'annihilation of the self' (*fana'*) and its corollary, the goal of becoming one with divine being, which would of course be inconsistent with traditional Islamic theism, and he repudiated such popular practices as the veneration of saints, while at the same time bringing about a major revival and reorientation of traditional Islamic thought and practice. Al-Ghazali's impressive synthesis in his famous *Ihya' 'ulum al-din* (The revival of the religious sciences) helped to provide a permanent bond between Sunni and Sufi Islam. W. Montgomery Watt writes: 'The main aim of al-Ghazali in his greatest work, the *Ihya*' . . ., was to show how a punctilious observance of the duties imposed by [Islamic law] could be the basis of a genuine Sufi life' [51: 92].

Al-Ghazali also brought about a synthesis between Islamic theology and philosophy, deeply affecting the course of subsequent Islamic religious thought. In his work, *The Inconsistency of the Philosophers*, he attacked certain conclusions of the essentially Neo-Platonist thought of earlier Islamic philosophers such as al-Farabi and Ibn-Sina (see above), while accepting some aspects of their thought and the philosophers' rationalist methods, especially Aristotelian logic. Just as al-Ash'ari overcame the first wave of Greek influence on Islam by combining Mu'tazili rational methods with Hanbali traditional beliefs, so al-Ghazali overcame the second wave, that is, the Islamic philosophical movement that culminated in the writings of Ibn-Sina, by mastering their thought and methods and then using these to defend and refine orthodox, Sunni beliefs. Al-Ghazali's accomplishment in bringing together Sunni theology,

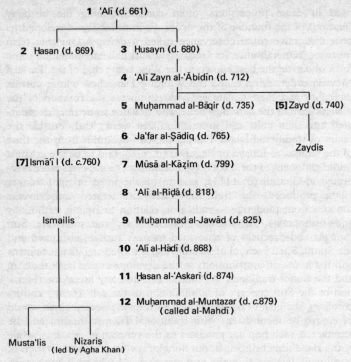

Figure 3.6 *The line of succession of Shi'i Imams*

especially that of al-Ash'ari's school, and elements of Neo-Platonist philosophy and Sufi mysticism brought about the second great synthesis in the dialectical process that established the Sunni thought of the great majority of Muslims today [16: 217–33, 246–51].

Some Muslims, however, chose to remain outside the fold of Sunni Islam. The largest minority group, the Shi'is, take their name from their identification as the 'party of 'Ali' (*shi'at 'Ali*), the cousin and son-in-law of Muhammad. The Shi'is began as a political movement among those who supported 'Ali and his descendants through Muhammad's daughter, Fatima, as the only legitimate successors of Muhammad as heads of the Muslim community. With the success of the Umayyads and the 'Abbasids and the rise of Sunni Islam, the Shi'is gradually formed a separate religious community, eventually centring their activities in Iran. They rejected the Sunni view that proper beliefs and practices should be determined by a 'consensus' (*ijma'*) of the *ulema*, the religious authorities, and developed in its place the doctrine that there was an infallible Imam ('leader' or 'guide') for each generation. These Imams, 'Ali and a direct line of his descendants, were the only source of religious instruction and guidance. According to the majority of Shi'is, called Imamis or Twelvers, the line of succession of Imams proceeded as shown in figure 3.6 to the Twelfth Imam, Muhammad al-Muntazar. When he mysteriously disappeared around 879 the Twelver Imamate came to an end, and a collective body of Shi'i religious scholars or *ulema* assumed his office awaiting his return as the 'Rightly Guided one' (*al-Mahdi*). The present ayatollahs (meaning 'signs of God') see themselves as joint caretakers of the office of the Imam, who is to return at the end of time. The Shi'is also developed their own theology, Qur'an commentaries, legal system and distinctive manner of performing the various Islamic rituals. They are thus by intention clearly set apart from the majority Sunnis [46; 51: 122–40].

The second largest group of Shi'is, considerably fewer in number than the Imamis or Twelvers, are called Ismailis or Seveners, because of their contention that the rightful Seventh Imam was not Musa al-Kazim, but his elder brother Isma'il (Ishmael), who died a few years before his father. The Ismailis developed their own distinctive beliefs, influenced by Neo-Platonism and the concept of gnosis or hidden knowledge that was passed down from God or Divine Being through a series of emanations to Prophets and Imams. The Ismailis flourished from the early tenth century, when they established the Fatimid dynasty in Egypt, to the late eleventh century, when, as a result of internal strife, they split into their two main branches, the Musta'lis (named after al-Musta'li, who became the Fatimid caliph and Ismaili Imam in 1094) and the Nizaris (who claim that his elder brother, Nizar, was the rightful caliph and Imam). The Fatimid dynasty (909–1171) ruled an area from Tunisia through Egypt and Palestine to Syria, and it was from them that the Crusaders captured Jerusalem in 1099. The Crusaders, apparently adopting local usage, called the Nizari Ismailis 'Assassins' (from the Arabic, *hashshashin*, 'users of hashish', allegedly because they used this drug in initiation ceremonies or in preparation for 'assassin', suicide missions). The Nizaris, a small sect, continued to use militant tactics against their enemies until this phase of their history came to an abrupt end in 1256 with the Mongol capture of their mountain fortress headquarters in Alamut, near the Caspian Sea. Victims of Nizari assassins include two 'Abbasid caliphs, a Seljuk sultan, the famous Persian vizier Nizam al-Mulk and a Crusader king of Jerusalem named Conrad. Through the centuries the Ismailis have been active missionaries, spreading Shi'i Islam especially to southern Arabia, East Africa and parts of India. The headquarters of the Musta'lis are now in Bombay. Since the early nineteenth century the leader of the Nizaris has had the title Agha Khan. Other offshoots of the Ismailis include the Druzes and the 'Alawis, also known as Nusayris. The Druzes broke away from the Ismailis in the eleventh century and came to believe in the deification of the Fatimid caliph and Imam, al-Hakim (d. 1020), whose return they seek in the same way as the Twelver Shi'is await the Mahdi. The Druzes are an esoteric sect, meeting on Thursdays (instead of observing the customary Muslim Friday congregational worship), holding firmly to monogamous marriage, and having their own strict ethical code and distinctive beliefs such as that 'Ali was an incarnation of God [46: 78–83].

In addition to the sects that broke away from Ismaili, Shi'i Islam, a wide variety of other groups either arose from Sunni Islam or combined Islamic and non-Islamic beliefs and practices to form syncretistic groups that came to be regarded as independent religions. Two quite different examples of such syncretistic communities are the Sikhs of India and Pakistan, who combine Islamic and Hindu beliefs and practices, and the Babis and Baha'is, whose roots go back to nineteenth-century Persia. Other groups began as Islamic reform movements, but then developed so far from traditional beliefs and rituals that many Muslims no longer accept them within the fold of Islam. Examples include the Ahmadiyyans, especially the branch often called Qadians, founded in the 1880s in India.

Modern Developments

In modern times traditional Islam has been challenged by a bewildering array of forces from both outside and inside the Muslim community. The strongest outside forces have been political, economic and social, and have come from the West. A large part of the Islamic world, from North Africa to Indonesia, came under European colonial rule. With the rise of nationalism among Islamic peoples and the establishment of independent states, there has been a continuing struggle for control among the various factions, some wanting secular states with Western-style law, education, etc., while others demand some form of Islamic state where traditional Muslim life can continue unhampered. The most vigorous outside forces challenging traditional Islam in the twentieth century have been secularism and various forms of socialist ideology, some Marxist and others non-Marxist. Muslim responses to these external forces have taken a wide variety of forms, and the struggle within the Muslim community has given rise to a number of competing movements and trends.

Early Revivalist Reform

After several centuries of relative stagnation within the previously
flourishing Islamic civilization, indigenous revivalist reform movements arose within the Muslim community during the late eighteenth and the nineteenth centuries, especially in Arabia and parts of
Africa. These indigenous movements are sometimes called 'pre-
modernist' with the connotation that they did not arise as reactions
to European or Western modernist influence, as was the case with
the movements discussed in the next section. One of the first and
most influential of the pre-modernist revivalist movements, sometimes called Wahhabism, was established in north central Arabia
through the tireless efforts of Muhammad b. 'Abd-al-Wahhab
(d. 1792), who set out to purify Islam from what he regarded as
various forms of heresy or 'innovation' (bid'a). He argued that
Muslims should cease such practices as venerating saints and making pilgrimages to their tombs, and instead should return to the
original beliefs and practices that prevailed during Muhammad's
lifetime. Modern historians counter such claims by Wahhabis and
other revivalists by pointing out that much that is perceived as
Islamic orthodoxy and orthopraxis developed gradually over a
period of several centuries after the time of Muhammad. In their
fervent puritanism the Wahhabis are not unlike the early Kharijis in
their impassioned call for a pure Islam based on a literal interpretation of the Qur'an. The Wahhabis breathed new life into the conservative legal school of Ahmad b. Hanbal and elevated it to a position
of influence it had never previously enjoyed. They joined forces with
the family of Su'ud, adding a religious fanaticism to the militancy of
the Su'udis who sought to conquer large portions of the Arabian
peninsula. From their capital, Riyadh, in central Arabia, the
Su'udis, with the sanction and support of the Wahhabis, captured
and 'purified' Mecca in 1806, but lost control of the holy city in
1818 when their power was broken by the famous Turkish governor
of Egypt, Muhammad 'Ali. At the beginning of the twentieth century Su'udi power was restored in central Arabia, and in 1932 'Abd-
al-'Aziz Ibn-Su'ud established the present Kingdom of Su'udi (or
Saudi) Arabia. Since then Wahhabis have dominated religious life,
and to a large degree education, in Arabia. This control has been
especially important in the holy cities of Mecca and Medina, which
have provided invaluable settings for global Wahhabi influence.
Thousands of young Muslims from all over the world spend years
pursuing Islamic education in Mecca and Medina and then return
to their home countries to become religious leaders and teachers. In
addition to their teaching that it is polytheism to visit the graves of
saints or to seek intercession through a prophet or saint, the
Wahhabis are staunch opponents of the annual celebration of the

Birthday of the Prophet (*mawlid al-nabi*), which they regard as *bid'a* although it is popular and widely accepted throughout most of the Islamic world. They also hold that it is unbelief to employ allegorical or non-literal interpretations of statements in the Qur'an, especially in order to avoid religious obligations or legal penalties simply because they are regarded as outdated or harsh by many modern Muslims. In more recent times the Wahhabis have also denounced such 'Western' innovations as tobacco, cinemas, American (and many Egyptian) television programmes and videos, Western dancing, nightclubs, and similar non-Islamic forms of entertainment, thus justifying the label that is often applied to them – the Puritans of Islam.

Indigenous Islamic reform or revivalist movements in India began as early as the seventeenth century. After a period during which Sufis enjoyed widespread popularity and significant influence in the Indian subcontinent, where they were responsible for large-scale conversions of Hindus to Islam, traditional Muslims found a champion in Ahmad Sirhindi (d. 1625) who attacked the philosophical monism of Sufis such as Ibn-al-'Arabi, but retained certain Sufi views and techniques in a system that stressed traditional Islamic law and values. Sirhindi's reforms were later espoused and enforced by the Mughal ruler and strong defender of Sunni Islam in India, Aurangzeb (d. 1707). A half-century later Indian Islam found a new intellectual leader in Shah Wali-Allah of Delhi (d. 1762), who, like Ibn-'Abd-al-Wahhab in Arabia, was concerned with 'purifying' Islam from non-Islamic beliefs and practices and returning to the original teachings of early Islam. His system stressed social and economic justice with a broad humanistic base, but, partly because of the cultural setting of Indian Islam, he also retained a Sufi interpretation of the universe. A later disciple, Sayyid Ahmad of Bareli, transformed this intellectual reform school into an active holy war crusade, which has sometimes been called the Wahhabi-Su'udi movement of India. After returning from a pilgrimage to Mecca, Sayyid Ahmad recruited an army and captured a large part of northwest India from the Sikhs, but his efforts had no lasting success. Muslim rule in India continued until 1858 when the great Mughal empire was brought to an end by the British.

The nineteenth century witnessed the birth of several indigenous reform movements in Africa. As in India, these movements combined the call to return to the simple teachings of early Islam with the use of Sufi methods of organization and propagation of ideas. The Idrisi order, founded by Ahmad b. Idris (d. 1837), rejected the Sufi idea of union with God, and instead proposed a union with the spirit of Muhammad as the only legitimate goal of Islamic mysticism. Ibn-Idris was not only a practising Sufi but also a specialist in Islamic law. Like Ibn-'Abd-al-Wahhab, he rejected the classical

Islamic concept of 'consensus' (*ijma'*) and insisted on the right of 'individual opinion' (*ijtihad*) for himself. From the Idrisi order sprang other independent orders, the most important being the Sanusiyya, founded in 1837 by the Algerian disciple of Ibn-Idris, Muhammad b. 'Ali al-Sanusi (d. 1859), who established his own Sufi-type ritual and organized over twenty centres or cells (Arabic sing. *zawiya*), mainly in North Africa. Like Ibn-Idris, al-Sanusi claimed the right to *ijtihad* and thus made legal rulings on economic and social matters for his followers. His teaching emphasized the goal of living the good life in this world, as contrasted with the otherworldly stress that often characterized traditional Islam. The Sanusi order provided an activist social reform programme that included political opposition to European colonial rule in Africa, including a campaign for the liberation of Libya from Italian rule. When Libya gained independence in 1951, the current leader of the Sanusi order became Idris I, the first king of the new nation.

Modernist Reform

In the mid-nineteenth century, reform of a definitely modernist mode began to make significant inroads into Muslim life and thought, especially in India and Egypt and admittedly under the influence of Western thought and culture. In India Muslims were boycotting the government schools and consequently shutting themselves out of government service and other employment, mainly because they considered British-ruled India to be a non-Muslim society, literally an 'abode of war' (*dar al-harb*). Sayyid Ahmad Khan (d. 1898) saw that by taking this approach Muslims were only hurting themselves, so he encouraged loyalty to the British, arguing that Muslims in India lived in a society in which they were free to practise their religion as they pleased. He urged Muslims to pursue modern education as a means of bringing themselves into the modern world, and in 1875 he founded a college, now the Islamic University of Aligarh, where all that was best in Western thought could be taught, to women as well as to men, in an Islamic atmosphere. He insisted that modern Muslims should be free to interpret and adapt traditional Islamic beliefs and practices in the light of reason and modern science, and he further argued that Islam and science could not be contradictory. For instance, he encouraged Muslims to rethink traditional Islamic practices regarding polygamy and slavery, which he saw as social evils. The influence of his thought and ideas continues to be strong among many Indian and Pakistani Muslims.

Another prominent Indian reformer was the Shi'i jurist, Amir 'Ali (d. 1928), who was also British-trained and educated. His book,

The Spirit of Islam, still widely read by Muslims and non-Muslims alike, has had widespread influence on contemporary Muslim life and thought. Many of his views are now generally accepted, at least by modernist or Western-orientated Muslims, even though he, like Sayyid Ahmad Khan, was severely criticized by the *ulema* of his day. Amir 'Ali remained traditional in most aspects, but he devised modern, rational explanations for the meaning of the Salat, fasting and other religious duties, and he called for sweeping changes in certain social institutions that had long characterized traditional Muslim life, for instance, the abolition of slavery and polygyny. His justification for these changes lay in his central thesis – later adopted and expanded by the Pakistani-born philospher, Fazlur Rahman – that Islam, properly understood, embodies certain moral and social values that tend towards modernization. He argued that, while the spiritual teachings of the Qur'an are eternal and changeless, the specific Qur'anic regulations of Muslim life were not intended to be permanent. They represented great steps forward in Muhammad's time, establishing a pattern of progress that God intended to continue through the centuries. Thus, when society as a whole had made sufficient progress, it was God's intention that such institutions as slavery and polygyny should be abolished. He also went further than any of his followers were prepared to go in regarding Muhammad as the author of the Qur'an, arguing that this was the view of the early generations of Muslims. And he urged Muslims to read the Qur'an on its own and interpret it for themselves, without the unnecessary burden of official interpretations that were placed upon it in medieval times [10: IV].

Meanwhile, in the Middle East similar concerns were being expressed by the leading Egyptian modernist thinker of the period, Muhammad 'Abduh (d. 1905), who argued that Islam and modern science were completely compatible. Influenced on this point by Jamal al-Din al-Afghani (d. 1897), 'Abduh urged Muslims to cultivate modern philosophical and scientific academic disciplines and expand the curricula of Islamic educational institutions. He was especially well situated to effect such reforms after being appointed head or Shaykh of the thousand-year-old mosque school, and now university, al-Azhar in Cairo. Trained as a theologian along traditional lines, 'Abduh became convinced not only that faith and reason were compatible, but that both must be utilized in order to understand the world and humankind. He sought to reform Islamic thought and modernize Islamic practice so that Islam could survive in the modern world and meet the needs of the younger generations of Muslims who were being introduced to Western ideas. 'Abduh set for himself the mission of restating the basic tenets of Islam in terms that were acceptable to the modern mind. One of the best-known examples of his social concerns and his rationalist or casuis-

tic method involves the question of the Qur'an's teaching on polygyny, where he gave a new interpretation to two well-known verses
on the subject. He argued that Sura 4. 3, which says that a Muslim
man may have up to four wives, 'but if you fear you cannot act
justly ('adala) [with two or more], then only one', must be interpreted in light of 4. 129/128, which urges a Muslim man to be fair
with his wives while acknowledging that he cannot treat them all
equally. Since the same verb ('adala) appears in both verses, 'Abduh
argued that the first means that a Muslim could have up to four
wives if he could treat them equally, but that the second says this is
impossible, so that the true teaching of the Qur'an is that a man
should have (or is allowed) only one wife ([18: 248–61] provides a
translation of his *fatwa* or legal ruling on polygyny).

These are only a few examples of prominent Muslim thinkers and
writers who adopted modern, Western thought and culture during
the period before these labels acquired the negative connotations
they have for so many Muslims today. They would have seen as
ludicrous the late twentieth-century enterprise commonly called the
Islamization of Knowledge whereby some scholars have attempted
to construct a distinctly Islamic body of scientific knowledge or a
distinctly Islamic understanding and interpretation of science.

The Search for Identity

It could be argued that virtually all of the major political and other
world events of the twentieth century – the two World Wars, the
collapse of the European colonial empires, the rise and fall of
Communist world influence, the vast increase in the number of
independent nation-states, the impact of technology and modern
communications, feminist movements, etc. – have had significant
repercussions on the Islamic world. One of the first was the dis-
integration of the Ottoman empire after the First World War and
the abolition of the caliphate at the instigation of Mustafa Kemal
Atatürk, the founder of the modern, secular state of Turkey. As
countries across Asia and Africa with majority Muslim populations
gained their independence, the struggle began between those who
favoured European-type secular constitutions, with religious and
personal status freedoms for peoples of all creeds and ethnic backgrounds, and those who insisted on establishing Islamic states, governed by traditional Islamic law. This Muslim search for identity in
a modern world where peoples could choose their own forms of
government spread from North Africa to Indonesia during the first
two-thirds of the twentieth century as the European colonial powers
gradually lost control of their former territories.

In this search for identity Muslims have organized into a wide variety of movements and parties that have continued, modified or reacted against the concerns of the nineteenth- and early twentieth-century revivalists and modernists discussed above. Several of these movements were, and some have continued to be, extremely active in political affairs and vocal in expressing their views through journals, pamphlets and a wide variety of other modern media. In Egypt the legacy of Muhammad 'Abduh continued for a while in a movement called the Salafiyya (the way of the ancestors), led by Muhammad Rashid Rida (d. 1935), who completed 'Abduh's Qur'an commentary and published it in an influential journal he founded, called al-Manar (The Lighthouse). The Salafiyya, a group of conservative reform leaders who saw themselves as Neo-Hanbalis, called for some social and legal reforms, while distrusting the freedom for radical change espoused by the modernists. After the death of its founder this movement drifted towards an anti-intellectual and fundamentalist position and gradually died out as an organized group, although some of its ideas and ideals have remained central to a wide variety of later movements. The direct heir of the Salafiyya was the Muslim Brotherhood (al-Ikhwan al-Muslimun), founded in 1928 in Ismailia, Egypt, by Hasan al-Banna' (d. 1949), who in his student days in Cairo was a follower of Muhammad Rashid Rida. Al-Banna' continued Rashid Rida's journal al-Manar for a while after the death of its founder, but he came to sense that the task of revitalizing Muslim society demanded a politically active campaign among the masses, rather than simply literary, intellectual endeavours. He organized some fifty centres throughout Egypt for classes and discussion groups, and eventually the movement spread to Syria, Palestine, the Sudan and other parts of the Arab world. In Egypt it became more and more political in its activities until 1954, when it was banned temporarily along with other political parties after the revolution led by Gamal Abdel Nasser. During the last quarter of the twentieth century, sentiment in Egypt and other countries for the aims and largely peaceful methods of the Muslim Brotherhood has ebbed and flowed. In some countries where the Brotherhood had been strong, it has been eclipsed by a variety of more radical Islamic groups, some of which are discussed briefly below [36; 10: 31–47, 110–20].

The most prominent equivalent of the Muslim Brotherhood outside the Arabic-speaking world has been Pakistan's Jama'at-i-Islami (Islamic Party), founded in British India in 1941 by the energetic Muslim leader and prolific writer Abu al-A'la al-Mawdudi (d. 1979). Pakistan, meaning the 'nation of the pure (pak)', was established in 1947 at the time of the partition of British India as a new experiment in modern Muslim statehood. The idea of establishing an Islamic state in the Indian subcontinent had been proposed over a decade earlier by the famous philosopher–poet

Muhammad Iqbal (d. 1938). The person most responsible for attempting to implement this goal was Muhammad Ali Jinnah, Pakistan's first President. Jinnah, who was not a particularly religious man and did not have in mind a theocratic state ruled by mullahs, died in 1948 before a constitution could be adopted. The absence of strong, positive leadership since then and the lack of a consensus among the politicians have prevented the realization of any of the various dreams of Pakistan as an ideal Islamic state. Al-Mawdudi's conservative Islamic Party at first opposed the idea of establishing an independent Pakistan, arguing that Islam was a universal force that should maintain its presence and strength in India. After the partition of British India in 1947, however, al-Mawdudi led the effort to enact a constitution that would make Pakistan a truly Islamic state, ruled by the principles of traditional Islamic law. With the repeated failure of efforts to establish such a constitution, al-Mawdudi and his followers began to devote a major part of their efforts to a vigorous educational campaign that rapidly gained widespread influence outside Pakistan. Al-Mawdudi developed a comprehensive theoretical basis for his party's social and political programmes, while providing a rationale for and defence of the maintenance of traditional Islam in the modern world. A number of his publications [e.g. 33] have been translated into many languages, including those of Europe and other areas where Muslim missionaries are active, making him one of the most popular proponents of traditional Islam [10: 120–4; 40: xiv]. As mentioned above, similar debates among Muslims regarding the type of government they prefer have characterized those states that have democratic or parliamentary systems. Those who favoured the establishment of European-type states won out virtually everywhere over conservative Muslims – like al-Mawdudi in Pakistani – who sought Islamic states governed in accordance with traditional Islamic law. However, the struggle is far from finished, as comments below will make clear.

Meanwhile, back in Egypt, the spiritual and intellectual centre of the Arab Islamic world at the time, the sparks of reform kindled by Muhammad 'Abduh continued to burn, although slowly, through the tireless and often fruitless efforts of some of his successors as Shaykh al-Azhar, head of the most prestigious Sunni institution of higher learning in the world. By the 1920s the Azharis, both faculty and graduates, had lost much of their former influence, partly because of an antiquated curriculum and partly because of their failure to communicate with the masses of often ill-educated Muslims. A consensus developed within al-Azhar, the venerable thousand-year-old institution, that changes were needed, but the faculty could not agree on the extent of the desired reforms. Mustafa al-Maraghi (d. 1945), who was appointed as head of al-Azhar in 1928, was the first Shaykh al-Azhar to prepare and promote a detailed proposal for a series of substantive reforms. His ideas, presented in the form of a memorandum to King Fu'ad, received broad support from progressive *ulema* and raised their hopes that al-Azhar would regain its former prestige as the leading educational institution in Egypt and the Middle East. However, a combination of political forces (involving dissatisfaction with the British, the king, the political influence of the clerics, etc.) and a lack of support from the majority of the *ulema*, along with what some perceived as a loss of perseverance and fortitude on the part of al-Maraghi, resulted in his failure to implement his far-reaching reform proposals. The person who appears to have had the greatest impact on the present status and role of al-Azhar as a pivotal institution in the complex religious and political environment of Egypt and the Middle East today is Mahmud Shaltut (d. 1963). In some ways he was a product of his traditional education, never studying a foreign language or culture, never travelling abroad or taking any interest in philosophy, mysticism or religious traditions other than Islam. In other ways he was an heir of the modernist tradition initiated by Muhammad 'Abduh, strongly supporting the reforms proposed by al-Maraghi and some say the leading architect behind the 1961 Reform Law that clarified the status of al-Azhar and formalized its relationship with the government and its role within Egyptian education and religious life. In addition to his scholarly and administrative activities – serving as Shaykh al-Azhar for the last five years of his life was the culmination of a long, productive and prolific career – Shaltut was heavily involved in reform issues that affected Muslims throughout the world. After becoming disaffected with the leadership of al-Maraghi, Shaltut initiated his own reform agenda in two well-publicized proposals in 1941 and 1943. As an active member of al-Azhar's prestigious Fatwa Commission, inaugurated in 1935, he helped maintain the tradition of studying and answering legal queries from Muslims all over the world. Finally, Shaltut was one of the pioneers of a movement that worked to reconcile differences among the four Sunni *madhahib* (see p. 179 above) and to improve relations between Sunnis and Shi'is. He and like-minded Muslim reformers in countries across the Muslim world continued to be criticized from both the right and the left, some decrying their concerns as caving in to modernism while others viewed their efforts as insignificant variations of traditionalism [57].

Muhammad 'Abduh's extensive influence took an interesting form in the activities of several Muslim women in the early part of the twentieth century, especially in Egypt and other Arab countries of the Middle East. For example, when the upper-class Egyptian, Huda Sha'rawi (d. 1947) became aware that veiling the face and female seclusion in the home are not required by the Qur'an, the canonical hadiths or Islamic law – as women had been and still are led to believe – she became active in the international women's movement, acknowledging on a number of occasions the influence and inspiration she received from the ideas of Muhammad 'Abduh. After helping to form a women's union and also a society to improve female literacy in 1914, Sha'rawi led the first organized feminist movement in the Arab world through her work with the Egyptian Feminist Union, created in 1923. In the same year, as an act of protest against male dominance in Islamic political and religious affairs in her country and others, she removed her face veil in public while returning home from a conference on women's suffrage rights in Rome. Primarily an activist rather than a writer, she was denied certain opportunities of Muslim women scholars today. For instance, although she was taught French, the social language of the upper classes in Egypt in her day, her male guardians used every means to keep her from learning classical Arabic, so that the written sources of Islam were closed books for her. Huda Sha'rawi recognized from an early stage in her activist career that Christian women in her country and others suffered similar discrimination and deprivation of basic human rights, so she worked tirelessly to improve the legal status and living conditions of all women, but this does not diminish her place in history as a pioneer in the quest for total equality for women in Muslim societies.

Continuing Struggle

During the last quarter of the twentieth century increasing dissatisfaction among traditional Muslims with their secular governments has brought about a resurgence of Islam that has taken a variety of forms ranging from terrorist activities to a revival of the veil even among school-age girls. It was in the context of this resurgence that the originally Christian term 'fundamentalist' began to be applied to Muslims. Since this occurred at about the same time that conservative discontent began to express itself in the form of violence, including terrorist activities and even suicide missions, many in the West came to equate Islamic fundamentalism with terrorism. This is a grievous misconception, since the vast majority of Muslims who hold what could very well be called fundamentalist beliefs are not proponents of violence. Although the concept of 'fundamentalism' has been adopted by its Arabic-speaking proponents in the term *usuliyya*, it is disliked by English-speaking Muslims because of its Protestant Christian origins and perceived pejorative connotations. A new term, 'Islamism' (*islamiyya* in Arabic), arose in the early 1990s as a synonym for 'fundamentalism' and is generally preferred by English-speaking Muslims. 'Islamists' and 'Islamism' are becoming widely accepted terms intended to convey positive connotations and the aspirations of the groups they designate, including the ideas of revival (*tajdid*), reform (*islah*), struggle (*jihad*) and a return to the beliefs and practices of the first generations of Muslims, the so-called 'forefathers' or ancestors (*salaf*) [13].

The Islamic revolution best known in the West was the Shi'i clerical takeover of the government of Iran in 1979, led by the Ayatollah (a title of a higher-level Shi'i religious scholar meaning 'sign of God') Ruhollah Khomeini (d. 1989). To the surprise of many, both inside and outside Iran, the clerics who have controlled the government since the time of the revolution in 1979 did not abolish all modern Iranian laws and return the country to a medieval form of government. Instead, they left intact a number of the key social and economic reform laws enacted under the government of the former shah and attempted to maintain a balance between fundamental Islamic principles and the needs of a modern government. Thus, the widespread perception of Iran as an oppressive society dominated by antiquarian religious laws – symbolized by the black robes of the clerics and veils of the women, which the media are so fond of capturing for Western audiences – is to a large degree a matter more of appearance than of substance.

Developments in the Sudan, on the other hand, especially for a short period during the 1980s, were not as favourable for the people as in Iran. Ja'far al-Numayri established an Islamic revolutionary regime in the Sudan in 1969. After years of failed attempts to enact conservative Islamic laws and thus establish a model Islamic state through constitutional means, al-Numayri decreed harsh Islamic laws in 1983 that were so unpopular that they brought about his overthrow two years later. A second military coup in 1989, led by Omar Hassan al-Bashir with the support of the National Islamic Front, promised 'Islamic participatory democracy', which, however, has been slow to take effect. Although most observers believe the new regime has failed both in its own goals and in its attempts to preserve popular support, traditional Islamic laws continue to be maintained there, and supporters of the regime argue that the Sudan is one of only two or three countries in the world today that can rightfully claim to be truly Islamic states. In Libya a different type of revolutionary regime was established in 1969 by Colonel Mu'ammar al-Qadhdhafi, who was widely assumed in the beginning to have aspirations for an international leadership role among conservative Muslims. Over the years, however, it became clear that his vision and ambition extended far beyond the Muslim community, as he hoped to inspire people throughout the so-called Third World to unite in resisting the last vestiges of European and American colonialism. After failing in his efforts to establish formal political ties between Libya and certain of its African Muslim neighbours – notably Egypt and the Sudan – al-Qadhdhafi gradually found himself ostracized or simply ignored by other Muslim leaders, even though he has continued to present himself as a champion of Islamic causes. His position within the Muslim community is now complicated by the fact that he has opposed fundamentalists or Islamists except in some of their anti-Western activities and rhetoric.

The varieties of religious, social and political struggles that persist today throughout the Islamic world are so complex that any generalization would be misleading at best. The following are just a few examples of the types of issues that characterize Islamic *jihad* in the late twentieth century.

In **Egypt** the Muslim Brotherhood, the oldest of the contemporary Islamist movements, continues to be a strong rival of the largely secularist government. It does not advocate violence to establish an Islamic state, and some Brotherhood members have served in key ministerial positions in the government. It is the more extreme Islamists in Egypt such as the Organization for Holy War (*Jama'at al-Jihad*) who oppose the government and engage in terrorist activities against senior government officials – for instance, claiming responsibility for the assassination of President Anwar Sadat in 1981 – as well as against moderate Muslim leaders, Coptic Christians and Israelis [13: 93–100].

In **Tunisia** the Islamic Tendency Movement (MTI, from its French name), which had been Tunisia's major Islamist organization, was gradually transformed into the Islamic Renaissance Party (Hizb al-Nahda) between 1979 and 1989 under the leadership of Rashid al-Ghannushi. Political activity by members of al-Nahda was banned in 1990 in response to anti-regime activities, and some members were tried as revolutionaries. Al-Ghannushi, one of the leading theorists and proponents of the establishment of modern Islamic states, remained al-Nahda's leader and continued to direct opposition to the government from exile.

In **Algeria** the Islamic Salvation Front (FIS, from its French name) became the dominant Islamist movement from the time it was legalized in 1989. In the first round of the elections for the National Assembly in 1991, the FIS gained more votes than all other political parties combined. After this stunning success by the Islamists, the government cancelled the second round of elections, scheduled for early 1992. The military intervened and installed a ruling council that declared a state of emergency, banned the Islamic Salvation Front, and then tried and convicted some of its leaders for revolutionary activity. This only increased anti-regime violence, notably by a militant movement called the Armed Islamic Group, which began anti-foreign terrorist activities in 1993.

In **Lebanon** the most active group seeking to establish an Islamic republic is Hizbullah (the Party of God), a Shi'i organization supported by Iran. Hizbullah has waged a vigorous military campaign against Israel and Israeli-backed groups in southern Lebanon, but also cooperated in the 1992 elections with the more moderate Shi'i party called AMAL (an acronym for Afwaj al-Muqawimat al-Lubnaniyya, 'Lebanese Resistance Battalions'). AMAL, also a word meaning 'hope' in Arabic, was founded just before the 1975–6 Lebanese civil war by Musa Sadr, a Shi'i religious leader who disappeared mysteriously in 1978 while on a trip to Libya to meet with Mu'ammar Qadhdhafi. Unlike Hizbullah, AMAL has continued to support the Lebanese government and the idea of a multi-confessional state, although with a more equitable sharing of power [13: 140–51].

In the **West Bank** and **Gaza**, where the political situation has been changing rapidly from year to year, the major Islamist group among Palestinians since 1987 has been Hamas (the Islamic Resistance Movement), founded mainly by Shaykh Ahmad Yasin, who was then also the leader of the Muslim Brotherhood in Gaza. Hamas has continued to reject Israel's right to exist and to seek an Islamic state in Palestine, thus setting a separate course from the largely secular Palestine Liberation Organization (PLO), which, under the leadership of Yassir Arafat, reached a peace agreement with Israel in 1994. The second most influential Islamist group in the West Bank and Gaza is the Islamic Jihad Movement, established in the early 1980s under the leadership of Fathi al-Shaqaqi and 'Abd-al-'Aziz 'Awda, like Hamas as an offshoot of the Muslim Brotherhood. These two groups have eclipsed the older Islamic Liberation Party, which was established in Jerusalem in 1953 by Taqi al-Din al-Nabhani and had a large following until the 1967 Arab–Israeli war. It re-emerged in the late 1980s and has been a vocal opponent of all Arab peace negotiations with Israel and a continuing voice for an Islamic state in Palestine.

A different type of continuing Islamic 'struggle' that is just as fiercely fought and widely disputed today as the activities people usually associate with *jihad* involves the changing roles of women in Muslim societies throughout the world. A growing number of Muslim women scholars have expressed their impatience with the slow pace of improvement in women's rights and living conditions in Islamic countries. Some writers, such as the Moroccan sociologist Fatima Mernissi, have demonstrated that a number of regulations of Islamic family law regarding the rights of women are much more restrictive than the teachings of the Qur'an, the hadiths and, in some cases, privileges women already had in Arabia in Muhammad's time [34; 35]. Scholars in women's studies – especially historians, sociologists and anthropologists – are gathering evidence that reveals a wide disparity between the ideals and the realities of women's lives in Islamic cultures [5; 29; 49]. Differences of opinion among Muslims vary widely on issues involving the roles of women in modern societies. The following illustrations are just a few examples.

The extent to which the daily lives of Muslim men and women remain separate, and women are kept in seclusion (*purdah*), varies from country to country and according to class and living conditions. Confinement to the home has always been unrealistic for women who are agricultural workers, domestic servants and urban poor, while employment opportunities for modern Muslim women make seclusion equally impractical for many middle-class workers. The custom of keeping women in partial seclusion in some countries seems just as oppressive to many modern Muslims, both men and women, as it does to most Westerners [34; 35], but is seen by others as a way of being respectful towards and protective of women [44: XII]. Customs also vary today regarding the seemingly innocuous issue of women worshipping in the mosques. In some countries women are still prohibited from full participation in regular mosque services, whereas in others, especially in times of war (for instance, in Iran during the period of its war with Iraq in the 1980s), more women might be found in some mosques than men. Customs of dress among Muslim women vary in different parts of the Islamic world, often influenced by local culture. In the Arabian peninsula and especially in the villages and smaller towns of some other countries women cover themselves completely from head to toe. In many countries throughout the world, especially in the larger cities, Muslim women often dress in the usual Western manner. In the Balkans, parts of Turkey and some other countries they simply cover their heads discreetly with scarves. The most common type of veiling, however, existing in a wide variety of styles, includes a head covering (often white, black, or blue) and either a gown or long dress with long sleeves for adult women, or some type of uniform for students. The gown or uniform is often of a different colour and in some cases is not unlike some styles of habit worn by Christian nuns. An interesting twentieth-century phenomenon is that veiling by Muslim women declined rapidly during the middle decades of the century, but then, during the so-called resurgence of Islam since the time of the Iranian revolution, was just as rapidly revived, so that many younger women are now emulating a practice their grandmothers' generation eschewed.

Many Muslims today, both men and women, continue to defend the traditional practices regarding polygyny, partly because it is sanctioned by the Qur'an and the hadiths and partly on the basis of reason. One argument that is often presented is that polygyny provides the comforts and security of married life and having children of their own for many women who want them but otherwise could not have them, especially in times when eligible men are not available, for instance when large numbers are killed in battle [44: XIV]. Some modernists such as the Egyptian Sunni theologian Muhammad 'Abduh and the Indian Shi'i jurist Sayyid Amir Ali have used rationalist arguments in attempts to demonstrate that polygyny has no place in modern Muslim life or was never part of true Islam (see pp. 212–13 above). Although these arguments have been accepted by many Muslims, both men and women, a growing number are no longer satisfied with continuing to debate with the traditionalists or attempting to come up with additional modernist arguments. Writers such as Fatima Mernissi are going back to the classical Arabic sources and are employing arguments from modern sociology and anthropology in efforts to demonstrate that Muslim women should be able to participate fully in modern life, including government and business as well as the professions, in which women have been more widely accepted. So the struggle continues. Muslim feminists and other modernists continue to work for reforms in Islamic family and public life, while traditionalists argue just as fervently in favour of what they regard as the permanent divine law or Shari'a [38; 44].

Each country and geographical region has its own unique problems and opportunities for Islam, which is continuing to spread as witnessed by conversions, increasing populations and, more significantly, increasing percentages of the total populations in areas such as Africa, Europe and North America. The rapid rise of the world Muslim population is caused primarily, however, by the high birth rates in countries with the largest numbers of Muslims (see appendix B). It is clear that Islam is today a vibrant, living force that will continue to hold its own against the socialist and secularist pressures of modern society. At the present time we are witnessing dramatic changes in the religious, social and political structures of Islamic countries from Morocco and Senegal to Indonesia and the Philippines, so that the Islamic world of future decades will appear just as different from that of today as today's Islamic world appears from that of past centuries.

Appendix A:

Key Dates (Julian and Gregorian) in the History of Islam
            (d. = 'death of')
  *c.*570   Birth of Muhammad
    622   The Hijra or Emigration of Medina and beginning of Islamic era
    624   Battle of Badr, first major Muslim victory in battle
    630   Battle of Hunayn, last battle led by Muhammad

632	d. the Prophet Muhammad
632–4	Caliphate of Abu Bakr, Muhammad's first 'successor' (caliph)
634–44	Caliphate of 'Umar; Arab conquest of Fertile Crescent and Egypt
644–56	Caliphate of 'Uthman; Arab conquest of Iran and raids into North Africa
c.651	Official recension of the Qur'an issued by the Caliph 'Uthman
656–61	Caliphate of 'Ali, cousin and son-in-law of Muhammad
661–750	Umayyad dynasty, ruled from Damascus
680	Battle of Karbala and death of Husayn b. 'Ali
691	Building of Dome of the Rock in Jerusalem begins
705	Building of the Great Mosque of Damascus begins
711	Arabs invade Spain and also cross Indus River into South Asia
728	d. the theologian Hasan al-Basri
732	Franks halt Arab advance in western Europe at Battle of Tours
748	d. Wasil b. 'Ata', early rationalist, Mu'tazili theologian
750–1258	'Abbasid dynasty, ruled from Baghdad
756–1037	Umayyad dynasty in Spain, ruled from Cordova
762	Building of Baghdad begins
767	d. Abu Hanifa, founder of the Hanafi legal rite
785–987	Great Mosque at Cordova built
786–809	Caliphate of the famous Harun al-Rashid
795	d. Malik b. Anas, author of *Muwatta* and founder of the Maliki legal rite
813–33	Caliphate of al-Ma'mun and era of pivotal controversies between Mu'tazili and traditionalist theologians led by Ahmad ibn Hanbal
820	d. al-Shafi'i, founder of the Shafi'i legal rite
827	Arabs begin conquest of Sicily
834	d. Ibn-Hisham, author of the biography of Muhammad
845	d. Ibn-Sa'd, author of the *Tabaqat*
847	d. al-Khwarizmi, the Arab mathematician who discovered logarithms
855	d. Ahmad b. Hanbal, theologian and founder of the Hanbali legal rite
861	d. the caliph al-Mutawakkil, with whom Sunni orthodoxy triumphed
870	d. the Traditionist (hadith specialist) al-Bukhari
875	d. the Traditionist Muslim
c.879	Twelfth Shi'i Imam, Muhammad al-Mahdi, dies or disappears
886	d. the Traditionist Ibn-Maja
888	d. the Traditionist Abu-Dawud
892	d. the Traditionist al-Tirmidhi
909–1171	Fatimid dynasty rules in northern Africa
910	d. the great Sufi master, al-Junayd

915	d. the Traditionist al-Nasa'i
923	d. the historian and Qur'an commentator, al-Tabari
925	d. the physician al-Razi (Rhases)
929	d. the astronomer al-Battani
935	d. the Sunni theologian al-Ash'ari
944	d. the Sunni theologian al-Maturidi
950	d. the Neo-Platonic philosopher al-Farabi
969	Fatimids conquer Egypt
990–1013	Al-Hakim Mosque in Cairo built
1001–21	Mahmud of Ghazni conquers the Punjab
1013	d. the theologian al-Baqillani
1031	Fall of the caliphate of Cordova
1037	d. the Neo-Platonic philosopher Ibn-Sina (Avicenna)
1037–1492	Moorish (North African) dynasties rule parts of Spain
1055	The Seljuk Tughrul Beg takes over rule in Baghdad
1099	Crusaders capture Jerusalem
1111	d. the theologian al-Ghazali
1138	d. the philosopher Ibn-Bajja (Avempace)
1154	Idrisi completes his geography of the world
1174–93	Saladin rules the Ayyubid dynasty from Cairo
1187	Saladin captures Jerusalem from the Crusaders
1198	d. the philosopher Ibn-Rushd (Averroës)
1206	Qutb-ud-din becomes first Muslim sultan in India
1209	d. the theologian and Qur'an commentator, Fakhr al-Din al-Razi
1240	d. the Sufi master Ibn-al-'Arabi
1254–1517	Mamluks rule in Egypt
1258	Hulegu the Mongol captures Baghdad and ends 'Abbasid rule
1273	d. the Sufi poet Jalal al-Din al-Rumi, founder of the Whirling Dervishes
1277	d. the Traditionist al-Nawawi
1286	d. the Qur'an commentator al-Baydawi
1289	Mamluks capture Tripoli from the Crusaders
1326	d. the theologian Ibn Taymiyya
1333–91	Alhambra built in Granada, Spain
1336	Compilation of the hadith compendium, *Mishkat al-Masabih*
1406	d. the historian Ibn-Khaldun
1453	Ottomans capture Constantinople, which becomes Istanbul
1492	Fall of Granada and end of Moorish rule in Spain
1505	d. the historian and Qur'an scholar, Jalal al-Din al-Suyuti
1517	Ottoman sultan, Selim I, assumes title of caliph
1526	Babur conquers Hindustan and founds Mughal dynasty in India
1550–6	Suleymaniye (Mosque of Suleyman the Magnificent) built in Istanbul
1625	d. Ahmad Sirhindi of India
1628–58	Reign of Shah Jahan, Mughal emperor
1632–52	Taj Mahal, mausoleum of Shah Jahan's widow, built in Agra, India

1644–58	Jami' Masjid built in Delhi
1762	d. Shah Wali-Allah of Delhi
1792	d. Ibn-'Abd-al-Wahhab, founder of Wahhabis
1837	d. Ahmad b. Idris, founder of the Idrisi order
1858	Muslim rule in India ends with banishment of last Mughal emperor
1859	d. al-Sanusi, founder of the Sanusi order in North Africa
1875	Islamic university founded in Aligarh, India by Sayyid Ahmad Khan
1881	Muhammad Ahmad declares himself Mahdi in the Sudan
1897	d. pan-Arabist and pioneer anti-colonialist Jamal al-Din al-Afghani
1898	d. Indian Muslim reformer Sayyid Ahmad Khan
1902	Ibn-Su'ud begins conquest of Arabia
1905	d. the Egyptian Muslim reformer Muhammad 'Abduh
1922	Last Ottoman sultan deposed by Mustafa Kemal Atatürk
1923	Standard edition of the Qur'an published in Cairo
1923	Egyptian Feminist Union founded under leadership of Huda Sha'rawi
1924	Ottoman caliphate abolished by Atatürk and Turkish parliament
1928	d. Indian Muslim reformer Sayyid Amir 'Ali, author of *The Spirit of Islam*
1928	Mohammed Arkoun, major Muslim reform intellectual, born in Algeria
1929	Muslim Brotherhood founded in Egypt by Hasan al-Banna'
1932	Islamic, Wahhabi kingdom of Saudi Arabia established
1935	d. the Egyptian Muslim reformer Muhammad Rashid Rida
1935	Hasan Hanafi, major Muslim reform philosopher, born in Egypt
1941	Jama'at-i-Islami founded in India by Abu al-A'la al-Mawdudi
1945	d. Muhammad Mustafa al-Maraghi, reform Shaykh al-Azhar
1947	Pakistan founded as a Muslim state after partition of British India
1947	d. Huda Sha'rawi, Egyptian activist for women's rights and education
1949	Hasan al-Banna', head of Muslim Brotherhood, assassinated in Egypt
1960	Higher Council of Islamic Affairs founded in Cairo
1962	Muslim World League founded in Saudi Arabia
1963	d. Mahmud Shaltut, renowned Egyptian teacher, reformer and jurist
1966	Sayyid Qutb, martyr of Islamic revivalism, executed by Egyptian government
1969	Islamic socialist regime established in Libya by al-Qadhdhafi
1973	Islamic Foundation established in Britain by Khurshid Ahmad

1975	World Council of Mosques founded
1975	Shi'i Lebanese Resistance Battalions (AMAL) created by Musa Sadr
1977	First World Conference on Muslim Education held in Mecca
1977	d. Ali Shariati, Iranian Muslim social and revolutionary thinker
1979	Shi'i Islamic revolutionary regime established in Iran by Khomeini
1979	d. Abu al-A'la al-Mawdudi, most influential Pakistani Islamist leader
1980s	Renaissance Party (Hizb al-Nahda) established in Tunisia
1980s	Islamic Jihad Movement established in the West Bank and Gaza
1981	Anwar Sadat, President of Egypt, assassinated by Muslim militants
1982	Islamic Society of North America founded
1982	Shi'i 'Party of God' (Hizbullah) established in Lebanon
1983–5	President Ja'far al-Numayri imposed harsh Islamic law in the Sudan
1983	International Islamic University at Kuala Lumpur, Malaysia founded
1984	International Solidarity Network of Women Living under Muslim Laws founded
1985	International Islamic University at Islamabad, Pakistan founded
1987	Islamic Resistance Movement (Hamas) founded in Gaza by Ahmad Yasin
1989	Islamist regime established in the Sudan by a second military revolution
1989	d. Ayatollah Ruhollah Khomeini
1991	Islamic Salvation Front banned in Algeria after winning national elections
1992	Islamic Jihad parties install interim government in Afghanistan struggle
1992–5	Bosnian Muslims suffer massive 'ethnic cleansing' in former Yugoslavia
1990s	Arab–Israeli treaties bring hope for peace to many Muslims in Middle East
1990s	Islamists in Algeria, Egypt etc. continue struggle (jihad) for Islamic governments

Appendix B: The Muslim World

Approximate Muslim populations and percentages of total populations in countries where Islam is dominant or is a significant minority. (Sources: [30; 53] and *Europa World Year Book 1992*, London; estimates for 2000 assume same percentages as in 1990.)

Region and country	1990 millions	%	2000 (est.) millions
A: South-West Asia			
Iran	56.5	98	72.4
Turkey	55.4	99	65.2
Afghanistan	18.4	99	24.2
Iraq	17.1	95	25.2
Saudi Arabia	14.1	95	20.6
Syria	10.5	87	15.0
Yemen Arab Republic	6.4	99	9.9
Jordan	3.7	93	5.3
Democratic Yemen	2.0	90	3.2
Lebanon	1.9	70	2.8
Kuwait	1.9	93	2.5
United Arab Republics	1.6	92	1.7
Oman	1.5	99	2.0
West Bank and Gaza	1.4	92	1.7
Israel	0.7	14	0.8
Bahrain	0.5	91	0.7
Qatar	0.3	99	0.5
B: South Asia			
Pakistan	108.6	97	140.9
India	101.5	12	121.5
Bangladesh	91.6	86	125.4
Sri Lanka	1.2	7	1.4
C: Rest of Asia			
Indonesia	155.3	87	185.9
Central Asian Republics*	54.0	19	59.1
China	19.0	2	20.3
Malaysia	10.3	58	12.0
Philippines	3.0	5	4.3
Thailand	2.2	4	2.6
Burma	1.5	4	2.0
Singapore	0.4	15	0.5
Mongolia	0.2	10	0.3
Brunei	0.2	60	0.2

*Former parts of USSR.

Region and country	1990 millions	%	2000 (est.) millions
D: Northern and Saharan Africa			
Egypt	47.8	90	64.1
Morocco (and Western Sahara)	25.1	99	31.0
Algeria	24.3	97	32.7
Sudan	17.2	73	24.4
Tunisia	7.9	99	9.8
Mali	7.6	90	11.0
Niger	5.9	85	9.0
Libya	3.7	98	5.5
Chad	2.3	50	3.1
Mauritania	1.8	96	2.9
E: Rest of Africa			
Nigeria	39.8	45	50.4
Ethiopia	16.9	35	21.8
Tanzania	7.7	30	9.7
Somalia	7.5	99	9.7
Senegal	6.6	90	8.6
Guinea	5.1	70	8.0
Ivory Coast	2.8	23	4.4
Cameroon	2.6	22	3.4
Ghana	2.1	14	2.7
Mozambique	2.0	13	2.6
Kenya	1.8	6	2.3
Sierra Leone	1.5	35	1.9
Malawi	1.3	14	1.7
Uganda	1.0	6	1.3
Zimbabwe	0.9	1	1.1
Madagascar	0.8	7	1.0
Benin	0.7	15	1.0
Gambia	0.7	85	1.0
Rwanda	0.6	8	0.8
Togo	0.5	15	0.8
Liberia	0.5	20	0.7
Djibouti	0.5	99	0.7
Comoro Islands	0.5	99	0.6
South Africa	0.3	1	0.4
Guinea-Bissau	0.3	30	0.4
Maldive Islands	0.2	99	0.3
F: Europe and North America			
Republics of former Yugoslavia	3.7	16	3.9

| Region and country | 1990 | | 2000 (est.) |
	millions	%	millions
United States of America	3.5	2	4.3
France	2.5	4	2.6
Albania	2.3	70	2.8
Germany	2.3	3	2.7
Britain	1.5	3	1.6
Bulgaria	1.2	13	1.2
Canada	0.3	1	0.4
Spain	0.3	1	0.3
Cyprus	0.2	25	0.2

Totals for these six geographical areas in millions for 1990:

South-West Asia	194
South Asia	303
Rest of Asia	246
Northern and Saharan Africa	144
Rest of Africa	105
Europe and North America	18

These figures show that the world Muslim population in 1990 was over one billion.

Appendix C: The Islamic Calendar

Months of Islamic, lunar calendar

1 Muharram (formerly, Safar I)	7 Rajab
2 Safar (formerly, Safar II)	8 Sha'ban
3 Rabi' I	9 Ramadan
4 Rabi' II	10 Shawwal
5 Jumada I	11 Dhu-l-Qa'da
6 Jumada II	12 Dhu-l-Hijja

Principal events of the Islamic year

1 Muharram	New Year's Day
10 Muharram	Ashura Day, voluntary fast day for Sunnis; commemoration of battle of Karbala for Shi'is
16 Muharram	Imamat Day (for Ismaili Khojas only)

12 Rabi' I	Mawlid al-Nabi (Birthday of the Prophet)
23 Jumada II	Birthday of Agha Khan IV (Ismailis only)
27 Rajab	Laylat al-Mi'raj ('Night of the Ascent' of Muhammad to heaven)
1 Ramadan	Beginning of the month of fasting
27 Ramadan	Laylat al-Qadr ('Night of Power', commemorating the sending down of the Qur'an to Muhammad)
1 Shawwal	'Id al-Fitr (Feast of the Breaking of the Fast)
8–13 Dhu-l-Hijja	Annual Pilgrimage ceremonies in and near Mecca
10 Dhu-l-Hijja	'Id al-Adha (Feast of the Sacrifice); also called 'Id al-Hajj (Feast of the Pilgrimage)

Appendix D: Islamic and Christian Calendars

Prevailing Christian calendar dates for the first day of Islamic (AH) centuries, assuming Gregorian dates from 1582 to present:*

1	16 July 622	801	12 September 1398
101	23 July 719	901	20 September 1495
201	30 July 816	1001	7 October 1592
301	6 August 913	1101	15 October 1689
401	14 August 1010	1201	24 October 1786
501	22 August 1107	1301	1 November 1883
601	28 August 1204	1401	9 November 1980
701	5 September 1301	1501	17 November 2077

The Gregorian calendar dates equivalent to the first day of the Islamic year and the first day of Ramadan, the month of fasting, are approximately as follows:

*All dates in appendix D were computed using HDATE, a calendar conversion programme developed by Dr Waleed A. Muhanna as part of Release 2.1 (August 1994) of his IslamicTimer© software package, which assumes the change from the Julian to the Gregorian calendar from 15 October 1582. Although most Roman Catholic countries accepted Pope Gregory XIII's reform of the Christian calendar – dropping ten days and improving the leap-year algorithm – from that date, Britain and its colonies did not adopt it until 1752. Other European countries made the change at various times, some (for example Greece) not until the twentieth century.

	1st Muharram	*1st Ramadan*
1400 AH	21 November 1979	14 July 1980
1401	9 November 1980	3 July 1981
1402	30 October 1981	23 June 1982
1403	19 October 1987	12 June 1983
1404	8 October 1983	31 May 1984
1405	7 September 1984	21 May 1985
1406	16 September 1985	10 May 1986
1407	6 September 1986	30 April 1987
1408	6 August 1987	18 April 1988
1409	14 August 1988	7 April 1989
1410	4 August 1989	28 March 1990
1411	24 July 1990	17 March 1991
1412	13 July 1991	5 March 1992
1413	5 July 1992	23 February 1993
1414	21 June 1993	1 February 1994
1415	11 June 1994	1 February 1995
1416	31 May 1995	22 January 1996
1417	19 May 1996	11 January 1997
1418	8 May 1997	31 December 1997
1419	28 April 1998	20 December 1998
1420	18 April 1999	9 December 1999
1421	6 April 2000	27 November 2000
1422	26 March 2001	17 November 2001
1423	15 March 2002	6 November 2002
1424	4 March 2003	27 October 2003
1425	22 February 2004	15 October 2004
1426	10 February 2005	5 October 2005
1427	31 January 2006	24 September 2006
1428	21 January 2007	13 September 2007
1429	10 January 2008	1 September 2008
1430	29 December 2008	22 August 2009
1431	18 December 2009	12 August 2010
1432	7 December 2010	1 August 2011
1433	27 November 2011	21 July 2012
1434	15 November 2012	10 July 2013
1435	5 November 2013	29 June 2014
1436	25 October 2014	18 June 2015
1437	14 October 2015	6 June 2016
1438	2 October 2016	27 May 2017
1439	22 September 2017	17 May 2018
1440	11 September 2018	6 May 2019
1441	1 September 2019	24 April 2020
1442	20 August 2020	13 April 2021
1443	10 August 2021	3 April 2022

	1st Muharram	1st Ramadan
1444	30 July 2022	23 March 2023
1445	19 July 2023	12 March 2024
1446	7 July 2024	1 March 2025
1447	27 June 2025	19 February 2026
1448	16 June 2026	8 February 2027
1449	6 June 2027	28 January 2028
1450	26 May 2028	16 January 2029

Bibliography

1 ABDUH, MUHAMMAD, *The Theology of Unity* (tr. I. Musa'ad and K. Cragg), London, Allen & Unwin, 1966

2 ABU DAWUD, *Sunan Abu Dawud* (tr. A. Hasan), 3 vols, Lahore, Muhammad Ashraf, 1984

3 ADAMS, C. J., 'Islamic Religious Tradition', in L. Binder (ed.), *The Study of the Middle East*, New York/London, Wiley, 1976, pp. 9–87

4 AYOUB, M. M., *The Qur'an and its Interpreters*, 2 vols to date (on Suras 1–3), Albany, NY, State University of New York Press, 1984, 1992

5 BECK, L., and KEDDIE, N. R. (eds), *Women in the Muslim World*, Cambridge, MA, Harvard University Press, 1978

6 BOSWORTH, C. E., *The New Islamic Dynasties: A Chronological and Genealogical Manual*, Edinburgh, Edinburgh University Press, 1996; 1st edn publ. 1980 as *The Islamic Dynasties: A Chronological and Genealogical Handbook*

7 BRENNER, L. (ed.), *Muslim Identity and Social Change in Sub-Saharan Africa*, Bloomington, Indiana University Press/London, Hurst, 1993

8 AL-BUKHARI, *The Translation of the Meanings of Sahih al-Bukhari*, Arabic–English (tr. M. M. Khan), 6th rev. edn, 9 vols, Lahore, Kazi Publications, 1983; first publ. Medina, Dar al-Fikr, 1976–9; rev. edn, Lahore, Kazi, 1979

9 CALVERLEY, E. E., *Worship in Islam, Being a Translation, with Commentary and Introduction, of al-Ghazzali's Book of the Ihyā' on the Worship*, London, Luzac, 1925, 1957

10 CRAGG, K., *Counsels in Contemporary Islam*, Edinburgh, Edinburgh University Press, 1965

11 DANIEL, N., *Islam and the West: The Making of an Image*, rev. edn, Oxford, Oneworld Publications, 1993

12 EICKELMAN, D. F., *Moroccan Islam: Tradition and Society in a Pilgrimage Center*, Austin, TX/London, University of Texas Press, 1976

13 ESPOSITO, J. L., *The Islamic Threat: Myth or Reality?*, New York /London, Oxford University Press, 1992

14 ESPOSITO, J. L. (ed.), *Islam in Asia: Religion, Politics, and Society*, New York/London, Oxford University Press, 1987

15 ESPOSITO, J. L., *Women in Muslim Family Law*, Syracuse, NY, Syracuse University Press, 1982

16 FAKHRY, M., *A History of Islamic Philosophy*, 2nd edn, New York, Columbia University Press/London, Longman, 1983; 1st edn 1970

17 FRISHMAN, M., and KHAN, H. (eds), *The Mosque: History, Architectural Development and Regional Diversity*, London/New York, Thames & Hudson, 1994

18 GÄTJE, H., *The Qur'an and its Exegesis: Selected Texts with Classical and Modern Muslim Interpretations* (tr. and ed. A. T. Welch), London, Routledge/Berkeley, CA, University of California Press, 1976

19 GEERTZ, C., *Islam Observed: Religious Development in Morocco and Indonesia*, New Haven, CT, Yale University Press, 1968; author provides reflections on this classic in a series of Harvard University lectures later publ. as *After the Fact: Two Countries, Four Decades, One Anthropologist*, Cambridge, MA, Harvard University Press, 1995

20 GOITEIN, S. D., 'The Origin and Nature of the Muslim Friday Worship', *Muslim World*, 49, 1959, pp. 183–95

21 GOODWIN, G., *A History of Ottoman Architecture*, London, Thames & Hudson, 1971

22 GUILLAUME, A. (tr.), *The Life of Muhammad: A Translation of Ibn Ishāq's Sīrat Rasūl Allāh*, Karachi/London, Oxford University Press, 1955

23 HODGSON, M. G. S., *The Venture of Islam: Conscience and History in a World Civilization*, 3 vols, Chicago/London, University of Chicago Press, 1974

24 HUMPHREYS, R. S., *Islamic History: A Framework for Inquiry*, rev. edn, Princeton, Princeton University Press, 1991; first publ. 1988

25 IBN SA'D, M. *Ibn Sa'd's Kitab al-Tabaqat al-Kabir* (tr. S. M. Haq), 2 vols, Karachi, Pakistan Historical Society, 1967, 1972

26 JEFFERY, A. (tr. and ed.), *A Reader on Islam: Passages from Standard Arabic Writings Illustrative of the Beliefs and Practices of Muslims*, The Hague, Mouton, 1962; repr. New York, Arno, 1980 and Salem, NH, Ayer Company, 1987

27 KAMALI, M. H., *Principles of Islamic Jurisprudence*, rev. edn, Cambridge, Islamic Texts Society, 1991; prev. publ. in Selangor Darul Ehsan, Malaysia, Pelanduk Publications, 1989

28 KEDDIE, N. R., *Roots of Revolution: An Interpretative History of Modern Iran*, New Haven/London, Yale University Press, 1981; Persian trans. publ. Tehran, Qalam, 1990 or 1991 (1369 AH)

29 KEDDIE, N. R., and BARON, B. (eds), *Women in Middle Eastern History: Shifting Boundaries in Sex and Gender*, New Haven, Yale University Press, 1991

30 KURIAN, G. T., *Encyclopedia of the First World*, 2 vols, *Encyclopedia of the Second World*, 2 vols, *Encyclopedia of the Third World*, 4th edn, 3 vols, New York/Oxford, Facts on File, 1990, 1991, 1992

31 LINGS, M., *Muhammad: His Life Based on the Earliest Sources*, London, Allen & Unwin/New York, Inner Traditions International, 1983

32 MALIK IBN ANAS, *Al-Muwatta of Imam Malik ibn Anas: The First Formulation of Islamic Law* (tr. A. A. Bewley), London/New York, Kegan Paul International, 1989 (the translator, Aisha Abdurrahman Bewley, is also the author 'Abdul Rahman I. Doi, whose useful booklet,

Women in Shari'ah (Islamic Law), 2nd edn, was publ. London, Ta-Ha Publishers, 1989)

33 MAUDOODI (al-Mawdudi), A. A., *Towards Understanding Islam*, 3rd edn, London, Islamic Foundation/New York, The Message Publications, 1988; 5th impr., updated version, 1993

34 MERNISSI, F., *Beyond the Veil: Male–Female Dynamics in Modern Muslim Society*, rev. edn, Bloomington, University of Indiana Press, 1987; first publ. Cambridge, MA, Schenkman, 1975; later edns incl. Paris, Editions Tierce, 1983, and London, Al Saqi Books, 1985

35 MERNISSI, F., *Women and Islam: An Historical and Theological Inquiry* (tr. M. J. Lakeland), Oxford, Blackwell, 1991

36 MITCHELL, R. P., *The Society of the Muslim Brothers*, with Foreword by. J. O. Voll, New York/London, Oxford University Press, 1993; first publ. 1969

37 MUSLIM IBN HAJJAJ, A. H., *Sahīh Muslim* (tr. A. H. Siddiqi), 4 vols, Lahore, Muhammad Ashraf, 1973–5

38 NASIR, J. J., *The Status of Women under Islamic Law and under Modern Islamic Legislation*, 2nd edn, London/Boston, Graham & Trotman, 1994; 1st edn publ. with slightly different title ('in' twice instead of 'under' twice) in 1990

39 RAHMAN, F., *Islam*, 2nd edn, Chicago, University of Chicago Press, 1979 (only minor changes to 1st edn, 1966; virtually no references to literature or historical developments after early 1960s, hence not really an updated edn)

40 RIPPIN, A. (ed.), *Approaches to the History of the Interpretation of the Qur'ān*, Oxford, Clarendon Press/New York, Oxford University Press, 1988

41 RIPPIN, A., and KNAPPERT, J. (eds and trs), *Textual Sources for the Study of Islam*, Manchester, Manchester University Press, 1986

42 ROBSON, J. (tr.), *Mishkat al-Masabih: English Translation with Explanatory Notes*, 4 vols, Lahore, Muhammad Ashraf, 1965–6; prev. publ. 1960–5

43 SCHIMMEL, A., *And Muhammad Is His Messenger: The Veneration of the Prophet in Islamic Piety*, Chapel Hill, NC/London, University of North Carolina Press, 1985; rev. and expanded tr. of *Und Muhammad ist Sein Prophet*, Düsseldorf, Diederichs Verlag, 1981

44 SIDDIQI, M. I., *The Family Laws of Islam*, new edn, Delhi, International Islamic Publishers, 1988; 1st edn publ. Lahore, Kazi Publications, 1984

45 AL-ṬABARĪ, *The History of al-Tabarī*, ed. Ehsan Yar-Shater, 40 vols, Albany, NY, State University of New York Press, 1985– (in progress)

46 TABĀTABĀ'Ī, M. H., *Shi'ite Islam* (tr. S. H. Nasr), 2nd edn, Albany, NY, State University of New York Press, 1977; 1st edn of Eng. tr. publ. 1971

47 TRIMINGHAM, J. S., *A History of Islam in West Africa*, London/New York, Oxford University Press, 1962

48 TRIMINGHAM, J. S., *Islam in East Africa*, Oxford, Clarendon Press, 1964

49 WALTHER, W., *Women in Islam: From Medieval to Modern Times*, with intr. (pp. 3–11) by G. Nashat (tr. C. S. V. Salt), rev. edn, Princeton, Markus Wiener, 1993; first publ. in Eng. (without subtitle), London, George Prior, 1981; tr. of *Die Frau im Islam*, Stuttgart, Kohlhammer, 1980

50 WATT, W. M., *The Formative Period of Islamic Thought*, Edinburgh, Edinburgh University Press, 1973

51 WATT, W. M., *Islamic Philosophy and Theology*, rev. edn, Edinburgh, Edinburgh University Press, 1985; first publ. 1962

52 WATT, W. M., *Muhammad: Prophet and Statesman*, London, Oxford University Press, 1961, 1974

53 WEEKES, R. V. (ed.), *Muslim Peoples: A World Ethnographic Survey*, 2nd edn, Westport, CT, Greenwood, 1984; 1st edn 1978

54 WELCH, A. T., 'al-Ḳur'ān', *The Encyclopaedia of Islam*, new edn, vol. 5, fasc. 85–6, Leiden, Brill, 1981, pp. 400–29; French edn, Paris, vol. 5, pp. 401–31, 1981

55 WENSINCK, A. J., *The Muslim Creed: Its Genesis and Historical Development*, Cambridge, Cambridge University Press, 1932; repr. London, Cass, 1965, New Delhi, Oriental Books Reprint Corp., 1979

56 WILLIAMS, J. A. (tr. and ed.), *The Word of Islam*, Austin, TX, University of Texas Press, 1994

57 ZEBIRI, K., *Mahmūd Shaltūt and Islamic Modernism*, Oxford, Clarendon Press, 1993

58 ZIAD ABU-AMR, *Islamic Fundamentalism in the West Bank and Gaza*, Bloomington, Indiana University Press, 1994

An excellent source for concise articles on virtually all aspects of the modern Islamic world (movements, countries, rituals, biographies, etc.) is J. L. Esposito (ed.), *The Oxford Encyclopedia of the Modern Islamic World*, 4 vols, New York/Oxford, Oxford University Press, 1995. For longer and more technical articles, see C. E. Bosworth et al. (eds), *The Encyclopaedia of Islam*, new edn, 8 vols. to 1995 (up to 'Sam-'), Leiden, Brill, 1960–; for the remainder of the alphabet and other articles on Islamic religion and law reprinted from 1st edn, see H. A. R. Gibb and J. H. Kramers (eds), *Shorter Encyclopaedia of Islam*, Ithaca, NY, Cornell University Press, 1953. For articles in journals and anthologies see J. D. Pearson et al. (eds), *Index Islamicus 1906–1955*, thereafter five-year Supplements, Cambridge, W. Heffer & Sons, 1958, 1962, 1967, 1972, then London, Mansell, 1977, 1983; *The Quarterly Index Islamicus*, 17 vols to 1993, 1977–.

4

Zoroastrianism

MARY BOYCE

Introduction

Sources

Zoroastrianism has a long oral tradition. Its prophet Zarathushtra (known in the West as Zoroaster) lived before the Iranians knew of writing, and for many centuries his followers refused to use this alien art for sacred purposes. The Avesta, their collection of holy texts, was finally set down in a specially invented alphabet in the fourth/fifth centuries CE. Its language, known simply as Avestan, is otherwise unrecorded. The small corpus of 'Old Avestan' texts is attributed to the prophet himself, and consists of the seventeen *Gathas* (hymns), *Yasna Haptanhaiti* ('Worship of the Seven Chapters', a short liturgy accompanying the daily act of priestly worship), and two very holy *manthras*.[1] All 'Young Avestan' texts are the composite works of generations of anonymous priestly poets and scholars. The whole Avesta was written down in Iran, under the Sasanian dynasty, and was then a massive compilation in twenty-one books. Only a few copies were made, and in the destruction which later attended the Arab, Turkish and Mongol conquests of Iran all were destroyed. The surviving Avesta consists of liturgies, hymns and prayers. The manuscript tradition goes back to Sasanian times, but the oldest existing manuscript was written in 1323 CE. The Avesta has been printed [13], and translations exist in German, French, English, Gujarati and Persian.[2] None can be regarded as authoritative, since research is still constantly producing new insights.

Some Avestan manuscripts have a running translation in Pahlavi, known as the Zand or 'Interpretation'. Pahlavi, the language of Sasanian Iran, was written in a difficult script. There exist in Pahlavi translations and summaries of lost books of the Sasanian Avesta, and also a considerable secondary religious literature [5]. This too is mostly anonymous. Almost all Pahlavi works have been edited and translated, but some of the translations badly need revision.[3] The later religious literature is in Persian, Gujarati and English.

Short Introduction to the History of the Faith

The internal evidence of the Old Avestan texts shows that Zoroaster lived before the Iranians conquered the land now named after them, probably, that is, around 1200 BCE [8: 27–51]. The Iranians then, as settled pastoralists, inhabited the inner Asian steppes east of the Volga. The prophet succeeded in converting one of the tribal princes, Vishtaspa, and saw his faith take root. It spread among the eastern Iranians, and eventually reached western Iran, which had been settled by the Medes and Persians (see figure 4.1). It became the state religion of the first Persian empire (550–331 BCE), founded by Cyrus the Great, its western priests being the famed magi [3]. Its doctrines had great influence then on some of the Persians' subjects, notably the Jews. Direct evidence for Zoroastrian beliefs and practices at this time comes mainly from Persian monuments and inscriptions and from Greek writings. The conquest of the empire by Alexander seems to have done much harm to the oral tradition, with sacred texts being lost through the deaths of priests.

In due course the Parthians, a people of north-eastern Iran, founded another Iranian empire (c.129 BCE–224 CE), which again had Zoroastrianism for its state religion [9: 78–100]; and this was succeeded by the second Persian empire, that of the Sasanians. They created for the faith a strong ecclesiastical organization, with a numerous priesthood and many temples and colleges [9: 101–44]. With the Arab conquest in the seventh century Islam supplanted Zoroastrianism as the state religion of Iran, but it was some 300 years before the Semitic faith became dominant throughout the land.

According to tradition, it was towards the end of the seventh century that a group of Zoroastrians sailed east in search of religious freedom, settling eventually, in 716, at Sanjan in Gujarat. Others joined them there, forming the nucleus of the 'Parsi' (Persian) community of India. For generations the Parsis prospered only modestly, as farmers and petty traders, spreading northward along the coast as far as Broach and Cambay. But from the seventeenth century, with the coming of European merchants, they advanced rapidly, and by the nineteenth century individuals had amassed huge fortunes. By contrast, the mother-community in Iran (then concentrated around the desert cities of Yazd and Kerman) was enduring ever greater poverty and oppression. The Parsis played a notable part in the development of Bombay, and by the twentieth century had become a predominantly urban community, with a well-educated middle class. Partly through their help the Iranis were freed from persecution and were able to follow suit, with a thriving community developing in Tehran. With the end of British rule in India in 1947 a number of Parsis settled abroad, notably in cities in England, Canada, Australia and the United States, and increasingly, after the establishment of the Islamic Republic of Iran in 1979, Iranian Zoroastrians joined them. Although prosperous, the community is numerically very small (see figure 4.2).

Scholarly Studies of Zoroastrianism

The Zoroastrians, enclosed as tiny minorities within Muslim and Hindu societies, were unknown to Western scholars until the seventeenth century, when merchants and other travellers brought back accounts of them. In 1700 an English divine, Thomas Hyde, published a study in Latin of the religion, drawing on these accounts and on meagre literary sources. He respected Zoroaster as a great seer and tried to prove that he had been a strict monotheist, and that Greek evidence about his dualism was misleading. In the eighteenth century a French scholar, Anquetil du Perron, travelled to India and persuaded a Parsi priest to part with Avestan and Pahlavi manuscripts, and to teach him how to read them. His published translations startled Europeans, since they gave evidence not only of dualism, but of the worship of many divine beings through intricate rituals [9]. Most were unwilling to abandon Hyde's interpretation, and so they concluded that Zoroaster's followers must have distorted their prophet's teachings. This theory was strengthened when it was discovered through linguistic studies of the Avesta that the Parsi priests no longer fully understood their holy texts. This was especially true of the *Gathas*, which present enormous difficulties. In the mid-nineteenth century a German philologist, M. Haug, realized that these hymns were the actual words of Zoroaster. (It was more than another century before the *Yasna Haptanhaiti* was also recognized to be by him.) Because of their many obscurities it was possible at that stage to interpret the *Gathas* very freely, so owing to his preconceptions Haug translated them in a way that supported the idea of Zoroaster's strict monotheism and rejection of rites [15]. Thereafter the theory that all the remaining Avestan and Pahlavi texts represented a corruption of the prophet's teachings became for a long time the dominant academic dogma in the West.

In the twentieth century a Swedish scholar, H. S. Nyberg, influenced by ethnographic studies, suggested that Zoroaster had been a 'shaman', who composed his hymns in inspired trances [26]; and a

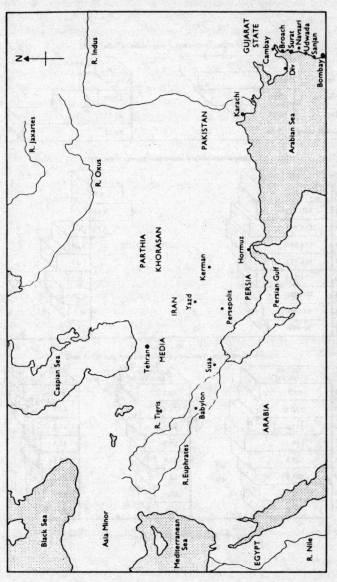

Figure 4.1 Zoroastrianism: some ancient and modern sites

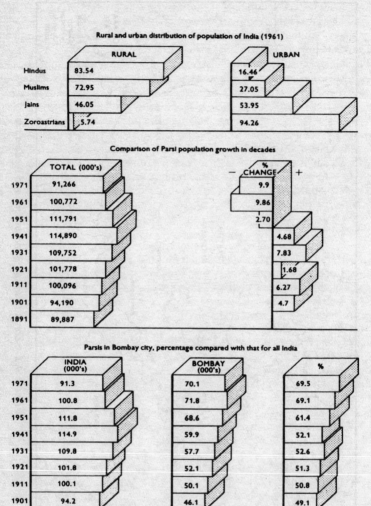

Rural and urban distribution of population of India (1961)

	RURAL	URBAN
Hindus	83.54	16.46
Muslims	72.95	27.05
Jains	46.05	53.95
Zoroastrians	5.74	94.26

Comparison of Parsi population growth in decades

	TOTAL (000's)	% CHANGE (− / +)
1971	91,266	9.9 −
1961	100,772	9.86 −
1951	111,791	2.70 −
1941	114,890	4.68 +
1931	109,752	7.83 +
1921	101,778	1.68 +
1911	100,096	6.27 +
1901	94,190	4.7 +
1891	89,887	

Parsis in Bombay city, percentage compared with that for all India

	INDIA (000's)	BOMBAY (000's)	%
1971	91.3	70.1	69.5
1961	100.8	71.8	69.1
1951	111.8	68.6	61.4
1941	114.9	59.9	52.1
1931	109.8	57.7	52.6
1921	101.8	52.1	51.3
1911	100.1	50.1	50.8
1901	94.2	46.1	49.1

Figure 4.2   *Some Parsi statistics*

Frenchman, G. Dumézil, sought to apply to Zoroastrianism his idea
that Indo-European peoples grouped their gods according to three
'functions', corresponding to the social roles of priest-king, warrior
and farmer. Much scholarly energy was spent on working out this
theory, without generally convincing results. (For an application of
his theories to Zoroastrianism see [12: 38ff.])

Meanwhile, some scholars who visited the Parsis were impressed
by their high ethical standards and philosophy of life, which seemed
to accord with Gathic teachings; and they began to question
whether there could really have been a serious break in the tradition. Then philologists discovered allusions to existing beliefs and
practices in the *Gathas* themselves, as their vocabulary and style
became better understood. The case was thus slowly built up for
regarding the Zoroastrians as having been, in fact, strikingly stead-
fast – as having maintained over three millennia an unbroken tradition, handed down by precept and practice as much as by holy
texts. Earlier interpretations of the history of the faith had prevailed
too long, however, to be easily discarded, and they still claim their
adherents.

Another problem dividing scholars was the date of Zoroaster.
Certain Pahlavi texts yield a date for him equivalent to 588 BCE, and
in the absence of any other firm tradition this was accepted by a
number of Western scholars, while as many others maintained that
it was far too late to be authentic. A convincing case has by now
been made for its being wholly artificial, evolved among the Greeks
in connection with the fiction that Pythagoras studied astronomy
with Zoroaster, and calculated evidently after the establishment of
the Seleucid era (312/311 BCE) [21]. It was then evidently adopted
by some Persian Zoroastrian scholastics.

Basic Doctrines

Inhabitants of vast empty steppes, the Iranian priests evolved a
severely simple creation myth [2: 130ff, 192ff; 9: 19ff]. They saw
the world as having been made by the gods, from formless matter,
in seven stages: first the 'sky' of stone, a firm enclosing shell; then
water, filling the bottom of this shell; then earth, lying on the water
like a great flat dish; then at its centre the original Plant, and then
by it the uniquely created Bull, and the First Man, Gayo-maretan
('Mortal life'); and finally the sun, representing the seventh creation, fire, which stood still above them. Fire was thought to be present too in the other creations, as a hidden life-force. Then the gods
made sacrifice. They plucked and pounded the Plant and scattered

its essence over the earth, and other plants grew from it. They slew the Bull and Gayo-maretan, and from their seed sprang other animal and human life. Then a line of mountains grew up along the rim of the earth, and at the centre rose the Peak of Hara, around which the sun began to circle, creating night and day. Rain fell, so heavily that the earth was broken into seven regions (*karshvars*). Humankind lives in the central region, cut off by seas and forests from the other six. One great sea, called Vourukasha ('Having many bays'), is fed by a huge river which pours down ceaselessly from the Peak of Hara (see figure 4.3). These final details the priestly thinkers evidently took from still more ancient myths, while the threefold sacrifice reflected the three offerings they themselves once made, of a pounded plant (*haoma*), cattle and human victims. Their belief, it seems, was that as long as men continued pious sacrifices and worshipped the gods the world would endure, governed by the principle of *asha*. This represents order in the cosmos and justice and truth among men. As well as venerating 'nature' gods, the Iranians worshipped three great ethical beings whom they called the

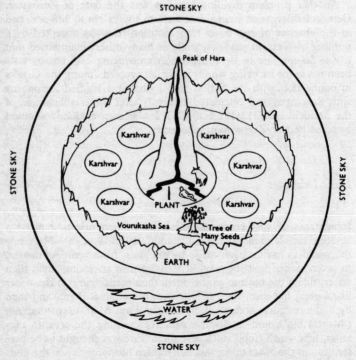

STONE SKY

Peak of Hara

Karshvar   Karshvar

Karshvar   Karshvar

STONE SKY   STONE SKY

Karshvar   Karshvar

PLANT

Vourukasha Sea   Tree of Many Seeds

EARTH

WATER

STONE SKY

Figure 4.3 *The Iranian world picture*

Ahuras ('Lords'): Ahura Mazda, Lord of Wisdom, and beneath him Mithra and Varuna, Lords of the covenant and oath which, duly kept, bound men together according to *asha*.

Zoroaster was himself a priest, born into this hereditary calling; but in his lifetime, it appears from the *Gathas*, the long-established pastoral society of the Iranians was being shattered. The Bronze Age was then well advanced among them, and warrior-princes and their followers, equipped with effective weapons and the war chariot, were indulging in continual warfare and raiding. The prophet's own people seem to have been victims of more advanced and predatory neighbours; and the violence and injustice which he thus saw led Zoroaster to meditate deeply on good and evil, and their origins. In due course he came to experience what he perceived as a series of divine revelations, which led him to preach a new faith. He taught that there was only one eternal God, whom he recognized as Ahura Mazda, a being wholly wise, good and just, but not all-powerful, for in his own words: 'Truly there are two primal Spirits, twins renowned to be in conflict. In thought and word, in act they are two: the good and the bad' (*Yasna* 30.3). God, that is, had an Adversary, Angra Mainyu (the Evil Spirit), likewise uncreated; and it was to overcome him and destroy evil that Ahura Mazda made this world, as a battleground where their forces could meet. He accomplished this through his Holy Spirit, Spenta Mainyu, and six other great beings whom he evoked, the greatest of the Amesha

Table 4.1 The six great Amesha Spentas and Spenta Mainyu: the great heptad

Avestan (Pahlavi)	Approximate English renderings	Creation
1 Khshathra Vairya (Shahrevar)	Desirable Dominion/ Power	Sky
2 Haurvatat (Hordad)	Wholeness/Health	Water
3 Spenta Armaiti (Spendarmad)	Holy Devotion/Piety	Earth
4 Ameretat (Amurdad)	Long Life/Immortality	Plants
5 Vohu Manah (Vahman)	Good Purpose/Intent	Cattle
6 Spenta Mainyu (Spenag Menog)	Holy Spirit	Man
7 Asha Vahishta (Ardvahisht)	Best Truth/ Righteousness, Order	Fire

Spentas, 'Holy Immortals'. Each of the seven protects and dwells within one of the seven creations; and each is at once an aspect of God, and, as his emanation, an independent divinity to be worshipped. Ahura Mazda is transcendent; but through the Holy Spirit he can be immanent in his especial creation, humanity. Table 4.1 gives the great heptad's names, in the order of their creations.

All those who seek to be *ashavan*, that is, to live according to *asha*, should try to bring the great Amesha Spentas into their own hearts and bodies, and should serve them by caring for their physical creations. With regard to the creation of humankind, this doctrine underlies a sustained and generous philanthropy. As for Khshathra's creation, this came to be regarded as including metals as well as the stony sky (no firm distinction being made between metals and stone among many ancient peoples), and so he could be honoured by caring for metal in all its forms (including eventually coins, to be put to good charitable uses).

The heptad evoked the other Holy Immortals, also, like them, called *yazatas*, beings 'worthy of worship'. Among them were many of the beneficent old gods, including the two lesser Ahuras. Angra Mainyu countered by bringing into being evil spirits, including the *daevas*, ancient amoral gods of war; and with them he attacked the good creations. By Zoroastrian doctrine it was he who destroyed the first Plant, Bull and Man, bringing death into the world, while the Amesha Spentas turned evil to good by creating more life from death. This is their function, to combat evil and strengthen good. Their creations strive instinctively to this same end, all except humans, who should do so by deliberate choice, in the light of Zoroaster's revelation. At death all individuals will be judged. If their good thoughts, words and deeds outweigh their bad, their souls cross a broad bridge and ascend to heaven. If not, the bridge contracts and they fall into hell, with its punishments.

The ultimate aim of all virtuous striving is to bring about the salvation of this world. According to Zoroaster's teachings, the combined efforts of all the righteous will gradually weaken evil and so bring about the triumph of the good, and this is the constant expectation of his followers. For various reasons, however [4: 382–7], another strand of belief developed, that the last days will be marked by increasing wretchedness and cosmic calamities. Then, it is generally believed, the World Saviour, the Saoshyant, will come in glory. He is to be born of the seed of the prophet, miraculously preserved within a lake, and a virgin mother. There will be a great battle between *yazatas* and *daevas*, good people and bad, ending in victory for the good. The bodies of those who have died earlier will be resurrected and united with their souls, and the Last Judgement will take place through a fiery ordeal: metals in the mountains will melt to form a burning torrent, which will destroy the wicked and purge

hell. (By a later softening of this doctrine, first attested in the ninth
century CE, the wicked, purified by the agony of this ordeal, will survive to joint the blessed.) The saved will be given ambrosia to eat,
and their bodies will become as immortal as their souls. The kingdom of Ahura Mazda will come on an earth made perfect again, and
the blessed will rejoice everlastingly in his presence.

Only one major Zoroastrian heresy is known: Zurvanism, which
probably arose in Babylon (then a Persian possession) in the fifth
century BCE [3: 231–42]. It was a monism, and its central doctrine
was that there was only one uncreated being, Zurvan ('Time'),
father of both Ahura Mazda and Angra Mainyu. This was grievous
heresy, since a common origin was thus postulated for good and
evil. But the Zurvanites held that Zurvan, a remote god, bestowed
his powers on his good son, who then created this world. Hence
Zurvanites and the orthodox were able to worship together in common veneration of the Creator, Ahura Mazda, despite this basic
doctrinal differnce.

Basic Observances

A Zoroastrian has the duty to pray five times daily (at sunrise, noon,
sunset, midnight and dawn) in the presence of fire, the symbol of
righteousness. He prays standing, and while uttering the appointed
prayers (which include verses from the *Gathas*) unties and reties the
kusti. This is the sacred cord, which should be worn constantly. It
goes three times round the waist and is knotted over the sacred shirt
(*sedra*). Before praying, the Zoroastrian performs ritual ablutions,
for the faith makes cleanliness a part of godliness, seeing all
uncleanness as evil. The Zoroastrian purity laws are comprehensive
but are now largely neglected by urban dwellers. Nevertheless even
they abhor pollution of earth or water, and maintain the strictest
cleanliness in their persons and homes. The conviction that unbelievers are necessarily unclean still operates among Parsis and prevents non-Zoroastrians entering fire-temples or being present at
Zoroastrian acts of worship.

The ancient veneration of fire among the Iranian peoples evidently centred on the ever-burning hearth fire. The temple cult of
fire was, it seems, instituted as late as the fourth century BCE [3:
221–5]. It, too, centres on an ever-burning wood fire, set either in
the top of an altar-like pillar or in a metal vessel. There are three
grades of sacred fire: the Atash Bahram ('Victorious fire'), which is
consecrated with many rites and kept blazing brightly; the Atash-i
Aduran ('Fire of fires'), more simply installed and allowed at times

to lie dormant beneath its hot ashes; and the Dadgah ('[Fire] in an appointed place'), which is virtually a hearth fire placed in a consecrated building. This may be tended, if necessary, by laypeople. There is no obligation on a Zoroastrian to visit a fire-temple, since he may pray before any 'clean' fire; but the sacred fires are much beloved, and in devout families children are taken to them from an early age. Some believers pray regularly at a temple (see figure 4.4), others attend only on special occasions. Some offering is always made, usually of wood or incense for the fire, with often a money gift for the priests.

Men and women have equal access to the temples, and boys and girls undergo the same initiation into the faith. This usually takes

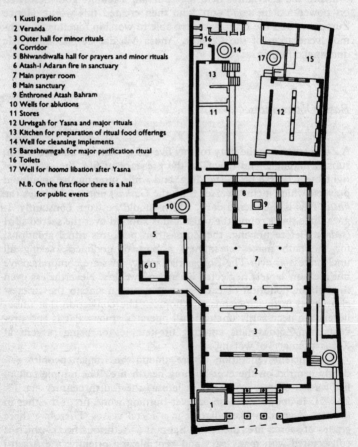

1 Kusti pavilion
2 Veranda
3 Outer hall for minor rituals
4 Corridor
5 Bhiwandiwalla hall for prayers and minor rituals
6 Atash-i Adaran fire in sanctuary
7 Main prayer room
8 Main sanctuary
9 Enthroned Atash Bahram
10 Wells for ablutions
11 Stores
12 Urvisgah for Yasna and major rituals
13 Kitchen for preparation of ritual food offerings
14 Well for cleansing implements
15 Bareshnumgah for major purification ritual
16 Toilets
17 Well for *hooma* libation after Yasna

N.B. On the first floor there is a hall
    for public events

Figure 4.4 *Ground plan of Anjuman Atash Bahram, Bombay*

place between the ages of seven and nine among Parsis, twelve and fifteen among Iranis. The occasion, called by Iranis *sedra-pushun* ('putting on the sacred shirt'), by Parsis *naojote* (probably 'being born anew'), is an important family event. The child has already learnt the *kusti* prayers. On the day he bathes, drinks a consecrated liquid for inward cleansing and puts on the sacred shirt. The priest then performs the simple ceremony of investing him with the *kusti*, after which relatives dress him in new clothes and give him presents amid general rejoicing. This ceremony takes place at home or in some public hall or gardens, as do weddings. Again, before marriage bride and groom undergo a ritual purification and put on new garments. Iranis and Parsis share a common ceremony of marriage, in which Avestan and Pahlavi words are spoken by the officiating priest in the presence of assenting witnesses from the two families. Both communities have in addition a wealth of popular customs, and the festivities last several days.

A birth is also naturally rejoiced at, but there is then concern for purity, and in a few strictly orthodox families the mother is still segregated for forty days. Formerly the infant was given a few drops of consecrated *haoma*-juice soon after birth; but its naming is a simple matter of declaration by parent or priest.

Ceremonies at death are far more important and have a double aim: to isolate the impurity of the dead body and give help to the soul. The body is given into the charge of professionals, who live to some extent segregated lives, as unclean persons. Wrapped in a cotton shroud it is carried on an iron bier, after due prayers by priests, to a stone tower (*dakhma*), where the polluting flesh is quickly devoured by vultures and the bones are bleached by sun and wind. Mourners follow the bier at a distance, two by two, and afterwards make ablutions. Some families now prefer cremation (by electrical means), or burial, with the coffin set in cement to protect the good earth. The funeral should take place within twenty-four hours of death; but the soul is held to linger on earth for three days, during which time priests say prayers and perform ceremonies to help it. Before dawn on the fourth day family and friends gather to bid it farewell. They pray and undertake meritorious acts for its sake, for example say extra prayers or give gifts to charity. Religious ceremonies are performed for the departed soul monthly during the first year, and then annually for thirty years. After that it is held to have joined the great company of all souls, and is remembered by name at the annual feast in their honour, called by Parsis Muktad, by Iranis Farvardigan or Panje. Some of these ceremonies for the dead go back to before Zoroaster's day, and are only uneasily reconciled with his teaching of each person's own accountability at Judgement Day. Muktad is observed on the last five days of the year. In Irani villages the festival is still celebrated in the home, with the family priest going from house to house to bless the offerings. In urban communities the offerings are usually sent to the fire-temple, where the people gather. Zoroastrianism has 'outer' ceremonies, which may be performed in any clean place, and 'inner' ones, which may be solemnized only in a ritual precinct (usually attached to the fire-temple). To be able to perform the 'inner' ceremonies priests undergo an ancient purification rite (the *barashnom*), followed by a nine days' retreat. Until recently some Irani villagers also tried to undergo this great cleansing at least once in their lives, and this used at one time to be the general practice.

Zoroastrianism has many holy days, joyfully celebrated. There are seven obligatory ones, traditionally founded by Zoroaster himself, in honour of Ahura Mazda and the creations. These are now known as the six *gahambars* and No Ruz ('New Day'), which, celebrating the seventh creation, fire, looks forward to the final triumph of good. It is the greatest festival of the year, with communal and family celebrations, religious services, feasting and present-giving. The *gahambars* are now fully kept only in Irani villages, with everyone joining in five-day festivals. Among holy days which it is meritorious to keep are those of the Waters (Aban Jashan) and Fire (Adar Jashan), when many people go to pray at river-banks or the sea-shore, or at fire-temples. Through a series of calendar reforms, not universally observed, there are currently three calendars of holy days (see appendix A). In Iran an ancient tradition is maintained of seasonal pilgrimages to sacred places in the mountains, where large gatherings take place for worship and festivities. In India pilgrimages are regularly made to the oldest Parsi sacred fire at Udwada, a village on the coast.

Priests and laity remain two distinct groups, though they intermarry. Priests wear white, the colour of purity, and some Parsi laymen also do so on religious occasions. Parsi women wear the sari. In Iran, Zoroastrian village women keep a distinctive traditional dress, but in towns all Zoroastrians have now adopted standard clothing. Zoroastrian women have never worn the veil. In dietary matters their religion gives Zoroastrians great freedom, in that they are required only to refrain from anything that might belong to the evil counter-creation (e.g. a hideous fish). Under Muslim and Hindu pressures many now refrain, however, from pork and beef, and some Parsis are vegetarians by choice.

Popular Customs

Underlying some popular customs is the belief that light is good, darkness evil. A blessing is generally murmured when a light is lit.

In traditional homes the housewife would sprinkle incense on a pan of embers and carry this through all the rooms at dawn and before sunset, in purification. No cock is killed after it has begun to crow, since it is then a holy creature, announcing daybreak. Water is not drawn in villages after dark, nor money exchanged.

Other popular customs arise from respect for the creations and their immanent divinities. A flame is not blown out, but allowed to die. Care is taken not to spill anything on a fire, and if this happens, a penance is performed. Offerings are regularly made and prayers said at sources of pure water (there is one very holy well in Bombay), and in Iran noble trees are venerated. It is held a sin to cut a sapling or kill a young animal (since neither has yet fulfilled its part in the scheme of things). Animals are treated well, especially dogs. By custom, still locally observed, bread is given regularly to a dog before the family eats; and in Vahman month Hindus drive cows into Parsi quarters and the Parsis acquire merit by feeding them.

The devout feel the presence of the *yazatas* everywhere. In Iran at *sedra-pushun* a child takes one of them as its especial guardian, and individual Parsis do the same, praying often to him and lighting lamps at the fire-temple on his feast day. The Iranis have many small shrines dedicated to individual *yazatas*, and on great holy days will visit all the local ones, kindling fire and lamps, and offering incense and prayers. They also regularly dance and sing at the shrines, believing that gladness pleases the divine beings. There are special rites to heal the sick, to restore lost purity, or to help a woman conceive a child. When performed by priests these always include Avestan prayers, in the presence of fire; but village women sometimes perform their own rites, verging on magic, without these elements. Such practices are strongly discouraged by the community elders.

Modern Developments

From about the ninth century Zoroastrians were cut off from contact with general advances in learning, and could do no more than practise and preserve their own faith. Increasing wealth among the Parsis did not bring any real change in this position until the early nineteenth century, when the laity were able to send their sons to Western-type schools in Bombay [17]. A Parsi priest then set up the first printing-press in that city, and Parsi newspapers were published. Soon afterwards a Scottish missionary, J. Wilson, made a determined effort to convert the Bombay Parsis, whom he admired, to

Christianity. He had studied Avestan and Pahlavi texts in translation, and now made use of the new newspapers for scornful attacks on their contents, especially their dualism. The Parsi laity had had no knowledge of these ancient texts, for they themselves used their Avestan prayers as holy *manthras*, potent but not literally understood. So, much startled, they turned to their priests to rebut Wilson's criticisms. But the priests, who were still trained in wholly traditional fashion, were ill-equipped to meet his challenge. One high priest simply published a restatement of orthodox beliefs, without making any attempt to reinterpret the ancient myths which they incorporated, and which Wilson had mocked; and the laity felt accordingly that he had failed them. Two other priests took refuge in occultism, interpreting the Avesta allegorically in the light of Sufi and Hindu concepts. Its 'inner' teachings, they declared, concerned a remote, almighty God, while 'Ohrmazd and Ahriman' were no more than allegories for man's own better and worse selves. The *yazatas* they held to be a series of intermediate intelligences; and they found that Zoroaster had implied the doctrine of reincarnation, with salvation to be achieved by self-denial and fasting. Although all this was in fact alien to Zoroastrianism, a number of Parsis accepted it as offering an escape from the perplexities suddenly thrust upon them.

Others tried to modernize their faith more rationally; and in 1851 the Zoroastrian Reform Society was founded, 'to break through the thousand and one religious prejudices that tend to retard the progress . . . of the community'. Some of its members adopted the extreme Western theory (publicized by Wilson) that Zoroaster had preached a simple monotheism, rejecting virtually all rituals; and their position was strengthened when Haug, lecturing in Bombay in the 1860s, expounded his own interpretation of the *Gathas*. Those who held to traditional observances received their share of Western support later, when Theosophy, with its occultism and regard for the esoteric value of rituals, was brought to Bombay from the US in 1885. A number of Parsis joined the Theosophical Society, and came into danger of adulterating their own beliefs and practices with alien (largely Hindu) ones. For this they were censured by adherents of Ilm-i Khshnoom ('Science of (Spiritual) Satisfaction'). This is an exclusively Zoroastrian occultist movement which was founded in 1902 by an uneducated Parsi, Behramshah Shroff. He interpreted the Avesta in the light of his own visions and again taught of one impersonal God, and of planes of being and reincarnation, with much planetary lore intermixed. He showed a total disregard for textual or historical accuracy, but stressed the importance of exactly performed rituals and adherence to the purity laws. There are some Ilm-i Khshnoom fire-temples, but the movement, though it has grown, is now subdivided into contending factions.

Reformists had earlier published, in Gujarati script, cheap printed copies of the Khorda (Little) Avesta, the Zoroastrian prayer-book, so that every Parsi now had direct access to the sacred texts. This further diminished the role of the priests, who had fallen rapidly from being respected for their learning to being despised as ignorant, not only of the new secular knowledge but also of the true meaning of the holy books. The need for better understanding of the latter led a layman, K. R. Cama, to introduce their study on Western philological principles. His pupils, all young priests, worked admirably at editing and translating Pahlavi and Avestan texts, but attempted no fundamental theological studies. The Parsis, who lack any one recognized ecclesiastical authority, remained perplexed and divided into contending religious groups. The old dualistic orthodoxy persisted mostly in the small towns and villages of Gujarat, but in Bombay it was largely overlaid by declared monotheisms of either the Western or the occultist type. In the 1970s, however, a new Western respect for Zoroastrian dualism began to exert an influence, and yet another movement was launched among the laity to revive more traditional beliefs, and to reconcile ancient myths with current scientific knowledge.

From the late nineteenth century the Parsi reform movement influenced the urban community in Iran, but an unquestioning orthodoxy survived in country regions there until well into the second half of the twentieth century. In cities outside Iran and India Parsis and Iranis mingle and every shade of religious opinion is represented, together with widespread secularism. Survival of the faith is often seen as part of the preservation of communal identity, and both for this and for truly devout reasons vigorous efforts are often made locally to maintain the religious life. Special efforts are now made to publish attractive books of instruction for children, and to ensure that they are initiated into the faith. Whether those with a non-Zoroastrian mother or father may properly be admitted, or converts made, are controversial matters, discussed all the more urgently because of the community's dwindling numbers, due both to a falling birth-rate and to absorption into surrounding societies.

Despite doctrinal confusions, the traditional moral theology can be seen still shaping the lives of Zoroastrians. Their prophet taught the need for each of his followers to be constantly active in furthering the good creation; and from the time the Zoroastrians first re-emerged into general history individuals can be seen exerting themselves to benefit others, through charitable gifts, public works, medical care and the like. Latterly they have entered local and national politics, caring thus not only for their own communities but for society at large. As three Parsis have sat in the British House of Commons [16: 69ff], and others have been active in Indian politics, so an Iranian Zoroastrian was a founding member of the first Iranian parliament, established in 1906. The strikingly parallel achievements of the two Zoroastrian communities, separated since the ninth century, and both for a long time impoverished and oppressed, appear to result from the two factors which they have in common: valiant ancestors, prepared to sacrifice almost everything for their faith; and that faith itself, demanding of them courage and integrity, love of God and their fellow creatures, and an undaunted active opposition to evil in every form.

The Modern Zoroastrian Diaspora

The dynamic role of Paris traders in British India resulted in the establishment of numerous Zoroastrian centres around the world. The first Parsi known to travel overseas for trade was Naoroji Rustomji, who went to Britain in 1723 to press his family case against the injustice of British officials of the East India Company. He was vindicated and returned to India a richer and renowned man who went on to become one of his Bombay community's leaders. From the middle of the eighteenth century Parsis were prominent in the China trade, and established formal associations in Canton, Shanghai and Hong Kong. After the 1947 Communist revolution all the communities regrouped in Hong Kong, where, at the close of the millennium, with the return of Hong Kong to China, there is a small Parsi community (approximately 150). It is a closely knit group with little cultural contact with the outside world, except back home to the old country, India, where its members have undertaken some significant charitable work. As a result of their relative cultural isolation they have generally preserved a traditional nineteenth-century code of practice and belief, relatively free from Western intellectual or religious influences.

Formal Parsi communities were established in East Africa from the 1870s, specifically in Zanzibar, Mombasa and Nairobi. They too remained culturally distanced from other communities and were thus free from modernizing Western influences, more so than the communities in India. After the Second World War all Asian communities in East Africa flourished in trade and the professions and their numbers consequently grew rapidly, including those of Parsis. By the 1960s Asians were so dominant that African jealousies were aroused and policies of Africanization followed, putting pressure on most Asians, including Parsis, to leave. A very small number went to India and a few travelled to Canada, but most moved to Britain, where their traditional staunch piety had quite an influence on the Zoroastrians already settled there.

From the mid-nineteenth century Parsis had moved from Bombay and Gujarat to Sind as middlemen in trade and as brokers and agents of the British forces [22]. They became wealthy and in the twentieth century were influential in local politics and noted for their considerable cosmopolitan charities, especially in the fields of education and medicine. As partition approached, and the Islamic nation of Pakistan emerged, some Parsis feared for their future, recalling their experiences in Iran. But others were close to the Independence leaders. Jinnah, the founder of Pakistan, for example, had a Parsi mentor (Sir Pherozeshah Mehta), and a Parsi wife, and it was a Parsi doctor who cared for him in his struggle with terminal cancer during the negotiations for partition. Since 1947 several Parsis have been influential in Pakistani politics and in the diplomatic and legal professions, as well as in business. But as a more fundamentalist, or extremist, form of Islam has become vocal, a number of Parsis have migrated, fearing for their future in the old country and seeking opportunities in the West. Because of the high profile of religion in Pakistan, the level of religious knowledge, practice and commitment typical of the communities there, mainly in Karachi, has been carried westwards with migrants from that city.

The Zoroastrian community in Britain is concentrated mainly in London, which houses the largest Zoroastrian population of any city in the Western world [18]. The community was formally founded in 1861 and consisted not only of travelling businessmen but also of students, mostly of law and medicine. In 1892 and 1895 two Parsis (Dadabhai Naoroji and Sir Muncherji Bhownagree) were elected Members of Parliament at Westminster, the first Asians to hold this position. A third, Shapurji Saklatvala, was elected an MP in 1920. The majority of British Zoroastrians have their ancestry in India, though there is a substantial proportion from Pakistan. Most of them arrived in Britain in the 1960s, and later in that decade were joined by the migrants from East Africa; but approximately one-third have been born in Britain. In 1979, following the fall of the Shah and the establishment of the Islamic Republic in Iran, they were joined by a number of Zoroastrians from Iran. The British community is, therefore, a microcosm of the macrocosm of the Zoroastrian world, and subject to a whole range of internal religious pressures, with traditional, reformist, Iranian and Indian groups. Whereas outsiders and scholars in the 1960s prophesied that Asian migrants to the West would inevitably assimilate, the British Zoroastrians now have a more vigorous programme of religious ceremonies, classes and social functions than they did in the earlier years. Religion appears to be of growing importance as a marker of the community and of individual identity, despite the problems of preserving the ancient faith in the modern West when their numbers are so small – 5,000 at most.

Zoroastrian individuals settled in North America at the start of the twentieth century, but it was not until the 1960s that they came in any numbers, first from India and Pakistan, and then around 1979 from Iran [30]. The earliest associations were in Vancouver and Toronto in Canada, and Chicago and New York in the US, all in the mid-1960s. Numbers have grown steadily into the 1990s, when there were approximately 6,000 on the continent with the largest concentrations in California and British Columbia. In both of these centres there is a roughly equal mixture of Parsis and Iranian Zoroastrians. The other smaller settlements (each below 1,000), mainly Parsi-dominated, are in Washington and Houston, Texas, as well as in the older centres already mentioned. Typically the Zoroastrians in the US are highly educated scientists; in Canada almost as highly educated but more in the professions. In both countries they have developed effective infrastructures for religious education, youth groups and camps, and have established religious buildings in several cities. Over twenty formal Zoroastrian bodies in Canada and the US have grouped themselves under an umbrella body, the Federation of Zoroastrian Associations of North America (FEZANA), which seeks to harness the resources of the scattered groups. They are a particularly active and dynamic section of the Zoroastrian world, and may have a role in shaping the future of the religion and its teaching, although there are some tensions with traditional religious authorities in India (less so with those in Iran).

The latest destination for Parsi migration is Australia, mainly Sydney, where a purpose-built centre was opened in the 1990s, and Melbourne. Although some individuals are going in search of education, most are migrating for career opportunities. Since most Australian Zoroastrians have only recently settled there, their ties with India and Pakistan (there are relatively few Iranian Zoroastrians) are close, and some traditional voices remain influential.

Several consequences for the history of the religion arise from this dispersion. The first is the draining away from India and Iran of some outstanding talents and dynamic potential leaders, making the problem of declining numbers there even more serious. The numbers and natures of the diaspora Zoroastrians mean that important developments for the future of the religion will take place outside the old countries. As religions move from one culture to another it is natural that they should change to some extent. Christianity in Africa has altered from its European forms; and if Zoroastrianism is to be meaningful for the second and third generations of American or British or Australian believers, so its teachings and practices too may need to be adapted. Yet such adaptations are inevitably going to cause tensions with religious leaders in India. How far can a religion change yet retain its identity? These broad issues will be discussed in chapter 25 below.

The position is somewhat different for Iranian Zoroastrians. For them there is still no doubt that Iran remains their true home, even though those in the diaspora are currently reluctant to return permanently. As the third millennium approaches, more are going back for visits, so that the ties are far from broken; indeed, Iranian Zoroastrians are stronger in the retention of many of their identity markers (especially language, music and food) than the Parsis. The Iranian Zoroastrians are more concentrated in the diaspora, mainly in California and British Columbia. Many of those who remain in Iran feel vulnerable and suffer discrimination in education and careers as well as socially. But official government figures there claim that the community's numbers are growing and those whose forebears have withstood oppression for over a millennium are likely themselves to face the future with determination to preserve the ancient religion of their prophet.

Notes

1 That *Yasna Haptanhaiti* is to be attributed to Zoroaster was established only late in the twentieth century. See Narten [25], and further Boyce [8: 62–100].
2 Darmesteter and Mills [10] is still the only complete English translation, but is badly in need of revision. For the *Gathas* it is best to look at more than one translation, e.g. Moulton [24], Duchesne-Guillemin [11], Insler [20] and Humbach [19].
3 This includes the pioneer translations of West [28], which are still valuable for their introductions and notes.

Appendix A: The Seven Holy Days of Obligation

Gahambar is the Middle Persian term for six of the seven obligatory Zoroastrian festivals, neglect of which was formerly held to be a sin. The *gahambars* appear to have been ancient seasonal festivals, refounded (tradition says by Zarathushtra himself) to honour Ahura Mazda and the six great Amesha Spentas, together with the seven creations. Each festival probably lasted originally one day, but after a calendar reform, it seems in the later Achaemenian period, they were extended to six days, later reduced to five. The seventh festival is called in Middle Persian No Roz ('New Day'), and celebrates the beginning of the year. The dates of the celebration of the festivals according to the three existing Zoroastrian calendars are shown in the table below.

The seven holy days of obligation

Festival/Ancient name		Dates celebrated	
		In 1980–3	In 1984–7
1 Midspring/Maidhyoizaremaya	S	5–9 October	4–8 October
Associated 'Holy Immortal':	K	5–9 September	4–8 September
Dominion	F	30 April	30 April
Associated creation: Sky		to 4 May	to 4 May
2 Midsummer/Maidhyoishema	S	4–8 December	3–7 December
Associated 'Holy Immortal':	K	4–8 November	3–7 November
Wholeness	F	29 June	29 June
Associated creation: Water		to 3 July	to 3 July
3 Bringing in corn/Paitishahya	S	18–22 February	17–21 February
Associated 'Holy Immortal':	K	19–23 January	18–22 January
Devotion	F	12–16 September	12–16
Associated creation: Earth			September
4 Homecoming (of the herds)/	S	19–22 March	18–21 March
Ayathrima	K	19–22 February	17–21 February
Associated 'Holy Immortal':	F	12–16 October	12–16 October
Immortality			
Associated creation: Plants			
5 Midwinter/Maidhyairya	S	7–11 June	6–10 June
Associated 'Holy Immortal':	K	8–12 May	7–11 May
Good Intent	F	31 December	31 December
Associated creation: Cattle		to 4 January	to 4 January
6 All Souls (Parsi Muktad,	S	21–25 August	20–24 August
Irani Farvardigan)/	K	22–26 July	21–25 July
Hamaspathmaedaya	F	16–20 March	16–20 March
Associated 'Holy Immortal':			
Holy Spirit/Ahura Mazda			
Associated creation: Man			
7 New Day/No Ruz	S	26 August	25 August
Associated 'Holy Immortal':	K	27 July	26 July
Righteousness	F	21 March	21 March
Associated creation: Fire			
'Old' No Ruz (Hordad Sal,	S	31 August	30 August
celebrated on day Hordad,	K	1 August	31 July
see Appendix B)	F	26 March	26 March

Appendix B: The Zoroastrian Calendar

From ancient times the Iranians had a year of twelve months with
thirty days each. The Zoroastrian calendar, created in pre-
Achaemenian times, was distinctive simply through the pious dedication of each day and month to a divine being. During the
Achaemenian period five days were added after the last month, to
make a 365-day calendar; and three extra days were devoted to
'Ahura Mazda the Creator (Dadvah)', making four in all dedicated
to the Deity. This was probably as an esoteric acknowledgement
of Zurvan, who was worshipped as a quaternity. In later usage
the first of these days is named 'Ohrmazd', the other three 'Dai'
(for Dadvah); the three 'Dai' days are distinguished by adding
to each the name of the following day, e.g. 'Dai-pa-Adar',
'Dai-by (the day)-Adar'. The names are given here in their Persian
forms.

The thirty days

1	Ohrmazd	16	Mihr
2	Bahman	17	Srosh
3	Ardibehisht	18	Rashn
4	Shahrevar	19	Farvardin
5	Spendarmad	20	Bahram
6	Khordad	21	Ram
7	Amurdad	22	Bad
8	Dai-pa-Adar	23	Dai-pa-Din
9	Adar	24	Din
10	Aban	25	Ard
11	Khorshed	26	Ashtad
12	Mah	27	Asman
13	Tir	28	Zamyad
14	Gosh	29	Mahraspand
15	Dai-pa-Mihr	30	Aneran

The twelve months

1	Farvardin (March/April)	7	Mihr (September/October)
2	Ardibehisht (April/May)	8	Aban (October/November)
3	Khordad (May/June)	9	Adar (November/December)
4	Tir (June/July)	10	Dai (December/January)
5	Amurdad (July/August)	11	Bahman (January/February)
6	Shahrevar (August/September)	12	Spendarmad (February/March)

Every coincidence of a month and day name was celebrated as a name-day feast. There was thus one such feast in every month but the tenth, when four feasts were celebrated in honour of the Creator, Ohrmazd. The chief name-day feasts still celebrated by the Parsis are Aban and Adar. The Iranis also celebrate the festivals of Spendarmad, Tir and Mihr with special observances.

The five 'extra' days

Among the Persions the five extra days at the year's end were named after the five groups of Zoroaster's hymns. (All but the first of these are known by the opening word of the first hymn in the group. *Gatha Ahunavaiti* is called after the 'Yatha ahu vairyo' *manthra*, also composed by Zoroaster, which precedes it in the liturgy.)

1 Ahunavad
2 Ushtavad
3 Spentomad
4 Vohukhshathra
5 Vahishtoisht

The *gahambar* of Hamaspathmaedaya is celebrated throughout these five days.

Various later calendar reforms were directed at trying to stabilize the 365-day calendar in relation to the seasons. (The ancient 360-day calendar had been adjusted from time to time by the intercalation of a whole extra month.) It is these attempts which have led to the existence of three Zoroastrian calendars today.

Bibliography

1 ANQUETIL DU PERRON, A. H., *Zend-Avesta, Ouvrage de Zoroastre*, 2 vols in 3, Paris, Tilliard, 1771
2 BOYCE, M., *A History of Zoroastrianism*, vol. 1, *The Early Period*, Leiden, Brill, 1975 (Handbuch der Orientalistik, ed. B. Spuler, I. viii. 1.2); repr. with corrs 1989, 1996
3 BOYCE, M., *A History of Zoroastrianism*, vol. 2, *Under the Achaemenians*, Leiden, Brill, 1982 (Handbuch der Orientalistik, ed. B. Spuler, I. viii. 1.2)
4 BOYCE, M., with GRENET, F., *A History of Zoroastrianism*, vol. 3, *Under Macedonian and Roman Rule*, Leiden, Brill, 1991 (Handbuch der Orientalistik, ed. B. Spuler, I. viii. 1.2)

5 BOYCE, M., 'Middle Persian Literature', in *Iranistik*, Leiden, Brill, 1968, pp. 31–66 (Handbuch der Orientalistik, ed. B. Spuler, I.iv.2.1)

6 BOYCE, M., *A Persian Stronghold of Zoroastrianism*, Oxford, Clarendon Press, 1977; repr. Lanham, University Press of America, 1989

7 BOYCE, M., *Textual Sources for the Study of Zoroastrianism*, Manchester, Manchester University Press, 1984; pb Chicago University Press, 1990

8 BOYCE, M., *Zoroastrianism: Its Antiquity and Constant Vigour*, Columbia Iranian Lectures 7, Costa Mesa, Mazda Publishers, 1992

9 BOYCE, M., *Zoroastrians: Their Religious Beliefs and Practices*, London/Boston, Routledge, 1979; pb 1984

10 DARMESTETER, J., and MILLS, L. H., *The Zend-Avesta*, Oxford, Clarendon Press, 1883–95 (Sacred Books of the East, vols 4, 23, 31); prev. publ. 1880–7; repr. Delhi, Motilal Banarsidass, 1965; New York, Krishna, 1974

11 DUCHESNE-GUILLEMIN, J., *The Hymns of Zarathustra* (tr. M. Henning), London, John Murray, 1952 (Wisdom of the East)

12 DUCHESNE-GUILLEMIN, J., *The Western Response to Zoroaster*, Oxford, Clarendon Press, 1958

13 GELDNER, K., *Avesta: The Sacred Books of the Parsis*, 3 vols, Stuttgart, Kohlhammer, 1896 (text with introduction)

14 GNOLI, G., *Zoroaster's Time and Homeland*, Naples, Istituto Universitario Orientale, Seminario di Studi Asiatici, Series Minor, VII, 1980

15 HAUG, M., *Essays on the Sacred Language: Writings and Religion of the Parsis*, Bombay, 1862; 3rd edn, London, Trübner, 1884; 4th edn 1907; repr. Amsterdam, Philo Press, 1971

16 HINNELLS, J. R., 'Parsis in Britain', *Journal of the K. R. Cama Oriental Institute* (Bombay), vol. 46, 1978, pp. 65–84

17 HINNELLS, J. R., 'Parsis and British Education, 1820–1880', *Journal of the K. R. Cama Oriental Institute* (Bombay), vol. 46, 1978, pp. 42–59

18 HINNELLS, J. R., *Zoroastrians in Britain*, Oxford, Clarendon Press, 1996

19 HUMBACH, H., *The Gāthās of Zarathushtra*, 2 vols, Heidelberg, Carl Winter, 1991

20 INSLER, S., *The Gāthās of Zarathustra*, Leiden, Brill, 1975 (Acta Iranica, 8)

21 KINGSLEY, P., 'The Greek Origin of the Sixth-century Dating of Zoroaster', *Bulletin of the School of Oriental and African Studies*, vol. 53, 1990, pp. 245–65

22 KULKE, E., *The Parsees in India*, Munich, Weltforum Verlag, 1974

23 MODI, J. J., *The Religious Ceremonies and Customs of the Parsees*, 2nd edn, Bombay, J. B. Karani's Sons, 1937, repr. Bombay, 1986; 1st edn Bombay, British India Press, 1922, repr. New York, Garland, 1980

24 MOULTON, J. H., *Early Zoroastrianism*, London, Williams & Norgate, 1913; repr. Amsterdam, Philo Press, 1972; New York, AMS, 1980

25 NARTEN, J., *Der Yasna Haptanhāiti*, Wiesbaden, Reichert, 1986

26 NYBERG, H. S., *Die Religionen des Alten Iran* (tr. into German by H. H. Schaeder), Leipzig, Hinrichs, 1938; repr. Osnabrück, Zeller, 1966

27 SEERVAI, K. N., and PATEL, B. B., 'Gujarāt Pārsīs', *Gazetteer of the Bombay Presidency*, vol. 9, no. 2, Bombay, Government Central Press, 1899

28 WEST, E. W., *Pahlavi Texts*, Oxford, Clarendon Press, 1882–1901, first publ. 1880–97 (Sacred Books of the East, vols 5, 18, 37, 47); repr. Delhi, Motilal Banarsidass, 1965; New York, Krishna, 1974

29 WILSON, J., *The Pārsī Religion: As Contained in the Zand-Avasta and Propounded and Defended by the Zoroastrians of India and Persia*, Bombay, American Mission Press, 1843
30 WRITER, R., *Contemporary Zoroastrians: An Unstructured Nation*, Lanham, University Press of America, 1994

5

Hinduism

SIMON WEIGHTMAN

Introduction

What is Hinduism?

The word Hinduism is used to refer to the complex religious tradition which has evolved organically in the Indian subcontinent over
several thousand years and is today represented by the highly
diverse beliefs and practices of more than 650 million Hindus.
Apart from communities in neighbouring states, and those communities in such places as Bali, South-West Africa and the Caribbean
that have been created by migration (together forming less than 10
per cent of the totality), the majority of Hindus live in India, where
they constitute over four-fifths of the entire population. Hinduism is
so diverse internally that the only way of defining it acceptably is
externally, in terms of people and places; the term 'Hindu' is, in origin, simply the Persian word for Indian. The land of India is crucial
to Hinduism; its sacred geography is honoured by pilgrimages and
other ritual acts and has become deeply embedded in Hindu
mythology and scriptures.

There are two principal reasons why it is preferable to regard
Hinduism as an evolving religious tradition rather than as a single,
separate 'religion' in the sense that the term is usually understood.
The first reason is that Hinduism displays few of the characteristics
that are generally expected of a religion. It has no founder, nor is it
prophetic. It is not creedal, nor is any particular doctrine, dogma or
practice held to be essential to it. It is not a system of theology, nor
a single moral code, and the concept of god is not central to it.
There is no specific scripture or work regarded as being uniquely
authoritative. Finally, it is not sustained by an ecclesiastical organization. Thus it is difficult to categorize Hinduism as a 'religion'
using normally accepted criteria.

The second reason for this preference is the extraordinary diversity of Hinduism, both historically and in the contemporary situation. Such diversity is scarcely surprising when it is remembered that Hinduism refers to the mainstream of religious development of a huge subcontinent over a period of several thousand years, during which time it has been subject to numerous incursions from alien races and cultures. The subcontinent is not only vast, but is also marked by considerable regional variation. Regions differ from one another geographically, in terms of terrain, climate, natural resources, communications etc., and also ethnographically, in terms of the many and varied ethnic, cultural and linguistic groupings that inhabit them. Diversity is, therefore, to be expected in almost every domain.

Hinduism evolved organically, with new initiatives and developments taking place within the tradition, as well as by interaction with and adjustment to other traditions and cults which were then assimilated into the Hindu fold. These two processes of evolution and assimilation have produced an enormous variety of religious systems, beliefs and practices. At one end of the scale are innumerable small, unsophisticated local cults known only to perhaps two or three villages. At the other end of the scale are major religious movements with millions of adherents across the entire subcontinent. Such movements have their own theologies, mythologies and codes of ritual and could, with justice, be regarded as religions in their own right.

It is, then, possible to find groups of Hindus whose respective faiths have almost nothing in common with one another, and it is also impossible to identify any universal belief or practice that is common to all Hindus. Confronted with such diversity, what is it that makes Hinduism a single religious tradition and not a loose confederation of many different traditions? The common Indian origin, the historical continuity, the sense of a shared heritage and a family relationship between the various parts: all these are certainly important factors. But these all equally apply to Buddhism, Jainism and Sikhism, each of which arose within the Hindu tradition but separated from it to become an independent religion. Crucial, however, is the fact that Hindus affirm it is one single religion. Every time a Hindu accepts someone as a fellow Hindu, in spite of what may be radical differences of faith and practice, he is making this affirmation. Whatever its seeds, Hindu self-awareness certainly developed in early confrontations with Buddhists and Jains, acquired greater potency as Hinduism was confronted by Islam and then Christianity, and finally was considerably strengthened in recent times by the growth of nationalism and political identity. It is Hindu self-awareness and self-identity that affirm Hinduism to be one single religious universe, no matter how richly varied its contents, and make it a significant and potent force alongside the other religions of the world.

Approaches to Hinduism

The first attested usage of the word 'Hinduism' in English was as late as 1829. This is not to say that the beliefs and practices of the Hindus, or 'Gentoos' as they were referred to in the eighteenth century, had not been previously studied. Indeed, serious work had already begun, spurred on by the exciting 'discovery' of Sanskrit and the realization that it was related to Latin and Greek [1: 1]. Philological work, the editing and translation of texts, has been a continuing and major scholarly concern. Because the corpus of religious and philosophical works is so vast, however, there still remains much that awaits thorough investigation. Nevertheless the huge body of religious writings, sometimes referred to as Hindu scriptures, has helped to form a mistaken view of Hinduism. Certainly these works are of primary importance. But it must be remembered that they were written by a priestly elite, the Brahmans, and are, of necessity, unrepresentative of the beliefs and practices of the great majority of Hindus at any given time. They are, moreover, not a coherent corpus, but as diverse as the history of Hinduism itself. Some authors, through excessive reliance on texts, and through failing to place these texts in their overall contexts, have perpetuated an image of Hinduism as being concerned solely with the higher realms of metaphysical and theological teachings when, in fact, a very great deal more is entailed.

Early observers in contact with the everyday realities of Hinduism, understanding the writings, beliefs and practices of the Brahmans to represent the true 'orthodoxy', were thus obliged to relegate much of what they found to the status of folklore and superstition. More recently, ethnographic and anthropological research has gone a long way towards removing this misleading polarization and has partly succeeded in integrating both aspects into a single totality. This process has itself generated further dualities, however, such as 'the great tradition' and 'the little tradition', which may prove in the long run to be equally unhelpful.

The Christian missionaries were highly critical of most of what they encountered in India, although they welcomed monotheism wherever they found it as providing further evidence of the universality of this phenomenon. Subjected to the scorn of the missionaries, the more Westernized and educated Hindus took the opportunity that the new word 'Hinduism' offered to reinterpret and project Hinduism almost as they wished, since it was never clear precisely what the term referred to. As will be seen later,

Hinduism came to be projected as 'the most ancient and mother of all religions', and through being, by implication, the best of all religions, it was naturally the most tolerant. This new mythology was coupled with the notion of the spiritual East and the materialistic West, as if there were no spirituality in the West and no materialism in the East. Such dubious popular images were supported by the equally false notion of the changelessness of India. In fact Hinduism and India are characterized by both continuity and change, and no single image can be appropriate either to so complex an agglomeration as Hinduism or to so vast a continent as India.

There is still a relativism in the use of the word Hinduism. To someone reading the literature it becomes clear that there are almost as many 'Hinduisms' as there are authors who write about it. Recently one scholar has commented trenchantly on the term Hinduism, describing it as 'a particularly false conceptualization, one that is conspicuously incompatible with any adequate understanding of the religious outlook of Hindus'. While the arguments cannot be rehearsed here, there is much validity in them, although it is improbable that his wish to have the word dropped will ever be fulfilled. The word is here to stay. In this chapter it will be used as many now use it to embrace the totality of beliefs and practices of all Hindus, both as they are now, and as they have evolved over the centuries [1; 2; 3; 5; 15].

History and Sources of Hinduism

All that is known of the earliest stage of religious life in India – designated by some as protohistoric Hinduism – is derived from excavated seals and statuettes belonging to the Indus valley civilization (?4000–1750 BCE) [1: I] (see figure 5.1). These are usually interpreted as indicating that veneration was shown to a male god, seated in a yogic posture and displaying characteristics of the god known in later Hinduism as Shiva (see figures 5.4–5.6 below); also to female goddesses, phallic symbols and certain animals and trees. Ritual purification with water seems also to have been an important element. Fragmentary as these details are, however, all of these features reappear in classical Hinduism and are widespread in current belief and practice – testimony to the persistence of religious forms in India [1: II].

The second historical phase, that of Vedism or Vedic religion, is usually taken to extend from about the middle of the second millennium BCE to about 500 BCE. It was ushered in by the arrival of the semi-nomadic Aryan tribes who, by conquest and by settlement and assimilation, spread during these centuries across north India. The Aryans were that branch of the Indo-European peoples who moved

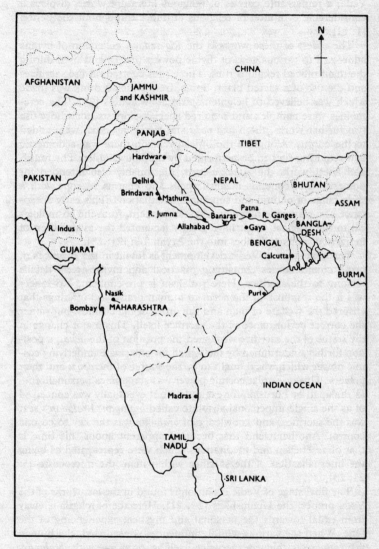

Figure 5.1   *General map of India*

down into Iran and Afghanistan and then into India. What is known of their religion when they were in India derives mainly from the Veda, a remarkable corpus of religious literature which displays a considerable evolution of religious attitudes throughout the period [1: 11].

The oldest of these works is the *Rig-veda*, a collection of hymns addressed to various gods or divine powers (*devas*) and used during the main official religious rites. These rites centred on fire sacrifices and the use of a sacred plant, Soma, from which a drink was made which was believed to heighten spiritual awareness [24]. The ceremonies were complex and required specialist priests, for whose use two further works, the *Sama-veda* and the *Yajur-veda*, were added to the corpus. Alongside the official religion there was a domestic cult requiring rites to be performed by the householder. The fourth and latest work, the *Atharva-veda*, presumably also intended for domestic use, contains magical spells and charms to cope with a wide range of natural and supernatural situations. This early acceptance of a very wide range of religious concern, from the cosmological to the magical, must have greatly facilitated the assimilation of indigenous cults and tribes into the Aryan fold [21; 23].

The next stage in Vedic development is found in the *Brahmanas*, prose commentaries containing practical and mythological details relating to the sacrifice. Here ritualism is pre-eminent. No longer was it the response of the *devas* to human praise and offerings that ensured the welfare of man and the order of the cosmos, but rather the correct performance of the sacrifice itself. This major change in the status of the sacrifice weakened the position of the *devas*, a position further undermined by the search for one single underlying cosmic power which was thought to be the source of the *devas* and their powers. This one great cosmic power was sometimes personalized – as Prajapati or Purusha, for example – but eventually was conceived of as the single impersonal absolute called *brahman*. *Brahman's* seat was the sacrifice, and knowledge of *brahman* was the key to cosmic control. Another trend that becomes apparent about this time is that of asceticism and meditation, which were represented as being the internalization of the sacrifice within man, the microcosm [5; 21; 23].

The final stage of Vedic evolution is found in the last works of the Veda proper, the Upanishads [20; 21]. Here the emphasis is away from ritual towards the personal and mystical experiencing of the One. When the various worldly influences are reduced, the human self (*atman*) is able to experience itself as, or at one with, *brahman*. Here for the first time too the very important doctrine of *samsara* appears. *Samsara* is the endless cycle of birth and rebirth to which each soul is subject until it obtains liberation (*mukti* or *moksha*) in *brahman*. The conditions of each birth are determined by the acts

(*karma*) performed during the previous life. Whereas the early
hymns were little concerned with the afterlife, now the major preoccupation is how to escape from the cycle of birth and rebirth [1: VII;
5; 21; 23].

The ten centuries from about 500 BCE to 500 CE are the period of
classical Hinduism. Because the chronology is problematic it will be
better to review the main religious developments thematically.
Certainly the period began in a time of great ferment. The Vedic
cult was in decline. The Upanishads and the quest for *moksha*
represented a turning away from the world. Meanwhile a new merchant class was flourishing whose members either supported their
own non-Vedic cults or else followed the new sects that were then
arising, of which Buddhism and Jainism were to become the most
important. The Brahmans, as priests, could well have lost much
influence in consequence, but they were also the educated elite, sole
guardians of Sanskrit and the textual traditions. It is they who were
the principal agents in creating a sufficiently flexible religious and
social framework within which they were able to assimilate the new
classes, peoples and cults. One of the main powers and functions of
the Brahmans at this time was that of legitimation. Perhaps the first
really significant exercise of that power, as well as the first affirmation of Hindu self-awareness, was to establish allegiance to the
Veda, however contrived, as the criterion of orthodoxy. In consequence, some of the newly arisen sects, notably Buddhism and
Jainism, were treated as heterodox and separated to go their own
way, although cross-fertilization continued for many centuries [1: II,
VII].

The change of emphasis to living-in-the-world was firmly established in the religious law books, *dharma sutras* and *dharma shastras*,
which codified how Hindu society should be and how Hindus
should live, at least according to Brahmanical prescription. The
essential concept was *varnashrama dharma*, that is, the duties or
right way of living of each of the four classes of society (*varnas*) in
each of the four stages of life (*ashramas*). Although there is also a
general *dharma*, righteousness or moral code, incumbent on all, this
relativist code of behaviour was founded on the belief that people
are not the same and that their duties or ethics vary according to
who they are and where they are in life. The four *varnas* –
Brahmans (priests and teachers), Kshatriyas (rulers and warriors),
Vaishyas (merchants and cultivators) and Shudras (menials) – were
ordered hierarchically on Vedic authority; the first three, the 'twice-
born', had full religious rights, while those of the menials were
much restricted. Unsubjugated tribes or groups with unacceptable
practices were considered 'untouchables' and outside the Hindu
pale. These prescriptive works, the *dharma shastras*, deal with
domestic rituals, life-cycle rites, sin, expiation, ritual pollution,

purification and many other matters fundamental to the Hindu way of life [13]. The three aims of life were *dharma*, the acquisition of religious merit through right living, *artha*, the lawful making of wealth, and *kama*, the satisfaction of desires, thus embracing the major aspects of human life. Only later was *moksha*, the quest for liberation, added as the fourth. Right living in this world, *dharma*, had displaced *moksha*, liberation from this world, at the very centre of Hinduism [1; 13; 28; 30; 32]. But *moksha* was never ignored. It was explored by schools of speculative philosophy, often with very sophisticated metaphysical systems, all purporting to be valid means of salvation. Six of these *darshanas* (doctrines) were accepted as

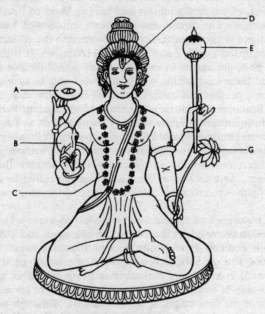

A *Cakra* (discus), a weapon and a symbol of kingly power

B *Shankha* (conch), used as a trumpet in both war and ritual

C *Vana-mala* – a garland of forest flowers. Often worn by Vishnu and Krishna.

D Sectarian mark, as worn by Vishnu's devotees

E *Gada* (mace)

F *Yajnopavita*, the sacred thread

G *Padma* (lotus), representing beauty and purity, often associated with Vishnu's wife
   Lakshmi and other goddesses

A, B, E and G are the four most usual attributes
by which Vishnu is identified

***Figure 5.2** Vishnu and his attributes*

orthodox, but only one of them, Vedanta, was to evolve and play an important part in the later development of Hinduism [5; 29].

There is ample evidence that non-Vedic theistic cults were widespread throughout the Vedic period. The process whereby these cults and divinities were brought within Hinduism and somehow connected to the Veda is both complex and little known. Suffice it to say that, for Hinduism, the rise, or re-emergence, of theism was one of the most profound developments of the period. Two gods, Vishnu and Shiva, both relatively unimportant in the Veda, became pre-eminent, although many other gods were also worshipped [4; 7; 16].

Vishnu (see figures 5.2 and 5.3) came to be identified with various existing deities, and this syncretism has given him the character of a benevolent god, concerned for the welfare of the world, who periodically, in times of moral decline, descends to the world in various forms and guises to restore righteousness. There are believed to be ten such descents (*avataras*) of Vishnu. Some of these are in the form of giant animals: the Fish, the Boar and the Tortoise. Then there is a Man-Lion and a Dwarf. But the most important in terms of devotion are Krishna and Rama, the seventh and eighth *avataras*. The mythology of these two is very elaborate. Krishna is worshipped in three forms: as a divine infant; as a mischievous youth who plays the flute and wins the hearts of the cowherd girls (*gopis*); and as a mighty hero. Rama, who like Krishna is a prince, restored righteousness to the earth by destroying the demon Ravana who had abducted his wife Sita. The word for a devotee of Vishnu, however he is worshipped, is Vaishnava (also an adjective meaning 'relating to Vishnu') and the entire cult of Vishnu is referred to as Vaishnavism [1: vii; 4; 7; 16; 31].

Shiva is also syncretic, but the various elements that go to form the mythology of Shiva are not represented as being separate *avataras* as in the case of Vishnu, but rather as different aspects of the god's complex character. In fact, Shiva is not thought to descend to the earth and take on a form; rather, he intervenes to help those who worship him. Shiva's character has various facets (see figures 5.4, 5.5 and 5.6). He is to some a loving god, full of grace towards his devotees. But there is also the dark side, Shiva the destroyer, who is fearsome and frequents cremation grounds and other frightening places. Shiva is also represented as the Lord of the dance (figure 5.6), as a great ascetic god meditating on the Himalayan Mount Kailash and, as the Lord of the beasts, also as a god of procreation. The word for a devotee of Shiva is Shaiva, which is also an adjective meaning relating to Shiva, and the cult of Shiva is referred to as Shaivism.

Vishnu's wife is Lakshmi, goddess of prosperity (see figure 5.7). The wife of Shiva is Durga (figure 5.8) in her fierce aspect, and

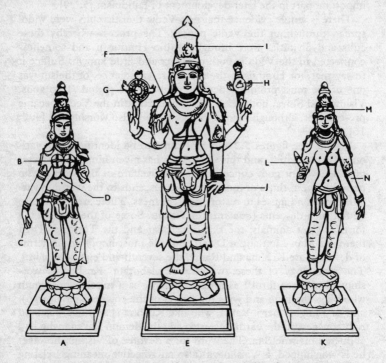

A Shridevi (Lakshmi), goddess of good fortune, standing as the first wife on the right

B Breast band, sign of the senior wife

C Hand in pose of relaxation

D The elaborate arrangement of threads on the chest is characteristic of Lakshmi. Vishnu and Bhudevi both wear the simpler form of sacred thread (*yajnopavita*). Although mortal women do not wear the thread, goddesses can be so shown

E Vishnu as 'Abode of Shri' (splendour, good fortune)

F *Shrivatsa* ('beloved of Shri') mark on Vishnu's chest

G *Cakra* (discus or quoit), decorated with flames

H Conch, decorated with flames

I Kingly crown (*kirita mukuta*) and ornaments

J Hand on thigh, symbolizing that for his worshippers the ocean of *samsara* is only thigh deep

K Bhudevi (Prithvi), the Earth Goddess, the second wife

L Water-lily bud (the Earth Goddess flower)

M Queen's crown (*karanda-mukuta*)

N Pose of relaxation

Figure 5.3   *Vishnu as Shrinivasa with consorts (south Indian bronzes from Srinivasanallur, Tiruchirapalli district, fifteenth/sixteenth century* CE)

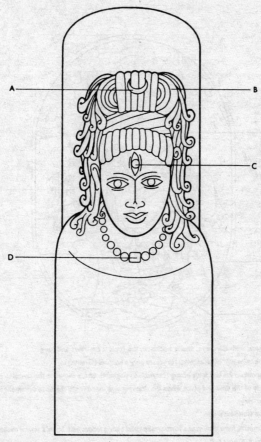

A Crescent moon

B *Jata*, the ascetic's unkempt locks of hair

C Third eye, representing Shiva's wisdom but also his power of destruction – he can blast
enemies with fire from it. It is a sign of yogic power

D *Rudraksha-mala*, a rosary of Rudraksha (eye of Shiva) seeds, sacred to Shiva.

Only the upper part of the sculpture would have been visible: it was made to fit into a pedestal
(possibly representing the *yoni*)

Figure 5.4 *Eka-mukha-linga* (lingam *with one face of Shiva*)

A Shiva, with third eye, snake necklace, the typical ear-rings and long
    unkempt hair of an ascetic. He wears only a *kaupina* (G-string)
B Parvati serves him with bhang (cannabis in yoghurt). She is shown in the costume of a
    lady of the time and place when the drawing was made (note the nose ornament and
    ear-ring)
C The Goddess's lion
D Ganesha, here shown as a four-armed child eating *laddus* with Shiva's animal mount
E Nandi, Shiva's bull
F Karttikeya, the six-headed, six-armed war god shown here as a child, feeding his
    peacock mount

Figure 5.5   *The domestic life of Shiva and Parvati (from a late
eighteenth- or early nineteenth-century Kangra drawing for a miniature
in the British Museum)*

A — H
G
B — I
J — K
D — O
C — J
E — L
F — M

P
N
Q —

A Goddess of River Ganga, which flows from Shiva's hair. She is here shown as a snake-tailed woman in the gesture of *namaskara* (to honour Shiva)

B Drum, giving the rhythm of the dance of creation

C Cobra

D *Abhaya-mudra*, the gesture granting freedom from fear

E Hand pointing to the raised foot signifies salvation

F The upraised foot, coming forward from the circle, represents salvation

G Skull, symbol of the ascetic

H Moon

I Third eye

J Long swirling locks full of flowers and snakes

K One male, one female ear-ring because Shiva combines attributes of both sexes

L Sacred thread

M Short dhoti of the ascetic

N The dance steps are the creation and destruction of universes. Shiva dances on one spot, at the centre of the universe/the human mind-heart

O Fire, the periodic destruction and re-creation of the universe

P Ornamental *prabha-mandala*, the circle of glory, representing the universe/human heart

Q Demon of Ignorance, who is glad to be trodden on by the God

Figure 5.6   *Shiva as Nataraja, king of dancers*

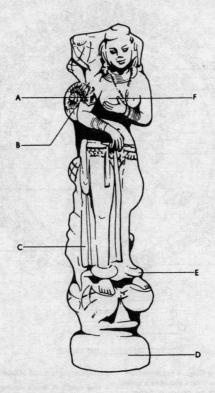

A Armband in the shape of a peacock

B The back of the image is carved with peacocks and lotuses. Peacocks are associated with the rainy season, hence fertility

C Diaphanous skirt, characteristic of the style from Mathura

D Pedestal, taking the form of the *purnaghata* ('full vase') of lotuses, which is still associated with Lakshmi

E Heavy anklets – the goddess is shown richly adorned

F She offers her breast and unfastens her garment, suggesting her power of fertility

Figure 5.7 *Lakshmi, as goddess of prosperity (Kushana, second/fourth centuries CE). This early image represents Lakshmi (who is Kamala, the lotus goddess) in association with symbols of water, fertility and female beauty*

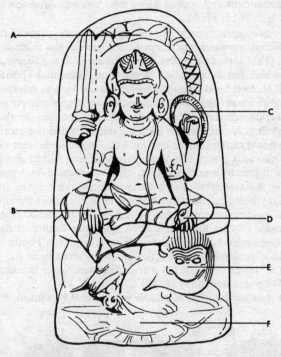

A halo (*prabha-mandala*)

B *Varada-mudra*, the gesture of granting favours (the small round object in the palm is
   perhaps a wishing gem). This suggests her benevolence to her worshippers

C The sword and the buckler (seen from the inner side) represent the goddess in her
   fierce aspect, in which she fights demons. The image combines fierce and gentle
   aspects

D Conch shell, showing that Durga is a *shakti* of Vishnu as well as of Shiva (in mythology
   she is Vishnu's sister, and Shiva's wife)

E Lion, the mount (*vahana*) of Durga

F Lotus footstool and pedestal

Figure 5.8   *Durga and her attributes (from a c. tenth-century relief*
from eastern India)

Parvati in her benevolent form (figure 5.5). It was around Durga–Parvati that, at the end of this period, the Mother Goddess cult re-emerged. Its followers were called Shaktas because they believed the goddess to be the immanent active energy (*shakti*) of the transcendent and remote Shiva who was otherwise inaccessible [1: VII; 4; 5; 7; 16; 17; 31].

The two great epics, the *Ramayana* and, particularly, the *Mahabharata*, are rich encyclopedic sources for the religion of this period [19]. Included in the *Mahabharata* is the *Bhagavadgita*, a poem which has become one of the most influential Hindu scriptures [14]. In it Lord Krishna speaks of three ways to salvation: that of enlightenment; that of action, including religious rites; and, the most highly recommended, that of loving devotion to the Lord (*bhakti*). It is *bhakti* that has inspired and informed the greater part of Hinduism to the present day [5; 14]. Other consequent developments also took place. The Vedic sacrificial rites had to give ground to new forms of worship (*puja*), often performed in front of an image or a statue symbolizing or representing the deity in question. A rich mythological literature evolved in works called Puranas, and temple-building began, so that, by the end of this period of classical Hinduism, temples must have been a familiar feature of the landscape (see figure 5.9). The characteristic features of Hindu temples are: (1) a 'sanctuary' housing the image, referred to as the *garbhagriha* (or 'womb-house'); (2) a spire (*shikhara*) over the sanctuary; and (3) a porch or canopy [4; 15].

The next period, that of middle or medieval Hinduism, from the

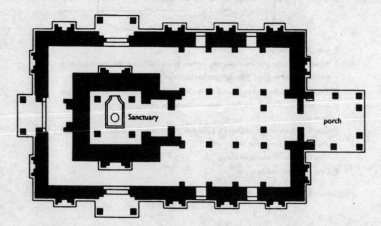

Sanctuary

porch

Figure 5.9 *Plan of the Svarga Brahma temple, Alampur (seventh century CE). In the appropriate niches of the outer walls are positioned the Dikpalas, the guardians of the eight directions of space*

sixth century to the nineteenth century of our era, is characterized by proliferation in almost every domain. It is also interesting that many of the major initiatives, especially in the earlier centuries, took place in the south of India where Buddhism and Jainism were in decline and new Hindu kingdoms arose fostering Hindu self-awareness [1: III, VII]. At a social level this period saw the proliferation of castes (*jatis*), but no theory as to their origin is, as yet, conclusive. It is not thought that they arose through the mixing of the four classes (*varnas*), from which they differ substantially, but clearly the *varna* model of hierarchy, specialization of functions and social separation provided an ideological backing. Whatever the defects of the system, and various sects attacked it vehemently, it served to provide social stability in times of political turbulence, to ensure the continuity of a richly diversified culture, and, above all, to give Hindus a social identity, even if it was not the identity that they themselves wished [1; 40].

The major developments in religious philosophy, the *darshanas*, or schools of salvation, took place within Vedanta. Shankara (?788–850 CE), who advocated the way of knowledge (*jnana*), formulated his system of Advaita, non-duality, as an exposition of Upanishadic thought, and also founded a monastic order which was to be the forerunner of many others [9; 22]. The Advaita position is held by many Hindus to this day. Briefly, Shankara asserted that only *brahman* was real; all else, including the phenomenal world, the sense of individuality, even the *devas*, was unreal, only appearing to be real because of *maya*, *brahman*'s power of illusion. When the human spirit, through meditation and enlightenment, realizes that it is itself of the substance of *brahman* and has no separate identity, then it merges with *brahman*, as the drop is absorbed in the ocean. This non-dualistic position, that the soul and God are of the same substance, is unsatisfactory for theists, because it does not allow for there to be a relationship between the individual soul and God. Thus in the twelfth century Ramanuja produced a system called Vishishtadvaita, differentiated non-duality, which, while accepting that the soul and God were of the same essence, also taught that the individual soul retained its self-consciousness, and hence was able to exist in an eternal relationship with God [8; 9; 22]. This new system of Ramanuja opened the way for theism, especially Vaishnavism, within Vedanta, and provided the initial theological impetus for later schools such as those founded by Madhva (thirteenth century), Nimbarka (fourteenth century), Vallabha (sixteenth century) and Caitanya (sixteenth century), all of whom followed and advocated the way of *bhakti*, devotion [29].

As the three principal currents of theism evolved, so each diversified and produced its own literature. The main genres, the Vaishnava *Samhitas*, the Shaiva *Agamas* and the Shakta *Tantras*, are primarily handbooks dealing with doctrine, yoga and meditation, temple-building and the consecration of the image of the deity in the temple, worship and festivals and the conduct expected of the adherent. At a less institutional level, *bhakti* was transformed from a restrained respect into a passionate and ecstatic experience by the Tamil devotional poets, the Vaishnava Alvars and the Shaiva Nayanars. These saint-poets in the south of India expressed their impassioned spirituality in hymns to Vishnu and Shiva respectively, not in Sanskrit but in Tamil, from the eighth to the tenth century. It has been said that, with them, *bhakti* ceased to be a way to salvation, but became salvation itself [25].

Within Vaishnavism this new attitude was reflected in the Sanskrit *Bhagavata Purana* (*c.* ninth century), which became a powerful source of inspiration for Krishna *bhakti* (devotion to Krishna) in the north [6]. Numerous new sects arose and many fine devotional poets used the vernacular languages such as Hindi, Marathi, Gujarati and Bengali for their verses, thus enabling millions to come into direct contact with the scriptural traditions for the first time [26]. Devotion to the other important *avatara* of Vishnu, Rama, found powerful expression in the *Ramacaritamanasa* of Tulsidas (sixteenth century), which is one of the most loved works in north India [18].

Shaivism, too, developed strongly. A distinctive school of Shaivism arose in Kashmir, certainly before the ninth century, which was much influenced by Advaita [10]. The devotional outpourings of the Nayanars of the south were incorporated into a theological system called Shaiva-siddhanta which was formulated in the twelfth century [12]. Also in the twelfth century, a movement came into being called Vira-Shaivism whose followers were called Lingayats. Vira-Shaivism, which rejected both the caste system and temple worship, exists to this day in a somewhat modified form [11; 12].

Shaktism also developed and proliferated. One aspect of Shaktism that had a strong influence on both Shaivism and Buddhism was called Tantrism. The movement was of a highly esoteric nature and had its own form of yoga, a secret language, a psychophysiological theory and characteristic modes of worship and practice designed to lead to self-realization and liberation. Although some of its practices have been much criticized, Tantrism, whose boundaries are difficult to define, is now generally thought to have added a new vitality to much of medieval Hinduism [17].

There remains one movement of major significance: the Sant tradition. The *sants*, themselves mainly from the lower castes, rejected the caste system and all forms of external religion, both Muslim and Hindu. They preached a form of interior religion based on constant awareness of and love for a personal God who was without attributes. Kabir, Raidas and Dadu, all of whom lived in the fifteenth and sixteenth centuries, were three of a long line of preacher-poets in whose name sects were later formed. One such sect, whose 'founder' was Guru Nanak, later developed into Sikhism [9; 27; and see chapter 6 below].

Thus during the Muslim period in India, and especially from the fifteenth century, Hinduism was vital and alive. *Bhakti* sects flourished, the vernacular languages were used, most of the population was involved at some level, and caste, however much loathed by certain groups, provided social stability and identity. In the face of this, Islam made surprisingly little headway, except perhaps to strengthen Hindu self-awareness. But it is in the modern period, in the nineteenth and twentieth centuries, which will be considered in the final section of this chapter, that Hinduism faced its greatest self-examination as it confronted Western culture and Christianity.

Hindu Presuppositions and Belief

It will be apparent from the above examination of the inherently diverse nature of Hinduism that any attempt to produce a concise exposition of 'basic teachings' or 'fundamental beliefs' could only be misleading and partial. Beliefs and teachings there are in abundance, but few command universal acceptance. Well-articulated systems of belief, theology and philosophy are found in specific sectarian traditions or philosophical schools, most of which have their own recommended *sadhana* (method of practical realization) for their adherents. But these are the particulars, not the universals, of Hinduism. At the most general level there are, however, certain underlying presuppositions which together constitute a kind of received understanding, although this understanding is modified for each individual by personal, family, caste, regional and, maybe, sectarian viewpoints. The most important of these presuppositions will now be examined, together with certain other areas of Hindu concern and belief.

One of the most important and potent concepts for all Hindus is that of *dharma*. *Dharma* has various levels of meaning, but no single English equivalent. The word 'Hinduism', though, is often rendered in Indian languages by the term *Hindu dharma*, the *dharma* of the Hindus. Here it signifies the religion or the right way of living for Hindus. At the cosmic level *dharma* is *sanatana dharma*, the eternal *dharma*, which is the unchanging universal law of order which decrees that every entity in the universe should behave in accordance with the laws that apply to its own particular nature. Coming to the world of man, *dharma* is the source of moral law. There is, on the one hand, *sadharana dharma*, the general code of ethics that applies to everyone. This includes injunctions to perform meritorious acts such as going on pilgrimages, honouring Brahmans and making charitable endowments, as well as prohibitions against causing injury, lying, etc. On the other hand there is the relativist *varnashrama dharma*, which has already been discussed above. In fact, today, *varnashrama dharma* is understood as accepting and following the customs and rules of one's caste (*jati*). Thus *dharma* means, among other things, eternal order, righteousness, religion, law and duty. The central importance of *dharma* has led some to state that Hinduism is a way of life, a proposition that has much, but not total, validity [28; 30; 32].

A person is a Hindu because he is born to Hindu parents, and thereby into their caste. Caste is the principal factor that determines an individual's social and religious status. Caste is too complex a subject to discuss in any detail here, but it is underpinned by, or expresses itself by means of, the religious notion of purity and pollution which is one of the most fundamental Hindu ritual concerns [40]. Nobody can escape from pollution, since the natural functioning of the body produces sources of pollution. All human emissions, for example, are polluting: saliva, urine, perspiration, faeces, semen, menstrual flow and the afterbirth. Menstruating women, and women for a period around childbirth, are considered impure and are subject to restrictions, which vary from caste to caste, to prevent them from polluting others, especially by means of food. But perhaps the most powerful source of pollution is death. Not only are those who handle corpses heavily polluted, but a dead person's household and certain of his relatives are also polluted by the death and have to observe various types of prohibition for varying periods. There are many ways of coping with the different types of pollution, but a particularly common one is the use of running water. A pious Hindu's morning bathing is not simply a wash, but a ritual purification to bring him to the state of purity considered necessary in Hinduism before approaching a deity [31].

A caste is a separate, hereditary group which is normally endogamous: that is, marriage takes place usually only within the caste. A caste protects its corporate purity by restricting various types of contact with other castes it considers to be polluting, and hence impure. Thus the attribution of 'pure' or 'impure' to castes is, to some extent, relative to the status of those making the judgement. The Brahman castes, though, are always at the top of the hierarchy, being the most pure, and hence the most vulnerable to pollution. At the bottom are those castes who, for example, handle dead animals or skins, or function as menials at funerals. The middle-ranging castes in any locality rank themselves hierarchically between these two extremes. Food is a major area subject to restrictions, because it readily carries pollution. The intercaste hierarchy in any locality is clearly demonstrated in food transactions, since it quickly becomes apparent which castes or group of castes will accept or reject water, cooked food and raw food from which other castes. Physical contact used to be another sensitive area, hence the 'untouchable' castes, now called Harijans, but this is much less of an issue nowadays, perhaps because of legislation making untouchability illegal. The Harijan castes, however, still remain at the very bottom of the hierarchy. In a close-knit community, for example in a multi-caste village, the system results in the most minute discriminations being made in the sphere of interpersonal relations, but in the looser society of a town there is much greater relaxation. If a member breaks his caste's purity rules, the pollution he incurs can affect the whole caste group, so the social sanctions against the offender can be severe, and he can be required to perform various ritual acts of purification before he is entitled to resume full caste rights. An individual's ritual status is determined by the status of the caste group into which he is born [32; 40].

But caste-linked *dharma* is not solely concerned with whom a person may marry and with purity rules that affect interpersonal behaviour. It can also determine, for example, what work a person may do, whether meat may be eaten or alcohol drunk, or whether widows may remarry. What one caste finds acceptable another does not, so that, at this level, *dharma* produces a relative morality, based on conformity to custom backed by social sanctions and scriptural authority. This by no means exhausts *dharma*. The most intimate group to which a Hindu belongs is the family. It is mainly within the family that *dharma* is transmitted from one generation to another, by custom and example in the normal process of growing up, by stories and myths which are usually highly moral and contain idealized relationships and situations, and finally by scripture and precept, although this is probably the least significant in practice. The handing down of *dharma* to the next generation is made easier by the extended nature of the Hindu family, which results in a greater exposure to adult moral and religious influences than is usually found in Western families. The Hindu family ethic is very strong, so the structure of authority and the roles and responsibilities of different relationships are usually strictly adhered to. The Hindu life-cycle rites as well as various lineage and caste cult observances take place within the family and form an important part of its religious life. Thus the Hindu is initiated into both the specific and the generalized *dharma* as a natural thing from his earliest years [40].

Dharma is more than an ethical system, but, in so far as it is viewed as such, it contrasts with the moral systems of those theistic religions which posit an ethical god. *Dharma* is ideologically sup-

ported by other important presuppositions, the already mentioned
doctrine of *samsara* (the endless cycle of birth and rebirth to which
the soul is subject), the allied doctrine of *karma*, that every action
produces its inevitable result so that one's status in this life is determined by one's conduct in a former birth, and the notions of *papa*
(sin) and *punya* (merit). Actions that deviate from *dharma*, whether
by omission or commission, are *papa*, sin, and increase an individual's store of demerit. To follow *dharma* is meritorious, and especially meritorious are such acts as pilgrimage, making gifts to
Brahmans or sponsoring a religious recitation. The merit, *punya*, so
attained adds to one's own store, or can be transferred to, say, a
departed ancestor. Certain expiatory rites, such as bathing in the
Ganges, reduce *papa* and hence increase the merit balance. It is the
balance between sin and merit that will eventually determine,
through the law of *karma*, how a person is born in a future life, as
an insect, animal or human, and, if human, with what status. The
law of *karma* is used by most Hindus to explain people's present
status and situation, but thoughts of future lives do not, on the
whole, act as a factor in determining immediate behaviour, since the
acquisition of merit through following *dharma* is an end in itself,
being one of the four Hindu aims of life [28; 30; 32].

If there are many restrictions for a Hindu in the domain of conduct, in belief there is almost total freedom. Provided that a Hindu
observes the rites and cults inherent in his *dharma*, he may believe
what he likes. There are, however, certain metaphysical presuppositions, like *samsara* and *karma*, to which Hindus are heir, reject them
or modify them as they may. (For a broad study of Indian beliefs
see [3; 28; 29]). Primary among these is the concept of *brahman*,
the impersonal absolute or world soul that underlies the phenomenal diversity of the universe and is, at once, both immanent and
transcendent. Questions about God can produce the answer *brahman*. Other answers represent *brahman* in a more personal form as
bhagvan or *ishvara*, the Lord. Those who worship Vishnu or Shiva
may replace *bhagvan* with their chosen deity. Broadly speaking, the
Hindu position, in so far as there is a single position, can be
described as a mixture of pantheism and monotheism, the blend
being determined by the emphasis given to the concept of *brahman*
as World Soul or to that of *bhagvan* as High God.

There are certain other aspects of the Hindu approach to the
divine that need to be considered. One is the principle of the *ishtadeva*, the chosen deity, which accepts that individuals worship
their preferred deity exclusively as the supreme god. Connected
with this is the inclusiveness of the Hindu approach. Other deities
and beliefs are not denied or opposed, but are accepted as valid for
others, although not regarded as of the same order of excellence as
one's own. Thus a devotee of Vishnu, for example, will subordinate

all the other major gods, seeing them as servants or manifestations of the one supreme Vishnu. A devotee of Shiva will do likewise. While, therefore, to enumerate all the various deities worshipped in India would produce a formidable list, and perhaps be suggestive of polytheism, to do so would be misleading without taking into account the position of the individual worshipper. For the individual there is one supreme God, however conceived or named, and various other *devas*, gods or spiritual powers. These merit respect and perhaps worship, but are conceived of as subordinate manifestations, often with specialized functions. One author has rightly pointed out that one could spend a lifetime in India and never find a 'polytheist' in Western terms, because even an unlettered peasant who has just made offerings at several shrines will affirm that 'Bhagvan ek hai', God is one. Finally, the divine is also seen in men of great sanctity, in animals such as the cow, in certain trees, rivers and mountains, and in countless sacred sites across the subcontinent (figure 5.10).

Another concept central and essential to Hinduism is *moksha* (liberation), which is also one of the four Hindu aims of life. That from which liberation is sought is *samsara*, the cycle of birth and rebirth. The part of the human individual which is immortal – variously described and designated by different schools of thought – passes at death to diverse heavens and hells where it works out its karmic debt and is then reborn in the form it has deserved. This cycle continues endlessly unless it merits, or is blessed with, a lifetime during which, through spiritual efforts, the intervention of a *guru* or the grace of God, *moksha* is attained, whereby it passes out of the cycle altogether. *Samsara* is generally described as unbearable and characterized by *dukkha* (grief). *Moksha*, and how to attain it, has been a major Hindu concern for over two and a half millennia. One of the oldest methods of achieving *moksha* is *sannyasa*, renunciation, whereby the renouncer (*sannyasi*) abandons home, society, the world and all its bondage. Through this renunciation, and usually by performing extreme austerities and practising some form of the spiritual exercises now generally known as *yoga*, the *sannyasi* seeks to become *jivanmukta*, liberated while still alive. In India today there must be hundreds of thousands of *sannyasis*, most belonging to one or other of the ascetic orders, each of which has its own code, organization, disciplines and traditions.

If the *sannyasi* is one ideal Hindu type, the other is the householder (*grihastha*), whose major concern is living in the world, and for whom *sannyasa* is the final *ashrama* or stage of life. As has been mentioned, the *Bhagavadgita* describes three ways to *moksha*: the way of works (*karma*); the way of enlightenment (*jnana*); and the way of loving devotion (*bhakti*). Since works (*karma*) constitute a form of bondage in themselves, the renunciation necessary on this

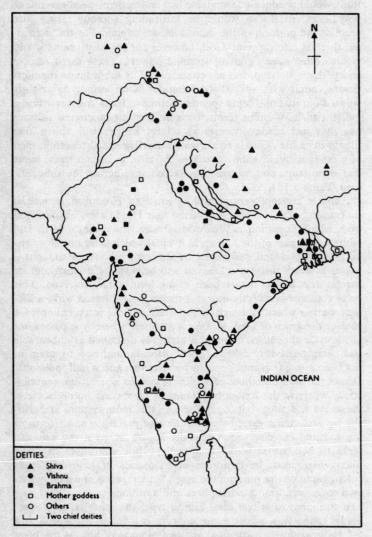

Figure 5.10 *Chief deities at sacred places in India*

path is of the fruits of actions. *Dharma* should be pursued and actions performed disinterestedly, without attachment to the outcome, and this renunciation is one way to liberation. The way of *jnana*, enlightenment, deals with another aspect of the problem. It is *avidya*, wrong knowledge or perception, or *maya*, illusion, that prevents man from knowing what is real and what is unreal, particularly with regard to that part of himself which is immortal. Through various *yoga* techniques and contemplation, man attains enlightenment whereby he perceives reality, renounces unreality, and, realizing his own immortal self, thus obtains liberation. The way of loving devotion, *bhakti*, is preferred by the theistic traditions. Here the renunciation is the total surrender of oneself to the Lord. The way also requires constant awareness of the Lord through devotions, meditation, prayer and the repetition of his name. The theistic traditions do not, of course, consider salvation to be solely a matter of human effort. Those who believe God to be loving and full of grace await God's grace as the means to salvation, to lift off the burden of their sins and to carry them safely across the ocean of existence, since, in the view of some, God's grace is able to override *karma*.

The state that obtains when *moksha* is achieved has been the subject of much speculation among the various sects and schools. At one end of the spectrum of opinion is the monist Advaita position of Shankara, which holds that the immortal self of man is identical with *brahman* and is absorbed into *brahman* as the drop of water into the ocean. At the other end of the spectrum are the theists, who hold that the immortal soul of man lives in an eternal relationship with God. Thus Vishnu, Shiva and Krishna each have their own abodes, heavens, in which selves retain their identity in various states of nearness to God. Between these two extremes there is a range of intermediate positions. For sinners, though, there is the certainty of hell, whose horrific tortures, matching the seriousness of different sins, are graphically described.

Just as humanity is subject to cycles of birth and rebirth, so the universe itself is thought to go through cycles of dissolution and recreation within immense time spans. The gods responsible for this cyclicity vary with the sectarian sources in which the myth is recorded. Within these cycles are lesser periods – *yugas*, or ages. The present age, the Kali-yuga, is thought to last 432,000 years and to have begun in the year 3102 BCE. The characteristics of this age are a decline in righteousness, piety and human prosperity. At the end of the age the world will be destroyed again by flood and fire, although there are alternative versions of what might happen [1; 28].

The presuppositions and concerns that have just been discussed form the central elements of the received Hindu religious understanding, at least at the most general level. There are, of course, other elements, of which astrology is one important example, but the essentials have been covered. At the level of the particular, one would need to examine the nature and the mythology of the various gods, and the theology and philosophy of the different schools and sects. It is, however, within the general conceptual framework just presented that the particular systems and beliefs are articulated, and the individual Hindu derives his or her personal faith.

Hindu Practice

The concept of *dharma*, and how it can affect almost every aspect of a Hindu's life, has already been discussed. One author refers to this as the 'ritualization of daily life', while others consider Hinduism itself to be primarily a way of life. There is another view that sees Hinduism essentially as a *sadhana*, a way, or ways, to self-realization and the attainment of *moksha*. In considering Hindu practice, therefore, one should remember that it has a far broader application than simply the performance of rites and rituals, being concerned with the practical realization of religious values at every level. That said, however, few religions have devoted so much attention to ritual as has Hinduism. From the earliest times, the ritual manuals contain details of the most astonishing complexity and elaboration [34]. Many of these works were, of course, produced for officiating Brahman priests, and absolute accuracy in performance is considered essential, since the smallest mistake invalidates the entire rite and brings retribution. It is, however, clear that the domestic rituals that the twice-born householder, in particular the Brahman, is expected to perform daily are no less complex and demanding [3].

A Brahman should perform a sequence of devotional rituals called *sandhya* three times a day, at dawn, at midday and in the evening. He should also worship his *ishtadeva*; make offerings to the *devas*, the seers of old and his ancestors; perform an act of charity; pay reverence to his teacher; and read from the scriptures. Some of these rituals are very elaborate. The morning *sandhya* includes rituals on rising, answering the calls of nature and brushing the teeth. The sequence continues with the Brahman purifying himself by bathing, purifying his place of worship, practising breath control, invoking the deity by the ritual touching of his limbs, meditating on the sun, making offerings of water and constantly uttering various prayers that he may be pure, free from his sins and strong enough to remain holy. One of the most important prayers, which may be repeated as many as 108 times, sometimes with the aid of a rosary, is called the 'Gayatri', a Vedic verse addressed to the sun as the Inspirer and Vivifier, and now understood as referring to the supreme God. It has been estimated that, if the enjoined rituals were performed in full, they would take at least five hours a day. Certainly there are some pious Brahmans who do in fact perform such rituals every day, but for most the daily rituals are very much abbreviated, and observance decreases proportionately as one descends the socio-ritual scale [36].

Of great importance among domestic rituals are the *samskaras*, or sacraments, which are the life-cycle rites that mark the major transitions of a Hindu's life. In the early texts there were as many as forty such rites, but now fewer than ten are generally performed. Their purpose is to sanctify each transition of an individual's life, to protect such individuals from harmful influences and to ensure blessings for them. The pre-natal rites have nowadays fallen from use and the first observances are those attending birth. These are designed primarily to contain the pollution generated by the birth and to protect the mother and child, who are considered to be particularly vulnerable to harmful influences. The exact time of birth is noted so that a horoscope may be drawn up. On the sixth day, or sometimes on the twelfth, there is the *namakarana*, or name-giving ceremony; the house is purified and a number of the restrictions on the mother are lifted. Some castes and families observe rites on the child's first sight of the sun, and the first taking of solid food. More widely observed is the rite of ritual tonsure, when the child's head is shaved. This can take place in the child's first year or later and is often done at a temple or religious fair, sometimes as the fulfilment of a vow made by the mother to a *deva* in return for the *deva* having kept the child healthy. Another rite, that of ear-piercing, is also fairly common, although there is wide variation as to when it is performed.

The next rite, the *upanayana*, initiation, has great traditional importance, because it is the rite by which the three highest *varnas*, or classes, become 'twice-born' through receiving initiation into the Hindu fold. Nowadays, however, the rite is not regarded with the same importance as previously, and it appears to have become mainly the concern of the Brahman castes. At this ceremony the young man is invested with the sacred thread, *janeu*, which must be worn at all times and kept free from impurity. He is also initiated into the 'Gayatri' prayer by the presiding Brahman priest, who thereby often becomes his *guru*, or spiritual preceptor. In some castes a different kind of initiation takes place when, for example, a Vaishnava ascetic acts as the *guru* and whispers a *mantra*, sacred formula, to those being initiated.

The rite that signals the ritual climax of the life-cycle is *vivaha*, marriage. Standing midway between the impurity produced at birth and death, it represents the point of maximum ritual purity, in token of which the couple are treated as gods. It is a Hindu's religious duty to marry. Through marriage the religious debt to the ancestors is paid off by the production of progeny. Marriage is, therefore, a sacrament of the utmost social and religious significance in Hinduism, and usually the greatest expense a Hindu incurs is that arising from having his children married. The elaborate complex of marriage rituals can take a week or more. Because of this there is great variation in practice. The actual marriage is sealed by a rite called *phera* during which the couple walk seven times round the sacred fire, although this is only one small part of the extremely elaborate series of social and religious rituals that constitute Hindu marriage.

The *antyeshti samskara*, the funeral sacrament, is the last of the rites performed. Again there is variation in practice, but the observances have a twofold purpose. The first is to enable the departing spirit (*preta*) to leave this world and attain the status of an ancestor (*pitri*) so that it does not remain as a ghost (*bhuta*) to trouble the living but can pass to its next destination. The second is to deal with the massive pollution that is released at death, which automatically affects certain of the deceased's relatives. The body is cremated on a pyre lit preferably by the eldest son of the departed. Then begins a period of ten or eleven days of ritual restrictions on the relatives, at the end of which offerings of milk and balls of rice or barley (*pindas*) are made. These offerings, which are made at ceremonies called *shraddha*, usually take place between the tenth and twelfth days and thereafter annually. Their purpose is to enable the departing spirit, the *preta*, to acquire a new spiritual body with which it can pass on. The funeral rites should properly by performed by a son so that the deceased may best be assured of a good rebirth. It is for this reason that Hindus long above all to have a son [3; 36].

One of the major differences in the style of domestic ceremonies is whether or not they are conducted by a Brahman priest. Not all Brahmans are priests – in fact, few are; nor are all religious practitioners Brahmans. The Brahman becomes a priest first because of his ritual purity, a necessary condition for acting as an intermediary between man and God, and second because of his specialized knowledge of ritual and sacred prayers and utterances. When a priest presides the rite will be more elaborate and in accord with scriptural prescription than when a head of household officiates. Rites without a priest are not invalid, but are less prestigious. An experienced priest can perform highly complex rituals and deliver a stream of sacred utterances and instructions at great speed, but many have to resort to handbooks to guide them through the ceremonies. A Brahman priest who serves a family is called a *purohita*. He will serve a number of families, usually by hereditary right, in return for an annual fee. After each ritual he will be paid a sum called *dakshina*, but this is not thought of as a fee, rather as a meritorious gift made to a Brahman. Brahmans will normally only serve as priests to twice-born castes.

Hindu worship (*puja*) falls into three categories: temple worship; domestic worship; and a form of congregational worship. This last type, *kirtana*, mainly consists of hymn-singing, and is the characteristic mode of *bhakti* devotion. It has to be said that the majority of temples in India are small, although there are a significant number of large ones, especially in the various sacred centres. A temple is the home of the enshrined deity, who will have been installed by a rite of consecration in the inner sanctuary. The god's consort may also be present, and other associated deities are often represented in different parts of the temple. Vishnu and his *avataras*, mainly Rama and Krishna, are usually represented by images – statues, often of considerable complexity – portraying many of the god's mythological attributes. This is also the case with the Goddess in her various forms. Shiva, however, is usually represented by the *lingam*, an object (usually a black stone) shaped like the male organ, and often set in the *yoni*, the shaped form of a female organ; these are the universal symbols of Shaivism [35].

Temple priests called *pujaris* serve the deity, treating him or her either as royalty or as an honoured guest, or both. They carry out, at set times of the day, a schedule of worship and attendance which begins before dawn. The deity is awakened, bathed and fed; holds court; rests; is anointed, decorated, and finally retired for the night. This schedule is accompanied by various ceremonies such as *arati* (the waving of lamps), the sounding of bells, the performance of music, hymns, prayers, the offering of flowers, fruit, grain, food and incense, together with other forms of worship and supplication. On festival days connected with the deity there are often spectacular ceremonies and processions which draw people from far around. There is no requirement for any Hindu to go to a temple, although many do, and worship is private. A Hindu goes to a temple in the hope of obtaining a *darshana* – a sight or experience – of the deity, to make offerings, to pray to or petition the deity, or perhaps to make or fulfil a vow. Often food which has first been offered to the deity and hence has become consecrated (*prasada*) is available for worshippers for whom it is a much desired blessing [35].

Domestic worship takes place in most households, but rarely with the elaboration of the temple routine. In most houses there is an area set aside for worship and maintained in a state of ritual purity. Here the *ishtadeva* of the household is represented by an image, by some symbol of the deity concerned, even by a poster. It is usually the women of the household who attend the deity and carry out the various rituals. These can comprise *arati*, offerings, prayers and acts of supplication. Geometrical designs called *yantras* and *mandalas* are sometimes used as symbols for worship. These range from fairly complex mystical symbols, used mainly in Tantric rites, to simpler designs made on the ground with different-coloured powders which can be used in the worship of any deity [3].

The devotees who gather together to worship by chanting *bhajanas* or hymns are usually, but not necessarily, affiliated to a sect. The chanting, the music, the rhythm and the atmosphere of fervent devotion can produce a deep effect and some enter a state of trance. At these gatherings there is also sometimes an *arati* ceremony and the distribution of *prasada*. Groups who gather together in this way to worship through hymn-singing occur all over India and at most levels of society. In those parts of Assam where *bhakti* has become institutionalized, *bhajanas* are the principal mode of worship.

A different kind of communal worship is the *katha*, or recitation of a work of scripture. It is meritorious to sponsor such a recitation, and priests are commissioned and an audience invited. Each text normally relates in specific terms exactly what benefits will accrue to those who hear the text and to those who sponsor its performance.

Another highly meritorious and widely practised religious act in Hinduism is pilgrimage [33]. All over India pilgrimages are taking place daily, on every scale and in every region (see figure 5.11). There are local and regional pilgrimage sites as well as all-India pilgrimage sites like Banaras and Conjeeveram. Each site has its own characteristics, its own benefits to offer the pilgrims. There are regional sites, for example, which offer help to the blind, to the childless or to those suffering from skin complaints. Banaras and Gaya are particularly concerned with salvation, the absolution of sin and the making of offerings for ancestors. Mathura and Brindavan are associated with Krishna, and hundreds of thousands of pilgrims go every year in the hope of obtaining *darshana*, an experience, of their Lord Krishna of whom they are devotees. Thus people undertake pilgrimages for a mixture of motives: for merit and salvation; for absolution of sins; to worship or experience the divine; to propitiate ancestors or to appease an angry deity; to obtain relief from illness or misfortune; or to ensure prosperity or some more specific blessing. The consequence of hundreds of thousands of Hindus mingling together away from their own localities is to reinforce the sanctity of the sacred geography of India to which Hinduism is so closely tied, and to continue to foster the sense of Hindu unity and self-awareness.

Pilgrimage sites are usually very well organized, with guides and priests who receive the pilgrims and then take them through the round of locations and ceremonies. There are booklets describing the various features and temples of each site, detailing their respective mythological associations, praising their merits and enumerating the benefits that accrue from each. Sometimes pilgrimages take place on particular days of the year when there is some great festival

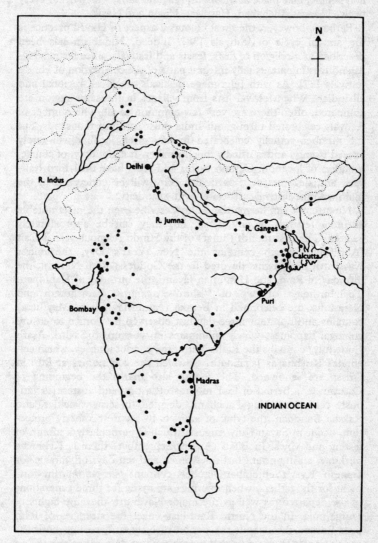

Figure 5.11 Important pilgrimage sites in India

or religious ceremony at a certain site, such as the Jagannatha festival at Puri. By far the largest gatherings, which run into several million people, take place at the *melas*, religious fairs, which occur every twelve years at Allahabad, Hardwar, Ujjain and Nasik.

Perhaps, however, the most colourful aspect of Hindu practice is the annual cycle of festivals [38]. Indeed, Hinduism has been described as a religion of fasts, feasts and festivals, since fasting, vigils and feasting are usually integral parts of the celebration of Hindu festivals [37]. As with pilgrimage, festivals are local, regional and all-Indian. When festival lists from villages in the same region are compared, often there are very few common to all. The number of festivals celebrated throughout India must run into thousands, but the number actually celebrated in any given locality will rarely exceed twenty, and is usually much smaller. It is not only, of course, a matter of location. Certain castes and sects have their own festivals, and devotees of a particular deity will be concerned in the main with the festivals associated with that deity.

No attempt can be made here to describe even the most notable all-India festivals in any detail, but they can be approximately located. The first month (lunar) of the Hindu religious year is Cait (April/May) which contains the New Year's Day, the minor Navaratri, nine nights devoted to the Goddess, Ram Navami, the birthday of Ram, and Hanuman Jayanti, the birthday of Hanuman. The birthdays of two of Vishnu's *avataras*, Parashuram and Narasinha, are celebrated in Besakh (April/May). Jeth (May/June) contains an important three-day fast observed by women to ensure conjugal happiness which culminates in worship to Savitri. Asarh (June/July) contains the Ratha Yatra, the chariot journey, which celebrates Krishna as Jagannath, of which the ceremonies at Puri in Orissa are renowned. The month also marks the beginning of Caturmasa, a period of four months of fasting and austerities variously celebrated. Nag Panchami, devoted to serpent deities, and Raksha Bandhan, the tying of amulets to secure brotherly protection, occur in Savan (July/August) which is particularly a month of fasting and vows. In Bhad (August/September) there is Krishna's birthday, an important fast for women and ten days of worship for Ganesh. Kvar (September/October) contains *pitri-paksha*, the fortnight for the fathers, when offerings are made for three generations of the departed, as well as the major Navaratri, the nine nights of Durga-puja. In the North, Ram-lilas enact the struggles of Ram over Ravana throughout the period of Navaratri, so that both the conclusion of Durga-puja and the triumph of Ram are celebrated on the same day, Dassahra, which is a major festival. Katik (October/November) is marked by Divali, a four- or five-day festival of lights, of which the day of Divali itself is considered auspicious for all new beginnings and the start of the new financial year, and also by the end of the period of Caturmasa. Sometimes in the month of Pus (December/January) but always on 14 January, is Makara Sankranti, which marks the entry of the sun into Capricorn and is an important festival, especially in the south. The month of Magh (January/February) is important for ritual bathing and fairs. Phagun (February/March) contains two major festivals, Mahashivaratri, the Great Night of Shiva, and Holi, the boisterous spring festival.

Even with these major all-India festivals there is considerable regional variation in the manner of their celebration, in the mythology and sometimes even in the deity connected with a particular date. Although this treatment of Hindu festivals has been short and it has not been possible to include description, this should not be taken to imply that their significance is small. They bring vitality to Hindu life; they provide an annual renewal of religious values; and they are often occasions for great joy and celebration.

Many sweeping generalizations have been made about the position of women in Hinduism, but the diversity of sources and the contradictory nature of their pronouncements cannot sustain a single view. Apart from the omission of certain Sanskrit *mantras* from some of the life-cycle rites, and the fact that marriage is regarded as such a significant event in a woman's life that initiation (*upanayana*) is not performed, there are almost no major areas of Hindu practice from which women are excluded. A woman is held to be an equal partner in *dharma* with her husband, and thought to share his destiny, which is why many Hindu women fast regularly for the welfare of their husbands. As the mistress of the household, ritual purity is in her charge, as are many of the household rituals. Women go on pilgrimages, sponsor *kathas*, visit temples, fast, and make vows and offerings. In fact, much of the living practice of Hinduism is dependent on the participation of women.

One of the ideals of Hindu womanhood is Sita, the wife of Rama, who is portrayed as ever obedient and subservient to her Lord's wishes [4]. But although the Hindu woman is expected to show public deference to her husband, this in no way indicates the nature of their private relationship. As manager of the household, and as mother, the Hindu woman wields considerable authority. Child marriage is now illegal and the remarriage of widows lawful. The practice whereby a widow immolated herself on her husband's funeral pyre (*sati*) – which was always the exception rather than the rule – has been forbidden in law for over a century. The battle to overcome prejudice against the education of girls was won in the nineteenth century. In short, there is little reason to think that the Hindu woman is at any greater disadvantage than women elsewhere in the world, as the presence of women in many leading positions in India conclusively demonstrates.

Hinduism in the Villages

Of the total Hindu population of India, over 80 per cent, that is over 500 million Hindus, live in villages. The number of villages is over 500,000. Thus the Hinduism of the villages must certainly be regarded as the religion's most prevalent if not its most characteristic form. It is in the villages that one meets the full diversity of Hinduism. Some have regarded the religion of the villages as a 'level' of Hinduism, as folk or popular religion, but this is a mistake. There is no separate 'village Hinduism' any more than there is a separate 'village Christianity'. The entire spectrum of Hinduism, from its most sophisticated to its most unsophisticated manifestations, can be found in the villages.

There is certainly a specific emphasis. The majority of villagers are simple, unlettered folk who struggle for their livelihood in the face of poverty, disease, climatic uncertainty and many other kinds of threats and difficulties. As is to be expected, such people are concerned not so much with the higher realms of metaphysical speculation, nor with elaborate ritualism, but rather with the practical, pragmatic side of religion. This latter aspect of religion, which seeks to attain ends in this world – a son, a good crop, recovery from illness, etc. – is as much a part of Hinduism as any other aspect, and has been since at least the time of the *Atharva-veda*. This is, however, only a matter of emphasis. Dispersed and localized in the villages of India, the continuing tradition of Hinduism flourishes and is still evolving in all its multiplicity and diversity [39, 41, 42].

There is no such thing as a typical Indian village. Almost every village is different from any other. This is not surprising given the great regional variations of the subcontinent, especially with regard to terrain, climate, ethnic and linguistic groupings and cultural traditions. The population of India, moreover, is not wholly Hindu. There are Muslims, Christians, Sikhs, Jains, Buddhists, Parsis and some Jews. Thus in religious terms, too, the population of the villages is not homogeneous. This lack of homogeneity is further increased by the segmentation of the Hindus into castes. There are single-caste and multi-caste villages. The nature and number of castes, and the strength of their representation, crucially affects the types of religious beliefs and practices found in a village, as well as determining its social structure. It is often the case in a multi-caste village that the pattern of residence reflects the caste composition, with, perhaps, each caste having its own quarter, and sometimes the Harijans occupying a separate hamlet.

The effect of having a number of different caste groups and also maybe households, sometimes hamlets, of adherents of other religions, is to produce considerable religious diversity within a single village. It may be that some of the castes are high, aspiring to Brahmanical norms in their behaviour and practices. Other castes, like the Harijans, who are denied the service of Brahman priests, have had to develop their own forms of religious expression. Not only are their customs quite different from those of the higher castes, but the deities they venerate are usually more local and tend to be more specific in their functions (like, for example, a smallpox goddess). Some castes have a traditional association with a particular deity, who functions rather like a patron saint, and in large castes which have a complex internal organization there are also clan and lineage deities. These caste cults add further diversity to the religious life of any particular village. It is because of this range and diversity that one must reject the notion of there being a special 'village Hinduism' [42].

The hierarchy into which the castes arrange themselves is determined at the village level. But, usually, unless there are some special factors, there will not be a marked difference between the ranking of a caste in one village and the way the same caste is ranked in the villages around, provided that the caste composition of the villages is more or less the same. The hierarchy is not, however, fixed, except that the Brahman is always at the top and the Harijan at the bottom. If a caste group does well economically and seeks to have its newly won material position ritually recognized in an enhanced position in the hierarchy, it will abandon those of its customs and religious practices which are considered 'low', adopting instead those of the castes above it in the hierarchy. In a generation or two it will have established itself higher up and become accepted in its new ritual status. Likewise a caste group might, for some reason, lose prestige or standing and slowly slip down in the hierarchy. Although at any one time the hierarchy seems fixed, in fact there is perceptible and constant movement when measured over decades. Low castes do not humbly accept their lowly status. There is generally much bitterness, and continual effort to improve their position [40; 42].

It used to be thought that villages were somehow self-contained units; but this is not the case and probably never has been. In the religious sphere, as in every other, villages are integrated into the locality and the region of which they form a part. There are considerable differences between the varieties of Hinduism found in the major regions of India: between, for example, Bengal, Gujarat and Tamil Nadu. Not only do these regional forms determine the religious outlook of the villagers, the location of a village within a region can also be influential. It could be situated near a major temple, the centre of a sect or an ascetic order, a place of regional pilgrimage, or some other sacred site with a long mythological pedigree. These can create sub-regional influences that again colour the beliefs and practices of the villagers in that locality. Some of the villagers might be drawn to join a sect whose centre was near by, or become disciples of a *guru* who had taken up residence in the vicinity. Local cults can develop around the tomb of a man who was considered to be of great holiness. Those elements of Hinduism that are considered to have an all-India spread, like certain festivals, in fact are mediated through regional and sub-regional traditions to the individual villagers. Although the names and dates may correspond, there are major differences in the rationale and significance of such festivals in different regions, and even greater differences in the significance they might hold within the total structure of each village's sacred year [38].

It is often the case that there are several small temples in a village, perhaps Rama, Shiva or Hanuman temples, but by far the most numerous structures are the small shrines that house the *grama devatas*, the village deities. If the various divine beings of Hinduism were to be ranked in terms of importance or power, *brahman* or *bhagvan*, the Godhead or God, would come first, in second place would come the *devas*, the major gods of Hinduism, and lastly would come the *grama devatas*, the village deities. If the ranking is in terms of immediacy and the amount of attention received from the villagers, then the order is reversed. The reason for this is that, in the unsophisticated understanding of a substantial proportion of the village population, *bhagvan*, God, is too transcendent, too remote, too concerned with the cosmos to be interested in a villager's problems. The *devas* too, who do *bhagvan's* work at a universal level, are also thought to be too busy or too grand to be concerned with humble peasants. But the various *devatas* or local deities are believed to be the supernatural powers which not only affect a villager's life and welfare, but which also demand his attention and can be extremely angry if they are not given it, with dire results for the villager.

The term *grama devata* is generic, and refers to all the deities of this category associated with a village. In a sense they all have a general function as guardian or tutelary deities of the village and they are all considered powerful and liable to bring disaster if not suitably propitiated. In fact, though, they are very varied. Some have specialized functions, like the goddesses of hydrophobia or smallpox. Others are associated with a specific part of the village for which they are the guardians. Many come into being as deifications of natural forces or the spirits of both the benevolent and the malevolent dead. One type of *grama devata* which is common to almost all parts of India is called *mata*, mother. In reality this is a euphemism, because *matas* are far from being maternal. Some are positively bloodthirsty, demanding animal sacrifices and offerings. They are among the most feared and most propitiated spirits in the villager's experience.

Not all *devatas* have shrines. Those that do, such as the special deity of a caste group, are usually represented by a statue or a brightly decorated figure of some kind. Sometimes, however, it is only possible to know that a *devata* lives in a thorn-bush or a clump of bamboos because rags are tied to it as votive offerings by the villagers. Sometimes bricks placed in a particular way or stones painted with lead oxide are the only indications of a *devata* [42]. It should not be thought that all villagers are entirely convinced about the power, even the existence, of many of the *devatas*. The higher castes in particular usually have little to do with them, regarding them as just the sort of thing that low castes would believe in. But the higher castes and the sceptical apart, this still leaves a substantial proportion of the village population who do accept that they live in an environment peopled with supernatural powers and spirits who can help them or harm them, and who require attention, propitiation and worship, as a matter of prudence if nothing else. No villager, however, will confuse this type of supernatural presence with *bhagvan*, although sometimes an identification is made between a particular *devata* and one of the *devas*.

When a villager is in some kind of difficulty, facing a crisis or an illness, he will first exhaust natural causes and remedies. If the problem persists, he may decide that supernatural causes are at work and turn to one of the village specialists in the supernatural. All villages have some such specialists, maybe one of the informal priests who tend the *grama devatas*, or perhaps an exorcist or a diviner. A quite different idiom operates here from that of the *devas*, who are approached by Brahman priests and in purity. The informal priests are nearly always from the lower castes and they have a special relationship with the village *devatas*, of whom they are the instruments through which the deities speak to the villagers. In many parts they are ecstatics and become possessed by their tutelary deity or some other deity who is then able to speak directly to the villager. These informal priests or ecstatics attain the trance state, in which they become possessed, often by means of drumming, flagellation or the use of intoxicants. Sometimes the worshippers and petitioners standing around also enter a trance and nod or collapse or howl [38; 42]. The kind of answer that a villager with a problem will be given by these priests is that such and such a deity is angry with them for some reason, usually neglect, and demands an offering, or that they are troubled by a hostile spirit or a ghost, or that their problem is caused by the effects of the evil eye on their crops or on a child. Whatever the diagnosis, the priest will prescribe a remedy which is usually the performance of rituals of various kinds that the villager must carry out. If the ecstatic is possessed by the deity that is causing the problem, then it speaks directly to the person concerned explaining what is required and why.

Exorcists are another kind of supernatural specialist commonly resorted to in the villages. They deal with people possessed by a spirit or, more usually, a ghost. A ghost is the spirit of someone who has died an unnatural or untimely death and for whom the funeral rites were not effective (in which case ghosts remain on earth haunting people and places). The most powerful male ghosts are the ghosts of Brahmans and the most feared female ghosts are those of women who died childless or in childbirth. When a possessed person comes to an exorcist, the exorcist, having enlisted the aid of his own tutelary deity, will perform a few rituals and then ask the ghost to leave. A long conversation might then ensue with negotiations about the offering the ghost will require before it consents to leave the victim. Whatever the technique of the exorcist, he will usually try to coax the ghost out and confine it in a clove or small object. Later he will 'seat' the ghost elsewhere. The patient will have to provide offerings for the ghost and the tutelary deity, and also some form of payment for the exorcist [38; 42].

But a villager's contact with the *devatas* is not always through these kinds of intermediaries. The most common religious act in villages is a simple act of worship, like the making of an offering, by a single person in private. Sometimes it is made out of piety, sometimes in thanksgiving, sometimes as propitiation. One of the most common practices is the making of vows. This is very much like a contract between a villager and a *devata* made in the villager's head. It will specify that if a desired event comes about, then the villager will worship the *devata* by making a special offering, keeping a vigil or some such act. The desired event might be that the villager finds a spouse for an offspring, has a good harvest or locates a lost animal. If the event does not take place, then there is no obligation on the villager. If it does, then the vow must be fulfilled otherwise there could be serious consequences. Many of the troubles of villagers are attributed by the *devatas'* priests to the non-performance of vows and the resulting anger on the part of the deity concerned.

These local deities and their cults have been treated at length because they constitute an important part of many villagers' religious life. But they are by no means all of it. Those selfsame villagers might also venerate one or more of the *devas*, the major gods of Hinduism. That this should not be thought of as polytheism has already been explained. The major events in the religious life of a village are the festivals that punctuate the year and are observed usually with great enthusiasm according to the manner of the place. Life-cycle rites too, a birth, a wedding or a funeral, provide important ceremonial occasions which are remembered for years and often bring relatives from far and near. Sometimes a wandering holy man or singer comes to the village and attracts much interest with *bhajanas*, recitations or preaching. Then there are the occasions when the villagers go out on small-scale pilgrimages or to visit a temple or some other sacred spot. All of this, both what is seen and what is unseen, forms part of the living Hinduism of the villages [39; 41].

Finally, it should again be stressed that the entire range of Hinduism is to be found in the villages, from the most orthodox Brahmanical observance to the purely local lower-caste cult. Also, it must be remembered that it is the entirety that constitutes Hinduism, not just those elements that are Brahmanical or which have an all-India spread.

Modern Developments

The very great changes that have taken place in the Indian subcontinent between the late eighteenth century and the present were matched by developments in the Hindu religious tradition, which underwent a series of major transformations. The causes that wrought these changes are multiple and complex: the demise of the Mughal empire; the arrival, rule and departure of the British; the expansion of communications and the arrival of the printing press; the development of the modern vernacular languages and the use of prose; Western education and the use of English; and the challenges from Christianity and its missionaries – all of these were factors. Equally important were the growth of political awareness, nationalism, the pressure of national and international events and the final development into independent nationhood and partition. Since independence, there has been a great expansion of the Hindu diaspora and Hindus are spread over most parts of the globe, creating new forms of the tradition, while a number of new religious movements or teachers coming from within Hinduism have gained many thousands of followers in India, Europe, Britain, America and elsewhere. These and many other factors have all been profoundly influential in various ways in bringing about the changes that have resulted in a tradition which is certainly far more self-aware, self-confident, even self-assertive, than it was in the final decades of the eighteenth century.

In looking first at the transformations in the century and a half prior to 1947, it is possible to identify two major intertwined directions of change: first, the developments which came from a revival and renewal within the tradition itself; second, the emergence of 'Neo-Hinduism', a form or representation of the highly diverse Hindu tradition created largely by the English-speaking educated elite, but within the Western concept of 'a religion', 'Hinduism', which was to be the face the tradition presented when it went public on the world stage. It is the second current, naturally, which has received the most attention in Western writing. The first current was more localized and lower-profile, expressing itself in vernacular tracts, in the formation of local associations and in countless other unobtrusive and more parochial ways; but, in so far as it produced a widespread revitalization and a restatement, even a re-creation, of the tradition itself, it has the greater long-term significance. The two currents were in constant interaction and should perhaps be seen as the internal and external manifestations of the same transformation, but since this is not yet how they are dealt with in the literature it is necessary to treat each separately.

The late eighteenth century saw the rise of a mercantile class which proved to be a new source of patronage for Hindu institutions and traditions, and this was certainly one important factor in the revitalization of Hindu religious life. The European 'discovery' of Sanskrit led to the production of grammars and dictionaries and the printing of Sanskrit and other religious texts and translations, thereby providing material for a restatement of the tradition and its past. In this restatement the tradition was referred to as Sanatana Dharma, which in the discourse of the time has the sense of 'old-style religion'. Many local associations were set up to protect Sanatana Dharma, and issues such as caste, image-worship and cow-protection were debated, often heatedly. The creation of 'Hindi' from a de-Persianized Urdu written in the Devanagari script and the demand for its use became a religious as well as a political and nationalistic issue. All of these processes resulted in a new self-awareness and self-identity, and in new formulations and developments in the many and diverse forms of the tradition. It is only now being realized just how much of the contemporary Hindu tradition and its manifestations were the results of this nineteenth-century redefinition and re-creation of Sanatana Dharma.

In contrast to this far-reaching inner transformation there remains the second current of change, the creation of 'Neo-Hinduism' [see in general 46; 52; 55]. At the beginning of this process stands Ram Mohan Roy (1772–1833) [5; 51]. He was born into a well-to-do Bengali Brahman family and was educated first in Patna, a centre of Muslim learning, where he formed an intense dislike of image-worship. In 1814 he joined the East India Company in Calcutta. There he embarked on a study of the Upanishads, from which he concluded that they contained a pure theism and certainly provided no justification for idol-worship. He learnt English and was deeply influenced by Western culture and scientific thought. He also had much contact with Christian missionaries. While thoroughly approving of the ethical teachings of Christianity, he could not, however, accept the divinity of Christ. He brought a rationalist approach to Hinduism and rejected not only image-worship but the doctrine of reincarnation as well. Appalled by certain Hindu practices, he became an active social campaigner. So effective was his campaigning against *sati*, the practice where widows immolated themselves on their husbands' funeral pyres, that in 1829 it was made illegal. A strong advocate of Western education, for women and girls as well as men and boys, he founded the Hindu College in Calcutta, which opened in 1819. In 1828 he founded the Brahmo Samaj, a society that met once a week to hear readings from the Upanishads and sermons and to sing theistic hymns. Prayer, or any attempt to approach the divine, formed no part of this rather cold, austere approach, which appealed mainly to the educated intellectual elite. Reminiscent of eighteenth-century deism, and also peculiarly un-Indian, Roy felt this to be a return to the former purity of Hindu worship.

The next effective leader of the Brahmo Samaj after the death of Roy was Debendranath Tagore, father of the famous poet, who joined the society in 1842. He was an intensely religious man who added prayer to the Samaj service. He initiated a study of the Veda and concluded that its claim to inerrancy and to be the unique scriptural authority could not be accepted. From then on reason and conscience became the primary sources of authority for the Samaj, and Debendranath himself compiled an anthology of passages taken from various scriptures, mainly the Upanishads, which accorded with the position of the Samaj. A book, the *Brahma Dharma*, became the principal sacred work for the Samaj [51].

In 1857 a young radical reformer called Keshab Chandra Sen joined the Samaj and quickly became part of the leadership, greatly impressing Tagore. At his instigation the Samaj rejected the Hindu sacraments, the *samskaras*, and produced rites of its own. It was the question of caste, however, that led Tagore and Sen to separate, and the Samaj to split. Sen wished to repudiate caste and for the twice-born to abandon the sacred thread. This was too much for the more conservative members of the Samaj. They remained with Tagore while Sen and his followers left to found the Brahmo Samaj of India. Sen thereafter became increasingly influenced by Christianity, and he compiled a scriptural work for the new Samaj drawing on sources some of which were not Hindu but were taken from other religions, particularly Christianity. He also made various changes in the service, incorporating elements of Bengali *bhakti*. But his greatest achievements were in the field of social reform. He campaigned strongly to improve the position of Hindu women and girls, and against child marriage. Under his leadership the Samaj celebrated inter-caste marriages and also the remarriage of widows, both revolutionary moves to the orthodoxy of the day.

The Brahmo Samaj was to split yet again, and Sen to found

another movement called the Church of the New Dispensation. This was even more eclectic, and included a great deal from Christianity, but it did not survive his death in 1884. Meanwhile the Samaj itself continued and had a certain amount of influence in Bengal and in missionary centres elsewhere. Its real importance, however, is that it began the process of Hindu self-examination and heralded the awakening of the Hindu social conscience. The campaigning eventually proved to be successful. Not only were Brahmo marriages recognized in law, but so were inter-caste marriages and the remarriage of widows, while child marriage was made illegal [5; 51].

Mention should also be made of the Prarthana Samaj in Maharashtra, which was not dissimilar to the Brahmo Samaj with which it had links. Its members, too, were theists, opposed image-worship, and rejected the authority of the Veda and the doctrine of reincarnation, but they saw their theism to be a continuation of medieval Maharashtrian *bhakti*. Under the leadership of Mahadev Govind Ranade (1842–1901) their main effort was in the field of social reform and social welfare, particularly with regard to the depressed castes. In this their achievement was considerable.

Quite different from both the Brahmo and the Prarthana Samaj was the Arya Samaj which was founded in 1875 by Dayananda Sarasvati (1824–83) [54]. Dayananda, after a childhood experience, had become disillusioned with image-worship. Eventually he found a *guru* under whom he studied and to whom he gave a pledge to remove from Hinduism all the corruptions and accretions that had entered it after the Veda. Whereas the trend of previous reform movements had been towards Westernization, here was a movement that was Hindu through and through, intent on returning Hinduism to its Vedic purity. Dayananda's view, however, of what constituted the message of the Veda was highly idiosyncratic and is beyond the scope of this account. What is really significant about the Arya Samaj is that it marked the movement of Hinduism on to the offensive. Dayananda fiercely attacked both Islam and Christianity since he saw them as threats to Hinduism in that they were attracting converts, especially from the lower castes. The Samaj instituted a ceremony for reconversion to Hinduism, and began to invest untouchable castes with the sacred thread, a procedure not recognized by the orthodox. The Samaj had some success, particularly in Punjab and the north. Colleges were established and the use of Hindi encouraged. Seeking to establish itself as a universal church, the Arya Samaj was militant, dogmatic and aggressive. It still exists in various parts of the world. Most Hindus did not like either its message or its methods, but it gave Hinduism a boost of self-confidence when it was needed.

A further boost came from an unlikely quarter. In 1877 Mme

Blavatsky and her helper Colonel Olcott arrived in India. They had opened the Theosophical Society two years earlier in New York, but with little success. However, there is no doubt that both Mme Blavatsky and her successor Mrs Annie Besant (1847–1933) greatly raised the self-confidence of Hindus. Hailing Hinduism as a repository of ancient wisdom and the source of all religions, these two formidable ladies travelled round India, lavish in their extravagant and uncritical praise of all things Hindu, awakening pride in the religious heritage of Hinduism and removing any feelings of inferiority that had developed following the activities of Christian missionaries, about whom they were scathing.

The next really significant influence came from deep within Hinduism. In 1852 Gadhadhar Chatterji, the son of poor Brahman parents, became a priest at the Kali temple near Calcutta. Here, in his longing for the Mother, he went through endless trances and mystical states until finally he was granted a vision of the Goddess. He turned to Tantric disciplines to control the stream of spiritual experience he was passing through and eventually was initiated by a monk of the Advaita school into the Vedantic teaching of pure monism. The name he received on initiation and by which he is generally known is Ramakrishna Paramahansa. Ramakrishna's deep spirituality made a powerful impact on all who came in contact with him, often producing in them some form of spiritual experience. Many came to see him, including Keshab Chandra Sen and other reformers, and they found that what they could only speak of from their minds, he spoke of from the depth of his own spiritual experience. Much that he said was not new, but his own consciousness enabled him to see God in every man and in every religion. He affirmed that all religions were true and that everyone should follow their own as their way to God realization. He was also insistent on the need to serve one's fellow men [5; 53].

Among Ramakrishna's disciples was a young Bengali called Narendranath Datta who had received a Western education in Calcutta and had been hovering on the edge of the Brahmo Samaj until he had met Ramakrishna. This meeting transformed his life. After Ramakrishna's death he became a *sannyasi* with the name of Vivekananda and travelled throughout India [45]. In 1893 he went as the representative of Hinduism to the first session of the World's Parliament of Religions in Chicago. Here he made a very great impact, presenting Hinduism for the first time to the world as a universal faith. His message, although questionable in part, was that all religions were true, that Hinduism is the most ancient, the noblest and the mother of all religions, that India was spiritual and the West materialistic, though he believed that India should use Western science and methods to improve its lot. His philosophical position was that of Advaita. He spent four years lecturing in America and

England and as a result Vedanta centres were set up in several cities. His return to India was greeted with great enthusiasm, for Hinduism had found an outstanding exponent and it was even thought that he had converted most of America. He immediately set up the Ramakrishna Mission, which devoted itself to social work and the relief of suffering as well as to promoting its religious message [45]. The Ramakrishna Mission has not had a great impact, although it still exists. But Vivekananda had made an unprecedented contribution. He had raised Hinduism to the status of a world religion in the outside world, and he had affirmed to Hindus that all parts of Hinduism were good, though some had been misunderstood and distorted. It was on these foundations that Mahatma Gandhi was to build.

Mohandas Karamchand Gandhi (1869–1948) was born to a family of Gujarati Vaishyas and, after a somewhat unsettled education, he was sent to London to study law, being called to the Bar in 1891 [47; 49]. After two years in India he went to South Africa where he remained for twenty years. He worked with the Indian community there and led them with some success in their struggle for justice, and against oppressive measures. By the time he returned to India in 1915, Gandhi was forty-six. Most of the values, convictions and techniques for which he later became famous in India had already been formed and tested. He had already formulated his concept of *satyagraha*, adherence to the truth, which he combined with *ahimsa*, non-violence, and *sarvodaya*, universal uplift or the welfare of all, as the three main essentials of his approach. His passionate belief in human equality and justice he had demonstrated in his work, and by personally taking an untouchable to live in his house in South Africa. His favourite religious reading was the *Bhagavadgita*, the *Ramacaritamanasa* of Tulsidas and the Sermon on the Mount. He was greatly influenced by the writings of Tolstoy, Ruskin, Thoreau and William Morris. He had established a community in a farm near Durban which sought to achieve simplicity of life, and it could be that it is to these authors that he owed his belief in the virtue of manual labour and his aversion to large-scale industry. Also deeply rooted in him was the belief that *brahmacarya*, total self-control, was essential to the pursuit of truth.

On his return to India, Gandhi established an ashram, or spiritual community, and set about both his political activities and also his campaign to improve the position of the untouchables, initially fasting until temples were opened to them for the first time ever. The history of the national movement, the winning of independence and Gandhi's central part in this cannot be chronicled here, but what must be realized is that Gandhi was a religious leader first, and a political leader second. He came to the masses of India as an ascetic, a *sannyasi*, and they regarded him as a *mahatma*, a saint or great soul, and even as an incarnation of Vishnu. He called himself a follower of *sanatana dharma*, the eternal *dharma* or righteousness, and he believed that the soul of India must first become liberated from its vices before there could be freedom from the British [49]. That is why he campaigned so strongly against untouchability, calling the untouchables Harijans, the people of God; that is why he fasted and prayed endlessly that there should be neither violence nor inter-communal hatred between Hindus and Muslims; and that was why partition and the blood-bath that followed were for Gandhi failure, even though the British had gone and India had achieved nationhood.

But if Gandhi felt this to be a failure, and if his efforts to remove untouchability have not succeeded, still his achievement is immense. Gandhi was truly a *mahatma*, a great soul, for he embraced within himself the entire people of India, imbuing them with his own deep spirituality, and led them to independent nationhood. Certainly this was a major political triumph, but, more important, it was the realization of religious values in the hearts and minds of men and women on a prodigious scale. In the process he, perhaps more than any other before, brought Hindu self-awareness and self-identity to a new maturity.

It is now more than half a century since Gandhi died and the Republic of India became an independent secular state. One feature of this period has been a hardening of that current which can be called political Hinduism, mainly right-wing and Hindu nationalist, which opposes the very secularism of the state and seeks to establish a 'Hindu nation'. This tendency can be traced back to 1909 when Mohan Malaviya and other members of the Arya Samaj established the Hindu Maha-sabha which was to turn into a right-wing Hindu nationalist party. One of its members, K. V. Hedgewar, in 1925, founded the Rastriya Svayam-sevak Sangh (RSS), a tightly organized and highly influential Hindu nationalist body, which remains extremely active to this day and is the subject of considerable controversy. Although itself not a political party, the RSS has nevertheless been closely associated with the Jana Sangh Party (founded in 1951), the Janata Party, and, finally, the Bharatiya Janata Party, the BJP, which has recently been attracting international attention through its involvement in the demolition of Babri Masjid, the mosque at Ayodhya which was destroyed in 1992 on the grounds that it was built over the birthplace of Rama. India, however, is as diverse politically as Hinduism is diverse religiously, so it will be as hard for the BJP to command nationwide acceptance as it will be for the Hindu nationalists to articulate a single form of 'Hinduism' which is universally acceptable as a unifying ideology. None the less, these are powerful forces which have certainly led to an increase in inter-communal tension, and they cannot be ignored.

Meanwhile the main body of the tradition has continued to evolve. New temples have been built, pilgrimage sites have been expanded, new deities have emerged as others have become neglected, new *gurus* and movements have arisen as others have given way. Among the movements, one, coming from within Vaishnava Krishnaite tradition and founded by Swami Narayan (1781–1830), has become particularly influential among Gujaratis both within India and in the Hindu diaspora. Among *gurus*, often regarded by their followers as incarnations of the deity, one of the most popular, again both in India and in the diaspora, is Sathya Sai Baba. Born in 1926, he announced early on that he was an incarnation of the Maharashtrian saint Sai Baba of Shirdi, whose name he took. In 1963 he declared he was Shiva. He is particularly renowned for the miracles he performs, but his inclusivist stance means he has a large following in the urban middle classes. These are but two examples among many. Some figures and movements have been influential in the West as new religious movements: Maharishi Mahesh Yogi with transcendental meditation, which has been a particularly successful transplantation of a yogic technique to the West; Prabhupada and ISKCON, or Krishna Consciousness, which comes as a Westernized version of Chaitanya's form of Vaishnavism; the followers of Rajnish; Sahaj Yoga, a restrained middle-class form of Tantrism; the Radhasoamis, who are firmly within the Sant tradition; and the Brahma Kumaris, an international Shaivite millenarian movement deriving from Sindh, are among the most notable. Whether in India or in the diaspora, the tradition is continually unfolding in new transformations, some local, some regional, all testimony to the diversity, the richness and the creativity of Hindu religious life and spirituality. The Hindu tradition, Hinduism, stands now as an equal alongside other world religions. Whatever the future holds, there can be no doubt that the contribution of Hinduism will be rich and valuable and will mark yet another stage in its continuing evolution.

Bibliography

General

1 BASHAM, A. L., *The Wonder that Was India*, London, Sidgwick & Jackson, 1954, 3rd rev. edn 1967; New York, Taplinger, 1968; London, Fontana, 1971
2 DE BARY, W. T., et al. (eds), *Sources of Indian Tradition*, New York, Columbia University Press, 1958; repr. 1969
3 KLOSTERMAIER, K. K., *A Survey of Hinduism*, 2nd edn, New York, State University of New York Press, 1994

4 O'FLAHERTY, W. D. (ed.), *Hindu Myths: A Sourcebook, Translated from the Sanskrit*, Harmondsworth, Penguin, 1975

5 ZAEHNER, R. C., *Hinduism*, London/New York, Oxford University Press, 1962; new edn 1966

Introduction to Hinduism

6 ARCHER, W. G., *The Loves of Krishna in Indian Painting and Poetry*, London, Allen & Unwin/New York, Macmillan, 1957

7 BHATTACHARJI, S., *The Indian Theogony: A Comparative Study of Mythology from the Vedas to the Purāṇas*, Cambridge, Cambridge University Press, 1970; repr. Columbia, MO, South Asia Books, 1978

8 CARMAN, J. B., *The Theology of Rāmānuja*, New Haven, Yale University Press, 1974

9 CARPENTER, J. E., *Theism in Medieval India*, London, Constable, 1926; first publ. London, Williams & Norgate, 1921 (Hibbert Lectures, 2nd ser., 1919)

10 CHATTERJII, J. C., *Kashmir Śaivism*, Srinagar, Research Department, Kashmir State/London, Luzac, 1914

11 DESAI, P. B., *Basaveśvara and His Times*, Dharwar, Kannada Research Institute, Karnatak University, 1968

12 DHAVAMONY, M., *The Love of God According to Śaiva Siddhānta: A Study in the Mysticism and Theology of Saivism*, Oxford, Clarendon Press, 1971

13 DONIGER, W., with SMITH, B., *The Laws of Manu*, Harmondsworth, Penguin, 1991

14 EDGERTON, F., *The Bhagavad-Gita, Translated and Interpreted*, Cambridge, MA, Harvard University Press/London, Oxford University Press, 1944, 1952; prev. publ. Chicago, Open Court Publishing, 1925

15 FARQUHAR, J. N., *An Outline of the Religious Literature of India*, London/New York, Oxford University Press, 1920

16 GONDA, J., *Viṣṇuism and Śivaism: A Comparison*, London, Athlone Press, 1970; New Delhi, Oriental Books, 1976

17 GUPTA, S., HOENS, D. J., and GOUDRIAAN, T., *Hindu Tantrism*, Leiden, Brill, 1979

18 HILL, W. P. D. (tr.), TULASĪDĀSA, *The Holy Lake of the Acts of Rāma: An English Translation of Tulasī Dās's Rāmacaritamānasa*, Bombay, Oxford University Press (India), 1952, 1971

19 HOPKINS, E. W., *Epic Mythology*, Strasbourg, Trübner, 1915; Ann Arbor, University Microfilms, 1961

20 HUME, R. E., *The Thirteen Principal Upanishads*, London, Oxford University Press, 1921; 2nd edn 1931, repr. 1934; Madras, Oxford University Press (India), 1949, repr. 1958

21 KEITH, A. B., *The Religion and Philosophy of the Veda and Upanishads*, Cambridge, MA, Harvard University Press/London, Oxford University Press, 1925

22 LOTT, E. J., *Vedantic Approaches to God*, London, Macmillan/Totowa, Barnes & Noble, 1980

23 MACDONELL, A. A., *Vedic Mythology*, Strasbourg, Trübner, 1897

24 O'FLAHERTY, W. D., *The Rig Veda: An Anthology*, Harmondsworth, Penguin, 1981

25 RAMANUJAN, A. K., *Speaking of Śiva* (Kannada poetry, tr. with introduction), Harmondsworth, Penguin, 1973
26 RANADE, R. D., *Indian Mysticism: Mysticism in Maharashtra*, History of Indian Philosophy, ed. S. K. Belvalkar and R. D. Ranade, vol. 7, Poona, Aryabhushan, 1933
27 VAUDEVILLE, C. (tr.), *Kabir*, vol. 1, Oxford, Clarendon Press, 1974

Hindu presuppositions and belief

28 BOWES, P., *The Hindu Religious Tradition*, London/Boston, Routledge, 1978
29 DASGUPTA, S. N., *A History of Indian Philosophy*, 5 vols, Cambridge, Cambridge University Press, 1922–55; repr. Atlantic Highlands, 1975; Delhi, Motilal Banarsidass, 1976
30 KANE, P. V., *The History of Dharmaśāstra*, 5 vols in 7, Poona, Bhandarkar Oriental Research Institute, 1930–62
31 MONIER-WILLIAMS, SIR M. B. H., *Brahmanism and Hinduism*, 4th edn, London, John Murray/New York, Macmillan, 1981
32 PRABHU, P. N., *Hindu Social Organisation*, new edn, Bombay, Popular Book Depot, 1954, repr. 1972; first publ. as *Hindu Social Institutions*, London/New York, Longmans, 1939

Hindu practice

33 BHARDWAJ, S. M., *Hindu Places of Pilgrimage in India*, Berkeley, University of California Press, 1973
34 DIEHL, C. G., *Instrument and Purpose: Studies on Rites and Rituals in South India*, Lund, Gleerup, 1956
35 MICHELL, G., *The Hindu Temple: An Introduction to its Meaning and Forms*, London, Elek/New York, Harper & Row, 1977
36 STEVENSON, M. S., *The Rites of the Twice-Born*, London/New York, Oxford University Press, 1920; repr. New York, International Publications Service, 1971, New Delhi, Oriental Books, 1971
37 UNDERHILL, M. M., *The Hindu Religious Year*, London/New York, Oxford University Press; Calcutta, Association Press, 1921

Hinduism in the villages

38 BABB, L. A., *The Divine Hierarchy: Popular Hinduism in Central India*, New York, Columbia University Press, 1975
39 CROOKE, W., *The Religion and Folklore of Northern India*, London, Oxford University Press, 1926; first publ. as *The Popular Religion and Folklore of Northern India*, 2 vols, Westminster, Constable, 1896; republ. Delhi, Munshiram Manoharlal, 1968 and (as *The Religion . . .*) New Delhi, Chand, 1972
40 HUTTON, J. H., *Caste in India: Its Nature, Function and Origins*, Cambridge, Cambridge University Press, 1946; 4th edn Bombay, Oxford University Press (India), 1963
41 O'MALLEY, L. S. S., *Popular Hinduism: The Religion of the Masses*, Cambridge, Cambridge University Press/New York, Macmillan, 1935
42 POCOCK, D., *Mind, Body and Wealth: A Study of Belief and Practice in an Indian Village*, Oxford, Blackwell/Totowa, Rowman & Littlefield, 1973

Modern developments

43 BABB, L. A., *Redemptive Encounters*, Oxford, Oxford University Press, 1987

44 BROCKINGTON, J. L., *The Sacred Thread*, Edinburgh, Edinburgh University Press, 1981

45 DEVDAS, N., *Swāmī Vivekānanda*, Bangalore, Christian Institute for the Study of Religion and Society, 1968

46 FARQUHAR, J. N., *Modern Religious Movements of India*, New York, Macmillan, 1915, repr. 1919; New Delhi, Munshiram Manoharlal, 1967

47 FISCHER, L., *The Life of Mahatma Gandhi*, London, Cape, 1951

48 FULLER, C. J., *The Camphor Flame*, Princeton, Princeton University Press, 1992

49 GANDHI, M. K., *Autobiography: The Story of My Experiments with Truth* (tr. from the original Gujarati by M. Desai), Ahmedabad, Navajivan, 1962; first publ. in English as *The Story of My Experiments with Truth*, 1927–9. Other edns include Washington, DC, Public Affairs Press, 1948, 1954; London, Phoenix, 1949

50 KINSLEY, D. R., *Hindu Goddesses*, Delhi, Motilal Banarsidass, 1987

51 KOPF, D., *The Brahmo Samaj and the Shaping of the Modern Indian Mind*, Princeton, Princeton University Press, 1978

52 LUTGENDORF, P., *The Life of a Text*, Berkeley, University of California Press, 1991

53 NIKHILANANDA, *The Gospel of Sri Ramakrishna*, Madras, Sri Ramakrishna Math., 1947, 1957

54 RAI, L. L., (LAJPAT RAI, L.), *History of the Arya Samaj*, New Delhi/Bombay, Orient Longman, 1967; first publ. as *The Arya Samaj*, London, Longman, 1915

55 SHARMA, D. S., *The Renaissance of Hinduism*, Benares, 1944

56 WILLIAMS, R. B., *A New Face of Hinduism*, Cambridge, Cambridge University Press, 1984

6

Sikhism

W. OWEN COLE

Introduction

Name

The term 'Sikh' is derived from the Punjabi verb *sikhna*, to learn. The first Sikhs were the followers of Guru Nanak (1469–1539), who lived in the Punjab region of north-west India. At first 'sikh' had no more precise meaning than 'disciple' or 'follower', but with the passage of time the movement has developed into a distinct religion with its own scriptures, beliefs, practices and values. The term has now a more precise definition, though some Sikhs themselves dispute its appropriateness. The *Rahit Maryada*, the Sikh Code of Conduct (see below, p. 333), defines a Sikh as 'any person who believes in God; in the ten Gurus; in the Guru Granth Sahib and other writings of the Gurus, and their teaching; in the Khalsa initiation ceremony; and who does not believe in the doctrinal system of any other religion' [5: appendix 1]. What all Sikhs agree on is the belief that their religion is distinctive and divinely revealed; it is not a form of Hinduism.

Sources for the Study of Sikhism

The principal primary sources for the study of the Sikh religion during its formative period, the time of the Gurus from 1469 to 1708, are Sikh. In common with other religious movements which have become established independent religions it was not until later in its development that it attracted wider literary attention [27: II].

These Sikh documents fall into two categories. First, there are the scriptures, the Guru Granth Sahib and the Dasam Granth. Of these the former, also called the Adi Granth, is the better known.

It consists of spiritual teachings expressed in metrical form composed by six of the ten Gurus, the first five and the ninth (see p. 315), as well as the verses of some Hindu and Muslim teachers who shared a similar religious outlook [5: III]. Though anthologies of the *gurbani*, as Sikhs describe the hymns, were made during the period of the second Guru and possibly in the time of the founder, Guru Nanak, the first definitive collection, the Adi Granth, was compiled only in 1603–4 under the supervision of Guru Arjan. The final recension was made in 1706 by the last Guru, Guru Gobind Singh. He included verses composed by his father, Guru Tegh Bahadur, at many places within the existing scripture, but none of his own. Two years later, on the eve of his death, he installed the Adi Granth as his successor, since which time the names Adi Granth and Guru Granth Sahib have been used synonymously and the book has become the authoritative guide and scripture of the Sikhs.

In theory the Dasam Granth, compiled some years after the death of Guru Gobind Singh by one of his disciples, Mani Singh [2: III; 22: 6–7] is also scripture, but it is rarely if ever installed as such in Sikh places of worship (*gurdwaras*) or studied or quoted as frequently as the Guru Granth Sahib. It is by no means certain that all its contents are authentic compositions of the Guru. Guru Gobind Singh was a scholar fluent in many languages. Persian, Sanskrit and Hindi are all employed in the Dasam Granth, although the script is *gurmukhi*, the one used in the Guru Granth Sahib. This makes it difficult for Sikh congregations to understand.

Some historical information is contained in the Dasam Granth but more is available in the Vars of the bard Bhai Gurdas (1551–1637). These are ballads or epic poems, epitomizing the work of the early Gurus and providing an insight into the Sikh way of life at an important stage of its development. Bhai Gurdas's father was a cousin of the third Guru, Guru Amar Das. Guru Arjan respectfully called him 'mamaji', maternal uncle, and chose him to be his scribe when he was compiling the Adi Granth. His compositions, together with those of Bhai Nand Lal (1633–1713), a companion of the tenth Guru, may also be read and used as commentaries in *gurdwaras* [22: 7–8].

For information about the life of Guru Nanak (1469–1539) it is necessary to turn to the *janam-sakhis* [15; 18: II; 19]. These are hagiographic biographies, the main purpose of which may be gleaned from the following closing declaration by the compiler of the Adi Sakhis: 'He who reads or hears this *sakhi* shall attain to the supreme rapture. He who hears, sings, or reads this *sakhi* shall find his highest desire fulfilled, for through it he shall meet Guru Baba Nanak. He who with love sings of the glory of Baba Nanak or gives ear to it shall obtain joy ineffable in all that he does in this life, and in the life to come salvation' [17: 243]. Similar traditional accounts exist of the lives of the other Gurus.

Sikhism is a religion which possesses a strong sense of community. The Gurus frequently counselled their followers upon matters of social as well as spiritual conduct. In 1699 Guru Gobind Singh instituted the Khalsa, a Sikh order which has developed into a community within Sikhism and is entered through an initiation ceremony [5: vi]. Codes of Khalsa discipline issued during the eighteenth and nineteenth centuries add to our knowledge of the concerns of the Sikh community during this period. (The *Chaupa Singh Rahit-Nama*, translated and edited by W. H. McLeod [16], is the most accessible.)

Short Introduction to the History of Sikhism

Sikhism owes its origins and early impetus to the sense of mission and dynamism of a man known reverentially as Guru Nanak. He was born on 15 April 1469 in Talwandi, now called Nanakana Sahib in his honour. This village is not far from Lahore in present day Pakistan (see figure 6.1). The *janam-sakhis* portray him as a precocious child who outstripped his teachers in knowledge while questioning the traditional standards and practices of piety which he encountered, both Hindu and Muslim [15: 4–9]. When he was thirty years old he underwent an experience which resulted in his becoming a religious teacher. This is described in the *janam-sakhis* [e.g. 15: 18–21], but the earliest account is his own, which is preserved in the Adi Granth:

I was a minstrel out of work.
I became attached to divine service.
The Almighty One commissioned me,
'Night and day sing my praise'.
The master summoned the minstrel
To the High Court, and robed me with the clothes of honour,
    and singing God's praises. Since then God's Name has
    become the comfort of my life.

Those who at the Guru's bidding feast and take their fill of the
    food which God gives, enjoy peace.
Your minstrel spreads your glory by singing your Word.
By praising God, Nanak has found the perfect One.

(Adi Granth, p. 150. Hereafter the abbreviation AG is used. All printed copies of the Adi Granth/Guru Granth Sahib are 1,430 pages long, so the provision of page numbers is an adequate and usual way of providing scriptural references.)

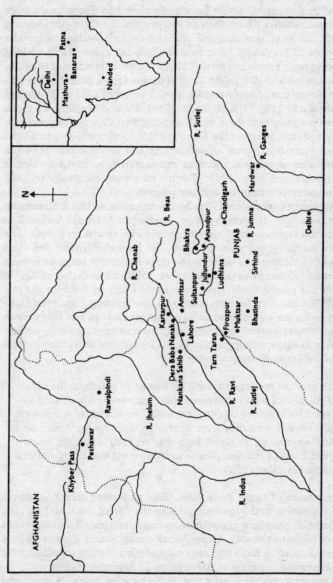

Figure 6.1 Sites in India relating to the Sikh religion

What form this experience took is not precisely known. One morning Guru Nanak took his customary bath in the river near his home in Sultanpur, where he was employed by the local Muslim governor, Daulat Khan; then he disappeared for three days, during which the river was dragged and the banks searched. When he returned to his family he remained silent for a day before making the enigmatic pronouncement: 'There is neither Hindu nor Muslim, so whose path shall I follow? I shall follow God's path. God is neither Hindu nor Muslim and the path I follow is God's' (Miharban Janam-Sakhi [19: 54]). A study of the life and teaching of Guru Nanak suggests that these words indicate that God lies beyond religious systems. Whether the Guru felt that God could also be found within them is a matter of debate. He was severely critical of the expressions of religion which he encountered, so much so that it must sometimes seem ironic that his own work eventually resulted in the development of yet another religion.

For over twenty years Guru Nanak travelled widely, encouraging women as well as men to follow 'God's path'. He felt inspired to establish *sangats*, communities of people who shared his beliefs. The *janam-sakhis* record visits to Tibet, Sri Lanka, Baghdad and even Makkah (Mecca) as well as to the most important religious centres of India. Then, in or shortly before 1520, he built the village of Kartarpur on the bank of the river Ravi. There he lived for the rest of his life, building his own home and also erecting a *dharmsala* (the early name for a *gurdwara*) and a hostel for visitors. His followers as householders worked tending their fields and meeting family obligations and other requirements. Bhai Gurdas described the spiritual aspect of life in Kartarpur thus:

> He gave his message through his hymns to enlighten the minds of his disciples and to remove their ignorance. These were followed by religious discussions while the echoes of the mystic and blissful melodies were heard. In the evening Sodar and Arti were sung, at dawn Japji was recited. Thus the Guru's word enabled the disciples to overthrow the burden of ancient traditions. (Var 1: 38)

The custom of using these *banis* daily and going to the *gurdwara* every morning and evening, and also the life of work and service, rather than practising renuciation, remains integral to the lifestyle of many Sikhs to this day. Guru Nanak made further journeys which were confined to India but gave most of his attention to establishing the Kartarpur community. He died on 22 September 1539.

The attractive personality and teaching of Guru Nanak, and probably his status as a Khatri, the most influential *jati* in Punjab, naturally won him many disciples. Their immediate needs were met

by his own example, leadership and teaching. However, at some
point in the development of the community Guru Nanak decided to
make provision for its continuation after his death, for his work of
preaching God's message to the so-called *Kal Yug* was not complete.[1] He groomed one of his disciples, Lehna, for leadership and
eventually designated him his successor, renaming him Angad,
which means 'my limb' [2, vol. II: 1–11]. The name was intended
to convey continuity. Bhai Gurdas wrote:

> During his own lifetime he [Guru Nanak] installed Bhai Lehna
> as his successor and confirmed his position as Guru. He
> passed on his light to his successor in such a manner, as if his
> spirit had moved from one body to another. None could
> understand his secret, for it was nothing short of a miracle. For
> Guru Nanak had spiritually transformed Guru Angad into the
> likeness of himself. (Var 1: 45)

This strategy ensured the safety of the message, the permanence of
the Panth (the Sikh community) and, eventually, the emergence of
Sikhism as a distinct religion.

In all there were ten Gurus (see figure 6.2). They were:

1 Guru Nanak, who was born in 1469 and died in 1539;
2 Guru Angad, who was born in 1504 (Guru 1539–52);
3 Guru Amar Das, who was born in 1479 (Guru 1552–74);
4 Guru Ram Das, who was born in 1534 (Guru 1574–81);
5 Guru Arjan, who was born in 1563 (Guru 1581–1606);
6 Guru Hargobind, who was born in 1595 (Guru 1606–44);
7 Guru Har Rai, who was born in 1630 (Guru 1644–61);
8 Guru Har Krishan, who was born in 1656 (Guru 1661–4);
9 Guru Tegh Bahadur, who was born in 1621 (Guru 1664–75);
10 Guru Gobind Singh, who was born in 1666 (Guru 1675–1708).

The later Gurus All the Gurus came from the same important Khatri
mercantile *jati* (Punjabi *zat*). With the fourth Guru the office came
to the Sodhi family [18: v] with which it was to remain, though it
was never automatically handed down from father to son. Sikhism
considers each of the Gurus to be of equal standing with all the
others. Two Sikh bards expressed this belief in the following words:
'The divine light is the same, the life form is the same. The king has
merely changed his body' (AG 966). The concept is also expressed
by the use of the word Mahala followed by the appropriate number
instead of a personal name when assigning a passage in the Guru
Granth Sahib to its author. The formula Mahala I denotes Guru
Nanak; Mahala V is Guru Arjan. Sometimes this is abbreviated to
MI or MV, or even simply I or V. One of the later Gurus as well as

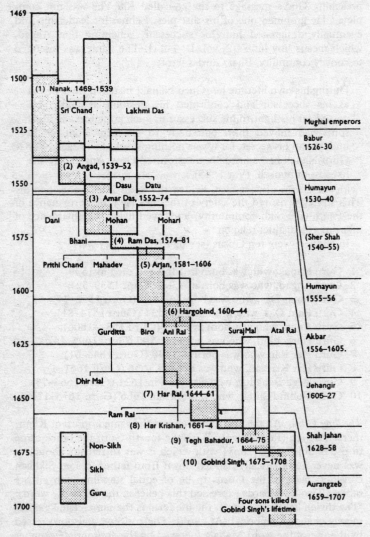

Figure 6.2 *The place of the ten Gurus in the Sikh religion*

The figure shows a timeline from 1469 to 1700 with the ten Sikh Gurus and related figures:

(1) Nanak, 1469–1539
Sri Chand
Lakhmi Das
(2) Angad, 1539–52
Dasu
Datu
(3) Amar Das, 1552–74
Dani
Mohan
Mohari
Bhani
(4) Ram Das, 1574–81
Prithi Chand
Mahadev
(5) Arjan, 1581–1606
(6) Hargobind, 1606–44
Gurditta
Biro
Ani Rai
Suraj Mal
Atal Rai
Dhir Mal
(7) Har Rai, 1644–61
Ram Rai
(8) Har Krishan, 1661–4
(9) Tegh Bahadur, 1664–75
(10) Gobind Singh, 1675–1708
Four sons killed in Gobind Singh's lifetime

Legend:
Non-Sikh
Sikh
Guru

Mughal emperors:
Babur 1526–30
Humayun 1530–40
(Sher Shah 1540–55)
Humayun 1555–56
Akbar 1556–1605.
Jehangir 1605–27
Shah Jahan 1628–58
Aurangzeb 1659–1707

Guru Nanak may end a verse with the phrase 'Nanak says'. Occasionally the same idea is conveyed by calling Guru Amar Das, for example, the third Nanak [15: 3].

Some Gurus played a more important part than others in the development of the Panth [5: II; 18: III]. Guru Angad's task was to consolidate the Panth which he did by writing down Guru Nanak's hymns in a script developed by himself or his predecessor. Now called *gurmukhi*, literally 'from the mouth of the Guru', it has become the script of written Punjabi. He may also have encouraged the compilation of the first *janam-sakhi*. This would provide scattered congregations, known as *sangats*, with an example to follow, instruction to study, and a collection of material for use in worship. Guru Amar Das established himself in the village of Goindwal on the river Beas. He summoned Sikhs to assemble in his presence three times a year, at Vaisakhi, Magha Shivatri and Divali [14: II, 79] in order to wean them away from Hindu practices associated with these festivals. He also divided the Sikhs into twenty-two districts known as *manjis*, each supervised by a *masand*, and used women missionaries especially for work among Muslim women. The fourth Guru began the building of Amritsar, then called Ramdaspur. It now lies on the Grand Trunk Road between Kabul and Calcutta but was then some miles to the north of it. His reason for choosing the site may have been related to its association with Guru Nanak, but he encouraged merchants and businessmen to establish themselves there, so it may be assumed that his motives combined commerce and piety. The brevity of his leadership, however, prevents scholars from adducing his purpose with certainty.

Guru Arjan, his younger son, built other towns in the region at Taran Taran, Sri Hargobindpur, named after his son, and Kartarpur (not to be confused with the village associated with Guru Nanak). He also made Amritsar into a religious centre, building a place of worship there called Harimandir Sahib, also known today as the Golden Temple, and authorizing the compilation of the Adi Granth which he formally installed in it, prostrating himself in front of it and thus acknowledging the message of the *gurbani* to be more important than the human messenger.

During the reign of the Emperor Akbar (1556–1605) the Sikh Panth prospered and enjoyed good relations with the state. Indeed, it may have been the interest that he showed in the movement (as well as other expressions of religious feeling) which encouraged the Sikhs to hope that they might be the reconciling agent between Islam and Hinduism for which Akbar seemed to be searching. In 1595, on the birth of his son, whom he named Hargobind ('world lord'), Guru Arjan composed the following words, which may have a significance beyond the natural expression of pleasure in the birth of a first child after a long period of childlessness during which his elder brother had been conspiring to contest the succession:

> The True Guru has sent the child. The long awaited child has been born by destiny. When he came and began to live in the womb his mother's heart was filled with gladness. The son, the world-lord's child, Gobind, is born. The one decreed by God has entered the world. Sorrow has departed, joy has replaced it. In their joy Sikhs sing God's Word. (AG 396)

Within two years of the installation of the Adi Granth in the Harimandir Sahib, Akbar had been succeeded by Jehangir, and the Guru had been imprisoned on suspicion of being implicated in a move to support Khusrau, the emperor's rival, and had died in captivity, providing the Sikhs with their first martyr. This dramatic change in fortune has affected the Panth to the present day. Guru Arjan's martyrdom is never forgotten. No matter how prosperous and hopeful the times may be which Sikhs are currently enjoying, there is a belief that a renewal of persecution is inevitable.

Guru Hargobind armed himself in obedience to his dying father's instructions. He lived and ruled as a temporal as well as spiritual leader, keeping court and enjoying hunting while remaining the Sikh Guru, though unlike his predecessors he did not compose religious verses. Doubtless there was some shift in focus from the living Guru to the Adi Granth during his lifetime. Hargobind's relations with the Emperor Jehangir were somewhat ambivalent: they hunted together, yet Jehangir also imprisoned him in Gwalior fort. At Divali Sikhs celebrate the Guru's release, along with that of fifty-two rajahs which he also secured, and his return to Amritsar. Sikhs associate with Hargobind the doctrine of *miri* and *piri*, that of wielding two swords, one of temporal justice, the other of spiritual authority.

The seventh and eighth Gurus did not make outstanding contributions to the Panth's development. With the ninth Guru, respectively their uncle and grand-uncle, leadership seems to have reverted to a more traditional form in the person of Guru Hargobind's surviving son, Guru Tegh Bahadur, now forty-three years old. A devout poet as well as a man of strong character, he succeeded to the *gaddi*, or seat of authority, at a time when Emperor Aurangzeb was introducing his policy of Islamization which included closing Hindu schools (1672) and demolishing temples, which were sometimes replaced by mosques. In 1679 the poll tax (*jizya*) imposed on non-Muslim subjects was reintroduced. Guru Tegh Bahadur was among the opponents of the emperor's policy. In 1675 he was executed in Delhi and is revered by Sikhs as a martyr who died not only for the Sikh faith but also for the principles of religious liberty.

The tenth Guru, his son, also experienced fluctuating relationships with the Mughals. His importance for the development of

Sikhism lies in two decisive acts. In 1699 at the Vaisakhi assembly at Anandpur he founded the Khalsa [5: vi; 18: i]. 'Khalsa' may be translated as 'pure', but the land which is the personal property of a sovereign is also called *khalsa*. The term therefore denotes a community of the Guru's own people. The *masands* (see above, p. 317) had often set themselves up in rivalry to the Gurus; this was a way of renewing sole allegiance to the Guru after destroying their power. Those who responded to the Guru's call for obedience received initiation through a ceremony known as *Khande ka amrit* or *Amrit Pahul* (sometimes the single word *amrit* is used). A mixture of sugar and water was stirred with a two-edged sword (a *khanda*) while a number of hymns were recited. Those initiated took certain vows and adopted five 'Ks' – five symbols which in Punjabi begin with the letter K. They are *kes* (unshorn hair), *kangha* (comb), *kirpan* (sword), *kara* (steel wristlet) and *kachch* (short trousers), often worn as an undergarment. To these male, and some female, members of the Khalsa add the turban worn by the Gurus. The result was the distinctive appearance which has marked the Sikh ever since. Male Khalsa replaced their sub-caste or family (*got*) name by Singh and women used the name Kaur. The theoretical significance of these names, meaning 'lion' and 'princess', is the elimination of caste identity which *got* names reveal, and the raising of everyone to the status of Kshatriya (warrior class). The Guru, formerly Guru Gobind Rai, now became known as Guru Gobind Singh. The creation of the Khalsa was a device for sanctioning the use of disciplined force under the Guru's personal control. Guru Hargobind had kept a small standing army, and irregular forces had existed under the *masands* [19, vol. I: v]. Now allegiance was to the Guru alone, who would only call upon them to fight in a *dharam yudh*, a struggle on behalf of justice and in defence of religious liberty [3: 63]. Sikhs regard this restrained use of force as the final development in a policy against injustice which had begun with Guru Nanak [e.g. 19: 44], who is sometimes described as being a pacifist: there seems to be no evidence for this view.

The last Guru's final act was to install the Adi Granth as his successor. Since then it has been called the Guru Granth Sahib, though the name Adi Granth is still used almost as a synonym. This decision was intended to prevent succession disputes, as his four sons had all predeceased him, but it also indicates that he considered that the mission begun by Guru Nanak was now ready to be developed in a different way. He had always taught that the Khalsa was his *alter ego*. Now he affirmed that belief by placing authority in the scripture and the community.

Later Sikh history The year 1708 marks the end of what might be called the canonical period of Sikhism. The scripture, the Khalsa and the tradition were now in place. Many Sikhs would deny that any further significant developments in these have taken place since. This is not completely correct. The stress upon the Khalsa form and ideal, of which students of the Sikh religion and uninitiated members of the Sikh Panth are very much aware today, belongs to the period of resurgence initiated by the Singh Sabha movement (see below).

The eighteenth century witnessed bitter struggles between Sikhs, Mughals and Afghans, which ended only when Maharaja Ranjit Singh [14, vol. I: x, xɪ] captured Lahore in 1799 and subsequently established an independent state; this lasted until 1849, when his son Maharaja Dalip Singh surrendered it and the Koh-i-noor diamond to the British.

Several other events in Sikh history must be mentioned if present-day Sikhism is to be understood fully. First, in the nineteenth century, the influential Singh Sabha movement emerged (2: 138–41; 22: 14–15), partly in response to successful Christian evangelism among young educated men in Punjab, but even more to the activities of the Arya Samaj (see p. 302). In 1877 Dayananda Saraswati came to Punjab and a branch of the Arya Samaj was opened in Lahore. His movement was well received by Sikhs until they realized that he held their Gurus in low esteem. Sikhs responded by increasing their support for a Singh Sabha (Sikh Society) which had been founded in Amritsar in 1873 to counter Christian missions, and to extend its work to Lahore and other cities. Its main function was to revive Sikhism through literary and educational activities, especially the founding of Khalsa colleges. This recovery also took the form of political agitation, leading to the Anand Marriage Act (1909), which gave legal recognition to the Sikh wedding ceremony, as well as emphasis upon Khalsa identity. With the Gurdwaras Act (1925) the protracted struggle to regain control of *gurdwaras* which had often passed into the ownership or custody of Hindus during the reign of Maharaja Ranjit Singh finally came to a successful conclusion.

Two other developments are of such magnitude as to deserve separate sections to themselves. They are the dispersion of Sikhs throughout the world, and the rise of the movement for an independent Sikh state.

Sikh Migration and the Diaspora

Sikhs never tire of saying that Neil Armstrong's pride at being the first man on the moon was severely dented when a taxi drew up and its Sikh driver asked him, 'Where to, sir?'

Migration is one of the most important aspects of Sikhism in the last 150 years and especially the latter half of the twentieth century. Only now is it really receiving the academic attention it deserves [1].

The movement of some Sikhs within India pre-dated overseas migration. This is fairly remarkable if we bear two things in mind. First, Sikhs were fighting for their survival during much of the eighteenth century until Maharaja Ranjit Singh established an independent Sikh state in 1801. There was nevertheless an established Khatri tradition of trading beyond Punjab. Secondly, cultural diversity might have been inhibiting. Among Hindus even a brahmin Sikh might have been suspected of being slack in observance of purity rules. Linguistic difficulties may have been slight. Even today many Sikhs speak Hindi and older ones have Urdu as well. The armies of Bombay and Madras did not recruit Sikhs before 1857, but that of the Calcutta Presidency did when the Anglo-Sikh wars ended in 1849 [39: 172]. The result of such recruitment would be the dispersal of some of the soldiers to a region at least 2,000 km from their homeland. Awareness of this migration might make the world-wide phenomenon of the Sikh diaspora more explicable.

An important date for Sikh migration beyond India was 1857, the year of the first independence struggle, known to British historians as the Mutiny. Sikhs stood aside from the uprising because they had no wish to reinstate the Mughals or any other Muslim rulers, and that seemed to them the likely consequence of its success. This won favour with the British, who began recruiting Sikhs into their army. By 1870 Sikh soldiers were serving overseas. There were also Sikh members of police forces in such British colonies as Hong Kong and Malaya. During the First World War they fought in Europe as well as Africa.

Sikh civilians were also migrating, perhaps individually but also in groups, by the end of the century. Kessinger notes that twenty men left Vilyatpur for Australia in the 1890s and that this had risen to about thirty-five by 1903, perhaps a third of the village's menfolk [12: 90, 92; 1: 32–3]. Sikhs were especially prominent in the development of East Africa in the 1890s, helping to build the railways. They were Ramgarhias for the most part, a group mainly of *tarkhans* (carpenters), but including some smiths (*lohars*), masons and brick-layers (*raj*), who have become a distinct Sikh *zat* which takes its name from Jassa Singh, a Sikh army commander of the eighteenth century who built the Ramgarh fort in Amritsar.

In 1902 Sikh soldiers from Hong Kong went to Canada to take part in celebrations marking the coronation of Edward VII. They eventually returned as settlers working in British Columbia's lumber mills. Sikhs were also to be found in California before the outbreak of the First World War. Most Sikhs migrated to America after the Second World War and claims are sometimes made that they now number more than a million there. The Canadian census of 1991 gives the country's Sikh population as 147,000. It is said that in 1985 there were forty-seven *gurdwaras* in the US and eighty-five in Canada. The number of *gurdwaras* does not, of course, necessarily indicate the size of Sikh population; but it provides some guide to population distribution, for a Sikh community will establish a *gurdwara* as soon as it can, following the tradition established in Guru Nanak's day and in keeping with its nature as a religion in which assembling together for worship is essential.

Migration to the United Kingdom The first known Sikh to arrive in Britain was Maharajah Dalip Singh, son of Ranjit Singh, the last ruler of the Sikh empire. When this was annexed by the British in 1849 its eleven-year-old ruler was placed in the custody of Sir John Login of the Bengal army, in whose care he converted to Christianity. Five years later he came to England, was received by Queen Victoria and bought an estate in Elvedon, Suffolk. As time passed he became increasingly dissatisfied with his treatment and attempted to return to India where he intended to be readmitted to the Sikh faith. He was stopped at Aden and returned to Europe, but not until he had taken *amrit*. In 1893 he died in Paris and was buried in the churchyard near his Suffolk estate. Dalip Singh and Ram Singh, builder of the Indian rooms in Queen Victoria's Osborne House, were among a very few but, in their cases, notable nineteenth-century Sikh visitors to Britain.

In 1911 the first *gurdwara* in Britain was established in Putney with financial support from the Maharajah of Patiala; others appeared only after the Second World War. Until then, Britain was apparently too far away; also, it must be remembered, Britain was at this time still an exporter of labour and the first immigration legislation had just been passed to curb the influx of Jews fleeing east European pogroms. Sikhs have never willingly migrated into inhospitable areas. Sikh eyes were still on the Pacific region which had already been pioneered, to which travel may have been easier and where work prospects were good.

Sikh and other Indian traders did, however, come to Britain between the two world wars. Many of them were pedlars belonging to the Bhatra *zat*. They would arrive at a port, set up base in rented rooms, buy small domestic items and go from door to door with their immense cases. Women might buy some goods on credit and provide the salesman with a regular if hard-earned living. Other Sikhs might work in the open-air markets. These were not settlers. Their families remained in Punjab and the men returned to them when they had made enough money to go back to their villages with pride (*izzat*) and the financial means to give them some prosperity. Their success encouraged others to take their chance.

Real settlement in Britain began in the late 1950s with a large-scale movement of economic migrants from Punjab, especially the Hoshiarpur district of the Jullundur *doab*, the area between the rivers Beas and Sutlej. They were augmented later by families from East African countries which, having gained their independence, pursued policies of Africanization. In the 1990s the British Sikh population stands at about 400,000, two-thirds of whom were born in Britain. (The UK does not include a religious question in censuses, so no accurate statistics exist. [See 13: 13.]) This is probably the largest Sikh population outside India. Britain's Sikhs chose to go to the UK because they were British; they had British passports. Some were war veterans who had served in Europe, others learned that there was plenty of work to be had, sometimes through newspaper advertisements. They went to the traditional industrial areas and parts of London. Not many went to Scotland, Wales, or Northern Ireland, where there was still unemployment, or to the coal-mining areas of south Yorkshire or the north-east, where the industry was fully manned. In brief, in common with all economic migrants through the centuries, they went where they were needed, not where they would compete with the existing labour force. They had little intention of staying permanently in the UK, but legislation during the 1960s confronted them with the choice of either bringing their families to join them or eventually leaving Britain. The vast majority decided to stay and sent for their immediate relatives. They still maintain close ties with India, sending money to improve the family home or to build *gurdwaras*, dispensaries or schools. Their children, now grown up and themselves parents, may visit Punjab less frequently, and declare themselves to be British Sikhs, though experience of racial discrimination and harassment make them uneasy about their status and future, and events in India since 1984 have reminded them that Punjab is the Sikh homeland.

Migration to North America Sikhs who migrated to the US, Canada and Australia in the second half of the twentieth century differed from most of those who went to Britain in that they were often well qualified and quickly found their way into white-collar employment.

Sikhism is not a religion which looks for converts, but a feature of the American diaspora is the large number of 'white' (*gora*) Sikhs. In January 1969 an Indian *sant*, Harbhajan Singh Puri (Yogi Bhajan, to give him his popular name), began teaching kundalini yoga in the US. Some of his students were attracted by his lifestyle, which included vegetarianism as well as the usual *amrit-dhari* discipline of the initiated Khalsa Sikh, daily *nam simran*, the prohibition of alcohol, tobacco, drugs and sex outside marriage, as well as by his Sikh world-view stressing equality and service. In November 1969 the first converts took *amrit*. Some doubts were expressed by Punjabi Sikhs when they saw *gora* Sikhs for the first time, dressed from head to foot in white Punjabi clothes and wearing turbans, including children as well as men and women. They have, however, turned out to be not hippies in transit from one fad to another but serious Sikhs. Their children have been brought up in the Sikh way; some have even been educated at Sikh schools in India. The movement is sometimes known as 3HO, Healthy Happy Holy, and by the end of 1975 had 110 centres and 250,000 people involved in its activities [24]. Its preferred title is Sikh Dharma of the Western Hemisphere; it is also known as the Sikh Dharma Brotherhood. A declared aim of the *sant* and his followers is to revive Sikh commitment to Khalsa ideals in Western countries where they have often become neglected. These converts could have an important role to play, together with other diaspora Sikhs, in enabling the Panth to distinguish universal Sikh values from those which are Punjabi.

Cultural changes among Sikhs in the diaspora Distinction between religion and culture tends to be a Western division unfamiliar and incomprehensible to many people of the East. There are, however, second- and third-generation settlers in the West who are beginning to compartmentalize religious belief and practice and secular life, at least to the extent of separating their understanding of the essence of Sikhism from a Punjabi/Indian lifestyle in respect of diet, dress, arranged marriages and language. Their neglect of these latter elements cuts them off from their spiritual heritage in the form of worship in the *sangat* and ability to understand the Guru Granth Sahib, as well as from converse with family elders who are often custodians of the tradition at the popular level, transmitting it to their grandchildren. Some Sikhs who perceive this trend as a danger respond by reinforcing Punjabi culture, particularly in retaining Punjabi as the language of the *gurdwara* and continuing to encourage arranged marriages. Usually, these are now more assisted than arranged, with young people having some say in the choice of partner. The practice of bringing in a bride or groom from India is becoming less frequent not so much because of legal hurdles but because of an awareness of changes in lifestyle among Western Sikhs. The prospect of a partner from Punjab reinforcing parental values may be seen to pose a threat to the bride or groom who was born in the diaspora. This is not to say that arranged marriages in themselves are proving unacceptable. On the contrary, many young Sikhs appreciate the stability they can bring and recognize their advisability in a system where one is marrying into an extended family.

Changes in religious practice Sikhs possess a strong sense of community. The Gurus spoke frequently of the *sangat*, the fellowship of believers which was essential for spiritual and moral development. Guru Ram Das said: 'Just as the castor oil plant imbibes the scent of the nearby sandal wood, so wrong doers become emancipated through the company of the faithful' (AG 861). In Punjab, however, this does not necessarily mean regular congregational worship of the kind found every Sunday in countries where it is a holiday. Sikhs have no weekly holy day. They should go regularly to the *gurdwara* and remember God in paying their respects to the Guru Granth Sahib, but much of their daily prayer takes place in the home, meditating every morning and evening upon specified compositions found in the scripture. It is at *gurpurbs* (anniversaries of the birth or death of one of the Gurus) or at the festivals of Vaisakhi or Divali or more regular occasions such as *sangrand*, the first day of the month, when Sikhs are likely to gather as a religious community.

In the diaspora the *gurdwara* has become the focus of Sikh life. Rooms in private houses were used by the first settlers; now, warehouses, redundant churches or former schools have been converted into *gurdwaras* and many purpose-built ones have been constructed. Weddings, held in the open or under marquees in India, usually take place in *gurdwaras* at weekends. The formal educational role of the *gurdwara* exceeds even its importance as a social centre where the elderly gather often for much of the day. For the young, Punjabi classes, training in playing the musical instruments used in worship, formal education in religion, all things unnecessary in Punjab, are essential functions of many diaspora *gurdwaras*.

The establishment of caste *gurdwaras* has occurred in some countries. One can only speculate upon reasons for this. One may be the settlement of several groups in an area whereas in India a village might have only one *zat*. Affluence and numbers might provide further explanations. The existence of sufficient Ramgarhia or Jat Sikhs in a town makes the financing of separate *gurdwaras* feasible.

Sants, spiritual teachers, have an important role in Sikhism where, in the absence of a regular professional ministry, the only practical authority is the Guru Granth Sahib. They provide personal leadership and may become the focus of devotion, though they take care not to be seen as in any way rivalling the scripture's authority or being regarded as *gurus* in the Hindu sense of the word. In India a Sikh will go to a *sant*'s *dhera* or encampment which is the equivalent of a Hindu ashram. In the diaspora, *sant gurdwaras* have taken root. Some *sants* now spend much of their time travelling the world ministering to the needs of their devotees. They often teach their own particular interpretation of Sikhism, perhaps the importance of taking *amrit* initiation, of holding regular continuous readings of the Guru Granth Sahib known as *akhand paths*, or of being vegetarian; or they may have a healing ministry.

Culture clashes in the diaspora All male Sikhs are expected to wear the turban. For those who have been initiated it is essential, as is the *kirpan*, the sword often worn as a sheath-knife about twelve centimetres long. Some migrant Sikhs made the error of cutting their hair and abandoning the turban when they arrived from India, being assured by Sikhs already there that they would not find employment otherwise. On the contrary, in fact, sometimes the turban-wearing Sikh had been highly respected by those alongside whom he had fought in Italy or Asia, and discarding this mark lost him the identity to which respect was attached. Colour, not race, was the real bar to employment and accommodation. Sikhs gradually became more confident and often, discovering that the initial advice had been unsound, readopted the turban and uncut hair. Some schools, transport authorities and other employers refused to recognize the right of Sikhs to wear the turban, but these disputes were normally resolved quickly. After all, Sikhs had worn turbans in the British army. The first clash with national authority in Britain occurred in 1972 when Parliament legislated that crash helmets should be worn by motor-cyclists. In 1976 Parliament passed the Motor-Cycle Crash Helmets (Religious Exemption) Act 'to exempt turban-wearing followers of the Sikh religion from the requirement to wear a crash helmet when riding a motor-cycle'. Since then the right to wear the turban has been generally accepted in all areas of British life. It is worn instead of a wig, for example, by a High Court judge and, in accordance with an exemption granted in the Employment Act of 1989, instead of a hard-hat on construction sites. There have also been disputes in Canada and the US relating to the right of Sikhs to wear turbans.

The Sikh *kirpan* is recognized as having a ceremonial and defensive purpose and to be an essential part of Sikh dress. Sikh responsibility has ensured that few people have questioned the right of Sikhs to wear it. A few years ago the British government signalled its intention of bringing in legislation to ban the carrying of knives. The Home Office assured Sikhs and Scots that their right to wear, respectively, the *kirpan* and the *skean dhu* would be safeguarded. Less newsworthy has been a development relating to the use of Sikh names. It took some years for application forms to change 'Christian name' to 'forename' or 'given name' but even longer for some employers, especially the British Nursing Council, to accept that a Sikh woman's surname should be 'Kaur' even though her father's name 'Singh' appeared on her birth certificate.

Khalistan

This is the name of a concept and aspiration which some Sikhs hope will be realized in the establishment of an independent Sikh country based on the historical and geographical Punjab, not the present small north-west Indian state of that name. The idea goes back beyond the partition of India in 1947. In 1945 the Shromani Akali Dal, a Sikh political party, put forward the Azad Kashmir scheme when it became clear that the British government accepted the principle of partition. This province would remain within the India Union [32: 9, 10]. Negotiations with Jinnah for predominantly Sikh areas of Punjab to be incorporated in Pakistan came to nothing when Muslims attacked Sikhs [32: 33].

Sikhs now express their view of these events tersely in the sentence: 'The Muslims got Pakistan, the Hindus got India, what did the Sikhs get?' Faced with the choice of belonging to India or Pakistan, Sikhs say, they chose India because Nehru offered them virtual autonomy whereas Jinnah had offered a religious freedom which he could not guarantee. That promise, however, has never become a reality. The federal India which Nehru and Gandhi envisaged, as well as Ambedkhar who drafted its constitution, has never matched their ideal. It was to have been a secular nation in the Indian sense of one in which all religions enjoyed equal respect and none was privileged. To protect the secular ideal against his great fear of communalism, Nehru deferred granting Sikh demands for a Punjab state defined along linguistic lines, a quite proper request within the constitution. In 1966, as a reward to Sikhs for their loyalty during the 1965 Indo-Pakistani war, his daughter Indira Gandhi, by then prime minister, granted it in the form of the Punjabi Suba. This, however, did not satisfy the aspirations of those who wanted a Sikh state, albeit within the Union, so opposition continued.

Sant Jarnail Singh Bhindranwale was the man the Congress Party hoped to use to embarrass the dominant Sikh Akali Dal. He proved to be beyond manipulation, however, and was eventually destroyed in June 1984 by an Indian army assault upon the Golden Temple complex which he had been openly fortifying for at least six months. On 31 October Mrs Gandhi was assassinated by Sikh members of her bodyguard, and in Delhi and elsewhere Sikhs were attacked; many were killed. Rajiv Gandhi, who replaced his mother as premier, attempted to solve the Punjab crisis by drawing up the Punjab Accord with a Sikh leader, Sant Harchand Singh Longawal, in July 1985; but he lacked the personal authority to implement the agreement.

The Punjab crisis remains unresolved. Most Sikhs recognize that their future lies within the Indian Union, but in a modified federation in which central authority is curbed and cannot be imposed upon the regions. A growing number of Sikhs, however, do not believe that an Indian government will ever have the will to relinquish central power and the patrimony which goes with it. At present the militants seem to have been checked in Punjab, though they are still active. Outside India, the Washington-based Council of Khalistan, under its President, Dr Gurmit Singh Aulakh, seeks to influence the US and other governments and draw attention through such organizations as Amnesty International and the United Nations to what they describe as the continued repression of the Sikh nation. In 1991 the Bharatiya Janata Party won many seats in India's general election on the basis of a clear religious appeal to Hindus to make India a Hindu nation. Sikhs are fearful of the rise of Hindu militancy for two reasons. If the Hindus tell them that they are really Hindus, as the nationalist Vishnu Hindu Parishad, for example, claims, calling them 'Keshadhari Hindus', their distinctive identity, which involves far more than an attachment to uncut hair, is threatened. If churches and mosques are attacked, Sikhs fear that *gurdwaras* will be the next chosen targets. Some Sikhs have moved to Punjab from other parts of India anxious to avoid this danger. Occasional Sikh attacks on Hindus in Punjab should be seen in the context of creating a an exclusively Sikh state *de facto*, if the Hindu government, as they see it, will not grant them one *de jure*.

The solution to the Punjab problem may lie in a radical redrafting of the Indian constitution to produce a federation which gives more regional autonomy.

Teachings

The most distinctive concept of Sikhism is its doctrine of *guru*-ship. The Srimat Bhagavata (11.3.21) advises the spiritual seeker who wishes to achieve liberation to 'find proper instruction at the feet of a *guru* who is well versed in the Vedas that lead to a knowledge of God'.[2] The first known *gurus*, or spiritual preceptors, in the Indian tradition were imparters of Vedic knowledge and many of them were Brahmans. There is, however, another parallel tradition in India, that of spiritual teachers whose authority lay not in their membership of the brahman *varna* or in the Vedas but in a personal awareness of enlightenment and belief that they had been commissioned directly by God. Often they saw their responsibilities as being to guide to liberation anyone, man or woman, regardless of caste, who approached them. Such a teacher was Guru Nanak; but the Sikh concept of *guru*-ship is far richer than that of merely believing in an enlightened teacher. God, Akal Purakh, the Timeless Being, is beyond human comprehension and can only be known by gracious self-revelation. The form of that revelation is as Adi Guru, or Primal Guru, often named as 'Sat Guru' (True Preceptor) which becomes the Word (*shabad*) or *gurshabad*, the message of enlighten-ment. The ten human Gurus of Sikhism were emphatic that God was the Guru and that any importance they might have had was as faithful messengers through whom the Word was revealed. Here they were taking hold of an ancient Indian idea of *shabad* as sound, the sound associated with *brahman*. What they believed was that this sound was the manifestation of *brahman* which became articulate and coherent in the words which they uttered. Thus the terms which are used for the verses in which the teaching is enshrined, *shabad* or *bani*, are often prefixed by the syllable *gur* to give expres-sion to this view (*gurbani*, *gurshabad*). When the tenth Guru installed the Adi Granth as Guru (whence its alternative name Guru Granth Sahib), he was doing no more than reaffirming the original doctrine that *guru*-ship belonged to the divine author and that the message was received from God rather than from the person con-veying it. Sikhs attempt to make this point firmly in *gurdwaras*, where pictures of the human Gurus should never be located in such a position that Sikhs bowing in front of the Guru Granth Sahib may be perceived to be sharing that honour with them. No Sikh should ever bow towards the portrait of one of the Gurus.

This is not the end of the story of *guru*-ship. When Guru Gobind Singh created the Khalsa in 1699 he was initiated as its sixth mem-ber and recognized its guruship. During the eighteenth century *guru*-ship seems to have been shared between the community and the scripture, being complete when the Khalsa gathered in the pres-ence of the Guru Granth Sahib. Such assemblies were eventually terminated, and awareness of the *guru*-ship of the Khalsa became more a memory than a present, practical reality. In the late twenti-eth century, at a popular level, *guru*-ship is sited in the ten Gurus and the scripture. Though that of God is acknowledged and explored by theologians, that of the community has been neglected, though some scholars are now beginning once more to turn their attention to it, and attempts have been made to revive the Sarbat Khalsa, a decision-making assembly of the Panth.

Western scholars frequently associate Guru Nanak with the north Indian Sant tradition [19: 151–8; 23: IV, s. 3]. The unifying core of Sant belief was, first, that God is *nirguna* (unconditioned, without qualities) rather than *saguna* (manifested, possessing qualities and form, usually as a divine incarnation (*avatara*, see p. 269)). God is therefore beyond the categories of male and female, though per-sonal in the sense that all the *sants* were aware of entering into a per-sonal relationship with the divine based upon grace. Secondly, Sant belief stressed that God is one without a second, the only ultimate reality. The Sant tradition was uncompromisingly monotheistic and was often critical of the polytheism which it saw in many aspects of Hinduism. From these ideas, realized through personal experience, other teachings were derived. *Avataras* were rejected; so was the efficacy of ritual acts, pilgrimages and asceticism, as well as the concept of ritual purity and pollution. The ministrations of Brahmans were considered unnecessary and the authority of the Vedas was implicitly denied. *Varna* and *jati* were thought to be illusory distinctions as, ultimately, were sexual differentiations. Sant teachings were open to Brahmans and untouchables, women as well as men, so spiritual liberation was open to everyone.

'Sant tradition' is, however, a convenient way of referring to a group of teachers and mystics united by a similarity of ideas, though not by any proven historical connection. Some of those who are assigned to the Sant group, such as Namdev (1270–1350), Ravidas (fifteenth century) and Kabir (d. 1518), are often described as disciples of Ramanand (c. 1360–1470), but this must be seen as no more than an attempt to provide them all with a Brahman guru, to offset *smarta* criticisms of unorthodoxy in the seventeenth century. A so-called sixteenth-century *smarta* reaction to the many *bhakti* teachers of north India was led by brahmins who emphasized traditional authority based upon the the Vedas (*shruti*) and *smirti* (the *Bhagavadgita*, the Laws of Manu and other texts). The *smartas* seem to have had no influence upon the Sikh Panth, though some heterodox groups responded to them. Guru Nanak explicitly rejected the authority of the Vedas and their Brahman interpreters. His successors endorsed this view. Many Sant views are to be found within Sikhism, but more coherently expressed and more fully developed in the life of the Panth than by members of the Sant tradition.

The relationship between Guru Nanak and Kabir has often excited the interest of Western scholars. One *janam-sakhi*, the Hindaliya, asserted that Guru Nanak was Kabir's disciple, but this was written by a disaffected former Sikh and is clearly an attempt to discredit the Sikh tradition and establish his own leadership [19: 23 n. 2]. The relation of Guru Nanak to Kabir, as of Kabir to the *sants*, is to be explained by an affinity of ideas. Guru Nanak was not Kabir's disciple [5: 41].

There has been no brahmanizing of the Sikh tradition. The principles and precepts taught by Guru Nanak remain intact. God, Akal Purakh, is beyond the categories of male and female, though scholars are fond of using male personal pronouns when writing about the divine being. God is *saguna* as well as *nirguna* [5: 75], a personal God, the divine Guru and inner teacher. Whoever, through grace, becomes aware of the inner activity of the immanent God as Guru, and responds to that voice by living in obedience to God's command (*hukam*), attains spiritual liberation while in the body. The effects of *karma* must still be worked out but no more will be accumulated (see p. 282). At death the soul (*atman* or *jot*) will live in the divine presence, never to be reincarnated. Effort cannot induce this revelation of God as immanent – it is a sovereign act of God's will; but Sikhs do believe that effort demonstrates earnestness of intention. Without it there would be no basis for the moral conduct which Sikhs consider important. However, there is a popular saying, 'Take one step towards God and God will take a hundred towards you.'

Once having received grace, truthful living, making an effort to serve humanity, becomes an imperative. Inner spiritual experience is developed by meditation until a person's whole being is God-permeated. The name given to the discipline which brings this about is *nam simran* [5: v], calling to mind God's name and thereby becoming so immersed in the divine unity that the illusion of duality is overcome.

Corporate worship as well as individual meditation is a means of achieving God-realization. The bard Bhai Gurdas wrote: 'One is a Sikh, two is a *sangat* [community or congregation], where five are God is present' (Var 13, 19). This line accurately reflects the teaching of Sikhism about the importance of the congregation. Guru Nanak himself said: 'The company of those who cherish the True One within them turns mortals into holy people' (AG 228). The emphasis which is placed upon becoming God-oriented (*gurmukh*) instead of self-centred and self-reliant (*manmukh*), which is a person's natural state, does not require the Sikh to turn to asceticism; on the contrary, domestic life, engagement in commerce, farming and industry, in fact any work which is honest and especially that which is beneficial to society, is to be pursued. In serving one's fellow human beings one serves God. At the same time the Sikh should live uncontaminated by the five evils of lust, covetousness, attachment, wrath and pride, like a lotus in a pond. The duties of a Sikh have been summed up in three phrases: *nam japna*, *kirt karna*, *vand chakna* – keeping God continually in mind, earning a living by honest means and giving to charity. *Seva*, service, not only to fellow Sikhs but to anyone, is not only a highly praised virtue, it might be said to be as essential a part of spiritual development as *nam simran*.

The ideals and teachings of Sikhism are such that it may be said that the *varnashrama dharma* of Hinduism (see p. 267) is reduced to one lifestyle in an ethical monotheism fully open to women and men alike, living as a householder (*grihastha*).

These words of Bhai Gurdas may sum up the Sikh ideal better than any others:

At dawn a Sikh wakes up and practises meditation, charity and purity.
A Sikh is soft-spoken, humble, benevolent, and grateful to anyone who asks for help.

A Sikh sleeps little, eats little, and speaks little, and adopts the
  Guru's teachings.
A Sikh makes a living through honest work, and gives in charity; though respected a Sikh should remain humble.
Joining the congregation morning and evening to participate in
  singing hymns, the mind should be linked to the *gurbani* and
  the Sikh should feel grateful to the Guru.
A Sikh's spontaneous devotion should be self-less for it is
  inspired by the sheer love of the Guru. (Var 28, 15)

Guru Nanak sanctified the way of life to which most peasants had
no alternative, and at the same time provided the villagers of north
India and beyond with an alternative to Islam. The egalitarian
monotheism of Islam must have been attractive to those classes of
Hindu society which, according to Brahmanical teaching, had no
hope of attaining *moksha* (see p. 283) in this present round of existence. In a Punjab under Muslim rule, Islam may also have offered
the hope of social improvement. Not surprisingly, there were many
conversions to Islam in that region. If the development of *bhakti*,
devotion, may be seen as the response of Hinduism to this threat, so
the work of Guru Nanak might be regarded as a carefully conceived,
broadly based movement providing an indigenous alternative to
Islam. The Guru Granth Sahib contains not only the *bani* of the
Sikh Gurus, but also many compositions by Muslims such as
Sheikh Farid, Hindus such as the Brahmans Ramanand and Jai
Dev, Pipa, the Rajput prince, low-caste men, for example Namdev,
a tailor or calico printer, and outcastes, Ravidas, the cobbler, and
Sadhna, a butcher, as well as Kabir the weaver, whose family had
become Muslim, perhaps to improve their status, but who refused
to class himself as either Hindu or Muslim. Their inclusion is seen
by Sikhs as making the important theological statement that truth
knows no sectarian limits. As Guru Nanak said, God is neither
Hindu nor Muslim. It would be wrong, therefore, to describe
Sikhism as theologically syncretistic, a pick-and-mix combining the
best of Hinduism and Islam, a view which neglects to address the
question of what criteria should be used to determine the 'best',
fails to comprehend the uncompromising nature of Islam, and
ignores many of the tenets of Sikh teaching outlined above.

Religious Practices

Although Sikhs may claim that the practices described below may
be traced to the Gurus, in fact many became neglected or corrupted

by Hindu influence between the period 1708 and the emergence of the Singh Sabha movement in the late nineteenth century which, among other achievements, did much to purify Sikh practices. Their response was eventually codified in the form of the *Rahit Maryada* (sometimes the spelling *Rehat Maryada* is used). [It can be found in 5: appendix 1; 22: 79–86].

The focal point of religious life and worship is the Guru Granth Sahib. Sikh worship is essentially congregational and takes place in its presence. Selections from the compositions which it contains should be sung by the *sangat* led by musicians (*ragis*). Readings and talks (*kathas*) are also the responsibility of the congregation. There are no priests; Sikhism rejects the whole of Vedic sacrificial practice. Its ministers (*granthis*) may be trained and paid, but in theory anyone may be one. The term really means one who is competent to read the Guru Granth Sahib.

The place where these acts of worship are held is called a *gurdwara* – literally the door (*dwara*) or abode of the Guru (see figure 6.3). In fact this name may be applied to a room in a private house as well as a place of public worship owned by the community, providing it contains a copy of the scripture. A family possessing a Guru Granth Sahib should consult, it, that is read from it, every day, and will probably do so in the evening. A feeling of not being able to care for it adequately may be one of the reasons why not all families have their own copy. On special domestic occasions they will borrow one from the *gurdwara*; meanwhile, for regular use, they will read from and meditate upon selected passages in a *gutka* or *nitnem*. Various names are used for such anthologies.

Public worship (*diwan*) may take place on any day. As already noted, Sikhs observe no weekly holy day, but as *ekadeshi*, the eleventh day of a lunar month, is important to Vaishnavite Hindus (see p. 269), and *sangrand* too (the day when the sun moves from one sign of the zodiac to another) is a day of customary significance in northern India, special *gurdwara* services are often held on these days. *Puran-mashi*, the evening of the full moon, is also kept in the same way by some Sikhs. According to one widely accepted tradition, Guru Nanak was born at that time.

Sikhs may visit the *gurdwara* at any time convenient to them to make an offering, listen to the words of the Guru Granth Sahib, receive *karah prasad* (sacramental food) and take *langar* (common food and drink) in the community kitchen. At the Golden Temple, daily worship begins before dawn and continues well into the night, and many major *gurdwaras* conduct worship from five or six in the morning until about eight in the evening. Overseas, some *gurdwaras* open only at the weekend when people can be present to attend the scripture and conduct services. The aim, however, is to make the *gurdwara* available every day and all day.

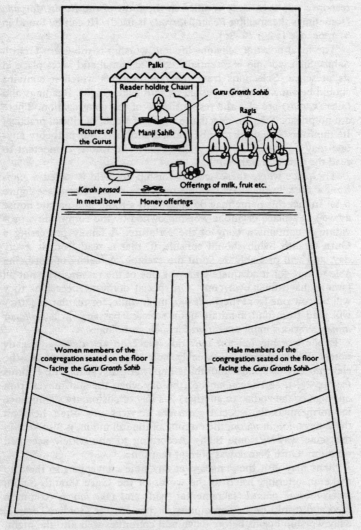

Labels within the figure:

Palki

Reader holding Chauri

Guru Granth Sahib

Ragis

Pictures of the Gurus

Manji Sahib

Karah prasad in metal bowl

Money offerings

Offerings of milk, fruit etc.

Women members of the congregation seated on the floor facing the *Guru Granth Sahib*

Male members of the congregation seated on the floor facing the *Guru Granth Sahib*

Figure 6.3 *Plan of a typical gurdwara*

There are times when the Adi Granth is read from beginning to end without a break (*akhand paths*). These occasions include *gurpurbs*, anniversaries of the birth or death of one of the Gurus, when the reading is held as a public, communal activity. These are Sikhism's only distinctive festivals: its others – Vaisakhi, Divali, and Hola Mohalla – can be traced to Hindu roots, though each has a distinctive meaning for Sikhs. Sometimes families will organize such continuous readings as an act of piety before a wedding or at the opening of new business premises. *Akhand paths* are carefully timed to last about forty-eight hours and normally to end in the early morning. As the Guru Granth Sahib is 1,430 pages long in the printed form now universally used, families cannot always organize *akhand paths*; instead, a normal reading (*sidharan path*) may be arranged. This will take place over a period of one or two weeks, family and friends assembling daily, usually after work, to participate in the spiritual exercise.

The scripture is also used when a child is named and at a wedding [37: 106–9; 2: 53–6, 59–64]. At the naming of a child someone should open the Guru Granth Sahib at random and read out the first word of the first hymn on the left-hand page. The first letter of the word should provide the initial letter of the name. When a couple have agreed to marry one another the marriage ceremony consists of circumambulating the scripture in a clockwise direction four times while the four verses of the wedding hymn (*lavan*), composed by Guru Ram Das, are sung. Consent and marriage in the presence of the Guru Granth Sahib is all that is required to legitimize a marriage in Sikh eyes. Funerals consist of readings from the scripture [37: 109–10; 2: 66–9], but bodies should not be taken into the presence of the holy book. In Indian villages, of course, cremations usually take place in the open, though large towns now have crematoria.

At some point in most services two features will occur which conclude the act of worship. The first is the saying of a formal prayer (*ardas*) [5, appendix 2; 22: 103–5] spoken by a member of the congregation facing the Guru Granth Sahib; the second is the sharing of *karah prasad*. This is a warm pudding of gram flour (semolina), water, sugar and ghee (melted butter), which is distributed to everyone who is present. It symbolizes equality and the rejection of caste restrictions, frequent bars to commensality in Hindu society.

The distinctive Sikh rite of initiation [5: vi; 37: 112–17], *amritpahul* or *khande ka amrit*, is also centred upon the Guru Granth Sahib, in the presence of which it must take place. It is the re-enactment of the ceremony which was held in 1699 when the Khalsa was founded. Five Khalsa members, wearing the distinctive insignia of the Five Ks (*kes*, uncut hair; *kangha*, comb; *kara*, wristlet; *kirpan*, sword; and *kachch*, shorts [5: v; 2: 31–6]) and, in the case of men, the turban, dissolve sugar crystals in water with a *khanda*, a short double-edged sword, while they chant prescribed hymns from the Adi Granth and some verses composed by the tenth Guru. The nectar (*amrit*) is then administered to the eyes and hair of the male or female initiate, who is then given some of it to drink. They then take certain vows, including the promise to practice *nam simran*, meditation on the Gurus' hymns, daily, and to wear the Five Ks, and then repeat the words of the *Mul Mantra*, a terse statement of faith composed by Guru Nanak. A paraphrase of it reads: 'There is One Supreme eternal reality; the true one; immanent in all beings; sustainer of all things; creator of all things; immanent in creation; without fear or enmity; not subject to time; beyond birth and death; self-manifesting; known by the Guru's grace.' In the *Mul Mantra* the Guru is God-manifest.

Sikhism has never succeeded in separating itself completely from its Hindu milieu. In fact, most Hindus would regard Sikhs as heterodox Hindus. As a minority faith existing in the midst of such a great tradition, not to mention the strong presence of Islam, it may seem remarkable that the Sikhism has survived at all. That it has done so must be in no small part due to the centrality of the Guru Granth Sahib as a basis of belief and focus of practice, and to the development of a fierce pride in the Sikh heritage. In practice, however, Sikhs have never entirely freed themselves from the influence of caste [18: v], especially, for example, in marriages. The theoretical equality of women is no more a complete reality than in other societies boasting the same egalitarian ideology. The Hindu concept of pollution has not yet been fully eradicated from Sikh life, despite the teachings of the Gurus. This can be seen from the use of *akhand paths* to purify a building and the reasons which some Sikhs give for being vegetarian. The experience of the eighteenth century, the martyrdom of two Gurus, and the recent memory of Muslim–Sikh tensions before and during the partition of India at the end of the Raj still affect relations between the two religions, although the emphasis of Sikhism is upon tolerance and coexistence based upon mutual respect and its attitude to other faiths is pluralist. It has no difficulty in accepting that all ethical monotheistic religions come from God [4: xii].

Notes

1 *Kal Yug* is the fourth Hindu *kalpa* or age, characterized by spiritual and moral decline. It encompasses the present time.

2 The Srimat Bhagavata is one of the Puranas, a Hindu text of perhaps the tenth century CE. It is divided into twelve books, with a total of 18,000 stanzas; the quotation is from book 11, chapter 3, verse 21.

Bibliography

1 BARRIER, N. G., and DUSENBERY, V. A. (eds), *The Sikh Diaspora*, New Delhi, Chanakya Publications, 1988 (the first detailed study of Sikhs world-wide)

2 COLE, W. O., *Teach Yourself Sikhism*, London, Hodder & Stoughton, 1994

3 COLE, W. O., and SAMBHI, P. S., *A Popular Dictionary of Sikhism*, London, Curzon Press; Glenn Dale, Riverdale, 1990

4 COLE, W. O., and SAMBHI, P. S., *Sikhism and Christianity*, London, Macmillan, 1993

5 COLE, W. O., and SAMBHI, P. S., *The Sikhs: Their Religious Beliefs and Practices*, 2nd edn, Brighton, Sussex Academic Press, 1995

6 GREWAL, J. S., *Guru Nanak in History*, Chandigarh, Punjab University, 1969

7 GREWAL, J. S., *The Sikhs of the Punjab, New Cambridge History of India*, vol II. 3, Cambridge, Cambridge University Press, 1990

8 HAWLEY, J. S., and MANN, G. S. (eds), *Studying the Sikhs: Issues for North America*, Albany, State University of New York Press, 1993 (examines some of the issues raised by studying Sikhism in a Western university)

9 KAPUR, R. A., *Sikh Separatism*, Delhi, Vikas, 1987

10 KAUR, M., *The Golden Temple, Past and Present*, Amritsar, Guru Nanak Dev University, 1983

11 KAUR SINGH, N-G., *The Feminine Principle in the Sikh Vision of the Transcendent*, Cambridge, Cambridge University Press, 1993

12 KESSINGER, T., *Viliyatpur, 1848–1968*, Berkeley/Los Angeles, University of California Press, 1974

13 KNOTT, K, *Sikh Bulletin*, no. 4, 1987 (available from West Sussex Institute of Higher Education, College Lane, Chichester PO19 4PE)

14 MACAULIFFE, M. A., *The Sikh Religion*, 6 vols, Oxford, Clarendon Press, 1909; repr. Delhi, Chand, 1970 (a faithful and comprehensive account of the Sikh tradition covering the period of the Gurus, 1469–1708)

15 MCLEOD, W. H., *The B40 Janam-sakhi*, Amritsar, Guru Nanak Dev University, 1980

16 MCLEOD, W. H. (tr. and ed), *Chaupa Singh Rahit-Nama*, University of Otago Press, 1987

17 MCLEOD, W. H. *The Early Sikh Tradition*, Oxford, Clarendon Press, 1980

18 MCLEOD, W. H., *The Evolution of the Sikh Community*, Oxford, Clarendon Press, 1976; Indian edn Delhi, Oxford University Press, 1975

19 MCLEOD, W. H., *Guru Nanak and the Sikh Religion*, Oxford, Clarendon Press, 1968; Indian edn Delhi, Oxford University Press, 1976

20 MCLEOD, W. H., *Popular Sikh Art*, Delhi, Oxford University Press (India), 1991

21 MCLEOD, W. H., *The Sikhs: History, Religion and Society*, New York, Columbia University Press, 1989

22 MCLEOD, W. H., *Sources for the Study of Sikhism*, Manchester, Manchester University Press, 1984; Chicago, Chicago University Press, 1990

23 MCLEOD, W. H., *Who is a Sikh?*, Oxford, Clarendon Press, 1989

24 MANSUKHANI, *Spokesman*, Baisakhi number, no. 4, 1976

25 O'CONNELL, J. T., ISRAEL, M., and OXTOBY, W. (eds), *Sikh History and Religion in the Twentieth Century*, Toronto, University of Toronto Press, 1988

26 SHERGILL, N. S., *International Directory of Gurdwaras and Sikh Organisations*, privately published, 1985; available from Virdee Brothers, 102 The Green, Southall, Middlesex, UB2 4BQ, UK

27 SINGH, DARSHAN, *Western Perspective on the Sikh Religion*, New Delhi, Sehgal, 1991

28 SINGH, GOPAL, *A History of the Sikh People, 1489–1988*, New Delhi, World Book Centre, 1979; rev edn 1988

29 SINGH, H. (ed.), *The Encyclopedia of Sikhism*, Patiala, Punjabi University; vol. 1, 1992; vols 2–5 forthcoming

30 SINGH, SIR JOGINDRA, *Sikh Ceremonies*, Chandigarh, Religious Book Society, 1968; first publ. Bombay, International Book House, 1941

31 SINGH, KHUSHWANT, *A History of the Sikhs*, 2 vols, 1963; rev edn Delhi, Oxford University Press (India), 1991

32 SINGH, KIRPAL, *The Partition of the Punjab*, Patiala, Punjabi University, 1972

33 SINGH, N., *The Sikh Moral Tradition*, New Delhi, Manohar, 1990

34 SINGH, P. *Gurdwaras*, New Delhi, Himalayan Books, 1992

35 SINGH, SHER, *Philosophy of Sikhism*, Lahore, Sikh University Press, 1944

36 SINGH, TARAN (ed.), *Guru Nanak and Indian Religious Thought*, Patiala, Punjabi University, 1970

37 SINGH, TEJA, *Sikhism: Its Ideals and Institutions*, London/New York, Orient Longmans, 1938; new edn Bombay, 1951; repr. several times

38 TATLA, D. S., and NESBITT, E., *Sikhs in Britain: Annotated Bibliography*, rev. edn, Ethnic Relations Unit, University of Warwick, 1994 (an essential publication for anyone studying Sikhs in the UK)

39 YADAV, *Punjab History Conference*, 1966

Translations of the Guru Granth Sahib

These tend to be written in sixteenth-century English or metrical poetry, apart from passages included in [14] above, an incomplete but substantial anthology still widely used which has the additional value of including considerable extracts from the Dasam Granth not easily available elsewhere.

Complete translations of the Adi Granth are:

Sri Guru Granth Sahib, ed. Gopal Singh: New Delhi, World Book Centre, 1962

Sri Guru Granth Sahib, ed. Manmohan Singh: Amritsar, Shromani Gurdwara Parbandhak Committee, 1969

Sri Guru Granth Sahib, ed. Gurbachan Singh Talib: Patiala, Punjabi University, 1990

Other Sikh texts

A compendium of many of the most frequently used and important Sikh texts is [22] above.

Kaur Singh, Nikky-Guninder, *The Name of my Beloved, Verses of the Sikh Gurus*, London, HarperCollins, Sacred Literature Series, 1996 is a modern English translation of important *banis* from the scriptures, published as part of the Sacred Literature Series sponsored by the International Sacred Literature Trust.

Dr Jarnail Singh of Canada has completed a French translation of the Guru Granth Sahib, privately published, 1996; available from 70, Cairnside Crescent, Willowdale, Ontario M2J 3M8, Canada.

7

Jainism

KENDALL W. FOLKERT
Revised and expanded by John E. Cort

Introduction

Jains have been present in India's religious life for at least 2,500 years, and continue to be a visible and active community. At present this community includes slightly more than 3 million people (less than 1 per cent of India's population), and its relative size has been small throughout its history. Yet the influence of the Jains on Indian culture and the continuity of their history have been such that Jainism is commonly and properly regarded as one of India's major indigenous religious traditions.

One of the hallmarks of Jainism is an ascetic ideal. Jains take their name from the term 'Jina', which means 'conqueror'. 'Jina' is an honorific term, not a proper name (cf. 'Buddha'); it is bestowed by Jains on twenty-four great religious teachers and leaders. The message and example of these teacher–conquerors is that the human being, without supernatural aid, is capable of conquering the bondage of physical existence and achieving freedom from rebirth; and that this conquest is to be achieved only by the most rigorous renunciation of all physical comforts and social constraints. These teachers are also called Tirthankaras, a title meaning 'crossing-maker', which points to their role as teachers and exemplars for others who seek the same goal. The title Tirthankara is also interpreted as meaning 'community-maker', indicating that they established the fourfold Jain community of monks, nuns, laymen and laywomen. They are further called Arhats, 'worthy ones', for they are the beings most worthy of emulation and veneration in the universe.

Though relatively small numerically, Jainism is not monolithic. Regional and linguistic divisions, and differences in religious practice, have been present in Jainism since at least the beginning of the Christian Era. Jains are, by and large, divided into Shvetambaras (so named because their monks and nuns are 'white-clad') and Digambaras (so named because their male ascetics are 'sky-clad', i.e. naked), each of which is further subdivided by movements which have arisen in recent centuries. It is also important to note that, while Jainism has an ascetic basis, the majority of those who call themselves Jains are laypersons whose religious life is not monastic.

Primary Sources for the Study of Jainism

Sources for study are best treated as three categories of literature: (1) early Prakrit texts; (2) later Sanskrit and Prakrit writings; and (3) more recent vernacular literatures. The first category comprises the oldest texts of Jainism, which were composed in various Prakrits (early Indian vernacular languages). By the fifth century CE, the Shvetambara Jains had assembled a collection of important texts, commonly called the Agama [7: 61-9]. The oldest and most venerated texts are the Angas, which present early accounts of Jain monastic discipline and contain sermons and dialogues of Vardhamana Mahavira (sixth century BCE), the last of the twenty-four Tirthankaras. By the thirteenth century these texts had been categorized into a sort of canon of forty-five texts, although the specific texts varied from one list to another [12: 47-77].

Not all Jains, however, regard these forty-five texts as normative. In the seventeenth century CE a Shvetambara movement called the Sthanakavasis rejected some of them, adopting as authentic only thirty-two of the forty-five, and the Digambara Jains, while not repudiating most of the dogmatic content of the Agama, hold that the language and form of this canon are not authentic. The Digambaras preserve two very old Prakrit texts that are contemporary with later Shvetambara canonical texts. These earliest Digambara texts, the *Shatkhandagama* ('Scripture in Six Parts') and the *Kashayaprabhrta* ('Treatise on the Stain of Passion') were supplemented by commentaries and writings which, together with the older texts, give the Digambaras their own body of normative literature, called the *Anuyoga* ('Expositions').

The second category of primary source literature, written in Sanskrit and Prakrit largely from the fourth century CE onwards, signals a major change in Jainism. Alongside commentaries on older texts, this large body of literature contains new didactic texts, philosophical writings, and narrative and technical works. An important feature of this literature is that much of it deals with the lay community, and includes writings (resembling the Hindu Puranas) that give a Jain view of world history and of the origins of basic human institutions and everyday religious activity. These Sanskrit sources thus point beyond themselves to a major development in

Jainism, namely the elaboration and ideological systematization of lay life, including religious discipline and temple, home and life-cycle rituals. These sources are, therefore, important for understanding the full range of Jain religious life. (For the reader's guidance, a list of major works in several categories is provided in appendices A and B at the end of this chapter.)

The third area of primary source material, of more recent origin, consists of works in modern Indian languages (including early forms of such languages as Gujarati, Hindi, Marathi and Kannada) and, since the late nineteenth century, in English. The vernacular works cover a range of religious material, including translations of doctrinal texts and recastings of Prakrit and Sanskrit narratives. There are also works written in recent decades that are directed towards Jain renewal and contemporary problems.

Jain writings in English were often aimed at European and American audiences, and include efforts at presenting ancient Jain texts and ideas to the Western world. Notable in this connection, though many more examples could be cited, are the works of J. L. Jaini, a Digambara layman and lawyer, and Professor P. S. Jaini, a Digambara layman who taught Buddhist studies at the University of California, Berkeley. J. L. Jaini's 1916 *Outlines of Jainism* and P. S. Jaini's 1979 *The Jaina Path of Purification* both present something of modern apologetics for Jainism.

Jain History

Many standard works refer to Vardhamana Mahavira, who lived from 599 to 527 BCE (the traditional dating), as the 'founder' of Jainism, and regard Jain history as beginning with him. However, Jains hold that the universe is eternal and uncreated and, as do Hindus, conceive of time in vast, cyclic terms. A full cycle of time consists of two main periods of some 600 million years, each subdivided into six parts. One of these main periods is a period of ascent, in which all conditions improve; the other is a time of descent, in which knowledge, behaviour, human stature, etc. all decline. In each main half-cycle there appear twenty-four great teachers, the Jinas or Tirthankaras referred to above.

In the current cycle of cosmic time (which is a period of decline), twenty-four such teachers are thus held to have lived. The last of these was Vardhamana Mahavira. His predecessor in the series was Parshva, whom the Jains place in the ninth century BCE, and for whose life there is some (but very little) historical evidence. Modern scholarly accounts of Jain history thus begin with Mahavira, but Jain literature and religious life include all twenty-four Tirthankaras.

Mahavira was born Vardhamana Jnatrputra in north-east India, near modern Patna. (Jnatrputra is his clan-name; 'Mahavira' is an honorific title meaning 'great hero'.) At thirty years of age, he abandoned his life as a member of the warrior (Kshatriya) class, and took up the life of a possessionless mendicant. For more than twelve years Mahavira devoted himself to renunciation and detachment from all physical needs and comforts. At the end of this time, having reached complete understanding of the nature of the universe and absolute detachment from worldly desires, he began teaching others. By Jain accounts, he had assembled a following of several hundred thousand by the time of his death at the age of seventy-two.

Leadership of the Jains thereafter passed to Mahavira's senior disciples, and under these men and their successors the movement began to spread from north-eastern India into eastern and northwestern population centres. The Jains, like the Buddhists, benefited from the support for monastic ideals of the Mauryan dynasty (third century BCE), and the growth and geographical spread of Jainism accelerated, carrying it into central and southern India.

In the period after Mahavira's death, divisions emerged within Jainism, in particular the Shvetambara–Digambara schism mentioned above. The two groups disagreed largely over monastic practice. The Digambaras maintained that an ascetic who had truly renounced the world would also renounce clothing, and go naked, as Mahavira apparently had done. The Shvetambaras maintained, however, that Mahavira's life and teachings did not make nudity an absolute requirement, and that the wearing of simple white garments would be a sufficient act of renunciation. From this particular disagreement, which gradually crystallized in the early centuries CE, have come the names (see above) that characterize this lasting division within Jainism.

Other areas of disagreement also arose, no less significant than the matter of clothing, but often more technical and less subject to popular debate. These included the question of scriptures, as detailed above; there were also disagreements over other particulars of monastic life, and differing versions of the life story of Mahavira, plus a significant and lasting disagreement concerning the status of women [11]. Shvetambaras admit women to full monastic vows, but Digambaras do not, arguing that women are not capable of attaining liberation and must await rebirth as males in order to pursue full ascetic careers.

All these differences were accentuated (and may well have been partly caused) by the fact that the two groups were concentrated in different regions and subcultures of India during Jainism's period of growth. The Digambaras were the principal Jains in south and central India, while the Shvetambaras concentrated in the north and west. Thus it is appropriate to think of the Shvetambara–Digambara division as being in many ways like the difference between Orthodox and Roman Catholic Christians.

Internal divisions notwithstanding, the Jains entered a period of growth and influence by the fifth century CE. In central and southern India, the Digambaras won royal patronage and were a notable cultural force, especially in such matters as the development of vernacular literatures. A few centuries later the Shvetambaras played much the same role in the north, and even more so in western India.

This was the period, as noted above, that gave a coherent and lasting pattern to the Jain lay community. As Jainism had moved into diverse regions and had grown in numbers, the absorption of laypersons into the movement required that the lay Jain be given a distinctive identity. Thus narrative texts and models of lay discipline are prominent in the literature of this period.

By the eleventh and twelfth centuries CE Jainism was beginning to retreat geographically into its present areas of concentration (see figure 7.1). The Digambaras gradually retreated to the north and west, leaving behind only a shadow of their earlier presence in the central and southern regions. In the Shvetambara-dominated areas less contraction occurred, although the Shvetambaras also declined in influence as new Hindu movements gained a following. The Shvetambaras also experienced the increasing presence of Islam in India from the twelfth century onwards.

By 1500 CE, Jainism had largely reached its current geographical distribution, and from this time onwards began to see various movements of reform and renewal. Prominent among these was a seventeenth-century Shvetambara movement called the Sthanakavasis. Still active today, its members are recognizable by their practice of wearing a cloth or mask over the mouth and nose. This group objected to the veneration of images as practised by Jains, and to the entire complex of temple-cultus and activity that had developed in Jainism by that time. From the Sthanakavasis developed the similar eighteenth-century Shvetambara Terapantha movement; the remaining, numerically dominant Shvetambaras are known as Murtipujakas, 'Image-Worshippers'.

Jainism has thus passed through periods of formative, largely monastic life (from Mahavira to the early Christian Era); of spread, growth and engagement with laity (early Christian Era to twelfth century); and of contraction, reform and redevelopment.

Scholarly Study of the Jains

The Jains came to the notice of Western scholarship largely through the efforts of Albrecht Weber, Georg Bühler and Hermann Jacobi. Weber and Bühler combined efforts in the 1880s to present to scholars a comprehensive account of the Jain scriptures, and Jacobi

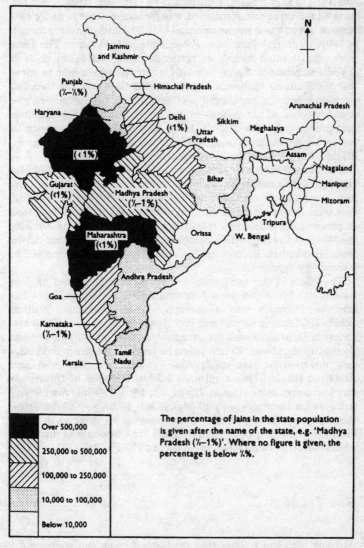

The percentage of Jains in the state population is given after the name of the state, e.g. 'Madhya Pradesh (½–1%)'. Where no figure is given, the percentage is below ¼%.

Scale:
- Over 500,000
- 250,000 to 500,000
- 100,000 to 250,000
- 10,000 to 100,000
- Below 10,000

Figure 7.1 *Distribution of the Jain population in India, by number and as percentage of state population*

pioneered the translation of Jain Prakrit texts into European languages. A number of other scholars, too numerous to catalogue here [see 15: 1–13; 8: 23–33], contributed to early Jain studies, but the work of the three just mentioned was formative. This is so for two reasons. First, it was not uncommon for nineteenth-century scholars of India to portray Jainism as subordinate to Buddhism. The Jains were often treated merely as predecessors of Buddhism or as a schismatic offshoot. Some scholarly attempts were made to show that Vardhamana Mahavira and Siddhartha Gautama, the Buddha, were one and the same, the Jain schismatics having altered the founder's portrait just enough to make it appear that they had their own unique origin [9: ix–xlvii]. It was Jacobi who put this notion to rest by his tireless translation and assembling of evidence, and since his time the Jains have been accorded appropriate recognition.

The second formative dimension of the work of Weber, Bühler and Jacobi was that their interests, typical for the nineteenth century, were heavily textual, philological and historical. Given this, they were drawn first to the Shvetambara tradition, which appeared to preserve the oldest and most complete set of texts. As a result, the Western world's earliest complete picture of Jainism was drawn from Shvetambara sources, while the Digambaras were portrayed in a secondary light.

The effect of this early focus on the Shvetambaras and on Jain texts is still felt. Subsequent Jain scholarship, by such eminent figures as Helmuth von Glasenapp, Ernst Leumann, Walther Schubring, Ludwig Alsdorf and P. S. Jaini, remained textual and historical in focus, and with the exception of Jaini placed an emphasis on the Shvetambaras. Recent years, however, have seen a promising new direction in Jain studies, as a number of European and American scholars have conducted fieldwork studies of contemporary Jain communities [see 1; 2; 3; 4; 13; 14; 17]. While there is still some disjunction between philological and anthropological studies, these recent scholarly developments promise to result in a much fuller understanding of the Jain tradition. The first fruit of this interaction is seen in Paul Dundas's excellent 1992 *The Jains* [7].

Basic Teachings

As noted, Jainism teaches that the human being can conquer the limitations of physical existence and attain immortality by means of rigorous ascetic discipline. Jainism bases its teaching on a fundamental division of all existing things into two classes: *jiva*, i.e. that which is sentient; and *ajiva*, that which is not. Every living thing consists of a *jiva* (often translated as 'soul', but better understood as a 'sentient essence') and of *ajiva*, i.e. a non-sentient, material component that has become associated with the *jiva*. This association with *ajiva* prevents the *jiva* from realizing its true nature, which is immortal, omniscient and absolutely complete in itself.

There is an infinite number of *jivas*, and each is an eternal and discrete entity, not linked to other *jivas* in any fashion. The *jivas* neither emanate from a common source nor in any way merge with one another upon liberation. There is no single 'supreme *jiva*' or supreme creator deity, and the Jinas are not regarded as creator gods. They are venerated and worshipped as divine, but this is by virtue of their status as beings who have attained spiritual liberation and perfection, not because of any primordial creation. Jains are not atheists, however, and they do freely talk of God, by which they refer to the sum total of the Jinas and other liberated *jivas*. Since these liberated beings are indistinguishable one from another, there is a sense in which they blend into a single entity, a single Jina, in the religious understanding of the Jains.

Jains also hold that each *jiva* has eternally been associated with *ajiva*, i.e. that there was no 'fall' of the *jiva* into an impure state. The *jiva*'s association with *ajiva* is beginningless, like the universe, yet the condition is not unchangeable. The association of the two is understood to be the work of *karma*, a concept that the Jains share with the larger Hindu tradition (see pp. 282, 283), but understand in a unique fashion. In the Jain view, *karma* is a subtle form of matter that clings to the *jiva*, obscuring (but not actually altering) the *jiva*'s innate capacities. This obscuring of its faculties causes the *jiva* to be reborn into an infinite series of physical existences, another basic premise that Jainism shares with Hinduism as a whole.

There is only one way in which the *jiva* can be set free of this karmic bondage and resultant physical rebirth, and that way involves the ascetic life. The goal of ascetic discipline is to stop any further association of the *jiva* with *karma*, and to hasten the decay of such *karma* as has previously obscured the *jiva*. When the *jiva* is at last rid of all karmic association, it is held to be freed of rebirth, and to rise to the uppermost reaches of the universe, the *siddha-loka* (see figure 7.2), to abide there eternally in its innate perfection of total knowledge and self-containment.

An interesting dimension of the Jain consideration of *jiva* and *ajiva* is the system of philosophical analysis known as *anekantavada*, the teaching of 'non-one-sidedness', which Jain philosophers developed as a way of dealing with the multiple dimensions of reality. Jain metaphysics considers the soul to be both essentially unchanging and yet capable of various qualitative alterations, and seeks to synthesize conflicting analyses of reality (e.g. either as permanent or

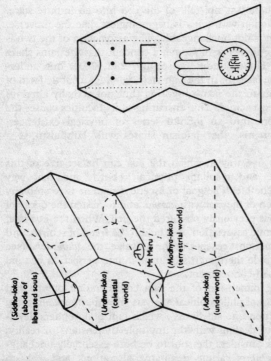

The portion shown inside the dotted rectangle is a sign commonly made during *puja*. The palm of the hand carries a stylized version of the word *ahimsa*:

(*Jain pratika*, symbol of Jain faith, officially adopted in 1975 at celebration of the 2,500th anniversary of *Mahavira's nirvana*.)

The symbol clearly reflects the archaic view of the universe (see left).

(*The archaic view of the universe, representing in rough outline the human form, and its four levels of abode*.)

Humans dwell in the *Madhya-loka*. The celestial world and underworld comprise many internal levels corresponding to the type of celestial or infernal being.

Siddha-loka (abode of liberated souls)

Urdhva-loka (celestial world)

Mt Meru

Madhya-loka (terrestrial world)

Adho-loka (underworld)

Figure 7.2 Loka-akasha: *the Jain conception of the universe*

as constantly changing). In the Jain view, any philosophical system that holds reality to be ultimately reducible to one ontological dimension (e.g. to permanence, or to constant change) is an *ekantavada*, a 'one-sided view', and is condemned to error by its very failure to take account of the several equally important dimensions of being. Thus the Jains insist on 'non-one-sidedness'.

These core teachings contain certain key elements related to basic Jain values. The first such matter is the nature of the *jiva*. Jains infer the existence of the *jiva* from its function as 'knower' and agent of activity in living things, and argue that the *jiva*'s innate nature must be whole and complete, or else there would be an inconsistency in its existence, even though it has been eternally associated with *karma*. Thus it is that the *jiva* is held to be innately omniscient and eternal. It is this capacity for omniscience that gives authority to Jain teachings, for the Tirthankaras are held to have attained omniscience in virtue of their ascetic detachment from all physical things. There being no supernatural agency, there can be no divine revelation; the truth of a Tirthankara's teaching thus ultimately rests on the Jain conviction that all *jivas* are capable of total knowledge [18: 61–4]. The work of a Tirthankara is to show the way, to 'make a crossing', based upon his attainment, which is, properly speaking, the recovery of his own *jiva*'s true nature, not the discovery of something new.

A second key element in Jain teachings is the nature of *ajiva* and the working of *karma* [see 7: 83–7; 18: 220–60]. All insentient existents are included in the category of *ajiva*, particularly space, time and matter, the latter conceived of as atoms. It is important to note that the actual existence of *ajiva* is not denied by Jains, and that matter is therefore real and eternal. *Karma*, then, as a subtle form of matter, is not an illusion or a result of perceptual error. It is real, and must be dealt with in a physical way, as must all components of worldly existence.

Dissolution of the *jiva*'s association with *karma* thus requires the cultivation of actual and extreme detachment from all that is not-*jiva*. No purely 'spiritual' or 'mental' exercise will suffice. In the second or third century CE, the Digambara philosopher Kundakunda taught that karmic bondage is a mental illusion, not a physical fact, and so promoted inner spiritual self-realization instead of physical asceticism. While Kundakunda's teachings have been influential throughout succeeding centuries, they have always represented a minority view, and have been harshly criticized by the majority of Jain authors. Jain monastic life has always had, and has today, a quality of concreteness and actual physical rigour to it.

A third key element is the practice of *ahimsa*, 'non-harm'. As Jainism evolved, *ahimsa* came more and more to the fore as a key component of detachment from *ajiva*, from the material world of *karma.* For Jains, *ahimsa* has come to embody one's willingness to separate oneself altogether not merely from acts of injury or killing, but also from the entire mechanism of aggression, possession and consumption that characterizes life in this world. Thus *ahimsa* has come to be a hallmark of the Jain commitment to detachment. It is not only an ethical goal, but also a metaphysical truth for Jains that non-harm is part of the path to liberation. In contrast to the relativistic tendencies seen in the doctrine of *anekantavada*, for the Jains *ahimsa* is a moral absolute. A common Jain phrase is 'non-harm is the supreme ethical principle' (*ahimsa paramo dharmah*), meaning that for the Jains *ahimsa* provides a measuring stick by which all actions and all religious traditions can be judged.

The central place given to this teaching has resulted in a number of characteristic Jain practices, including the monastic practice of carrying a small broom or whisk with which to brush away gently any living creatures before one sits or lies down. The Sthanakavasi and Terapanthi practice of permanently wearing a mask stems from a desire to prevent even the accidental ingestion of invisible creatures. The concern for *ahimsa* has also involved the entire community, monastic and lay, in a characteristic insistence upon vegetarian diet, and opposition to animal slaughter in general, as important dimensions of non-harm. Jain laypersons are enjoined to engage only in occupations that minimize the destruction of living beings, and thus most Jains are members of mercantile or professional classes.

The achievement of such detachment, in total reliance upon one's innate capacities, is an arduous task, and has been attempted by only a minute fraction of the Jain community at any one time. The Jain layperson has no expectation of final liberation. Living outside of monastic orders means that release from physical existence can come only in some future life. Moreover, even the ascetic is understood to live many lifetimes of renunciation before achieving total conquest. The casting of this rigorous teaching into day-to-day practice has been a dominant factor in the history of Jainism and its concrete everyday life.

Characteristic Jain Practices

Introduction

In matters of religious practice Jainism presents an interesting case. Since Jain teachings give priority to the ascetic ideal, monastic practice is the most direct outcome of the teachings. At the same time, one cannot quickly and sharply draw a line between monastic and lay religious practice in Jainism, and treat the former as orthopraxis and the latter as the 'little' tradition in Jainism. Such a bifurcation fails because there is a body of lay Jain practice that is modelled on the monastic life; because Jainism has regularly sought to link together monk and layperson, ascetic and lay life; and because the majority of Jains have always been laypeople.

Therefore, Jain religious practices are best seen as being of two basic types: first, those practices – monastic and lay – that are most informed by the ascetic ideal; and second, those practices – largely of laypersons, but also of monks – that are less directly linked to asceticism, and instead include practices based on devotion and veneration of the Jinas.

The more ascetic model is framed by a vision of the complete path to liberation as consisting of fourteen stages, called *gunasthanas* [12: 272–3; 18: 268–80]. These stages trace the progression of the *jiva* from a state of total karmic bondage to its final release and the regaining of its full capacities. Only at the fourth *gunasthana* is the *jiva* sufficiently free of bondage to enable one to live as a pious layperson, and the monastic path proper begins at the sixth *gunasthana*. Thus the formal orthopraxis of Jainism assumes a continuity between the lay and monastic careers.

Monastic Asceticism

Entry to the sixth *gunasthana* is marked by the taking of monastic vows. Jains have always taken the specifics of monastic practice with great seriousness; as noted above, differences over monastic practice have led to divisions within Jainism. Despite these differences, however, there is a basic set of monastic practices that is widely shared [7: 129–60; 6: 139ff]. The aspirant to monastic orders must be physically and morally fit, and will have prepared for entry into orders by studying under a chosen preceptor who is already in orders. When the aspirant is ready, a formal ceremony of initiation is conducted.

In this ceremony, the new ascetic takes five great restraining vows (*mahavratas*): to observe *ahimsa*, and to avoid lying, taking what is not freely given, sexual activity and ownership of any possessions. He or she will be given a new name, which sometimes includes the name of the preceptor's monastic lineage. (Beginning early in the movement's history, Jain ascetics formed themselves into monastic lineages, called *gacchas* among the Shvetambaras and *sanghas* among the Digambaras. For details of monastic organization, see [7: 103–24; 2].)

If the aspirant is entering a Digambara order, he gives up all his possessions and clothing, and is given a small whisk of peacock feathers as his only possession. A Shvetambara initiate is given three pieces of cloth to wear, a whisk made of wool, and a begging-bowl and staff. The Sthanakavasis and Terapanthis add a face-mask to this set of items. Thereafter, the new monk or nun is expected to join with at least two or three others and to live a life of increasingly rigorous discipline. Such a small group of ascetics generally remains relatively mobile for eight months of the year, spending periods of time in various temples, study centres and places of pilgrimage, or simply travelling. They beg for all their food and accept no possessions beyond those given them at their initiation. During the four remaining months, specifically in the rainy season (late June to early October), monks and nuns congregate in various towns and villages, to be with their preceptors and the leaders of their larger monastic groups. Here the monks and nuns are instructed, formally confess their transgressions of monastic discipline to their superiors, and in turn instruct and assist the lay community that hosts them for this period of time.

At the historical core of Jain monastic practice are a set of six Obligatory Actions (*avashyakas*). These rituals, performed in some cases constantly, in other cases at set times of the day, and in further cases whenever appropriate, comprise a mix of ascetic and devotional activities that provide a well-rounded rhythm of ritual life. The first of these is *samayika*, a state of perpetual meditative equanimity that so pervades the monks' lives that even while sleeping they are always aware of their movements. The second is *caturvimshati-stava*, the recitation of a devotional hymn of veneration to the twenty-four Jinas. The third, *vandana*, is related to the second, but consists of veneration of the monastic leaders rather than the liberated Jinas. Fourth is *pratikramana*, a rite of veneration and atonement for improper actions. This rite, which lasts several hours, is performed every morning and evening, with special versions in fortnightly, four-monthly and annual cycles. The fifth Obligatory Action is *pratyakhyana*, the ritual statement of the monk's intention to perform certain *karma*-destroying austerities. The final Obligatory Action is *kayotsarga*, literally 'abandoning the body'. This is not a separate rite, but rather is found as a constituent of each of the other Obligatory Actions. It is a form of standing meditation, with the arms at one's side, and the eyes fixed on the tip of the nose.

In the course of this day-to-day life, the monk or nun strives to further the *jiva*'s continuing dissociation from the bonds of *karma* and to advance it along the subsequent *gunasthanas*. As noted above, many lifetimes of monastic discipline are required to traverse these stages; and as the Jain ascetic reaches old age, he or she may choose to die voluntarily, undertaking a ritual death by fasting, which is called *sallekhana*. Performed under the close supervision of one's preceptor, this ideally passionless death ensures that one will not void one's spiritual progress by clinging to material existence at the end of one lifetime. It is a powerful sign of Jainism's dedication to the conquest of material existence by renunciation.

Lay Asceticism

As noted above, Jainism passed through a period of change from c.500 to 1300 CE, particularly in respect of its lay community. While there is evidence for the presence of laypersons in Jainism from early on, their role *vis-à-vis* the monastic orders probably remained somewhat fluid until the early centuries of the Christian Era. Growth in royal patronage, the influence of charismatic monks, and Jainism's presence among new populations in the Deccan and western India led to the accomplishments of this period, namely, the development of a distinctive lay Jain religious identity.

One of the foci of this development was the ordering of an ideology of lay discipline modelled on monastic practice. To further this, some forty texts and manuals of lay discipline (called *shravakacaras*) were produced [19: xxvii–xx]. A basic pattern of lay requirements emerged from these texts, consisting of a set of prescribed disciplines that leads the Jain layperson through eleven stages of heightened renunciation.

These eleven stages, known as *pratimas*, are essentially a lay version of the monastic career, and all Jain laypersons are expected to reach at least some point of progression through these stages. The stages are: (1) right views; (2) taking vows; (3) practising equanimity through meditation; (4) fasting on certain holy days; (5) purity of nourishment; (6) sexual continence by day; (7) absolute continence; (8) abandoning household activity; (9) abandoning possessions; (10) renouncing all concern for the householder's life; and (11) renouncing all connections with one's family [12: 186].

Linked to the *pratimas* is a collection of some twelve lay restraining vows. These are also modelled on monastic vows, and involve restraint in diet, travel, clothing and the like. These vows are taken at the second *pratima*, and full practice of them is attained as one moves through the stages. There is even a thirteenth and final vow, recommended but not obligatory, that is a lay version of the ascetic death by starvation.

The *pratimas* clearly carry the layperson along a path of increasing ascetic rigour, leading at the eleventh stage to virtual ascetic renunciation. There is nothing here of the Hindu or Buddhist notion that the layperson can find salvation through alternative disciplines or devotional religion. The lay discipline of the Jains can have only one of two results: (1) rebirth in circumstances that permit an ascetic life, brought about by partial progression through the stages; or (2) full ascetic renunciation in one's present life. In neither case will the lay vows and stages themselves lead to liberation.

There is, thus, great consistency between Jainism's basic ascetic teaching and this view of lay life. Given that the authors of these manuals of lay discipline were by and large monks, this consistency should not be surprising. Arising as it did in Jainism's period of greatest growth and change, the lay programme represents a major effort to bind together the lay and monastic community.

Daily Religious Life

Notwithstanding the significance of formal lay discipline, a great many Jains do not practise only the ascetic model of lay piety, but rather participate in the Jain tradition by means of other religious activities that are often the more visible features of Jainism. These include temple worship, pilgrimage, observance of holidays, veneration of monks and participation in Jain 'rites of passage'. From the outside many of these would appear to have only a tenuous connection with Jain asceticism; yet the ascetic model has at least penetrated these to some extent, and long historical association has woven them into a ritual and philosophical whole that exhibits great continuity with Jainism's earliest teachings.

Temple Worship

The most visible non-ascetic practice is the temple cult. Although Jainism teaches no creator deity, Jains do venerate the Jinas as humans who have attained a god-like perfection. There is an extraordinary profusion of Jain temples to be found in India, so that few Jain communities, however small, are likely to be without one or more. Evidence of a cult of images as old as the first century BCE, and votive slabs from the early Christian Era, found at Mathura, show images of Tirthankaras in standardized forms identical to those in later temples: seated in deep meditation or standing erect, arms and hands held at the side, in an attitude of immobile bodily discipline (cf. the great statue of Bahubali (Gommateshvara) at Shravana-Belgola in Karnataka, Mysore).

The seated image came to dominate Jain iconography, and at least one such image is the focal point of each Jain temple. This image is offered *puja* ('worship', i.e. homage shown by acts of symbolic hospitality) by laypersons according to their private patterns of temple attendance. Jains are enjoined to perform *puja* especially in the early morning, after bathing and before breakfasting.

The ceremony itself is constructed around a basic rite known as the 'eightfold worship', though it can be much more elaborate [see 1]. For the purpose of discussion, the ritual can be divided into four basic parts.

1 Before coming to the temple, the worshipper bathes and dons clean clothes. Upon entering the temple, the worshipper approaches the central shrine, and with hands folded in a gesture of prayer bows down before the image of the Jina while reciting verses of obeisance to the Jina's teaching. In many cases the central shrine is a discrete room in the middle of the temple; if this so, the worshipper circumambulates the shrine three times clockwise, while singing hymns of praise.

2 Now the worshipper enters the central shrine and begins the eightfold worship proper. The worshipper offers the image a symbolic bath, dabs it at nine places with cooling sandalwood paste, places whole flowers on the image, waves incense before it, and waves a lamp before it. These five actions are collectively known as the 'limb worship', for in them the worshipper physically touches the limbs of the image.

3 The worshipper leaves the shrine room and performs the second part of the eightfold worship, known as the 'facing worship', because the actions are done while facing, but not touching, the image. On a small table the worshipper makes the final three offerings of unbroken grains of rice, food (usually in the form of a hard sweet) and fruit. The rice is formed into the Jain *svastika* (as shown in the area within the dotted rectangle of figure 7.2). Jains interpret the four arms of the *svastika* as representing the four possible levels of existence within the round of rebirth: divine, human, nether world, and animal/vegetable; the three dots are the religious virtues of insight, knowledge and conduct, that collectively constitute the religious path to liberation, which is represented by the crescent [7: 108, 200].

4 The eightfold worship is known as physical worship (*dravya puja*), for in it the individual offers physical substances to the image. The final part of the ceremony is known as spiritual worship (*bhava puja*), for rather than making physical offerings, the person engages in spiritual veneration. The worshipper sings his or her own favourite hymns, and recites the universal Jain prayer known as the Litany of Reverence (Namaskara Mantra):

I revere the Jinas.
I revere the [other] liberated souls.
I revere the monastic leaders.
I revere the monastic preceptors.

I revere all monks in the world.
This fivefold reverence
    destroys all demeritorious karma
    and of all holies
    is the foremost holy.

Many, but by no means all, Jains perform temple *puja* daily, and there is great variation in the style of its performance from one individual to the next. The temples more commonly draw the entire community to them on festival occasions, particularly those that celebrate events in the lives of the Tirthankaras or other cardinal events in Jain history. On such occasions elaborate *puja* ceremonies are staged, often including decorations and renewal of a temple's images.

This act of worship is related to ascetic Jainism in that its stated purpose is to focus the layperson's desires on detachment from material existence as represented by the virtues of renunciation and dispassion, physically symbolized in the Tirthankara's image, and thus to reduce karmic bondage. But it is doubtful that its significance ends there. It is also fruitful to see *puja* in Jainism as an institution that gives the lay community a sense of identity in addition to the identity derived from the ascetic ideals and monastic lineages. The temple cult is largely the province of laypersons. Monks and nuns may not serve as temple officiants, nor is their presence during *puja* even welcomed. Temple servants, who may assist with *puja* and who care for the images and the temple itself, are from the lay community and in the case of the Shvetambaras are usually not even Jains, but rather high- or middle-caste Hindus. Nevertheless, ascetics have often attached themselves to temples for purposes of study and teaching, are centrally involved in the consecration of images and the propagation of the temple cult, and among southern Digambaras have become almost a class of temple specialists. As noted in the introduction to this chapter, the Sthanakavasis and Terapanthis object to the temple complex and the veneration of images. In place of the temple cult, they focus on meditative veneration of the Jinas, instruction by monks and nuns, confession and study [7: 215–24].

Briefly put, the temple-cultus in Jainism, while penetrated by the ascetic ideal and orthodox Jain teachings, is also kept apart from asceticism by being – at least ideally – outside the domain of monastic control. Thus the Jain layperson, while being drawn towards the rigorous ideals of an ascetic tradition, also has an institutional arena in his or her religious life in which lay control is dominant.

Pilgrimage and Holidays

Pilgrimage to holy places is an important act for Jains, and is closely related to the purposes of temple *puja*. Pilgrimage sites are associated with events, especially the attainment of final liberation, in the lives of Tirthankaras and other great Jain saints, and pious laypersons have endowed such sites with great complexes of temples and shrines. Among major sites of pilgrimage are Sammeta Shikhara and Pavapuri (in Bihar), and Mt Girnar (in Saurashtra), all of which are sites where Tirthankaras attained liberation; also Shatrunjaya (in Gujarat), Mt Abu (in Rajasthan) and Shravana-Belgola (Karnataka), which are sites of major temples and monuments celebrating the asceticism of Tirthankaras and other Jain saints.

Jains also celebrate a complex calendar of holidays whose principal festivals are, like many pilgrimage rites, linked to five major events in the lives of the Tirthankaras, especially Rishabha (the first Tirthankara), Mahavira and his predecessor Parshva. The events are: (1) descent into the mother's womb; (2) birth; (3) ascetic renunciation; (4) attainment of omniscience; (5) physical death and final liberation. Many of these events are particularly celebrated by pilgrimage to sites associated with the Tirthankaras; and the birth date and death/liberation date of Mahavira (March/April in Caitra and October/November in Karttika) are widely celebrated by all Jain communities. A wide range of other celebrations and monthly fast-days are also observed [see 12: 146–225]. Notable among these is Akshayatritiya ('the immortal third', celebrated on the third day of the waxing moon in Vaishakh (April/May)), commemorating the first giving of alms to the first Tirthankara, Rishabha, and emphasizing the virtue of alms-giving to ascetics in general.

But perhaps the most significant holiday period is Paryushana, held for eight days (by Shvetambaras) or ten days (by Digambaras) in the months of Shravana and Bhadrapada (August/September), while the monks and nuns are in their rainy-season retreat [8: 189–211; 4: 157–85]. In this period, laypersons particularly seek to perform fasting and austerities on the ascetic model, and to spend time with monastic leaders. The holiday thus takes advantage of the rain-retreat, which brings ascetics and laypersons together for a protracted period. It also serves the lay community itself, for on the final day of Paryushana, known as Samvatsari, laypersons make a general confession for the transgressions of the past year, not only to their monastic confessors but also to each other. Letters are written and visits paid for the purpose of asking and extending forgiveness. Persons will often return to home villages and towns for these holidays and the accompanying activities. Thus Paryushana, while it emphasizes the layperson's efforts to participate in ascetic activities, also serves to bind together the lay community and strengthen its identity.

Rites of Passage

As one would expect in a tradition whose fundamental basis is ascetic and which counsels absolute detachment from social values and material existence, the oldest Jain teachings do not establish norms in the area of religious life to do with life-cycle rites, an area of great importance for communal identity in a social setting. In the period after 500 CE, when Jainism was growing vigorously, the problem became critical. Various efforts at defining the Jain relationship to Hindu day-to-day religious culture came to full fruition in the eighth century CE in the Digambara Jinasena's *Adipurana*, a Jain *purana*, or 'account of ancient things'. In it, Jinasena sought to establish a Jain version of the Hindu *samskaras*, or life-cycle rites (see pp. 287–8).

In this case, however, the ideal has not fully penetrated day-to-day practice. Jinasena's vision of the life-cycle rites extends to fifty-three 'sacraments', of which the first twenty-two cover the life-cycle of the lay householder, while the remaining thirty-one 'sacramental' stages trace one's life through post-householder ascetic renunciation, rebirths on the ascetic path and, finally, absolute liberation. But Jains, by and large, use a series of life-cycle rites only somewhat different from its Hindu counterpart.

One significant difference does remain between the Jain and Hindu rites, in that most Jains do not observe the rites of *shraddha*, the post-funeral rites that Hindus observe in order to effect the transition of the deceased's soul from one existence to the next. These rites have been sharply decried by Jain teachers as being contrary to Jain views concerning the *jiva* and the workings of *karma* [12: 302–4]. Jains thus cremate their dead ceremonially, and might performa commemorative *puja* in the temple, but there the formal life-cycle rites end. Hence, even where Hindu practice appears to have been adopted by Jains, at least one characteristic sign of Jain orthodoxy remains, enough perhaps to mark a distinctive identity even in this area where the Jain lay community most resembles its larger Hindu context.

Nineteenth- and Twentieth-Century Developments in Jainism

Remarkably little is known about the actual condition of the Jain community at the beginning of the nineteenth century. Lay Jain communities appear to have been thoroughly embedded in the broader Indian cultural milieu, and to many outside observers such as early British merchants and administrators the Jains appeared to be merely a subsect of the Hindu merchant castes. The number of fully fledged monks, who observed the letter of the five great vows, was quite small: perhaps several dozen each among the Shvetambara Murtipujakas, Sthanakavasis and Terapanthis, and even fewer among the Digambaras. The dominant monastic form among Murtipujakas and Digambaras was that of quasi-priestly resident monks, known as *yatis* among the Murtipujakas and *bhattaraks* among the Digambaras. These resident monks held legal title to their monasteries, and in some cases also controlled extensive landed estates. The monks fulfilled a number of social roles, from acting as hereditary caste priests to performing magical and healing rituals.

Reform Movements

Through a process the origins of which are still obscure, a number of monks and lay Jains came to criticize the existing state of the Jain community and instituted a vigorous movement of reform. This reform was not without precedents, however. Periodically throughout Jain history influential laymen and monks have criticized their contemporary Jain community as lax and debased in its religious observances, and called for a return to Mahavira's original teachings of non-harm, renunciation and asceticism. The history of many of the Shvetambara *gacchas* (mendicant lineages) revolved around charismatic reforming monks, assisted at some times by leaders of the lay community, and at other times by kings.

The nineteenth- and twentieth-century reform movement was led by both monks and laity. The leading Murtipujaka monk was one Acharya Vijay Anandsuri (1837–96), who began his monastic career as a Sthanakavasi monk named Atmaramji (the name by which he continued to be known). Through studying Jain texts he became convinced that the Sthanakavasi opposition to image worship was wrong, and so in 1876 in Ahmedabad he and eighteen of his Sthanakavasi disciples were reinitiated as Murtipujaka monks in the Tapa Gaccha, the dominant Murtipujaka lineage, in a public ceremony. Atmaramji spent the remaining twenty years of his life preaching against the *yatis* and for reform of monastic praxis, initiating monks, converting Sthanakavasis to the Murtipujaka position, and encouraging laity to build and renovate temples. He also came to the attention of Western scholars, and was even invited to the 1893 World's Parliament of Religions in Chicago, but declined to attend since to do so would violate his monastic vow of non-harm. (In his stead he educated and sent a young layman named Virchand Gandhi, who was one of the foreign stars of the Parliament.) The number of fully fledged Murtipujaka monks increased greatly under Atmaramji, and continued to increase dramatically under his successors, so that in the mid-1980s the number of monks in the Tapa Gaccha was nearly 1,200, and the number of nuns nearly 3,700 [4: 491–4]. At the same time, the institution of the *yati* has nearly disappeared in little over a century. Similar revivals of the monastic orders also occurred among the Digambaras and Sthanakavasis, although the growth in the number of monks has not been as dramatic.

While Atmaramji and other monks were preaching reform, leading members of the laity were also aroused to reinvigorate their tradition. In part they were inspired by the joint challenge of British colonial rule and Christian missionary efforts, but these reformers also had before them the memory of the earlier and totally indigenous reforms. What was new about the nineteenth- and twentieth-century movement was not the idea of reform, but rather certain aspects of the methods and the content of reform, as well as the rhetoric of modernity in which the reforms were couched. The principal vehicles for the lay reform efforts were well-funded lay conferences, founded around the turn of the century. They were organized along sectarian lines, except for the All-India Jain Association, which remains as an effort to bridge the long-standing and deep sectarian divides within the Jain community. These conferences published magazines and newspapers in both English and vernacular languages to spread their message of reform. They also held large conventions every few years, attended by thousands of laypeople. These conventions were organized along Western lines, with chairmen, subcommittees, delegates and the adoption of formal resolutions.

The resolutions tell us much about the thrust of this reform movement. Some were concerned with advancing the legal position under the British colonial government; but most were aimed inwardly at the community itself. They called for the establishment of commercial, religious and women's educational institutions. They urged financial support for the restoration of the traditional Jain manuscript libraries, the publication of critical editions of ancient and medieval texts, and the distribution of vernacular religious literature. Among the Murtipujakas there were calls for the restoration and rebuilding of famous old temples. Laity were urged to withdraw their support of *yatis*, and in many cases lay congregations filed lawsuits against *yatis* to gain control over the monasteries, temples and libraries controlled by the latter. Finally, Jains were urged to abandon a wide array of 'harmful practices' and return to a more strictly Jain ceremonial life in accordance with the Jain emphasis on *ahimsa*. These practices included social customs such as child marriage, polygamy, intermarriage with Hindus, and paying bride-price, as well as religious practices such as excessive mourning at funerals, worshipping Hindu deities and observing Hindu or Muslim festivals. The end result was to engender in the Jain community a sense of 'Jainness' in contrast to Hinduism and the surrounding Indian culture.

While the Jain community was consciously trying to change itself, broader currents in Indian society were effecting changes with far-reaching consequences. The fact that the offices of several of the sectarian conferences were in Bombay, rather than in older centres of Jain population, indicates the extent to which even in the nineteenth century the Jains were migrating within India. Bombay, in Maharashtra, is now far and away the largest Jain population centre (see figure 7.1), and many villages and small towns in Gujarat and Rajasthan in which Jains lived for over a thousand years have lost as much as 90 per cent of their Jain population. This migration to Bombay (as well as other metropolitan centres such as Madras, New Delhi, Calcutta, Bangalore, Ahmedabad and Jaipur) has been in search of the greater economic possibilities these cities provide. The Jains have on the whole been very successful in fields such as manufacturing, wholesale marketing and gemstones, so that per capita they now are one of the wealthiest communities in India. This increase in wealth has allowed the Jains to pay for many of the reform projects, such as renovating temples, establishing research institutes and schools, and underwriting publication of Jain texts. In addition, since many newly wealthy Jains attribute their wealth in part to their devotion to individual charismatic monks, this money has been channelled into public expression of that devotion through building new temples and donating large sums on public occasions such as festivals and monastic initiations.

The Jain tradition has also seen several new movements in the twentieth century. One was initiated by a Shvetambara layman named Raychandbhai Mehta, known as Shrimad Rajchandra (1867–1901) [7: 224–7]. He was influenced by the spiritual writings of the second- or third-century Digambara philosopher Kundakunda, and devoted the final years of his life to intensive meditation and fasting. Rajchandra also had a significant influence on his slightly younger contemporary, Mohandas K. (Mahatma) Gandhi, through whom the Jain ideals of *ahimsa* were brought into the political sphere. Another movement influenced by the writings of Kundakunda was that started by Kanjisvami (1889–1980), a Sthanakavasi monk who in 1934 declared himself to be a Digambara layman [7: 227–32]. In recent years these two movements, both of which are centred in Saurashtra in Gujarat, have come together as a new community of Digambara laity known as the Kanjisvami Pantha, from which monks are conspicuously absent, although there is a small number of lifelong celibates who are accorded respect.

Jainism, like all religious traditions, has exhibited a range of responses to the problems posed by modernity and secularism to a world-view based not upon the post-Enlightenment Western principle of doubt and scientific method, but rather upon a notion of absolute truth expressed in the omniscience of Mahavira. The Shvetambara Terapanthis, under their charismatic leader Acharya Tulsi (b. 1924), have launched a number of vigorous programmes designed both to revitalize the Terapanthis and to reach a larger audience [7: 218–24]. In 1949 Tulsi inaugurated the Anuvrat Movement, designed to purify Indian social life of corruption through the application of the twelve lay vows of Jainism. Another innovation is *prekshadhyana*, associated with Tulsi's successor Acharya Mahaprajna. This is a form of meditation, aimed at both monks and laypeople, that claims to revive the Jains' long-lost meditation system. A third development under Tulsi has been the creation of a new class of temporary monks and nuns, known as *samans* (monks) and *samanis* (nuns). While they take the five great vows, the vows are modified so that they can travel abroad and thus minister to the growing overseas Jain population.

A rather different response to the challenges of modernity can be seen in what might be called 'Jain fundamentalism'. One expression of this trend has been a rejection of Western astronomy and an affirmation of the traditional Jain cosmographical teachings, found in Prakrit and Sanskrit texts, of a flat earth at the centre of the universe. Under the guidance of the late Shvetambara Murtipujaka monk Abhaysagar (1924–86), a temple was built at Palitana, Gujarat, designed to illustrate the Jain cosmography, and a research institute was founded with the task of scientifically proving this cosmography. A similar temple and research institute were founded at Hastinapur, Uttar Pradesh, under the guidance of the Digambara nun Jnanmati (b. 1933). A more far-reaching rejection of many aspects of modern society has been initiated by the Shvetambara Murtipujaka monk Chandrashekharvijay (b. 1934). At Navsari, Gujarat, he has established a boarding school called Wealth of Asceticism (Tapodhan) to raise Jain youth on strictly Jain lines. His teachings have been spread throughout the Shvetambara community through his many books, a monthly magazine called *The Messenger of Liberation* (*Muktidut*) and a voluntary organization of young men known as Vir Sainik, 'Mahavira's Army'. Chandrashekharvijay emphasizes physical discipline, respect of elders, self-sufficiency and personal piety. He has also engaged in various social campaigns emphasizing a reliance upon Jain virtues of asceticism and frugality in the face of a society perceived to be materialistic and morally decadent.

The Jain Diaspora

Perhaps the most significant change in the later twentieth century has been the emigration of Jains from India. While medieval narratives are full of accounts of Jain merchants travelling to south-east Asia, and during the British empire period Jain merchants went to Burma, Malaya and Africa to pursue business opportunities, in almost all cases the men went alone, and considered their natal village or town as home. In the early years of this century Jains in eastern and southern Africa began to bring their families to settle with them, but the flow of emigrants did not swell until the 1965 liberalization of US immigration laws allowed South Asians more easily to settle permanently in America [16]. In recent years the number of Jains in North America has grown dramatically, from some 1,900 families in 1979 to over 5,000 families in 1992. The Jain community is relatively affluent, with over half being in professions such as engineering and medicine, and the rest being businessmen. The number of Jain centres has grown accordingly, from the first centre in 1966, to nine in 1979, to sixty-eight in 1992 [10]. Several dozen of these centres have temples, some housed in converted churches, some in structures shared with local Hindu communities, but increasingly built from the ground up as temples. A significant Jain population also resides in England. Most English Jains live in London, but the major English temple is in Leicester. The majority of the English Jains came not directly from India but via East Africa, many being forced out of Uganda by Idi Amin [2]. Other centres of diaspora Jains are Antwerp, Belgium, with a small but wealthy population of diamond traders; Kobe, Japan, where a community of pearl merchants has built a temple; and Nairobi, Kenya, which also has a temple.

The strictures of the monastic code make it impossible for a monk to follow the monastic rules fully and travel abroad. As a result, the diaspora Jain community, for perhaps the first time in Jain history, is almost exclusively a lay community. In 1971 the Shvetambara Murtipujaka monk Chandraprabhsagar (b. 1922), better known by his pen-name Chitrabhanu, broke with tradition and travelled to New York. He was joined three years later by the late Sthanakavasi monk Sushilkumar (1926–94). For many years their followers were largely young Americans, but in recent years their American following has fallen off and they have become the leading ascetics of the diaspora community. Chitrabhanu formally renounced his monastic status, but Sushilkumar did not, which has caused some controversy among the Jains both in India and abroad. In recent years they have been joined by several other Murtipujaka and Sthanakavasi monks. In addition, Digambara *bhattaraks* from south India, and Shvetambara Terapanthi *samans* and *samanis*, whose vows do permit them to travel, have filled an important role as occasional travelling preachers in Europe and North America.

Most of the diaspora Jains are Shvetambara Murtipujakas from Gujarat, but there are also many Sthanakavasis, Terapanthis, Kanjisvami Panthis and Digambaras from throughout north and western India. As a result of this cultural and sectarian diversity, coupled with the small size of the Jain population in any one city, the Jain centres in North America are consciously non-sectarian, and have worked to harmonize differences in temple ritual and the annual calendar. This downplaying of sectarian differences has been championed by the Federation of Jain Associations in North America (JAINA), the umbrella organization founded in 1981. Through its quarterly magazine and biennial conventions JAINA has worked to create a single Jain identity in North America. Almost 10,000 Jains attended the eighth JAINA Biennial in Chicago in July 1995.

The question of Jain identity has been at issue throughout the history of the tradition, and never more so than today among diaspora Jains. To a significant extent Jain self-identity has been tied to the monks, and the very terms of sectarian identification are drawn from matters of monastic praxis. In the absence of any significant monastic community, the diaspora Jains have had to seek new emblems of self-identity. A further problem faced by the diaspora community is the lack of its traditional intellectual resources, the monks, so that the laity have to fill new roles in the propagation and passing on of the religious teachings. In India, Jain identity is a matter of monastic affiliation on the one hand, and familial and cultural milieu on the other. Without either of these, the Jains in the West could easily blend into the larger Hindu diaspora community. In recent years Jains have come to identify their tradition as being centred on three basic expressions of the cardinal principle of *ahimsa*: non-violence, vegetarianism and ecological harmony. Non-violence is expressed through support for animal rights and similar causes; but the Jains to date have not entered into dialogue with the Western pacifist tradition of socially engaged non-violence. Vegetarianism is expressed through support for organizations that publicly espouse vegetarianism, but is more of an emblem of personal identity and religiosity. Ecological harmony is a new expression of the Jain principle of *ahimsa*, largely dating from 1990, when Jains from throughout the world presented 'The Jain Declaration on Nature' to Britain's Prince Philip, the president of the World Wildlife Fund, as part of the Jains' entry into WWF's Network on Conservation and Religion. This declaration reviews the Jain teachings of *ahimsa*, *anekantavada*, meditative equanimity, karmic compassion, cosmography and the twelve lay vows to show how they represent a proto-ecological ethic of interdependence and harmony.

This rhetoric of ecological Jainism has been accorded a prominent place in Jain newsletters and at the recent JAINA conventions. While it remains to be seen whether ecology becomes an enduring and meaningful part of the self-identity of diaspora Jains, the vibrancy and creativity of the Jain encounter with ecology indicate the resources the tradition can bring to bear in its encounter with the pervasive forces of change and modernity.

Appendix A: Major Texts of the Shvetambara Agama

The texts listed below were all written in Prakrit, but, following the common practice, the Sanskritized forms for their titles are given here. An asterisk indicates that the work is available in translation in a European language (see bibliography below).

Aṅgas	*Other important texts*
*Ācārāṅga	*Ācāradaśāḥ
*Sūtrakṛtāṅga	*Bṛhatkalpa
Sthānāṅga	*Vyavahāra
Samavāya	Niśītha
*Vyākhyāprajñapti (Bhagavatī)	*Mahāniśītha
*Jñātṛdharmakathāḥ	*Daśavaikālika
*Upāsakadaśāḥ	*Uttarādhyayana
*Antakṛddaśāḥ	Āvaśyaka
*Anuttaraupapatikadasah	Nandi
Praśnavyākaraṇa	*Anuyogadvāra
Vipākaśruta	
Dṛṣṭivāda (extinct)	

Appendix B: Major Prakrit and Sanskrit Works

What follows is a highly limited selection of works by major authors, divided according to subject-matter. An asterisk indicates that the work is available in translation into European languages (see bibliography). The most comprehensive account of this literature in general is contained in Maurice Winternitz, *A History of Indian Literature*, vol. 2, *Buddhist Literature and Jaina Literature* [20]. The literature concerning lay disciplines is best surveyed in R. Williams, *Jaina Yoga* [19]. See also the bibliographies to P. Dundas, *The Jains* [7], and K. W. Folkert, *Scripture and Community* [8].

Narrative literature, including Jain Puranas

Paümacariya, Vimalasūri (claimed by both Digambaras and Śvetāmbaras), c. fifth century CE
Ādipurāna, Jinasena (Digambara), eighth century CE
Uttarapurāna, Gunabhadra (Digambara), ninth century CE
*Triṣaṣṭiśalākāpuruṣacaritra, Hemacandra (Śvetāmbara), twelfth century CE

Writings on lay discipline

Ratnakaranda, Samantabhadra (Digambara), fifth century CE
Yaśastilaka, Somadeva (Digambara), tenth century CE
Srāvakācāra, Amitagati (Digambara), eleventh century CE
Yogaśāstra, Hemacandra (Śvetāmbara), twelfth century CE
Sāgāradharmāmrta, Āśādhara (Digambara), thirteenth century CE
Commentary on Mānavijaya's *Dharmasamgraha*, Yaśovijaya (Śvetāmbara), seventeenth century CE

Didactic and philosophical writings

*Tattvārthādhigamasūtra, Umāsvāti (claimed by both Digambaras and Śvetāmbaras), second century CE(?)
Mūlācāra of Vaṭṭakera (Digambara), c. second century CE
*Pravacanasāra of Kundakunda (Digambara), second–third century CE
Āptamīmāmsā, Samantabhadra (Digambara), fifth century CE
*Nyāyāvatāra, Siddhasena (claimed by both Digambaras and Śvetāmbaras), fifth century CE
*Saddarśanasamuccaya, Haribhadra (Śvetāmbara), eighth century CE
*Pramānamīmāmsā, Hemacandra (Śvetāmbara), twelfth century CE
*Anyayogavyavacchedikā, Hemacandra (Śvetāmbara), twelfth century CE
*Syādvādamañjarī (a commentary on the foregoing), by Malliṣeṇa (Śvetāmbara), thirteenth century CE
*Jaina Tarka Bhāṣā, Yaśovijaya (Śvetāmbara), seventeenth century CE

Bibliography

Works cited in the text

1 BABB, L. A., *Absent Lord: Ascetics and Kings in a Jain Ritual Culture*, Berkeley, University of California Press, 1996
2 BANKS, M., *Organizing Jainism in India and England*, Oxford, Clarendon Press, 1992
3 CARRITHERS, M., and HUMPHREY, C., (eds), *The Assembly of Listeners: Jains in Society*, Cambridge, Cambridge University Press, 1991
4 CORT, J. E., 'Liberation and Wellbeing: A Study of the Śvetāmbar Mūrtipūjak Jains of North Gujarat', PhD thesis, Harvard University, 1989
5 CORT, J. E., 'The Śvetāmbar Mūrtipūjak Jain Mendicant', *Man*, n. s. vol. 26, 1991, pp. 549–69

6 DEO, S. B., *History of Jaina Monachism*, Poona, Deccan College, 1956

7 DUNDAS, P., *The Jains*, London, Routledge, 1992

8 FOLKERT, K. W., *Scripture and Community: Collected Essays on the Jains* (ed. J. E. Cort), Atlanta, Scholars Press, 1993

9 JACOBI, H., *Jaina Sūtras*, vol. 1, Oxford, Clarendon Press, 1884 (Sacred Books of the East, vol. 22)

10 *Jain Directory of North America, 1992*, Norwood, MA, Jain Center of Greater Boston, 1992

11 JAINI, P. S., *Gender and Salvation: Jaina Debates on the Spiritual Liberation of Women*, Berkeley, CA, University of California Press, 1991

12 JAINI, P. S., *The Jaina Path of Purification*, Berkeley, CA, University of California Press, 1979

13 LAIDLAW, J., *Riches and Renunciation: Religion, Economy, and Society among the Jains*, Oxford, Clarendon Press, 1995

14 MAHIAS, M. -C., *Délivrance et Convivialité: Le Système Culinaire des Jaina*, Paris, Éditions de la Maison des Sciences de l'Homme, 1985

15 SCHUBRING, W., *The Doctrine of the Jainas* (tr. W. Beurlen), Delhi, Motilal Banarsidass, 1962

16 SEELING, H., 'The Jain Tradition in America: Centers, Organizations, and Temples', paper prepared for The Pluralism Project, Committee on the Study of Religion, Harvard University, 1992

17 SHĀNTĀ, N., *La Voie Jaina: Histoire, Spiritualité, Vie des Ascètes Pèlerines de l'Inde*, Paris, OEIL, 1985

18 TATIA, N., *Studies in Jaina Philosophy*, Banaras, Jain Cultural Research Society, 1951

19 WILLIAMS, R., *Jaina Yoga: A Study of the Mediaeval Śrāvakācāras*, London, Oxford University Press, 1963

20 WINTERNITZ, M., *A History of Indian Literature*, vol. 2, *Buddhist Literature and Jaina Literature* (tr. S. Ketkar and H. Kohn), Calcutta, University of Calcutta Press, 1933

Translations of Jain texts listed in the appendices

21 *Ācāradaśāh*: JACOBI, H., *Jaina Sūtras*, vol. 2, Oxford, Clarendon Press, 1895 (Sacred Books of the East, vol. 45)

22 *Acaranga*: JACOBI, H., *Jaina Sutras*, vol. 1, Oxford, Clarendon Press, 1884 (Sacred Books of the East, vol. 22)

23 *Antakṛddaśāh*: BARNETT, L. D., *The Antagaḍadasāo and Anuttarovavāiyadasāo*, London, Royal Asiatic Society, 1907

24 *Anuttaraupapātikadaśāh*: BARNETT, L. D., *The Antagadadasāo and Anuttarovavāiyadasāo*, London, Royal Asiatic Society, 1907

25 *Anuyogadvāra*: HANAKI, T., *Anuogaddārāiṁ*, Vaishali, Research Institute of Prakrit, Jainology, and Ahimsa, 1970

26 *Anyayogavyavacchedikā*: THOMAS, F. W., *The Flower-Spray of the Quodammodo Doctrine*, Berlin, Akademie-Verlag, 1960

27 *Bṛhatkalpa*: SCHUBRING, W., *Das Kalpa-sūtra, die alte Sammlung jinistischer Monchsvorschriften*, Leipzig, G. Kreysing, 1905; Eng. tr. M. S. Burgess, 'The Kalpa-Sutra: An Old Collection of Disciplinary Rules for Jaina Monks', *Indian Antiquary*, vol. 39, 1910, pp. 257–67

28 *Daśavaikālika*: LALWANI, K. C., *Daśavaikālika-sutra*, Delhi, Motilal Banarsidass, 1973

29 *Jaina Tarka Bhāṣā*: BHARGAVA, DAYANAND, *Jaina Tarka Bhāṣā*, Delhi, Motilal Banarsidass, 1973

30 *Jñātṛdharmakathāḥ*: VAIDYA, N. V., *Nāyādhammakahāo*, 2 vols, Poona, author, n.d.

31 *Mahāniśītha*: DELEU, J., and SCHUBRING. W., *Studien zum Mahānisīha*, Hamburg, Cram, de Gruyter & Co., 1963, chs 1–5

32 *Nyāyāvatāra*: UPADHYE, A. N., *Siddhasena's Nyāyāvatāra and Other Works*, Bombay, Jain Sahitya Vikasa Mandala, 1971

33 *Pramāṇamīmāṃsā*: MOOKERJEE, S., and TATIA, N., *Pramāṇamīmāṃsā of Hemacandra*, Varanasi, Tara Publications, 1970

34 *Pravacanasāra*: UPADHYE, A. N., *Śrī Kundakundācārya's Pravacanasāra (Pavayaṇasāra), a Pro-Canonical Text of the Jainas*, Bombay, Shetha Manilal Revashankar Jhaveri, 1935

35 *Saddarśanasamuccaya*: SATCHIDANANDA MURTY, K., *Shad-Darsana Samuccaya (A Compendium of Six Philosophies)*, Tenali, Tagore Publishing House, 1957

36 *Sutrakṛtaṅga*: JACOBI, H., *Jaina Sutras*, vol. 2, Oxford, Clarendon Press, 1895 (Sacred Books of the East, vol. 45)

37 *Syādvādamañjarī*: THOMAS, F. W., *The Flower-Spray of the Quodammodo Doctrine*, Berlin, Akademie-Verlag, 1960

38 *Tattvārthādhigamasūtra*: JAINI, J. L., *Tattvārtha-sūtra of Umāsvāti*, Arrah, Central Jaina Publishing House, 1920

39 *Triṣaṣṭiśalākapuruṣacaritra*: JOHNSON, H. M., *The Lives of Sixty-Three Illustrious Persons*, 6 vols, Baroda, Oriental Institute, 1930–62

40 *Upāsakadaśāḥ*: HOERNLE, A. F. R., *The Uvāsagadasāo, or The Religious Profession of an Uvasaga*, 2 vols, Calcutta, Bibliotheca Indica, 1888–90

41 *Uttarādhyayana*: JACOBI, H., *Jaina Sūtras*, vol. 1, Oxford, Clarendon Press, 1884 (Sacred Books of the East, vol. 22)

42 *Vyākhyāprajñapti (Bhagavatī)*: LALWANI, K. C., *Bhagavatī Sutra*, 4 vols, Calcutta, Jain Bhawan, 1973–85

43 *Vyavahāra*: French and German tr. C. Caillat in W. Schubring (ed.), *Drei Chedasūtras des Jaina-Kanons*, Hamburg, Cram, de Gruyter & Co., 1966, pp. 49–89

8

Buddhism

L. S. COUSINS

Introduction

A Vast Expanse

The history of Buddhism extends over two and a half millennia. It has spread into a number of originally unrelated cultures and exercised great influence over much of Asia. No other religion has existed in such disparate cultures as a major influence for so long. Over 50 per cent of the population of the world lives in areas where Buddhism has at some time been the dominant religious force. Inevitably it has responded to differing circumstances, and local customs and ideas have influenced it in many ways. Adaptability has historically been a marked feature, arising no doubt from some of Buddhism's most distinctive and central notions. Yet there is also continuity.

All forms of Buddhism today derive from the same roots. The approach adopted here is to begin with this common source in ancient Indian Buddhism and then go to describe separately the Buddhism of the three main twentieth-century geographical areas. This treatment of the subject should not blind us to the fact that most kinds of Buddhism are motivated by similar concerns. The aim is nearly always to create conditions favourable to personal meditational or spiritual development. The general understanding is that insights of the right kind can transform the individual in ways usually expressed in terms of 'liberation', 'freedom' or 'spontaneity'. This is generally seen as requiring a long period of training. Underlying this practice is an elaborate classification of states of mind as they relate to the path leading to liberation and a rather exact methodology of spiritual training – a kind of 'spiritual technology'. No two schools of Buddhism describe these matters in precisely the same way, but there is a constant similarity of concern and parallelism of method. An underlying common purpose has been adapted to different situations with great flexibility.

Three Great Traditions

The three great traditions of Buddhism are distinct historically and geographically (figure 8.1).

Southern Buddhism, often known as Theravada Buddhism, has about 125 million adherents, most of whom live in the five countries of Sri Lanka (Ceylon), Burma, Cambodia, Laos and Thailand (Siam). Smaller numbers are found in bordering parts of China, Vietnam, Malaysia, Bangladesh and India, and as relatively recent emigrants elsewhere (e.g. in the United States).

Eastern Buddhism is practised in China, Japan, Korea, Vietnam and among various emigrant populations. A meaningful estimate of numbers cannot be given. The close relationship between Buddhism and various indigenous religions (Confucianism, Shinto, Taoism, folk religion) is such that a family or individual may adhere simultaneously to various practices. Moreover, Communist rule in much of the area has made reliable information unobtainable. Some estimates give numbers of actively committed Buddhists, but this is misleading when set beside the figures for nominal adherence commonly quoted for other religious traditions. It may be said that Buddhism is one of the most widely influential religious traditions within a population of the order of 1,500 million.

Northern Buddhism is current in Tibet, Mongolia, the Himalayas, parts of China and the Soviet Union, and among a scattered emigrant population, with perhaps 10 or 20 million adherents. Its influence has been greater than numbers might suggest, since it has preserved a rich and independent cultural, spiritual and philosophical tradition derived directly from classical Indian Buddhist teachings.

Older names for these areas that reflect particular prejudices are best avoided and have not been used here. In particular, it should be noted that the terms 'Lamaism' for Northern Buddhism and 'Hinayana' for Southern Buddhism are considered insulting by many adherents of those traditions.

For more detailed general introductions to the whole of Buddhism, see [4; 47; 55].

Incompleteness

One common feature of the three great traditions should be noted. Everywhere it has penetrated, Buddhism coexists with indigenous

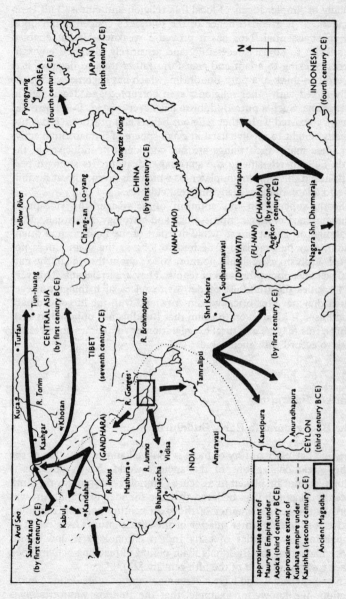

Figure 8.1 The expansion of Buddhism

religious traditions in complex ways. This is true both of elaborate and varied systems such as Hinduism, Confucianism or Taoism and equally of simpler forms of local folk religion and cultus. This is no accident. It is a consequence of the founder's concentration upon the most essential. Nor has it proved a weakness. It has enabled Buddhism to adjust successfully and sensitively to varied environments, seeking to adapt and transform rather than to destroy. It is an error to think of a pure Buddhism, which has become syncretistically mixed with other religions, even corrupted and degenerate in later forms. Such a pure Buddhism has never existed. Buddhism has always coexisted with other religious beliefs and practices. It has not usually sought to involve itself in every sphere of human ritual activity, since many such things are not considered 'conducive to' the path, i.e. not relevant to the spiritual endeavour. Its strength perhaps lies in this very incompleteness which has given it great flexibility and adaptability in many different cultures.

So the superstition and 'animism' of the villager, the widespread Asian interest in magic, numerology and astrology, the rituals of the Brahman or Taoist priest, while not part of the fundamental orientation, may be practised if desired so long as the main aim is not lost. Buddhism as such has no more to say about them than the natural scientist about the laws of tennis. They are irrelevant. This very fact entitles the Buddhist modernist to reject such things however much they have historically been entwined with the life of ordinary Buddhists. If he goes on to claim that Buddhism is opposed to such things, this may be a natural exaggeration or sometimes an excessive wish to accord with alien values.

Ancient Buddhism

The Background to Early Buddhism

Origins The early history of India is less well known than that of the other great civilizations of the ancient world. Much of what is known cannot be placed in a secure chronological framework. Until recently most scholars believed that the founder of Buddhism was born in the second quarter of the sixth century BCE and remained active well into the first quarter of the fifth century. As a result of important new studies of early Indian chronology it now seems more likely that the Buddha's main period of teaching activity took place towards the end of the fifth century [27].

None the less we do have a certain amount of more definite information. We know, for example, that the Buddha was certainly a contemporary of the founder of Jainism; and we also know the names of most of the important kings ruling in northern India during his lifetime. So the context in which the Buddha lived and taught is clear. Most of northern India seems to have been inhabited by people speaking early forms of the Middle Indian languages, still rather close to Sanskrit. These dialects were probably mutually comprehensible; so communications across India would have been easier at this time. Outside India important developments had taken place. During the latter part of the sixth century Cyrus the Great was completing the extension of the Persian empire into Central Asia and perhaps what is now known as Afghanistan (see p. 237). Within two decades Darius had made the Indus valley into the richest province of the empire. Henceforth the Middle Indian world was in a situation similar to that of the Greek world to the west. Overshadowed by the enormous territories of the Great King, both experienced great cultural and economic impact. Skills, techniques and ideas from the ancient civilizations of the area could spread more rapidly than ever before. The similarity with Greece is striking in other respects also. In both these frontier areas we find a proliferation of ideas and systems of belief, offering different prescriptions for life. Just as the Greek philosophical tradition afterwards emerged to influence the subsequent intellectual history of Western civilization, so too Buddhism later emerged to influence the intellectual and religious history of Asian civilization.

The Buddha appears to have made a conscious attempt to avoid the dogmatism of competing religious systems. He aimed to teach only what was essential for spiritual development and carefully excluded from his system everything not directly relevant to that purpose. The result is radically unusual. The Buddha set out a middle way, based mainly upon pragmatic considerations, in which one-sided viewpoints and aims were rejected. Materialistic views of life and spiritually oriented beliefs in personal immortality were considered equally misleading. Mistaken too were extreme goals, seeking either self-satisfaction through indulgence in pleasure or self-purification through ascetic discipline. Traditional religious beliefs, rites and customs were re-evaluated, on the basis not so much of 'reason' as of what might be called 'spiritual common sense'. Extreme forms of superstition and ritualism were opposed, but so was a naïve materialism which sought to deny the real experiences of the spiritual path.

Buddhism and Hinduism It is sometimes suggested that the Buddha was a Hindu. If by Hindu is meant 'anyone adhering to a religion of Indian origin', then he obviously was. However, if Hinduism is understood as that synthesis of various traditions oriented towards the Brahmanical Vedic tradition which has been the religion of most educated Indians since at least the fifth century CE, then the Buddha was certainly not a Hindu. Indeed, Buddhism was one of the influences which led to the formation of the Hindu synthesis. If Hinduism is taken as synonymous with 'Brahmanism', then it is uncertain what exactly was the Buddha's relation to that. During the period of the formation of Buddhism there were at least three major sources of religious authority in India:

1 the hereditary priestly class of the Brahmans, preserving the scriptures of the Vedic tradition and much ancillary learning;
2 the naked ascetics, emphasizing ascetic practices;
3 the clothed wanders (*parivrajakas*) with a less extreme discipline.

While some in groups (2) and (3) may have adhered to the Vedic tradition, it is clear that many did not. From the naked ascetics developed the religions of the Jains and Ajivakas. Buddhism may have been more closely related to the third group.

Some scholars believe that the non-Brahmanical traditions derive from indigenous Indian beliefs stemming from the Indus valley civilization (*c.*2000 BCE), before the entry of the speakers of Indo-European languages who brought the beginnings of the Vedic tradition to India. More probably native and immigrant elements had become inextricably mixed long before the fifth century BCE.

Buddhism is clearly influenced by and aware of all three contemporary tendencies. The Vedic tradition was certainly important, but not yet fully formed. The classical spiritual literature of that tradition contained in the Upanishads is not easily datable. The very earliest Upanishads are probably pre-Buddhist, others may be contemporary with early Buddhism, but probably the majority of the fourteen or so major Upanishads are post-Buddhist and perhaps influenced by Buddhism [101: 28–42; 39: 32–59].

The Three Jewels

The Buddha The reliability of the accounts we have of the life of the Buddha is a matter of much scholarly debate. Our sources cannot be shown with certainty to be sufficiently close in time for absolute reliability. It is not that we know nothing. The traditional life story handed down largely in common among all Buddhists is quite full. We may be fairly sure that it contains much accurate information of a historical kind. We are quite sure that it contains later elaboration and additions. What we often do not know is which is which.

The future Buddha was born as a princeling named Siddhattha (Sanskrit: Siddhartha)[1] in the Gotama clan among a people known as the Sakkas, who dwelt near the present-day border of India and

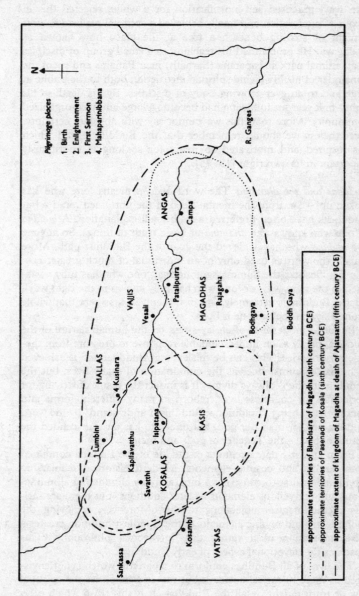

Figure 8.2 The political background to early Buddhism in north-east India

Pilgrimage places
1. Birth
2. Enlightenment
3. First Sermon
4. Mahaparinibbana

N

R. Ganges

ANGAS

Campa

VAJIS

Pataliputra

Vesali

MAGADHAS

Rajagaha

2 Bodhgaya

Buddh Gaya

MALLAS

4 Kusinara

Lumbini

Kapilavatthu

3 Isipatana

Savatthi

KOSALAS

KASIS

Kosambi

Sankassa

VATSAS

.... approximate territories of Bimbisara of Magadha (sixth century BCE)
– – – – – approximate territories of Pasenadi of Kosala (sixth century BCE)
– – – – – approximate extent of kingdom of Magadha at death of Ajatasattu (fifth century BCE)

Nepal (see figure 8.2). After a royal upbringing he renounced family life, studied under various spiritual teachers, went on to seek his own way, practised self-mortification for a while, rejected this in favour of moderation and finally achieved a spiritual realization after a night of striving beneath a tree at the place now known as Bodhgaya. He proclaimed his teaching to a small group of disciples in an animal park at Isipatana (Sarnath) near Banaras and spent the remainder of his life giving spiritual instruction both to the public at large and to an ever-growing body of disciples. By his death in his eighty-first year his following had become a large and well-organized community. More than this we cannot say with absolute certainty. Nevertheless we should remember that the Buddha legend which has inspired and motivated so many for so long is enormously important in its own right [13; 75].

Buddhas and the dhamma The word *buddha* means 'one who has woken up' – i.e. from the mental sleep of the untrained mind – but Buddhists have often preferred a traditional explanation. A *buddha* is 'one who knows' the *dhamma* or basic truth of things. So anyone is a *buddha* who has achieved the goal of the Buddhist path. More usually the word is used only of an individual of much greater cosmic significance: the Samma-sambuddha, 'one who has fully awakened in the right way' or 'one who has fully known in the right way'. Such a Buddha is extremely rare in the universe, so rare that whole aeons may pass before one is born.

Buddhist modernists often lay stress on the human nature of the Buddha, partly as an understandable response to pressure from theistic missionaries. This can be misleading. Buddhahood is achieved in human circumstances as the culmination of many lives, but the penultimate life is always divine. It is in fact the result of striving for perfection for countless lives, reborn in many different forms and conditions of being. Traditional Buddhism understands by the word Buddha neither man nor god, but one who has far transcended the nature of both – the Teacher of gods and men.

From an early date accounts of the life of the Buddha contained both human and cosmic elements. Modern historical scholarship attempted at first to construct a biography by eliminating all miraculous and marvellous elements as later additions, but there are serious methodological objections to this. Moreover, removing the more poetic and mythic elements of the Buddhist tradition creates a false impression of a rather dry, intellectual philosophy. This obscures the devotional aspect of early Buddhism.

The lives of all Buddhas conform to a pattern, which is not envisaged as mere historical accident but rather exemplifies the spiritual law or truth taught by all the Buddhas. It is this truth which early Buddhists called *dhamma* (Sanskrit: *dharma*). In practice the word was used in a number of slightly differing ways. *Dhamma* is the law of the cosmos – the true nature of things, their intrinsic lawfulness as it were. It is also the law of the mind, of the good life and of the spiritual path. The understanding gained by the Buddhas enables them to be the embodiment of this. To realize *dhamma* is at once to comprehend the law of the spiritual life and to achieve its goal. So the Buddha declared: 'Who sees *dhamma* sees me. Who sees me sees *dhamma*.' The teachings and texts of Buddhism are the outward embodiment of *dhamma*. They are *dhamma* to be learnt as opposed to *dhamma* to be practised or *dhamma to* be penetrated in the moment of liberation [14: 131–5; 36: 146–54].

The Sangha Many Buddhist ceremonies begin with the act of going for refuge to the 'three jewels'. The third, added to the Buddha and the *dhamma*, is the community, or Sangha. In its more universal aspect this refers to those who have realized the transcendental *dhamma* – the holy community of the noble ones or *ariyasangha*. In its more historical sense it is the community of *bhikkhus* or religious mendicants. It is often mistakenly supposed that it is the latter which is taken as refuge. In fact, however, in the context of the refuges it is the community of those who have achieved some degree of enlightenment who are the object of refuge. The monastic order stands as a symbol for the *ariyasangha* and as such both the monks themselves and often also the robes that they wear are given great reverence, especially in the Southern Buddhist tradition.

It is not known how much of the organization of the community evolved during the Buddha's long life, how much was already current in earlier Indian mendicant groups and how much developed during the following century. However it happened, it was a remarkable achievement. No other religious or non-religious community combines so long a history with so wide an influence and spread. As late as the mid-twentieth century members of the Buddhist Sangha numbered well over one million and although the hostility of Communist governments reduced that number considerably, it probably still exceeds a quarter of a million and is now again growing in numbers.

The secret of the success of the Buddhist Sangha lies in the set of training rules known as the *Patimokkha*. This is now current in three distinct recensions among Southern, Eastern and Northern Buddhists respectively (others are preserved but no longer in use). It is enlarged from a common core of 150 major rules, but differing social conditions have led to a fairly wide variation in the way in which the rules are now applied.

In ancient India the most distinctive feature of the Buddhist Sangha was probably its adoption of a compromise between the settled lifestyle of many orthodox Brahmans and the wandering characteristic of other traditions. We do not know if this practice had been adopted by earlier groups of ascetics, but by establishing fixed residences for three months in the rainy season, the Buddha ensured that the life of the *bhikkhu* would provide both for the establishing of local centres of operation and for the retention of at least something of the simplicity necessitated by the life of the wandering religious beggar. Larger, settled institutions tended to develop later, but great individual mobility usually remained possible. This kind of inherent compromise is natural to the Buddhist 'middle way' and quite characteristic of the training rules of the *Patimokkha*. A similar balance is clearly expected between the demands of discipline and a relaxed approach, as well as between respect for seniority and individual autonomy. Authority was collective rather than hierarchical, but a certain minimum observation was enforced. Only the breach of four specific rules led to expulsion (*parajika*, i.e. 'defeat'): the act of sexual intercourse; taking human life; theft; or dishonest claim to some spiritual attainment. The majority of the lesser rules are concerned either with ensuring simplicity of lifestyle or with maintaining a disciplined deportment.

The *Patimokkha* can be approached fairly laxly and each *bhikkhu* is in principle free to leave the Sangha if he wishes. Yet taken with a full commitment it represents a most demanding training, requiring great attention and awareness in every action – especially for the inexperienced. Such, of course, is its purpose. It is part of the spiritual training directed towards the Buddhist goal, intended to arouse constant awareness throughout life [20: 86–110; 49; 77; 107].

The Development of Ancient Buddhism

Ashoka The Buddhist scriptures were not committed to writing until the first century BCE. The earliest independent evidence for Buddhist ideas is therefore found in the inscriptions of the Emperor Ashoka (Sanskrit: Ashoka) of the Mauryan dynasty in the third century BCE. Ashoka states that he turned to a serious commitment to Buddhist practice as a result of revulsion at the horrors of war. His authority extended over the greater part of South Asia and his prestige must have greatly aided the wider extension of Buddhism. In subsequent Buddhist tradition Ashoka is portrayed as the ideal Buddhist ruler, strongly committed to the spread of the teaching. Reacting against this, some writers have tried to present him as hardly Buddhist at all, but more concerned with the general moral values of Indian society.

In fact, Ashoka's personal position is quite clear. He worshipped at Buddhist shrines, enlarged Buddhist monuments, went on Buddhist pilgrimages and formally expressed adherence to the

Sangha. Nevertheless he spoke always of *dhamma* in his edicts and avoided the more abstract forms of Buddhist teaching. While *dhamma* can be interpreted in terms of the general background of Indian religion as good or right behaviour and need not have any specifically Buddhist import, this view should not be taken too far. Ashoka was following the Buddha's own example in seeking to find common ground and to conciliate without conceding essentials. His edicts are similar in content to Buddhist texts addressed to the ordinary layman. If they also differ little from comparable Jain and Brahmanical works, this is quite natural in a philosophy which aims at consensus, at a 'middle way'. Ashoka's attitude to other religions is set out clearly in his Twelfth Rock Edict:

> His Majesty . . . gives praise to all religious teachers whether monks or householders . . . both by giving (*dana*) and by various kinds of worship (*puja*). But his Majesty does not think giving or worship to be as valuable . . . as strengthening the real essence . . . the foundation of this is control of speech so that praising one's own religious teachers or criticism of other people's should not occur without reason or, if there is reason, it should be mild. Other people's teachers should be given praise in every way. By doing so one profits one's own religion and benefits the other's religion. By doing otherwise one damages one's own religion and does harm to the other person's.

Ashoka's edicts evince a concern for animal and human welfare both on a practical and on a moral level: 'This will profit in this life and also in the next life.' He tried to set an example of diligent endeavour and non-violence to his successors, and apparently adopted vegetarianism, but was clearly not an outright pacifist. He was hostile to animal sacrifice even though this could not have been welcome to traditional Brahmans. He was, above all, concerned with moral purification and self-awareness. He gave his own definition of *dhamma*: 'Few faults, many good deeds, pity, generosity, truthfulness, purity.' So *dhamma* is what you are and do, rather than what you believe. This emerges directly from his Buddhism. If he conceived of it as strengthening the 'real essence' of all religion, perhaps this was because he conceived of Buddhism in the same way, as the Buddha before him certainly did [101: 242ff].

Early Buddhist literature During the early period a considerable body of oral literature had developed in vernacular Middle Indian. Eventually this was organized into three sections or 'baskets': the Tipitaka. When later it was set into writing, slightly different dialects were used in different localities. The general tendency was to use a more 'learned' style closer to classical Sanskrit. In north

India a highly Sanskritized form of Middle Indian, sometimes referred to as Buddhist Hybrid Sanskrit, was widely used. In the south Sanskrit was not so important until a much later date; so in Sri Lanka a much less Sanskritized but stylish form became current, known traditionally as the Magadha language but now usually referred to as Pali. (Strictly the word *pali* means scriptural text and only became used as a name for the language of the texts around the seventeenth century CE.) In fact the Pali Canon or Tipitaka in Pali appears to have been written down rather earlier than elsewhere (first century BCE) by a conservative group which relegated later material to commentaries. Some other branches incorporated such material directly into their recension of the canon.

The three sections are distinct in subject-matter and method. The *Vinaya-pitaka* or 'Basket of Discipline' is concerned with the order and discipline of the Sangha. It contains an elaborate case-law, based upon the convention that each rule was established by the Buddha as a result of a specific incident. The *Vinaya-pitaka* must be rather early in date as, apart from various appendices, it is fairly similar in the different recensions. Still earlier is the *Patimokkha* code, which is likely to have been laid down by the Buddha himself, at least in its main portion.

The second section – the *Sutta-pitaka* – consists for the most part of discourses attributed to the Buddha and given at specific places to specific people. Those discourses are called *suttas*, a word later rendered into Sanskrit, probably erroneously, as *sutra*. In fact, as has been recently pointed out, it is more likely that it comes from a different Sanskrit term (*sûkta*) which means literally something 'well-said'. (Properly speaking, the word *sutra*, literally a 'thread', originally refers to a mnemonic phrase or sentence used to summarize a particular rule, e.g. in grammar.)

The *Sutta-pitaka* is organized in four or five *nikayas* ('parts'), later known as *agamas* ('traditions'). The fifth *nikaya* is probably a later addition. It varies considerably in different recensions, but usually contains some quite early works as well as some much later compositions. A number of recensions of the discourses survive – complete in Pali, partial in Sanskrit and in Chinese and Tibetan translations. Although there are differences as to details and many variations of arrangement, the four *nikayas* contain more or less the same fundamental ideas in all recensions. Such variation as exists is probably due to chance rather than sectarian differences. Indeed, this is wholly to be expected in an oral literature. The texts contain much repetition of stock passages and formulaic patterns. This is a technique to ensure accurate preservation of oral traditions, but it is one which allows considerable variation of the exact form. Such oral works, we know from studies elsewhere, are rarely recited identically. Their content, however, is very traditional and conservative [33; 72: 1–10].

The abhidhamma movement The third section of the Ancient Buddhist canon is the *Abhidhamma-pitaka*. Here the case is rather different. Each of the main recensions of the canon seems to have included different works in this section; so it is probable that the *abhidhamma* works are later than the four *nikayas*. However, it is important to distinguish the *abhidhamma* movement from the *abhidhamma* literature; for while particular works differ, the *abhidhamma* method differs much less. The movement of thought and practice which brought the *abhidhamma* approach into prominence probably occurred during the Mauryan period (third century BCE), if not earlier. Indeed, the *nikayas* already show signs of influence from such a movement.

Abhidhamma classifies experience in terms of fleeting groups of events. These events are called *dhammas* because in aggregate they constitute the *dhamma* or truth realized by the Buddha and because they are, as it were, the constituent parts of his teaching. In later *abhidhamma* each *dhamma* is something unique and indivisible in its nature. Like the quarks of modern physics, *dhammas* do not exist separately but always occur in groupings. They cannot be subdivided, but strictly speaking they are changing events, not static realities. Philosophically this leads to a process-oriented view of experience in which only properties are recognized. There is no substantial core which owns the properties. Above all, there is no permanent and unchanging soul or ground of being in man or the universe. In fact, however, the earlier *abhidhamma* is concerned not so much with ultimate events as to show the fluidity and subtle structuring of experience. The aim is to produce a changed perception of reality. So an elaborate map of psychological states and spiritual levels was constructed on the basis of earlier traditions. The whole subsequent history of Buddhism is coloured by the *abhidhamma* endeavour. All the later systems of Buddhist thought are constructed upon an *abhidhamma* edifice [101:218ff].

Other developments Ancient Buddhism was not static. We can identify a number of developing tendencies. Naturally these had roots in the earliest form of Buddhism known to us; equally naturally, they are related to the general evolution of Indian thought. Brahmanical religion was slowly moving from its earlier sacrificial and intellectual emphases towards an approach based on devotion (*bhakti*; see pp. 276-9). So too was Buddhism, although devotional elements had probably always been present in both. Emphasis on such elements was not, then, a sectarian move, but rather a climate of opinion that led gradually to new practices. The natural tendency to use more and more exalted language in praise of the Buddha inevitably brought about a more and more exalted conception of his status. No doubt the founder had never been conceived of as an 'ordinary' human being any more than many living Indian holy men are today. Devotional practices, based upon the worship of various kinds of relic, gradually increased in importance. Initially a matter mainly, but not exclusively, for the laity, they later came to involve the Sangha too.

If the Buddha was radically superior to his enlightened disciples, then the path to buddhahood must necessarily also be superior. Gradually this began to be explained in detail as the path of the *bodhisatta* (= Sanskrit *bodhisakta*). The term *bodhisatta*, which originally meant 'one bound for awakening' or 'one seeking awakening' was in the earliest sources applied by the Buddha to himself in the past while on the quest for enlightenment. This meaning remains current in Southern Buddhism (e.g. in the voluminous canonical and post-canonical literature on the *jatakas* or past lives of the Buddha). Later a different interpretation became widespread and the word *bodhisatta* was interpreted as equivalent to the Sanskrit word *bodhisattva* (literally, 'being of enlightenment'), which soon became widely used. Probably the intention was to imply that there was some qualitative difference from the very beginning in an individual destined for full buddhahood.

The explanation of the new way was based upon older conceptions of the path. The same terms were used but viewed as 'perfections', i.e. exalted to the highest possible degree. Since the Buddha had always been seen as motivated by concern for the welfare of all beings, the path to buddhahood is naturally viewed as based upon compassion. Just as the Prince Siddhattha was depicted as striving heroically over many lives, so every *bodhisatta* must strive similarly. The same general tendency led eventually to the introduction of the Buddha image in the early centuries of the Christian Era. In early Buddhism Buddhas were represented not in human form but by symbols (see figure 8.3). This is perhaps because prior to Greek influence such representation was characteristic of the cult of the inferior deities. Later a rich artistic heritage of iconographic forms was to develop, expressing some of the central spiritual ideals in visual form (see figure 8.4) [86: 1–82; 60].

The early Mahayana The developments outlined so far are the heritage of all later forms of Buddhism, but it was from this milieu that a new kind of Buddhism was to emerge and develop in a different direction. At first it was simply a convergence of these existing tendencies. Although some scholars have seen the new direction, usually referred to as the Mahayana, as a highly radical departure, this is clearly wrong. It is only true, if at all, of later, fully developed Mahayana Buddhism. The early Mahayana literature developed over a period of centuries and did not at first differ greatly from the forms of Buddhism which already existed. It was simply another

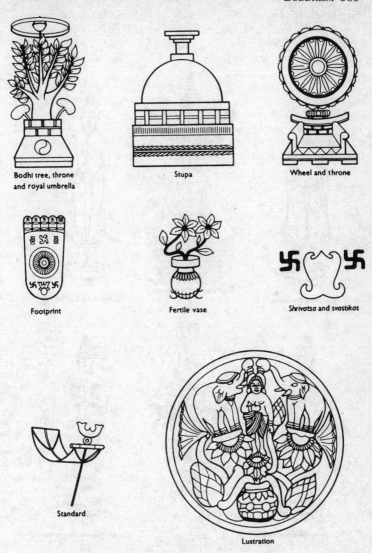

Figure 8.3 *The symbols of ancient Buddhism*

step in the same general line of development. Since existing institutional forms were not altered by the early Mahayanists, both the Sangha and its lay supporters continued to function in much the same way as before. Most of such change as occurred came much later and as part of general trends affecting the whole of Indian

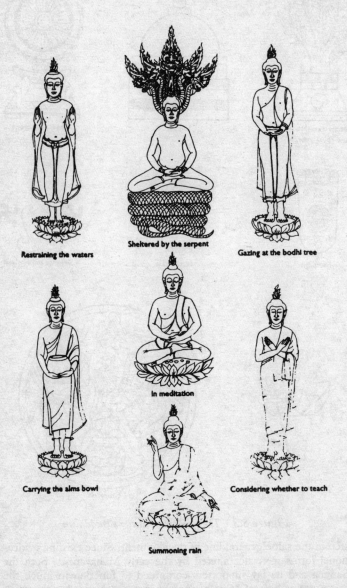

Restraining the waters

Sheltered by the serpent

Gazing at the bodhi tree

Carrying the alms bowl

In meditation

Summoning rain

Considering whether to teach

Figure 8.4   *The Buddha figure in Thai tradition*

Contemplating the corpse

Practising austerities

Revealing the worlds

Defeating Mara

Conferring ordination

Releasing the life faculty

Mastering his illness

Buddhism. Down to the twelfth century, at least, the great centres of Mahayana Buddhism tended also to be centres for schools adhering to the earlier traditions. Given Buddhism's rather pragmatic orientation, it should not surprise us that many monks seem to have studied or practised both.

Indeed, as late as the early fifth century CE the Chinese pilgrim Fa-hsien did not distinguish an exclusive Mahayana. Throughout India he describes either monasteries with monks studying only the older form of Buddhism or those where the monks studied both the old and the new. Only in the capital city of Pataliputra (modern Patna) did he find entirely separate colleges for the two, built by the king. These must have been something more like universities [108: 20–33].

The Place of the Mahayana

The essence of the Mahayana What, then, did the new departure involve? Three main tendencies can be identified: the full adoption of a heroic ideal; a new cosmology closely related to visualization practices; and a new philosophical expression based upon the experience of 'emptiness' in insight meditation. The heroic ideal of the *bodhisattva* path was not new. What was new was the claim, explicit or implicit, that this should be adopted by all. Immediate personal enlightenment (arahatship) was now to be seen as an inferior goal. Greater stress was laid on altruistic action based upon 'skilful means' and compassion. This too was not new, but was now emphasized more than ever before.

The background world picture of early Buddhism was that of Indian religion in general but modified to fit the Buddhist meditational 'map' (see p. 398). Meditation practices included recollection of the qualities of the Buddha and various kinds of visualization exercise. The Mahayana took these earlier cosmological and meditational elements and combined them in a new way. The final result was much more specifically Buddhist in form. Such earlier Indian deities as Brahma and Indra were overshadowed by new figures – Buddhas and spiritually advanced *bodhisattvas*. Their names and much of their nature derive from earlier devotional responses to the Buddha. They could and did become much more closely associated with the most spiritual and uniquely Buddhist teachings.

The philosophy of emptiness develops from earlier insight meditation and the related *abhidhamma* thought. The aim of both is to dissolve rigid views (*ditthi*) and bring about a fresher perception of the world. Apparent entities such as the mind are merely changing collections of evanescent events – a direct intuition of this is the experiencing of emptiness. *Abhidhamma* developed detailed analyses of this ever-changing world. The aim was to break down the apparent unity of things and so free the mind from rigidity.

The Mahayanists felt that these analyses had themselves created a prison similar to the old one: the constituent parts were being taken as fixed entities, and this was just as entrapping as older notions of soul or spirit. They emphasized the complete emptiness of all phenomena including all parts. Nothing has real existence in that nothing exists independently and nothing which has come into being has any permanence. This is from their standpoint not nihilism or pessimism; it is this very non-fixity which makes liberation possible. Indeed, liberation is precisely the recognition of this emptiness. It is not an escape to somewhere else: rather, it is a transformed understanding of this world itself.

A dynamic balance These three tendencies arise from different aspects of the earlier tradition, in which they were part of a dynamic whole; in the Mahayana, too, they are skilfully interconnected. The heroic ideal of the *bodhisattva* path begins with the undertaking of a resolve to attain buddhahood. The commitment required in such a resolve is seen as an act of great spiritual and kammic potency (see p. 396) productive of enormous results. Hence the realm of wondrous paradises and awe-inspiring spiritual beings to be visualized. Conversely, such wondrous results can only reinforce the desirability of the *bodhisattva* path. To follow that path it is necessary to develop the perfections, last and greatest of which is the perfection of wisdom. That perfection of wisdom is nothing other than the realization of emptiness.

Between the emotionally attractive realm of vision and the inspiring but detached knowledge of emptiness is a necessary complementarity. Each is needed to balance the other. Without devotion and visionary experience, emptiness is cold and dry. Without perfect wisdom, such marvellous visions can only entrap. In this way the Mahayana sought to preserve the balanced synthesis so characteristic of the Buddhist spiritual path from its beginning [21: 121–40].

Mahayana and Hinayana The new movement gradually became systematized. There was a gain in precision but perhaps some loss of the initial freshness and insight. Gradually it diverged more and more from the earlier tradition. The two were distinguished in terms of the goal at which they aimed. So they became known as the *bodhisattva-yana*, 'vehicle of the *bodhisattvas*', and the *sravaka-yana*, 'vehicle of the disciples'. As the superiority of the former became more emphasized (by its adherents), the terms Mahayana, 'Great vehicle', and Hinayana, 'Inferior vehicle' or 'Incomplete vehicle', became increasingly common. There is great confusion over the different senses in which these terms are used. In later Eastern and Northern Buddhist usage it is mainly a distinction of spiritual level. The Mahayana is superior in three ways: in its motivation (greater compassion); its goal (buddhahood); and its level of understanding (supreme wisdom). Teachings on these subjects represent a deeper level of exposition of the Buddha's message. The Hinayana is correspondingly seen as selfish in motivation, inferior in goal (arahatship) and lacking depth of understanding.

Too often these distinctions have been uncritically applied to early Buddhism or to Southern Buddhism. In both cases there are problems. Early Buddhism places a high value on the motivation of concern (*anukampa*) for others and never views the *arahat* as selfish: rather, he 'goes forth for the welfare and benefit of the world'. Both in early Buddhism and in later Southern Buddhism the superiority of altruistic action ('both for one's own benefit and for the benefit of others') is recognized; so all branches of later Buddhism have traditionally recognized the legitimacy of the *bodhisatta* path and its goal of buddhahood. In fact, some Southern Buddhists do aspire to practise the perfections of the *bodhisatta*. They do not, however, consider this suitable for all and they do not accept the authority of the Mahayana literature. Indeed, many Southern Buddhists have great faith in the depth of understanding of their teachers and would certainly not accept the Mahayana claim to superiority.

The later Southern tradition is not monolithic. It contains various traditions from both the earliest and subsequent periods as well as important elements reflecting both influence from and reaction against the Mahayana. Moreover, all forms of modern Buddhism have been influenced in their assessments of the past (and of their more distant co-religionists) by Western historical scholarship. Unfortunately this has introduced inappropriate issues and value judgements derived from European Protestant–Catholic controversy. This is particularly noticeable in attitudes towards the devotional, the ritual and the magical on the one hand and towards monasticism on the other.

The traditional Protestant antipathy towards both the practice of celibacy in general and towards religious orders in particular has been adopted, often rather unconsciously, by movements which have developed in a Protestant milieu, such as Marxism/ Communism and various forms of scientific rationalism. As a result such attitudes easily come to be identified with being modern and up-to-date and have been taken on board by some groups and movements in the Buddhist world. This development has been most noticeable in the tendencies towards Buddhist modernism which have been particularly strong in Japan and among the emergent middle class in the Southern Buddhist countries.

The Disappearance of Ancient Buddhism

The decline of Buddhism in India Buddhism flourished in India for a very long time: certainly as long as Christianity has so far done in England, or Islam anywhere. Sometimes a model is adopted which suggests that Buddhism had a highpoint in the last centuries BCE or the early centuries CE and then declined continuously until its final disappearance in the twelfth century. Such a model must be mistaken. Indeed, it probably exaggerates both the highpoints and the lows. Buddhism was probably at no stage dominant in mainland India and its support was always patchy. It is more likely that there were certain areas where Buddhism was influential and others where this was less so. In addition, some of these localities varied greatly at different times. Certain dynasties were very supportive of Buddhism; others less so. This too varied over time. Archaeological data tend to give information mostly about such aspects as Buddhist monuments, that is, about locations and periods where Buddhism was supported by the wealthy classes. Peripatetic mendicant monks by their very nature do not leave much in the way of archaeological remains, nor do small wooden monasteries. Yet these must have been the norm.

It is clear that Buddhism remained widespread in India well after the destruction of the largest monastic centres and their great libraries in northern India by invading Muslims in the late twelfth century CE. We know less about it after that date because Chinese and Tibetan pilgrims had less motivation to visit India after the destruction of the major centres and less to write about if they did. There is, however, sufficient scattered evidence to suggest that Buddhism remained active for some centuries or more in such areas as Bihar, Orissa, the Andhra country and south India. We should think of a very slow rate of decline over a long period of time. Sometimes the case of Buddhism is contrasted with that of Jainism, but this is perhaps misleading; for Jainism too was very much reduced in numbers and influence during this period. The similarities are much greater than the differences.

The Buddhism of Nepal Part of the problem here is the tendency to use the anachronistic term 'India' in ways which are somewhat influenced by the boundaries of the modern state. Buddhism did in fact survive in parts of the Indian subcontinent: in Sri Lanka, perhaps in parts of Bangladesh and in Nepal. No doubt, at least in the case of Sri Lanka, it is partly because Buddhism survived there that the island is not part of the Republic of India today. Sri Lanka, however, is a subject for the next section. Of special interest here is the case of Nepal where a form of ancient north Indian Buddhism survives to this day.

Present-day Buddhism in Nepal survives among the Newars of

the Katmandu valley. Many Sanskrit Buddhist texts which would otherwise have been lost were preserved by them, as well as many rituals and particular traditions. Some have seen their particular form of Buddhism as degenerate. While there is no doubt some truth in this claim, recent work by scholars investigating Nepalese religion has shown that it perhaps overstates the case. It is certainly not a monastic form of Buddhism in the usual sense, although relatively recently Southern Buddhist monastic traditions have been introduced to Nepal and have had some success there. There are also various peoples in parts of Nepal who traditionally practise Northern Buddhism, and many refugees from Tibet [35].

Southern Buddhism

Introduction

Sources The Pali Text Society (founded by T. W. Rhys Davids in 1881) has published most of the Pali Canon in the Roman alphabet, as well as many translations and a great deal of commentarial material. Much remains to be done, although the Pali Text Society has continued to be very active under its most recent presidents, K. R. Norman and R. F. Gombrich. Especially valuable are the translations of I. B. Horner [50; see also 71] and T. W. Rhys Davids [78; see also 100]. The most influential later work is the *Visuddhimagga* of Buddhaghosa (fifth century CE) [11]. The traditional manual of *abhidhamma* is the *Abhidhammatthasangaha* of Anuruddha (*c.* eleventh century) [3]. The main historical sources are the *Ceylon Chronicles*, admirably studied by Wilhelm Geiger. They can be compared with archaeological and epigraphic evidence [72].

The recent history of Southern Buddhism is essentially the history of Sri Lanka (Ceylon) and South-East Asia. This is based partly upon local traditions and chronicles and partly upon outside sources, notably travellers' accounts and missionary writings. Much information on the modern practice of rural Buddhism is to be found in studies which utilize the methods of social anthropology [63]. Important are the works of M. E. Spiro [89] for Burma, S. J. Tambiah for Thailand, F. Bizot for Cambodia and R. F. Gombrich for Sri Lanka [41]. The last of these integrates the present-day picture with that given in the ancient Ceylon commentaries. More recently a number of studies have attempted to examine new trends and developments in particular countries [9; 40; 51; 95; 97].

History The *Ceylon Chronicles* inform us that Buddhism was introduced into the island by a mission sent by the Emperor Ashoka and led by his son Mahinda. The dominant school was the Vibhajjavada 'separative teaching' or 'teaching which distinguishes', which came to be one of four main divisions of the Sangha in Ancient Buddhism [29]. In the first century BCE its canon of scriptures was written down in Pali in Sri Lanka. Indeed, archaeological evidence establishes that Sri Lanka was a major centre of South Asian Buddhism at this time. The early history of Vibhajjavada outside the island is little known, but it is quite possible that it remained widespread in India and had already missionized parts of South-East Asia.

Certainly by the fifth century CE various forms of Vibhajjavada using Pali were widespread in southern India and among the Pyu and Mon peoples of present-day Burma and Thailand. The capital city of Sri Lanka at Anuradhapura was a centre of Vibhajjavada learning to which monks came from far afield. Indeed, most of the leading writers in Pali during the first millennium CE came from outside the island. The prestigious Mahavihara ('great monastery') claimed to preserve authoritative commentaries brought by Mahinda and later written down in the local dialect. In the fifth century Buddhaghosa came to the island and rendered these into Pali in order to make them more widely available. A considerable literature followed, continuing down to the present day. Provided with a strong sense of historical continuity through their chronicles, the followers of the Mahavihara proved very resistant to Mahayana ideas and preserved their own independent traditions with great tenacity. Although north Indian Buddhist ideas are known to some Pali writers, especially Dhammapala, they are utilized only so far as is compatible with Mahavihara traditions [2]. The name of Theravada, which at first meant something like 'original teaching', came to be interpreted as the teaching of the Elders as opposed to the teaching of other (later) schools. Strictly applicable to all surviving Buddhist schools, it came after about 600 CE to be used exclusively by this tradition as a result of their claim to represent the unaltered teaching of the Elders in the undivided Sangha of old. As a result the older term of Vibhajjavada now faded from usage.

The first half of the second millennium saw a series of attempts by monarchs to unify the Sangha under the leadership of the orthodox Mahavihara tradition, which ultimately came to be accepted, especially at court and in government, as the most authentic form of Buddhism. There remained, however, much local variation. Traditions deriving from other branches of Theravada, from ancient north Indian Buddhism and even from the Mahayana continued to be influential down to modern times. Theravada was strikingly successful during this period. One reason for this was probably the simplicity of the relatively uniform Mahavihara tradition. Although the ancient centres in south India slowly declined, in South-East Asia the decline of other schools was matched by the growth of

Theravada. Large areas formerly dominated by Mahayana Buddhism or Hinduism became the preserve of Theravada. By the fifteenth century Theravada Buddhism was dominant among the Burmese, the Mons, the Thai peoples and even the Khmers, covering most of its present-day territory. The subsequent period saw various attempts at unification, centralization or reform and various hazards of war or invasion but nevertheless the overall picture altered little down to the nineteenth century.

In Sri Lanka Buddhism had a more difficult time. Invasions from mainland Asia and, more seriously, conquest of much of the island by the Portuguese and Dutch, with consequent missionization, persecution and destruction, weakened the economic base of Sinhala culture and severely damaged Buddhist institutions. Yet, despite such problems, Buddhism retained the allegiance of most Sinhalese and was able to recover much ground in a revival during the eighteenth century [64].

Academic study of the Theravada We do not know how much the hellenistic Greeks and Romans knew of Buddhism, although the name of the Buddha is mentioned a few times in surviving sources. There is reason to believe that the occasional travelling monk may have reached the Mediterranean, and Buddhist layfollowers must have visited Egyptian ports where there was a lively trade with India. Of course, Buddhism was certainly well known to the later Asiatic Greeks and in the Iranian world further east. Even if more than is generally supposed was known about Buddhism in the classical world, at any rate almost no knowledge of Buddhism survived the decline of classical learning. Thereafter Europe was dependent upon travellers' reports, from a few missionary monks travelling in Asia, and occasional envoys and traders, the most famous of whom is Marco Polo. It was only in the sixteenth and seventeenth centuries that more became known of the Asian countries through trade and conquest and a number of travellers' accounts of various Buddhist countries appeared. Such writings, however, treat of religion only incidentally. The first accurate knowledge of the Indian cultural background came only with the gradual development of Sanskrit studies. In the early nineteenth century this led to the first studies of Sanskrit Buddhist literature, mostly Mahayana, as preserved especially in Nepal.

The study of Ancient Buddhism had to await the creation of the linguistic tools necessary for the study of the Pali texts. To the traditional scholarship of Sri Lanka was applied the method of classical philology. English colonial officers and missionaries played some part in this pioneering work; so, too, did Danish travellers and scholars, among others. Valuable though this was, it went hand in hand with a missionary-based account of Buddhism. Despite making available much important information both on the texts and on contemporary practice, this account was unsatisfactory, focusing attention upon areas where European opinion would consider Buddhism defective and propagating far-reaching negative evaluations which remain influential in certain circles: Buddhism was portrayed as 'pessimistic', 'life-denying' and so on. These judgements were partly based upon selective attention to particular statements taken out of context and a tendency to disregard the great variety of practice and attitude in Buddhism.

A reaction followed. The Pali Text Society made the Pali Canon fully accessible. The work of its founder, Rhys Davids, and a number of other scholars, mainly from England, Germany and Scandinavia, established a new school of Buddhist studies. It was believed that in the Pali texts an authentic early version of the Buddhist canon was preserved, more reliable than any other and providing accurate and detailed information as to the life and teachings of the Buddha. A rather favourable picture of Ancient Buddhism emerged, strongly influenced by rationalist and Protestant ideas. Miraculous, ritual and devotional elements in the literature were viewed as later innovations. Influences from Sri Lanka played an important part in the formation of this school, but ultimately it was itself to exercise a strong influence on Buddhist modernism [103; 31: 15–26, 69ff].

The Structure of the Teaching

Many observers have found difficulty in reconciling Buddhist theory with the actual practice of the ordinary villager in the countryside. Much of the apparent discrepancy is due to an unbalanced presentation of Buddhist thought in which elements connected with popular practice tend to be minimized. They may be thought of as less interesting or not significant for the Western reader, or sometimes as later introductions of peripheral importance. Often, too, there is a bias towards the intellectual as opposed to the emotional. The result is a very misleading picture. This is quite clear if the traditional structure of Buddhist teaching is examined.

A passage which occurs about twenty times in the Pali Canon sets this out explicitly:

Then the Lord gave a step-by-step discourse . . . as follows: discourse on giving, discourse on precepts, discourse on the heaven worlds; he made known the danger, the inferior nature and the tendency to defilement of sense desires and sense objects and the advantage in being without them. When the Lord knew that the heart of the listener was fit, open, free from hindrances, happy and at ease, then he revealed the elevated *dhamma* teaching of the Buddhas: suffering, arising, ceasing, path.

Usually the listener gains direct perception of *dhamma* 'just as a clean and dirtless cloth would easily take a dye'.

There are distinct levels to the teaching given here:

1   Step-by-step discourse: (a) first part: giving (*dana*), precepts (*sila*) and the heavens; (b) second part: the defects of sensuality and positive gain in freedom from it.
2   The particular or elevated teaching, i.e. the Four Noble Truths: suffering; its arising; its cessation; and the path to its cessation.

The step-by-step discourse does not contain anything specifically Buddhist. It was common ground in ancient Indian religion. The first part is mainly concerned with outward behaviour and way of life. The second is more to do with inner purity of heart. For those interested in spiritual practice it would be highly inspiring and lead to a transformed state of mind. Only in such a state is the hearer ready for the more profound elevated teaching, usually known as the Four Noble Truths.

The Four Noble Truths are well known (see p. 399 below). Too often they are approached out of context. They are intended for the spiritually advanced hearer who has both ordered his outer life in accordance with the harmony of things and cleansed his heart from fear and the grosser forms of attachment – he is now ready for a life which unifies compassion and experiential knowledge of *dhamma*. As we shall see, to expound the Four Noble Truths as a purely rational philosophy is to miss much of their purpose. The exposition here follows the sections of the traditional teaching, beginning with the first part of the step-by-step discourse.

Step-by-step discourse: first part
Giving. *Dana*, or giving, is the foundation of Buddhist practice. Charity and hospitality, although valued, are not what is meant here. Buddhist *dana* is a religious act, performed with great care and a sense of purpose. It is usually directed towards a person of religious commitment, especially a member of the Buddhist Sangha. Giving to such an individual is felt as a special and awesome act of great potency. It explicitly replaces the Brahmanical sacrifice with its strong magical and religious quality. Indeed, *dana* retains something of this magical element. No doubt the Buddha aimed to retain the religious power of the sacrifice while rejecting its superstitious and life-destroying elements. The power of *dana* as a sacrifice of one's own possessions is attributed not to the intervention of divine beings or divine power, but to the workings of mental law. It is held

that *dana* can transform the mind. The inner intention of the giver is reflected in the care, attention and joy with which the giving is performed. The higher the state of mind, the more powerful the action (*kamma*). Also important is the state of mind of the recipient, made infectious as it were by the special nature of the act of giving. Either of these is sufficient to make the act effective. The two together are even more powerful.

Dana is usually explained in terms of its future effects, especially those in subsequent lives. Careful questioning of the practitioner soon reveals more immediate rewards too. The giver (*dayaka*) often has an enjoyable or moving experience, made stronger by the slightly formalized or ritual context in which *dana* usually occurs. In Buddhist theory this is a short-lived experiencing of a higher state – a foretaste of later stages of the path. Buddhist texts and sermons are fulsome in praise of *dana* precisely because it leads simply and naturally to the more advanced stages. Above all, it reduces possessiveness and selfishness, leading naturally to sensitivity for the needs of others. This makes possible a correctly motivated commitment to control of one's external actions – the next stage.

Precepts. The first stage of the step-by-step discourse now turns to *sila*, or 'precept'. In this context what is meant is the act of undertaking precepts or training rules, especially the set of the five precepts. The formal undertaking of these normally follows the act of 'going for refuge' to the 'three jewels' (see p. 377 above). The two together amount of declaring acceptance of Buddhist teaching as one's guide and undertaking to put it into practice in one's daily life. In some ways they represent the act of becoming a Buddhist, although in Southern Buddhism they are not given on a single occasion in life, but tend to accompany every Buddhist activity, especially at the beginning, to set the right atmosphere. The repetition of the formula 'I undertake the training rule of refraining from . . .' is a purposive act (*kamma*), effective in its own right. The intention involved is an action which helps to condition one's future and so its frequent repetition accumulates merit. Mere lip-service would be of only limited value, but an impressive ritual context is normal. This is intended to improve the state of mind at the time of undertaking *sila*, since the better that state then is, the better will be the future effect.

The precepts are explained by the principle of 'doing to others as you would be done by'. In Southern Buddhism the emphasis is on avoiding harm either to oneself or to others. This is considered superior to a one-sided concern for either, perhaps because of a sense of the ultimate unity of life. If all living beings are in some way linked, then harming oneself also harms others. The five precepts represent the fundamental discipline of external behaviour to which the Buddhist aspires. They entail refraining from: (1) destroying life; (2) taking what is not given; (3) wrong behaviour in regard to sense pleasures; (4) untrue speech; (5) causes of intoxication such as wines, beers and spirits. Additional precepts are taken with varying frequency in different areas. So eight precepts are often taken on special days connected with the lunar cycle: full-, new- and quarter-moon days. They involve a mild, temporary restriction of adornment, entertainment and physical comfort and are specifically intended as an opportunity for the ordinary person to partake of the lifestyle of the Sangha. Sometimes a white cloth or scarf is worn around the shoulders to indicate that eight precepts have been taken. Overall, the aim is to create conditions which favour a better state of mind [83: 87ff; 54].

Kamma. A great part of popular Buddhism is based upon the performance of *dana* and *sila.* Each of these is only fully effective when accompanied by the appropriate understanding, i.e. the operation of the law of *kamma* (Sanskrit *karma* – see p. 282) or action must be understood. It is this which determines the future condition of the individual, both in this life and in future lives. Every act of will is considered a seed which will one day bear fruit in results of like kind to the original act. Our own actions in the past have created much of our present life and environment. This includes the material and social conditions in which we are born, the physical condition of our body and even much of our mental capacity. In modern terms, both environment and genetic inheritance are the result of past actions. They are the wages of our deeds. This week's wages are based upon last week's work. Next week's depend upon what we do now. Comprehension of this law is known as 'knowledge of the ownership of deeds'. Such knowledge reinforces *dana* and *sila,* since awareness of personal responsibility affects the whole calibre of an action. Such understanding liberates the mind from fatalistic or superstitious views. Past actions, environment, genetics, history – none of these totally determines the individual's fate; for he himself creates his own future.

A modern analogy may perhaps make this clearer. When the laws of gravity and motion are understood, it is no longer necessary to explain the movements of the heavenly bodies by means of angels or divine intervention. So, too, for the spiritual life. If the laws of the mind are comprehended, it is not necessary to imagine constant supernatural intervention. Of course, in practice the sun 'rises' and 'sets'. There is nothing wrong with this as figurative or conventional language. The case is similar in spiritual matters. Moreover, we assume that the law of gravity is operating throughout the universe at the present time, although for most scientific laws there is no way of absolutely proving that this is the case. Similarly, the law of *kamma* applies to all conscious experience, past, present and future. Human, subhuman or above-human – all are subject to it. Since actions produce states and states produce conditions of being, all living beings are subject to change of state and change of being. It follows that conscious existence necessarily leads to birth and death [50: vol. 3: 248–62].

The cosmos. The Buddhist conception of the universe is large-scale: worlds are organized into a spatial hierarchy, grouped in 'clusters' which are grouped in 'galaxies' which are grouped in 'super-galaxies' each containing billions of worlds. Each of these comes into being and passes away again and again over a very long period of time. None of this corresponds exactly with modern scientific cosmology, although Buddhist modernists find it quite possible to reconcile the two. After all, the Buddhist conception is at least on the right sort of scale and compares very favourably in this respect with the rather parochial single world of the semitic religious.

For the more traditional, however, such a cosmos is only a part of the whole. The universe also has many levels. The inferior levels are the four descents (*apaya*), populated by: (1) *asuras* or fallen *devas*; (2) *petas*, literally, the dead; (3) animals; (4) *niraya* or hell-dwellers. The last of these inhabit numerous states of torment located on eight major levels. Each of these levels is surrounded by sixteen annexes with such pleasant abodes as acid rivers or sword-leaved forests. Since there are also cold hells and hells in the darkness between universes, this rather outdoes Dante and the classical Hades combined! The other three inferior levels are intended to accommodate the vast variety of the spirit world and the animal kingdom, considered as existing at or near the same level as human beings. Superior levels are more numerous. They are best set out in a simplified form (see table 8.1). Higher in some respects are the

Table 8.1 The twenty-one heavenly realms

No. of	Name and nature	Corresponding states	Method of attainment
Five	*Pure abodes*: inhabited by Brahmas of great spiritual attainments	Transcendent states	*Samatha* and *vipassana* meditation
Ten	*Brahmas*: each overlord of a universe	*Jhana*	*Samatha* meditation
Six	*Devas*: enjoyment of paradisaical pleasures	Skilful states	*Dana* and *sila*

Formless Brahmas, who have transcended the limitations of bounded existence.

A detailed correspondence between heaven worlds and states of consciousness is traditional: parallelism of psychology and cosmology is a fundamental feature of Buddhist thought. Indeed, most Buddhist statements about the cosmos can be converted into statements about individual spiritual experience. Some Buddhist modernists argue that the traditional cosmology is merely symbolic. Hell realms, for example, are states of guilt and self-torment. This interpretation has considerable support even in ancient literature, given Buddhism's marked concern with psychology. While most Buddhists still accept a more literal interpretation based upon the law of *kamma*, it is also not unusual to find both the symbolic and the literal understanding accepted as valid.

The heavens. The first stage of the step-by-step discourse culminates in description of the realms of the *devas* who enjoy heavenly pleasures. For, the more subtle and refined are the acts of *dana* and *sila*, the more subtle will be the resultant level of consciousness and the ensuing state of rebirth. The lower heavens may be depicted quite concretely – filled with palaces and gardens, places of beauty and wonder with marvellous wishing-trees to fulfil every desire. Many ordinary Buddhists are quite happy to aim at such a goal. It is often wrongly supposed that this is somehow improper. It should rather be seen as the necessary basis for the commencement of the spiritual path proper. The renunciation and quest of the Buddha-to-be began from the luxuries of the royal palace. So, too, the good life with full experience of wholesome pleasures is the ideal starting-place for dissatisfaction with them.

Indeed, this notion is clearly expressed in the famous story of the Buddha's cousin Nanda who was virtually tricked into the life of a monk on his wedding day. When, not surprisingly, his motivation began to flag, he was shown a vision of the beautiful nymphs in the heaven worlds which could be his if he remained. Of course, the outcome in fact is that both Nanda and his wife eventually become enlightened. The story illustrates what later tradition refers to as the Buddha's skilful means in teaching [65].

Step-by-step discourse: second part This part deals with the world of sense and the higher heavens.

The world of sense. The step-by-step discourse now turns to sensory experience (cf. p. 394 above). The aim is to show how the attractions of colour, sound, smell, taste and touch take possession of the mind and distort it both in waking life and in dream and imagination. On the most concrete level the search for wealth and possessions leads either to envy at others' possessions (if unsuccessful) or to possessiveness and fear of loss (if successful). This search is the ultimate cause of much violence, dishonesty and theft and too easily undermines generosity and *sila*. This is the danger in sensory experience. Compared with the higher achievements to come, the sensual is inferior even as a source of pleasure and happiness, and the mind preoccupied with it loses contact with its own central nature.

Freedom from too much concern with sensory experience brings real advantage. The functioning of the mind is no longer obstructed by partialities and graspings which interfere with spontaneity of action. Free from cares and concerns, it returns to a simpler and cleaner kind of functioning. The natural result is greater openness towards other living creatures and a more universal type of conduct. This is summed up as the four Brahma abidings: loving-kindness to all beings; compassion for their sorrow; joy in their joy; and balanced observation of their faults and virtues.

The higher heavens. Such states open the way to the Brahma heavens. These are reached by some form of calm meditation (*bhavana*). Their inhabitants dwell in power, radiance and beauty. The senses play a much smaller role there, but since the inhabitants are still subject to the law of action, they may eventually fall to some lower level. The danger of their state is that it may be too satisfying. Yet it has one overwhelming advantage: the mind has the kind of sensitivity, receptivity and stability necessary for the full comprehension of the profoundest teaching [65].

The elevated teaching The phrase here can in fact be translated either as the *dhamma* teaching particular to the Buddhas or as the elevated *dhamma* teaching of the Buddhas. In the first case it would mean the part of the Buddha's teaching which is special and unique to the Buddha (as opposed to the step-by-step discourse shared with other spiritual traditions), while in the second case it would mean the higher part of the teachings. In either case it consists of the Four Noble Truths and Buddhist meditation.

The Four Noble Truths. The four truths are often referred to as the *ariya* or noble truths, because they bring one to true nobility – attained not by birth but by inner purification. They are traditionally explained by the simile of the physician: a doctor recognizes illness, diagnoses its cause, removes the cause and prescribes treatment to bring about health. The four truths apply the same method to the general human condition. But the matter is not quite as simple as that. In a famous passage the Buddha reproves his disciple Sariputta for suggesting that the Four Noble Truths are clear and easy to understand. Knowledge of the idea is not enough. Only a full and existential comprehension can bring about the hoped-for transformation. Hence the need for the right prior state. The four truths are not so much *descriptive* as *prescriptive* truth. The important thing is not that the universe is this way; rather, when the mind is suitably at peace, one should see things in this way in order permanently to change the mind for the better [76; 82].

1   The first truth is usually given as *dukkha*, or suffering, but other terms are sometimes substituted. For example, the first truth can be given as 'the world', the second as 'the arising of the world' and so on. In fact, the first truth is meant to include most of ordinary human life. So the word 'suffering' must be interpreted with care. Even the most pleasurable experiences are *dukkha*. When life is described as suffering, it does not mean that pleasurable experiences are not pleasurable. It is simply that they remain subject to change and loss. By comparison with spiritual pleasures they are not satisfying. Indeed, the human condition is unsatisfactory so long as it lacks the lasting harmony and balance of the mind which contacts the transcendent.

Suffering is taught to arouse *samvega*. This is a kind of inner stirring and stimulation which motivates the individual to spiritual effort and, if prevented by cheerfulness from turning to depression, leads to mental awakening. So the first truth is usually explained by the great shocks of life: birth, sickness, old age and death. In normal life it is often these which arouse *samvega*, but it can equally be the result of a vision of the unending process of birth and death or of the transitoriness of things.

2   The second truth is the arising of suffering. The cause of suffering is *tanha* ('thirst'), explained as craving for sense pleasure, for being and for non-being. *Dukkha* arises because we desire to have or control things, to experience in one way rather than another. We are dissatisfied with the way things are because we seek something different. This is a rather simplified explanation, albeit far-reaching. The full account of the second truth is given by the formula known as *paticcasamuppada*, 'conditioned origination'. The history and interpretation of conditioned origination is a matter of much debate, but as far as later Buddhism is concerned, the basic principles are quite clear. Our present life and circumstances are largely due to past acts (*kamma*). These acts arose from ignorance (*avijja*) of *dhamma*. They must, then, be distorted in some way and create distorted results. Even now we continue to try to force experience into a false mould, by our craving. So our likes and dislikes generate attachment and rejection, forming a more or less fixed pattern made rigid by habitual desires and prejudices. These form the prison of our future. Yet understanding the nature of the process makes possible an escape from that prison.

3   The escape is *nibbana* (Sanskrit *nirvana*), for the Buddhist the supreme bliss and the final liberation. This is the ceasing of suffering: the third truth. Craving and ignorance are ended. Just as when the cause of disease is removed the state of health returns, so when the cause of suffering is removed *nibbana* ensues. The

individual who reaches this final goal experiences great joy and happiness. All doubts and burdens are gone. His mind is free from prejudice and complication. He has a firm knowledge of freedom and liberation.

Many Western observers have seen something negative in *nibbana* as a goal. This seems perverse to the Buddhist, for whom *nibbana* is above all supreme happiness. Indeed, the main schools of Indian Buddhism all agree that *nibbana* is not a mere negation. Rather, it is the unconditioned *dhamma*, not expressible in spatial or temporal terms; knowledge of it dissolves ignorance and ends craving. The question of the subsequent fate of the individual who achieves the goal is often raised in this context. This is an 'unanswered question'. Such matters as the temporal and spatial extent of the universe and the precise relationship between living being and body are placed in the same category. The reason given for the Buddha's silence is practical: such matters are time-wasting and distracting; they do not conduce to the aim.

It might seem that this could not apply to the spiritual goal itself, but in fact it is even more important here. Buddhism is a middle way between eternalism (belief in personal immortality) and annihilationism (belief that death is the final end). If eternalism is a rigid view (*ditthi*), motivated by craving and obstructing the path to liberation, it is counter-productive to describe the goal as if it were some permanent state of being. If annihilationism is another such view brought about by a different form of craving, then the opposite description is equally unhelpful. Buddhist teaching is primarily prescriptive. There is no point in including in the prescription anything which will diminish the chances of health.

4   The fourth truth is the truth of the path leading to the ceasing of suffering: the eightfold *ariya* path. If one looks at table 8.2, it is easy to see that the fourth truth includes a much wider range of Buddhist

Table 8.2   The fourth truth: the way

	Faculties (*indriyas*)	Factors of the path (*maggangas*)	Factors of awakening (*bojjhangas*)	
3 Wisdom	5 Wisdom	1 Perfect view 2 Perfect thought	2 Investigation of *dhamma*	Insight (*Vipassana*)
1 *Sila*	1 Faith	3 Perfect speech 4 Perfect action 5 Perfect livelihood		
2 Concentration	2 Strength	6 Perfect effort	3 Strength 4 Joy	Calm (*Samatha*)
	3 Mindfulness	7 Perfect mindfulness	5 Tranquillity 6 Concentration 7 Equipoise	
	4 Concentration	8 Perfect concentration	1 Mindfulness	

teachings about the spiritual path than just the eight factors. All these teachings should be seen as forming an intricate and harmonious whole which naturally tends and inclines towards the goal – 'just as whatever great rivers there be, all tend and incline towards the ocean' [36].

The way can be divided into an ordinary (*lokiya*) and a transcendent (*lokuttara*) path. The Buddhist path is not so much a series of stages or steps as a particular grouping of states of mind with the property of flowing naturally towards the goal. In the ordinary path they have not yet reached a full and harmonious balance. When they do, the mind transcends ordinary understanding and acquires direct knowledge of the unconditioned truth. It is this knowledge which brings permanent change and leads to freedom of heart and understanding.

Buddhist meditation. Each of the four truths requires some activity. The first truth is to be *fully comprehended*; the second is to be *abandoned*; the third is to be *made visible*; the fourth is to be *brought into being*. The four are symbolized (in three aspects or 'turnings') by a twelve-spoked wheel: the wheel of *dhamma*. No doubt this is intended to emphasize the interrelatedness of the truths. The activity of the fourth truth is then *bhavana*, 'bringing into being', often rendered as 'meditation'. What is meant is the bringing into being of the path and the training necessary for this. Two types of *bhavana* exist, based upon calm and insight respectively.

The normative method is to take calm or *samatha* as one's vehicle (*yana*) and seek first to develop the higher states of consciousness which lead to the Brahma realms (p. 397). The *samatha* meditator tries to purify his mind from distractions and hindrances in order to reach mental absorption of a very subtle kind in one of the four meditations or *jhanas*. This could then be developed to the fourth *jhana* which is the basis for even subtler states or for various psychic abilities. Since the fourth meditation is a state of well-established mindfulness and equipoise, it is very suitable for the arousing of insight, and in fact insight may spontaneously arise at this point. If not, he must eventually turn to the systematic development of insight in order to achieve the balance necessary for the transcendent path [26].

The alternative is to take insight or *vipassana* as one's vehicle. This was at one time unusual, but the decades after the Second World War saw a strong revival of insight meditation, especially in Burma. Insight meditation needs a special type of self-observation which remains slightly detached in order to avoid interfering with the natural flow of mental and physical phenomena. With clarity and alertness, greater awareness of mental and physical events and processes will arise. This leads to experiential knowledge of the four truths. There are some difficulties on this route: a false belief that one is enlightened can arise and, if this is overcome, a type of existential crisis must be gone through. Ultimately, however, a poised and equable state of great understanding will be constantly present. Now the mind will naturally tend towards stillness and great inner peace, bringing about the necessary balance of *samatha* and *vipassana*.

Such a balance completes the ordinary path, and the transcendent path will arise when conditions are appropriate. At the moment of its arising there is contact with the truth which is not a product of causes or conditions: the *ariya dhamma*. The meditator attains the stage known as 'stream-entry'. He is freed from doubt and superstitious religious practice, as well as from identification with the body. He has joined the family of the Buddha and won through to the *ariya* lineage. He cannot be reborn in the four descents nor break his observance of the precepts. A permanent change has occurred and henceforth he will always tend towards the final goal. The stream-enterer may train his mind to experience at will the transcendent attainment and can seek to unite it with his every action. He is now an *ariya*, noble by purification, and within seven lives will attain the final and highest state of the *arahat*. In Southern Buddhism the *arahat* is a rare and lofty ideal man, who has attained the goal of ending every kind of mental defilement. He has done all that is to be done (to achieve liberation). He is the full embodiment of the *ariya* path – his actions accord fully with the needs of the situation. Henceforth, in most but not all cases, he may be expected to dedicate his life for others. The Buddha set the model for this, when he sent the first of his *arahat* disciples to wander the world 'for the benefit and welfare of the manyfolk' [82: 61–87; 56; 57; 70].

Buddhism in Ordinary Life

Merit-making Traditional Buddhism plays an important part in village life. Custom is important, but in principle it is a question of making merit by giving, taking precepts (*sila*) and sometimes a little meditation. Giving here includes transferring merit in order to benefit others, and above all 'rejoicing' (*anumodana*). Taking pleasure in the good deeds of others is a mental act, productive of beneficial future results. So giving, undertaking precepts and so on potentially benefit the onlooker almost as much as the doer. In other words, these are inherently participatory activities by way of joyful approval.

A wider sense can be given to the notion of keeping the precepts by including conscious acts of service to others and the act of deliberately honouring or paying respect to others. Similarly, meditation practice can also include teaching *dhamma* and hearing *dhamma*. Hence listening to the chanting of Pali texts is a meritorious activity. This is partly independent of comprehension. Provided the listening produces a positive response or recalls

previous meritorious acts it will still be effective. Of course, understanding is even better [89: 92ff; 41].

Paritta Such chanting is especially common in the form of 'protection' (*paritta* or *rakkha*) discourses. The practice is mentioned only
rarely in the Pali Canon and always in contexts of healing and protection. There is a recognized manual of such discourses, selected
from the more awe-inspiring and potent contexts. Similar material
is current in sources of Sanskrit origin, so this kind of ritual use of
discourses must be well over 2,000 years old and perhaps even older
than that. At some point (we do not know when) many new Pali
verses and formulae were added in order to create a complex set of
recognized forms for ritual purposes. Indeed, its strong ritual component has been a major factor in the growth and success of
Southern Buddhism. Together with other merit-making activities,
the chanting of Pali discourses accompanies ceremonial occasions of
many kinds, including some of the major events of the individual
life-cycle. There are also many traditional ceremonies in which
specifically Buddhist ritual plays little part. Chanting *paritta* comes
into its own, however, with events which are in some way dangerous
or potentially so: death, illness, possession, danger, embarking upon
some new activity or entering a new house. It may take place on
quite a small scale, but often there is an impressive and colourful
ceremonial context, involving a great deal of careful preparation, all
of which is, of course, also meritorious activity [32: 109ff; 41: 201ff;
46].

Worship Worship is often supposed to be unimportant in Southern
Buddhism. This is not true for the step-by-step discourse, though it
may be for the elevated teaching. Focusing on the latter allows
Buddhist modernists to minimize ritual and worship. So, for example, the claim of the texts that from the very first seeing of *nibbana*,
'excessive belief in precepts and vows' is abandoned, is sometimes
explained (incorrectly) as giving up 'rites and rituals'. This is in part
a modern exaggeration under the influence of Protestant criticisms
of Catholic ritualism, but in fact there has probably always been an
element of caution towards ritual forms, especially theistic ones, in
Southern Buddhist teaching. The usual result, even among modernists, is in practice a relaxed attitude to traditional devotion,
although there are a few small groups more strongly opposed to
such practices. Nevertheless it is probably more common among
Buddhists in general to view worship as a necessary preliminary.

Southern Buddhism recognizes three kinds of object of worship:
corporeal relics of a Buddha or *arahat*: relics of use (i.e. those made
use of in some way by such an individual); and symbolic relics
which remind one of the Buddha or *dhamma*. The cult of relics has

canonical sanction and certainly considerably pre-dates the reign of Ashoka, since Ashoka enlarged a pre-existing relic shrine of a former Buddha. (Indeed, it may even be in part pre-Buddhist.) Offerings to a relic and any act honouring or paying respect to a relic are held to be forms of giving and of *sila* respectively.

Relic shrines may be very large buildings, often of historical significance, or smaller buildings – they may even be portable. These are most frequently referred to by the Sanskrit term, *stupa* (Pali *thupa*), but other names are current in different localities. The best known are probably the Sinhalese *dagaba* and its possible derivative, 'pagoda'. Pagodas themselves often acquire great sanctity and become cult centres. They may also enshrine the remains of respected teachers or renowned leaders of society. Also important, especially in Sri Lanka, is the bodhi tree (a relic of use), usually planted in the monastic precincts. In principle this should be a descendant either of one of the trees planted by Mahinda, especially the one at Anuradhapura, or of the original tree at Bodhgaya. The Buddha image is also very important, especially if it contains relics. Such images may be enshrined in large halls, for worship, in the environs of pagodas or in small shrines at home or workplace. Archaeology shows that the Buddha image is a later introduction to Buddhism, but Buddhist tradition hardly recalls its earlier aniconic phase (see pp. 382–3). It is meritorious to worship any relic. Offering of appropriate substances (incense, oil lamps, candles, even water, food or clothing are all common); paying respect by act or gesture, especially prostration; service by cleaning, adorning or embellishing; chanting appropriate verses or sounding musical instruments – all these things give merit and so simultaneously give hope of advantageous future results and lead towards readiness for the path [41; 32: 79ff].

Festivals Southern Buddhism has its own traditional lunar calendar, varying only slightly from country to country. Most of the full-moon days have some special association in the life of the Buddha or in the history of Buddhism (see table 8.3). Together with three other special days in the lunar month they are known in Pali as *uposatha* days and are important in the life of the Buddhist monastery. Laypeople may often visit the monastery on these days. Special clothes, usually white, may be worn, particularly in Sri Lanka, and additional precepts may be undertaken (see p. 395 above). Although considered highly meritorious, such observances are not in any way compulsory, but most village Buddhists probably do attend at least a few times a year, especially on the more important full-moon days. Annual festivals vary considerably, both locally and nationally. Festivals connected with the agricultural year (ploughing, sowing), with particular deities or spirits and with particular

Table 8.3 Annual festivals of Southern Buddhism[a]

Season	Pali name of month	Significance of full-moon day	Other festivals in this month
Summer	1 Citta	Birth, enlightenment and final enlightenment of the Buddha	Solar New Year festivals Rocket festival (Laos)
	2 Vesakha		
	3 Jettha	Arrival of Mahinda in Sri Lanka	Local festivals (Sri Lanka)
	4 Asalha	Conception, renunciation, first sermon and ascent to the second heaven of the Buddha	
	An intercalary month (second Asalha) is sometimes added to reconcile the lunar and solar calendars		
Rains	5 Savana[b]		Ancestor festival (Thailand)
Period when monks remain in one place ⎱	6 Potthapada[b]	Descent from second heaven after preaching abhidhamma	Sowing festival (Sri Lanka)
	7 Assayuja[b]		
	8 Kattika[b]	Sending forth of the first Buddhist missionaries	Robe-offering ceremonies (Kathina)
Winter	9 Maggasira	Establishment of the community of nuns	Harvest festival
	10 Phussa		
	11 Magha	Assembly of disciples and Buddha's renunciation of his life-span	
	12 Phagguna	Origin of world in each world cycle	Festival of sand pagodas (Burma) Vessantara festival (Thailand)

[a]Each month ends on the full-moon day. The length is alternately thirty and twenty-nine days. The year begins near the spring equinox.
[b]Three of the four months of the rainy season are kept as a period of intensified activity by the Sangha who remain in one location during this period.

localities are widespread. The Buddhist element in these varies greatly. All of the Southern Buddhist countries have a New Year festival in the spring, fixed by a solar calendar, although the exact date varies slightly.

In Sri Lanka the two most important full-moon days are those of Wesak (Pali Vesakha) and Poson (Jettha). The latter commemorates the arrival of Mahinda in Sri Lanka and is naturally of greater significance there. Of more general importance in the Southern Buddhist countries as a whole is Wesak, which is associated with the birth, enlightenment and death of the Buddha. Indeed, the Vesakha festival has been adopted, at least in theory, by the international Buddhist movement as a universal Buddhist celebration ('Buddha Day'). In fact, the centrality of Vesakha appears to be a relatively recent phenomenon, influenced by celebrations of Christmas. More important in ancient India and still in South-East Asia are three full moons connected with the *vassa* (rains) when Buddhist monks remain domiciled in the same monastery for three months. Asalha full moon begins the *vassa* and commemorates the first sermon of the Buddha. Assayuja commemorates the Buddha's return from preaching the *abhidhamma* to his mother in the second heaven and is the usual end of the *vassa*. Kattika recalls the sending forth of the first Buddhist missionaries and the permissible end of a late *vassa*. Both may be festivals of lights. The ending of the *vassa* is associated with elaborate presentations of robes to the Sangha.

Most Buddhist festivals may be taken in more serious or less serious ways. There is usually much festivity and merry-making, an air of enjoyment and gaiety. There may be a great deal of colourful and careful decoration. Different festivals may involve the use of lights or fireworks, dramatic representations, entertainments, fairs, processions, model-making or water sports. A few more committed individuals will use the occasion as an opportunity for more serious religious practice. Typically, it is very much a matter of individual preference [38].

Pilgrimage The ancient tradition of pilgrimage to the Buddhist centres in India associated with the life of the Buddha fell largely into abeyance after the Muslim conquest of north India. It has revived considerably in the last century. More local pilgrimages are very widespread. In particular, the many sites on the island of Sri Lanka connected with Buddhist history and monuments have long been centres of pilgrimage. Some have their own season and special activities. Pilgrimages are usually seen as enjoyable as well as virtuous activities [41: 108ff; 15: 35ff].

Buddhism and the spirit world Buddhism has had little difficulty in accommodating a large number of local beliefs concerning various gods, spirits and the like, although naturally the powers of such entities are seen as circumscribed by the law of *kamma* and other laws. The Buddhist perceives the universe as vast enough to encompass many such entities. Numerous different cults coexist with Buddhism – some barely tolerated, some irrelevant and ignored, some incorporated to a greater or lesser degree into the larger scene. Such cultic activities may play a considerable part in the life of the villager.

There has been much discussion among scholars as to the precise relationship between Buddhism and such cults. Some see a supernatural hierarchy with the Buddha at the summit. Others contrast the 'great tradition' with the 'little tradition'. Or, the profane or secular level of spirit cults can be set against the superior sacred level of the Buddhist teaching. Many early European observers, followed by some Buddhist modernists, saw the existence of such cults as deriving from a corruption of the original 'pure' Buddhism [63]. In actual fact, Buddhism is not concerned with such matters. They are not rejected; they are simply a different sphere of human activity. Provided there is no direct opposition to Buddhist teaching, they can be left to regulate themselves.

It is sometimes thought that there is an inconsistency between believing in the law of *kamma* and at the same time making offerings to a deity to obtain some desired result. This is mistaken; it is no different from asking aid of a king or doctor. Such aid is itself part of a complex set of relations and subject to various causes and conditions. The help given by a deity is a matter of fact or falsehood. So the striking contrast between the role of spirit cults in Buddhist villages and the tendency of Buddhist modernists to minimize or deny such elements is only superficially a problem. Contact with Western scientism often leads to the supposition that such spirits or deities do not exist. In that case they are not a fact and can be discarded. Buddhism in general is committed to the notion that various entities and levels of being exist, but not to most particular names, although in practice Buddhist traditionalists tend to observe at least a part of their local spirit cult [48; 73; 85; 94].

Modern Developments

The nineteenth and twentieth centuries have been a period of great economic, social and political change in the Southern Buddhist countries. Buddhist thought and institutions have responded to an influx of ideas and practices from elsewhere. The linguistic and cultural diversity of these countries makes the identification of general tendencies unusually difficult. Three important trends are best characterized as reformism, 'ultimatism' and modernism.

Reformism A notable feature of the recent history of the Buddhist Sangha is the growth of reformist fraternities (*nikayas*): the Shwegyin, Dvara and Veluvan *nikayas* in Burma; the Thammayut *nikaya* in Thailand and Cambodia; the Ramanna *nikaya* in Sri Lanka. The general aim of such groups is closer conformity to the ideals of the Sangha. This is not an entirely new phenomenon. In Sri Lanka both the largest fraternity, the conservative Siam *nikaya*, and the second largest, the Amarapura *nikaya*, trace their origins to earlier reformist movements. In time such movements become less homogeneous and overall discipline may decline.

The great majority of monks in Burma have remained in the much larger and more diverse Sudhamma *nikaya*. The same is true for the Maha (or Syam) *nikaya* in Thailand, Cambodia and Laos. These two fraternities, and to some extent the Siam *nikaya*, in fact represent the mass of the Sangha, grouping monasteries and traditions of diverse origins and long-standing local roots. Their membership includes monks and groups of monks very similar in practices and views to those of the reformist fraternities as well as many who would be considered lax and even corrupt by the committed reformist.

In Sri Lanka and Burma the ending of the monarchy and its replacement by foreign non-Buddhist rulers tended to undermine the discipline of the Sangha. This did not occur to the same extent in Thailand and Indo-China, where traditional governmental control was maintained and even in some cases strengthened. Some caution is necessary here, however, as accusations of laxity are often based upon a rather exacting spiritual ideal, seeking to restore an idealized situation of poverty and simplicity of lifestyle [67: 66ff; 97].

'Ultimatism' It seems useful to adopt the term 'ultimatism' to identify the tendency to take what is true from the viewpoint of ultimate truth or at an advanced level of spiritual practice as if it were the whole of Buddhism. In effect 'ultimatism' discards, ignores or even rejects the step-by-step discourse in favour of the elevated teaching (p. 399). This is a perennial possibility, frequent also in the history of Mahayana Buddhism. In Southern Buddhism today it takes the form of a rejection of much traditional practice and ceremonial as well as of many of the outward forms customarily associated with merit-making activities. It is often supported by reference to early Buddhism, while in more extreme forms it may be associated with symbolic interpretation of rebirth and of supernatural elements in Buddhist tradition. The emphasis tends to be directed towards insight meditation and more rigorous interpretation of the Four Noble Truths [96].

Buddhist modernism During the modern period a certain amount of institutional change has taken place. Particularly striking is the development of lay Buddhist organizations based upon European models. Some customs and values based upon Christian practices have been introduced. Non-Christian strands of thought (notably scientific rationalism, but also theosophy) exercised a marked influence. A tendency arose to see Buddhism as essentially scientific and not really a religion at all. If religion is defined in theistic terms, as was usual in the nineteenth century, then this is quite clearly the case. Perhaps, however, it is better to widen the definition of religion. At all events, the result was a movement, often associated with ultimatist ideas, to reject ritual and superstition as later accretions to the pure original teaching [10: 191ff; 53].

Esotericism Less well known, although quite pervasive especially in South-East Asia, is the tradition of esotericism in Southern Buddhism. Some scholars in fact prefer to use the term Theravadin Tantrism to describe this trend. Although it can be seen as related to the pan-Indian phenomenon of Tantra, the connection is rather loose and it may be better to avoid so specific a terminology. A series of works by a French scholar, François Bizot, has made known a number of short texts belonging to this tradition and there is some reason to believe that it may have been quite influential in the past. Among the practices involved are forms of meditation based upon ritual, visualization and the use of letters and sounds. An elaborate set of correspondences is employed, relating such things as parts of the body, sections of the Buddhist canon and the process of gestation. One tradition, for example, describes the search for *nibbana* in terms of the quest of two children for the crystal sphere which grants entry to the city of *nibbana*, to be found in the flower of 'the four-branched figtree' [6; 7; 28; 95].

The present-day situation Among the general population in the Southern Buddhist countries a rather traditional form of Buddhism is still the norm, but diluted influences stemming from reformist, ultimatist and modernist trends are widespread. In those groups that have been exposed to Western education and a middle-class lifestyle some form of Buddhist modernism is common, often combined with ultimatist notions and support for reformist groups within the Sangha. These tendencies do not usually become sectarian, perhaps because of a general dislike of extremism and a theoretical adherence to the 'middle way'.

Meditation revival It is often suggested that the twentieth century has seen a considerable revival in the practice of Buddhist meditation, but in fact the situation is a little more complex. It is necessary to distinguish between the situation in the Sangha and among laypeople, as well as to examine the differences between countries and meditation schools. A large number of practices and methods are current among the Sangha and, at least in South-East Asia, this has probably always been the case. In Burma the modern period has seen widespread growth in the practice of *vipassana* meditation [51]. More traditional schools, usually laying more emphasis on *samatha* meditation, remain strong in Thailand and Indo-China. In the Thammayut *nikaya* this is often combined with reformism and some degree of modernism.

There has been a considerable increase in numbers of centres for the practice of lay meditation in recent years. In Sri Lanka this is, perhaps, an innovation, but in South-East Asia, where almost all youths traditionally spend a period of weeks or months as members of the Sangha, lay mediation practice has probably always been present. Such centres have also been established in many other Asian and Western countries [57: 116ff; 59: 303–13].

Eastern Buddhism

Introduction

The Buddhism of China, Vietnam, Korea and Japan was influenced by the cultural background, the existing religious beliefs and practices and the historical development of the region. Understanding of it has been affected by the presuppositions of study in the area generally. These matters are discussed in the sections of this volume concerned with Chinese and Japanese religions (chapters 9 and 10).

Sources The Chinese Buddhist canon is very large. The first printed edition, made between 971 and 983 CE, used more than 130,000 wood-blocks. Many other editions have since been made in China, Korea and Japan. The nineteenth-century Japanese scholar Nanjio compiled a catalogue based upon the arrangement which had been usual in recent times, listing some 1,662 items (see table 8.4). A more historical arrangement is used in the modern standard edition, published in Japan over the decade 1924–34. The vast majority of works included are translations from Sanskrit, Middle Indian and, just possibly, from Central Asian languages. The modern edition contains about 1,700 such translations [31: 77–101].

The first three sections in the table are the three main divisions of the Ancient Buddhist canon. Works drawn from various recensions of this are the main content of the Hinayana sections. North Indian Buddhism distinguished between *sutra* – works attributed to an enlightened being – and *shastra* – later works of exposition. Many *shastra* works were included in the first part of the third section. The

Table 8.4   Number of items in Nanjio's catalogue

1	*Discourses (sutra)*	
	(a) Mahayana	541
	(b) Hinayana	240
	(c) Later additions	300
2	*Vinaya*	
	(a) Mahayana	25
	(b) Hinayana	60
3	*Abhidharma*	
	(a) Mahayana	94
	(b) Hinayana	37
	(c) Later additions	23
4	Miscellaneous	
	(a) Indian works	147
	(b) Chinese (and Korean) works	195
Total		1,662

beginning of the fourth section is very diverse but includes a number of Mantrayana works (see p. 429 below), while the second part contains a number of works belonging to Chinese schools [69].

Unlike South Asia, East Asia has a well-developed tradition of historical studies. Moreover, Eastern Buddhism itself has a considerable historical literature [31: 101ff].

History The historical background to Eastern Buddhism may be considered under the following headings: early history; developments in India; the second turning of the wheel of *dharma*; the third turning; consolidation in China; and later times.

Early history. Although south China was probably influenced by forms of Buddhism coming from Indo-China, Buddhism initially entered the Chinese heartland mainly from Central Asia and eastern Iran. This occurred during the Han dynasty (206 BCE–220 CE), not later than the first century CE. Some form of Ancient Buddhism, probably still mainly an oral tradition, was introduced at a time when a clear distinction between the nascent Mahayana and the earlier schools had probably not yet developed. Central Asian influence predominated until the end of the period of the three kingdoms (220–65 CE). The two main approaches were the Meditation school of the Iranian An Shih-kao (fl. 148–68), which was less interested in the Mahayana, and the more specifically Mahayanist Wisdom school of the Kushan Lokaksema (fl. 168–88), concerned with the early Mahayana *sutras*. Both of these trends continued for many centuries. Since Buddhism was at first popular mainly among immigrant communities and with ordinary people outside the governing class, traditional Chinese historiography, always focused on the literate and governing sectors of society, tells us relatively little about the earliest period.

Early Chinese Buddhism tended to employ native Chinese terms, especially Taoist ones. Indeed, the Chinese probably saw Buddhism as a strange, foreign kind of Taoism. The development of new trends in Chinese thought, especially the 'Dark Learning' based upon the *Book of Changes* (*I Ching*), provided the opportunity for Buddhism to penetrate the ruling circles. By the end of the third century a Chinese 'gentry Buddhism' oriented towards the Mahayana had developed and at the same time contact had grown up with Buddhist centres in Kashmir, closer to the Indian mainstream. In the fourth century Buddhism achieved full official recognition in both China and Korea [68; 98; 110; 1: 182ff].

Developments in India. The date, geographical location and sectarian affiliations of the early Mahayana have each been the subject of considerable discussion. Much depends on how the term 'Mahayana' is defined; for the trends from which Mahayana emerged may well be considerably older than the distinctive Mahayana. Probably its origin cannot be much before the first century BCE or later than the first century CE. As to its geographical source, plausible arguments have been advanced for east India, for south India or for the north-west. Similarly, it can be related to three of the four major groups in the Sangha. The most likely explanation for so much evidence pointing in different directions is that the early Mahayana very quickly became a pan-Indian and non-sectarian movement [108: 20–33].

New *sutras* proliferated. It was not claimed that these had been known previously, although most were expounded as the 'word of the Buddha'. They had been preserved in some realm other than the human because they dealt with matters of great profundity which earlier generations had not been able to comprehend or even remember. Only now had teachers of sufficient calibre arisen – men able to journey to such realms and understand the teachings found there. In other words, the early Mahayana works were written down by spiritual teachers as a result of some kind of meditational or spiritual attainment – a type of 'inspired literature' [101: 352ff; 108: 37 ff].

The second turning of the wheel of dharma. Two distinct phases of the Mahayana can be identified. Later Indian Buddhism distinguishes these as the second and third 'turnings of the wheel of *dharma*', where the first turning was the first sermon of the Buddha and the whole canon of Ancient Buddhism. (This was a reformulation of the original 'three turnings' which referred to phases in the understanding of the Four Noble Truths.) The most noticeable feature of the new 'second turning' is its emphasis upon 'emptiness'

(Sanskrit *shunyata*). In the third 'turning' there is a more positive assertion of ultimate truth, reacting against the apparent nihilism of emptiness teachings when inadequately understood. Stress is placed upon such notions as *tathata* ('thusness'), *dharmata* ('*dharma*-ness') and *buddhata* ('Buddha-ness'), and more importance is given to the role of mind. By and large the Mahayana *sutras* represent a creative outflow and not a rigid systematization; so consistency is not a strong feature. Inevitably more philosophically sophisticated expositions arose in the form of *shastra* literature.

The *sutras* of the second 'turning' provided the inspiration for the first great *shastra* system – the Shunyatavada ('emptiness teaching'), also known as the Madhyamaka ('of the Middle'). Earlier scholars often refer to the Madhyamika philosophy, but strictly this form of the word is best reserved for individuals belonging to this school. The chief exponent of the Shunyatavada was Nagarjuna (second or third century CE), but there were many later authorities. The Shunyatavada used the systematic method of the *abhidharma* (p. 381) to support the teachings of the Mahayana. The aim was to prove that all positions and supposed realities are purely arbitrary. If the earlier teaching is that the apparent world is a fragile house of cards, the Shunyatavada went further and suggested that there were not even any cards. Reality is like a shifting palace made out of soap bubbles! The aim is to create an attitude of flexible spontaneity – a more natural and flowing response to life [101: 373–92; 22: 381–2; 62; 81; 108: 37–76].

The third turning. It is the last phase of the Mahayana *sutra* literature which is connected with the formation of the second great *shastra* system – the doctrine of Vijnaptimatra ('information only'). This emphasized meditation practice and so acquired its second name: Yogacara ('practice of yoga'). The school was probably founded by Asanga and his younger brother Vasubandhu (*c.* fourth century). Some scholars believe that the true originator of the Yogacara was Maitreyanatha, the teacher of Asanga, but it is more likely that this is a reference to the *bodhisattva* Maitreya as the inspirer of Asanga.

The Yogacara may be seen as uniting the teachings of the Mahayana with those of the earlier *abhidharma* schools. The result was a kind of Mahayanist *abhidharma*, giving an elaborate map of the Buddhist path and offering quite detailed descriptions of the stages of meditational experience [19: 233ff]. The diverse teachings of the Mahayana *sutras* were brought within a single all-embracing system. More extreme interpretations of the notion of emptiness were rejected. In this respect Asanga certainly considered that he was remaining faithful to Nagarjuna's intention of adopting a middle position. Not all later Madhyamikas agreed, but many still made use of Asanga's teachings. The most characteristic teaching of the Yogacarins was the idea of 'information only'. In a dream we have many apparent experiences, but on waking we realize that they are only valid as experiences. We truly received them as information, but they do not correspond to any external reality. The Vijnaptimatra school extends this to waking life; only the information itself is 'real'. This is often described as idealism, although strictly speaking even mental events are purely 'information'. However, the school does speak of mind as more real than matter [101: 392–447; 22: 382–3; 44: 250–60; 108: 77–95; 43].

Both of the great *shastra* systems have had many exponents in Eastern and Northern Buddhism down to modern times. Each has influenced the later forms of the other. They are the two great orientations of the Mahayana. Indeed, they continue the two great traditions of Ancient Buddhist meditational practice. The Shunyatavada represents the insight or wisdom-oriented approach, while the Yogacara returns rather to the calm or concentration-oriented approach (p. 402).

Consolidation in China. Influences from Kashmir increased markedly in China during the fourth and fifth centuries. More systematic attempts to introduce Indian Buddhist ideas and literature began to take place. The pilgrimage of Fa-hsien to India (399–413 CE) increased contact still further, while the arrival of Kumarajiva (401 CE) led to the large-scale introduction of Shunyatavada literature [31: 77–101]. By the sixth century relations with India had increased greatly. For some centuries monks from all over India came to China and Chinese pilgrims visited Indian Buddhist centres, especially the large-scale monastic universities in the ancient heartland. The arrival of Paramartha (546 CE) signalled the introduction of many Yogacara works. Still more were brought back from India by the Chinese pilgrim Hsüan-tsang, who returned in 645 CE [98].

A massive quantity of Buddhist texts and practices of varying provenance were brought to China. Not surprisingly the Chinese found this confusing. So they began to develop schools of thought which sought to make overall sense of the many different traditions. Indeed, similar processes were at work in India too. The result was the emergence of the two great theoretical traditions of Eastern Buddhism: the T'ien-t'ai and the Hua-yen (see below).

During the T'ang dynasty (618–907 CE) Buddhism reached a very high level of influence not only in China and Korea, but also in Japan where it had been introduced in the sixth century. The period saw the introduction to China of the last phase of Indian Buddhism: the Mantrayana (see p. 429). Most important of all, the dynasty saw the formation of two new movements which gradually came to dominate the Chinese Buddhist scene: the Pure Land school, emphasizing devotion to the Buddha Amitabha, and the Meditation school, laying stress on an individual breakthough to illumination [23; 102: 66–74].

Later times. Towards the end of the T'ang period, in 845 CE Buddhism experienced a severe persecution. Partly due to this and partly due to civil disorders towards the end of the dynasty, many of the smaller and older groups were severely weakened and never recovered their former strength [102]. From the beginning of the T'ang dynasty onwards native Chinese religious traditions began to regain much of the ground previously lost, partly because they had successfully incorporated elements learnt from Buddhism and renewed their own vitality. Although under some emperors Buddhism continued to receive great favour, increasingly it was disapproved of as a foreign and non-Chinese cult. Attempts to harmonize the different schools seem to have increased in the medieval period. Indeed, some efforts were made to provide a basis for unity between Buddhism, Confucianism and Taoism. Eventually many Chinese came to believe in the harmony of the three religions and even more tended to practise it. Although a slow decline in its social role and importance did take place, Chinese Buddhism retained considerable strength into the twentieth century. The period of maximum influence came rather later in Korea and Japan, but there too a reaction in favour of Confucian and Shinto notions ultimately occurred.

Academic study of the Mahayana Early interest in the Mahayana, stimulated by the discovery of Sanskrit texts from Nepal and the work of Eugène Burnouf and other scholars, had rather weakened by the end of the nineteenth century. This was due to the natural enthusiasm at the discovery of the Pali literature (see pp. 392–3). A number of scholars active during the first half of the twentieth century sought to re-emphasize the value of works available in Chinese and Tibetan translation, many of which represent north Indian traditions just as ancient as that from Sri Lanka. One group of scholars working in Russia is especially associated with the name of T. Shcherbatsky. Influenced by contact with the living tradition of Northern Buddhism, they sought to comprehend Buddhist thought in terms of European philosophical development.

A second group, composed mainly of Belgian and French scholars, was more interested in the Mahayana as a religion and in the history of Buddhism. The most influential writer of this group was probably Louis de La Vallée Poussin. Eastern Buddhist traditions and studies of Hinduism were more influential. The period since the Second World War has seen a strong continuance of this Franco-Belgian school, most notably with the work of Étienne Lamotte. Moreover, the researches in Tibet of the Italian scholar, Giuseppe Tucci, gave a new impetus to studies of Northern Buddhism. Important contributions have been made by scholars from India, especially in the study of Buddhist philosophy and history, and by Japanese scholarship, notably in the field of Eastern Buddhism.

At the same time new discoveries from the sands of Central Asia, the caves of Tun-huang, Gilgit in Kashmir and from the libraries of Nepal and Tibet have recovered lost Buddhist literature and opened up new fields for research. Text-critical and historical critical studies using these new materials have developed, especially in Germany and Italy. The recent expansion of Buddhist studies in North America has led to much new work, particularly in the field of Eastern Buddhism [31: 15ff; 23: 1–32].

The Schools of Eastern Buddhism

Eastern Buddhism is much more diverse than the Northern and Southern traditions. It contains a number of distinct schools which have tended on occasion to form separate sects (see table 8.5). Originally there were rather more such schools, including a number

Table 8.5 Eastern Buddhist schools

India	China	Korea	Japan	English
A Ancient traditions				
1 *Vinaya*	Lu	Yul	Ritsu	Discipline
2 *Abhidharma-kosa*	Chu-she	Kusa	Kusha	
B Indian Mahayana theory				
3 Shunyatavada or Madhyamaka	San-lun	Samnon	Sanron	'Nihilist' or 'Three Treatise school'
4 Yogacara or Vijnaptimatra	Fa-hsiang or Wei-shih	Popsang or Yusik	Hosso	'Idealist'
C Chinese Mahayana theory				
5 Based on the *Nirvana sutra*	Nieh-p'an	Yolban or Sihung		
6 Based on the *Lotus sutra*	T'ien-t'ai	Ch'ont'ae	Tendai	Lotus
7 Based on the *Avatamsaka sutra*	Hua-yen	Hwaom	Kegon	Totalism
D New modes of practice				
8 Mantrayana or Vajrayana	Chen-yen	Milgyo {Ch'ongji, Sinin}	Shingon or Mikkyo	Esoteric
9 Based on the Pure Land *sutras*	Ch'ing-t'u	Chongt'o	{Jodo, Shin}	Pure Land
10 Dhyana	Ch'an {Lin-chi, Ts'ao-tung}	Son or Chogye	Zen {Rinzai, Soto}	Meditation

stemming directly from Ancient Buddhism. Indeed, the schools listed in group A are really just two of these, one specializing in *vinaya*, the other in *abhidharma*. Only the former continues as a living tradition in some temples – few in number but influential. The second is now merely an object of study. The two schools of the Indian Mahayana are widely influential, although only the Yogacara survives as a distinct, but minor, organized sect [22: 381–6; 93: 14ff; 79: 148ff].

T'ien-t'ai The T'ien-t'ai school is named after the mountain on which Chih-i, its most famous teacher, established himself. Chih-i (538–97CE) may be accounted the founder of the school, even if he derived much of his teaching from various predecessors. Indeed, T'ien-t'ai gathered into itself a number of earlier lines of teaching based upon the *Lotus sutra* and the Mahayana *Nirvana sutra*. Although the school is usually considered as primarily intellectual, it is important to note that it emphasized very traditional forms of meditation practice. Important works concerned with calm and insight meditation derive directly from the teachings of Chih-i himself [90].

The most characteristic feature of T'ien-t'ai is the elaborate classification of the Buddha's preaching into the 'five periods and eight teachings'. Different levels of teaching and different methods of giving that teaching are related to distinct periods in the Buddha's life and to the various forms of Buddhist literature. In this way a hierarchy is defined, giving an appropriate place to every extant form of Buddhism. The result is a comprehensive and encyclopaedic system. In Japan the T'ien-t'ai school had great success and remains an important sect there. From it emerged the specifically Japanese school of Nichiren (see chapter 10 below). Eclectic by nature, Japanese Tendai was influenced by a number of other Chinese schools, notably the Mantrayana and the Pure Land [23: 303–13; 37: 437–96; 52; 90].

Hua-yen Although traditionally founded by Tu-shun (557–640 CE), the Hua-yen or Garland school received its most complete form with Fa-tsang (643–712). Its inspiration came from a group of Indian *sutras* known in Eastern Buddhism as the *Avatamsaka* or *Garland sutra*. Hua-yen gave systematic form to a group of Indian teachings which are not quite so systematized in any surviving Indian text. Traditional Chinese philosophy also influenced Hua-yen. Perhaps partly for this very reason it is widely regarded in Eastern Buddhism as philosophically the most advanced school and has had wide influence.

Hua-yen developed its own classifications of the different kinds of Buddhist teaching on similar lines to T'ien-t'ai, but it is best known for its 'philosophy of totality'. A rich and striking symbolism verging on extravagance is employed. Everything in the universe is connected and harmoniously related to everything else. Indeed, the result may be described as a 'hologram universe' in which every part contains the whole. This is all set out in some detail and pursued in great depth [23: 313–20; 17; 24; 108: 116–38].

Pure Land teachings One branch of early Indian Buddhist meditation seems to have concentrated upon the visualization of the figure of the Buddha. In the early Mahayana this took the form of visualizing the Buddha Amitabha ('boundless radiance') in his pure land of Sukhavati ('land of happiness') and reciting his name. The practitioner aspired to a vision of Amitabha and rebirth in his paradise. Reciting the name eventually became widely popular far outside the circle of meditation specialists, so that in East Asia the cult of Amitabha became the most widespread form of Buddhist devotion. Eventually a specific school came into being, known in China as the Ch'ing-t'u.

The Indian authority for this school lies in three texts: the two *Sukhavati-vyuha sutras* ('*sutras* on the vision of the land of happiness') and the *Sutra of meditation on the Buddha of Boundless Life*, although the last of these may have been written in China. At first it was simply one popular form of meditation and devotion, but later it came to displace many of the earlier forms. It is sometimes suggested that the emphasis on devotion as providing a special kind of salvation is unnatural in Buddhism and alien to the earlier tradition. Yet even the earliest form of Buddhism known to us taught that faith in the Buddha was able both to bring about a heavenly rebirth and to set one firmly on the path to liberation. The difference lies in the Mahayana emphasis on the 'power of resolve' of a Buddha, which is capable of creating enormously favourable conditions. This gradually became a doctrine of grace, reaching its most extreme development in Japan [108: 215–76; 25: 273–80].

Devotion to Amitabha as part of the general Mahayana is very ancient. Many Chinese teachers played an important role in furthering both meditation on Amitabha and recitation of his name. But the Ch'ing-t'u does not really become a distinctive school until later. This was mainly the work of Tao-ch'o (562–645) and his disciple Shan-tao (613–81). They laid emphasis on the power of simply 'reciting the name' to ensure rebirth in Amitabha's paradise. This was considered to be a simple approach, easy for ordinary people to adopt and still effective even in a period in which the original teaching was in decline. As a result of the work of Honen (1133–1212) and his disciple Shinran, Pure Land had great success in Japan, eventually becoming the largest single school (see pp. 489–90) [23: 338–50; 92].

The Meditation school The traditions of meditation practice begun by An Shih-kao continued for many centuries. They were constantly augmented by new lines of teaching from India and Central Asia. During the T'ang dynasty a new Ch'an 'Meditation' school arose (best known in its Japanese form as Zen). No doubt it derived much from earlier schools, but by the end of the dynasty it had developed a kind of genealogy tracing its lineage of teachers through a series of six patriarchs. The first patriarch was considered to have been Bodhidharma, an Indian monk supposed to have arrived in China *c.*520 CE. Around the lives of these patriarchs a rich and colourful spiritual literature came into being. So vital was this tradition that it absorbed into itself numerous other traditions and almost all later Chinese meditation schools claimed affiliation to a lineage deriving from the Ch'an patriarchs.

Already by the end of the T'ang period five such lineages had arisen. The two most important of these were the Lin-chi (Japanese: Rinzai) and the Ts'ao-tung (Japanese: Soto). Although both claimed to derive their tradition from the sixth and last patriarch – Hui-neng (638–713) – they differ somewhat in approach. In fact, recent studies based upon materials found in the caves of Tun-huang have shown that the traditional picture of the history of Ch'an Buddhism is somewhat over-simplified and that more account needs to be taken of previously little-known branches such as the Northern School founded by Shen-hsui (606?–706) and the Ox-head School of Fa-jung (594–657), both of which continued for some centuries after their foundation [34; 66; 109].

Ch'an Buddhism has become well known for its emphasis on spontaneity and for a certain tendency towards iconoclasm. The teachers of this school were wary of any kind of routine or habitual spiritual practice. Similarly, they showed a measure of hostility to ritual and to scriptural or scholastic literature. None of this should be exaggerated. Ch'an taught 'not clinging to written words and not separating from written words'. The aim was to undermine *attachment* to particular religious forms; there was no wish to abolish the forms themselves – such a wish would itself be seen as a form of attachment. Indeed, Ch'an eventually developed a very large literature of its own, concentrating on stories of the sayings and deeds of the Ch'an masters.

The main aim is to re-emphasize the immediate accessibility of direct realization. Enlightenment is to be striven for and realized in this very life. The Ch'an teachers claimed 'a special transmission outside doctrines' – a direct and wordless communication between teacher and pupil. Later tradition lays great stress on this transmission. Practical action was preferred to study. Ch'an often stresses the suddenness of the realization of enlightenment, but in fact different degrees of realization were usually recognized. It is sometimes suggested that Ch'an represents a radically new development, even one which is no longer Buddhist at all. This is an exaggeration. In reality, there is almost nothing in Ch'an which cannot be paralleled in earlier Indian Buddhism. The difference is in *style* rather than *content*. Ch'an adopted unconventional and unusual forms of expression. Probably the example of Taoism is very important here, especially for its tradition of simplicity and naturalness [18; 34; 91].

Diffusion and Adaptation

Chinese Buddhism Buddhism has been changed by the culture and customs of every country to which it has come. Equally, it has brought change to those countries. Yet China is a special case. Here Buddhism was the medium of contact between two of the great civilizations of the ancient world. There was no question of replacing the existing culture; inevitably Buddhists had to adapt to Chinese forms and customs. Chinese people asked new questions and offered new problems. Native Chinese religion and philosophy influenced and mingled with the new teachings.

It is customary to speak of Buddhism becoming Chinese, but this should not be taken too far. Even before it arrived in China Buddhism was a rich and varied religious tradition. It is not so much that it adopted Taoist or other Chinese ideas wholesale; rather, it selected from a rich repertoire those elements which appealed in the Chinese situation. Naturally this led to a measure of convergence – the more so as the native traditions also brought to the fore elements which resembled Buddhist ideas or methods.

Buddhism in Korea Although Korean Buddhism had some direct contact with India, it is chiefly derived from Chinese sources. Prior to the arrival of the Ch'an school in the eighth century, Korean Buddhism had become dominated by the O-kyo or 'five doctrines'. These were the Vinaya, Yogacara, Nirvana (a precursor of T'ien-t'ai), Hua-yen and Haedong schools. The two last were the most important. The Haedong (or Popsong) is an eclectic school founded in Korea by Wonhyo (617–86). Ch'an (known in Korea as Son) eventually established nine branches, known as the nine mountains after the location of many of the leading temples. In the eleventh century T'ien-t'ai, which had previously played a relatively minor role, was revived with the aim of reconciling the existing trends. Ch'an was then reorganized under the name of Chogye and stimulated by the introduction of Lin-chi traditions. Some forms of Esoteric Buddhism were also present from a relatively early date. Buddhism was very influential under the Koryo dynasty (918–1392), but less so under the Choson dynasty (1392–1910) when Neo-Confucianism gained in importance and Buddhism sometimes suffered fairly severe restrictions [12; 42: 22–3].

Despite such difficulties Buddhism has survived and is today very much a vital presence in Korea. It is perhaps best seen as character-ized by a synthesis of Ch'an meditation with doctrinal studies, espe-cially but not exclusively centred on Hua-yen thought, but there are also important strands deriving from Pure Land devotion and from Esoteric Buddhism. The monastic tradition is that of the Vinaya (Yul) school.

Sectarianism and syncretism There is some doubt as to the precise nature of the schools of Chinese Buddhism in the T'ang period (618–907 CE). It may be guessed that the Sangha at large was more than merely the sum of the different schools. If the schools had a certain independence of organization and action, they yet remained very much part of the larger grouping. For this reason the gradual decline of most of the schools as separate entities did not necessarily mean the complete elimination of their influence. Teachings deriv-ing from other schools remained widespread even when the vast majority of temples were committed to the two practical schools of Ch'an and Pure Land.

Korean Buddhism took a slightly different direction, partly as a result of government intervention. A reform in the sixteenth century reduced the numbers of monks and grouped the existing schools into two administrative sects: the Son and the Kyo. The former, meditation-oriented grouping was dominated by Ch'an but included also T'ien-t'ai, Vinaya and the Mantrayana. The Kyo con-tained the remaining doctrinal schools. This division continued until the twentieth century, when it was replaced by a single umbrella organization. In fact, separate schools continued within this body; at present no fewer than nineteen are officially recognized and more are unofficial [42].

In Japan the ancient schools grew more and more into indepen-dent sects with their own organization and separate lay following. It is important not to read this Japanese development back into the classical Chinese situation. The ancient Chinese schools were much less institutionalized sectarian entities than their successors in Japan. In China there arose a movement towards syncretism which tended to unite the Buddhist sects and in some cases sought to harmonize the teachings of Buddhism with those of Taoism and Confucianism. This led to a much more integrated and united form of Buddhism. Japanese writers tend to view this as a degeneration, but it can also be viewed as a successful victory for ecumenism over sectarian intol-erance [106: 395–407].

The religion of ordinary people Buddhism in East Asia is closely connected with the native religious traditions in many ways, as is only natural when religions have been in such close contact for so long. For treatment of the religious situation as a whole in two of those countries, China and Japan, see chapters 9 and 10 below. Here mention will be made only of some specifically Buddhist elements.

Most of the Chinese population before Communist rule took part occasionally in Buddhist activities of one kind or another. These might include festivals, ceremonies, pilgrimages and various kinds of merit-making activity. In this they perhaps differed little from the population of most other Buddhist countries – except perhaps in greater willingness to take part similarly in activities associated with other religions. Things can have been no different in ancient India. Of course, many of the above activities could equally be undertaken with serious intent by the more committed, who constituted a relatively small percentage of the population [106: 357ff].

Buddhist festivals Buddhist monasteries theoretically celebrate between thirty-five and forty events, but most are of minor importance. Apart from festivals common to all Chinese, especially the New Year festival, five are particularly significant for Buddhists (see table 8.6).

In Eastern Buddhism the traditional dates for the enlightenment and death of the Buddha are the eighth of the twelfth month and the fifteenth of the second month respectively, but these are not widely celebrated. It should be noted that in the traditional lunar calendars the fifteenth day would be the full-moon day, but sometimes this connection has been obscured as a result of official adoption of some form of the Christian solar calendar. The rains retreat (see table 8.3) runs from the fifteenth of the fourth month to the fifteenth of the seventh month, but this is now of less importance in Chinese Buddhism. Nevertheless it is the festival which terminates the rains retreat which is the most important specifically Buddhist festival. The same is the case quite widely in the Buddhist world, although calendar differences tend to obscure this [106: 108–10].

Table 8.6 Major Eastern Buddhist festivals

Month	Day	Event
Second	19	Birth of the Bodhisattva Kuan-yin (Avalokiteshvara)
Fourth	8	Birth of the Buddha
Sixth	19	Enlightenment of Kuan-yin
Seventh	9–15	Ullambana ('Festival of Hungry Ghosts')
Ninth	19	Death of Kuan-yin

Recent Developments

The Sangha in Eastern Buddhism The monastic community in China probably came from three main sources: the Sarvastivadins, the Mahasanghikas and the Dharmaguptakas. The Dharmaguptakas were either a branch of the Sarvastivadins or an early branch of the Vibhajjavadins (see figure 8.5). The order of nuns was also transmitted to China from various sources, including Sri Lanka. In fact, since the lineage of the nuns was not preserved either in Southern Buddhism or in Northern Buddhism, it is only in Eastern Buddhism that it has continued to the present day. However, it is probable that the Eastern Buddhist lineage is a synthesis of various earlier ordination lines. In any case it was ultimately the Dharmaguptaka recension of the *Vinaya* which was the most influential in China and its Sangha today, both monks and nuns, can be viewed as belonging to that school.

In modern times, before Communist rule, the Chinese Buddhist Sangha was quite large – of the order of half a million monks and a quarter of a million nuns. About 5 per cent of these lived in larger public monasteries, which were generally well ordered and disciplined. The remainder lived in a large number of very small temples. Some of these were also occupied by monks with a strong personal commitment to the lifestyle of the Sangha. Others, we are told, were very nominal, even lax in their observance of the monastic discipline. Of course, some criticism of this kind comes from sources hostile to any form of monasticism and must be treated with caution.

A set of rules created by the Ch'an monk Pai-chang (d. 814 CE) was widely accepted as authoritative, at least in theory (in addition to the fundamental rules of the *Vinaya* and the Mahayana *Brahmajala-sutra*). Some of the minor rules of the Indian *Vinaya* had fallen into abeyance, but by and large the basic principles of Ancient Buddhist monasticism were still acknowledged in China, Vietnam and Korea. Indeed, the peripatetic nature of the ancient Sangha was perhaps better preserved in China than elsewhere. Many monks, especially in their youth, spent several years wandering from province to province studying and practising in different temples [106].

In Japan the situation changed most noticeably after the Meiji restoration in 1868. The requirement for celibacy was abolished by law and eventually marriage became widespread. This should not be confused with the much older tradition of a married priesthood in some branches of the Japanese Pure Land school. The new practice was also introduced into Korea under Japanese rule but has met opposition there. The vast majority of non-Japanese Buddhists regard a married monk as a contradiction; so, too, did the Japanese

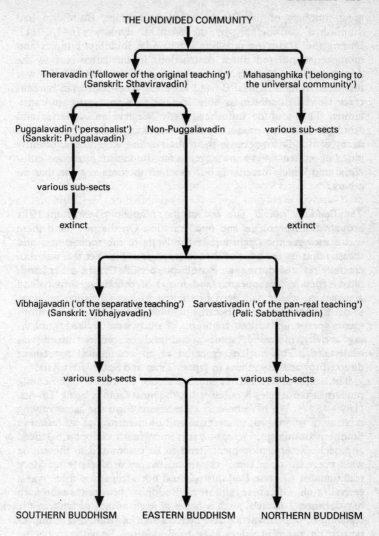

THE UNDIVIDED COMMUNITY

Theravadin ('follower of the original teaching')
(Sanskrit: Sthaviravadin)

Mahasanghika ('belonging to the universal community')

Puggalavadin ('personalist')
(Sanskrit: Pudgalavadin)

Non-Puggalavadin

various sub-sects

various sub-sects

extinct

extinct

Vibhajjavadin ('of the separative teaching')
(Sanskrit: Vibhajyavadin)

Sarvastivadin ('of the pan-real teaching')
(Pali: Sabbatthivadin)

various sub-sects ———————— various sub-sects

SOUTHERN BUDDHISM   EASTERN BUDDHISM   NORTHERN BUDDHISM

Figure 8.5   The main divisions of the Sangha

founders of most of the sects which now practise it. No doubt
Protestant Christian attitudes to celibacy have given some outside
reinforcement to monastic marriage.

Chinese Buddhism in the nineteenth century Compared with its cultural and intellectual importance during the T'ang period or the

great numbers of the Sangha in Mongol times, Buddhism had diminished considerably by the Manchu dynasty (1644–1911). During the T'ai-p'ing rebellion (1850–64), Buddhist temples and monasteries suffered much destruction. In the latter part of the dynasty the government was not sympathetic and Buddhism was restricted in its activities. By and large the Neo-Confucian bureaucracy viewed Buddhism as non-Chinese, non-productive and anti-family. This attitude influenced early Western missionaries and scholars, who then produced somewhat exaggerated reports of the decay of Buddhism because their observations were not sufficiently based upon first-hand knowledge. In fact Buddhism remained influential and widely practised, but more so in some regions than in others.

The Buddhist revival The fall of the Manchu dynasty in 1911 brought both problems and opportunities. On the one hand there was a movement to expropriate the lands of the monasteries and thereby destroy the basis of Buddhist religious life. Yet this was successfully resisted during the Republican period. On the other hand, old restrictions disappeared and forms of preaching activity and association, which had been prohibited to non-Christian religions under the Manchus, now became possible. A number of new movements sprang up; various traditions of study were revived; publishing activity increased; some social and educational work was undertaken. The nucleus emerged of an ecumenical movement directed towards Buddhists in Japan, Tibet and South-East Asia.

The work of a relatively small number of monks representing modernist tendencies is noteworthy, the most famous being Tai-hsu (1890–1947). We have here in a Mahayana form the same varying mixture of reformism, modernism and ultimatism that we found in Southern Buddhism. Here, too, it is important to adopt a balanced approach. Reform movements tend to be committed to presenting what preceded as in some way unsatisfactory or degenerate. More traditionalist Chinese Buddhists would not accept that there was a revival at all. Of course, almost all Buddhists believe that the faith has declined – indeed, such a belief is itself an act of faith in the teaching of impermanence and hence a sign of vitality. It is important to be aware of values alien to Buddhism. Social activities by monks can be seen as an admirably modern innovation, but many Buddhists would see this as a wholly inappropriate imitation of Christian missionaries and destructive of the proper role of the Sangha. Outsiders have tended to be unsympathetic towards the values of silence and contemplation, yet these are as essential to Mahayana Buddhism as the giving of material help to others, which is primarily the task of the lay Buddhist. Buddhism in both the Manchu and Republican periods was still a lively and powerful force in Chinese religious affairs. What is referred to as a revival is best seen as a form of Buddhist modernism – part of the response of Buddhism to the arrival of European religious and secularist ideas and practices [23: 455–60; 16; 105].

The situation in Korea Much that has been said about the difficulties of Buddhism in China under the later Manchus applies equally to the state of Buddhism under the Choson dynasty (1392–1910) in Korea. Here too the removal of restrictions brought about a revival and modernization of activities. However, the growth of Japanese influence and the eventual Japanese seizure of Korea led to a rather different situation. On the positive side the elimination of Neo-Confucian controls and the widespread social influence of Buddhism in Japan tended to strengthen Korean Buddhism. On the other hand, the Japanese government was strongly influenced by a revived form of Shinto with a pronounced hostility towards Buddhism and tried to bring Korean Buddhism into line with Japanese practices. Most strikingly, the attempt was made to introduce by force the practice of so-called married monks: for example, senior positions were restricted to married monks and other such measures were adopted. This is, of course, much against the overall traditions of Eastern Buddhism and was resented by many Koreans.

After the Second World War and the overthrow of Japanese rule there was a strong move to restore traditional Korean practices in South Korea. Notably, there was a fairly fierce conflict on the specific issue of monastic celibacy. Ultimately the celibate monks (who clearly had the support of the bulk of the Buddhist population) were successful in obtaining control of most of the major monasteries and generally revitalizing Korean Buddhism on traditional lines. A small order of married monks does still continue, but seems to be declining fairly rapidly [12: 25–33].

The Communist period With Communist rule established in China, North Korea and Vietnam a very different situation emerged. In China during the 1950s a policy of moderate restriction, modelled on Soviet policies developed in a Christian context, was initially adopted. Russian practice was much more hostile to monasticism than to the clergy, and the application of the Soviet model in Buddhist areas with 'monks' and no married clergy was necessarily very destructive. (The extreme case was Outer Mongolia where almost the whole monastic order was put to death.) Monastic lands were nationalized and monks required to support themselves by some kind of work. Although such a policy was already severe and destructive of the spiritual training of the monks, many other activities were also restricted. The government for its part claimed to be engaged in a programme of reform which, no doubt, was sometimes justified. Some Buddhist cultural activities received government support; so, for example, Buddhist temples and monuments considered to be of cultural importance were repaired. According to government figures there were 100 million Chinese Buddhists in the 1950s.

From about 1958 the situation worsened markedly. By the climax of the Cultural Revolution a decade later Buddhism was totally prohibited throughout China, at least in theory. Buddhist monasteries and temples were closed and in many cases suffered damage at the hands of Marxist fanatics. How far this was universal is uncertain. It seems likely that there was some variation in different areas. With the abatement of the more extreme tendencies came a move back towards the pre-1958 situation. By about 1980 many of the leading centres were again functioning and there was some action to repair damage. The following decade saw a new policy of tolerance, leading to some revival of monastic ordination. Moreover, at a grassroots level outside the purview of officaldom there was some revival of lay Buddhist activity (see p. 438 below) [104].

The 1990s began with a slight tightening of official control, due to alarm at the collapse of European Communist regimes. The future is obviously uncertain. Yet after all Buddhism has survived persecutions in the past and doubtless it still has many centuries of activity to come. Outside the Chinese mainland the post-war period has seen an increase in Buddhist activities in Taiwan, in Hong Kong and in the Chinese diaspora. This seems attributable in part to Buddhist refugees from Communist rule, but also to influences from other Asian countries and even from the West.

Northern Buddhism

Introduction

Sources Tibetan Buddhism possesses two great canonical collections: the *bKa' 'gyur* and the *bsTan 'gyur*.[2] The former contains translations of Indian scriptures and is usually arranged under six headings: (1) *Vinaya*; (2) *Prajna-paramita* ('perfection of wisdom'); (3) *Avatamsaka* ('garland'); (4) *Ratna-kuta* ('jewel heap'); (5) *Sutra*; (6) *Tantra*. It consists of about 100 volumes and contains around 700 works. The *bsTan 'gyur* has over 200 volumes and more than 3,600 works. These are mainly the works of Indian authorities – in effect, *shastra* literature of various kinds. The three main sections are: (1) a short collection of hymns; (2) commentaries on *tantras*; and (3) commentaries on *sutras*. Tibetan also has an enormous literature of its own, much of which is known only to Tibetan scholars.

History The history of the formation of Northern Buddhism may be divided into four periods: early history; developments in India; the spread of Mantrayana; and the second diffusion of Buddhism in Tibet.

The early period. According to Tibetan tradition Buddhism was introduced to Tibet in the reign of Srong btsan sgam po (d. 649 CE) by two of the king's wives, one from Nepal and one from China. This can only have been on a small scale, since it was not until the reign of Khri srong lde brtsan (756–97?) that Buddhism made significant progress, culminating in the foundation of the monastery of bSam yas. The inspiration for this came from the Indian scholar Shantarakshita. Later tradition gives a major role to the yogi and sage Padmasambhava, said to have been invited by Shantarakshita to overcome supernatural opposition to the spread of Buddhism.

In fact Buddhism came from various sources. We hear of a contest between followers of the Chinese Ch'an tradition and supporters of Indian schools, to some extent a contest between gradualist and sudden approaches to enlightenment. Tradition would suggest that the Indian tradition was completely victorious. More recent historical research, however, has shown that tendencies derived from the Ch'an school persisted for a long time and indeed may have played an important part in the formation of some forms of traditional Tibetan practice. There were probably also important influences from Central Asian Buddhism (figure 8.6) [80].

In due course resistance arose from followers of the native Tibetan religious tradition known as Bon. This led to some persecution of Buddhism in the reign of gLang dar ma, but after the death of this king in 842 CE the Tibetan kingdom broke up and Tibet lost control of Central Asia. Buddhism was affected by the general chaos and largely disappeared from historical view. Yet it continued to develop, especially in outlying areas, and gradually penetrated Tibetan culture, both influencing and being influenced by the Bon religion [88: 66–110; 99: 1–15].

Developments in India. The religious creativity of Indian Buddhism had produced another great flowering of sacred literature: the *tantras*. Like the earlier Mahayana *sutras*, these claimed to be the teaching of a Buddha or equivalent figure. They represent the third and last major phase in Indian Buddhist thought and practice. Just as the Mahayana did not replace the teachings of Ancient Buddhism, so too the new school did not displace the Mahayana, but developed within the old and was superimposed upon it.

The movement based upon the *tantras* is known as the Mantrayana, 'Vehicle of the *mantra*'. A *mantra* is a word or phrase used for meditation and devotion. According to a widely used explicatory 'etymology' it 'protects the mind'. An alternative name is Vajrayana ('Vehicle of the diamond'), i.e. the indestructible vehicle.

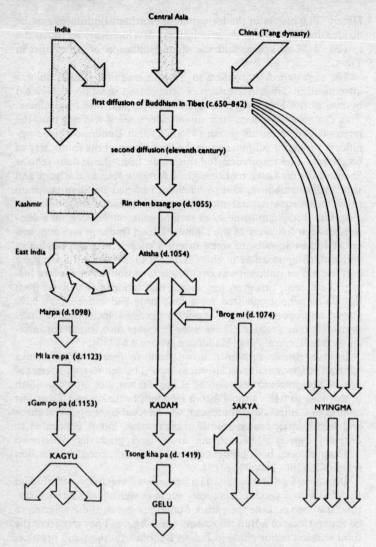

Figure 8.6 *The evolution of Northern Buddhism*

The origin of much of the early tantric literature is still obscure; there were certainly parallel developments in both Hinduism and Buddhism. Much folk tradition and magical technique was incorporated in the new movement, including materials of very ancient origins. It is now known that some of the later Buddhist tantras were borrowed wholesale from Shaiva sources, although modified to accord with Buddhist rather than Hindu philosophy.

Two features of the Mantrayana are perhaps the most important. First, it involved the elaborate use of magical methods – esoteric teachings, ritual and ceremonial, initiations, incantations, sacred circles, etc. – in effect, the skilful and joyful use of sense experience and imagination to bring about individual transformation. Secondly, it emphasized the possibility of enlightenment in this very life, claiming that its special methods could provide a direct path to the goal in contrast with the more gradual approach of the later Indian Mahayana. Necessarily, great importance was given to the role of the teacher. A rich and vivid symbolism was employed. At first this probably emerged from and formed part of visualization exercises, but it soon began to take artistic form. Especially noticeable is the use of imagery connected with sexuality or with death. Eventually a new pantheon of specifically Mantrayana deities comes into existence, including many goddesses and female consorts or aspects of Buddhas and *bodhisattvas*.

Mantrayana developed into an articulated and sophisticated system. Elaborate correspondences were established between the pantheon, the body, meditational experiences and the world at large. In some schools the ritual performance of sexual acts seems to have taken place, but (at least in Buddhism) this should not be exaggerated. It can only have played a minor part in the Mantrayana movement as a whole. It should perhaps be noted that several distinct types of such sexual practice occurred. So we can distinguish the introduction of a ritual and meditational element into the sexual life of a lay couple from ritual acts with an unusual partner. The performance of any kind of sexual act by monks was always controversial and usually so hedged around with restrictions as to make it unlikely in practice. In effect most schools did not permit it.

Tantra has a marked tendency to make use of activities which are psychologically 'loaded', especially in its visualization methods. Death, sexuality, any kind of taboo act or substance are all grist for its mill. The aim is partly to free the mind from ambivalent attractions and partly to startle the mind out of rigid habits. In this there is some similarity with the methods of Ch'an Buddhism [101: 482–502; 22: 386–7; 79: 116–23].

The spread of Mantrayana. In the last part of the first millennium CE the Mantrayana spread widely over most of the Buddhist world. It was present in Sri Lanka and South-East Asia as well as influential in Indonesia. In none of these places did it endure into modern times, although it left many traces of its influence. It was primarily in the area influenced by the Buddhism of Tibet that the Mantrayana remained important.

Yet there are some exceptions; for the Chinese Mantrayana

school was introduced into Japan by Kukai (774–835), best known as Kobo daishi. The school which he founded, the Shingon, remains one of the larger Japanese sects. Shingon may be seen as a synthesis of an earlier phase of Mantrayana with the Chinese theoretical schools. Its practice, however, is essentially tantric in nature, although not deviating from conventional morality. Tendai (the Japanese branch of the T'ien-t'ai school) also adopted major elements of tantric ritual and practice, both from Kobo daishi himself and directly from China. Finally, it should be noted that the tantric tradition continues also to some extent in Korean Buddhism [22: 389–90; 23; 45; 58].

The second diffusion of Buddhism in Tibet. The end of the tenth century and the course of the eleventh saw renewed contacts between Tibet and Indian Buddhism. Relations were established with Kashmir and the centres of Buddhism in eastern India. New translations were made from the large body of Buddhist literature still available in the Indian monastic universities, soon to be destroyed by the invading Muslims. A number of Tibetan translators who had studied in India or Kashmir were at work in this period, notably Rin chen bzang po (d. 1055), 'Brog mi (d. 1074) and Marpa (d. 1098). Just as important were Indian teachers who came to Tibet. Particularly notable was Atisha (982–1054), one of the leading figures of contemporary Indian Buddhism.

The following century saw the rapid growth of Tibetan monasticism and the formation of the principal schools. This culminated in the thirteenth century when the Mongols established the head of the Sakya school as ruler of Tibet. Later a new school was formed by the reformer Tsong kha pa (1357–1419), known as the Gelu. The heads of the Gelu school eventually acquired the title of Dalai Lama and gradually became rulers of Tibet. In the eighteenth century the Manchu rulers of China established effective suzerainty. Tibetan Buddhism showed great vitality, not only spreading throughout the Tibetan cultural area but also winning over the Mongols and establishing itself on a small scale quite widely in northern Asia. Indeed, it was showing definite signs of expansion in the period just before the arrival of Communism [99: 16–28; 88: 160ff].

Changing assumptions Tibetan religion was very little known before the influx of Tibetan refugees into Western countries during the 1960s and later. Many very distorted accounts had become current. On the one hand Tibet was seen as a country in the grip of medieval religious superstition, dominated by demonolatry and a completely decadent and corrupt form of Buddhism. On the other hand it was portrayed as the home of the mystical, the spiritual and the magical – a land of great Masters filled with occult lore and profound knowledge. No doubt there is a measure of truth in each of these pictures,

but they have made it more difficult to arrive at a balanced understanding.

It is now quite clear that Tibet was the direct heir of later Indian
Buddhism. It had both preserved the learning of the great monastic
universities of India and added to that learning in a creative and
constructive, if rather conservative, way. As a result the monasteries
of Tibet were the repositories of a very considerable and unique heritage – not only in such subjects as religion, philosophy and logic,
but also in artistic and cultural products. The growth of Tibetan
studies in the twentieth century has begun to bring real knowledge
of that heritage and has replaced more extreme notions with a realistic and balanced assessment of Tibetan religion.

The Nature of Northern Buddhism

The structure of the teaching Tibetans sometimes argue that their
teaching includes all three vehicles: the Hinayana, the Mahayana
and the Vajrayana. There is some truth in this, although it can
sometimes be a polemical claim, implying that other forms of
Buddhism are redundant. The oldest Buddhism is represented in
the Vinaya discipline and the practice of moral restraint. Moreover,
the Tibetan monastic curriculum sometimes included quite detailed
study of the *abhidharma* and there are in any case many elements
surviving from an early period. Yet it is clearly with the second and
third vehicles that most Northern Buddhist teaching is concerned.
Tibetan Buddhism contains large elements both of Mahayana and
of Mantrayana. The former, often referred to as the 'Vehicle of the
perfections', Tibetans see as the *bodhisattva* path, developing perfections over many lives, as set out in the Mahayana *sutras* and the
great *shastra* systems of the Shunyatavada and the Yogacara. These
two *shastra* systems were widely known and studied in the Tibetan
schools [30; 84].

The vehicle of the *mantras* is seen as a direct route, utilizing specific practices as a skilful means enabling buddhahood to be reached
in years rather than lives. On one level this is reserved for the experienced practitioner at a relatively advanced stage. On another level
it can be said to pervade the whole of Tibetan religion. Tibetan art
and devotion are filled with the figures of deities, *bodhisattvas* and
Buddhas whose origins lie in the *tantras* or who are presented in a
guise based upon the *tantra* [87].

Perhaps the most striking feature of Tibetan Buddhism to the
observer is the part played by ceremony and ritual, especially the
public conferment of various kinds of blessing and initiation. This
aspect of Northern Buddhism is in fact immensely successful and
popular, even quite outside the normal limits of the religion.

Recently such ceremonies have been performed fairly widely in both
Europe and North America with visible effectiveness and impact.
Their form and arrangement, however, are based upon Mantrayana
theory of a quite detailed and sophisticated kind [61].

The role of the Lama Mantrayana Buddhism emphasizes the role of
the teacher (Sanskrit *guru*; Tibetan *blama*), as any religious tradition
which stresses initiations and esoteric teachings is likely to do. So
much is this the case that the Lama is often added as a fourth refuge
to the 'refuge in the three jewels' usual in Eastern or Southern
Buddhism. It is incorrect to apply the term Lama to any Northern
Buddhist monk, as is sometimes done. Indeed, Tibetans understandably tend to object to the name 'Lamaism' for their religion
because it implies that it is not authentic Buddhism.

One significant innovation that certainly has been made in Tibet
is the introduction of the institution of so-called 'incarnate lamas' or
tulkus (Sanskrit *nirmanakaya*). Originally the idea was simply that a
past teacher might return to new life as a child or might be especially connected to a child. The first Karmapa Lama (Dus gsum
mkhyen pa: 1110–93) introduced a new notion by predicting his
own immediate rebirth after death. Eventually the custom of finding
a child to succeed a dead teacher became widespread. In some cases
such 'lines' of succession were considered to act as the vehicle for
the manifestation of the power of a *bodhisattva* or Buddha. The
most famous example is of course the Dalai Lama, considered to be
a focus for Avalokiteshvara, the *bodhisattva* of compassion [99:
134–5].

Meditation methods The same combination of Mahayana and
Mantrayana applies in the realm of meditation practice. There is
basic training in calm and insight meditation (see p. 402), modelled
especially on the accounts of the Yogacara school. This is widely
practised but is often, though not always, regarded as only a preliminary stage. More typical is some kind of meditative ritual. This is
essentially some combination of an appropriate *mantra* with a corresponding visualization exercise. So, for example, one may visualize
oneself as taking the form of a Buddha while picturing that Buddha
before one in an appropriate context (e.g. surrounded by circles of
attendant Buddhas, *bodhisattvas* and deities). Such a practice will
usually be initiated by ceremonial authorizations from a teacher,
preferably one who has himself mastered that particular method.
The practitioner must thereafter repeat a series of chants and visual-
izations, make offerings, repeat the relevant *mantra*, make appropriate gestures (*mudra*) at intervals and so on. Eventually the
visualization should come joyfully alive, only to be dissolved again
in emptiness. Such methods occur in many different forms using a

multiplicity of different techniques. Successful ritual service of a given deity is seen as bringing both inner and outer rewards, as well as advancing one on the path to liberation. It is almost impossible to separate this kind of meditation from more general popular devotion and cult, since each can lead into the other. Indeed, rituals performed by Tibetan monks are based upon the patterns and theoretical structure of tantric meditation and are at the same time intended to create conditions in the participant favourable for meditation, as well as accomplishing more immediate results [99: 47–109; 74: 148–58; 8; 5: 25ff].

The schools of Northern Buddhism Tibetan Buddhist schools differ as to precisely which texts they hold to be authoritative and to which deities they pay most attention; in some cases they possess particular teachings or practices in which they specialize. They remain quite similar in general features and perhaps do not amount to distinct sects. Three general groups can be distinguished: (1) the tradition deriving from the first diffusion of Buddhism in Tibet – the Nyingma ('old ones'); (2) the schools stemming from the second diffusion – especially the Kadam, the Sakya and the Kagyu; and (3) the reform which gave rise to the Gelu or New Kadam school, often known as the 'Yellow Sect'. The earlier Kadam was absorbed by the Gelu school. This left four main schools as well as a number of less well-known ones.

The Sakya and Kagyu may perhaps be seen as the intellectual and yogic wings of the same many-branched tradition. The latter in particular is well known for its cotton-clad yogis, going back to the teachings of the poet-saint Milarepa (1040–1123). Especially important for this school are the Six Doctrines attributed to the Indian yogi Naropa (the teacher of Marpa), leading to the spiritual achievement known as *Mahamudra*.

The Nyingma is partly a response to the success of the schools belonging to the second diffusion. On the one hand, it retains many ancient traditions and practices of varying origin. On the other hand, it has been one of the most creative schools. It gives authority to texts supposedly hidden during the period of persecution and later found by clairvoyant masters, even to some which are openly the product of contemplation. In this, of course, it simply continues the practice of the ancient Mahayana. The Nyingma school underwent a considerable renaissance in the fourteenth century, creating its own collection of *tantras* and developing a cult based upon the legendary figure of Padmasambhava, seen as its founder.

The Gelu school represents an attempt to return to the tradition of Atisha, re-emphasizing monastic discipline, which its founder Tsong kha pa (1357–1419) felt had become lax. Tsong kha pa had studied in all three of the schools of the second diffusion and stressed the importance of following authentic Indian tradition. The school had great success and founded large monastic universities in Lhasa and elsewhere, requiring a long and impressive period of study. Shunyatavada teaching played an important role and unusual emphasis was placed on the study of logic and on public debate [22: 388–9; 99: 33–9, 47–109].

The Sangha Only one Vinaya tradition was established in Tibet – that of the Mulasarvastivada. In principle it is adhered to by all schools, but in practice it is overlaid to some extent by various Mahayana and Mantrayana traditions. A fairly complex organization had naturally developed in the larger monasteries. Before 1959 Tibet had a rather larger Sangha, according to some accounts as much as 25 per cent or more of the population. Such a high figure is probably an exaggeration, since observers may have been confused by the presence of married lay disciples at monasteries, wearing similar robes to the monks. There were certainly a few very large monasteries, especially in Lhasa and at the principal centres of various sects [88: 237ff; 99: 110ff].

Festivals The Tibetan calendar is related to the Chinese, with some differences. It is a lunar calendar, each month beginning at the new moon with the full moon on the fifteenth day. New Year and harvest festivals play an important part everywhere, as do festivals of sect founders and tutelary deities in particular monasteries. Those generally recognized are shown in table 8.7 [99: 146ff; 38: 53–6].

Table 8.7 Tibetan Buddhist festivals

Month	Day	Event
One	10–15	Great miracle at Shravasti (following the New Year celebrations)
Four	7	Birth of the Buddha
Four	15	Enlightenment and entry into *nirvana* of the Buddha
Six	4	First sermon of the Buddha
Nine	22	Descent of the Buddha from heaven (end of the rains retreat)
Ten	25	Death of Tsonkhapa (offering of robes)

Recent History

The Manchu rulers of China had established suzerainty over Tibet and their representatives exercised a measure of authority in Lhasa throughout the nineteenth century. The fall of the Manchu dynasty in 1911 ended that suzerainty as far as the Tibetans were concerned. Tibetan culture and religion continued to remain largely out of contact with the rest of the world until the Chinese Communist invasion in 1950 established Chinese overlordship under an agreement providing for Tibetan self-government. This collapsed in 1959, the Dalai Lama fled to India and direct Chinese colonial rule was forcibly imposed. Eventually the Cultural Revolution led to an attempt to destroy Tibetan religion totally. This appears to have involved the large-scale destruction of Tibet's artistic, sculptural and architectural heritage – probably one of the worst cultural crimes of one people against another in recent centuries. At present there are intermittent signs of a return to more moderate policies.

Tibetan religion is still active in the Himalayan territories of India and Nepal as well as in the small kingdom of Bhutan and among refugee communities in India and elsewhere. With the decline of Communism in the former Soviet Union, Northern Buddhism has revived considerably in its former territories, both in Mongolia and among the Buriat, Tuvan and Kalmuk peoples of Russia, recovering for example its former 'Cathedral' in St Petersburg. Moreover, it has had some success in the field of missionary endeavour.

Afterword: The Three Traditions in the World Today

The twentieth century has brought mixed fortunes for Buddhism. Communist rule has meant wholesale destruction, especially to the Sangha, first in the Asian territories of the Soviet Union and in Mongolia, then successively in North Korea, China, Tibet, Vietnam, Laos and Cambodia. Each of the three traditions has suffered. The same period saw a revival of activity and a return to lands long lost. Notably in Indonesia and in India, Buddhism has re-established its presence and won new support.

More remarkably, new fields for expansion have emerged. In Europe, Southern Buddhism began to establish itself on a small scale as early as the beginning of the century. Eastern Buddhism in its Zen form started to attract a significant following outside the Asian immigrant communities in the 1950s, especially in North America. The work of Tibetan refugee teachers in the 1960s and 1970s won support for Northern Buddhism. By the early 1980s some hundreds of Buddhist groups and centres were widely scattered across the Western world. Much of this activity is on a fairly small scale, but in many cases quite well established. All three major traditions have been increasing in numbers fairly rapidly. Membership figures are rarely available, even for groups that have a formal membership (many do not), but it is clear that the number of groups is increasing quite rapidly both in Europe and in the Americas. In Germany, for example, the number of centres grew fivefold (to a couple of hundred) between 1975 and 1991. The situation is similar in a number of other countries, including the UK [79: 198ff; 74: 248–58; 4: 273–85].

The Buddhist Diaspora

It is important to note that there has been a considerable emigration from the traditional Buddhist countries over recent decades. This has brought a substantial population into a number of areas where Asian Buddhists were not previously present in large numbers. The US now has a population of approaching half a million people claiming descent from the Southern Buddhist countries; not all of these will be Buddhists, but many must be. Similar immigration has taken place in Europe, but on a smaller scale; for example, there are some 40,000 Buddhist immigrants in Germany.

The Buddhist Revival of the 1980s

It is perhaps important to note that from the 1980s there has been a considerable revival of Buddhist activity in much of its traditional territory. Despite many earlier predictions to the contrary, Buddhism looks highly likely to outlast Communism, which had earlier presented the appearance of a most lethal enemy. Its position is now much stronger in the Southern Buddhist lands of Laos and Cambodia, in the Eastern Buddhist territories of China and across the greater part of the territorial range of Northern Buddhism. Setting this trend alongside the continuing growth in Europe, the Americas and elsewhere, it seems that a genuine Buddhist revival has been in process. No doubt Buddhism faces many difficulties as a result of the social changes arising with rapid growth and industrialization in Pacific Asia, but it is clear that it is likely to continue to be able to respond to such problems in the medium term.

Notes

1 Where Buddhist names and terms are current in both a Sanskrit and a Pali form (see p. 380), only one form is generally given in the text: Sanskrit where dealing with Northern or Eastern Buddhism or with specifically Mahayana notions, Pali in the case of Southern Buddhism or the remainder of Ancient Buddhism.

2 The written form of the Tibetan language is unusually different from the present-day spoken forms. Although a correct form has been generally used here, simplified forms have been given for words which already have some current usage in English, e.g. names of sects.

Bibliography

1 *Encyclopaedia Britannica*, 15th edn, *Macropaedia*, vol. III, Chicago, Encyclopaedia Britannica, 1974

2 ADIKARAM, E. W., *Early History of Buddhism in Ceylon*, Colombo/Migoda, M. D. Gunasena/Puswella, 1953 [1946]

3 ANURUDDHA, *Compendium of Philosophy* (tr. S. Z. Aung), London, Pali Text Society, 1910; repr. 1979

4 BECHERT, H., AND GOMBRICH, R., *The World of Buddhism: Buddhist Monks and Nuns in Society and Culture*, London, Thames & Hudson, 1984

5 BEYER, S., *The Cult of Tārā: Magic and Ritual in Tibet*, Berkeley, University of California Press, 1973

6 BIZOT, F., *Le Chemin de Laṅkā*, Textes bouddhiques du Cambodge, Paris, École française d'Extrême-Orient, 1992

7 BIZOT, F., *Le Figuier à Cinq Branches. Recherche sur le bouddhisme khmer*, Publications de l'École française d'Extrême-Orient vol. CVII, Paris, École française d'Extrême-Orient, 1976

8 BLOFELD, J. J., *The Way of Power: A Practical Guide to the Tantric Mysticism of Tibet*, London, Allen & Unwin, 1970

9 BOND, G. D., *The Buddhist Revival in Sri Lanka: Religious Tradition, Reinterpretation and Response*, Studies in Comparative Religion (ed. F. M. Denny), Columbia, University of South Carolina Press, 1988

10 BUDDHADĀSA, BHIKKHU, *Toward the Truth*, (ed. D. K. Swearer), Philadelphia, Westminster Press, 1971

11 BUDDHAGHOSA, *The Path of Purification*, 2nd edn (tr. Ñāṇamoli, Bhikkhu), Colombo/Berkeley, Semage/Shambhala, 1964, 1976

12 BUSWELL, R. E., JR, *The Zen Monastic Experience: Buddhist Practice in Contemporary Korea*, Princeton University Press, 1992

13 CARRITHERS, M., *The Buddha*, Oxford/New York, Oxford University Press, 1983

14 CARTER, J. R., *Dhamma: Western Academic and Sinhalese Buddhist*

440 L. S. COUSINS

Interpretations: A Study of a Religious Concept, Tokyo, Hokuseido Press, 1978

15 CARTER, J. R. (ed.), *Religiousness in Sri Lanka*, Colombo, Marga Institute, 1979

16 CHAN, W. T., *Religious Trends in Modern China*, New York, Columbia University Press, 1953

17 CHANG, C. C. *The Buddhist Teaching of Totality: The Philosophy of Hwa Yen Buddhism*, London, Allen & Unwin, 1972

18 CHANG, C. C. (CHANG CHEN-CHI), *The Practice of Zen*, New York/London, Harper/Rider, 1959/1960

19 CH'EN, K. K. S., *Buddhism in China: A Historical Survey*, Princeton, Princeton University Press, 1964; repr. 1972

20 CH'EN, K. K. S., *Buddhism: The Light of Asia*, Woodbury, NY, Barron's Educational Series, 1968

21 CONZE, E., *Buddhism: Its Essence and Development*, Oxford/New York, Cassirer/Philosophical Library, 1951

22 CONZE, E., *Buddhist Thought in India*, London, Allen & Unwin, 1962

23 CONZE, E., 'Recent Progress in Buddhist Studies,' in *Thirty Years of Buddhist Studies* (ed. E. Conze), Oxford/Columbia, Cassirer/University of South Carolina Press, 1967/1968

24 COOK, F. H., *Hua-yen Buddhism: The Jewel Net of Indra*, University Park, Pennsylvania State University Press, 1977

25 CORLESS, R. J., *The Vision of Buddhism: The Space under the Tree*, New York, Paragon House, 1989

26 COUSINS, L. S. 'Buddhist Jhāna: Its Nature and Attainment According to the Pali Sources', *Religion*, vol. 3, 1973, pp. 115–31

27 COUSINS, L. S. 'The Dating of the Historical Buddha', *Journal of the Royal Asiatic Society*, vol. 5, 1996

28 COUSINS, L. S., 'Esoteric Southern Buddhism', in S. Hamilton (ed.), *Indian Insights: Buddhism, Brahmanism and Bhakti: Papers from the Spalding Seminars on Indian Religions*, Luzac Oriental, 1996

29 COUSINS, L. S., 'The "Five Points" and the Origins of the Buddhist Schools', in T. Skorupski (ed.), *The Buddhist Forum*, vol. II, London, Soas, 1991, pp. 27–60

30 DALAI LAMA, X. (NGAWANG LOBSANG YISHEY TENZING GYATSO, DALAI LAMA, 1935–), *The Opening of the Wisdom-Eye and the History of the Advancement of Buddhadharma in Tibet*, Bangkok, Social Science Association Press of Thailand, 1968

31 DE JONG, J. W., *Buddhist Studies*, Berkeley, Asian Humanities Press, 1979

32 DE SILVA, L., *Buddhism: Beliefs and Practices in Sri Lanka*, 2nd edn, Colombo, 1980

33 DENWOOD, P., AND PIATIGORSKY, A., *Buddhist Studies – Ancient and Modern*, London/Totowa, Curzon Press/Barnes & Noble, 1983

34 DUMOULIN, H., *Zen Buddhism: A History: India and China*, New York, Macmillan, 1994

35 GELLNER, D. N., *Monk, Householder, and Tantric Priest: Newar Buddhism and its Hierarchy of Ritual*, Cambridge, Cambridge University Press, 1992

36 GETHIN, R. M. L., *The Buddhist Path to Awakening: A Study of the Bodhi-*

Pakkhiyā Dhammā, Leiden, Brill, 1992

37 GODDARD, D., *A Buddhist Bible*, 2nd edn, Thetford, Vt, Author, 1938

38 GOMBRICH, R., 'Buddhist Festivals', in A. Brown (ed.), *Festivals in World Religions*, London/New York, Longmans, 1986, pp. 31–59

39 GOMBRICH, R., *Theravāda Buddhism: A Social History from Ancient Benares to Modern Columbo*, The Library of Religious Beliefs and Practices (ed. J. Hinnells and N. Smart), London/New York, Routledge & Kegan Paul, 1988

40 GOMBRICH, R., and OBEYESEKERE, G., *Buddhism Transformed: Religious Change in Sri Lanka*, Princeton, Princeton University Press, 1988

41 GOMBRICH, R. F., *Precept and Practice: Traditional Buddhism in the Rural Highlands of Ceylon*, Oxford, Clarendon Press, 1971

42 GRAYSON, J. H., *Korea: A Religious History*, Oxford, Clarendon Press, 1989

43 GRIFFITHS, P. J., *On Being Buddha: The Classical Doctrine of Buddhahood*, SUNY Series, Towards a Comparative Philosophy of Religions (ed. F. E. Reynolds and D. Tracy), Albany, State University of New York Press, 1994

44 GUENTHER, H. V., *Philosophy and Psychology in the Abhidharma*, 2nd edn, Berkeley, Shambhala, 1974

45 HAKEDA, Y. S., *Kūkai: Major Works. Translated with an Account of his Life and a Study of his Thought*, 4th edn, New York, Columbia University Press, 1972

46 HARVEY, P., 'The Dynamics of Paritta Chanting in Southern Buddhism', in K. Werner (ed.), *Love Divine. Studies in Bhakti and Devotional Mysticism*, Richmond, Curzon Press, 1993, pp. 53–84

47 HARVEY, P., *An Introduction to Buddhism: Teachings, History and Practices*, Cambridge/New York, Cambridge University Press, 1990

48 HOLT, J. C., *Buddha in the Crown*, Oxford, Oxford University Press, 1991

49 HOLT, J. C., *Discipline: The Canonical Buddhism of the Vinaya-pitaka*, Delhi, Motilal Banarsidass, 1981

50 HORNER, I. B. (tr.), *Middle Length Sayings*, London, Pali Text Society, 1954–9; repr. 1975–7

51 HOUTMAN, G., 'Traditions of Buddhist Practice in Burma', PhD thesis, London University, 1990

52 HURVITZ, L. 'Chih-i', *Mélanges chinois et bouddhiques*, vol. 12, 1962

53 JACKSON, P. A., *Buddhadasa: A Buddhist Thinker for the Modern World*, Bangkok, Siam Society, 1988

54 KEOWN, D., *The Nature of Buddhist Ethics*, London, Macmillan, 1992

55 KEOWN, D., *A Very Short Introduction to Buddhism*, Oxford, Oxford University Press, 1996

56 KHANTIPALO, B., *Calm and Insight: A Buddhist Manual for Meditators*, London, Curzon Press, 1981

57 KING, W. L., *Theravāda Meditation: The Buddhist Transformation of Yoga*, University Park/London, Pennsylvania State University Press, 1980

58 KIYOTA, M., *Shingon Buddhism: Theory and Practice*, Los Angeles/Tokyo, Buddhist Books International, 1978

59 KORNFIELD, J., *Living Buddhist Masters*, Santa Cruz, Unity Press, 1977

60 LAMOTTE, E., *History of Indian Buddhism: From the Origins to the Śaka Era*, Louvain, Institut Orientaliste, 1988

61 LESSING, F. D. and A. W. (trs), *Introduction to the Buddhist Tantric Systems*, 2nd edn, Delhi, Motilal Banarsidass, 1978

62 LINDTNER, C., *Nagarjuniana*, Delhi, Motilal Banarsidass, 1987 [1982]

63 LING, T. O. 'Sinhalese Buddhism in Recent Anthropological Writing: Some Implications', *Religion*, vol. 1, 1971, pp. 49–59

64 MALALGODA, K., *Buddhism in Sinhalese Society, 1750–1900: A Study of Religious Revival and Change*, Berkeley, University of California Press, 1976

65 MARASINGHE, M. M. J., *Gods in Early Buddhism*, Vidyalankara, University of Sri Lanka, 1974

66 MCRAE, J. R., *The Northern School and the Formation of Early Ch'an Buddhism*, Studies in East Asian Buddhism 3, Honolulu, University of Hawaii Press, 1986

67 MENDELSON, E. M., *Sangha and State in Burma: A Study of Monastic Sectarianism and Leadership*, Ithaca, Cornell University Press, 1975

68 MORGAN, K. W. (ed.) *The Path of the Buddha: Buddhism Interpreted by Buddhists*, New York, Ronald Press, 1956

69 NANJIO, B., *A Catalogue of the Buddhist Tripitaka*, Oxford, Clarendon Press, 1883

70 NARĀSABHO, P. M. S., *Buddhism: A Guide to a Happy Life*, Bangkok, Mahachulalongkornrajavidyalaya Buddhist University, 1971

71 ÑĀNAMOLI, BHIKKHU (tr.), *The Middle Length Discourses of the Buddha: A New Translation of the Majjhima Nikāya* (ed. Bhikkhu Bodhi), Boston, Wisdom Publications, 1995

72 NORMAN, K. R., *Pāli Literature, A History of Indian Literature*, vol. 7, fasc. 2 (ed. J. Gonda), Wiesbaden, Harrassowitz, 1983

73 OBEYESEKERE, G., *The Cult of the Goddess Pattinī*, Chicago, University of Chicago Press, 1984

74 PREBISH, C. S. (ed.), *Buddhism: A Modern Perspective*, University Park, Pennsylvania State University Press, 1975

75 PYE, M., *The Buddha*, London, Duckworth, 1979

76 RAHULA, W., *What the Buddha Taught*, 2nd edn, Bedford, Gordon Fraser, 1967 [1959]

77 RAY, R. A., *Buddhist Saints in India: A Study in Buddhist Values and Orientations*, New York/Oxford, Oxford University Press, 1994

78 RHYS DAVIDS, T. W. and C. A. F., *Dialogues of the Buddha*, vol. 3, London, Pali Text Society, 1899–1921; repr. 1977

79 ROBINSON, R. H., and JOHNSON, W. L., *The Buddhist Religion: A Historical Introduction*, 2nd edn, Encino, Dickenson, 1977

80 RUEGG, D. S., *Buddha-nature, Mind and the Problem of Gradualism in a Comparative Perspective: On the Transmission and Reception of Buddhism in India and Tibet*, Jordan Lectures in Comparative Religion XIII, London, School of Oriental and African Studies, University of London, 1989

81 RUEGG, D. S., *The Literature of the Madhyamaka School of Buddhist Philosophy in India, A History of Indian Literature*, vol. 7, fasc. 1 (ed. J. Gonda), Wiesbaden, Otto Harrassowitz, 1981

82 SADDHĀTISSA, H., *The Buddha's Way*, London/New York, Allen &

Unwin/Braziller, 1971/1972

83 SADDHĀTISSA, H., *Buddhist Ethics*, London/New York, Allen & Unwin/Braziller, 1970/1971

84 SGAM. PO. PA, *Jewel Ornament of Liberation* (tr. H. V. Guenther), London, Rider, 1971 [1959]

85 SLATER, R. H. L., *Paradox and Nirvāna*, Chicago, University of Chicago Press, 1951

86 SNELLGROVE, D. L. (ed.), *The Image of the Buddha*, London/Paris, Serindia/Unesco, 1978

87 SNELLGROVE, D. L., *Indo-Tibetan Buddhism: Indian Buddhists and Their Tibetan Successors*, Boston, Shambhala, 1987

88 SNELLGROVE, D. L., and RICHARDSON, H. E., *A Cultural History of Tibet*, London/New York, Weidenfeld and Nicolson/Praeger, 1968

89 SPIRO, M. E., *Buddhism and Society: A Great Tradition and its Burmese Vicissitudes*, London/New York, Allen & Unwin/Harper & Row, 1971

90 STEVENSON, D. B., 'The Four Kinds of Samādhi in Early T'ien-t'ai Buddhism', in P. N. Gregory (ed.), *Traditions of Meditation in Chinese Buddhism*, Honolulu, University of Hawaii Press, 1986, pp. 45–97

91 SUZUKI, D. T., *An Introduction to Zen Buddhism*, London, Rider, 1969 [1934]

92 SUZUKI, D. T., *Shin Buddhism*, London/New York, Allen & Unwin/Harper & Row, 1970

93 TAKAKUSU, J., *The Essentials of Buddhist Philosophy*, 3rd edn, Honolulu, Office Appliance Co., 1956

94 TAMBIAH, S. J., *Buddhism and the Spirit Cults in North-East Thailand*, Cambridge, Cambridge University Press, 1970

95 TAMBIAH, S. J., *The Buddhist Saints of the Forest and the Cult of Amulets: A Study in Charisma, Hagiography, Sectarianism and Millennial Buddhism*, Cambridge Studies in Social Anthropology 49 (ed. J. Goody), Cambridge, Cambridge University Press, 1984

96 TAMBIAH, S. J., *World Conqueror and World Renouncer: A Study of Buddhism and Polity in Thailand against a Historical Background*, Cambridge Studies in Social Anthropology 15 (ed. J. Goody), Cambridge, Cambridge University Press, 1976

97 TAYLOR, J. L., *Forest Monks and the Nation-State: An Anthropological and Historical Study in Northeastern Thailand*, Singapore, Institute of Southeast Asian Studies, 1993

98 TSUKAMOTO, Z., *A History of Early Chinese Buddhism from its Introduction to the Death of Hui-yüan*, Tokyo/New York, Kodansha International, 1985

99 TUCCI, G., *The Religions of Tibet* (tr. G. Samuel), London/Berkeley, Routledge & Kegan Paul/University of California Press, 1980

100 WALSHE, M., *Thus Have I Heard: The Long Discourses of the Buddha*, London, Wisdom Publications, 1987

101 WARDER, A. K., *Indian Buddhism*, Delhi, Motilal Banarsidass, 1970

102 WEINSTEIN, S., *Buddhism under the T'ang*, Cambridge Studies in Chinese History, Literature and Institutions (ed. P. Hanan and D. Twitchett), Cambridge, Cambridge University Press, 1987

103 WELBON, G. R., *The Buddhist Nirvana and its Western Interpreters*, Chicago, University of Chicago Press, 1968

104 WELCH, H., *Buddhism under Mao*, Cambridge, MA, Harvard University Press, 1972

105 WELCH, H., *The Buddhist Revival in China*, Cambridge, MA, Harvard University Press, 1968

106 WELCH, H., *The Practice of Chinese Buddhism*, Cambridge, MA, Harvard University Press, 1967

107 WIJAYARATNA, M., *Buddhist Monastic Life, According to the Texts of the Theravāda Tradition* (tr. Claude Grangier and Steven Collins), New York, Cambridge University Press, 1990

108 WILLIAMS, P., *Mahāyāna Buddhism: The Doctrinal Foundations*, London/New York, Routledge, 1989

109 YAMPOLSKY, P. B., *The Platform Sutra of the Sixth Patriarch*, New York, Columbia University Press, 1967

110 ZÜRCHER, E., *The Buddhist Conquest of China*, Leiden, Brill, 1959

9

Chinese Religions

MICHAEL SASO

Introduction

Religion, in the modern Chinese context, is festive, celebrating the passage of men and women in the Chinese community through the cycle of life and death. Chinese religion is traditionally defined by the rites of passage, i.e. birth, maturation, marriage and burial, and the annual cycle of calendrical festivals. Membership of the Chinese social community is demonstrated by participation in the rites of passage and the annual festivals, rather than by intellectual assent to a body of revealed scripture. Chinese religion is therefore a cultural rather than a theological entity. All of the religious systems coming from abroad into the Chinese cultural complex found it necessary to accommodate to the religious and cultural values of China in order to survive and function. The success of Western religions especially has depended upon acceptance of the strong Chinese values of family and social relationships, and adaptation in some way to the customs of the Chinese people. The seasonal festivals as well as the rites of passage have equally survived the iconoclastic rigours of the socialist state of mainland China and the even more devastating secularized education and industrial revolution of maritime China. ('Maritime China' and 'diaspora China' are almost synonymous: maritime China refers to all Chinese living outside of mainland China on the Pacific basin or the islands of South-East Asia, while China of the diaspora refers to all Chinese living abroad owing to the political and economic situation on the mainland.)

The term for religion in China, *tsung-chiao*, refers literally to a *tsung* or lineage of *chiao* or teachings, of which the common men and women of China have traditionally admitted three: the Confucian system of ethics for public life; the Taoist system of rituals and attitudes towards nature; and the Buddhist salvational concepts concerning the afterlife. The three teachings, Buddhist, Taoist and Confucian, act as three servants to the faith and needs of the masses, complementing the social system. Confucius regulates the rites of passage and moral behaviour in public life; Taoism regulates the festivals celebrated in village and urban society, and heals the sick; Buddhism brings a sense of compassion to the present life and salvation in the afterlife, providing funeral rituals for the deceased and refuge from the cares of the world for the weary. But the Chinese commonly say that 'the Three Religions all revert to a common source' (*San-chiao kuei-i*), meaning in modern times that in fact the functionaries or priests of the three religions are dependent on the beliefs and needs of the common people of China, and attain meaning and livelihood as servants of the people. Religion is therefore a celebration by and for the people.

The Main Primary Sources

The main primary sources for the study of Chinese religion are: (1) the Confucian ritual classics, histories and local gazetteers; (2) Taoist canonical writings, popular manuals and fiction; and (3) Buddhist canonical texts and popular devotional *shan-shu* books. The Confucian sources for religious custom and the rites of passage include later dynastic summaries in the form of sumptuary or ritual laws governing provincial and local variations in the rituals used at birth, maturation, marriage and burial [25]. Local and provincial officials frequently summarized the state-approved ritual laws in popular manuals commonly known as *Complete Home Rituals*, still available in temple and village bookshops in maritime China [6]. Though the variations found by anthropologists throughout mainland and maritime China often seem too disparate for systematic comparison, in fact at the deep structural level the Chinese rites of passage always follow the Confucian model.

The primary source for public ritual where a Taoist priest or liturgical expert is required is the Taoist canon, now available in inexpensive photo-offprint for scholarly and ritual use [5]. The canon contains hundreds of *chiao* rituals of renewal and *chai* funeral liturgies used today for festival and for burial. The canon also preserves philosophical treatises, exorcisms and healing rituals, internal 'alchemy' or meditative tracts, alchemical formulae, medicine and herbal texts, and other rich sources of myth and popular Chinese religious practices. Field research in East and South-East Asia has uncovered a vast quantity of primary materials concerning the modern practice of Chinese religion in mainland and maritime China of the diaspora (South-East Asia). These modern sources are now in the process of publication [34; 35].

Popular Buddhist sources of Chinese religious practice are found in the *shan-shu* publications, privately funded treatises on meritorious lives, legends and myths for public distribution [10; 18]. (For other sources of Buddhist practices, see chapter 8 on Buddhism in this volume.) Popular fiction dating from the Ming and the Ch'ing dynasties onwards, available in corner bookstores and penny lending libraries throughout maritime China, has been used as a first-hand source for popular beliefs and practices. The pioneering work in these vernacular publications has been done by the noted sociologist and sinologist Wolfram Eberhard [10].

An Introduction to the History of Chinese Religion

Chinese religious history is divided into four major periods, listed traditionally as the spring, summer, autumn and winter of cultural development [2; 33]. The birth of Chinese religion is traceable to the oracle bones: prognostications were made by inscribing questions to the spirits on the carapace of a tortoise or the leg bone of an ox, and then applying heat to the bone to obtain an oracle reading. The cracks appearing in the bones gave the negative or positive response of the spirit to the problems posed by the Kings of Shang, *c.*1760–1100 BCE, China's first historically documented period [19]. The religious cosmology depicted in the oracle readings is not unlike the cosmology of later summer and autumn Chinese history.

The later spring of China's religious history extends from the beginning of the Chou kingdom, *c.*1100 BCE, through the Warring States era to the beginning of the Han dynasty in 206 CE. During this extended period six ways of thought are generally recognized to have formed the core of the Chinese cultural/religious system. Three of these, the moral/ethical directives of Confucius, the penal codes of the legalists, and the secular agnosticism of the logicians, form what came to be called the Confucian way (*Ru-chiao*). The teachings of the Confucian school are traditionally considered to be collected in the *Four Books* and the *Five Classics* [24]. The legalist writings and the works of the logicians, along with the writings of the Confucian classics, are well summarized in the *History of Chinese Philosophy* of Feng Yu-lan, translated and annotated by Derk Bodde [11].

The second set of three teachings from ancient China, the Taoist, Muoist and *yin–yang* Five-Element schools, form what came to be called spiritual Taoism (*Tao-chiao*) in the summer of Chinese religious history. The works of Lao-tzu (sixth/fifth century BCE), and Chuang-tzu (fourth century BCE) are the fundamental mystical and theoretical sources for religious Taoism [23]. The treatise on the brotherhood of man and universal love of Muo-tzu is now included as a part of the Taoist canon, providing inspiration for the sworn brotherhood and fraternal societies of modern China [47]. The yin–yang Five-Element (or Five-Mover–Five-Phase) cosmology which derives from the Tsou Yen school of ancient China formed the theoretical system of the so-called 'New Text' Confucian liturgists of the Han dynasty and inspired the first converts to religious Taoism [20].

In a more holistic sense such generalizations, which create a false dichotomy between the philosophical and the religious, the Confucian and the Taoist, are purely academic, i.e. simple heuristic devices to explain the richness of the Chinese religious/cultural heritage. In practice the Confucian statesman, Taoist poet and master of ceremonies for popular household ritual were often the same person. Like two sides of the same precious coin, Confucian social ethics and Taoist communion with nature formed the core of the Chinese religious spirit [29].

The second period of Chinese religious history, extending from 206 BCE to 900 CE, the summer or maturity of the three religions of China, witnessed the introduction of Buddhism into China from India; the formation of liturgical or spiritual Taoism as the priesthood of the popular religion; and the supremacy of Confucianism as custodian of the moral/ethical system of Chinese social culture. The rites of passage summarized by the New Text Confucianists of the early Han period, and the grand Taoist liturgies of renewal, became standardized for all of China [15].

The third period of Chinese religious history, the autumn or religious reformation, extended roughly from the beginning of the Sung dynasty c.960 CE to the end of the Ch'ing dynasty and the imperial system, 1912 CE. During this period a true reformation of the religious spirit of China occurred, some 500 years before the reformation of European religious systems. The Chinese religious reformation was typified by lay movements in both Buddhism and Taoism, a syncretism, even ecumenism, between Buddhist and Taoist spiritual elements, and the growth of local popular cultures [15]. Secret societies, religious cults, clan and temple associations, merchant groups or huikuan flourished throughout China. Christianity was brought to China by Jesuits in the sixteenth century, and by increasing waves of missionaries in the nineteenth and twentieth centuries, but owing to the inability of Christian missionaries to adapt to the religious cultural system of China, it never equalled the popularity of Buddhism in the Chinese context [15].

The modern period of Chinese religious history is compared to winter in the four seasons of nature's constant cycle. Like a phoenix rising from the ashes of a burnt-out fire, or the drop of yang in the sea of yin which brings about cosmic rebirth in the depths of winter, the spirit of Chinese religion is at present experiencing a new vitality and rebirth both in the People's Republic and the maritime diaspora of China. To study Chinese religion in the modern era is indeed illuminating, since the structure of the religious system, which was often hidden by the proliferation of local customs and rituals in the recent past, is now laid bare by the necessities of secular society, and the exigencies of cultural continuity in a world filled with political as well as technological upheaval. Chinese religion continues to be a vehicle of self-expression and identity for the people who comprise China's masses, whether in continental, maritime or emigrant China overseas.

The Main Phases and Assumptions of Scholarly Study of Chinese Religion

The modern study of Chinese religion can be broken down into three main phases, namely: (1) the nineteenth-century scholars who approached the study of China from the superior colonialist attitude or as missionaries who saw Chinese practices as gross superstition; (2) the early and mid-twentieth-century scholars who as historians of religion or anthropologists approached the Chinese experience from the 'objective' or 'scientific' viewpoint; and (3) the structural phenomenologists who by participatory observation attempt to see Chinese religion from its own experiential 'eidetic' perspective.

The major works of the first group of sinologists who studied Chinese religions were published between the late nineteenth and early twentieth centuries. De Groot's massive *The Religious System of China* and Henri Doré's *Superstitions chinoises* are classics of this period [7; 14]. The second group – historians of Chinese religion and anthropologists, with extensive fieldwork published during the past thirty years – are typified by the British social anthropologist Maurice Freedman and the American positive school of anthropology, represented by Arthur Wolf [49]. Where Freedman holds for the structured systematic view of Chinese religious practice, Wolf emphasizes the local, non-systematized and eclectic nature of field evidence. The excellent bibliography of Chinese religion prepared by Lawrence Thompson and the textbook of Chinese religion by the same author summarize modern studies in the field [42; 44].

The third and most modern form of Chinese religious studies is typified by the intensive participation of the scholar in the religious life of the Chinese environment, an approach to Chinese religion based on laying aside one's own cultural assumptions and adopting the eidetic vision of the subject. This approach, which is basically structural in nature, owes much to the insights of Claude Lévi-Strauss, who in the study of South American myths first proposed a deep-structure theory underlying the seemingly contradictory nature of field evidence. The works of Kristofer Schipper, Emily Ahern, David Jordan and Liu Chih-wan are typical of scholars who have gone deeply into field experience to explain their insights into Chinese religion [1; 17; 28; 40]. To the above names and titles must be added the impressive work of Professor Kubo Noritada, whose field experiences in China (both maritime and mainland), and publications, are significant [22].

The Basic Assumptions of the Chinese Religious System

Chinese religion as practised in the twentieth century is based solidly on the *yin–yang* Five-Element theory of nature. This is a composite of the Taoist, the Tsou-yen and the Fang-shih schools of the late spring period of Chinese religious history [27].

Cosmic Gestation

From the Taoist tradition, specifically the forty-second chapter of the *Lao-tzu*, is taken the definitive statement of cosmic gestation:

> The Tao gave birth to the One.　*(T'ai-chi)*
> The One gave birth to the Two.　*(yin and yang)*
> The Two gave birth to the Three.
> The Three gave birth to the myriad creatures.

The meaning of this text (see figure 9.1) is dramatically expressed in Taoist ritual, seen throughout maritime China, South-East Asia, Taiwan, Hong Kong and modern Honolulu. The ritual is called Fen-teng ('Dividing the new fire') and is an essential part of the Taoist Chiao rites of cosmic renewal [37].

Yin and Yang

From a new fire struck from a flint is lit a first candle, representing the immanent, visible Tao, *T'ai-chi* or primordial breath within the (head) microcosm of man. From the *T'ai-chi* is lit a second candle, representing primordial spirit, or soul within man, the chest or heart of the microcosm. A third candle is lit symbolic of vital essence, the gut or intuitive level within man. These three candles represent *T'ai-chi*, the immanent, moving Tao of nature, *yang* and *yin*. They also represent the Three Spirits of the Transcendent Tao's working

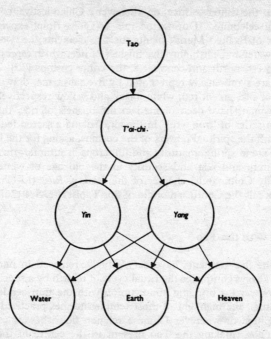

Figure 9.1 *A structural view of the Chinese cosmos (from the* Lao-tzu, *chapter 42). The Tao gives birth to the One:* T'ai-chi *or primordial breath. The One gives birth to the Two:* yin *and* yang. *The Two give birth to the Three: watery underworld, earth and heaven. The Three give birth to the myriad creatures.*

in nature: *San-ch'ing*, Primordial Heavenly Worthy who governs heaven; *Ling-pao*, Heavenly Worthy who governs earths; and *Tao-te*, Heavenly Worthy who rules water and rebirth. Thus the Tao gestates on the macrocosmic level, heaven, earth and water; on the microcosmic level, head, chest and belly (intellect, love, and intuition). On the spiritual level the Tao is seen to be ever gestating, mediating and indwelling within man [39].

The Five Elements

Just as the cosmic gestation chapter of the *Lao-tzu* is dramatically expressed in modern ritual, so the *yin–yang* Five-Element theory is still enacted during the annual celebration of cosmic renewal, in modern maritime China. The ritual is called Su-ch'i and occurs on or about the winter solstice, or whenever a Chiao festival of renewal is being celebrated. During the rite, a Taoist ritual expert, called 'Master of Exalted Merit', plants the five elements, i.e. wood, fire, metal, water and earth, into five bushels of rice, which represent east, south, west, north and centre, i.e. the entire cosmos [32]. The elements are symbolically represented by five talismans, drawn on five pieces of silk, green, red, white, black and yellow respectively. Once the talismans have been planted in the bushels of rice, the Taoist draws a series of 'true writs' in the air, striking a sacred feudal contract with the spiritual powers of the cosmos, asking for the blessings of new life in spring, maturity and full crops in summer, rich harvest in autumn, and rest and security in the old age of winter. (The 'Monthly Commands' chapter of the *Book of Rites* (Li-Chi; Yüeh-ling) reveals the Confucian origin of this Taoist rite. See [36].)

Union with the Tao

After the five elements have been ritually renewed in nature, the Taoist always completes the ritual cycle of rebirth by a special meditative prayer for bringing about union with the transcendent Tao. This ritual, the highlight of most temple liturgies practised in maritime China or wherever Chinese religion flourishes, is called the Tao-ch'ang (making the Tao present in the centre of the microcosm) or the Cheng-chiao (attaining true mystical union with the Tao). The ritual is the converse of the Su-ch'i described above. Having planted the five talismans in the five bushels of rice on the first day of the Chiao festival of renewal, on the last day the Taoist dances the sacred steps of Yü (playing the role of China's Noah who stopped the floods of antiquity) and 'harvests' the talismans, one by one, ingesting them meditatively into the five organs within his body. The five organs (liver for east and wood, heart for south and fire, lungs for west and metal, kidneys for north and water, spleen/stomach for centre and union) act as a sort of divine mandala making the presence of the gestating Tao felt within the centre of the microcosm. The mystic experience of union with the Tao is thus taught by ritual performed in the village temple for the men and women of the village to see. What could not be taught by the theologian verbally is understood by the peasant through the visible expression of liturgical drama [32, last segment].

The theory of Chinese religion is, therefore, seen as an eternally cycling progress outward from the Tao to the myriad creatures, and returning to the Tao for renewal by the very process of the seasons in nature. By following the path of nature, humans attain eternal union. Ritual acts as a dramatic, non-verbal source of instruction for the laity in the Chinese religious system.

Confucian Virtue

Ritual is to Taoist cosmology as behavioural norms are to the Confucian ethic; just as the theory of Chinese religion is demonstrated in the liturgies of the Taoist Chiao festival, so the definitions of the Confucian ethic are drawn directly from the experience of the human encounter at the practical level of everyday experience. The Confucian norms for behaviour, written down in the spring of the ancient Chinese cultural system, are very much alive in the winter of the modern present. *Li* or respect, *hsiao* or family love, *yi* or mutual reciprocity among friends, *jen*, benevolence towards the stranger, and *chung*, loyalty to the state, are values deeply embedded in the hearts of the men and women of China, equally valid for mainland and maritime communities [23: LXVI].

Li is, like many Chinese characters, a symbol not limited by a single linear definition. The word means religious ritual as well as heartfelt respect, an attitude which is basic to the ego in approaching human relationships. The word reflects the virtue of the *chun-tzu*, the man or woman of outgoing, giving nature, who imitates heaven in generous liberality, and like the great ocean conquers by 'being low', letting all things flow into its embrace [25, bk I: 62, 116, 257]. *Hsiao* is the virtue governing family relationships. Its definition embraces the love of children for parents and parents for children, making the family the very centre of Chinese social life. *Yi* represents the sense of deep commitment that friend must give to friend, and reciprocity governing the transactions of honest business. *Jen*, literally all the good things which happen when two humans meet, is best translated by the word 'benevolence', from a Latin root, *bene-volens*, meaning 'wishing good things' for others. The comment of tourists coming back from mainland China, 'how kind everyone is', reflects the modern sense of *jen*, welcoming the stranger (*hao-k'o*), for which the great cities of China were traditionally famous. Finally *chung*, the sense of loyalty to the reigning power of state, coupled with an immense sense of democratic vote or common decision at the village and community level, makes China one of the most stable cultural systems in human history [12].

The Cosmos

The *yin–yang* Five-Element theory governs not only the rituals of religious Taoism, but also the concepts of the present and the afterlife of the ordinary men and women of China. The principles of *yang* and *yin*, when joined together in harmonious union – often represented as a dragon and a tiger in a sort of cosmic struggle of gestation – form the visible earth. Separated, *yang* floats upwards to form the heavens,

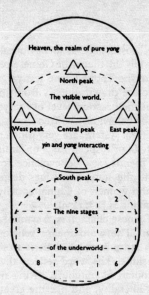

Figure 9.2 *The spatial structure of the Chinese cosmos. Heaven is pure, separated* yang; *earth is the visible world, where* yin *and* yang *interact. The watery or fiery underworld is the realm of pure* yin, *divided into the nine sections of the magic square.*

and *yin* sinks downwards to form the watery and fiery underworld [12: 42–8]. The three stages of the cosmos, heaven, earth and underworld, are reflected in the head, chest and belly of the microcosm (see figure 9.2). Upon death the soul, which has completed its life-cycle, is thought to sink downwards into the realms of *yin*, where it is purged of its darkness and sins for a period before release to the heavens [30]. During this period the soul can cause sickness in the family or other calamity if unattended by the prayers and food offerings of the living. The function of the medium, or shaman, in China as in Japan, Korea and South-East Asia, is to descend to the underworld (shaman) or act as a channel for the voice of the deceased (medium) to inquire about the needs of the unattended or sickness-causing soul. Buddhist ritual, especially, is thought to be efficacious in freeing the soul from the tortures of hell to ascend to the western heavens and paradise [13].

Hell

Hell is seen in the drawings of modern temple frescoes and devotional books to have nine cells or stages of punishment, each governed by a

demon king [9]. The role of Buddhist and Taoist ritual is to lead the
soul through these stages, paying off the evil politicians whose role in
the afterlife, as in the present, is to tax and punish the common man
and woman. In the Chinese system, only politicians stay eternally in
hell, in charge of the tortures of the damned. The paper money
burned at funeral and other rituals in China is symbolic of the merits
of the living whose acts of love and giving are like banknotes in hell,
drawing interest to free the souls of the deceased into eternal life [48].

Life-cycles

Finally, the theory of cyclical growth and renewal is equally
reflected in the annual cycle of festivals of the lunar almanac, and
the cycle of life of humankind in the cosmos. Birth, maturation,
marriage, old age and death in the cycle of life are reflected in the
planting of spring, growth of summer, harvest of autumn, and
old age or rest of winter (figure 9.3). The annual cycle of festivals

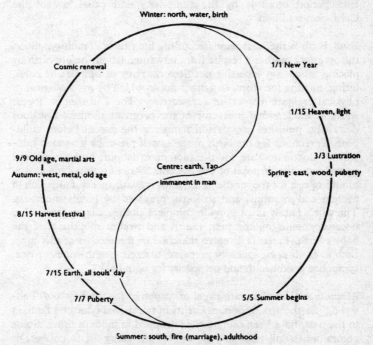

Figure 9.3 *The temporal structure of the Chinese cosmos. Yang is born
at the winter solstice,* yin *at the summer solstice. The human life-cycle
and the annual cycle of festivals follow the same pattern.*

liturgically celebrates these natural events of life, as explained below. Chinese religion is therefore eminently practical, integrating the individual into family and community, celebrating the passage of men and women through the cycle of life and of nature. Though the secular mind of the modern Chinese intellectual tends to deny the influence of the religious cultural system on the individual, the contemplative mystic of the Taoist and Buddhist community and the banquets of the common people of the Chinese community draw the politician and the academician into the joys of festive celebration.

Characteristic Practices of Chinese Religion

The Rites of Passage

Birth, maturation, marriage and burial have been regulated from the Han period onwards by the sumptuary and ritual law of the Confucian tradition.

Birth Birth is the least regulated of the life rituals. Tradition allows the pregnant mother a respite from unwanted labour before birth by placing taboos on excessive needlework, tying of bundles or bales, lifting, moving furniture, and other duties which by psychological or physical pressure may cause a miscarriage. The *T'ai-shen* or 'foetus spirit' is made ritual protector of the pregnant mother, a jealous deity who punishes any person harassing the parent before childbirth. Directions for the birth process itself prescribe a woman midwife or doctor to care for the mother in labour, and pay special attention to the disposal of the placenta. Strict custom decrees one month of rest for the mother after delivery, with special foods rich in protein and vitamins, and so forth, prepared by family members. The wife's family must provide complete clothes, diapers and other necessary items on the first, fourth and twelfth months after the baby's birth. Presents given to the child or the mother at this time, such as fresh eggs, specially prepared chicken, health wines or rice, symbolize good health and prosperity for both [41].

Maturation The elaborate ritual of 'capping' for the boy and 'hairstyling' for the girl, important events in traditional educated families in the past, have been more or less dropped in modern times. Some communities still celebrate the boy or girl going off to college, or commemorate the *kuan* maturation rituals as a part of the marriage festivities. Otherwise the rite of puberty, or maturation, is only celebrated in the more traditional families, and often only by a banquet in which a chicken is served to the young adult to commemorate approaching maturity [48].

Marriage Marriage in modern China of the diaspora is still a most elaborate affair, with the six stages observed in a fashion adapted from the traditional past. The stages or steps of Chinese marriage are as follows [16]:

Proposal, consisting in the exchange of the 'eight characters' – the year, month, day and hour of birth for both parties. The eight characters of the boy are placed by the family altar of the girl's household, and any untoward event in the family during a three-day waiting period signals that the girl rejects the marriage.

Engagement is announced by the bride's side sending out invitations for the auspiciously chosen wedding day, with a box of moon-shaped biscuits.

The bride's dowry is sent to the groom's home in a solemn procession through the streets. The entire community sees the gifts *en route*, and notes whether the bride's vanity box is prominently displayed. The groom-to-be opens the vanity box with a special key, symbolizing that the love of the young couple is sincere. The bride-price is usually sent by the groom's family, counted, and sent back at this time. The groom's gifts to the bride, in the form of jewellery, clothes and other items, match the value of the dowry.

The bridal procession, formerly carried out by means of a bridal palanquin, now makes use of a limousine or taxi. The groom must go to meet the bride at her home, and accompany her back to his residence to the accompaniment of music, fireworks and streamers. On arrival at the groom's home, the bride pretends to be weak as crossing the threshold she steps over a smoking *hibachi* or cooking-pot, a saddle and an apple at the gate, symbolizing (by homonyms) a pure and peaceful crossing into the new household.

The exchange of marriage vows frequently takes place in a Christian church in the modern setting. The bride and groom toast each other with a small cup of rice wine, and then proceed to an extensive banquet. During the banquet the bride and groom must toast each table of guests. Tea coloured to look like whisky is taken by the young couple, while each guest must swallow a complete glass of spirits. The traditional custom of reciting poetry and giving long speeches is frequently but not always shortened.

The morning after is celebrated by the young bride serving breakfast to her new parents-in-law, and in turn being served breakfast by them. A basket of dried dates and seeds is given to the new parents-in-law, a homonym for 'many children' (many seeds) from the bride. The bride returns home to her own parents 'for the first time as a guest' on the third day after marriage.

Burial Funeral rites in modern China of the diaspora may be extensive and costly, using Taoist and Buddhist forms as in the past, or completely Westernized in mortuary and church-burial form. Even when performed in a mortuary or church, certain aspects of the traditional rites of burial are observed, however, as noted in the following traditional account, taken from Chinese manuals [26].

The moment of death. When death occurs at home, or sometimes in a modern hospital, the dying person often asks to be put on the floor, as near as possible to the ancestor shrine in the main hall of the room. Death is signalled to the neighbours by wailing. The family immediately goes into mourning, by removing all jewellery and fine clothes, and dressing in coarse cloth, hemp or muslin, as custom decrees. The burial day is chosen, and invitations are sent out to all paternal relatives to the sixth degree, and all maternal relatives to the third degree, to attend the funeral.

Preparing the corpse and coffining. The corpse is washed ritually and put in a coffin. Layers of white paper money or talismans are put over the corpse, symbolizing purification and protection from harmful germs or baleful influences after death. Even when done in a mortuary with an open coffin, the custom of laying white paper talismans across the body of the deceased is observed. Mourning visitors put incense in the incense pot and offer the bereaved family condolences and money gifts to help meet the expense of a funeral. The family altar and all decorations in the front room are covered with white cloth during the entire funeral. Food and precious belongings are put into the coffin before the closing and sealing.

Mourning at home or in the funeral parlour. A Taoist or Buddhist priest, or a Christian minister (sometimes all three), is asked to perform the funeral ritual at home or in the funeral parlour. Paper houses containing complete furnishings, symbolic clothes and paper money for the bank of merits in hell are burned. The burning of paper signifies the merits of the living, and the prayers of the community for the eternal salvation of the deceased. Flowers, incense and paper items, funeral wreaths and a special ancestor shrine for the deceased are presented during the funeral rite.

The funeral procession. Chinese and Western bands, playing traditional and modern dirges, children portraying the twenty-four scenes of filial piety as burial drama, a willow branch symbolizing the soul of the deceased, and the entire mourning family accompany the coffin to the grave. All of the invited mourners pause before the cemetery, with only the immediate family and the officiating ministers or priests going to the grave-side. After burial the willow branch is carried back to the family altar and used ritually to 'install' the soul of the deceased in the memorial tablet. The ancestor shrine, less and less frequently seen in the families of maritime China, acts as a reminder to the living of the central place of family and its virtues of love and mutual care in the present life.

Post-funerary liturgies are performed for the deceased by Buddhist, Taoist or Christian ministers on the seventh, ninth and forty-ninth days after burial, and on the first and third anniversaries of death in a special manner. The Taoist rituals are especially colourful, depicting a journey of the Taoist high priest into the underworld where the demonic politicians of hell are tricked and cajoled into releasing the soul into paradise. A huge funerary banquet is provided for all guests, relatives and coffin-bearers who attended the funeral when the burial is completed.

Through much of the diaspora of maritime China, ancestor worship within the family has been supplanted by ancestor tablets which are kept for a fee at a Buddhist shrine, pagoda or temple. The altar in the main room of the traditional Chinese household, with the patron spirits of the family in the centre and the ancestor shrine on the left or 'west' side, is less and less frequently seen in Honolulu and South-East Asia. Education in Chinese religion at the college level, however, and the influx of Chinese from mainland China (who are, as a rule, more religious than those from secularized Taiwan or Hong Kong) tend to restore the practice of such traditional religious customs.

The Annual Cycle of Festivals

The festive cycle of Chinese religious life follows the farmer's almanac, reflecting the busy time of the planting, weeding and harvesting process when religious festivals are relatively infrequent, and the rest periods when festivals predominate. Cyclical festivals fall in the odd-numbered or *yang* months, and farming activity in the even-numbered or *yin* (earth) months. The festivals are doubly symbolic, representing the progress of men and women through life as well as the ripening, harvesting and storing of crops. The calendar is followed enthusiastically by Chinese communities of the diaspora, and recognized cognately by mainland communities [3; 8; 33].

First (lunar) month, first day The lunar New Year, or festival of spring, is a family banquet in honour of the ancestors and the living members of the family who assemble from distant places to affirm identity. The New Year festival is the most important and widely celebrated of Chinese festivals today. Five or seven sets of chopsticks, wine, tea and bowls of cooked rice are laid out in memory of the ancestors on the family altar or table. Then a sixteen- or twenty-four-course banquet is served. Flowers, freshly baked cake, sweets, sweet dried fruit, three or five kinds of cooked meat, fish, noodles, bean curd, and various kinds of vegetable dishes, all with homophonic meaning for blessing and prosperity in the New Year, are served at the banquet. Women wear flowers in their hair, children receive presents and cash in a red envelope, new clothes are donned and fireworks signal the beginning of the first lunar month of spring. Good-luck characters are pasted by the door and the lintels, and visits made to friends, shrines and churches on New Year's Day.

First month, fifteenth day This is the festival of light. The first full moon of the New Year is celebrated by a lantern procession and a dragon dance. Children carry fancy lanterns in the streets, and contests are held for the best lantern, best poems and best floats in the lantern parade.

Third month, third day The lustration festival is celebrated from the beginning of the third lunar month until 105 days after the winter solstice, in the fourth lunar month, as a sacrificial cleaning of the graves and the celebration of the bright and clear days of spring. The graves are cleaned and symbolically 'roofed' or covered with talismanic tiles, begging for blessing in spring. The family holds a picnic in the hills after offering food at the grave.

Fifth month, fifth day The beginning of summer is celebrated by the eating of *tseng-tzu* (rice cakes), by dragon boat races on the river and by rituals to keep children healthy and safe from the colds of summer. The colourful Taoist ritual exorcising the spirits of pestilence is seen throughout the coastal areas of south-east China and the diaspora.

Seventh month, seventh day The festival of puberty, or the seven sisters day, is celebrated throughout maritime China, Japan and the diaspora with the charming tale of the spinning-girl and the cowherd boy, whose eternal tryst is commemorated on this evening.

Seventh month, fifteenth day 'All souls' day' or the Buddhist Ullambhana is celebrated throughout Asia as a pre-harvest festival. The souls are freed from hell in a ritual of general amnesty before the rice and other crops are harvested from the soil. As on New Year's Day, the entire family celebrates with a banquet.

Eighth month, fifteenth day The full moon of autumn marks the harvest festival, celebrated with a banquet of fresh fruits and round mooncakes eaten under the rising harvest moon. Poetry reading and family evenings after the harvest express thanks for nature's bounteous plenty.

The winter festivals From the ninth month, ninth day until the eleventh month, eleventh day, various festivals celebrate the autumn and the winter period of rest and recycling. The Taoist rite of cosmic renewal or Chiao is most frequently celebrated at this time, up until the winter solstice [37]. Besides the cyclical festivals, various birthdays celebrating the heroes or saints of the folk religion occur at even and odd month intervals throughout the year, according to local custom. These patron saints' festivals include the festivals of the local patron saints of the soil, on the first and fifteenth day of each month; the Heavenly Empress Ma-tsu, who protects fishermen, sailors and immigrants, on the fourth month, twenty-third day; Kuan-kung, patron of merchants and martial arts, on the sixth month, fifteenth day; and Tz'u-wei the patron of the pole-star, on the ninth month, ninth day. Taoist, Buddhist and popular temples usually offer rituals on all festive occasions. The spirit of Chinese religion, ecumenic or irenic rather than syncretistic,[1] moulds all religious systems to the needs of the people for ritual to celebrate the rites of passage.

Religious Functionaries

Three functionaries assist the people of the village in the practice of the rites of passage and the festivals. These are the Buddhist monk, the Taoist priest and the possessed medium or shaman. The Buddhist monk provides Pure Land-motivated chants, Ch'an (Zen) meditation and tantric, that is, mantric chant, *mudra* (hand gesture) and eidetic visualization[2] as regular services in the local Buddhist monasteries. The majority of the temples (*miao*) of popular Chinese religion are ministered by Taoist priests under the direction of a lay temple board of directors. Taoists provide various rituals for healing and blessing, including the universally popular ritual asking blessing from Ursa Major, the constellation of the Pole Star. Both Buddhist and Taoist temples offer a modernized version of the method of prognostication of the yarrow stalk and *I Ching* book (that is, numbered wooden sticks are drawn from a wooden container by chance, and the corresponding hexagram is read by a monk or nun in the temple) for reading one's fortune or common-sense advice in practical home and business matters. The temple or religious centre in the Chinese village is truly a cosmic as well as a cultural axis, providing fairs, opera, puppet shows, storytellers and meeting-places as well as religious services. As with the medieval cathedrals of Europe, the villagers build their own temples from local donations, and spend years, decades even, in making these cultural focal points into objects of artistic pride and functional meaning.

The medium, shaman and oracle are three different functionaries within the Chinese system, with a different word for each role. The medium, whose body is occupied by a spirit while in trance, the shaman, who travels into the afterlife, whether the underworld or the heavens, and the oracle, who speaks in the words of a bystanding spirit, fulfil the roles of seer, healer and keeper of justice in villages where the spiritual power of the temple and the religious system provides more stability than the rapidly changing political and industrial forces of change. The medium and the shaman have tended to multiply in those areas where political stability is repressive or lacking (such as Taiwan, Korea, the Philippines and South-East Asia) and practically to disappear where economic growth or strictly enforced political discipline is dominant, as in Japan or mainland China [45].

Conclusion

The power of the folk religion in modern China, whether in the diaspora or on the mainland, has not been destroyed but rather simplified and strengthened by modernization and political change. Proto-scientific systems such as *feng-shui*, or the placing of buildings to utilize the wind and the sun, and *di-li* or the placing of graves so as to preserve natural watersheds, are quite visible throughout maritime China. The festivals and their paraphernalia such as incense, paper money and paper clothes are still seen in the countryside and outlying areas of mainland China. Religion dies hard in modern Asian society because it is a vehicle for self-expression and cultural identity, giving the ego a firm place in family, society and nation. Just as the Chinese who have emigrated to South-East Asia and America are finding new meaning in asserting the festivals of the past, so the peasants and masses of mainland China will restore the celebrations of life's cycle which give meaning to existence in a vital socialist society. Such a phenomenon is possible because religion is a cultural force in China, affirming and strengthening the smooth working of human relationships in the difficult struggle for survival in a hard-working peasant and industrial environment. Religion brings joy and meaning to the passage of life and death in a truly social context.

The Mystic Tradition in China

The Chinese mystic tradition is perhaps one of the most fascinating aspects of the study of Asian religion. From the early Taoist texts of the *Lao-tzu* and *Chuang-tzu* (*Laozi* and *Zhuangzi*, fifth to fourth centuries BCE) to late Ming dynasty (sixteenth century CE) forms of

Ch'an (Zen) meditation that combined breathing techniques and Pure Land chant with sitting, Chinese 'mystic' writers have inspired more than two millennia of ascetic and monastic practice. The mystic tradition in China merits a separate detailed study, the basic elements of which are itemized below.

Mysticism is defined in the Taoist ascetic (*hsiu-yang*) tradition as the practice of 'heart–mind fasting' and 'sitting in forgetfulness'. These two terms, taken from the *Chuang-tzu Nei-p'ien*, chapters 4 and 5, name the method for practising the emptying of the mind of all judgement and the heart of all desires, a requisite precondition for realizing the presence of the Transcendent Tao (Wu-wei chih Tao/Wuwei zhi Dao). The Western term for such a practice is kenosis, i.e. the emptying of the mind of conceptual imagery and judgement. The mind which does not judge can 'hear the music of the Tao of Heaven', in the words of the *Chuang-tzu* (*Zhuangzi*).

The *Chuang-tzu Nei-p'ien* (the first seven chapters of the *Book of Chuang-tzu*) distinguishes clearly between the *wu* 'kataphatic' possessed medium tradition and the 'apophatic' mystic. In the last lines of chapter 7, Chuang-tzu describes how the fledgling mystic Lieh-tzu goes in search of a master. He finds *Hu-tzu*, the 'Empty Gourd' Taoist on the top of a hill, and the *wu* trance medium/psychic Chi-hsien (Zixian). Chi-hsien is a popular healer, while Hu-tzu is a master of kenotic (emptying) prayer. Chi-hsien is taken by Lieh-tzu to meet the mystic 'Empty Gourd'. Three encounters take place, after which (the fourth meeting) Chi-hsien flees and never comes back. The mystic (emptying all thoughts and images) and the psychic (filling the mind with images, resulting in spirit-possession) are two diametrically opposed traditions.

The prayer method of apophasis or kenosis invoked for mystic prayer is a simple technique without doctrinal or other religious content. It can be practised in any religious tradition, and is in fact found in many Western prayer systems.[3] The methods of apophatic or kenotic prayer are very highly developed in both the Chinese Buddhist and Taoist traditions. They are described in simple-to-follow form in a number of well-known texts.

The first of these meditative texts is the well known *Lao-tzu Tao-te Ching* (*Laozi Daode Jing*), attributed to the mystic of the sixth/fifth centuries BCE, Lao-tzu (Laozi). The work is sometimes called 'the 5,000 Character Book' because its eighty-one brief chapters contain about that many Chinese written characters. The work is divided into two sections, the 'Tao' (Dao, Transcendent, unmoved gestator) and the 'Te' (De, the primordial first mover, seen as female 'breath' or primal energy). A second-century BCE version of the work was discovered at Ma Wang Tui (Mawangdui) in Hunan province in 1974. In this early version the 'Te' section of the book is placed first, and the 'Tao' last. This arrangement suggests the title 'The

Classic for Attaining the Tao (Way)' i.e. the way of kenotic prayer that leads to union with the eternal Transcendent.[4]

Lao-tzu warns in the very first chapter of the *Tao-te Ching* that the conceptualization and verbalizing of the mystic experience is completely relative, if not impossible. One can use words to describe the infinite, such as 'mysterious' and 'gateway to all mysteries', but the experience itself is intuitive, beyond words. Yet the *Tao-te Ching* attempts to describe the experience of union with the Transcendent in terms of nature, using such symbols as water, wind, the empty hub of a wheel to describe what the words generated by intellectual judgement fail to convey.

> Water is the best of all. Without contention,
> It does good for all things.
> It goes to the lowest place, that others avoid.
> Because of this it is closest to Tao.

The simplicity of the Taoist way makes no distinction between the high and the lowly, is not elated by praise or discouraged by criticism. Possessions and wealth are things to be given away and a life of simplicity is to be pursued, because such a way of life is closest to Tao. It is only when mind and heart are freed from images and desires that the mystic can indeed be one with the transcendent Tao. Like the empty hub of a wheel, the mystic is centred on the Tao when intellect and will are unimpeded by the relative.

> A thirty-spoked wheel has a single hub.
> It is because its centre is empty
> That it can be used on a cart.

Greatness is judged not by praise and acclaim, but by finding the lowest position, like water, which is closest to Tao.

> The great river and ocean are the greatest
> Of all creatures,
> Because they are the lowest.
> Thus all things flow into them.

Lao-tzu teaches that the person who is a true mystic, far from being an anti-social recluse, brings good to all who come in need of help. The success of the contemplative life is measured by the ability to give and to heal.

> Be like Tao,
> [*Wu-wei*, Transcendent Act]
> Make little things important.

Make the few many,
Requite anger with goodness.
Long ago Taoists took Goodness as their master,
Touched the subtle, wondrous mysteries of Tao . . .
Such as shivering when wading in a winter creek,
Careful not to disturb the neighbours,
Polite and thoughtful when invited as a guest,
Sensitive as ice beginning to melt;
Simple as an uncarved block of wood,
Unspoiled as a wild valley meadow,
Cleared of mud and silt like a placid pond.
One can only keep this kind of Tao
By not getting too full,
Staying new and fresh like sprouting grass.

Beauty for the mystic is found in the act of giving, just as Tao from an eternal unmoving first act gestates 'one', 'two', 'three' and all the myriad creatures. The mystic not only avoids argument and contention, but in the very act of emptying and giving does not put down or harm those who receive healing.

Words in contracts are not beautiful,
Beautiful words are not found in contracts.
Good people don't dispute,
Disputes do not bring good.
Knowledge isn't always wise.
Wisdom isn't something learned.
The Taoist . . . finds joy in giving to others.
The more given, the more happiness.
Heaven's Tao gives,
Without harm or discord.

The depth of Lao-tzu's words is expanded and clarified by the humorous stories and wisdom of *Chuang-tzu* (*Zhuangzi*).[5] Except for chapter 2, which is quite long, and chapter 3, which is short, the *Nei-p'ien* chapters are of even length, and move consistently through a series of humorous tales which describe a method of interior 'emptying' or kenosis.

Chapter 1 shows that the relative action of the great and the small must not be judged as good or bad. The great bird P'eng (a symbol of heaven/*yang*) flies for six months with one flap of the wings. The great fish Ao (water/*yin*) swims for six months with one flap of its tail. A small bird flies from the ground to a tree branch with many flaps of its wing. A small mouse needs many sips of water to fill its belly. The human mind judges one thing good and another bad on the basis of a relative judgement of size or accomplishment. The Taoist sage Lieht-zu learned to ride on the wind, while the sage of Mt Ku-yi (Guyi) could ascend to the clouds on a dragon. The accomplishments of one person do not make another person less good. True goodness is measured by the bringing of interior peace and blessing to all who come in contact with the Tao.

The second chapter, entitled 'Abstain from Arguing about Things',[6] opens with the story of the sage *Nan Guo-tzu Chi (Nanguozi Ji)* who could make 'the body like dry wood and the mind like ashes', i.e. one with the Tao, by abstaining from all judgements. The simple rule for the meditation of union is to abstain from any sort of judgement, including good as well as bad. When verb is not put to noun, and the heart–mind is at peace, then the meditator can 'hear the music of heaven'. Judgements are at any rate relative. The monkeys in a zoo were angry because the zoo-keeper gave them only three bananas in the morning, and four in the evening. So the zoo-keeper gave them four in the morning, and three in the evening. The monkeys were then quite happy. Winning or losing an argument does not make the winner correct or the loser wrong.

Once a Chinese princess was married by her father the king to a prince who lived in a far-off land. She cried and cried when leaving her home, but when arriving in her new kingdom she repented her tears. Her new life was filled with peace and happiness. For the Taoist, the entire cosmos is home. Eternity has already begun, and death is only a change of residence.

The fourth chapter teaches the Taoist meditative method called 'heart–mind fasting', that is, keeping the heart and mind focused on Tao's presence in nature, and in the interior of the meditator, rather than on thoughts and judgements within the mind. This simple technique is achieved by focusing awareness on the 'lower cinnabar field', the centre of the physical body, rather than on thoughts in the mind or desires in the heart. The Tao's presence is experienced in the body's physical centre. Tao's act of eternal gestation is seen, heard and felt with the intuitive powers of the belly rather than with the logical faculties of mind or the self-seeking powers of the will in the heart. The heart stops listening to the ears or the mind when it is focused on the Tao.

> Only the Tao dwells in the void. Fasting in the heart means that the heart–mind is emptied, so that only the Tao may dwell there.
>
> Keep the ears and eyes focused on the Tao within, so that the mind is not engaged in the human struggle for fame. Shut out all worldly knowledge and judgements, so that spirits and demons will not come and dwell inside.

The conviction that judgements and forces both inside and outside the human mind and body are spiritual energies that must be
exorcised in order to be aware of Tao's presence is essential to
Taoist mysticism. To the fourth-century CE woman Taoist Wei
Huacun is attributed the authorship of the Yellow Court Inner
Chapters (*Huang-t'ing Nei-ching*).[7] In this text of the later monastic
ascetic Taoist tradition, the meditator is given the names of hundreds of spirits and their energies that reside in every crevice and
section of the body's microcosm, reflecting the spiritual energies of
the outer cosmos.[8] As in the Buddhist Tantric tradition, the meditator is taught to envision each spirit and send it out of the body, thus
voiding the interior before the meditation of union with the Tao.

Chapter 5 uses the symbol of the *Fu*, the royal talisman of
China's ancient kingdoms, to explain the method of union with the
Tao. In ancient China, kings and loyal courtiers swore fealty by
breaking a jade seal in half. The king kept one half, and the duke,
lord or marquis kept the other half. At the winter solstice festival the
loyal knights returned to the king's banquet table, and matched
their talismans to those of the king, proving loyal service.

In the same manner, the Tao is the heavenly half of a talisman
(*Ling*), and the meditator is the other half (*Bao*). When judgement
is stopped, when the meditator 'sits in forgetfulness' (*dzuowang*),
then the two halves of the talisman can be joined.[9]

The Tao-realized person is called in chapter 6 a *Chen-jen*
(*Zhenren*), i.e. a 'true person'. The meditation of 'sitting in forgetfulness' is described as follows:

My limbs do not feel, my mind is darkened
I have forgotten my body, and discarded my knowledge
By so doing, I have become
One with the Infinite Tao.

The final chapter, 7, tells two stories: (1) the story of Empty
Gourd (related above) and (2) the story of Mr Hundun (the person
united to the Tao) who did not have the five sense apertures of ordinary humans. Each day the Lord of the Southern Ocean (*yang*) and
the Lord of the Northern Ocean (*yin*) came to play inside Hundun's
warm interior (i.e. the meditation of 'heart–mind fasting' and 'sitting in forgetfulness'). They felt sorry for Hundun, and decided to
give him the seven apertures of an ordinary human being: two eyes,
two ears, two nostrils, and a mouth. Each day they drilled one hole.
On the seventh day Hundun died.

So, too, meditation on the Tao's presence dies when we fill our
hearts and minds with judgements, and do not let go. The meditator must be like a mirror, not holding thoughts or worries inside:
'The person who has touched the Tao uses the heart–mind like a

mirror, not reaching out and grabbing, not holding on, responding, but not storing inside. Thus s/he can bring healing without harming self or others.'

The later Taoist religious tradition, which has developed from the second century CE up to the present, relies on these ideas for inspiration and enlightenment. All truly Taoist ritual is initiated by a meditation called *Fa-lu* in which the Taoist high priest (man and woman can equally perform this role) empties all of the spirits and images out of the heart–mind, before inviting the Transcendent Tao to be present. All of the spirits of the cosmos, including images of the Tao as gestating, mediating and indwelling, are exorcised or sent out of the body. A grand 'mandala' or cosmic design is constructed around the meditating Taoist. The spirits of the heavens are seen to be in the north, facing the Taoist (who stands with his/her back to the south). The spirits of *yang* (Blue Dragon, spring and summer) are in the east, to the right of the Taoist. The spirits of *yin* (White Tiger, autumn, winter) are to the west. The spirits of the water and underworld, the 'orphan souls' (images from the past filling the mind with worries) are left outside of the sacred temple or meditative area. These spirits of past memories, unrequited ancestors, all those who suffered because of the individual or the community offering prayer, are released from memory. These rites are enacted throughout the villages of south-east China, Taiwan, South-East Asia and Hong Kong in the modern period. (For a fuller explanation of the Taoist ritual process, see [33].)

The kenotic tradition is also preserved in modern Chinese and Tibetan Buddhist practice. It is to be found in three separate forms: (1) the combined Pure Land chant and Ch'an (Zen) meditations of the Chinese Buddhist monastery; (2) the practice by the laity of a popular form of *Chih-kuan* (*Zhiguan*), i.e. Samatha-vipassana centring meditation from the T'ien-t'ai Buddhist tradition; and (3) the Tibetan Tantric forms of mandala chant ritual and Dzog-chen sitting meditation.

The first of these methods, the Chinese form of Ch'an (Zen) which uses Pure Land chant (*nianfuo*) along with quiet sitting meditation in the lotus position, can be found in most traditional Buddhist monastic centres. Monks and nuns on Mt Chiu-hua (Jiuhua Shan) in Anhui province, the Xixia monastery outside of Nanjing, and a great number of mountain retreats in Fujian and Gwangdong provinces continue to practise and transmit the teachings of the traditional Chinese Ch'an tradition. The chanting of the Amida Sutra, the Heart Sutra, the *P'u-men P'in* chapter (26) of the *Lotus Sutra*, the *Great Compassion Sutra*, and other traditional texts are combined with daily sitting in the *dhyana* or *vipsyana*, with the mind focused on the *Hsia Tan-t'ien* (*xiadantian*) or 'lower cinnabar' region, about three inches below the navel and three or so inches within. The laity who attend Buddhist temple services on the first and fifteenth of each lunar month, days which the government has declared to be officially sanctioned for Buddhist services, spend a great part of the morning listening to the monks and nuns chant *sutras*, a practice which the Buddhist monks say is a more sure and expedient way to attain 'mind and heart emptying' than sitting meditation. The laity as well as most monks set more store by Pure Land chant than by 'sitting'. The older Buddhist masters teach their modern disciples that this latter practice, if done without a spiritual guide, can lead to pride, distractions, and self-aggrandizement.

A second popular form of emptying meditation is practised by a widespread lay movement in modern China. A great number of private lay masters teach a form of *zhiguan* or 'centring' prayer based on the Greater and Lesser Vipassana *sutras*, i.e. the *Ta Chih-kuan* (*Da Zhiguan*) and *Hsiao Chih-kuan* (*Xiao Zhiguan*) healing texts of the T'ien-t'ai (Tiantai) tradition. This phenomenon is found everywhere in modern China, and is not limited to Buddhist texts. Pseudo-Taoist Ch'i-kung (Qigong) masters and self-styled Buddhist *zhiguan* experts are so numerous that government attempts to control their spread (sometimes by arresting popular leaders and forbidding unapproved public Qigong demonstrations) have been ineffective. The majority of such masters and their followers are often quite highly motivated. No fees are asked for the transmission of meditative teachings. The goal of the teacher and of the meditator is for the most part healing rather than the pure meditation of emptying. The purpose of learning Vipassana or Qigong meditation is almost always to heal some illness. Men and women who are accomplished masters must be able to free themselves and their followers from illness.

The third form of kenotic prayer practised widely throughout Tibet and parts of Mongolia, Gansu, Qinghai, Szechuan and Yunnan provinces is Tantric Buddhism. This powerful form of visualization and emptying through the use of *mudra, mantra* and *mandala* meditation is based firmly on the philosophy of Madhyamaka, the 'empty' middle way. The Tantric method of prayer is totally non-judgmental, freeing the mind from conceptual images and the will from any form of assent or denial. Whereas Ch'an (Zen) sitting focuses on emptying the mind, and Pure Land chant on purifying the devotional heart, Tantric prayer uses mind to contemplate (*mandala*), mouth to chant (*mantra*) and body and hands to dance (*mudra*) in a form of total bodily kenosis. Tantric prayer in its Tibetan form achieves kenosis by overload, i.e. by visualizing such powerful sacred images that the mind is no longer drawn by any form of judgement or the heart by desires. The state of absolute detachment elicited by the stark beauty of the Tibetan highlands that gave birth to this unique form of prayer changed warlike Tibet and Mongolia into nations whose cultures became focused on prayer and devotion, rather than war and conquest. Up to the present Tibet rejects the modernization imposed by the polluting Han Chinese socialist technocracy in favour of the spiritual abundance of a simpler form of life based on pastoral nomads, quiet farming and Tantric meditation.

The above is only a brief summary of a marvellously rich tradition. Many excellent works exist in English that can assist the reader to learn more of Ch'an (Zen) meditation, Pure Land chant and Tantric contemplation. Modern bookshops are filled with treatises on and translations of Buddhist prayer. Fewer works are available on the Taoist tradition of kenosis, due to what is conceived as 'Taoist' in Western book markets rather than to the reality of Taoist practice in China. Though there are many translations of the *Laozi* and *Zhuangzi*, treatises on Taoist liturgical prayer in English are less well known. The opening of China to the modern world since 1960 has begun to alleviate this situation. (For an excellent bibliography of Taoist literature, see [4]; for descriptions of Taoist ritual, see [33]; for a detailed bibliography on every aspect of Buddhism, Taoism and popular religion up to the early 1980s, see [43].)

Religion in Modern China

Perhaps one of the most volatile and unpredictable areas in modern Chinese life is the status of religion under 'socialism with a special Chinese flavour'. After the opening of China to Western investment and economic progress in 1979–80, the enlightened policies of Deng Xiaoping have brought about a certain amount of freedom of religious practice in China, which was again curtailed to some extent after the democracy movement and demonstrations in Tiananmen Square in May–June 1989.[10] The condition of religion in China from June 1989 to 1996 is quite different from the period 1980–9.

The opening of China to the market economy in the early 1980s brought with it, in Deng Xiaoping's words, 'files and insects', i.e. a certain amount of religious freedom, which was seen as unavoidable with the coming of free markets, private small businesses and individual enterprise. Scholars of the Academy of Social Sciences were quick to point out that the restoration of the 'freedom of religion' clause allowed by the first Chinese socialist constitution constituted an improvement in Chinese social and cultural values. Surveys done by the Academy between 1984 and 1988 showed that where religion was practised, 'production was high, divorce was low, family values were maintained, and loyalty to the state and its principles upheld' [33: 193–212]. The survey of religion published by the Shanghai branch of the Academy of Social Sciences, entitled *The Religious Question in the Socialist Era* [31],[11] pointed out that religion in China could no longer be called the 'opiate of the people' because socialist China no longer had a capitalist class which could use religion as a tool to oppress the proletariat. Religion for the Chinese was for the most part a festive rather than a doctrinal system.

The five great religions officially recognized by the Chinese state are the Buddhist, Taoist, Islamic, Catholic and Protestant faiths. Monks, priests, ministers and mullahs from each of these traditions are educated at state expense in state-constructed and subsidized seminaries. In spite of the official attitude of the state and the Communist Party to religion, the Marxist–Leninist principle of the 'united front' (i.e. the unifying of party goals with religious faiths) is used as the guiding principle for handling religious questions in China. Since 1980 the re-promulgation of ethnic minority as well as religious rights has inspired a more open attitude towards religious belief and practice in China. The fact that religious rights are seen as analogous to ethnic minority rights has brought about both an opening and a restricting of religious practice at the official level. To understand this phenomenon, it is necessary to examine each of the religious traditions as a separate entity, since the state and the Party handle each religion in a different fashion.

The first and most obvious area of scholarly study and state–Party concern is with Islam in China. The Yuan dynasty (1261–1365) policy of using Islamic and other minorities to govern the Han Chinese brought a huge influx of Arab, Persian, Turkish and other military officials into thirteenth- and fourteenth-century China. These Yuan-sponsored officials for the most part married Han Chinese women, and became a separate ethnic group (of multi-ethnic origin) classified as Hui i.e. of Islamic origin, in China. The Ming dynasty (1365–1644) did not employ this diverse ethnic group in the capacity of civil officials, but continued to use the Hui as military experts. The Qing (Ch'ing) dynasty, on the other hand, discriminated against and completely eliminated the Hui from all posts, civil or military, causing great unrest among Islamic peoples in China, which resulted in uprisings, wars and massacres during the foreign (Manchu) Qing rule. An enlightened socialist China decided after the 1980 reforms to allow a certain amount of autonomy for all of the Islamic areas in China, built seminaries and schools that taught the Qur'an, Islamic, Arabic and Iranian studies, and trained mullahs at state expense. This policy was implemented not only for the Hui minority, a term used to name people of Islamic belief or descent in such widely separate places as Yunnan,

Hunan, Fujian, Shandong, Beijing, Gansu and Ningxia (a Hui autonomous region), but also among the Uighur, Khazak, Salah (an immigrant Islamic group coming to Qinghai province from Samarkand during the Yuan dynasty), Bao'an and other Islamic minorities. These groups are remarkable for their maintaining of ancient divisions, such as the 'loud' and 'quiet' method of reading the Qur'an, Sufi, Sunni and even Shi'a beliefs (such as among the Kirgiz ethnic group of Persian origin). Ties between the Islamic groups of China and the Middle Eastern Islamic nations are close. The Chinese government grants travel permits for the annual pilgrimage to Mecca.

Buddhism is also a very obvious area of concern in and support by official state policy. The Buddhist Studies Association supports the restoration of Buddhist shrines, the gathering of immense financial profit from tourism to Buddhist sacred places, and the education of Buddhist monks and nuns to staff chosen monastic and temple environments in places of popular devotion throughout China. Great Buddhist centres such as Putuo Shan, with its devotion to Guanyin (Avalokiteshvara; symbol of compassion), Jiuhua Shan (and its shrine to Dizangwang, Ksitigharba; symbol of salvation from suffering), Xixiashan outside Nanjing, Omei Shan, Wutai Shan and other great centres have continued the tradition of Ch'an meditation, Pure Land Chant, and popular devotion including the rites of *zhaodu*: praying for the ascent of deceased souls from Buddhist purgatory to the Pure Land.

Tibetan Buddhism is a special case, because of the delicate question of Tibetan cultural and religious independence as against complete political separation, which the Chinese government does not consider to be a question open to discussion. For this extremely sensitive reason, the rebirth of Tibetan religion, with the flocking of monks and nuns to traditional monasteries, the rebuilding of the great temples (destroyed completely during the Cultural Revolution) and immense numbers of pilgrims turning prayer wheels, circumambulating and prostrating in the old fashion, makes Tibet, Qinghai, Gansu, Yunnan and western Szechuan (which comprised the ancient Tibetan kingdom) appear to have undergone an almost complete restoration of the traditional religious system. The Jhokang temple in Lhasa, Drepung, Kumbun, Labrang, Rongwo and other great monasteries have restored the 'living Buddha' tradition of the past. Foreign visitors to Tibet are everywhere asked for pictures of the Dalai Lama, the spiritual leader of Tibet and winner of the Nobel Peace Prize, now in exile in India. The revival of religion in all Tibetan-speaking areas is found among old and young alike.

Taoism is the least noticed of China's traditional religious systems, due to the rigours of the celibate monastic life and the long years of training required for popular Taoist priests who perform the rites of passage for China's villages and cities. The state keeps a close watch over Taoist mountains, collecting fees from tourists and pilgrims who come to these famous sacred shrines. Taoists are trained at the state-run White Cloud monastery (Baiyun Guan) in Beijing, in the Quanzhen (Ch'uan-chen) style rather than the more traditional liturgies of the Celestial Master, the meditations of the Shangqing (Shang-ch'ing) and the popular rites of the Lingbao (Ling-pao) traditions. (For a more detailed description of these various Taoist schools, see [4; 33; 43].) The great Taoist centres of Mao Shan, Lunghu Shan, Qingcheng Guan, Wudang Shan and many others have been restored and support communities of Taoists in their scenic environs. Popular 'fireside' (married) Taoist priests who act as ritual experts for villages and cities are found throughout Fujian, Zhejiang, Gwuangzhou, Zhiangxi, and other south-eastern provinces.

Christianity in its Protestant and Catholic forms has registered the greatest growth of any of the religions of modern China. Candidates flock to seminaries, where they are educated at state expense. Political control over the Protestant faith is maintained by an internal organization called the 'Three Self' movement, while Catholics are carefully watched by the 'Patriotic Association' (Aiguohui). Though this latter state-sponsored group has officially declared itself a schismatic church, not recognizing papal authority in Rome, in fact all of the faithful, almost all of the priests and more than 70 per cent of the state-appointed bishops do recognize the authority of Rome. Belonging to the Patriotic Association for most of the clergy is simply a means of being allowed some form of religious freedom. A good number of Catholics and Protestants, however, maintain an 'underground' church, that does not accept any form of activity classified as 'United Front' by the state. The underground churches have been officially declared illegal, and their members are arrested and gaoled when their activities become public. In spite of such difficulties, Christianity in China flourishes as it never did under the dominance of the foreign missionary in the past. More people attend churches in China than in Taiwan, Hong Kong, Japan, Korea, or city parishes in the United States and Europe.

Three separate bodies of officials watch over religious growth in China. The highest of these is the United Front Association (Tongjanbu), the official Party organ. The second is the Religious Affairs Bureau, nominally a local or provincial organization with headquarters in the central government in Beijing. In fact the majority of the Religious Affairs Bureau officials are Communist Party members dedicated to the eventual elimination of religion in the perfected socialist state of the future. There is however a small body of dedicated cadres who in fact work for the freedom and growth of religion in China. Finally, each of the five religious groups has a control organ working from within: the above-mentioned 'Three Self' Christians, the 'Patriotic' Catholics, and the Buddhist, Taoist and Islamic Studies associations. Within each of these groups, Party, state, and religious body, are dedicated men and women who see religion in China as part of its cultural heritage, and thus, in spite of opposition, work for its growth and smooth functioning within the market economy and increasingly consumer-oriented society of 'socialism with a special Chinese flavour'. In fact, the number of people practising religion of some sort is approximately equivalent to the number of Party members in China, each standing at 6 per cent of the population. In one of his last addresses, Zhou Enlai predicted that 'religion would be present for at least the next 200 years in China'. The prediction of the insightful Premier, as in so many other instances, is proving to be correct.

Notes

1 'Irenic' signifies an attitude of peace and acceptance towards other people and their ideas, stemming from the self. 'Ecumenic' connotes a positive effort to understand points held in common between two opposing religious systems. Thus, to the Chinese, Buddhism is a system for the afterlife, Taoism for the present (natural) life and Confucianism for moral virtue. The self is inwardly irenic, outwardly ecumenic with regard to the three religious teachings. There can never be an ecumenism of dogma, only of religious experience.

2 'Eidetic visualization' means the constructing of an imaginative picture of the Taoist heavens, the arrival of Taoist spirits, or other imaginative contemplations rather in the style of the Ignatian Spiritual Exercises known in Western Christian terms. 'Eidetic' means that the outlines of the meditation are drawn by the classical text, while the meditator himself or herself fills in the outlines with a complete devotional experience of the text. Thus the *eidos* or substantial form of the meditation is fixed by custom, whereas the qualitative or devotional aspects are determined by the meditator.

3 The 'dark night of the soul' and 'dark night of the senses', terms found in the writings of the Western mystics Teresa of Avila and John of the Cross, are examples of apophatic or kenotic forms of prayer. Also included within this tradition are the works of the Pseudo-Dionysius, the *Cloud of Unknowing*, and Meister Eckhardt. Though the analogy between these forms of Western mystic prayer and the Buddhist Taoist tradition in China have often been pointed out by scholars and mystics in Asia and the West, official church authorities, Protestant and Catholic alike, have been slow in recognizing the significance of inter-religious prayer and dialogue.

4 There are many excellent translations of both versions of the text. The standard works of D. C. Lau are an excellent introduction. The romanization of Chinese characters used here includes the Wade–Giles as well as the modern Pinyin, where both forms seem helpful.

5 The first seven chapters of the *Chuang-tzu*, called the 'Inner Chapters' (*Chuang-Tzu Nei-p'ien*), are thought to be the most authentic part of the thirty-three-chapter text.

6 The chapter is also called 'Making All Things Equal'. The Chinese *Zhi wu lun*, 'Equalizing Discourse on Things', or an alternative reading, 'Zhai Wulun' ('Abstention from Arguing about Things'), have the same meaning.

7 Note that the Inner Chapters of the *Chuang-tzu* and the Inner Chapters of the Yellow Court Canon both contain the basic directions for the practice of mystic contemplation; the *Chuang-tzu* teaches the exorcism of judgement, while the Yellow Court Canon's Inner Chapters teach the exorcism of all images and spiritual energies from the mind and body.

8 The head, chest and belly of the meditator are seen to respond to heaven, earth and the underworld in the macrocosm. Taoist ritual also uses this meditative method [33].

9 Note that the term *Ling-pao* (*Lingbao*) used in religious Taoist ritual preserves this meaning. The Taoists use talismans in ritual to join heaven and earth, humans with the Tao of Transcendence. The talisman must not be seen as a superstitious fetish, but as a sign of meditative process practised by the Taoist, that preceded the act of public ritual. In a deeper sense, *Tao* is the heavenly or *Ling* half of the talisman, and *Te* (of the *Tao-te Ching*) is the earthly or human half, the *Bao*.

10 The official term used for the incident of 4 June 1989, *dongluan*, 'political disturbance', reflects the psychological turmoil caused by the students and others during the events of May–June 1989. The officially recognized causes of the Tiananmen incident are attributed to foreign influence, especially on the students of Beijing who participated in the demonstrations. The demise of socialism in the USSR and the dissolution of the Soviet Union is officially attributed to the freedom of religion allowed by Moscow in the 1980s. Much of the freedom of religion allowed by the Chinese government during the 1980s has been subtly curtailed during the early 1990s.

11 An edition of 8,000 volumes sold out within the first month of publication, and has not yet appeared in a second printing.

Bibliography

1 AHERN, E., *The Cult of the Dead in a Chinese Village*, Stanford, Stanford University Press, 1973
2 BODDE, D., *Festivals in Classical China*, Princeton, Princeton University Press, 1975

476 Michael Saso

3 BODDE, D. (ed. and tr.), Li-Chen Tun, *Annual Customs and Festivals in Peking, as Recorded in the Yen-ching Sui-shih-chi*, 2nd edn, Hong Kong University Press, 1965

4 BOLTZ, JUDITH, *A Survey of Taoist Literature*, Berkeley, University of California Press, 1986

5 *Cheng-t'ung Tao-Tsang* and *Wan-li Tao-tsang*, Ming dynasty versions of the Taoist canon, are reprinted in Taiwan and readily available for library and private use: e.g. Taipei, I-wen Press, 1961

6 *Complete Home Rituals* (Chia-li Ta-ch'eng), Hsinchu, Chu-lin Press, 1960. This and similar volumes are found throughout maritime China, as popular summaries of the works cited in item 25 below.

7 DORÉ, H., *Researches into Chinese Supersititions* (tr. M. Kennelly et al.), 13 vols, Shanghai, T'usewei, 1914–; repr. Taipei, Ch'eng Wen, 1966

8 EBERHARD, W., *Chinese Festivals*, Taipei, 1964; prev. publ. New York, H. Schuman, 1952; London/New York, A. Schuman, 1958

9 EBERHARD, W., *Guilt and Sin in Traditional China*, Berkeley, University of California Press, 1967

10 EBERHARD, W., *The Local Cultures of South and East China* (tr. A. Eberhard), Leiden, Brill, 1968

11 FÈNG, YU-LAN, *A History of Chinese Philosophy* (tr. D. Bodde), 2 vols, Princeton, Princeton University Press, 1952–3

12 FÈNG, YU-LAN, *A Short History of Chinese Philosphy* (tr. and ed. D. Bodde), New York, Macmillan, 1962; prev. publ. 1948

13 GROOT, J. J. M. DE, *Buddhist Masses for the Dead at Amoy: Acts of the Sixth International Conference of Orientalists*, Leiden, 1885

14 GROOT, J. J. M. DE, *The Religious System of China*, 6 vols, Leiden, Brill, 1892–1910; Tapiei, Literature House, 1964; Ch'eng Weng, 1976

15 GROOT, J. J. M. DE, *Sectarianism and Religious Persecution in China*, 2 vols, Amsterdam, Müller, 1903–4; Taipei, Literature House, 1963; other edns Shannon, Irish University Press, 1973; New York, Barnes & Noble, 1974

16 IKEDA, T., *Taiwan no Katei Seikatsu* (Daily Life and Customs in Taiwan), Taipei, Toto Press, 1944

17 JORDAN, D. K., *Gods, Ghosts and Ancestors*, Berkeley, University of California Press, 1972

18 KARLGREN, B., 'Legends and Cults in Ancient China', *Bulletin of the Museum of Far Eastern Antiquities*, vol. 18, 1946

19 KEIGHTLEY, D., *Sources of Shang History: The Oracle-Bone Inscriptions of Bronze Age China*, Berkeley, University of California Press, 1978

20 KU, CHIEH-KANG, *Ch'in-Han de Fang-shih yü Juei-shih* (Proto-Taoists and Confucianists of the Ch'in-Han Period), Shanghai, Chun-lien Press, 1954

21 KUBO, NORITADA, *Chugoku no Shukyo Kaikaku* (The Religious Reformation of China) Kyoto, Hozokan, 1966

22 KUBO, NORITADA, *Dōkyō-shi* (A History of Taoism), Tokyo, Yomakawa Press, 1978

23 LAO, D. C. (tr.), *Lao Tzu: Tao te Ching*, Harmondsworth/Baltimore, Penguin, 1963

24 LEGGE, J., *The Chinese Classics*, 4 vols, Taipei, 1961; prev. publ. 5 vols, Hong Kong, author/London, Trübner, 1861–72; 2nd edn Oxford,

Clarendon Press, 1893–5; London, Oxford University Press, 1935; also Hong Kong University Press, 1960, repr. 1970; New York, Krishna, n.d.

25 *Li-Chi* (*Lĭ Kĭ*) (Book of Rites) (tr. J. Legge), Oxford, Clarendon Press, 1885 (Sacred Books of the East, vols 27, 28); Delhi, Motilal Banarsidass, 1966. For a translation of the text of Lin Po-T'ung, *Kuan-hun-Sang-Chi*, Canton, 1845, see item 33 below, summarizing the modern adaptations of the *Li-Chi* and the *Ta-T'ang K'ai-yüan Li*, Szu-ku Ch'uan-shu, Toyo Bunka, Tokyo, Iwanami Press, 1972

26 LIN, PO-T'UNG, *Kuan-hun-Sang-Chi* (The Rites of Passage), 3 vols, Canton, 1845 (wood-block prints; for the rites of marriage and burial)

27 LIU, CHIH-WAN, *Chung-kuo Min-chien Hsinyang Lun-chi* (A Treatise on Chinese Popular Religion), Nankang, Academia Sinica, 1974

28 LIU, CHIH-WAN, *Rites of Propitiation* (Sung-shan Ch'i-an Chien Chiao Chi-tien), Nankang, Academia Sinica, 1967

29 LIU, TS'UN-YEN, *Selected Papers*, Leiden, Brill, 1976, ch. 3, pp. 76–148

30 MORGAN, E., *Tao, The Great Luminant*, Shanghai, Kelly & Walsh, repr. Taipei, Ch'eng Wen, 1966 (translations from the Huai-nan-tzu); London, Trübner, 1935; New York, Paragon, 1969

31 *The Religious Question in the Socialist Era*, Shanghai, Shanghai Academy of Social Sciences, 1987

32 SASO, M., *Gold Pavilion* (A Manual for Taoist Meditation), Boston, Tuttle Press, 1995

33 SASO, M., *Blue Dragon, White Tiger*, Honolulu, University of Hawaii Press, 1990

34 SASO, M., *Chuang-lin Hsü Tao-tsang* (The Chuang and Lin Family Collections of the Lung-hu Shan Taoist Canon), Taipei, Ch'eng-wen Press, 1975)

35 SASO, M., *Dōkyō Hiketsu Shusei* (A Collection of Taoist Esoterica), Tokyo, Ryukei Shosha, 1978

36 SASO, M., 'On the Ling-pao Chen-wen', *Tōhō Shūkyō* (Tokyo), vol. 50, November 1977, pp. 22–40

37 SASO, M., *Taoism and the Rite of Cosmic Renewal*, Pullman, Washington State University Press, 1972

38 SASO, M., *The Teachings of Taoist Master Chuang*, New Haven, Yale University Press, 1978, ch. 1 (for a traditional Taoist view of its history, using Chinese and Japanese sources)

39 SASO, M., and CHAPPELL, D. (eds), *Buddhist and Taoist Notions of Transcendence*, Honolulu, University of Hawaii Press, 1977 (Buddhist and Taoist Studies, 1)

40 SCHIPPER, K. M., *Le Fen-teng, rituel taôiste*, Parise, École Française d'Extrème-Orient, 1975

41 SUZUKI, S., *Kan-kon-so-sai* (The Chinese Rites of Passage), Taipei, Nichinichi Press, 1934

42 THOMPSON, L. G., *Chinese Religion: An Introduction*, 3rd edn, Belmont, CA, Wadsworth, 1979

43 THOMPSON, L. G., *Chinese Religion in Western Languages*, Tucson, University of Arizona Press, 1985

44 THOMPSON, L. G., *Studies of Chinese Religion: A Comprehensive and Classified Bibliography . . .*, Encino, CA, Dickenson, 1976

45 WALEY, A., *The Nine Songs: A Study of Shamanism in Ancient China*, London, Allen & Unwin, 1955

46 WATSON, B. (tr.), *Chuang Tzu: The Complete Works*, New York, Columbia University Press, 1968

47 WATSON, B., (tr.), *Mo Tzu: Basic Writings*, New York, Columbia University Press, 1963

48 WOLF, A., 'Gods, Ghosts and Ancestors', in A. Wolf, (ed.), *Religion and Ritual in Chinese Society*, Stanford, Stanford University Press, 1974, pp. 179–82 (discusses the various uses of paper money)

49 WOLF, A. (ed.), *Religion and Ritual in Chinese Society*, Stanford, Stanford University Press, 1974 (the views of Wolf and Freedman are expressed in the introduction and chapter 1 respectively)

10

Japanese Religions

DAVID REID

Introduction

Religion is frequently studied as a matter of personal belief. This is not always possible in Japan, where religious phenomena include many dimensions to which faith is irrelevant. Shinto festivals and Buddhist mortuary rites, for example, are not commonly thought of as part of personal religion. None the less, there are also dimensions where personal belief is essential, as in the majority of sects (Shinto, Buddhist, Christian and others). Yet again, a few sects (mainly Buddhist) place no emphasis whatever on faith, preferring a 'try-it-and-see' attitude. One thing that these disparate religious phenomena have in common is behaviour. In this discussion, behaviour will be recognized as 'religious' if it expresses a relationship with a divine being or beings, as in Shinto, popular Buddhism, Christianity and folk religion, or with a life-transforming ultimate/immanent principle, as in elite forms of Buddhism.

Living religion in Japan, as in other countries, includes an organizational dimension. Religious organizations have their own internal histories, to be sure, but for the student of Japanese religion and society more important is the question of the changing relationships between religious organizations and the state. Throughout most Japanese history, the state has set the terms within which such organizations could exist. It is important, therefore, to give a brief account of the continuing story of the interplay between religious organizations and state power.

Religious Studies in Japan

Broadly construed, the term 'religious studies' as used in Japan includes every academic discipline that takes religion as its object of study. Narrowly construed, the term excludes not only theological and philosophical studies but also historical and textual studies. It is limited to disciplines in which contemporary religious phenomena are studied empirically and, at least in principle, comparatively. Phenomenology of religion, anthropology of religion, psychology of religion and sociology of religion constitute the principal disciplines.

The 'Little Tradition' Matrix

'Great' traditions are usually distinguished from 'little' traditions by the existence of highly developed systems of thought and doctrine in the former and the relatively weak development of such systems in the latter. On this basis, the term 'little tradition' will be applied to Shinto in its three principal forms: folk Shinto, Shrine Shinto and Sect Shinto. The term 'great traditions' will refer to Buddhism, Confucianism and Christianity.

Shinto has a highly complex history of its own. It resists systematic portrayal. One may identify, however, two general tendencies in Japanese ways of thinking that have their roots in Shinto. One deep-seated and far-reaching motif is the emphasis on Shinto as something that unifies. Ideally, its festivals unite people with the *kami*, the divine beings, more immanent than transcendent, who desire to see their people enjoying a life of communal harmony and abundance, filled with dynamic vitality and purity of heart. Socially, this unity is sought primarily at two levels: the local community and the national community. In both cases the expectation is that the oneness achieved, whether interpreted religiously or not, will lead to increasing productivity, creativity and prosperity. In all this, the role of the emperor is central. For historical reasons to be touched on later, the emperor is the chief priest of the Shinto world. In modern Japan (from 1868 onwards), he has also played a key role in the Japanese state. Together, these two roles helped shape the stubborn problem of the relationship between religion and state power. From 701 CE, when the law of the land was first codified, until 1945, when defeat in war led to the institutionalization of the hitherto alien value of government neutrality in respect of religion, the dominant assumption was that upright religion was properly at the service of the state [18: 162]. This centuries-old feature of the 'little tradition', issuing as a general tendency, strongly affected the way people perceived, evaluated and modified the imported 'great traditions'.

The other motif of Shinto thought to be considered here is the emphasis on different kinds of divinities or *kami*. Ichiro Hori distinguishes between two main types: clan *kami* and charismatic *kami* [16: 30–4]. Clan *kami*, associated with rites for the ancestors, were initially the ritual focus of territorially limited and mutually exclusive quasi-genealogical bodies. Generally beneficent, *kami* of this type had no clearly defined personalities or functions. Charismatic *kami*, associated with local shrines, were originally objects of faith who united people from different social groups. Such *kami* had sharply defined personalities and performed specific functions, such as healing. Over the years, these two types became intertwined. In modern Japan, Shrine Shinto can be viewed as a religion of clan *kami* in an enlarged, more comprehensive sense. The *kami* of local communities have their parishes, and the *kami* associated with the imperial household embrace the entire nation. In both cases they unite people in a sense that transcends the genealogical nexus. The charismatic *kami* come into view primarily in the new religious movements. These movements will receive consideration later, but here it should be emphasized that for centuries people with urgent personal problems have sought help from one charismatic *kami* or another, one shamanic leader or another. Such practices and expectations have given rise to the general tendency to assume that religion oriented to a 'living *kami*' should provide tangible, this-worldly benefits. This tendency has likewise guided people's perceptions, evaluations and modifications of the imported 'great traditions'.

Religious Traditions in Japanese History

The story of the interaction between religious traditions and the state is a continuing one. Borrowing the administrative classifications employed in the organization of statistical data (see table 10.1), we shall divide this history into four periods representing cumulative layers of religious tradition.

Shinto Period (Pre-Sixth Century CE)

The key development in the first period was the regionally limited establishment, about the middle of the fourth century CE, of a hereditary priestly rule that, exceptions aside, continues to the present day in the imperial household. The religious practices later given the name 'Shinto' are closely tied to the priestly role of the empresses and emperors in this line. These practices, fundamentally concerned with food and the sun, involved priestly tasks not only for the chief ruler but also for the heads of the many clans. The beings whose favour they sought, the *kami*, were of many

Table 10.1 Numbers of adherents to major classes of religious tradition in Japan between 1953 and 1978

Annual numbers of adherents by tradition

Year	Shinto	Buddhist	Christian	Other	Total	Population of Japan
1953	77,780,324	47,714,876	485,399	3,419,471	129,400,070	86,981,463
1958	76,844,827	48,974,838	652,518	4,010,745	130,482,928	91,767,079
1963	80,284,643	69,843,367	711,636	5,350,790	156,190,436	96,155,847
1968	83,458,684	83,278,496	831,335	6,768,042	174,336,557	101,330,883
1973	87,414,779	84,573,828	879,477	10,002,986	182,871,070	109,103,610
1978	98,545,703	88,020,880	950,491	13,729,376	201,246,450	115,174,112

Sources: Figures on adherents are taken from the Ministry of Education, *Shukyo Nenkan* (Religions Yearbook). They represent the numbers of people claimed by religious organizations as of 31 December in a given year. The population figures are estimates prepared by the Bureau of Statistics, Office of the Prime Minister. They represent the situation as of 1 October in a given year.

kinds: *kami* of nature, *kami* of ideas, *kami* in outstanding people, ancestral *kami*, etc. [15: 672]. Two major festivals were held, one in the spring to pray for a successful harvest, the other in the autumn to celebrate the harvest granted. Divination and purification were important features. The reigning empress or emperor, who had to observe many taboos, was regarded as possessing the mystical power to receive influences from the sun goddess, augment the food supply, and thereby control the well-being of the people.

Shinto–Buddhist Period (538–1549)

In the sixth century (538 according to the *Jogu Shotoku ho'o teisetsu* but 552 according to the *Nihongi*, or *Nihon shoki*, of 720), when Buddhism was introduced from Korea, the political situation in Japan was unsettled. Clan heads were in effect the heads of village states. Imperial court control, though growing, was by no means complete. Buddhism was seen, on the one hand, by the court as a way of promoting a spiritual outlook that would support its claims to 'universality' with magico-religious power, but, on the other hand, by village-state heads as a threat to autonomy and tradition. Confucian morality, entering Japan in the fifth century together with the Chinese system of writing, weakly complemented Buddhism as an ordering of human relationships that strengthened the hand of male power-holders. Efforts to centralize political power included the development of official compilations of Shinto myth and legend, so organized as to centre on the imperial house.

Between 538 and 1549, Buddhism took deeper root in successive waves of sectarian tradition (see figure 10.1). The Nara, Tendai and Shingon sects were imported from China between the seventh and ninth centuries, when political power resided in the imperial court. The Pure Land, Zen and Nichiren sects, more interested in winning believers among the masses, began just before and during the Kamakura period (1185–1333) when leading men of the military or samurai class were seizing political power and the emperor was sinking into obscurity. The changing relationships between Shinto and Buddhism reflect these political conditions. When power was held by the court, Buddhist thinkers, then in favour, accommodated Shinto to Buddhism. When power fell to the Kamakura military government, Shinto thinkers, in reaction, accommodated Buddhism to Shinto. In time, the two became interwoven both doctrinally and institutionally.

Shinto–Buddhist–Christian Period (1549–1802)

Christianity entered the scene in 1549. The shogunate (government under the shogun or leading general) was then at a low ebb. Fief heads or *daimyos*, relatively autonomous, warred with one another to enlarge their domains. Tendai, Nichiren and Pure Land soldier-monks armed themselves, fortified their monasteries and took sides in the fray. Under Nobunaga Oda (1534–82) order was restored in central Japan, but in the process opposing monasteries were razed and thousands of monks killed. His successor, Hideyoshi Toyotomi (1536–98), established a military dictatorship over the entire country. Christianity was outlawed in a series of inconsistently enforced edicts that began with Hideyoshi's expulsion of Catholic missionaries in 1587 and his crucifixion of twenty-six Japanese and foreign Christians in 1596. It grew under Ieyasu Tokugawa (1542–1616) to include the exiling of Japanese Christians to Manila and Macao in 1612 and the further executing of Christians under his son Hidetada (1578–1632). The opposition to Christianity culminated in an absolute prohibition following the abortive Shimabara Revolt of 1637–8.

Buddhism was put into government service with the establishment of the *danka seido* (1638), a system that required every

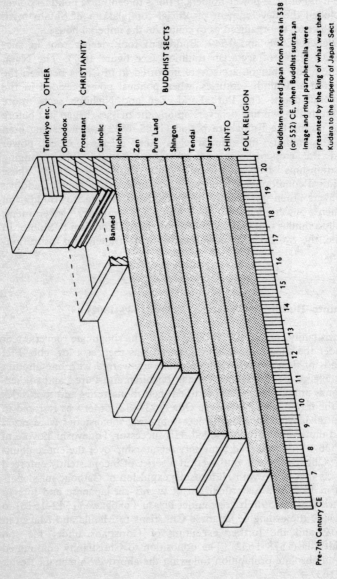

Figure 10.1   Layers of Japanese religion: major sect traditions and when they began

OTHER { Tenrikyo etc.

CHRISTIANITY { Orthodox
Protestant
Catholic

BUDDHIST SECTS { Nichiren
Zen
Pure Land
Shingon
Tendai
Nara

SHINTO

FOLK RELIGION

Banned

Pre-7th Century CE   7   8   9   10   11   12   13   14   15   16   17   18   19   20

*Buddhism entered Japan from Korea in 538 (or 552) CE, when Buddhist sutras, an image and ritual paraphernalia were presented by the king of what was then Kudara to the Emperor of Japan. Sect tradition began as shown.

Japanese household to affiliate with a local temple, and the *terauke seido* (1662), where every adult was required to obtain annually from this temple a certificate attesting that he or she was innocent of association with subversive religion. These developments led to the formation of underground Christian congregations – some of which persist today. Not surprisingly, mandatory ties to Buddhist temples, the only institutions then authorized to conduct mortuary rites, weakened voluntary interest in Buddhism. Temple ties became more a matter of obtaining ritual services for the household dead than a matter of seeking enlightenment.

One stream of religious tradition conspicuous in this period is *shugendo*, the way that leads to magico-religious power through ascetic practices in the mountains (see figure 10.2). A blend of folk Shinto, esoteric Buddhism and *yin–yang* Taoist magic (see pp. 450–6), this tradition traces its origin to the legend-surrounded shaman En-no-Gyoja of the Nara period (710–94). Several centuries later, under the hereditary Tokugawa shogunate, the formerly unregulated ascetics were brought under government control as part of an overall policy towards religious movements and organizations.

During the seventeenth century, Neo-Confucianism came to play an influential role. The Tokugawa shogunate encouraged Confucian studies both in its own schools and in fief schools throughout the nation in order to mould samurai ideas and behaviour. In the eighteenth century, through private schools for commoners, Confucian principles spread among craftsmen, merchants and farmers. In the Mito fief (part of what is now Ibaraki prefecture, located just northeast of Tokyo) these studies led to the *Dai Nihon Shi*, a multi-volume history of Japan inculcating the idea of the *kami*-descended imperial line as the only legitimate basis of authority and enlarging the principles of loyalty and filial piety by identifying the emperor as the supreme object of such virtues. These ideas, transmuted into Shinto restorationism, helped bring an end to seven centuries of samurai rule.

Shinto–Buddhist–Christian–Other Period (1802–)

Since 1802, two major developments affecting the Japanese people and their institutions have taken place. One was the restoration of the emperor (1868), the other defeat in war (1945). (Post-1945 developments are treated in a later section of this chapter.)

During the turbulent closing years of the Tokugawa shogunate and the early years of the restoration government, a number of new religious organizations appeared (see table 10.2). The harbinger of this development appeared in 1802, which thus marks the turn from the preceding to the present period. Nyorai-kyo, a body classified as

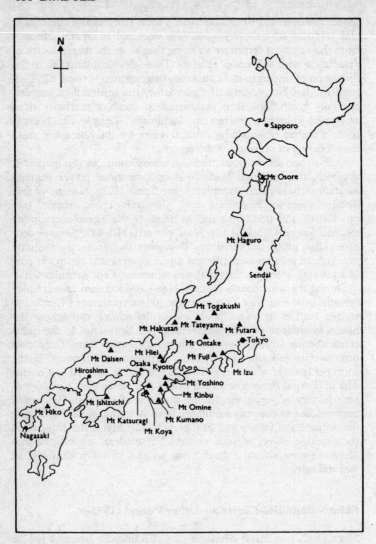

Figure 10.2 *Japanese mountains historically associated with magico-religious powers*

Buddhist, began as a faith-healing sect based on the belief that its founder, a peasant woman named Kino (1756–1826), was a living *kami* and prophet of a better life in the next world. When the restoration government took control, it disestablished Buddhism and established Shinto in its place, identifying it not as a religion,

Table 10.2 Some surviving new religious organizations in Japan: year of origin, classification and current membership

	Shinto			Buddhist			Other		
Period	Origin	Name	Members	Origin	Name	Members	Origin	Name	Members
1801–1900	1814	Kurozumi-kyo	218,240	1802	Nyorai-kyo	34,030	1838	Tenrikyo	2,525,759
	1840	Misogikyo	124,960	1857	Honmon Butsuryushu	465,158			
	1843	Shinrikyo	266,120						
	1859	Konkokyo	480,072						
	1873	Maruyama-kyo	3,251						
	1873	Ontake-kyo	734,390						
	1873	Izumo Oyashirokyo	1,051,206						
	1892	Omoto	163,760						
1901–45	1913	Honmichi	480,072	1914	Kokuchukai	22,706	1919	Ennokyo	306,975
				1917	Nihonzan Myohoji	1,120	1924	P L (Perfect Liberty) Kyodan	2,658,872
				1923	Reiyukai	2,838,000	1930	Seicho no Ie	3,242,911
				1925	Nenpo Shinkyo	862,030	1934	Sekai Kyuseikyo	803,841
				1929	Gedatsukai	216,528			
				1930	Soka Gakkai	16,539,375			
				1935	Kodo Kyodan	417,636			
				1938	Rissho Koseikai	5,081,286			
Post-1945	1949	Ananaikyo	201,360	1948	Shinnyo-en	543,959	1945	Tensho Kotai Jingukyo	401,572
				1950	Myochikai Kyodan	686,205	1947	Zenrinkai	602,153
				1950	Bussho Gonenkai	1,354,662			
				1951	Saijo Inari-kyo	286,270			

Sources: Membership figures, voluntarily reported, are for 31 December 1978, as found in the 1979 edition of the *Shukyo Nenkan* (Religions Yearbook). The list of organizations follows Murakami [25: 170–1].

which would have made it voluntary, but as an ethic, obligatory for all the emperor's subjects. Institutionally intertwined for centuries, Shinto and Buddhism were forcibly separated. The *shugendo* organizations, an inseparable amalgam of traditions, were ordered to disband. Many *shugendo* ideas, however, were taken up into the new religious organizations – ideas such as spirit-possession, exorcism, faith-healing and leaders deemed living *kami* or living buddhas.[1]

The government classification for most of the new religious organizations of these years was (and is) Sect Shinto, a term coined to distinguish them from 'non-religious' State Shinto. The movements thus grouped together can be understood as belonging to four types:

Shinto revivalism: Shinrikyo, Izumo Oyashirokyo;
purification: Misogikyo;
mountain worship: Maruyama-kyo, Ontake-kyo;
faith-healing: Kurozumi-kyo, Tenrikyo, Konkokyo, Omoto (Tenrikyo, in order to emphasize its universality, was reclassified as 'Other' at its own request in 1970).

Honmon Butsuryushu, founded in 1857 by the Nichiren Buddhist priest Nissen Nagamatsu (1817–90), is significant as the first of the lay Buddhist associations to emphasize commitment to the *Lotus Sutra* as essential to the welfare of individuals and of the nation.

From 1859 on, Christian missionaries reintroduced Christianity. Churches, schools and medical care were the main forms through which Christians, Japanese and foreign, sought to plant the new faith. Christianity found a moderate welcome as Japan ended over two centuries of seclusion from the West, but met with disapproval as nationalistic feeling and war fever began to mount from about 1890. It remains a minority religion.

The anti-Buddhist iconoclasm that occurred in many areas with the turn to State Shinto lasted only a few years. When cooler heads prevailed, Buddhism was given government protection. Until 1945, however, the mythology of State Shinto became an increasingly rigid norm. New religious bodies were required to conform or be crushed by state power [25: 48–51, 95–109].

It can be seen that continental Buddhism entered Japan during the shift from clan government to imperial government when a difficult reorientation of values was in process. Buddhism as a popular religion took hold during the shift from imperial to military government, another reorientation. Christianity arrived during a temporary shift to domain government, was ousted soon after the restoration of centralized military rule when Neo-Confucian influence was strong, and returned during the swing to a new imperial government under the aegis of Shinto restorationism. The new religious organizations came into being during the decades bracketing the restoration of imperial rule, during the economic depression and totalitarian controls following the First World War, and, to anticipate, during the period of economic and spiritual distress following the Second World War. In broad perspective, then, it appears that significant religious developments have tended to coincide with periods of political unrest and value-confusion. This finding is reinforced when one turns to the religious leaders of these times.

Religious Leaders and their Teachings

One cultural thread evident throughout Japanese history is the tendency to honour only what has a clearly traceable lineage. Arguments supporting the legitimacy of the imperial house rarely fail to mention its 'direct and unbroken succession' – a cultural norm even if not a historical fact. In the same way, a person recognized as an outstanding religious leader is frequently revered not only for what he taught but also because he founded a sect that takes pride in tracing its origin back to 'the founder'.

Saicho (767–822), who founded the Japanese Tendai sect tradition in 805 after studying it in China, exemplifies a tendency now common among Japanese Buddhists: to seek the absolute not beyond but within the present world. He gave currency to the phrase *sokushin jobutsu*, 'to become a living buddha'. This has come to mean that one need not await countless rebirths or undergo endless austerities in order to achieve buddhahood; one can become a living buddha in this lifetime. This teaching has had an immense influence on new Buddhist organizations in the modern period, particularly those that, with Tendai, attach special importance to the *Lotus Sutra* and its doctrine that all forms of existence, animate and inanimate, are filled with – and can realize – the Buddha nature.

Kukai (774–835), after studying Tantric Buddhism in China, founded the Japanese Shingon sect in 816. He taught that the entire universe is the body of the Supreme Buddha, Vairocana, and thus that absolute truth and this-worldly phenomena are essentially identical. Synthesizing Buddhist and non-Buddhist philosophies into ten stages of realization culminating in Tantrism, he further taught that meditation, ritual postures and mystical syllables are uniquely important as symbolic representations of, and channels for, the living substance of the cosmos. This teaching appears to underlie the widespread ritual practice of chanting the title of the *Lotus Sutra*.

Honen (1133–1212) and his disciple Shinran (1173–1262) lived at a time when the idea of the impending dissolution of the world was current. Like earlier itinerant holy men, they sought to make the way of enlightenment available to people of all classes and conditions. Both taught that the way of enlightenment most appropriate for 'this degenerate age' was not that of ascetic exercises but rather that of simple reliance on the power and compassion of Amitabha (Japanese: Amida) Buddha, who had vowed to help people and was sure to welcome them into his Pure Land. Honen, urging people to call on Amida and gain enlightenment, founded the Pure Land sect in 1175. Shinran, more radical, held that Amida had already fulfilled his vow and that people only needed to accept their enlightenment through faith. This made the celibate monastic life, till then deemed essential to salvation, logically unnecessary. Shinran therefore renounced it, married, and demonstrated that Amida's way applied unconditionally to laypeople in the secular world. His organization, the True Pure Land sect, dates from 1224.

The two main forms of Zen Buddhism, Rinzai and Soto, were introduced from China by the Japanese priests Eisai (1141–1215) and Dogen (1200–53). Eisai, favoured by the Kamakura shogunate, taught a way of enlightenment through enigmatic questions that threw the seeker into a quandary but could lead to a flash of liberating insight. His ties were mainly with the newly dominant samurai class. Dogen, less reliant on political patronage but more reliant on scriptural authority, taught that the way to enlightenment is through *shikan taza*, 'seated meditation alone'. His ties were mainly with the unlettered and often superstitious peasant class. The present influence of Zen is seen not only in chastely styled architecture and gardens that communicate a oneness with nature and ultimate reality, but also in cultural and martial arts groups where mastery of techniques goes hand in hand with spiritual training (rarely thought of as religious).

Nichiren (1222–82) is by far the most confrontational of Japanese religious leaders, and the sect tradition that bears his name has been the most prone to schism. Like many before him, including Saicho and Dogen, Nichiren treated the *Lotus Sutra* as the highest scriptural authority, but unlike his predecessors, he taught that it was imperative for the welfare of Japan that the government rid the nation of false ways (primarily the Shingon, Zen and Pure Land sects) and establish as the state religion the true Buddhism he proclaimed. This teaching, in subsequent variations, looms large in the development of several new religious organizations.

In the Shinto world Kanetomo Yoshida (1435–1511), founder of Yoshida Shinto, took as his point of departure a thirteenth-century school of thought called Ise Shinto. In contrast with Buddhist thinkers who had interpreted the Shinto *kami* as demigods in need of enlightenment or, later, as *avataras* (see p. 269) of specific buddhas and *bodhisattvas*, Ise Shinto had declared that the basic reality of the universe was a *kami* through whom the buddhas and *bodhisattvas* had their being. Yoshida, going a step further, sought to develop a Shinto free of Buddhist influences by emphasizing purity of heart as a mystical form of worship.

Japanese Neo-Confucianism began with Seika Fujiwara (1561-1619). Both he and his illustrious disciple Razan Hayashi (1583-1657), one of the most influential Confucian advisers to the first Tokugawa shogun, taught that the way of Confucius was virtuous in so far as it fitted into the way of the *kami*, the way of the emperor. They regarded Buddhism as inferior for teaching a universal law that concealed differential obligations according to social rank. As often noted, the traditional Confucian doctrines of abdication and justifiable rebellion could not be accommodated in Japan. Under Mitsukuni Tokugawa (1628-1700), founder of the Mito school, Neo-Confucian teachings were recast in such a way as to uphold the superiority of the emperor over *daimyo* and shogun, yet also in such a way as to soften the distinction between ruler and ruled by presenting the Emperor as a caring father.

Norinaga Motoori (1730-1801) was the founder of a movement to purify Shinto of all Buddhist and Confucian accretions. Atsutane Hirata (1776-1843) went even further, developing into an anti-foreign chauvinist as he promoted restoration of power to the imperial house. The influence of these and other leaders – Buddhist, Confucian and Shinto – who cannot all be dealt with here, lives on in modern Japan.

The Religious Population of Contemporary Japan

Some Statistics

The estimated population of Japan on 1 October 1978 was 115 million. Of this number, how many people belonged to religious organizations and, more broadly, how many regarded themselves as religious?

To answer the first question, data from the *Shukyo Nenkan* (Religions Yearbook) are usually employed. But immediately one confronts an anomaly. In 1978 the total number of adherents to the major classes of religious tradition was 201 million, a figure almost 75 per cent larger than the population (see figure 10.3 and table 10.1). This 'discrepancy' is generally accounted for by reference to two factors: dual or multiple affiliation; and inflated membership reports. Whatever the case, it is useless to compare these figures (population and adherents) in the expectation of determining what proportion of the population belongs to religious organizations and

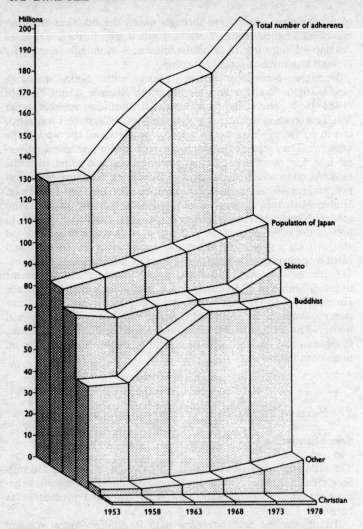

Figure 10.3 *Adherents to major classes of religious tradition in Japan between 1953 and 1978 (see also table 10.2)*

what proportion does not. One can, however, consider survey findings. One survey, published in 1979, asked people about their membership in organizations of various kinds. With regard to religious organizations, only 13.6 per cent said they were members [14: 133]. This percentage, applied to the 1978 population, suggests that only

15.6 million out of 115 million people counted themselves as adherents of religious organizations.

Living religion is by no means limited to members of religious organizations. Another survey, conducted in 1979, asked people if they professed any religious faith. Affirmative replies to this question amounted to 33.6 per cent [14: 133]. Most people replying in the affirmative went on to identify their faith as Buddhist (78.4 per cent). Only a handful (3.3 per cent) identified their faith as Shinto – almost certainly Sect Shinto rather than the district-organized Shrine Shinto in which the question of faith rarely occurs. But since most Japanese people of religious persuasion are both Shinto parishioners and Buddhist temple supporters, it is perhaps not unreasonable to suppose that about the same number of people can be found in both camps. If so, the religious population of present-day Japan can be reckoned at about one-third of the total population.

Contemporary Religious Practices

Before 1945 Japanese households traditionally had both a *kami* altar (*kami-dana*) and a buddha altar (*butsudan*). To a lesser extent, the same holds true today. Rural households, especially, often have several *kami* altars: one main altar and other minor altars. In a rough division of labour, the *kami* altar is generally associated with life and the avoidance of whatever impedes vitality and productivity, the buddha altar with death and the veneration of those who are becoming or who have become ancestors. On both, offerings of food and drink are reverently presented at the beginning of each day.

The Shinto and Buddhist practices of ordinary people may be grouped under two headings: the annual cycle and the life-cycle. (For a list of major festivals see table 10.3; for a picture of the pattern they form see figure 10.4.)

The New Year season involves a number of activities now largely associated with Shinto. Some of these activities are oriented to the household, some to the national community. At the end of a year, households throughout the land 'clean the slate' by giving the house, yard and adjacent road a thorough cleaning and by paying off all debts due. Entrances are decorated with evergreens and shafts of cut bamboo. (According to the widely accepted theory of Kunio Yanagita, New Year was originally a festival to welcome the ancestral spirits, apparently conceived of as diminutive, like songbirds or fireflies. He saw the bamboo shafts as their 'landing sites'.) For three days or so, people lay aside their daily work in order to be with their families, send out New Year's greetings, call on and give gifts to elderly relatives, teachers and others. They wear their best clothes and eat special foods. Today, any awareness of the

Table 10.3 Annual major festivals (see also figure 10.4)[a]

Date or period	Japanese name	English paraphrase
1–6 January	Shogatsu	New Year
3 February	Setsubun	Turn of the seasons
3 March	Hina Matsuri	Doll festival
21 March	Haru no Higan	Vernal equinox
8 April	Hana Matsuri	Flower festival; Buddha's birthday
April–May	Taue Matsuri	Rice-planting festivals[b]
15 June	Suijin Matsuri	Water *kami* festival
30 June	Oharai	Grand purification
13–16 July[c]	Bon	Feast of lights
15 August[c]	Tsukimi	Moon-viewing
August[c]	Kaza Matsuri	Wind festivals[b]
23 September	Aki no Higan	Autumnal equinox
October–November	Shukaku Matsuri	Harvest festivals[b]
1 December	Suijin Matsuri	Water *kami* festival
31 December	Oharai	Grand purification

[a]For explanations of these and other festivals, see Hori [18: 126–32]; for a remarkable essay on one local festival, see Yanagawa [38].
[b]Where the word 'festivals' occurs, festival observance dates vary with the locality.
[c]These dates and periods are those of the lunar calendar, presently about one month ahead of the solar calendar.

purported connection between New Year and the ancestors is dim, except that if a family loses one of its members, it will not celebrate the next New Year and sends postcards advising people not to send New Year's greetings to the house. Closer to the spirit of national community is the practice of visiting a big-name shrine or temple at New Year. According to police estimates, the number of people who went to such institutions rose from 25 million in 1965 to 60 million in 1976. In 1979 some 56 per cent of the total population made such visits.

The midsummer feast of lights or Bon festival is a community-wide activity in which, traditionally, individual households welcome their visiting ancestral spirits and entertain them communally. At this time the house is cleaned and decorated with fresh fruit and flowers. Meat foods are generally taboo. A small welcoming fire is built just outside the gate in order to guide the spirits. People dress up in light, summer-weight kimonos, and entire communities hold outdoor dances and displays of fireworks to celebrate the occasion.

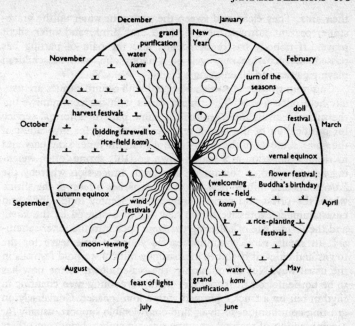

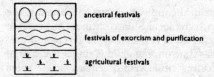

O O O O ancestral festivals

∿∿∿∿ festivals of exorcism and purification

⊥ ⊥ ⊥
⊥ ⊥ ⊥ agricultural festivals

Figure 10.4 *Annual pattern of major Japanese festivals (see also table 10.3)*

It closes with 'seeing-off' fires, in some areas prepared on hundreds of tiny floats set adrift on streams or lakes at nightfall – a spectacular sight. Most of today's urban residents or their recent forebears came from a rural area where the 'old homestead' is still located and where the ancestral tablets are kept. Millions of people, therefore, travel to the country for these family reunions and, a few days later, return to the cities. Officially, the Bon festival is not a national holiday. Some idea of its importance to ordinary people can be gained, however, from the realization that over half the industries in Japan give workers a few days off at this time.

The spring and autumn equinoxes are also times when the ancestors are honoured. Trips to the 'old homestead' are not necessary. Instead, a few relatives get together and visit the family grave in their area. They clean and sweep the site, pour water on the grave-stone, present flowers, incense, food and drink, and offer silent prayer. If nobody has died recently and the pain of parting has passed, the occasion may well be a happy one, with the children playing games and all enjoying a picnic.

Community-wide festivals associated with Shinto shrines are usu-ally held once a year. The timing varies with the community, but the major festivals follow much the same pattern: a formal service for purification of the parish representatives and for invocation of the *kami*; removal of the *kami*-symbol from the inner sanctuary and its ritual installation in a scaled-down portable shrine (often weigh-ing several tons); a solemn or boisterous procession whereby the *kami* tours and infuses new life into the parish; a feast at the shrine where the priest and parish representatives enjoy food, drink and entertainment expressive of the new vigour bestowed by the *kami*; and the formal rite of ushering the *kami* back into the inner sanctu-ary. In small, rural communities, as young people leave for the towns and cities, it becomes increasingly difficult to hold festivals in the usual way. Not uncommonly, the scaled-down shrine now has to be borne not on the shoulders of stalwart young men chanting in rhythm but on a truck equipped with a loudspeaker. Conversely, in growing communities festivals find considerable support, usually for a combination of reasons, at some times mainly religious, at others mainly secular.

The life-cycle has its focus in the individual, but its context is the family. *Birth* is associated with the local Shinto shrine. On or about the thirtieth day after birth, the child is taken to the shrine and pre-sented to the *kami*. From that time on, the child is under the care of the divinity. This point receives ritual reinforcement a few years later when girls of three and seven years of age, and boys of five, are dressed up and taken to the shrine in mid-November.

Marriage did not become a religious ceremony until the twentieth century. Since 1901, when the first Shinto wedding was performed, Shinto rites have gradually become the accepted way of uniting households through matrimony, though Christian rites (not necessarily requiring faith) are becoming increasingly popular.

Death is by far the most complex rite of passage. Buddhism is the main religious tradition involved, but the legal abolition of the extended family and its replacement by the nuclear family is leading to a different way of identifying the ancestors. Until 1945 the ances-tors in the paternal line were the principal objects of veneration. Women who married out of the family had their names struck out of the family record, and affines were treated, in death, more as guests than as family members. Since 1945, however, many people, especially those in their thirties and forties, are coming to venerate both the paternal and maternal lines. As before, the process of becoming an ancestor calls for thirty-three to fifty years of ritual observances, some at the Buddhist temple, others before the buddha altar in the home.

Post-1945 Developments

In 1945, as a direct result of defeat in war, religious freedom supported by government neutrality *vis-à-vis* religion became a reality for the first time in Japanese history. In this new situation hundreds of new religious organizations sprang up. Most proved ephemeral, some downright fraudulent. Most of the sizeable groups trace their origin to the years between the First and Second World Wars, but it was after 1945 that they grew by leaps and bounds (see figures 10.5 and 10.6). This growth provided part of the stimulus for internal reform movements among several older bodies.

With regard to the surviving new religious organizations, some of which are listed in table 10.2, those mentioned may be considered representative of many [18: 89–104]. The most conspicuous organizations, like Honmon Butsuryushu before them, are associations of lay Buddhists who give pride of place to the *Lotus Sutra* and seek to reform Japanese society. Two streams may be distinguished. The first is Soka Gakkai. Largest of all, it is theoretically under the Nichiren Shoshu, a monastic organization that claims exclusive legitimacy as heir to the teachings of Nichiren. One of the fundamental goals of the Nichiren Shoshu is to see the emperor and the government converted to the form of Buddhism it proclaims as exclusively true. Religious freedom and government neutrality towards religion have no place in its world-view. But its independently formed lay association, Soka Gakkai, has come out in favour of religious freedom and separation of state and religion. The short history of the relationship between Soka Gakkai and the Nichiren Shoshu, not to mention the latter's other lay associations, has been one of tension and near-schism. Through its network of neighbourhood groups, however, Soka Gakkai has brought help to millions of people more concerned about personal problems than about abstract questions of principle and authority.

The second stream runs through the tradition connecting Reiyukai and one of its many offshoots, Rissho Koseikai. The importance of memorial rites for ancestors and faith in the *Lotus Sutra* are the two main tenets of Reiyukai. Particularly notable in this group is its practice of having members venerate ancestors in both the paternal and maternal lines. Some scholars derive this practice from the circumstance that in its early days Reiyukai drew

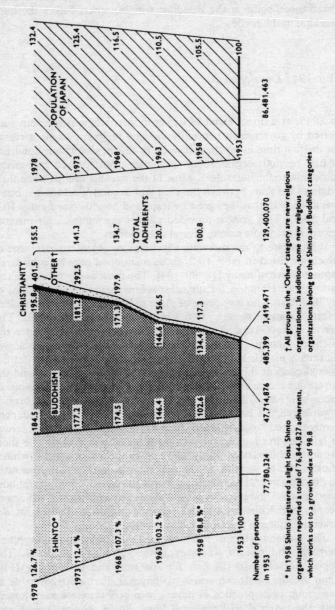

Figure 10.5 Growth indices for major classes of religious tradition in Japan between 1953 and 1978

POPULATION OF JAPAN

1978 — 132.4
1973 — 125.4
1968 — 116.5
1963 — 110.5
1958 — 105.5
1953 — 100

86,481,463

TOTAL ADHERENTS

155.5
141.3
134.7
120.7
100.8

129,400,070

CHRISTIANITY   OTHER†

1978 — 195.8 401.5
1973 — 181.2 292.5
1968 — 171.3 197.9
1963 — 146.6 156.5
1958 — 134.4 117.3

485,399   3,419,471

† All groups in the 'Other' category are new religious
organizations. In addition, some new religious
organizations belong to the Shinto and Buddhist categories

BUDDHISM

184.5
177.2
174.5
146.4
102.8

47,714,876

SHINTO*

1978 — 126.7 %
1973 — 112.4 %
1968 — 107.3 %
1963 — 103.2 %
1958 — 98.8 %**
1953 — 100

77,780,324

Number of persons in 1953

* In 1958 Shinto registered a slight loss. Shinto
organizations reported a total of 76,844,827 adherents,
which works out to a growth index of 98.8

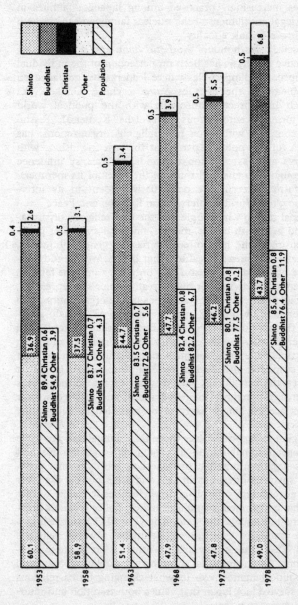

Figure 10.6 Percentages of adherents to Japanese traditions between 1953 and 1978. For each year shown, the upper bar represents the number of adherents claimed for the four classes of religious tradition (Shinto, Buddhist, Christian and Other), while the lower bar represents the size of the total population of Japan. If the upper bar is treated as 100 per cent, the numbers of adherents claimed for the four classes of religious tradition break down into the percentages shown. If, on the other hand, the lower bar is treated as 100 per cent, the percentages for the four classes of religious tradition become larger, as indicated.

its members from economically peripheral families in which both parents had to work for pay. At any rate it anticipated the bilateral memorial rites increasingly practised among Japanese families in general since legal entitlement of the nuclear family and the growth of the idea of male–female equality.

Rissho Koseikai also honours the *Lotus Sutra* and the ancestors, but its distinctive emphasis has been on perfection of the individual through group counselling circles where leaders give guidance on personal problems in the light of *Sutra* teaching. Unlike Soka Gakkai, which has direct connections with the political world through its formally autonomous party (the Komeito), Rissho Koseikai, in company with other new religious organizations, has chosen not to form a political party but to form friendships with political figures and, as occasion demands, to exercise influence indirectly through dialogue and through the votes of its members. Its social reform concerns are particularly evident in its inter-religious agency, the World Conference on Religion and Peace.

The principal reason why people join the new religious organizations is to find help with health, marital, financial and other problems. The nature of the help offered varies. In general, however, one can perceive a tendency to affirm that health, wealth and happiness can be obtained if a person will only have implicit faith in the leader, and in the divinity or divine reality he or she represents, participate wholeheartedly in the activities of the organization, and win other members by holding out the promise of the help available through this supportive fellowship. Because they often blended doctrinal interpretations with elements of folk religion and even magical practices, the new religious organizations were at first viewed with suspicion and disdain by educated people. In recent years, however, the new bodies have to some extent rid themselves of such features, rationalized their operations, and reached a stage where leaders are no longer likely to be regarded as near-divine wonder-workers.

Living religion in Japan involves more than annual and life-cycle rites of passage, internal reform in established organizations and new religious organizations that promise help with personal problems. It also involves questions of law and state power. For over 1,000 years, government officials and religious leaders alike took it for granted that government could legitimately police religious organizations in the interests of the state. The year 1945 brought imposition of the value of government neutrality towards religious organizations. This value is only half a century old in Japanese institutional history. Its meaning is a subject of public debate, legal action and political manoeuvre. In what changing forms religious freedom will survive in a Japan that values both tradition and internationalism remains to be seen.

Postscript: Developments since the Early 1980s

Scholars of Japanese religion and society would probably agree that
the decade ending in 1993 has seen four noteworthy developments.
One has to do with the character of the recent new religions; the
second with the schism between Soka Gakkai and its parent organization, the Nichiren Shoshu; the third with the rituals surrounding
the death of the Emperor Showa and the enthronement of Emperor
Akihito; and the fourth with the issues arising from the Aum
Shinrikyo case.

A New Type of New Religion

The recent new religions, regrettably tagged 'new new religions',
show certain traits of character that set them apart from the organizations generally spoken of as 'new religions'. The difference may
perhaps best be brought out by contrasting Rissho Koseikai with
Agonshu.

When it began in 1938, Rissho Koseikai, like many new religions,
had two founders: a woman and a man. In Rissho Koseikai the
woman was Myoko Naganuma (1889–1957), who had been a
Reiyukai medium and is often characterized as a shaman. The man
was Nikkyo Niwano (1906–), the organizer and systematizer. At this
early stage Rissho Koseikai included many magical features.
Criticisms in the newspapers, however, led it to divest itself of these
magical elements, particularly after Naganuma's death.

When the mantle of leadership fell to Niwano, Rissho Koseikai
assumed a different character. It now emphasized the rational,
objective articulation of *Lotus Sutra* doctrine, offered help to members through small group 'counselling' sessions in which people presented their problems and received guidance from the group leader
in light of the Buddhist law, and began to work for world peace in
concrete ways such as assisting refugees and initiating agricultural
projects. In a word, the development of Rissho Koseikai can be seen
as a trajectory that begins with socially disapproved shamanistic
spiritualism and moves towards socially respectable, anti-magical,
rationally oriented teaching and practice. Other new religions follow
different trajectories, but tend to end up in the same place.

Agonshu, which did not become a legally incorporated religious
organization until 1981, was founded by Seiyu Kiriyama (1921–)
and stands in the Tantric, or esoteric, Buddhist tradition. Together
with Aum Shinrikyo, GLA (God Light Association), the Mahikari
organizations, Kofuku no Kagaku and similar bodies, Agonshu has
a decidedly magical character. These groups hold in common the

idea that spirits (*kami*, the spirits of dead humans, animal spirits and the like) can possess living people and bring them good or evil fortune. Yet even though evil spirits cause the living to suffer business setbacks, family strife, painful illnesses, etc., all will be well if the sufferer simply follows the secret teaching of the sect, for this will cause the possessing spirit to depart. More particularly, the Agonshu Star Festival (*Hoshi matsuri*) held annually in Kyoto features the burning of two huge mounds of *gomagi*, wooden sticks that people purchase and inscribe with prayers and requests. One mound is for the ancestors, the other for the satisfaction of immediate needs. In the presence of half a million people Agonshu assistants, dressed as *yamabushi*, or mountain ascetics, burn the *gomagi* to the accompaniment of chanting, drumming and dramatic music. The implicit message is that this ritual, if carried out by Agonshu people according to Agonshu precepts, will assure ancestral spirits that they are not forgotten by the living, and will almost certainly result in the tangible benefits that people have requested. Such teaching, combined with high-tech media such as satellite technology, makes for an exotic mix that has proven attractive to many.

Some scholars claim that people used to join the new religions in order to receive help with tangible problems such as poverty and disease, but that the motivation for joining these more recent new religions is simply attraction to the occult. This view seems difficult to reconcile with the Star Festival ritual described above, but it may be that the ritual is more spectacle than petition. If so, Agonshu may well represent what these scholars say it is: a form of mysticism that draws people suffering from the straitjacket of economic rationalism by packaging the the occult–irrational in a composite of traditionalism, universalism and high-tech extravaganza.

It remains to be seen whether Agonshu and other more recent new religions, like Rissho Koseikai and others before them, will follow a trajectory that leads them to discard magical elements and accommodate their rituals and teachings to the anti-magical social standards held up as normative by most educated people in Japan today. For the time being, however, the rise of this type of new religion strikes many as a significant development [24: 224–6].

Schism

The conclusion was reached in the mid-1980s that 'the short history of the relationship between Soka Gakkai and the Nichiren Shoshu . . . has been one of tension and near-schism.' Today the schism has become a reality. Key differences between the monastic parent organization and Soka Gakkai may be posed in contrasting columns, as shown in table 10.4.

Table 10.4 Contrasting features of Nichiren Shoshu and Soka Gakkai

Nichiren Shoshu	Soka Gakkai
Adherents: 200,000	Adherents: 1,262,000
Maintains that the form of Buddhism it proclaims as exclusively true should be adopted by the emperor and the government	Recognizes religious freedom and separation of religion and state
Regards other forms of religion as evil teachings	Has abandoned the view that other religions are evil
Insists that *shakubuku*, or conversion through browbeating, is the best proselytization method	Has chosen to engage in dialogue with other religions

The occasion for the schism, however, was rather mundane: a tape-recording of a November 1990 speech to Soka Gakkai leaders by Daisaku Ikeda, honorary chairman of Soka Gakkai. In this speech he allegedly called in question the integrity of the head priest of Nichiren Shoshu. This tape came into the hands of Nichiren Shoshu leaders, who first demanded an explanation, but when they found the explanation unsatisfactory, revised Nichiren Shoshu rules in such a way as to relieve Ikeda and other Soka Gakkai leaders of their posts as heads of Nichiren Shoshu lay organizations. By November 1991 Nichiren Shoshu had ordered the dissolution of Soka Gakkai, and when this was rejected, it formally expelled Soka Gakkai and all its international affiliates.

Until its expulsion, Soka Gakkai depended on the Nichiren Shoshu for legitimate copies of the mandala kept at the Nichiren Shoshu head temple and distributed to members, for priestly ministrations at funerals and memorial rites, for a *kaimyo* (a posthumous name identifying the deceased as a disciple of the Buddha), and also for the *doshi honzon*, a special copy of the *gohonzon* used at funerals. Since the expulsion, Soka Gakkai has begun to revise its teachings and practices in such a way as to make this dependence unnecessary. In essence, the new teaching emphasizes the importance of faith in the *Lotus Sutra* rather than in a copy of the mandala, calls for lay funerals, and attacks the priests for inventing *kaimyo* and *doshi honzon* to augment their wealth and power.

This development is being carefully watched by scholars of Japanese religion. If, as is probable, the rupture cannot be healed, the parent organization will lose much of its lay support and perhaps become once again a small eddy in the massive stream of Japanese Buddhism. More important is the question whether Soka Gakkai can formulate the concepts and teachings it will need in order to legitimize its existence and become a fully autonomous lay Buddhist movement. If it does, it could become a powerful force for religious and social reform.

The Emperor is Dead, Long Live the Emperor!

Emperor Hirohito died on 7 January 1989. This brought the Showa period to an end, and it was formally decided that the emperor of that period should henceforth be known as the Showa emperor. Crown Prince Akihito succeeded him immediately, the Heisei period thus beginning on 8 January 1989. The formal Sokui-no-Rei enthronement ceremony and the subsequent Daijosai, or Great Food Offering, were not held, however, until November 1990.

For the most part, scholars of Japanese religion and society tend to consider the Showa emperor's funeral and the Heisei emperor's enthronement from one of two points of view. Some focus strictly on the complex of rituals themselves – a highly specialized study that few are competent to undertake. Others direct their attention to the question of religious freedom and constitutionality implied in state funding for these explicitly Shinto rituals. This question is an important dimension of the general theme of the interaction between religion and politics.

The Constitution of Japan promulgated in 1946 states that 'no public money or other property shall be expended . . . for the use, benefit or maintenance of any religious institution or association . . .' (Article 89). On the face of it, this article would appear to make it impossible for the government to spend money for Shinto, Buddhist or Christian rituals without violating the constitution. But with regard to the Showa emperor's funeral and its Shinto rituals, the government, faced with demands from one side that funds be provided so as to uphold tradition and with demands from the other that funds be withheld so as to uphold the constitution, decided on a compromise course. It tipped its hat to supporters of the constitution by dividing the funeral into two parts: a religious 'private' part, and a secular 'public' part, with a separate invitation for each. But it gave its substantive backing to the traditionalists by deciding that both parts would be paid for from public funds.

A similar strategy reappears in relation to government funding for the enthronement ceremony and the Daijosai ceremony that followed. The Daijosai is a rite in which the newly enthroned emperor assumes spiritual power by spending part of one night in a specially constructed Shinto shrine and by symbolically sharing new rice and new rice-wine with Shinto deities. (Some go so far as to say that he assumes divinity through this rite.) The government announced that the enthronement ceremony, or Sokui-no-Rei, would be a state affair, to be paid for with state funds. As for the Daijosai, the government announced that it would pay for the construction of the necessary shrine, but that funds for the rite itself would be allocated from the *kyutei*, or Imperial Court budget for Imperial Family affairs of a public nature. But since this budget comes from the government anyway, the question whether funds for the rite come from public funds is open to more than one interpretation.

Differing views as to what the government had done or should have done in view of the constitutional prohibition on the use of public funds for the benefit of any religious institution led to a flurry of court cases. As if to exemplify 'the law's delay', no final rulings have yet (March 1996) been handed down, but few expect rulings that will find the government guilty of violating the constitution.

Difference of opinion, however, does not always lead to litigation. Sometimes it leads to harassment, sometimes to violence. Probably few Christians in Japan think of themselves as 'leftists', but Japanese Christians who have opposed government funding for the Daijosai on the grounds that it violates the constitution are often lumped together with Communists and Socialists by the media and branded as liberals. This in turn makes them 'fair game' for rightist terrorism. The president of a Christian women's college, after issuing with three other Christian university presidents a statement to the effect that public money for the Great Food Offering violates the constitutionally mandated separation of religion and the state, found that gunshots had been fired through a window in his house, narrowly missing his wife. Again, the United Church of Christ in Japan (Kyodan), specifically its Information Center on Imperial Succession, has received a number of harassing telephone calls with messages such as 'Get out of the country' and 'Japanese are not supposed to criticize the Emperor's enthronement ceremony and Great Food Offering ceremony'. Such behaviour is typical of the intolerance of loyal opposition that threatens religious freedom in Japan.

Not surprisingly, many who feel threatened by such opposition see the source of the problem in the constitution. Maintaining that the present constitution was forced on Japan by the Occupation, they have formed a National Congress for Enacting an Autonomous Constitution. Opposition groups maintain, conversely, that the present constitution must be protected. This is a controversial area that will no doubt consume Japanese energies for years to come.

Behind this division of opinion regarding the Constitution lies a more fundamental problem, namely whether Shinto is a religion, and if so, in what sense and to what extent. Those who wish to protect the present constitution hold, by and large, that Shinto is a religion and that when the government provides funds for Shinto rites, it undermines its own legitimacy. Among those who call for revision of the present constitution, conversely, many maintain explicitly that Shinto is not a religion but a way of life, the implication being that the government should therefore be legally free to dispense funds to maintain what is traditional and customary in Japan. This deep-seated division is reflected in surveys which show that only a fraction of the Japanese people identify their religion as Shinto, even though, from a point of view common in the Shinto world, all Japanese citizens should 'naturally' be supporters of their local shrine and participants in its festivals. Vested interests being what they are, it is questionable whether a generally persuasive resolution to this question will ever appear. If not, the chances are strong that future court rulings on religious freedom will tend to interpret it in ways that depart from the literal meaning of the constitution and strengthen the dominant view that Shinto is not so much a religion as a matter of custom and tradition [29: 33–58].

This is not to say, however, that a return to the wartime policy of defining Shinto as a non-religion is just around the corner. Shinto itself has no principled basis on which to resist such a return, but the Japanese people as a whole are extremely sensitive about their reputation in the world at large, especially the Western world. Internationalism, despite its threats to tradition, exerts a powerful attraction. With regard to the question of the religious status of Shinto and the related question of revising the constitution, it may be the lever of autonomously valued international reputation that will guide Japan not to a principled conclusion but to a negotiated accommodation.

Aum Shinrikyo Issues

Details of Aum Shinrikyo's criminal involvement in the sarin gas attack in the city of Matsumoto in June 1994, in the sarin gas attack on the Tokyo subway system in March 1995, and in the murders of several individuals have been widely reported in the news media and need not be repeated here. The news reports have occasioned a number of Aum Shinrikyo studies that consider the life of its founder, explain its teachings and ascetic practices, and indicate points of friction with the larger society. Acquaintance with these matters will be taken for granted. The focus here will be on issues that have recently become important among the Japanese people because of the Aum Shinrikyo case. These issues may be identified as follows: moral education for young people; revision of the Religious Corporation Law; and the question of invoking the Antisubversive Activities Law.

Particularly shocking to the Japanese public was the realization that the upper echelons of Aum Shinrikyo leaders were peopled by brilliant graduates of the most elite universities in Japan. But the fact that graduates of leading universities could have lent themselves to such immoral and anti-social actions has cast a pall over people's hopes for the future of Japanese society. Calls for educational reform are already being heard, since educational institutions are widely regarded as training grounds not only for mind and body but also for moral character. If these calls issue in concrete guidelines for the reform of moral education, it is probable that such guidelines will be framed and issued to the schools by the Ministry of Education. This is something to watch for.

Aum Shinrikyo applied for religious corporation status in 1989, three years after its founding as Aum Shinsen no Kai and two years after its founder, Asahara Shoko (1955–), gave it its present name. It became an independent religious corporation under the jurisdiction of the Tokyo metropolitan government, maintaining a head office in Tokyo, but with branch offices in major cities throughout Japan. It also maintained a general headquarters and training centre in Shizuoka prefecture and a complex of buildings on land in neighbouring Yamanashi prefecture. Because it was under the jurisdiction of the Tokyo metropolitan government rather than the Ministry of Education, the police found themselves at a disadvantage when they wanted to search Aum Shinrikyo premises, for the metropolitan government could give orders only to Tokyo police. If searches were required outside Tokyo, local authorities had to make the arrangements. Central coordination was next to impossible.

Revisions to the Religious Corporation Law enacted by the Diet in December 1995 addressed this problem. Key points include the following: (1) all religious corporations that operate in more than one prefecture now come under the jurisdiction of the Ministry of Education rather than the governor of the prefecture where the group first registered; (2) all religious corporations have to submit lists of their senior officials and financial assets to competent authorities every fiscal year; (3) members of the group and other interested parties may inspect the documents submitted to the authorities; and (4) in cases where suspicions lead to calls for a group's dissolution, authorities now have the right to demand reports and question corporation officers after receiving permission from a Ministry of Education panel. In December 1995, under the provisions of the Religious Corporation Law, the Tokyo High Court ordered Aum Shinrikyo to disband.

Fear of religious terrorism is so strong, however, that many people are pressing for even stronger action: invocation of the Antisubversive Activities Law. This law, if invoked, would ban Aum Shinrikyo from conducting any activities as an organization and would prohibit adherents from all 'acts for the group'.

Opponents of this action argue that application of the Antisubversive Activities Law to an organization, for which there is no precedent, would allow police to interfere in the lives of citizens as they did for years under the notorious wartime Peace Preservation Law and the Religious Organizations Law.

The Public Security Investigation Agency is currently holding hearings as to whether the Antisubversive Activities Law should be invoked. But so far there has been little public discussion of how the government can at once protect public security when it is threatened by religious terrorism and still be neutral in respect of religion as required by the constitution. Without such discussion, there is a strong likelihood that the government may revert to the centuries-old tradition that religion is to be regulated in the interest of the state – a dismal prospect for democracy and religious freedom in Japan.

In 1984 this analysis concluded with the words: 'in what changing forms religious freedom will survive in a Japan that values both tradition and internationalism remains to be seen.' These words seem, if anything, even more appropriate today.

Note

1 Capital letters have been employed for *the* Buddha (and its derivatives, Buddhism, Buddhist etc.), lower-case for all others (a 'living buddha', 'buddha altar' (the altar for the household dead) etc.) who become buddhas, whether through enlightenment or through death (death-related attribution of buddhahood is unique to Japan).

Appendix: Sources for Study

The brief list of primary sources that follows is limited to texts of Japanese provenance. Omitted, therefore, are the pre-Japanese *sutras* on which Japanese Buddhist schools rely. For the convenience of the reader, works available in English translation predominate, but it should be remembered that such works constitute only a fraction of the whole. For more complete bibliographical information on Western-language works, see: J. M. Kitagawa, 'The Religions of Japan', in C. J. Adams (ed.), *A Reader's Guide to the Great Religions* (New York, Free Press/London, Collier-Macmillan, 1965), pp. 161–90; J. Swyngedouw, 'A Brief Guide to English-language

Materials on Japan's Religions', *Contemporary Religions in Japan*, vol. 11, nos 1–2, 1970, pp. 80–97; H. B. Earhart, *The New Religions of Japan: A Bibliography of Western-Language Materials*, 2nd edn, Ann Arbor, Center for Japanese Studies, University of Michigan, 1981.

Early period (prior to 1185)

To begin with materials generally associated with Shinto, the *Kojiki*, drawing on traditions that antedate its completion in 712, is the earliest cultural source-book. See the D. L. Philippi translation (University of Tokyo Press, 1968). A close second is the *Nihongi* (720), still available in the 1896 translation of W. G. Aston (London, Allen & Unwin, 1956). About one-fourth of an anthology of some 4,000 poems reflecting life in seventh- and eighth-century Japan may be found in *The Manyōshū* (New York, Columbia University Press, 1965). The *Izumo Fudoki*, translated by M. Y. Aoki (Tokyo, Sophia University, 1971), is an eighth-century compilation of factual and etymological information that includes a unique collection of myths. Of the fifty books specifying administrative regulations of the tenth century, the first ten, covering festivals, deities, rituals etc., are now accessible in the *Engi-Shiki*, 2 vols, translated by F. G. Bock (Tokyo, Sophia University, 1970, 1972).

Buddhist and Confucian influences converge in Prince Shōtoku's 'Seventeen-Article Constitution' of 604, translated in R. Tsunoda et al., *Sources of the Japanese Tradition* (New York, Columbia University Press, 1958). Excerpts from the works of Saichō may be found in the same source. Some works of his contemporary Kūkai appear in Y. S. Hakeda's *Kūkai* (New York, Columbia University Press, 1972). Another important Buddhist work of this period, often compared to the *Divine Comedy*, is Genshin's *Ōjōyōshū*, a partial translation of which was published by A. K. Reischauer in the *Transactions of the Asiatic Society of Japan* (2nd ser., vol. 7, 1930).

Medieval period (1185–1868)

Neither Hōnen's central work, the *Senjaku Hongan Nenbutsu Shū* (Collection of passages on the original vow of Amida), nor the main scriptures and commentaries of the Pure Land school are yet available in a commendable translation, but Shinran's *magnum opus*, the *Kyōgyōshinshō* (Teaching, practice, faith and attainment), appeared serially in annotated translation in the *Eastern Buddhist* (beginning with vol. 8, no. 3, November 1957). The chief scriptures of the True Pure Land school exist in a difficult translation by K. Yamamoto entitled *The Shinshu Seiten* (Honolulu, Honpa Hongwanji Mission of Hawaii, 1955). Important in this connection is the *Tannishō* (Notes lamenting differences), a good translation of

510 DAVID REID

which is that by R. Fujiwara (Kyoto, Ryukoku Translation Center,
Ryukoku University, 1962). For Zen Buddhism see Eisai's *Kōzen
Gokoku Ron* (Propagation of Zen for the protection of the country),
the preface to which is translated in *Sources of the Japanese Tradition*,
and Dōgen's *Shōbō Genzō: The Eye and Treasury of the True Law*, 3
vols, translated by K. Nishiyama and J. Stevens (Tokyo, Nakayama
Shobō, 1975, 1977, 1982). Nichiren's noted *Risshō Ankoku Ron*
(Treatise on the establishment of the orthodox teaching and the
peace of the nation), together with other primary materials, appears
in L. R. Rodd, *Nichiren: Selected Writings* (Honolulu, University
Press of Hawaii, 1980). Also to be noted is the remarkable thirteenth-century work *Gukanshō* (Some modest views), a rare
Buddhist interpretation of Japanese history, now available in
English as *The Future and the Past: A Translation and Study of the
Gukanshō* by D. M. Brown and I. Ishida (Berkeley, CA, University
of California Press, 1979).

Shinto, overshadowed in religion by Buddhism and in philosophy
by Confucianism, sought to redress the balance from about the
fourteenth century. Here we find the purportedly archaic 'Five classics of Shinto' (*Shintō gobusho*) associated with Ise Shinto, but
unfortunately still untranslated, as are: (I) K. Yoshida's *Yuiitsu
Shintō Myōhō Yōshū* (Essentials of the eminent law of pure Shinto),
an early argument for Shinto primacy; (2) the *Dai Nihon Shi*
(History of Japan), a 397-volume work which, though not completed until 1906, was begun in 1657 and is said to have exercised
great influence on Shinto 'restorationist' thought and action; (3) the
highly regarded works of N. Motoori, a leading scholar of Japanese
classical literature and thought; and (4) the works of his chauvinistic
disciple A. Hirata.

The latter years of this period mark the beginning of several new
religious organizations. The primary sources for the study of such
groups, however, are treated below in connection with the modern
period.

Modern period (1868–)

A list of the scriptures of the new religious organizations (which is
not easy to come by) is presented here. It covers only the better-
known organizations and is adapted from N. Inoue et al.,
Shinshūkyō Kenkyū Chōsa Handobukku (Handbook for the study of
new religious organizations) (Tokyo, Yūzankaku Shuppan, 1981,
pp. 220–43): (1) Ananaikyō: *Reikai de Mita Uchū* (The cosmos seen
in the spirit world); (2) Iesu no Mitama Kyūkai Kyōdan: *Seisho*
(The Bible); (3) Izumo Taishakyō: *Kyōshi Taiyō* (Essentials of the
teaching), plus eleven other titles; (4) Ennōkyō: *Ennōkyō Kyōten*
(Ennōkyō scriptures), plus three other titles; (5) Ōmoto: *Reikai
Monogatari* (Tales of the spirit world), eighty-one vols, plus one

other title; (6) Ontakekyō: *Ontakekyō Nagomi no Oshie* (The Ontakekyō 7–5–3 doctrine); (7) Kyūsei Shukyō: *Mioshie* (The eminent teaching); (8) Kurozumikyō: *Kyōso no Mikunsei* (Admonitions of the founder); (9) Gedatsukai: *Hannyashin-gyō* (Essence of wisdom *sutra*); (10) Kōdō Kyōdan: *Hoke Sanbukyō* (*Lotus Sutra* trilogy); (11) Konkōkyō: *Konkōkyō Kyōten* (Konkōkyō scriptures), plus two other titles; (12) GLA (God-Light Association) Sōgō Honbu: *Shinkō Kiganbun* (Prayerbook of spirit and action); (13) Shinshūkyō: *Uchū no Seishin* (Spirit of the universe), plus four other titles; (14) Shinnyoen: *Ichinyo no Michi* (The way of indivisible reality); (15) Shinrikyō: *Kyōso no Dōtō* (The lineage of the founder's path); (16) Shinreikyō: *Akeyuku Sekai* (The dawning world); (17) Seichō no Ie: *Seimei no Jissō* (The reality of life), forty vols, plus four other titles; (18) Sekai Kyūseikyō: *Tengoku no Ishizue* (The cornerstone of heaven), plus eight other titles; (19) Sekai Mahikari Bunmei Kyōdan: *Miseigenshū* (Sacred utterances), plus one other title; (20) Zenrinkai: *Seikyō* (Sacred scripture) plus one other title; (21) Sōka Gakkai: *Nichiren Daishōnin Gosho* (Writings of the great Nichiren), plus one other title; (22) Daijōkyō: *Hokekyō* (*Lotus Sutra*); (23) Tenshō Kōtai Jingūkyō: *Seisho* (Words of life); (24) Tenrikyō: *Ofudesaki* (Tip of the divine writing brush), plus three other titles; (25) Nakayama Shingo Shōshū: *Gozabun* (Writings from the dais); (26) Nyoraikyō: *Okyōsama* (Sacred scriptures); (27) Nenpō Shinkyō: *Nenpō Hōgoshū* (Nenpō teachings), plus one other title; (28) PL (Perfect Liberty) Kyōdan: *P L Kyōten* (P L scriptures), plus one other title; (29) Bussho Gonenkai Kyōdan; *Kunyaku Hokekyō Heikaishi* (*Lotus Sutra* in Japanese translation with commentary); (30) Bentenshū Myō'ōji: *Shūso Sonjo Okotoba Shūsei* (Collected sayings of the foundress); (31) Honmichi: *Ofudesaki* (Tip of the divine writing brush), plus three other titles; (32) Honmon Butsuryūshū: *Hokekyō* (*Lotus Sutra*); (33) Maruyamakyō: *Oshirabe* (The quest); (34) Misogikyō: *Yuiitsu Mondōsho* (The pure catechism); (35) Myōchikai Kyōdan: *Asayu no Otsutome* (Daily tasks), plus one other title; (36) Myōdōkai Kyōdan: *Myōhō Rengekyō* (The lotus of the wonderful law), plus one other title; (37) Risshō Kōseikai: *Hoke Sanbukyō* (*Lotus Sutra* trilogy), plus one other title; (38) Reiyūkai: *Namu Myōhō Rengekyō* (*Lotus Sutra*), plus one other title.

Some of these works are doubtless available in English. Those interested may consult the organizational headquarters of the relevant group, the addresses for nearly all of which are given in Hori [18: 170–232].

Bibliography

1 ABE, Y., 'Religious Freedom under the Meiji Constitution', *Contemporary Religions in Japan*, vol. 9, no. 4, 1968, pp. 268–338 (and serially in the next five issues of this journal)

2 ANDREWS, A. A., *The Teachings Essential for Rebirth: A Study of Genshin's Ōjōyōshū*, Tokyo, Sophia University, 1973

3 ANESAKI, M., *History of Japanese Religion*, Rutland, Vt, Tuttle, 1963; first publ. London, Kegan Paul, 1930

4 BELLAH, R. N., *Tokugawa Religion: The Values of Pre-Industrial Japan*, Glencoe, IL, Free Press, 1957

5 BERTHIER-CAILLET, L., *Fêtes et rites des quatre saisons au Japon*, Paris, Publications Orientalistes de France, 1981

6 BLACKER, C., *The Catalpa Bow: A Study of Shamanistic Practices in Japan*, London, Allen & Unwin/Totowa, NJ, Rowman, 1975

7 CALDAROLA, C., *Christianity: The Japanese Way*, Leiden, Brill, 1979

8 COLLCUTT, M., *Five Mountains: The Rinzai Zen Monastic Institution in Medieval Japan*, Cambridge, MA, Council on East Asian Studies, Harvard University, 1981

9 CREEMERS, W. H. M., *Shrine Shinto after World War II*, Leiden, Brill, 1968

10 DAVIS, W. B., *Dojo: Magic and Exorcism in Modern Japan*, Stanford, CA, Stanford University Press, 1980

11 DRUMMOND, R. H., *A History of Christianity in Japan*, Grand Rapids, MI, Eerdmans, 1971

12 EARHART, H. B., *Japanese Religion: Unity and Diversity*, 3rd edn, Belmont, CA, Wadsworth, 1982

13 ELIOT, SIR CHARLES, *Japanese Buddhism*, London, Routledge/New York, Barnes & Noble, 1959; first publ. London, Arnold, 1935

14 FUJII, M., 'Gendaijin no Shūkyō Kōdō' (The Religious Behaviour of Contemporary Japanese People), *Jurisuto*, no. 21, 1981, pp. 132–8

15 HIRAI, N., 'Shinto', *Encyclopaedia Britannica*, 15th edn, *Macropaedia*, vol. 16, Chicago, EB, copyr. 1974, 1982

16 HORI, I. I., *Folk Religion in Japan: Continuity and Change*, Chicago, IL, University of Chicago Press, 1968, 1974; University of Tokyo Press, 1968

17 HORI, I. I., 'Japanese Religion', *Encyclopaedia Britannica*, 15th edn, *Macropaedia*, vol. 10, Chicago, IL, EB, copyr. 1974, 1982

18 HORI, I., et al. (eds), *Japanese Religion*, Tokyo/Palo Alto, CA, Kodansha International, 1972

19 KITAGAWA, J. M., *Religion in Japanese History*, New York, Columbia University Press, 1966

20 LEBRA, T. S., *Japanese Patterns of Behavior*, Honolulu, University Press of Hawaii, 1976

21 MATSUMOTO, S., *Motoori Norinaga: 1730–1801*, Cambridge, MA, Harvard University Press, 1970

22 MORIOKA, K., *Religion in Changing Japanese Society*, University of Tokyo Press, 1975

23 MORIOKA, K., and NEWELL, W. H. (eds), *The Sociology of Japanese Religion*,

Leiden, Brill, 1968 (repr. from *Journal of Asian and African Studies*, vol. 3, nos 1–2, 1968)

24 MULLINS, M. R., SHIMAZONO, S., and SWANSON, P. L. (eds), *Religion and Society in Modern Japan: Selected Readings*, Berkeley, CA, Asian Humanities Press, 1993

25 MURAKAMI, S., *Japanese Religion in the Modern Century* (tr. H. B. Earhart), Tokyo, University of Tokyo Press, 1980

26 NAKAMURA, H., 'Japanese Philosophy', *Encyclopaedia Britannica*, 15th edn, *Macropaedia*, vol. 10, Chicago, IL, EB, copyr. 1974, 1982

27 NAKAMURA, H., *Ways of Thinking of Eastern Peoples: India, China, Tibet, Japan* (rev. English tr., ed. P. P. Wiener), Honolulu, East–West Center Press, 1964

28 NORBECK, E., *Religion and Society in Modern Japan: Continuity and Change*, Houston, TX, Tourmaline Press, 1970

29 REID, D., *New Wine: The Cultural Shaping of Japanese Christianity*, Berkeley, CA, Asian Humanities Press, 1991

30 ROTERMUND, H. O., *Die Yamabushi: Aspekte ihres Glaubens, Lebens und ihrer sozialen Funktion im japanischen Mittelalter*, Hamburg, Cram & De Gruyter, 1968

31 SMITH, R. J., *Ancestor Worship in Contemporary Japan*, Stanford, CA, Stanford University Press, 1974

32 SMITH, W. W., *Confucianism in Modern Japan: A Study of Conservatism in Japanese Intellectual History*, 2nd edn, Tokyo, Hokuseido Press, 1973

33 SPAE, J. J., *Itô Jinsai: A Philosopher, Educator and Sinologist of the Tokugawa Period*, New York, Paragon Book Reprint, 1967; first publ. Peiping, Catholic University of Peking, 1948

34 SUGIMOTO, M., and SWAIN, D. L., *Science and Culture in Traditional Japan: AD 600–1854*, Cambridge, MA, MIT, 1978

35 SWYNGEDOUW, J., 'Japanese Religiosity in an Age of Internationalization', *Japanese Journal of Religious Studies*, vol. 5, nos 2–3, 1978, pp. 87–106

36 TAKAKUSU, J., *The Essentials of Buddhist Philosophy* (ed. W. T. Chan and C. A. Moore), 2nd edn, Honolulu, University of Hawaii, 1949

37 TAMARU, N., and REID, D. (eds), *Religion in Japanese Culture: Living Traditions Meet a Changing World*, Tokyo/Palo Alto, Kodansha International, 1996

38 YANAGAWA, K., 'Theological and Scientific Thinking about Festivals', *Japanese Journal of Religious Studies*, vol. 1, no. 1, 1974, pp. 5–49

11

Native North American Religions

ARMIN W. GEERTZ

Introduction

When Europeans arrived on the American continent 500 years ago, they found people bearing the modern phase of what archaeologists have called the 'archaic culture'. This type of culture spread from the north to the south during the climatic changes that occurred around 8000 BCE. The strength of this particular type of culture lay in a total utilization of natural resources. Agriculture made its first real impact around the beginning of this era, but even then the variegated use of natural resources did not cease, and we still find hunting and foraging together with agriculture throughout the Americas.

Throughout this long history numerous languages and cultures arose. In North America alone 200 separate languages with countless dialects were being spoken shortly before the arrival of the Europeans. Approximately 2,000 separate languages were being spoken on the whole continent, roughly equivalent to one-third of the world's languages. The systematic study of the relationships between these languages is still in progress, but scholars have identified at least seventeen languages families as different from one another as Indo-European is from Sino-Tibetan. Furthermore, most of the 2,000 individual languages are still being spoken today.

The cultural variety of Native Americans is just as striking. Cultural diversity can even be found within common linguistic groups (such as the Athapaskans of the woodlands and the prairies). On the other hand, striking cultural similarities can be found between mutually incomprehensible linguistic groups (such as the Pueblo culture or the North-west culture). Religions have demonstrated a curious independence of their own, sometimes closely bound to localities, at other times sweeping across linguistic and cultural barriers. Examples of the latter are the newer religious movements such as the Ghost Dance among the Plains tribes and the more widespread Native American Church or the use of the sacred pipe or sweatbaths in ritual contexts. Even though religion, culture and language are intimately related to each other, various theories that attempt mechanically to equate religious types with cultural or ecological types have failed to explain the diversity.

Obviously, a chapter on the religions of Native North Americans can only be selective. In what follows, characterizations of selected groups in various regions are *not* meant to promote certain tribes as paradigmatic for whole regions, rather as characteristic for them. The map insets in the following pages can help give the reader a compact overview of the multiplicity of languages, cultures and religions of Native North Americans in relation to their geographical locations. The caption to each map inset contains information on examples of language families followed by examples of specific peoples. Information on the kind of technology used is followed by information on social and religious aspects of the area. I will in the following restrict this chapter to four areas: the North-west Coast, the Eastern Woodlands, the Plains and the South-west.

The Sources on Native North American Cultures and Religions

There is an enormous amount of literature on Native North America going back to the seventy-three volumes of the *Jesuit Relations*, produced in the seventeenth and eighteenth centuries. The best modern overview of the sources and literature is found in Åke Hultkrantz's book *The Study of American Indian Religions* [13] and in the recent multi-volume *Handbook of North American Indians* [34].

When the Smithsonian Institution was established in 1846, Henry R. Schoolcraft submitted his plan for the investigation of the American Indians in which all of the main concerns of later anthropology were already present, especially the importance of native folklore in its social function. During the latter half of the century, the museums became centres of anthropological activities by sponsoring fieldwork, research and publications, and thus took on the dual role of educating anthropologists as well as the public. Museums were key institutions of civil society, crucial to the production and legitimation of moral and cultural values. Today many of these same museums are struggling with difficult ethical and political issues concerning the repatriation of Native American material culture and burial remains.

All of the concerns developed during the nineteenth century were synthesized, intensified and made more scientific through the efforts of the Bureau of American Ethnology under the leadership of the great pioneer John Wesley Powell (1834–1902), but it was the World Columbian Exposition and associated Congresses in 1893 which had the greatest influence on American anthropology. A special building was built for the ethnological exhibits and named the 'Anthropological Building'. Since that time, the word anthropology came to be used as the label for the entire study of humankind. The exhibits were grouped according to Powell's linguistic classification to show the genetic relationships among the tribes. At the same time the arts and crafts were grouped together by natural region to demonstrate the effects of natural resources on manufacture and to show the 'culture areas' of the tribal groups. The theory of culture areas stemmed directly from this arrangement of museum exhibits.

By 1900 American anthropology had become an academic discipline. Franz Boas (1858–1942) introduced to anthropology rigorous standards of proof and a critical scepticism towards all generalization. He preached the radical German empiricism of his early training and disdained the use of theory, being content to collect 'objective' data. He substituted the historical method for the discredited comparative method of evolutionists. Boasian anthropologists have since been criticized for mostly eliciting idealized memories of what indigenous cultures had been like a generation or more before the time of fieldwork. By the end of the 1920s every major university department of anthropology was chaired by Boas' students.

New developments in American anthropology during the 1930s and 1940s laid emphasis on the individual in relationship to his or her culture in terms of gestalt psychology, psychoanalytical conceptions and learning theory. This period also saw an increase in the biographical approach which has produced many fine studies and autobiographies of memorable Native American personalities, such as the Hopi Don Talayesva [31], the Winnebago Sam Blowsnake [28] and the Yahi Ishi [18].

The period 1930–60 witnessed the rise of social anthropology and the decline of ethnology in Britain and the US. The Second World War caused new orientations everywhere, and in the postwar US a synthesis of social and cultural anthropology developed with new relationships between the social sciences and history. Since the 1960s many superb ethnographies have been written about Native North American religions. Linguistic studies and collections of religious and mythical texts have also seen a renaissance, such as the excellent work of Ekkehart Malotki on the Hopi [21], Dennis Tedlock on the Zuni [36] and Donald Bahr on the Pima and Papago [1]. It should also be noted that important contributions to the study of Native North America have been made by distinguished European ethnographers such as Werner Müller [22], Wolfgang Lindig [19] and Horst Hartmann [8]. Now taking over their mantle are younger scholars such as Christian F. Feest [4; 5], who is the founding editor of the *European Review of Native American Studies*, published in Vienna.

From 1960 on there developed a sharpened awareness of the role that theory plays in scientific work, as a result of strong influences from French and German philosophy. One of these is the structuralist method introduced by the French anthropologist Claude Lévi-Strauss. Taking his point of departure in linguistic theory, Lévi-Strauss became one of the most significant interpreters of the mass of ethnographic material left by Boas and his students. His method of analysing Native American myths has demonstrated the startling complexity of indigenous classification systems, and his classic four-volume work entitled *Mythologique* (*Introduction to a Science of Mythology* in English), published between 1964 and 1971, has become a classic in his own lifetime.

The most renowned historian of religions in the study of Native North Americans is the Swedish scholar Åke Hultkrantz. Hultkrantz placed emphasis on beliefs, the ideology of rites and the function of religion [9; 10; 12]. The emphasis on beliefs and conceptions was formulated in order to counterbalance American behavioural studies.

Hultkrantz has influenced several generations of scholars in the US as well as in Europe; his American students include Joseph Epes Brown, Daniel Merkur, Guy H. Cooper, Thomas McElwain and Paul B. Steinmetz. Other historians of religions have been developing parallel or alternative strategies in the study of Native North Americans. Karl W. Luckert established the excellent bilingual text series called *American Tribal Religions*. Sam Gill, Christopher Vecsey and Jordan Paper have dealt with comparative issues, and I have dealt with theoretical problems in the study of Native American religions [20; 7; 25; 6].

In order to overcome insider/outsider problems, Boas encouraged educated natives to write down spontaneously in the vernacular what they knew or what they could gather from their elders. The results were many excellent bilingual collections [e.g. 14; 15; 16]. More recent scholars in linguistics have found that encouraging trained native speakers to analyse their own languages can bring rewarding results. In the field of social and cultural anthropology, there are a number of outstanding cultural informants and editors, and many Native American scholars such as the renowned Edward P. Dozier, Alfonso Ortiz and Emory Sekaquaptewa have served as mentors for generations of graduate students, both native and non-native [see e.g. 3; 24].

518 Armin W. Geertz

Relations between Native Americans and outside scholars have not always been cordial, but the era of conventional researcher–informant relations has now ended. Not only are many native peoples tired of intruders, anthropologists especially, they have also become aware of the political and ethical impact they have on the American public. Many have university educations and are trying to help their people accommodate themselves to American society. Consequently, educated native people are demanding equal status in academic publications, and an ever-increasing number of peoples and tribes, such as the Pueblos, are claiming the exclusive right to represent their own cultures and aggressively pursue non-natives who write about them. The 'living laboratories' of early anthropology that spawned scholarly monographs, encouraged tourism and inspired popular culture have now become angry Native American writers. Recent examples are the outrage of the Hopis at the publication of the sensationalizing *Book of the Hopi* by Frank Waters during the 1960s, the official banishment of Judith Fein by the Eight Northern Pueblos for her popularizing *Indian Time* (1993) and the heated attack on the highly acclaimed scholarly monograph *When Jesus Came, the Corn Mothers Went Away* by Ramón A. Gutiérrez (1991). Publications on Native American cultures are no longer just interesting additions to contemporary literature; such work has become the focus of ethical and political issues.

North-west Coast Cultures

The North-west Coast cultures extend more than 1,500 miles from Alaska to California [35; 38]. The peoples of the North-west Coast have developed a distinctive material culture which justifies a common classification. Its primary characteristic is a highly developed

Figure 11.1 (a) *Back and side of a Kwakiutl long-bench illustrating a man and a hawk. The man has animal ears and face-paint. The hawk's head is split into two parts on either side of the man and its wing is shown along the side to the left. (b) A Tsimshian hat used during ceremonial dances. The hat is made of wood and symbolizes the killer whale. (c) A Tshimshian drumskin on which is painted an eagle simultaneously viewed from the front and sides. It is surrounded by a human-like figure also simultaneously viewed from the front and sides.*
(d) A Tlingit club used for killing seals and halibut. The carving represents the killer whale, the dorsal fin being bent down along the side of the body to conform to the functional requirements of the instrument.

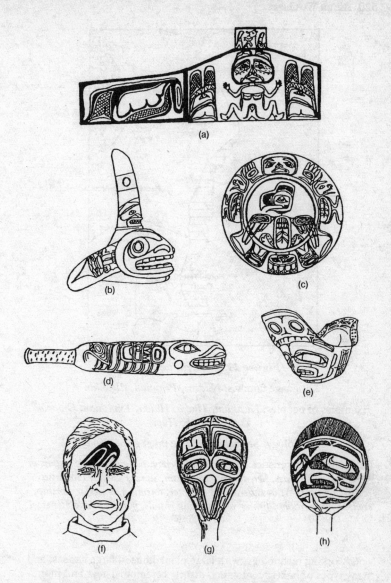

(e) Tlingit dish made of the horn of the bighorn sheep. The figure is that of a hawk. (f) Haida face-painting representing the beak of a hawk. (g) Horn spoon, tribe unknown, representing the raven. (h) Tlingit rattle with hawk head.

Source: *Collage drawn by Birgit Liin, based on Franz Boas,* Primitive Art, *Oslo, 1927, figs 167–9, 173, 211, 218, 241, 288d.*

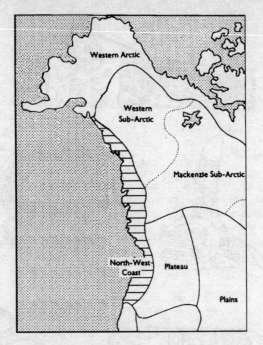

Figure 11.2 *North-west Coast*

Language families: *Nadene, Penutian, Algonkin*

Examples of peoples: *Kwakiutl, Tlingit, Haida, Tsimshian, Chinook, Yurok, Karok, Hupa*

Technology: *Sea fishing and hunting; game hunting*

Religious characteristics: *Hierarchical society, potlatch rituals as part of central ceremonies, hereditary shamanism, secret societies, Hamatsa ceremony to the Man Eater deity, trickster, totemism, ancestor worship, stylized iconography, fishing and hunting rituals, masks, World Renewal Ceremony*

woodworking technology, with large plank houses, large canoes, and many types of boxes, containers, dishes, ceremonial gear and monuments such as the well-known funerary poles.

The natives first met Europeans in the late eighteenth century, but it was not until the nineteenth century that colonization, missionization and governmental coercion began to have its long-term effects on Native North-west Coast cultures. The greatest tragedy of this period came with the epidemics by which 80 per cent of the population died from smallpox, measles and malaria, brought by the Europeans. Today an estimated 100,000 people live along the North-west Coast speaking over forty-five languages belonging to thirteen different language families. Most of the languages of the southern regions were extinct by the late twentieth century and a sizeable number in the north were on the verge of disappearing until programmes of language learning were established during the 1960s.

The North-west Coast peoples live in permanent villages organized socially in three major classes: the wealthy elite, the commoners and their slaves. Class was generally a matter of birth and wealth: even slaves had a hereditary status. Principles of descent, however, vary from region to region. The elite maintained their status by their wealth, especially through the well-known extravagant gift-giving rituals called 'potlatch', which were held during communal ceremonies. The potlatch phenomenon has been the object of much speculation among researchers who have proposed interpretations claiming that the excessive destruction and distribution of wealth reflects, on the one hand, the exorbitance of megalomania or, on the other hand, the benign distribution of wealth and goods.

Even though rituals and beliefs among the North-west Coast peoples vary greatly, there are themes common to most of the cultures. One of the basic ideas is that humans are situated in a complex web of relationships reaching into the animated world of the physical habitat, the animals, the spirits and the dead. Life and death are in constant flux, and survival depends on ritual and kinship relations with a variety of creatures. Like prey fed upon by humans, humans are also prey to a variety of man-eating birds, animals and monsters as well as other kinds of danger. Relationships to these beings are controlled through ritual, and protection against them can be obtained through a guardian spirit, the activities of a shaman, the concerted efforts of the head of the family or village, or the ceremonies of the secret brotherhoods.

Guardian spirits are gained through fasting and isolation, and communication with them is through trance, dreams and visions. They can also possess their human partners. High-ranking social positions usually mean that the family has a special permanent relationship with a superhuman entity. Thus iconographic crests served not only as coats of arms but also as potent symbols of relationship to greater powers. Poles are raised in honour of the ancestors either in front of the family house (sometimes with the door of the house placed in the mouth or belly of one of the spirits in the family line) or as the central or corner post in the house itself, thus signifying the close relationship between pole and house, the ancestors and their living relatives. This relationship is a totemic one. The symbols also serve in ritual contexts as means of transformation. Like the flow of iconic imagery transforming the shape of one creature into another, humans could also flow into other forms. For instance, one of the crucial moments in the initiation of a new member of the Hamatsa brotherhood occurs when the initiate crawls through the mouth of the image of the Man-Eater deity. Masks play an important role in this respect, especially the so-called transformation masks. These masks are complex constructions that open up revealing not the wearer but another mask or another being inside the mask. In Kwakiutl mythology the gods use masks to transform themselves, and one myth relates that humanity came to earth as gods who took off their masks and became human.

The Kwakiutl have shamans who function just like other shamans around the world. Shamans are religious specialists who through ecstatic behaviour fly to various regions of the cosmos in order to heal the sick, divine the future and ensure the fertility of humans and animals alike. Kwakiutl shamans can be of either gender, and their helping spirits follow the family line. Shamans must follow stringent rules of behaviour and ritual, their families sometimes following them in this. Shamans wear transformation masks and costumes during their seances. With the help of their guardian spirits, they serve to heal the sick and restore souls by battling against witches and other beings who cause the illness. They also serve as intermediaries between humans and non-humans, prophesying coming events, controlling the weather, and affecting the outcome of war and the hunt. The art of transformation is their particular domain. Myths and tales are filled with descriptions of shamans and others taken prisoner by animal spirits who then become those animals and after suffering many adventures return to human society through a painful retransformation process.

Complex ceremonies are held during the winter where the origins of the clan or some other significant event are dramatically re-enacted. The Kwakiutl Cedar Bark Dance can serve as an example here. This festival is the more important of the two major ceremonial complexes still practised among the Kwakiutl. Basically, the dances are re-enactments of the primordial activities of the ancestors and demonstrations of their powers. The most important spirit performed in the dance is Baxbakwalanuxsiwe, Man-Eater Spirit. A public sign that the dance is soon to be held is the sudden disappearance of a novice dancer prior to the dance. The novice or initiate is thought to have been spirited away by the Man-Eater Spirit. In the old days, when the time was right, the inviters, dressed in full ceremonial attire, sailed by canoe to the village to be invited and called upon them from the boat as the chief gave a dramatic and poetic speech. After receiving a festive meal, they sailed back home and reported dramatically on their journey. Today, however, invitations are sent on printed cards bearing crest designs.

(a)

(b)

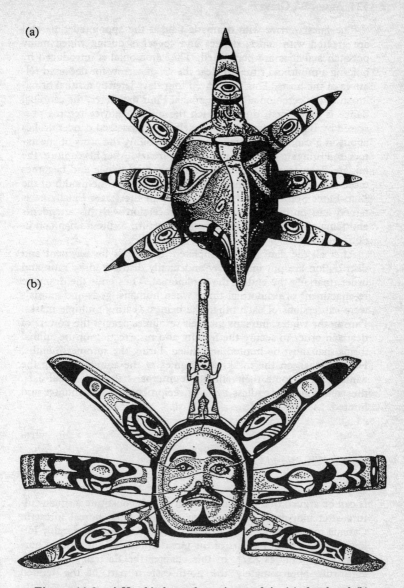

Figure 11.3 *A Kwakiutl transformation mask in (a) closed and (b) open positions. The figure in the closed position is the Thunderbird. The face in the opened position is probably the deity's human form.*
Source: *Drawing by Poul Nørbo, based on Deborah Waite, 'Kwakiutl Transformation Masks', in Douglas Fraser (ed.),* The Many Faces of Primitive Art, *Englewood Cliffs, 1966, fig. 7.*

The guests arrive with dramatic flair at the appointed time and are greeted with songs, dances and speeches during which many potlatch activities are performed. The ceremonial is introduced by holding a mourning ritual to clear the air of sorrow for deceased relatives of the hosts. This is followed four days later by a ritual bringing in of the ceremonial paraphernalia. Four days later, the cannibal dance is performed, during which the missing novice returns possessed by Baxbakwalanuxsiwe himself. The possessed dancer dashes about in a cannibalistic craze, apparently biting the arms of spectators and bringing everyone into intense frenzy. After his capture, the initiate then demonstrates his newly inherited dance and becomes more tame by, among other things, going through the mouth of the Man-Eater Spirit painted on the screen of the stage. Finally he is tamed and purified and returns in procession with his attendants and female relatives, thus signifying his return to the human condition.

After all the dances are completed, the goods for payment and distribution are put on display and finally distributed by rank and order, marking the end of the ceremonial. Thus ends the dramatic re-enactment of primordial times when humans, gods and animals were expressions of each other like beings wearing multiple masks. During the winter, humans pit their resources against the powers of death in order to secure the fertility and resurrection of the animal forms that must be hunted and killed during the summer months. Humans take on the masks and names of the animals during the winter and become their animal counterparts through ritual acts, thus renewing the endless cycle of reciprocity between hunter and hunted.

Eastern Woodland Cultures

It can be argued that the Eastern Woodlands constitute a single culture stretching from the southern margin of the boreal forest in Canada to the southern tip of Florida, and in the west roughly following the western borders of the Great Lakes and the eastern borders of the Prairies [37]. In this chapter the Eastern Woodlands constitute approximately the north-eastern part of the United States.

All of the tribes of the Eastern Woodlands depended on maize, hunting, fishing and foraging. The peoples around the northern regions of the Great Lakes, however, depended on gathering wild rice rather than maize horticulture. Women universally had the duty of horticulture and foraging while the men went hunting and fishing.

Figure 11.4   *Eastern Woodlands*

Language families: *Algonkin, Hokan-Siouan*

Examples of peoples: *Illinois, Miami, Penobscot, Iroquois, Shawnee, Delaware, Cherokee*

Technology: *Hunting, agriculture*

Religious characteristics: *Sun god, sacred fire ritual, sacred drink, New Year's ceremony, sacred kingship*

The Atlantic seaboard cultures tended to have a pattern of seasonal movement in exploiting the rich resources of the coastal and riverine areas.

The archaeological record seems to indicate that the region has a long history of dynamic change. Although Europeans were in contact with the tribes of the Eastern Woodlands since 1497, they had less impact culturally and demographically than the Spaniards had on the natives of the south-east until the seventeenth century. Recent scholarship has shown that the influence of Europeans penetrated the Eastern Woodland regions before they actually appeared, resulting in the establishment of large native political organizations

1 Sayewi talli wemiguma wokgetaki,

At first, in that place, at all times, above the earth,

 2 Hackung kwelik owanaku wak yutali Kitanitowitessop.

On the earth, [was] an extended fog, and there the great Manito was.

 3 Sayewis hallemiwis nolemiwi elemamik Kitanitowit-essop.

At first, forever, lost in space, everywhere, the great Manito was.

 4 Sohalawak kwelik hakik owak awasagamak.

He made the extended land and the sky

 5 Sohalawak gishuk nipahum alankwak.

He made the sun, the moon, the stars.

 6 Wemi-sohalawakyulikyuchaan.

He made them all to move evenly.

 7 Wich-owagan kshakan moshakwat kwelik kshipehelep.

Then the wind blew violently, and it cleared, and the water flowed off far and strong.

 8 Opeleken mani-menak delsin-epit.

And groups of islands grew newly, and there remained.

9 Lappinup Kitanitowit manito manitoak.

Anew spoke the great Manito, a manito to manitos,

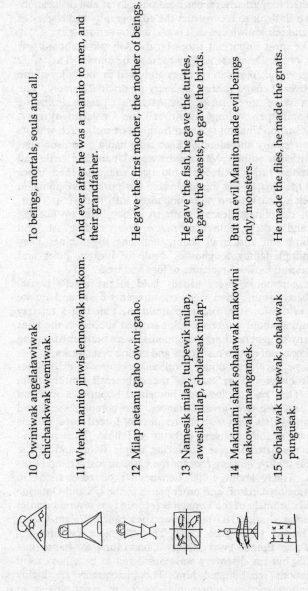

10 Owiniwak angelatawiwak chichankwak wemiwak.

To beings, mortals, souls and all,

11 Wtenk manito jinwis lennowak mukom.

And ever after he was a manito to men, and their grandfather.

12 Milap netami gaho owini gaho.

He gave the first mother, the mother of beings.

13 Namesik milap, tulpewik milap, awesik milap, cholensak milap.

He gave the fish, he gave the turtles, he gave the beasts, he gave the birds.

14 Makimani shak sohalawak makowini nakowak amangamek.

But an evil Manito made evil beings only, monsters.

15 Sohalawak uchewak, sohalawak pungusak.

He made the flies, he made the gnats.

Figure 11.5 *The first verses of the Walum Olum*

Source: *Daniel G. Brinton, The Lenâpé and their Legends, Philadelphia: D. G. Brinton, 1885.*

designed to protect territories and trade routes. However, the main experience of the peoples of the Eastern Woodlands, especially in the areas suited for agriculture, has been one of war and dislocation. This makes it difficult to reconstruct the ethnography and history of the region, and our knowledge of it is plagued by serious gaps.

One of the most important tribes on the Atlantic seaboard was the Lenape, or the Delaware as they came to be known. They were the largest group of Algonkin speakers and lived in the valley of the Delaware River. Lenape means 'ordinary or original person'. The Lenape consist of three tribes: the Munsee ('person from the island'), Unami ('person from downriver') and Unalachtigo (translation unknown) or Unalimi ('person from upstream'), each with its own dialect, territory and identity. Each tribe had a totemistic relation to a particular animal: Munsee the wolf, Unami the turtle and Unalachtigo the turkey. Chieftainship over the combined tribes belonged to the Unami, but this leadership was purely ceremonial in nature. Their social systems were organized into thirty-four clans, mainly with matrilineal descent patterns. They lived by hunting deer, bear and turkeys, cultivating maize, beans and squash, and fishing in both salt and fresh water, including shellfishing. They lived in multiple-family longhouses made of hickory poles and sheets of chestnut bark in stockades of logs and trees.

Religious ceremonies were usually held in the chief's house. During puberty, young men were encouraged to fast and isolate themselves in the forest in order to attain the vision of a tutelary spirit. Dreaming about a tutelary spirit secured success in the hunt and prosperity in general. Large ceremonies were performed during the year in connection with first fruits and curing ceremonies.

The Lenape have been under continual pressure: in early times from the Iroquois and as early as the eighteenth century from Europeans. They had to flee their homeland because of war and have been displaced over great distances. The complex social and cultural changes that went with the traumas of forced travel to new and unknown regions are very difficult to follow. Thus we find Lenapes in the eastern areas producing maple syrup and in the western areas trading ginseng root for the Chinese market and hunting buffalo. Today about 4,000 Lenape live on reservations in Oklahoma (mainly Unami) and other places in the US and Ontario.

The tribal chronicle of the Lenape is recorded on several bundles of sticks engraved with 183 red pictographs called Walam Olum, 'red paint record' (see figure 11.5). This chronicle was first discovered by the French-born scholar Constantine S. Rafinesque around 1825, but his discovery was considered to be a hoax until later generations rehabilitated him. The pictographs are highly stylized symbols used as mnemonic devices to assist singers in remembering the five-part epic on the creation of the world, the adventures of the tutelary deity Nanabush, 'The Great White One' (manifesting himself as a white hare) and the wanderings of the Lenape bands and tribe. The epic is thought to have originated from a Munsee chief who received it through divine revelation.

The Lenape had a priesthood with two branches. One was called Powwow, 'one who dreams'. Their job was to interpret people's dreams with the help of their own tutelaries. They could also foresee the future, discern the causes of accidents and illness, and discover the whereabouts of the game animals. The other was called Medeu, 'herbal doctor', who were both priests and medicinemen. There was probably a third group called Gitschi achkook, 'the great one-horned serpent', who were wandering exorcists and also performed burial ceremonies.

In the ethics, rituals and theology of the Lenape, humans have the job of humbly following the Weelipeleexing, 'the good (or beautiful) white path', established for humanity by the creator Kitanitowit. The most important way to do this in recent times was to perform the annual ceremony called Ngamwin, 'Big House Ceremony', which developed during the late nineteenth and early twentieth centuries out of the aboriginal harvest and first fruits ceremonies. One of the main rituals during the Ngamwin was the treading of the symbolic white path in the ritual house. The ceremony was held in connection with the harvest in a specially built longhouse. The twelve-day ceremony consisted mainly of songs reciting the puberty visions of the men. The last day was reserved for the recitals of the women and younger men. These recitations were accompanied by processions around the centrepost to the accompaniment of the drum. Every evening ended with a festive meal. Masked dances were also performed for the guardians of the game animals.

According to tradition, the Ngamwin was instituted after the Lenape were hit by an earthquake during which the earth opened and spewed black tar, smoke and steam from the underworld. Someone had a vision showing how Kitanitowit could be appeased by building the 'Big House' and performing the rituals of the Ngamwin. The Big House symbolized the universe in many ways. The earthen floor was the earth, the walls the four quarters, the ceiling the firmament, the space beyond the ceiling the twelve heavenly regions, the earth under the floor the Underworld, and the twelve carven masks on the walls and posts the spirits of the four quarters. The participants were the three divisions of mankind relating to the universe and its inhabitants and to the creator through the centrepole. This pole was believed to pierce the heavenly regions and serve as the creator's handrest. The pole was engraved with a human face said to be the image chipped into a mountainside by Kitanowit himself.

Figure 11.6 *The interior of the Lenape Big House: the central pole is believed to pierce the heavenly regions, serving as a handrest for the creator whose human visage is carved into the pole. The roof is open on the left.*
Source: *Drawing by Armin W. Geertz based on Frank G. Speck,* Concerning Iconology and the Masking Complex in Eastern North America, *Philadelphia, University of Pennsylvania, 1950, plate X.*

Every action performed in the House had cosmological significance, and when the assistant priest swept the paths between the two open fires, he symbolically swept the road to heaven. The main objective was to benefit the whole world. A central ritual was the New Fire ritual in which the new, purified fire was ignited in order to renew life and secure health, long life and the general welfare of the people. Lenape ethics holds nature to be clean and without blemish. That which is given by nature to humans, such as game animals, is pure, whereas human cultural products and domesticated animals are not. By attaining a vision during puberty, humans can return to a state of purity without blemish. Each year humanity returns to this state through the celebration of those visions during the Big House Ceremony and the lighting of the New Fire. In this manner the participants become transformed into spiritual heroes singing the praises of their tutelaries.

Plains Cultures

The Great Plains cover the vast region of unbroken grassland on an elevated steppe from northern Alberta and Saskatchewan to the Rio Grande [33: 337–83; 27]. The Plains and Prairies formed the ecological frameworks for two basic types of cultures, namely the nomadic and the sedentary tribes. These cultures are found in thirty ethnic groups speaking languages from several linguistic families not restricted to the Plains. The Plains cultures developed a unique sign language which served as a lingua franca for the entire area and

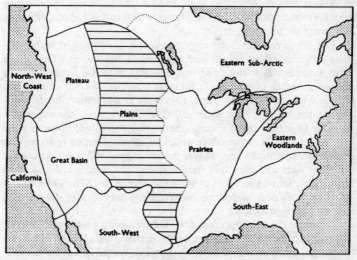

Figure 11.7 *Plains*

Language families: *Algonkin, Athapascan, Kiowa-Tanoan, Siouan*

Examples of peoples: *Blackfoot, Cheyenne, Crow, Arapaho, Teton, Pawnee*

Technology: *Big game (buffalo), use of horse*

Religious characteristics: *Buffalo altar, individual tutelary spirits, visions, medicine men, sacred bundles, sacred objects such as the arrow, pipe, spear and hat, Wakan Tanka, Sun Dance, Ghost Dance*

helped the thriving trade relations. There are today 225,000 Native Americans on the Plains.

Even though the bison is native to the Plains, and nomadic cultures have existed since the end of the Ice Age, the nomadic Plains cultures of the historic period which reached a high point by the 1850s had developed a specialized way of life centred on the bison and on a European import, the domesticated horse. The sedentary cultures, on the other hand, represented an extension of hoe horticultures developed in late prehistoric times.

The best-known nomadic Plains culture is that of the Teton or Western Sioux. The term Sioux is a French corruption of an Algonkin pejorative meaning 'lesser, or small, adder or enemy'. The correct term is Oceti Sakowin, 'the Seven Fireplaces', referring to the seven divisions of the Teton who moved out of the Minnesota area on to the Great Plains in the early eighteenth century. The natives themselves, however, now use the term Sioux. The Teton belong to the largest of the Sioux divisions and are the second most populous Native American tribe in the United States, numbering today around 100,000 people. They are also called Lakota, which is the name of their dialect.

The horse nomads lived in portable skin tipis painted with symbols describing the visions and exploits of the owner. They have been regarded ever since the first contacts with the French during the seventeenth century as formidable warriors. When not engaged in war with the Algonkin tribes, they were at war with tribes belonging to the other Sioux divisions. The Teton were known as the scourge of the northern Plains, dominating the village horticulturalists and the trade of the whole area and offering armed resistance to American riverboats and wagon trains. Indeed, they are renowned for their wars and especially for the defeat of Custer's army in 1876 and their own tragic defeat at Wounded Knee in 1890. The century of their greatness ended on reservations, where they live today, mostly in South Dakota.

Teton social organization and kinship principles are bilateral. Marriage is exogamic and residence is patrilocal. In the old days, the family lived in one or more tipis and consisted of a man, his wife or wives, unmarried children and sometimes elderly parents. Mobility for the bands or residential groups within the tribe was absolutely essential to the survival of these nomadic hunters. The patterns of fusion and fission of the bands were mostly based on affiliation with one or more men who were adept hunters and warriors. The social organization is much the same today. Chiefs are elder men elected on the basis of their achieved prominence, their maturity and judgement, and their generosity. They appoint younger leaders and soldiers to take care of the camps and enforce the resolutions of the council. When the bands gather together as a unit in camp circles during the summer months, they are under the single authority of a military society appointed for the task. The Teton also have many male and female religious and social societies.

The camp circles, or hoops, as they also are called, symbolically encircle the camp as one unit, defining the group in relation to the rest of the world. The summer camps are clearly the highpoint of the Teton year, where friends and relatives catch up on the gossip of the year and pursue matchmaking, competitive games, contests, oratory and debate and, in the old days, communal bison hunts and war parties. It is also the time to perform the great religious ceremonies under the leadership of the wicasa wakan, 'the holy men', those who are adept at communicating with superhuman spirits and powers.

In the following account, the religion of the Oglala is used to exemplify Teton religion. According to Oglala thought, all natural and cultural phenomena have the potential to be transformed from a secular to a sacred state. This potential is called wakan, 'sacred'. Those who have become permanently sacred are collectively called Wakantanka, 'Great Sacred'. Wakantanka consists of sixteen superhuman beings and powers, half of whom created the universe and the other half of whom came into existence when the earth was created. The first eight are the Sun and Moon, Sky and Wind, Earth and Falling Star, and Rock and the Thunder-being. The second eight are the Buffalo, the Bear-man, the Four Winds, the Whirlwind, the Shade, Breath, Shadelike and Potency.

There are many other superhuman beings and powers, both good and evil. Wakantanka is primarily concerned with the good aspect of universal energy, and the counterpart Wakansica, 'Evil Sacred', is concerned with the evil aspect. Humans may harness either aspect through propitiation of Wakantanka or Wakansica. Sacred humans gain the innate power of animate and inanimate objects through visions of superhumans and thereby gain also the ability to ward off sickness and evil. These are to be distinguished from medicine men and medicine women who heal through the use of herbal medicines. Sacred men and women serve as intermediaries, foreseeing the results of the hunt and war, or serving as instructors and interpreters of the myths, or as directors of the ceremonies. They instruct others on how to gain visions, and take on apprentices who become sacred persons in their own right.

All of the sacred ceremonies of the Oglala were given to them during a period of famine by White Buffalo Calf Woman. These consisted of seven major rituals, all of which are integrated in the symbolism of the pipe. The bowl of red stone represents the earth. It contains carvings of a buffalo calf representing four-legged animals. The stem of wood represented the flora, and the twelve feathers the eagle and winged creatures. In smoking the pipe all creatures and things are joined to the smoker. The pipe, being sacred, is handled with great care by persons fully initiated in the protocol of pipe-smoking. The bowl and stem are kept separated unless in use because the potency of the assembled and loaded pipe is considerable. The pipe is smoked in a circle of seated individuals, men and women, noted for their integrity and purity. Each person smokes the pipe in turn in order to invoke the desired powers or super-human beings.

White Buffalo Calf Woman also had a stone in her bundle with seven circles carved on it. These are the seven rites in which the pipe is to be used. The seven rituals are not the only ceremonies performed by the Oglala, but they form central themes in Oglala religion. They are the sweat lodge, the vision quest, ghost-keeping (vigil for departed relatives), the Sun Dance, the making of relatives (a type of blood-brother ritual), girl's puberty ritual, and throwing of the ball (a religious ball game).

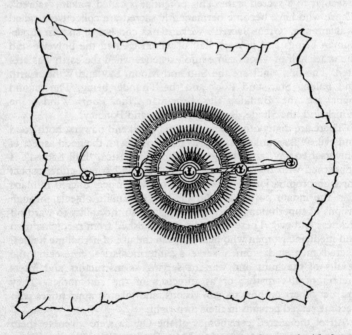

Figure 11.8 *A typical Teton female skin cape decorated with the bursting sun motif. The motif is made of porcupine quills sewn on to the skin.*

Source: *Drawing by Birgit Liin based on Norman Feder,* American Indian Art, *New York, 1965*

The Sun Dance warrants special mention. It is called Wi wanyang wacipi, 'sun-gazing dance' and is the only calendrical ceremonial, usually performed in June or July. The dance is under the authority of the sacred persons, and one of them is appointed Sun Dance leader. The dance itself lasts four days. The first day is spent constructing the sacred lodge around the central hole and the buffalo skull altar. The second day is spent chopping down in a careful ritual manner the tree which will serve as the central pole. The third day is spent decorating the pole with, among other things, the effigies of a man and a buffalo. It is also during the third day that the pole is placed in the central hole and raised. When this is accomplished the warrior societies dance the 'ground-flattening dance', during which they stamp a cross from the pole out to the four directions and shoot at the effigies hanging from the pole.

The men who have pledged to sacrifice themselves during the Sun Dance have been given instructions in a separate tipi during the first three days. They choose one of four types of sacrifice: gazing at the sun from dawn to dusk, piercing the breasts with skewers attached to the pole, piercing of the breasts and scapulae with skewers attached to rawhide ropes in order to hang suspended from four posts, and piercing of scapulae with skewers attached to thongs with one or more buffalo skulls to be dragged around the dance area. The idea of the latter three types is to dance until the flesh is torn through. They dance without food or drink all day while blowing on eagle bone whistles. Others also offer bits of their own flesh to Wakantanka while the dancers go through their ordeals. After the dance is concluded, the camp circle breaks up and the paraphernalia is given away, but the lodge itself is left to deteriorate as a gift to Mother Earth.

South-west Cultures

Two things strike the mind and imagination when visiting the South-west [23]. First, one is struck by the immensity of the natural environment, its sometimes otherworldly shapes and colours, and the remarkable variety of ecological niches. Second, one is equally struck by the impressive variety of native cultures, and even more so by the fact that in spite of the violence of its contact history, the peoples of the South-west still live at or near the spots where the Spaniards found them in 1540. This continuity is reflected in the cultures down to the present day.

In 1960 there were roughly 200,000 Native Americans in north-western Mexico and the south-western US, gathered in twenty-five

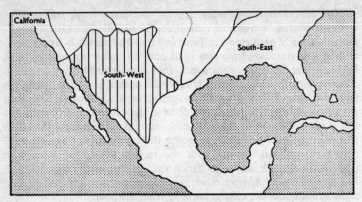

Figure 11.9 *The South-west*

(a) Pueblos

Language families: *Utaztecan, Hokan-Siouan*

Examples of peoples: *Hopi, Zuni, Tanoan, Keresan, Acoma*

Technology: *Agriculture, hunting, foraging*

Religious characteristics: *Creator deity and trickster, tutelary spirits, sweathouse, recitations of myths with long songs, Kuksu initiation ceremony, ceremonies for the bear and the deer*

(b) Nomads

Language families: *Athapaskan*

Examples of peoples: *Navaho, Apache*

Technology: *Hunting, foraging, sheep herding*

Religious characteristics: *Medicine men, elaborate sand-paintings, elaborate healing rituals, mountain deities, female puberty ceremony, Mountain Dance*

groups or 'tribes'. Looking at Arizona and New Mexico alone, we find representatives of six major language families. But this language diversity did not hamper cultural exchange.

Pueblo Cultures

The approximately 50,000 Pueblo people are divided into two major groups: the eastern Pueblos, along the Rio Grande valley, and the Western pueblos, consisting of the Zunis and the Hopis. Although there are a great many similarities in the religions of the

Pueblos, the kinship, political and world-view systems can be divided into two types: (1) the bilateral type (inheritance through either line) of the eastern Pueblos, and (2) the matrilineal type (inheritance through the female line) of the western Pueblos. The bilateral type divides all of society, and ultimately the cosmos, into two equal groups. This dual system reflects itself in village planning, in governmental structure and in ceremonial system, where all facets of life operate within the boundaries of one of the two groups. The system involves the assumption of governmental and ritual responsibilities which change hands between the two groups at or near the equinoxes or the solstices. The matrilineal type rests on interrelationships between matriclans (that is, clans which calculate kinship and inheritance through the female lines) grouped into phratries (large groups of clans) and the delegation of political and religious power through cooperation between ritual brotherhoods and priesthoods.

Among all of the Pueblos, political power is an integral part of the indigenous ceremonial hierarchy. The organizations of the hierarchies were different from Pueblo to Pueblo, and from east to west, but one of the key common aspects of these organizations is that secret ritual knowledge brings social power. This can be knowledge about primordial times, insight into ritual matters, the owning of powerful songs or powerful ceremonies, knowledge about powerful beings, or other similar matters. This knowledge is revealed through a long series of initiations into ritual brotherhoods or priesthoods, and, as intimated, the most important knowledge is literally held as property – equivalent to Western notions of material possession. It is this knowledge and its practical applications which decide the order of the hierarchy. Thus, among the Hopis and the Zunis, social prestige and power are based on the order of arrival of the clans in primordial times and the particular rituals which they claim to have owned at the time.

The main focus of the ceremonial organization is the calendrical observance of large-scale dramatic ceremonies ranging from four to sixteen days in length which ensure and guard the life-cycle of the maize plant. By securing the cooperation of solar, astral and geo-physical powers, the maize maintains its stages of life and death, thereby securing parallel stages in the cycles of human life and death. In a variety of ways, the metaphor of the maize plant guides the creative genius of the Pueblo people and informs the fabric of their social lives.

The Pueblo people live in a world alive with creatures of all types, from the subhuman to the superhuman, all of which are conceived of as belonging to an intricate series of reciprocal relations, where human groups are related to groups of flora and fauna, and gods, demons, and spirits claim allegiance from those who know their secrets. The worlds of these various beings are conceived of as being located in a systematic cosmos of storied worlds, one on the other, which are further divided into directional zones, sometimes four, sometimes six, usually consisting of the cardinals and the zenith and nadir. Thus, the idea of the centre or at least of a central world axis is prominent, and the whole structure constitutes a powerful frame of reference for mythical and ritual actors, as well as for the ideology of phratry and dual group relations. The Pueblo cosmos is further symbolized by the squarely built cult houses, called kivas, which represent the various underworlds that are connected by the axis, called in Hopi the Sipaapuni.

Cross-cutting the powerful clans, priesthoods, and ritual brother-hoods are other groups such as the mask cult (called by the Hopi term 'Kachina'), ritual clown societies, curing societies, war soci-eties and hunting societies. The Kachina Cult is the most famous Pueblo cult because of its open-air performances with dancing troupes arrayed in colourful, highly codified masks and costumes.

Figure 11.10 *Hopi Kachina dancers representing the Hemis Kachina. This Kachina opens and closes the Kachina dance season which covers the period from late winter to midsummer*
Source: *Photograph from the Forman Hanna collection, courtesy of the Arizona Historical and Archaeological Association, Tucson, Arizona (date and village unknown).*

The Kachinas are ancestral spirits, some animal, some human or superhuman, whose arrivals and departures usually follow seasonal fluctuations. During these and other ceremonies, the important core narratives are told often in the form of liturgical dialogue between priests and the masked representatives of important deities. These narratives relate the story of the emergence of mankind from subterranean worlds and their migrations to the centre of this world.

Against this array of societies, ceremonies and beings stand the forces of evil. The Pueblos do not conceive of any god containing the essence of evil. Some gods are more malevolent than others, but all superhuman beings are dangerous. On the other hand, the Pueblo people concern themselves mostly with human evil. A witch is by definition the exact opposite of everything that is considered sacred, good and – especially – sociable. The Pueblos do not conduct witch-hunts, but they do have specialists, such as medicine men and medicine women, who actively combat the diseases caused by witches and sorcerers and who sometimes engage in occult battles with them. Pueblo conceptions of power are such that power in itself is neither good nor evil, but becomes one or the other through usage. Thus, even medicine men or powerful priests are often suspected of using their power for sorcerous activities.

Navajo Culture

Navajo social organization and religious world-view seem to represent a bridge between the Pueblo world and the older residues of Athapaskan life. Navajos live in isolated clusters, and the fundamental principle of organization is the house, herds and fields of the resident female. Social identity is based on some sixty matriclans loosely organized in fifteen unnamed phratries. Navajo identity is further determined, even in matters of political status and leadership, by the size and appearance of the sheep herd. In earlier times, there was no clearly defined group larger than the residence group, except for loosely organized groups under the leadership of one or more headmen for dealing with outsiders.

The Navajo universe is divided into 'holy-people' and 'earth-surface people'. These beings live within the confines of a circular cosmos bounded by four sacred mountains. As with the Pueblos, the Navajos believe that they too have emerged from a series of subterranean worlds, of which the present world is the fifth. But the Navajo universe is neither mythically nor socially structured in the strict hierarchy of the Pueblos.

Navajo ceremonies are famous for their delicately produced sand-paintings which depict the universe in intricate symbol systems. Although this art is obviously borrowed from the Pueblos, it has

Figure 11.11 *A Navajo sand-painting concerning the mythical activities of the War Twins who established the 'Shooting Chant' during which the sand-painting is made. The picture was revealed to the younger Twin by the Thunder People, who instructed him in its ritual use. It illustrates the watery regions of the gods and powers and the four plants – blue maize, blue beans, black squash and blue tobacco – which grow out of the lake in the centre of the painting. The painting is open to the east and is protected by the beaver and the adder.*
Source: *Drawing courtesy of Dover Publications, Inc., New York, from Gladys A. Reichard,* Navajo Medicine Man Sandpaintings, *New York, 1939, fig. 8.*

none the less been refined by the Navajos. Navajo ceremonies clearly show the adoption of Pueblo ceremonies by Athapaskan shamanism. The Navajo 'singer' who performs complicated ceremonies over up to nine nights is a priest and not a shaman: he has learned his craft not through visions but through apprenticeship under a local singer, from whom he learns the songs, medicines, techniques and rituals. All of these matters have their source and patterns in the adventures of culture heroes or gods who have experienced misfortunes and illness, and through them have learned how to resolve such crises.

The interesting thing about Navajo ceremonies as opposed to Pueblo ceremonies is that while Pueblo ceremonies address cosmic powers on behalf of communal needs and crises, Navajo ceremonies do so on behalf of only one individual patient. Thus, the elaborate sand-paintings are prepared in order to vivify and invoke the gods on the rim of the universe and to bring them to the patient who is physically placed in the centre of the painting. Contact with the gods ensures that the patient becomes sacred and strong, and when they leave, they take his or her sickness with them, after which the sand-painting is discarded in the bush. One sand-painting is made and destroyed every twenty-four hours for the duration of the healing ceremony.

A strong religious factor among the Navajos is membership in the Native American Church of North America. Its appeal did not gain force until the devastating experience of forced stock reduction by the Bureau of Indian Affairs during the 1930s. Various estimates indicate that roughly half of the Navajo population are members of the Church today. The Native American Church is a pan-Indian religious movement that combines Christian symbolism with indigenous symbols and ritualism, with the addition of the ritual eating of the psychotropic peyote cactus (*Lophophora williamsii*), that contains among other alkaloids the well-known mescaline. Through the peyote ritual and its accompanying visions, the believer receives insight into his or her problems, as well as cures for sickness and misfortune.

Revitalization and Modern Native American Philosophy

The sources at our disposal seem to indicate a dynamic history in Native American religiosity. For instance, in the South-west we find clear indications of major influences from ancient Mexico which swept through the Pueblo areas. Even the masked Kachina rituals are a relatively recent addition to Pueblo religions. We have also seen how the invading Navajos acquired Pueblo cosmology and ritual. On the North-west Coast we find the spread of the Hamatsa ceremonial complex throughout the religions of the area. But one of the most important sources of religious dynamism was Christian missionizing. It is difficult to give a brief overview of the role of Christianity among Native Americans [see 39]. From John Eliot (1604–90) among seventeenth-century New England Natives to the

Moravian inter-racial utopian communities among the eighteenth-century Lenape, Christianity has left its indelible mark on Native American religiosity. Many followed the traditional Christian denominations, but are now reformulating Native theologies. Even more have developed new religious movements with more or less Christian characteristics.

Generally the religious movements inspired by Christianity combine earlier shamanistic elements, the desire to return to the old ways and the hope for the return of the game animals. Most were millennial movements founded by prophetic visionaries receiving revelations from the Master of Life on how to live and what ceremonies to perform. These movements encouraged higher morals and attempted to fight poverty, alcoholism, immorality and witchcraft. Thus prophets such as the Tewa Popé (1680s; the Pueblo Rebellion), the Delaware prophet Neolin (1760), the Seneca Handsome Lake (1799), the Shawnee prophet Tenskwatawa (1811), the Salish John Slocum (1840?–1898?; Shaker), the Wanapum Smohalla (1855; the Prophet Dance), the Paiute Wodziwob (1870; the Ghost Dance), the Paiute Wovoka (1889; Ghost Dance revival), and many others demonstrate these features [11; 17]. Today many attempts to return to aboriginal religion actually constitute exercises in creative syncretism. The American Indian Movement, the Sun Dance movements and others attempt to reinstitute conceived primordial traditions.

One of the most significant developments in recent years has been that of a pan-Indian philosophy by Native American writers and thinkers. Much of it springs from romanticizations by white Americans, but there are also serious attempts to formulate an all-encompassing philosophy which has its primary frame of reference in opposition to American philosophy. It includes ideas of nature as continually unfolding, of time as being cyclical, of the presence of superhuman power, of a space–time continuum, of the elements, of metaphysical ontology, of truth based on oral tradition, of ethics based on reciprocal relations with all beings, and of trust in the truth value of dreams and visions [2; 32].

Inter-cultural Dynamics

Native Americans have long been the object of Euro-American romanticizations. Many of these can be shown to be historically false, such as the Thanksgiving story of Squanto, the supposed Indian origin of maple syrup, the idea that the Hopi language lacks abstract notions of time and space, or that Long Lance was an

Indian. Similarly, the famous Black Elk was not a spokesman for traditional Lakota culture as most people think, Jamake Highwater was very likely a Greek-American film-maker, Hyemeyohsts Storm's supposed Indian ancestry has been contested by Native Americans, and Chief Seattle, who supposedly gave the ecology speech admired and repeated by Americans and Europeans since the 1970s, never gave that speech: it was a film script written in 1970 for a film on ecology produced by the Southern Baptist Convention.

Many Euro-Americans have more or less adopted a conceived 'Native American' ideology as their own, enacting, as it were, their own fantasies about the Native Americans. They are jokingly called 'Wannabes' by Native Americans because they 'wannabe' Indians. The various types of Euro-American Wannabe styles are explicit identification, symbolization, creative syncretism, activism and tourism/hobbyism. The term wannabe is now also being applied to young Native Americans searching for their roots.

Native Americans have become core symbols in New Age thought and activities. This position is clearly based on Euro-American primitivism. If any one author has been an accessory to the convergence of New Age expectations with its stereotypes of Native Americans, it is Carlos Castaneda. Starting as a UCLA doctoral candidate in anthropology who was to specialize in Yaqui ethnomedicine, Carlos Castaneda at first enthralled his readers with the magic of psychotropic experiences under the expert and mysterious guidance of his Yaqui teacher don Juan Matus. Through each subsequent novel, one detects a keen attunement to the expectations of his American audience: from the use of *Datura* and peyote, the reader follows Castaneda's growing maturity and his realization that don Juan's teachings have nothing to do with drugs and everything to do with New Age ideals, i.e. a holistic world-view, strict attendance to the miraculous in nature, concerted efforts at self-development which ultimately lead to liberation even from death, and – especially in his most recent volumes – the creative manipulation of energy fields and cosmic light rays. Even though many critics have doubted the existence of don Juan and his team of 'impeccable warriors', he has nevertheless had an undeniable impact on the New Age public through eight volumes of powerful narrative. Castaneda became a cult figure himself, and has conducted innumerable workshops on his occultistic techniques. Many have tried to emulate his success, and some are currently challenging his integrity on the Internet and in New Age magazines, claiming that he is draining the energy of his pupils in order to pursue his own evil plans. One of Castaneda's friends, Michael Harner, also moved from ethnography to 'going native' by establishing the Center for Shamanic Studies in Connecticut. His particular form of shamanic therapy has enjoyed popularity the world over. Indians have become highly marketable in New Age circles, and Harner's White Shamanism has become a standard feature in the New Age US.

Native American reactions vary. Native American writer Wendy Rose called it another kind of cultural imperialism [29]; only this time, the imperialist is the rootless white suddenly become a presumptuous 'expert' through eclectic misunderstandings of Native American thought. The American Indian Movement (AIM) has responded with hostility to the New Age use of Native American culture. The Traditional Elders Circle has also condemned the exploitation of their sacred symbols. Their anger is especially directed towards 'shamanistic' courses and courses in 'Native American' rituals. But not all Native Americans feel that way. An interesting modern phenomenon is that of well-educated younger Indian shamans, 'the New Native Shamans', as they are called. Leslie Gray from the California Institute of Integral Studies in San Francisco and Native American Studies Department at the University of California in Berkeley combines many ideals and professions: a university professor, shamanistic consultant, healer, shaman, sophisticated and young. She represents a new generation of Native Americans who have lost their traditional roots and yet function as bridge-makers between two worlds. Leslie Gray's therapy is called 'self-help shamanism' in which she teaches her patients how to enter altered states of consciousness and to travel to the upper and/or lower worlds in order to gain information, health, or personal empowerment [30].

Will the religions of Native Americans withstand the contemporary wave of New Age missionization? I believe they will. Native Americans have withstood 500 years of European domination in each their own way, and they will most likely continue to do so. Perhaps the greatest threat to their native lifestyles and world-views is posed by agents beyond the control of even the mightiest, namely, television, videos, technology, American and world economy, the English language, and American habits of food, clothing and lifestyle. These factors will be crucial in the development of Native American religions and cultures in the coming millennium.

Bibliography

1 BAHR, DONALD M., et al., *Piman Shamanism and Staying Disease*, Tucson, University of Arizona Press, 1981

2 CALLICOTT, J. BAIRD, *In Defense of the Land Ethic: Essays in Environmental Philosophy*, Albany, State University of New York Press, 1989

3 DOZIER, EDWARD, *The Pueblo Indians of North America*, New York, Holt, Rinehart & Winston, 1970

4 FEEST, CHRISTIAN F., *Indians and Europe: An Interdisciplinary Collection of Essays*, Aachen, Rader Verlag, 1987

5 FEEST, CHRISTIAN F., *Native Arts of North America*, London, Thames & Hudson, 1980

6 GEERTZ, ARMIN W., *The Invention of Prophecy: Continuity and Meaning in Hopi Indian Religion*, Los Angeles, University of California Press, 1992, 1994

7 GILL, SAM, *Mother Earth: An American Story*, Chicago, University of Chicago Press, 1987

8 HARTMANN, HORST, *Kachina-Figuren der Hopi-Indianer*, Berlin, Museum für Völkerkunde, 1978

9 HULTKRANTZ, ÅKE, *Belief and Worship in Native North America* (ed. Christopher Vecsey), Syracuse, Syracuse University Press, 1981

10 HULTKRANTZ, ÅKE, *Conceptions of the Soul among North American Indians*, Stockholm, Ethnographical Museum, 1953

11 HULTKRANTZ, ÅKE, 'Ghost Dance', in Lawrence E. Sullivan (ed.), *Native American Religions: North America*, New York, Macmillan, 1987, 1989, pp. 201–5

12 HULTKRANTZ, ÅKE, *The North American Indian Orpheus Tradition*, Stockholm, Ethnographical Museum, 1958

13 HULTKRANTZ, ÅKE, *The Study of American Indian Religions*, Chico, CA, Scholars Press, 1982

14 HUNT, GEORGE, and BOAS, FRANZ, *Kwakiutl Texts*, 2 vols, New York, *Memoirs of the American Museum of National History*, 5 and 10, 1902–5, 1906

15 JONES, WILLIAM, *Fox Texts*, New York, American Ethnological Society Publications, 1, 1907

16 JONES, WILLIAM, *Ojibwa Texts*, New York, American Ethnological Society Publications, 7, 1917–19

17 JORGENSEN, JOSEPH G., 'Modern Religious Movements', in Lawrence E. Sullivan (ed.), *Native American Religions: North America*, New York, Macmillan, 1987, 1989, pp. 211–17

18 KROBER, THEODORA, *Ishi in Two Worlds: A Biography of the Last Wild Indian in North America*, Berkeley, University of California Press, 1961

19 LINDIG, WOLFGANG, *Geheimbünde und Männerbünde der Prärie- und der Waldlandindianer Nordamerikas*, Wiesbaden, Franz Steiner, 1970

20 LUCKERT, KARL W., *Coyoteway: A Navaho Holyway Healing Ceremonial*, Tucson, University of Arizona Press, 1979

21 MALOTKI, EKKEHART, and TALASHOMA, HERSCHEL, *Hopitutuwutsi Hopi Tales: A Bilingual Collection of Hopi Indian Stories*, Lincoln, University of Nebraska Press, 1978

22 MÜLLER, WERNER, *Die Religionen der Waldlandindianer Nordamerikas*, Berlin, Dietrich Reimer Verlag, 1956

23 ORTIZ, ALFONSO, *Southwest*, Washington, DC, Smithsonian Institution, 1979, 1983 (*Handbook of North American Indians*, vols 9, 10)

24 ORTIZ, ALFONSO, *The Tewa World: Space, Time, Being and Becoming in a Pueblo Society*, Chicago, University of Chicago Press, 1969

25 PAPER, JORDAN, *Offering Smoke: The Sacred Pipe and Native American Religion*, Moscow, University of Idaho Press, 1988

26 POWERS, WILLIAM K., *The Oglala Religion*, Lincoln, University of Nebraska Press, 1975, 1982

27 POWERS, WILLIAM K., 'The Plains', 'Lakota', in Lawrence E. Sullivan (ed.), *Native American Religions: North America*, New York, Macmillan, 1987, 1989, pp. 35–43

28 RADIN, PAUL, *The Autobiography of a Winnebago Indian*, Los Angeles, 1920; repr. New York, Dover, 1963

29 ROSE, WENDY, 'Just What's All This Fuss about Whiteshamanism Anyway?', in Bo Schöler (ed.), *Coyote Was Here: Essays on Contemporary Native American Literary and Political Mobilization*, Aarhus, University of Aarhus, 1984, pp. 13–24

30 SHAFFER, CAROLYN R., 'Dr Leslie Gray, Bridge between Two Realities', *Shaman's Drum*, vol. 10, 1987, pp. 21–8

31 SIMMONS, LEO W. (ed.), *Sun Chief: The Autobiography of a Hopi Indian*, New Haven, Yale University Press, 1942

32 SIOUI, GEORGES E., *For An Amerindian Autohistory: An Essay on the Foundations of a Social Ethic*, Montreal, McGill-Queen's University Press, 1992

33 SPENCER, ROBERT F., and JENNINGS, JESSE D., *The Native Americans: Prehistory and Ethnology of the North American Indians*, New York, Harper & Row, 1965

34 STURTEVANT, WILLIAM C. (ed.), *Handbook of North American Indians*, 20 vols, Washington, DC, Smithsonian Institution, 1978–

35 SUTTLES, WAYNE (ed.), *Northwest Coast*, Washington, DC, Smithsonian Institution, 1990 (*Handbook of North American Indians*, vol. 7)

36 TEDLOCK, DENNIS, *Finding the Center: Narrative Poetry of the Zuni Indians*, Lincoln, University of Nebraska Press, 1978

37 TRIGGER, BRUCE G. (ed.), *Northeast*, Washington, DC, Smithsonian Institution, 1978 (*Handbook of North American Indians*, vol. 15)

38 WALENS, STANLEY, 'The Northwest Coast', in Lawrence E. Sullivan (ed.), *Native American Religions: North America*, New York, Macmillan, 1989, pp. 89–98

39 WASHBURN, WILCOMB E. (ed.), *History of Indian–White Relations*, Washington, DC, Smithsonian Institution, 1988 (*Handbook of North American Indians*, vol. 4)

12

Religions of the Pacific

BRIAN COLLESS AND PETER DONOVAN

Introduction

The Pacific Ocean covers nearly a third of the earth's surface. Geographically and historically its island inhabitants form four main groups: Indonesian, Australian, Melanesian and Polynesian (see figures 12.1, 12.2). Apart from Indonesia, which has been subject to Indian influences for nearly 2,000 years and Islamic contact for over 1,000, the remaining Pacific territories have enjoyed many centuries of isolation from the rest of the world. In their small, remote communities, the native peoples have developed cultures in which religious belief and practice play a vital and distinctive part. They provide some of the world's best examples of primal religions. Modern history of religion in the Pacific, however, is dominated by the increasing intrusion of Europeans since the sixteenth and seventeenth centuries, and the response of native societies to European culture, including its Christian religion. Writing about the Pacific has largely reflected European viewpoints and concerns. Only recently have indigenous writers and scholars begun to emerge, recording Pacific islanders' own reactions to the foreign impact, and attempting to recover and appreciate afresh their ancient beliefs and ways.

Sources for Study

Primal religions of the Pacific have no written traditions. Reducing to writing their myths and teachings, and recording their practices, has been the work of a wide variety of foreigners (including explorers, missionaries and colonial officers), for many of whom scholarly objectivity was not a primary concern. Some descriptions by

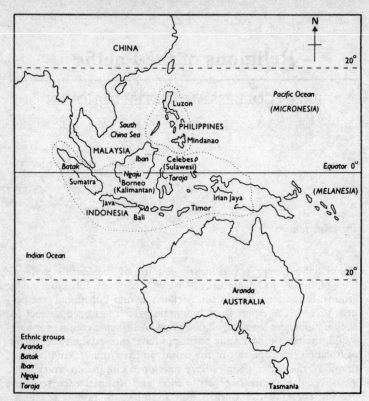

Figure 12.1 *Western islands of the Pacific Ocean*

colonists and missionaries, however, provide invaluable records of native beliefs at a stage before the invading world seriously altered their character. Among these are the collection of Polynesian legends and myths by Sir George Grey [15], R. H. Codrington [8] on the beliefs and practices of Melanesians, and Carl Strehlow [27] on the myths of central Australia. Emerging modern anthropology, with its systematic and analytical fieldwork, had notable representatives, including Bronislaw Malinowski [21], F. E. Williams [31], Sir Baldwin Spencer [25] and A. P. Elkin [11]. Classical descriptions of the culture of Polynesian peoples were produced by the Maori scholar Sir Peter Buck [5]; E. S. C. Handy [17] and R. W. Williamson [32] recorded in detail the religion and mythology of Central Polynesia; and Elsdon Best [4] compiled records of the traditions of the New Zealand Maori.

Greater justice has been done to local and regional diversity

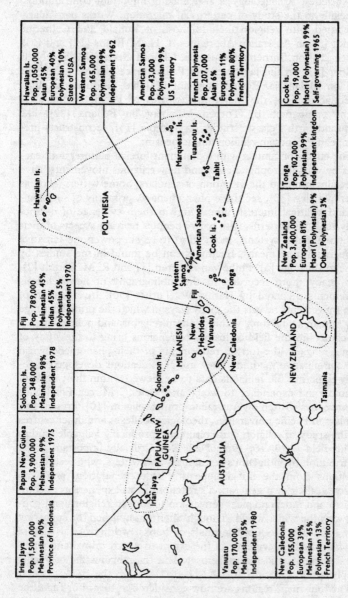

Figure 12.2 Eastern islands of the Pacific Ocean

Hawaiian Is.
Pop. 1,050,000
Asian 45%
European 40%
Polynesian 10%
State of USA

Western Samoa
Pop. 165,000
Polynesian 99%
Independent 1962

American Samoa
Pop. 43,000
Polynesian 99%
US Territory

French Polynesia
Pop. 207,000
Asian 6%
European 11%
Polynesian 80%
French Territory

Cook Is.
Pop. 19,000
Maori (Polynesian) 99%
Self-governing 1965

Tonga
Pop. 102,000
Polynesian 99%
Independent kingdom

New Zealand
Pop. 3,400,000
European 81%
Maori (Polynesian) 9%
Other Polynesian 3%

Fiji
Pop. 789,000
Melanesian 45%
Indian 45%
Polynesian 5%
Independent 1970

Solomon Is.
Pop. 348,000
Melanesian 98%
Independent 1978

Papua New Guinea
Pop. 3,900,000
Melanesian 99%
Independent 1975

Irian Jaya
Pop. 1,500,000
Melanesian 90%
Province of Indonesia

Vanuatu
Pop. 170,000
Melanesian 95%
Independent 1980

New Caledonia
Pop. 155,000
European 39%
Melanesian 45%
Polynesian 13%
French Territory

POLYNESIA

MELANESIA

Marquesas Is.

Tuamotu Is.

Tahiti

Hawaiian Is.

American Samoa

Cook Is.

Western Samoa

Tonga

Fiji

New Hebrides (Vanuatu)

New Caledonia

Solomon Is.

PAPUA NEW GUINEA

Irian Jaya

AUSTRALIA

NEW ZEALAND

Tasmania

through the many ethnographic studies in Oceania in recent years, by scholars eager to record information about these rapidly changing societies. Archaeology is also making important contributions, especially to the study of patterns of migration. Works particularly concerned with religion include those of Ronald and Catherine Berndt [3] on Australian Aborigines, I. H. N. Evans [12] and Erik Jensen [18] on Borneo tribespeople, Clifford Geertz [14] and Niels Mulder [23] on the Javanese, and P. Lawrence and M. J. Meggitt [20] on Melanesia. Roslyn Poignant [24] has produced an illustrated account of the major mythologies of Pacific islanders. A recent monograph by Torben Monberg on Bellona [22], like Raymond Firth's classic studies on Tikopia [13], reconstructs pre-European Polynesian religion in microcosm.

The effects of contact with a dominant foreign culture, and reactions by way of prophetic cults and new religious movements, have especially attracted the attention of scholars. Some writers, such as Peter Worsley [33], see these phenomena as primarily of sociological and political interest; others find in them evidence of distinctively religious patterns, with native peoples reviving aspects of their traditional belief-systems, in an effort to regain power and initiative through spiritual means. Examples can be found in the studies by Kenelm Burridge [6], Philip van Akkeren [1] and R. M. Berndt [2], with many more recorded in the bibliography of new religious movements prepared by Harold W. Turner [30]. Investigation of such movements reveals the many ways in which the primal heritage may remain a vital force within modern religious and political life.

Scholars in the field of history of religions bring to the study of primal religions the further refinements of their phenomenological and comparative method. They use classifications developed especially to permit the religious data to be viewed within the worlds of meaning and experience to which they belong. Mircea Eliade, for instance, has written on Australian primal religion [10]. Present-day scholars in Pacific universities, theological colleges and other centres for the study of religion and culture are producing valuable studies in this field [7; 9; 16; 19; 26; 28; 29]. Crucially important is the contribution by indigenous researchers and writers, who record oral traditions from the fast-disappearing older generation, and who reflect on their own generation's reactions to its experiences of colonialism and independence, conversion to foreign religions and contact with the wider world. Though often unpublished, or appearing only in locally produced journals or books, writing of this nature provides the best evidence of the extent to which primal and traditional elements still assert themselves in the religious life of Pacific peoples [9].

The four main regions are now considered in turn. For each, the general features of the beliefs and practices of Pacific primal religions are discussed; foreign influences, which have produced major disruptions of traditional life, are considered; and an account of modern developments, showing the ways in which underlying primal elements remain alive, is given.

Indonesia

Beliefs

Throughout the Pacific region we encounter myths of a marriage between Earth (Mother) and Sky (Father), and their eventual separation (it is usually their children who break their creative embrace, as in Polynesia). Indonesia is no exception, but here we also find sacred marriage in the context of the production of the staple food. In Java it is Sri and Sadono (the Hindu Lakshmi and Vishnu; see pp. 269–76) who unite to produce rice, the divine plant of life. For tribespeople and village farmers a mystical relationship between man and rice establishes the unity of society and its symbiosis with nature. The Indonesian world is inhabited by humans and spirits whose wishes sometimes clash, and propitiation is required. The word *adat* is widely used for the correct behaviour expected of people, as also of spirits and animals, to maintain cosmic order. Conceptions of an impersonal supernatural power (like Polynesian *mana*) are widespread. In Javanese mysticism (*kebatinan*) the idea of *rasa* or *roso*, intuitive inner feeling leading to higher knowledge, is cultivated. The belief in a soul is usually complex, involving a substance which can be increased, by certain techniques, alongside a personal spirit. An afterlife is everywhere acknowledged and is not an innovation from Islam or Christianity; nor have Hindu or Buddhist ideas of reincarnation had much influence here, save in Hindu Bali.

Practices

In Indonesia the religious year revolves round the life-cycle of rice. In Borneo, for example, the cycle begins with divination to find the right place in the jungle for farming, followed by slashing and burning; rituals accompany planting, growth, ripening, harvesting and storing. In Java and Bali the ritual pattern is similar, but there the grain is cultivated in irrigated terraces. Great reverence is shown to the spirit or soul of the rice; it is treated as a person. In many places the 'rice mother' (a bundle from the harvest) is set up to represent the whole field and be ritually cared for.

Spirits of many kinds have to be propitiated in every part of the village and landscape, and at every turn in life. In Java every significant occasion is marked with a *slametan*, a religious meal aimed at producing *slamet*, peace and well-being, in the community and in the spirit world; the spirits eat the essence of the food and are satisfied. There is a Muslim prayer in Arabic to solemnize the ceremony, but the purpose is propitiation of spirits. In funerary rites, burial is the normal method of disposal of the dead body, but in Hindu Bali it is cremation. Ritual specialists are on hand to ensure a good departure for the soul of the deceased.

Foreign Influences

The legacy of India to Indonesia is evident from the monuments and temples on the landscape of Sumatra, Java and Bali. Hindu–Buddhist images of metal and stone are always being discovered. There are traces of Muslim iconoclasm, which has made archaeologists' work more difficult, but there is general tolerance between religions. Whereas Sunni Islam of the Shafi'ite school (see pp. 178–9) is firmly established in the archipelago, Bali remains Hindu and Java is not prepared to jettison its old and proven tradition when it accepts new faiths. In Java's ricefields the God of the new religions must allow a place for the rice goddess, who goes under the Hindu name Dewi Sri. In Java and Bali those who espouse exclusive Islam or Christianity are not at home in the village and must live in the cities or establish new settlements.

Modern Developments

The ideas of 'modernity' and 'development' are in great vogue in the Republic of Indonesia today, as the diverse religious and ethnic groups strive to build a modern developed nation. Its motto is 'Unity in Diversity' (a phrase of religious origin from the Hindu past) and the first of its five principles of nationhood (the *Panca Sila*) is 'belief in God'. In the 1970s the government actually fostered religion, declaring that the development of religion and belief in the oneness of God were necessary to create harmony as the various communities sought to build the new society together. Christianity has its independent churches, notably the Batak churches of Sumatra and the indigenous church of East Java, and the mosque is the centre of countless communities; but *gurus* are rising up in increasing numbers in Java to teach Javanese mysticism. Some of these *gurus* mix Muslim and Christian ideas into their Hindu–Javanese teachings, but go on to offer day-by-day revelations. Admittedly some of these intuitions relate to the national lottery, but more significantly these specialists of the sacred (who are usually also involved in the secular world as mechanics, teachers, soldiers, politicians and so on) offer their disciples individual and social harmony.

Australia

Beliefs

Aboriginal myths usually recount the wanderings of supernatural beings in the creative period, conventionally known as 'the Dream Time' or 'the Eternal Dreaming'. In south-eastern Australia there are traces of a male supreme being who now lives in the sky but once walked upon the earth to establish it. In the north, however, instead of this All-Father we find Earth as Mother of all. The Rainbow Snake is widely represented in the mythology, sometimes as male, sometimes as female. It is associated with rain or water, and is often held to be the first creator, as the maker of all living creatures.

Australian religion is said to be totemic. Totemism involves a relationship between a person or group and some natural object, phenomenon or species. It is an affirmation of a kinship bond between mankind and nature: they share the same life essence and exist for the mutual imparting of life. Totemism is also a declaration of strong attachment to one's own land and people, and a symbolic expression of Aboriginal social values and relationships. Aboriginal Australians are not materialistic; their possessiveness extends only to their personal totem and a few sacred objects. They cultivate the spiritual life religiously. The person's spirit exists before birth and survives after death, but there is no heaven or hell. The spirit simply remains on or in the land.

Practices

The greater part of sacred lore and law is in the hands of males, especially older men and medicine men. Males also direct most of the religious rituals in Aboriginal religion, but women take part in some of them and have their own secret ceremonies. Myth and rite are complementary: rituals are either enactments of myths or validated by myths (for example, stories giving the origin of circumcision and subincision as performed on boys at initiation). Of vital importance are the increase rituals, for stimulating spirit beings to augment food supplies, or fertility, or love between a woman and a man. In the case of food or weather, each totemic group (kangaroo, honey-ant, sun, rain and so on) has its own special dance ritual for increasing the supply.

A potent ingredient in ritual practices is human blood (obtained not from sacrificial victims but from a man's own subincised urethra or arm veins) or its substitute, red ochre. For ceremonial occasions human bodies are decorated with feathers, fat, clay, colouring and blood. Thus arrayed, the people dance and sing. Typical ritual objects are secret and sacred carved boards (often used as bullroarers); thread crosses (wool and hairstring threaded on a frame of two or three sticks, worn on the hair or on the back in dances, but sometimes large and elaborate, with sacred boards and spears as the framework); and symbolic designs drawn on the ground or painted on walls.

Foreign Influences

Before the coming of the European to Australia in 1788, the Aborigines had lived in isolation. In the north there had been contacts with Melanesians and Indonesians (reflected in songs, rituals and paintings), but the surface was only ruffled at the edges by such encounters. The invasion of the British was more catastrophic. From the very start their diseases spread with ease; smallpox ravaged the black population for half a century. Disseminating their Christian religion was not so easy; Aborigines saw no spiritual or political relevance in it to their own well-ordered world. Iconoclastic missionaries found no heathen idols to smash, and some inclined to the prevailing opinion that they were dealing with savages who had no religion and were beyond redemption. Though the European missionary could not impose his morals on the Aboriginal, he nevertheless imparted demoralization. One of this apparently dying race said with grave humour to the anthropologist W. E. H. Stanner: 'When all the blackfellows are dead all the whitefellows will get lost in the bush, and there'll be no one to find them and bring them home.' Aboriginal religion contains, however, the sacred secret of survival on the dry southern continent.

Modern Developments

Christianity has made a few conquests. Part-Aborigines who have no clear relation to a tribe or locality can find a sense of belonging and unity in Christian conventions which bring them together to sing and pray. The Bandjalang of northern New South Wales offer an example of a syncretistic movement, a synthesis of Pentecostal Christianity with their own myth and ritual (which had been branded as the work of devils by the missionaries who had taught them). The whites with their prosperity and power are linked with the Romans who crucified Jesus. When Christ returns it will be the blacks that he favours. While the whites are thus denigrated and demoted, Aboriginal women are promoted to sharing in knowledge of religious lore, since they too are 'baptized in the Spirit'. In general, though, Aboriginals are disturbed that so much of their secret heritage is being published in books and magazines, exposing women and uninitiates to danger or disaster from breaking taboos. Aboriginal Australians are not acquisitive, and not prone to cargo cults. So far they have not shown themselves desirous of gaining the whole world at the cost of losing their own soul.

Melanesia

Beliefs

Central to all Melanesian religion is belief in ancestor-spirits who through their access to supernatural powers can bring good or ill to their living descendants. Gods, demons, land-spirits (*masalai* in pidgin) and other forces of the unseen environment also intervene in human affairs. While there is little speculation about the origins of the wider world, creative gods and culture heroes are credited with having given both the local culture and the means of livelihood. Animals, reptiles or fish may be regarded as totems, providing a bond between clan groups and their natural habitat.

Prosperity and order in the small communities depends on effective control of spiritual power (sometimes called *mana*) which shows itself in practical achievements such as successful warfare, trading, pig-rearing or crop-growing. Gods and spirits are believed to supervise communal morality, bringing illness or accident to those who misbehave or break taboos. Magic and sorcery are widely believed in and practised. Spirits of the recently dead are commonly sought by the living, through divination, in order to discover why their death occurred. Premature deaths and suicides raise the suspicion of sorcery, for which pay-back (appropriate recompense) must be sought, before the spirit will be free to journey to its final destination.

Practices

Through individual and communal rituals, spirits of ancestors are honoured and their help is sought in the affairs of life. Male cult rites take place at the ceremonial house (*haus tambaran*), where the spirits make their presence known through sacred masks, musical instruments, dreams, prophecy and trance-mediums. In these rites, young men are introduced to the inner secrets of tribal lore. Birth, puberty, marriage, trade exchanges and funerals are all marked by communal ceremonies, commonly involving feasts and dances (*singsings*). Ceremonial distributions of wealth and food strengthen ties among the living and with the unseen powers.

Techniques of sympathetic magic, spells, incantations and herbal medicines, known to sorcerers and other religious specialists, are used in private rituals for healing, divination and success in hunting or courting, as well as for protection from dangerous animals, malicious ghosts and demons, and the effects of sorcery.

Foreign Influences

In the past century, Melanesia has been invaded by European trade, government and religions. The new sources of power which foreigners brought (wealth, weapons, medicines) deeply disrupted communities in which status rested on traditionally recognized achievements. Colonial governments brought an end to tribal warfare, depriving village societies of an important customary source of prestige, and of the need for much religious ritual.

However, since power is believed to be essentially a religious matter, native people assumed that by adopting European beliefs and practices they could share the higher levels of power and prosperity which Europeans appeared to enjoy. Christianity, then, was found by many to be a peaceful means of attaining the traditionally sought religious goal, a safer and more prosperous life in harmony with nature and society. In some cases, the impact of foreign culture was resisted by an established means of defence, namely religious revival and ritual. 'Nativistic' movements, often led by prophets (male or female), have been accompanied by mass enthusiasm and ecstatic behaviour, sometimes involving total rejection or selective reinterpretation of mission teachings. Of such movements, the widely discussed 'cargo cults' form only one of several distinct types (see chapter 14 below).

Modern Developments

Melanesia has experienced vigorous missionary activity since the middle nineteenth century. Converts from other Pacific islands, brought by some of the missions, played an important part. Melanesian converts themselves actively spread Christianity. Under colonial administration, foreign missions helped establish communications, were responsible for health and education, and provided a spiritual rationale for the adoption of European ways. The Pacific War of 1941–5 brought great changes: missions lost property and personnel; European prestige and control declined; and, of necessity, Melanesian initiative and experience in church affairs increased. In the post-war period, foreign missions have increasingly given place to autonomous national churches, among which ecumenical cooperation is extensive. Many smaller evangelical missions have been introduced, and other groups, including Jehovah's Witnesses, Latter-day Saints, and the Baha'i faith, are active. Indonesian rule of Irian Jaya (Western New Guinea) will mean increasing contact with the religion of Islam.

Despite major foreign influences, the cultural roots of primal religion remain vital, not only underlying cults and independent churches but contributing generally to the identity and aspirations of Melanesia's newly independent peoples. The 'localization' of theology, as well as of liturgy and church administration, is actively promoted by Christian leaders. They point to similarities between their own primal heritage and the biblical world; a pragmatic and communal experience of life; respect for forefathers; guidance from prophets, dreams and visions; and salvation through a fruitful relationship with higher powers. From this common basis Christian leaders seek to develop an indigenous Christianity, freed from association with colonialism and white cultural dominance.

Polynesia

Beliefs

For the Polynesians, life is lived within a world peopled by supernatural beings. The great creator god Tangaroa (or Io, in Maori religion) brought the cosmos into existence out of an original void. Earth and Sky begot lesser gods (*atua*) who in turn produced humans and continue to preside over important human concerns (Tane is god of forests and woodcutting; Tu, god of warfare; Hina, goddess of motherhood and weaving). Lesser spirits, ghosts and demons abound. Gods stand at the head of long lines of noble ancestors, transmitting through them the creative power (*mana*) which brings life and prosperity to their living descendants. Genealogies and migration stories trace family histories back to the mythical homeland Hawaiki, where spirits of the dead return to rest.

Although gods and ancestor-spirits are felt to be close at hand, mystery and awe lie at the heart of Polynesian religion. Direct access to the power and favour of the gods was traditionally reserved for chiefs (themselves once divinized) and for priests (*tohunga*), who possessed secret knowledge of lore and ritual.

Practices

Gods and ancestor-spirits were invoked by the *tohunga* with sacred chants at a shrine or on a *marae* (gathering place for communal occasions). Honoured by rituals of offering, feast and dance, the gods in return granted *mana* to the chiefs, their people and their tribal lands. Food to nourish the gods and ensure their favour included the offering of human sacrifices. The first enemy killed was, for instance, offered to the god of war. First-fruits from freshly gathered foods or a catch of fish were likewise returned to the patron god. Human sacrifice was also commonly used in the consecration of buildings, war canoes and other types of sacred object.

Equally important were rites of purification from the effects of *tapu* (taboo). (*Tapu* formed a system of restraints and prohibitions to preserve the effectiveness of *mana*.) Water, the chief purifying agent, was sprinkled on new-born children, bloodstained warriors and those contaminated by sickness or death, in order to free them from *tapu* and make them safe for contact with other people. Priests used a variety of further rituals and chants for healing and divination, protection from sorcery or evil spirits, and for the burial of the dead to ensure their peaceful departure to the spirit-land.

Foreign Influences

The impact of European culture brought new diseases and weapons, reducing island populations and altering the balance of inter-tribal rivalry. Foreign trading undermined the native economies; dependence on foreign political and religious leadership destroyed the *mana* of chiefs; and the destruction of sacred objects and places by converts to Christianity challenged the authority of priests and the efficacy of traditional beliefs. Missionaries appropriated local languages for preaching and translating the Bible. Mission stations became centres for the spreading of foreign ways of life, while former villages and sacred places were abandoned.

Sometimes, when chiefs were befriended by missionaries and embraced the new faith, conversions of whole tribes followed. Native converts, trained as teachers and preachers, became the chief agents of further expansion.

Disillusionment came for many when the expected benefits did not all follow conversion. Conflicts between different churches, the neglect of Christian moral teachings by other Europeans, and the involvement of missionaries in colonialist politics all contributed to a loss of confidence in the new religion's claims. However, after customary priestcraft, ritual and sacred places had been outlawed by mission decree or government law, it was not possible for the ways of the past to be completely reinstated. Resurgences of primal beliefs have from time to time occurred in the form of nativistic movements which either rejected foreign ways (as with the Mamaia cult in Tahiti in the 1820s) or, under prophet leaders, drew on biblical and traditional sources to produce indigenous versions of Christianity (as with the Ringatu and Ratana movements, which have become major churches among New Zealand Maori today).

Modern Developments

Although Christianizing helped bring peace and stability during two centuries of disruption, European missionary attitudes and policies inevitably resulted in the Polynesian peoples becoming ashamed of and abandoning many valuable features of their own heritage. Recovering those features (while protecting them from debasement by tourism) is a concern of leaders in Pacific culture today. A Pacific Conference of Churches actively promotes a local theology and a sense of continuity with the faith of non-Christian ancestors and their religion. The Pacific Theological College in Suva, Fiji, is a centre for such developments. Universities in Hawaii, Fiji, Australia and New Zealand have departments concerned with Pacific history and culture, including religion.

Mormonism (active in the Pacific since the 1840s), the Baha'i faith (introduced in the 1950s) and other new religions compete with post-Christian and secular ideologies for the support of the rising generation. But whether in scattered island villages or among migrant communities in city suburbs, the patterns set by the main missions – Congregationalist, Wesleyan, Roman Catholic, Anglican and Seventh-day Adventist – remain, for the foreseeable future, the familiar forms of religion for the great majority of Polynesians. In New Zealand, a current revival of Maoritanga (Maori culture) includes an emphasis by Maori Christian leaders on retaining traditional ways and concepts within Christian faith and practice. Among these are healing and exorcism rites, ceremonies of burial and mourning, respect for elders and ancestors, and other values embodied in the custom of the *marae*. To this extent, at least, primal religion remains alive.

Bibliography

1 AKKEREN, P. VAN, *Sri and Christ: A Study of the Indigenous Church in East Java* (tr. A. Mackie), London, Lutterworth, 1970

2 BERNDT, R. M., *An Adjustment Movement in Arnhem Land, Northern Territory of Australia*, The Hague/Paris, Mouton, 1962

3 BERNDT, R. M. and C. H., *The World of the First Australians*, London, Angus & Robertson, 1964; 2nd edn Sydney, Ure Smith, 1977

4 BEST, E., *Maori Religion and Mythology*, Wellington, 1924 (*Dominion Museum Bulletin*, no. 10); repr. Wellington, Government Printer, 1976; New York, AMS, 1976

5 BUCK, SIR PETER (Te Rangi Hiroa), *The Coming of the Maori*, Wellington, Maori Purposes Fund Board/Whitcombe & Tombs, 1949; 2nd edn 1950

6 BURRIDGE, K., *New Heaven, New Earth: A Study of Millenarian Activities*, Oxford, Blackwell, 1969

7 CHARLESWORTH, M. et al. (eds), *Religion in Aboriginal Australia*, St Lucia, University of Queensland Press, 1984

8 CODRINGTON, R. H., *The Melanesians*, Oxford, Clarendon Press, 1891; repr. New York, Dover, 1972

9 DEVERELL, G. and B., *Pacific Rituals*, Institute of Pacific Studies of the University of the South Pacific, Suva, 1986

10 ELIADE, M., *Australian Religions: An Introduction*, Ithaca, Cornell University Press, 1973

11 ELKIN, A. P., *The Australian Aborigines: How to Understand Them*, Sydney/London, Angus & Robertson, 1938; 5th edn 1974

12 EVANS, I. H. N., *The Religion of the Tempasuk Dusuns of North Borneo*, Cambridge, Cambridge University Press, 1953

13 FIRTH, R., *Tikopia Ritual and Belief*, London, Allen & Unwin, 1967

14 GEERTZ, C., *The Religion of Java*, Glencoe, IL, Free Press, 1960; Chicago, University of Chicago Press, 1976

15 GREY, SIR GEORGE, *Polynesian Mythology*, London, John Murray, 1855; repr. Christchurch, Whitcombe & Tombs, 1956; repr. of 1906 edn New York, AMS, 1976

16 HABEL, NORMAN C. (ed.), *Powers, Plumes and Piglets*, Bedford Park, South Australia, Australian Association for the Study of Religions, 1979

17 HANDY, E. S. C., *Polynesian Religion*, Honolulu, 1927 (*Bernice P. Bishop Museum Bulletin* no. 34); repr. New York, Kraus, 1971

18 JENSEN, E., *The Iban and their Religion*, Oxford, Clarendon Press, 1974

19 KING, M. (ed.), *Te Ao Hurihuri: The World Moves On: Aspects of Maoritanga*, Wellington, Hicks Smith, 1975

20 LAWRENCE, P., and MEGGITT, M. J. (eds), *Gods, Ghosts and Men in*

Melanesia, Melbourne/London/New York, Oxford University Press, 1965

21 MALINOWSKI, B., *Argonauts of the Western Pacific*, London, Routledge, 1922, 1978; New York, Dutton, 1922, 1961

22 MONBERG, T., *Bellona Island Beliefs and Rituals*, Honolulu, University of Hawaii Press, 1991 (Pacific Islands Monograph Series, no. 9)

23 MULDER, N., *Mysticism and Everyday Life in Contemporary Java*, Singapore, Singapore University Press, 1978

24 POIGNANT, R., *Oceanic Mythology: The Myths of Polynesia, Micronesia, Melanesia, Australia*, London, Hamlyn, 1967; Melbourne, Sun Books, 1970

25 SPENCER, SIR BALDWIN, and GILLEN, F. J., *The Arunta: A Study of a Stone Age People*, London, Macmillan, 1927

26 STEPHEN, M. (ed.), *Sorcerer and Witch in Melanesia*, Melbourne, Melbourne University Press, 1987

27 STREHLOW, C., *Die Aranda- und Loritja-Stämme im Zentral-Australien*, Städtisches Völker-Museum, Frankfurt, Baer, 1907–20

28 SWAIN, T., and TROMPF, G., *The Religions of Oceania*, London/New York, Routledge, 1995

29 TROMPF, G. W., *Melanesian Religion*, Cambridge, Cambridge University Press, 1991

30 TURNER, H. W., *Bibliography of New Religious Movements in Primal Societies*, vol. 3, *Oceania*, Boston, G. K. Hall, 1990

31 WILLIAMS, F. E., *Drama of Orokolo*, Oxford, Clarendon Press, 1940

32 WILLIAMSON, R. W., *Religious and Cosmic Beliefs of Central Polynesia*, vols 1, 2, Cambridge, Cambridge University Press, 1933; repr. New York, AMS, 1977

33 WORSLEY, P., *The Trumpet Shall Sound: A Study of 'Cargo' Cults in Melanesia*, 2nd edn, London, MacGibbon & Kee, 1968

13

African Religions

AYLWARD SHORTER

Introduction

The term 'African religions' is used here to refer to the indigenous, ethnic religions of sub-Saharan Africa. The concept of tribe or ethnic group is a fluid one in Africa, for ethnic identities shade into one another and there have been continual migrations and amalgamations throughout African history. Basically the tribe is a category of interaction among heterogeneous peoples, but it has a cultural core which consists of a human tradition in a given physical environment. Such an environment offers a limited number of choices for solving the problems of daily living and each society has developed its social and cultural institutions in accordance with a chosen economy. Within the framework provided by physical environment and human tradition, African societies have interrogated human existence, have developed their own religious imagery and symbolic classifications and have evolved their own organic universe. Any attempt to classify the tribes of Africa is necessarily arbitrary. One such attempt has been that of G. P. Murdock, who lists 742 sub-Saharan tribes [22]. This conservative estimate conveys some idea of the size and complexity of the subject.

Nevertheless, indigenous religion in Africa is not strictly identifiable with the tribe, however it is defined, even though beliefs and values are articulated within tribal structures and traditions. Religious concepts and practices have been shared over wide areas in the history of Africa and certain religious institutions, such as ancestor veneration, have a near-universal currency. Particularist or holistic studies inevitably present a false picture although they are a necessary stage in our understanding of African religion and provide the primary sources of information. Such studies have been made by social anthropologists, early travellers and explorers, and scientifically minded missionaries. Participant observation, as a method, is required by the oral and ritual nature of the material. Subsequent comparative studies by scholars of religion have been based on this ethnographic material, particularly on recorded prayer-literature. The recent development of oral history has carried the study of African religions considerably further, providing, as it does, hard evidence for the interaction of peoples and the spread of ideas. Finally, modern African poets, novelists, playwrights and political philosophers have added their interpretations to the growing literature on African religion.

Students of African religion were at first sceptical about the possibility of historical studies. Today there is no doubt that they are both possible and worthwhile. Religion permeated every aspect of life in traditional African societies and its history is inseparable from that of their social and political institutions. Over much of the continent, particularly eastern, central and southern Africa, populations have been small and scattered, and poverty of resources has imposed a subsistence economy in the shape of hunting-gathering, shifting cultivation and pastoralism. Such societies did not elaborate rich material cultures, but discovered parables for the spiritual realities of existence in the phenomena of an all-embracing nature. The theologies of such religions, though often subtle, were not elaborate. In the lake regions and forest fringes where soils are richer and rainfall more plentiful, settlement has been more dense and culture technologically more advanced. In such societies theology has been patterned more on the interplay of personalities, divinities and deified human beings, while religious practice has centred on holy places, graves, shrines, temples and mausoleums. All over the continent territorial and royal cults are found which have played an important role in politico-religious history.

In the colonial era (late nineteenth century to mid-twentieth century) ritual leaders were mostly secularized, and immigrant religions, such as Islam and Christianity, acted as catalysts in an enlargement of social and theological scales. They also added to the doctrinal repertory of African traditional religion and stimulated reinterpretation, particularly with regard to belief in a supreme being or 'High God'. Certain indigenous belief-systems crossed the Atlantic as a result of the slave trade and survive in recognizable form in Cuba, Brazil and the Caribbean [3]. Such are the well-known *vodun* snake cult from Benin (see figure 13.1), which has become the Voodoo of Haiti and Jamaica, and the religious traditions from Nigeria, Zaire, Angola and Mozambique which survive as the Candomblé brotherhoods in Brazil, the Umbanda and Macumba spirit cults and the syncretic Batuque traditions.

Within Africa itself, ethnic religious values and traditions have lent a special colour to Islam and Christianity in their orthodox or

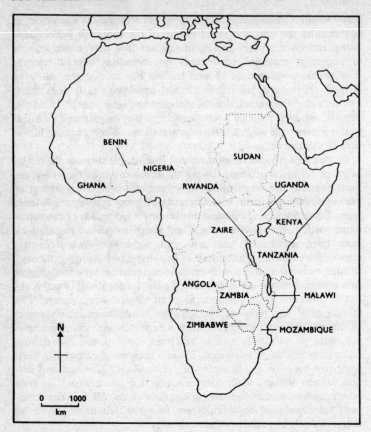

Figure 13.1 *African countries referred to in the text*

mission-related forms. They have also taken new forms of their own
in the so-called Independent church movements, some of which are
not so much neo-Christian or neo-Judaic as neo-traditional, a good
example being Elijah Masinde's Religion of the Ancestors (*Dini ya
Misambwa*) in Kenya. Finally, contemporary Africa is witnessing the
appearance of numerous communities of affliction, practising spirit
mediumship therapy and also witch eradication movements.

Racial and religious prejudice often bedevilled early accounts of
African religions, and it was felt that peoples who were technologically inferior were incapable of 'higher' religious feelings and behaviour. Symbolism and mythology were held in contempt by
Westerners, who considered scientific facts to be the only realities.

Naïve evolutionism was replaced by misguided missionary progressionism and the effort to find vestiges of a 'primitive revelation'. It was social anthropology that began to appreciate African religions on their own terms, but even then Eurocentric criteria were responsible for concepts such as the 'withdrawn' or 'lazy' God (*deus otiosus*), the so-called 'High God' and for dualistic or polytheistic interpretations. With regard to comparative analysis, Evans-Pritchard advocated the 'limited comparative method' [10] (the study of dissimilarities among contiguous and historically related peoples) while Mary Douglas has proposed categorization on the basis of 'definable social experience' [8: IX]. Theologians, such as J. S. Mbiti [20] and E. B. Idowu [16], believe in the essential comparability of all ethnic religions, a 'super-religion' which purports to belong to all Africans, while historians, such as B. A. Ogot [24], I. N. Kimambo, T. O. Ranger [26] and R. Gray [14], advocate a more factual, but necessarily more restricted, analysis. Finally, African writers such as Chinua Achebe [1], Ngugi wa Thiongo [23] and Wole Soyinka [31] have chronicled the destruction of the old organic universe; used African religion as an allegory for modern sociopolitical processes; replaced it with an alien, Marxist ideology; or sought to secularize it in modern, tragic theatre.

The Teachings of African Religions

Africa's approach to the numinous is both personal and 'transpersonal'. In many instances 'spirit' is a category which includes inanimate medicines and fetishes as well as personal beings. Sometimes the concept is unified and the different levels of spirit are seen as 'refractions' of an ultimately powerful being, symbolically associated with the sky. This is the case for the northern Nilotes of Sudan, the Nuer [11] and Dinka [19]. In other instances a supreme being is more clearly and exclusively personalized as a creator and/or life-giver, again employing sky-symbolism: sun, rainbow or lightning, for example (see figure 13.2). The supreme being has also been associated with mountains and high hills, Mts Kenya and Kilimanjaro (the latter in Tanzania) being the most celebrated examples, and it is possible that hill-symbolism represents an older stratum of belief than sky-symbolism (see figure 13.3).

Generally speaking, African experience of nature is classified as being either life-fulfilling or life-diminishing; and there is a third, enigmatic category of natural phenomena which seem to share human life or characteristics [7: 9–26; 9]. Thus classified, nature reveals the existence of spiritual realities, beings and powers, as well

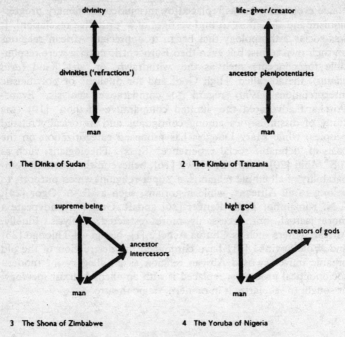

Figure 13.2 *Contrasting African theologies*

as means of human communication with the numinous. Very often nature spirits are thought to control the wild animals, as well as the trees and plants that grow in the wilderness, or are associated with lakes, streams or rock-formations. A special place is reserved for the Earth and its (usually female) personalization in African cosmology. Occasionally, Sky–Earth opposition results in a clearly bisexual representation of the supreme being. The ultimate source of evil and disorder in the world is rarely personalized as a spirit, but more commonly traced to the witch, a human being who possesses preternatural powers to harm others secretly and malevolently.

Although there are well-documented instances of totemic spirits who are invoked as the guardians of clans and lineages, the patrons of society are usually the spirits of the dead, the ancestors. The spiritual world of the ancestors is patterned after life on earth. The recently dead and the unremembered collectivity of the remotely deceased are invoked by, and on behalf of, the family community. The territorial spirits who are the ancestors of chiefs or who are eminent personalities of the past are invoked on behalf of larger social groupings. Ancestors are thought to be mediators in one

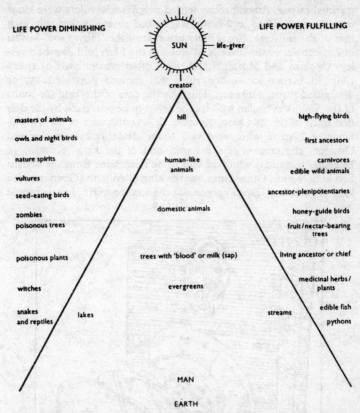

LIFE POWER DIMINISHING

LIFE POWER FULFILLING

SUN — life-giver

creator

masters of animals	hill	high-flying birds
owls and night birds		first ancestors
nature spirits	human-like animals	carnivores
vultures		edible wild animals
seed-eating birds		ancestor-plenipotentiaries
zombies	domestic animals	honey-guide birds
poisonous trees		fruit/nectar-bearing trees
poisonous plants	trees with 'blood' or milk (sap)	living ancestor or chief
witches	evergreens	medicinal herbs/plants
snakes and reptiles	lakes	edible fish
	streams	pythons

MAN

EARTH

Figure 13.3 *Cosmology of the Kimbu of Tanzania: pattern of symbols representing spiritual powers*

sense or another. They are perhaps seldom conceived of as intercessors, like the Christian saints. More often they are plenipotentiaries of the supreme being, mediating his providence and receiving worship in his name. Occasionally they are seen as mankind's companions in the approach to the supreme being, guarantors of authentic worship [5; 18]. Much of traditional morality is concerned with pleasing the ancestors and living in harmony with them, since they are the most important members of the total community.

Leadership in traditional Africa was basically ritual leadership, whether of divine kings, or of prophet-arbitrators or spirit-mediums. In the shifting political situation of the pastoralists the leaders were members of prophet-clans which were credited with exceptional spiritual power. Among more settled peoples, the rulers were kings whose own life and well-being was linked cosmo-biologically with that of the universe. Royal cults like that of the 'High God' Mwari in Zimbabwe, or the divinity M'Bona in the Shire and Zambezi valleys (Malawi and Mozambique), were often manipulated by rulers [28]. In certain cases, the ruler was himself possessed by, or descended from, a divinity. This was the case of the king (or Reth) of the Shilluk in Sudan who was believed to be possessed by the deified spirit of the first king, Nyikang. It was also true of the Yoruba kings of Nigeria who were said to be descended from the god Odudua, the creator of the Earth, and of the king (Kabaka) of Buganda (Uganda) who was said to be descended from the deified first king, Kintu. Other kings like the king of Ashanti (Ghana) or the king of Ankole (Uganda) possessed the soul or spirit of their people

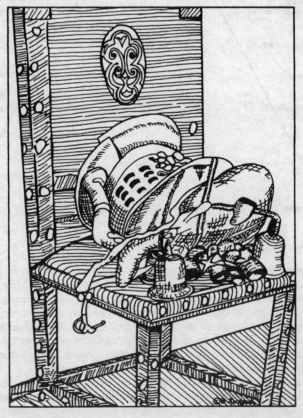

Figure 13.4 *The Golden Stool of the Ashanti, Ghana*

in an important item of their regalia, the 'Golden Stool' or the royal drum (figure 13.4).

It is particularly in the highly developed, monarchical societies that the greatest theological pluralism is encountered. When Christian missionaries appeared on the scene, it was sometimes difficult for them to select a supreme divinity with which they could identify the Christian God. In Buganda, for example, there were three candidates – the god of the sky, the creator god and the first god-king – while in the Yoruba religion the supreme being was king of the gods, but he was the creator neither of the Earth nor of mankind. Such pluralism was basically unsystematic and the question of which divinity was supreme was often unimportant to those concerned. The experience of the numinous consisted in the dialectical interplay between the various spiritual beings. This was expressed mythologically and acted out in various ritual forms. Thus the tensions of human society were reproduced at the spiritual level.

In the precarious existence led by members of traditional African society, life and the transmission of life were important values. Death presented a paradox, since it was both a diminution of life and the gateway to a more powerful participation in life as an ancestor. Generally, one could only qualify for ancestorship by becoming oneself a life-giver, and the afterlife was bound up with a person's remembrance by the living. Humans could become ancestors, and in certain cases ancestors could become humans again. Peoples like the Ashanti of Ghana have a very clear concept of reincarnation. For them a person is reincarnated again and again until his life-work is complete and he is qualified to enter the world of the ancestors [27: 39–41]. Literal reincarnation is rarer than forms of nominal reincarnation whereby the living benefit by a special protection from their ancestor namesakes. Many people, like the Shona of Zimbabwe, believe that ancestral spirits can possess the living.

African Religious Practices

Foremost among the religious practices of traditional Africa is sacrifice. Among pastoralists it tends to have a markedly piacular or expiatory character and to be offered wholly or mainly to the supreme being. It is, typically, cow-sacrifice and is a feature of the cattle-culture complex. Sacrifice in other groups, however, is far from being reserved to the supreme being alone. It is modelled on human gift-exchange and on customs connected with the sharing of food and drink. First-fruits sacrifices are very common, from the first portions of meat set aside by the hunter when he butchers his quarry, or the first portions of harvested grain, to the first mouthfuls of cooked food or the first mouthfuls of beer. Formal sacrifice at graves and shrines is usually a gift-oblation and is mostly a foodstuff or a libation. However, non-edible goods are also offered, and sometimes living animals, cows, goats or chickens are dedicated without immolation. When sacrifice is made to ancestors it is often likened to the feeding of, and caring for, old people, but it clearly goes beyond purely human ideas of eating and drinking. Ancestors are credited with exceptional knowledge and power, and sacrifice to them is an acknowledgement of their powerful role in human society. Misfortunes are very frequently attributed to a failure to offer sacrifice in due form or due time.

A very great proportion of African religious ritual is ancestral or funerary. This is especially true of territorial cults. The chief is often in some sense a 'living ancestor', ruling on behalf of his forebears and ensuring that a regular ancestral cult takes place. The rulers of chiefdom societies in western Tanzania were responsible for periodic offerings at their ancestors' graves. The rulers of the East African lake kingdoms also regulated the ritual that took place in the tomb-houses of their predecessors and at the shrines where their jaw-bones and umbilical cords were preserved. The Divine King (Oba) of Benin in Nigeria is still obliged to venerate the funerary altars of his ancestors, while in the kingdom of Ashanti the ritually blackened stools of deceased local chiefs are assembled before the king and his Golden Stool, in an important rite of national solidarity. In Ashanti also the embalmed bodies of former kings are preserved in a special mausoleum and continually repaired with gold-dust.

Mention has already been made of royal, ritual objects such as the Golden Stool of Ashanti, believed to have been conjured from heaven by the priest Anokye, and of royal drums like Byagendanwa of Ankole (Uganda). Such objects are often personified. The Golden Stool, for example, has its own stool, umbrella and attendants, and the Ankole drum has its own wives, servants and household. The ghost-horn blown during the territorial rituals of the Kimbu in western Tanzania is also symbolically identified with the country itself.

In traditional Africa practically every element of life had a religious aspect, and this was the case especially with the rites of passage. Religious invocations and offerings played a part in birth-rites and naming ceremonies, in puberty rituals and other forms of initiation, as well as in marriage ceremonial and in funerals, mourning and inheritance ceremonies. There were numerous professional associations with their own religious rituals. In the more pluralistic societies, where ego-centred networks were as strong as, or stronger than, group loyalties, there were numerous particular cults of spirits or divinities with their own ceremonial repertory of song and dance, and their own traditions of ethical behaviour.

African notions of moral evil include the factual breaking of taboos and the ordinary laws of life, as well as the more grave anti-social actions. The first may be regarded fairly lightly, with only the culprit himself to blame. In the second case, it has to be remembered that traditional society in Africa included the dead as well as the living. An offence against society was, therefore, also an offence against the guardians of society. Redressive and reconciliatory rituals consequently often contained prayer for salvation from sin and its social effects. Although sickness, suffering and misfortune were thought to reveal such offences, a clear distinction was drawn between the state of sin and its effects. Redressive rituals were typically communal, since anti-social behaviour incurred collective guilt and punishment [34]. These rites often involved public confession of faults and symbolic purification. Sometimes they included a communal gesture of renouncing the evil that had brought the misfortune.

Liminal rituals are very common in Africa. These celebrate – and, indeed, try to re-create – the liminal or marginal phase in rites of passage [33: 94–203]. It is an experience of temporary loss of status and social distinctions in which the deep springs of human interrelatedness are rediscovered. In the past, such rituals were performed by secret or semi-secret dance societies or mask societies. Often they acted out traditional cosmological myths or impersonated ancestors and historical personalities. Such were the Nyau societies of Central Malawi and the Egungun society of the Yoruba (Nigeria).

Whether it took a magical or a religious form, divination was always an important stage in the celebration of rituals in Africa. It was the divination process that decided which ritual was appropriate, and thus many religious ceremonies began with divination. If divination itself was a religious ritual it could take the form of spirit-mediumship. In some cases there was a god or divinity of divination who was thought to be the spokesman of the spirit world and who could identify which spirits or ancestors should be approached on a given occasion. Ifa, in the Yoruba pantheon, was such a god of divination.

Popular Manifestations of African Religion

At the popular level the African believer is often more engrossed in the identification of human sources of evil, and in counteracting them, than in the acknowledgement and worship of superior forces of good. The African, it has been said, is 'naked in front of evil' [17: 32]. Principally, this means that witch-finding is an important activity, and it involves recourse to the diviner and medicine man. The client approaches the diviner with certain presuppositions and suspicions, and these are rendered explicit in the divination process. The latter affords social approval for a retaliatory course of action against his enemies, and the medicine man provides protective rituals and medicines, as well as retaliatory ones.

The application of magic to areas of religious belief and practice is as rife in Africa as it is in the popular forms taken by religions elsewhere. There are societies, for example, in which it is believed that nature spirits and ancestors can be manipulated through magical processes. The Ganda (Uganda) believe that ancestral spirits can be conjured into medicine horns and then 'sent' to harm an enemy or rival. There is also the belief that a troublesome spirit can be disposed of by conjuring it into a pot which is then totally burnt and destroyed. There is also the possibility that prayer and sacrifice may take on the character of a magical technique with infallible results, if it is correctly performed.

Spirit-mediumship occurs sometimes as a popular form of prayer. It is obviously satisfactory for the worshipper to feel that he is in direct contact with the spirit he addresses and that he can obtain an immediate answer to prayer, even though the message may be somewhat enigmatic. Spirit-mediums may be possessed by nature spirits who are objects of propitiation or by ancestors and hero divinities. In some cases the medium is mentally dissociated and speaks in trance; at other times, he or she simply speaks unfalteringly from the heart, believing that what is said in perfect truth and sincerity is the message of the spirit. This is the case with the Kubandwa mediumship of Rwanda and of the Lubaale spirit-mediumship (personally observed at Kampala, 31 July 1975) in Uganda. Worshippers seek information and guidance from the spirits in this way, and they also give gifts and offer praise to them.

Popular worship takes place in the family context, chiefly through ancestral or totemic rituals. Graves and ancestor shrines or figures play an important part in this worship (figure 13.5). The wearing of protective charms and emblems is also often thought to be a means through which ancestors exercise their guardianship, and territorial rites of passage, the arrival and departure of travellers, house-moving or the opening up of new cultivation are also occasions for invoking the ancestors and possibly other spirits. Birth-rites, weddings and funerals are fundamentally family celebrations, and in many areas puberty initiation has become a family, rather than a community, affair as a result of the breakdown of traditional social structure. Reconciliation ceremonies take place at neighbourhood

Figure 13.5 *Yoruba ancestor shrine, Nigeria*

level when disputes have to be settled, and these may have a religious, even a sacrificial, character. Although on formal community occasions prayer takes the form of a lengthy praise-poem, or of litanic song, in the ordinary household the typical prayer formula is a short and familiar petition, directly stating the needs of an individual or family. Religious values enter into much of the oral literature of African peoples. Not only are there cosmological and moral themes in myth and etiological folk-tales, but religious ideas underlie proverbs and other didactic forms. Spontaneous oaths and blessings also take a religious form.

Modern Developments in African Religions

It has been estimated that between 30 and 40 per cent of the population of contemporary Africa still practise traditional African religion [2]. If Christians and Muslims who also resort occasionally to traditional practices are included, then the percentage might reach 70 per cent. It remains true, nevertheless, that African religion in its visible form, that is, as structured through pre-colonial tribal institutions, has been severely weakened. As far as ritual is concerned, the trend has been away from communitarian forms and towards individual and familial ones. With regard to concepts, beliefs and values, traditional religion is more tenacious than might be thought. Old ideas survive in new forms. Religion in Africa has always been highly absorbent and prone to syncretism, if not to reinterpretation. The playwright Wole Soyinka has described African religious symbolism as 'protean' [31: 122]. Certainly African religion has a remarkable resilience and a surprising capacity to survive in a submerged form.

Islam and Christianity have undoubtedly helped to bring about a monotheistic reinterpretation of traditional theology in some clear instances. Monica Wilson has shown how Kyala, the hero-divinity of the Nyakyusa (Tanzania) developed, under missionary influence, into the Christian God [35: 187ff], while Soyinka has argued that Idowu's concept of 'diffused monotheism', as applied to the Yoruba pantheon (Nigeria) is a Eurocentric reinterpretation [31: 108]. It is generally agreed that Christian eschatology has made a strong impact on traditional religious thought in Africa, and the idea of a bodily resurrection and future bodily existence is certainly attractive to people for whom bodily life and physical generation are important values. It may be that the conceptual formulations of Christian theology have unwittingly encouraged a literal and materialistic understanding of heaven and hell among Africans [21].

Accelerated organizational change has encouraged the growth of new forms for African traditional religion. One of these is the witch-eradication movement, which has been a recurring phenomenon in Central Africa and southern Tanzania. This is, in a sense, a millenarian phenomenon in which a group of 'experts' who are possessed of a new and effective technique claim to be able to cleanse a whole community or countryside of witches and sorcerers. Travelling from place to place, they organize collective rites of purification and reconciliation in which people renounce their witchcraft and their evil powers are neutralized. A new golden age is proclaimed in which people will be free from the fear of witchcraft and sorcery. However, disillusionment usually follows, and there may eventually be further visits from the eradicators. Tomo Nyirenda's Mwana Lesa movement and Alice Lenshina's Lumpa Church (both in Zambia) are perhaps the most famous of modern, millenarist eradication movements, but there have been numerous others ([25: 45–75]; and see chapter 14 below).

Some so-called 'Independent churches' are also traditionalist revivals rather than splinter groups from established mission churches. Other neo-traditional 'churches' are racially or ethnically conscious movements which attempt to purge foreign elements, while still other modern religious movements are frankly syncretist. Even an Independent church like the Maria Legio Church of Kenya, which is ostensibly a schism from the Roman Catholic Church, inspired by the lay association known as the Legion of Mary, is in fact better understood in terms of the *juogi* spirit beliefs of the Luo tribe. But even those independent movements like the Religion of the Ancestors (*Dini-ya Misambwa*, also in Kenya) or the ethnically conscious Kikuyu churches which nurtured the Mau Mau protest that precipitated Kenyan independence, were reinterpretations of traditional religion under the influence of Christianity.

Of equal interest is the way in which traditional values and institutions have shaped or affected religious movements which are demonstrably Christian and even orthodox Christianity itself [12]. Many Christian Independent churches have an organization which derives from traditional models of ritual or prophetic leadership. Dreams, mythology and spirit-mediumship may also play an important part in the life of these churches. In the mission-related churches, now under African leadership, the exercise of authority, as well as liturgical and musical adaptations, owes much to non-Christian traditions. Moreover, since Christian missionaries refused to accept African traditional religion as a coherent philosophy (albeit couched in symbolic and mythological language), neophytes have not been required to renounce their previous religion effectively. The result, as Robin Horton indicates, is a process of 'adhesion', rather than 'conversion', resulting in a crypto-traditionalism [15].

An interest which unites traditional religion, independent church movements, mission-related Christianity and the various forms of Islam is undoubtedly spirit-mediumship and spirit-healing. Among Christians the Pentecostal movement has exerted a strong influence, but the exorcism of evil spirits is also gaining popularity and even official approval. In the case of exorcism, the practice owes more to traditional ideas about morally neutral, but none the less malevolent, personifications of misfortune, than to Christian demonology. The Islamic jinn are also comparable to these traditional spirits. Many independent churches are basically Pentecostal, and it has been conjectured that the Pentecostalism which is now influencing Africa derives in part from spirit-possession cults which were carried to the New World by African slaves in the first place [4]. Certainly the neo-African and syncretic cults in Brazil and elsewhere tend to emphasize spirit-mediumship [3].

Finally, it cannot be denied that politicians and statesmen in independent African countries have exploited traditional beliefs as well as the politico-religious character of traditional leadership in order to consolidate their power. This opportunism has been denounced by – among others – Wole Soyinka as a trivialization of the essential, 'with catch-all diversionary slogans such as "authenticité"' [31: 109]. In spite of such false prophets of retrieval, traditional religious values continue to exert their influence both within and outside the religious organizations of contemporary black Africa and to presage the transformation even of Islam and Christianity.

More Recent Developments

African religions have retained their importance during the last quarter of the twentieth century, especially through their increased influence on the mainstream churches and faiths and on new religious movements in the continent. Traditional religious rituals are still performed in many contexts by educated and even 'Westernized' Africans. Often these contexts relate to marriage, childbirth, burial, inheritance or royal succession. Three outstanding examples which took place in 1986 can be cited here as examples. In April of that year, a young teenager was whisked from his college in England to the throne of Swaziland in southern Africa. The young monarch, Mswati III, underwent elaborate secret rituals in which he was symbolically sacrificed for the nation. In August a Tanzanian bank manager and Member of Parliament went through a complicated series of rituals at his father's graveside. During the ceremonies he was introduced to his ancestors as the new senior chief of the Kimbu tribe and was empowered to communicate with them. In December of the same year a five-month legal tussle began in Kenya between relatives by marriage, belonging to different tribes, over the burial of a prominent Nairobi lawyer. The traditionalists won. Such examples abound, and they demonstrate the tenacity of traditional religion.

In July 1993 the traditional kingdoms were restored in Uganda, chief among them being the Kingdom of Buganda. Twenty-seven years after his father fled the country, Ronald Muwenda Mutebi II became the thirty-sixth Kabaka of Buganda. Lengthy traditional ceremonies took place in secrecy on the royal hill of Budo, during which the new king struck the *kyebabon*, or royal drum. This was followed by a Christian coronation ceremony. The restoration of these monarchies is another example of a public return to traditional ritual and of a cultural recovery affecting many parts of Africa.

There is also abundant evidence of continuing witchcraft practices and beliefs. Witchcraft cleansing is increasingly popular, especially in Central Africa, and it often takes on the character of a new religious movement. It tends to be directed against anti-social elements, as well as against mainstream Christianity, especially

Catholicism. Puritanical Protestant attitudes help the adepts to recognize Catholic devotional objects as instruments of witchcraft. Witchcraft is generally believed to be an ever-present reality and it continues to command the attention of traditional healers and diviners in both rural and urban areas.

The massive influx of migrants to the towns and cities of Africa over the past decade has increased the tensions which give rise to accusations of witchcraft. It has also probably encouraged traditional healers to adopt a more modern appearance. Frequently, they stress the 'scientific' character of their practice, and like to claim proficiency in palmistry, astrology or herbal medicine. They also adopt the titles of 'Doctor' 'Professor' or 'Sheikh'. However, their techniques still include traditional religious rituals, the interpretation of dreams and the propitiation of spirits.

The mainstream Christian churches have taken a more serious interest in traditional African religion. Greater pastoral attention to traditional religion has been called for, and some attempts at formal dialogue with its practitioners have even taken place. Most of the interest, however, centres on the concept of inculturation, the idea that the Christian Gospel should engage in dialogue with traditional religion from within and that Christianity should be re-expressed in African cultural and religious forms. Two well-known instances in which the Catholic church has formally come to terms with African religious ideas are the Zaire Mass and the Zimbabwe Second Burial Rite.

At the same time, the Independent churches, which have always been vehicles for the beliefs and values of traditional religion, have tended to become more sophisticated. This is partly due to urbanization, and it is noticeable that these movements flourish in African towns and cities. In some cases, as in Kenya, they have become organized into associations of churches. Although they still cater mainly for the poorer classes, there is a considerable fluidity of membership between them and the mainstream churches. This suggests that they have a wider, if not a growing, appeal, and that they cater for certain religious needs more successfully than mainstream Christianity.

Much of this new sophistication derives from the Pentecostalist explosion of the 1980s. On the one hand, a fundamentalist form of evangelical Christianity, which reflects the response of the southern United States to modern social and geopolitical trends, has begun to affect Africa. On the other hand, African Independent churches have been finding among the proponents of this form of Christianity sponsors for their own foundations. The popular form of this fundamentalism, promoted by crusades and Bible schools, ascribes individual and social evils to demons. To this is added the faith-gospel promise of health and wealth to all who believe and who support evangelism.

Such teachings have found an immediate echo in the African religious mentality. One widespread consequence has been the demonization of traditional alien spirits, and the proliferation of Christian exorcists – even in the mainstream churches – one of the most celebrated of whom is Emmanuel Milingo, former Catholic Archbishop of Lusaka, called to Rome in 1982. Another consequence has been to strengthen the preoccupation with health and healing, and to encourage a form of faith which virtually transforms new religious movements into African 'cargo cults'.

So far from encouraging Independent churches to become protest movements, the millenarianism and dispensationalism of the new trends from America have made them submissive and docile to brutal totalitarian regimes, and have helped to entrench the rule of corrupt and inhuman dictators. There has been little evidence, so far, of a traditionalist backlash against this new form of American and/or Western religious influence.

The most fruitful prospects for the visible survival of traditional religion in Africa probably lie in the tolerance now being shown by mainstream Christianity and the latter's desire for genuine dialogue and coexistence.

Bibliography

1 ACHEBE, C. *Things Fall Apart*, London, Heinemann, 1958; New York, McDowell, Obolensky, 1959

2 ARINZE, F., and TSHIBANGU, T., 'Rapport du groupe des religions traditionelles africaines', *Bulletin: Secretariatus pro non-Christianis* (Vatican City), vol. 14, nos 2–3, 1979, pp. 187–90

3 BASTIDE, R., *The African Religions of Brazil* (tr. H. Sebba), Baltimore/London, Johns Hopkins University Press, 1978; first publ. As *Les Religions africaines au Brésil*, Paris, Presses Universitaires de France, 1960

4 BECKMANN, D. M., *Eden Revival: Spiritual Churches in Ghana*, St Louis, Concordia, 1975

5 BERNARDI, B., *The Mugwe, A Failing Prophet: A Study of a Religious and Public Dignitary of the Meru of Kenya*, London/New York, Oxford University Press/International African Institute, 1959

6 DE HEUSCH, L., *Sacrifice in Africa: A Structuralist Approach*, Manchester, Manchester University Press, 1985

7 DOUGLAS, M., *Implicit Meanings: Essays in Anthropology*, London/Boston, Routledge, 1975

8 DOUGLAS, M., *Natural Symbols: Explorations in Cosmology*, London, Barrie & Rockliff/New York, Pantheon, 1970; 2nd edn London, Barrie & Jenkins/New York, Vintage, 1973

9 DOUGLAS, M., *Purity and Danger: An Analysis of Concepts of Pollution and Taboo*, London, Routledge/New York, Praeger, 1966

10 EVANS-PRITCHARD, SIR EDWARD E., *The Comparative Method in Social Anthropology*, London, Athlone Press, 1963 (L. T. Hobhouse Memorial Lecture no. 33)

11 EVANS-PRITCHARD, SIR EDWARD E., *Nuer Religion*, Oxford, Clarendon Press, 1962; 1st publ. 1956; new edn London, Oxford University Press, 1970

12 FASHOLÉ-LUKE, E. W., et al. (eds), *Christianity in Independent Africa*, London, R. Collings/Bloomington, Indiana University Press, 1978

13 GIFFORD, P., *Christianity and Politics in Doe's Liberia*, Cambridge, Cambridge University Press, 1993

14 GRAY, R., 'Christianity and Religious Change in Africa', in *The Church in a Changing Society*, Stockholm, Almqvist & Wiksell (distr.), 1978 (CIHEC Conference, Uppsala, 1977), pp. 345–52

15 HORTON, R., 'On the Reality of Conversion in Africa', *Africa*, vol. 7, no. 2, 1975, pp. 132–64

16 IDOWU, E. B., *African Traditional Religion: A Definition*, London, SCM/Maryknoll, NY, Orbis, 1973

17 ILIFFE, J., *A Modern History of Tanganyika*, Cambridge/New York, Cambridge University Press, 1979

18 KENYATTA, J., *Facing Mount Kenya: The Tribal Life of the Gikuyu*, London, Secker & Warburg, 1938, repr. 1953; school edn Nairobi, Heinemann, 1971

19 LIENHARDT, G., *Divinity and Experience: The Religion of the Dinka*, Oxford, Clarendon Press, 1961

20 MBITI, J. S., *African Religions and Philosophy*, London/Ibadan, Heinemann; New York, Praeger, 1969

21 MBITI, J. S., *New Testament Eschataology in an African Background*, London, Oxford University Press, 1971

22 MURDOCK, G. P., *Africa: Its Peoples and their Culture History*, New York, McGraw-Hill, 1959

23 NGUGI WA THIONGO, *Petals of Blood*, London, Heinemann, 1977

24 OGOT, B. A., *History of the Southern Luo*, vol. 1, *Migration and Settlement, 1500–1900*, Nairobi, East African Publishing House, 1967

25 RANGER, T. O., 'The Mwana Lesa Movement of 1925', in T. O. Ranger and I. N. Kimambo (eds), *The Historical Study of African Religion*, London, Heinemann, 1972; Berkeley, University of California Press, 1972, repr. 1976, pp. 45–75

26 RANGER, T. O., and KIMAMBO, I. N., *The Historical Study of African Religion*, London, Heinemann, 1972; Berkeley, University of California Press, 1972, repr. 1976

27 SARPONG, P. K., *Ghana in Retrospect: Some Aspects of Ghanaian Culture*, Tema, Ghana Publishing Corporation, 1974

28 SCHOFFELEERS, M., 'The Interaction of the M'Bona Cult and Christianity, 1859–1963', in T. O. Ranger and J. Weller (eds), *Themes in the Christian History of Central Africa*, London, Heinemann/Berkeley, University of California Press, 1975, pp. 14–29

29 SHORTER, A., *The Church in the African City*, London, Geoffrey Chapman, 1991

30 SHORTER, A., *Jesus and the Witchdoctor: An Approach to Healing and Wholeness*, London, Geoffrey Chapman, 1985

31 SOYINKA, W., *Myth, Literature and the African World*, Cambridge, Cambridge University Press, 1978; 1st edn 1976

32 TER HAAR, G., *Spirit of Africa: The Healing Ministry of Archbishop Milingo of Zambia*, London, Hurst, 1992

33 TURNER, V. W., *The Ritual Process: Structure and Anti-Structure*, London, Routledge/Chicago, Aldine, 1969

34 TURNER, V. W., *Schism and Continuity in an African Society: A Study of Ndembu Village Life*, Manchester, Manchester University Press, 1957

35 WILSON, M., *Communal Rituals of the Nyakyusa*, London/New York, Oxford University Press/International African Institute, 1959

14

New Religious Movements in Primal Societies

HAROLD W. TURNER

Introduction

In the last few centuries, and notably in the twentieth, the tribal peoples of the Americas, Asia, Africa and the Pacific have responded to their increasing interaction with the more sophisticated and powerful societies and religions by developing their own new religious movements. These usually differ at some important points from both the local tribal (here called primal) religion and the more universal religion concerned. Such movements have arisen in the interaction with Western culture and the Christian religion following the expansion of the European peoples across the world, but they also occur in relation to Hindu, Buddhist and, to a lesser extent, Islamic contacts.

Most of these religious movements possess no written sacred texts or other sources and have depended instead on a new oral tradition. This oral tradition enshrines the account of the origins of the movement, often the story of the founder's call and early struggles. These may also have been recorded in a diary or journal, or as a written testimony, and they can then assume the status of an authoritative canon or incipient scriptures. Sometimes this material is presented as having been given in written form from heaven, or otherwise divinely revealed. The oral tradition may also include new forms of old myths, and very often a body of sacred songs and prayers that may become the basis for a printed hymn-book or liturgy, as commonly in Africa and among New Zealand Maoris. In general, however, much earlier information comes not from such primary sources but from the rather hostile accounts of outsiders – colonial government agents or soldiers, travellers and missionaries. Since the mid-twentieth century there has been an increasing flow of scholarly information from more systematic and sympathetic academic studies.

There seem to have been few if any equivalent movements among the tribal peoples of North Africa and Europe during the earlier Christian expansion into these areas. The history of these movements may be said to start with European colonial and missionary expansion into Central and South America. Probably the earliest recorded movement occurred in Guatemala in 1530, followed by others in Colombia, Brazil, Paraguay, Bolivia, Peru, etc., up to the present day. In the sixteenth century similar movements appeared in west central Africa after the conversion of the old Kingdom of the Kongo by Portuguese missionaries. Few of these movements lasted long, and it is in North America that the first of the movements still surviving appeared: the Narragansett Indian Church in Rhode Island in the 1740s, and the Handsome Lake Religion among the Seneca from 1800. These were followed by the Peyote cult or Native American Church, which has spread over much of North America in the last 100 years and is now the main Indian example (see p. 515 above). Although the first Caribbean movement was George Liele's Native Baptist Church in Jamaica in the 1780s, most movements – Pocomania, Revival Zion, Bedwardism, Convince, Santeria, Shango, Spiritual Baptists, Rastafarianism, etc. – were later nineteenth- and twentieth-century developments. Modern movements in black Africa trace back to Ntsikana and Makanna, Xhosa prophets at the beginning of the nineteenth century, but the great proliferation of Independent churches (as most intend to be) began late in the century and has continued ever since. Similar developments occurred in the Philippines and in Oceania throughout the nineteenth century, especially among the New Zealand Maoris, as in the Pai Marire and Ringatu religions. But it is in Melanesia, and since the 1930s, that most movements have appeared – usually small, short-lived and of the cargo-cult form [6]. In Asia, the new religions of Japan are rather different phenomena, but the 200 that have appeared in Korea in the past century or more are somewhat close to the new tribal movements. Elsewhere in Asia these have occurred in Siberia, in India among the scheduled tribes interacting with Hindu or Christian traditions since the eighteenth century, and in Burma and South-East Asia among the hill tribal peoples influenced by Buddhist culture or Christian missions in the same period. Indonesian movements have appeared in the later nineteenth and the twentieth century, either in relation to Christian contacts, or with an Islamic background, but the latter shade off into Islamic mystical movements that differ from new tribal religions.

The first major scholarly study in this field was James Mooney's on the Ghost Dance religion, in 1896 [5]; this also included substantial accounts of most other movements among Indians in the United States. Other anthropologists developed the study further, both in the Americas and in other parts of the world, giving us the common terms 'nativistic' [4] and 'revitalization' [10] for these movements, seen as acculturation phenomena, together with various systems of classification. Other human sciences have produced major studies, each in terms of its own categories. Sociologists have seen the movements as products of social change and in relation to traditional social structures; economists have been concerned with material wants, with relative deprivation, and hence with cargo cults as a search for wealth in irrational ways; political scientists have studied the effects of colonialism and spoken of 'protest' movements, and indeed earlier movements often did come into violent clashes with governments and were suppressed; psychologists have used the categories of neurosis and crisis, and investigated the psyche of founders and leaders; and historians have sought to place these new movements in their wider context and trace their development over the years, as well as to stress the place of the individual in the appearance and shaping of the movement. By contrast, the first major study of African movements was that of the missionary–scholar, B. G. M. Sundkler, in 1948 [7]; while using many of the above categories, he also gave attention to the religious features and the spiritual search apparent in the Zulu prophet movements he surveyed. Other scholars in the religious disciplines produced most of the major African studies until the more recent advent of the historians and social scientists [8; 9].

Since these movements are now better understood as religious developments, although necessarily conditioned by the various other factors identified above, a classification may be offered in terms of the degree of interaction between the two religious traditions concerned. Those seeking to remodel the existing primal religion with some borrowed elements may be called neo-primal; those deliberately rejecting the local and the invading traditions in favour of a new composite form drawn from both of the others may be called synthetist; in the case of those related to Christianity a third type of movement which resembles the religion of ancient Israel and stresses the Hebrew scriptures or 'Old Testament' may be called hebraist; those which go beyond this point in their biblical content and possess some form of Christology may be called Independent churches (see figure 14.1). Some movements, of course, overlap these analytic categories. Various names have been used – 'millennial' and 'messianic' movements, 'prophet', 'syncretist' or 'separatist' cults, etc. The term 'adjustment movements', commonly used of Melanesia, is useful, but the best working name is probably 'new religious movements' (i.e. in primal societies interacting with more powerful societies and their universal religions).

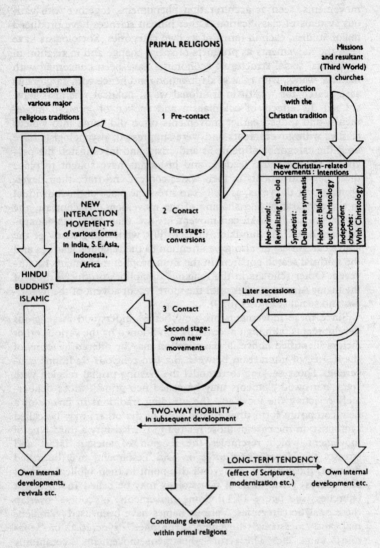

PRIMAL RELIGIONS

Interaction with various major religious traditions

Missions and resultant (Third World) churches

Interaction with the Christian tradition

1 Pre-contact

NEW INTERACTION MOVEMENTS of various forms in India, S.E. Asia, Indonesia, Africa

2 Contact

First stage: conversions

New Christian-related movements: Intentions

Neo-primal: Revitalizing the old

Synthetist: Deliberate synthesis

Hebraist: Biblical but no Christology

Independent churches: With Christology

HINDU BUDDHIST ISLAMIC

3 Contact

Second stage: own new movements

Later secessions and reactions

TWO-WAY MOBILITY in subsequent development

Own internal developments, revivals etc.

LONG-TERM TENDENCY (effect of Scriptures, modernization etc.)

Own internal development etc.

Continuing development within primal religions

Figure 14.1 *Varieties of religious content and intentions in new religious movements in primal societies*

Basic Beliefs

Common to most movements is the belief in a new revelation specially given from the spirit world to a local founder or leader. This often occurs through a dream or a mystical experience of dying, visiting heaven and being commissioned to return to earth with a new ritual and moral code, and with divine power, especially for healing. There is usually an emphasis upon a single supreme and personal God, either as a development from a possibly remote High God in the traditional primal religion, or in replacement of the former spirits and divinities. Some of the latter may be transposed into angels or saints, or else demoted as the devil. Reliance on this supreme and powerful God usually results in rejection of the use of magic, although belief in its effectiveness when used by others may continue.

The new religion usually offers definite practical blessings, here and now, in the form of mental or physical healing, further individual revelations for guidance from the spirit world, or promises of success and prosperity, or of protection from evil forces. These blessings may be set within the wider promise of a new social or world order that is shortly to appear, perhaps through some cataclysmic event or messianic leader. This new order may introduce a paradisal era of peace, health and plenty; lost lands or a previous state of sinlessness may be recovered; oppression and humiliation at the hands of conquerors or colonial powers will cease, and the tables may even be turned with the tribal peoples in a dominant position. Such millennialism is common in some regions, as in Melanesian cargo cults, but is rarer in other regions, as in Africa where the emphasis is upon immediate practical benefits.

These promised blessings lead to a new, hopeful and confident attitude to life, as well as to a new self-respect, a sense of dignity and of identity among peoples whose morale has been undermined by the traumatic effects of interaction with the invading society. This confidence rests upon the belief in the new authoritative revelation given especially for themselves, and upon the conviction that supernatural help is to be given towards these various blessings. This help may come from God or Jesus or some other being in the spirit world, such as guardian angels, ancestors or culture heroes, or the deceased founder returning from the dead once again. Receipt of the blessings also depends upon faithful observance of the new forms of worship, perhaps upon extensive performance of the new ritual dances (as in the 'Ghost', i.e. ancestor, dances of Native Americans or of prayers, fastings and other disciplines, and the observance of a strict moral code.

Whereas primal religions are characteristically confined to one tribal group, the new religious movements show various degrees of a more universal outlook. The revelation and the blessings are then regarded as given for other adjacent tribes, for all of their own race, or even for the whole world including the whites, who will then depend upon the tribal people for their full salvation. Thus while Godianism, a sophisticated neo-primal religion in eastern Nigeria, promotes a single God of Africa and rejects Christianity as for whites only, another Nigerian movement calls itself 'The Church of the Lord (Aladura) Throughout the World', and has had the occasional white member and branches in Britain.

Two of the basic drives at work in these new religious movements are the search for meaning and the quest for spiritual power. On the one hand, confidence in the traditional primal world-view with its religious beliefs and practices has been eroded, for it cannot cope with the new inter-cultural situation or defend its adherents against the religious system and world-view of the invasive society. On the other hand, there are many for whom the new religion, in the foreign form in which it arrives, also fails to provide the necessary meaning and spiritual power for daily living in a situation of great cultural change. (See figure 14.2.) Peoples across the tribal world have therefore created new religious systems of their own, combining in various degrees something of their existing world-view and cultural forms with the new views and practices of the more powerful invasive religion. Sets of beliefs from the two systems may merely coexist somewhat incongruously; in other cases there is a creative synthesis into a new belief-system that brings meaning and power to its adherents. The new system of belief will be implied and expressed in concrete popular forms of prophecy, ritual, dance, song, story, healing, code of conduct, etc.; it is less likely to articulate the analysis used here or to take the form of theology, doctrine or creed in a Western Christian manner.

Characteristic Practices

Many movements engage in a selective and dramatic rejection of some of the old ways, in preparation for the expected new order. Cargo cultists may kill the pigs, cease gardening and even destroy the food stores in view of the imminent supernatural abundance; Siberian shamans' drums have been burnt and Native American medicine bags thrown away. These are more extreme examples, but it is common to destroy ritual objects or shrines and especially magic paraphernalia, for the power formerly sought in this way is now derived from faith in the new God.

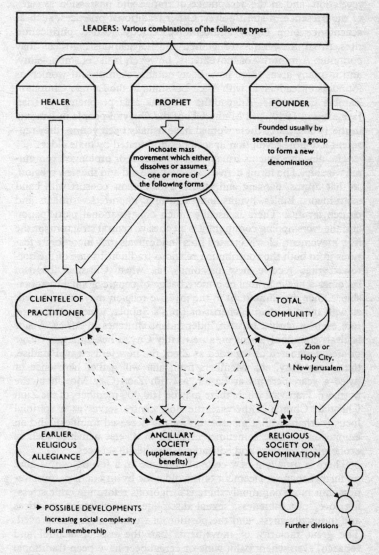

LEADERS: Various combinations of the following types

HEALER

PROPHET

FOUNDER

Founded usually by
secession from a group
to form a new
denomination

Inchoate mass
movement which either
dissolves or assumes
one or more of
the following forms

CLIENTELE OF
PRACTITIONER

TOTAL
COMMUNITY

Zion or
Holy City,
New Jerusalem

EARLIER
RELIGIOUS
ALLEGIANCE

ANCILLARY
SOCIETY
(supplementary
benefits)

RELIGIOUS
SOCIETY OR
DENOMINATION

- - - ► POSSIBLE DEVELOPMENTS
  Increasing social complexity
  Plural membership

Further divisions

Figure 14.2   *Variety of social forms in new religious movements in primal societies*

There are, however, substantial retentions of the old ways, especially in the continued reliance on dreams and visions as a means of revelation, and in the acceptance of trance and possession as signs of the presence of spirit power. Other traditional practices, such as acceptance of a highly authoritative 'chiefly' leader, purification rites, ritual uncleanness of women and polygamous marriage, may continue. A minority of movements, however, insist on monogamy, and in many areas there have been notable examples of women as founders or leaders, as with Alice Lenshina in the Lumpa Church in Zambia from 1953, Angganitha the Biak area prophetess in Irian Jaya around 1940, and Mama Chi of the Guaymi people in Panama in the 1960s. Since these women have usually been young, they represent a double revolution in societies dominated by male elders.

The new movements usually stress frequent or prolonged communal worship. The forms derive from both the old and the new religion, so that drums, dancing and reporting of dreams consort with band instruments, Bibles, hymns and preaching, imported vestments and church layouts. There is usually much congregational participation and the worshipping community is a cohesive central structure for the new movement. Newly created rites and festivals may incorporate features from both the contributing religious traditions; some of the borrowed rites receive new meanings, as when Christian baptism becomes a healing ritual or a mere badge of congregational membership. Other rites important in the invasive religion may be neglected, as with the Christian eucharist or Lord's Supper, which tends to be rare even in fairly Christian Independent churches in Africa. Major festivals commonly focus on a new Holy City, a headquarters village or area designated or regarded as Zion, the new Jerusalem, Paradise, the Happy City, etc. Members from afar will gather here once or twice a year, perhaps at Easter, as with Zion City Moriah in the northern Transvaal where there may be 100,000 members of the Zion Christian Church. Otherwise the holy centre serves as a spiritual focus (perhaps with a mausoleum for the deceased founder), and an administrative base sometimes involved in diverse activities such as economic enterprises and educational and health services.

There is usually a new code of conduct. In a few cases this goes no further than replacement of the old code by an era of permissiveness, but more commonly there is a rigorous reforming ethic stressing love, peaceableness, sexual discipline, humanitarian practices and industriousness, and the position of women is often improved. The great majority of movements ban the use of alcohol and tobacco, even where palm wine or cereal beer have been traditional and local missions have allowed smoking and drinking. In newly developing countries, where alcohol and tobacco manufacturing are most inappropriate forms of economic development, this ascetic ethic is of considerable value.

The chief practical blessing offered by the new movements is usually mental and physical healing, for this deals with the most urgent problem of many tribal peoples, often accentuated rather than diminished by Western contacts. The central methods used are religious, such as confession, prayer, fasting, anointment with holy water or other rituals, together with the support of the believing community. Western physical treatment is usually rejected but some traditional herbal and purgative treatments may be retained. These methods have considerable efficacy within the cultural and social situation, especially for the more psychosomatic ailments, and with people for whom modern scientific medical treatment is either inaccessible or unsuitable. The tendency, however, is to accept the modern scientific treatment along with continued use of the traditional religious methods.

A more general benefit lies in the new religious communities which replace or transcend the old tribal groups and, where these are disrupted, offer a new 'place to belong', with new roles, especially for women and for young men. There are often many official positions with ranks, titles, uniforms and insignia. The social structure ranges from loosely associated decentralized groups such as the Native American Church or the Rastafarians to highly integrated and centralized bodies with hierarchical systems such as some of the larger African Independent churches. Either social form may span many tribal peoples within the one movement, and especially in Africa may transcend international boundaries; some Nigerian independent churches have spread around West Africa and to Britain, and the Kimbanguist Church in Zaire has many members in a number of central African countries. This expansion as a more universal faith reveals a remarkable missionary zeal once a movement breaks from its original tribal context, something that was quite unknown in the original primal ethnocentric religion. Some movements, however, remain essentially tribal, such as the great Nazarite Church of Shembe among the Zulu, and gain part of their strength from revitalization of the local culture.

In their early stages many movements have clashed with governments, often violently, and have been repressed as subversive, rebellious or harmful to their adherents. In the case of the more exotic movements, or of founders who were charlatans, this has been unavoidable, but too often the authorities have failed to appreciate the genuine religious motivations embedded in the new forms. The age-old conflict between rulers and prophets is seen again in these movements, but once they are established many settle down to an apolitical existence, concentrating on worship, pastoral functions, the spreading of the movement and any associated economic or developmental activities.

Recent Developments

The considerable amount of study given to these movements since the 1950s has assisted governments (and others) to a better understanding, although clashes are still possible. In the New Hebrides of the 1970s there was tension between the Nagriamel movement of Jimmy Stevens and the authorities, culminating in an attempted secession from the new Vanuatu state in 1980. This had to be dealt with by military means; what is not as widely known is that there was a new syncretistic Christian dimension to this movement and that this continued in a more apolitical form.

In the Philippines the potential for conflict remains, but the largest of the new movements, the Iglesia ni Cristo, has had an understanding with the government, to their mutual advantage, since the late 1960s. Similarly in South Africa some of the Independent or Zionist churches cooperated with the government in spite of the apartheid policy, and for some years in the 1970s the government even provided a theological training college for their ministers. The Kimbanguist Church in Zaire has been regarded favourably by the government, and even the much-persecuted Peyote cult or Native American Church in the US is securing religious freedom as state bans and other types of opposition are being removed. In contrast, during the 1970s there were several African countries where governments proscribed a wide range of indigenous movements, even if not always very effectively, and in Melanesia new cargo cults or revival movements that conflict with public order or welfare will continue to pose problems to government.

The great majority of movements, especially in more recent times, have arisen by interaction with the Christian tradition, and since about 1960 there has been considerable change in the attitudes of churches and missions towards them. Hostility, suspicion and ignorance are giving way to a better appreciation and a desire to cooperate with the new movements where possible. These are seen as extensive forms of grass-roots indigenization of the Christian faith, showing considerable creativity in forms of worship and styles of life, with a valuable if sometimes unorthodox evangelistic achievement, and performing a pastoral function in local cultural terms. Some of the African Independent churches have been admitted to the World Council of Churches and to national Christian councils, and in West Africa, Zimbabwe, Kenya, etc., various mission bodies have entered into partnership with some of the independent churches for Bible study and leadership training. Elsewhere fraternal relations may be established, as with the Ratana and Ringatu faiths in New Zealand, the Daku community in Fiji, the

Hallelujah religion in Guyana, and even with the Rastafarians in Jamaica and the Peyote cult in the US.

One sign of the developing interest in these movements was the establishment in the University of Aberdeen in 1973 of a documentation centre for this subject. In 1981 this unique collection of resources, covering all continents, was transferred to the Selly Oak Colleges, Birmingham, England, as a Study Centre for New Religious Movements in Primal Societies, and microfilmed copies of its resources were made available across the Third World. Doctoral candidates in the latter, as well as in Western countries, commonly choose one of these new movements for their research, and academic interest in many disciplines has been increasing. It is realized that many of the processes and problems of social, cultural and religious change in the developing world or among tribal peoples can fruitfully be studied through these specific and spontaneous manifestations of such changes. Development agencies, however, have not shown interest in the modernization and development potential of these new movements; this is considerable, for all such movements represent local transitions, at the grass-roots level and in varying degrees, from the old order to the new. The movements themselves also show changes in their religious content. There is a tendency for those towards the left of the four-point spectrum shown in figure 14.1 to move to the right, becoming more acculturated and identified with the religious forms and contents of the invasive religion, especially where this is the Christian tradition. Here the influence of the scriptures and the association with Western modernization contribute to this result. Examples of the opposite movement are less common, as with the hebraist movement, the Bayudaya of Uganda, which is now clearly an African Judaism whereas in the 1920s it began as a Christian movement. In general, and contrary to the interpretations of earlier observers before the 1960s, these movements function as bridges into the future rather than back to the past.

In Africa, new religious movements have been profoundly affected by influences from the United States during the 1980s. Not only have American and Western evangelists addressed huge rallies in various African countries, but crusades, using TV satellite and local radio, as well as Western-trained local evangelists, have taken place. American churches and congregations have also offered financial sponsorship to African Independent churches, and these have often been encouraged to form associations among themselves.

The major influences have come from the Pentecostalist and Faith Gospel traditions. They have tended to strengthen the prophetic and healing tradition of new religious movements in Africa, but they have also helped to marginalize them politically, since they discourage socio-political involvement and lay heavy emphasis on personal, rather than social, sin, as well as on health and wealth for the righteous. They also encourage an understanding of the Bible as a book of prophecies concerning contemporary events, and interpret them as anticipating the imminent coming of Christ.

The new religious movements also represent a massive response to the traumatic changes experienced by the tribal peoples in the twentieth century, although statistics are somewhat uncertain. The greatest proliferation has been in Africa, where there could be upwards of 10 million people in 8,000–10,000 movements, some 3,000 of them in South Africa alone, and over 500 in Ghana. Many are small and some are ephemeral, but their places are taken by others and the larger ones dating from earlier in the century are well established. The largest is the Kimbanguist Church: the 3 million adherents claimed for it may not be too inaccurate. The Iglesia ni Cristo in the Philippines may have the 1 million members it claims, and there are probably well over 500 other movements there. The Ratana and Ringatu movements in New Zealand have some 40,000 census members, about one-seventh of the Maori population. It is probably safe to say that there are between 12 million and 20 million people involved in this development across the continents, although any figure depends on how these movements are defined. What is clear is that they are extensive, still growing, and of considerable significance from religious as well as from other viewpoints [3].

Bibliography

1 BASTIDE, R., *The African Religions of Brazil* (tr. H. Sebba), Baltimore/London, Johns Hopkins University Press, 1978; prev. publ. as *Les Religions africaines au Brésil*, Paris, Presses Universitaires de France, 1960

2 BINNEY, J., CHAPLIN, G., and WALLACE, C., *Mihaia: The Prophet Rua-Kenana and his Community at Maungapohatu*, Wellington, NZ, Oxford University Press, 1979

3 HESSELGRAVE, D. J. (ed.), *Dynamic Religious Movements: Case Studies of Rapidly Growing Religious Movements around the World*, Grand Rapids, MI, Baker Book House, 1978

4 LINTON, R., 'Nativistic Movements', *American Anthropologist*, vol. 45, no. 2, 1943, pp. 230–40

5 MOONEY, J., *The Ghost Dance Religion and the Sioux Outbreak of 1890*, Washington, DC, Government Printing Office, 1896; abr. edn, Chicago, Chicago University Press, 1965; originally formed part 2 of the *Fourteenth Annual Report of the Bureau of Ethnology, 1892–3*

6 STEINBAUER, F., *Melanesian Cargo Cults: New Salvation Movements in the South Pacific* (tr. M. Wohlwill), London, George Prior/St Lucia, University of Queensland Press, 1979

7 SUNDKLER, B. G. M., *Bantu Prophets in South Africa*, London, Lutterworth, 1948; 2nd edn London/New York, Oxford University Press/International African Institute, 1961

8 TURNER, H. W., *Bibliography of New Religious Movements in Primal Societies*, Boston, G. K. Hall: vol. 1, *Black Africa*, 1977; vol. 2, *North America*, 1979; vol. 3, *Oceania*, forthcoming

9 TURNER, H., *Religious Innovation in Africa*, Boston, G. K. Hall, 1980

10 WALLACE, A. F. C., 'Revitalization Movements', *American Anthropologist*, vol. 58, no. 2, 1956, pp. 264–81

15

Modern Alternative Religions in the West

J. GORDON MELTON

During the twentieth century, the West has experienced a phenomenon it has not encountered since the reign of Constantine: the growth of and significant visible presence of a variety of non-Christian and non-orthodox Christian bodies competing for the religious allegiance of the public. This growth of so many religious alternatives is forcing a new situation on the West in which the still dominant Christian religion must operate in a new pluralistic religious environment.

Recognition of what was happening was slow in coming. Early in the twentieth century, conservative religious leaders, primarily fundamentalist Christians, felt the presence of some alternative religions such as Spiritualism and Christian Science and new religious perspectives such as humanism and modernism. Seeing a threat to orthodoxy, they attacked the alternatives as heresies, apostasy and the influence of Satan, and developed the 'cult' model for understanding these groups. Each author assailed those groups that offered the greatest threat to his or her particular orthodox perspective. Social scientists also lumped these different religions together as 'the cults', rather than calling them churches or sects, but did little research on them. During the last generation, in response to the rapid growth of the alternative religions since the Second World War, a new group of scholars has arisen who see these alternative and non-conventional religions as 'new' religions or new religious movements (NRMs) and who have devoted several decades to extensive research on them and the people who have joined them. The area has proved so fruitful in extending our knowledge of the dynamics of religious life that what amounts to a subdiscipline in the sociology of religion has emerged among scholars who have specialized in studying them.

The designation 'new religions' properly conveys the recognition of the manner in which fresh religious expressions are competing with secularizing forces in directing the future of Western society. The emergence of new spiritualities is not unique to this generation, however, and some historical perspective is needed to grasp the significance of the current presence of NRMs.

Beginnings

As both political and intellectual forces in the eighteenth century freed the religious environment from the control of the state church, and fostered initially a climate of religious tolerance, and then genuine religious liberties, alternative religions began to appear. First came the Quakers, then the perfectionists (i.e. the Wesleyans), the Deists, the Swedenborgians and the Millennialists. By the beginning of the nineteenth century, new patterns of religious growth were evident. Periodically, the West convulsed with religious revivals as the churches, no longer always supported by state taxes, were forced to find ways to gain the voluntary support of the populace. Each wave of religious fervour, beginning with the well-known 'Second Great Awakening' at the start of the nineteenth century, saw the birth of new alternative churches and religions. Older, minuscule groups often seized the opportunity of the revivals to jump into prominence. The 'Second Great Awakening' in America launched the Methodists, Baptists, Disciples of Christ and Cumberland Presbyterians into the prominent position they attained during the rest of the century and initiated an era of prosperity for the Shakers. Later periods of revival saw the rise of Spiritualism, Latter-day Saints, the Holiness Churches, New Thought, Christian Science and Pentecostalism. From their American beginnings, each soon travelled abroad, some gaining their greatest acceptance in a European (Spiritualism) or South American (Pentecostalism) home.

Until the end of the nineteenth century, the alternatives were basically indigenous to the West. England (with Ann Lee, 1736–84; Joanna Southcott, 1730–1814), the European continent (Swedenborg; the German Brethren) and the New World (Joseph Smith, 1805–44; Mary Baker Eddy, 1821–1910) each contributed new leadership. However, in 1893 a very different set of 'alternatives' arrived in the West. In that year, the League of Liberal Clergymen of Chicago, Illinois, sponsored the World's Parliament of Religions, when for the first time representatives of all the major world faiths assembled in a large Western city for a religious showcase without precedent. Buddhists, Hindus, Sikhs, Muslims, Confucians and Jews joined Spiritualists, Taoists, Parsis and Christians of every perspective for this giant conclave. Some saw the gathering as merely a big religious show, with little future significance. Yet the Parliament initiated some profound changes, especially among the religions of the East. The enthusiastic welcome given to Eastern thinkers such as Vivekananda, A. R. M. Webb and Shaku Soyen led directly to the founding of centres of Hinduism, Islam and Buddhism in the United States and to the spread of these religions in the West. Spurred by the warm experience, Eastern religious leaders began to see the West as a fertile mission field and set as their goal the returning of the favour accorded them by the nineteenth-century Christian missionary movement into Asia.

The mere fact of the Parliament being held underscored a new attitude of respect among Western scholars and religious leaders for the non-Christian religions of the world. Although many years were to pass before a majority of Christians would move beyond the view that other religions were at best pagan and heathen (and those of Asia a major source of degradation), the Parliament gave many the opportunity to see at first hand the depth and sophistication of non-Christian religious thought. After the Parliament, the various Eastern religions began to appear in the urban landscape, despite strong anti-Asian prejudice in many parts of the West. The growth of Eastern religions suffered a severe blow in 1917 when the United States passed an immigration law which stopped all immigration from Asia except by a small number of Japanese.

While Asian religions grew slowly in the West, metaphysical and occult religions expanded rapidly following the founding of the Church of Christ, Scientist (1875), the National Spiritualist Association of Churches (1893) and the International New Thought Alliance (1914). At the same time 'ritual magick' re-emerged on the European continent and spread to England and subsequently to North America. The earliest metaphysical and occult groups tended to be Christian in orientation and to use Christian symbols, though in unfamiliar ways; but as the century progressed, newer branches tended to drop any Christian veneer, with the exception of occasional references to Jesus as a great teacher.

The growth of the metaphysical and occult religions, and the presence, especially in the Asian communities in the West, of Hindu and Buddhist groups, set the stage for 1965. In that year, without fanfare, President Lyndon Johnson opened the United States once again to Asian immigrants, an act which had grown out of an attempt to pacify new American allies in southern Asia who felt insulted by the anti-Asian immigration policies of the United States. The results were quite unexpected, however, as large numbers of Japanese, Indians and, in fact, Asians from Korea to Sri Lanka took advantage of the new situation and filled the quotas. Among all the Asians, gurus, swamis and Zen masters travelled to their compatriots' new homelands ready to meet the spiritual needs not only of the immigrants. Even prior to 1965, Eastern teachers had been moving into Europe; now, stimulated by the new opportunities in North America, they also increased their presence in the more open of the European nations. Following the fall of the Berlin Wall in 1989, numerous teachers have opened centres in eastern Europe and the countries of the former Soviet Union.

Having founded various movements in the 1960s, the Eastern religions were ready to reap the harvest when a period of general religious enthusiasm swept the West in the early and mid-1970s (see figures 15.1 and 15.2). New movements in the United States grew to national proportions and quickly spread to Europe, while movements previously established in Great Britain and on the European continent soon set up branches in North America. Eastern religions were joined by Jewish and Islamic groups. These Middle Eastern groups, displaced by the Nazi onslaught, found haven in England

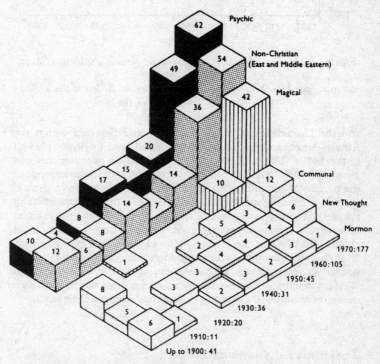

Figure 15.1 *Alternative religions in the United States: growth by decades, 1900–1970*

Source: *After J.G. Melton,* A Directory of Religious Bodies in the United States, *New York, Garland, 1977.*

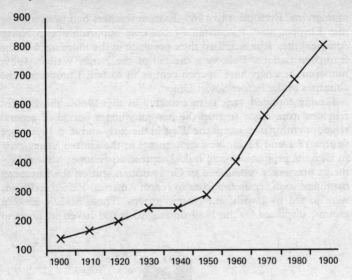

Figure 15.2 *Growth rate of alternative religions in the United States,*
1900–1990
Source: *After J. G. Melton*, A Directory of Religious Bodies in the United
States, *New York, Garland, 1977 (updated)*

and the United States. Islam took root and flowered within the
African-American community from a small seed originally planted
in the 1930s. The religious revival of the 1970s gave impetus and
growth to every family of 'alternative religion' and the emergence of
the pluralistic situation allowed all kinds of deviation from the old
norm of mainstream Christianity. Once a new form of faith
appeared it soon found cause to splinter, thus enlarging the number
of available religious options from which a new believer could
choose. By 1990, in the United States alone, over 1,000 Christian
sects and 600 alternative religious bodies competed for members. A
similar situation, if on a lesser scale, could be found in most
Western countries, the few exceptions being those which took legal
measures to hinder the spread of alternative religious organizations.

The Families of Alternative Religions

Over 700 alternative religions, religious communities quite distinct
from the main branches of Christianity and Judaism in the West,

have appeared in the United States. Simultaneously, a like number have also emerged and are active in Europe. While many of these newer groups have become international bodies with local communities in both Europe and America, just as many have yet to develop ties across the Atlantic. The seeming chaos of beliefs and practices that meets the first cursory glance at the alternative religions masks the fact that the overwhelming majority of the new religions cluster into a relatively small number of denominational 'families'. Groups of each family share a common *thought-world* of ideas they believe to be important, a similar *lifestyle* with predictable behaviour patterns and a *heritage* which can be traced to a common root. These families represent the major directions that alternative religious groups have taken.

Table 15.1 New religious movements in Europe and America (early 1990s)

	Cult movements per million	No. cult movements
Switzerland	16.7	108
Iceland	12.0	3
United Kingdom	10.7	604
Austria	7.9	60
Sweden	6.8	57
Denmark	4.5	23
Netherlands	4.4	64
Ireland	3.9	14
West Germany	2.5	155
Belgium	2.4	24
Norway	1.9	8
Greece	1.5	15
Italy	1.2	66
Portugal	1.0	10
France	0.9	52
Finland	0.8	4
Spain	0.7	29
Poland	0.5	17
Europe[a]	3.4	1,317
United States	1.7	425

[a]Total based only on the nations listed in the table.
Source: R. Stark, 'Europe's Receptivity to New Religious Movements', *Journal for the Scientific Study of Religion*, vol. 31, 1993, pp. 389–97

The Latter-day Saint Family

The Latter-day Saints are held together by a shared belief in the revelations of Joseph Smith, Jr, which they collected into a set of books that now serve as authoritative literature alongside the Bible. The most famous piece of Latter-day Saint scripture, the *Book of Mormon* (from which they take their more popular designation as Mormons), stands beside other volumes, the *Doctrines and Covenants* and the *Pearl of Great Price*. Smith also produced an inspired version of the Bible which some Mormon groups use.

Central to Latter-day Saint belief is the idea of the Restoration. According to Smith, true Christianity died with the death of the last original apostles, but was restored through Joseph Smith's ordination by God and subsequent ministry. The Restoration found its earthly visible manifestation in Zion, the gathered community of saints, and a new temple (complete with new ceremonies) to replace the one destroyed many centuries ago. Also, in the first generations, the Saints adopted the United Order, a communal self-help structure (which was, however, abandoned by most Mormons soon after the move to Utah in 1847).

Over the years no fewer than fifty distinct Latter-day Saint bodies have appeared and disappeared, while almost as many again survive to the present day. Most of these emerged in the United States, but a few, such as the Independent Church of Jesus Christ of Latter-day Saints, developed originally in Europe. A disruption in the Reorganized Church of Jesus Christ of Latter-day Saints in the late 1970s led to the emergence of ten new independent church groups, most of which survived their first decade. The majority of the twentieth-century Mormon groups began with a prophet providing new revelations to supplement those left by Smith. In Utah, polygamy, practised and then abandoned by the main body of Mormons, arose anew as young Fundamentalists, i.e. those who practise polygamy, became more vocal and visible during the 1970s.

The Communal Family

The communal impulse constantly reappears in all religious traditions, but, even in its more accepted monastic form, it implies a lifestyle that separates its practitioners from the mainstream of culture and religion. Among those groups which thrived in the nineteenth century by far the most successful (in length of existence) were the religious communities such as the Shakers and the Perfectionists of Oneida. The single most successful communal group of recent centuries are the Hutterites, who migrated from Russia into the American north-west and western Canada just across the border. The Hutterian agricultural lifestyle proved remarkably resilient in the face of the modern world, and by the early 1990s there were over 300 Hutterite colonies in existence. In the 1960s and 1970s a new wave of communalism swept the younger generation, who established a range of communities in every country of the Western world. Most that survived into the 1990s were overtly religious in nature.

The major groups formed in the twentieth century were either Christians who took a very literal approach to Scripture, and particularly the injunction to hold all things in common (*Acts* 2), or groups with a distinctly Eastern mystical perspective (though they seem very eclectic theologically). In either case, they agree that the main fact of their life and thought is the challenge of communal existence. Most communal groups have a very low profile and are not well known, though a few, like The Farm and the Church of Armageddon, have become visible because of their activism and their brushes with the legal authorities. Living almost invisibly through the 1980s, The Family, known in the 1970s as the Children of God, emerged out of seclusion with approximately 9,000 members in some thirty countries.

The New Thought Metaphysical Family

New Thought, a very eclectic movement, draws inspiration from mesmerism, New England Transcendentalism, *laissez-faire* economics and a basic intuition that religion must be practical and applied to the major problems of everyday life – illness, poverty, unhappiness. The modern metaphysical church, which exists in two rather distinct wings, Christian Science and New Thought, can best be traced to the New England Transcendentalist movement of the mid-nineteenth century. Ralph Waldo Emerson, reacting to both orthodox Christianity and a cold rationalism, developed an idealistic philosophy which placed its faith in an underlying invisible spiritual reality that gave depth to the visible world and could be apprehended more easily by direct intuition than by reasoning.

In the 1870s, Mary Baker Eddy gave a distinctly religious, even Christian, slant to Emerson's idealistic spiritual world. She added a practical twist in suggesting that an apprehension of the Oneness underlying the visible world led to a realization of one's unity with God and of God's perfection. In God, illness and even poverty could not exist. Eddy not only advocated a Christianized version of Emersonian thought, but called those who had experienced the Oneness she talked about and its healing effects into a community of faith, the Church of Christ Scientist. The movement spread quickly after the publication of her textbook, *Science and Health with a Key to the Scriptures* (1875).

Eddy's church was a tightly run organization with little room for creative variations in either theology or practice. Thus it was inevitable that some of her strongest leaders would feel constrained under the system and break away from it to create variations. This happened almost from the beginning. However, the most important of those who separated from Eddy and established independent work was Emma Curtis Hopkins. The first person to whom Eddy entrusted the editorship of the *Christian Science Journal*, Hopkins broke with Eddy after a little more than a year and began rival work in Chicago. She soon emerged as the leader of the independents, and by 1887 the Hopkins Metaphysical Association had established affiliated centres across America from Maine to San Francisco. Hopkins opened the Christian Science Theological Seminary in Chicago, and sooner or later all of the founders of what were to become the important New Thought groups came to sit at her feet. Among her hundreds of students were Melinda Cramer (Divine Science); Annie Rix Militz (Homes of Truth); Charles and Myrtle Fillmore (Unity School of Christianity); Ernest Holmes (Religious Science); and Frances Lord, who first brought New Thought to England in the 1880s. The numerous New Thought groups were finally able to find some unity in the International New Thought Alliance, formed in 1914.

The Spiritualist/Psychic Family

Possibly the largest of the alternative families contains the groups built around the experience of various forms of psychic phenomena. They have a continuous history in the West, at least since the time of Scandinavian seer Emanuel Swedenborg (1688–1772). These groups are the most ahistorical in their perspective, and few contemporary leaders of psychic groups know about, or seem willing to acknowledge their debt to, the thought and practices of their predecessors. The psychic groups share a common relationship to science, in that they believe that psychic phenomena demonstrate 'scientifically' the truth of their religious perspective. They look to parapsychology for a verification of their religion, and have grown as the recognition of psychical research has grown. They might be said, however, to have an attitude better labelled 'scientism', that is, they have a love of things scientific accompanied with little actual knowledge, or appreciation, of science or of scientific methodology.

Historically, the psychic community traces its lineage not only from Swedenborg but also from his later contemporary Austrian Franz Anton Mesmer (1734–1815), whose ideas about animal magnetism fosteted a movement that, while not being directly religious itself, gave content and an early rationale to the psychic groups. From the thin thread of mesmerism and Swedenborg's New Church, Spiritualism emerged in New York. Andrew Jackson Davis (1826–1910), Spiritualism's great prophet, counted Swedenborg among his main spirit contacts. From New York, Spiritualism quickly spread across North America and to Europe, where it enjoyed a much greater acceptance in England and France than it did in the land of its origin. Once Spiritualism had spread and provided a base, other psychic groups could emerge.

Spiritualism centred upon the presentation of 'scientific' evidence of life after death, demonstrated in the practice of mediumship. Mediums were special people, capable of contacting, often while in a state of trance, the realm of the dead. If one accepted the reality of mediumship then a logical possibility emerged: the medium could not only contact the spirits of the dead and prove that they survived, but could explore in some detail the nature of the life to come and even locate accomplished teachers who could, having experienced and survived the veil of death, speak authoritatively about the great human questions of origins, meaning and destiny. Such attempts to turn to the spirit world to find the answers to philosophical, cosmological and ethical issues began with Spiritualism's first generation. Many of the volumes of Andrew Jackson Davis's books include the results of such probing. By the end of the nineteenth century, mediums whose work specialized in the bringing forth of new teachings from the spirit realm emerged. Such mediums are today called channels.

Through the twentieth century, the psychic/occult movement has grown and diversified widely. Each generation has produced a host of psychics with variant revelations and a wide range of attitudes towards the dominant Christian perspective in society. Through the 1960s and 1970s, groups founded upon psychedelic drug experiences and 'flying saucer' sightings created even more variations. The splintering of psychic groups can be traced to the complete lack of any central authority system or support from the dominant culture, coupled with a drive among members for an immediate experience of some form of psychic phenomenon, an impulse not unlike the Pentecostal drive to experience the gifts of the Spirit. Leaders rest their claim to authority on their ability to produce psychic phenomena or on their relation to someone who can.

The impact of psychic alternatives in the West has been measured during the last decade by the spread of belief in astrology, reincarnation and the efficacy of meditation. Since the 1970s, over 20 per cent of the American public profess to practising meditation, to believing in reincarnation and to holding some faith in astrology. From so large a base, it is no surprise that over 300 of the alternative religions are psychic/occult groups.

The Ancient Wisdom Groups

Closely related to and deriving from Spiritualism are the 'ancient wisdom' groups. These groups are recognizable by their adoption of a mythical story placing their origin at some point in the far past, frequently Atlantis or ancient Egypt. At this olden time a pure spiritual teaching existed but was overthrown by a corrupt religiosity, frequently identified with the Christian Church. The pure teaching went into hiding but was preserved by a small group of evolved beings, the masters, most of whom have been reincarnated on earth periodically, and now exist in a disembodied state. Collectively they are called the Great White Brotherhood, and from their evolved state they attempt to guide the destiny of humanity in the godly direction. The members of the ancient wisdom groups are their instruments of their working in the visible world.

Among the groups which have a form of the ancient wisdom story at the heart of their understanding of the world are the Rosicrucians, Theosophy, the I AM Religious Activity, the Church Universal and Triumphant, and many additional occult orders.

The modern New Age movement combines influences from both the ancient wisdom and Spiritualist psychic groups. The New Age movement began in Great Britain among some independent Theosophical groups. Through the twentieth century Theosophists had looked for the coming of a New Age, though the vision of what form such a new society might take varied. However, in the 1960s some of these groups began to talk about the emergence of the New Age during the next generation. The New Age was to be brought about by the release of new spiritual energies resulting from the change of astrological cycles, popularly referred to as the beginning of the Age of Aquarius. These early New Age groups linked together with groups internationally who shared a common commitment to receiving the new spiritual energy and transmitting it to the world. The vision of a possible imminent new age became a vitalizing message to members of the older metaphysical, Spiritualist/psychic and ancient wisdom communities.

During the 1980s the New Age movement became an important force which raised the standing of these alternative communities in the West and reached far beyond them to bring many hundreds of thousands of new adherents to its member organizations. Study of the New Age has been hampered by its decentralized structure, which has made it difficult to measure. Also, the New Age differs from other groups in that rather than attracting young adults, it has tended to attract an older group (age 35–45), those making the transitions of mid-life. By the 1990s, the New Age vision had largely been spent, but it left behind millions of people who had found meaning in New Age/occult belief. Recent surveys indicate that

Table 15.2 Percentage of acceptance of New Age beliefs[a] by adherents of Protestant denominations in the United States[b]

	CC/DC	ELCA	PCUSA	SBC	UCC	UMC	Total
HumNat	75	71	72	47	79	76	72
Reincr	7	10	10	3	11	7	8
Astro	13	8	10	4	9	9	9
TruthinMe	34	31	30	27	33	34	32
Be Anything	57	54	54	40	59	56	54
TalktoDead	6	8	6	5	8	7	7
OwnBeliefs	34	29	31	28	36	30	32

[a]New Age statements measured:
  HumNat = Human nature is basically good
  Reincr = I believe in reincarnation, that I have lived before and will experience other lives in the future
  Astro = I believe in astrology
  TruthinMe = Through meditation and self-discipline I come to know that all spiritual truth and wisdom is within me
  Be Anything = I am in charge of my life, I can be anything I want to be
  TalktoDead = It is possible to communicate with people who have died
  OwnBeliefs = An individual should arrive at his/her own beliefs independent of any church
[b]From a national sample of 3,349 respondents of adult members of the following denominations:
  CC/DC = Christian Church Disciples of Christ
  ELCA = Evangelical Lutheran Church in America
  PCUSA = Presbyterian Church (USA)
  SBC = Southern Baptist Convention
  UCC = United Church of Christ
  UMC = United Methodist Church
Source: M. Donohue, 'Prevalence and Correlates of New Age Beliefs in Six Protestant Denominations', *Journal for the Scientific Study of Religion*, vol. 32, 1993, pp. 177–84.

many people who have accepted such beliefs have remained attached to older churches where they can make a personal adjustment.

The Magical Family

The magical family consists of those groups which include as a significant element in their life the practice of magic, which can be defined as the art of employing cosmic, paranormal forces (believed to underpin the universe) in order to produce desired effects at will. Magic has two major forms. In working high magic, the major focus of change is the magician's own consciousness. Low magic refers to the production of alterations in the everyday world, such as healing the body, locating a better job, improving one's love life or cursing an enemy. While the practice of magic in itself is not necessarily religious, in the modern West its practice is most commonly found as an integral aspect of magical groups which provide all the traditional religious functions for their members.

Almost eliminated from the West in the eighteenth century, magic began a remarkable comeback in the nineteenth century, culminating in the formation of the Hermetic Order of the Golden Dawn (OGD) in the 1880s. From that group, and in particular from one of its members, Aleister Crowley (1875–1947), the second stage of the magical revival began. First Crowley, and his secretary/student Israel Regardie, published the majority of the OGD material, thus making it available to the wider occult community. Then, through his voluminous writings, Crowley provided occultists with perhaps their single most coherent digest of magical practice and most widely accepted presentation of magical thought. All three major groupings of modern magical 'religions' draw heavily upon the work of Crowley (even in those cases where groups and individuals openly separate themselves from Crowley and his more controversial and objectionable emphasis upon sex magic).

This revival of magic concentrated on its ceremonial form, centred upon the disciplined practice of ritual invocation and evocation for the working of high magic. The OGD assembled the work of prior magical teachers such as Eliphas Lévi (1810–75), added the writings of their own scholar–teacher S. L. MacGregor Mathers (1854–1918), and formed the first magic group to spread throughout the British Isles, on to the European continent and across the ocean to America. While several groups, such as the California-based Builders of the Adytum and the Fraternity of the Inner Light and the Servants of the Light, both British-based, carry on the Golden Dawn tradition, most ceremonial magic groups can be traced to Aleister Crowley. After leaving the OGD, Crowley joined the German-based Ordo Templi Orientis (OTO) and eventually became its Outer Head. He imposed his unique brand of magic, 'thelema' (from the Greek word for 'will'), upon the Order (which led to a split in the German section). Through his travels and writings he expanded the Order into a world-wide organization. In the early 1980s, the OTO branch headed by Grady McMurty of Berkeley, California, was the single largest magical group in the West, with centres in North America, New Zealand, Australia, Europe and even behind the Iron Curtain. Several other OTO branches, such as that founded by British thelemite Kenneth Grant, also have an international membership. More recently, new offshoots of thelemic magic based upon Maat, the Egyptian goddess of truth and justice, have appeared, such as the London/Chicago-based Ordo Adeptorum Invisiblum. Together the various OTO and Maatian organizations include the overwhelming majority of ritual magicians in the West.

Witchcraft, the second major grouping of magical religion, presents a confusing picture to the average observer. The word 'witchcraft' is popularly used to describe at least four distinct phenomena, frequently if mistakenly equated with each other. Anthropologists use the word to refer to the art of the tribal shaman in the pre-technological (or primal) societies. Biblical scholars use it to describe the *ob*, such as the famous *ob* of Endor (1 *Samuel* 28), whose accomplishments included knowledge of herbs and poisons and the art of mediumship. The Western historian usually means the worship of the Devil, i.e. Satanism, with all of its associated practice of malevolent sorcery, the black mass and witch-hunters. However, modern witchcraft, as practised in Western technological society, is none of these. Rather, it is a form of polytheistic nature religion based upon the worship of the Mother Goddess. This new witchcraft, more properly called Neo-Paganism, was created during the 1940s and 1950s by Gerald Gardner (1884–1964), a retired British civil servant who had spent most of his life in southern Asia. Gardner attempted to develop a popular magical religion. He combined elements of both Western and Asian magic, Masonic rituals, nudity and Goddess worship with liberal doses of Aleister Crowley. First made public in the 1950s, Gardnerian witchcraft spread quickly in England and came to America in the 1960s. It subsequently spread to Ireland and Europe. Numerous variations of Goddess worship, which (in spite of claims to the contrary) can be traced almost entirely to Gardner, appeared, and by 1980 included literally hundreds of covens and groves (the small groups which meet together to practise their nature-oriented faith) in Europe, North America, Australia and South Africa. The Neo-Pagan witches view their task as reviving the old religion(s) of pre-Christian Europe. With the movement's growth into its second generation, it has experienced constant change as different covens have put various ethnic facades (Scandinavian, Welsh, Greek) on to their practice and have experimented with newly written rituals and new alternative magical techniques. Low magic predominates in witchcraft's rituals and practice, an emphasis that generally differentiates Neo-Pagans from ceremonial magicians.

Originating in the 1970s, Dianic Witchcraft, a form of Wicca which emphasized not only the femaleness of the deity, but the role of Witchcraft as a religion of female liberation, emerged as an important segment of the Neo-Pagan community in the 1980s. Feminist Wicca serves as a bridge between the larger Neo-Pagan world and the community of Goddess worshippers who have found in the proclamation of a female deity a rallying cry behind which women can assert their equality in what they perceive to be a male-dominated world.

The third group of magical religionists flashed into prominence momentarily in the late 1960s, and was heard from with less and less frequency during the 1970s and 1980s. The Satanists, those who actually worship the Devil and whose magic consists of the invocation of him or one of his demonic legion, have gradually faded from the occult world. Generally occultists, including ceremonial magicians and witches, dislike and fear the worshippers of Satan as much as Christians do. Contemporary Neo-Pagans consistently try to separate themselves from the taint of satanic images constantly being thrown at them. Neo-Pagans assert that they practise a positive religion with their own Pagan deities, rather than a negative religion based upon the Devil of Christianity. Satanism is a magical religion which has as its central dynamic the rejection of and an attack upon Christianity. Modern Satanists have drawn their image of his Infernal Majesty from the snake in the Garden of Eden, the bringer of knowledge, and Lucifer, the light-bearer. This modern Satan is seen as the giver of wisdom and builder of the individual ego. His worshippers, though few in number, can be found throughout the Christian world in small disconnected groups.

During the late 1980s, beginning on the west coast of the United States, and expanding to Great Britain in the early 1990s, claims of a large Satanist conspiracy caught the attention of many law officials, social workers and psychological counsellors. A decade of investigation, however, has produced little of substance to verify these claims, and as any official support for such claims was withdrawn, the crusade to stamp out Satanism has largely died.

The Eastern Family

Since 1965 the high level of visibility of Buddhism, Hinduism, Sikhism and Jainism has indicated a significant proliferation of Eastern religion in the West. Several hundred different Eastern groups now operate in Europe and America; and, most significantly, they have broken out of the Asian ethnic communities which provided their initial base of support to serve both Caucasian and African constituencies. To a large extent, it is the spread of Asian religion among American and European young adults that has been at the core of concern over alternative religions and has given rise to what is popularly termed the 'cult' controversy.

Typically, the Eastern groups each have a single teacher, a guru, though the title varies from group to group. The guru teaches the spiritual techniques by which the members can gain enlightenment or mystic vision, and members view the guru as an accomplished master of the system s/he teaches. Within Eastern groups, systems and practices vary as widely as they do within the whole of Western Christianity. Some are ascetic (Hare Krishna), some philosophical (Vedanta), some indulgent (Tantra) and some rigorous (certain types of yoga). While nominally led by the guru, the groups also present a wide variety of organizational strengths, and ask for differing degrees of commitment from their members. Among the Hare Krishna, an ascetic monastic model of life has been adopted; some siddha yoga groups are based on the absolute obedience given to the guru; other groups merely respect the guru as a learned teacher, and have formed a rather loose organization. Some groups seek almost total commitment of the members' time, money and energy; others seek only a few hours a week and a modest donation of financial resources and labour.

The rather sensationalized media coverage given to these exotic groups, which most Westerners still find strange in the extreme, masks two very different trends among those groups serving the non-ethnic community. First, the success of these groups is much more limited than media coverage would tend to suggest. After almost half a century of their infiltration of the West, the largest guru-oriented group still numbers fewer than 50,000 members, and the majority count their members in the hundreds. Secondly, there has been a steady stream of new Eastern groups through the 1980s and into the 1990s. Thus, while the numerical success of any single group might be limited, the number of groups is constantly growing. Many of the newer gurus and teachers receive little attention from the media unless they become involved in a scandal. As the twentieth century comes to a close, the Eastern religious groups have established a permanent base in the West from which to expand through the next century.

The Middle Eastern Family

Judaism has been in the West longer than Christianity, but, for a variety of historical and theological reasons, has remained a minority religion. The events of the Second World War dramatically reshaped the total Jewish community and scattered most of what was not destroyed of east European Jewry. That war brought many Jews to the United States and Canada, and they brought with them varieties of Judaism never before seen in North America in the many Chasidic groups. (Chasidism is a mystical Orthodox form of Judaism – see p. 20 above.)

The post-1945 era has also seen many Muslims coming to the West, building upon the smaller immigration efforts that began in the late nineteenth century. Large Islamic communities are currently appearing in American and European metropolitan centres for the first time. The proliferation of both Judaism and Islam has been remarkable, with over thirty mystical Jewish groups and almost as many Islamic groups establishing communities. There have, however, been important differences in their patterns of growth. Jewish groups have tended to grow primarily within the Jewish community. The Chasids have promoted large families and advocated the conversion of more liberal Jews and of non-practising Jews. Muslims, on the other hand, have bolstered their immigrant communities by spreading Islam among African Americans and by the penetration of mystical Islam (Sufism) among young adult middle-class whites, the group most attracted to Eastern faiths in general.

Opposition to Alternative Religions

The growth of alternative religions in the twentieth century generated a counter-movement headed by those who saw the establishment of alternative religious communities as a threat. In the early part of the century, opposition started within conservative Christian bodies which saw their members being seduced by exotic forms of faith. For many years these bodies produced books, pamphlets and tracts warning of the dangerous beliefs of such groups – primarily Mormonism, Christian Science, Spiritualism, Theosophy and Seventh-day Adventism. Several organizations, such as the Christian Research Institute founded by Baptist minister Walter Martin and the Religious Analysis Service in Minneapolis, Minnesota, were established to coordinate anti-cult activity and channel literature to Christians engaged in a ministry to cults.

In labelling the alternative religions as 'cults', anti-cultists assumed that in some measure the alternative religions were essentially all alike, an assumption that has proved completely false. The only characteristic they share is a negative evaluation; they each present an alternative to traditional Christianity. The assumption of similarity has also been used to attack the 'cults', by attributing to all of them the faults and excesses of any one of them. This practice, along with the highly polemic motivation underlying most anti-cult literature, makes such materials the least useful in understanding the nature of life in alternative religions, though of immense usefulness in understanding the climate in which NRMs have had to operate.

In the early 1970s a new form of opposition to alternative religions developed: the deprogramming movement. Ted Patrick, whose son had briefly associated with the Children of God in south-

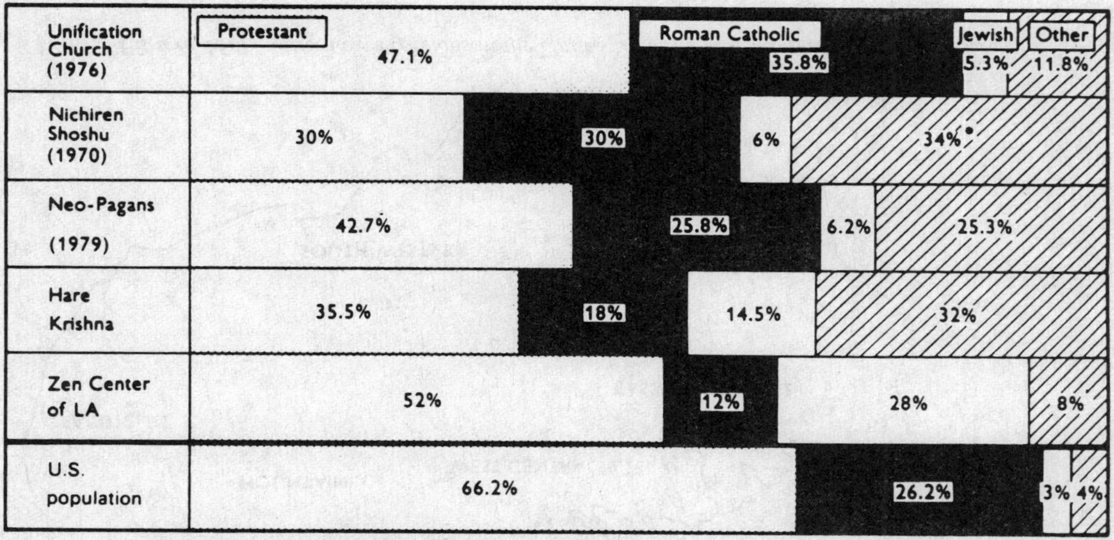

Figure 15.3 Religious backgrounds of members of alternative religions in the United States, early 1990s

Sources: Based on J. S. Judah, The History and Philosophy of the Metaphysical Movements in America, Philadelphia, Westminster Press, 1967; E. M. Layman, Buddhism in America, Chicago, Nelson Hall, 1976; J. G. Melton, 'The Neo-Pagans of America: An Alternative Religion?', paper presented to the American Academy of Religion, 1970.

* Includes large percentage of Buddhists. (West Coast Buddhists were original Nichiren Shoshu target population)

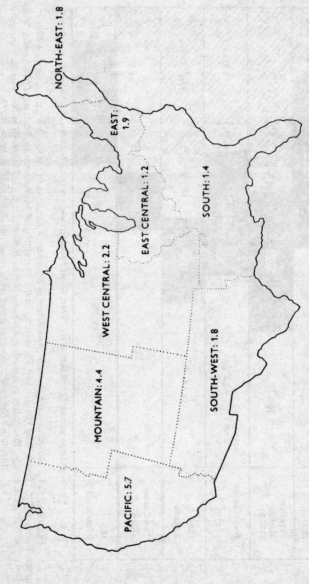

NORTH-EAST: 1.8

EAST: 1.9

EAST CENTRAL: 1.2

SOUTH: 1.4

WEST CENTRAL: 2.2

MOUNTAIN: 4.4

SOUTH-WEST: 1.8

PACIFIC: 5.7

Figure 15.4 Alternative religions in the United States, 1979: number per million residents

ern California, soon found other parents who had offspring in the same group. They formed FREECOG (Free Our Children from the Children of God) and attacked the group for its communal lifestyle and odd beliefs. They were, in turn, joined by parents who had sons and daughters in other alternative religions, with whom they formed the Citizens' Freedom Foundation, the first of a number of similar groups across North America. The Citizens' Freedom Foundation gradually transformed itself into the Cult Awareness Network (CAN) and during the 1980s absorbed the energy of most of the earlier activist anti-cult organizations. CAN also inspired similar anti-cult organizations in Europe and South America. Anti-cultism is represented in England primarily by Family, Action, Information, and Rescue (FAIR) and in France by the Association pour la Défense de la Familie et de l'Individu (ADFI). Similar organizations can be found in most European countries, and around the world, such as the SPES Foundation in Argentina and the Association Exposing Pseudo Religious Cults in Australia. These organizations are joined by groups of former members of some of the more controversial new religions (the Unification Church, Nichiren Shoshu, the Children of God/The Family).

These anti-cult groups have developed a working rationale in which they see cult members as passive victims of recruitment processes through which the alternative religions brainwash and hypnotize members to the point that they lose their freedom to think and make decisions. To alleviate this problem, it is argued, it may be necessary to kidnap the 'victim' and keep him or her locked away from the group for a number of days, during which he or she is subjected to a high-powered counter-indoctrination process. While seen as freeing the mind, the process centres on the manipulation of powerful emotional forces applied with great pressure. This process typically includes fatigue, the desecration of sacred symbols, the pleas of parents and family members, and intense interrogation; depending on the degree of resistance of the person being deprogrammed, it can also include the absence of privacy, physical confinement in ropes and physical abuse.

The major target of the anti-cult movement during the 1970s was the Unification Church, a small group built around the charisma and visions of Sun Myung Moon, a Korean prophet who has expounded a version of Christianity called the Divine Principle. In 1975 the anti-cult movement took the Unification Church as its target and directed the majority of its efforts to inhibiting its activity. Second only to the Unification Church as anti-cult targets were the Church of Scientology, the Way International, Hare Krishna, the Church Universal and Triumphant, and the Children of God (now known as The Family).

In the United States anti-cult efforts have included de-programmings, attempted anti-cult legislation, civil suits, and a campaign of vilification directed through the media. Unable to obtain legislative support through the 1980s, the anti-cult movement found some success in civil courts. Representatives were frequently able to convince juries that cults engaged in 'brainwashing'. However, that approach was stymied by the end of the decade when psychologist Margaret Singer, the major exponent of the brainwashing theory, was denied status as an expert witness in a case in US federal court after several of her colleagues argued effectively that her ideas about mind control were not supported by the findings of the scientific community. Sociologist Richard Ofshe, also turned out of court in the same case, and several other experts who based their testimony on Singer's opinions, have since been unable to testify in support of suits brought against the non-conventional new religions. Various attempts to reverse the courts' view, including suits by Singer and Ofshe against the scholars who opposed them, proved unsuccessful. By the mid-1990s it appeared that the cult wars were slowly coming to an end.

The New Religious Situation

Religious observers have for many years spoken of Western society moving into a post-Christian era, and certainly Christian leaders have experienced a marked erosion of power in directing culture. That downward turn was initially seen in terms of articulate unbelievers, pushing an assertive secularism, emerging as the Church's major competitor. Through the twentieth century, the older churches, which had previously enjoyed state support, have largely failed to keep up as population grew. Decade after decade they commanded the allegiance of a smaller and smaller percentage of the population. However, the public did not so much turn to atheism as to a host of religious alternatives, especially Christian sectarian movements and the NRMs. During the 1970s the alternative faiths, while not growing nearly so much as the anti-cultists would have us believe, did grow enough to create a qualitative shift in the religious environment. They penetrated society to the point where they can no longer be dismissed as an odd phenomenon on the edge of society. Their members, drawn from the educated middle to upper-middle class, including professionals and career business executives, can no longer be dismissed as merely the alienated and oppressed. They see themselves as full, active participants in Western culture.

The visible impact of the alternative religions is highest in urban areas (see table 15.3), where their worship centres dot street cor-

Table 15.3 Alternative religions in the United States (early 1990s)

State [a]	Number of new religions	New religions per million residents	New religions per million (mid-1970s)
Dst. of Col.	12	20.0	15.7
California	191	9.1	6.0
New Mexico	10	7.8	9.1
Utah	12	6.9[b]	1.7
Arkansas	16	6.8	1.0
Hawaii	7	6.3	4.4
Missouri	31	6.0	3.1
South Carolina	4	5.9	0.4
Connecticut	5	5.0	1.6
Idaho	5	5.0	1.3
Colorado	13	4.8	6.0
New York	68	3.9	3.3
Washington	19	3.9	2.9
Louisiana	4	3.9	0.3
Arizona	14	3.6	5.9
Oregon	9	3.6	4.8
Vermont	2	3.5	0.0
Nevada	4	3.3	10.0
Montana	2	2.5	0.0
Illinois	26	2.3	3.0
Massachusetts	14	2.3	1.9
West Virginia	4	2.2	0.0
Rhode Island	2	2.0	1.0
Florida	25	1.9	2.4
New Hampshire	2	1.8	2.5
Pennsylvania	18	1.5	1.5
Minnesota	6	1.4	1.0
Virginia	8	1.3	1.6
Maryland	6	1.3	0.5
Texas	20	1.2	1.2
Michigan	11	1.2	1.1
North Carolina	8	1.2	0.6
Oklahoma	3	1.0	0.7
Tennessee	4	0.8	1.0
Wisconsin	4	0.8	0.7
Alabama	3	0.7	0.6
Indiana	4	0.7	0.5
Ohio	7	0.6	0.8
Georgia	3	0.5	0.4

[a]The remaining states had either 1 or 0 groups headquartered in the state.
[b]Mormon groups included in count.
Sources: J. G. Melton, *Encyclopedia of American Religions*, Detroit, Gale Research, 1992; R. Stark, W. S. Bainbridge and D. P. Doyle, 'Cults in America: A Reconnaisance in Space and Time', *Sociological Analysis*, vol. 4, 1979, pp. 347–59

ners, their stores open their doors in shopping districts, and their books rest on bookstore shelves beside Christian devotional texts. Their children now attend state schools in which Buddhists, Scientologists, Hindus, Unificationists, Jews, Sikhs and an occasional Pagan sit beside all varieties of Christians. The alternative religions moved quickly to institutionalize and prepare future leaders. Hastily prepared training sessions in the 1960s have given way to the Unification Theological Seminary, the Religious Science School of Ministry, the Dharma Realm Buddhist University and the California Institute of Asian Studies.

Dialogue between the leaders of these alternative religions and those of mainstream churches proceeded at a snail's pace through the 1970s and 1980s, but obviously bore some fruit. In 1993, at the centennial of the World's Parliament of Religions, the event which marked the beginning of religious pluralism in the West, the new religions participated as full members in dialogue. In addition, religious and social science scholars, led by the Institute for the Study of American Religion in Santa Barbara, California, CESNUR (Center for Studies on New Religions) in Turin, Italy, and INFORM in London, now draw on three decades of new religions studies. There is every sign that as the twenty-first century approaches the new alternative religions, having become a familiar part of the Western religious landscape, will be fully accepted as members of the religious community.

Bibliography

1 ADLER, M., *Drawing Down the Moon*, Boston, Beacon, 1987
2 BARKER, E., *New Religious Movements*, London, HMSO, 1990
3 BECKFORD, J., *Cult Controversies*, London, Tavistock, 1985
4 BROMLEY, D. G., and HAMMOND, P. E., *The Future of New Religious Movements*, Macon, GA: Mercer University Press, 1987
5 BROMLEY, D. G., and SHUPE, A. D., *Strange Gods*, Boston, Beacon, 1981
6 DONOHUE, M., 'Prevalence and Correlates of New Age Beliefs in Six Protestant Denominations', *Journal for the Scientific Study of Religion*, vol. 32, 1993, pp. 177–84
7 ELLWOOD, R. S., and PARTIN, H. B., *Religious and Spiritual Groups in America*, Englewood Cliffs, Prentice-Hall, 1988
8 GALANIER, M., (ed.), *Cults and New Religious Movements*, New York, American Psychiatric Association, 1989
9 JUDAH, J. S., *The History and Philosophy of the Metaphysical Movements in America*, Philadelphia, Westminster Press, 1967
10 MELTON, J. G., 'Another Look at New Religions', *Annals of the American Association of Political and Social Science*, vol. 527, May 1993, pp. 97–112.

11 MELTON, J. G., *Encyclopedia of American Religions*, Detroit, Gale Research, 1992

12 MELTON, J. G., *Encyclopedia Handbook of Cults in America*, New York, Garland, 1993

13 MELTON, J. G., CLARK, J., and KELLY, A., *New Age Encyclopedia*, Detroit, Gale Research, 1990

14 MILLER, T. (ed.), *When Prophets Die: The Post-charismatic Fate of New Religious Movements*, New York, State University of New York Press, 1991

15 NELSON, G. K., *Spiritualism and Society*, New York, Schocken/London, Routledge, 1969

16 SALIBA, J. A., *Perspectives on New Religious Movements*, London, Geoffrey Chapman, 1995

17 SHEPARD, L., *Encyclopedia of Occultism and Parapsychology*, Detroit, Gale Research, 1990

18 SHUPE, A. D., and BROMLEY, D. G., *Anti-cult Movements in Cross-cultural Perspective*, New York, Garland, 1994

19 STARK, R., 'Europe's Receptivity to New Religious Movements', *Journal for the Scientific Study of Religion*, vol. 31, 1993, pp. 389–97

20 STARK, R., BAINBRIDGE, W. S., and DOYLE, D. P., 'Cults in America: A Reconnaissance in Space and Time', *Sociological Analysis*, vol. 4, 1979, pp. 347–59

21 WUTHNOW, R., *The Consciousness Reformation*, Berkeley, University of California Press, 1976

22 WUTHNOW, R., *Experimentation in American Religion: The New Mysticisms and their Implications for the Churches*, Berkeley, University of California Press, 1978

23 WRIGHT, S., *Leaving Cults: The Dynamics of Defection*, Washington, DC, Society for the Scientific Study of Religion, 1987

16

Baha'ism

DENIS MACEOIN

Introduction

Among the new religious movements clamouring for attention in the modern West, Baha'ism (the Baha'i faith) stands out as something of an anomaly in being both sufficiently independent to be regarded as a religion in its own right and yet small enough to be treated as a sect or church in the sociological sense.

The movement originated in the 1860s as a faction within Babism (founder: the Bab, 1819–50), a messianic sect of Shi'a Islam (see p. 206 above) that began in Iraq and Iran in 1844. The founder of Baha'ism, Baha' Allah (1817–92), claimed to be a new prophet and expounded his religion as the latest in a long line of divine revelations. Had it remained confined to the Middle East, it is likely that Baha'ism would have joined the ranks of the numerous heterodox Islamic sects there, with most of which it shares common features. But in 1894 the movement became one of the first missionizing Eastern religions to reach the West, arriving in the United States while still in a state of flux after its emergence from Shi'a Islam.

Unlike the Ahmadiyya and some recent Sufi groups that have sought converts in Europe and America, the Baha'is had consciously broken their connection with Islam and were in search of a means of defining their identity as a community based on a separate revelation, something which had proved difficult in Islamic countries but which they found possible in more pluralist societies. The original move to North America was the initiative of a single individual, but the moment was perfect, and early successes among fringe-group adherents encouraged the Baha'i leadership to divert considerable energies to the promulgation of Baha'ism in the West as a 'new world faith' destined to supersede all established religions.

This development was given considerable impetus by the Western preaching journeys of 'Abd al-Baha' (1844–1921), Baha' Allah's son and successor. The head of the movement from 1921, Shoghi Effendi (1897–1957), accelerated this process of Westernization, and by the time of his death in 1957 the religion had changed its character enormously.

Although the Baha'i conversion rate in Europe and North America has been severely limited and is likely to remain so, since the 1960s the movement has had remarkable success in establishing itself as a vigorous contender in the mission fields of Africa, India, parts of South America and the Pacific, thus outstripping other new religions in the extent of diffusion, if not in numbers. With a world-wide membership of perhaps 4 million and an international spread recently described as second only to that of Christianity, the place of Baha'ism among world religions now seems assured.

The most important Baha'i community is probably still that of Iran, where adherents constitute the largest religious minority. The history of Baha'ism in Iran has been chequered, however, with periodic bouts of persecution and a continuing pattern of discrimination. The community has never succeeded in winning official recognition, and since 1979 Iranian Baha'is have been under threat from the Islamic regime: over 200 have been killed, many have been imprisoned and property has been confiscated [27].

The outsider seeking a relatively unbiased approach to Baha'ism is faced with ambiguity. In terms of numbers, influence, social position, voluntariness of membership and so on, it is most usefully treated as a sect or denomination (with major regional fluctuations), rather than as a wholly independent tradition. But Baha'is themselves emphasize other criteria, such as the lives of the movement's founders and saints, the richness of its scriptural literature, the breadth and rapidity of its geographical expansion, and the ontological assumption of a divine revelation subsequent to and abrogatory of Islam.

The informed observer must try as far as possible to shift between these and other approaches. Perhaps the central focus of interest lies in the conscious promulgation of an alternative religion, not primarily as an outgrowth of an existing major tradition, but as a new tradition *in potentia* and, increasingly, in reality. In its earliest phases, Baha'ism experienced the normal processes of small-scale religious development and, in terms of internal routinization, high participation, and zeal to convert and to confirm new adherents, it has continued to do so. But the use of aggressive, centrally planned missionary tactics since the late 1930s has made it possible increasingly to transform theological assumptions about status into empirical realities or (which may be as significant) into assumptions in the minds of the public, moulded by careful presentation of data. What we are witnessing, in other words, is the planned construction of a 'world religion' according to objectives derived from external theories about what actually constitutes such a phenomenon.

Sources

The question of sources for Baha'i history and doctrine is a vexed and complicated one, in spite of the comparative modernity of the movement. In the case of historical materials in particular there has been sharp controversy since the late nineteenth century, and, if anything, this seems to be increasing. There are several reasons for this. The first is that, almost from the inception of the religion, Baha'is themselves have been deeply concerned with historical issues, and numerous general 'official' histories have been written, including some either penned or vetted by leaders of the movement [e.g. 3; 23; 32; 42]. Valuable as they are, these and other works by adherents are normally tendentious. Independent scholars since E. G. Browne (d. 1926), have criticized this central tradition of Baha'i historiography, but until recently limited access to primary source materials and lack of scholarly interest have restricted the production of alternative versions.

A second problem is that Baha'i history is characterized from the very beginning by factionalism, some of it severe. With the exception of the Azali Babis in Iran and the small grouping of Orthodox Baha'is in the United States, alternative or sectarian groupings have tended to fade out. At the same time, idealizing tendencies in what is now the mainstream of the movement have played down or concealed the historical significance of earlier disputes and the personalities associated with them. Useful factional literature is scarce, while many crucial documents remain in private hands or are kept in official archives to which the researcher has little or no access.

Nevertheless, ample primary materials do exist and, in recent years, many of these have been used as the basis for radical reinterpretations of Baha'i and, in particular, Babi history. Many important manuscripts were obtained by European scholars in the late nineteenth century, the main collections being in Cambridge, London and Paris. Unfortunately, the largest manuscript collections are those of the National Baha'i Archives in Iran and the International Baha'i Archives at the Baha'i World Centre in Haifa, Israel, neither of which is accessible to the public. In general, more primary materials are available for the earlier than for the later period. The introduction of a rationalized administrative system from the 1920s onwards has meant that crucial materials have gone straight into official archives, while printed materials have tended to become blander and less inclined to reveal the full range of developments or events behind the scenes. This is noticeably true of recent volumes of the official yearbook, *The Baha'i World* [6].

In the case of scriptural writings, the problems are fewer and less critical. Strictly speaking, Baha'i scripture consists of the Arabic and Persian writings of the Bab, Baha' Allah and 'Abd al-Baha', the first two representing 'revealed' scripture (in the Qur'anic sense of direct verbal inspiration), the third infallible commentary on and extension of the former two. The writings of the Bab fall into an ambiguous position, in that they are technically regarded as abrogated by those of Baha' Allah. Although not regarded as scripture, the writings in Persian and English of Shoghi Effendi are deemed infallible interpretations of the sacred text and occupy a high position in the religion (especially in Iran, where prayers written by him are used in devotions). Taken together, these materials constitute one of the largest canons in any religion, the full extent of which is difficult to gauge because so much remains in manuscript form. The main collection of original manuscripts is at Haifa, but reliable copies may be found elsewhere.

The works of the Bab [see 25] were composed over only six years, but they fall, nevertheless, into at least two distinct periods, with major shifts in his thought between the two. These works are couched in highly ungrammatical Arabic and idiosyncratic Persian, and are at times almost unreadable, leading to serious problems of interpretation. Modern Baha'is, even Iranians, are almost wholly ignorant of these works, except in the form of selective quotations in later books. There are French translations by Nicolas of works from the later period [33–35]. A recent Baha'i publication [50] provides interpretative translations of carefully selected and not very representative passages from major works.

The writings of Baha' Allah also fall into two main periods: works between about 1852 and 1867 (up to his break with Babism), and those from 1867 to 1892. Works from the first period [e.g. 4; 40; 41] are largely concerned with ethical issues, mysticism and scriptural interpretation; those from the second [e.g. 17; 38] increasingly with apologetics for his new religion, and with the formulation of laws, rituals and so on. Compilation volumes including early and late writings have been published [e.g. 39].

'Abd al-Baha's works consist principally of collected letters and lectures, many of which have been translated into English [e.g. 2; 11; 19]. Shoghi Effendi wrote in both Persian and English, but his best-known works are in the latter language [e.g. 42; 44; 45]. His rhetorical and exaggerated English style has become a model for later Baha'i writing, particularly that produced by official bodies. Three collections of English letters from the Universal House of Justice have been published [51–53].

Two problems concerning scriptural materials deserve mention.

The first is that no critical editions of any original-language texts have been published. The second relates to translations. Baha'i sources state that translations exist in about 700 languages, but this is misleading in that these often consist of no more than a tiny prayer-book or less. Significantly, however, all current translations are made, not from original Arabic or Persian texts, but from the English translations of Shoghi Effendi. These latter are written in fluent if somewhat archaic English, highly interpretative and wholly lacking in critical apparatuses. For the majority of Baha'is, therefore, access to scriptural authority is possible only in mediated form.

Recent translations made at Haifa adopt both the style and the technique of Shoghi Effendi. Apologetic and polemical literature is extensive and easily obtained in most languages. Material in English has been comprehensively summarized in a recent bibliography [15]. A straightforward example of contemporary Baha'i apologetics, which presents historical and doctrinal material uncritically, is [22]. There is a large body of anti-Baha'i polemic in Persian and Arabic. Early materials emphasize the movement's heterodoxy, while more modern works attempt to place Baha'ism alongside Zionism and Freemasonry as part of a wide, Western-backed conspiracy against Islam. There is a much smaller corpus of anti-Baha'i writing from a Christian perspective, a recent example of which is [29]. Sectarian writing within the movement is limited; most current titles are published by the New Mexico-based Orthodox Baha'is: see [15: 294–302; 36].

History

Baha'is have inherited from Islam a view of history as a linear process directed by the divine will and marked by the periodic appearance of major and minor prophets, some of whom bring books and laws and found religious communities. Whereas Muslims see Muhammad as the 'Seal of the Prophets' and Islam as the final religion, for Baha'is this is only true in the sense that Islam completes a series of revelations that together comprise a 6,000-year 'prophetic cycle', the first part of a much longer 'universal cycle' (see figure 16.1). According to modern Baha'i theory, the second part of the 'universal cycle', the 'cycle of fulfilment' (i.e. of prophecy) or 'Baha'i cycle', was initiated on 22 May 1844 by the declaration of a young Iranian, the Bab (1819–50), to be the 'promised one' of Islam. Although regarded as an independent prophet by Baha'is, the Bab's central function is that of a herald for the advent of Mirza Husayn 'Ali Baha' Allah (1817–92), who announced his mission in Baghdad in 1863.

Baha' Allah is regarded as the promised saviour of all ages and

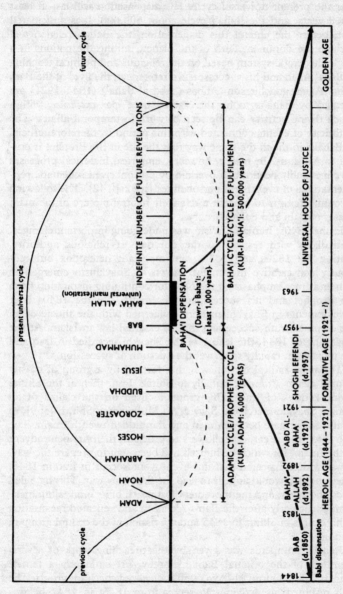

Figure 16.1 The Bahá'í view of history

The labels within the figure:

previous cycle

present universal cycle

future cycle

ADAM

NOAH

ABRAHAM

MOSES

ZOROASTER

BUDDHA

JESUS

MUHAMMAD

BAB

BAHÁ' ALLÁH (universal manifestation)

INDEFINITE NUMBER OF FUTURE REVELATIONS

BAHÁ'Í DISPENSATION
(Dawr-i Bahá'í:
at least 1,000 years)

ADAMIC CYCLE/PROPHETIC CYCLE
(KUR-I ADAM: 6,000 YEARS)

BAHÁ'Í CYCLE/CYCLE OF FULFILMENT
(KUR-I BAHÁ'Í: 500,000 years)

1844   1853   1892   1921   1957   1963

BAB (d.1850)   Babí dispensation

BAHÁ' ALLÁH (d.1892)

'ABD AL-BAHÁ' (d.1921)

SHOGHI EFFENDI (d.1957)

UNIVERSAL HOUSE OF JUSTICE

HEROIC AGE (1844 – 1921)   FORMATIVE AGE (1921 –)

GOLDEN AGE

religions, the 'universal manifestation' of the divinity, who presides over the present universal cycle. His dispensation will last at least 1,000 years, and the Baha'i cycle about 500,000. It is anticipated that, before the end of this dispensation, the Baha'i religion will become the dominant faith of the planet, uniting the nations in a single theocratic system based on the religious and political teaching of Baha' Allah and his successors. In retrospect, the lives of the Bab, Baha' Allah, and his son 'Abbas ('Abd al-Baha') (1844–1921) are deemed by Baha'is to be the 'sacred time' *par excellence*, within which divine activity can be seen at work in temporal affairs. The historicity of events connected with this period is, therefore, crucial to Baha'is in much the same way that the life of the Prophet is crucial to Muslims. In reality, however, empirical historical processes have inevitably been much overlaid by preconceived schematic representations of events and personalities [see esp. 42]. The following account attempts to present a relatively neutral picture of the main phases of Babi and Baha'i history.

In the 1840s, Iranian Shi'ism was undergoing important changes, particularly with respect to the question of religious authority. During the 1820s and 1830s, an important heterodox but religiously conservative movement known as Shaykhism emerged in Iraq and Iran, emphasizing the need for continuing inspiration from the Prophet and his successors, the Imams. By the 1840s later developments in Shaykhism were concerned with the theme of an age of inner truth succeeding that of external law in Islam. At the beginning of 1844, the leader of the Shaykhi sect died in Iraq and the movement rapidly split over the question of succession.

The most radical faction was that formed by a group of mostly Iranian clerics ('*ulema*), initially in Shiraz, Iran, then at the Shi'ite shrine centres of Iraq. This group focused on the claims of an Iranian Shaykhi merchant, Sayyid 'Ali Muhammad Shirazi [3; 9], to be the *bab* or gate between men and the hidden twelfth Imam. The Bab directed his earliest followers to proclaim the imminent advent of the Imam, for which he himself had been sent to prepare the way. It was widely expected that this event would occur in Iraq in 1845, when the Bab would appear to lead the final holy war. This he failed to do, however, and the movement lost much of its original momentum, particularly after the Bab's seclusion and repeated recantation of his claims in Shiraz in 1845 and the fission of the central group in Iraq.

Renewed impetus was given by the preaching work of several members of the original Babi hierarchy, pre-eminently a female scholar called Qurrat al-'Ayn, who radicalized the Iraqi group. The Bab resumed his activities in secret from 1846; in 1847 he was arrested and subsequently transferred to prison in Adharbayjan province, where he continued to write prolifically. Effective control of the movement was, however, by then in the hands of several provincial leaders. In late 1847, the Bab claimed to be the hidden Imam in his persona as the Mahdi (see p. 207), and in 1848 a conclave of his followers met in Mazandaran to abrogate the outward laws of Islam and inaugurate the age of inner truth. These activities were soon followed by outbreaks of mass violence between militant Babis and state troops in Mazandaran (1848–9), Nayriz (1850) and Zanjan (1850–1), in the course of which some 3,000–4,000 Babis were killed, including most of the leadership. (Modern Baha'i sources increase this figure to 20,000, but all the contemporary evidence speaks of lower numbers.) The Bab himself was executed by firing squad in Tabriz on 8 or 9 July 1850.

Following a Babi attempt on the life of the king of Iran, Nasir al-Din Shah, in August 1852 and the execution of several remaining leaders, a largely non-clerical group chose voluntary exile in Baghdad from early 1853. Leadership of this group initially fell to the son of an Iranian state official, Mirza Yahya Nuri Subh-i Azal (c.1830–1912), regarded by many as the Bab's appointed successor. Even during the Bab's lifetime, however, there had been problems in the movement concerning authority, and later theories of theophany had encouraged a veritable rash of conflicting claims to some form of divinity.

The question of authority was concentrated by the early 1860s in a growing power struggle between Yahya and his half-brother, Mirza Husayn 'Ali Baha' Allah [10], who had by then become the *de facto* leader of a large section of the Baghdad community. Whereas the Azali faction was essentially conservative, seeking to preserve the late doctrines and laws of the Bab, the Baha'i sect sought radical modifications in doctrine and practice. In his early writings, Baha' Allah effectively restructured the Bab's highly complex system, simplifying it and preaching tolerance and love in place of the legalism and severity of the later Babi books. In this, he seems to have been much influenced by close contact with Sufi circles. Perhaps the most crucial change, however, was the explicit repudiation of Babi militancy in favour of political quietism and obedience to the state.

In 1863, most of the Baghdad community was exiled via Istanbul to Edirne in European Turkey. Whether or not he had actually made his claims semi-public before leaving Baghdad, Baha' Allah now proclaimed himself a divine manifestation and set about the task of dismantling the Babi system and remaking it as the Baha'i faith.

The last twenty-four years of Baha' Allah's life were spent in exile in Palestine, first in Acre, then in its vicinity, where he died at Bahji on 29 May 1892. Curiously and significantly, remarkably little is known of his life there, in spite of the considerable freedom he possessed after leaving Acre. He continued to write extensively, drawing up laws and ordinances for his community, and incorporating into his teachings various European ideas which had gained some currency in educated circles through the Ottoman empire. Though not a recluse, he had little contact with the outside world, living a somewhat remote existence surrounded by numerous Iranian followers, by whom he was regarded with extreme deference.

Before his death, he followed the Shi'ite system of directly appointing his eldest son 'Abbas [8] as the head of the community and inspired interpreter of the sacred text. A split nevertheless occurred between the followers of 'Abbas and those of his younger half-brother, Mirza Muhammad 'Ali, the effects of which lasted for some time. Both sides used excommunication as a weapon, but in the end the largely progressive faction of 'Abbas succeeded in gaining control, largely through the superior charismatic appeal of 'Abd al-Baha' himself and his greater openness to a move beyond the Near East.

The first Western converts came into the movement in 1894, and during the early years of the twentieth century small groups were established in the United States, Britain, France and Germany. These were, for the most part, drawn from the cultic milieu of the period, often combining membership with continued affiliation to churches or cult movements such as Theosophy. But following 'Abd al-Baha's Western travels (1911, 1912–13) and the dispatch of orthodox teachers to America, Western Baha'ism became increasingly exclusive, while methods of routinized administration began to take precedence over earlier metaphysical and occult concerns. Several factional disputes led to the eventual predominance within the movement of those concerned mainly with social and moral issues and committed to organizational restructuring.

The appointment of Shoghi Effendi Rabbani (1897–1957) [37] as first Guardian of the Cause of God (wali-ye amr Allah, originally a Shi'i term for the Imam) proved singularly important for the later development of the movement. In his first years as Guardian, Shoghi made strenuous efforts to demystify and organize the communities under his centralized leadership. Between 1921 and 1937, he concentrated on the establishment of local and national administrative bodies throughout the Baha'i world, had by-laws drawn up for their operation, instituted the regularization of publications, and began to create an image of Baha'ism as a dynamic new world religion. Having consolidated his own authority and firmly established the principles of Baha'i organization, he turned his attention to missionary enterprise, which he directed through a series of 'plans' designed to introduce Baha'ism into all parts of the globe.

Shoghi Effendi's death in 1957 provoked a serious crisis in the movement, the details of which remain unclear. He had been appointed first of a line of Guardians intended to lead the Baha'i community in parallel with the then unestablished legislative body, the Universal House of Justice, but had died without issue and without leaving any instructions as to the future leadership of the religion. He had, moreover, by then excommunicated all his living male relatives, so that there did not seem to be any way of perpetuating the Guardianship through a collateral line. 'Abd al-Baha' had been explicit about future Guardians in his will and testament, and Shoghi himself had stressed that, without the Guardianship, the Baha'i system would be 'mutilated and permanently deprived of [the] hereditary principle' [45: 148]. The effective termination of a hereditary Guardianship thus called into question certain basic assumptions about the workings of the system and left open the possibility of future factionalism, an eventuality which the present Baha'i leadership has come to regard as particularly threatening. It is, however, a measure of Shoghi Effendi's success in creating a functional religious bureaucracy that, in 1963, the National Assemblies elected the first Universal House of Justice with virtually no opposition. The centralizing authority of this institution, combined with others since created at the Baha'i World Centre in Israel, has so far proved an effective means of preserving the unity of the Baha'i community in the face of occasional factionalism (see figure 16.2).

Developments in Scholarship

Popular and academic interest in Babism was sparked off by the extensive account given of the sect by Gobineau in 1865 [20], but the first serious research on the subject was carried out after 1889 by the Cambridge orientalist, E. G. Browne, who met Baha' Allah, Subh-i Azal and 'Abd al-Baha', corresponded with numerous Baha'is and Azalis, and built up an impressive collection of manuscripts. Although now dated, Browne's work [e.g. 14; 16; 31; 32; and see 30: 29–36] is still immensely useful for its detailed examination of selected historical and scriptural materials.

It was Browne and his French contemporary A. L. M. Nicolas [see 30: 36–40] who first drew attention to the controversial character of much Baha'i historical writing, a point which continues to be a focus of scholarly interest. Inevitably, such early studies approached the subject from an 'orientalist' perspective, seeing it purely in its Iranian and Islamic contexts; but, with significant changes in the nature and distribution of Baha'ism, such an approach became increasingly less satisfactory. At the same time, there was little scholarly interest in the contemporary cultic milieu,

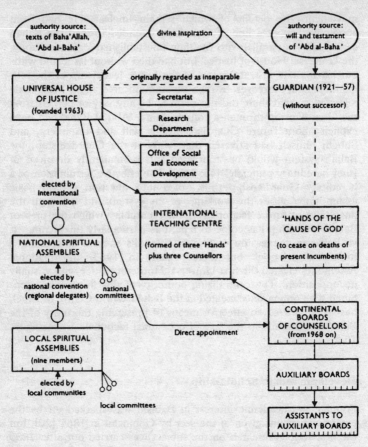

Figure 16.2 Baha'i organization

and techniques for the study of small-scale movements were still undeveloped, so it is not altogether surprising that after Browne's death in 1926 there was a significant hiatus in academic work on the subject. Orientalists lost interest in a movement that had in most ways passed out of their field, and the apologetic nature of contemporary Baha'i writing did little to inspire fresh interest elsewhere.

Beginning with Peter Berger's doctoral dissertation on Baha'ism in 1954 [13], a number of broadly sociological studies of the movement as a whole have been produced in the West [21; 24; 47]. At the same time, several recent studies have revived serious research on Babism and Shaykhism [5; 6; 12; 26], incorporating a wide body of previously unused primary sources and analysing the material within the context of modern scholarship on Islam, Shi'ism and Iranian history. For the most part, such studies present an interpretation of the origins of Baha'ism radically different from that provided within the movement itself, and it seems likely that future research will continue to emphasize this disparity.

Whereas official Baha'i doctrine conflates the two movements of Babism and Baha'ism (and makes Shaykhism a prophetic movement preparing for the Bab), academics are increasingly stressing the significance of Babism as an extremist movement within nineteenth-century Shi'ism, with only tenuous links to what developed outside Iran as Baha'ism. It seems, therefore, that, although studies of the overall Babi to Baha'i development are both possible and desirable, the main thrust of future research is likely to be in two directions, one towards Babism and its Shi'i roots, the other towards Baha'ism and its move away from Islam, particularly in the West.

A tradition of Baha'i scholarship was built up in Iran throughout the twentieth century, notably by Gulpaygani, Mazandarani and Ishraq-Khavari. This adopted the standard methodology of contemporary Islamic scholarship, with little or no room for radical historical or textual criticism, and it continues to dominate Baha'i writing, not only in Iran but in the West as well, where a knowledge of sources rather than an ability to analyse them is the main scholarly criterion. This problem has been exacerbated by the priority given in the movement to works of propagation, so that writing is either openly apologetic or produced with apologetic criteria in mind, and by the mandatory vetting by special committees of all materials to be published by Baha'is. Recent years, however, have seen the beginnings of moderately serious scholarship within the movement, with a shift of focus away from history towards doctrine, administration and scriptural exegesis. This process has been encouraged by official bodies like the Association for Baha'i Studies, the 'Studies in Babi and Baha'i History' series of publications, a number of periodicals and the imminent publication of a Baha'i encyclopaedia.

Internal scholarship of this kind is strictly controlled, mainly by panels for the review of publications, and attempts to introduce more radical approaches have met with criticism and led to the closure of some journals and a publishing house. Nevertheless, there are still signs that some younger Baha'i academics are willing to question official assumptions and that a crisis of some sort will in time develop between them and representatives of the orthodox camp. The outcome of such a debate is likely to be crucial to the future shape of a religion which makes the harmony of faith and reason one of the central bases for its appeal.

Teachings

The characteristic doctrines of Baha'ism have been succinctly described by Shoghi Effendi as follows:

> The Baha'i Faith upholds the unity of God, recognizes the unity of His Prophets, and inculcates the principle of the oneness and wholeness of the entire human race. It proclaims the necessity and inevitability of the unification of mankind . . . enjoins upon its followers the primary duty of an unfettered search after truth, condemns all manner of prejudice and superstition, declares the purpose of religion to be the promotion of amity and concord, proclaims its essential harmony with science, and recognizes it as the foremost agency for the pacification and the orderly progress of human society. It unequivocally maintains the principle of equal rights, opportunities, and privileges for men and women, insists on compulsory education, eliminates extremes of poverty and wealth, abolishes the institution of priesthood, prohibits slavery, asceticism, mendicancy, and monasticism, prescribes monogamy, discourages divorce, emphasizes the necessity of strict obedience to one's government, exalts any work performed in the spirit of service to the level of worship, urges either the creation or the selection of an auxiliary international language, and delineates the outlines of those institutions that must establish and perpetuate the general peace of mankind. [43: 3–4]

It is vital to the faith of Baha'is that these and other doctrines contained in their scriptures be regarded as wholly original, not merely in the sense of being largely 'new', but as emanating directly from God. This view owes much to the Islamic theory of divine revelation as a unidirectional process whereby the uncreated Word is conveyed to men unaltered through the inert medium of the prophet. The Bab and Baha' Allah are regarded as 'manifestations of God', a term borrowed from Shi'ism and theosophical Sufism. They are, in other words, incarnations of the eternal Logos, which has appeared in all previous major prophets, and as such possess the dual conditions of humanity and divinity. In the later writings of Baha' Allah, however, this comes close to a doctrine of incarnationism (e.g. 'the essence of the pre-existent has appeared'). The knowledge of God can be obtained only through recognition of his manifestations, a recognition which in turn entails absolute obedience to their laws [39: 49–50, 329–30].

Divine revelation is progressive (though sporadic rather than continuous), in accordance with the exigencies of changing human circumstances. At the same time, all developments in the human sphere are ultimately generated by the creative power of the divine word in each age [39: 141–7]. This doctrine entails the more problematic corollary that the teachings of a prophet must be chronologically prior to expressions of the same ideas in the world at large (in itself evidence that the prophet has not been influenced by the thoughts of others). Such a view, while clearly important as a means of establishing the credentials of Baha'ism for its followers, is equally clearly difficult to sustain empirically and has the disadvantage of obscuring the actual process through which the Baha'i teachings developed. The following remarks may help to clarify that process.

The majority of Baha'is today are converts from non-Islamic backgrounds and, as a result, there is widespread ignorance within the community of the extent to which the basic doctrines of the religion are Islamic (and, in particular, Shi'ite) in origin. Leaving aside for the moment the question of individual doctrines, it is incontrovertible that the context within which these operate differs in no radical sense from the central presuppositions of Islam. History is a process directed by periodic divine intervention, the purpose of which is to reveal the will of God in the form of a *shari'a*, a comprehensive ethical, legal and social system designed to fashion and regulate the affairs of society at all levels. Western distinctions between church and state, religion and politics, do not strictly apply here, for the sacred law embraces all areas of human experience. The Baha'i *shari'a* is derived from two primary sources: the sacred text and the legislation of the Universal House of Justice. In practice, only a small portion of Baha'i law is either known or acted on outside Islamic countries, though the recent publication of an English translation of the *Kitab al-aqdas* [7] suggests that the authorities now consider it appropriate to start introducing legislation more widely.

Yet another central theme developed from Shi'ism is the notion of the 'covenant', through which the authority of 'Abd al-Baha', Shoghi Effendi and the present leadership is guaranteed and the unity of the religion in theory assured. Thus Baha' Allah appointed 'Abd al-Baha', who in turn appointed Shoghi Effendi; the Universal House of Justice is similarly elected on the authority of a statement by Baha' Allah to the effect that such a body would be divinely guided. As in Shi'ism, this concept involves the corollary of the expulsion from the community and the subsequent shunning of those who have rebelled against the authority of the appointed head of the faith.

Even several apparently modernist teachings, such as the harmony of religion and science, the oneness of humankind or the unity of revealed religion are, in essence, typically Islamic. This primary Islamic stratum in Baha'ism was modified in two ways: first, in Baha' Allah's reaction against Babism; and second, in his response to external influences, particularly modernist and Western ideas. Although Baha' Allah retained and simplified most of the religious and metaphysical teachings of the Bab, he reacted strongly against many of his laws and ordinances, especially those which underpinned the fanaticism and exclusivism that characterized the Babi movement. Many of Baha' Allah's earliest writings speak of the reforms he had instituted among the Babis, notably in the abrogation of laws directed against non-believers, above all the waging of holy war. 'Abd al-Baha' was later to characterize Baha'ism as, in a sense, the diametrical opposite of Babism. Whereas the latter emphasized 'the striking of necks, the burning of books and papers, the destruction of shrines, and the universal slaughter of all save those who believed and were faithful', the former stressed compassion, mercy, association with all peoples, trustworthiness towards others and the unification of humankind [1]. Later, however, Shoghi Effendi's wholesale conflation of Babism and Baha'ism served to obscure this important distinction, and modern Baha'i writing often describes as 'the teachings of the Bab and Baha'u'llah' what are, in fact, mainly doctrines of the latter [e.g. 30: XXIII–XXV].

Baha' Allah may have been influenced in this direction by Sufi and Christian doctrines. His early writings contain quotations from Sufi writers and the New Testament, and he himself was for a time a Sufi dervish. In his later exile in Turkey and Palestine, he came into contact with Europeans and Islamic modernists, as did 'Abd al-Baha', and seems to have been extremely receptive to the Western ideas then gaining currency in the Middle East. As a result, his writings in Acre incorporated notions such as collective security, world government, the use of an international auxiliary language and script, universal compulsory education and so on. 'Abd al-Baha' seems to have been particularly interested in these and related matters, as is obvious from an early work [18], and in his later talks and letters he addressed himself increasingly to topics of interest to Western converts. He spoke at length concerning the equality of the sexes, the need for an independent search after truth, the harmony of science and religion, and the solution of economic problems, and frequently referred to issues such as evolution, social and scientific progress, labour relations, socialism and education.

Having been an essentially progressivist movement in the early years of the twentieth century, Baha'ism is still portrayed as such in contemporary literature, and Baha'is continue to identify themselves with what are seen as 'progressive' causes, such as world government or religious and racial harmony. The Baha'is possess non-governmental observer status with the UN and are regular participants at international conferences on human rights, women, and environmental and Third World issues. However, until the 1980s direct Baha'i participation in movements for social change was severely limited by a long-standing prohibition on involvement in politics. This was reinforced by Shoghi Effendi's conviction that believers should leave the outside world to collapse, while building a new Baha'i order to take its place.

Although this remains the underlying position, in 1983 the Universal House of Justice announced that social action was now to be incorporated into Baha'i community life and set up an Office of Social and Economic Development in Haifa to coordinate such activities. This shift towards a more activist policy is a direct response to the growth of the religion in the Third World, and projects are now being undertaken in several spheres, including literacy, social development, agriculture and medicine. As with similar programmes sponsored by other religious groups, Baha'i development projects are closely linked to the movement's broader missionary enterprise.

Development issues apart, the Baha'is seem to be experiencing problems similar to those faced by Catholics and other conservative churches in responding to broader social change, particularly in the West. While Baha'i doctrine emphasizes the need for periodic adjustments of religious law and practice to accommodate change in other spheres, such adjustment can only be made through the appearance of a new prophet. The Universal House of Justice can legislate on matters not already dealt with in Scripture, but it is powerless to abrogate existing rulings. This leaves the Baha'is upholding illiberal attitudes on numerous issues of modern social concern, such as homosexuality, cohabitation, abortion, the use of alcohol and drugs, euthanasia and capital punishment. In the Third World, the most likely area of conflict between Baha'i progressivism and conservatism lies in the movement's commitment to the principle of absolute obedience to established authority.

At a deeper level, there is a marked strain of authoritarianism within the movement itself, something which has caused tensions and even division in the past. Preservation of Baha'i unity remains an overriding concern, with unquestioning loyalty to the institutions of the faith seen as the best means to secure and maintain it. Further crises over this issue are, therefore, almost inevitable as the movement grows and diversifies.

Practices

The question of contemporary religious practice in Baha'ism is complicated by the existence of a gap between prescriptive regulations (which are extensive) and actual practices (which are limited), particularly outside Iran, although as time goes on more and more ritual and other prescribed practices are being introduced [see 28]. The basic pattern is again Islamic, the main religious obligations being those of ritual prayer (*salat*), annual fasting (*sawm*) and pilgrimage (*hajj* and *ziyara*) (see pp. 181–97). Many customary rites in Islam (such as the rites of passage) tend to be prescriptive in Baha'ism, although the forms tend to follow Islamic practice quite closely.

Salat is private, with three alternative versions to be performed (once in twenty-four hours, once at noon, or thrice daily), with ritual ablutions. The prayer-direction (*qibla*) is the tomb of Baha' Allah near Acre. Fasting takes place during the last month of the solar Baha'i year (2–20 March) on the Islamic pattern. As in Islam, there are exemptions for certain categories, such as the sick and pregnant women. Pilgrimage is less well defined. Strictly speaking, the Islamic *hajj* to Mecca has been replaced by two pilgrimages, both of which are restricted to men. These are to the house of the Bab in Shiraz and to that of Baha' Allah in Baghdad, and both involve elaborate ritual ceremonies. In practice, it has never been possible for Baha'is to perform these *hajj* rites, and the destruction of the house of the Bab in 1979 following the Iranian revolution has introduced a fresh complication. 'Abd al-Baha' made obligatory what may be termed 'lesser pilgrimage' (*ziyara*) to the tombs of Baha' Allah and the Bab (now in Haifa), this being the form of visitation made by Shi'is to the tombs of Imams and their relatives or by Sunnis to the shrines of saints. Visitation to the shrines in Israel has become the standard Baha'i pilgrimage; indeed, most non-Iranian Baha'is are unaware that other forms exist, and even imagine the *ziyara* to be the ritual equivalent of the Islamic *hajj*, which it is not. *Ziyaras* can also be made to numerous other Baha'i holy sites, particularly in Iran, and special prayers exist for recitation at these. The grave of Shoghi Effendi in London has become an important pilgrimage site in recent years.

Devotional and ceremonial practices are generally informal. At the local level, communal activities are organized by local assemblies, which are elected annually. As in Islam, there is no priesthood, but recent years have seen the emergence of a semi-professional appointed hierarchy responsible for the propagation of the faith and protection from external attacks and internal dissent. In Arabic, these individuals (who include women) are known as *'ulema*, although their functions are not currently comparable to those of the Islamic clergy. They perform no ceremonial or intercessory functions. The principal communal gatherings are those held for the Nineteen-day Feast on the first day of each Baha'i month (of which there are nineteen, each of nineteen days) and for the nine principal holy days during the year (on which work has to be suspended) (see appendix to this chapter). Feasts, which are preferably held in the homes of individuals, consist of three portions: the reading of prayers and sacred texts; administrative consultation; and the sharing of food and drink. Holy-day meetings generally consist of readings of prayers and devotional texts designated for the occasion, sometimes with sermons or historical readings relevant to commemorative festivals.

Most Baha'i communities meet in private homes or halls rented or purchased for the purpose. There are in existence only a handful of houses of worship (*Mashriq al-adhkar*), which are show-pieces built on a continental basis and at present used largely for public gatherings. They follow a common pattern of circular design incorporating nine entrances and a dome, but are otherwise architecturally diverse and, in several cases, represent fine examples of modern religious architecture. The seven temples now in use are located in the United States (Wilmette, Illinois), Germany, Panama, Australia, India, Uganda and Samoa.

Rites of passage are limited to naming ceremonies for babies (circumcision is not mandatory), marriage and funeral rites. Marriage is conditional on the consent of both parties and all living parents; arranged marriages are permitted and are common in Iran and elsewhere. The ceremony is flexible, the minimum requirement being the recitation by the bride and groom in the presence of witnesses of two verses adapted from the Persian Bayan. Simplicity is preferred, but ceremonies are usually expanded with music and readings from sacred texts and tend to follow cultural norms. The preparation and burial of the dead are carried out according to complex regulations. Cremation is not prohibited but is regarded as undesirable. The place of burial is to be no more than one hour's journey from the place of death and the plot is to be arranged so that the feet of the dead face the Baha'i *qibla*. The ritual *salat* for the dead (used only for adults) is the only occasion on which communal recitation of prayer is permitted.

Babism followed popular Shi'ism in being particularly rich in thaumaturgical and magical practices, such as the use of talismans, engraved stones and incantatory prayers. There are fewer such practices in Baha'ism, but they have not been wholly eradicated. There are numerous thaumaturgical, protective and supererogatory prayers, most of them as yet little known outside Iran. A calligraphic representation of the 'greatest name of God' in Arabic is found in most Baha'i homes:

Ya baha' al-abha – *O splendour of the most splendid*

Equally common is the much stylized representation of the name Baha', designed to be engraved on ringstones, which owes much of its form to magical symbols found in popular Islam:

Strictly speaking, the symbol of the Baha'i religion is a five-pointed star, but it is much more common to find a nine-pointed star on jewellery and publications, as well as on gravestones.

Distribution

The key element in the growth of Baha'ism since the 1930s has been careful planning – a theme developed by Hampson [21] in the only full-length study of the subject. Since 1937, a series of national, regional and global missionary 'plans' have been conceived to coordinate the expansion and consolidation of the religion. Growth has been assessed in terms of ethnic groups, territories and localities represented, administrative bodies founded, assemblies legally incorporated, property purchased or constructed, literature translated or published, and so on. The result has been an impressive overall increase in all these areas, laying the base for future expansion. Significant gains have been made since the 1960s in several Third World countries, with expansion currently most rapid in India, South Vietnam, South America, the Pacific and parts of sub-Saharan Africa, to the extent that Baha'ism is now 'overwhelmingly a "Third World" religion' [48]. Although Iranians, Americans and Europeans remain the most active in missionary and administrative work, they now form a very low percentage of the Baha'i population world-wide: Westerners form 3 per cent of the total, while Iranians (94 per cent in 1954) now account for only 6 per cent. Conversion to Baha'ism is extremely rare in Muslim countries, where restrictions are often severe, and there is no reason to think this situation will improve in the foreseeable future.

There is no question that Baha'ism is very widely distributed, to the extent that the *Britannica Book of the Year* for 1988 described it as the second most widely spread religion after Christianity. Until recently, however, it has been difficult to interpret this spread in more precise terms, since available statistics have been restricted to 'assemblies' or 'localities' rather than individuals. In the past few years, however, figures for individual adherents have been made public. Although these are still open to question on several counts, they do provide researchers for the first time with a solid basis on which to make calculations (for a detailed analysis, see [48: 69–74]). The most recent estimate of Baha'i populations was carried out for 1988. According to these rounded figures, the total number of Baha'is in the world was then 4,490,000 [48: 72].

Table 16.1 Statistics on Baha'ism

Year	Total countries opened	Total national assemblies	Total local assemblies	Total localities (with or without assemblies)
1921	35			
1954	128	12	708	3,117
1964	240	56	4,566	15,186
1973	335	113	17,037	69,541
1979	343	125	23,624	102,704
1992	218[a]	165	20,435[a]	120,046

[a] Reduction owing to administrative changes.

These statistics are, however, distorted in a number of ways, most importantly by the lack of accurate figures for disaffiliated and inactive believers. The Baha'i administration sets low requirements for membership but insists on formal withdrawal. Understandably, this latter is seldom forthcoming and, as a result, large numbers of individuals and even localities may be officially registered long after informal disaffiliation. That figures for disaffection may be high is suggested by Hampson's finding that, in 1976, mail was returned unopened from the addresses of 31 per cent of US adherents [21: 230]. It is also difficult to estimate how successful post-registration consolidation has been in mass-conversion areas in the Third World. In some places, there appear to be problems of multiple affiliation.

Another factor that should be taken into account when comparing current figures with those for earlier periods is the 1979 decision of the Universal House of Justice that all newly born children of Baha'is be automatically registered as Baha'is.

Conclusion

The development of Baha'ism may prove to be an important exemplum for future trends in the religious sphere. In the past, religious traditions have developed self-consciousness as distinct, reified systems only after lengthy periods of growth. With the partial exception of Islam, no major tradition has been founded or initially developed as a self-defined entity separate from others. The notion of 'world religions' is itself relatively recent. (On these and related points, see [49].)

In the modern period, however, it does not seem possible for unselfconscious development of this kind to take place. New movements emerge into a universe of already reified and competing systems. In order to compete, they are obliged to define themselves within terms of the prevailing norms. Baha'ism would seem to be the first of the new religious movements that shows signs of developing as an independent tradition. In origin, it belongs wholly to the pre-modern world of nineteenth-century Iran, but the significant phases of its development are marked by various responses to Western ideas and methods. Since the 1920s, its leaders have planned, systematized and organized in order to make it conceptually and actually a 'new world faith'. It has, in Hampson's words, 'managed its own development' [24: 2]. The future progress of Baha'ism must remain matter for speculation, but without doubt a firm basis has been laid for continued expansion in some regions. It will be surprising if the movement succeeds in resisting tendencies towards fission, heterodoxy and popularization if it moves much beyond its present sectarian dimensions. But there is already much to learn from its progress so far. Conscious planning, rational organization and long-term strategies have, it seems, become keys to religious growth in the modern age.

Appendix: The Baha'i Calendar

The Baha'i calendar is known as the Badi' Calendar and was devised by the Bab. It is based on a solar year of nineteen months, each of nineteen days, plus four intercalary days (five in leap years). There are also cycles (*vahids*) of nineteen years, nineteen of which constitute a *Kullu shay'*. Baha'is date the commencement of the Badi' era from the New Year's Day (21 March) preceding the announcement of the Bab's mission in May 1844.

Days of the week

Day	Arabic name	English name	Translation
1st	Jalal	Saturday	Glory
2nd	Jamal	Sunday	Beauty
3rd	Kamal	Monday	Perfection
4th	Fidal	Tuesday	Grace
5th	Idal	Wednesday	Justice
6th	Istijlal	Thursday	Majesty
7th	Istiqlal	Friday	Independence

Names of the months

Month	Arabic name	Translation	First day
1st	Baha'	Splendour	1 March
2nd	Jalal	Glory	9 April
3rd	Jamal	Beauty	28 April
4th	'Azamat	Grandeur	17 May
5th	Nur	Light	5 June
6th	Rahmat	Mercy	24 June
7th	Kalimat	Words	13 July
8th	Kamal	Perfection	1 August
9th	Asma'	Names	20 August
10th	'Izzat	Might	8 September
11th	Mashiyyat	Will	27 September
12th	'Ilm	Knowledge	16 October
13th	Qudrat	Power	4 November
14th	Qawl	Speech	23 November
15th	Masa'il	Questions	12 December
16th	Sharaf	Honour	31 December
17th	Sultan	Sovereignty	19 January
18th	Mulk	Dominion	7 February
19th	Ala'	Loftiness	27 March

Ayyam-i-Ha' (intercalary days): 26 February to 1 March inclusive.

Feasts, anniversaries and days of fasting

Feast of Ridvan (Declaration of Baha' Allah), 21 April to 2 May
   1863
Feast of Naw-Ruz (New Year), 21 March
Declaration of the Bab, 23 May 1844
The Day of the Covenant, 26 November
Birth of Baha' Allah, 12 November 1817
Birth of the Bab, 20 October 1819
Birth of 'Abd al-Baha', 23 May 1844
Ascension of Baha' Allah, 29 May 1892
Martyrdom of the Bab, 9 July 1850
Ascension of 'Abd al-Baha', 28 November 1921
Fasting season lasts nineteen days beginning with the first day of the
   month of 'Ala', 2 March – the Feast of Naw-Ruz follows
   immediately thereafter.

Holy days on which work should be suspended

The first day of Ridvan
The ninth day of Ridvan
The twelfth day of Ridvan
The anniversary of the declaration of the Bab
The anniversary of the birth of Baha' Allah
The anniversary of the birth of the Bab
The anniversary of the ascension of Baha' Allah
The anniversary of the martyrdom of the Bab
The feast of Naw-Ruz

Bibliography

1 'ABD AL-BAHA, *Makatib-i 'Abd al-Baha'*, vol. 2, Cairo, 1912, p. 266
2 'ABD AL-BAHA, *Talks by Abdul Baha Given in Paris*, London, Baha'i
   Publishing Society/East Sheen, Unity Press, 1912; 4th edn London,
   G. Bell, 1920; US edn as *The Wisdom of Abdu'l-Baha*, New York,
   Baha'i Publishing Committee, 1924; also publ. as *Paris Talks*, London,
   Baha'i Publishing Trust, 1961
3 'ABD AL-BAHA', *A Traveller's Narrative Written to Illustrate the Episode of
   the Bab* (ed. and tr. E. G. Browne), 2 vols, London, Cambridge
   University Press, 1891; repr. Amsterdam, Philo Press, 1975; new edn
   Wilmette, IL, Baha'i Publishing Trust, 1980
4 ALI-KULI KHAN (tr.), Baha'u'llah, *The Seven Valleys and the Four Valleys*,
   Wilmette, IL, Baha'i Publishing Committee, 1945 (New York, 1936);
   3rd rev. edn London, Baha'i Publishing Trust, 1978

5 AMANAT, ABBAS, *Resurrection and Renewal: The Making of the Babi Movement in Iran, 1844–1850*

6 *The Baha'i Yearbook, 1925–1926*, New York, Baha'i Publishing Committee, 1926; subsequently publ. as *The Baha'i World*, vols 1–7, New York, 1928–39; vol. 8, Wilmette, IL, 1942; vol. 9, New York, 1945; vols 10–12, Wilmette, IL, 1949–56; vols. 13–18, Haifa, 1971–82

7 BAHA'U'LLAH, *The Kitáb-i-Aqdas, The Most Holy Book*, London, Baha'i Publishing Trust, 1993

8 BALYUZI, H. M., *'Abdu'l-Baha*, London, George Ronald, 1971; Wilmette, IL, Baha'i Publishing Trust

9 BALYUZI, H. M., *The Bab*, Oxford, George Ronald, 1973

10 BALYUZI, H. M., *Baha'u'llah*, Oxford, George Ronald, 1980

11 BARNEY, L. C. (tr.), 'Abd al-Baha, *Some Answered Questions*, London, Trübner/Philadelphia, Lippincott, 1908; London, Baha'i Publishing Trust, 1961; Wilmette, IL, Baha'i Publishing Trust, 1981

12 BAYAT, M., *Mysticism and Dissent: Socioreligious Thought in Qajar Iran*, Syracuse, NY, Syracuse University Press, 1982

13 BERGER, P., 'From Sect to Church: A Sociological Interpretation of the Baha'i Movement', PhD dissertation, New School for Social Research, New York, 1954

14 BROWNE, E. G. (ed.), *Materials for the Study of the Babi Religion*, Cambridge, Cambridge University Press, 1918

15 COLLINS, W. P., *Bibliography of English-Language Works on the Bábi and Bahá'í Faiths 1844–1985*, Oxford, George Ronald, 1990

16 COOPER, R., *The Baha'is of Iran*, London, Benjamin Franklin House, 1987 (Minority Rights Group Report no. 51); 4th edn with revisions by the Minority Rights Group, 1991

17 ELDER, E. E., and MILLER, W. MCE. (trs), Baha'u'llah, *Al-Kitab al-Aqdas, or, The Most Holy Book*, London, Royal Asiatic Society, 1961 (= 1962)

18 GAIL, M. (tr.), 'Abd al-Baha, *The Secret of Divine Civilization*, Wilmette, IL, Baha'i Publishing Trust, 1957; 2nd edn 1970

19 GAIL, M. (tr.), 'Abd al-Baha, *Selections from the Writings of 'Abdu'l-Baha* . . . (tr. by a committee at the Baha'i World Centre and by Marzieh Gail), Haifa, Baha'i World Centre/Wilmette, IL, Baha'i Publishing Trust, 1978

20 GOBINEAU, J. A. DE, *Les Religions et philosophies dans l'Asie centrale*, Paris, Didier, 1865; 10th edn Paris, Gallimard, 1957

21 HAMPSON, A., 'The Growth and Spread of the Baha'i Faith', PhD dissertation, Honolulu, University of Hawaii, 1980 (University Microfilms 80–22, 655)

22 HATCHER, W. S., and MARTIN, J. D., *The Bahá'í Faith: The Emerging Global Religion*, San Francisco, Harper & Row, 1984

23 HUSAIN HAMADANI, M., *The New History (Tarikh-i-Jadid) of Mirza 'Ali Muhammed the Bab by Mirza Huseyn of Hamadan* (tr. and ed. E. G. Browne), Cambridge, Cambridge University Press, 1893; repr. Amsterdam, Philo Press, 1975

24 JOHNSON, V., 'An Historical Analysis of Critical Transformations in the Evolution of the Baha'i World Faith', PhD dissertation, Waco, TX, Baylor University, 1974 (University Microfilms 75–20, 564)

25 MACEOIN, D. M., *Early Babi Doctrine and History: A Survey of Source Materials*, Leiden, Brill, 1992

26 MACEOIN, D. M., 'From Shaykhism to Babism: A Study in Charismatic Renewal in Shi'i Islam', PhD dissertation, University of Cambridge, 1979 (University Microfilms 81–70, 043)

27 MACEOIN, D. M., A *People Apart: The Baha'i Community of Iran in the Twentieth Century*, London, School of Oriental and African Studies, Occasional Papers, 1989

28 MACEOIN, D. M., *Ritual in Babism and Baha'ism*, London, I. B. Tauris, 1994

29 MILLER, W. MCE., *The Baha'i Faith: Its History and Teachings*, South Pasadena, William Carey Library, 1974

30 MOMEN, M. (ed.), *The Babi and Baha'i Religions, 1844–1944: Some Contemporary Western Accounts*, Oxford, George Ronald, 1981

31 MOMEN, M. (ed.), *Selections from the Writings of E. G. Browne on the Bábí and Bahá'í Religions*, Oxford, George Ronald, 1987

32 NABIL-I-A'ZAM (Mulla Muhammad Zarandi), *The Dawn-Breakers: Nabil's Narrative of the Early Days of the Baha'i Revelation* (tr. and ed. Shoghi Effendi), New York, Baha'i Publishing Committee, 1932; British edn (abr.) London, Baha'i Publishing Trust, 1953

33 NICOLAS, A. L. M. (tr.), *Le Béyân arabe* (by 'Ali Muhammad Shirazi, called the Bab), Paris, Leroux, 1905

34 NICOLAS, A. L. M. (tr.), *Le Béyân persan* (by 'Ali Muhammad Shirazi, called the Bab), 4 vols, Paris, 1911–14

35 NICOLAS, A. L. M. (tr.), *Le Livre des sept preuves de la mission du Bab* (by 'Ali Muhammad Shirazi, called the Bab), Paris, Maisonneuve, 1902

36 *The Orthodox Baha'i Faith: The Cause for Universal Religion, Brotherhood and Peace: A Sketch of Its History and Teachings*, Roswell, NM, Mother Baha'i Council of the United States, 1981

37 RUHIYYIH RABBANI, *The Priceless Pearl*, London/Wilmette, IL, Baha'i Publishing Trust, 1969

38 SHOGHI EFFENDI (tr.), Baha'u'llah, *Epistle to the Son of the Wolf*, Wilmette, IL, Baha'i Publishing Committee, 1941; rev. edn Baha'i Publishing Trust, 1976

39 SHOGHI EFFENDI (tr.), Baha'u'llah, *Gleanings from the Writings of Baha'u'llah*, Wilmette, IL, Baha'i Publishing Committee, 1948; New York, 1935; London, 1949; 2nd rev. edn Wilmette, IL, Baha'i Publishing Trust, 1976

40 SHOGHI EFFENDI (tr.), Baha'u'llah, *The Hidden Words*, London, Baha'i Publishing Trust, 1932, 1944; Wilmette, IL, Baha'i Publishing Trust, 1939; rev. edn 1954

41 SHOGHI EFFENDI (tr.), Baha'u'llah, *The Kitab-i-Iqan. The Book of Certitude*, 1931, New York, Baha'i Publishing Committee, 1937; 2nd edn London, Baha'i Publishing Trust, 1961; rev. edn Wilmette, IL, Baha'i Publishing Trust, 1974

42 SHOGHI EFFENDI, *God Passes By*, Wilmette, IL, Baha'i Publishing Committee, 1944; rev. edn 1974

43 SHOGHI EFFENDI, *Guidance for Today and Tomorrow*, London/Wilmette, IL, Baha'i Publishing Trust, 1953

44 SHOGHI EFFENDI, *The Promised Day is Come*, Wilmette, IL, Baha'i

Publishing Committee, 1941, rev. edn Baha'i Publishing Trust, 1980; Bombay, Baha'i Assembly of Bombay, 1942

45 SHOGHI EFFENDI, *The World Order of Baha'u'llah*, New York, Baha'i Publishing Committee, 1938; rev. edn Wilmette, IL, Baha'i Publishing Trust, 1965, copyr. 1955

46 SMITH, P., *The Babi and Baha'i Religions: From Messianic Shi'ism to a World Religion*, Cambridge, Cambridge University Press, 1987

47 SMITH, P., 'A Sociological Study of the Babi and Baha'i Religions', PhD dissertation, University of Lancaster, 1982

48 SMITH, P., and MOMEN, M., 'The Baha'i Faith 1957–1988: A Survey of Contemporary Developments', *Religion*, vol. 19, 1989, pp. 63–91

49 SMITH, W. CANTWELL, *The Meaning and End of Religion*, New York, Macmillan, 1962, 1963; London, New English Library, 1965; London, SPCK, 1978

50 TAHERZADEH, M. (tr.), *Selections from the Writings of the Báb* (by 'Ali Muhammad Shirazi, called the Bab), Haifa, Baha'i World Centre, 1976

51 UNIVERSAL HOUSE OF JUSTICE, *Messages, 1968–1973*, Wilmette, IL, Baha'i Publishing Trust, 1976

52 UNIVERSAL HOUSE OF JUSTICE, *Wellspring of Guidance: Messages, 1963–1968*, Wilmette, IL, Baha'i Publishing Trust, 1969; rev. edn 1976

53 UNIVERSAL HOUSE OF JUSTICE, *A Wider Horizon: Selected Messages of the UHJ 1983–1992*, Riviera Beach, FL, Palabra Publications, 1992

Part II

Cross-Cultural Issues

17

Religion and Gender

URSULA KING

Introduction

The religions of the world have been studied in great detail but until recently little attention has been paid to gender differences and their impact on religious teaching and practice. Yet religions are an important source for the understanding of gender. This may not be self-evident but on closer examination it becomes clear that all religious traditions contain prescriptive teachings on gender roles, and religious beliefs and practices are themselves significantly shaped by gender perspectives.

The critical gender analysis which has grown up since the 1970s has gained great importance in all contemporary scholarship, including the study of religions. A new critical awareness of gender differences, linked to the existing asymmetry in the power relations, representation, knowledge and scholarship between men and women, challenges the traditional practice and study of religion and is thus setting a new research agenda for both theology and religious studies.

The debates about feminist theology in particular have attracted much public attention in Western countries. This is primarily due to their importance in influencing the reform of liturgical practices and language, and in advocating the ordination of women. Such developments, however, are not restricted to religion in the West, but have an international and even global dimension. All religions, whether of ancient or modern origin, are beginning to be affected by debates about gender issues which are raised by the new consciousness and voices of women who in the light of their own experience have undertaken to re-examine critically all existing social, cultural and religious practices.

Conceptual Clarifications

The notion of religion is a complex one and not always easy to apply cross-culturally. Thus there is always much room for interpretation and debate as to the precise meaning of the concept *religion* in different contexts. Similar debates surround the meaning of *gender*, though for different reasons. The notion of gender is much discussed in contemporary sociology and anthropology, where gender identity and gender relations are seen as central for the understanding of any social order. Gender ideologies are frequently hierarchically organized so that sexual inequalities are embedded in thought, language and social institutions, including religious roles and institutions. Yet the more we know about the complex and sometimes contradictory male and female roles which exist in different societies, the more difficult it becomes to state insights about gender in universal terms.

The idea of *genderedness* is an important new insight of feminist thought and represents a breakthrough in the history of human consciousness. Gender is a primary source of individual and social identity, but it interacts closely with other factors such as race, class, age and ethnicity. But what is meant by gender? Contemporary writers distinguish *sex*, as the biologically given differences between women and men, from *gender*, as the historically, socially and culturally developed 'construct' or interpretation of what it means to be a woman or man in different religions and cultures. Though applicable to both sexes, the notion of gender is currently mostly debated with regard to women. Feminist scholars have developed a substantial body of new theory and knowledge which has already become an integral part of many women's studies courses. However, these generally make little reference to religion and often deal with women's changing experience in an entirely secular context without taking into account that the origin of different gender constructions and inequalities is often deeply enshrined in religious teachings, especially in sacred scriptures which are considered as foundational and normative in particular religious traditions. Similarly, many current debates about the experience and self-understanding of women, their role, image and status in society, are still shaped or affected by religious teachings even when these are sharply criticized or vehemently rejected. It is therefore especially important to address gender-specific inquiries to the whole field of religion.

The feminist critique of society focuses particularly on the close and complex relationship between gender and power, expressed everywhere through the marginalization and subordination of women, frequently experienced by them through different forms of exploitation, oppression and violence. The prevalence of such experiences is a proof of the pervasiveness of *patriarchy*, understood as an all-male power structure and universal male dominance, so clearly present in many social institutions, assumptions and attitudes. Patriarchy is the major focus of all feminist critique and the term is used not only to describe the understanding and practice of sex roles and the formation of separate gender identities, but also to refer to women's past and present dependence on and subordination to fathers, husbands, brothers and all men in positions of influence, power and privilege. Rarely commented upon is the religious origin of the word patriarchy itself, which in the Christian tradition has for centuries described the dignity, see or jurisdiction of an ecclesiastical patriarch. Not only the word, but the reality and existence of patriarchy are inextricably connected with religious roots and ramifications. All historical religions are inherently deeply patriarchal.

Another focus of women's critique is *sexism*, which has been defined as an exclusive ordering of life by way of gender or rather by sharply differentiated gender roles and by the assumption that one sex is essentially superior to the other, resulting in discrimination against members of the supposedly inferior sex. Sexism is currently endemic in all social and religious institutions. Almost everywhere women are kept in subordinate positions whereas men hold most, and often all, positions of power and authority. This male-centredness in human history and institutions has meant that male experience has been taken as the universal human norm and become an integral part of our thought structures, concepts and language.

This hidden dimension of patriarchy in our conscious and unconscious mind is also referred to as *androcentrism*, a word which means that men or male experience are at the centre of reality. In the past, men have named things and people, have thought and shaped the world, have created religion, history and culture. They have mapped out reality for themselves and established its boundaries according to their own experience alone, whereas women have been assigned a place within the scheme of things invented by men without being acknowledged as agents and participants in their own right.

Wherever one looks in the world, religious institutions are affected by patriarchy, sexism and androcentrism. Women are either invisible or marginal to the public positions of power, hierarchy and authority. Whereas women represent almost everywhere the majority of religious practitioners in the ordinary day-to-day religious life at grass-roots level, they are hardly ever the official 'spokeswomen' of religious institutions and organizations. This is also clearly the case in the current inter-faith activities around the globe, though mention may be made of the positive developments in Christian ecumenical circles associated with the World Council of Churches (WCC). The WCC is making considerable efforts to increase the proportion of women among its official representatives and on its working committees. Its 'Decade of Churches in Solidarity with Women' (1988–98) is intended to accord women also greater visibility and participation in local churches around the globe. Though widely varying in its effectiveness, this is a pioneering programme which provides a model for similar positive affirmation and action programmes which need to be launched by religious groups elsewhere.

Much feminist critique is addressed to the wider issue of the *masculinity* of contemporary culture, understood to be associated with competitive, exploitative, manipulative and destructive aspects of human behaviour which are seen as a great threat to the future of humankind and the planet. Similarly criticized are unexamined assumptions of 'value neutrality' and 'objectivity' underpinning the research work of many scientists and scholars. These concerns have important implications for the debates about the most appropriate methodology for the study of religions.

Contemporary women have developed a new critical consciousness grounded in their own experience. This has empowered them to define their own agenda, to find their own voice, but also to rediscover the voices and experiences of women hidden in the cultural and religious artefacts of the past. Whereas previously male scholars of religion have occasionally made women's religious roles and experiences an object of their study, the growth of feminist critical awareness and the possibility of women's own scholarly training up to the highest academic level have now enabled women to be themselves both subjects and objects of their own scholarly analysis. This development has produced rich new data, insights and perspectives of inquiry in the study of religions while at the same time challenging some of the dominant paradigms in theology and religious studies.

Historical Overview

'Religion and gender studies' is a fast-growing field where some of the most innovative and creative developments in the contemporary study of religion are taking place. Women scholars in religion are developing a different kind of methodology where the researcher's existential participation and commitment enter into the interpretation of what is being researched and call into question much of the assumed 'objectivity' of previous methods, thus inviting a new critical reflection on what religion is about and for.

So far most of the feminist analysis and challenge of religion has been concerned with Christianity and Judaism, but a growing number of studies are dealing with women in other religions too. Historically, religion was an important dimension of the first wave of the women's movement in the nineteenth century when many women working for social, legal and political equality drew inspiration from the Judeo-Christian belief that both men and women are created in the image of God and are called to be equal heirs of God's kingdom. In their fight to gain access to higher education and the professions, women also asked for the right to theological training. The Free Churches in the United States granted this right to women as well as that of ordination. Reverend Antoinette Brown Blackwell (1825–1921), the first woman theology graduate at Oberlin College, also became the first woman ever to be ordained, in 1853, at the age of twenty-eight, by the Congregational Church in New York; soon thereafter other women were ordained by the Universalist Church, the Unitarians and the Adventists [27: 333-5]. Without such access to theological education women would never have become theologically literate and sufficiently well trained to criticize the androcentric assumptions of their discipline.

In the history of religions, too, women sought professional training early and made important contributions to the study of religion which up to now have unfortunately been given little official recognition in the standard reference works of religious studies [26]. Some women scholars, together with several ordained women, were highly acclaimed plenary speakers at the historical 1893 World's Parliament of Religions held in Chicago [27], and when the international history of religions congresses were organized from 1900 onwards, women scholars regularly participated, although they were not specifically concerned with gender issues as such at that time.

Feminist theology and feminist studies of religion only began to come into their own in the 1970s, at first in the United States, then in Europe and the rest of the world. An important focus and catalyst for these developments has been the section on 'Women and Religion' which has been regularly convened at the Annual Meeting of the American Academy of Religion since 1972. Much work has come out of the United States where feminist theology and women in religion courses have become an integral part of many university and college curricula. A landmark was the publication in 1979 of *Womanspirit Rising: A Feminist Reader in Religion* by Carol P. Christ and Judith Plaskow [12]. Now considered a classic, it was republished in 1992. The vigorous growth of women's critical scholarship is best demonstrated by the pages of the *Journal of Feminist Studies in Religion*, published in the US since 1985. A number of other, more popular journals on women and religion have come into existence since then. In Britain, *Feminist Theology* has been published three times a year since 1982, while the only feminist theological journal in Asia, *In God's Image*, has appeared regularly since 1982 and is now followed by additional titles published in other parts of Asia.

In Europe the European Society for Women in Theological Research was founded in 1985 and has held several bi-annual conferences since then, complemented since 1993 by the publication of an annual *Yearbook*. Women's theological work in the countries of the so-called Third World has been much stimulated and supported by the Women's Commission of the Ecumenical Association of Third World Theologians (EATWOT) which was founded in 1983 and has initiated several national and international conferences [16; 29: 1–20].

Among women scholars in religion, rather less numerous than Christian women theologians around the world, interest in feminist methodological debates and topics can also be documented, especially since the 1980s. It is indicative that the fourteenth Congress of the International Association for the History of Religions (IAHR), held in Winnipeg, Canada, in 1980, included a section on 'Femininity and Religion', but this was not continued subsequently. A decade later, however, at the seventeenth IAHR Congress in Rome in 1990, a lively debate on gender issues took place at a specially organized panel on 'Religion and Gender'. A selected number of papers given at this panel have now been published together with a survey of the current state of debate and a bibliography of recent publications [30: 1–38].

New courses are being introduced and new conferences held; new publications in the field of women and religion continue to appear; new dictionaries and encyclopedias are being planned. Thus the religious experience of women in past and present times is being more and more closely examined, made known and critically evaluated. When Mircea Eliade edited his *Encyclopedia of Religion* in sixteen volumes in 1987 [15], only two articles dealt specifically with current gender issues. One was Rosemary Ruether's examination of 'Androcentrism' [38]; the other a helpful and succinct survey of 'Women's Studies' in religion by Constance H. Buchanan [9]. In it Buchanan discusses the critical and constructive tasks of women scholars in religion, showing that the development of feminist theory on gender, religion and culture is thoroughly cross-disciplinary (one might add, even trans-disciplinary), with women scholars from different religious backgrounds working on diverse religious traditions and drawing on methods and insights from several disciplines. This enables them to gather a new body of data which then in turn can form the starting-point for further theoretical debates.

Anne E. Carr has maintained that the innovative research of women in religion means that:

much of past scholarship is placed on a new map of religious reality. Less than half the story has been told. To begin to tell the other part is to acknowledge that women have always been involved (even when excluded or ignored) in everything human, in everything religious. As the distinct subject matter of women's studies is the experience of women, that of women's studies in religion is the religious experience, expression, and understanding of women. But the concept of gender reminds us that the experience of women has been and always is in relation to men in the whole of human society. Thus women's studies affects the study of men (now seen as part of the whole), the study of the human in its wholeness, and religious studies generally [11: 93].

Women in World Religions

Faced with a vast area of investigation and a proliferation of data about women in the different religions of the world, it is both necessary and helpful to distinguish some major lines of inquiry. To begin with, a 'hermeneutics of suspicion' (Paul Ricoeur) has to be applied to all traditional knowledge about religion. Religious teachings and practices have to be meticulously deconstructed into their constituent and original elements so that due attention can be paid to the emergence of unequally weighted gender differences. Women attempt to analyse and critically deconstruct past materials so that they can reconstruct them in a new and different way. June O'Connor describes this as 'rereading, reconceiving and reconstructing religious traditions'. By 'rereading' she means re-examining religious data with regard to women's presence and absence, their words and their silences, whereas 'reconceiving' requires the retrieval and recovery of lost sources and suppressed visions, sometimes also described as 'reclaiming women's heritage'. The final aim of reconstruction involves the task of reconstructing the past on the basis of new information and with the help of the historical imagination as well as the use of new paradigms for thinking, seeing, understanding and valuing [35: 102–4].

Another way of looking at women in world religions is by asking systematic and comparative questions. Here it is possible to point to three major clusters of inquiries. The first concerns women's role and status as prescribed by different religious traditions, their scriptures and teachings. What is women's role and nature as defined by those teachings? What is women's participation in ritual and liturgy? In which rites can women participate and from which ones are they excluded? Do women possess rites of their own different from those of men? What religious and spiritual authority can women exercise? What access do they have to priesthood, monasticism or religious leadership, for example? What kind of religious communities are open to women?

The second cluster of inquiries, though not entirely separate, focuses more distinctly on the image rather than the role of women. How are women represented in religious language and thought? What kind of images are associated with women in different sacred writings and theological texts? Do such texts project empowering or debilitating images, images of equality and partnership or negative, stereotypical images of women's weakness, inferiority and subordination? Are feminine images and symbols used in relation to ultimate reality, in referring to the divine or transcendent, and if so, do such images have any positive effect on the lives of actual women?

These two clusters of inquiries deal with mainly androcentric material because they are concerned with what world religions have traditionally believed and taught *about* women. Thus they indicate how women have been treated by men rather than what women have experienced and said themselves. A third, exciting area of inquiry is concerned with women's own religious experiences and their distinct articulation, in so far as this has been possible at all. This involves the historical task of rediscovering women's voices in the past and recovering women's spiritual and mystical experiences. How far are these experiences possibly different from those of men or at least expressed in a different way? When women have been able to describe their own religious experiences, this has usually not been through a conceptually well-defined theological language but much more through a rich devotional and mystical literature of a more personal or autobiographical nature. To what extent are the images and symbols used in such literature created by women distinct from and in contrast to those used by male authors?

Until now studies on religious experience have paid little attention to gender differences; their primary data are often dealt with as if derived from asexual beings. This is a rich field inviting comparative investigation, yet at present the comparative study of female and male saints and mystics is still in its infancy. However, such religious figures, women of strong devotion and deep spiritual insight, are found in all religious traditions. They exercise a considerable fascination on contemporary women because they provide such inspiring role models in terms of female identity, autonomy and strength, even though their living conditions were in many respects very different from those of today. Here, more than anywhere else, women ask searching questions about which elements of the past remain usable for a viable religiosity and spirituality today.

Specific Studies

A close examination of the teachings of almost any religious tradition usually reveals a profound ambivalence towards women. Most religions seem to work with a double typology, presenting both negative and positive traits about women so that on one hand women feel subordinate and rejected while on the other they can discover religious elements which can inspire and transform, empowering them to seek equal space and participation in religious life and institutions. Many contemporary women's voices challenge traditional religion by expressing protest and anger, but there also exist voices of promise and prophecy which speak of women's newly found freedom and spiritual power and are of the utmost importance for the renewal of religion today.

I have explored these comparative themes in *Women and Spirituality: Voices of Protest and Promise*, which also contains a bibliography of over 500 titles on women and world religions [28: 229–59]. It is impossible to attempt to make even a small selection of books which might claim to be representative of this fast-growing area of religion and gender. All I can do here is to direct the reader's attention to some significant recent studies which contain again further bibliographical references.

Quite a few books now provide brief introductory surveys on women in different religions, but most of these remain descriptive of what religions have traditionally taught about women without including a critical analysis of these teachings. Wherever possible, it is preferable to study primary sources in a critical perspective. An excellent source book with texts from different religious traditions is Serenity Young's *Anthology of Sacred Texts By and About Women* [47]. This includes a general introduction discussing cross-cultural themes followed by texts from Judaism, Christianity, religions from the ancient Near East, Greece and Rome, northern European paganism, shamanism and tribal religions, Hinduism, Buddhism, Confucianism, Taoism and alternative religious movements. This unusually wide collection shows clearly how the image and status of women have often been prescribed, idealized and vilified in a very similar manner in the sacred literature of different religions. An examination of the images and roles of women in specific religions is found in the earlier pioneering essays edited by Rosemary Radford Ruether under the title *Religion and Sexism: Images of Woman in the Jewish and Christian Traditions* [39] and in the more recently published papers on *Roles and Rituals for Hindu Women* by Julia Leslie [32].

The task of feminist reconstruction can be applied to particular aspects or periods of a religion or to the rethinking of the whole of a religious tradition. A radical rethinking of Christian origins through the reinterpretation of New Testament texts is found in Elisabeth Schüssler Fiorenza's *In Memory of Her: A Feminist Theological Reconstruction of Christian Origins* [17], whereas the whole of Christian theology is reinterpreted from a woman's perspective in Rosemary Radford Ruether's *Sexism and God-Talk: Toward a Feminist Theology* [40]; both were published in 1983. A fundamental contrast is represented by the work of Mary Daly who, ever since her ground-breaking book *Beyond God the Father* first appeared in 1974 [14], has devoted all her intellectual and publishing efforts to the radical deconstruction of Christianity. This has earned her the description of being a 'post-Christian', a designation shared by a number of other women writers, including Daphne Hampson with her study on *Theology and Feminism* (1990) [21].

A theological reconstruction of Judaism is offered by Judith Plaskow in her well-known book *Standing Again at Sinai: Judaism from a Feminist Perspective* [36], while the voices of Jewish women from past and present have been collected by Ellen M. Umansky and Dianne Ashton in *Four Centuries of Jewish Women's Spirituality* [44]. This is another book with excellent source material, a quarter of which is drawn from contemporary Jewish women writing after 1960.

Quite a few publications deal with women in Islam, either in general or with reference to particular aspects of Islamic belief and practice, or describing the situation of Muslim women in particular countries. Very helpful are the critical studies by Fatima Mernissi, *Women and Islam: An Historical and Theological Enquiry* [34] and Leila Ahmed, *Women and Gender in Islam* [2]. Comparative studies are provided in *Women's Studies of the Christian and Islamic Traditions* by Kari Elisabeth Børresen and Kari Vogt [7].

An important book for the feminist reappraisal of central aspects of the Buddhist tradition is the study by Rita M. Gross, *Buddhism After Patriarchy: A Feminist History, Analysis and Reconstruction of Buddhism* [19], whose significance is enhanced by its methodological appendices which discuss feminism both as an academic method and as a social vision with an important impact on the study of religion.

Relevant texts from Jainism are examined by Padmanabh S. Jaini in *Gender and Salvation: Jaina Debates on the Spiritual Liberation of Women* [22], while a feminist analysis of traditional and contemporary Sikh writings is found in Nikky-Guninder Kaur Singh's book *The Feminine Principle in the Sikh Vision of the Transcendent* [43]. Traditional aspects of different religious traditions are critically analysed in *After Patriarchy: Feminist Transformations of the World Religions* edited by Paula M. Cooey, William R. Eakin and Jay B. McDaniel [13], and Catherine Wessinger's collection of essays on *Women Outside the the Mainstream: Female Leaders in Marginal Religions in America* [46] explores the little-known world of women founders and leaders of small religious groups outside the major religious traditions.

The number of specialized studies dealing with women in Chinese, Japanese or African religions, or with women in new religious movements, though small, is also steadily growing so that the traditional imbalance in our knowledge about men and women in different religions is slowly being modified. It is no exaggeration to say that the whole area of religion and gender is one of the richest and most rewarding fields of investigation in the contemporary study of religions. The intellectual importance of these developments is nowhere more apparent than when one examines some of the specific issues and themes common to several studies on women and religion.

Specific Themes

Contemporary feminist thinking is not only changing *what* we know but also challenging *how* we come to know by giving special attention to women's different experiences and ways of knowing. This has consequences for all disciplines and leads to an epistemological shift, that is to say a shift in the theory of knowledge, which has implications for practical action and ethics. New empirical observations on women and religion are closely related to the development of new theoretical reflections which are leading more and more to what Rosalind Shaw has called 'the gendering of religious studies' [30: 65–76].

In spite of women's general subordination and oppression through most of human history, empirical investigations of past and present lives reveal numerous women as active agents and religious subjects in their own right. Researchers have developed a special interest in women as religious actors – as shamans, witches, healers, nuns, ascetics and mystics. Such figures, widely found throughout the religions of the world, are often considered and revered as women apart who, although they possess little or no official, institutional authority, personally enjoy a high moral and spiritual authority among a wide group of followers to whom they give much help and counsel. Such female religious specialists are often recruited from among women who eschew traditional female social roles as wives and mothers or who have reached the biological limits of their womanhood through being beyond childbearing age. It is in fact extremely rare to find women who are at the same time both religious officiants of one kind or another and also wives and mothers.

There exist not only many examples of women religious actors but also of women religious innovators. Throughout the history of religions one can find numerous women leaders and participants in dissident and so-called heretical religious movements. Of particular interest is the role of women in new religious movements, sects and cults where their equal status and participation can by no means always be taken for granted. Women often take part in wider religious and social protest movements, but they also develop strategies of resistance for coping with their own situation of oppression. Some of these strategies draw much inspiration from different religious ideas and practices, such as specific beliefs about human destiny and salvation or practices such as prayer, fasting, religious songs and rituals, vows and pilgrimages.

Women's actual participation in religious life is one issue; the symbolic representation of women in the world of the religious imagination is quite another. Here again the double typology of the denigration and idealization of women is widely prevalent. Sometimes women are seen as sacred or as especially spiritual, whereas at other times they are considered as demonic and taboo. Serenity Young's analysis of persistent cross-cultural themes about women across different religious traditions mentions the particularly striking contrast of representing women as both evil and wise [47: xviii–xxii]. The symbolism of evil is tied up with other themes such as woman's body and sexuality, menstruation taboos, the figure of the witch and the fear of death. In opposition to these negative images many religions also possess the positive image of woman as a figure of wisdom. The feminization of the spirit of wisdom exists as Sophia in the Judeo-Christian traditions, in the goddess of wisdom in Mediterranean and Indian religions, and as the female *boddhisattva* of compassion found in the Far East.

Interest in the human body and in sexuality is a dominant cultural theme in present-day society. However, the revaluation of human physical existence, of sexuality and marriage, has not necessarily brought about the positive affirmation of women, nor has it led to the much-needed revision of traditional religious teachings on sexual ethics. The theme of sexuality and embodiment is central to contemporary feminist thought and there is much interest in feminist ethics, especially in the moral problems raised by new reproductive technologies and genetic engineering. The wide range of views and taboos associated with female sexuality and bodily functions and the need for many reforms are well brought out in the reports on *Women, Religion and Sexuality: Studies on the Impact of Religious Teachings on Women* initiated by the WCC [4].

Moving from bodily existence to symbols of the sacred and transcendent, one must ask which experiences of the sacred, whether those of men or women, have been described by reference to female forms and images? Where are the female faces of the divine, and what kind of gender-related symbols are associated with what some authors call the human constructs of ultimate reality? Some religions abound in feminine imagery and symbolism, none perhaps more so than Hinduism; but the symbolic ascendancy of the feminine, particularly noticeable in Asian religions, often stands in inverse relation to the actual status of women in society, where it can go together with their denigration and subordination. The symbolic order is never a guarantor of empirical reality; on the contrary, it can often function as a compensatory projection of what is unattainable at the level of concrete reality constrained by numerous social norms and conventions.

Much contemporary feminist debate in Judaism and Christianity concerns the central challenge of whether traditional symbols, so heavily orientated towards the masculine, can be reformed or reconstructed, or whether they must be radically rejected and perhaps be replaced by new ones. A large amount of work has been done on the use of language and metaphor in relation to the image and concept of God. The dominant model of God in the Judeo-Christian traditions, almost to the exclusion of all other models, has been that of God the Father, but women theologians are now also exploring other models, such as those of mother, lover and friend [33: 91–180].

Some debates about the understanding of God explore the meaning of divine motherhood, but however empowering and affirming they are to some, the experience and image of motherhood are not necessarily always positive. Like God the Father, God the Mother can be an ambivalent model for the transcendent. Much writing is concerned with the nature of the Goddess, her historical and contemporary importance [3]. The theological reconstruction surrounding the Goddess has been termed 'thealogy' in order to distinguish it from traditional theology, largely centred on the perception of a divine male figure. The re-emergence of the Goddess as a vibrant religious and spiritual symbol among people in the West is linked to the contemporary reaffirmation of the body and sexuality, to the 'Goddess within' who is seen as a source of empowerment for women, and to an earth-based spirituality connected with 'Gaia', the sacred earth which needs to be revered to ensure the continuing renewal of life on our planet [18: 225–377]. This earth-centred spirituality, sometimes also understood as 'creation spirituality', is very significant in the contemporary search for ecological wisdom and has special importance in the ecofeminist movement too.

Besides exploring the different meanings of father and mother in relation to the understanding of God and representing the divine as

Goddess, some women writers also recommend the conceptualization of divine life in androgynous forms or prefer a completely monistic approach to ultimate reality which transcends all human forms and images.

The relation between gender models and images of God is of great significance. This is particularly true in the Judeo-Christian traditions which teach that male and female are created 'in the image of God' (*Genesis* 1: 27). If this is truly so, then both women and men must be able to reveal something about this image. Yet throughout the ages the biblical texts on this matter have been interpreted in a very androcentric way whereby the human male on his own, or at best male and female together, but never woman alone, have been said to embody the image of God. The unsatisfactoriness and injustice of such an interpretation has only been recognized in recent times so that the holistic interpretation, whereby women and men are equally, and independently, defined as a God-like image, is a very modern development due to recent new insights into the meaning of human genderedness [6].

The lively discussions about the 'imago dei' – about being created in the image of God – indicate the crucial importance of reflecting critically on the question of what it means to be human as well as sexually differentiated. But they also show that gender-related symbols do not always provide an appropriate answer to this question, because such symbols function differently in different religious traditions. The perception of the transcendent may or may not include a gender component, but even where this is understood as a supreme being which is male, the dominant soteriology or message about human salvation seems to be ultimately gender-inclusive. Discussions around the theme of symbols and gender therefore demonstrate that it is not enough to look at female images and experiences alone, but that religious thought, language and practice have to be studied with reference to both genders and to the way in which they interrelate.

The emergence of feminist theology and spirituality provides powerful themes in the contemporary women's movement, also leading to changes in religious practice and to the creation of new prayers, songs and rituals. The existence of feminist theology, however diverse and pluralistic in orientation, indicates a lively struggle and includes many creative moments whereby positions of traditional faith and those of modern feminism have to be negotiated and brought together. In its widest, most inclusive sense the term 'feminist theology' can refer to all religious and spiritual developments in the women's movement, but its narrower and more precise meaning refers specifically to new theological developments in both Christianity and Judaism (each of which contains further distinct strands of traditional, reformist or revolutionary leanings). The term 'feminist spirituality' is often considered to refer to a separate religious development which is new and mainly occurring outside traditional religious institutions, but the boundaries are often fluid.

The situation of feminist theology has become more complex still through the development, mostly in the United States, of black 'womanist theology' by African-American women (a development also found in South Africa), of '*mujerista* theology' (developed by women members of Hispanic groups in the US) and the distinct theological voices of Asian-American women. Thus one now has to speak of feminist theologies in the plural, a situation further enhanced by other distinct theological developments among women from different cultures around the globe [29].

Some women have changed their religious position from being practising Christians to a 'post-church' or even 'post-Christian' commitment, whereas others have taken a more active step and joined the lively new spirituality groups associated with the worship of the Goddess, or have become members of the modern Wicca movement or other alternative new religions.

Women's spirituality is an often-encountered theme in contemporary feminism and in its most inclusive sense is sometimes referred to as the 'womanspirit movement'. It is worth pointing out that secular feminism contains already an implicit spiritual dimension; its struggle for the full humanity of women, for liberation from oppression, for peace and justice points not only to political, social and economic, but also ultimately to spiritual aims [28: 5–9].

Much has been written on women's spiritual quest and women's new empowerment from within. Prominent themes among others are women's discovery of their own self and its agency, their experience of bonding and networking, of creative re-imaging and renaming of the sacred, their growth in sensitivity to the interdependence and sanctity of all life, of experiments with new relationships and different community-building. Many of these topics are powerfully explored in contemporary feminist novels, some of whose main characters sensitively exemplify women's wide-ranging spiritual search for wholeness and integration and their struggle for the fullness of life. The rich texture of such experiences is also well reflected in the essays edited by Judith Plaskow and Carol P. Christ, *Weaving the Visions: New Patterns in Feminist Spirituality* [37] or those by Carol J. Adams on *Ecofeminism and the Sacred* [1]. The theme of spirituality also figures in many books on feminist theology, not least those by Asian women theologians who are speaking of a newly emerging spirituality arising from their encounter with the riches of their own indigenous spiritual heritage which is such an integral part of the religious pluralism of Asia.

Current Debates

The above summary of studies and themes conveys something of the tremendous range of developments which characterizes the field of women in religion. As the discussion has shown, however, it is not enough to pursue simply a historical and phenomenological approach to the study of women in different religions, for such studies raise perhaps as many questions as they answer. The field of religion and gender requires a much more comprehensive perspective, and when this is pursued numerous new and very rewarding theoretical, philosophical and methodological questions are opened up and yield new insights. It is evident that women scholars of religion are helping us to gain a more differentiated understanding of the nature of the self, of religious experience and practice, and of our symbols and constructs of ultimate reality. Such work raises fundamental questions about the nature of religion as traditionally defined by Western philosophy, theology and sociology, but it also shows that cultural and religious definitions of femininity – of what it means to be a woman – cannot be critically examined without taking a new look at the dominant definitions of masculinity. Contemporary gender studies also include the new men's studies which apply the insights and results of critical feminist theory to a thorough re-examination of male genderedness, considered problematic in its traditional understanding and expression [8; 22].

The pluralism of questions and methods, together with the feminist perspective or angle of vision, distinguish contemporary women's studies from any traditional study of women. By now the field is growing larger still by focusing on the broader issues of gender rather than simply on contemporary women's studies. The radical feminist theologian Mary Daly has disparagingly dismissed such gender studies as being simply 'blender studies', but traditional androcentric presuppositions which underpin all past knowledge, in religion and elsewhere, cannot be fully dismantled without analysing the whole project of gender construction to its fullest extent. This requires a critical focus on both male and female gender roles.

Although the new men's studies make use of the insights and results of feminist scholarship, they lack at present the social and political urgency and existential commitment of women's scholarship. So far, too, they have not influenced the field of religious studies, but the complexity of gender-related symbols also requires a comprehensive rather than an exclusively woman-centred analysis. As Caroline Walker Bynum has pointed out: 'Gender-related symbols, in their full complexity, may refer to gender in ways that affirm or reverse it, support or question it; or they may, in their basic meaning, have little at all to do with male and female roles. Thus our analysis admits that gender-related symbols are sometimes "about" values other than gender' [10: 2].

The truth of this statement is clearly brought to light in the many case studies collected together in the volume *Gender and Religion: The Complexity of Symbols* [10]. Other publications which open up more inclusive religion and gender perspectives are *With Both Eyes Open: Seeing Beyond Gender* [24] and *After Eden: Facing the Challenge of Gender Reconciliation* [45]. The latter is concerned with 'decentring' white, Western feminism and challenges the concepts of masculinity and femininity by laying bare the sources of gender brokenness in the Western world. Committed to a Christian theological perspective, the authors examine various ways of dealing with human difference by proposing a model of gender reconciliation grounded in a Christian feminist vision which embraces both women and men.

For historical and practical reasons the discussion on religion and gender focuses at present primarily on a woman-centred approach which is itself part of the existing gender polarization, or what Sandra Lipsitz Bem [5] calls 'the lenses of gender'. These lenses filter the hidden assumptions about sex and gender that are embedded in our cultural discourses, social institutions and individual minds. Religions have provided the fundamental matrix for many of these discourses, sacralized power and authority, and upheld a hierarchy of gender and social relations which now requires critical dismantling and creative transformation. Religious studies around the world have much to contribute to the theoretical and practical tasks involved in doing this, as is evident from the more than a dozen papers presented by an international group of women scholars in the collection on *Religion and Gender* [30].

Although critical work on religion and gender is at present still in its early stages, much territory has been mapped out already which indicates that these new and exciting explorations 'will inevitably alter perceptions of female and male, the masculine and feminine, and perceptions of gender in religious studies as a whole' [11: 94].

Bibliography

1 ADAMS, CAROL J. (ed.), *Ecofeminism and the Sacred*, New York, Continuum, 1993

2 AHMED, LEILA, *Women and Gender in Islam*, New Haven/London, Yale University Press, 1992

3 BARING, ANNE, and CASHFORD, JULES, *The Myth of the Goddess: Evolution of an Image*, London, Penguin, 1993

4 BECHER, JEANNE (ed.), *Women, Religion and Sexuality: Studies on the Impact of Religious Teachings on Women*, Geneva, WCC Publications, 1990

5 BEM, SANDRA LIPSITZ, *The Lenses of Gender: Transforming the Debate on Sexual Inequality*, New Haven/London, Yale University Press, 1993

6 BØRRESEN, KARI ELISABETH (ed.), *Image of God and Gender Models in Judaeo-Christian Tradition*, Oslo, Solum Forlag, 1991

7 BØRRESEN, KARI ELISABETH, and VOGT, KARI, *Women Studies of the Christian and Islamic Traditions*, Dordrecht, Boston/London, Kluwer Academic, 1993

8 BROD, HARRY (ed.), *The Making of Masculinities: The New Men's Studies*, London, Allen & Unwin, 1987

9 BUCHANAN, CONSTANCE H., 'Women's Studies' in M. Eliade (ed.), *The Encyclopedia of Religion*, New York, Macmillan/London, Collier Macmillan, 1987, vol. 15, pp. 433–40

10 BYNUM, CAROLINE WALKER, HARRELL, STEVAN and RICHMAN, PAULA (eds), *Gender and Religion: On the Complexity of Symbols*, Boston, Beacon Press, 1986

11 CARR, ANNE E., *Transforming Grace: Christian Tradition and Women's Experience*, San Francisco, Harper & Row, 1990

12 CHRIST, CAROL P., and PLASKOW, JUDITH (eds), *Womanspirit Rising: A Feminist Reader in Religion*, New York, Harper & Row, 1979; Harper-SanFrancisco, 1992

13 COOEY, PAULA M., EAKIN, WILLIAM R., and MCDANIEL, JAY B. (eds), *After Patriarchy: Feminist Transformations of the World Religions*, Maryknoll, Orbis, 1991

14 DALY, MARY, *Beyond God the Father: Toward a Philosophy of Women's Liberation*, Boston, Beacon Press, 1974

15 ELIADE, MIRCEA (ed.), *The Encyclopedia of Religion*, 16 vols, New York, Macmillan/London, Collier Macmillan, 1987

16 FABELLA, VIRGINIA, and ODUYOYE, MERCY AMBA (eds), *With Passion and Compassion: Third World Women Doing Theology*, Maryknoll, Orbis, 1988

17 FIORENZA, ELISABETH SCHÜSSLER, *In Memory of Her: A Feminist Theological Reconstruction of Christian Origins*, London, SCM, 1983

18 GADON, ELINOR W., *The Once and Future Goddess: A Symbol of Our Time*, San Francisco, Harper & Row, 1989

19 GRAHAM, ELAINE, *Making the Difference: Gender, Personhood and Theology*, London, Mowbray, 1995

20 GROSS, RITA M., *Buddhism after Patriarchy: A Feminist History, Analysis and Reconstruction of Buddhism*, Albany, State University of New York Press, 1993

21 HAMPSON, DAPHNE, *Theology and Feminism*, Oxford, Blackwell, 1990

22 HOFMAN, GRETA (ed.), *Women and Men: Interdisciplinary Readings on Gender*, Nemiroff, Montreal, Fitzhenry & Whiteside, 1987

23 JAINI, PADMANABH S., *Gender and Salvation: Jaina Debates on the Spiritual Liberation of Women*, Berkeley, University of California Press, 1991

24 JOHNSON, PATRICIA ALTENBERND, and KALVEN, JANET (eds), *With Both Eyes Open: Seeing Beyond Gender*, New York, Pilgrim Press, 1988

25 JOY, MORNY, and MAGEE, PENELOPE (eds), *Claiming Our Rites: Studies in*

Religion by Australian Women Scholars, Adelaide, Australian Association for the Study of Religions, 1994

26 KING, URSULA, 'A Question of Identity: Women Scholars and the Study of Religion', in Ursula King (ed.), *Religion and Gender*, Oxford, Blackwell, 1995, pp. 219–43

27 KING, URSULA, 'Rediscovering Women's Voices at the World's Parliament of Religions', in Eric J. Ziolkowski (ed.), *A Museum of Faiths: Histories and Legacies of the 1893 World's Parliament of Religions*, Atlanta, Scholars Press, 1993, pp. 325–43

28 KING, URSULA, *Women and Spirituality: Voices of Protest and Promise*, 2nd edn, London, Macmillan/University Park, Penn State Press, 1993

29 KING, URSULA (ed.), *Feminist Theology from the Third World: A Reader*, London, SPCK/Maryknoll, Orbis, 1994

30 KING, URSULA (ed.), *Religion and Gender*, Oxford, Blackwell, 1995

31 KLOPPENBERG, RIA, and HANEGRAAFF, WOUTER J. (eds), *Female Stereotypes in Religious Traditions*, Leiden, Brill, 1995

32 LESLIE, JULIA (ed.), *Roles and Rituals for Hindu Women*, London, Pinter, 1991

33 MCFAGUE, SALLIE, *Models of God: Theology for an Ecological, Nuclear Age*, London, SCM, 1987

34 MERNISSI, FATIMA, *Women and Islam: An Historical and Theological Enquiry*, Oxford, Blackwell, 1991

35 O'CONNOR, JUNE, 'Rereading, Reconceiving and Reconstructing Traditions: Feminist Research in Religion', *Women's Studies*, vol. 17, no. 1, 1989, pp. 101–23

36 PLASKOW, JUDITH, *Standing Again at Sinai: Judaism from a Feminist Perspective*, San Francisco, Harper & Row, 1990

37 PLASKOW, JUDITH, and CHRIST, CAROL P. (eds), *Weaving the Visions: New Patterns in Feminist Spirituality*, San Francisco, Harper & Row, 1989

38 RUETHER, ROSEMARY RADFORD, 'Androcentrism', in M. Eliade (ed.), *The Encyclopedia of Religion*, New York, Macmillan/London, Collier Macmillan, 1987, vol. 1, pp. 272–6

39 RUETHER, ROSEMARY RADFORD (ed.), *Religion and Sexism: Images of Women in the Jewish and Christian Traditions*, New York, Simon & Schuster, 1974

40 RUETHER, ROSEMARY RADFORD, *Sexism and God-Talk: Toward a Feminist Theology*, Boston, Beacon Press/London, SCM, 1983

41 RUETHER, ROSEMARY RADFORD, *Women Healing Earth: Third World Women on Ecology, Feminism and Religion*, London, SCM/Maryknoll, Orbis, 1996

42 SHAW, MIRANDA, *Passionate Enlightenment: Women in Tantric Buddhism*, Princeton, Princeton University Press, 1994

43 SINGH, NIKKY-GUNINDER KAUR, *The Feminine Principle in the Sikh Vision of the Transcendent*, Cambridge, Cambridge University Press, 1993

44 UMANSKY, ELLEN M., and ASHTON, DIANNE (eds), *Four Centuries of Jewish Women's Spirituality: A Sourcebook*, Boston, Beacon Press, 1992

45 VAN LEEUWEN, MARY STEWART, et al. (eds), *After Eden: Facing the Challenge of Gender Reconciliation*, Grand Rapids, Eerdmans/Carlisle, Paternoster Press, 1993

46 WESSINGER, CATHERINE (ed.), *Women Outside the Mainstream: Female Leaders in Marginal Religions in America*, Illinois, University of Illinois Press, 1993
47 YOUNG, SERENITY (ed.), *Anthology of Sacred Texts By and About Women*, London, Pandora/New York, Crossroad, 1993

18

Spirituality

URSULA KING

Introduction

Many contemporary writings speak about spirituality, but the word
is used in widely different contexts and is not easy to define. Some
people feel uneasy with references to spirituality or 'the spiritual'
because they understand it in dualistic terms, as standing in contrast
to 'matter' or 'the material', the physical or the 'world'. Others prefer the notion of 'the spiritual' to that of 'the religious' because it is
less institutionalized and more diffuse. Others again consider the
spiritual and spirituality as the heart of religion or its highest ideal,
encountered particularly in religious and mystical experience.

The subject-matter of spirituality is of perennial human concern.
The spiritual quest has found numerous cultural expressions
throughout history, yet the way in which this concern is now studied, through critical and comparative reflection in a global, cross-
cultural context, is a specific development of the twentieth century.
It comes as a surprise, however, that many contemporary dictionaries and encyclopedias, while referring to spiritualism, spiritualist
groups, spiritual experience or spiritual disciplines, do not include
an entry on spirituality as such – a sign that this is still a newly
emerging subject area.

The widespread contemporary interest in spirituality is linked to
the emphasis placed on the subject, on the discovery of the self and
a more differentiated understanding of human psychology. Many
religions do not possess a precise word for the term 'spirituality',
which originated in the Christian tradition, where it has a long history in theology and religious practice. But today the notion of spirituality is applied across different religious traditions; it is used inside
and outside particular religions as well as in many inter-faith and
secular contexts. Thus spirituality has become a universal code

word to indicate the human search for direction and meaning, for wholeness and transcendence. In contemporary secular society spirituality is being rediscovered as a lost or at least hidden dimension in a largely materialistic world. This process is both facilitated and heightened through the exploration of numerous traditional writings on spirituality, now made widely available across the different religious traditions.

In order to consider spirituality in a wider cross-cultural context, it is important to understand more precisely what spirituality is, what ideals and teachings are connected with its practice, and how these can best be studied. Each of these aspects will be examined in the following sections.

What is Spirituality?

From a historical and comparative point of view one can only speak of spirituality in the plural. Many different spiritualities and schools of spirituality exist which represent specific cultural expressions of the particular religious ideals of different religious traditions. The way in which religious ideals find concrete expression varies greatly from one culture and religion to another. Spirituality in the singular, not only as a lofty ideal, but as lived and taught by individual persons and whole communities, is part of the history of the human spirit and its being called beyond history. The history of spirituality is resonant with longings for the permanent, everlasting and eternal, for wholeness, peace, joy and bliss, which have haunted human beings through the ages, and for which many people are still searching today.

Spirituality has been defined in a general, inclusive manner as an exploration of what is involved in becoming human. This is a neutral definition which makes no reference to religion as such. In somewhat more detail, spirituality has been called an 'attempt to grow in sensitivity, to self, to others, to non-human creation and to God who is within and beyond this totality' [29: 3]. Spirituality has also been described as 'the way in which a person understands and lives within his or her historical context that aspect of his or her religion, philosophy or ethic that is viewed as the loftiest, the noblest, the most calculated to lead to the fullness of the ideal or perfection being sought' [26: 136]. These definitions emphasize the understanding of spirituality as an integral, holistic and dynamic force in human life, both for the individual and for communities.

In the preface to the important series *World Spirituality: An Encyclopedic History of the Religious Quest* (25 vols; see [5]) the general editor, Ewert Cousins, describes spirituality as being concerned with the inner movements of the human spirit towards the real, the transcendent, the divine. Spirituality is here understood as wisdom and wise counsel intended to help one follow a path, guiding the human being on a journey towards the goal of spiritual realization. Cousins characterizes spirituality as a faith's wisdom to live that faith, but following such a path today must also include dialogue with other spiritual traditions in the world. While spirituality encompasses a universal human quest, one must recognize the often close relationship between faith and spirituality; but spirituality also relates to an intellectual discipline of critical study and reflection, and such study has grown considerably over the last few decades. There is also the question of the relationship between spirituality and mysticism. A variety of specific spiritual disciplines and practices exist, particularly those of purification, meditation and contemplation, which can lead their followers to higher states of mystical experience and consciousness. Theistic traditions speak of unitive experiences of love and communion with God, whereas non-theistic traditions stress the realization of the ultimate oneness of all things or even refer to an absorption or fusion with the One. The term spirituality covers a wide range of religious orientations and experiences, whereas the different types of mysticism represent very specific spiritual experiences.

Walter Principe distinguishes three distinct but interdependent levels in the understanding of spirituality: first, spirituality as lived experience or praxis; second, spirituality as a teaching that grows out of this praxis and guides it in turn (i.e. the spiritual disciplines and guidelines to holiness and perfection found in different religions); third, the systematic, comparative and critical study of spiritual experiences and teachings which has developed recently in a new way. These three levels are closely intertwined with numerous socio-cultural factors which shape the practice and understanding of spirituality during particular historical periods, in different religions, and in different places where the same faith is practised.

Spiritual Ideals and Teachings

Evelyn Underhill has said that the spiritual life is 'the heart of all real religion and therefore of vital concern to ordinary men and women'; it is 'that full and real life for which humanity is made' [36: 8, 33]. Spiritual writers, theologians and scholars over the centuries have taken different positions on this question. Spirituality is deeply grounded in human experience, but it is also linked to the belief that there is a greater, fuller reality which surrounds, beckons and calls us. Spirituality can thus be understood as a calling as well as a process and a goal. Christians, for example, speak of the call to holiness and perfection implicit in the gospel which says 'You must be perfect as your Father in heaven is perfect' (*Matthew* 5: 48). From the beginning of Christianity the search for spiritual perfection, of life lived in the spirit of God, has led to new forms of life, to asceticism, monasticism and mysticism. Countless Christian writers, from the desert fathers and mothers to medieval and modern saints and mystics, have written about their spiritual quests and struggles, left instructions and teachings, and provided us with models of Christian discipleship and holiness. Thus spirituality has also been described as 'the theory and practice of the Christian life' [30: 32].

This broad general definition is given from within one particular religious tradition; it is not as wide-ranging and inclusive as the description by Evelyn Underhill quoted above. The interest in spirituality, in its history and interpretation, has been particularly marked among Christians, who have long distinguished between different 'schools of spirituality', such as the spirituality of the Spanish or Flemish mystics, or of Russian Orthodoxy, for example. It is interesting to note that in Eliade's *Encyclopedia of Religion* [8] the only entry on spirituality is an article on 'Christian Spirituality' [38]; there is no discussion of the important comparative usage of 'spirituality' in the practice and study of other religious traditions, so prominent in contemporary writings. In fact, some Western writers mistakenly believe that the term 'spirituality' has only come into use in recent decades. Yet it was already applied in a comparative context in the nineteenth century when Hindu reformers, beginning with Swami Vivekananda, contrasted Indian spirituality with Western materialism and proclaimed that India possessed treasures of spirituality which the West still had to discover.

The same *Encyclopedia of Religion* includes, however, entries on 'Spiritual Discipline' [21] and the 'Spiritual Guide' [31]. These entries indicate some of the topics associated with spirituality in many religious traditions. Almost all religions recognize the need for spiritual direction in some form, whether provided by the teaching of the elders, as in many primal religions, or by a spiritual counsellor, guide, master or guru who by instruction can initiate the adept into the teachings and disciplines linked to a particular path of spiritual perfection. Such paths often include multiple stages ranging from general acts of renunciation and purification to very specific intellectual and physical practices. Spiritual exercises and disciplines undertaken to attain specific spiritual goals are found in all religions. Such practices can range from individual and communal prayer to the practice of silence, the stilling of the mind, meditation, contemplation, the reading or recitation of sacred texts and mantras, to fasting, penances, pilgrimages and many others. They may also be associated with specific rituals and bodily postures, on all of which extensive religious literature exists. In terms of general disposition and particular practices, one can distinguish between disciplines of the body, the mind and the heart, for which different religions provide different prescriptions.

Widely discussed topics are whether the call to spiritual perfection and holiness is a special vocation or a general vocation applying to all human beings; whether the spiritual quest is best pursued individually, as a solitary quest in isolation from society, or whether it is more appropriately followed within a communal setting, such as a religious order, but still set apart from society; or whether spirituality can be practised while living in the midst of society and going about one's ordinary daily business. Other questions concern the relationship between human effort and non-human powers (sometimes described as divine action or grace) in attaining a spiritual goal, and also whether such attainment requires much practice or can be reached suddenly and quite unexpectedly. Furthermore, what social consequences arise out of particular individuals and groups following a spiritual path or teaching?

Much of spirituality, as lived and taught in the past, was developed by a religious elite which alone possessed the necessary leisure for cultivating mind and spirit. One always has to enquire into the social context in which particular spiritual teachings developed and ask which were the social strata most likely to produce the 'man and woman of the spirit', the *perfecti*, whether they were monks, nuns, yogis or *pirs*. As a rule, two main models of spirituality can be distinguished: (1) an ascetic/monastic model of renunciation spirituality, setting the adept apart from society; and (2) a model of 'householder spirituality', practised within the context of one's ordinary life where asceticism is less pronounced. During much of Christian history the predominant locus of sanctification, the place to seek holiness and spiritual perfection, was the cloister. But after the Reformation the emphasis shifted from the cloister to ordinary life in society; a new 'spirituality-of-being-in-the-world' developed which, however, was not without precedents in earlier Christian centuries. In Hinduism and Buddhism the idea of the world-renouncer as model of spiritual perfection is paramount. Parallel examples of householder spirituality also exist in these traditions, but they are not valued as highly as renunciation. By contrast, Sikhism, Judaism and Islam focus on the householder model of spirituality and reject asceticism and monasticism.

Spiritual ideals, though ultimately gender-transcendent, are not gender-neutral. It is striking how many traditional spiritual teachings and practices contain sexist and anti-women elements. Spiritual advice, given to apparently asexual spiritual seekers, is often anti-body and anti-woman. Male models of holiness and perfection often imply not only a contempt for the body in general, but especially for women's bodies. Thus they do not hold much attraction for women seeking to pursue the spiritual life. These differences have become much more apparent today when many feminists critically evaluate previous forms of spirituality and seek to develop new and more appropriate ones for our own time. The complex history and early Christian roots of our Western attitudes to the body and human sexuality have been traced in great detail in Peter Brown's magisterial study *The Body and Society: Men, Women, and Sexual Renunciation in Early Christianity* [3].

Ultimate spiritual goals and ideals of spiritual perfection vary considerably across the religious traditions. Human beings may seek union with God or the Divine; they may strive for the ultimate oneness that is *brahman*; they may hope to attain the enlightened state of *nirvana*, find salvation or liberation (*moksha*), or reach paradise. Such ideals depend directly on the doctrinal teaching and philosophical structure of each religion. There exists also much debate on whether these spiritual goals can be attained in this life or only in a life to come.

The spiritual path implies movement and transformation. It is often likened to a journey of the soul along a particular way, under the guidance of a teacher and a set of teachings. Jewish tradition speaks of religious norms as *halakhah*, 'the way to go', and the early Christians referred to Christ's teachings as 'the way'. In China ultimate reality itself is known as Tao, 'the Way'. Sacred Hindu literature speaks of three paths to liberation, those of action, meditation and worship. Both Buddhism and Hinduism teach the need for *sadhana*, for spiritual exercises and discipline, in order to reach the realization of the ultimate spiritual goal. Some of the most ancient and best known instructions, still followed today, are found in the *Yoga-sutras* of Patanjali which teach an eightfold path for self-control and meditation in order to reach an ultimate state of utter freedom and absolute independence.

Hinduism knows many different spiritual schools with quite different, and sometimes mutually exclusive, teachings about the nature of the self and the world, and the absolute goal of human beings. These teachings are transmitted by the *guru*, who has a particularly important position in Hinduism. It is said that the spiritual bonds between *guru* and disciple are as strong as a blood relationship; in fact, in some cults the *guru* takes the place of God for the disciple. In Islam the spiritual guide or teacher is found in the person of the *shaykh* or *pir* who leads his followers on the Sufi path with its principles of purification.

Christians know the figure of the spiritual director, but in following 'the way of the Lord' the supreme teacher has been Christ him-

self. His life and actions have provided a rich store for the spiritual
life of Christians, sometimes more focused on the cross and at other
times more on the resurrection, or on Christ's acts of healing and
his parables. The 'imitation of Christ' has produced a rich spiritual
and devotional literature throughout the centuries. However,
Eastern and Western Christianity have developed quite different
devotional and prayer practices for Christian disciples seeking spiritual perfection and holiness. The spirituality of the Orthodox East is
shaped by the Byzantine legacy which 'integrated into one vision:
the writings of the Christian Fathers, the monastic doctrine and
experience of prayer and the ascetical way of life whose *summa* is the
Philakolia' [14: 519].

The long history of Buddhism has also produced a rich heritage
of spiritual practices based on the *dhamma*, the teaching of the
Buddha. A major volume on *Buddhist Spirituality* edited by
Takeuchi Yoshinori [40] opens with the bold statement:

> Of all the great religions, it is Buddhism that has focused most
> intensively on that aspect which we call spirituality. No reli-
> gion has set a higher value on states of spiritual insight and lib-
> eration, and none has set forth so methodically and with such
> a wealth of critical reflection the various paths and disciplines
> by which such states are reached, as well as the ontological and
> psychological underpinnings that make those states so valuable
> and those paths so effective. [40: xiii].

From a Buddhist perspective spirituality is seen as most closely akin
to the Sanskrit term *bhavana* or 'cultivation', which points to a profound process of transformation whereby human existence is freed
from illusions and passions, rooted in ignorance and suffering.
Much of Buddhist spiritual practice centres on meditation, which is
the path to the enlightenment of the mind and to the transformation
of the affective life by replacing attitudes of clinging with those of
letting go. Different Theravada and Mahayana schools have developed a wide range of meditation techniques. *Vipassana* and Zen
meditation practices, to name some of the best known, are designed
to cultivate tranquillity, mindfulness and insight, leading to the cardinal Buddhist virtues of wisdom and compassion. Also central is
the teaching on emptiness, focusing on the realization that all things
are 'empty', that nothing exists independently, autonomously or
eternally. The doctrinal teachings of Buddhism draw a very different
map of spiritual reality from those of theistic religions, so that one
can even speak of a Buddhist 'spirituality of emptiness' [40: 373;
22]. The powerful transformative resources of Buddhist spirituality
are clearly evident in contemporary Buddhist debates about social
reform and modernization, as for example in Thailand [40: 112–19]

and in the vigorous growth of Buddhism in various Western countries.

Islamic spirituality is rooted in the Qur'an and the instructions of the Prophet Muhammad as Messenger of God. Islamic languages possess a range of expressions for the Western term 'spirituality'; these connote inwardness, the real, the world of the Spirit, the presence of divine grace, a sense of moral perfection, of the beauty of the soul, and the recollection of God. For the Muslim the spiritual life is based on both the fear and the love of God, on obedience to God's will, and on a search for the knowledge of God, the ultimate goal of creation. Islamic spirituality is closely connected with the pattern of Islamic rites as constituted by the 'pillars of faith', which have both an outward and an inward meaning. The inner meaning has been most developed by Sufism, the Islamic tradition of mysticism, which includes many esoteric spiritual teachings and practices. But whether ordinary or esoteric, the essence of Islamic spirituality is concerned with divine unity. In the view of Seyyed Hossein Nasr, spirituality is at the heart of Islam and is the key to understanding its many aspects. It 'has rejuvenated Islamic society over the ages, . . . caused the flowering of some of the world's greatest art, ranging from gardening to music, and made possible the appearance of some of the most outstanding philosophers and scientists whom the world has known. It has also carried out a discourse with other religions when circumstances have demanded' [23: xviii].

Each religious tradition possesses such rich spiritual resources – ideals of holiness and perfection, teachings on justice, love and compassion, on peace and human unity, visions of true freedom and wholeness of being, wells of wisdom and experiences of contact with the eternal – that it is impossible to provide here more than a glimpse of the spiritual universes enshrined in the world's religions. It is important to underline, though, that it is only at the present time, with the global means of communication at our disposal, that the human community is in a position to get to know these resources across different traditions and draw on an immense storehouse of spiritual and practical wisdom. Thus we live in a particularly exciting period which provides new opportunities for great creativity in the field of spirituality.

Sources for the Study of Spirituality

In the early decades of the twentieth century Roman Catholic scholars in France developed a particular interest in studying spirituality and the characteristics of the spiritual life in relation to religious experience and consciousness. They founded the important *Dictionnaire de spiritualité, ascetique et mystique, doctrine et histoire* which has been published since 1937 and has only just been completed [37]. It provides articles of great scholarly depth, but its overall focus, as that of so many other publications, is the history and practice of Christian spirituality. Though not truly comparative, a somewhat more comprehensive approach is found in the more accessible one-volume work on *The Study of Spirituality* edited by Cheslyn Jones, Geoffrey Wainwright and Edward Yarnold [14], which deals with the theology and history of Christian spirituality from earliest times to the present day, including an informative section on Orthodox Christianity from the tenth to the twentieth century. Other brief chapters deal with the spirituality of Judaism, Islam, Hinduism, Buddhism and African religion as well as Amerindian spirituality, always accompanied by bibliographies on sources and further studies. The book also contains some interesting contributions on 'Current Spirituality' which deal among others with Christian ecumenical spirituality, that of Pentecostals and the charismatic movement, contemporary trends in Christian Orthodoxy and on the 'Interplay with Other Religions', written by the Japanese theologian Kosuke Koyama, who maintains that such interplay – or what others might describe as inter-faith encounter and dialogue – belongs to the essential nature of religious spirituality. He writes:

> The interplay between the religions of the world and the spirit of Western civilization (modernization) in our time presents an agonizing ambiguity of destructive and creative implications. Christian spirituality which has been historically a constitutive element of Western civilization is bound to go through re-formation not in terms of the Christian humanity of the West, but in the name of all humanity. This cannot be done without Christian spirituality interacting with the teaching and spiritualities of other religious traditions.
>
> The spirituality of dominance will be challenged. A spirituality of interdependence informed by Christian theology and ministry must appear. [14: 560]

This is how a Christian theologian from the Far East expresses the challenge of contemporary religious pluralism for the understanding of Christian spirituality. Members of other faiths will have to meet this challenge from a different perspective, drawing on the spiritual resources of their own religious tradition. Examples of Christian responses to the spiritualities of different faiths are Diana Eck's book *Encountering God* [7] and Donald W. Mitchell's *Spirituality and Emptiness: The Dynamics of Spiritual Life in Buddhism and*

Christianity [22] as well as the collected essays on *Spirituality in Interfaith Dialogue* edited by Tosh Arai and Wesley Ariarajah [2]. More substantial studies of greater length are found in the different volumes of the previously mentioned series on *World Spirituality: An Encyclopedic History of the Religious Quest* [5], in which studies on Jewish, Islamic, Hindu, Buddhist, Christian, Native Mesoamerican and North American spirituality have already appeared.

The resources on Christian spirituality are vast. For an excellent selection of newly edited primary sources see the series on *Classics of Western Spirituality* published since 1978 [24]; succinct information can be obtained from the *Dictionary of Christian Spirituality* [39]. The *World Spirituality* series contains three volumes of detailed studies on all aspects of Christian spirituality. Volume I deals with developments from the origins of Christianity to the twelfth century [18], volume II with the high middle ages and Reformation up to 1600 [27] and volume III with numerous aspects of post-Reformation and modern spirituality [6], including substantial sections on Eastern Orthodox spirituality and on twentieth-century developments such as Pentecostal spirituality, Christian feminist spirituality, and the implications of ecumenism for Christian spirituality. All essays list extensive bibliographical resources.

For an initial acquaintance with and overview of the wide range of Christian spiritual writings through the ages, beginning with the church fathers and including excerpts from most of the well-known spiritual classics with special attention given to twentieth-century authors, the large one-volume anthology on *Christian Spirituality: The Essential Guide to the Most Influential Spiritual Writings of the Christian Tradition* [20] is especially helpful. For a critical reassessment of Christian spirituality and its interpretation from a contemporary scholarly perspective see Bradley C. Hanson (ed.), *Modern Christian Spirituality: Methodological and Historical Essays* [13] and especially the highly acclaimed study on *Spirituality and History: Questions of Interpretation and Method* by Philip Sheldrake [30].

If one seeks not a scholarly but a brief, popular introduction to spirituality in the contemporary world, one of the most accessible texts is Evelyn Underhill's *The Spiritual Life: Great Spiritual Truths for Everyday Life*. These four broadcast talks, given in 1936, are now available in print [36]. The general anthropological foundations for spiritual development in relation to human psychological growth are examined in James W. Fowler's study *Stages of Faith* [10].

An exciting new publishing venture, which will make available many previously unknown texts on spirituality, are the translations of hitherto mainly untranslated (or poorly translated) sources from the different world faiths made possible through the International Sacred Literature Trust, founded in 1985. The Trust encourages scholarly translators from within different faith communities to present the wisdom of their traditions within accessible contemporary textual editions, published world-wide by HarperCollins [42]. Such publications encourage new discussions within, across and beyond the different faiths and can help to promote a new awareness of our global interdependence in spiritual as well as material matters.

Contemporary Perspectives on Spirituality

Many people today are asking what kind of spirituality might bring about the profound personal and social transformations the world so desperately needs. Many are the voices that speak out on spirituality, however differently understood. Spirituality is a topic as much addressed by new religious movements as it is by the ecological, the peace and the women's movements; it is raised by those interested in psychotherapy and the transformation of consciousness, and by people working for the renewal of Christianity or in inter-faith dialogue. Yet contemporary understandings of spirituality can sometimes appear too nostalgic and imitative of the past, not sufficiently linked to today's society. Much current interest in spirituality, especially in traditional religious circles, is too individualistic and static, too much focused on revival rather than creativity and renewal. It is often more concerned with the individual self and personal inwardness, and with an outright rejection of materialism and hedonistic consumerism, than with a truly balanced transformation of both the inner and the outer world.

Yet there are also many creative new developments in the contemporary understanding of what spirituality is really about – understandings which capture the dynamic, transformative quality of spirituality as lived experience, as the struggle for the fullness of life lived in justice and peace, as the great adventure of human beings, of body, mind and soul, in seeking and discovering the all-encompassing horizon of transcendence, of the graciousness, goodness and abundance of life. Such new understandings are linked to a new awareness of and new inquiries into our spiritual energy resources – as much needed for our survival as our material ones – and the importance of our global religious heritage for the future of humankind.

A pioneer in thinking about human spiritual energy resources and the function of spirituality in an interdependent world was the French Jesuit, Pierre Teilhard de Chardin (1881–1955), who as early as 1937 wrote an essay on 'The Phenomenon of Spirituality' and its meaning within human social evolution [16]. His own life as a scientist, priest and mystic provides an inspiring example of

Christian spirituality in the contemporary world [17], and one of his writings, *Le Milieu Divin* [34] is considered a modern spiritual classic.

Other important new developments are the growing interest in native spiritual traditions and the spiritual heritages of indigenous peoples and cultures. These are being newly discovered and praised because of their inherent reverence for life and nature, so greatly valued by the contemporary ecological movement and enhanced by a new kind of creation spirituality, particularly associated with the work of Matthew Fox [11]. A rediscovery of the sacred and the development of new forms of spirituality are also present in contemporary ecofeminism [1], and newly emerging spiritualities figure as an important theme in some writings of liberation theology [32] and in the theology of women from the Third World [15]. Liberation and women theologians from different parts of the world draw much inspiration from the indigenous cultural and religious traditions of their own regions. They criticize the Eurocentric character of Christian thought and practice imported from the West, and are seeking for new expressions of spirituality which they can truly claim as their own.

Spirituality is a central theme in the contemporary women's movement too, not in a traditional, dualistic sense where the world of work and matter is divided from that of the spirit, but where spirituality is understood as a search for wholeness and integration through radically transforming traditional patriarchal attitudes to gender, work, the environment, and many other aspects of personal and social experience. Such spirituality has profound political implications and is deeply empowering for women. This close link has been explored in an important set of essays on *The Politics of Women's Spirituality*, published in 1982 [33], and is further developed in more recent publications [25; 41]. Besides the explicit interest in spirituality among contemporary women – sometimes referred to as the womanspirit movement or as spiritual or metaphysical feminism, and often linked to the worship of the Goddess – there also exists an important implicit spiritual dimension in the feminist movement, as I have argued in *Women and Spirituality* [18]. The feminist aims of liberation, peace and justice, of seeking to realize the full humanity of women, are ultimately not only social, economic and political but also spiritual aims.

Feminist spirituality includes women's new awareness of their own empowerment from within to effect personal, social and political changes. Such spirituality is deeply rooted in women's discovery of their own self and its agency, their experience of bonding and power-sharing, the creative reimaging and renaming of the sacred, and a growth in sensitivity to the interdependence and sacredness of all forms of life. Many of these themes are reflected in contemporary women's literature, which through poetry and fiction explores different aspects of women's spiritual needs and quest, themes of loss and pain, of oppression and freedom, of intimacy and mutuality, of the connections between sexuality and spirituality. Women are also discovering a rich spiritual heritage in the women saints and mystics of the past and in the female imagery and symbolism present in many religions of the world. In the case of Judaism, for example, a rich collection of sources can be found in *Four Centuries of Jewish Women's Spirituality* [35]. (See also chapter 17 in this volume on 'Religion and Gender'.)

Yet another important contemporary theme is the place of spirituality in education. Understood as a process of growth and transformation, spirituality is not only for adults but concerns also the development of the young. Spirituality is linked to an expanded and deepened awareness which needs to be fostered and nurtured in many different ways. In Britain, for example, both the Education Act (1944) and the Education Reform Act (1988) refer to the spiritual development of pupils which must be promoted not only through religious education but across the entire curriculum. This explicit requirement has led to a great deal of discussion among educationists and to publications on new approaches and methods in RE [12]. In many countires around the world the place of religious education in a situation of cultural and religious pluralism is at present widely discussed. Such discussion must of necessity include a reflection on the importance of the spiritual dimension in human life. Different policy options regarding religion in public education raise many controversies about the kind of society people deem desirable, as is evident from current debates in the new South Africa [4].

Spirituality is a theme which has even figured in discussions at the United Nations. Different spiritual teachings and practices differ much in meaning, content and value, so that traditional African and Native American spiritualities, for example, are markedly other in character to some of the classical spiritualities from East and West. This adds to the rich variety and complexity of spirituality as lived and experienced today. Spirituality, however understood, is of considerable significance, given the growing cross-cultural and inter-religious encounters around the globe. It is not only a subject of great historical depth and richness, important in the religious life of the past, but also of great contemporary relevance in shaping the lives of individuals and societies. The interest in the study and teaching of spirituality is growing fast; the comparative, critical study of spirituality therefore deserves a central place in the study of religions today.

Bibliography

1 ADAMS, CAROL J., (ed.), *Ecofeminism and the Sacred*, New York, Continuum, 1993

2 ARAI, TOSH, and ARIARAJAH, WESLEY (eds), *Spirituality in Interfaith Dialogue*, Geneva, WCC Publications, 1989

3 BROWN, PETER, *The Body and Society: Men, Women, and Sexual Renunciation in Early Christianity*. New York, Columbia University Press, 1988

4 CHIDESTER, DAVID, et al., *Religion in Public Education: Policy Options for a New South Africa*, University of Cape Town, Institute for Comparative Religion in Southern Africa, 1992

5 COUSINS, EWERT (gen. ed.), *World Spirituality: An Encyclopedic History of the Religious Quest*. New York, Crossroad, 1985–/London, Routledge & Kegan Paul, 1986–

6 DUPRÉ, LOUIS, and SALIERS, DON E. (eds), *Christian Spirituality: Post-Reformation and Modern*, London, SCM, 1989

7 ECK, DIANA L., *Encountering God: A Spiritual Journey from Bozeman to Banaras*, Boston, Beacon Press, 1993

8 ELIADE, MIRCEA, (ed.), *The Encyclopedia of Religion*, 16 vols, New York, Macmillan/London, Collier Macmillan, 1987

9 ELLER, CYNTHIA, *Living in the Lap of the Goddess: The Feminist Spirituality Movement in America*, Boston, Beacon Press, 1995

10 FOWLER, JAMES W., *Stages of Faith: The Psychology of Human Development and the Quest for Meaning*, San Francisco, Harper, 1981

11 FOX, MATTHEW, *Creation Spirituality: Liberating Gifts for the Peoples of the Earth*, San Francisco, HarperSanFrancisco, 1991

12 HAMMOND, JOHN, et al., *New Methods in RE Teaching: An Experimental Approach*, Harlow, Oliver & Boyd, 1990

13 HANSON, BRADLEY C. (ed.), *Modern Christian Spirituality: Methodological and Historical Essays*, Atlanta, Scholars Press, 1990 (American Academy of Religion Studies in Religion, no. 62)

14 JONES, CHESLYN, WAINWRIGHT, GEOFFREY, and YARNOLD, EDWARD (eds), *The Study of Spirituality*, London, SPCK, 1986

15 KING, URSULA (ed.), *Feminist Theology from the Third World: A Reader*, London, SPCK/Maryknoll, Orbis, 1994

16 KING, URSULA, *The Spirit of One Earth: Reflections on Teilhard de Chardin and Global Spirituality*, New York, Paragon House, 1989

17 KING, URSULA, *Spirit of Fire: The Life and Vision of Teilhard de Chardin*, Maryknoll, Orbis, 1996

18 KING, URSULA, *Women and Spirituality: Voices of Protest and Promise*, 2nd edn, London, Macmillan/University Park, Penn State Press, 1993

19 MCGINN, BERNARD, and MEYENDORFF, JOHN (eds), *Christian Spirituality: Origins to the Twelfth Century*, London, Routledge & Kegan Paul, 1986

20 MAGILL, FRANK N., and MCGREAL, IAN P. (eds), *Christian Spirituality: The Essential Guide to the Most Influential Spiritual Writings of the Christian Tradition*, San Francisco, Harper & Row, 1988

21 MAHONEY, WILLIAM K., 'Spiritual Discipline', in M. Eliade (ed.), *The Encyclopedia of Religion*, New York, Macmillan/London, Collier Macmillan, 1987, vol. 14, pp. 19–29

22 MITCHELL, DONALD W., *Spirituality and Emptiness: The Dynamics of Spiritual Life in Buddhism and Christianity*, New York, Paulist Press, 1991

23 NASR, SEYYED HOSSEIN (ed.), *Islamic Spirituality: Foundation*, London, Routledge & Kegan Paul, 1987

24 PAYNE, RICHARD J. (ed.-in-chief), *Classics of Western Spirituality: A Library of Great Spiritual Masters*. New York, Paulist Press/London, SPCK, 1978–

25 PLASKOW, JUDITH, and CHRIST, CAROL P. (eds), *Weaving the Visions: New Patterns in Feminist Spirituality*, San Francisco, Harper & Row, 1989

26 PRINCIPE, WALTER, 'Towards Defining Spirituality', *Studies in Religion/Sciences Religieuses*, vol. 12, 1983, pp. 127–41

27 RAITT, JILL (ed.), *Christian Spirituality: High Middle Ages and Reformation*, London, Routledge & Kegan Paul, 1987

28 RAPHAEL, MELISSA, *Theology and Embodiment: The Post-Patriarchal Reconstruction of Female Sacrality*, Sheffield, Academic Press, 1996

29 SCOTTISH CHURCHES COUNCIL, Working Party Report on 'Spirituality', Dunblane, Scottish Churches House, 1977

30 SHELDRAKE, PHILIP, *Spirituality and History: Questions of Interpretation and Method*, New York, Crossroad, 1992/London, SPCK, 1991

31 SMITHERS, STUART W., 'Spiritual Guide', in M. Eliade, ed., *The Encyclopedia of Religion*, New York, Macmillan/London, Collier Macmillan, 1987, vol. 14, pp. 29–37

32 SOBRINO, JON, *Spirituality of Liberation: Toward a Political Holiness*, Maryknoll, Orbis, 1988

33 SPRETNAK, CHARLENE (ed.), *The Politics of Women's Spirituality: Essays in the Rise of Spiritual Power within the Feminist Movement*, New York, Anchor Press/Doubleday, 1982

34 TEILHARD DE CHARDIN, PIERRE, *Le Milieu Divin*, London, Collins, 1960

35 UMANSKY, ELLEN M., and ASHTON, DIANNE, (eds) *Four Centuries of Jewish Spirituality*, Boston: Beacon Press, 1992

36 UNDERHILL, EVELYN, *The Spiritual Life: Great Spiritual Truths for Everyday Life*, Oxford, Oneworld, 1993

37 VILLER, M., CAVALLERA, F., DE GUIBERT, J., and RAYEZ, A. (founder eds), *Dictionnaire de spiritualité, ascetique et mystique, doctrine et histoire*, Paris, Beauchesne, 1937–94

38 WAINWRIGHT, GEOFFREY, 'Christian Spirituality', in M. Eliade, ed., *The Encyclopedia of Religion*, New York, Macmillan/London, Collier Macmillan, 1987, vol. 3, pp. 452–60

39 WAKEFIELD, GORDON (ed.), *A Dictionary of Christian Spirituality*, London, SCM, 1983

40 YOSHINORI, TAKEUCHI (ed.), *Buddhist Spirituality: Indian, Southeast Asian, Tibetan, Early Chinese*, New York, Crossroad, 1994

41 ZAPPONE, KATHERINE, *The Hope for Wholeness: A Spirituality for Feminists*, Mystic, CT, Twenty-Third Publications, 1991

42 Up to 1996 nine books with texts from eight different religions had been published and three further books are forthcoming in 1997. Details of the publications can be obtained directly from the International Sacred Literature Trust, 6 Mount Street, Manchester M2 5NS, UK

19

The Study of Diaspora Religion

JOHN R. HINNELLS

Teachers of religion have for decades emphasized the importance of the study of 'world religions', partly because of the subjects' own inherent importance, but also because of their relevance to Western society, especially in view of the fact that in recent years, as a result of migration, Hindus, Muslims and members of other religions live and worship in Western cities. Yet encyclopedias and introductory books continue to look at these religions solely in their old countries; any mention of them in the West has generally treated the Western groups as marginal to the main history and phenomenon of that religion. This section of the *New Handbook* (chapters 19–25) represents the first serious attempt to look at the Western forms of these religions as important in themselves and as showing something important about the Western societies they are found in, and to do so in a comparative international perspective. In recent years American universities have begun to engage in the study of black African, or Afro-Caribbean, religion, but these areas are rarely included in general introductions, are ignored by British universities, despite the size and significance of black groups in the UK, and are not (yet) part of the Australian scene. This section seeks to fill those lamentable gaps. Some preliminary remarks are necessary to explain the logic behind this new section of the book.

People have carried their religions around the globe for millennia, but this has become a far more common phenomenon since the middle of the twentieth century, partly because of improved travel and communications, and also because of the huge migrations which followed the Second World War. It has been an era of unparalleled international change and religions have been part of, and affected by, these changes. There have been countless studies of migrant groups in the West, but in the United States these have tended to focus on groups not particularly associated with the religions covered in part I of this book, and in Britain such studies have mostly focused on the problems of racial discrimination, housing, employment and welfare. Undoubtedly these are major issues, but this emphasis has had two consequences. First, it has meant that the migrant groups are seen almost wholly as 'problems'; secondly, it has implied that their religion is something they left behind in the old country, whereas, as the following chapters make clear, recent studies and the migrants themselves often assert that they are more rather than less religious after migration. It is only in the 1990s that scholars have begun to write about the place of religion in these groups. The subject is, therefore, a new one. Certain consequences flow from this newness. First, there are major areas of great importance yet to be researched. Chapter 25 seeks to identify a few of these. Secondly, little headway has so far been made in developing broad theories about the impact of migration of non-Western religions to the West. Again, the concluding chapter attempts to point to some broad issues. Thirdly, the 'technical' vocabulary remains fluid, debated, sometimes not even thought through. This introductory chapter must include a preliminary account of some of the terms and the debates. Some of the opinions expressed below are my own, and others would argue differently. I have therefore used the personal expression 'I think' more often than academics are schooled to do, so that the reader may be alerted to which arguments are personal ones. But first it is necessary to explain the selection of topics.

Most religions have been associated with migrations; Judaism, Christianity and Islam are obvious examples for well over a thousand years. Europeans have migrated around the globe, as adventures, traders, imperial powers and missionaries. In recent centuries many have migrated to Australia, and numerous races have migrated to the United States of America. But a global history of religion in migration is not feasible in the size of book that is viable in this context. Some selection was, therefore, necessary. After much reflection, it was decided to focus on (1) the black African diaspora, because of its importance and previous neglect, and (2) migration from South Asia, or essentially what was termed the Indian subcontinent, the old British India, now divided into several nations, notably India, Pakistan, Bangladesh and Sri Lanka. This focus merits further justification. Whatever their modern differences, these countries have, in the past, formed some kind of unit, as part of the British empire, where one language (English) was common throughout, and governed, for better or for worse, by a common judicial and government system. Yet within this region there is an exceptional variety of religions, including Hindus, Muslims, Sikhs, Jains, Parsis, Buddhists (though these are few in number in modern times) and Indian Christians.

There is another aspect of what is meant by South Asian religion.

Obviously Islam, Christianity and Buddhism are global religions, and Parsis typically do not see themselves as South Asian but ultimately as true Persians. Muslims, for example, might legitimately want to protest that in a real sense Islam is not a South Asian religion. It does, however, have distinctive and important South Asian dimensions, as do the other religions listed. This section focuses on those branches of these religions which have migrated to the West from South Asia. It is a pity that scholars generally have not engaged more in internal comparisons within the religions (a classic exception to this is Geertz [5], who compared Islam in Morocco and South-East Asia). Typically, scholarship on religions tends to view the traditions as monolithic wholes and anything that is different as deviant, or to labour in one small corner, ignoring the rest. My own personal opinion is that, just as 'He who knows one, knows none' (i.e. the study of any one tradition cannot be said to be the study of religion), so also the study of any one part of a tradition cannot be said to be a study of that religion. The study of, say, Protestantism is not the study of Christianity. The first section of this *Handbook* looked at the religions in their old countries; here it examines them in migration, making comparisons both between countries and between religions.

The 'Western' countries studied, Australia, Britain, Canada and the United States, also have a degree of similarity despite their diversity. There is a common language, a common dominant religious culture (Christian) and an approximately similar level of economic development. Three of the four countries even belong to one Commonwealth of Nations. This practical example of 'comparative religion' at work thus compares what has happened to a number of major religions in moving from one reasonably defined region into another group of varied, but not dissimilar, countries. To a certain extent, therefore, like is being compared with like. (Continental Europe was excluded because of its significant differences, for example in language, although such a comparison would be interesting.)

This comparison can tell us much about the religions, about the ethnic groups which migrate and about the new countries into which the migrants bring their religions. In view of the number of and interest in studies of the Jewish diaspora it was tempting to include that subject; but it seemed wise, at this stage of research, to restrict the comparison to a tighter unit, especially when it already involves so many religions and such large countries and populations as those proposed. The material on the black African diaspora is occasionally used in the concluding chapter 25, but, for now, that has been left as a separate topic. Perhaps future editions of the book may extend the field of comparison, though the range of options is huge. Not only might one include, say, East and South-East Asians in the West, but also one might address questions such as: 'How similar are the sort of religious/ethnic issues involved in white migration to white areas, e.g. Swedish people in Australia?' For the present, however, a comparative study of how even seven major religions have migrated to four important countries is an enormous undertaking in the study of living religion. Because living necessarily involves change, as does migration, the whole subject is one of central importance in the study of contemporary religion, albeit one that has been neglected.

South Asian migration is not simply a modern phenomenon. As Bilimoria shows in chapter 21, it has been suggested that South Asians migrated to Australia millennia ago. Archaeologists have established that there was trade between the Indus valley civilization and Mesopotamia and probably further west. Similarly, Indian traders have travelled to East Africa and throughout much of the Pacific for centuries. In the nineteenth century Indians were used as 'the coolies of the empire', being deployed in Africa, the Caribbean and elsewhere (see among others [9]). The twentieth-century South Asian diaspora is not something restricted to Australia, Britain, Canada or the US. There were, for example, more South Asians in South-East Asia in the 1980s than in Europe (including Britain); more in the Middle East, or Africa, than in America; more in the Caribbean than in the Pacific (see table 19.1). Although these figures indicate that in the 1980s there were 8,691,490 South Asians living overseas, the popular stereotype perpetrated in the Western media of overwhelming numbers of South Asians 'swamping' other countries is, as Clarke et al. [3] emphasize, entirely false, for it is estimated that there are 350 million Europeans living outside Europe. Thus, while less than 1 per cent of South Asia's population

Table 19.1 The South Asian diaspora, 1987

Country of residence	No.
South-East and East Asia	1,862,654
Europe	1,482,034[a]
Middle East	1,317,141
Africa	1,389,722
Caribbean and Latin America	957,330
Pacific (Fiji, Australia, New Zealand)	954,330
North America	728,500

[a]Of these, 1,260,000 were in the UK.
Source: C. Clarke, C. Peach and S. Vertovec, *South Asians Overseas: Migration and Ethnicity*, Cambridge, Cambridge University Press, 1990, p. 2.

live outside South Asia, something like a third of Europeans populate other areas of the world. If any group of people have swamped others, then it is the Europeans who have been doing the 'swamping'.

So far the terms 'migrants' and 'religion in migration' have been used. But that vocabulary is unsatisfactory. In the four countries under discussion there are important, substantial and obviously increasing numbers of second- and third-generation South Asians. They clearly are not migrants. Equally, their religion, Hinduism, Islam or whatever it may be, is not in migration. It is now part of the respective national scenes. My own preference is for the term 'diaspora religion'. That term has generally been associated with Jews outside Israel, but it is applicable to the religion of any people who have a sense of living away from the land of the religion, or away from 'the old country'. In some senses, therefore, Christianity is a diaspora religion, but the Catholic and Protestant churches (black-led churches are perhaps different) are so indegenized in the West that they do not really have a sense of living away from the country of the religion. For them the 'Holy Land' may be a place of pilgrimage, but it is not the centre of the religion in the same way as, for example, India is for Hindus or Jains, or Punjab is for Sikhs. Similarly, Islam in Pakistan and Bangladesh, while distant from the land of pilgrimage, is not perhaps a diaspora religion in that these nations are, and see themselves as, Muslim countries. One feature of a diaspora community is that it is not only away from the old country, but is also a minority phenomenon. To a certain extent the diaspora experience for Muslims in the West is of an ethnic diaspora, the experience of Pakistanis, or of smaller groups such as Gujaratis, away from the old country. In what follows, 'diaspora religion' indicates a religion practised by a minority group, conscious of living in a culturally and religiously different, possibly hostile, environment, away from the old country of the religion. It is a convenient term, though not one without difficulties [4]. The alternatives, such as 'migration', do an injustice to the people who wish to see themselves not only as Muslims or Pakistanis but also as Australian, British, Canadian or US citizens. The question of identity is one which will recur.

A much used, and abused, term in this subject is 'race'. From the days of empire, and of Hitler's Germany, this term has been used to imply a biologically determined set of fixed characteristics, genetically conveyed, marking out different groups and establishing a hierarchy of peoples. The quest for racial 'purity', however, has not been confined to Europe. American attitudes to blacks and Australia's 'white as snow' policy, which excluded all non-whites from the continent [6], have been as racist as the Europeans. But 'race' remains part of scholarly, as well as popular, vocabulary and is used to indicate groups which are treated as if they were biologically different, in their organization, or by their exclusion of others, or which are marked out by outside societies as biologically distinctive for exclusionary motives. It is a term fraught with dangers because of its lack of 'hard' scientific justification and the social ills with which it has been associated [1; 7; 8]. In much modern political discussion the old biological racism is replaced by a cultural racism which argues that certain groups should be excluded, or restricted, because their culture is (allegedly) incompatible with that of the rulers.

Another common term that requires questioning comment is 'ethnic(ity)'. In common practice it has come to be associated with coloured, or black, minorities, or 'Third World' peoples, for example in department stores selling 'ethnic jewellery'. Most academics use 'ethnicity' to refer to a sense of cultural distinctiveness, with culture taken to include both secular and religious features, a consciousness of a specific history or of common origins, possibly language; it is a consciousness of identity worked out in a sense of distinctiveness from, if not hostility to, others. Whereas race alludes to (alleged) biological differences, commonly ethnicity alludes to perceived cultural distinctiveness. But which boundaries people draw around themselves may differ from one context to another. To give a personal example, in one context I may define myself as a Derbyshire person, or as English, or British, or European (and in others as male, or by profession, age or hobby). 'Ethnics' is a term generally used to describe 'others', but we all have our own ethnicity. The phrase 'ethnic minorities' has become code for African or Asian, or coloured minorities, but that is not a reasoned, or reasonable, use of the term. Sometimes the idea of perceived deprivation is associated with 'ethnic minorities', but usage remains inconsistent. Many groups who have a sense of common history and language and a sense of deprivation are not in practice referred to as ethnic groups – Derbyshire people have all these features and commonly feel deprived by the government in London of resources and consideration! What is happening in practice, and illegitimately in my opinion, is the substitution of 'ethnic minorities' for 'coloured/black races'.

The terms 'acculturation', 'assimilation' and 'integration' are often used unthinkingly. In this book acculturation is used to indicate a person's acquiring the characteristics of another culture, e.g. Hindus in the US internalizing certain values, norms or ideals from the majority population. But it must be stressed that this is not a simple process. It is common for a person to take on some features of the culture (e.g. language, political or economic values) but not others (e.g. family values). People may also acculturate differently at different times; they change as they go through life, and may act differently in different company. Acculturation is not, therefore, a simple process. Assimilation is generally used to indicate a broader range of features than acculturation, suggesting the dropping of features of the old tradition in becoming similar to the majority population. But again, the phenomenon is not simple. Individuals or groups may assimilate the dominant tradition in some aspects of their lives and not others, and this may change with the passage of time. It would be wrong to assume that any one group assimilates uniformly. Integration is perhaps at the opposite end of the scale from assimilation and indicates simply the observance of laws and social requirements (e.g. attending school between certain ages or paying taxes) to respect the laws of the country (on these and other related terms see [2]).

Community is another term meriting comment. There is rarely a clearly defined entity corresponding to this term. Hindus, Muslims, etc. in any of the four countries are likely to have their own divisions – by region, say Gujarati or Punjabi, Pakistani or Bangladeshi (as well as Arab or Indonesian, or black Muslims); by language or class/caste; by 'sect', or as devotees of a particular figure. Even as small a community as the Zoroastrians have numerous internal groupings, Indian, Pakistani, East African or Iranian, and of course many would assert that they are Australian, British, Canadian or American. There is, therefore, no such thing as the Jain, Hindu, Sikh etc. community in any of these countries, any more than there is a unitary Christian or Jewish community. What there is, is a sense of 'us' as opposed to 'them', non-Hindus, non-Parsis, etc. Although 'the community' is a myth, it is, like most myths, a powerful concept.

Other terms that have been popular, but are now seen as mistaken, are 'host' (and implied 'guest') communities. This is inappropriate thinking, for second and further generations are hardly any longer 'guests', and the people who are actually hosts to any newcomers are rarely members of the wider society, but rather the existing members of the local Hindu, Muslim, etc. groups. It has also been argued, reasonably, that it is unhelpful to refer to 'waves' of migration, because of the fears, however unjustified, that term triggers in the minds of wider society of being 'swamped'.

The words 'black' and 'white' are not as clear as they appear. Some people use 'black' to mean 'coloured' and therefore under the label 'black' include not only people of African descent, but also people from Asia. The logic, it is argued, is that all suffer from prejudice because they are 'not white'. My own opinion is that subsuming all non-whites under one label fails to do justice to the distinctiveness of the diverse cultures. It also ignores the tensions that have existed between Asians and black Africans, for example throughout East Africa in the 1960s which triggered the policies of

Africanization and the subsequent migration of Asians from the region. Black/Asian conflict has also arisen in the West. Furthermore, defining people simply in terms of their relationship to 'whites', I think, fails to define them in their own terms. But the term 'white' is also an oversimplification. It generally means people of European descent, but even in Europe that is not a clear concept as one considers nations further east of the Mediterranean. Despite the moves towards European union the internal divisions are considerable, even between neighbouring countries, for example Britain and France. The complexities of 'white' meaning 'of European descent' are even greater when discussing Australia, Canada and the US.

'East' and 'West' are also much abused terms. What is East or West depends on where one stands. Britain is east of the US, which is east of Australia. In this context West is a convenient umbrella term for the four countries under discussion because of their shared language, religion and culture, but as a geographical term it is meaningless.

Language, however necessary, is a very imprecise tool.

Bibliography

1 BANTON, M., *Racial Theories*, Cambridge, Cambridge University Press, 1987

2 CASHMORE, E. ELLIS, *Dictionary of Race and Ethnic Relations*, London/New York, Routledge, 1988; 2nd edn repr. 1991

3 CLARKE, C., PEACH, C., and VERTOVEC, S., *South Asians Overseas: Migration and Ethnicity*, Cambridge, Cambridge University Press, 1990

4 CLIFFORD, J., 'Diasporas', *Cultural Anthropology*, vol. 9, no. 3, 1994, pp. 302–38

5 GEERTZ, C., *Islam Observed: Religious Developments in Morocco and Indonesia*, New Haven, Yale University Press, 1968; Chicago, University of Chicago Press, 1971

6 JUPP, J., *Immigration*, Sydney, Sydney University Press (Australian Retrospectives series, 1991

7 MILES, R., *Racism after 'Race Relations*, London/New York, Routledge, 1993

8 REX, J., *Race and Ethnicity*, Milton Keynes, Open University Press, 1986

9 TINKER, J., *The Banyan Tree: Overseas Emigrants from India, Pakistan and Bangladesh*, Oxford, Oxford University Press, 1977

20

African Diaspora Religion

OSSIE STUART

Introduction

People of African origin have endured a dispersal perhaps unprecedented in terms of numbers and degree of brutality in modern times. This African dispersal was the direct result of the slave trade; its lasting legacy, the creation of an African diaspora. Though slavery and the traffic in slaves in Africa preceded European involvement in the trade, it was the fabulous profits to be had from European plantation economies of tobacco, sugar and, later, cotton in the New World which dramatically increased the numbers of slaves involved. As a direct result of the slave trade, people of African ancestry are now to be found as far afield as North America, Brazil, the Caribbean and, most recently, Europe. However, this event must be placed in context, as it was just one aspect of the dramatic European expansion which transformed a situation in which Europe was merely a branch of world history to one in which the world was part of European history [29].

The African slave trade displaced substantial numbers of black people to Latin America (principally to Brazil), the Caribbean and North America. It is impossible to be accurate about the numbers, but between the sixteenth and the nineteenth century over 10 million people arrived as slaves in these territories from the Senegambia, what was called the 'Gold Coast' and East Africa [7]. The statistics speak for themselves, and table 20.1 showing the numbers of slaves who arrived at various destinations in the New World and Europe during this period is just a guide to the human scale of the trade. When considering these figures it should be remembered that there was a 30 per cent mortality rate among those forced to make the passage.

The impact of this trade upon the West African societies is prob-

Table 20.1 Numbers of slaves taken from Africa to the New World and Europe, sixteenth to nineteenth centuries

Destination	No. (millions)
Spanish Americas	1.5
British Caribbean	1.5
French Americas	1.5
Brazil	3.5
Dutch Americas	0.5
United States and British North America	1.0
Europe	0.5

Source: P. Curtin, S. Freierman, L. Thompson and J. Vansina, *African History*, London, Longman, 1978.

ably incalculable. However, it is known that the movement of so many people transformed the cultures of North America, the British and French Caribbean and Brazil. Indeed, this social transformation in both Africa and the New World was accompanied by a similar religious one. Regardless of whether the slave-importing religious culture was Catholic or Protestant, the transmission of African culture, especially African religions, shaped the religion of former slaves and their descendants, first in the New World and subsequently wherever people of African origin are to be found in the West.

Throughout the New World religion played an essential role among African slaves and their descendants. This is because it was a reminder of the Africa whence they came; it provided the medium through which to tell subsequent generations that their origin was a different place. Religion, whether African folk or Christianity, is the only universal language of aspiration throughout the New World. It was the only permitted language in which Africans could formulate the dream of becoming free subjects. This allows us to talk about an African diaspora, black people who share a common cultural affinity and, equally important, patterns of oppression.

Beginning with Africa, this section of the chapter will explore the characteristics which enable us to draw links between the numerous Christian and non-Christian African-influenced religions found in the Caribbean and Brazil, North America and the United Kingdom, as a European country with a significant black population. The syncretic links between Christianity and African religions are the principal characteristic of the new black religions inside and outside Africa. In predominantly Catholic countries some integration between African religions and the cult of saints has taken place. In Protestant countries, on the other hand, the devotion of saints is disapproved of, limiting the opportunity for similar developments. Nevertheless, even in Protestant countries, such as the United States and the United Kingdom, the characteristics of African diaspora religion can be found. Whether in Protestant or Catholic countries, these include spirit-possession, song and dance, folklore and myth, healing and charismatic worship.

Following on from the section on Africa is a study of diaspora religion in the United States. This section emphasizes the political and social roles which are also a characteristic of African diaspora religion. In this case Africa has benefited, and continues to benefit, from ideas formulated in the New World. Africa's liberation struggles, not to mention the overthrow of the apartheid South African state, were motivated by ideas which originated among African Americans and their response to the racism they experienced in the United States [16]. The continued dynamism of African diaspora religion, both in Africa and in the New World, can be partially accounted for by discrimination. However, as will become apparent in the subsequent sections on the Caribbean and Britain, this is not a complete explanation. The creation of new religions will be explored with an emphasis upon the important roles played by social status, community identity, gender and social class. African religion is characterized by its great diversity within the African diaspora. This diversity disguises the common features shared by black religions across the world, a commonality which enables us to talk about an African diaspora religion.

African Religions

Christianity is the major modern religion practised today throughout Africa south of the Sahara. This can be accounted for by contact with European nations, which began in the fifteenth century. The original European intervention remained on the periphery of the continent until the nineteenth century, when the interior of Africa, called the 'dark continent', was explored and then colonized. By the early twentieth century nearly all of Africa had been subjected to European rule and Christianity was established as the predominant religion [7].

Any description of African religion must begin with Christianity. The other important religions in Africa – Islam, classical religion and the syncretic new religious movements – have been deeply affected by the rise of Christianity on the continent. Islam is largely absent south of the Sahara, except in West Africa, where marabouts and Sufi orders were the agents of conversion. Likewise, in East

Africa Swahili culture – the language reflecting the mix of Afro-Arab shared heritage – along with the various slave trade routes helped to establish Islam in a number of centres along the East African coast as far south as Tanzania; but further expansion was checked by the presence of European missionaries [7]. For this reason, Islam does not feature prominently in this section.

Non-Christian and syncretic African religions, however, do figure prominently in this section. In response to Western Christianity. African theologians have embraced a new single African identity which relies heavily upon a celebration of African traditional culture. New religious movements and the reassertion of African classical religion are important parts of this theology. The relationship between the African theologies and both African culture and the colonial legacy will also be explored in this section.

Christianity

European expansion and Christianity At the beginning of the nineteenth century the interior of Africa was still untouched by the Europeans who had penetrated at various points along the shoreline. Portuguese trading posts on the east and west coasts and Dutch settlers around the Cape shared a presence in Africa with those European nations involved in the slave trade. Black Africa was still in the hands of people who wielded traditional powers and maintained a social structure which would be unrecognizable 100 years later. Yet the slave trade had left its mark upon African society. An estimated ten million people were enslaved and sent to the New World as a vital component in the economies of the Caribbean, Brazil and North America [7].

The slave trade and the Dutch and British settlement in the Cape were precursors of the 'scramble for Africa'. Intense British and French rivalry in Europe initiated the partition of Africa, with a literal race across the continent which drew in both Belgium and Germany. By the beginning of the twentieth century the majority of Africa was controlled by European nations. In the following years those parts of Africa left unmolested by the initial partition were consumed by Italy, France and Spain, with the sole exception of Ethiopia, which resisted Italian attempts to colonize it at the end of the nineteenth century. An Africa was created with national boundaries which bore little relation to the linguistic and cultural divisions which existed at that time. This legacy was confirmed when African nations, created by colonial *fiat*, achieved independence during the 1950s and 1960s and declared these boundaries to be inviolable. This decree has meant that each and every former colonial state has had to invent itself and to imagine its identity. Classical African religion has played a key role in this construction.

European Christian missionaries came to Africa in advance of the main partition of the continent. In the west, on the slave coast, Christian anti-slavery activists established a Christian community of freed slaves in Sierra Leone. This was to become a centre of learning and the propagation of Christianity across the region using, initially, black catechists (untrained converts) and, later, trained African priests. Fourah Bay College in Freetown, Sierra Leone was one of the first colleges founded to train an African clergy [7]. David Livingstone, a missionary and explorer, was celebrated by his contemporaries for his 'discoveries' rather than his success as a missionary. However, his life did capture the imagination of the British public, underwriting support for British participation in the 'scramble for Africa'.

Missionaries from France, Germany and Britain, both Catholic and Protestant, began to translate the Bible into vernacular languages and establish schools. These, with the aid of African catechists, became powerful tools of conversion. Catechists aided missionaries in a number of crucial ways, teaching them the local languages, assisting in translation of the Bible and aiding the missionaries in the establishment and running of the missions. The pace of Christian expansion in Uganda, for example, was dictated by the role of the catechists and was far more rapid than originally envisaged by the missionaries [7]. The missions were attractive to the local populations because of the education they offered. Quite simply, African communities, confronted with the impact of the European expansion, perceived education to be the route to modernization. At the height of the colonial period conversion and access to education provided an opportunity to learn a European language and to obtain a skilled job. Unlike classical African religion, Christianity was able to provide a sense of stability at a time of traumatic and dramatic change.

The Christian message missionaries brought to Africa was both radical and potent because the Bible spoke about the African condition in a way that related directly to its people. The Bible addressed themes with which black Africans could easily identify, such as circumcision, the prophecy of healing, Mount Carmel and the rainmaking contest, and the suffering of the people of Israel. The explicit message that all were equal before God took on a particular meaning within the context of oppression represented by both colonialism and slavery [16].

In spite of the strong implications in Christian doctrine concerning equality, most missionaries in the early twentieth century were deeply influenced by pseudo-scientific racism. They preached spiritual equality but were reluctant to train African clergy to replace themselves. Though some Africans were ordained and trained by both Catholic and Protestant churches, overt discrimination against the African clergy in the actual administration of the churches lasted until the end of colonialism. This discriminatory double standard on the part of European missionaries both galvanized Africans and aroused their resentment from the beginning of the colonial period, especially within the Protestant churches. The result was that whole congregations broke away from parent missionary churches and created independent churches. These new Africanized churches, of which more will be said later, are a potent phenomenon right across Africa and an indication of the continuing importance of Christianity to many African communities, outside the mainstream church. These independent churches also preceded the general Africanization of Christianity which took place once colonialism was overcome [18].

The mainstream churches in black Africa Christianity has expanded dramatically in Africa: today, the Christian churches claim a membership of some 140 million Africans. Catholicism is the dominant religion in Africa, even in many of the territories not colonized by either France or Portugal [30]. However, the Africanization of the clergy, whether Catholic or Protestant, has not resolved the problem of a shortage of trained priests. As a result, the catechists continue to play a vital role in the churches across Africa [7]. In consequence the church hierarchy remains fluid and the laity are encouraged to play a central role in the day-to-day running of the more remote church congregations. Nevertheless, the leadership of the Christian churches in Africa is now in the hands of Africans [16]. Today, African Catholics are represented by six Cardinals. South Africa has a legacy of gross discrimination based upon racial difference; nevertheless, white South African Anglicans, of whom there are a substantial number, are also headed by a black African leadership. The new leadership in Africa has begun to influence church policy at the both the regional and the global level; at ecumenical and other global Christian meetings African Christian views and perspectives are heard and upheld [16].

African and black theologies African theology places African culture and religion at the centre of Christian worship, directly challenging the assumption that Christian salvation can only be achieved by a rejection of African traditional culture. A unified Africa and a sense of a common African or black experience was created by colonization. The universal contempt in which Africans were held throughout the colonial period was shared by peoples right across the continent. The early Christian church in Africa also contributed to this shared experience. Indeed, white missionaries assumed that Western civilization and Christianity were the same thing and essential for the salvation of the African people [16; 18]. Racism still persists today, despite the overthrow of European rule in Africa since the 1960s. As a result, the modern African identity is shaped by the perception that theirs is a backward and inferior cultural identity and by the experience of racism. African theology seeks to place African culture at the centre of Christian worship on the continent.

There is evidence of differing strands of theological thought across the numerous African churches. The clearest distinction, however, is that between black theology, as articulated in South Africa, and African theology, adhered to by independent countries further to the north. Much of both African and black theology is based upon the common experience of oppression all Africans share. Nevertheless, it is important to explore the distinctiveness of 'black' and 'African' theology, while accepting the shared context from which each is derived.

African theology The roots of an African theology began with the nineteenth-century North American African-American activists, such as W. E. B. Dubois and E. W. Blynden [16]. Though primarily concerned with politics, these African Americans were early pan-Africanists and linked the promotion of black peoples with a reaffirmation of African culture and religion. This approach was taken up by Africans in the early years of the twentieth century within the context of resistance to colonialism and the imposition of a Christianity interpreted from a solely European perspective. It was in this context that African religious thinkers began to rebel against the assumption that adoption of Christianity necessarily involved a rejection of the African personality and traditional culture, and that there was no continuity between African traditional religion and the Christian message [16].

Young Africans educated in seminaries and schools in both Europe and Africa began to question the assumptions behind colonialism and Christianity in Africa. The Négritude Movement, a literary grouping that began in the 1930s in Paris, led by Léopold Senghor and Aimé Césaire, was an affirmation of black cultural identity in history, literature and art. Placide Tempels wrote a seminal work which affirmed the existence among the African peoples of a coherent system of thought and a positive philosophy of existence, of life, death and life after death. Subsequent writers have disputed his analysis as being too Eurocentric, yet they too accepted his basic notion that the African way of life has a valid philosophy. The following years saw the creation of an Africanized Christian doctrine, cult, pastoral practice and art, based upon African culture and religious traditions. The Zairean T. Tshibangu made the most significant contribution to this development. He reasoned that it was possible to have a 'theology with an African colour'. While acknowledging that divine revelation and principles of human reasoning are shared universally, he argued that there are special African characteristics which allow for a theology done in an African way [16].

African theology challenges and refutes the notion that traditional cultures and religions are inferior and to be abandoned. In contrast, African theology raises the question of what unity of Christian faith means, as opposed to uniformity, and how the universality of the one Christian faith is to manifest itself in concrete forms. The main themes of African theology are those aspects of Christian faith which Africans especially value, but which Western culture has neglected or failed to emphasize [20; 23; 8; 14]. These include the important of community and communion; the value of solidarity and human relationships, both among the living and with the deceased (especially the ancestors); and the constant interaction with the invisible (God, minor deities and spirits). Life is considered holistically, a view which is closely associated with traditional African conceptions about health and sickness, good and evil. African theologians find the Old Testament, with its disposition towards symbolism and ritual, to be most representative of African lives. Ultimately, because Africa is a continent of the oral tradition rather than the written word, the most dynamic elaboration of African theology is articulated by the congregation rather than by theologians. This means that African theology is the authentic and original expression of the celebration, song, dance, prophecy, dreams, sermon and healing ritual within the Independent African churches. It is also elaborated in small Christian communities or the revival groups within mainstream churches [17; 21].

This process was supported by the Second Vatican Council between 1962 and 1965 and became standard thinking among progressive Catholic thinkers during the following decade. Protestant thinkers were also influenced by the radical departure in thinking of African theology. The All Africa Council of Churches was formed in 1963 and provided a vehicle through which new African religious leaders could share ideas and encourage the Protestant churches to respond to African theology. Since the establishment of the Ecumenical Association of African Theologians in 1977 in Accra, this body has become the major forum in which African theology is being developed [29].

South African black theology Dramatic changes have taken place in South Africa in the early 1990s, culminating in universal elections which swept the African National Congress into power with Nelson Mandela as President. These events have placed a question mark against the future form of South African black theology, based as it was on the long tradition of protest against racial discrimination, appropriation of land and economic exploitation to which communities not of European origin have been subjected. The Calvinist perspective of the early Dutch settlers in the Cape, from whom the Afrikaner communities are descended, was at the heart of white justification for the occupation of this region and the confrontation with the people they found there. This was a view which assumed that God chose white people as his own possession and ordained them to subject the heathens (black people), making them the hewers of wood and the drawers of water. With the construction of the apartheid system in 1948, the state formalized the organization of people on the basis of colour and race. These became powerful symbols of distinction and the apportioning of power and privilege [16].

The reaction to this institutionalized racism among black people and other peoples of non-European descent was both similar to that of African peoples throughout the continent south of the Sahara and also quite distinct. The rapid development of African Independent churches in the first decades of the twentieth century was just as prolific in South Africa as it was across the rest of the continent. Dissatisfied with the levels of autonomy given to both catechists and trained African priests, African leaders broke with mainstream missions to establish Independent churches. However, the particular South African context in which African people lived also evoked a specific political response, in which the churches also participated. The religious form this response took has at its core South African black theology.

The apartheid system not only classified people on the basis of race, it also had an economic logic. Its purpose was to sustain a cheap and disenfranchized labour force for the mines and industries. The consequence was the impoverishment of the vast majority of South Africa's population. Africans were confined to huge urban townships, such as Soweto, which did not enjoy even the most basic of facilities; or they were isolated in 'Bantustans', territories under nominal black control which were nothing more than dormitories for the unemployed and the families of migrant labourers. The response of the African National Congress to this extreme form of exploitation was to abandon its originally non-violent methods and instead to adopt more forceful methods to challenge the apartheid state. Likewise, black theology began to take shape during the 1970s, a time of extreme oppression against African leaders such as Mandela and Steve Biko [22; 18; 16]. This decade was a time when Africans were seeking to establish black consciousness, rejecting the apartheid system which defined Africans as foreigners in their own land and, instead, beginning to assert their own identity [22]. For African church leaders, who were closely associated with this new consciousness, black theology was of central importance.

Archbishop Desmond Tutu, Bishop Mana Buthelezi and the Reverend Allan Boesak were able to articulate the suffering of both their congregations and the wider black community [31]. Indeed, the strength of black theology was its ability to create a sense of shared experience between religious leaders and the people. In the face of a system of extreme oppression based upon the colour of an individual's skin, the central theological question became one concerning the necessity of condoning more extreme methods than mere reform to overthrow an unjust system. Can the support of violence be reconciled with Christianity? [15]

This question lay at the heart of South African black theology, a liberation theology which has been at variance with African theology and its project to revalorize African traditional culture. This is very understandable, as black South Africans were confronted by an apartheid ideology which had given great prominence to the ascribed national characteristics of communities to divide and keep separate non-European communities. Today, however, South Africa has entered a new era, one in which the apartheid system has been dismantled and the differences within society are no longer underwritten by the state. This means that, for all its success in challenging apartheid, the main tenets of South African black theology have, like apartheid, been consigned to history.

Over recent years there has been a move to reconcile the differences between African theology and South African black theology. Theologians representing both traditions realized that they had much to learn from each other. South Africans have come to accept that Africans will not be able to liberate themselves unless they first regain their culture and human identity. In return, theologians further north were obliged to give more attention to the present-day problems confronting modern Africa. Whether they agree or not, it is the congregations rather than the theologians who will determine the shape and pace of theological change in South Africa. This is nowhere more apparent than in Africa's Independent churches, which are part of the trend towards new religious movements in modern Africa [16].

New religious movements in modern Africa The most dynamic phenomenon in modern Africa has been the growth of Independent churches or new religious movements across the continent south of the Sahara. They are examples of how Christianity has been adapted to the African condition, rejecting foreign structures, especially those proffered by Western missionaries. There are thought to be over 10,000 of these new movements across Africa, in Nigeria, Ghana, Kenya, Zaire, South Africa and elsewhere. Fifteen per cent of all Christians in Africa, between ten and twelve million people, belong to such groups [29].

The origins of these movements can be traced back to colonialism and the problems Africans had with European traditional religion. The paternalistic mission churches and the perception held by missionaries that ancestor cults and polygamy, for example, were idolatrous, as well as Africans' reluctance to accept Western medicine unconditionally, were all sites of conflict between Africans and European missionaries. The new religious movements have dealt with these issues with varying degrees of success, some by splitting from mainstream churches, others by replacing the European missionary with a black leadership. The worship of a black prophet or Messiah in place of the white symbolism usually accompanies such splits. These new churches incorporated features of African society and religious practice, including, for example, methods of faith healing, traditional medicine and polygamy – which, with the Bible now at their disposal, Africans could see was part of ancient Israelite religion [18; 29].

It is very difficult to classify these new religious movements, with few religions falling into any neat system. There are, however, three widely recognized general types of movement. The most numerous and the fastest-growing consists of the Zionist Independent churches, the prophet-healing or spiritual churches. These churches are described as being broadly Pentecostalist in character and with an emphasis upon charismatic leadership and healing. They derive their name from the close relationship between these churches and American missions in South Africa, especially the Evangelical Christian Catholic Church of Zion City, Illinois. These churches are found both in South Africa and in the rest of the continent [18]. One of the most influential Zionist Independent churches is the Aladura church in Nigeria and other countries in West Africa [7]. 'Aladura' is Yoruba for 'owners of prayer'. This prayer and healing movement is represented by societies such as the Celestial Church of Christ and the Brotherhood of the Cross and Star, as well as numerous Cherubim and Seraphim societies all over West Africa. These churches were first founded in 1918, but saw considerable expansion throughout the middle decades of the twentieth century under Joseph Babalalo's mass healing movement. Since Nigeria's independence in 1960 this movement has received official recognition and continues to make converts among the Muslim population in Nigeria's north. The Aladura churches still draw most of their members from former mission churches, providing opportunities for women, in particular, to achieve positions of leadership. Though no formal union has been established between these West African churches, most have relationships with Western Pentecostal churches. For example, the Church of the Lord, Aladura is affiliated to the World Council of Churches [29].

The similar Ethiopian churches, known also as Separatist or Orthodox churches, form the second group of new religious movements. Ethiopian churches, in contrast to the Zionist churches, are African Independent churches which have largely maintained the patterns of worship and doctrine of the European churches from which they have broken off. Not to be confused with the ancient Ethiopian Orthodox Church, these churches were founded during the first decades of the twentieth century in reaction against the paternalism and discrimination within the European-run mission churches [18]. Again, these churches are closely associated with South Africa, but can be found right across the African continent. The Jamaa Movement in Zaire, Maria Legio in Kenya and the Catholic Church of the Sacred Heart in Zambia originated in Roman Catholic missions [7]. The Providence Industrial Mission in Malawi and the Cameroon Baptist Convention originated in Protestant missions [29].

The third group of movements are eschatological, such as Alice Lenshina's Zambian Lumpa Church. Christian in ethos, this movement predicted the ending of the world, emphasized the role of music and perceived witchcraft as a danger. Other movements revived classical religion through the mission structure. All these movements adopted traditional functions but altered their content. Healing, for example, though prominent, is stripped of its traditional methods and theories. The syncretic nature of these movements is also a major characteristic, as is visionary experience [7; 29]. Yet without doctrinal underpinnings these movements rarely survive the death of their charismatic leadership. They wane, become a distinctive African Christian church or create a new syncretic movement based upon Christian and classical religious concepts combined.

African Classical Religions

African classical or 'traditional' religions are an important aspect of Africa's past. The very term 'traditional' reinforces the sense of authenticity enjoyed by these religions. As a consequence, religion continues to play a significant role in the creation of contemporary African identity. This is ironic, because this identity emphasizes the common experience shared by Africans, and yet the concept of a unified African identity did not exist prior to colonialism, when African traditional religions were at their height. Successful resistance to colonialism and the construction of a new independent Africa relied upon resistance to oppression and the assertion of a new African culture, in which traditional religion played a key part. A discussion of African classical religions, therefore, far from being a discussion of a dead past, is a description of modern African cultural identity.

The evidence for African classical religions is derived from the period of dramatic transformation during the fifteenth and sixteenth centuries. This was a time of the West, Southern and East Africa empires. These included, in the west, the interior empire of Ghana and its fourteenth-century successor, Mali, the state of Songhay, the Hausa trading cities, and the forest kingdoms of Oyo, Benin and Akan. In the east, the Funji empire spread over what is now Sudan and Ethiopia. In southern Africa there were the Zimbabwe kingdom, the Kongo state and a similar empire in what is now Zaire. These states were agricultural and trading empires and, as a result, were influenced by circumstances beyond their border. The West African states, for example, owed their strength to contacts with the trans-Saharan trade routes and, later, with Europeans and the slave trade on the coast [7].

The absence of written evidence makes it impossible to construct accurate historical accounts of these kingdoms. However, it is with these empires that African classical religions are closely associated. Far from being fixed and stable religions, they were evolving at a time of considerable transformation in the regions in question. As the empires asserted themselves, what is today recognized as traditional African religion superseded the previous local cults. European intervention at this point had a profound impact upon these ritual-based religions. The purpose of a discussion of African classical religion here is accordingly to emphasize its contemporary role in Africa, not to subscribe to a notional ancient authenticity.

Until recently some Western scholars were reluctant to accept that religion existed among people who relied upon an oral, rather than a written, tradition. It is now accepted that what 'religion' is has been circumscribed by its having been understood hitherto from a solely Western cultural perspective [16]. Scholars now accept that African 'religiosity' exists in many forms and, unlike Western religion, is based upon a cosmology in which the entire world can be viewed as a source of power to be held in balance and controlled. This is in contrast with Western notions which distinguish between sacred and secular [18].

It is not clear whether it is possible to talk about a single African traditional religion, or of a multitude of different religions on the African continent. Scholars, especially anthropologists, have taken the latter view; African theologians, in contrast, have taken the former view and have sought to map out common ground between these African religions. The question of an artificially constructed African past culture and the absence of a definition of culture remains [16]. The great diversity in geography, history and language across Africa, not to mention the varying social forces, has resulted in many distinct forms of religious custom on the continent. Nevertheless, underlying assumptions about the role and nature of the human's place in the world represent common characteristics which these religions share. Rather than address individual religions, it seems therefore more appropriate to provide a brief summary of some of the common features shared by African classical religions.

Common to all these religions is the belief in a supreme being; they are therefore described as theisms. Usually beneficent, such a being can be appealed to in times of crisis, most often through intermediaries such as lesser divinities and ancestors; yet the supreme being plays little part in the cults or mystic imagination of the people. The intermediaries, who may take the form of deities, spirits or ancestors, relate closely to the daily concerns of people. They may act as the agents of the One, but they also have their own independence and power inherent in the world, as expressed through their actions [29].

Myths within African classical religion convey a sense of an original order which became disturbed during the creative process, as a result of which death and disorder entered the world. As cosmology, these religions are explanatory: they describe the human condition, including the world as it is experienced, mortality and regeneration, rather than apportioning blame and suggesting a means of salvation, or the hope of restoring the primordial state. The world as it is experienced is thus the starting-point for ritual and worship [29].

The period in which African classical religion established itself was an era of political and economic centralization in African states. The development of religious authority in West Africa, Sudan and Zimbabwe supported the notion of divine kingship and served to accommodate the older and more diffuse forms of authority. Among the West African religions, for example, modern rituals re-enact the struggles between local cults and centralized imperial religion. Within agriculturally based imperial states the ritual of sacrifice was performed by the king, who was closely associated with the fertility of the land. Southern African states, such as the Zulu, associated the fertility of the land with a female deity. These patrilineal societies have elaborate female initiation ceremonies and women form the links between clans through marriage. As a result, women play an important role in these societies as healers and ritual specialists, mediating between human society and the spirits [29]. On the other hand, the more decentralized societies such as the Nuer or the Dinka in southern Sudan, or the Mbuti of Zaire, do not acknowledge central spiritual authority or create shrines with religious specialists to support them [7].

Ancestors also play the important role of maintaining the continuity between life and death. Recently deceased ancestors (described as 'shades') have power to intervene in the affairs of the society. Also common is the belief in multiple 'selves' within an individual. Thus part of a person can represent continuity with a family or a clan, or can be the reincarnation of a dead individual who continues to retain their position as an ancestor. Witchcraft is important in manifesting previously known or unknown 'selves' within an individual. Witchcraft can be used positively to support an individual or community, or for anti-social ends. The notoriety associated with witchcraft is the result of the attention paid to the anti-social activities associated with this practice, including sorcery, shape-changing, cannibalism and 'beasts of the forest'.

In recent years the witch-curing cults which counteract the activities of sorcerers have gained in popularity. This development has coincided with increased interest in healing and divination cults in general. Sickness and ill health are perceived as resulting from a diminution of personal power as a consequence of possession by a deity or ancestor, or the effects of witchcraft. Healers, using oracles and other forms of divination, determine the source of the illness and proffer remedies. The holistic approach to the body, which is a characteristic of African religion, means that divination has a prominent position in these religions. Divination in Yoruba society has developed considerably in recent years; in particular, deities are perceived to make themselves known through sickness [29].

Music and art are central in African classical religions. Music plays many roles. It can have an important part in ritual and worship; the spirit world is thought to be amenable to music, especially that derived from divine sources. There is a distinction between sacred and other forms of music, in particular between the repertoire of hymns and songs associated with the gods and ancestors and those used for healing, fertility and celebration. In contrast, much of African religious art is symbolic rather than representative. The locations of shrines found in regions where classical religion is practised are either places thought to be charged with power by, perhaps, the presence of spirits, or sites where sacrificial offerings might be made. Carved bronzes, as among the Edo in West Africa, are symbolic of individual kings; likewise, masks and body paint display temporary spirit-possession. Sculpture of the human form can reflect the devotees themselves, symbolizing the human response to divine power [29].

To conclude, single-tradition religion in Africa, whether modern classical religion, Christianity or Islam, serves to bring together the disparate cultures on the continent. Yet we know that the era of single-tradition religion in Africa south of the Sahara only began with, first, the arrival of Europeans, and then the imposition of colonialism. The survival of African classical religions into the modern age betokens more than merely a revival of interest in ancient tradition: it is a reassertion of a new African identity, one which has deeply affected all the single-tradition religions south of the Sahara.

One sign of this is the emergence of an African Christian theology, which seeks to spell out Africa's distinctive contribution to the world's cultural heritage, ideas and institutions, both in the past and in the future. Another sign is, of course, the impact of African culture overseas. Within the African diaspora in North America, the Caribbean, South America and Europe, African culture lives on.

African Diaspora Religion and the United States of America

Introduction

The United States and Brazil share a legacy of African slavery, yet religion among the former slaves and their descendants differs markedly between the two countries. The United States is a plural society in which the division of church and state was a novelty at the time of its inclusion in the American constitution, with no European states having such legislation. Slavery and Protestantism form the context within which we can understand the distinct development of African diaspora religion in the United States. Black religion in the United States is a strongly emotional faith, based upon evangelical Protestantism. In recent years, and in a further departure from their Brazilian neighbours, many African Americans have embraced Islam. Yet, despite the overtly anti-white rhetoric of the early Islamist organizations, the character of African-American Islam originally resembled that of fundamentalist Protestantism rather than that of mainstream Islam. To understand the unique and influential development of African-American diaspora religion it is necessary to begin with a description of the wider development of Christianity in North America. As the freed slaves streamed north after the Civil War and emancipation they encountered a Protestant European religious and ethical environment which was to have a lasting impact. Into this environment the descendants of slaves and former slaves brought their distinct African identity.

Protestantism comes to North America

The fall to the British in 1664 of New Amsterdam, renamed New York, influenced the nature of Christian religion during America's early European history. By this date the eastern seaboard was settled principally by members of the Church of England and others whose allegiance was to organizations of a dissenting character. For example, the southern colonies of Virginia, Maryland and the Carolinas were Church of England, while the northern colonies of

Massachusetts, Connecticut, Rhode Island, Pennsylvania and New Jersey were associated with the dissenting tradition [1]. Baptists, inspired by Roger Williams, were predominant on Rhode Island. Quakers were to be found in both New Jersey and Pennsylvania, but were in the majority in these colonies only for a short period. The New England Puritans were, in the main, Congregationalists. Rejecting the more bureaucratic Presbyterian organization, they governed themselves through independent congregations, as their name implies. As a great pioneer of separatism, Roger Williams made his mark on the American constitution with the enactment of the First Amendment, separating church from state. Nevertheless, the hostility of the northern colonists to slavery, their pacifism and their simplification of worship have had a major influence upon modern North American puritan thinking. The 'Great Awakening' of the eighteenth century added new vigour to this strand of thought, as Jonathan Edwards and, later, George Whitefield introduced a passionate and charismatic intensity which was well received by all the Protestant organizations. Indeed, this made their doctrines and practices more relevant to their lives as they began to move away from the east coast into America's hinterland. It was at this time that Methodism, named for the idea that one should live according to a 'method' laid down in the Bible, also gained in popularity [9].

The nineteenth century, a period characterized by the European expansion westwards, saw a second 'Great Awakening' among the temporary camps of the new settlers. These pioneers, confronted with huge, open tracts of land, were susceptible to evangelical fervour, from which the Baptists, Methodists and Congregationalists drew most benefit. It was during this period, too, that the first original North American religion, Mormonism, was created in Upper New York State. Its cohesiveness, puritanism and emphasis upon family values attracted many followers to the Mormon church. Once it had abandoned its more bizarre practices, Mormon became another conforming evangelical Protestantism [1; 9].

The importance of the Protestant religious movement across North America lies in its impact upon general North American values and outlook. Separatism, pacifism, egalitarianism, tolerance, independence, thrift and the importance of the family are all conspicuous puritan values; they are all found in strands of American thinking. These values would be tested during the days of mass immigration from Catholic Europe during the earlier decades of the twentieth century. Of more importance in the present context, however, is the impact of puritanical beliefs upon the many hundreds of thousands of former slaves as they began to move north out of the former slave colonies into the industries of central and eastern America in the nineteenth century. The adoption of Protestantism by African Americans has had a significant influence upon their identity.

African Americans and Slavery

The slave trade was the sole reason for the presence of Africans and their descendants on the American continent. As can be seen from table 20.2, African Americans have been a significant minority of the total population of the United States since the end of the eighteenth century.

Table 20.2 African American population of the United States, 1790–1994

Year	Slave	Free	Total	% of US population
1790	697,681	59,527	757,208	19.3
1800	893,602	108,435	1,002,037	18.9
1810	1,191,362	186,466	1,377,828	19.0
1820	1,538,022	233,634	1,771,656	18.4
1840	2,487,355	386,293	2,873,648	16.1
1860	3,953,760	488,070	4,441,830	14.1
1880			6,580,793	13.1
1900			8,833,994	11.6
1920			10,463,131	9.9
1940			12,866,000	9.8
1960			18,871,831	10.5
1970			22,672,570	11.0
1980			26,488,219	11.7
1991			29,986,060	12.1
1994			33,000,000	12.9

Source: United States Commerce Department, Census Bureau.

Though the original slaves brought with them their customs, language and, most importantly, their religions, force of necessity meant that the majority of these importations were quickly abandoned. As commodities in an extremely brutal trade, African slaves were open to widespread and pervasive exploitation and abuse and were not accorded the dignity of being considered human beings. Slavery helped to manufacture the myth of the inferiority of black people in comparison to whites. It was in this context that Africans, forbidden to practise their own religions, were introduced to Protestantism. Slaves were taught a version of Christianity designed to legitimize their the situation and to promise escape from this enslaved misery into eternal life. Yet the use of religion as a form of social control was only partially successful, for the Christian message also offered the hope of freedom and equality. Furthermore, in secret societies and meetings on slave compounds across the American South, the scriptures were reinterpreted and synthesized with African expression in stories, song and dance, bringing new meaning and energy to the Christian way [19].

African American Protestantism

The passage of the Thirteenth Amendment to the Constitution on 18 December 1865 guaranteed the emancipation of slaves originally promised by President Lincoln's 1863 Proclamation. Former slaves were free to move out of the southern slave states and north into the industrial heart of the United States, and to follow white settlers west over the Alleghenies. As they did so they encountered new Protestant denominations. African Americans in slavery from the mid-eighteenth century onwards had found the Baptists to have the greatest appeal for them of all the puritan groups, because of their warm and charismatic nature and the emphasis upon the conversion experience. The advocating of adult baptism, though not unique among Protestant groups, helped the Baptists to become the most popular form of Christianity among Africans in the South [19]. However, emancipation brought new opportunities and a growing dissatisfaction with white-led churches [31]. Though they preached liberation and egalitarianism, these churches largely failed to extend these values to their black members. As a consequence, African Americans established their own independent churches. Methodism, with its emphasis upon devotional worship and music, enjoyed a significant black following and it was from this religion that the most important schism took place. As early as 1787, Richard Allen formed the first black Methodist congregation, the Free African Society. In 1793 this society became Bethel Church, an independent Methodist church. In 1816 representatives of a number of black Methodist churches met in Philadelphia and organized the African Methodist Episcopal Church as the first national black denomination, choosing Allen as their bishop [19]. Emancipation heralded a similar break with other white-led churches. Outside the South, blacks established separate churches and, eventually, denominations within Protestantism, including many black Baptist churches.

Black Protestantism is evangelical. In the North American context, this means a belief in the authority of the Bible, salvation only through close personal faith in Christ, experience of conversion and emphasis on a moral life, with abstention from smoking, drinking and promiscuity. This orientation can be described as leaning towards fundamentalist rather than liberal Protestantism, but it suited black communities under siege from extremes of poverty and racism. Black Protestantism became the cornerstone of African-American identity. The Azusa Street Revival in Los Angeles headed by the black preacher William J. Seymour in 1906, which inaugurated the new evangelical Pentecostalism, is a case in point. Black Protestantism also played a central role in the political struggle against discrimination [32].

Evangelicalism remained a potent force within black Protestantism throughout the 1930s, 1940s and 1950s. Out of this period came Martin Luther King, Jr, a Baptist minister and one of the most important Christian leaders in the United States during the twentieth century. Educated at Boston University, King studied the life and teachings of Mahatma Gandhi and further developed the Indian leader's doctrine of *satyagraha* ('holding to the truth') and non-violent civil disobedience [32]. The bus boycott in Montgomery, Alabama, began a political career of campaigning for civil rights and for better education for Southern blacks which ended only with his assassination in 1968. The death of Dr King coincided with attacks by white extremists upon black churches. Four black children were murdered in the bombing of 16th Street Baptist Church in Birmingham, Alabama, in 1963; dozens of black churches throughout the South were burned or bombed. The death of Dr King and the attacks upon black churches were indications of the important political role black Protestantism played at this time [32].

Today African-American Christians are found in most of the major Christian denominations in the United States, with the number of members of the Roman Catholic Church reaching 855,000 in 1978; the United Methodist Church had 500,000. However, the majority of African-American Christians are members of over 140 denominations which have split either from white or white-controlled denominations or from other black groups during the past two centuries [2]. These can be roughly divided into three separate Christian traditions: Baptist, Methodist and Pentecostal.

The majority of black Americans are Baptists. Indeed, many prominent African Americans in the United States have been Baptist ministers. As well as Martin Luther King, these include Rev. Jesse Jackson and Ralph David Abernathy. Abernathy was a Baptist clergyman who helped establish the Southern Christian Leadership Conference and served as its president from 1968 to 1977. The largest black-led Baptist denomination is the National Baptist Convention, USA, which emerged out of a schism with the National Baptist Convention of America in 1915. In 1978 it had 30,000 congregations and 6,426,000 affiliated members. The second largest is the National Baptist Convention of America, which in 1978 had 15,200 congregations and 3,300,000 affiliated members. The other significant Baptist churches are the Progressive National

Baptist Convention, formed in 1961, which had 655 congregations and 636,000 members, and the 1865 National Primitive Baptist Convention, which had 2,198 congregations and 207,000 affiliated members at the end of the 1970s [2].

The second largest church tradition which has substantial black allegiance is Methodism. Like the Baptist tradition, African-American Methodism was one of the major churches slaves and former slaves joined. The largest denominations are the African Methodist Episcopal Church and the African Methodist Episcopal Church of Zion. The former had 6,000 congregations with 1,529,000 members in 1978; the latter, 4,500 congregations and 1,307,000 members. The other large African-American Methodist church is the Christian Methodist Episcopal Church; in 1978 it had 2,598 congregations and 600,000 affiliated members [2].

The third major black tradition is the Pentecostal movement. The black Pentecostal community, which has little to do with the white Pentecostals or Neo-Pentecostal (charismatic) movement among whites, numbered over 2.7 million adherents in 1970. The largest body is the Church of God in Christ, with 7,000 congregations and 1,600,000 affiliated members. A schism within this organization in 1969 produced the Church of God in Christ International. This is now the second largest Pentecostal denomination, with 1,041 congregations and 501,000 members in 1978. Other major denominations are the Pentecostal Assemblies of the World, with 550 congregations and 60,000 members, and the United Holy Church of America, which had 470 congregations and 70,000 members in 1978. The former was formed in 1914, the latter in 1886 [2].

North American Black Theology

The development of a distinct black theology was influenced by a number of factors. The most important were the civil rights movement, the rise of the Black Power movement in response to the perceived failings of Martin Luther King's non-violent struggle, and, finally, the continuing absence from mainstream North American Christianity of the black experience and the theological content it might have contributed. These influences challenged black religious leaders to examine the relationship between black religion and the struggle for power and identity among the people. A distinct black theology was the principal outcome of their response [16].

The works of D. J. Roberts and J. H. Cone were central to the creation of a black theology during the 1970s. This theology has at its core the social and historical context which defines not only the questions black people address to God but also the answers to those questions. Though black theology is based upon biblical revelation, the study of the scriptures is determined by the social context within which people live, in order, as Roberts described, to 'contribute to a faith beyond discursive reason, and one which is based upon "reasons of the heart"' [26]. This is why, according to Cone, 'white' theology interprets the divine Word differently from black religious thought. The emphasis upon the black experience means that North American black theology, with its roots in slavery, promotes the distinction between black and white. Political struggle, which might condone violence, and a preoccupation with social and political issues, might be criticized as negative and narrow. Indeed, Cone's works have been criticized as being too combative, making it difficult to imagine an eventual reconciliation between black and white Christians. Roberts addressed this issue head-on, reasoning that, for Christians, separation must eventually give way to reconciliation [25]. Yet it is important not to assume a weakness in the black Christian position. Reconciliation can only be achieved through liberation.

James Cone has the reputation of a radical black theologian. Of white liberal Protestantism, he said, 'American theology is racist! It identifies theology as dispassionate analysis of the "tradition", unrelated to the suffering of the oppressed' [5]. Roberts was equally critical, but Cone's language was the more combative. Cone supported and advocated Black Power, by which he meant freedom, self-determination and the restoration of dignity among African Americans [6]. His words challenged the ecclesiastical establishment in the United States. More importantly, both Roberts and Cone, as well as other black theologians, helped black theology to emerge as an important dimension of North American theology.

Islam and African Americans

During the mid-1960s, a time when black American Christianity was extremely powerful at the forefront of the civil rights movement, African Americans were being attracted to an alternative religion, Islam. Yet this was not the orthodox Islam which many slaves had brought with them from Africa. Instead, until the 1970s an unorthodox grouping, the Nation of Islam, won most adherents among African Americans. The history of the Nation of Islam consists of its transformation from the unorthodox to the orthodox and its continuing political importance as a radical African-American organization.

Like most of the black Protestant groupings, the Nation of Islam owes its roots to the perceived injustices within North American society during the middle years of the twentieth century.

Established by Wallace D. Fard in Detroit in 1930, the organization was taken over by Elijah Poole, later known as Elijah Muhammad, in 1934. Elijah Muhammad, declaring Fard to be Allah, took the title of Allah's messenger and taught an extremely unorthodox doctrine. This was that blacks had been usurped by the evil race of whites who were allowed to rule for thousands of years, at the end of which chaos would follow, from which would emerge a kingdom ruled by black people. Segregation of blacks from whites was advocated, as was abstinence from drink, pork, smoking and even cosmetics [12].

This radical doctrine was challenged by one of the organization's most charismatic representatives, Malcolm X. On his return from a *hajj* (pilgrimage) to Mecca, during which he discovered the incompatibility of the teachings of Elijah Muhammad with those of orthodox Islam, Malcolm X split with the Messenger of the Nation of Islam. It was an act for which he would pay with his life, but the momentum for change had been started. In 1975, ten years after the murder of Malcolm X, Wraithudden Muhammad, son of Elijah, took over the movement and eventually brought it into line with orthodox Islam. Changing its name to the American Muslim Mission, Wraithudden Muhammad, now an orthodox Muslim, opened up the membership to whites and renounced any separatist pretensions. However, many members of the Nation of Islam remained loyal to the teachings of Elijah Muhammad and, under the militant leadership of Louis Farrakhan, the Nation of Islam lives on. It remains a significant black radical religious group and, like its former organization, continues to attract African-American adherents who live in a society with a legacy of slavery and continuing racism [12].

African Diaspora Religion in Latin America and the Caribbean

African Diaspora Religions in the Caribbean

Introduction In contrast to the United States, African diaspora religions in the Caribbean and Latin America serve to express aspects of the Africanness of the descendants of former slaves. Unlike North America, Latin America and the Caribbean were colonized by predominantly Catholic countries. This provided the opportunity for African rituals and ideas to mingle with Catholic practices. Indeed, the conquest of the New World was a Catholic crusade within the context of the sixteenth-century Counter-Reformation which firmly established this religion in the major countries of Latin America and the Caribbean, such as Brazil, Mexico, Cuba, Haiti, the Dominican Republic and Puerto Rico. The former Dutch and British colonies in the region are predominantly Protestant countries, yet the refusal to convert slaves to mainstream Christianity has enabled nonconformist and syncretist traditions to fill the void in these islands too. Nonconformist churches, such as the Baptist, Methodist and Pentecostal, are found in the former British colonies such as Jamaica and Barbados. These are the most important Christian churches among blacks in the Caribbean. Like the other nonconformist churches, Pentecostalism is a popular, charismatic grouping with a distinctive style of worship. Worship through songs, conversion, faith-healing, speaking in tongues and ecstatic experiences of the Spirit are all part of the evangelical spirit which was derived from the United States, fired by fundamentalist missionaries. However, other, non-Christian, religions are also of significance in the Caribbean. These religions are derived from the African slave legacy and express those aspects of African culture which remain throughout the Caribbean. The religions described below are the most influential in the region, but they are by no means the only such religions.

Santeria Of the many religions in the Caribbean to make direct reference to African culture, Cuban Santeria is perhaps the most significant. Many aspects of Yoruba rites feature in this religion, which is a syncretic mix of Catholicism and Yoruba. Deities and holy figures from each are identified with one another, integrating the two religious traditions. Thus, for example, the Shango god of thunder becomes St Barbara; Orunmila, of divination, becomes St Francis; Obatala is Our Lady of Mercy; Elegba is St Peter. The life and power of the gods reside in stones secured beneath the altar. Animal sacrifice and spirit-possession are also elements of Santeria. Fidel Castro's repression of religion makes it difficult to assess the number of adherents to Santeria [27].

Voodoo Voodoo is burdened with an extremely sinister reputation as a religion replete with heathen, supernatural and evil practices. It is perceived by many to be the very antithesis of Christianity. Indeed, reference to this religion is rarely made without emphasis upon its darker side. This means that the central role Voodoo, and similar African folk religions, plays in the lives of the people of the Caribbean is generally overlooked [28]. The traditional view of Voodoo is that it is a syncretic mix of African and Catholic religion which is predominantly found in Haiti. Voodoo has indeed been exploited by most of Haiti's leaders. François Duvalier, who was president of Haiti from 1957 until his death in 1971, used the religion both to stifle dissent and to win the support of poor Haitians.

Duvalier was able to use Voodoo in this way because it is so deeply embedded in the ordinary everyday religious life of the people as a whole. The positive role Voodoo plays in the lives of Haitians must, however, be understood alongside its more negative aspects.

Voodoo owes its origins to the Benin religion, from which it derived its name. Brought over with slaves to the Caribbean, the religion can be found throughout the region. Its predominance in Haiti is accounted for by the brutal plantation colony run by the French. In this extremely oppressive environment 25,000 slaves died every year. This high mortality meant that more slaves went to Haiti than anywhere else; 300,000 in the last twenty years of the colony's existence. Voodoo sustained many through this extreme oppression and became the organizing principle of the eighteenth-century slave rebellions. The defeat of the French and the creation of the first independent black state in the New World in 1804 was an extraordinary achievement. However, the centrality of Voodoo to this success has fixed its notoriety in Western minds.

Like many African religions, Voodoo emphasizes human relationships, both between the living and the deceased (especially the ancestors), and with invisible deities and spirits, with whom humans are in constant interaction. Life is considered holistically, and the religion is closely associated with traditional African conceptions of health and sickness, good and evil. As a consequence, in ritual worship spirit-possession, animal sacrifice and music and dance feature prominently. The holistic approach to life is reflected in the importance attached to the natural cycle of life and death. The fear of Zombies is evidence of this importance. People who have had their souls stolen by sorcery are described as Zombies in Voodoo tradition. Those so affected have committed crimes against society and are placed in a state of perpetual purgatory, where they cannot complete the natural cycle of life and death, as a form of retribution. The fear is not of Zombies, but of becoming one. Its power as a social sanction depends not on how often it has occurred, but that it can occur and has done.

To dwell upon Voodoo's sanctions is to misunderstand its positive role in Caribbean society. The real power of Voodoo lies in its capacity for good, in particular for healing. Traditional Voodoo cures remove bad spirits (called the 'spirits of death') which cause sickness and death. Traditional healing is claimed to be as effective as modern medicine, and is especially important in an impoverished society such as Haiti where access to good modern medicine is denied to many. Traditional healers and priests remain accessible to even the poorest in Haitian society. In a society where there is a massive discrepancy in wealth between the poor majority and the tiny, rich, ruling elite, Voodoo is one of the few common languages, expressing the sense of shared Haitian identity [28].

The Rastafarian movement The Rastafarian movement is one of the most important religious movements among people of African descent, both in the Caribbean and wherever black communities are to be found. It has also had a dramatic impact upon the wider societies and cultures with which it has come into contact. In Britain during the 1970s, for example, the Rastafarian movement became a key symbol of black youth identity and had both a negative and a positive effect upon British society as a whole. The perception of the Rastafarian movement includes that of a deviant phenomenon, Rasta adherents being closely associated with drug-taking and trafficking. By the 1970s, nevertheless, it was a hugely popular religion among both black and white youth, with reggae music at the centre of British popular culture. Yet the world-wide adoption of Rastafari belies its Caribbean context.

The Rastafarian movement is a millenarian movement; its adherents believe that a process of transformation is to be engineered and executed by a supernatural agency. Its origins stems from the work of the Jamaican Marcus Garvey, who established the Universal Negro Improvement Association in 1914. This organization was the vehicle for Garvey's aim to return blacks to Africa. His organization was active in both the United States and Jamaica for two decades, spreading his message that the evil system of colonialism had scattered blacks all over the world where they were unable to express themselves fully, intellectually and culturally. The restoration of their lost pride was to be brought about, in Garvey's opinion, by a complete rupture with the white world and the return of blacks to Africa, which for Garvey was synonymous with Ethiopia. Nevertheless he failed in his stated aim, with neither black Americans nor Jamaicans taking up his invitation to return to Africa [4].

Crucially, Garvey's doctrine depicted evil as not only the white race which continued to subordinate black people, but also blacks themselves who accepted this inferiority. Evil lay both inside and outside black people. Garvey argued that blacks had to recognize their potential. To achieve this, people had to awake from a slumber of centuries to a life revealed through God. Garvey's conviction that this 'awakening' was to occur in the near future and would result in a social transformation in which all blacks would gravitate to a great African homeland survived the decline of his organization and his death in 1940. Despite Garvey's failure, by the early 1930s groups of Jamaicans had been inspired by his doctrine, none more so than early Rastafarian leaders. A great deal of mythology surrounds Garvey and his alleged words, 'Look to Africa when a Black king shall be crowned, for the day of deliverance is near.' Nevertheless, this phrase served to create a new belief-system [4]. In November 1930 the Prince Regent, Ras ('Prince') Tafari, was crowned as

Emperor Haile Selassie of Ethiopia. This event coincided with Garvey's attempts to generate interest in the Ethiopian royalty and at the same time it was perceived as portending a transformation in which colonial rule would be overthrown and blacks returned to Ethiopia. These ideas coincided with a world economic depression, which helped to create the powerful idea of a symbolic millennial return to the paradise of Ethiopia. The symbolic importance of Ethiopia stemmed from its being the only black-ruled state in existence at a time of universal European colonization of African territories and subjection of black peoples. In the early 1930s Rastafarians took on Garvey's blueprint. Though the Rastafarian movement is considered to be at variance with Garvey's own set of beliefs, his teaching remains the key influence upon this black religion [4].

By the time Haile Selassie was overthrown in 1974 the beliefs and symbolism of the Rastafarian movement had been more or less established, as had its anti-establishment reputation. The modern characteristics of the Rastafarian movement include a loosely defined belief-system due to its lack of a single authoritative voice. This is in contrast to its early years, with Leopold Howells, Archibald Dunkley and Nathaniel Hibbert active before the Second World War and Claudius Henry after it. During this later period the Rastafarian movement became strongly associated with intrigue, violence and revolution in Jamaica. Ironically, these events helped to create great interest in the movement and to imbue it with a political dimension: it became the voice of the oppressed Jamaican. It is this perspective which served to propagate Rastafarian beliefs, symbols, motifs and emblems across the world. In Jamaica, the use of Rastafarian symbols by the Premier Michael Manley in his 1972 and 1976 election campaigns, during which the reggae artist Bob Marley played concerts on his behalf, indicated both the incorporation of the Rastafarian movement into Jamaican identity and its wider popularity within the majority black population [4]. Since then the Rastafarian movement has become a universal language of aspiration in Jamaica and the wider New World alike.

The number of Rastafarians in Jamaica is estimated to be about 100,000 [29]. Within Rastafarian belief God is both a deity and inherent in all people. The acceptance of Ras Tafari as a living manifestation of God is a central aspect of adherents' belief. Lacking in central authority, Rastafarians are unable to organize themselves on sectarian models; indeed, the membership is more appropriately described as a loose aggregation. Yet the Rastafarian movement has a shared and clear conception of evil as embodied in the white colonial system, described as 'Babylon'. The shared focus on the source of evil and on the perceived ways of alleviating it is universal throughout the movement. Rastafarians regard themselves as a very exclusive and elite body of people, admittance being restricted to those who accept the divinity of Haile Selassie. This emphasis upon the individual has made the Rastafarian movement appear extremely enigmatic to observers, but is perhaps the reason for the success of its world-wide propagation and its continuing survival [4].

African Diaspora Religions in Latin America

Latin American, like Caribbean, religion is influenced by both Christianity and African classical religions. Brazil reflects this mix clearly, with large numbers of the poorer parts of the population, who are predominantly of African slave origin, adopting non-Christian religions. As in the Caribbean, the non-Christian religions described below are probably the most important in Brazil, but do not constitute an exhaustive list.

Winti Winti, also known as Alfodré, is a folk religion practised by the Creole population in Surinam. Some do not describe this as a syncretic religion, but instead see Christianity and Winti as juxtaposed, with adherents of Winti behaving in certain contexts as sincere Christians. This might be explained by the predominance of Protestantism in Surinam as a consequence of the work by Moravian missionaries.

Winti is of African origin, however, and is a spirit-possession cult which deals with everyday concerns including illness and misfortune. Winti conceives the world as being replete with various spirits and forces in the classical African way. These wintis – deities – and also spirits of the dead need to be honoured and placated, and their help can be sought. The intervention of these deities in human affairs is frequent; they communicate with the participants in the rite by means of the possession of male and female mediums. The rites are usually overseen by the bonoeman, a religious mediator, who has a supervisory role and is skilled in traditional medicine. Winti is also practised within Surinamese communities in the Netherlands. A religion akin to Winti, but with a more systematic African expression, is practised by the descendants of African slaves who are isolated in the interior of Surinam [3].

Candomblé Candomblé is the name of a religion which, like Voodoo, came to Brazil with African slaves. Recognized as a religion during the nineteenth century in the states of Bahía, Maranhão and Pernambuco, it too has come to represent a universal language among African Brazilians who are largely from the most underprivileged groups in Brazil's society. It is known as Shango, the Yoruba god of thunder, in Pernambuco; Macumba in Rio, in the south-east of Brazil; Tambor de Mina in Maranhão; Nagô in Pajelança; and Catimbó or Batuque in the central regions of Brazil. These diverse names reflect the local specificity of this African folk religion. Far from tending towards cohesion, the different congregations have remained independent of each other. This reflects Candomblé's origins as the continuation in Brazil of African traditional religions, centred upon worship and the rites of spirit-possession.

Candomblé is syncretic in that it mixes (some would say juxtaposes) African and Roman Catholic beliefs, such as African deities with Catholic saints. Amerindian beliefs have also been incorporated, though to a lesser extent. As with other African folk religions, the relationship with the deceased (especially the ancestors) and the constant interaction with invisible deities and spirits, are central features of Candomblé. In Bahía women hold an important role as mediums of the Yoruba gods. These cults endured considerable persecution in both the late nineteenth and the mid-twentieth centuries. Today they have a significant following; now legal, participation in them is fully recognized [3].

Umbanda Umbanda is often described as an African Brazilian folk religion. However, unlike Candomblé, it is not confined to the poorest groups in north-east Brazil. Found in the south of Brazil, its members are more affluent and many are from Euro-Brazilian communities. Established in the early twentieth century, Umbanda is a much more cohesive and better-organized movement than Candomblé, producing publications to promote its cause. The 200,000 adherents also have significant political influence, with members in local and central government. At election time the support of this religion is seen as an important electoral prize. However, although attempts have been made to create a federation out of the various congregations throughout the country, as with Candomblé this has been largely unsuccessful, and Umbanda congregations remain independent of each other.

Umbanda is described as a syncretic religion which incorporates African, Amerindian and Catholic features. In terms of both content and membership, less emphasis is placed on African traditional religion than in Candomblé. However, spirit-worship forms an important element of this religion. Ritual includes placating harmful spirits through sacrifice to numerous deities. The belief in reincarnation is also a salient part of Umbanda. Reincarnation, in either a higher or a lower economic position, is one of the major forms of social sanction. Favourable or unfavourable rebirth is thought to give reward or punishment for conduct in this life. Belief in reincarnation is closely associated with the spiritualism of Allan Kardec and Kardecismo [3].

Conclusion With, perhaps, the exception of Umbanda, the adherents of the non-Christian Caribbean and Latin American African-derived cults summarized above come from the poorest sections of their country's population. As is the case in the United States, the United Kingdom and even Africa, poverty and racism are strong catalysts for the growth of these alternative religious groupings. It would be a mistake, however, to focus on this negative image to account for the popularity of these African diaspora religions. They also play a very important role in creating a sense of cohesion, of belonging and identity in communities which, in many cases, consist merely of the dispossessed. They also help to create a sense of status and purpose for sections of the population, for example women, who would not otherwise receive equivalent opportunities. To view these diaspora religions as bizarre or even dangerous, as many observers do, particularly in the case of Santeria, Rastafari and Voodoo, is to misunderstand their vital role as a central feature of the identity of the countries in which they are found. That they evoke the past should not mislead one to think that they are not part of the future of both the Caribbean and Latin America.

African Diaspora Religion in Britain

Background

People of African origin have been resident in Britain for more than four centuries. However, for the majority of this period they were few in number. Nevertheless, these early 'black Britons' were active Christians as members of mainstream and nonconformist churches. There has been a black Pentecostal independent church in London since 1908 [10]. However, significant black congregations were only formed with mass immigration, mainly from the British Caribbean, which began in 1948. Britain was facing a labour shortage in its service industries, such as health and transport, at this time and encouraged West Indians to migrate to Britain with the promise of work in these industries, which were less popular with white workers, in the major industrial conurbations of London, Birmingham, Manchester, Leeds and Bristol [24].

The proliferation of independent organizations within the British black church movement can be partly accounted for by the Caribbean Christian experience which the migrants brought with them and the rejection of migrant Christians by the white established churches. The prevalent racism within the established church, combined with a method of worship perceived as sober and boring, drove migrant Christians away from white-led churches.

The consequence was the phenomenal growth of black-led churches in Britain. According to Roswith Gerloff [11], by 1990 there were approximately 1,000 assemblies and initiatives in 300 organizations in Britain. These assemblies are thought to have 70,000 members and an estimated 120,000 adherents. The growth rate of black churches in Britain is thought to be 103 per cent from 1970 to 1985, or 113 per cent from 1970 to 1990: approximately 5 per cent annually since 1970. This phenomenal growth far exceeds that for other denominations, and is attributable to a number of factors. In the 1970s continuing immigration helped to build congregations. Once immigration had been curtailed by legislation, these churches continued to grow as a result of natural growth among the under-12 and over-35 age groups. Finally, the churches also received 'converts' from established churches. The vast majority of people who have joined these churches are of African descent [11].

The Caribbean and African Diaspora in Britain

Today Britain, like other European nations that had a colonial empire, has an ethnically diverse population. The rich cultural traditions brought to Britain with migrants from the former colonies are now a feature of British identity. You will find people from white, African Caribbean and African Christian traditions on the same street in London and in Britain's other major cities. Black and minority ethnic communities make up 20 per cent of London's population. Similar proportions apply to Britain's other major conurbations. Furthermore, while white church-goers number a mere 1 or 2

Table 20.3 London's population by racial group, 1991

Racial group	No.
White	5,490,000
Indian	362,000
African Caribbean	304,000
Black African	170,000
Other	128,000
Other Asian	118,000
Pakistani	88,000
Black Other	85,000
Bangladeshi	85,000
Chinese	59,000
Total	6,889,000

Source: London Research Centre.

per cent of the total white population, the dynamism among African Caribbean Christians is such that 20 per cent of their communities are churchgoers [11]. A significant proportion of these are adherents of the black independent churches.

One vital role played by the independent churches is the affirmation of the cultural identity of their congregations. These churches are representative of the diverse theological traditions which have come to the United Kingdom with people of African, African-Caribbean and North American descent. It is important to remember that no black Christian church in modern Britain is directly the result of white Christian mission. It is true that white American headquarters or white American mission agencies were active in the Caribbean; yet the Caribbean churches established an indigenous black leadership of their own long before their arrival in the United Kingdom. Free from the subservience of being 'overseen' by a white authority, these churches have grown in a climate in which the established churches rejected members from the Caribbean purely on the grounds of race. In an environment where the black communities have felt the full force of poverty and deprivation, these independent churches have proved especially appealing. Consequently the Native, Revival, Holiness, Adventist or Pentecostal traditions, in being transplanted to Britain, have themselves been transformed by coming into contact with people whose needs are influenced by their experience as British citizens. Meeting those needs has meant that these Christian traditions have been made anew and become an important part of the British Christian tradition [13].

Black Theologies in Britain

It is not possible to talk about the black church movement in Britain as if it were a single entity. The diversity of denominational and national backgrounds of migrants and the contexts in which they now find themselves is mirrored by the variety of theological expression in the United Kingdom. Gerloff has identified eleven different independent black traditions, some of them further subdivided, some intermingling and creating new families [11]. Each has had to come to terms with British society and, as a consequence, develop a new theology. These new theologies both transform British society and are themselves transformed in turn.

The Pentecostal movement The Pentecostal movement, by far the largest group of African-Caribbean Christians, is directly related to the Azusa Street Revival under the leadership of William J. Seymour in Los Angeles from 1906. This reasserted African elements in African American Christianity, of which two characteristics are 'speaking in tongues', believed to include actual languages given to improve communication between God and people, and divine healing, understood as redemption of the individual and the community [11]. Today several groups belong to the National Association of Evangelicals in the United States and to the World Council of Churches. The largest multi-congregational Pentecostal body in the United States is the Assemblies of God, with an inclusive membership of about 2.1 million in 1988. Today the Pentecostal movement is spread over the world; it is particularly strong in South America and has an estimated 500,000 adherents in Russia and states formerly within the USSR.

Gerloff has identified three different families of the black Pentecostal movement in Britain. The family with the largest number of adherents is the Trinitarian Pentecostals. This organization is subdivided into those who teach a 'two-stage-crisis experience', in the Assemblies of God tradition, and those who teach a 'three-stage-crisis experience', in the Church of God tradition. The former group is small in Britain because of the racist policies of the white American Assemblies of God movement; it had little impact in the Caribbean, only reaching Britain via the indigenous movement called Pentecostal Assemblies of the West Indies. The latter group has the largest percentage of African-Caribbean Christian adherents in Britain. Their teaching is represented by two sister organizations, the New Testament Church of God, a name adopted in Jamaica from the Church of God, Cleveland, and the Church of God of Prophecy. Both these organizations have their headquarters in Cleveland, Tennessee [11; 13]. Today the leadership of the New Testament Church of God in Britain is younger and more radical. As a result, these organizations have become more concerned with current political, social and racial issues, in contrast to the policies adopted by their white American headquarters. Many smaller splinter organizations are connected with the indigenous black headquarters in Jamaica, such as the New Testament Assemblies and the Assemblies of the First Born. The oldest and largest, the Calvary Church of God Christ in Nottingham, has long had links with the oldest black Pentecostal tradition in African America. Members of the Church of God in Britain have replaced earlier usage with an evangelical language of their own which better reflects their social and political needs. Trinitarian Pentecostal churches have been members of the Afro-West Indian Council of Churches since 1977 [11].

The second family of black Pentecostals in Britain is the Oneness (Apostolic) Pentecostals. This organization also has connections with the Azusa Street Revival, and was popular among the black and urban poor in the United States. It was adopted by the rural poor in the Caribbean, especially in Jamaica, and is also popular in Latin America [11]. In the United Kingdom approximately one-third of all Pentecostals are members of this movement. The movement's outreach work, ecumenical relations and community projects mean that it is still attracting adherents. The largest member churches are the First United Church of Jesus Christ (Apostolic), the Bibleway Church of Our Lord Jesus World-wide, and the Shiloh United Church of Christ Apostolic (World-wide).

The third black Pentecostal family is the Revival (Healing) Pentecostals. This movement is influenced by American healing evangelists such as A. A. Allen, Oral Roberts, Morris Cerullo and others. It may also have been influenced by the Latter Rain Movement, which teaches a new kind of revivalism different from the Caribbean indigenous religion. In Britain congregations in London, Nottingham and Ireland worship at churches such as Latter Rain Outpouring and Miracle Revival Fellowship. Gerloff has found that healing campaigns unite black and white interracially more easily than other activities [11].

The African Methodist Episcopal The African Methodist Episcopal (AME) and the African Methodist Episcopal Zion (AMEZ) are the parent organizations of numerous African-American independent churches. They were formed as the first Christian protest movement against inequality and racial discrimination within North American Methodism at the beginning of the nineteenth century. While both the AME and the AMEZ can be described as 'African' in leadership and outreach, they retain the original Methodist doctrine and liturgy. Though they had a considerable impact in South America and South Africa, in comparison to Pentecostalism they have not had a similar effect in the United Kingdom. Of the two, the AMEZ has the larger presence in Britain. Its relative success is thought to derive from its tolerance of charismatic features [11].

Revivalist and Spiritual Baptists The Great Jamaican Revival of 1861–2 created the first synthesis between African cultural symbols, including expressions such as shouting, dancing, dreams and visions, with the Christian message of deliverance. The British congregations are historically and theologically linked with the Native Baptist tradition led by figures such as George Liele and Moses Baker. Revivalist features were apparent in the 1970s in Britain within AMEZ and Church of God congregations in the West Midlands and London. Today Pentecostalism has absorbed this heritage by emphasis on the one Holy Spirit in the matter of spirit-possession. Spiritual Baptists are still flourishing, however. Originating in Trinidad, several Spiritual Baptist churches have joined the London-based United Council of Spiritual Baptist Churches [11].

Sabbatarians Three streams, the Seventh-day Baptists, the Seventh-day Adventists and the Church of God (Seventh Day) are represented in Sabbatarianism. The Seventh-day Baptists are one of the oldest nonconformist groups in England, beginning in the seventeenth century. With its proud history of religious liberty, Seventh-day Baptism was revived by Jamaican immigrants in Britain in the 1950s. However, the Seventh-day Baptists have a small presence in Britain in comparison with the Seventh-day Adventists, who form, alongside the Pentecostals, the largest African-Caribbean Christian group. The Adventists, with a history of opposition to racism in the United States in the nineteenth century, are followers of 'Third World' Adventism and form half the membership of the British Union Conference of Seventh-day Adventists. The African-Caribbean Seventh-day Adventist congregations have a community-orientated and socially innovative lay membership. This is in contrast to the British white bureaucratic administration, a difference which creates tension among the Seventh-day Adventists in Britain [11].

The Holiness Movement The Holiness Movement's history precedes that of Pentecostalism. The movement was formed when the Wesleyan Holiness Church split from the American Methodists in 1843 over the issues of the abolition of slavery, emancipation of women, poverty and non-hierarchical church structures. These ideas made this movement attractive to adherents in the Caribbean, and also to British congregations. In the 1970s the Wesleyan Holiness Church merged with Pilgrims. While still important in the West Indies, the movement's significance in Britain has waned [11].

African indigenous churches So far we have only described the main Caribbean-influenced Christian movements within the African diaspora in Britain. However, in Britain there is also a sizeable presence of African indigenous churches. These churches are divided into Nigerian and Ghanaian congregations and are found mainly in London. There are a few multi-cultural congregations such as the London Aladura International Church, Musama Disco Christo Church in Waterloo and the Church of Cherubim and Seraphim in Birmingham. The Ghanaian, Nigerian and multi-cultural congregations emphasize African cultural symbols such as dreams and visions, prayer for healing, dancing and water symbolism, alongside a straightforward social and ecumenical consciousness. These congregations are derived from the Nigerian Aladura and the Ghanaian Prophetic groups, each of which began as problem-solving and healing churches, similar to the African Caribbean Revivalist and Spiritual Baptist churches. The largest churches are Cherubim and

Seraphim, the Divine Prayer Society, the Church of Universal Prayer Fellowship and numerous Ghanaian assemblies.

In recent years the composition of the African population in Britain has changed. Refugees from East Africa, for example Somalia and Ethiopia, now make up a significant proportion of the African community. The African population in London is projected to double to nearly 400,000 by 2000. This will have an important impact upon black British religion. Alongside African indigenous churches and the Pentecostalist groups, an 'African' Islam will also become more common in the large cities of the United Kingdom. It remains to be seen whether the style of worship at African mosques – for example, oral liturgy, narrativity of theology, a high degree of participation in worship and decision-making and an urge for the salvation of the lives of individuals and communities – indicates that they are derived from a similar cultural and religious tradition as other African religions in Britain.

The British Rastafarian movement Much of what has been said about the Rastafarian movement in the Caribbean also applies to the United Kingdom. In Britain the movement, which merges religious/spiritual, artistic/cultural and radical political aspects, influenced African Caribbean youths in particular during the 1970s [4]. The association of black spiritual renewal with the politics of race and discrimination attracted many black British adherents who felt alienated by British society. Today, the popularity of the Rastafarian movement is long past its peak. It is impossible to assess the current number of adherents in Britain, but members of the Rastafarian movement can be found in all the major conurbations, such as Manchester, London and Birmingham. This religion, perhaps more than any other, served to create a universal language through which disparate populations of African-Caribbean descent could share beliefs and experiences and forge a common black British identity.

Conclusion

There are similarities between black religion in the United States and Britain. The Act of Toleration in 1689, after the 'Glorious Revolution' in Britain, guaranteed a Protestant religious tradition in much the same way as the First Amendment to the American Constitution, separating church from state, enabled a nonconformist tradition to develop in the United States. Both countries have dynamic black-led independent churches among their poorest regions. Along with their straightforward social and ecumenical consciousness, these churches play an important social and political role. However, in contrast to developments in the United States, a black British theology has yet to evolve. Indeed, despite there being a long history of an 'African' presence in Britain, the black experience has yet to emerge as an important dimension of British theology.

Bibliography

1 ALBANESE, C., *America: Religion and Religious*, California, Belmont, 1981
2 BARRETT, D. B. (ed.), *World Christian Encyclopaedia of Comparative Christian Religions*, Nairobi, Oxford University Press, 1982
3 BASTIDE, R., *The African Religions of Brazil*, Baltimore, Johns Hopkins University Press, 1978
4 CASHMORE, ERNEST, *'Rastaman': The Rastafarian Movement in England*, London, Allen & Unwin, 1983
5 CONE, J. H., *A Black Theology of Liberation*, Philadelphia, Lippincott, 1970
6 CONE, J. H., *Theology and Black Power*, New York, Seabury, 1969
7 CURTIN, P., FREIERMAN. S., THOMPSON, L., and VANSINA, J., *African History*, London, Longman, 1978
8 DICKSON, K., 'Towards a Theologia Africana', in M. E. Glasswell and E. Fasholé-Luke (eds), *New Testament Christianity for Africa and the World*, London, SPCK, 1974
9 ELLWOOD, R. S., *Religious and Spiritual Groups in Modern America*, Englewood Cliffs, Prentice-Hall, 1973
10 FRYER, P., *Staying Power*, London, Pluto Press, 1987
11 GERLOFF, R., *A Plea for British Black Theologies: The Black Church Movement in Britain in its Transatlantic Cultural and Theological Interaction*, Frankfurt am Main, Peter Lang, 1992
12 HADDAD, Y. Y., *A Century of Islam in America*, Washington, DC, Islamic Affairs Program, Middle East Institute, 1986
13 HOWARD, V., *A Report on Afro-Caribbean Christianity in Britain*, Leeds, University of Leeds Department of Theology and Religious Studies, 1987
14 KABASELE, F., et al., *Chemins de la christologie africaine*, Paris, 1986
15 KAIROS DOCUMENT, *A Theological Comment on the Political Crisis in South Africa*, London, 1986
16 KALILOMBE, P., 'Black Theology', in D. F. Ford (ed.), *The Modern Theologians: An Introduction to Christian Theology in the Twentieth Century*, Oxford, Blackwell, 1995, vol. 2
17 KALILOMBE, P., 'Doing Theology at the Grassroots: A Challenge for Professional Theologians', *The African Ecclesial Review*, vol. 27, 1985, pp. 148–61, 225–37
18 KRETZSCHMAR, L., *The Voice of Black Theology in South Africa*, Johannesburg, Ravan Press, 1986
19 LINCOLN, C. E., and MAMIYA, L. H., *The Black Church in the Afro-American Experience*, Durham, NC, Duke University Press, 1990

20 MBITI, J. S., *African Religion and Philosophy*, Garden City, NY, Praeger, 1970

21 MILINGO, E., *The World In Between*, London, 1984

22 MOORE, B., *The Challenge of Black Theology in South Africa*, London, 1974

23 POBEE, J. S., *Toward an African Theology*, Nashville, Abingdon, 1979

24 RAMDIN, R., *The Making of a Black Working Class in Britain*, Aldershot, Wildwood House, 1988

25 ROBERTS, D. J., *Black Theology in Dialogue*, Philadelphia, Westminster Press, 1980

26 ROBERTS, D. J.., *A Black Political Theology*, Philadelphia, Westminster Press, 1974

27 SIMPSON, G. E., *Religious Cults of the Caribbean: Trinidad, Jamaica and Haiti*, London, 1980

28 SINGER, A., and SINGER, A., *Divine Magic: The World of the Supernatural*, London, Box Tree, 1996

29 SMART, N., *The World's Religions*, Cambridge, Cambridge University Press, 1995

30 TURNER, H. W., 'New Studies of New Movements: Some Publications on Independent Churches since 1973', *Journal of Religion in Africa*, vol. 11, no. 2, 1980, pp. 121–33

31 TUTU, D., 'Whither African Theology?', in E. Fasholé-Luke et al. (eds), *Christianity in Independent Africa*, London, Rex Collins, 1978

32 WILMORE, G. S., *Black Religion and Black Radicalism*, Maryknoll, Orbis, 1983

21

The Australian South Asian Diaspora

PURUSHOTTAMA BILIMORIA

Introduction: A Historical Overview of Migration

A general perception persists that South Asian migration to Australia is a post-1960s phenomenon. In fact, it began in the early nineteenth century, when some Indian servants boarded trading ships or accompanied their European masters to Australia, and a few Ceylonese (Sri Lankans) sailed on convict ships, destined for the penal colony [7]. When labour was sought for the opening up of the hinterlands, tribesmen from Chotanagpur were successfully recruited. As more workers arrived they dispersed into adjacent states. Official apprehension towards Indian cultural practices saw Indian 'coolie' labour restricted following the Indian Emigration Act of 1839. Nevertheless a few itinerant merchants and 200 Anglo-Indian apprentices arrived subsequently.

Among the migrants, Hindus outnumbered Muslims and Sikhs from Punjab; a Parsi was recorded in the 1881 census [2]. After the 1850s came the 'Ghans' (short for Afghans). Though dubbed 'Hindoos' (i.e. coloured Indian nationals), they were turbaned Pathans or Punjabi Muslims from the North-West Frontier provinces, camel men who came to support explorers crossing the deserts westward. Later, some ventured to the goldfields and a few gained pastoral work, while others became hawkers and pedlars in rural outposts and a handful managed caravanserais.

Opposition to the introduction of Asian labourers on cotton and sugar-cane plantations in Queensland led to the 1862 Indian Coolie Act, restricting the intake of Indian labour. The Sikh workers went south to settle in the coastal towns of New South Wales, where they later established a significant presence, with the first Sikh shrine in Australia. A few free immigrants took up work in banana plantations in the 1880s, including 500 Sinhalese who warded off a violent protest against their arrival from local Anglo-Australian residents [9]. Only a few spouses were permitted entry.

The total number of ethnic South Asians in Australia rose from a few hundred in 1857 (the year of the Indian Mutiny) to approximately 4,500 in the entire continent-colony at the turn of the century.

The 'White Australia' Policy

Australia's entry into the twentieth century was marked by anti-Asian xenophobia. Bitter opposition to the presence of coloured labourers intensified; though directed in particular at the Chinese, it affected Indian workers. Disturbances in other Crown colonies, and a near diplomatic impasse between India and Australia, did not help. The 1901 Immigration Restriction Act effectively promulgated the infamous White Australia policy. Racial exclusiveness was one way of asserting the superiority of the 'white race' and its presumed supporting religious base, Christianity. This made it impossible for all but a handful of students, travellers and merchants on temporary permits to enter Australia, while the entry of women and dependants almost ceased. The 1911 population census counted a mere 3,698 'Hindoos', including their Australian-born offspring. Employment became increasingly hard to obtain. In 1914 Totaram Sanadhya, a Hindu activist returning to India from Fiji, commented

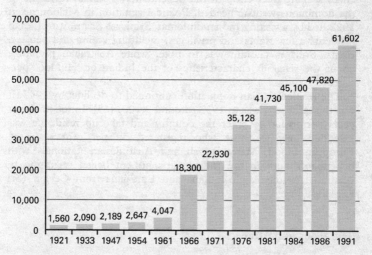

Figure 21.1 *Indians migrating to Australia: cumulative numbers, 1921–1991*

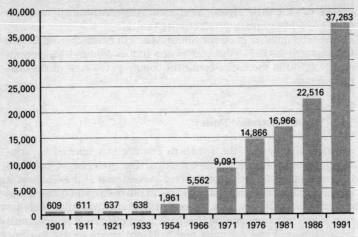

Figure 21.2 *Numbers of Sri Lankans arriving in Australia,*
1901–1991

on the absence of community cohesion and religious identity among
the Indians scattered in different parts of Australia. Most Indians
survived by intermarrying and assimilating with the host society. By
1921 there were barely 2,200 South Asians in Australia.

Submissions by Mahatma Gandhi and others at imperial conferences seeking freer entry of the dependants of Indian residents to
the dominions went unheeded. Political agitation in Melbourne in
1922, led by a visiting Indian diplomat, Srinivasa Sastri, won Indian
residents a few rights and privileges, including voting and pension
rights. Still, as Gandhi was to note, white Australian prejudice
about the religious characteristics of the Indian or 'Hindoo' persisted.

The resident Indian population continued to decline: by 1947, it
was the same as it was in 1933 (around 2,100) [13]. In the post-war
years permission to enter the country and take up residence was
extended only to those who registered 50 per cent or more
European blood. Many British and Australasian nationals with
dependants born in the Indian subcontinent began migrating to
Australia, as did Anglo-Indians and Eurasians from Ceylon (Sri
Lanka).

The 1960s and After

Indian media and Asian leaders persistently criticized Australia's
'white-as-snow' ideology. Australian intellectuals, too, voiced

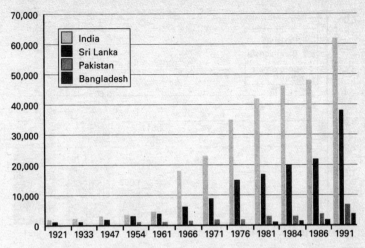

Figure 21.3 *South Asian migrants to Australia, by year of arrival and country of origin, 1921–1991*

increasing concerns on humanitarian grounds, which intensified during the Vietnam War. Other Western nations had already begun to liberalize their immigration policies. This had a benign influence on Australian attitudes towards non-white immigration. Colonialism was over and Australia could not afford to strain trading relations with the dominant Western nations by its stance on non-white people. The White Australia policy was therefore abandoned in the early 1970s; and although reservations about admitting people with 'different standards of living, tradition and culture' have persisted in some quarters, the official change of policy marked a turning-point in the migration of South Asians. A more relaxed stance on immigration and new opportunities facilitated the arrival of professionals, such as doctors, engineers, teachers and technicians. Between 1954 and 1971, Sri Lankan-born immigration to Australia increased significantly among both the major ethnic groups, Sinhalese and Tamil. Dutch Burghers and Eurasians of mixed Sinhalese and Dutch, Portuguese or British descent also arrived in large numbers. By 1986 Sri Lankan-born residents numbered 22,516 (see figure 21.2). In 1982, 850 Sri Lankans arrived in Australia; the average annual intake between 1989 and 1991 was approximately 3,200.

The proportion of Christians arriving from Sri Lanka remained higher than those of Buddhists and Hindus, although the proportion of Hindus increased after civil unrest in Sri Lanka during the 1980s. These differences in proportion reflected, especially among

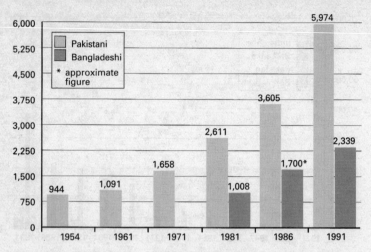

Figure 21.4 *Pakistani and Bangladeshi migrants to Australia, 1954–1991*

Burghers and Sinhalese Christians, the uncertainty that followed independence, and Tamil disenchantment with a predominantly Sinhalese regime.

Migration from Pakistan remained small in comparison to that from Sri Lanka: the total number of Pakistan migrants grew from 1,000 in the 1950s to over 3,000 in the 1980s. Most of the incomers were Urdu-speaking Muslims; only a handful were Christians, Sikh Punjabis and Sindhi Hindus. The Bangladeshi population was recorded separately at around 1,008 in 1981; most were Muslims, with some Hindus and Christians [14]. This trend continued into the 1990s as employment and educational opportunities attracted more urban, middle-class migrants.

The largest among the subcontinental immigrant groups is that of Indians. In the 1960s, the numbers increased markedly. By 1971 there were 22,930; by 1991, the Indian-born population in Australia reached 61,602 [8]. (These figures, of course, include people of European descent born in India.) Including migrants from other regions of the subcontinent, namely Sri Lanka, Pakistan, Nepal and Bangladesh, there was a 320 per cent increase in migration from South Asia in just two decades after the abolition of the White Australia policy. Figures for all South Asian arrivals (at airports) of permanent residents continued to show a steady increase, from 7,000 in 1989 to 11,000 in 1991 [8].

People of Indian ancestry came not only from the subcontinent but also from Malaysia, Singapore, Fiji, Mauritius, the UK and

New Zealand. There was an upsurge in arrivals following political disturbances in East Africa during the 1970s. Two military-style coups in Fiji in the late 1980s and political upheavals in Sri Lanka and South Africa attracted more people to the safer haven of Australia. These immigrants have tended to be wealthy and resourceful, and thus able to secure good employment, or set up lucrative businesses, and procure homes in 'blue ribbon' suburbs.

The 1991 Census

The 1991 census recorded numbers of people by birthplace from South Asian regions as follows: India 61,602; Sri Lanka 37,318; Pakistan 5,974; Bangladesh 2,339; Bhutan, Nepal and the Maldives together 1,239. Discounting people of European descent, and adding those of the second generation, born in Australia – 15,000 of Indian ancestry and 2,500 of Sinhalese descent – along with migrants of South Asian descent born in other parts of the world and their Australian-born offspring, we arrive at a total of 125,300 as the upper limit for people of South Asian origins domiciled in Australia up to 1995.

South Asians are, on average, much younger than the European Australian population, 83 per cent having arrived after 1981; 50 per cent of them are in the 25–44 age group, compared with 31 per cent of the population as a whole. Correspondingly, there is a higher

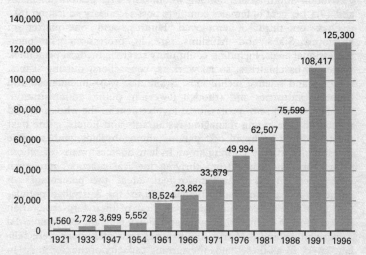

Figure 21.5 *Numbers of people of South Asian ancestry in Australia, 1921–1995*

proportion of children between one and fourteen years of age than in the population as a whole. The majority tend to be married, the proportion being higher than in the Australian population (65 per cent compared with 53 per cent); Hindus, Sikhs and Muslims have a lower rate of de facto relationship (the legal term used to describe two adults living together in a relationship on a par with that of a married couple), and they also have a low divorce rate of between 2 and 3 per cent, compared with almost 5 per cent in the European Australian population. This also accounts for lower numbers of one-parent families among South Asian immigrants.

Education is highly valued by South Asian immigrants. People of Indian and Sri Lankan descent are among the highest-qualified groups in Australia, after Jewish and non-diaspora Chinese (that is, those who have become acculturated, speak only or mainly English and have no persisting connections with China). Among the former, Hindus are the most highly qualified: 20 per cent of them hold at least a bachelor's degree, and a further 10 per cent have postgraduate qualifications, compared with 12.8 per cent for the total Australian population. Overall, the men have a higher level of education than the women – in a ratio of 3:2 for post-secondary qualifications. However, a much higher proportion of South Asian women, especially of Indian ancestry, have such qualifications, including university degrees, than is the case in the Australian population as a whole, including other overseas-born groups. But the high educational profile is not maintained among the second-generation South Asians, among whom only 17.2 per cent of males and 17.1 per cent of females complete post-secondary education [8].

Over one-third of employed Hindus, and one-quarter of employed Sikhs and Muslims, are in professional or para-professional areas, including community services: medical personnel, surgeons, psychiatrists, social workers, counsellors, nursing sisters, teachers and science technicians. Some also work in financial and property industries and (though fewer) in public administration. Managerial and semi-professional involvement in the wholesale and retail trade, including managing restaurants and hotels, is the next most favoured group of occupations among Indians, with sizeable investments usually coming from Indian doctors, many of whom divert surplus income from thriving medical practices into such enterprises. In all these employment areas the percentages of participants are significantly higher than for the Australian population as a whole. Not surprisingly in view of their former agrarian background in Punjab, Malaysia and Fiji, Sikhs are also employed in agriculture and forestry. About 5 per cent of Indians were self-employed. In all these fields the earning capacity of the South Asian migrants is higher than that of the Australian population as a whole.

For all Indians, female representation in community services is higher than for males. However, fewer women hold higher specialist qualifications (such as surgeons, paediatricians, psychiatrists), the majority being nurses, occupational therapists, counsellors, teachers and librarians. Among all South Asian women, however, Sri Lankan Buddhist and Hindu women (regardless of place of origin) have a proportionally higher-level occupational record in the professional sector.

A higher percentage of Hindus than of all other religious groups except Jews claim an annual income in excess of $50,000, which makes Hindus and Sri Lankan Buddhists among the most affluent groups of all South Asian immigrants. Jains and South Asian Muslims, though fewer in number, have relatively the same levels of education and income as their Hindu and Buddhist counterparts. However, some Muslim women are more restricted in their movement outside the home than Hindu and Jain women. Forty-nine per cent of Sikh families claim an annual income greater than $40,000.

Unemployment among South Asian migrants is relatively low. However, since 1986 the situation has changed due to an increased intake of migrants from all regions of South Asia who may not possess qualifications currently in demand in Australia. The 1990s recession led well-qualified immigrants to seek employment in trading stores, warehouses, factories, transport and restaurants. By the mid-1990s there was a significant increase in the number of Indian immigrants joining computer software and advanced electronic industries.

The generally high level of education is also reflected in the high

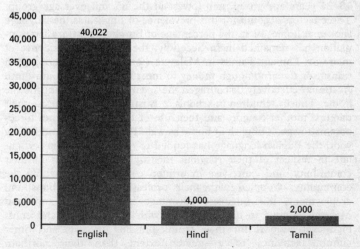

Figure 21.6 Language spoken at home by Indian-born migrants, 1991

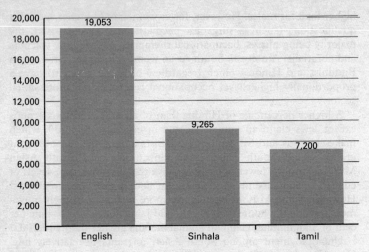

Figure 21.7 *Language spoken at home by Sri Lanka-born migrants, 1991*

proportion of South Asian migrants who indicated speaking English at home in comparison to the smaller proportion who indicated speaking a regional language at home. The percentage of those who speak only English is high: approximately 22 per cent or 10,000 in the total Sri Lankan population. It is proportionately largest in the 15–24 years age group, and lowest in the 65 and over age group. Three factors account for this prevalence of English as the language spoken at home. First, the percentage of Burgher and Eurasian population has remained high. Secondly, the short-term residence of many Sri Lankan Tamils in Malaysia (for safety, education, or in transit; or to earn enough money to meet the criteria for entry into Australia) effectively discouraged the speaking of Tamil outside the home. Thirdly, children in schools in Australia tend not to use their parents' mother tongue, and their use of English sometimes forces parents to speak English at home as well. Proficiency in, and facility with, the English language has tended to make Sri Lankans articulate in respect of their religious identity and the needs of their community, and expressive in printed communication within the community. Coupled with their professional qualifications and employment, this linguistic advantage has enabled Tamil and Malayali Hindus to deal effectively with bureaucracies and enlist high-level support for their temple-building projects and other cultural activities to a greater extent than their northern co-religionists.

Among Sikhs, 910 indicated exclusive use of English and 457

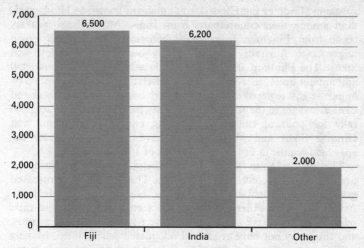

Figure 21.8 *Hindi speakers in Australia, by country of origin, 1991*

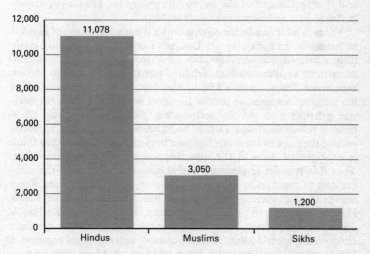

Figure 21.9 *Religions of Fijians in Australia, 1991*

that they spoke Hindi. Punjabi, the lingua franca of Sikhs, is not flagged in the census data. The large number choosing 'other language' seems to indicate that close to 90 per cent of Sikhs use Punjabi at home. Among Hindus, 15,000 or 34 per cent reported speaking Hindi at home. Most Hindus are bilingual. A proportionally higher number of migrants of Indian descent from Fiji reported speaking Hindi, or the Hindi–Urdu amalgam known as Hindustani, than among their counterparts from India. More Hindi-speakers come from Fiji than from the subcontinent, and of all Fijian migrants to Australia, Hindus greatly outnumber Muslims and Sikhs. The Fiji-born Indians have shown little organizational skill and are not united as a group. Their differences are compounded by linguistic and regional divisions that hark back to communalism and caste cleavages in the subcontinent. They have shown little desire to rally for political causes, despite the enormous problems that Hindus, Sikhs and Muslims alike have experienced under the apartheid regime in Fiji since the coups of 1987 and 1989.

The figures given above do not include people of European descent who have converted to a Neo-Hindu sect or guru-based group such as Vedanta or Hare Krishna. Nor do they include South Asians who were either too shy or too secularized to disclose their religion, or who have used a distinct sect-name, such as Lingayat, and thus may not have registered adequately as 'Hindus'. Making adjustments to take account of these factors, it would be safe to say that by mid-1995 there were close to 46,500 Hindus in Australia, and that by the end of the twentieth century the Hindu population in Australia may be approximately 60,000.

There is a further factor complicating the identification of Hindus in Australia. Indians and Sri Lankan Tamils have generally come from educated, semi-middle-class urbanized backgrounds in which, as in most secular contexts, religion and matters of public life are kept apart. Thus, while a Hindu may not outwardly display his or her religious leanings, in private life there would be a place for spiritual pursuits and identity reclamation. Some Indians who come from a relatively strong Hindu background have chosen to disassociate themselves from this heritage because that is what they think is expected of them in the new, supposedly secular environment. They find it easier to pursue a liberal existence without all the associations of the Hindu tradition. However, occasionally even these non-practising Hindus will support the activities of their fellow Hindus, especially in public deliberations. They may sponsor Hindu functions, take family visitors to a local temple, encourage their children to learn Indian classical dance, and perhaps organize a Hindu wedding ceremony for a son or daughter. Many of these people play a major role in the various Indian associations [1].

While most Hindus are of Indian descent, like all Indians they have come to Australia from a variety of places: in addition to those from India (approximately 25 per cent), Fiji and Sri Lanka, from Malaysia, Singapore, the UK, South and East Africa, and Nepal. Only 17 per cent of Hindus in Australia were born there.

In 1991, just over half of all Hindu residents in Australia lived in New South Wales. The proportion of Sikhs in New South Wales

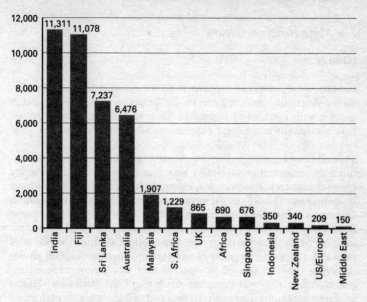

Figure 21.10 *Hindus in Australia, by country of origin, 1991*

was also high: 43 per cent of the total, with another 34 per cent living in Victoria and Queensland. About one-quarter of all Hindus, Sikhs and Muslims lived in Victoria and around 10 per cent in Queensland, with much smaller numbers in the other states. New South Wales has continued to be the favoured destination of Hindus and Muslims, but not of Sikhs [6].

Buddhists from the South Asian region have mostly been of Sinhalese extraction; some are Burmese. As many Buddhist migrants from South Asia as Hindus from the region are recorded. This is partly because of a steady arrival in Australia of Tibetan Buddhists who had taken refuge in India or Nepal, or were born there. The presence of Tibetan Buddhists has been quite visible in Australia, especially after the two visits by the Dalai Lama during which he led Buddhist seminars and met politicians. In 1995 there were some 6,500 Buddhists among the Sri Lankan population. Of the 142,000 Buddhists in Australia in 1995, fewer than 8,000 (including some from Burma, Nepal, India, Bhutan, etc. as well as Sri Lanka) were of South Asian origin.

The Main Religious Groups

Hindus

Hindus, who constitute the largest South Asian religious community in Australia, also appear to be better organized than other groups, with established structures for religious and cultural activities, community service and expressions of a public 'voice'.

Traditions and practices Ideally, Australian Hindus aspire to continue the entire range of Hindu beliefs and practices, but there are many constraints. For instance, elaborate Vedic/Agamic rituals have been performed only on the rare occasions of temple inauguration ceremonies. For these special occasions teams of priests have come from India. During the most auspicious days in the Hindu almanac, such as Maha Shivaratri, or the Great Night of Lord Shiva, rites based on the Vedic fire altar (*homa*) are also performed. But rituals involving the sacrifice of living creatures would not be contemplated. Vedic rites still comprise the bulk of the traditional Hindu wedding ceremony (*vivaha*), although these are usually performed in one afternoon rather than over several days. They are usually followed by a secular reception. Some Hindus take their marriageable children to India to benefit from the ceremony performed in full regalia and with attention to the details of customary practice. Talks may have been conducted over a sequence of visits, as a result of which a religious engagement has already been made. Funerary rites (*antyeshti*) are more substantially changed in Australia in order to adhere to health regulations. The body of the deceased is not allowed to be returned to the home, unless the funeral agency agrees to it. Cremation is preferred by most Hindus. The traditional practice of the eldest son torching the funeral pyre is not permitted by local authorities; instead, an incense stick is placed on top of the coffin-lid as it is lowered into the high-voltage furnace. The ashes are returned to the family for scattering in holy rivers in India, or in the nearby Indian or Pacific Oceans. The priests available for private ceremonies outside the temples are not necessarily well equipped to perform the major life-cycle rites in prescribed detail. Nevertheless, the commitment of the key participants and sponsors (*yajaman*) of such rites is strong, and the task is carried through with a sense of duty and reverence for tradition.

Arya Samajis account for some 30 per cent of the Hindus in Australia and are more orthodox than most other Hindus. They congregate in homes to perform Vedic *homa* or sacrificial offerings to Agni. No form of representation (printed image, sculptured icons, etc.) is permitted in Arya Samaj homes or ceremonies. On the other hand, Sanatani Hindus congregate to offer *archana* and *arati* (lamp-lit worship), and perform major *pujas* (worship using chants and offerings) to Vishnu-Narayana, Ganesha or Subramaniya, or honour some guru-incarnate, whose colourful life-size image adorns the petalled *mandapa* or worship-altar.

Festive days and important astronomical configurations, particularly the four phases of the moon, are observed assiduously by Hindu households. Families earmark days for observing fasts and strict purity in the household, which usually means refraining from consuming non-vegetarian food and alcohol. Women are generally discouraged from participating in worship during their menstrual periods. Major festivals such as *dussera* (the ten-day goddess worship), *diwali* (the festival of light) and the New Year, along with the 'birthdays' of Rama and Krishna and days dedicated to Ganesha, Shiva and the Goddesses, are celebrated with *pujas*, sweets, family gatherings and exchanges of greetings.

Most Hindu homes will have a mini-altar set aside in a corner of the house for the purposes of *puja*, or meditation, by the members of the household. In terms of doctrinal emphasis, neither the Gita nor Gandhi plays a significant role. The emphasis is usually on a mixture of popular Hinduism and *bhakti*, with a smattering of Vedanta teachings, and some reference to *karma* and and its corollary rebirth, but with little of the moral overtone of the classical teachings. Most Hindus are educated in Western systems and motivated towards achievement, which may run counter to the fatalistic presuppositions of *karma*, rebirth and related doctrines. Little interest is shown in explanations for the beliefs and practices or different forms of worship. However, participants will happily sit through extended 'discourses' on Vedanta and the more subtle nuances of *dharma* by visiting swamis and gurus. Such *bhashans* or teaching-speeches are reproduced in the respective societies' newsletters, or distributed on amateur videos. These, together with Indian films on secular or religious narratives (such as the *Mahabharata*) are important popular means of transmitting traditions.

There are, however, signs of what might be termed 'Protestantization' evident in the Hindu community in Australia. There are various reasons for this development. First, the secular Western context makes even the devout Hindu somewhat circumspect about the extent to which orthodox traditions can be maintained. Few are willing to draw attention to themselves in such a way, despite the rhetoric of multiculturalism. The younger generation, in particular, have aspirations towards a secure career and want to be part of the host society. Secondly, within the subcontinent itself changes in religious orientation have taken place in the broader context of nationalist discourses and communal tensions. An element of politicization has entered the fabric of everyday

Hindu life. From Gandhi's home-rule movement to the social and political turbulences of the late twentieth century, Hindus in the diaspora have not been spared this fervour. Indeed, some claim that the ferment is largely fuelled by elements in the diaspora – the so-called NRIs (non-resident Indians). There are Hindus in North America, the UK, Africa and Australia who harbour a zeal for reform in India and the preservation of Hindu civilization and the rights of Hindu citizens against other ethnic or caste-based claims.

Similar sentiments appear to inform the activities of Tamil Hindus from Sri Lanka who have developed relations with Tamil, Telugu and Kannada-speaking immigrants from south India. There is no evidence of a direct link between any segment of the Australian Tamils and, say, the Tigers or radical Tamil elements in Sri Lanka (or Tamil Nadu). However, there have been reports of Tamils and liberal Sri Lankan immigrants being approached for funds in support of the Tamil liberation cause in Sri Lanka. Literature distributed, supposedly unofficially, during major temple gatherings has included locally produced Tamil newspapers highly critical of the Sri Lankan ruling regime. A major cause of schism and eventual split within the first broad-based Hindu temple association in Victoria was attributed to differences between moderate and radical factions within the Tamil community.

These factors combine to colour the emphasis on the doctrinal and devotional aspects of a multi-faceted Hindu tradition. At the same time, for practical reasons the community has developed a centralized structure and defined lines of authority similar to those in church or political organizations. There has also been a shift from worship in the home to the temple. Patrons are encouraged to 'sponsor' regular as well as special *pujas*, in return for public acknowledgement. The quantity of the donation itself can become a measure of one's dedication to, or esteem within, the congregation. These developments bear on the issue of leadership patterns in the Hindu community. Priests conduct *pujas* and certain life-cycle rites; temple priests are respected for keeping a tradition alive. Beyond these roles, the priests have no significant voice in the community on matters relating to values, disputes, official family or community affairs, or representation in the wider society. Business is conducted by the temple executive, drawn from within the ranks of the local temple association. Eminent community members, such as local representatives of the Indian government, have played an active part in giving cultural and even spiritual shape to the community. They have brought together diverse community groups, promoted cultural and artistic events, and supported scholarly meetings. The dedicated work of these non-aligned leaders who attempt to preserve the honour of their secular office by not taking the part of any particular group is not always reciprocated by Indian or Hindu organizations.

The importance of transmitting cultural traditions, for which language and classical learning are indispensable vehicles, is not widely recognized in the community. Two Australian universities teach in the specialist areas of Sanskrit and three in Hindi–Urdu, and tuition in Tamil is also available. While there is much discussion of the need to promote teaching of Indian religions, languages and philosophies in schools and universities, negligible effort has been forthcoming from the community itself. However, in 1994 the Bengali community succeeded in having Bengali included in the high school curriculum as a non-English language option.

It is said that caste is endemic to Hindu society, which tends to be hierarchical and, to that extent, exclusivist. Among pre-1960s immigrants, it was common to be identified by one's place of origin and caste. Thirty years on, caste is almost never discussed openly; much less does it determine the make-up of social and religious gatherings. However, caste considerations may play a significant role in marriage plans. Most Hindu marriages continue to be arranged. The suitable boy or girl is generally selected along caste lines, though not necessarily along sub-caste or *jati* lines. A compromise may be reached if the level of education and socio-economic standing of the partner is deemed higher than that of the local suitor, or than expectations. A Hindu family in Australia will happily marry their son or daughter to a comparable boy or girl resident in North America rather than entertain dowry and immigration sponsorships for an eligible caste partner in India. In arranging marriages, Hindus are concerned about supposedly lax moral and sexual attitudes in Western society. However, despite these concerns, some families leave the search for a suitable partner entirely to the young people themselves.

Organization and temple culture Over the centuries of bitter struggle for internal control and against foreign intrusions, Hinduism has come to be grouped around *sampradayas* or sectarian lineages, led by *acharyas* (pontifical heads) or increasingly nowadays by gurus and swamis. Most Hindu organizations in Australia are self-governed by a *kendra* or committee formed from among the members, with an elected executive. Some temple associations seek links with individual temples (*devasthanam*) in South Asia, or with bodies such as the official Hindu Charitable and Endowment Board of a south Indian government, or with the popular Vishwa Hindu Parishad (VHP or World Hindu Council).

In the mid-twentieth century organizational structures were developed not so much to serve the immigrant community as in response to the growing appeal of Hinduism, Buddhism, yoga and meditation among youth in Western societies. In the 1960s and 1970s a number of gurus with a strident universalist outlook began to travel to the West. An assortment of yogis, babas, swamis, monks, lamas, tantric advocates, Matajis or spiritual mothers, and harbingers of universal brotherhood spread the 'good word' and enlisted converts, or rekindled faith in the diaspora Indian. This was part of the 'counter-culture' movement which later spilled into the New Age phenomenon.

There is in Australia no umbrella organization that can legitimately claim jurisdiction over the religious affairs of the many Hindu and Neo-Hindu organizations. However, in several of the major cities in Australia, Hindus have organized themselves into collectives and built temples. Curiously, the initial organizational initiative almost invariably arises among the north Indian Hindus. Tamil groups have assumed responsibility for organizing temple structures and the attendant rites that are more traditional and grounded in Sanskritic or Agamic injunctions. The cooperative spirit that is also a feature of Hindu communities is illustrated in the successful completion of four Hindu temples in Sydney and Melbourne; another three were under construction by early 1996. Each temple project, including the provision of Tamil priests trained in the shastric tradition, was supported financially and spiritually by a trust that controls the most popular temple and pilgrimage centre in India, which is on the hills of Tirupathi in Andhra Pradesh reached via Madras. To this day the Sydney temple is largely patronized by Hindus from south India and Sri Lanka. This temple has been a source of inspiration for similar projects in other states [7].

One group of north Indians, mostly upper-caste Gujaratis, predominantly worshippers of Shiva, organized themselves under the aegis of the India Heritage Research Foundation (sponsors of the *Encyclopedia of Hinduism*, in progress) to build the world's first 'Underground Hindu Temple'. Going 'underground' was a strategy adopted in the face of an intransigent local council which had earlier rejected the temple plans, following opposition from local church bodies. The major deity to be housed is Sri Vishvanatha (Shiva in a *linga* form), after the famed Vishvanath temple in Varanasi. The temple was projected to be completed by early 1997. In the meantime, foundations for a third temple in the Sydney metropolitan region had been laid. This was organized predominantly by south Indian Shaivites of Tamil and Telugu background from Malaysia and elsewhere. It was to be a modest temple dedicated to Murugan or Subramaniya; work on it was still in progress in 1996.

A Hindu Society of Victoria was incorporated in the late 1970s. A major temple project incorporating adjacent shrines to Vishnu, Shiva and Devi under one massive structure was planned, to cost an estimated one million dollars. Again, help came from the Tirupathi temple endowment charity. The planning and building of this temple spanned some ten years, with periodic disruptions due to internal dissensions and management issues within the Hindu Society of Victoria, Inc. Meanwhile, a breakaway group commenced construction of a second Hindu temple in the outskirts of Melbourne, dedicated to Ganesha (or Vinayaka). The *Mahakumbhabhisheka* or grand temple dedication ceremony of Sri Vakrathunda Vinayagar Temple, built in a quasi-traditional style, was held in October 1992. Regular prayers and celebrations take place in the temple, conducted mostly in Tamil. Eventually, the Hindu Society of Victoria reorganized itself under strong Tamil leadership and completed construction of its massive temple by mid-1994. Traditional craftsmen or *shilpis* produced stylistic embellishments and fine aesthetics which the temple design embraces. The gala dedication ceremony of this temple and the icons of the gods took place in May 1994.

In the nation's capital, Canberra, there are two different Hindu organizations, the Mandir Society of Australia and the Hindu Temple and Cultural Centre of the Australian Capital Territory. Both declare allegiance to Vedanta and the *bhakti* tradition, and each group has been constructing its own Hindu temple on the outskirts of Canberra. The division in the Canberra Hindu societies is not clearly defined along the north/south Indian divide, but rather reflects personal and ideological differences. However, a third group of more orthodox Shaiva south Indians have recently begun work on their own temple, as in Sydney. North Indian Hindus in Australia have growing links with the Vishwa Hindu Parishad and the Bharatiya Janata Party (BJP), and occasionally also with the RSS (Rasthriya Swayam-sevak Sangh). This connection with politically conservative Hindu movements has caused divisions within the north Indian Hindus. Anti-Muslim sentiments exist among some Hindus, although these are hardly ever expressed publicly.

The building of temples in response to a perceived religious need also resulted in the coming together of Hindus in the southern diaspora in an organized way. The temple has both a private and a public face. As an emblem for prescribed ritual and interiorized spiritual practice, the temple makes it possible for Australian Hindus to continue their cultural activities with greater confidence. The temple signifies a permanent fixture and a powerful presence which makes Hindu identity tenacious and publicly visible. The temple also opens up a space for negotiating tensions among the different sectarian and regional groups.

Muslims

The percentage of Muslims in the total Australian population who have indicated place of birth in South Asia or are of Indian ancestry

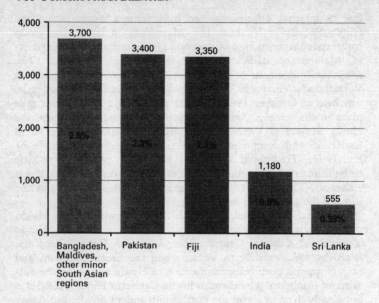

Figure 21.11 *Muslims in Australia, by country of origin, 1991:
numbers and percentage of total Australian population*

is as follows: Pakistan 2.3 per cent, India 0.8 per cent, Sri Lanka
0.38 per cent, Bangladesh and other South Asian regions such as
Burma and the Maldives 2.6 per cent, Fiji 2.2 per cent and Africa
approximately 1 per cent. Curiously, the Muslim migration from
Fiji is higher than from India, the country with the second highest
proportion of Muslims after Indonesia. The age distribution for
Muslims is relatively the same as for other South Asians, although
the educational profile, especially among females, is low.
Demographically, Muslims tend to be diffused among other Indian
groups as similar factors pertaining to employment, housing assistance, trade opportunities and children's education determine the
choice of residence. Among long-term residents and parents with
high educational and/or professional backgrounds restrictions on
girls' participation in education and career opportunities are less-
ened.

The percentage of Urdu-speakers among the Australian Muslim
populations is highest for the Pakistani and Bangladeshi groups,
followed by Fiji-born Muslims and Indian-born Muslims.

On the issue of religious practice, the Muslim situation is somewhat more complex, as Muslims from whatever part of the world
will attend a mosque if it is sufficiently close to the order they

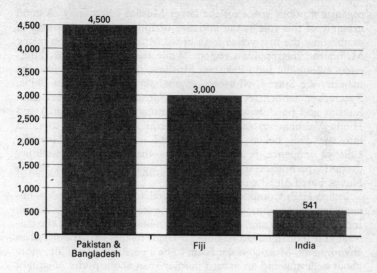

Figure 21.12   *Urdu speakers in Australia, by country of origin, 1991*

belong to (e.g. Sunni or Shi'ia). The first mosques in Australia were erected (from makeshift tin sheds) by the Afghans and Punjabi Muslims in the late nineteenth century. Nowadays, prominent minarets rise above the Australian suburban skyline on mosques erected with the support of Muslims mostly from the Middle East, Turkey, eastern Europe, Malaysia and Indonesia. South Asian Muslims happily involve themselves in the activities of these mosques and attend for prayers.

Pakistani, Indian and Bangladeshi Muslims each maintain a distinctive community sense. Their unity is reinforced by the language they speak, Urdu for Pakistanis and Indians, Bengali for Bangladeshis, and other cultural and perhaps ideological values they trace back to their ancestral roots. Indian Muslims, who would have migrated from India or the pre-partition provinces, or from Africa, Malaysia and Fiji, generally speak Urdu, Hindustani or Gujarati, and tend to identify closely with other South Asian communities, while also maintaining links with the Islamic group they find doctrinally acceptable. The majority of the Muslims in present-day Australia come from Turkey, the Middle East, Afghanistan, eastern Europe, and neighbouring Indonesia and Malaysia. Muslims from South Asia and Fiji constitute a significant minority within the wider South Asian diaspora and have played a significant role in organizing public space for the larger Muslim community. A good example of this role is the initiative of Indo-Pakistani Muslims in establishing the first venue for a broad Muslim congregation in the Melbourne metropolitan region. While there are religious differences among the Indo-Pakistani Muslims, these are not radical; the majority are Sunnis, with only approximately 2–3 per cent Shi'is. Syncretistic tendencies are also in evidence, with elements from Sufism, and possibly also Sikhism (among Punjabi Muslims) and Hindu Vaishnavism (among Bangladeshi Muslims), incorporated into the daily beliefs and practices of the Australian Muslims. Chistiya influence is also evident as the Pakistani community devoutly patronizes the visits of the well-known Chistu singer, Nusrat Fateh Ali Khan.

Indian High Commissioners in Australia have often been prominent Indian Muslim diplomats with a secular outlook. Overall, Indo-Pakistani Muslims appear to take a liberal approach to the cultural and individual expressions of Islam in the secular Australian environment. Most consider Islam to be a personal way of life, more about believing and an inward journey than about purity of rituals, faultless observances or absolute authority (*hukm*). They may not all offer prayers five times a day, especially if they are employed in a demanding job, and they may not read the Qur'an or attend the mosque with any regularity. The women may not wear the face-covering veil (though they may drape the dress shawl over their heads). They would not call themselves devout Muslims, but they are as likely to observe Ramadan as Muslims from other regions, at least for part of the thirty days, and at the end of it join in celebrating 'Id al-Fitr and 'Id al-Adha (Festival of Sacrifice) with much festive camaraderie and a deepening of religious experience [11].

Australian Muslim liberalism is demonstrated in other ways. When widespread agitation overseas followed publication of Salman Rushdie's *The Satanic Verses*, protests were made by a small gathering of Pakistani Muslims in Sydney, and in Melbourne forceful comments were made publicly by a leading Muslim scholar of Pakistani origin. But nothing comparable to the violence that took place in Pakistan or the public burning of the book in the UK occurred in Australia. Nor was there any public condemnation of the Hindu destruction of the Babri Masjid in Ayodhya. The Muslim neo-modernist influence from Sayyed Ahmad Khan to Muhammad Iqbal perhaps tempers reactions. There is no *ulama* or Islamic legal authority, no Deobandi or Barelwi clerics to demand adherence to the *Shar'ia* (religious law) derived from the Qur'an and *hadith*. Elements of what one might call fundamentalist tendencies, such as the Council of Islamic Ideology in Pakistan, are largely absent among Australian-based subcontinental Muslims, with the exception of one group. In what is perhaps the largest Australian centre of

Muslim population, Lakemba, a suburb of Sydney, with its mosques, *halal* food stores, cultural activities centres and much else that draws Muslims of all persuasions to settle there, the presence of Jama'at Tablighi is strong [11]. This 'religious caravan' goes back to a nineteenth-century Indian reactionary movement against the assimilation of Hindu spiritual practices into Islam. It also corresponds to the Islami Jami'iyyat-i-Tulaba set up as a student wing of Mawdudi's programme for the Islamization of Pakistan (and by subterfuge also in Bangladesh) in the late 1970s. It was vigilant in maintaing traditional law and order and what it considered the proper observance of Islamic precepts and conduct. Tablighis are favoured among some Pakistani and Indian Muslims in Lakemba, generally to keep womenfolk and new converts to Islam in check. The colloquial use of the judgment *kafir* (or *takfir*, infidel) is not uncommon in Lakemba, although no one has been pronounced an apostate deserving a *fatwa*.

There have been efforts to encourage the reading of the Qur'an by women and to increase women's knowledge of the principles underpinning Islamic religious habits. Often, however, the (male) *imam* will decide which passages of the Qur'an and Sunna are to be read by the women, with no interpretations allowed. Some South Asian Muslim women activists believe that the tradition allows for women to develop critical skills and a knowledge base from which to reform Islamic society and to contribute to social reforms in a secular society. But a strong Muslim women's group is conspicuous by its absence in Australia.

State-run ethnic radio broadcasts provide time slots for each of the South Asian national groups to transmit cultural programmes in their own languages. Pakistani volunteers use the opportunity to inform the community about important developments within the community, give daily prayer times, and conduct dialogue between lay members and religious leaders (*imams, maulwis*) about such matters as the significance of festive days in the calendar, the propitious time to plan for Hajj or pilgrimage to Mecca, and other issues. Women take the opportunity to ventilate issues of local welfare and the need to provide community support and network facilities for Muslim women who are victims of abuse at home, or who have been estranged from their families or have suffered bereavement. There is frequent emphasis on family values, generosity and the welfare of dependants.

The community leadership maintains that there is no emphasis on missionary activities as there are too few people to proselytize. What resources there are tend to be directed towards providing information and support, welfare for the disadvantaged, and schools for the young across the region, which extends to New Zealand and Fiji. A further reason for tolerant coexistence is that the community is numerically too small and scattered to be able to organize its adherents in any threatening way, despite the voice of the larger Muslim groups. Because of their predominantly middle-class, urbanized and educated background, as well as a shared cultural and linguistic base, South Asian Muslims in Australia tend to identify closely with other South Asians irrespective of their religious affiliations.

Sikhs

The 1991 census records 7,795 Sikhs in Australia but the writer's estimate is that there are some 9,300. The discrepancy arises because many do not declare themselves to be Sikhs, fearing prejudice, some having arrived as refugees and a few as illegal immigrants. Since 1984 Sikh migration has declined with the rise of political tensions in Punjab. After the storming of the Harimandir Sahib in Amritsar, and the subsequent assassination of Indira Gandhi, Australian immigration authorities introduced tougher screening measures for Sikhs looking for refugee and migrant status in Australia. These strictures did not adversely affect Sikh migration from other regions, especially Malaysia, as they have an identity distinctive from that of Indian Sikhs. Half of all Sikhs living in Australia were born in India. A few have come from Malaysia, Singapore, Fiji, Africa and the UK.

In some ways, the 'new Sikhs' who migrated in the later part of

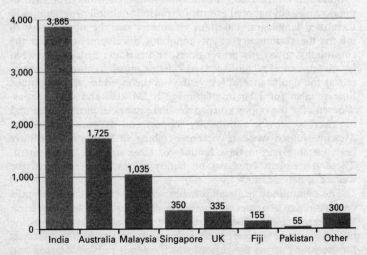

Figure 21.13   *Sikhs in Australia, by country of origin, 1991*

the twentieth century are not very different from the earlier Sikh immigrants. In the closing years of the nineteenth century, Sikhs gathered to offer prayers to their Gurus in a makeshift shrine in Woolgoolga on the northern border of New South Wales, close to Queensland. They struggled against both internal conflicts and the low esteem accorded them by the host community. In this way they grounded their continuity within tradition, while also adjusting to change [10]. There is another feature, especially among Indian Sikhs, which makes them quite distinctive: the very strong religious sense that Sikhs have. While as a social group Sikhs are active, progressive and enterprising, they are also highly conscious of their religious tradition and remain devout in their adherence to the principles promulgated by the Gurus. Indeed, in a survey conducted among people of Indian descent in Victoria, Sikhs rated strongly, following closely the Indian Christians, in terms of involvement in their religious tradition. Each city may have more than one *gurdwara*.

There are some important differences between Punjabi Sikhs and those of Malaysian origin. Sikhs from the subcontinent exhibit strong leanings towards the Punjab. Malaysian Sikhs, although they continue to wear the symbolic turban, tend to be more liberal and inward-looking, and are culturally at some remove from Punjab. Most are in the business, technical and rural sectors, find it difficult to compete with the more professionally qualified subcontinental Sikhs, and keep somewhat aloof from their Punjabi counterparts. More significantly, the Malaysian Sikhs, in the wake of the political crises in Punjab, distanced themselves from the subcontinental Sikhs, fearing their impact on the Australian community. However, the recently reorganized Sikh Association of Victoria provides a particular incentive, especially for all adolescent Sikhs, to become involved in community activities, ranging from cultural dinners to sporting events to 'Bangra Beat Nite', which is a fusion of traditional Punjabi music and dance with reggae and rap rhythm.

Many diaspora Sikhs are concerned about the political situation in Punjab. The Indian Sikhs in Australia, like those in Britain and North America, have tried to form a lobby to monitor and respond to events connected with the Sikh struggle for greater autonomy from central government control in Punjab, and with the plight of Punjabi Sikhs in Pakistan. The issue of a separatist movement intent on establishing Khalistan has not been welcomed by all Sikhs in Australia; nevertheless, a handful of Sikh spokesmen behave as though the entire Australian Sikh community has a political stake in the struggle against 'Hindu dominance' in India.

Sikhs remain grounded in their tradition. However, some compromises are made in their practices in the new environment; and while leadership issues earlier on marred the unity of Sikhs, especially in Melbourne, by the early 1990s there seemed to be greater community stability. In December 1993 one of the three Sikh groups in Melbourne invested $1.3 million in converting a massive former mail-sorting centre to house a congregation of 1,000. Each weekend, *langar* (community food) is served to all guests at the *gurdwara*, routinely sponsored by different families. Three priests are brought from India on a rotational basis to perform regular worship centred on the Adi Granth and to lead prayers and the singing of *kirtans* (semi-devotional songs to the Ultimate based on the sayings of the Sikh Gurus and Bhakti-Sufi saints). By the mid-1990s Victoria boasted three major Sikh groups, each with its own *gurdwara* and slight variations in worship and Gurubani or recitations from the Adi Granth. An earlier worship-hall was abandoned after an unresolved legal dispute in 1992, and the congregation relocated to another site in the outskirts of Melbourne where it has built a modern *gurdwara*. Likewise, the Sydney Sikh community is organized around four collectives. Each group anywhere attracts a cross-section of Sikh immigrants from the different regions. The political overtones of Sikh congregations of the 1980s have largely disappeared as liberal and more orthodox Sikhs together have taken control of the local Sikh organizations. The emphasis is increasingly on maintaining cultural identity, conducting ceremonies and rites according to the Sikh scriptures, and strengthening normative ties with India, whose unity the Sikhs now fear to be under greater threat from Neo-Hindu nationalism than from the diminishing Sikh agitations.

Parsis

The Parsi community in Australia is much smaller in size than those of most other South Asian groups. They number approximately 1,100, mostly urban professionals who have retained something but not all of the traditional forms they brought with them from Bombay or rural Gujarat, Pakistan and, lately, Sri Lanka. The community in Sydney and Melbourne gathers regularly for festival and social functions. However, not all Parsis self-consciously identify themselves as Zoroastrians or voice public concern at the absence of a 'fire temple' in their midst. Factors which may weaken religious and cultural ties have to do with the professional preoccupations of the established migrants, their isolation from each other in the expansive metropolis, their earlier urban and anglicized education, and the increasing number of out-marriages among the younger generation. Recent studies suggest the group in Melbourne, like its counterpart in New Zealand [13], is more traditional than that in Sydney, but generally relations with the host community are good [12].

Buddhists

In the decades when the White Australia policy virtually stopped migration from Sri Lanka, a few Sinhalese Buddhist families kept the flame of Dhamma burning by setting up a small temple inaugurated by invited Sinhalese monks. Thus the Brisbane Buddhist Vihara survives from the turn of the century. Remnants of Buddhist doctrines imported by Theosophists and (falsely) identified with J. Krishnamurti (who visited Australia in 1922 and again in 1974) continued to echo in different circles. Meanhile, Chinese Mahayana and later Zen Buddhism captured the imaginations of a long chain of contemplative Australians, locally and abroad. A major Aboriginal poet–novelist was ordained in Buddhism for three out of the seven years he spent in north India, later studying Pali and Sanskrit in Melbourne [9].

Through the efforts of local converts to Buddhism and with the guidance of itinerant Buddhist teachers and monks (some of whom were Europeans), Buddhist societies espousing Theravada teachings were established first in Sydney and then in Melbourne in 1953. Regular meditation classes and lecture or discussion meetings were organized, and publicized in their magazine called *Metta*. The presence of Sri Lankan monks attracted lay members of the Sinhalese community as well. They brought *dana* or offerings for the monks, participated in meditation and were present during *Vesakha* or Buddha's enlightenment day ceremonies.

Divisions among Australian Buddhists over emphasis on meditation or observances, doctrine verses practice, Theravada versus Mahayana, the authority of the monk over reason or conscience, not to mention personality clashes, did not accord with the quieter demeanour of the Sinhalese Buddhists, whose patronage of societies accordingly diminished. Sinhalese Buddhists have not moved to establish their own meditation centres or shrines, preferring to pursue the Dhamma (moral teachings) and the attendant practices in the privacy of their own homes. Community gatherings are organized during Vesakha, usually with an established Buddhist *vihara* or society.

Jains

Jainism is not prominent in Australia, where numbers have always been very small even compared with the Parsis. Some Jains arrived from Africa, Gujarati-speaking entrepreneurs and teachers who have adjusted themselves to living for two or three generations outside the subcontinent. Jain families from India have expressed moral concern about adjusting to the dominant Western environment.

They have brought certain basic skills in business and technology. They conduct their worship and religious rites mostly at home and occasionally visit Hindu temples. By early 1994, an estimated fifty Jain families were settled in Australia.

Conclusion

In the early nineteenth century South Asian migrants were few and restricted to menial labour. The tight controls on immigration had specific inbuilt biases in respect of gender and skills, for example. The migrants suffered double alienation: from the distant mother-country and in the uncertain environment in which they had now settled. Indians, as British subjects, gained a few rights and liberties. This ironically gave the community a sense of cohesiveness which enabled them to maintain their language and cultural base. The lingering White Australia policy and the post-Second World War depression interrupted further migration from anywhere in Asia. After the 1960s, demand for professional skills, regulations favouring reunion of families and temporary visas for merchants, travellers and students helped to increase the numbers of South Asians in Australia. What attracted most to the country was not the promise of an open and encouraging environment where religion and spiritual aspirations could be freely pursued; rather, for many of the urban-educated professionals, newly exposed to secularism and modernity, the sixth (island) continent appealed as a safe refuge from the religious orthodoxies and caste-based life back home in the subcontinent.

South Asians in Australia have endured considerable hardship, persevering despite social and cultural alienation and prejudice on account of their colour or religious background. Only in recent times have the communities been able to resist the pressures of an assimilationist ideology that had all but erased their earlier distinctive presence in the vast empty landscape. The communities have been slow in affirming their diversity and ethnic distinctiveness while also reinforcing traditional values. In the broader context of mainstream Australian society, the Hindu temple, the Islamic minaret, the Sikh *gurdwara* and the Sinhalese-patronized Buddhist *vihara* symbolize the struggles of disparate communities within a decidedly multi-cultural and ethnically plural environment. The leaders of the communities and of the nation at large have faith that the resulting interaction of cultures promises to produce a society that is more tolerant, more enlightened, more artistically thriving and more democratic than was the case in its earlier colonial history into the third millennium [4]. Religious diversity is a fact of life that the relatively young nation of Australia is no longer prepared to ignore, despite the occasional consternation it causes in segments of the society still anxious about preserving the dominant Anglo-Celtic-Christian identity against the challenges of cultural pluralism. But it has taken some two centuries to reach this more sanguine state of affairs, in which the contribution of the diasporic South Asians is beginning to be registered as a significant factor.

Bibliography

1 BILIMORIA, P., *Hinduism in Australia: Mandala for the Gods*, Melbourne, Spectrum Publications/Deakin University Press, 1988

2 BILIMORIA, P., and GAHGOPADHYAY, R., *Indians in Victoria (Australia)*, Ethnic Affairs Commission of Victoria, with Deakin University, Victoria, 1988

3 BOYD, JAMES W., and KOTWAL, F. M., 'The Indian Parsis in New Zealand', in Kapil N. Tiwari (ed.), *Indians in New Zealand: Studies in a Subculture*, Wellington, Price Milburn/New Zealand Indian Central Association, 1980, pp. 163–82

4 *Bureau of Immigration and Population Research Bulletin* (Canberra), no. 9, July 1993

5 *Census of Population and Housing, 1991*, State Comparison Series, Canberra, Australian Bureau of Statistics, cat. no. 2731.0

6 *Census Profile on Religion in Australia, 1991*, Canberra, Australian Bureau of Statistics, cat. no. 2510.0

7 CLARK, MANNING, *A History of Australia*, vol. 1, Melbourne, Melbourne University Press, 1971; first publ. 1962

8 *Community Profiles 1991: Census Sri Lanka Born*, Canberra, Bureau of Immigration, Multicultural and Population Research, Australian Government Publishing Service, 1995

9 CROUCHER, PAUL, *A History of Buddhism in Australia, 1848–1988*, Sydney, University of New South Wales Press, 1989

10 DE LEPERVENCHE, MARIE, *Indians in a White Australia: An Account of Race, Class and Indian Immigration in Eastern Australia*, Sydney, Allen & Unwin, 1984

11 DEEN, HANIFA, *Caravanserai Journey among Australian Muslims*, Sydney, Allen & Unwin, 1995

12 HINNELLS, JOHN, 'South Asian Diaspora Communities and their Religion: A Comparative Study of Parsi Experiences', *South Asia Research*, vol. 14, Spring 1994, pp. 62–108

13 JAYARAMAN, R., 'Indians', in James Jupp (ed.), *The Australian People: An Encyclopedia of the Nation, its People, and their Origins*, Sydney, Angus Robertson, 1988, pp. 542–5

14 JUPP, JAMES (ed.), *The Australian People: An Encyclopedia of the Nation, its People, and their Origins*, Sydney, Angus Robertson, 1988, sections on 'Sri Lankans' and 'Pakistanis'.

22

The Religions of South Asian Communities in Britain

KIM KNOTT

Religion was not a significant factor in the decision of South Asians to migrate to Britain, but during the principal period of settlement and community development, from 1950 to the present, it has become a matter of central importance. The various symbols of the religions of South Asians, whether these are aspects of dress, festivals, religious buildings or artefacts, have provided strong identifying features, and South Asians in the 1990s are often referred to as Muslims, Hindus and Sikhs rather than, for example, Indians or Pakistanis, or Asians. Many places of worship have become congregational and now function as social and cultural centres as well as places for the performance of ritual and prayer. Many have civic status. They attract local government grants, and provide representatives and leaders for police panels, community relations councils, equal opportunity agencies, education committees and welfare initiatives.

In contrast to the largely undifferentiated view which persisted among all but a few white Britons in the 1960s and 1970s of migrants from the Indian subcontinent as 'Asians' with a common and alien culture, there is now, at the turn of the millennium, a somewhat more informed perception of differences in regional background, religion and culture. Resulting from a liberal multiculturalist tendency, which unfortunately has not succeeded in combating racial violence or disadvantage, this has had the effect of placing religious and cultural institutions in a prominent position in terms of the engagement of South Asian communities with the wider society in Britain. To a large extent, religion has become a defining characteristic for people whose initial objectives in migrating were primarily financial, educational and social.

Religion and Migration

The process of migration, which uproots individuals and communities from the familiarity of known geographical, social and cultural locations and institutions, forces a reassessment of the meaning and nature of religious practices and ideas [1; 2; 7]. A new self-consciousness emerges. Rituals performed previously as routine in appropriate locations have to be undertaken afresh, making the best of an alien environment. Places of worship that were once an unquestioned part of normal surroundings have to be created, often by those who have few skills and little experience for the task. Philosophical and social ideas which were held in common as a framework for daily action are set in tension with those of other, more well-established communities who see little reason to challenge their own verities. And, as a new community begins to develop and feel more settled, questions of what to tell the children arise. Do the much-loved stories of deities, gurus and prophets with their associated values and ideals have the same meaning to children schooled partially in a different culture with its own traditions?

The extent and nature of the changes to religions after migration depend on several general factors such as the size and character of the immigrant community (including its cultural traditions), its expectations and intentions, and the milieu – political, social, legal and cultural – in which it must establish itself. Communities manage this process of transplantation in different ways. Some – such as those migrating for a second time or those coming from other urban locations – have useful resources to draw on [1; 21]. Others, for example those from rural locations, find the reproduction of their culture and social institutions extremely difficult. Adherence to religious traditions is often helpful to individuals and communities in the process of settlement in so far as it may provide continuity, and a sense of unity and coherence. In the longer term, however, this adherence in novel circumstances provokes new questions and a need for different future strategies. The way in which South Asians in Britain from different religions have dealt with these challenges will be examined in the following sections.

The History of the Religions of South Asians in Britain

During the nineteenth century a number of professional Indians, many educated in English-language schools in India, came to Britain to study or work. Many Parsis were among their number, and the first Indian firm to be established in Britain was founded by several members of the Cama family in 1855 [26]. In the 1860s and 1870s a number came for higher education, several of them later becoming leaders in Indian society. The first Asian Member of Parliament was also a Parsi, the Liberal Dadabhai Naoroji, elected in 1892. In addition, the first religious institution set up by and for South Asians was the Religious Society of the Zoroastrians of Europe, established in 1861 principally to secure a burial ground to enable proper Zoroastrian funeral practices to be conducted.

In addition to the arrival of professional Indians in this period, a small number of visitors came, not with the motive of settling, but with the intention of promoting Indian interests, either political or religious. Ram Mohan Roy, a prominent Hindu reformer, came to Britain in the 1830s and discussed issues of common concern with many Unitarians; he died in Bristol in 1833. Gandhi studied in London in the 1890s. Members of Vivekananda's Ramakrishna Mission and of the Gaudiya Vaishnava Math came to England in the 1930s. They gathered small numbers of interested followers around them, but had little real impact at that time [17]. Several Sikh maharajas also visited Britain, as a result of which the first Sikh *gurdwara* was formed in 1911 in Putney.

The migration process which' led to the development of Muslim, Hindu and Sikh communities did not begin in the nineteenth but in the twentieth century. The causes and context of this emigration from the subcontinent were colonial, rooted in the Indian experience of British rule. Although there was a strong tradition of migration westwards to Africa for the development of trade in earlier times, later emigrations have been driven by the need to find work. Whereas early, pre-1914, migrants were indentured and sent to British or Dutch colonies, those who came to Britain entered freely (until 1962) in the hope of finding work to improve family conditions back in the subcontinent. The rumour of Britain's unsurpassed wealth and glory, and the unsurprising assumption by Indians that their British citizenship would open all the necessary doors for them, led many to expect 'streets paved with gold' and a more generous welcome than they in fact received on arrival in Britain.

Accounts of the immigration of Muslim, Hindu and Sikh South Asians are plentiful [1; 2]. In short, early pioneering migrants arrived in Britain from the 1920s onwards. Muslim Sylhetis from Assam jumped ships on which they had worked as lascars, Asian merchant navy seamen. Many settled in the East End of London, often working in cafés or the boilerhouses and kitchens of hotels. Punjabis who came at this time generally made a living as pedlars, moving on later to market trading or wholesaling. These types of work, along with the factory jobs taken by later settlers, only confirmed the negative, colonialist perception of the British that South Asians were mere labourers.

The pioneers acted as hosts to many Indian males arriving in Britain just before and after the Second World War. In the 1950s, this male migration grew with the labour boom. However, few cultural or religious organizations were developed, though some welfare societies were formed. The men were in Britain to work hard and earn good money. Ties with home were strong, and it was there that the religious festivals, life-cycle rites and other rituals of the community were maintained. In some areas where Sikh men were concentrated, such as Gravesend and Leeds, devout individuals soon opened rooms in their homes for worship [23; 24]. These early ventures led to the hiring of public buildings for festivals such as *Baisakhi* or the Gurus' anniversaries, and ultimately to the purchasing in the late 1950s of houses to be used as *gurdwaras*. Pakistani organizations were also formed at this time, and a small number of places of worship were opened. By 1960, there were nine registered mosques [12].

It was the arrival of women, children and other dependants which brought about the more rapid formation of religious organizations. In the early 1960s, men were joined by other family members, partly because wives were keen to join their husbands in order to reassert their domestic influence, to help in the process of remitting wealth to the family in India or Pakistan, and to obtain a good education for their children [11; 14; 15]. In addition, in 1962, the British government introduced an Immigration Act whose effect was to slow the entry of those from the subcontinent. Many 'beat the ban' by arriving before the legislation was in place. The 1960s, then, was a period of family consolidation and community development. In this decade some thirty mosques were opened as well as many *gurdwaras* [11; 12].

The first Hindu temple was established in Leicester in 1969. The Hindu population was slower than the Sikh and Muslim to settle and develop religious institutions. It was not until the small number of Indian Hindus, mostly from Punjab, were joined by 'twice migrants', Gujaratis from East Africa, that this process began in earnest [16, 17; 19, 20]. The East African Asians comprised chiefly Gujarati Hindus and Punjabi Sikhs who came to Britain from the mid-1960s onwards from Tanzania, Malawi, Uganda and Kenya as a result of post-independence Africanization policies. They were experienced migrants who had already developed religious and social centres and sectarian movements while in Africa [1; 21]. They were accustomed to arranging the visits of holy people, *sants* and *sadhus*, obtaining religious specialists, and arranging life-cycle rites and festival programmes.

In addition to the formation of many South Asian religious and cultural centres in British cities in the 1960s and 1970s, patterns of domestic religious practice were developed along the lines of family traditions in the subcontinent. This had not been possible in the all-male households which existed before the arrival of wives and older relatives. Therefore, in addition to assisting in the development of public organizations, women maintained those practices they themselves had learnt from their mothers and mothers-in-law of food preparation, feasting and fasting, the religious nurture of children, the conducting of rituals and prayers, and the keeping of holy days [5; 6; 14; 15; 17; 21]. They also began women's gatherings for the purposes of singing, prayer, recitation, or food sharing.

The 1980s in Britain saw the proliferation of religious organizations among Muslims, Hindus and Sikhs. Old alliances made in difficult times of financial stringency between West and East Pakistanis (now Bangladeshis), Sikhs of different caste backgrounds, and Hindus from different regions of India began to disintegrate. Diversification became evident in most communities, with religious and cultural centres being formed by particular caste associations, sects, regional or even kinship groups. There have been occasional attempts to promote unity, either nationally by bringing together mosque or temple organizations to find a unified Muslim or Hindu voice (e.g. the Council of Mosques and the National Council of Hindu Temples), or locally through the formation of overarching associations which can tackle general questions of racism or social provision, or host major cultural programmes.

The other major change which has been witnessed from the early 1980s onwards is the impact of a British-born second generation. Over half the current South Asian population, 51.9 per cent in 1991, was under twenty-five. The majority of these young people, and some older than this, have received a British education and have had English as their first language (though many have continued to use the mother tongue with their close families). In general, they have achieved higher than average success at all levels of the education process. The challenges facing Muslim, Hindu, Sikh and other South Asian communities in Britain as a result of the needs of this generation will be discussed in a later section.

The Religions in the 1990s

At the time of the 1991 population census there were 1,476,900 South Asians in Britain, representing 2.7 per cent of the population. Neither the census itself nor any other national survey provides statistics on religious affiliation, so estimates must suffice. Judging

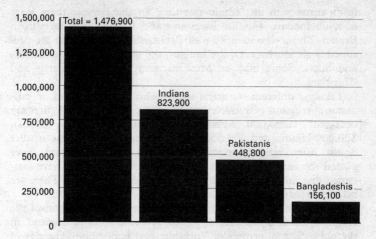

Figure 22.1 *South Asian groups in Britain, by ethnic origin*
Source: *1991 Census Statistical Papers, Centre for Research in Ethnic Relations, University of Warwick.*

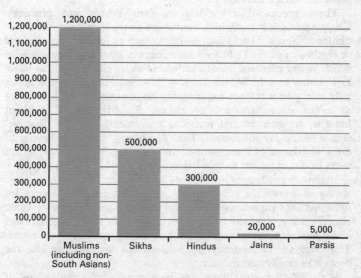

Figure 22.2 *Estimates of religious community membership, 1992*
Source: *Runnymede Trust and other sources.*

from answers to an 'ethnic question' in the census, there were 823,900 Indians, 448,800 Pakistanis and 156,100 Bangladeshis in Britain. Those who identify with Pakistan and Bangladesh are presumably all Muslims. Of the Indians, the great majority are Hindus and Sikhs. Some may be Muslims, and some Jains, Parsis and Christians.

Taking a different statistical source, this time one based on estimates of religious community membership, the following figures are obtained: 1,200,000 Muslims (including non-South Asians), 300,000 Hindus and 500,000 Sikhs (with no figures for the smaller South Asian religious communities) [8]. Other estimates have placed the number of Sikhs somewhat below this, and have estimated that there are about 20,000 Jains and 5,000 Parsis. There are no figures for South Asian Christians.

Looking briefly at the national character and distribution of the religions, Islam is most strongly present in the north of England, in the old industrial centres of Yorkshire and Lancashire. The city of Bradford, with its predominantly Mirpuri Pakistani population, has some forty mosques representing all the major sectarian groups: Deobandi, Tablighi Jama'at, Barelwi, Jama'at-i-Islami, Ahl-i-Hadith and Shi'a, as well as the Ahmadiyya movement which is not recognized as truly Islamic by other South Asian Muslim groups [10; 11]. Birmingham also has a large Pakistani Muslim population divided along similar lines, whereas the Bangladeshi Muslims are centred primarily in East London.

These groups differ widely in their beliefs and practices. Characteristic features which contribute to the rich diversity of traditions of South Asian Islam in Britain are as follows: the *madrasa* or seminaries of the Deobandi movement in Bury and Dewsbury, in which young men are trained as *'ulama* along similar lines to those in Pakistan and India; the Barelwi devotional focus on the *pir* or holy man who is at once a spiritual guide, counsellor and healer; the *da'wa* or missionary activity among the Muslims of Tablighi Jama'at, an international revivalist movement; and the 'Islamist' stance of the lay movement, Jama'at-i-Islami, linked in Britain to the UK Islamic Mission with its headquarters in Leicester, which seeks to return people to true Islamic doctrine [11; 12; 14; 15].

Islamic organizations, as well as Muslim families, have retained strong links with the subcontinent. Generally, religious leaders are imported for temporary periods, and materials for children's Islamic education are obtained from there. Individuals make regular visits and many continue to remit money to family members back home. The Bangladeshi community has been the last to complete the process of family reunification.

Both mosque and home are important in the daily lives of Muslims. Both are places of prayer for those who practise Salat

Key and principal areas of settlement

Muslims (Bengali) ○ :
   East End, London

Muslims (Pakistani) ○ :
   Birmingham
   Bradford

Hindus △ and *Jains* ✳ :
   North and Greater London
   Leicester

Sikhs □ :
   West London
   West Midlands
   West Yorkshire

Parsis ▽ :
   London
   Manchester

South Asian Christians † :
   London

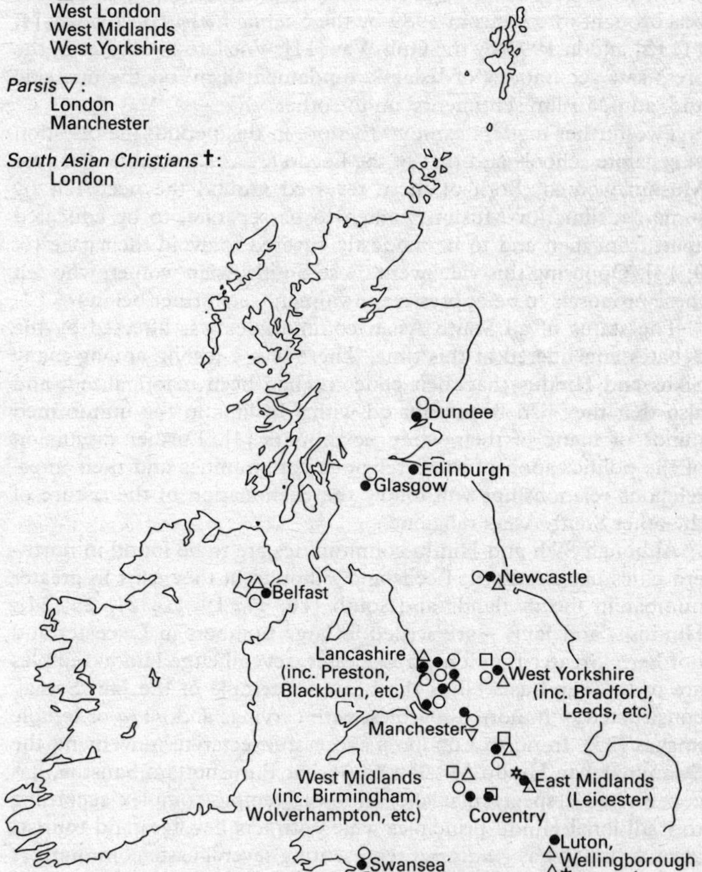

Figure 22.3 *Areas of settlement of South Asians in Britain, by religion*

regularly. Few women attend the mosque, even during the fast of Ramadan, though facilities are now improving for them in a number of the larger mosques. For many men, choice of a mosque is governed by questions of local geography, although sectarian allegiance is important for some. Keeping the fast annually and celebrating with the festival of 'Id are important for the majority, and most Muslim children attend classes regularly in which they learn to recite the Arabic of the Qur'an. Consciousness of Muslim identity was brought into focus in 1989 by the *Satanic Verses* controversy [4; 11; 13] and in 1991 by the Gulf War [11]. Vociferous debates in the press saw accusations of 'Islamic fundamentalism' on the one side and 'anti-Muslim sentiments' on the other.

Two further matters came to the fore in this period: the question of separate schools and that of the headscarf as acceptable dress for Muslim women. Both of these revolved around the need felt by some Muslims for Muslim women to be separate, to be educated apart from men and to be modestly covered to avoid their gaze [6; 9; 13]. Opposing this view were those South Asian women who felt these proposals to be oppressive to women (see further below).

The status of all South Asian communities was affected by the debates engendered at this time. There was a feeling among many Sikhs and Hindus that their concerns had been marginalized, and also that they had been equated with Muslims in the uninformed minds of many of their white neighbours [4]. Further discussion of the politicization of these religious communities and their inter-religious relationships will follow the examination of the nature of the other South Asian religions.

Although Sikh and Hindu communities are to be found in northern cities like Bradford, Leeds and Edinburgh, they exist in greater number in the midlands and south [16; 17; 19; 20; 21; 23; 24]. Hindus – and Jains – are settled in large numbers in Leicester and northern Greater London. In Leicester, several large Hindu temples are to be found as well as the beautiful temple of the Jain Samaj, constructed of imported marbles, with carvings and *murti* or temple images [25]. In north London a successful sectarian movement, the Swaminarayan Hindu Mission or Akshar Purushottam Sanstha, has constructed a spectacular and imposing temple complex according to traditional Hindu principles which attracts devotees and tourists alike. Southall has *gurdwaras* representing several caste communities and sectarian divisions. One of its largest is associated with the movement which calls for a separate, independent state for Sikhs.

Places of worship have different significance for Hindus and Sikhs. Most of the former see their homes as the primary location for regular worship (*puja*) of the deities. Generally, women are the ritual specialists in this context, passing on to children their knowledge of fasting, vows, domestic festival rites and Hindu stories [17;

18]. Temples or *mandirs*, which are dedicated to a variety of deities, particularly Radha and Krishna, are visited at the time of festivals such as the anniversaries of Shiva (Mahashivaratri), Rama (Ramnavmi) and the goddesses (Navaratri) [17; 18; 19; 20]. They are used as centres for cultural and educational activity.

Gurdwaras, too, are used in this capacity, not least for the teaching of Punjabi and, increasingly, Sikh religious education. Sikhs appear to be more congregational in their practice than Hindus. Many attend the Sunday *diwan*, a regular service in which the Sikh holy book, the Guru Granth Sahib, is central in providing readings and songs, spiritual inspiration and guidance [22; 24]. Remembrance services for the ten Sikh Gurus, *gurpurbs*, are performed in the *gurdwara* and sometimes accompanied by local processions. *Gurdwaras* are also used for the personal initiation or *amrit* at which Sikhs commit themselves to maintaining Sikh symbols and ethical teachings in a ceremony with powerful communal significance reminding all Sikhs of events in their early history when the Khalsa or Sikh fellowship was first established by Guru Gobind Singh.

The community life of British Sikhs and Hindus is organized not only by participation in the life of a place of worship, but also through their membership of caste groups and their commitment to religious teachers or to sectarian movements. It is not uncommon for *mandirs* and *gurdwaras* to serve these socio-religious groups. The operation of caste practice has altered with migration, but it is still of great importance in the arrangement of marriages [1; 17; 21; 24]. Principal castes represented in Britain include, among the Gujarati Hindus and Jains, the Patidars, Lohanas and Oshwals, all mercantile communities, and, among the Punjabi Hindus, the Khatri, also now a caste of traders. Among Punjabi Sikhs, the principal castes are Jats, Ramgarhias and Bhatras. Although many of the problems of caste hierarchy are less evident here than in India, caste communities perceived by others as low continue at times to be stigmatized [1; 24].

Membership of some sectarian groups is affected by caste, although religious leaders, *gurus*, *arcaryas* and *sants*, often preach against it, and discipleship is formally open to all. Important groups present in Britain include devotional movements such as the Swaminarayan Hindu Mission, Pushti Marg, the Hare Krishna Movement and the devotees of Sathya Sai Baba among the Hindus, and the followers of Sant Baba Puran Singh among the Sikhs. Most of these groups, and the Punjabi Namdharis, Nirankaris and Radhasoamis, are characterized by their focus on a living teacher. The Hindu reformist Arya Samaj, the revivalist Hindu Swayam Sevak Sangh and the pro-Khalistani 'Sikh Youth Federation' are also represented in Britain. A number of these movements remain

Table 22.1 Principal sectarian movements in Britain and their primary characteristics

MOVEMENT	CHARACTERISTICS						Includes non-Asian membership	PLACE AND DATE OF ORIGIN
	Devotional	Charismatic authority	Reformist	Revivalist	Missionary	Caste-related		
Muslim and Muslim-related								
Young Muslims UK					✓		✓	Britain, 1970s
Barelvis	✓	✓						UP, India, 1870s
Deobandis			✓					UP, India, 1860s
Tablighi Jama'at			✓		✓			India, 1920s
Ahl-i-Hadith			✓	✓				India, 1870s
Jama'at-i-Islami			✓	✓				India/Pakistan, 1940s
Ahmadiyya		✓					✓	Punjab, India, 1880s
Hindu and Hindu-related								
Swaminarayan movement	✓	✓						Gujarat, India, 1800s
Pushti Marg	✓							India, 1500s
Arya Samaj			✓	✓				Punjab, India, 1875
Ramakrishna Mission	✓		✓		✓		✓	Bengal, India, 1897
Sathya Sai Baba Fellowship	✓	✓					✓	AP, India, 1940s
ISKCON (Hare Krishna)	✓	✓			✓		✓	USA, 1960s
Brahma Kumaris		✓						Sindh, India, 1930s
Sikh and Sikh-related								
Sikh Missionary Society			✓		✓			Britain, 1960s
Sikh Youth Federation			✓	✓				Britain, 1980s
Nanaskar Movement			✓	✓				Punjab, India, 1910s
Baba Puran Singh movement	✓	✓						E. Africa, 1930s
Namdharis		✓	✓					Punjab, India, 1850s
Nirankaris		✓	✓					Punjab, India, 1840s
Radhasoamis		✓						UP, India, 1860s
Ravidasis						✓		Britain, 1960s
Valmikis						✓		Britain, 1970s

UP = Uttar Pradesh; AP = Andhra Pradesh

strong in India, to which their British Asian adherents make periodic visits [17; 19; 24].

The smaller religious populations, of Jains, Parsis and Asian Christians, have also been active in community-building since their arrival. The Jains are noted for their beautiful Leicester temple and their European-wide publications [25]. Like the larger religious communities, they have been tested with the question of what it is to be a Jain in the context of secular, nominally Christian Britain. The Parsis, the smallest and oldest community with its centre in London's St John's Wood, fear the future in the face of secularization and the out-marriage of young people [26]. The Asian Christians, with families scattered throughout England, experience the difficulties of maintaining internal cohesion as a result of their social, ethnic and denominational differences [27]. Questions of leadership and representation are a particular challenge for this growing religious population.

Emerging Trends in the Reproduction of the Religions of South Asians in Britain

Between 1970 and the end of the 1980s, the religious initiative of Britain's South Asian communities was focused largely on establishing converted or purpose-built centres for worship and cultural activity. From the mid-1980s various other trends have emerged, relating both to the experience of South Asians as recently settled minorities in Britain and to their response to the processes of late modernity, such as globalization, religious revivalism, feminism and the rise of ethical and ecological concerns.

Migration and the stages of settlement, as shown above, encouraged various socio-religious developments. In these it was possible to observe elements of both continuity and change. Attempts were made to establish places of worship which fulfilled the same functions as those in the Indian subcontinent, and privately many of the same ritual practices were continued. However, the formation of organizations, the stress on lay initiatives, the adoption of Western bureaucratic processes and committee procedures were new to the majority, that is, to all but those who had had similar experiences in East Africa. Activities including the laying of the first foundation stone, the donation of money and voluntary effort, the hiring of ritual specialists, negotiations with local planners, financial agencies and neighbourhood groups, and the opening of new centres were novel to most South Asians.

While traditional forms of worship were reproduced in a general way with a consciousness of ritual continuity, many adaptations occurred to suit new contexts. Some of these were simply designed to meet changes resulting from new physical locations, different working weeks and public holidays, and available resources. In addition, the necessary engagement with a Western socio-cultural context challenged South Asian settlers to develop strategies that protected participants, particularly women and young people, from its full force. The threat of Western secularity, amorality and promiscuity was countered with informal policies which sheltered the vulnerable from their influence and often resulted in the development of a conservative and protective stance [9].

The division between South Asians (and Afro-Caribbeans) and the dominant white culture, focused on the experience of racism and the legacy of colonialism, contributed to a sense of *otherness*. South Asians were characterized as 'immigrants', 'black', 'Asian', and as 'Muslim', 'Hindu' and 'Sikh'. They were seen as separate and different from the majority of white British residents, even if they themselves were British citizens born in Britain [1; 2]. Racially motivated attacks and discrimination were facts of life for them.

Well-intentioned but naïve multiculturalist policies in local government and education helped further to separate South Asians into different 'faith communities' or 'ethnic minorities' for the purposes of management and resourcing. This complemented certain South Asian communalist trends, thus helping to produce an identity for many of belonging to a particular religious community. It became common to speak, for example, of 'the Muslim community' and individuals referred to themselves as 'a Sikh' or 'a Hindu' as distinct from 'a Christian'. In addition, the character of British Christianity helped in defining the reproduction of the religions of South Asians. In inter-faith meetings, religions were expected to be typologically comparable, with Christianity as the principal template. As a result, South Asians were frequently expected to give an account of their traditions which would conform to existing ideas about the nature of religion as perceived in the West. In the verbal or written accounts presented to outsiders certain ideas were often stressed such as monotheism, the role of holy books, common religious practices, priestly and congregational activity, rites of passage, and in more recent years the roles of women and ecological consciousness. Issues relating to purity, pollution and caste, popular or folk traditions, and the veneration of holy people, for example, were less often mentioned. A standardizing process often referred to in sociological accounts as 'Protestantization' occurred [6; 11; 19; 20; 26].

Irrespective of the outward, generic presentation of these religions by their representatives, in practice they have retained many vernacular elements [1; 14; 15; 17; 18; 22]. The challenge in respect of these is how to transmit them meaningfully to a young generation. This is achieved less through the formal nurture which takes place in supplementary language or religious classes, where children are often introduced to the principal stories and teachings of their religions, and more through observation, imitation, repetition and discussion, generally from mothers or other female kin. The continuity of regional and family traditions is evident to a limited extent in public places of worship in the form of visiting holy teachers, particular practices or visual images, but is principally manifested in the home [18].

The maintenance of local traditions represents an indirect link with the region of the subcontinent from which their practitioners derive. For example, particular Gujarati traditions of celebrating Norta or Navaratri (the annual festival of the goddesses) link Gujaratis in India and Britain, though changes have occurred in both locations. It is frequently noted that British Gujaratis maintain more conservative and less dynamic traditions than their Indian counterparts, a criticism also directed at other South Asian religious groups in Britain.

Socio-religious links with the subcontinent depend on the process of migration, the length of settlement in Britain, numbers of surviving relatives and the degree of involvement in organizations active there. Many Pakistani and Bangladeshi Muslims retain strong links and make frequent visits. For many East African Hindus and Sikhs there may be no direct family ties, though an active engagement with a religious movement such as the Swaminarayan Hindu Mission or the Radhasoamis, with its principal centre in India, might encourage visits to be made and would certainly result in a continuing interest in Indian religious affairs. For many South Asians, Britain is in all senses the centre of their lives. They may make a trip to the subcontinent to affirm their identity as Indian, but they have no formal ties with it. For a smaller number, the principal allegiance is not to India but to another country where kin are resident. Parsis world-wide retain close ties, and Jains, Sikhs and Hindus often have family members in Canada or North America. Finally, there are those who identify strongly with a global movement whose members hail from different national and ethnic backgrounds. Revivalist Islamic groups, for example Young Muslims UK, look outward to Muslims world-wide who claim shared objectives and attitudes.

What these examples show is the variety of operational maps which exist for South Asians in Britain. Not only do these differ, but they change as the individual matures and develops new interests, and as events occur in the subcontinent and elsewhere. Events in India in 1984, when the Golden Temple or Harimandir Sahib in Amritsar was besieged, Bhindranwale shot and Mrs Gandhi later assassinated, had an immense impact on the feelings of British Sikhs and Hindus. This led to an increased politicization, particularly of many young Sikhs who became involved with the Sikh Youth Federation and later in the running of certain *gurdwaras*. From a position of ignorance about Sikhism, Punjab and its politics, many became active spokespersons for Sikh initiation or *amrit* and a pure Sikh way of life, and for Khalistan, a separate Sikh state. Events in Ayodhya in 1992 following the destruction of the Babri mosque and the resultant communal riots affecting both Muslims and Hindus in India have also had repercussions in Britain, both in attacks on places of worship and in a rise in interest among young Hindus in learning about their religion and participating in the revivalist movement, Hindu Swayam Sevak Sangh.

A similar trend followed the publication in 1988 by Viking Penguin of *The Satanic Verses* by Salman Rushdie and the ensuing *fatwa* or ruling by Ayatollah Khomeini in Iran which called for the death of the author. The political circumstances which lay behind this trend were, however, British rather than subcontinental. They included matters of unemployment, racial discrimination and harassment, media stigmatization and a lack of political representation for Muslims. Together with the offence caused by Rushdie's provocative defamation of the prophet Muhammad, who is deeply venerated in South Asia, these injustices encouraged Muslims, particularly the young, to move towards a more outspoken demonstration of their feelings than hitherto [4; 11].

The controversy which followed raised profound intellectual questions about liberalism, freedom of speech, blasphemy, the relations between religion, state and citizenship, and the nature of ethnic and religious coexistence in a plural society. It also evoked a range of Muslim responses. Kalim Siddiqui, founder of the Muslim Parliament in Britain in 1992, and Shabbir Akhtar, author of *Be Careful with Muhammad* (1989) and other articles criticizing the liberal defence of *The Satanic Verses*, both took a radical line in promoting Islam and opposing British secular culture. A moderate voice was that of Zaki Badawi, chairman in 1989 of the Council of Imams and Mosques, who decried the *fatwa* as ungodly while uniting with other Muslim spokespersons in a fear for the future of the British Muslim communities.

A very different voice heard at this time was that of a group of women who, in May 1989, ran a counter-demonstration in solidarity with Salman Rushdie and in opposition to Muslim fundamentalism. Later to form the feminist group Women Against Fundamentalism, they criticized the claim of religious leaders and male spokespersons to speak for all Asians; they raised the issue of women's unheard voices, often those of battered women, girls unwillingly forced to marry, and women shackled by tradition, custom and community pressure; and they challenged policy-makers, the media and educators alike over their uncritical assumption that the agendas of religious communities were representative of all Asian interests [9].

Women's perspectives on religion and its implications varied considerably. Some, like Niggat Mirza, who in the 1990s was Head of the Muslim Girls' School in Bradford, and Rana Kabbani, author of an autobiographical response to the Rushdie controversy (*Letter to Christendom*, 1989), adopted what was sometimes referred to as a Muslim feminist perspective in which such things as the *hijab* or headscarf and the separation of girls and boys for education were seen as consonant with Muslim women's interests. Some young Hindu and Sikh women, particularly those in revivalist movements, took a similar position, interpreting traditional roles as a form of liberation for women. This perspective was seen as wholly misguided by the members of Women Against Fundamentalism, for whom even moderate, egalitarian strategies for improving women's representation and participation in religious life represented an effort to silence potential opposition. A range of Asian women's voices were portrayed in Zerbanoo Gifford's study, *The Golden Thread* [5].

Moral issues were frequently debated in this period, not least those relating directly to an Asian social and cultural agenda such as arranged marriage and dowry abuse. In relation to the former, every kind of response was heard from positive support to radical dissent. In the case of the latter, while few people agreed publicly with the idea of dowry and none with its abuse, its social embeddedness made it difficult to challenge in practice. Women's counselling agencies and refuges were set up to enable women's silence to be broken on these difficult issues. Other ethical debates, on issues such as abortion, AIDS, sexuality (including homosexuality), war and peace, and ecology were rarely addressed in public by the elders of religious communities, but more frequently by young people, in schools and youth groups, and in media debates. Magazines such as the Muslim *Trends* and *The Sikh Reformer* attempted to tackle these issues in a realistic and constructive way.

One forum where difficult questions were raised by religious communities was the Interfaith Network UK, an organization set up in 1987 to facilitate inter-religious discussion and the formulation of common responses on matters of mutual interest. All the religions of Britain's South Asians were represented, and the issues discussed included young people and the future, religious education and worship in schools, faith communities and the media, shared values in a multicultural society, dealing with conflict, and women's religious concerns. A consultative document, *Mission, Dialogue and Inter-Religious Encounter*, was produced in 1993 during the Christian churches' Decade of Evangelism following fears by non-Christians that they might be seen as targets for conversion.

The Interfaith Network engaged the participation of a minority of British Muslims, Hindus and Sikhs and other religious Asians at a national level, but others were involved locally in inter-faith groups where open discussions, cultural programmes, shared meals and, on occasions, joint worship took place [7]. Similar initiatives included meetings between Muslims and Christians during the Gulf War and the war in Bosnia, Sikh–Christian discussion groups, and a Jain–Christian conference on 'Reverence for Life'.

The engagement by religiously committed British Asians with other religions and with secularity has taken many forms, some of which have been explored here. In addition, a scholarly and artistic engagement has occurred in which they have reflected upon their own identity or that of their community in relation to the British plural context in late modernity. Tariq Modood, in *Not Easy Being British*, has examined the issue of citizenship raised by the presence of British Asians, while Shabbir Akhtar in *A Faith for All Seasons* and Akbar Ahmed in *Postmodernism and Islam* have sought to evaluate contemporary Islam in the light of modernity. Parminder Bhachu and Sewa Singh Kalsi, in empirical studies, have raised difficult questions for the Sikhs concerning the issues of caste and sect [21; 24]. Novelists, poets and artists, such as Farrukh Dhondy, Leena Dhingra, Salman Rushdie, Debjani Chatterji, Hanif Kureishi and Sutapa Biswas, have reflected on the meaning of their religious traditions in the context of British secularity. The 1993–4 film *Bhaji on the Beach*, written by Meera Syal, raised the issue of the interplay between the traditional (Hindu) values held by an older generation with those of younger, Asian women born and brought up in Britain. The conflicts and reconciliations, and the interweaving of Indian social and religious images and ideas with those of British secular culture, were indicative of some of the experiences of British Asians in the 1990s.

The future of British Islam, Sikhism, Hinduism and other religions from South Asia depends on the dynamism of this inter-relationship, as well as on the continuing development of religious organizations, practices and representations. This evolutionary process has already brought forth new religious forms, different from subcontinental varieties and from those growing up in other parts of the diaspora (see chapters 21 and 24 in this volume). The principal challenges now faced by South Asian religious communities in Britain include the following: the cultural competence of lay and religious leaders and their ability to formulate satisfactory future strategies; the use of English as well as vernacular and sacred languages in religious practice and communication; the engagement of young people's interests in spiritual and moral questions; and the call by an increasing number of women to be involved in all aspects of religious practice, theology, organization and management. The manner in which these issues are faced is of great interest not only for the religious future of Britain, but also in terms of its political representation, social organization and cultural character.

Bibliography

General

1 BALLARD, R. (ed.), *Desh Pardesh: The South Asian Presence in Britain*, London, Hurst, 1994

2 BAROT, R. (ed), *Religion and Ethnicity*, Kampen, Kos/Pharos, 1993

3 BOWKER, J., *Worlds of Faith: Religious Belief and Practice in Britain Today*, London, Ariel Books/BBC, 1983

4 COHN-SHERBOK, D. (ed.), *The Salman Rushdie Controversy in Interreligious Perspective*, Lewiston/Queenston/Lampeter, Edwin Mellen Press, 1990

5 GIFFORD, Z., *The Golden Thread: Asian Experiences of Post-Raj Britain*, London, Grafton Books, 1990

6 PARSONS, G. (ed.), *The Growth of Religious Diversity: Britain from 1945*, vol. 1, *Traditions*; vol. 2, *Controversies*, London, Routledge, 1993–4

7 *Religions in the UK: A Multifaith Directory*, Derby, University of Derby, 1993

8 RUNNYMEDE TRUST, 'Religious Observance and Affiliation: Estimates and Data', *Runnymede Bulletin*, no. 253, March 1992

9 SAHGAL, G., and YUVAL-DAVIS, N. (eds), *Refusing Holy Orders: Women and Fundamentalism in Britain*, London, Virago, 1992

Muslims

10 BARTON, S. W., *The Bengali Muslims of Bradford*, Community Religions Project Monograph, Leeds, University of Leeds, 1986

11 LEWIS, P., *Islamic Britain: Religion, Politics and Identity among British Muslims*, London, I. B. Tauris, 1994

12 NIELSEN, J., *Muslims in Western Europe*, Edinburgh, Edinburgh University Press, 1992

13 RAZA, M. S., *Islam in Britain: Past, Present and Future*, Leicester, Volcano Press, 1991

14 SHAW, A., *A Pakistani Community in Britain*, Oxford, Blackwell, 1988

15 WERBNER, P., *The Migration Process*, London, Berg, 1991

Hindus

16 BOWEN, D. (ed.), *Hinduism in England*, Bradford, Bradford College, 1981

17 BURGHART, R. (ed.), *Hinduism in Great Britain: The Perpetuation of Religion in an Alien Cultural Milieu*, London, Tavistock, 1987

18 JACKSON, R., and NESBITT, E., *Hindu Children in Britain*, Stoke on Trent, Trentham Books, 1993

19 KNOTT, K., *Hinduism in Leeds: A Study of Religious Practice in the Indian*

Hindu Community and in Hindu-Related Groups, Community Religions Project Monograph, Leeds, University of Leeds, 1986, repr. 1995

20 NYE, M., *A Place for our Gods: The Construction of a Temple Community in Edinburgh*, London, Curzon, 1996

Sikhs

21 BHACHU, P., *Twice Migrants: East African Sikh Settlers in Britain*, London, Tavistock, 1985

22 COLE, W. O., and SAMBHI, P. S., *The Sikhs: Their Religious Beliefs and Practices*, London, Routledge Kegan Paul, 1978

23 HELWEG, A. W., *Sikhs in England: The Development of a Migrant Community*, 2nd edn, Delhi, Oxford University Press, 1989

24 KALSI, S. S., *The Evolution of a Sikh Community in Britain: Religious and Social Change among the Sikhs of Leeds and Bradford*, Community Religions Project Monograph, Leeds, University of Leeds, 1992

Jains, Parsis and Christians

25 BANKS, M., *Organizing Jainism in India and England*, Oxford, Clarendon Press, 1992

26 HINNELLS, J. R., *Zoroastrians in Britain*, Oxford, Oxford University Press, 1996

27 JEFFERY, P., *Migrants and Refugees: Muslim and Christian Pakistani Families in Bristol*, Cambridge, Cambridge University Press, 1976

23

The Religions of the South Asian Diaspora in Canada

HAROLD COWARD

According to the 1991 census, there are some 420,000 South Asians in Canada, most of whom have arrived since the 1960s. The breakdown in terms of religions is as follows: Sikhs 135,000, Hindus 120,000, Muslims 90,000, Christians 55,000, Buddhists 3,000, Jews 70 and 16,930 assorted others, including Jains and Parsis. The vast majority came to Canada directly from India, Pakistan, Bangladesh and Sri Lanka; however, significant groups also arrived from Fiji, East Africa, Guyana and Trinidad. In Canada, South Asians have settled mainly in Ontario (131,000), British Columbia (104,000), Alberta (40,000) and Quebec (30,000), with the remainder spread across the other provinces and a few even locating themselves in the far north (the Yukon and North West Territories). Most South Asians are to be found in the cities of Toronto, Vancouver, Montreal, Calgary, Edmonton, Winnipeg and Ottawa.

Although they comprise less than 1 per cent of the total Canadian population, the South Asians, by virtue of their distinctive dress, food, culture and religion, are a high-profile element in Canada's multicultural mosaic. Table 23.1 offers a demographic profile of the Hindu and Sikh components of the South Asian community (figures for South Asian Muslims are not available). The median age group is 25–44 years, lower than that of the Canadian population, and there are fewer people over 65 years. Other characteristics of this community include an excess of males and higher proportions of married people and of persons in professional employment than the wider population [6]. They have developed the reputation of being hard-working and self-sufficient, many of them well-educated professionals or successful businesspeople. Their temples, *gurdwaras*, mosques and community centres have added a rich diversity to Canadian cities. South Asian classical music and dance has established itself as a part of Canada's cultural life. South Asian authors

Table 23.1 *Concentrations of Sikhs and Hindus in major Canadian cities*, by age

	Total population	Under 15 years	15–24 years	25–44 years	45–64 years	65 years and over
Toronto						
Hindu	90,100	21,625	13,925	37,925	13,625	3,040
Males	47,480	10,780	7,320	20,565	7,350	1,460
Females	42,665	10,840	6,605	17,360	6,275	1,580
Sikh	41,450	11,675	6,585	15,405	5,705	2,075
Males	21,540	6,090	3,160	8,385	2,890	1,015
Females	19,910	5,585	3,430	7,025	2,820	1,060
Montreal						
Hindu	13,775	3,540	1,900	6,030	1,925	375
Males	7,410	1,825	925	3,425	1,055	175
Females	6,370	1,715	980	2,610	870	195
Sikh	3,880	920	500	1,660	635	165
Males	2,175	430	320	1,025	330	70
Females	1,700	490	180	630	305	95
Vancouver						
Hindu	14,800	4,055	2,215	5,485	2,440	680
Males	7,365	2,010	1,020	2,695	1,290	345
Females	7,515	2,045	1,195	2,790	1,145	335
Sikh	49,625	14,275	8,215	16,700	7,550	2,890
Males	25,095	7,220	4,125	8,730	3,660	1,350
Females	24,530	7,050	4,085	7,965	3,885	1,535

Source: Statistics Canada, *Religions in Canada*, Ottawa, Industry, Science and Technology Canada, 1993, table 2. Comparable figures for South Asian Muslims and Parsis are not available because Statistics Canada totals for those groups include Middle Eastern as well as South Asian immigrants.

such as Michael Ondaatje (winner of the 1992 Booker Prize for his novel, *The English Patient*) and Rohinton Mistry (winner of the 1991 Governor-General's award for his novel *Such a Long Journey*) are ranked among the best of Canada's creative writers. In spite of its sometimes inhospitable climate, Canada has proved to be a place where South Asian immigrants have flourished. Unlike other immigrant groups such as the Chinese, South Asians usually arrive with some knowledge of the English language. In addition, many South Asians have come from Commonwealth countries where the legal and political institutions bear a marked similarity to their counterparts in Canada. This has enabled them to adapt quickly and successfully to life in Canada [1: 55–65].

History

Around 1900 Sikhs began to arrive in British Columbia, mostly single males who proved themselves hard workers in lumbering and farming. By 1908 there were 5,000 Sikhs in the province and, together with the Chinese and Japanese immigrants, they were perceived as a threat by the relatively small Anglo-Saxon population. The Sikhs responded to this hostility by establishing *gurdwaras* under the auspices of the Vancouver Khalsa Diwan Society. As British subjects, they had been able to vote; but the British Columbia legislature removed that privilege, denying South Asians municipal and federal voting rights and excluding them from serving as school trustees, on juries or in public service, holding jobs resulting from public works contracts, purchasing Crown timber or practising the professions of law and pharmacy.

By passing the 'continuous journey' legislation in 1908, the federal government effectively banned further South Asian immigration by requiring South Asians to purchase a ticket for a through passage to Canada from their country of origin. Since no shipping company covered both the India–Hong Kong and the Hong Kong–Canada legs of the journey, the purchase of a continuous ticket was impossible, effectively cutting off immigration to Canada from India. A celebrated test case occurred in 1914 when a ship chartered by Sikhs in Hong Kong, the *Komagata Maru*, arrived in Vancouver with 376 Indians on board. In Vancouver, the Immigration Department allowed only twenty-two, who were returning to Canada, to land. The remainder were held on board for two months and then were deported to India. In the aftermath of this event, many Sikhs either returned to India or left for the United States, so that by 1918 the Sikh population in British Columbia had dwindled to 1,000.

Between 1919 and 1924, however, wives and children of men living in Canada were allowed to immigrate from India. This established a basis for family life; now, with existing *gurdwaras*, Sikhs finally had a place of their own in Canada – but not the vote or full rights. In spite of hostility and rejection from a community that saw them as Indians in Canada rather than Indo-Canadians, these pioneer Sikhs established themselves by focusing on their own religious and cultural foundations [3: 67]. For the next twenty years, the community remained static: a small group of Sikhs, constantly called 'Hindus' by the Canadian public of the day. In spite of these

difficulties, the established Sikh families flourished economically
and maintained their religious foundation through the Khalsa
Diwan Society and its *gurdwaras*, which exerted continual pressure
on provincial and federal politicians to cancel the 'continuous journey' rule and restore the vote to South Asian Canadians.

After Britain gave independence to India in 1947, the Indian
government pressed Canada to institute an annual immigration
quota such as had been established in the United States. In 1951
only 2,148 South Asians lived in Canada, 1,937 of them in British
Columbia [3: 105]. Giving in to pressure from the government of
India without, and from the Khalsa Diwan Society within, the
Canadian government initiated a quota system for South Asian
immigrants. In 1957 a new immigration agreement between Canada
and India raised the Indian quota from 150 to 300 per year, of
which one-half was to be preferentially filled by relatives of South
Asians who were already Canadian citizens. By the end of 1961,
under this new policy, 2,338 immigrant visas had been issued and
2,000 others came to Canada as dependent relatives – mostly professors, engineers, doctors, teachers and technicians [3: 106]. This
pattern continued throughout the 1960s as Canada was then experiencing a shortage of professionals. Thus, while the earliest South
Asian immigrants to Canada had been well-off Sikh farmers, the
second influx, of their relatives arriving in the 1950s and 1960s,
were well-educated professionals.

There was, however, another important dimension of this later
group of South Asian immigrants: not all were Sikhs. Gradually,
during the 1950s and 1960s, other ethnic/religious groups began to
arrive: Muslims from Punjab and Pakistan; Hindus from Punjab,
Uttar Pradesh, Gujarat, Bengal and Madras; and a few Buddhist
Sinhalese from Sri Lanka. They spread out across Canada, establishing settlements in Toronto, Montreal and other cities. No longer
could the South Asians in Canada be equated with the Sikh communities in British Columbia. Like the Sikhs, most of the Hindus
and Muslims arriving during this period were professional people;
many of them settled in the Toronto area.

Further changes in Canada's regulations during the 1960s
resulted in a sharp increase in South Asian immigration. The
government removed almost all racial, national and ethnic restrictions and instead focused on economic and social criteria. As a
result the annual rate of South Asian immigration increased rapidly
to over twelve times what it had been in the 1950s and, rather than
being focused in British Columbia, spread into cities right across
Canada: Montreal, Ottawa, Toronto, Hamilton, Winnipeg, Calgary
and Edmonton. This pattern continued through the 1970s,
although the occupational range broadened in these years to include
many more skilled blue-collar workers. The countries of origin of

these immigrants also became more varied, as South Asians came from Africa (Uganda, Kenya, Tanzania and South Africa) as well as from Fiji, Mauritius, Guyana and the Caribbean. Many of those from Africa were political refugees [3: 121–45]. In the late 1970s and early 1980s economic recessions in Canada resulted in a general restriction on immigration; family-sponsored immigrants took priority, making it difficult for independent South Asian migrants to come to Canada. However, South Asians have established such a strong base population in Canada that family-sponsored immigration alone means that South Asians will never comprise less than 10 per cent of Canada's new immigrants each year. While the rapid expansion of the period 1965–82, during which over 250,000 South Asians arrived, is over, the Canadian South Asian community has now reached a size suitable for the establishment of a solid foundation for life in Canada. This large size also makes it a very visible community, which has drawn some backlash from Anglo-Canadians and French Canadians.

Sikhs in Canada

Development and Debate

From 1900 to 1950 one could fairly say that the South Asian community in Canada was the Sikhs of British Columbia. In the 1950s a major rift occurred within Canadian Sikh communities over the cutting of hair and beard and wearing of the turban. While there have always been those within Sikhism who did not find it necessary to undergo initiation into the Khalsa and wear the five *karkars* (i.e. the *Nanakpanth* or followers of the teachings of Nanak, the first Guru), many Sikhs have insisted on complete conformity to the Khalsa discipline. While the wearing of the turban in India is widely practised and has a long and respected historical legacy, no such understanding was present in Canada. Consequently, many Sikhs felt pressured to shave, cut their hair and discard the turban so as to fit better into Canadian society. This resulted in a conflict over what Sikh practice requires. In 1952 the election of a clean-shaven man to the executive of the Vancouver Khalsa Diwan Society led to a split, with those insisting on the beard and turban leaving to form the Akali Singh Society with its own *gurdwaras* in Vancouver and Victoria [17: 13].

A rupture of a different kind occurred in 1984 when the Indian Prime Minister Indira Gandhi sent troops into the Golden Temple in Amritsar. Until then Sikhs and Hindus in Canada had usually seen themselves as part of the same community, often sharing the

same facilities. Events in India now shattered this sense of commonality, Sikhs withdrawing from association with Hindus. The invasion
of the Golden Temple and the events that followed – namely, the
assassination of Indira Gandhi, the massacre of Sikhs in Delhi, the
crash of an Air India flight from Toronto, continuing controversies
over Khalistani separatism and alleged Sikh terrorist activity –
created formal disruptions in Canada–India trade and diplomatic
activity, and internal delays in Sikh developments within Canada.
For example, plans for a Chair of Sikh Studies at the University of
British Columbia, funded equally by the community and the
government of Canada, were put on hold by the government until
relations between India and Canada normalized again in 1987 with
the signing of a treaty of extradition. Only then did the Canadian
government release its portion of the funding, making the appointment of Dr Harjot Oberoi to the Chair possible [20: 120]. Sikh
studies in Canadian universities, particularly at the University of
British Columbia and the University of Toronto (where Professor
W. H. McLeod of New Zealand has been teaching one term each
year) have resulted in Sikh sacred texts being placed under the close
examination of modern historical and critical scholarship. This has
led to yet another rift in the community. Some Sikhs with deeply
held convictions find the suggestion that certain of those convictions
lack historical truth to be profoundly upsetting. In response they
have mounted attacks against Harjot Oberoi and the many writings
of Hew McLeod, as well as those of the Canadian Sikh students he
has supervised at the University of Toronto (e.g. the doctoral thesis
of Pashura Singh). As Gurinder Singh Mann has noted, this diaspora scholarship and the negative reaction to it is symptomatic of
the coming of age of Sikh studies [18: 108].

Influential Sikh leaders in North America have lined up in support of such historical scholarship. While some of McLeod's books
have been published in Punjabi translation by Guru Nanak Dev
University in India, it is in diaspora settings such as Canada that the
revolution in Sikh studies is taking place. In order to be credible in
the modern West, some Canadian Sikhs have felt the need to put
their own tradition under the microscope of critical scholarly analysis so that it will be in a position to hold its own alongside other religions which have exposed themselves to modern scholarship and
not only survived but been able to reassert themselves more effectively in the modern world as a result. In Gurinder Singh Mann's
view, work by Canadian Sikh scholars such as Harjot Oberoi and
Pashura Singh is helping 'the Sikh community to understand that a
distinction can and must be made between the teaching of Sikhism
in a university' and its promotion at the *gurdwara* level' [18: 108].
Yet these are not completely separate activities, for the teaching of
Sikhism in Canadian universities, it is maintained, is allowing

Canadian students and society to understand Sikhism better, and Sikh students who take these courses to understand and interpret their tradition better to their Canadian peers. At the level of the *gurdwaras*, however, debate continues as to the wisdom of allowing the sacred tradition to be exposed to critical academic analysis. On balance, Canadian Sikh communities, and especially the predominance of university-educated professionals in their membership, seem to be pleased to have their tradition fully represented in the university curriculum alongside the other great religions.

Gurdwaras and Home Life

For Sikhs in Canada, it is their religion, centred in the *gurdwara*, that provides a sense of identity and community solidarity [5: 142]. Thus, wherever Sikhs have settled, *gurdwaras* have rapidly appeared: first in Vancouver, Victoria and other British Columbia locations, then in Toronto and cities such as Windsor, Winnipeg, Calgary and Edmonton. In 1969 the first *gurdwara* in Ontario was opened in a converted warehouse in Toronto. Now there are some twenty-five *gurdwaras* in Ontario, the most recent being a new building in Malton (a Toronto district) that seats 15,000 people and is the largest *gurdwara* in North America [14: 65]. As the centre of the Sikh community, the *gurdwara* is a meeting-place for worship, religious and cultural education, the celebration of festivals, the collection of funds for charitable projects, and the discussion of issues important to Sikhs. When the Sikh community needs to respond to events in mainstream Canadian life, political or otherwise, it is at the *gurdwara* that such responses are organized. The *gurdwara* is also the place where family events such as births, weddings and deaths are shared with the community. While Sikhs have daily prayers and scripture readings at home, Sunday worship in the *gurdwara* brings the whole community out to worship and eat together. This Canadian pattern follows the practice established in India: a priest or *granthi* reads from scripture, the Adi Granth, preaches on the text which has been read, and leads in prayers and the singing of hymns or *kirtans*. The Indian Sikh pattern of worship has required little adaptation to fit its new Canadian setting. After the service, families take turns in providing the common meal in which everyone, including any visitors, shares.

One major change in the *gurdwara*'s function has occurred. In the early British Columbia Sikh communities, the *gurdwara* was not only the religious centre but also the locus of social service, political and cultural activities. Canadian public policy has adopted multiculturalism (*The Canadian Multicultural Act* 1990). This policy, however, has increasingly separated out the religious from these other activities and placed the latter into an ethnic rather than a religious context. While consistent with Canada's stated commitment to multiculturalism and religious pluralism, this policy has resulted in new government or government-supported institutions being established on an ethnic basis to provide social and cultural services in a non-religious context. Thus, whereas Canada's first *gurdwaras* provided food and shelter for homeless Sikhs, helped with immigration and employment, and offered educational and cultural programmes, these functions have now largely been taken over by government agencies or semi-governmental organizations like the Immigrant Services Centre and various ethnic health services organizations. Also, with the establishment of community groups such as the Punjabi Cultural Association, the Punjabi Literary Association and independent Punjabi schools, ethnic cultural and educational activities no longer belong exclusively to the *gurdwaras* [8: 89]. Now, *gurdwaras* are more closely focused on religious concerns and function increasingly like Western-style 'houses of worship'. Support for this differentiation between 'religion' and 'ethnicity' is especially strong among two groups: Canadian-born second- or third-generation Sikhs and a small but vocal group of white, non-South-Asian, Sikh converts.

Second- or third-generation Canadians of Punjabi Sikh ancestry are now a sizeable group and are marked by their strong ethnic identity. By and large they have not married outside their own group. While they have responded aggressively to increasing anti-South-Asian hostility in recent years, they have in the main kept their distance from recent Sikh religious revivalism, 'regarding it as an unfortunate return to aspects of life in "village India" with little relevance to, or positive implications for, the community's situation in Canada' [8: 90]. Many second- and third-generation Sikhs are comfortable in identifying more closely with ethnic cultural and political institutions than with religious organizations from which they may feel estranged. Thus, as Dusenbury observes, the idea arises that in Canada one can be 'ethnically Sikh' without being 'religiously Sikh' [8: 90]. This is, of course, consistent with Canadian public policy, where religious practice is seen as a matter of individual preference and quite separate from one's ethnicity. Equally, it is just such a 'Canadian' or 'Western' way of living that may properly cause concern among those who judge Sikhism to be a total way of life, not separable into religious and secular ethnic components.

Field studies with Sikhs living in Canada show that changes are occurring in their experience of scripture, the Adi Granth. The many distractions and pressures of modern Canadian society militate against the experience of 'village India'. The individualistic and rationalistic nature of modern society emphasizes intellectual study rather than the devotional approach to scripture. The crucial importance of being immersed in learning the singing of scripture as a child poses a major challenge to Sikh parents in Canada. Canadian Sikhs report that the pressures to amass material possessions, to drink and eat meat, and the fast pace which leaves little time for devotions, results in a life, as one respondent put it, which is 20 per cent Sikh and 80 per cent the other life [10: 29]. He feels himself pulled apart by the pressures towards egoism, selfishness and competition – all of which go against the teachings of the Adi Granth. Some respond by taking *amrit* or baptism and joining the Khalsa in the hope that that this commitment with its outward symbols will call forth a more complete dedication.

Sikhs are also experimenting with ways to make their Sunday services more attractive to their Canadian-born children. Although most children can understand some Punjabi, many cannot read the prayers in the original. Therefore English translations are sometimes offered, and at least one group is experimenting with home worship in which the prayers are said in English and Punjabi [14: 66]. Sikh youth camps are also common across Canada as one- or two-week summer events where Sikh traditions are taught to the young.

In recent years clashes between Sikh practice and Canadian public policy have achieved a high profile in the media. The red-coated Royal Canadian Mounted Police (RCMP) officer is a cherished Canadian symbol. Problems arose when the RCMP set out to recruit members of Canada's ethnic minorities. Sikhs selected for service wished to wear beard and turban, in conformity with Khalsa requirements, rather than the flat-brimmed stetson required as regulation dress by the force. Because they wished to recruit ethnic minorities and because they realized that the regulation requiring wearing of the Mountie dress hat would probably not withstand a court challenge based on the 1982 Charter of Rights and Freedoms which forbids religious discrimination of any kind, the Canadian government relaxed the regulation, allowing Sikhs in the RCMP to wear turbans. A subsequent court challenge of this ruling was brought by a group of RCMP veterans but was lost.

Such incidents are testing both the determination of Canadian Sikhs to participate fully at all levels in Canadian society – without sacrificing their religious beliefs – and the validity of the Canadian claim to a multicultural policy which respects ethnic and religious differences. An interesting consequence of these debates is the desire of some non-Khalsa Sikhs to make clear to Canadians that not all Sikhs are required by their religious beliefs to wear turbans in public. Media focus on Sikhs wearing turbans in the RCMP has misled Canadians into thinking that all Sikhs must wear turbans. This, the non-Khalsa Sikhs point out, applies only to a particular group of Sikhs, namely those initiated into the Khalsa; other Sikhs are not required by religion to wear the turban [15]. Whereas all Khalsa are Sikhs, not all Sikhs are Khalsas. This distinction, while correct, is certain to create further confusion among non-Sikh Canadians.

The above discussion of the Sikhs in Canada has been more lengthy and detailed than will be offered for the two other major religious groups of the South Asian diaspora in Canada, the Hindus and the Muslims. The reason for this is twofold. First, the Sikhs, historically, *were* the South Asian diaspora in Canada from 1900 to 1950, and they are still the largest group. Secondly, because of the distinctive appearance of the Khalsa Sikhs, they provide, in many ways, the 'acid test' as to how effective Canada's official policy of multiculturalism is in practice – as evidenced in the turban debate, discussed above.

Hindus in Canada

Unlike the Sikhs, who are virtually all ethnic Punjabis, Canadian Hindus have a variety of ethnic backgrounds. The earliest Hindus were also Punjabis and they came along with the Sikh migration. The next largest group of South Asians who came directly from India were Hindus from Uttar Pradesh and surrounding regions in northern India. They are Hindi speakers, largely from an urban middle-class background, and came as part of the large group of South Asian professionals who arrived in Canada as independent migrants in the 1960s. During the same period some Tamil Hindus from the Madras area came to Canada as teachers. Bengali Hindus began to arrive during the 1970s. Also during the 1960s and 1970s, substantial numbers of Hindus – as well as Muslims – arrived in Canada from former British colonies that were achieving independence and discriminated against South Asians, including East Africa, South Africa, Fiji, Mauritius, Guyana and Trinidad. While Hindus from East Africa tended to be professionals and business-people, those arriving from the other areas were mainly blue-collar workers [3: 212–47]. In Canada, Hindus spread themselves across the country, settling mainly in larger cities.

Unlike Sikhs, Hindus do not have a unified set of beliefs and practices shared by all believers. Nor is their religion so heavily focused on a community temple with weekly congregational worship. Hindu religious practice is more individual in nature and centred on the home and family. Thus Canadian immigrant Hindus at first felt no pressure for a public place of worship. However, by

1970 Hindus had extended their individual worship to include group prayer services held in one another's homes – especially if a visiting teacher from India was passing through. Such meetings, however, often remained specific to particular ethnic groups. In the 1970s secular issues surrounding marriage and death in Canada led Hindu groups to begin to think of erecting temples. In Canada, unlike India, marriage or death rites were public occasions, and a Hindu community without a temple had nowhere to celebrate them. This need drew diverse groups of Hindus together in the larger centres and buildings were constructed. One of the first was the Vishwa Hindu Parishad of Vancouver, which in 1974 opened a multi-use temple [3: 190]. As Hugh Johnston observes, 'The members of the Vishwa Hindu Parishad, who have been raised in many local Indian traditions, have made practical compromises to create a religious community in Canada; and they have created a place of worship which is as much a church or *gurdwara* as it is a temple' [17: 11]. Worship is congregational, taking place between 12 noon and 1.00 p.m. on Sundays, with people arriving and leaving on time in Protestant fashion, unless there is food in the kitchen below provided by a family, Sikh-style, for which people remain after the worship service.

Permanent multi-use facilities now also exist in Calgary, Edmonton and Toronto. In other locations, Hindus depend upon temporary arrangements, for example, renting the halls of Christian churches, for their religious celebrations. Unlike the Sikhs, where fund-raising to build a *gurdwara* involved an appeal to a single ethnic community, Hindus have had to span many different ethnic and religious groupings in order to raise the required funds. This has often been a difficult diplomatic task. Once a temple is established, its use is allocated by time to the various Hindu groups. General prayer services and religious lectures designed to serve all usually occur on Sundays; individual families book the temple for marriages, funerals and other special occasions. As Buchignani observes, 'This multi-use concept is a brilliant solution to the difficulties posed by divergent Hindu practice and belief' [3: 190]. It has helped draw Hindus together so that Hinduism has an organizational basis upon which to be recognized as a formal religion within Canada. Towards this end the Vishwa Hindu Parishad of Vancouver in 1983 organized a national conference to develop the constitution for a Hindu Council of Canada [3: 190]. Not all Hindus have been satisfied with this unifying approach, and in Toronto, where Hindu numbers are sufficiently large, various ethnic groupings have established their own institutional organizations and obtained their own buildings.

Milton Israel reports that there are now more than fifty Hindu temples and organizations in Ontario, most in the Toronto area.

The oldest Hindu temple there, the Prarthana Samaj, was established in 1967 when a former church was purchased. Immigrants from Guyana and Trinidad under the leadership of Dr Bhupendra Doobray, a cardiovascular surgeon who also served as priest, purchased a building on Yonge Street in 1981 that became their temple – the Vishnu Mandir. A new temple was built in 1984 and another in 1990. It draws 600–700 people to a Sunday service which is followed, Sikh-style, by a congregational meal sponsored by a family. The temple staff consists of six priests from India and Dr Doobray who preaches the sermon. The service proceeds in Sanskrit, Hindi and English. A variety of images are present in the temple and the front altar holds statues to the gods Durga, Hanuman, Ganesh and Rama; discussion is under way regarding the possible inclusion of the Buddha and Lord Mahavira of the Jains. The eclectic nature of this very successful Hindu temple is evident.

A contrasting pattern is evident in the Ganesh temple established by Tamil immigrants from south India, South Africa, Singapore and Malaysia and refugees from Sri Lanka. The emphasis of this group is on the purity of the building and its rituals from a Tamil perspective; for example, it celebrates the festival of Lord Murugan, the patron god of the Tamils. Building of the Ganesh temple complex (it also contains a senior citizens' facility, living apartments for priests, a wedding hall and a cafeteria) began in 1984 and is still continuing. Rather than adapting to a Canadian congregational style, as the Vishnu temple has done, the Ganesh temple attempts faithfully to recreate south Indian Hindu worship in Canada – as the Sri Venkateswara temple has done in Pittsburgh. Around the large hall are fourteen altars where *murtis* or images of individual gods such as Ganesh, Shiva, Durga and Murugan are installed, each with 'their own space where individual worshippers may come and pray, alone or with the mediation of a priest' [14: 57]. Thus several activities involving different worshippers, priests and gods may be going on simultaneously, producing the general cacophony of sound typical of a south Indian temple. Unlike the Vishnu temple, Sunday is not a special day at the Ganesh temple. Festival days, however, are, and on these occasions 10,000–15,000 people may attend [14: 58].

A third example of the variety of Hindu practice in the Toronto area is provided by the Arya Samajis. Followers of Dayananda Saraswati, they reject the use of images in worship and instead focus on a simple Vedic fire ritual which any member of the Samaj can perform. They also reject caste. Arya Samaj followers came to Canada mainly from East Africa and the Caribbean as well as from India. In Toronto there are two Arya Samaj communities which are part of a North American network with congregations in more than seventy cities including London, Windsor, Calgary and others in Canada. Linguistic differences separate the two Toronto groups.

One is made up of mainly Hindi speakers from East Africa or India and conducts worship in Hindi. The other is made up of immigrants from the Caribbean who do not know Hindi and conduct their services in English. Both groups, however, chant the Vedas in Sanskrit [14: 60].

The Toronto area, with its large concentration of close to 100,000 Hindus, offers a magnification of the patterns that exist in more or less developed form in other Canadian cities. While a multi-use temple with Canadian Protestant-style congregational worship may satisfy communities with smaller numbers of Hindus, ethnic and sectarian differences seem to manifest themselves once the population of Hindus becomes large enough to support such divisions. Ethnic languages play a major role in such separations, and it is an open question as to how successful these first-generation communities will be in passing their languages on to their children.

Another aspect of Hindu religion that was present in India, and has assumed increased importance in religious practice in Canada, is the role of the guru. Scholars have concluded that the enlightened guru is the dynamic sacred centre of Hinduism – that the guru's interpretation of scripture, tradition and experience is more sacred than the sacred texts or rituals themselves. At the home altar, photos or images of an individual's or family's guru often occupy centre stage in addition to the deities one would find in the temple. The role of the guru has been to restructure the traditional *puja* and ritual of village India to meet the challenge of modern life in both India and Canada [11]. However, modern Indian gurus such as Maharishi Mahesh Yogi, Prabhupada, Rajneesh and Sathya Sai Baba have attracted more occidental followers than South Asian Canadians.

Restructuring is especially evident in the ritual function of sacred language. In India, sacred Hindu texts were learned passively by being heard over and over again as part of one's daily activity until they were internalized and became part of one's consciousness. By this means, passages from the Vedas, Upanishads, Gita, Ramayana, etc. were memorized by oral repetition at a young age and through repeated rehearsal in ritual became a foundational part of the individual's mature consciousness. To some extent, audio and video presentations of the Ramayana and Mahabharata attempt to replace the traditional ways of learning these texts.

In Canada everything is different. No longer do the children rise at five in the morning to chant Sanskrit texts with parents and grandparents as they did in India. Some adults confess that they now do their morning chanting while running for the bus or while walking or driving to work. Gone is the leisurely pace of rural India. In Canada it is replaced by the Protestant work ethic. Within the home it is hard to find a time in either the morning or the evening when the whole family can gather for worship. Sometimes Saturday is set aside for family devotional practice. Often the absence of grand-parents or other members of the extended family further reduces the power of the family to transmit the sacred tradition. Outside the family, Hindus live as a minority group in a secular, materialistic culture, and so the contextual reinforcement of family practice, experienced in India, is simply absent in Canada. In the face of these difficulties a new practice, introduced by gurus, is appearing. It responds to the complexities and time problems of Canadians by simplifying home worship into a pattern which, in essence, consists in chanting a guru's name or *mantra* 108 times, two or three times a day [11: 103]. Whereas in India practice involved both traditional Sanskrit texts chanted in rituals *and* observances relating to a guru, in Canada much of this is collapsed into one simple flexible and effi-cient practice – chanting the guru's name or *mantra*.

While the *guru mantra* may prove effective for Hindus living in Canada, it does raise questions. The very simplicity of the approach and the 'blind faith' in the guru that is required may well produce a Hinduism with more dependence upon a priestly group (i.e. the gurus) than was the case in India. If Hindus no longer learn their scripture and ritual in childhood, the possibility of home religious practice independent of the guru may be largely lost; and without the foundation of daily worship at home, temple worship may rapidly become a shell of what it once was. Dependence upon a guru, however, may be the only way of continuing daily Hindu wor-ship in the modern Canadian context.

Following the lead of the Sikhs, Canadian Hindus also took advantage of the federal government's matching grant programme to establish a Chair of Hindu Studies at Concordia University in Montreal in the mid-1980s. The first appointment to the Chair was Dr Krishna Sivaraman, an internationally known scholar who had previously served McMaster University in Canada and Banaras Hindu University in India. This Chair gave Hindu studies a high profile.

Muslims in Canada

According to the 1991 census there are 253,000 Muslims in Canada, of which about 91,000 are South Asians. Of the South Asians, the largest groups came from Pakistan, Gujarat via East Africa, Bangladesh, Sri Lanka and the Caribbean. In Canada they are mostly concentrated in the urban centres of Montreal, Toronto, Calgary, Edmonton and Vancouver. The majority of South Asian

Muslims came to Canada during the period of open immigration in the 1960s and 1970s. A great many are well-educated professional people.

By far the best organized of all the South Asian Muslims in Canada are the Isma'ilis. They are Shi'i Muslims who follow the Agha Khan, whose headquarters are in France. Originally from Gujarat in India, the Isma'ilis moved to East Africa, where they prospered; expelled from East Africa, they came to Canada, where they refined and modernized their organization in a complex hierarchical structure that links small local groups, with individual prayer halls (*jamat khana*), into a national structure with headquarters in Toronto. Perhaps more than any other South Asian religious community, the Isma'ilis have successfully transferred a religious life of daily practice to Canada. Most families pay a tithe of 10 per cent of their income, so the community has flourished financially. Rather than building large central mosques, the Isma'ili pattern is to have small *jamat khana* within neighbourhoods to facilitate attendance at daily prayer meetings. The most important weekly meeting is on Friday, but in Canada it has been shifted from midday to the evening to accommodate Canadian work schedules [3: 187].

In Ontario there are *jamat khanas* in Unionville, Markham, Toronto and Brampton [14: 74]. Montreal has one *jamat khana* near the city centre and a small one on the West Island [19: 321]. In British Columbia there are thirteen *jamat khanas*; Alberta has five in Calgary and several in Edmonton. Most *jamat khanas* are open every day in the early hours of the morning for *dhikr* or personal meditation, and in the evenings for family prayers. In her study of Isma'ili worship patterns in Canada, Parin Dossa finds that there has been a significant change from the community's practice in East Africa. There, 80 per cent of families attended the *jamat khana* daily, whereas in Canada, with the faster pace and greater complexity of life, only 44 per cent of families manage daily attendance, with 23 per cent going two to three times per week and 33 per cent appearing on festive occasions only [7: 56]. An equally important aspect of Dossa's analysis is the added stress living in Canada has put on Isma'ili women. Whereas in East Africa women were at home all day and had ample time to prepare dinner and organize the family for attendance at evening prayers, in Canada most women work outside the home. As prayers at the *jamat khana* usually begin at 7.00 p.m., this means that Isma'ili women who go out to work typically have the following stressful schedule: simple meals are prepared the night before; a phone call is made from work to remind the children to take a bath (baths must be taken before going to prayers); on arrival home, the children are fed first and then the husband (who eats by himself while his wife gets herself ready to go out); after 7.00 p.m. prayers the wife eats alone [7: 57].

While this rigorous and highly organized schedule makes it possible for families to attend evening prayers, it is too hectic for many families to maintain daily; hence the decline from 80 per cent to 44 per cent in daily attendance at evening prayers since coming from East Africa. The shared family dinner, a highlight of life in East Africa, seems no longer possible. Isma'ili adaptation to life in Canada, while successful, has been at a cost to women and to family life. Its rigid hierarchical structure is also proving an irritant to the young, some of whom are shifting to the more democratic approach of the Canadian Sunni Muslims.

The Pakistani Sunni Muslim community is comparable in size to the Isma'ili. A few Punjabi-speaking Muslims arrived in Vancouver in 1904 with the first Sikhs; most, however, have migrated since 1967, settling mainly in Ontario, Quebec and Alberta. They are generally well-educated professionals, including doctors, university professors and teachers. Rather than remaining insular, they have joined together with Sunni Muslims from the Middle East in mosques and Islamic centres in Montreal, Toronto, Ottawa, Edmonton, Calgary and Vancouver [17: 19]. This same pattern has been followed by other South Asian Sunni Muslims arriving from Bangladesh, Fiji and the Caribbean, who either supported mosques already in existence or joined with other Sunnis to start mosques – as is the Sunni practice around the world. Ethnic divisions tend to surface only for special annual South Asian religious celebrations. In most of the above cities, permanent Sunni mosques have now been built. In addition to regular worship, Sunni organizations devote careful attention to educating the young in the Arabic language and the Qur'an. However, since South Asian Sunnis differ in language and culture from other Sunnis, and from each other, such teaching is usually carried on in ethnic associations rather than through mosques [3: 188].

Yet another group of South Asian Muslims should be noted in passing. The Ahmadiyyas, a nineteenth-century sectarian movement of Islam which began in India, claims some 10,000 adherents in Canada. About half of them are in Toronto with smaller groups in cities such as Montreal, Vancouver and Calgary. The Canadian Ahmadiyya headquarters is located in Maple, Ontario. There they have built the largest mosque in North America, which has prayer rooms with large television screens on which their leader's sermons are broadcast live from London (where he lives) by satellite [14: 75]. A trademark of the Ahmadiyyas across Canada is the inter-faith discussions on contemporary issues which they regularly sponsor.

Yvonne Haddad has concisely summarized the stresses and adaptations that life in Canada has caused for South Asian Muslims [12]. For Pakistani Muslims in Canada, the ideal of contiguity between religion and state (basic to the establishment of Pakistan as separate from India) seems an unlikely prospect in their new country where they are but a tiny minority. Despite the government policy of multiculturalism, Canada, like the whole of the Western world, seems hostile to those who are attempting to be faithful to the traditional practice of Islam. There are no minarets to call the faithful to prayer, nor is time provided for the performance of prayer during working hours. Interviews with Canadian Muslims indicate that those who had been faithful in spiritual practice in their home country often became negligent in their performance in Canada. Long working hours and television tend to keep people up later in the evening, making the early rising for prayers, which is customary in the Arab world and Pakistan, difficult. As a result, Muslim law has provided alternative times for prayer. But it appears that once Muslims begin to compromise on this they become less assiduous, and prayer is reduced to once or twice a day [12: 75]. Canada's northern geographical location adds an extra problem if Ramadan comes in the summer, for the dawn-to-dusk fast period can then be very long – from 4.00 a.m. until 11.00 p.m. in June in Edmonton; in the far north, night may never arrive. Some Muslims solve this problem by observing times of sunrise and sunset as they would be on the latitude of Mecca.

Like other Canadians, Muslims borrow from the bank to start businesses, to buy houses and, in at least three cases in Calgary, London and Windsor, to build mosques. Yet the practice of usury is banned in the Qur'an. Explanations offered to justify this practice include the idea that dealing with a bank is not the same as dealing with an individual, and that it is necessary for modern living. Other areas of stress for Muslims living in Canada include the sexual freedom of Canadian society, the presence of pornography, the difficulty in obtaining properly slaughtered meat, dating practices among young people and conflict between Canadian and Islamic inheritance and marriage laws. Muslim girls have had problems in Canadian schools; dress codes have ruled out the traditional head covering and required the wearing of shorts (thus exposing the legs) for gym. The courts, however, have decided against the schools and in favour of Muslim traditional dress for those who wish to wear it. Even in the mosque there is a sense of separation. Muslims of South Asian background tend to keep separate from Muslims of Middle Eastern origin. As one Pakistani leader put it, 'We worship together, but then the Pakistanis go back to their curries and the Arabs to their kebabs' [12: 80]. One wonders if this sense of separation will persist in young people of the second and third generation. As to the relationships between the three Muslim communities, they get on by ignoring each other. At the theological level, the Ahmadiyyas are not recognized as real Muslims by either the Sunnis or the Isma'ilis.

Other South Asian Religious Groups

In addition to the large groupings of Sikhs, Hindus and Muslims, South Asian immigrants to Canada have included Buddhists, Jains, Parsis, Jews and Christians. By far the largest of these groups are the South Asian Christians, numbering 31,385 Roman Catholics and 22,750 Protestants in the 1991 census. The Roman Catholics, like other Christian immigrants, have blended into local Canadian congregations. Some of the Protestants, however, especially those from Kerala, have created their own Malayali-language churches wherever sufficient numbers were present. For example, the first such Toronto congregation was established in 1968 and today there are eleven congregations in the city. In addition, the Canadian Mar Thoma Church and the New Grace Covenant Pentecostal Church have their own churches [14: 80]. The Mar Thoma Church claims to descend from Thomas the disciple of Jesus who, according to Indian tradition, arrived on the Malabar Coast from Palestine in the first century CE. The Mar Thomas have congregations in the other major Canadian cities of South Asian immigration.

Buddhists number some 3,000 and have mainly settled in Toronto. The majority are Theravadins from Sri Lanka. They have their own Sri Lankan Centre in Toronto, complete with monks, services on Sunday, and Sunday school classes for the whole congregation. A very small group of Indian Buddhists have formed themselves into the Ambedkar Mission, named after Dr B. R. Ambedkar of India. A Sri Lankan monk leads services for them on Saturdays. A small number of Jains, mainly from Gujarat, are spread across the major cities. To date they do not seem to have formed any separate organizations. Some 300 Baghdadi Jews left India (from the areas of Bombay, Calcutta, Puna and Surat) in the late 1940s to settle in Montreal and Toronto. They have integrated easily into existing Jewish congregations.

The Parsis are Zoroastrians who, oppressed under Islamic rule in their Iranian homeland, fled to north-west India in the tenth century. Although they first settled in Gujarat, they moved to Bombay in increasing numbers from the seventeenth century [13]. Parsis began to arrive in Canada in 1965, the earliest Parsi migrants settling in Montreal and Vancouver, but the major growth in numbers took place in the 1970s and Toronto quickly became the main centre. There are now more than 2,500 Parsis in Canada, the vast majority residing in southern Ontario. Hinnells points out that the backgrounds of Parsis arriving in Canada were quite variable [13]. Many came to Canada via East Africa, and tended to be highly educated professionals or businesspeople. Those in business were more traditional than the professionals; those who migrated from rural

Gujarat or from Karachi were more traditional than those from Bombay. Canada is seen by migrating Parsis as a less threatening host than either Britain or the United States due to its multiculturalism policy, which is perceived to encourage individuals and groups to preserve their religious and ethnic identities. For example, a government grant enabled the Toronto association to enlarge their building.

The history of the Parsis of southern Ontario, as reported by Milton Israel [14], may be taken as typical. Many Parsis responded to federal government advertisements in the late 1960s for professional and middle-class families. They established the Zoroastrian Society of Ontario and issued a regular newsletter. They rented halls for religious and cultural occasions. In the 1970s the community, with substantial help from the Iranian businessman Arbab Rustam Guiv, purchased an estate in North York for use as a temple. After a battle with the city over zoning restrictions was settled in favour of the Parsis, the temple was dedicated in 1980. The temple now serves as the religious, cultural and administrative centre for southern Ontario's Parsis. Currently there are fourteen hereditary priests in southern Ontario, six of whom are in active service [14: 76–8].

Hinnells [13: 66] notes that in Canada tensions sometimes arise between South Asians and Iranians in the Zoroastrian community, with the Iranians sometimes claiming to be truer to the tradition. Differences exist at both superficial and deeper levels. At community festivals, Parsis do not enjoy kebabs and Iranians dislike spicy Indian food. The Iranian Muslim environment has led them to emphasize the authority of the revealed words of the Prophet, whereas Parsis from the Hindu context 'commonly see the priest as a man of spiritual power and complex rituals as points of access to that power' [13: 66]. This has led to a situation in which many Parsis accept the authority of priests in Bombay but not in Iran, while Iranian immigrants will not accept the priests or leaders in India. To date this tension has not been successfully resolved.

Because many of the Parsis who migrated to Canada were highly educated and Westernized people they adapted quickly. They ensured that their children were highly educated in school and university. The professional nature of a large percentage of the community means that reason has been stressed sometimes to the detriment of religion. A study conducted by Hinnells finds that 'Those who undertake postgraduate studies in the sciences typically affirm what might be called their "ethnic links" (food, language, music) more strongly, but substantially fewer of them assert their religious links' [13: 71]. Against this, however, is Hinnells' own observation that a liturgical development is occurring among those in the diaspora. While it may not have the blessing of the Bombay leadership, who would see it as a corruption, the simplification of purity rituals, the making of prayers meaningful and the critical interpretation of the scripture, when combined with the 'young seeking for their roots', may well result in a religious revitalization. New Zoroastrian leadership may well be found in diaspora meetings of priests in Toronto, rather than in pronouncements from India or Iran.

Conclusion

South Asians are a high-profile part of Canada's cultural mosaic. They share an internal awareness of being a strong South Asian presence. A complex of communities embodying seven major religions and many more ethnic communities, South Asians provide a major challenge to Canada's multiculturalism policy. While South Asians have apparently adapted successfully to life in Canada, some signs suggest that this may have occurred at the expense of their religious practices. Changes are definitely taking place as traditional religion engages with the modern, secular pluralism that prevails in Canada. Judgement as to the positive or negative nature of these changes for the South Asian religious diaspora will be possible only in the second and third generations of these communities in Canada. Because religion provides the meaning and structure which undergirds these communities, the continued vitality of religion, in new or old forms, will be essential to the future viability of South Asian traditions in Canada.

Bibliography

1 BUCHIGNANI, NORMAN, 'South Asian Canadians and the Ethnic Mosaic: An Overview', *Canadian Ethnic Studies*, vol. 11 (1979)
2 BUCHIGNANI, NORMAN, 'Conceptions of Sikh Culture in the Development of a Comparative Analysis of the Sikh Diaspora', in J. T. O'Connell, M. Israel and W. G. Oxtoby (eds), *Sikh History and Religion in the Twentieth Century*, Toronto, Centre for South Asian Studies, 1988
3 BUCHIGNANI, NORMAN, INDRA, DOREEN M., and SRIVASTAVA, RAM, *Continuous Journey: A Social History of South Asians in Canada*, Toronto, McClelland & Stewart, 1985
4 *Canadian Multicultural Act, The: A Guide for Canadians*, Ottawa, Canadian Government Printing Office, 1990
5 CHADNEY, JAMES G., *The Sikhs of Vancouver*, New York, AMS Press, 1984

6   D'COSTA, RONALD, 'Socio-Demographic Characteristics of the Population of South Asian Origins in Canada', in Milton Israel and N. K. Wagle (eds), *Ethnicity, Identity, Migration: The South Asian Context*, Toronto, Centre for South Asian Studies, 1993, pp. 181–95

7   DOSSA, PARIN, 'Ismaili Space/Time: An Anthropological Perspective of Ismaili Immigrant Women in Calgary and Vancouver', *Canadian Ethnic Studies*, vol. 20, 1988

8   DUSENBURY, VERNE A., 'Canadian Ideology and Public Policy: The Impact on Vancouver Sikh Ethnic and Religious Adaptation', *Canadian Ethnic Studies*, vol. 13, 1981

9   *Globe and Mail*, 'Legion Controversy Riles Veterans Groups', 3 June 1994, p. A2

10 GOA, DAVID, and COWARD, HAROLD, 'Ritual Word and Meaning in Sikh Religious Life: A Canadian Field Study', *Journal of Sikh Studies*, vol. 13, 1986, pp. 13–32

11 GOA, DAVID J., COWARD, HAROLD G., and NEUFELDT, RONALD, 'Hindus in Alberta: A Study in Religious Continuity and Change', *Canadian Ethnic Studies*, vol. 16, 1984

12 HADDAD, YVONNE YASBECK, 'Muslims in Canada', in Harold Coward and Leslie Kawamura (eds), *Religion and Ethnicity*, Waterloo, Wilfrid Laurier University Press, 1977, pp. 101–14

13 HINNELLS, JOHN R., 'The Modern Zoroastrian Diaspora', in J. M. Brown and R. Foot (eds), *Migration: The Asian Experience*, London, Macmillan, 1994, pp. 56–82

14 ISRAEL, MILTON, *In the Further Soil: A Social History of the Indo-Canadians in Ontario*, Toronto, Organization for the Promotion of Indian Culture, 1994

15 JAIN, SUSHIL, 'Sikh or Khalsa? The Question of Identity or Definition', *Canadian Ethnic Studies*, vol. 22, 1990

16 JOHNSTON, HUGH, *The Voyage of the Komagata Maru: The Sikh Challenge to Canada's Colour Bar*, Bombay, Oxford University Press, 1979

17 JOHNSTON, HUGH, 'The Development of the Punjabi Community in Vancouver since 1961', *Canadian Ethnic Studies*, vol. 20, 1988

18 MANN, GURINDER SINGH, 'Sikh Studies and the Sikh Educational Heritage', in J. S. Hawley and G. S. Mann (eds), *Studying the Sikhs: Issues for North America*, Albany, State University of New York Press, 1993

19 MCDONOUGH, SHEILA, 'Muslims of Montreal', in Y. Haddad and J. Smith (eds), *Muslim Communities of North America*, Albany, State University of New York Press, 1994, pp. 317–34

20 O'CONNELL, JOSEPH T., 'Sikh Studies in North America: A Field Guide', in J. S. Hawley and G. S. Mann (eds), *Studying the Sikhs: Issues for North America*, Albany, State University of New York Press, 1993

21 SRINIVAS, KALBURGI M., and KAUL, SAROOP K., *Indo-Canadians in Saskatchewan: The Early Settlers*, Regina, SK: India-Canada Association of Saskatchewan, 1987

22 STATISTICS CANADA, *Religions in Canada*, Ottawa, Industry, Science and Technology Canada, 1993

23 *Time Magazine*, 'May Mounties Wear Turbans?', Canadian edn, 30 October 1989, p. 56

24

South Asian Religions in the United States

RAYMOND BRADY WILLIAMS

The first South Asian immigrants came to the United States in 1820, but not until the beginning of the twentieth century did more than 275 people arrive from India in a single decade. Punjabi Sikhs fled to California from serious anti-oriental riots in Vancouver, British Columbia, in 1907. They were part of a large oriental influx that caused a change in US government policy from the 'open door' characteristic of the nineteenth century to the restrictive Immigration Act of 1917 and the 'Asiatic Barred Zone'. During the Great Depression of the 1930s and the Second World War of the 1940s, immigration virtually ceased, and some reverse emigration even developed. Not until the Luce–Celler legislation in 1946 were migrants from South Asia allowed to enter (100 persons per year) and made eligible for citizenship. Only 13,607 persons immigrated legally from India between 1820 and 1960.

Large-scale immigration from India followed changes in the (Hart–Celler) immigration law of 1965, which opened the door to migrants from countries previously virtually excluded, including countries of South Asia. It stipulated that those admitted in the first few years would be those in professions needed in the United States, constituting the 'brain drain' from these developing countries – doctors, engineers, scientists, nurses – who quickly established themselves as upper-middle-class professionals. More recently, family members have been admitted under the family reunification provisions of the law. Many relatives do not possess the educational or professional qualifications of their sponsors and have to wait as long as ten years to enter. Nevertheless, the South Asian community is generally young, well-educated, prosperous and energetic. As part of the 'new ethnics', they are transforming cultural and religious life in the United States in ways that were unforeseen by those proposing changes in the immigration law (see table 24.1).

Table 24.1   South Asian population growth in the United States

	1980	1990	% change
Asian Indian	361,531	815,447	+125.6
Bangladeshi	1,314	11,838	+800.9
Pakistani	15,792	81,371	+415.3
Sri Lankan	2,923	10,970	+275.3

Source: US Department of Commerce, Bureau of the Census, 1990, CB91–215.

Canadian immigration laws, influenced heavily by Canada's position in the British Commonwealth, permitted earlier, less restricted immigration from Commonwealth countries. Admission of refugees holding Commonwealth passports, such as those from East Africa in the 1960s and early 1970s, created South Asian communities in Canada very different in economic, social, professional, educational and religious backgrounds from the South Asians in the United States (see chapter 23 in this volume). These new citizens and permanent residents represent many different South Asian regional, linguistic and ethnic groups, and they are active in several different religions. South Asian contributions to religious diversity are transforming the religious landscape of North America.

The Religions

Sikhs

Sikhs entered the United States from Canada as single male Punjabi agriculturalists early in the twentieth century. Shortly after they arrived, the Immigration Act of 1917 prevented Sikh men from sending to Punjab for brides, so only six Sikh women resided in the country from 1904 to 1947. Moreover, Sikhs were not eligible for citizenship and were not permitted to own land. Men married outside the community and were largely assimilated: they gave up the beard and turban; few children were initiated into Khalsa membership, and the second generation was raised with little knowledge of either the Punjabi language or the Sikh religion. Nevertheless, the first Sikh meeting was held in 1904, the first small prayer hall was built in 1906, and the Pacific Khalsa Diwan Society was formed in Stockton in 1912.

The Ghadar movement developed in this context in 1913 to support an uprising against the British in India and continued until the mid-twentieth century. Mark Juergensmeyer identifies the Ghadar syndrome as an emotional response to threats to Punjabi and Sikh identity in both India and the United States [8:173–90]. In spite of discrimination, the Sikh community in California prospered, and a second *gurdwara* was built in El Centro in 1948. Until the later phase of immigration and the groundswell of building of *gurdwaras* in the 1970s, Stockton and El Centro were the only two *gurdwaras* in the United States. Sikhs established networks for immigration to Canada after 1951 because of political turmoil in Punjab and in East Africa, accounting for approximately 30 per cent of all South Asian immigrants into Canada and increasing to approximately 100,000. They spread across eastern Canada as well as in British Columbia, and a large number of Sikh societies developed a couple of decades earlier than their counterparts in the United States.

During the 1970s Sikhs were often identified with the Hindu community and participated in general Indian cultural programmes. Then came the great crisis of the 1980s and conflict with the Indian government over issues that eventually led both to the Indian army entering the Golden Temple in Amritsar and to the call for the establishment of Khalistan as a separate homeland for Sikhs. Sikhs in the United States retain a close involvement with events in India and thus represent an immigrant group whose adaptation to the United States is dramatically affected by events in their home country. Almost every Sikh society experienced divisive annual elections pitting moderates, favouring negotiation with the Indian government hoping for a peaceful resolution of the Sikh problem, against radicals, supporting armed resistance and secession of Sikhs from India.

A 'Khalistan syndrome' developed that captured simultaneously the threat to Sikhs in India and the threat of secularism in the United States. Many individual Sikhs responded by becoming more religiously devout, more clearly identified by dress and custom as Sikhs, and more active politically. Nevertheless, Sikhs in the United States are less radical than those in Canada and England, due in part to the social, economic and educational status of American Sikhs. A branch of the Akali Dal party was formed in the United States in 1981. Immediately after the Amritsar incident, the World Sikh Organization was founded, with a first meeting hastily called for 28 July 1984, in New York. An American affiliate of the radical Sikh Students Association was also formed in 1984, and in the same year a Sikh Association of America was formed in Washington, DC to oppose policies and actions of the Indian government.

The Sikh Dharma Brotherhood began in 1969 when Harbhajan Singh Puri arrived from India and converted a number of young white Americans to a small Sikh sect emphasizing yoga. These 'white Sikhs' criticize the Westernization and lack of Sikh devotion of immigrants. Converts make a distinction between Sikh religion and Punjabi culture, and oppose some elements of Punjabi culture which they claim are antithetical to Sikh religion, such as caste distinctions and the subordination of women. The Sikh Dharma Brotherhood seems destined to continue for a time as a small, declining movement, primarily in California, separate from the larger group of Punjabi Sikhs.

Muslims

Muslims in the United States constitute a montage of nationalities, ethnic groups, languages and cultures not found anywhere else in the world except in Mecca during the Hajj, coming from more than sixty countries and identified with more than 100 subgroups. Dar al Islam ('the house of Islam', i.e. the world-wide community of Islam) incorporates all and officially recognizes no ethnic or racial boundaries, so that a difficulty in the study of South Asian Muslims is in distinguishing them from others. Nevertheless, some mosques in the larger cities can be identified as Arab (resulting from immigration early in the twentieth century), European (Yugoslavian), Asian (Indian and Pakistani) or black. Several Shi'i groups are also present.

Estimates of the number of Muslims in the United States vary widely, from 3 million to over 6 million, including black Muslims. Muslims support more than 600 mosques and Islamic centres. If current demographic trends in relative birth rates and immigration continue, Islam will surpass Judaism as the second largest religious community in the country early in the third millennium. Arabs (more than 460,000) and Iranians (more than 225,000) are the largest Muslim immigrant groups. Asian–Indian (c.50,000) and Pakistani Muslims (c.81,371) share the same mosques and languages and have similar ethnic backgrounds, so it is difficult to distinguish them statistically. Immigrants from Bangladesh are few in number (11,838), so they are almost invisible in the crowd at Asian mosques. Muslims from the Indian subcontinent are collectively the best-educated and most professionally advanced of the Muslims in the United States, and the Islamic community of North America is now the best-educated per capita of all Muslims in the world – at least, best-educated in Western, technological terms.

Prior to 1970 Friday prayers were often hold in universities where Muslim students gathered; later, many mosques and centres opened in most American cities. Two strategies have been followed in establishing mosques and centres. In Chicago, for example, some thirty mosques developed independently throughout the metropolitan area, and these can be identified as Asian, Arab, or even as specifically as Hyderabadi, signalled by the place of origin of the officers or the training of the *imam*. In other cities, associated centres developed in various parts of the city from a central mosque, as did the five regional centres in Houston. The centres provide occasions for worship and religious education, including learning Arabic. City-wide 'Id festivals occur in large rented halls or convention centres. Hyderabadi Muslims from Andhra Pradesh and Memon Muslims with roots in Gujarat join together for communal activities outside the mosques. The Consultative Committee of Indian Muslims, founded in Chicago in 1967, promotes unity among Indian Muslims residing in North America, provides information about the problems (communal tensions and riots) in India, and marshals resources to help the Muslim community in India preserve its constitutional rights and improve its social, educational and economic condition.

Muslims in the United States share with Muslims in India and many other countries the experience of living as a minority in a non-Muslim environment. One explicit goal for some Muslims in America is accordingly to evolve strategies for operating in a predominantly secular, non-Muslim environment. Strategies for educating children, maintaining social cohesiveness, arranging appropriate and effective marriages, planning for the propagation of Islam in secular, democratic states, and developing educational resources in an increasingly secular, pluralistic, modern culture could provide a model for solving the problems of contemporary minority status 'Islamicly'.

Islamic law permits marriages between Muslim men and women of other religious communities. Marriage to a US citizen provides opportunity for permanent residence, and a majority of brides convert to Islam. Anecdotal evidence suggests, however, that only a small number of South Asian Muslims marry outside the ethnic group. It is common for Muslim men and other South Asians to return to the subcontinent for brides because they fear that girls growing up in the West are 'spoiled' by Western dating customs and feminist attitudes. Community leaders and parents of girls are concerned about the imbalance created in the marriage pool by this tendency and the difficulty American-educated Muslim girls have in adjusting to husbands reared in the subcontinent.

A special challenge faced by Muslims in America is training *imams* and other religious specialists for the second and succeeding generations. Thus far, no institution exists to provide education that is both grounded in traditional Islamic scholarship and focused on the needs of these new immigrant families. As a result, much of the educational material is seen by the younger generation as inadequate to bridge the gap between the cultures and the generations. Application of Islamic law requires negotiation between Muslim leaders and local officials to permit observance of Shari'a – for example, school physical education requirements for Muslim children, appropriate institutional meals, chaplains in government institutions, and laws regarding family, divorce and inheritance. People from South Asia face a paradox: Pakistanis and Indians both have a positive position in public opinion because Pakistan has long been an ally and because India is the world's largest democracy, but discrimination exists against Muslims.

As many as 20 per cent of Muslims in America are Shi'a (who revere descendants of the Prophet's family), and those from South Asia are from three groups: the Ithna'Asharis (who revere the Prophet's first twelve descendants), the Bohora Isma'ilis (a merchant community loyal to a representative of Prophet's family, called the Dai), and the Nizari Isma'ilis (followers of the Agha Khan, a direct descendant of the Prophet's family). South Asian Ithna'Asharis in metropolitan areas generally meet separately from Iranian Shi'as. The Daudi Bohoras claim about 2,000 families with centres in Chicago (200 families), Detroit, Los Angeles, San Francisco, New York and Houston. Nizari Isma'ilis are expanding and number more than 30,000 in more than seventy-five *jamat khanas* (communal centres) in twenty-two states. They are the only group that came primarily from East Africa. Nizari Muslims have an extensive programme of religious, economic, educational, medical and professional development administered through the *jamat khanas*, which assist members in their adaptation to the United States.

The Ahmadiyya movement, founded in 1889 as a reform movement in Punjab, came to Chicago in 1921 as an aggressive missionary sect and now has a national headquarters in Washington. African-American converts form a majority in the twenty centres in eastern and central United States. Each of the centres is responsible to the Director-General of the Ahmadiyya Muslim Foreign Mission in Pakistan. Ahmadis are regarded as heretics because of the status they attribute to their founder, and Muslims officially excluded them from Islam at the Muslim World League in 1974. A decade later the military government of Pakistan curtailed the freedom of the Ahmadis. Ahmadis generally keep a low profile among immigrants in America, but they do organize protests against perceived repression in Pakistan.

Immigrants exercised a significant influence on the American Muslim Mission led by Wallace Muhammad in its move away from the doctrines and practices of Elijah Muhammad and the Nation of Islam towards a more orthodox form of Islam – a movement that began shortly after the new Muslim immigrants arrived in the late 1960s. Relations between immigrant Muslims and African-American Muslims (called Bilalians after an early companion of Muhammad) have become closer as the latter have become more orthodox, adopting Arabic prayers, ceasing to attribute divinity to Elijah Muhammad, and undertaking the disciplines of the Hajj and annual celebrations. More than 161 mosques of the American Muslim Mission are now called *masjids*, and their decor reflects orthodox patterns. Immigrants and Bilalians meet in the mosque, but in most social and cultural affairs do not interact. The socioeconomic differences between the two groups are so vast that mutual understanding is difficult. Out of the negotiations among the various ethnic groups will develop a community that occupies an Asian room in the American House of Islam.

Hindus

The centennial of the 1893 Chicago World's Parliament of Religions commemorated the activity of one of the most remarkable religious migrants since the apostle Paul. Following Swami Vivekananda's presentation of the 'wisdom of the east' at the parliament, he became a celebrity in both India and the United States and attracted some Americans to the Vedanta philosophy of the Ramakrishna Mission. After the Second World War, some prominent immigrants from Britain – Aldous Huxley, Gerald Heard and Christopher Isherwood – reinvigorated Vedanta on the west coast, and its influence continues through Vedanta centres in major American cities. The emphases of the Vedanta societies are on meditation and monistic philosophy (rather than on ritual) and on reaching people from the general population (rather than immigrants from India), which prevents them from becoming the primary religious centres for the new immigrants. Nevertheless, swamis of the Ramakrishna Mission are honoured by immigrants and on occasion lecture and provide religious leadership.

Vivekananda's most prominent successor was Abhay Charan De (A. C. Bhaktivedanta Swami Prabhupada) who arrived in the United States at about the same time as new immigration laws opened the door to many Hindu immigrants. He began to teach a north Indian form of Krishna devotion to young people in the parks of New York City, and in 1966 established the International Society of Krishna Consciousness (ISKCON). By the time of his death in 1977, he was the chief religious figure for thousands of young Americans who expressed their rejection of family and American values by looking eastward. He established temples containing images of Radha-Krishna. Full-time members, some under vows of celibacy and others married with children, lived in the temples and ashrams of the organization, performed the daily cycle of rituals in the temple, performed chants and bhajans, administered major Hindu festivals, and studied Bhaktivedanta's commentaries on the

Gita and the Sri Caitanya-caritamrita. They became active in the public propagation of Hinduism.

When new Hindu immigrants arrived from India, they were surprised to be greeted at the airport by a group of white Americans, dressed in saffron robes, dancing, selling books and chanting. ISKCON temples were the only Hindu centres in cities where the immigrants located. The irony is that the white American converts, who renounced family and wealth, became religious specialists for these immigrants, who were part of the scientific and technological 'brain drain' seeking their material fortune in the United States. Immigrants came to constitute the majority of congregational members. Nevertheless, North America is the only region where ISKCON has not shown growth since the death of the founder in 1977. Schism within and legal disputes without, including criminal charges, have led to many defections and to a decline in membership. Fewer than 2,000 full members are now affiliated with ISKCON in the United States and growth in overall membership since 1976 has been in countries outside North America.

Some missionary forms of Hinduism were transitory, such as the experiment at Rajneeshpuram in Oregon that became notorious in the 1980s because of reports of sexual and financial misdeeds and manipulation of political power. Negative public response to Rajneesh made it difficult for immigrants to gain respect for their religion to match the general positive image of India and of the immigrants themselves among the public. Other sects, such as the Radhasoami and Sai Baba groups, gained modest success in establishing small groups and centres; these were more successful because their disciplines are not antithetical to the American ethos. All these forms of missionary Hinduism are eclipsed in the United States by the Hindu institutions of the immigrants, which, while developing away from the glare of publicity, are far more significant for the future of religion in America.

Hinduism in the United States can be plotted on two related axes. The first is the size of the Hindu community, which dictates to some extent the shape of the religious groups and strategies of adaptation. Where only a few Hindus are present, they generally meet together for worship, discourses and rituals that may be identified as an ecumenical Hinduism. The common language is English, and the religious texts and rituals are those associated with the all-India Sanskrit tradition adapted for the American context. For example, pregnancy rituals become community 'baby showers', Brahmin chanting becomes communal singing, and the Bhagavadgita is treated like the Bible. As the community grows, it splinters into regional–linguistic or sectarian groups. The second axis is length of residence. When immigrants are new to an area, their primary concern is to achieve economic and social security. Religious activity takes place within the family or among friends. Once the family is established and children are present, attention turns to providing a more structured and permanent religious life.

Home shrines and family Hinduism are most important in preserving Hindu traditions among immigrants. Few immigrants have time to perform all the prescribed daily rituals, and fewer have the specialized training needed to perform elaborate rituals; nevertheless, families do engage in morning or evening worship, periods of meditation, and the reading of sacred texts and prayers. Brahmins are available in most large cities to perform life-cycle and family rituals, such as the first hair-cutting, weddings and funerals. Some are resident priests in established temples; others are independently employed. Occasionally these priests advertise in newspapers, listing the religious rituals they are prepared to perform and their fees. Some brahmins engaged in this work propose an association to certify persons qualified to act as such religious specialists and to establish a standard fee, but up to now those not affiliated with a temple act as independent agents.

A variety of nascent groups meet in homes. Gita study groups read and discuss portions of the Bhagavadgita and other religious texts; bhajan groups gather to sing devotional hymns; meditation groups based on the teachings of Sankara and other philosophers study and practise forms of meditation. In larger cities, groups form on regional–linguistic lines, providing Indians with the opportunity to share their vernacular language and culture. The Arya Samaj attracts north Indians in several cities, and Durga Puja societies join together to sponsor festivals attended by Bengalis, without intervening regular activities. When such groups outgrow members' homes, they meet in rented halls, churches, newly built India cultural centres or temples.

Hindu immigrants are temple-builders, as more than fifty major new Hindu temples in America attest. Several large temples in south Indian style constitute a pilgrimage cycle during vacations for some Asian Indians, moving from the Ganesh temple in New York (dedicated in 1977) to Venkateswara in Penn Hills near Pittsburgh (1976), to Venkateswara in Dayton, to Rama (1986) and Venkateswara (1986) in Chicago, to Meenakshi in Houston (1982), and on to Shiva–Vishnu in San Francisco (1986). Some stop at the ISKCON centre in West Virginia, called New Vindraban. Consultations have explored the feasibility of a national association of Hindu temples, but no effective association has been established.

One of the earliest and wealthiest, and the most prominent Hindu temple in the United States, is Sri Venkateswara temple in Penn Hills near Pittsburgh. It maintains an intimate association with the famous pilgrimage temple at Tirupati, with both negative and positive results. Many Asian Indians in the Pittsburgh area wanted an ecumenical temple that would house images of many deities and meet the religious, spiritual, cultural, humanitarian, educational and social needs of all its members. Negotiations with Tirupati precipitated a split when north Indians established a separate temple nearby in Monroeville. A positive result is that funding and advice were provided that enhanced the design and accoutrements of the temple. The Tirumala Tirupati Devasthanam and the Andhra Pradesh state government responded to an appeal from Pittsburgh by establishing a programme to support the construction of Hindu temples in foreign countries. They gave approximately US$150,000 to each temple for the services of temple architects, masons and craftsmen and to supply images, temple stones and worship implements.

A staff of brahmin priests brought from India perform the full range of daily, annual, life-cycle and occasional rituals as performed in south India. Several thousand nearby residents and pilgrims visit the temple each month, and three-quarters of the pilgrims have roots in four south Indian states: Tamil Nadu, Andhra Pradesh, Karnataka and Kerala. Sunday school classes in Hinduism and language instruction are provided each week. An annual summer camp for children is held in cooperation with the Chinmaya Mission West. The temple sponsors music and dance and contributes to scholarships, research programmes and relief work in both the United States and India. More than 10,000 people contribute annually to support a budget of approximately $1 million. Trustees of other temples across the country attempt to emulate its great success.

Swaminarayan temples are a different type, representing a distinct sect within Hinduism and drawing support primarily from a single Gujarati regional–linguistic group. As an early nineteenth-century Vaishnava reform movement, it combines a strict puritanical discipline, especially for its *sadhus*, with a fervent devotion to the founder, Sahajanand Swami (1781–1830), now called Swaminarayan, who is worshipped as the highest manifestation of the supreme being (*purushottam*). One branch of the Swaminarayan tradition initiated work in the United States by sending four *sadhus* there in 1970 with the names of twenty-eight followers, mostly students, who were in the country. After two decades the Bochasanwasi Swaminarayan Sanstha, which is obedient to Pramukh Swami as the chief devotee (*akshara*) of Swaminarayan, has over sixty centres and ten major temples, in New York (1977), Chicago (1984), Los Angeles (1984), Houston (1986), Dallas (1988; new building in 1994), Atlanta (1988), Boston (1990), San Jose, California (1991), Edison, New Jersey (1992) and Orlando, Florida (1994). Two other Swaminarayan organizations, called the

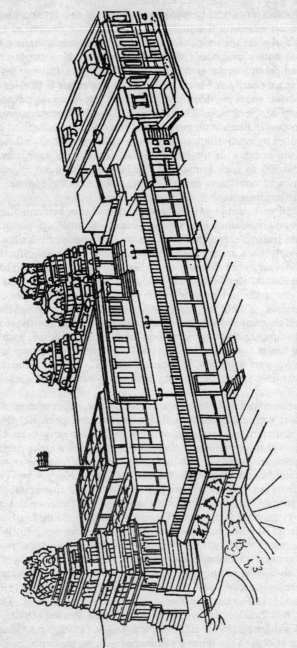

Figure 24.1 Sri Venkateswara Temple, Penn Hills, Pennsylvania

International Swaminarayan Satsang Organization and the International Swaminarayan Satsang Mandal, also have temples in Chicago, Dallas, Boston and Weehawken, New Jersey. The combination of ethnic identity and allegiance to a central hierarchy has proved to be very successful for the Bochasanwasi Swaminanayan Sanstha, which is one of the most visible and fastest-growing religious groups among Hindu immigrants.

Holy men and various religious specialists from India tour the United States each summer to visit homes of devotees, to lecture to large gatherings, to initiate followers, to give pastoral care and to provide advice and leadership to the Hindu community. These religious leaders are part of a seasonal cultural migration from India that includes musicians, dancers, astrologers, politicians, film stars and other artists. They provide a bridge back home to India but face an increasingly difficult task of maintaining ties with the second generation in America.

A reverse movement occurs when immigrants and their children return to South Asia for visits. For the devout, these visits become religious pilgrimages to visit sacred sites and holy people. Vows are taken in the United States to be fulfilled in India. Immigrants approach religious leaders in India for advice about personal and institutional affairs in the United States. Gifts from successful immigrants support religious and educational institutions in South Asia. Children are sent back to India for summer camps and tours led by *sadhus* and other religious specialists, which are coordinated with youth conventions and summer camps conducted in the United States by visitors. Such interaction has a double effect: on the one hand, it fosters the development of a form of Hinduism that can survive and be transmitted to future generations in the United States; and on the other, it produces and validates a type of religious leadership in India that is more responsive to the needs of people living in a developed, secular, scientific culture. Expatriates are having significant effects on religions in India, which is an aspect of the modern transnationalism of religion.

Jains

The venerable Jain tradition in India is that Jain monks travel only on foot and do not go abroad, because Jain discipline for monks requires a gradual restraining of bodily activities and functions that is generally thought to be antithetical to travel abroad. Nevertheless, the development of Jainism in the United States is associated with the arrival of two progressive Jain monks. Chitrabhanu Muni was the first to come, in 1971, for a series of lectures at Harvard University. He lectured widely on Jain philosophy, meditation and vegetarianism and established a Meditation International Centre in New York, mainly for white Americans. He was a Shvetambara monk when he arrived, and although he subsequently married, he exerts considerable influence on immigrant Jains. Sushil Kumar Muni was a Sthanakavasi Shvetambara monk from Delhi who came to the United States in 1975. He established an ashram in a large house on Staten Island provided by followers from both the settled and immigrant communities. In 1983 he established another ashram, called Siddhachalam, in the Pocono Mountains near Blairstown, New Jersey, where a new temple was dedicated in 1990 under the auspices of the International Mahavira Jain Association. He died in 1994.

As in India, where they make up only 0.48 per cent of the population, Jains in North America have an influence beyond their number (approximately 45,000 persons in the United States and 4,000 in Canada) because they are a prosperous community and exhibit respected virtues of non-violence and close family ties. Most, perhaps 70 per cent, are Gujaratis from the area of the old Bombay Presidency. Twenty Jain temples serve the community, about half of which are in larger Hindu temple complexes. The Jain population is so small that the various sects of Jains must meet together, and accommodations permit inclusion of several groups. Where only a few families live in an area, Jains meet in rented halls or private homes. Jains are so scattered that the major festivals are the only times when they get together and where Jain identity is asserted. The festivals of the Jain calendar common in the United States are the celebration of the birth of Mahavira (Mahavira jayanti, in April/May); the commemoration of the liberation of Mahavira (Vira-nirvana, in October/November); and the annual fasting and confession (Parsyusanaparva, for eight or ten days in September). Regular rituals are generally performed by Jain laymen, without the assistance of brahmins; patterns and schedules of worship are diverse and differ from those in Gujarat and Bombay.

Many aspects of doctrine, ritual and practice are more difficult to maintain as a minuscule minority, so some national organizations have been formed to preserve Jain identity and to transmit Jainism to new generations. A Federation of Jain Associations in North America (JAINA) was formed in 1983 to maintain unity and promote activities of local, independent associations throughout the country. The *Jain Study Circular*, begun in 1979 by the Jain Centre of Greater Boston, contains both serious articles on Jain philosophy and religion and news items. Jains are developing new symbiotic relationships with Hindus in the United States, with Jains in India and with the wider American society.

Christians

Christianity is centuries older in India than in America, and the majority of Christian immigrants from India are Keralites who trace their spiritual lineage to stories about the apostle Thomas's travels in south India. Modern Indian Christian hospitals and schools provided skills that facilitated immigration: the majority of Indian Christian migrants gained entry because the wives or mothers were nurses who came to urban hospitals in the 1970s. This created a gender difference among immigrants, because most Christian families accompanied women, whereas most other groups came with fathers, husbands or brothers who had qualifications to enter. Some of the husbands of Christian nurses are pastors, who established Christian congregations of immigrants; the immigration of Christian pastors was in any case facilitated because they had recognizable educational preparation and degrees, including some from American seminaries and graduate schools.

Congregations represent many Indian denominations and regional groups, and follow different strategies of adaptation. An attraction/repulsion phenomenon is present among South Asian Christians in that many feel an attraction to American churches and participate in local congregations of several denominations, but nevertheless are afraid of the secularizing influences of American churches that weaken family devotional life, discourage frequent attendance at worship, and focus on the individual rather than on the family. The programmes of the immigrant churches are intended to preserve ethnic traditions within the Christian family and also to save the children from the evil influences of drugs, illicit sex, materialism, and the breakdown of family ties that seem to immigrants to be all too prevalent in 'Christian' America.

Many Indian Protestants and Roman Catholics participate in local congregations and parishes with other Americans, while also attending worship services and fellowship meetings of Asian Indian religious groups. Indian Roman Catholics participate in Indian Catholic Associations in larger cities. A few dioceses have Asian Indian priests, and some larger dioceses, such as Chicago and Houston, support Indian priests to perform special services in three rites recognized by the Roman Catholic Church in India: Latin, Syro-Malabar and Syro-Malankara. Some immigrant families postpone rituals such as baptism, christening and first communion until they return for visits to the extended family in India, reflecting the transnational character of families and churches.

Indian Protestants in some cities join in national ecumenical Indian Christian fellowships, but as the communities grow, regional and denominational groups sap the strength of the ecumenical fellowships. Ethnic groups based on regional–linguistic identities are stronger, representing Tamil, Telugu, Hindi, Malayali and Gujarati Christians. Malayali Christians from the state of Kerala are the most active and successful in establishing churches and new denominations in the United States. Although Christians make up only one-fifth of the population of Kerala (which has the largest Christian population of all the Indian states) between 60 and 70 per cent of Malayalis in the United States are Christian.

The development in the United States of the Mar Thoma Church of India parallels that of other churches: a prayer group in Queens, New York, in the early 1970s; the first parish approved in 1976; a Zonal Council in 1982, becoming a diocese in 1988; and a resident bishop and a Diocesan Centre in Pennsylvania in 1993, serving thirty-seven parishes and two chapels, consisting of over 3,000 families or 11,400 members. The Mar Thoma Church prohibits priests from becoming permanent residents because all Mar Thoma priests, both in India and abroad, serve on three-year appointments; they come to America for three years and then return to Kerala. In the early days they served under the auspices of the Episcopal Church, which maintains close relations with several of the immigrant churches.

The Malankara Orthodox Church in America was the first Asian Indian Christian group to establish a bishop for the church in America, loyal to the Catholicos of the East in Kottayam, Kerala. More than fifty Malankara priests are permanent residents in the United States, some of whom received their professional education in American seminaries, and they serve fifty-six recognized parishes. Most have secular employment because congregations are too small to support a full-time priesthood. The Sunday schools follow a graded curriculum with study books that are prepared in English at the Sunday school centre at Kottayam, Kerala. Some churches conduct the Holy Eucharist in English one Sunday a month.

The liturgy and programmes of the Jacobite Syrian churches are the same as those of the Malankara Orthodox churches, but they have a different hierarchy loyal to the Patriarch of Antioch. The first Orthodox immigrants from India joined Syrian Orthodox believers in a manner similar to Zoroastrian temples, where immigrants from the two cultures of Iran and India are joined in a sometimes uneasy alliance. In 1993 the Patriarch of Antioch agreed to establish a separate diocese and to consecrate a bishop from Kerala for the Malankara congregations of Indian immigrants.

The continuation of the Knanayan Syrian Orthodox Church in the United States is testimony to the power of caste and ethnic identity. Knanaya claim descent from Persian refugees who emigrated to India in 345, called 'old Christians' to distinguish them from 'new Christians' in India, who are supposedly from lower castes. Knanaya are a separate endogamous community with seven small congregations in the United States (two in New York, one each in Philadelphia, Boston, Houston, Dallas and Chicago), served by priests who are permanent residents. Knanaya Catholics of the Syro-Malabar rite have approximately 2,000 registered families in nine societies (New York/New Jersey, Chicago, Houston, Washington, Philadelphia, Tampa, Miami, Detroit and Los Angeles). Although these St Thomas Christian groups are small, they are growing through both immigration and natural birth, and will eventually become a more significant feature of Orthodoxy and American Christianity.

Many Tamil, Gujarati and Hindi fellowships meet in church buildings across the country; for example, the Emmanuel Methodist Church in Evanston, Illinois contains a single congregation with services in English, Gujarati and Hindi. Although the Church of South India has no diocese outside of India, many of its pastors have migrated to the United States, where they have established congregations in several cities. In 1993 the Moderator of the Church of South India authorized the establishment of a North American Council for the church. Pentecostal churches are numerous, independent, difficult to identify and growing rapidly, both in India and in the United States. Pentecostals are generally 'converts' from the St Thomas churches in south India and belong to several groups: the New Testament Church (the name in America for the Ceylon Pentecostal Mission), the Indian Pentecostal Church, the Church of God and the Assemblies of God. Pastors and priests of all these churches generally come with the green card as permanent residents of the United States.

Buddhists

Thai and Sinhalese Theravada Buddhist temples and ashrams in the United States attract both immigrants and persons from the majority population. Generally, Thai and Sinhalese Buddhists maintain distinct institutions in order to preserve ethnic identity and cultural patterns, and there are six Sinhalese temples among the approximately 125 Theravada temples in the United States. In several temples the pattern is to have two 'congregations': one made up of immigrants who observe the rituals as closely as possible to those in Sri Lanka, and the other of white Americans who emphasize meditation and philosophy. Thai and Sinhalese Buddhists join a kaleidoscope of Buddhist groups in the United States resulting from the presence of 'old immigrants' from China and Japan and of 'new immigrants' from all over Asia, especially Vietnam, Laos and Cambodia. Some Korean immigrants are Buddhists – and all are influenced by Buddhism – but a surprisingly large number are

Presbyterian Christians. So few Buddhists from South Asia have arrived that it is difficult to characterize their process of adaptation.

Transnational Families and Religions

South Asian immigrants to the United States form transnational networks of families and religious institutions that reach to East Africa, Malaysia, the UK, the Gulf states, Australia and Canada. New forms of transnational association not available to earlier migrants have been made possible by the rapid mobility and communications of recent years. Many families have members in several countries, and religion constitutes a major aspect of creating and maintaining identities across geographical and national boundaries. These transnational relations at the close of the twentieth century generate a new transnational approach to the study of migration, which takes account of the multiple relations – familial, economic, social, organizational, religious and political – that cross national boundaries, and of the need for migrants to take actions, make decisions, feel concerns and develop identities within social networks that connect them to two or more societies simultaneously [3:1–24]. The transnational character of the associations of new immigrants also requires revisions of older analyses of citizenship, ethnicity, asimilation and pluralism in the United States, which take on different configurations because of the transnational character of families and religious organizations of new immigrants.

Hinduism, Jainism, Sikhism and the Parsi religion have become transnational in ways that could not have been conceived earlier. Christianity has become transnational through associations of South Asian migrants that are different from the missionary or church partnership models of earlier generations. Marriage contracts, financial resources, leadership transfers and festivals move across transnational networks to unite religious organizations. Resources have long moved from wealthy countries to South Asia to support Muslim and Christian activities; now significant resources – financial, personal and material – are being returned to South Asia to support Hindu, Jain and Sikh activities as well. Immigrants now create reverse impacts on religions and societies in South Asia in ways that were not possible for earlier immigrants.

The need of immigrants to re-establish their personal and group identities in the context of religious freedom in the United States is one of the reasons why Americans are more religious, by some measures, than citizens of other industrialized nations. The transnational nature of religions of immigrants is related to the development of families, the urban-village settlement patterns, conflicts in the communities, the language use of immigrants, tensions between the generations, and the development of leadership.

Families

United States immigration laws encourage family reunification by permitting residents to sponsor parents and siblings for immigration. The first group of immigrants came without the grandparent generation, which is religiously significant because grandparents in South Asia are primary transmitters of religious tradition. When immigrants are well established, they call parents to reside in the United States, so that an increasing number of the grandparents' generation attend religious meetings. They exercise a conservative influence by encouraging the use of ethnic languages, cuisines and mores and, in some instances, a yearning for an India that no longer exists. Some retired grandparents take up new positions, with or without pay, as priests, administrators and religious specialists.

Some American politicians call for restrictions on the admission of immigrants to the United States, but it seems likely that the number of immigrants from South Asia will remain at the current high levels or even increase. The constant stream of new entrants renews contacts with the religious traditions and institutions of South Asian villages, but it also creates disappointments, jealousies and difficulties in integrating these new immigrants into religious and social groups already established, many of which may have progressed on paths of integration and acculturation. Religious groups attempt to incorporate well-established early immigrants, their American children, relatives who are recently arrived and dependent, and a new wave of professionals – a complex and dynamic stream of generations.

Immigrants are led to establish religious institutions when their children reach the age when they face peer pressures to conform to the host society. The call to 'save the children' means protecting them from things most feared: drugs, casual relations with the opposite sex, moving in the wrong crowd, and the breakdown of family discipline and values, which for many immigrants means the loss of both religious and ethnic identity. Religious institutions help to shape and preserve the identity of the next generation, and the creation of programmes is correlated with the number and ages of the children: they include Sunday schools, language instruction, summer camps, residential schools, pilgrimages to South Asia, family conferences, package youth tours to India, and visits to festivals in other countries where the religious groups are established.

The most intense emotion and heated discussions between parents and children concern language use in religious services and arrangements for dating and marriage – emotional and heated because here the issue of assimilation is crucial. Parents and religious leaders support the South Asian restrictions on casual dating and provisions for arranged marriages. Parents prefer to arrange marriages within the ethnic group and, if possible, within the religious community. The networks and procedures available in India for negotiating marriages are not present in the United States, so new procedures are developing, with various adaptations that are called 'semi-arranged marriages'. The second generation matures in a society with very different expectations regarding dating and pre-marital sexual activity, so tensions exist. New patterns are developing, but religious groups lack strategies or procedures for incorporating spouses from outside the religious community or the ethnic group into the community. That remains a serious challenge and a flashpoint of conflict between generations and between religious leaders and youth.

Immigration to the United States is part of the transnational movement of modern technological elites to urban areas throughout the world. Although South Asians are spread throughout America, in small towns as well as cities, the religious institutions are urban. Moreover, most immigrants live in urban areas and even those from small cities and towns go to the urban temples, mosques, *gurdwaras* and shrines for religious ceremonies and festivals. Hence, urban areas manifest a religious diversity not found in the hinterland, thereby exacerbating tensions both within cities and between urban and non-urban America.

Conflicts and Tensions

These religious groups are part of an ever-changing kaleidoscope made up of small units that unite, divide and join new constellations. New immigrants are always on the move, geographically certainly, but also socially and religiously. They form new groups, make new allegiances and cherish various elements of their identities. Communalism in South Asia is an experience common to most immigrants, but schisms and conflicts, both internal and external, are newly created in the United States. As the number of South Asians grows in American cities, religious groups split, forming new groups based on sectarian, linguistic, ethnic and social distinctions. Tensions between Asian Muslims and black Muslims, divisions between regional linguistic groups over the style and rituals of new Hindu temples, conflicts in Sikh *gurdwaras* over Khalistan, and denominational negotiations between Christians have become burning issues in North America. Having entered the United States when a positive evaluation was placed on diversity and minority status, new immigrants are negotiating with other immigrants of the same religion, ethnicity or nationality over what minority identities will be preserved and affirmed, and also with the host society over what advantages or disadvantages are to be derived from forms of minority status. This is a multicultural conversation with many transnational participants.

Language

Religious groups face special problems relating to the use of both sacred and secular languages. South Asians use sacred languages in rituals – Arabic, Sanskrit, Syriac and Gurmukhi – in which very few of the immigrants have formal, traditional education. Immigrants received bilingual education in South Asia in English and the regional language, but it is difficult to educate children in both the written and oral regional languages, to say nothing of the sacred languages. Regional languages are important in rituals of several religious organizations that follow an ethnic strategy of adaptation. Religion is a cultural phenomenon that, along with poetry, is clothed in the native language in texts, rituals and doctrines difficult to translate with precision. Gujarati, Urdu, Malayali, Hindi, Punjabi and other regional languages are primary modes of communication and thereby become second-order sacred languages for immigrants. Moreover, complex ritual symbolism is equally difficult to translate in the absence of the fuller and richer symbolic structure present in India. Immigrants lack the theological competence to explain the details of their religion even in their native language, much less in English, and authentic religious leaders from India and Pakistan are rarely fluent in American English. Sunday school curricula, both those prepared by denominational leaders in India and those from commercial publishers in the United States, are perceived by many young people to be inadequate. Language selection, the absence of adequate translation, and the use of regional languages in ritual and in religious education are among the most difficult and emotionally laden problems religious groups face because they impinge directly on the transmission of tradition, identity formation, relations between generations, and most of the other problems faced by the immigrants. When and how to make the transition from regional languages to English are pressing questions.

Leadership

The success of immigrants in establishing many strong religious organizations in a relatively short time is remarkable given that the impetus, leadership and strong support has come from laypeople, not religious specialists. Indeed, many claim to have been less religious in India than they are in America. Most early immigrants did not bring religious specialists with them, the only exception being the Christians, whose pastors in the 1970s were primarily either husbands of nurses or students in American seminaries. Otherwise, the laypeople established strong organizations with only minimal advice, encouragement or support from South Asia. Most organizations relied upon retired specialists who gained entry for family reunification, priests on temporary visas, and leaders on frequent tours. Especially during the spring and summer, hundreds of groups of religious specialists from South Asia tour America. Visits to South Asia during the immigrants' vacations at New Year or in the summer take on the appearance of pilgrimages as people visit temples, shrines and holy people to obtain advice, inspiration and materials that will be useful in the United States. Nevertheless, one point of conflict is the amount of authority that institutions and leaders in India will have over groups and leaders in the United States.

New American immigration regulations in 1991 revised designations of 'religious workers' by including a new 'lay religious worker' category, thus making it easier for religious organizations to bring religious specialists to serve the community. The main qualifications are that the lay religious worker be sponsored by a religious organization, that he or she have been a member of that religious group for the last two years, and that the sponsoring organization provide sufficient compensation to prevent the person from taking another job in the United States. Volunteers with independent income or financial support from relatives or friends are also eligible. Groups search for specialists who are both trained in the traditional forms of the religion and able to communicate effectively with members and followers educated and assimilated in the United States; such leaders are bridges between the old and the new, the traditional and the modern, and between the generations.

Training for priests, *imams*, pastors and others able to minister to these new religious groups is not as yet available in either the United States or South Asia. This vacuum attracts all types of self-authenticated volunteers for positions as religious specialists, creating problems for the immigrants. Regulation of unwelcome visits is a difficult challenge, as are the schisms caused by leaders. A few nascent attempts have been made to train religious leaders for the new religious organizations. Swaminarayan Hindus recruit Asian Indian young men who return to India for training. The American Islamic University has study programmes and scholarships to send future *imams* to the Middle East for training, especially for the black American Muslim Mission. The Vishwa Hindu Parishad founded a Hindu university at Orlando, Florida in 1994. Christians support and use the facilities of seminaries both in the United States and in south India.

Future styles of leadership depend upon decisions regarding the most appropriate form of transmission of religious traditions, either by teaching through words or by gestures in rituals. These two strategies of transmission are emphasized to different degrees in religious organizations. Hindu temples provide rituals performed according to traditional Sanskrit *agamas* by traditionally trained brahmin priests; Gita study groups provide lectures in English on philosophy and theories of devotion. Learning by observing, in both senses of that term, or by hearing are common in religious communities, but they require different hermeneutics, different languages, different styles and different types of religious leaders. Ritual seems a compelling mode of transmission and preservation for people in the first generation, but words, preferably in English, seem more potent for people of the second and third generations. Religious groups can be charted on a continuum of emphasis from ritual to word, and the shift of emphasis through the stream of generations will determine what religious institutions will survive and prosper.

Conclusion

At the middle of the twentieth century, migration to the United States had been quiescent for two decades, and the informal but powerful Judeo-Christian pact hammered out earlier in the century provided a religious basis for civic life. At the end of the century, the situation is dramatically changed. New immigrants and their families contribute new energy, challenges and potential in civic life and expand horizons by providing vital and personal contacts with parts of the world previously largely absent from purview. New foods, languages, customs, rituals, beliefs, architectures and religions are becoming familiar. The buildings are changing the physical landscape of the country, just as the new ideas and customs are changing the common mental and spiritual landscape. Both the vitality and the uncertainty in the country at the turn of the century result in part from a breakdown of the pact among Protestants, Catholics and Jews that provided a common, transcendent basis for civic life and from the incipient negotiation about the shape of American life in the twenty-first century as religious people work out the two sides of the American coin: *E Pluribus Unum* and *In God We Trust*.

Bibliography

1 BUCHIGNANI, NORMAN, INDRA, DOREEN M., and SRIVASTIVA, RAM, *Continuous Journey: A Social History of South Asians in Canada*, Toronto, McClelland & Stewart, 1985

2 FENTON, JOHN Y., *Transplanting Religious Traditions: Asian Indians in America*, New York, Praeger, 1988

3 GLICK SHILLER, NINA, BASCH, LINDA, and BLANC-SZANTON, CHRISTINA (eds), *Towards a Transnational Perspective on Migration*, New York, New York Academy of Sciences, 1992

4 HADDAD, YVONNE YAZBECK, *Mission to America: Five Islamic Sectarian Communities in North America*, Gainesville, University Press of Florida, 1993

5 HADDAD, YVONNE YAZBECK, *The Muslims of America*, Oxford, Oxford University Press, 1991

6 HADDAD, YVONNE YAZBECK, and LUMMIS, ADAIR T., *Islamic Values in the United States: A Comparative Study*, New York, Oxford University Press, 1987

7 HINNELLS, JOHN R., 'South Asian Diaspora Communities and their Religion: A Comparative Study of Parsi Experiences', *South Asia Research*, vol. 14, 1994, pp. 62–104

8 JUERGENSMEYER, MARK, and BARRIER, N. GERALD (eds), *Sikh Studies*, Berkeley, Graduate Theological Union, 1979

9 KOSMIN, BARRY A., and LACHMAN, SEYMOUR P., *One Nation under God: Religion in Contemporary American Society*, New York, Harmony Books, 1993

10 KÖSZEGI, MICHAEL A., and MELTON, J. GORDON, *Islam in North America*, New York, Garland, 1992

11 ROCHFORD, E. BURKE, JR, *Hare Krishna in America*, New Brunswick, Rutgers University Press, 1985

12 WAUGH, EARLE H., MCIRVIN ABU-LABAN, SHARON, and BURCKHARDT QURESHI, REGULA (eds), *Muslim Families in North America*, Edmondon, University of Alberta Press, 1991

13 WILLIAMS, RAYMOND BRADY, *A New Face of Hinduism: The Swaminarayan Religion*, Cambridge, Cambridge University Press, 1984

14 WILLIAMS, RAYMOND BRADY, *Religions of Immigrants from India and Pakistan: New Threads in the American Tapestry*, Cambridge, Cambridge University Press, 1988

15 WILLIAMS, RAYMOND BRADY (ed.), *A Sacred Thread: Modern Transmission of Hinduism in India and Abroad*, Chambersburg, Anima Press, 1992

25

Comparative Reflections on South Asian Religion in International Migration

JOHN R. HINNELLS

Introduction

In the light of the last four chapters the falsity of many white stereotypes of South Asians, commonly grouped ignorantly under the single label 'Pakis', is evident. Similarly, the chapter on African diaspora religion dispels many stereotypes of the black African (or Afro-Caribbean) communities.

The first obvious feature is the high level of education characteristic of the South Asian communities in Australia, Canada and the US. In Britain many of the earliest migrants were uneducated manual workers, but the second and third generations are pursuing further education with vigour. Indeed, a higher proportion of South Asians and black Africans than of whites are staying on beyond the legal school leaving age [20]. In the US there is a high proportion of scientists. Throughout the diaspora the South Asian populations are generally climbing the social ladder to significant levels of professional responsibility. However, there remain, especially in Britain, high levels of unemployment, unnaturally high given the educational levels. The only obvious explanation can be prejudice on the part of the white majority.

Another false stereotype is the image of South Asians 'swamping' the white population. The numbers of South Asians are highest in Britain, the smallest of the four countries studied. But even here, although the numbers are significant, South Asians remain a small proportion of the total population and do not match the numbers of Europeans migrating overseas, or of the Irish living in the country. South Asians have commonly been stereotyped as 'problems' – in terms of housing, employment, etc. But, with the younger age profile and high levels of educational achievement, they are in fact likely to be contributing significantly more than their fair share to supporting the social services required by the ageing white population. This same point could also be made of the black African population. In Australia, Canada and the US, South Asians are providing educated professionals and business entrepreneurs needed by those countries.

The earlier literature on South Asians in the West focused on social concerns and neglected religion, reinforcing a stereotype of the migrants leaving their religion in the old country. In fact, numerous recent studies of South Asians in all four Western countries emphasize the considerable and increasing prominence of religion in the various communities, especially in comparison with the secularizing tendencies typical of many white societies. Linked to the earlier stereotype was the assumption, widespread in the 1960s, that Asians would inevitably assimilate as the second and third generations rejected their parents' cultural traditions. The media often gave prominence to stories of youngsters leaving home and either rebelling against restrictions or submitting to them unhappily. Although some have had difficulties, recent studies have made it clear that in the majority of cases the tight family unit has been positively appreciated and preserved. The family values mean that South Asians have far fewer divorces, separations and single-parent families and, therefore, have fewer of the social problems that often go with these situations. The white images of South Asians which dominated Australia, Britain, Canada and the US in the 1950s are almost all universally false.

The basic questions to be addressed are as follows. What are the overall patterns for change and continuity that may be observed in diaspora religions? What are the key features of the maturation of the South Asian religions in the West and what are the important areas for future research in this area? Is there a common diaspora experience, or are there distinctive Australian, British, Canadian and US South Asian experiences? What is distinctive about the Hindu/Muslim/Jain/Parsi (etc.) experience? In what ways are South Asian experiences the same as or different from those of the black African diaspora? The emphasis in this concluding chapter will be on the international South Asian diaspora, because of the extent of coverage elsewhere in the book and because South Asia encompasses a number of religions, thus facilitating some genuine 'comparative religion'. The example of the Parsis will be frequently cited, partly because they are the subject of my own fieldwork and so I know a little more about them, but also because they are an interesting and appropriate 'test case'. Their numbers are sufficiently small for it to be possible to gain a global perspective, yet because they have migrated from urban and rural India, Pakistan and East Africa, with a 'control group' of fellow Zoroastrians from Iran, they are associated with many of the old countries discussed in these chapters. In addition, they were among the earliest to migrate, indeed their presence in Britain dates back to the 1720s, giving them a longer trajectory of settlement for study. Readers may wish to reflect on the extent to which comments made regarding Parsis in what follows can be applied to other groups.

Factors for Change and Continuity in Diaspora Religion

It is helpful to develop some sort of framework within which to understand the subject of diaspora religion. Despite their relatively tight focus on the experiences of people from one subcontinent in four similar Western countries, the previous chapters have shown that there are substantial differences in terms of religion, nationality, ethnicity, group and individual identities. Three scholars have reflected on what such a structure for this study might be: Knott [21; 22]; Helweg [13]; and Hinnells [18]. Developing Knott's 1986 thesis [23], Hinnells suggested ten major factors for change and continuity in the preservation of a religion in the diaspora [8]. The factors affecting how people settle in the new country include the following.

1 *Where people come from* This can be interpreted in two ways:
   (a) *Which country people have migrated from*: India, Pakistan, Bangladesh or Sri Lanka. Typically, for example, Bangladeshi women have stayed at home, and have pursued higher education and careers to a lesser extent than women from India, including Muslim women. Especially significant is whether they are 'twice migrants', i.e. people who have migrated onwards, e.g. from South Asia to East Africa and then on to 'the West', or from Britain onwards to Canada and Australia. Several studies indicate that South Asians who migrated from East Africa have staunchly preserved many of the nineteenth-century Indian traditions, whichever religion they adhered to. In Britain and Canada in particular they have proved to be forces for the reassertion of 'orthodoxy' or tradition. In part this is because in East Africa they lived largely within the shell of their own community, whereas the different religions in the Indian subcontinent were subject to substantial forces for change. Direct migrants thus brought with them the evolved forms of their religions. Bilimoria has shown in chapter 21 above that Malaysian Sikhs, in contrast, have weakened their Punjabi ties. Minorities in a country where the majority tradition is seen as (potentially) hostile, for example Parsis in Pakistan, tend to draw tighter, stronger boundaries around themselves and these boundaries may be preserved in the new country.

(b) *Where in the old country people have migrated from.* Migrants from rural areas typically retain traditions more strictly than those from cosmopolitan urban areas, because the latter house greater educational and social resources which have prepared migrants for life in the West, and as a result such people often resist Western traditions less. Migrants from, say, Karachi and Bombay may therefore have more in common than rural and urban Pakistanis, or rural and urban Indians. A further factor in the respective settlement patterns is that in all four Western countries, South Asians have typically settled in urban areas (the early Sikh settlers in Canada and Australia being exceptional). The South Asian and black African religions are to be found among industrial workers or professionals in larger conurbations. Migrants have rarely settled in the rural areas of the West because of restricted opportunities for education and employment. It is therefore those who came from urban areas who were most prepared for life in urban centres and react against it least.

2 *The perceptions of the new country with which people come* The image of Britain as an imperial power, or as a racist society, or as a declining power, or as a land of religious freedom and justice can determine, to some extent, the level of resistance of the new settler to British ways. The same is, of course, true of other countries: America may be seen as a melting-pot which might threaten a person's heritage; as a Christian country with aggressive (tele-)evangelism; as sexually lax and dominated by drugs; or as the country of great opportunity, a country which opens its doors to people from all countries. Any one person is likely to have a mixture of perceptions, but the balance of those perceptions can affect attitudes to settlement. The more negative people feel about the new country, or the more hostile they perceive it to be, the less likely they are to adopt its ways quickly.

3 *The nature of the migration process* People who have migrated for their own self-perceived benefit, e.g. for higher education or career opportunities, generally resent the new country less than those who have felt compelled to migrate, by, say, policies of Africanization or persecution (e.g. Zoroastrians from Iran). The former group are, therefore, typically more willing to adjust to new ways whereas the latter, understandably, want to cling to the heritage which they felt was threatened and to assert their ethnic identity, for example by preserving their language, cuisine, dress and religion. Further change is often seen as a greater threat by those who have been compelled to migrate.

4 *What people were before they migrated* Those who had completed their education, and were therefore reasonably secure in their tradi-

tion, and those who had been educated (formally or informally) in their religion (e.g. older rather than younger people), are generally better equipped, in part at least, to perpetuate the religion.

5 *When people migrated* This refers not only to the stage they had reached in their own life, as discussed in point (4) above, but also to the decade in which they migrated, which may affect the pattern of settlement. Helweg [13], for example, compares the very different experiences among the South Asians who settled in Australia of the earlier manual workers and of their fellows who came later as educated professionals. The former generally came as part of a group, were uneducated and depended on leaders in their community to aid them in living, at work and in dealing with Australian bureaucracy. Their sense of community was strong and they retained strong links with the old country and kept at a distance from white Australians. The later educated professionals were less dependent on co-religionists, were more open to socializing with wider society and felt more links with the new than with the old country. Hinnells ([18]; to be elaborated in [14]) also found different patterns for those who had migrated in different decades. In general terms, Australian, British, Canadian and US societies are less hostile to South Asians in the 1990s than they were in the 1960s, and this attitude of the wider society can condition the attitude of the migrant to settlement. Later migrants move into a community which has elaborated an infrastructure (buildings, community gatherings, religious functions, classes, etc.) which make it considerably easier to, and more likely that newcomers will, practise the religion. The situation in the new countries is not static and the 'type' of person who migrates is not constant. It is, therefore, impossible to generalize about *a* (or *the*) process of religious migration. It changes with the passage of time.

6 *With whom people migrated* If people migrate as part of an extended family, as, for example, most did when compelled to leave East Africa, then they settle as part of a support group which encourages and reinforces respect for the tradition. Being part of an extended family of three generations can be important because of the role grandparents play in encouraging the tradition. People who migrate as part of a chain, moving from a region to a community where friends and relatives from the old country have already settled, tend to become part of a support network and therefore have encouragement in their preservation of the tradition. In contrast, people who migrate alone, for example as students or high-flying executives, are more vulnerable to cultural influences from the new country.

7 *To where people migrated* Similarities and differences between the

four countries will be discussed below, but there are also differences within any particular country, for two reasons.

(a) If people are able to settle in a locality where there are many co-religionists and with religious resources (temple/mosque; religious classes and leaders) it is easier and more likely that the religion will be preserved than if people live in isolation or in a scattered group.

(b) Different cities/towns in any of the countries develop South Asian communities with not only distinctive histories but also different religious characters. Williams [30] and Hinnells [16], working totally independently, found that the different groups they were researching were each rather traditional in Houston, Texas, and liberal or reforming in Chicago. In part this was the consequence of chain migration, where people of similar backgrounds followed each other and therefore established a distinctive community; in part because the Houston groups grew quickly in the early 1980s as a result of the oil boom, so that well-to-do people came. Most of these individuals made substantial amounts of money and were able to bring their extended families with them, including grandparents. Chicago, in contrast, has a very high proportion of students who live alone and are particularly subject to acculturating influences. Differences may similarly be found between British, Canadian or Australian cities [15]. It is, therefore, simplistic to talk just in terms of Australian, British, Canadian or US South Asians. It is necessary to distinguish to some extent between centres within each country.

8 *What people do in their lives after they have settled* For example, those who proceed to a postgraduate education, especially, but not only, if those studies are in the sciences rather than in the arts, tend to weaken their religious ties, but not necessarily the more secular aspects of their ethnicity (e.g. language, food and music [14; 16]). Similarly, high-flying executives tend to assimilate more than housewives or retired persons living at home. The friendships that are formed, both within and outside the community, and the frequency of contacts with the community and with the old country are all crucial elements in the preservation of tradition. Visits back to the old country, and the associated experiences, are important factors. It would be wrong to assume that it is always the older people who enjoy those visits most. According to Hinnells [18], some of the early 1960s settlers appear to have become emotionally, as well as physically, distanced from the old country and many of the respondents commented on, for example, the dirt, poverty and corruption in the subcontinent. Conversely, many young people born in the West who visited the old country in search of their roots found the experience stimulating and rewarding, commenting on the friendliness and hospitality they had experienced there. Some current

research also suggests that precisely which place in the country young people (especially of the second and third generations) visit affects their response. Young Asian New Yorkers may find, say, rural Bengal less appealing than, say, Delhi or Dacca or Lahore. The reaction can be very personal. Some would find rural tranquillity more appealing, despite the lack of material provisions, than the frantic pressures of Western city life. But by far the most powerful factor identified by Hinnells [18] in the preservation of the religion was that when young people married within the community and had children, a very strong bond is commonly developed with the religion.

9 *Who people are* There are two aspects to this:

(a) Gender. Men who go out to work in the 'outside' world inevitably come into closer contact with external influences. In some religions the religious duties associated with the home mean that the women preserve the tradition more actively. This would be true of many Hindu households, for example. But even where women do move widely outside the home, gender differences may still be observed. Among the Parsis studied by Hinnells [18], it was the women who were more concerned to preserve the purity laws, group identity and the community boundaries, e.g. through avoiding intermarriage. There was, however, no major difference between the genders on the mythical/cosmological dimensions of the religion (e.g. belief in the afterlife).

(b) The same research suggested that businessmen tend to preserve the tradition more than highly educated professionals. This is partly because (successful) businessmen can afford to provide the resources (communally or domestically) more than middle-class professionals, but also because the higher education (especially where this took place in the West) which provided the foundation for the careers of the professionals often taught them to be more critical, analytical and Westernized in their thinking. These trends are reinforced where the businessman's success is based within his own community, or with the old country, in contrast to the professionals whose success and work generally involves them in contacts beyond their community.

10 *External factors* These may be in either the old country or the new. Successive chapters have emphasized the impact that the invasion of the Golden Temple in Amritsar had on Sikhism in the diaspora, provoking many men to assert their Sikh identity more strongly and visibly by wearing turbans and growing their hair. Likewise, the international outcry against Salman Rushdie's *Satanic Verses* provoked many Muslims to reassert their Islamic identity, because they felt it had been threatened or devalued. Various

studies suggest that, similarly, perceptions of hostility within the new country through racial discrimination commonly lead not to assimilation (hoping to avoid prejudice) but rather to the reassertion of identity and community ties. Negative stereotypes in the media, misrepresentation by teachers, legislation that is seen as hostile (e.g. the ban on wearing turbans), all typically lead to a reassertion of the religious tradition that is thought to be under threat.

Of course, none of these ten factors operates in isolation and different individuals, or groups, are subject to all of them not only to different degrees, but in changing forms. Racial discrimination may increase, or an individual may have a career change, or move to another location in the new country. It is not only the diaspora groups which change. It is not uncommon for people to act differently in different company. There is nothing inevitable about how human beings react to their background or experiences, but there are common trends. It is these common trends, not inevitabilities, which have been identified. Future research may be expected to show that the situation is more rather than less complicated than this analysis has suggested. Inevitably, these contrasting factors for change and continuity sometimes result in communal tensions, between different generations or between individuals seeking power, but the media has probably exaggerated these, the former in particular. The generational differences are probably more acute where the parents come from a rural background with little educational opportunity, and where the second generation have achieved considerable success in higher education and their resulting careers. But it is not only in the diaspora that changes occur. Many people find in the course of visits that life and religion in the old country have changed in ways they themselves have not. Life in the subcontinent is not as static as Western stereotypes often suggest, and diaspora South Asians do not always change as dramatically as people have suggested.

The Maturation of Diaspora Religions and some Areas for Research

Knott [22] identified seven areas for future research concerning the maturation of South Asians in Britain, though the principles apply in other countries also. The following discussion focuses on, and develops, Knott's seven areas.

1 *The place of language* This involves both the classical sacred languages – Sanskrit, Arabic, Avestan, Gurmukhi, etc. – and the lan-

guages in daily use in the subcontinent – Urdu, Punjabi, Hindi, Gujarati, Bengali, etc. The former provide access to some of the authoritative literature, but they do more. In various religions from South Asia, more so than in Christianity, worship is conducted in the sacred language. In Hinduism, and among Parsis, the holy language is commonly seen as having sacred power; in Islam, Arabic is the very word of God. For many traditional members of these religions the holy language is an essential part of spiritual experience. It is not simply a question of understanding teaching (this subject will be discussed further below with respect to the understanding of prayer). As successive chapters above have shown, language classes are offered in various communities throughout the diaspora, but Jackson and Nesbitt [20] found in their fieldwork in central England that such language teaching was more prominent in some of the new groups associated with modern figures, notably Sai Baba, than with the classical 'big' traditions.

The modern languages are different in that they may form the means of communication within the home. This is the case not only between the elders, but also between the young and their elders and with other community members. Language is commonly a crucial element in the preservation of individual and group identity. The transmission of language is therefore a key factor in the future of the various religions in the diaspora. The role of language merits substantial research for other reasons. The vocabulary of different languages can determine patterns in the logic of thought. Some languages, for example, have no word for religion. The adaptation of English terms – God, prayer, priest, worship – may be appropriate for some religions, but may give subtle twists in meaning for others.

Very different practices and beliefs can be alluded to, for example, by the term 'prayer'. To a Protestant, prayer is essentially conversation with God, as intercession, adoration or expression of penitence. In this context, it is essential that the words of prayer are understood, otherwise the words become meaningless 'mumbo-jumbo'. For several religions from South Asia, prayer is the recitation of the words of sacred power. For Orthodox Parsis in India, for example, they are the very words uttered by the prophet Zoroaster in revelation. When they are recited in the totally pure context (moral and physical) of the ritual, by a consecrated priest, in absolute concentration and with devotion, they are believed to make powerfully present the spiritual realities invoked. Understanding the words may even be considered a hindrance, for then the worshipper thinks about their meaning, and that necessarily limits the experience to the low levels of human vocabulary, rather than being attuned to the holy forces. When the words are merely written down in a book, they are dead. They are activated and become living, powerful prayers when properly used. The one word 'prayer' may be inappropriate for two such different religious activities as those described of Protestants and Parsis. When young Western-educated Parsis use the word prayer it is possible that subconsciously their perception of their own tradition may become syncretized with that of the Protestant West.

Another dimension to the issue of language is that if the language in which a person thinks is so important, how does one evaluate, even identify, the language of thought? Many South Asians, especially those who settled in the West at an early age and those of the second or third generations, may move easily from one language to another, according to the company they are in, or the subject-matter of the conversation. For example, Parsis are more likely to discuss banking in English, but tell bawdy jokes in Gujarati. The language used for religion may vary. Even within one sentence people fluent in both languages may move from one to the other. When, why, with whom and with what consequences merits further research.

2 *The transmission of the tradition* In South Asia the religion is 'caught not taught': it is commonly (especially in rural areas) part of the total environment, and part of daily life in mixing with elders, family and co-religionists. Values and behaviour are learned through regular participation in domestic and communal rituals. Whole life patterns are generally determined by religious traditions. In the Western diaspora, even where South Asian family and religious groups live in reasonable proximity to one another, they are nevertheless part of a wider society which is not governed by Sikh, Hindu, Islamic, Zoroastrian, etc. traditions. The basic legal system in the West reflects a historically Christian foundation more than is generally admitted by the legislators. This was highlighted in Britain with the Rushdie affair, where the law of blasphemy was seen to be applied only to Christianity. The structure of the working week, with days off on Saturday and Sunday, and that of the year, centred around Christian festivals, reflect a Christian foundation of the culture. There are some severely practical problems in the West for religions from other countries, for example the unchangeable facts of daylight hours in northern Canada affecting the fast at Ramadan (see chapter 23, p. 791 above). The various authors above emphasize how the faster pace of life in the West, the working hours of both men and women, and the absence of servants or extended families, leaves few with the time needed for lengthy religious practice. Not only 'ordinary' acts of worship, but even the important and less common life-cycle rites, funerals for example, may have to be shortened (see chapter 21). Jackson and Nesbitt [20] also emphasize how outsiders' studies of South Asians all too often focus on aspects of

the religions which may have been part of traditional Western scholarly studies of them, e.g. the 'scriptures', whereas the young members of the religion are deeply affected by more 'popular' means of transmission, e.g. the visual arts, dance, drama and not least the video, either of events in the old country, Indian secular movies or productions of the great epics like the Mahabharata (see also [29] concerning aspects of South Asian arts in North America). It is important to appreciate the enjoyment young children experience through these activities, an aspect of South Asian diaspora religion not anticipated by many writers in the 1960s who forecast the inevitable assimilation of the groups and the erosion of the religion with succeeding generations.

There are, however, other factors in the transmission of South Asian religion in the West. In wider 'Christian' society questions of beliefs, doctrines, creeds are of central importance. The widespread use of such terms as 'inter-*faith* dialogue' reflect this Christian concern. South Asian children, and their elders, are often asked by outsiders 'What do you believe?' 'What does your religion teach about . . .?' an approach which is unfamiliar to many from the Indian subcontinent. The problem is more acute in countries like Britain where religious education is a core element of the school syllabus. This has often taken the form of inculcating Christianity, but even where a more open 'world religions' perspective has been taken, Hindu, Sikh, Muslim, etc. children have (a) heard an outsider's account of their religion which they have all too often not recognized and (b) been asked to give a rational, logical exposition of teaching which neither they nor their parents have been equipped to give. One consequence of this has been the provision in many South Asian religious communities, in all four Western countries, of 'Sunday schools' (or sometimes Friday schools for Muslims) to teach young people about the religion. The young who have experienced a Western education, especially those who in the process have attended Christian-style worship in school assemblies, have come to assume that it is important to understand the meaning of the words of prayer and to comprehend why specific rituals are performed and what is their meaning. A process has consequently emerged among some South Asians which scholars have often called 'Protestantization', the acquisition of Protestant assumptions about true/false teachings and about understanding prayer and the dismissal of complex, traditional, little (intellectually) understood rituals as superstitious. This process also involves seeing worship not so much as an individual act (as in many South Asian traditions) but rather as a congregational activity (because of the community development through socializing).

The means of transmission, and what is being transmitted, are therefore changing. Institutional forms are also subject to change in order to meet the perceived needs of members in a Western setting, for example youth groups and camps, weekend seminars, social and welfare committees and functions. Sometimes this involves these diaspora religions taking on additional roles not needed in the old country; but also, as Coward notes in chapter 23 with regard to Canada, the state sometimes takes over the caring roles which the religions have normally provided, with the result that the groups become simply 'faith communities' as many Christian churches are.

3 *Individual identity* Because of the influences described, will a distinctly Australian, British, Canadian, US Hinduism/Sikhism/Islam etc. emerge? Does religion have to change to remain meaningful to people in different environments, and how different will the religions from South Asia be from those in the old countries? Just as Christianity has indigenized in, say, Africa, so it is reasonable to suppose that religions from South Asia will indigenize in the West. How? In Western Islam, Hinduism, etc., what will the role of women be? How will a Western education affect attitudes to the veil, to divorce law, to the perception of the role of the 'good wife'?

There is another dimension to the issue of personal identity. In the 1970s academics and the media spoke of Asian migrants, particularly the second generation, as being 'caught between two cultures' – indeed, the vocabulary has become so common that it is used by members of the communities; but is the concept valid? Ballard [2; 29–31] argues that just as bilingualism does not produce psychological or personal stress, so similarly young South Asians may be better seen as 'skilled cultural navigators' as they move inside and outside their ethnic colony. My own research would support Ballard's contention as far as the majority are concerned, but something like 40 per cent of my respondents spoke of two dimensions to their personality, a Parsi/Zoroastrian side and a Western side. Those who felt least comfortable with this position were, on the whole, the offspring of intermarriages and individuals who were neither consciously Zoroastrian nor consciously British. Those who asserted either side of their personality strongly did not, they said, feel caught between cultures. The question of identity is clearly a topic on which more research is needed. What is important, and emphasized by all the writers in this section, including Stuart in connection with the black African diaspora, is that religion is a crucial means by which many assert their identity (see also [11]). Coward (chapter 23 above) refers to individuals who may consider themselves ethnically, but not religiously, Sikh. Fenton [9] comments on some American South Asian youth who are not religious believers nevertheless wanting to come together to assert an ethnic 'Indian' identity which ignores religious divides. A similar question might be whether one has to hold a corpus of religious beliefs to be a Jew.

Many Parsis believe that religion is something to do with one's genes, it is in the blood. It is what a person is, not what they believe. The parameters by which religious identity is marked out cannot be simple Western categories based on belief-systems.

4 *Group identity* Before migration, few people from South Asia thought of themselves necessarily as Hindus, but rather as Gujaratis, Punjabis or Bengalis, or members of a particular caste or *jati*, as devotees of a particular god such as Shiva, or followers of a particular holy man such as Sai Baba. As chapter 5 above indicated, 'Hinduism' is originally an outsider's term and concept and to some extent remains so in the old country. From schools, the media, scholars and legislators, many South Asians (especially the second generation) have begun to see themselves as Hindus, Zoroastrians (rather than in racial terms as Parsis) and Muslims. Will this trend towards internationalized perspectives of religious identity increase with successive generations, and will caste/*jati* divisions, or regional allegiances, disappear? Will young people with limited contact with the old country lose a sense of being Punjabi, Bengali or Gujarati and become part of a unitary religion, say Hinduism, as described in Western books rather than as lived on the ground in the old country?

There is, however, a contrary pressure. As successive chapters have noted, in the early days of Western migration Indian religious centres incorporated not only shrines to different deities but also different religions, e.g. pictures of the Sikh Gurus alongside Rama or Krishna, or statues of Shiva, or figures from Jainism. The early centres were often Indian cultural or religious centres, not particularly sectarian, or Hindu. This changed not only because of events in Amritsar, but also because, as numbers and resources have grown, so more 'sectarian' centres have been built in some places. In each of the four Western countries discussed the facilities are growing for people to follow particular branches of the South Asian religions. As the third millennium approaches, therefore, there are contrasting trends – towards the globalization of the religion as 'Hinduism', 'Zoroastrianism', etc., but also towards a reassertion of group differences. It is not clear how these pressures will balance out.

How group identity will be affected by changes of legislation is also a subject of interest, but one which none of the governments of the four countries has fully addressed. The example of blasphemy has already been noted. The laws are often illogical. For example, while racial prejudice is banned in Britain, religious discrimination is not. Sikhs wearing turbans are exempted from laws relating to the wearing of crash helmets for motorcyclists, or in some uniforms, not because, according to the courts, they are religious markers, but because they are indicators of race (even though many Sikhs do not wear them!). All four countries affirm the right of religious freedom, but how far does this freedom extend? Should rites considered by the practitioners to be religious (whether or not historians think they are) be permitted even when considered harmful, as Western doctors believe female circumcision is (especially in the way it is commonly performed)? What of public rites of animal sacrifice in association with certain Muslim festivals? Should polygamy be permitted? What of a Muslim man who three times declares he has divorced his wife, but does not go through the courts, and then remarries? Is that bigamy? How far can there be a plurality of laws in a religiously plural society? Can there be a Muslim (Hindu/ Sikh, etc.) law in the US (Canada, Australia, etc.) [25]? The four countries have hardly begun to consider seriously what provisions are necessary if a full account is to be taken of the nature of a multi-religious society.

Medicine is another obvious example of the wider implications of a multi-religious society. The various religions have different attitudes to suffering, its cause and management. Psychiatric illness is an area of particular difficulty for South Asians [26]. The rites of passage associated with the great turning-points of life, notably birth, puberty/marriage and death, are of importance in all cultures, but also moments where medical services are often required [10]. However, medical training rarely, if ever, includes any component to equip doctors to cope with the human problems of a multi-religious society. Western funeral services, in particular the limited time allowed at crematoria, make the observance of religious traditions especially difficult, as do hospital routines. In the course of my research I have lived with Parsi families at times of bereavement. Although I cannot prove my assertion, I have no doubt but that natural grief is further compounded by the feelings of the bereaved that they are not caring for the soul as they have been brought up to do, as they believe it is right and necessary to do. Grief blends with guilt, justified or not. The preservation of group identity is something requiring both internal community energy and external support from the wider society. Research is necessary not only on the religions, but also on what a sensitive, balanced and effective (and effective for what?) multicultural policy should comprise.

5 *Leadership* At present most South Asians, whatever their religion, in each of the four countries recruit their religious leaders from the old countries and support them in the diaspora. They also fund the visits of leaders and teachers from the subcontinent. But already there are signs that some of the Western-educated youth look for teachers who can communicate in the manner of Western (secular) teachers. Among diaspora Parsis, for example, the complaint is not

uncommon, how can the leaders in the old country understand, and therefore direct, what happens in the West? Occasionally young men born in the West travel to the old country to be trained and duly initiated so that they may function in diaspora rituals. Will the time come when such leaders are also expected to have a Westernized theological or academic training?

Banks [3] has noted a different trend, namely how traditional priestly authorities have been marginalized in community leadership, which has become dominated by successful businessmen, or professionals, individuals who have achieved success in the outside world and are therefore skilled in presenting the community to the outside. Such leaders have (often successfully) presented to outsiders the image of internal religious contrasts between the religion of the mystics (sometimes implied to be religious fanatics) and that of the ordinary Jain (Muslim, Hindu, etc.), implying that it is the latter which is the 'authentic' voice. Would the ordinary Australian, British, Canadian and US businessman be the authentic voice of Christianity in South Asia?

A different trend relating to leadership is the impact of external Christian understandings, as the media, and others, refer to, say, Muslim or Sikh leaders as the 'priests' of the religion, designating them by an inappropriate term with inappropriate colouring. The question of who will determine, from where, and by what measures, the policy, religious practice, etc. of the South Asian diaspora groups is a complex yet crucial one. Some of their Westernized leaders have attempted to evolve a simplified, practical, rational code of worship, but such radical reforming steps typically encounter hostility from the leaders in the old country. The informal, private use of tape recordings of prayers played in the car on the way to work, as described by Bilimoria (chapter 21 above), is a less contentious compromise.

6 *Universalization* The point has already been made that Western images of, say, Hinduism, which ignore caste, regional or spiritual ties, may well determine how the concept of a small group is internally affected as it absorbs the Western perceptions. A 'universal Hinduism' may replace the small groups of Krishna or Shiva or Kali devotees. Further, contacts between the diaspora communities may well lead to a new globalization of the religion. Williams in chapter 24 draws attention to what he calls 'transnational' families and religions, as networks are developed with co-religionists around the world, and not just with the old country. The globalization of South Asian religion is a growing phenomenon and does not only apply to the US. The Sikhs in Canada and Britain have been major contributors in the debate about Sikhs in India; educated Hindu or Muslim leaders in the West can have much honour when visiting the old

country. The lines of authority in the global network of South Asian religions may well become complex, if not conflicting.

There is another dimension to the issue of universalization and globalization. Will a diaspora (not just a British/Canadian, etc.) form of religion emerge? Attitudes to, and the needs met by, religious worship are different in the Western diaspora from those in South Asia. This has been alluded to with reference to the idea of the power of the sacred word, and the Protestantizing trend towards emphasizing the understanding of prayer. But there is more to it. In the diaspora, worship is a key focus for the coming together of co-religionists, sometimes from a wide area. This meeting, and the need for socializing, brings a congregational dimension to the religious activity which may not be common in the old country, especially for Hindus, Parsis and Jains. However, time pressures also mean that some lengthy rites, common in the old countries, are not favoured by many people in the diaspora. While, therefore, many have a deep yearning to preserve their heritage, there is also a common call for the streamlining as well as the translation of ritual and prayer. Further, some of the traditional rituals are impossible outside the old country. Parsis, for example, lacking a properly pure temple, cannot perform many of the 'higher' or 'inner' ceremonies which demand the proper physical setting and the involvement of a wholly pure priest, a level of purity very difficult to achieve in the diaspora. But what has emerged is not a new ritual, but rather a reassertion of a rite, the *jashan*, which has long been part of the religion. It is still practised in India and Iran, but it is much more the focus of religious activity in the diaspora because of the way in which it meets the needs of the people. It can be performed in a temple, or the home, or any clean place. It does not involve a permanently burning temple fire. Although it is performed by a team of priests, this may be a small team, and it is not uncommon in the old countries for the laity to attend. It has the potential, therefore, for use as a congregational rite which may be performed in rented church halls as well as homes. It is extremely rare in any religion for a wholly new ritual to be devised; rather, as in this case, liturgies evolve. There is a tension. Many, especially among the young, want shorter rituals and the translation of prayers, but if rites are to provide powerful spiritual experiences, they cannot lose their identity and character. The development of worship, and ritual practice in general, among diaspora communities is a crucial aspect of the maturation of the religion, and one which merits further study.

7 *The impact of Western religious ideas* In addition to the 'Protestantizing' trend already discussed, Knott (chapter 22) also notes the influence of secularization, atheism and inter-faith dialogue. These merit elaboration. In South Asia generally, and in cer-

tain religions in particular (especially Islam and Hinduism), there is a conviction that religion is not just a set of beliefs, or one part of life, but is rather a total way of life. In the West, however, religion has generally become merely a compartment of life, something reserved for the weekends, or for important communal gatherings. Working in outside firms, or in professional bodies, means that the religion can rarely be taken into the workplace on a daily basis. Not only are the national laws based on non-Islamic/non-Hindu, etc. principles, but also the ordering of family, social and personal life is determined by non-religious factors to a far greater extent than in the old country. In Britain especially, Parsis consider the eroding effect of secularization to be one of the greatest threats to their young people.

Knott's inclusion of inter-faith dialogue is interesting. The motives of Christians engaged in such activities are doubtless honourable, to increase tolerance and understanding, even to learn from each other. But what has also happened is that the Hindus/Muslims/Parsis/Sikhs who have been drawn into such dialogue have generally been the educated, the good communicators, often the Westernized, perhaps rather liberal, members of the traditions. Their role in inter-faith dialogue, especially when this has resulted in contact with significant social leaders, such as state governors or British royalty, has given these representatives a status, influence, even authority, back in the community, an authority they might not otherwise have had and sometimes despite the fact that they are not necessarily typical or traditional. (The point is similar to, but slightly different from, that discussed in (5) above on leadership.)

One of the most obvious areas of Western impact is the role of women already alluded to (see chapter 22 above; also [1; 27; 28]). The issue is not only women's opportunities for education and careers, but also their role in the religious life of the communities (in mosques for example) and the extent to which rising fundamentalism (or extremism) in many religions – including evangelical Christianity – is consistently seen to give them a subservient role in conflict with modern, liberalizing trends. Related questions, obviously, are marriage patterns, love or arranged marriages, caste restrictions in marriage and the widespread typical South Asian opposition to intermarriage. One might ask if it is less racist for Asian families to object to intermarriage with whites than it is for white parents to object to a black or Asian partner for their offspring?

The National Characteristics of the South Asian Diasporas

The above ten factors for change or continuity, and seven areas for research on the process of maturation, all have international dimensions. In the light of the individual chapters on Australia, Britain, Canada and US, what can be said of the distinctive features of South Asian religions in the respective countries?

The first obvious difference is in their histories. Britain has had the longest, and closest, contact with the Indian subcontinent. As a result South Asians and white Anglo-Saxons have a range of presuppositions about each other, and about their relations, which has affected the settlement. The reports of East India Company and government officials, or of missionaries, have been an important factor in Anglo-Indian relations since the seventeenth century. Some of those long-standing stereotypes of the 'natives' and the 'heathen' have not entirely disappeared, even if modern race relations laws make their expression illegal. They are almost certainly a hidden factor in race relations problems in Britain.

The modern history of the growth of South Asian communities in Britain is different from that of the other three countries. Although the respective authors rightly draw attention to the small communities of Sikhs in Canada and the US, and of pedlars and manual workers in Australia, early in the twentieth century, because of the empire Britain had a larger and more diverse South Asian presence prior to the 1960s. Students and businessmen, royals, diplomats and travellers were relatively numerous in the nineteenth century. The post-1960s settlers in Britain, therefore, had more of a network into which to move than did recent migrants to the other three Western countries.

The modern history of migration is also crucially different between continents. It is not simply that it started a decade earlier in Britain (in the 1950s rather than the 1960s and even later in Australia) but that the nature of the migration was very different. Essentially, Britain was seeking manual workers to take up the jobs which white Anglo-Saxons did not want but which were crucial in post-Second World War reconstruction because of the huge numbers of young men killed in the war. (The fact that Britain actively set out to persuade South Asians to come for Britain's own benefit is not part of popular British mentality, any more than Australians or Americans recognize their indebtedness to South Asian educational, scientific and professional excellence.) British imperial stereotypes of Asians as poverty-stricken, menial, manual workers were reinforced by the fact that the migrants of the 1950s and 1960s were employed as manual workers who took the lowest-paid work, worked long and unsociable hours and lived in cheap housing, all to save money to send 'home' because they envisaged returning to the old country. Not all early South Asian settlers in Britain were manual workers, however. A number of doctors, for example, settled in Britain after the Second World War, having served in the Army Medical Corps. Some professionals also came in the 1960s, but they have been generally ignored. At the dawn of the third millennium a substantial proportion of British medical students are second-generation South Asians, but my own respondents are convinced that the medical profession, more perhaps than any other, practises racial discrimination in senior appointments.

South Asian migration to Canada and the US was roughly contemporary (mid-1960s), and both admitted well-educated professionals rather than manual workers. But there are some differences between the two countries. (The following assertions are based on my own Parsi research; see [14; 15].) Because of its wealth and international power in trade, the US has drawn more heavily on the very well educated, especially scientists. The Canadian South Asian migration has more blue-collar workers than the US, but fewer than Britain. Like Britain, the educated people Canada has attracted have been graduates in the liberal arts rather than, as in the US, in science. South Asia's brightest scientists have been attracted more by the United States than by Canada or Britain. There is, therefore, a different recruitment pattern in the US. Compared with Britain, citizens of the United States tend not to think of South Asians as poverty-stricken labourers working in squalor. Second-generation South Asians in Britain have a higher proportion of their young people going to university than do white Anglo-Saxons, but that is not (yet) the public perception of them. The image is somewhat different in the US and Canada.

From the mid-1980s, new migration (as opposed to relatives of existing settlers) has become a mere trickle to Britain and reduced to the US and Canada. The new land of opportunity for people from South Asia has become Australia. Obviously there are exceptions, but preliminary studies suggest that people are not (yet) migrating there so much for higher education as for employment, once they have that education. Oxford, Cambridge and America's Ivy League universities still attract those able to gain entry. But my own informants suggest that Australia is seen as a more Asia-linked centre of Western opportunity, as the land of freedom and toleration (despite its past White Australia policy). The result is that while the South Asian population of Britain has a relatively wide age span (though South Asians remain typically younger than white Anglo-Saxons), their counterparts in Canada and the US are younger, and those in Australia younger still, with fewer second-generation South Asians there. The different continents are, therefore, at different stages in the history of South Asian migration.

The study of South Asian diaspora religion is still in its infancy, but my own work (especially [14]) suggests that the following religious patterns are likely to emerge from these different histories and demographic patterns. The highly educated scientists are more likely to assimilate quickly than manual labourers who have been part of a chain migration. So, too, are executive-class persons who have grown out of that educational group. However, in the early years after they have migrated people often affirm their religion more strongly than they did in the old country, because it is a stake of continuity in a sea of change (a point emphasized by Haddad [11] for American Muslims). One would, therefore, expect the newer groups in Australia to maintain closer ties with the old country and to be preserving their religion. However, religion is a high-profile phenomenon in America, especially with tele-evangelism, and has sufficient importance for it to be a factor in US presidential elections, unlike in the other countries under discussion. Although, Britain's head of state, the Queen, is officially also the head of the Church, Britain has the image of being a more secular state in practice. At least among my informants, the fear of conversion is greater in America than in Britain, where the greater fear is secularization. In Britain, the US and Canada alike, however, the greatest fears among South Asian parents are of the sexual immorality, neglect of the family and drugs which they associate with the West. Wider society would be mistaken to think that the South Asians have a wide-eyed uncritical admiration of Western life! (Such fears are not absent in Australia, but in my research I did not find them as prominent as in America.) As the opportunities are probably seen as greatest in the US, so too are the dangers of assimilation. In the early years of modern South Asian migration to the US, government policy was associated with what was known as 'the melting-pot', which anticipated that migrants would each contribute their distinctive flavour to the whole as they were melted down into the pot of American society. The intention may have been good; but from the perspective of many South Asians this was a threat, that their distinctive traditions would be lost [8: x]. The issue is addressed by D'Innocenzo and Sirefman:

> Some scholars argue that the symbol of the 'melting pot' is misleading. It has not reflected an equal fusion of newcomer and native, producing a stronger amalgam. Rather it represents a mold designed to force immigrants to conform to nativist standards. Despite enormous pressures 'to fit in', most immigrant and ethnic groups have retained distinctive aspects of cultural identity producing a 'salad bowl' effect, in which there is a larger entity, but in which each component can still be distinguished from the others. Just as one can discern the chicory

from the lettuce and tomatoes from the cucumber in a salad, so in the United States various ethnic groups stand out in particular ways. [8: x]

A number (though by no means all) of my US informants shared the scholars' assessment of the melting-pot, and were less convinced by the 'salad bowl' imagery. The melting-pot continued to be seen as a threat, and because of this the able, well-educated professionals who have characterized South Asian communities in the US have been particularly active in evolving community structures and strategies for the preservation of their ethnicity and particularly of their religion. Although Canadian groups are also well organized, my Canadian respondents were generally much more willing to be identified as Canadians than US respondents were to be identified as Americans. The Canadian policy of multiculturalism appears, from my research, to have been more effective in removing the perception of a threat of Westernization. The perception of government policy has a significant impact on attitudes to settlement and adaptation.

The interaction between the South Asian religions and scholarly study of those traditions is still in its very early days and it would be hazardous to draw too bold a picture. In Britain relations between Muslims and the wider community have been strained by the Rushdie affair, but that was not seen as a particularly academic prejudice. There have been occasional debates between Islamic intellectuals and Western Qur'anic specialists, but on the whole the majority of Muslims have ignored Western scholarship. The Palestinian Edward Said has attacked Western 'imperialist', Orientalist approaches to non-European religions, condemning what he sees as the insularity and cultural arrogance of grouping all the 'other' religions under a single heading 'Oriental', thus denying their individual integrity. He believes the treatment of Islam to be especially bad. Said's criticisms have provoked extensive international scholarly debate, but few Western Muslims have been involved in it. In some British universities an extremist, or fundamentalist, Muslim group, Hizbu-t-Tahrir, has, among other things, called for attacks on Jews. Attempts to curtail their activities, for example under legislation relating to incitement to racial hatred, have been labelled anti-Islamic by the group. This predominantly student group has clashed vigorously, and violently, with Western values.

British, Australian and US Sikhs have not been as alienated by scholars as Canadian Sikhs have been by the work of McLeod, but then few have learned from him to the same extent either (see chapter 23 above). His literary-critical analysis of Sikh scriptures replicates earlier work on the Jewish and Christian Bibles, fundamentally challenging traditional views of the unity or coherence of what had been seen as the divine word. His work is respected by some Sikhs around the world, but he has also been the focus of considerable hostility. In contrast to Canada and the US, at present no British university employs anyone who would describe themselves as a specialist on Sikhism, a remarkable gap given the size of the community. Some scholars have been discouraged from working on aspects of Sikh studies because of the treatment McLeod has received.

In Australia there has been little interaction between scholars and the South Asian communities, other than Bilimoria's constructive work within his own Indian community [4; 5].

The Parsis in all four countries have almost consistently good relations with Zoroastrian specialists, mostly because their community has had nearly 150 years of studying Western scholarship, and the battles over such issues as scriptural authority occurred in the early nineteenth century. Western Parsis (more than Iranian Zoroastrians) actively encourage Western scholars to speak to, and write for, their communities, but even that can have its problems. The writings of Boyce (especially her 1978 volume [6]) and Hinnells (particularly a 1981 booklet [17]) have been widely sold by Parsi organizations and used in the community religious education programme. How far should an outsider affect the minority group she or he studies?

The Jewish and black African diaspora experience, and developments in feminist theology (see Ursula King's chapter 17 above), suggest that it is in the US that new, distinctive and creative theologies may evolve. This has already begun in the case of Islam, especially with the university employment of Nasr and Rahman [12]. These two writers would not now be seen as orthodox in their old countries, and in that they may foreshadow a trend towards a more radical diaspora theology, perhaps in tension with that of the old country. In Britain and Australia, there is not, as yet, such a move towards the development of a diaspora theology. A pattern that has been noted is an emphasis, especially by the secular leadership, on those aspects of the religion most likely to be acceptable in the West, for example vegetarianism and non-violence among the Jains [3], or on Gandhi and the Gita among Hindus, rather than on, say, the purity laws, or the more mythological cosmology of the traditions, or (in public at least) caste traditions. But as the younger generation grows it is perhaps likely that the South Asian religious diaspora will become more doctrinally developed than a sanitized or simplified version of the old tradition.

In general it is the American communities which have the human and financial resources, as well as the suggested creative energies, to evolve a distinctive religious form. So far, however, it is only in Britain that South Asians have achieved significant political power, with the election of two South Asian Members of Parliament in the nineteenth century [18: v] and several more in the 1980s. It may not be too long before South Asians have seats in comparable governmental institutions in the other three countries.

The Experiences of the Different Religions

The internal constituencies of the religions are different in the various countries. Muslims in Britain are predominantly of South Asian provenance (especially outside London), whereas in Canada there is a proportionately stronger Middle Eastern presence. The latter is even greater in the United States, where black Muslims also have a high profile. Indeed, Islam is perhaps more ethnically diverse in the US than in any other country. As Islam may become the second largest religion, after Christianity, in the US early in the third millennium, the global political role of the US almost certainly means that the future of Islam is going to be significantly affected by developments in American Islam rather than by those in Australia or Britain. As many second-generation Muslims study their religion at Western universities, the interaction between scholarship and community members could result in productive interaction. Islam, more than any of the religions discussed here, has welcomed a number of converts. Many of these have been marriage partners, but not all. There has been some serious Western interest in the Sufi mystics, but also in more conventional Islam. Whether the tension between Islam and the West will prove to be confrontational or constructive is far from clear. It could well be both.

Since the invasion at Amritsar, the assassination of Mrs Gandhi and the blowing up of an Air India aircraft, Sikhism has been more politically aggressive in Britain, and especially Canada, than in the US. In Australia there are more South-East Asian Sikhs who distance themselves from the political strife of Punjab. Despite the controversy surrounding them, there are Sikh intellectuals in Canada who could give that country a unique and significant role in the future of Sikh theology. With Sikhs having a minority status in India, and in some areas perceiving themselves to be under threat, the Western Sikh diaspora could well have a more prominent role in the future of their religion than in, say, globally diverse Islam. Generally, relations between Sikhs and the West have been less confrontational than between Islam and the West.

Hinduism is not the same in each of the four countries. Whereas British Hindus come predominantly from northern India (Gujarat, Punjab and Bengal), in the US and Australia there are more south

Indians, and in the latter country many Hindus have migrated via South-East Asia, as have a significant proportion of Australian Muslims. Gujaratis are typically more public in the profession of their religion and have numerous important holy men, and usually describe Bengalis as not being very religious – a contrast not denied by Bengalis because institutional religion is not as evident there. South Indian Hinduism has a strong devotional strain. A number of Western Hindus from all parts of the subcontinent tend to follow the modern holy men, notably Sai Baba, rather than the great six philosophical schools. The religious education infrastructure is particularly effective among the followers of these modern exponents of the traditions. When Hindus began their major westwards migration in the 1960s, they were generally suspicious of the Westerners in the Hare Krishna movement, or International Society for Krishna Consciousness (ISKCON), but over the years mutual respect and cooperation has grown in a way which has not been so common with Muslim groups. Western scholarship has generally had little impact on Hindu communities. Given their relative sizes, it seems most unlikely that diaspora Hindus will have a fundamental effect on the development of the religion in the old country. Because Hinduism is a tradition transmitted through the home, to a greater extent, perhaps, than any other religion, it has not generally had such a powerful public image in the West as, say, Islam, though the building of magnificent Indian-style temples in Australia, Britain and the US has changed this to some extent in the 1980s and 1990s. Of all the religions discussed in these chapters, Hinduism probably faces more problems with identifying clear guidance on the proper format for religious practices, for example in association with funerals. In India there are different priestly roles for different settings, such as family and temple priests. In the West one priest, and usually one who is not fully trained, has to undertake all roles. Further, there is in Hinduism a much greater variety of practices and a less clear-cut idea of what is, and is not, essential than in other religions. Families can therefore be at a loss not knowing what to do. If they, especially the bereaved, later find they have not done the 'right' thing, distress and guilt can be considerable.

In stark contrast to Hinduism, it may well be the case that the future of Zoroastrianism is fundamentally affected by the diaspora groups in the West. In large part this is because of the diminishing size of the community in Bombay, the disproportionately high level of educational and professional achievers who have migrated, and the creative energy being shown by various Western groups, not least in America. There have been tensions with the old country, but at the approach of the third millennium a number of these are being worked out in international conferences, the exchange of visits of teachers and leaders, and the common sharing of much Western scholarly literature. Zoroastrianism will probably be more fundamentally affected by its Western expansion than any other of the religions from South Asia.

There are relatively few Indian Christians in Britain, but they are an important group in the US and Australia. They have a very different Western experience from the other religions, partly because they are moving from a minority status in the old country to being part of the dominant religion in the new world. They have also been, in relative terms, more successful at recruiting their own professionally trained religious leaders. In part this is because the primary migrants were often women, who came as nurses and paramedics from Christian mission hospitals, and whose husbands sometimes turned to the religious ministry. There is, of course, greater provision for Christian theological training in the West than there is for any other religion. Thus far there is little sign that South Asian Christian theology is impacting on the established Western churches [24], but as it becomes part of seminary syllabuses it is possible that it may percolate through to congregations or affect the development of Christian thought in the West. The danger for the Indian Christians may be that they will be swallowed up by the established churches and their distinctive features lost.

The Jain communities do not have a high profile in the West, often accepting the outsiders' perception of them as part of the Indian, or Hindu, scene rather than as something different. In part this is because of the small size of their communities, in part because they are not an aggressive group. Their public profile has increased in Britain since the opening of a magnificent temple, with traditional art from Indian craftsmen, in a disused church in Leicester. In the US the leading Jain scholar, Jaini, has shed lustre on his community perhaps to a greater degree than any other South Asian religious writer has done for their community. The historical and contemporary importance of Jainism is widely overlooked by Westerners; few university courses in any country do them justice and public ignorance is deeply regrettable. Whether Western Jains are likely to affect the long-term history of their religion seems doubtful.

Another important South Asian group which is unevenly represented across the four countries are the East African Asians. They are found predominantly in Britain, but also in Canada, and have been important elements in Hindu, Sikh, Jain and Parsi communities as 'orthodox' influences calling for the reassertion of traditions and warning against excessive assimilation. There has been trade between the Indian subcontinent and East Africa for hundreds, probably thousands, of years. Communities of traders grew in the nineteenth century, first in the island of Zanzibar and then on the mainland as the hinterland was opened up with the building of the East African railway at the turn of the century. Apart from the coolies who built the railway, most of whom returned to India, the Indian groups (mainly Punjabis and Gujaratis) who settled in Africa were successful traders, and in the twentieth century included many professionals. The main centres were in Zanzibar, Kenya, Tanzania and Uganda. Typically they lived in isolation from both the Europeans and the blacks and generally preserved staunchly the 'Victorian' forms of their religions. In the 1960s policies of Africanization led to their marginalization, even expulsion. When they migrated to Britain and Canada they brought their resources and talents, as well as their traditional religion, with them; hence their significant impact on the established South Asian groups in the West, whichever of the South Asian religions they followed.

Buddhism varies considerably across the four Western countries. In Britain there are very few South Asian Buddhists, just small numbers of Sri Lankans and Tibetans. British Buddhism is predominantly a white Anglo-Saxon phenomenon. The situation is different in the other three countries because each of them, Australia and the US in particular, has substantial numbers of East Asians, Vietnamese for example. The South Asian Buddhists in these three countries generally seek to remain separate from their co-religionists from the rest of Asia, partly for ethnic reasons, partly because of the differences between Mahayana and Theravada Buddhism. Nevertheless, Asian Buddhism has a higher profile in Australia, Canada and the US, in particular, than it does in Britain. In general, Buddhists, whatever their nationality, have had a less hostile attitude to Western scholarship than most other Asian religions, and it is possible that Western Buddhism will play an important part in the long-term global history of the religion. Buddhist monks and nuns are not unusual sights at many Western universities. The potential for Western impact is especially true in the case of Tibetan Buddhism, because its survival largely depends on Western groups following the Chinese invasion of Tibet, the exile of the Dalai Lama and the oppression of many Buddhists in the old country. The remarkable personal and spiritual qualities of the Dalai Lama have resulted in a considerable level of respect among most Westerners for what he stands for.

The internal constituencies of the various religions are therefore different in the four countries and those constituencies inevitably affect the beliefs and practices of the communities. There is, in short, no such phenomenon as the (South) Asian community, nor even a unitary South Asian Hinduism/Islam/Sikhism, etc. in the West.

Conclusion

These diaspora groups have their impact on others. In terms of the old countries, there may be concern at the 'bleeding away' of potential leaders, professionals, businessmen, social reformers, educationists, etc. In the days of empire, Britain was criticized for exploiting South Asia's natural resources. At the dawn of the third millennium the West is draining away the region's leading human resources. Mention has already been made of the potential religious impact the diaspora groups could have on the religion in the old country. What has not been seriously studied is the impact that the religions have on the religion of the new countries. The fact that religion is such an important aspect of the South Asian communities raises significantly the profile of religion, especially in a more secular country like Britain. It has, of course, fundamentally affected the study of religion in schools and universities, inspiring a move away from syllabuses dominated by Christian theology to a more pluralist approach [7]. Asian religions have influenced various new religious movements, or New Age groups. But they, and black-led churches especially, have also influenced the 'established' forms of religion. The visible vitality and value of the religions have challenged traditional Christian assumptions about the falsity of 'pagan' religion. Religious pluralism is not a subject confined to the halls of academia; it has entered some at least of the churches. The black-led churches have inspired the older established churches to rediscover the charismatic and healing movements that were part of early Christianity but have long been neglected in the West. Some aspects of feminist theology have been inspired by writers from Asia and Africa. Some Westerners have been attracted to the mystical quest of certain parts of Hinduism, and a few have converted to Islam. Even more have had their individual consciences challenged about their commitment to their own religion. The South Asian diasporas in the West are not simply 'problems' bound for inevitable assimilation and disappearance, as many saw them in the 1960s. They are important aspects both of the history of their own religion and of the mosaic of living religions in Western societies. The visibility of such a diversity of religions has made religious and non-religious people alike more conscious of diverse cultures and world-views and has provoked many to ask more searching questions about themselves. No longer can the study of religion be considered an esoteric subject. It is something which is vital for politicians, social workers, doctors, journalists and teachers, indeed for anyone who is not a recluse, whatever their own religion may or may not be.

Bibliography

1 AGNEW, V., 'Feminism and South Asian Immigrant Women in Canada', in M. Israel and N. K. Wagle (eds), *Ethnicity, Identity and Migration: The South Asian Context*, Toronto, University of Toronto Press, 1993, pp. 142–64

2 BALLARD, R., *Desh Pardesh: The South Asian Presence in Britain*, London, Hurst/University of British Columbia Press, 1994

3 BANKS, M., *Organizing Jainism in India and England*, Oxford, Oxford University Press, 1992

4 BILIMORIA, P., *Hinduism in Australia: Mandala for the Gods*, Melbourne, Spectrum, 1989

5 BILIMORIA, P., *Indians in Victoria (Australia): A Historical, Social and Demographic Profile of Indian Immigrants*, Victoria, Deakin University, 1988

6 BOYCE, M., *Zoroastrians: Their Religious Beliefs and Practices*, 3rd rev. edn, London, Routledge, repr. 1988

7 D'COSTA, G., 'Theology of Religions', in D. Ford (ed.), *The Modern Theologians*, vol. 2, Oxford, Blackwell, 1989, pp. 274–90

8 D'INNOCENZO, M., and SIREFMAN, J. P. *Immigration and Ethnicity: American Society – 'Melting Pot' or 'Salad Bowl'?*, Westport, CT, Greenwood Press, 1992

9 FENTON, J. Y., *Transplanting Religious Traditions: Asian Indians in America*, New York, Praeger, 1988

10 FULLER, J. H. S., and TOON, P. D., *Medical Practice in a Multicultural Society*, London, Heinemann Medical Books, 1988

11 HADDAD, Y. Y., *Islamic Values in the United States*, New York, Oxford University Press, 1987

12 HADDAD, Y. Y., *The Muslims of America*, New York, Oxford University Press, 1991

13 HELWEG, A. W., 'Indians in Australia: Theory and Methodology of the New Immigration', in S. Vertovec (ed.), *Aspects of the South Asian Diaspora*, Delhi, Oxford University Press, 1991, pp. 7–35

14 HINNELLS, J. R., 'Parsis in Britain, Canada and USA: A Comparative Study', in H. Coward, J. R. Hinnells and R. B. Williams (eds), *South Asian Religions in Migration: An International Comparison*, Albany, State University of New York Press, 1997

15 HINNELLS, J. R., 'South Asian Diaspora Religion: Comparative Parsi Experiences', *South Asia Research*, vol. 14, 1994, pp. 62–110

16 HINNELLS, J. R., 'Zoroastrian Migration to the American Continent', in M. Treasureywala (ed.), *Proceedings of the 6th North American Congress*, Toronto, Toronto Zoroastrian Association, 1988, pp. 19–49

17 HINNELLS, J. R., *Zoroastrianism and the Parsis*, London, Ward Lock Educational, 1981

18 HINNELLS, J. R., *Zoroastrians in Britain*, Oxford, Oxford University Press, 1996

19 ISRAEL, M., and WAGLE, N. K., *Ethnicity, Identity and Migration: The South Asian Context*, Toronto, University of Toronto Press, 1993

20 JACKSON, R., and NESBITT, E., *Hindu Children in Britain*, Stoke on Trent, Trentham Books, 1993

21 JONES, T., *Britain's Ethnic Minorities*, London, Policy Studies Institute, 1993

22 KNOTT, K., 'Bound to Change? Religions of South Asians in Britain', in S. Vertovec (ed.), *Aspects of the South Asian Diaspora*, Delhi, Oxford University Press, 1991, pp. 86–111

23 KNOTT, K., 'Religion and Identity, and the Study of Ethnic Minority Religions in Britain', in V. Hayes (ed.), *Identity Issues and World Religions*, Proceedings of the 25th Congress of the IAHR, South Australia, 1986, pp. 167–75

24 KOYAMA, K., 'Asian Theology', in D. Ford (ed.), *The Modern Theologians*, vol. 2, Oxford, Blackwell, 1989, pp. 217–34

25 MENSKI, W., 'Asians in Britain and the Question of a New Legal Order: Asian Laws in Britain', in M. Israel and N. K. Wagle (eds), *Ethnicity, Identity and Migration: The South Asian Context*, Toronto, University of Toronto Press, 1993, pp. 238–68

26 RACK, P., *Race, Culture and Mental Disorder*, London/New York, Tavistock, 1982

27 SAGHAL, G., and YUVAL-DAVIS, N., *Refusing Holy Orders: Women and Fundamentalism in Britain*, London, Virago, 1992

28 SRIVASTAVA, A., and AMES, M. M., 'South Asian Women's Experience of Gender, Race and Class in Canada', in M. Israel and N. K. Wagle (eds), *Ethnicity, Identity and Migration: The South Asian Context*, Toronto, University of Toronto Press, 1993, pp. 123–41

29 THAKKAR, R., 'Transfer of Culture through Arts: The South Asian Experience in North America', in M. Israel and N. K. Wagle (eds), *Ethnicity, Identity and Migration: The South Asian Context*, Toronto, University of Toronto Press, 1993, pp. 217–38

30 WILLIAMS, R. B., *Religions of Immigrants from India and Pakistan: New Threads in the American Tapestry*, Cambridge, Cambridge University Press, 1988

General Bibliography

BRANDON, S. G. F., *A Dictionary of Comparative Religion*, London, Weidenfeld/New York, Scribner, 1970

BROWN, A. (ed.), *Festivals in World Religions*, ed. on behalf of the Shap Working Party on World Religions in Education, London/New York, Longman, 1986

ELIADE, M., *The Encyclopedia of Religions*, 16 vols, London, Collier Macmillan/New York, Macmillan, 1987

ELIADE, M., *Patterns in Comparative Religion* (tr. Rosemary Sheed), London/New York, Sheed & Ward, 1958; new edn 1979

ELIADE, M., *From Primitives to Zen: A Thematic Sourcebook of the History of Religions*, London, Collins/New York, Harper & Row, 1967; new edn London, Fount Books, 1978

ELIADE, M., *The Sacred and the Profane: The Nature of Religion* (tr. W. R. Trask), New York, Harcourt Brace, 1959, repr. 1968; New York, Harper, 1961

EVANS-PRITCHARD, SIR EDWARDE E., *Theories of Primitive Religion*, Oxford, Clarendon Press, 1965; London, Oxford University Press, 1967

FOY, W. (ed.), *Man's Religious Quest*, London, Croom Helm/New York, St Martin's, 1978

GENNEP, A. VAN, *The Rites of Passage* (tr. M. B. Vizedom and G. L. Caffee), London, Routledge, 1960, new edn 1977; Chicago, Chicago University Press, 1960, 1961

HASTINGS, J., *Encyclopaedia of Religion and Ethics*, 13 vols, Edinburgh, T. & T. Clark, 1908–26; repr. 12 vols, New York, Scribner, 1961

HINNELLS, J. R. (ed.), *A New Dictionary of Religions*, Oxford/London, Blackwell/Penguin, 1995

HINNELLS, J. R. (ed.), *Who's Who of World Religions*, London, Macmillan, 1991; Penguin, 1996

LEEUW, G. VAN DER, *Religion in Essence and Manifestation: A Study in Phenomenology* (tr. J. E. Turner), London, Allen & Unwin, 1938; first publ. in German as *Phänomenologie der Religion*, 1933

LING, T., *A History of Religion East and West*, London, Macmillan/New York, St Martin's, 1968; New York, Harper Colophon, 1970

MOORE, A. C., *Iconography of Religions: An Introduction*, London, SCM/Philadelphia, Fortress, 1977

NOSS, J. B., *Man's Religions*, 6th edn, New York, Macmillan, 1980

PARRINDER, E. G., *A Dictionary of Non-Christian Religions*, Amersham, Hulton Educational, 1971; Philadelphia, Westminster, 1973

PARRINDER, E.G., *Man and His Gods*, Feltham, Hamlyn, 1971; repr. 1973

PYE, E. M. (ed.), *Macmillan Dictionary of Religions*, London, Macmillan, 1993

ROBERTSON, R., *Sociology of Religion: Selected Readings*, Harmondsworth/Baltimore, Penguin, 1969

SHARPE, E. J., *Comparative Religion: A History*, London, Duckworth, 1975, new edn 1976; New York, Scribner, 1976

SKORUPSKI, J., *Symbol and Theory: A Philosophical Study of Theories of Religion in Social Anthropology*, Cambridge/New York, Cambridge University Press, 1976

SMART, N., *The Phenomenon of Religion*, London, Macmillan/New York, Herder, 1973; 2nd rev. edn Oxford, Mowbray, 1978

SMART, N., *The Religious Experience of Mankind*, New York, Scribner, 1969; London, Fontana, 1971; repr. Fount, 1977

SMART, N. (ed.), *The World's Religions*, Cambridge, Cambridge University Press, 1989, 1992

SMITH, HUSTAN, *The Religions of Man*, New York, Harper & Row, 1965 (© 1958)

SMITH, W. CANTWELL, *Belief and History*, Charlottesville, University Press of Virginia, 1977

SMITH, W. CANTWELL, *The Faith of Other Men*, New York, Harper & Row, 1972

SMITH, W. CANTWELL, *The Meaning and End of Religion: A New Approach to the Religious Traditions of Mankind*, New York, Macmillan, 1963; New York, New American Library (Mentor), 1964; London/New York, SPCK, 1978; New York, Harper & Row, 1978

STRENG, F. et al., *Ways of Being Religious: Readings for a New Approach to Religion*, Englewood Cliffs, NJ, Prentice-Hall, 1973

SUTHERLAND, S. (ed.), *The World's Religions*, London, Routledge, 1988

WAARDENBURG, J. J., *Classical Approaches to the Study of Religion: Aims, Methods and Theories of Research*, 2 vols, The Hague/Paris/Hawthorne, NY, Mouton, 1973–4

WERBLOWSKY, R. J. Z., *Beyond Tradition and Modernity: Changing Religions in a Changing World*, London, Athlone, 1976; distr. in US and Canada: Atlantic Highlands, NJ, Humanities Press

WHALING, F. (ed.), *Religion in Today's World*, Edinburgh, T. & T. Clark, 1987

ZAEHNER, R. C. (ed.), *A Concise Encyclopedia of Living Faiths*, New York, Hawthorn Books, 1959; 3rd edn London, Hutchinson/Boston, Beacon Press, 1977; 4th rev edn publ. as *Encyclopedia of Living Faiths*, London, Hutchinson, 1988

The following three series of books have been published on religion around the world with wide-ranging coverage. The first two are designed to provide reliable and authoritative introductions to the various religions; the third consists of compendia of new translations of important texts from the different religions.

HINNELLS, J. R., and SMART, N. (eds), *The Library of Religious Beliefs and Practices*, London/Boston, Routledge

STRENG, F. (ed.), *The Religious Life of Man*, Encino, CA, Dickenson

HINNELLS, J. R., and DONIGER, W. (eds), *Textual Sources for the Study of Religion*, Chicago, Chicago University Press

Index

Muhammad 'Ali 209
Muhammad 'Ali, Mirza 626
Muhammad Ali Mosque, Cairo 190
Muhammad b. 'Abd-al-Wahhab
    209, 210
Muhammad, Elijah 712, 801–2
Muhammad al-Muntazar 207
Muhammad VI, Sultan 168
Muhammad, Wallace 801
Muhammad, Wraithudden 712
Muktād 247–8
muktī (liberation) 266–7, 268,
    283–5, 286, 332
Mūl Mantra 336
Mūlasarvāstivada tradition 436
Mulder, Niels 550
Müller, Werner 517
multiculturalism 832
  in Australia 741, 754–5
  in Britain 756, 768
  in Canada 775, 781–4, 791,
      793–4, 839
Muni, Chitrabhanu 807–8
Muni, Sushil Kumar 808
Muo-tzu 447–8
Murdock, G. P. 562
Murji'i Muslims 201
Murtipujaka Jains 344, 359–60, 362,
    363–4
Musama Disco Christo Church 724
music
  in African religions 704, 708, 714
  in Islām 204–5
  in Judaism 45–6
Muslim (scholar) 165
Muslim Brotherhood 214, 219, 220,
    225
Muslim World League 801
Al-Musta'li 207
Musta'li Shi'ites 207
Mu'tazili Muslims 202, 203, 205,
    223
Mwana Lesa movement 574
Myanmar
  and Christianity 90, 91
  and Islām 227, 746
  and new religious movements
      582
  and Southern Buddhism 370,
      392, 402, 409, 411
mysticism
  in Buddhism 456

  in Chinese religions 456, 462–70
  in Christianity 79, 80, 116–17,
      150, 474 n.3
  in Hinduism 278, 845
  in Islām 166, 203–4, 206, 210–11,
      610, 674, 841
  in Judaism 11, 18, 19–20, 21, 22,
      35–6, 610
  in Pacific religions 551
  Vedic 266–7
  see also spirituality

Al-Nabhani, Taqi al-Din 220
Nagamatsu, Nissen 488
Naganuma, Myoko 501
Nāgārjuna 414
Nago *see* Candomblé
Nagriamel movement 590
nāmakarana (name-giving) 287
Namaskara Matra 355–6
Nāmdev 330, 332
Nāmdhārī movement 765
namegiving
  in Bahā'ism 635
  in Hinduism 287
  in Sikhism 335
  in Zoroastrianism 247
Nanāk, Gurū
  hymns 317, 336
  life 311, 312–14, 319, 328, 332,
      333
  and Sant tradition 329–30
  and Sikh community 279,
      314–15, 322, 331, 779
Nand Lāl, Bhai 31
Nanda 398
Nanjio 411, *412*
Naoroji, Dadabhai 253, 758
Nara school of Buddhism 483
Narayan, Swami 306
Nāropa 435
Narragansett Indian Church 582
Nasr, Seyyed Hossein 674, 840
Nasser, Gamal Abdel 214
Nation of Islām 711–12, 801–2
nation-states 74, 149, 213
National Association of Evangelicals
    722
National Baptist Convention of
    America 709
National Primitive Baptist
    Convention 710

793–4, 827, 834
Roberts, D. J.   710–11
Roberts, Oral   723
Roman Catholic Church
  in Africa   476–7, 691–2, 695, 697,
    701
  in Caribbean   713
  and charismatic movement   125
  in China   81, 473–4
  and European Enlightenment
    99–100
  and festivals   118
  in India   809
  in Japan   81, 483
  in Latin America   712–13, 718
  and liberation theology   88–9
  and ministry   124
  and missionary movement   77,
    81–4, 88
  post-Reformation   77
  and priesthood   124
  and Reformation   75–6, 138–9
  and sacraments   120
  and spirituality   674–5
  and theology   94–5, 102, 105, 122,
    124, 139
  and Uniate churches   132, 134
  in USA   709
  see also First Vatican Council; Latin
    Christianity; Second Vatican
    Council
Roman Empire, and Christianity
  63–8, 70, 77, 79
Rome, in Western Christianity
  69–70, 73, 75, 136–7, 139, 140
Rose, Wendy   544
Rosh Chodesh festival   29
Rosh Ha-Shanah (New Year) festival
  25, 29
Rosicrucianism   604
Roy, Ram Mohun   89, 300–1, 758
royal cults, in African religions   563,
  568–9, 570, 576, 703
RSS (Rasthriya Swayam-sevak Sangh)
  305, 745
Ru-chiao see Confucianism
Ruether, Rosemary Radford   652,
  655–6
Rushdie, Salman, *The Satanic Verses*
  748, 764, 770–1, 772, 825, 828,
  839
Russell, C. T.   151

Russia
  Christianity in   71, 78–80, 87, 122,
    129–31, 132, 152, 722
  Judaism in   19
  see also Soviet Union
Rustomji, Naoroji   252

Sabbatarianism   724
  see also Church of God (Seventh
    Day); Seventh-day Adventism;
    Seventh-day Baptists
Sabbath (Shabbat)   29, 32, 34, 60,
  64, 117–18, 135
Sacks, Jonathan   50, 52
sacraments
  Christian   119–21, 139–40, 145–6,
    149
  Hindu   287–8, 301, 379
  Jain   358
  Jewish   24, 47
sacrifice
  in African diaspora religions   713,
    714
  in African religions   569–70, 576,
    703
  in Buddhism   394–5
  in Christianity   109, 120, 124
  in Hinduism   296
  in Islām   832
  in Judaism   32, 60, 64
  in North American native religions
    535
  in Pacific religions   558
  in Vedism   266, 276, 333, 740
  in Zoroastrianism   241–2
Sadat, Anwar   219, 226
sādhanā (way)   279, 286, 672
Sadhna   332
Sadr, Musa   220, 226
Sahaj Yoga   306
Sai Baba, Sathya   306, 765, 787,
  803, 827, 842
Saicho   489, 490
Said, Edward   839
saints
  in Christianity   69, 75, 111, 118,
    132, 139, 150, 691–2
  in Islām   204–5, 207
Saklatvala, Shapurji   253
Sakya school of Buddhism   432,
  435
Salafiyya movement   214

Index compiled by Meg Davies